Collins

Collins
Canadian
French
Dictionary

Collins Canadian French Dictionary
Copyright © 2007
All rights reserved

Published by Collins, an imprint of HarperCollins Publishers Ltd

HarperCollins books may be purchased for educational,
business, or sales promotional use through our
Special Markets Department.

HarperCollins Publishers Ltd
2 Bloor Street East, 20th Floor
Toronto, Ontario
Canada M4W 1A8

www.collinsdictionaries.ca

Cataloguing in Publication Data is available upon request

Typeset by Thomas Callan
Printed and bound in the United States

Acknowledgements
We would like to thank those authors and publishers who kindly
gave permission for copyright material to be used in the Collins
Word Web. We would also like to thank Times Newspapers Ltd.
for providing valuable data.

MANAGING EDITIOR
Maree Airlie

EDITORS
Caëlle Amiot-Cadey
Joyce Littlejohn

CONTENTS

Note on trademarks

Words which we have reason to believe constitute trademarks have been designated as such. However, neither the presence nor the absence of such designation should be regarded as affecting the legal status of any trademark.

USING THIS DICTIONARY

The *Collins Canadian French Dictionary* is designed specifically for anyone starting to learn French, and has been carefully researched with teachers and students. It is very straightforward, with an accessible layout that is easy on the eye, guiding students quickly to the right translation. It also offers essential help on French culture.

This section gives useful tips on how to use the *Collins Canadian French Dictionary* effectively.

▷ Make sure you look in the right side of the dictionary

There are two sides in a bilingual dictionary. Here, the **French-English** side comes first, and the second part is **English-French**. The middle pages of the book have a grey border so you can see where one side finishes and the other one starts.

▷ Finding the word you want

To help you find a word more quickly, look at the words in **black** at the top of pages. They show the first and last words on the two pages where the dictionary is open.

▷ Make sure you use the right part of speech

Some entries are split into several parts of speech. For example 'glue' can either be a noun ("Can I borrow your **glue**?") or a verb ("**Glue** this into your exercise book"). Parts of speech within an entry are separated by a black triangle ▶ and are given on a new line. They are given in their abbreviated form (*n* for noun, *adj* for adjective, etc). For the full list of abbreviations, look at page vi.

> **glue** [glu:] *n* colle *f*
> ▶*vb* coller

▷ Choosing the right translation

The main translation of a word is shown after the part of speech. If there is more than one main translation for a word, each one is numbered. You may also sometimes find bracketed words in *italics* which give you some context. They help you to choose the translation you want.

pool [pu:l] *n* ❶ *(for swimming)* piscine *f* ❷ *(pond)*
étang *m* ❸ *(puddle)* flaque *f* ❹ *(game)*
billard *m* américain ▷ *let's have a game of pool.*
Jouons au billard américain

Often you will see phrases in *italics*, preceded by a white triangle ▷.
These are examples of the word being used in context.

numérique [nymeʀik] *adj* digital ▷ *un*
appareil photo numérique a digital camera

Phrases in **bold type** are phrases which are particularly common and
important. Sometimes these phrases have a completely different
translation.

chausson [ʃosɔn] *nm* slipper; **un chausson aux**
pommes an apple turnover

Once you have found the right translation, remember that you may
need to adapt the French word you have found. You may need to
make a **noun** plural, or make an **adjective** feminine or plural.
Remember that the feminine form is given for nouns and adjectives,
and that irregular plural forms are given also.

dancer ['dɑːnsəʳ] *n* danseur *m*, danseuse *f*

horse [hɔːs] *n* cheval *m* (*pl* chevaux)

salty [sɔːltɪ] *adj* salé(e)

You may also need to adapt the **verb**. Verbs are given in the infinitive
form, but you may want to use them in the present, past or future
tense. To do this, use the **verb tables** in the last section of the
dictionary.

▷ **Remember!**
Never take the first translation you see. Always look to see if there is
more than one translation, or more than one part of speech.

ABBREVIATIONS

abbr	abbreviation
adj	adjective
adv	adverb
art	article
conj	conjunction
excl	exclamation
f	feminine
n	noun
nf	feminine noun
nm	masculine noun
nmf	masculine or feminine noun
nm/f	masculine or feminine noun
npl	plural noun
num	number
pp	past participle
pt	past tense
prep	preposition
pron	pronoun
sg	singular
vb	verb

SYMBOLS

▷	example
▶	new part of speech
◉	new meaning

Note that to help you decide whether to use **le**, **la** or **l'** in front of a word starting with 'h', the article is given for all the nouns in letter **H** on the **French-English** side of the dictionary.

PHONETIC TRANSCRIPTION

CONSONANTS

NB. **p, b, t, d, k, g** are not aspirated in French.

poupée	p	puppy
bombe	b	baby
tente thermal	t	tent
dinde	d	daddy
coq qui képi	k	cork kiss chord
gage bague	g	gag guess
sale ce nation	s	so rice kiss
zéro rose	z	cousin buzz
tache chat	ʃ	sheep sugar
gilet juge	ʒ	pleasure beige
	tʃ	church
	dʒ	judge general
fer phare	f	farm raffle
verveine	v	very revel
	θ	thin maths
	ð	that other
lent salle	l	little ball
rare rentrer	R	
	r	rat rare
maman femme	m	mummy comb
non bonne	n	no ran
agneau vigne	ɲ	
	h	hat rehearse
yeux paille pied	j	yet
nouer oui	w	wall wail
huile lui	ɥ	
	x	loch

MISCELLANEOUS

ʳ	in English transcription: final r can be pronounced before a vowel
'	in French wordlist: no liaison before aspirate h

vii

PHONETIC TRANSCRIPTION

VOWELS

NB. The pairing of some vowel sounds only indicates approximate equivalence.

ici vie lyrique	i i:	heel bead
	ɪ	hit pity
jouer été	e	
lait jouet merci	ɛ	set tent
plat amour	a æ	bat apple
bas pâte	ɑ ɑ:	after car calm
	ʌ	fun cousin
le premier	ə	over above
beurre peur	œ	
peu deux	ø ə:	urgent fern work
or homme	ɔ	wash pot
mot eau gauche	o ɔ:	born cork
genou roue	u	full hook
	u:	boom shoe
rue urne	y	

DIPHTHONGS

	ɪə	beer tier
	ɛə	tear fair there
	eɪ	date plaice day
	aɪ	life buy cry
	au	owl foul now
	əu	low no
	ɔɪ	boil boy oily
	uə	poor tour

NASAL VOWELS

matin plein	ɛ̃	
brun	œ̃	
sang an dans	ɑ̃	
non pont	ɔ̃	

In general, we give the pronunciation of each entry in square brackets after the word in question. However, on the English-French side, where the entry is composed of two or more unhyphenated words, each of which is given elsewhere in this dictionary, you will find the pronunciation of each word in its alphabetical position.

a

a [a] *vb see* **avoir**; **Elle a beaucoup d'amis.** She has a lot of friends.; **Il a mangé des frites.** He had some fries.; **Il a neigé pendant la nuit.** It snowed during the night.; **il y a (1)** there is ▷ *Il y a un bon film à la télé.* There's a good film on TV. **(2)** there are ▷ *Il y a beaucoup de monde.* There are lots of people.

à [a] *prep* ❶ at ▷ *être à la maison* to be at home ▷ *à trois heures* at 3 o'clock ❷ in ▷ *être à Truro* to be in Truro ▷ *habiter au Portugal* to live in Portugal ▷ *habiter à la campagne* to live in the country ▷ *au printemps* in the spring ▷ *au mois de juin* in June ❸ to ▷ *aller à Regina* to go to Regina ▷ *aller au Portugal* to go to Portugal ▷ *aller à la campagne* to go to the country ▷ *donner quelque chose à quelqu'un* to give something to somebody ▷ *Cette veste appartient à ma sœur.* This jacket belongs to my sister. ▷ *Je n'ai rien à faire.* I have nothing to do.; **Ce livre est à mon père.** This book is my father's.; **Cette voiture est à nous.** This car is ours. ❹ by ▷ *à bicyclette* by bicycle ▷ *être payé à l'heure* to be paid by the hour; **à pied** on foot; **C'est à côté de chez moi.** It's near my house.; **C'est à dix kilomètres d'ici.** It's 10 kilometres from here.; **C'est à dix minutes d'ici.** It's 10 minutes from here.; **cent kilomètres à l'heure** 100 kilometres an hour; **À bientôt!** See you soon! **À demain!** See you tomorrow! **À samedi!** See you on Saturday! **À tout à l'heure!** See you later!

abandonner [abɑ̃dɔne] *vb* ❶ to abandon ▷ *Elle a abandonné sa voiture à côté de la route.* She abandoned her car at the side of the road. ❷ to quit ▷ *J'ai décidé d'abandonner mes leçons de natation.* I've decided to quit swimming lessons.

abeille [abɛj] *nf* bee

abîmer [abime] *vb* to damage; **s'abîmer** to get damaged

aboiteau [abwato] (*pl* **aboiteaux**) *nm* aboiteau

abolir [abɔliʀ] *vb* (*law, custom*) to do away with

abonnement [abɔnmɑ̃] *nm* ❶ season ticket ❷ (*to magazine*) subscription

s'abonner [abɔne] *vb*: **s'abonner à une revue** to take out a subscription to a magazine

abord [abɔʀ] *nm*: **d'abord** first ▷ *Je vais rentrer chez moi d'abord.* I'll go home first.

aboyer [abwaje] *vb* to bark

abri [abʀi] *nm* shelter; **être à l'abri** to be under cover; **se mettre à l'abri** to take shelter

abricot [abʀiko] *nm* apricot

s'abriter [abʀite] *vb* to take shelter

absence [apsɑ̃s] *nf* absence; **Il est passé pendant ton absence.** He came while you were away.

absent [apsɑ̃, -ɑ̃t] (*f* **absente**) *adj* absent

Acadie [akadi] *nf* Acadia ▷ *Mes ancêtres étaient originaires de l'Acadie.* My ancestors were from Acadia.

acadien [akadjɛ̃, -ɛn] (*f* **acadienne**) *adj, n* Acadian; **un Acadien** (*man*) an Acadian; **une Acadienne** (*woman*) an Acadian; **les Acadiens** the Acadians

accélérateur [akseleʀatœʀ] *nm* accelerator

accélérer [akseleʀe] *vb* to accelerate

accent [aksɑ̃] *nm* accent ▷ *Elle a l'accent de Terre-Neuve.* She has a Newfoundland accent.; **un accent aigu** an acute accent; **un accent grave** a grave accent; **un accent circonflexe** a circumflex

accentuer [aksɑ̃tɥe] *vb* to stress

accepter [aksɛpte] *vb* to accept; **accepter de faire quelque chose** to agree to do something

accès [aksɛ] *nm* access ▷ *avoir accès à quelque chose* to have access to something; **être d'accès facile** to be approachable

accessoire [aksɛswaʀ] *nm* ❶ accessory ▷ *les accessoires de mode* fashion accessories ❷ prop

accident [aksidɑ̃] *nm* accident ▷ *un accident de la route* a road accident ▷ *Elle a eu un accident de ski.* She had a skiing accident.; **par accident** by chance

accompagner [akɔ̃paɲe] *vb* to accompany

accomplir [akɔ̃pliʀ] *vb* to carry out ▷ *Il n'a pas réussi à accomplir cette tâche.* He didn't manage to carry out this task.

accord [akɔʀ] *nm* agreement; **être d'accord** to agree ▷ *Tu es d'accord avec moi?* Do you agree with me?; **se mettre d'accord** to come to an agreement; **D'accord!** OK!

accordéon [akɔʀdeɔ̃] *nm* accordion ▷ *Il joue de l'accordéon.* He plays the accordion.

accorder [akɔʀde] *vb* ❶ to grant ▷ *accorder la permission* to grant permission ▷ *accorder une guitare* to tune a guitar ❷ (*grammatically*) to make agree ▷ *accorder un adjectif avec un nom* to make an adjective agree with a noun; **s'accorder** to agree ▷ *Ils s'accordent pour dire que le film est ennuyant.* They agree that the movie is boring.

accotement [akɔtmɑ̃] *nm* shoulder ▷ *Elle s'est stationnée sur l'accotement.* She parked on the shoulder.

accrochage [akʀɔʃaʒ] *nm* fender-bender

accrocher [akʀɔʃe] *vb*: **accrocher quelque chose à (1)** to hang something on ▷ *Il a accroché sa veste au portemanteau.* He hung his jacket on the coat rack. **(2)** to hitch something up to ▷ *Ils ont accroché la remorque à leur voiture.* They hitched the trailer up to their car.; **s'accrocher à quelque chose** to catch on something ▷ *Sa jupe s'est accrochée à une branche.* Her skirt got caught on a branch.

s'accroupir [akʀupiʀ] *vb* to squat down

accueil [akœj] *nm* welcome ▷ *un accueil chaleureux* a warm welcome.; **Elle s'occupe de l'accueil des visiteurs.** She's in charge of looking after visitors.

accueillant [akœjã, -ãt] (f **accueillante**) adj welcoming ▷ Ses parents ont été très accueillants. Her parents were very welcoming.

accueillir [akœjiʀ] vb to welcome

accumuler [akymyle] vb to accumulate; **s'accumuler** to pile up

accusé [akyze] nm accused ▷ L'accusé a déclaré que... The accused stated that...

accusée [akyze] nf accused

accuser [akyze] vb to accuse ▷ **accuser quelqu'un de quelque chose** to accuse somebody of something

achat [aʃa] nm purchase; **faire des achats** to do some shopping

acheter [aʃte] vb to buy ▷ J'ai acheté des livres à la librairie. I bought some books at the bookstore.; **acheter quelque chose à quelqu'un (1)** to buy something for somebody ▷ Qu'est-ce que tu lui as acheté pour son anniversaire? What did you buy her for her birthday? **(2)** to buy something from somebody ▷ J'ai acheté des œufs au fermier. I bought some eggs from the farmer.

achigan [aʃigã] nm (fish) bass

acide [asid] nm acid

acier [asje] nm steel

acné [akne] nf acne ▷ Elle a de l'acné. She has acne.

acquérir [akeʀiʀ] vb to acquire

acquis [aki] vb see **acquérir**

acquitter [akite] vb to acquit ▷ L'accusé a été acquitté. The accused was acquitted.

acrobate [akʀɔbat] nmf acrobat

acrobatie [akʀɔbasi] nf acrobatics

acte [akt(ə)] nm act; **un acte de naissance** a birth certificate

acteur [aktœʀ] nm actor ▷ Il est acteur. He's an actor. ▷ un acteur de cinéma a film actor

actif [aktif, -iv] (f **active**) adj active

action [aksjɔ̃] nf action; **une bonne action** a good deed

Action de grâce nf Thanksgiving

s'activer [aktive] vb ❶ to bustle about ▷ Elle s'activait à préparer le repas. She bustled about preparing the meal. ❷ to get moving ▷ Allez! Active-toi! Come on! Get moving!

activité [aktivite] nf activity

actrice [aktʀis] nf actress ▷ Elle est actrice. She's an actress. ▷ une actrice de cinéma a film actress

actualité [aktɥalite] nf current events; **un problème d'actualité** a current issue; **les actualités** the news

actuel [aktɥɛl] (f **actuelle**) adj present ▷ le système actuel the present system; **à l'heure actuelle** at the present time

actuellement [aktɥɛlmã] adv at present

adaptateur [adaptatœʀ] nm adapter

adaptation [adaptasjɔ̃] nf adaptation ▷ une adaptation télévisée d'un roman a TV adaptation of a novel

addition [adisjɔ̃] nf bill ▷ L'addition, s'il vous plaît! Can we have the bill, please?

additionner [adisjɔne] vb to add up

adhésif [adezif, -iv] (f **adhésive**) adj: **le ruban**

adhésif sticky tape

adieu [adjø] excl farewell!

adjectif [adʒɛktif] nm adjective

admettre [admɛtʀ(ə)] vb ❶ to admit ▷ Il refuse d'admettre qu'il s'est trompé. He won't admit that he made a mistake. ❷ to allow ▷ Les chiens ne sont pas admis dans le restaurant. Dogs are not allowed in the restaurant.

administration [administʀasjɔ̃] nf administration

admirable [admiʀabl(ə)] adj wonderful

admirateur [admiʀatœʀ] nm admirer

admiratrice [admiʀatʀis] nf admirer

admirer [admiʀe] vb to admire

admis [admi] vb see **admettre**

adolescence [adɔlesɑ̃s] nf adolescence

adolescent [adɔlesɑ̃] nm teenager

adolescente [adɔlesɑ̃t] nf teenager

adopter [adɔpte] vb to adopt

adoptif [adɔptif, -iv] (f **adoptive**) adj ❶ adopted ▷ un enfant adoptif an adopted child ❷ adoptive ▷ les parents adoptifs the adoptive parents

adorable [adɔʀabl(ə)] adj lovely

adorer [adɔʀe] vb to love ▷ Il adore le chocolat. He loves chocolate. ▷ J'adore jouer au tennis. I love playing tennis.

adresse [adʀɛs] nf address; **mon adresse électronique** my e-mail address

adresser [adʀese] vb: **adresser la parole à quelqu'un** to speak to someone; **s'adresser à quelqu'un (1)** to speak to somebody ▷ C'est à toi que je m'adresse. It's you I'm speaking to. **(2)** to go and see somebody ▷ Adressez-vous à la patronne. Go and see the boss. ▷ Adressez-vous au bureau de renseignements. Ask at the information desk. **(3)** to be aimed at somebody ▷ Ce film s'adresse surtout aux enfants. This film is aimed mainly at children.

adulte [adylt(ə)] nmf adult

adverbe [advɛʀb(ə)] nm adverb

adversaire [advɛʀsɛʀ] nmf opponent

aérien [aeʀjɛ̃, -ɛn] (f **aérienne**) adj: **une compagnie aérienne** an airline

aérobic [aeʀɔbik] nm aerobics ▷ Elle fait de l'aérobic. She does aerobics.

aérogare [aeʀɔgaʀ] nf (airport) terminal

aéroport [aeʀɔpɔʀ] nm airport

affaire [afɛʀ] nf ❶ case ▷ une affaire de vol a case of theft ❷ business ▷ Leur affaire marche bien. Their business is doing well.; **une bonne affaire** a real bargain; **Ça fera l'affaire.** This will do nicely.; **avoir affaire à quelqu'un** to deal with somebody

affaires [afɛʀ] nfpl ❶ things ▷ Va chercher tes affaires! Go and get your things! ❷ business ▷ Les affaires marchent bien en ce moment. Business is good at the moment. ❸ **Mêle-toi de tes affaires.** (informal) Mind your own business.; **une femme d'affaires** a businesswoman

affection [afɛksjɔ̃] nf affection

affectueux [afɛktɥø, -øz] (f **affectueuse**) adj affectionate

affiche [afiʃ] nf poster

afficher [afiʃe] vb (a notice) to post ▷ Ils ont affiché les résultats dans le couloir. They've posted the results in the hallway.; **« Défense d'afficher »** "Post no bills"

affilée [afile]: **d'affilée** adv at a stretch ▷ Elle a travaillé douze heures d'affilée. She worked 12 hours at a stretch.

affirmation [afiʀmasjɔ̃] nf assertion

affirmer [afiʀme] vb to claim ▷ Il a affirmé que c'était la vérité. He claimed it was the truth.; **s'affirmer** to assert oneself ▷ Il est trop timide, il faut qu'il s'affirme. He's too shy, he should assert himself.

affluence [aflyɑ̃s] nf: **les heures d'affluence** rush hour ▷ Durant les heures d'affluence, les autobus passent toutes les sept minutes. During rush hour, buses come every 7 minutes.

s'**affoler** [afɔle] vb to panic ▷ Ne t'affole pas! Don't panic!

affranchir [afʀɑ̃ʃiʀ] vb to stamp ▷ Elle a affranchi mon passeport. She stamped my passport.

affreux [afʀø, -øz] (f **affreuse**) adj awful

affronter [afʀɔ̃te] vb to face ▷ Vancouver affronte Montréal en finale. Vancouver will face Montréal in the final.

afin de [afɛ̃d(ə)] conj: **afin de faire quelque chose** in order to do something ▷ Je me suis levé très tôt afin d'être prêt à temps. I got up very early in order to be ready on time.

afin que [afɛ̃k(ə)] conj so that ▷ Il m'a téléphoné afin que je sois prêt à temps. He phoned me so that I'd be ready on time.

agacer [agase] vb to get on somebody's nerves ▷ Tu m'agaces avec tes questions! You're getting on my nerves with all your questions!

âge [ɑʒ] nm age; **Quel âge as-tu?** How old are you?

âgé [ɑʒe] (f **âgée**) adj old ▷ Mon grand-père est âgé. My grandfather's old. ▷ Elle est âgée de dix ans. She's 10 years old.; **les personnes âgées** the elderly

agence [aʒɑ̃s] nf agency ▷ l'agence pour l'emploi the employment agency; **une agence de voyages** a travel agency; **une agence immobilière** a real estate agency

agenda [aʒɛ̃da] nm (daybook) agenda ▷ J'ai perdu mon agenda. I've lost my agenda.

s'**agenouiller** [aʒnuje] vb to kneel down

agent [aʒɑ̃] nm: **un agent d'infiltration** a secret agent; **un agent de police** a police officer; **un agent de la GRC** a Mountie

agente [aʒɑ̃t] nf: **une agente d'infiltration** a secret agent; **une agente de police** a police officer; **une agente de bord** a flight attendant

agglomération [aglɔmeʀasjɔ̃] nf urban area; **l'agglomération de Toronto** Greater Toronto

aggraver [agʀave] vb to make worse; **s'aggraver** to get worse

agir [aʒiʀ] vb ❶ to act ▷ Il a agi par vengeance. He acted out of revenge. ❷ to take effect ▷ Ce médicament agit très vite. This medicine takes effect quickly.; **Il s'agit de...** It's about... ▷ Il s'agit du club d'art dramatique. It's about the drama club. ▷ De quoi s'agit-il? What is it about?; **Il s'agit de faire attention.** We must be careful.

agité [aʒite] (f **agitée**) adj ❶ restless ▷ Les élèves sont agités. The students are restless. ❷ rough ▷ La mer est agitée. The sea is rough.; **un sommeil agité** troubled sleep

agiter [aʒite] vb to shake ▷ Agitez la bouteille. Shake the bottle.

agneau [aɲo] (pl **agneaux**) nm lamb

agrafe [agʀaf] nf (for papers) staple

agrafeuse [agʀaføz] nf stapler

agrandir [agʀɑ̃diʀ] vb ❶ to enlarge ▷ J'ai fait agrandir mes photos. I got my photos enlarged. ❷ to extend ▷ Ils ont agrandi leur jardin. They've extended their garden.; **s'agrandir** to expand ▷ Leur magasin s'est agrandi. Their store has expanded.

agréable [agʀeabl(ə)] adj nice

agréer [agʀee] vb: **Veuillez agréer, Madame, l'expression de mes sentiments distingués. Jane Ormal.** Yours sincerely, Jane Ormal.

agressif [agʀesif, -iv] (f **agressive**) adj aggressive

agressivité [agʀesivite] nf aggression; **faire preuve d'agressivité envers quelqu'un** to be aggressive towards somebody; **l'agressivité au volant** road rage

agricole [agʀikɔl] adj agricultural ▷ le matériel agricole agricultural machinery; **une exploitation agricole** a farm

agriculteur [agʀikyltœʀ] nm farmer; **Il est agriculteur.** He's a farmer.

agricultrice [agʀikyltʀis] nf farmer; **Elle est agricultrice.** She's a farmer.

agriculture [agʀikyltyʀ] nf farming

ai [e] vb see **avoir**; **J'ai deux chats.** I have two cats.; **J'ai bien dormi.** I slept well.

aide [ɛd] nf ❶ help ▷ J'ai besoin de ton aide. I need your help. ▷ appeler quelqu'un à l'aide to call to somebody for help; **À l'aide!** Help! ❷ aid ▷ une aide financière financial aid; **à l'aide de** using ▷ J'ai réussi à ouvrir la boîte de conserve à l'aide d'un couteau. I managed to open the can using a knife.

aide-infirmier (pl **aides-infirmiers**) nm nurse's aid; **Il est aide-infirmier.** He's a nurse's aid.

aide-infirmière (pl **aides-infirmières**) nf nurse's aid ▷ Elle est aide-infirmière. She is a nurse's aid.

aider [ede] vb to help

aie [ɛ] vb see **avoir**

aïe [aj] excl Ouch!

aigre [ɛgʀ(ə)] adj sour

aigu [egy] (f **aiguë**) adj (pain) sharp ▷ J'ai ressenti une douleur aiguë dans le bas du dos. I felt a sharp pain in my lower back.; **e accent aigu** e with an acute accent

aiguille [eguij] nf needle ▷ une aiguille à tricoter a knitting needle; **les aiguilles d'une montre** the hands of a watch

ail [aj] nm garlic

aile [ɛl] nf wing

aille [aj] vb see **aller**

ailleurs [ajœʀ] adv somewhere else; **partout ailleurs** everywhere else; **nulle part ailleurs** nowhere else; **d'ailleurs** besides

aimable [ɛmabl(ə)] adj kind

aimant [ɛmɑ̃] nm magnet

aimer [eme] vb ❶ to love ▷ *Il aime ses enfants.* He loves his children. ❷ to like ▷ *Tu aimes le chocolat?* Do you like chocolate? ▷ *J'aime bien cette fille.* I like this girl. ▷ *J'aime jouer au tennis.* I like playing tennis. ▷ *J'aimerais aller en Grèce.* I'd like to go to Greece. ▷ **J'aimerais mieux ne pas y aller.** I'd rather not go.

aîné [ene] (f **aînée**) adj elder ▷ *mon frère aîné* my big brother
▶ nm oldest child ▷ *Il est l'aîné.* He's the oldest child.

aînée [ene] nf oldest child ▷ *Elle est l'aînée.* She's the oldest child.

ainsi [ɛ̃si] adv in this way ▷ *Il faut faire ainsi.* This is the way to do it.; **C'est ainsi qu'il a réussi.** That's how he succeeded.; **ainsi que** as well as; **et ainsi de suite** and so on

air [ɛʀ] nm ❶ air ▷ *l'air chaud* warm air; **prendre l'air** to get some fresh air ❷ tune ▷ *Elle a joué un air au piano.* She played a tune on the piano.; **Elle a l'air fatiguée.** She looks tired.; **Il a l'air d'un clown.** He looks like a clown.

aire de jeux [ɛʀ-] nf playground

aire de repos [ɛʀ-] nf (on highway) rest area

aise [ɛz] nf: **être à l'aise** to be at ease ▷ *Elle est à l'aise avec tout le monde.* She's at ease with everybody.; **être mal à l'aise** to be ill at ease; **se mettre à l'aise** to make oneself comfortable

ait [ɛ] vb see **avoir**

ajouter [aʒute] vb to add

alarme [alaʀm(ə)] nf alarm ▷ *donner l'alarme* to raise the alarm

Alberta nf Alberta

album [albɔm] nm album

alcool [alkɔl] nm alcohol ▷ *Je ne bois pas d'alcool.* I don't drink alcohol.; **les alcools forts** spirits

alcoolisé [alkɔlize] (f **alcoolisée**) adj alcoholic; **une boisson non alcoolisée** a soft drink

alentours [alɑ̃tuʀ] nmpl: **dans les alentours** in the area; **aux alentours d'Ottawa** in the Ottawa area; **aux alentours de cinq heures** around 5 o'clock

algèbre [alʒɛbʀ(ə)] nf algebra

algue [alg(ə)] nf seaweed

alibi [alibi] nm alibi

aliment [alimɑ̃] nm food ▷ *Le fromage est un aliment très nutritif.* Cheese is a very nutritious food. ▷ *les aliments solides* solid food; **les aliments naturels** health food ▷ *un magasin d'aliments naturels* a health food store

alimentaire [alimɑ̃tɛʀ] adj ❶ food ▷ *un groupe alimentaire* a food group ▷ *une banque alimentaire* a food bank; **Le guide alimentaire canadien** Canada's Food Guide ❷ eating ▷ *nos habitudes alimentaires* our eating habits

alimentation [alimɑ̃tasjɔ̃] nf diet ▷ *Elle a une alimentation saine.* She has a healthy diet.

allée [ale] nf ❶ path ▷ *les allées du parc* the paths in the park ❷ (in street names) drive; **les allées et venues** comings and goings

allégé [aleʒe] (f **allégée**) adj low-fat ▷ *un yogourt allégé* a low-fat yogurt

aller [ale] vb ❶ to go ▷ *Elle est allée à Edmonton.* She went to Edmonton. ▷ *Je dois y aller.* I've got to go. ▷ *Elle ira le voir.* She'll go and see him. ▷ *Je vais me fâcher.* I'm going to get angry.; **s'en aller** to go away ▷ *Je m'en vais demain.* I'm leaving tomorrow.; **aller bien à quelqu'un** to suit somebody ▷ *Cette robe te va bien.* This dress suits you.; **Allez! Dépêche-toi!** Come on! Hurry up!; **« Comment allez-vous? » « Je vais bien. »** "How are you?" "I'm fine."; **« Comment ça va? » « Ça va bien. »** "How are you?" "I'm fine."; **aller mieux** (after an illness) to be better
▶ nm ❶ outward journey ▷ *L'aller nous a pris trois heures.* The journey there took us three hours. ❷ one-way ticket ▷ *Je voudrais un aller pour Halifax.* I'd like a one-way ticket to Halifax.; **un aller simple** a one-way ticket; **un aller et retour** (1) a return ticket ▷ *Je voudrais deux allers et retours pour Montréal.* I'd like two return tickets to Montréal. (2) a round trip ▷ *Elle a fait l'aller et retour en dix heures.* She did the round trip in ten hours.

allergie [alɛʀʒi] nf allergy ▷ *J'ai des allergies.* I have allergies.; **une allergie alimentaire** a food allergy

allergique [alɛʀʒik] adj: **allergique à** allergic to ▷ *Je suis allergique aux poils de chat.* I'm allergic to cat hair.

allô [alo] excl (on phone) Hello! ▷ *Allô! Je voudrais parler à la directrice.* Hello! I'd like to speak to the principal.

s'allonger [alɔ̃ʒe] vb to lie down ▷ *Il s'est allongé sur son lit.* He lay down on his bed.

allophone [alɔfɔn] adj allophone
▶ nmf allophone

allumer [alyme] vb ❶ to turn on ▷ *Tu peux allumer la lumière?* Can you turn the light on? ▷ *Allume la radio.* Switch on the radio. ❷ to light ▷ *Elle a allumé une bougie.* She lit a candle.; **s'allumer** (light) to come on ▷ *La lumière s'est allumée.* The light came on.

allumette [alymɛt] nf match ▷ *une boîte d'allumettes* a box of matches

allure [alyʀ] nf ❶ speed ▷ *à toute allure* at top speed ❷ look ▷ *avoir une drôle d'allure* to look odd

alors [alɔʀ] adv ❶ then ▷ *Tu as fini? Alors je m'en vais.* Are you finished? I'm going then. ❷ so ▷ *Alors je lui ai dit de partir.* So I told him to leave.; **Et alors?** So what? ❸ at that time ▷ *Elle habitait alors à Vancouver.* She was living in Vancouver at that time.; **alors que** (1) as ▷ *Il est arrivé alors que je partais.* He arrived just as I was leaving. (2) while ▷ *Alors que je travaillais dur, lui se reposait.* While I was working hard, he was resting.

alphabet [alfabɛ] nm alphabet

alphabétique [alfabetik] adj alphabetical ▷ *par ordre alphabétique* in alphabetical order

aluminium [alyminjɔm] nm aluminum

amande [amɑ̃d] nf almond; **la pâte d'amandes** marzipan

amant [amɑ̃] nm lover

amante [amɑ̃t] nf lover

amateur [amatœʀ] (f **amateur**) adj amateur ▷ *Elle est pianiste amateur.* She's an amateur pianist.

▶ *nm* ❶ amateur; **en amateur** as a hobby ▷ *Il fait de la photo en amateur.* He takes photos as a hobby. ❷ fan; **C'est un amateur de jazz.** He's a jazz fan.

amatrice [amatʀis] *nf* ❶ amateur; **en amatrice** as a hobby ▷ *Elle joue du violon classique en amatrice.* She plays classical violin as a hobby. ❷ fan; **C'est une amatrice de sport.** She's a sports fan.

ambiance [ãbjãs] *nf* atmosphere ▷ *Je n'aime pas l'ambiance ici.* I don't like the atmosphere here. ▷ *Il y a de l'ambiance dans ce café.* This café has a lot of atmosphere.; **la musique d'ambiance** background music

ambitieux [ãbisjø, -øz] (*f* **ambitieuse**) *adj* ambitious

ambition [ãbisjõ] *nf* ambition ▷ *Elle a l'ambition de devenir première ministre.* Her ambition is to become Prime Minister.; **Il a beaucoup d'ambition.** He's very ambitious.

ambulance [ãbylãs] *nf* ambulance

ambulancier [ãbylãsje] *nm* ambulance driver

ambulancière [ãbylãsjɛʀ] *nf* ambulance driver

âme [ɑm] *nf* soul

amélioration [ameljɔʀasjõ] *nf* improvement

améliorer [ameljɔʀe] *vb* to improve; **s'améliorer** to improve ▷ *Le temps s'améliore.* The weather's improving.

amende [amãd] *nf* fine ▷ *une amende de cinquante dollars* a 50 dollar fine

amener [amne] *vb* to bring ▷ *Qu'est-ce qui t'amène?* What brings you here? ▷ *Est-ce que je peux amener un ami?* Can I bring a friend?

amer [amɛʀ] (*f* **amère**) *adj* bitter

ami [ami] *nm* friend; **C'est son petit ami.** He's her boyfriend.

amical [amikal, -o] (*f* **amicale**, *mpl* **amicaux**) *adj* friendly

amie [ami] *nf* friend; **C'est sa petite amie.** She's his girlfriend.

amitié [amitje] *nf* friendship; **Fais mes amitiés à tes parents.** Give my regards to your parents.; **Amitiés** (*in letter*) Regards

amour [amuʀ] *nm* love ▷ *l'amour paternel* paternal love; **faire l'amour** to make love

amoureux [amuʀø, -øz] (*f* **amoureuse**) *adj* in love ▷ *être amoureux de quelqu'un* to be in love with somebody

amour-propre [amuʀpʀɔpʀ(ə)] *nm* self-esteem

amplement [ãpləmã] *adv*: **Nous avons amplement le temps.** We have plenty of time.

ampoule [ãpul] *nf* ❶ light bulb ❷ blister ▷ *J'ai une ampoule au pied.* I have a blister on my foot.

amusant [amyzã, -ãt] (*f* **amusante**) *adj* amusing

amuse-gueule [amyzgœl] *nmpl* snacks

amuser [amyze] *vb* to amuse; **s'amuser (1)** to play ▷ *Les enfants s'amusent dehors.* The children are playing outside. **(2)** to enjoy oneself ▷ *On s'est bien amusés à cette soirée.* We really enjoyed ourselves at that party.

amygdales [amidal] *nfpl* tonsils ▷ *se faire opérer des amygdales* to have one's tonsils removed

amygdalite [amidalit] *nf* tonsilitis

an [ã] *nm* year; **avoir neuf ans** to be nine years old; **le jour de l'An** New Year's Day; **le Nouvel An** New Year's

analyse [analiz] *nf* ❶ analysis ❷ (*medical*) test ▷ *une analyse de sang* a blood test

analyser [analize] *vb* to analyse

ananas [anana] *nm* pineapple

ancêtre [ãsɛtʀ(ə)] *nmf* ancestor

anchois [ãʃwa] *nm* anchovy

ancien [ãsjɛ̃, -ɛn] (*f* **ancienne**) *adj* ❶ former ▷ *C'est une ancienne élève.* She's a former student. ❷ old ▷ *notre ancienne voiture* our old car ❸ antique ▷ *un fauteuil ancien* an antique chair

ancre [ãkʀ(ə)] *nf* anchor

âne [ɑn] *nm* donkey

ange [ãʒ] *nm* angel; **être aux anges** to be over the moon

anglais [ãglɛ, -ɛz] (*f* **anglaise**) *adj, n* English ▷ *la grammaire anglaise* English grammar ▷ *Est-ce que vous parlez anglais?* Do you speak English?

angle [ãgl(ə)] *nm* ❶ angle ▷ *un angle droit* a right angle ❷ corner ▷ *à l'angle de la rue* at the corner of the street

anglophone [ãglɔfɔn] *adj* Anglophone ▷ *une communauté anglophone* an Anglophone community

▶ *nmf* Anglophone ▷ *Beaucoup d'anglophones habitent à Montréal.* A lot of Anglophones live in Montréal.

angoissé [ãgwase] (*f* **angoissée**) *adj* anxious ▷ *Il était angoissé à l'idée de prendre l'avion.* He was anxious about flying.

animal [animal, -o] (*pl* **animaux**) *nm* animal

animal de compagnie *nm* pet; **« les animaux de compagnie ne sont pas acceptés »** "No pets"

animalerie [animalʀi] *nf* pet shop

animateur [animatœʀ] *nm* ❶ host ▷ *Il est animateur à la télé.* He's a TV host. ❷ youth leader ▷ *Il est animateur au centre sportif.* He is a youth leader at the sports centre.

animatrice [animatʀis] *nf* ❶ host ▷ *Elle est animatrice à la télé.* She's a TV host. ❷ youth leader ▷ *Elle est animatrice au centre sportif.* She is a youth leader at the sports centre.

animé [anime] (*f* **animée**) *adj* lively ▷ *Cette rue est très animée.* This is a very lively street.; **un dessin animé** a cartoon

anneau [ano] (*pl* **anneaux**) *nm* ring

année [ane] *nf* year ▷ *l'année dernière* last year ▷ *l'année prochaine* next year

anniversaire [anivɛʀsɛʀ] *nm* ❶ birthday ▷ *C'est l'anniversaire de ma sœur.* It's my sister's birthday. ❷ anniversary ▷ *un anniversaire de mariage* a wedding anniversary

annonce [anõs] *nf* ad ▷ *J'ai lu votre annonce dans le journal.* I saw your ad in the paper. ▷ *passer une annonce* to place an ad; **les petites annonces** the classified ads; **une annonce publicitaire** a commercial; **une annonce radiophonique** a radio ad; **une annonce télévisée** a TV commercial

annoncer [anõse] *vb* to announce ▷ *Ils ont*

annoncé leurs fiançailles. They've announced their engagement.

annuaire [anɥɛʁ] nm ❶ phone book ❷ yearbook

annuel [anɥɛl] (f **annuelle**) adj annual

annuler [anyle] vb to cancel

anonyme [anɔnim] adj anonymous

anorexie [anɔʁɛksi] nf anorexia

antenne [ɑ̃tɛn] nf ❶ aerial; **antenne parabolique** satellite dish; **être à l'antenne** to be on the air ❷ antenna

antibiotique [ɑ̃tibjɔtik] nm antibiotic

antigel [ɑ̃tiʒɛl] nm antifreeze

antimoustiques [ɑ̃timustik] (f+pl **antimoustiques**) adj insect repellent ▷ *une lotion antimoustiques* insect repellent lotion

antimoustiques [ɑ̃timustik] nm insect repellent

antipathique [ɑ̃tipatik] adj unpleasant ▷ *Je le trouve plutôt antipathique.* I find him rather unpleasant.

antiquaire [ɑ̃tikɛʁ] nmf antique dealer ▷ *Elle est antiquaire.* She's an antique dealer.

antiquité [ɑ̃tikite] nf antique ▷ *un magasin d'antiquités* an antique shop; **pendant l'Antiquité** in classical times

antivol [ɑ̃tivɔl] nm (on bike) lock

anxieux [ɑ̃ksjø, -øz] (f **anxieuse**) adj anxious ▷ *Il est anxieux de nature.* He's a born worrier.

août [u] nm August; **en août** in August.

apercevoir [apɛʁsəvwaʁ] vb to see ▷ *J'aperçois la côte.* I can see the shore.; **s'apercevoir de quelque chose** to notice something; **s'apercevoir que...** to notice that...

apparaître [apaʁɛtʁ(ə)] vb to appear

appareil [apaʁɛj] nm device; **un appareil orthodontique** braces; **les appareils ménagers** domestic appliances; **un appareil photo** a camera; **Qui est à l'appareil?** (on phone) Who's speaking?

apparemment [apaʁamɑ̃] adv apparently

apparence [apaʁɑ̃s] nf appearance

apparition [apaʁisjɔ̃] nf appearance ▷ *Il n'a fait qu'une brève apparition.* He appeared only briefly.

appartement [apaʁtəmɑ̃] nm apartment

appartenir [apaʁtəniʁ] vb: **appartenir à quelqu'un** to belong to somebody

apparu [apaʁy] vb see **apparaître**

appel [apɛl] nm ❶ cry ▷ *un appel au secours* a cry for help ❷ phone call; **faire appel à quelqu'un** to appeal to somebody; **formule d'appel** (in letter) salutation

appeler [aple] vb to call ▷ *Elle a appelé le médecin.* She called the doctor. ▷ *J'ai appelé mon cousin à Trois-Rivières.* I called my cousin in Trois-Rivières.; **s'appeler** to be called ▷ *Comment ça s'appelle?* What is it called? ▷ *Elle s'appelle Muriel.* Her name's Muriel. ▷ *Comment tu t'appelles?* What's your name?

appétissant [apetisɑ̃, -ɑ̃t] (f **appétissante**) adj appetizing

appétit [apeti] nm appetite; **Bon appétit!** Enjoy your meal!

applaudir [aplodiʁ] vb (applaud) to clap

applaudissements [aplodismɑ̃] nmpl applause

application [aplikasjɔ̃] (computer) application ▷ *lancer une application* to open an application

appliquer [aplike] vb ❶ to apply ❷ to enforce ▷ *appliquer la loi* to enforce the law; **s'appliquer** to apply oneself ▷ *Elle s'est appliquée à étudier.* She applied herself to studying.

apporter [apɔʁte] vb to bring

appréhender [apʁeɑ̃de] vb to dread ▷ *J'appréhende cette réunion.* I'm dreading this meeting.

apprendre [apʁɑ̃dʁ(ə)] vb ❶ to learn ▷ *apprendre quelque chose par cœur* to learn something by heart; **apprendre à faire quelque chose** to learn to do something ▷ *J'apprends à faire la cuisine.* I'm learning to cook. ❷ (news) to hear ▷ *J'ai appris son départ.* I heard that she had left.; **apprendre quelque chose à quelqu'un** (1) to teach somebody something ▷ *Ma mère m'a appris l'anglais.* My mother taught me English. ▷ *Elle lui a appris à conduire.* She taught him to drive. (2) to tell somebody something ▷ *Il m'a appris la nouvelle.* He told me the news.

apprentissage [apʁɑ̃tisaʒ] nm learning ▷ *On dit que l'apprentissage de l'arabe est très difficile.* They say learning Arabic is very difficult.

appris [apʁi] vb see **apprendre**

approbation [apʁɔbasjɔ̃] nf approval ▷ *donner son approbation* to give one's approval

approcher [apʁɔʃe] vb: **approcher de** to approach ▷ *Nous approchons de Fredericton.* We are approaching Fredericton.; **s'approcher de** to come close to ▷ *Ne t'approche pas, j'ai la grippe!* Don't get too close to me, I've got the flu!

approprié [apʁɔpʁije] (f **appropriée**) adj suitable ▷ *une réponse appropriée* a suitable answer

approuver [apʁuve] vb to approve of ▷ *Je n'approuve pas ses méthodes.* I don't approve of his methods.

approximatif [apʁɔksimatif, -iv] (f **approximative**) adj ❶ approximate ▷ *un prix approximatif* an approximate price ❷ rough ▷ *un calcul approximatif* a rough calculation

appui [apɥi] nm support ▷ *J'ai besoin de votre appui.* I need your support.

appuyer [apɥije] vb to lean ▷ *Elle a appuyé son vélo contre la porte.* She leaned her bike against the door.; **appuyer sur** to press ▷ *Appuyez sur le bouton.* Press the button.; **s'appuyer** to lean ▷ *Elle s'est appuyée contre le mur.* She leaned against the wall. ▷ *Il s'est appuyé sur la table.* He leaned on the table.

après [apʁɛ] prep, adv ❶ after ▷ *après le déjeuner* after lunch ▷ *après son départ* after he had left ▷ *après qu'il est parti* after he left ▷ *Nous viendrons après avoir fait la vaisselle.* We'll come after we've done the dishes. ❷ afterwards ▷ *aussitôt après* immediately afterwards; **après coup** afterwards ▷ *J'y ai repensé après coup.* I thought about it again afterwards.; **d'après**

according to ▷ *D'après elle, c'est une erreur.* According to her, that's a mistake.; **après tout** after all

après-demain [apʀɛdmɛ̃] *adv* the day after tomorrow

après-midi [apʀɛmidi] *m or nf* afternoon

arachide [aʀaʃid] *nf* peanut ▷ *le beurre d'arachide* peanut butter

araignée [aʀeɲe] *nf* spider

arbitre [aʀbitʀ(ə)] *nmf* ❶ referee ❷ umpire

arbre [aʀbʀ(ə)] *nm* tree; **un arbre généalogique** a family tree

arbuste [aʀbyst(ə)] *nm* shrub

arc [aʀk] *nm* bow ▷ *son arc et ses flèches* his bow and arrows

arc-en-ciel [aʀkɑ̃sjɛl] (*pl* **arcs-en-ciel**) *nm* rainbow

architecte [aʀʃitɛkt(ə)] *nmf* architect ▷ *Elle est architecte.* She's an architect.

architecture [aʀʃitɛktyʀ] *nf* architecture

aréna [aʀena] *nm* arena ▷ *On construit un nouvel aréna à Timmins.* They're building a new arena in Timmins.

arène [aʀɛn] *nf* bullring; **des arènes romaines** a Roman amphitheatre; **l'arène politique** the political arena

arête [aʀɛt] *nf* fish bone

argent [aʀʒɑ̃] *nm* ❶ silver ▷ *une bague en argent* a silver ring ❷ money ▷ *Je n'ai plus d'argent.* I have no more money.; **l'argent de poche** allowance ▷ *Est-ce que tu reçois de l'argent de poche chaque semaine?* Do you get a weekly allowance?; **l'argent liquide** cash

argile [aʀʒil] *nf* clay

argot [aʀgo] *nm* slang

arme [aʀm(ə)] *nf* weapon; **une arme à feu** a firearm

armée [aʀme] *nf* army; **l'armée de l'air** the Air Force

armoire [aʀmwaʀ] *nf* wardrobe

armure [aʀmyʀ] *nf* armour ▷ *un chevalier en armure* a knight in armour

arnaquer [aʀnake] *vb* (*informal*) to con

aromatisé [aʀomatize] (*f* **aromatisée**) *adj* flavoured

arôme [aʀom] *nm* ❶ aroma ❷ (*added to food*) flavouring; **arômes naturels** natural flavours

arpenter [aʀpɑ̃te] *vb* to pace up and down ▷ *Il arpentait le couloir.* He was pacing up and down the corridor.

arrache-pied [aʀaʃpje]: **d'arrache-pied** *adv* furiously ▷ *travailler d'arrache-pied* to work furiously

arracher [aʀaʃe] *vb* ❶ to take out ▷ *La dentiste m'a arraché une dent.* The dentist took one of my teeth out. ❷ to tear out ▷ *Arrachez la page.* Tear the page out. ❸ to pull up ▷ *Il a arraché les mauvaises herbes.* He pulled up the weeds.; **arracher quelque chose à quelqu'un** to snatch something from somebody

arranger [aʀɑ̃ʒe] *vb* ❶ to arrange ▷ *arranger des fleurs dans un vase* to arrange flowers in a vase ❷ to suit ▷ *Ça t'arrange de partir plus tôt?* Would it suit you to leave earlier?; **s'arranger** to come to an agreement ▷ *Arrangez-vous avec le patron.* You'll have to come to an agreement

with the boss.; **Je vais m'arranger pour venir.** I'll organize things so that I can come.; **Ça va s'arranger.** Things will work themselves out.

arrestation [aʀɛstasjɔ̃] *nf* arrest ▷ *en état d'arrestation* under arrest

arrêt [aʀɛ] *nm* stop ▷ *un arrêt d'autobus* a bus stop; **sans arrêt** (1) non-stop ▷ *Elle travaille sans arrêt.* She works non-stop. (2) continually ▷ *Ils se disputent sans arrêt.* They quarrel continually.

arrêter [aʀete] *vb* ❶ to stop; **Arrête!** Stop it!; **arrêter de faire quelque chose** to stop doing something ❷ to switch off ▷ *Il a arrêté le moteur.* He switched the engine off. ❸ to arrest ▷ *Ma voisine a été arrêtée.* My neighbour's been arrested.; **s'arrêter** to stop ▷ *Il s'est arrêté devant une vitrine.* He stopped in front of a store window.; **s'arrêter de faire quelque chose** to stop doing something ▷ *s'arrêter de fumer* to stop smoking

arrière [aʀjɛʀ] *nm* back ▷ *l'arrière de la maison* the back of the house; **à l'arrière** at the back; **en arrière** behind ▷ *Ils sont restés en arrière.* They stayed behind.

▶ *adj* (*f+pl* **arrière**) back ▷ *le siège arrière* the back seat ▷ *les roues arrière* the rear wheels

arrière-grand-mère [aʀjɛʀgʀɑ̃mɛʀ] (*pl* **arrière-grands-mères**) *nf* great-grandmother

arrière-grand-père [aʀjɛʀgʀɑ̃pɛʀ] (*pl* **arrière-grands-pères**) *nm* great-grandfather

arrivée [aʀive] *nf* arrival ▷ *l'arrivée des passagers* the passengers' arrival; **ligne d'arrivée** finish line ▷ *Elle a franchi la ligne d'arrivée.* She crossed the finish line.

arriver [aʀive] *vb* ❶ to arrive ▷ *J'arrive à l'école à huit heures.* I arrive at school at 8 o'clock. ❷ to happen ▷ *Qu'est-ce qui est arrivé à Mom?* What happened to Mom?; **arriver à faire quelque chose** to manage to do something ▷ *J'espère que je vais y arriver.* I hope I can manage it.; **Il m'arrive de dormir jusqu'à midi.** I sometimes sleep till noon.

arrogant [aʀogɑ̃, -ɑ̃t] (*f* **arrogante**) *adj* arrogant

arrondissement [aʀɔ̃dismɑ̃] *nm* district

arroser [aʀoze] *vb* to water ▷ *Il arrose ses tomates.* He is watering his tomatoes.

arrosoir [aʀozwaʀ] *nm* watering can

art [aʀ] *nm* art

artère [aʀtɛʀ] *nf* ❶ artery ❷ main road ▷ *les grandes artères de Calgary* the main roads of Calgary

article [aʀtikl(ə)] *nm* ❶ article ▷ *un article de journal* a newspaper article ❷ item ▷ *les articles en promotion* items on special; **un article de forum** (*on a listserv*) a post

articulation [aʀtikylasjɔ̃] *nf* joint ▷ *l'articulation du genou* the knee joint

articuler [aʀtikyle] *vb* to pronounce clearly

artificiel [aʀtifisjɛl] (*f* **artificielle**) *adj* artificial ▷ *des plantes artificielles* artificial plants

artisan [aʀtizɑ̃] *nm* (*self-employed*) crafter; **être artisan de quelque chose** to be the architect of something

artisanat [aʀtizana] nm crafts; **boutique d'artisanat** craft shop

artisane [aʀtizan] nf (self-employed) crafter

artiste [aʀtist(ə)] nmf ❶ artist ❷ performer

artistique [aʀtistik] adj artistic

arts plastiques nmpl fine arts

as [as] vb see **avoir**; **Tu as de beaux cheveux.** You have nice hair.
▷ nm ace ▷ **l'as de trèfle** the ace of clubs

ascenseur [asɑ̃sœʀ] nm elevator

aspect [aspɛ] nm appearance

asperge [aspɛʀʒ(ə)] nf asparagus

aspirateur [aspiʀatœʀ] nm vacuum cleaner; **passer l'aspirateur** to vacuum

aspirine [aspiʀin] nf aspirin

assaisonner [asɛzɔne] vb to season

assassin [asasɛ̃] nm murderer ▷ **Cette femme est un assassin.** This woman is a murderer.

assassiner [asasine] vb to murder

Assemblée des Premières Nations nf Assembly of First Nations

assembler [asɑ̃ble] vb to assemble; **s'assembler** to gather ▷ **Une foule énorme s'était assemblée.** A huge crowd had gathered.

s' asseoir [aswaʀ] vb to sit down ▷ **Asseyez-vous, s'il vous plaît.** Please sit down. ▷ **Assieds-toi à côté de moi.** Sit beside me.

assez [ase] adv ❶ enough ▷ **Nous n'avons pas assez de temps.** We don't have enough time. ▷ **Est-ce qu'il y a assez de pain?** Is there enough bread?; **j'en ai assez!** I've had enough! ❷ quite ▷ **Il faisait assez beau.** The weather was quite nice.

assiette [asjɛt] nf plate ▷ **une assiette à dessert** a dessert plate; **une assiette de charcuterie** assorted cold cuts

assis [asi, -iz] vb see **asseoir**
▷ adj (f **assise**) sitting ▷ **Elle est assise par terre.** She's sitting on the floor.

assistance [asistɑ̃s] nf ❶ audience ▷ **Y a-t-il un médecin dans l'assistance?** Is there a doctor in the audience? ❷ aid ▷ **l'assistance humanitaire** humanitarian aid ❸ assistance ▷ **avec l'assistance de quelqu'un** with the assistance of somebody

assistant [asistɑ̃] nm assistant

assistante [asistɑ̃t] nf assistant

assister [asiste] vb: **assister à un accident** to witness an accident; **assister à un cours** to attend a class; **assister à un concert** to be at a concert

association [asɔsjasjɔ̃] nf association

associé [asɔsje] nm (in business) partner

associée [asɔsje] nf (in business) partner

associer [asɔsje] vb to connect ▷ **J'associe l'été au camping.** I connect summer with camping.; **s'associer** to go into partnership

assommer [asɔme] vb to knock out ▷ **Un coup fort l'a assommé.** A heavy blow knocked him out.

assorti [asɔʀti] (f **assortie**) adj ❶ matching ▷ **des couleurs assorties** matching colours ❷ assorted ▷ **des chocolats assortis** assorted chocolates; **être assorti à quelque chose** to match something ▷ **Son sac à main est assorti à ses chaussures.** Her purse matches her shoes.

assortiment [asɔʀtimɑ̃] nm assortment

assurance [asyʀɑ̃s] nf ❶ insurance
▷ **une assurance maladie** medical insurance
❷ confidence ▷ **parler avec assurance** to speak with confidence

assurer [asyʀe] vb ❶ to insure ▷ **La maison est assurée.** The house is insured. ▷ **être assuré contre quelque chose** to be insured against something ❷ to assure ▷ **Je t'assure que c'est vrai!** I assure you it's true!; **s'assurer de quelque chose** to make sure of something ▷ **Il s'est assuré que la porte était fermée.** He made sure the door was shut.

asthme [asm(ə)] nm asthma ▷ **une crise d'asthme** an asthma attack

astronaute [astʀɔnot] nmf astronaut

astronome [astʀɔnɔm] nmf astronomer

astronomie [astʀɔnɔmi] nf astronomy

astucieux [astysjø, -øz] (f **astucieuse**) adj clever

atelier [atəlje] nm ❶ workshop ❷ (artist's) studio

athlète [atlɛt] nmf athlete

athlétisme [atletism(ə)] nm track and field ▷ **un championnat d'athlétisme** a track and field championship

atlas [atlas] nm atlas

atmosphère [atmɔsfɛʀ] nf atmosphere

atomique [atɔmik] adj atomic ▷ **la bombe atomique** the atomic bomb

atout [atu] nm ❶ asset ▷ **L'atout principal de ce joueur, c'est sa vitesse.** This player's main asset is his speed. ❷ trump card ▷ **J'avais quatre atouts dans mon jeu.** I had four trump cards in my hand.

atroce [atʀɔs] adj terrible

attachant [ataʃɑ̃, -ɑ̃t] (f **attachante**) adj lovable

attacher [ataʃe] vb to tie up ▷ **Elle a attaché ses cheveux avec un élastique.** She tied her hair up with an elastic band.; **s'attacher à quelqu'un** to become attached to somebody; **une poêle qui n'attache pas** a non-stick frying pan

attaquer [atake] vb to attack

atteindre [atɛ̃dʀ(ə)] vb to reach

attendant [atɑ̃dɑ̃]: **en attendant** adv in the meantime

attendre [atɑ̃dʀ(ə)] vb to wait ▷ **attendre quelqu'un** to wait for someone ▷ **J'attends d'avoir un appartement à moi.** I'm waiting until I have an apartment of my own. ▷ **Attends qu'il ne pleuve plus.** Wait until it stops raining.; **attendre un enfant** to be expecting a baby; **s'attendre à** to expect ▷ **Je m'attends à ce qu'ils soient en retard.** I expect they'll be late.

attentat [atɑ̃ta] nm: **un attentat à la bombe** a terrorist bombing

attente [atɑ̃t] nf wait ▷ **deux heures d'attente** a two-hour wait; **la salle d'attente** the waiting room

attentif [atɑ̃tif, -iv] (f **attentive**) adj attentive

attention [atɑ̃sjɔ̃] nf attention ▷ **à l'attention de** to the attention of; **faire attention (1)** to be careful **(2)** to pay attention ▷ **Ne fais pas attention à cette remarque-là.** Pay no attention to that remark.; **Attention!** Watch out! ▷ *Attention, tu vas te faire écraser!* Watch out, you'll get run over!

attentionné [atɑ̃sjɔne] (*f* **attentionnée**) *adj* thoughtful

attentivement [atɑ̃tivmɑ̃] *adv* ❶ carefully ▷ *lire attentivement* to read carefully ❷ closely ▷ *observer attentivement* to observe closely

atterrir [ateʀiʀ] *vb* to land

atterrissage [ateʀisaʒ] *nm* (*of plane*) landing

attirant [atiʀɑ̃, -ɑ̃t] (*f* **attirante**) *adj* attractive

attirer [atiʀe] *vb* to attract ▷ *attirer l'attention de quelqu'un* to attract somebody's attention; **s'attirer des ennuis** to get into trouble ▷ *Si tu continues, tu vas t'attirer des ennuis.* If you keep that up, you'll get yourself into trouble.

attitude [atityd] *nf* attitude

attraction [atʀaksjɔ̃] *nf*: **une attraction touristique** a tourist attraction; **un parc d'attractions** an amusement park

attraper [atʀape] *vb* to catch

attrayant [atʀɛjɑ̃, -ɑ̃t] (*f* **attrayante**) *adj* attractive

au [o] *prep* *see* **à**; **au printemps** in the spring

aube [ob] *nf* dawn ▷ *à l'aube* at dawn

auberge [obɛʀʒ(ə)] *nf* inn; **une auberge de jeunesse** a youth hostel

aucun [okœ̃, -yn] (*f* **aucune**) *adj*, *pron* ❶ no ▷ *Il n'a aucun ami.* He has no friends. ▷ *Aucun enfant ne pourrait le faire.* No child could do that. ❷ none ▷ *Aucun d'entre eux n'est venu.* None of them came. ▷ *Aucune de mes amies n'aime le football.* None of my female friends like football. ▷ *« Tu aimes ses films ? » « Je n'en ai vu aucun. »* "Do you like his films?" "I haven't seen any of them."; **sans aucun doute** without any doubt

au-delà [odla] *adv*: **au-delà de** beyond ▷ *Votre ticket n'est pas valable au-delà de cette limite.* Your ticket is not valid beyond this point.

au-dessous [odsu] *adv* ❶ downstairs ▷ *Ils habitent au-dessous.* They live downstairs. ❷ underneath; **au-dessous de** under ▷ *au-dessous du pont* under the bridge ▷ *dix degrés au-dessous de zéro* ten degrees below zero

au-dessus [odsy] *adv* ❶ upstairs ▷ *J'habite au-dessus.* I live upstairs. ❷ above; **au-dessus de** above ▷ *au-dessus de la table* above the table

audio [odjo] (*f+pl* **audio**) *adj* audio ▷ *des fichiers audio* audio files ▷ *le matériel audio* audio equipment; **un audioclip** an audio clip

audiovisuel [odjovizɥɛl] (*f* **audiovisuelle**) *adj* audiovisual

auditeur [oditœʀ] *nm* (*to radio*) listener

audition [odisjɔ̃] *nf* audition

auditionner [odisjɔne] *vb* to audition

auditrice [oditʀis] *nf* (*to radio*) listener

augmentation [ɔɡmɑ̃tasjɔ̃] *nf* rise ▷ *une augmentation de prix* a rise in prices; **une augmentation de salaire** a raise

augmenter [ɔɡmɑ̃te] *vb* to increase

aujourd'hui [oʒuʀdɥi] *adv* today

auparavant [opaʀavɑ̃] *adv* first ▷ *Vous pouvez utiliser l'ordinateur, mais auparavant vous devez taper le mot de passe.* You can use

the computer but first you have to key in the password.

auquel [okɛl] (*mpl* **auxquels**, *fpl* **auxquelles**) *pron*: ▷ *l'homme auquel j'ai parlé* the man I spoke to

aura, aurai, auras, aurez, aurons, auront *vb see* **avoir**

aurore boréale [ɔʀɔʀbɔʀeal] *nf* northern lights

aussi [osi] *adv* ❶ too ▷ *« Dors bien. » « Toi aussi. »* "Sleep well." "You too." ▷ *Elle aussi parle espagnol.* She too speaks Spanish. ❷ also ▷ *J'aimerais aussi que tu achètes le journal.* I'd also like you to get the paper. ▷ *Je parle anglais et aussi allemand.* I speak English and also German.; **aussi … que** as … as ▷ *aussi grand que moi* as big as me

aussitôt [osito] *adv* right away ▷ *aussitôt après son retour* right after his return; **aussitôt que** as soon as ▷ *aussitôt que tu auras fini* as soon as you're finished

autant [otɑ̃] *adv*: **autant de (1)** so much ▷ *Je ne veux pas autant de gâteau.* I don't want so much cake. **(2)** so many ▷ *Je n'ai jamais vu autant de monde.* I've never seen so many people.; **autant … que (1)** as much … as ▷ *J'ai autant d'argent que toi.* I've got as much money as you have. **(2)** as many … as ▷ *J'ai autant d'amis que lui.* I've got as many friends as he has.; **d'autant plus que** all the more since ▷ *Elle est d'autant plus déçue qu'ils le lui avaient promis.* She's all the more disappointed since they had promised her.; **d'autant moins que** even less since ▷ *C'est d'autant moins pratique pour nous que nous devons changer deux fois d'autobus.* It's even less convenient for us since we have to change buses twice.

auteur [otœʀ] *nm* author

auteure [otœʀ] *nf* author

auto [oto] *nf* car

autobus [otobys] *nm* bus ▷ *en autobus* by bus ▷ *l'autobus scolaire* school bus

autochtone [otɔktɔn] *adj*, *nmf* Aboriginal; **un autochtone** an Aboriginal man; **une autochtone** an Aboriginal woman; **les autochtones** the Aboriginal peoples

autocollant [otɔkɔlɑ̃, -ɑ̃t] (*f* **autocollante**) *adj* self-adhesive ▷ *une étiquette autocollante* a self-adhesive label; **une enveloppe autocollante** a self-seal envelope ▶ *nm* sticker

auto-école [otoekɔl] (*pl* **les auto-écoles**) *nf* driving school

automatique [otomatik] *adj* automatic

automne [otɔn] *nm* fall; **en automne** in the fall

automobile [otomɔbil] *adj*: **une course automobile** a car race ▶ *nf* car

automobiliste [otomɔbilist(ə)] *nmf* motorist

autoradio [otoʀadjo] *nm* car radio

autorisation [otoʀizasjɔ̃] *nf* ❶ permission ▷ *Elle m'a donné l'autorisation de sortir ce soir.* She's given me permission to go out tonight. ❷ permit ▷ *Il faut une autorisation pour camper ici.* You need a permit to camp here.

autoriser [ɔtɔRize] *vb* to give permission for ▷ *Il m'a autorisé à en parler.* He's given me permission to talk about it.

autoritaire [ɔtɔRitɛR] *adj* authoritarian

autorité [ɔtɔRite] *nf* authority

autoroute [ɔtɔRut] *nf* highway

auto-stop [ɔtɔstɔp] *nm*: **faire de l'auto-stop** to hitchhike

auto-stoppeur [ɔtɔstɔpœR] *nm* hitchhiker

auto-stoppeuse [ɔtɔstɔpøz] *nf* hitchhiker

autour [otuR] *adv* around ▷ *autour de la maison* around the house

autre [otR(ə)] *adj, pron* other ▷ *Je viendrai un autre jour.* I'll come some other day. ▷ *J'ai d'autres projets.* I've got other plans.; **autre chose** something else; **un autre** another ▷ *Tu veux un autre morceau de gâteau?* Would you like another piece of cake?; **l'autre** the other ▷ *Non, pas celui-ci, l'autre.* No, not that one, the other one.; **d'autres** others ▷ *Je t'en apporterai d'autres.* I'll bring you some others.; **les autres** the others ▷ *Les autres sont arrivés plus tard.* The others arrived later.; **ni l'un ni l'autre** neither of them; **entre autres** among other things ▷ *Nous avons parlé, entre autres, de nos projets de vacances.* We talked about our holiday plans, among other things.

autrefois [otRəfwa] *adv* in the old days

autrement [otRəmã] *adv* ❶ differently ▷ *Elle l'a fait autrement.* She did it differently. ❷ otherwise ▷ *Je n'ai pas pu faire autrement.* I couldn't do otherwise.; **autrement dit** in other words

autruche [otRyʃ] *nf* ostrich

aux [o] *prep see* **à** ▷ *J'ai dit aux enfants d'aller jouer.* I told the children to go and play.

auxquelles [okɛl] *pron*: ▷ *les revues auxquelles il est abonné* the magazines to which he subscribes

auxquels [okɛl] *pron*: ▷ *les enfants auxquels il a parlé* the children he spoke to

avaient, avais, avait *vb see* **avoir**; **Il y avait beaucoup de monde.** There were a lot of people.

avalanche [avalɑ̃ʃ] *nf* avalanche

avaler [avale] *vb* to swallow

avance [avɑ̃s] *nf*: **être en avance** to be early; **à l'avance** beforehand ▷ *réserver une place à l'avance* to book a seat beforehand; **d'avance** in advance ▷ *payer d'avance* to pay in advance; **l'avance rapide** fast forward

avancé [avɑ̃se] (*f* **avancée**) *adj* advanced ▷ *à un niveau avancé* at an advanced level; **bien avancé** well under way ▷ *Les travaux sont déjà bien avancés.* The work is already well under way.

avancer [avɑ̃se] *vb* ❶ to move forward ▷ *Elle avançait prudemment.* She was moving forward cautiously. ❷ (*date*) to move up ▷ *La date de l'examen a été avancée.* The date of the exam has been moved up. ❸ to put ahead ▷ *Il a avancé sa montre d'une heure.* He put his watch ahead an hour. ❹ (*watch*) to be fast ▷ *Ma montre avance d'une heure.* My watch is an hour fast. ❺ to lend ▷ *Peux-tu m'avancer dix dollars?* Can you lend me 10 dollars?

avant [avɑ̃] *prep, adj* ❶ before ▷ *avant qu'il ne pleuve* before it rains ▷ *avant de partir* before leaving ❷ front ▷ *la roue avant* the front wheel ▷ *le siège avant* the front seat; **avant tout** above all
▶ *nm* front ▷ *l'avant de la voiture* the front of the car; **à l'avant** in front; **en avant** forward ▷ *Elle a fait un pas en avant.* She took a step forward.

avantage [avɑ̃taʒ] *nm* advantage

avant-dernier [avɑ̃dɛRnje, -jɛR] (*f* **avant-dernière**, *mpl* **avant-derniers**) *adj* second-last ▷ *l'avant-dernière page* the second-last page ▷ *Ils sont arrivés avant-derniers.* They arrived second-last.

avant-hier [avɑ̃tjɛR] *adv* the day before yesterday ▷ *Il est arrivé avant-hier.* He arrived the day before yesterday.

avec [avɛk] *prep* with ▷ *avec ma mère* with my mother; **Et avec ça?** (*in store*) Anything else?

avenir [avniR] *nm* future; **à l'avenir** in future ▷ *À l'avenir, essayez d'être à l'heure.* Try to be on time in future.; **dans un proche avenir** in the near future

aventure [avɑ̃tyR] *nf* adventure

aventureux [avɑ̃tyRø, -øz] (*f* **aventureuse**) *adj* adventurous

aventurier [avɑ̃tyRje] *nm* adventurer

aventurière [avɑ̃tyRjɛR] *nf* adventurer

avenue [avny] *nf* avenue

averse [avɛRs(ə)] *nf* (*of rain*) shower

avertir [avɛRtiR] *vb* to warn; **avertir quelqu'un de quelque chose** to warn somebody about something

avertissement [avɛRtismã] *nm* warning

aveugle [avœgl(ə)] *adj* blind

avion [avjɔ̃] *nm* plane; **aller en avion** to go by plane ▷ *Il est allé en Alberta en avion.* He flew to Alberta.; **par avion** by airmail

aviron [aviRɔ̃] *nm* (*canoe*) paddle ▷ *un aviron en bois* a wooden paddle

avis [avi] *nm* ❶ opinion ▷ *J'aimerais avoir ton avis.* I'd like to have your opinion.; **à mon avis** in my opinion; **changer d'avis** to change one's mind ▷ *J'ai changé d'avis.* I've changed my mind. ❷ notice ▷ *jusqu'à nouvel avis* until further notice

avocat [avɔka] *nm* ❶ lawyer ▷ *Il est avocat.* He's a lawyer. ❷ avocado

avocate [avɔkat] *nf* lawyer ▷ *Elle est avocate.* She's a lawyer.

avoine [avwan] *nf* oats

avoir [avwaR] *vb* ❶ to have ▷ *Ils ont deux enfants.* They have two children. ▷ *Elle a les yeux bleus.* She has blue eyes. ▷ *J'ai déjà mangé.* I've already eaten. ▷ *Est-ce que tu as vu ce film?* Have you seen this film? ▷ *Je leur ai parlé hier.* I spoke to them yesterday.; **On t'a bien eu!** (*informal*) You've been had! ❷ to be ▷ *Elle a trois ans.* She's three. ▷ *J'avais dix ans quand je l'ai rencontré.* I was ten when I met him.; **il y a** (1) there is ▷ *Il y a quelqu'un à la porte.* There's somebody at the door. (2) there are ▷ *Il y a des chocolats sur la table.* There are some chocolates on the table. (3) ago ▷ *Je l'ai rencontré il y a deux ans.* I met him two years ago.; **Qu'est-ce qu'il y a?** What's the matter?; **Il n'y a qu'à partir plus tôt.** We'll just have to leave earlier.

avortement [avɔʀtəmɑ̃] *nm* abortion

avouer [avwe] *vb* to admit

avril [avʀil] *nm* April; **en avril** in April

ayez, ayons *vb see* avoir

b

babillard [babijaʀ] *nm* billboard; **un babillard électronique** (*computer*) a bulletin board

baby-foot [babifut] *nm* foosball ▷ *jouer au baby-foot* to play foosball

bac [bak] *nm* = **baccalauréat**

baccalauréat [bakalɔʀea] *nm* B.A. ▷ *un baccalauréat en histoire* a B.A. in history

bâcler [bakle] *vb* to botch ▷ *Je déteste le travail bâclé!* I hate work that's not done properly!

bagage [bagaʒ] *nm* luggage; **faire ses bagages** to pack; **les bagages à main** hand luggage ▷ *un bagage à main* a piece of hand luggage

bagarre [bagaʀ] *nf* fight ▷ *Une bagarre a éclaté dans la cour de l'école.* A fight broke out in the schoolyard.

se bagarrer [bagaʀe] *vb* to fight ▷ *Il s'est encore bagarré avec son frère.* He's been fighting with his brother again.

bague [bag] *nf* ring

baguel [begœl] *nm* bagel ▷ *un baguel grillé* a toasted bagel

baguette [baget] *nf* ❶ stick of French bread ❷ chopstick ▷ *manger des baguettes* to eat with chopsticks; **une baguette magique** a magic wand

baie [bɛ] *nf* ❶ bay ❷ berry

baie d'Hudson Hudson Bay

baignade [bɛɲad] *nf*: «**baignade interdite**» "no swimming"

se baigner [bɛɲe] *vb* to go swimming ▷ *Si on allait se baigner?* Shall we go swimming?

baignoire [bɛɲwaʀ] *nf* bathtub

bâiller [baje] *vb* to yawn

bain [bɛ̃] *nm* bath ▷ *prendre un bain* to take a bath ▷ *prendre un bain de soleil* to sunbathe

baiser [beze] *nm* kiss

baisse [bɛs] *nf* decrease ▷ *la baisse du taux de chômage* the fall in the unemployment rate; **être en baisse** to be falling

baisser [bese] *vb* ❶ to turn down ▷ *Tu peux baisser le chauffage.* You can turn down the heat. ❷ to fall ▷ *Le prix des lecteurs MP3 a baissé.* The price of MP3 players has fallen.; **se baisser** to bend down ▷ *Elle s'est baissée pour*

ramasser son cahier. She bent down to pick up her notebook.

bal [bal] *nm* dance ▷ *un bal populaire* a local dance

balade [balad] *nf* (*informal*) walk ▷ *faire une balade* to go for a walk

se balader [balade] *vb* (*informal*) to wander around ▷ *J'adore me balader dans les rues du Vieux-Québec.* I love to wander around the streets of old Quebec City.

baladeur [baladœʀ] *nm* personal stereo

balai [balɛ] *nm* broom ▷ *Je vais donner un coup de balai dans la cuisine.* I'm going to sweep the kitchen.

balance [balɑ̃s] *nf* (*for weighing*) scales; **la Balance** Libra ▷ *Elle est Balance.* She's a Libra.

se balancer [balɑ̃se] *vb* to swing

balançoire [balɑ̃swaʀ] *nf* swing

balayer [baleje] *vb* ❶ to sweep ▷ *J'ai balayé la cuisine.* I swept the kitchen. ❷ to sweep up ▷ *Va balayer les feuilles sur le patio.* Go and sweep up the leaves on the patio.

balbutier [balbysje] *vb* to stammer

balcon [balkɔ̃] *nm* balcony

baleine [balɛn] *nf* whale

balle [bal] *nf* ❶ ball ▷ *une balle de tennis* a tennis ball ❷ bullet

ballerine [balʀin] *nf* ❶ ballet dancer ❷ ballet shoe ▷ *une paire de ballerines rouges* a pair of red ballet shoes

ballet [balɛ] *nm* ballet

ballon [balɔ̃] *nm* ❶ ball ▷ *lancer le ballon* to throw the ball; **un ballon de football** a football; **le ballon chasseur** dodgeball ❷ balloon

balnéaire [balneɛʀ] *adj*: **une station balnéaire** a seaside resort

banal [banal] (*f* **banale**, *mpl* **banaux**) *adj* ❶ commonplace ▷ *La violence est devenue banale à la télévision.* Violence has become commonplace on television. ❷ clichéd ▷ *L'intrigue du film est très banale.* The plot of the film is very clichéd.

banane [banan] *nf* banana ▷ *La banane est un fruit.* The banana is a fruit.

banc [bɑ̃] *nm* bench; **le banc de neige** snowbank

bancaire [bɑ̃kɛʀ] *adj*: **une carte bancaire** a bank card

bandage [bɑ̃daʒ] *nm* bandage

bande [bɑ̃d] *nf* ❶ gang ▷ *une bande de voyous* a gang of thugs ❷ bunch ▷ *C'est une bande d'idiots!* They're a bunch of idiots! ❸ (*hockey*) boards ▷ *L'autre joueuse m'a poussée dans la bande.* The other player shoved me into the boards.; **une bande dessinée** a comic strip; **une bande magnétique** a tape; **la bande sonore** the sound track; **Elle fait toujours bande à part.** She always keeps to herself.

bandeau [bɑ̃do] (*pl* **bandeaux**) *nm* headband

bander [bɑ̃de] *vb* to bandage ▷ *L'infirmière lui a bandé la jambe.* The nurse bandaged his leg.

bandit [bɑ̃di] *nm* bandit

banique [banik] *nf* bannock

banlieue [bɑ̃ljø] *nf* suburbs ▷ *Elle habite en banlieue.* She lives in the suburbs.; **les trains de**

banlieue commuter trains

banque [bɑ̃k] nf bank; **la banque alimentaire** food bank

banquet [bɑ̃kɛ] nm banquet ▷ *le banquet annuel de l'association* the club's annual banquet

banquette [bɑ̃kɛt] nf seat ▷ *la banquette arrière de la voiture* the back seat of the car

baquet [bakɛ] nm (*laundry*) tub

barachois [baʁaʃwa] nm barachois

barbare [baʁbaʁ] adj barbaric

barbe [baʁb(ə)] nf beard ▷ *Il porte la barbe.* He has a beard.; **la barbe à papa** cotton candy

barbecue [baʁbəkju] nm barbecue ▷ *être invité à un barbecue* to be invited to a barbecue ▷ *faire griller du saumon au barbecue* to barbecue salmon; **du poulet grillé au barbecue** barbecued chicken

barbouiller [baʁbuje] vb to smear ▷ *Les murs étaient barbouillés de graffitis.* The walls were plastered with graffiti.; **J'ai l'estomac barbouillé.** (*informal*) I feel queasy.

barbu [baʁby] (f **barbue**) adj bearded ▷ *un grand barbu* a big, bearded man

baromètre [baʁɔmɛtʁ(ə)] nm barometer

barrage [baʁaʒ] nm dam; **un barrage de police** a police roadblock

barre [baʁ] nf (*metal*) bar ▷ *une barre de fer* an iron bar; **la barre d'outils** (*computer*) toolbar; **la barre oblique inverse** backslash

barreau [baʁo] (pl **barreaux**) nm (*on window*) bar ▷ *Il s'est retrouvé derrière les barreaux.* He ended up behind bars.

barrer [baʁe] vb to block ▷ *Il y a un tronc d'arbre qui barre la route.* There's a tree trunk blocking the road.

barrette [baʁɛt] nf barrette

barrière [baʁjɛʁ] nf fence

bas [bɑ, bɑs] nm ① bottom ▷ *en bas de la page* at the bottom of the page ▷ *en bas de l'escalier* at the bottom of the stairs ② stocking ▷ *une paire de bas* a pair of stockings ▶ adj, adv (f **basse**) low ▷ *parler à voix basse* to speak in a low voice; **en bas** (1) down ▷ *Ça me donne le vertige de regarder en bas.* I get dizzy if I look down. (2) at the bottom ▷ *Son nom est tout en bas.* His name is at the bottom. ▷ *Il y a une porte en bas de l'escalier.* There's a door at the bottom of the stairs. (3) downstairs ▷ *Elle habite en bas.* She lives downstairs.

Bas-Canada nm Lower Canada

base [bɑz] nf base ▷ *la base de la pyramide* the base of the pyramid; **de base** basic ▷ *Le pain et le lait sont des aliments de base.* Bread and milk are basic foods.; **à base de** made from ▷ *des produits de beauté à base de plantes* cosmetics made from plants; **une base de données** a database

basket-ball [basketbol] nm basketball ▷ *jouer au basket-ball* to play basketball

basse [bɑs] adj see **bas**

basse-cour [bɑskuʁ] (pl **basses-cours**) nf barnyard

bassin [basɛ̃] nm ① pond ▷ *Il y a un bassin à poissons rouges dans le parc.* There's a goldfish pond in the park. ② pelvis ▷ *une fracture du bassin* a fractured pelvis

bassine [basin] nf washbasin

bas-ventre [bavɑ̃tʁ(ə)] nm stomach ▷ *Elle se plaint de douleurs dans le bas-ventre.* She is complaining of pains in her stomach.

bataille [bataj] nf battle

bateau [bato] (pl **bateaux**) nm boat

bateau-mouche [batomuʃ] (pl **bateaux-mouches**) nm pleasure boat

bâti [bati] (f **bâtie**) adj: **bien bâti** well-built

bâtiment [batimɑ̃] nm building

bâtir [batiʁ] vb to build

bâton [batɔ̃] nm stick ▷ *un coup de bâton* a blow with a stick ▷ *un bâton de hockey* a hockey stick

battement [batmɑ̃] nm: **J'ai dix minutes de battement.** I've got ten minutes free.; **un battement de cœur** heartbeat

batterie [batʁi] nf ① battery ② (*car*) ▷ *La batterie est à plat.* The battery is dead. ③ drums ▷ *jouer de la batterie* to play the drums; **la batterie de cuisine** the pots and pans

batteur [batœʁ] nm drummer

battre [batʁ(ə)] vb to beat ▷ *Quand je la vois, mon cœur bat plus vite.* When I see her, my heart beats faster.; **se battre** to fight ▷ *Je me bats souvent avec mon frère.* I fight a lot with my brother.; **battre les cartes** to shuffle the cards; **battre les blancs en neige** beat the egg whites until stiff; **battre son plein** to be in full swing ▷ *A minuit, la fête battait son plein.* At midnight, the party was in full swing.

bavard [bavaʁ, -aʁd(ə)] (f **bavarde**) adj talkative

bavardage [bavaʁdaʒ] nm chat

bavarder [bavaʁde] vb to chat

baveux [bavø, -øz] (f **baveuse**) adj ① runny ▷ *une omelette baveuse* a runny omelette ② (*informal*) arrogant ▷ *Il est un peu trop baveux à mon goût.* I find him a bit too arrogant.

bavure [bavyʁ] nf blunder ▷ *une bavure policière* a police blunder

BD [bede] nf (= *bande dessinée*) comic strip ▷ *Elle adore les BD.* She loves comic strips.

béant [beɑ̃, -ɑ̃t] (f **béante**) adj gaping ▷ *un trou béant* a gaping hole

beau [bo, bɛl] (f **belle**, mpl **beaux**) adj, adv ① lovely ▷ *un beau cadeau* a lovely present ▷ *une belle journée* a lovely day ▷ *un bel été* a lovely summer ② beautiful ▷ *C'est une belle femme.* She is a beautiful woman. ③ handsome ▷ *C'est un beau garçon.* He is a handsome boy.; **Il fait beau aujourd'hui.** It's a nice day today.; **J'ai beau essayer, je n'y arrive pas.** No matter how hard I try, I just can't do it.

beaucoup [boku] adv ① a lot ▷ *Il mange beaucoup.* He eats a lot. ② much ▷ *Elle n'a pas beaucoup d'argent.* She doesn't have much money. ▷ *Elle est beaucoup plus grande que moi.* She is much taller than me.; **beaucoup de** a lot of ▷ *Il y avait beaucoup de monde au concert.* There was a lot of people at the concert. ▷ *J'ai fait beaucoup de fautes.* I made a lot of mistakes.; **J'ai eu beaucoup de chance.** I was very lucky.

beau-fils [bofis] (pl **beaux-fils**) nm ① son-in-law ② stepson

beau-frère [bofʁɛʁ] (pl **beaux-frères**) nm brother-in-law

beau-père [boрεʀ] *nm* (*pl* **beaux-pères**) *nm*
❶ father-in-law ❷ stepfather

beauté [bote] *nf* beauty

beaux-arts [bozaʀ] *nmpl* fine arts

beaux-parents [boparɑ̃] *nmpl* in-laws

bébé [bebe] *nm* baby

bec [bɛk] *nm* ❶ beak ❷ little kiss ▷ *un petit bec sur la joue* a little kiss on the cheek; **le bec sucré** sweet tooth ▷ *Ma petite sœur a le bec sucré.* My little sister has a sweet tooth.

bêche [bɛʃ] *nf* spade

bêcher [beʃe] *vb* to dig ▷ *Il bêchait son jardin.* He was digging the garden.

bégayer [begeje] *vb* to stammer

beige [bɛʒ] *adj* beige

beigne [bɛɲe] *nm* doughnut

bel [bɛl] *adj see* **beau**

bélier [belje] *nm* ram; **le Bélier** Aries ▷ *Elle est Bélier.* She's an Aries.

belle [bɛl] *adj see* **beau**

belle-famille [bɛlfamij] (*pl* **belles-familles**) *nf* in-laws

belle-fille [bɛlfij] (*pl* **belles-filles**) *nf* ❶ daughter-in-law ❷ stepdaughter

belle-mère [bɛlmɛʀ] (*pl* **belles-mères**) *nf* ❶ mother-in-law ❷ stepmother

belle-sœur [bɛlsœʀ] (*pl* **belles-sœurs**) *nf* sister-in-law

bénédiction [benediksjɔ̃] *nf* blessing

bénéfice [benefis] *nm* profit ▷ *On a réalisé un bénéfice de 170 $ sur la vente de chocolats.* We made a profit of 170 on the chocolate sales.

bénévole [benevɔl] *adj* volunteer ▷ *du travail bénévole* volunteer work
▶ *n* volunteer

bénir [beniʀ] *vb* to bless

benjamin [bɛ̃ʒamɛ̃] *nm*

benjamine [bɛ̃ʒamin] *nf*

béquille [bekij] *nf* crutch ▷ *Il marche avec des béquilles.* He walks on crutches.

berceau [bɛʀso] (*pl* **berceaux**) *nm* cradle

bercer [bɛʀse] *vb* to rock

berceuse [bɛʀsøz] *nf* lullaby

béret [beʀebask(ə)] *nm* beret; **les bérets bleus** peacekeepers

berge [bɛʀʒ(ə)] *nf* (*of river*) bank

bernache du Canada [bɛʀnaʃ-] *nf* Canada goose

besoin [bazwɛ̃] *nm* need; **avoir besoin de quelque chose** to need something ▷ *J'ai besoin d'argent.* I need some money. ▷ *J'ai besoin d'y réfléchir.* I need to think about it.; **une famille dans le besoin** a needy family

bétail [betaj] *nm* livestock

bête [bɛt] *nf* animal
▶ *adj* stupid

bêtise [betiz] *nf*: **faire une bêtise** to do something stupid ▷ *Je crois que j'ai fait une bêtise.* I think I've done something stupid.; **dire des bêtises** to talk nonsense ▷ *Tu dis des bêtises!* You're talking nonsense!

béton [betɔ̃] *nm* concrete; **un alibi en béton** a cast-iron alibi

betterave [bɛtʀav] *nf* beet

beurre [bœʀ] *nm* butter ▷ *une sauce au beurre* a sauce made with butter; **beurre d'arachide** peanut butter

beurrer [bœʀe] *vb* to butter

biberon [bibʀɔ̃] *nm* baby's bottle

bibliographie [biblijɔgʀafi] *nf* bibliography

bibliothécaire [biblijɔtekɛʀ] *nmf* librarian

bibliothèque [biblijɔtɛk] *nf* ❶ library ▷ *emprunter un livre à la bibliothèque* to borrow a book from the library ❷ bookcase ▷ *une bibliothèque en chêne massif* a solid oak bookcase

bicyclette [bisiklɛt] *nf* bicycle

bidon [bidɔ̃] *nm* can ▷ *un bidon d'essence* a can of gas

bidonville [bidɔ̃vil] *nm* shanty town

bidouiller [biduje] *vb* (*computer*) to hack ▷ *Il passe des heures chaque soir à bidouiller sur son ordinateur.* He spends hours hacking on his computer every night.

bidouilleur [bidujœʀ] *nm* (*computer*) hacker

bidouilleuse [bidujøz] *nf* (*computer*) hacker

bien [bjɛ̃] *nm* ❶ good ▷ *le bien et le mal* good and evil ▷ *Elle m'a dit beaucoup de bien de toi.* She told me a lot of good things about you. ▷ *C'est pour ton bien.* It's for your own good.; **faire du bien à quelqu'un** to do somebody good ▷ *Ses vacances lui ont fait beaucoup de bien.* His holiday has done him a lot of good. ❷ possession ▷ *son bien le plus précieux* her most treasured possession
▶ *adj, adv* ❶ well ▷ *Elle travaille bien.* She works well. ▷ *Je me sens bien.* I feel fine. ▷ *Je ne me sens pas bien.* I don't feel well. ❷ good ▷ *Ce restaurant est vraiment bien.* This restaurant is really good. ❸ quite ▷ *bien assez* quite enough; **Je veux bien le faire.** I'm quite willing to do it.; **bien mieux** much better; **J'espère bien y aller.** I very much hope to go. ❹ right ▷ *Ce n'est pas bien de dire du mal des gens.* It's not right to say nasty things about people. ▷ *Il croyait bien faire.* He thought he was doing the right thing.; **C'est bien fait pour lui!** It serves him right!

bien-être [bjɛ̃nɛtʀ(ə)] *nm* well-being ▷ *une sensation de bien-être* a feeling of well-being

bienfaisance [bjɛ̃fəzɑ̃s] *nf* charity; **une œuvre de bienfaisance** a charity

bien que [bjɛ̃k(ə)] *conj* although ▷ *Il fait assez chaud bien qu'il n'y ait pas de soleil.* It's quite warm although there's no sun.

bien sûr [bjɛ̃syʀ] *adv* of course

bientôt [bjɛ̃to] *adv* soon ▷ *À bientôt!* See you soon!

bienvenu [bjɛ̃vny] *nm*: **Vous êtes le bienvenu!** (*to visitor*) You are welcome! ▷ *Vous êtes tous les bienvenus!* You're all welcome!

bienvenue [bjɛ̃vny] *nf* welcome ▷ *Bienvenue à Calgary!* Welcome to Calgary! ▷ *Vous êtes la bienvenue!* You're welcome!

bifteck [biftɛk] *nm* steak

bijou [biʒu] (*pl* **bijoux**) *nm* jewel

bijouterie [biʒutʀi] *nf* jewellery store

bijoutier [biʒutje] *nm* jeweller

bijoutière [biʒutjɛʀ] *nf* jeweller ▷ *Elle est bijoutière.* She's a jeweller.

bilan [bilɑ̃] *nm*: **faire le bilan de quelque chose** to assess something ▷ *Il faut faire le bilan de la situation.* We need to assess the situation.

bilingue [bilɛ̃g] adj bilingual
bilinguisme [bilɛ̃gɥism(ə)] nm bilingualism
billard [bijaʀ] nm pool
bille [bij] nf (toy) marble
billet [bije] nm ❶ ticket ▷ un billet d'avion a plane ticket ❷ (paper money) bill ▷ un billet de dix dollars a 10-dollar bill
billion [biljɔ̃] nm trillion
binette [binɛt] nf (emoticon) smiley
biodégradable [bjɔdegʀadabl(ə)] adj biodegradable
biographie [bjɔgʀafi] nf biography
biologie [bjɔlɔʒi] nf biology
biologique [bjɔlɔʒik] adj ❶ organic ▷ des légumes biologiques organic vegetables ❷ biological ▷ des armes biologiques biological weapons
biscotte [biskɔt] nf (sold in packets) toasted bread
biscuit [biskɥi] nm cookie
bise [biz] nf kiss ▷ Grosses bises de Terre-Neuve. Love and kisses from Newfoundland.; **faire la bise à quelqu'un** (informal) to give somebody a peck on the cheek ▷ Elle m'a fait la bise. She gave me a peck on the cheek.
bison [bizɔ̃] nm bison
bisou [bizu] nm (informal) kiss ▷ Viens faire un bisou à maman! Come and give Mummy a little kiss!
bissextile [bisɛkstil] adj: **une année bissextile** a leap year
bizarre [bizaʀ] adj strange
blague [blag] nf ❶ (informal) joke ▷ raconter une blague to tell a joke; **Sans blague!** No kidding! ❷ trick ▷ Il nous a encore fait une blague! He's played a trick on us again!
blaguer [blage] vb (informal) to joke
blâmer [blame] vb to blame
blanc [blɑ̃, blɑ̃ʃ] (f **blanche**) adj ❶ white ▷ un chemisier blanc a white blouse ❷ blank ▷ une page blanche a blank page ▶ nm white ▷ Elle était habillée tout en blanc. She was dressed all in white.; **un blanc d'œuf** an egg white
Blanc [blɑ̃] nm white man
Blanche [blɑ̃ʃ] nf white woman
blanche [blɑ̃ʃ] adj see **blanc**
blé [ble] nm wheat; **le blé d'Inde** corn
blessé [blese] (f **blessée**) adj injured ▶ nm injured person ▷ L'accident a fait trois blessés. Three people were injured in the accident.
blessée [blese] nf injured person
blesser [blese] vb ❶ to injure ▷ Il a été blessé dans un accident de voiture. He was injured in a car accident. ❷ to hurt ▷ Elle a fait exprès de le blesser. She hurt him on purpose.; **se blesser** to hurt oneself ▷ Je me suis blessé au pied. I've hurt my foot.
blessure [blesyʀ] nf injury
bleu [blø] (f **bleue**) adj ❶ blue ▷ une veste bleue a blue jacket ❷ (steak) very rare ▶ nm ❶ blue ▷ J'aime le bleu. I like blue. ❷ bruise ▷ Il a un bleu au front. He's got a bruise on his forehead.
bleuet [bløɛ] nm blueberry ▷ la tarte aux bleuets blueberry pie

bleu marine (f+pl **blue marine**) adj navy blue ▷ des vêtements bleu marine navy blue clothes
bloc [blɔk] nm ❶ un bloc de papier à lettres a pad of writing paper; **un bloc de glace** a block of ice
bloc-notes [blɔknɔt] (pl **blocs-notes**) nm notepad
blogue [blɔg] nm blog
blond [blɔ̃, -ɔ̃d] (f **blonde**) adj blond ▷ les cheveux blonds blond hair; **blond cendré** ash blond ▷ Elle a les cheveux blond cendré. She has ash blond hair.
blonde [blɔ̃d] nf (informal) girlfriend ▷ Ma blonde a fait son propre site Web. My girlfriend made her own Web site.
bloquer [blɔke] vb to block ▷ bloquer le passage to block the way; **être bloqué dans un embouteillage** to be stuck in a traffic jam
se blottir [blɔtiʀ] vb to huddle ▷ Ils étaient blottis l'un contre l'autre. They were huddled together.
blouse [bluz] nf blouse
blouson [bluzɔ̃] nm jacket ▷ un blouson en cuir a leather jacket
bobettes [bɔbɛt] nfpl underpants
bobine [bɔbin] nf reel ▷ une bobine de fil a reel of thread
bocal [bɔkal, -o] (pl **bocaux**) nm jar
bœuf [bœf] nm ❶ ox ❷ beef ▷ un rôti de bœuf a roast of beef
bof [bɔf] excl ❶ « Le film t'a plu? » — « Bof! C'était pas terrible! » "Did you like the film?" — "Well... it wasn't that great!"; « Comment ça va? » — « Bof! Pas très bien. » "How is it going?" — "Oh... not too well actually."
boire [bwaʀ] vb to drink
bois [bwa] nm wood; **en bois** wooden ▷ une table en bois a wooden table
boisson [bwasɔ̃] nf drink ▷ une boisson chaude a hot drink ▷ une boisson non alcoolisée a soft drink
boîte [bwat] nf ❶ box ▷ une boîte d'allumettes a box of matches; **une boîte aux lettres** a mailbox ❷ can ▷ une boîte de thon a can of tuna; **une boîte de conserve** (of food) a can; **en boîte** canned ▷ des petits pois en boîte canned peas
boiter [bwate] vb to limp
bol [bɔl] nm bowl
bombarder [bɔ̃baʀde] vb to bomb
bombe [bɔ̃b] nf ❶ bomb ❷ spray can ▷ du déodorant en bombe aérosol spray deodorant
bon [bɔ̃, bɔn] (f **bonne**) adj, adv ❶ good ▷ un bon restaurant a good restaurant ▷ Le tabac n'est pas bon pour la santé. Smoking isn't good for you.; **être bon en maths** to be good at math; **sentir bon** to smell good; **Bon courage!** Good luck!; **Bon voyage!** Have a good trip!; **Bonne fin de semaine!** Have a good weekend!; **Bonne chance!** Good luck!; **Bonne journée!** Have a good day!; **Bonne nuit!** Good night!; **Bon anniversaire!** Happy birthday!; **Bonne Année!** Happy New Year! ❷ right ▷ Il est arrivé au bon moment. He arrived at the right moment. ▷ Ce n'est pas la bonne réponse. That's

not the right answer.; **de bonne heure** early; **bon marché** cheap ▷ *Les fraises ne sont pas bon marché en hiver.* Strawberries aren't cheap in winter.; **Ah bon?** Really? ▷ *« Je pars aux États-Unis la semaine prochaine. » « Ah bon? »* "I'm going to the States next week." "Really?"; **J'aimerais vraiment que tu viennes! » « Bon, d'accord. »** "I'd really like you to come!" "OK then, I will."; **Est-ce que ce yogourt est encore bon?** Is this yogurt still OK?
▶ *nm* **voucher** ▷ *un bon d'achat* a voucher; **le bon de réduction** coupon; **pour de bon** for good ▷ *Cette fois, c'est pour de bon.* This time it's for good.

bonbon [bɔ̃bɔ̃] *nm* candy; **les bonbons haricots** jelly beans

bondé [bɔ̃de] (f **bondée**) *adj* crowded

bondir [bɔ̃diʀ] *vb* to leap

bonheur [bɔnœʀ] *nm* happiness; **porter bonheur** to bring luck

bonhomme [bɔnɔm] (*pl* **bonshommes**) *nm*: **un bonhomme de neige** a snowman

bonjour [bɔ̃ʒuʀ] *excl* ❶ Hello! ▷ *Donne le bonjour à tes parents de ma part.* Say hello to your parents for me. ❷ Good morning! ❸ Good afternoon!; **C'est simple comme bonjour!** It's easy as pie!

bonne [bɔn] *adj see* **bon**

bonnet [bɔnɛ] *nm* ❶ hat ▷ *un bonnet de laine* a woolly hat ❷ (women's); **un bonnet de bain** a bathing cap

bonsoir [bɔ̃swaʀ] *excl* Good evening!

bonté [bɔ̃te] *nf* kindness

bord [bɔʀ] *nm* ❶ edge ▷ *le bord de la table* the edge of the table ❷ side ▷ *Jane a garé sa voiture au bord de la route.* Jane parked her car on the side of the road.; **au bord de la mer** by the sea; **au bord de l'eau** by the water; **monter à bord** to go on board; **être au bord des larmes** to be on the verge of tears

border [bɔʀde] *vb* ❶ to line ▷ *une route bordée d'arbres* a tree-lined street ❷ to trim ▷ *un col bordé de dentelle* a collar trimmed with lace ❸ to tuck in ▷ *Ma mère borde ma petite sœur tous les soirs.* My mother tucks in my little sister every night.

bordure [bɔʀdyʀ] *nf* border; **une auberge en bordure de mer** an inn right by the sea

bosse [bɔs] *nf* ❶ bump ▷ *Elle a une grosse bosse au front.* She has a big bump on her forehead. ❷ *La route est pleine de bosses.* The road is very bumpy.

botanique [bɔtanik] *adj* botanical ▷ *les jardins botaniques* the botanical gardens
▶ *nf* botany

botte [bɔt] *nf* ❶ boot ▷ *une paire de bottes* a pair of boots; **les bottes de caoutchouc** rubber boots ❷ bunch ▷ *une botte de radis* a bunch of radishes

bottin [bɔtɛ̃] *nm* phone book

bouc [buk] *nm* ❶ goatee ❷ billy goat; **un bouc émissaire** a scapegoat

bouche [buʃ] *nf* mouth; **une bouche d'égout** (in road) a maintenance hole; **une bouche de métro** a subway entrance

bouchée [buʃe] *nf* mouthful

boucher [buʃe] *vb* to plug ▷ *boucher un trou*

to plug a hole ▷ *L'évier est bouché.* The sink is clogged. ▷ *J'ai le nez bouché.* My nose is stuffed up.
▶ *nm* butcher ▷ *Il est boucher.* He's a butcher.

bouchère [buʃɛʀ] *nf* butcher ▷ *Elle est bouchère.* She's a butcher.

boucherie [buʃʀi] *nf* butcher shop

bouchon [buʃɔ̃] *nm* ❶ (of plastic bottle) top ❷ (of wine bottle) cork ❸ traffic jam ▷ *Il y avait beaucoup de bouchons sur l'autoroute.* There were a lot of traffic jams on the motorway.

boucle [bukl(ə)] *nf* (of hair) curl; **une boucle d'oreille** an earring ▷ *une paire de boucles d'oreilles* a pair of earrings

bouclé [bukle] (f **bouclée**) *adj* curly

bouclier [buklije] *nm* shield; **le Bouclier canadien** the Canadian Shield

bouddhiste [budist(ə)] *adj* Buddhist
▶ *n* Buddhist

bouder [bude] *vb* to sulk

boue [bu] *nf* mud

bouée [bwe] *nf* buoy; **une bouée de sauvetage** a life buoy

boueux [bwø, -øz] (f **boueuse**) *adj* muddy

bouffe [buf] *nf* (informal) food ▷ *La bouffe est infecte à la cafétéria.* The food in the cafeteria is revolting.

bouffée [bufe] *nf*: **une bouffée d'air frais** a breath of fresh air

bouffe-minute *nf* fast food

bouffer [bufe] *vb* (informal) to eat

bouger [buʒe] *vb* to move

bougie [buʒi] *nf* candle

bouillabaisse [bujabɛs] *nf* fish soup

bouillant [bujã, -ãt] (f **bouillante**) *adj* ❶ boiling ▷ *Faites cuire les pâtes à l'eau bouillante.* Cook the pasta in boiling water. ❷ piping hot ▷ *La soupe est servie bouillante.* The soup should be served piping hot.

bouillir [bujiʀ] *vb* to boil ▷ *L'eau bout.* The water's boiling.; **Je bous d'impatience.** I'm bursting with impatience.

bouilloire [bujwaʀ] *nf* kettle

bouillon [bujɔ̃] *nm* stock ▷ *du bouillon de légumes* vegetable stock

boulanger [bulãʒe] *nm* baker ▷ *Il est boulanger.* He's a baker.

boulangère [bulãʒɛʀ] *nf* baker ▷ *Elle est boulangère.* She's a baker.

boulangerie [bulãʒʀi] *nf* bakery

boule [bul] *nf* ball ▷ *une boule de cristal* a crystal ball; **une boule de neige** a snowball; **la machine à boules** pinball machine

bouleau [bulo] *nm* birch

bouleverser [bulvɛʀse] *vb* ❶ to move deeply ▷ *Leur histoire déchirante m'a bouleversée.* I was very moved by their heartbreaking story. ❷ to shatter ▷ *La mort de son ami l'a bouleversé.* He was shattered by the death of his friend. ❸ to turn upside down ▷ *Cette rencontre a bouleversé sa vie.* This meeting turned her life upside down.

boulimie [bulimi] *nf* bulimia

boulot [bulo] *nm* ❶ (informal) job ▷ *Elle a trouvé du boulot.* She has found a job. ❷ work ▷ *J'ai beaucoup de boulot en ce moment.* I've got a lot of work to do at the moment.

bouquet [buke] nm bunch of flowers ▷ *un bouquet de roses* a bunch of roses

bourdonner [buʁdɔne] vb to buzz

bourgeois [buʁʒwa, -waz] (f**bourgeoise**) adj middle-class ▷ *un quartier bourgeois* a posh area

bourgeon [buʁʒ5] nm bud

bourré [buʁe] (f**bourrée**) adj: bourré de stuffed with ▷ *un portefeuille bourré de billets* a wallet stuffed with bills

bourreau [buʁo] (pl **bourreaux**) nm: **C'est un véritable bourreau de travail.** He's a real workaholic.

bourrer [buʁe] vb to stuff ▷ *bourrer une valise de vêtements* to stuff clothes into a suitcase

bourse [buʁs(ə)] nf grant; **la Bourse** the Stock Exchange

bous [bu] vb see **bouillir**

bousculade [buskylad] nf rush ▷ *la bousculade de dernière minute* the last-minute rush

bousculer [buskyle] vb ❶ to jostle ▷ *être bousculé par la foule* to be jostled by the crowd ❷ to rush ▷ *Je n'aime pas qu'on me bouscule.* I don't like to be rushed.

boussole [busɔl] nf compass

bout [bu] vb see **bouillir**

bout [bu] nm ❶ end ▷ *Elle habite au bout de la rue.* She lives at the end of the street. ▷ *Il est assis en bout de table.* He is sitting at the end of the table. ❷ tip ▷ *le bout du nez* the tip of the nose ❸ little piece ▷ *un petit bout de fromage* a little piece of cheese; **un bout de papier** a scrap of paper; **au bout de** after ▷ *Au bout d'un moment, il s'est endormi.* After a while he fell asleep.; **au bout du compte** ultimately ▷ *Au bout du compte, c'est à toi de décider.* Ultimately, it's your decision.; **Elle est à bout.** She's at the end of her tether.

bouteille [butej] nf bottle ▷ *une bouteille d'eau* a bottle of water

boutique [butik] nf shop ▷ *une boutique de cadeaux* a giftshop ▷ *une boutique de souvenirs* a souvenir shop

bouton [but5] nm ❶ button ❷ pimple ▷ *J'ai un bouton sur le nez.* I've got a pimple on my nose. ❸ bud ▷ *un bouton de rose* a rosebud; **un bouton d'or** a buttercup

boxe [bɔks(ə)] nf boxing

boxeur [bɔksœʁ] nm boxer

boycotter [bɔjkɔte] vb to boycott

bracelet [brasle] nm bracelet

bracelet-montre [braslemɔ̃tr(ə)] (pl **bracelets-montres**) nm wristwatch

branche [brɑ̃ʃ] nf branch

branché [brɑ̃ʃe] (f**branchée**) adj (informal) trendy ▷ *avoir un look branché* to look trendy

brancher [brɑ̃ʃe] vb ❶ to connect ▷ *Le téléphone est branché?* Is the phone connected? ❷ to plug in ▷ *L'aspirateur n'est pas branché.* The vacuum cleaner isn't plugged in.

bras [bra] nm arm

brasse [bras] nf breaststroke ▷ *nager la brasse* to do the breaststroke

brave [brav] adj ❶ nice ▷ *C'est un brave type.* He's a nice guy. ❷ brave ▷ *Ta mère est une femme très brave.* Your mother is a very brave woman.

bravo [bravo] excl Bravo!

bref [brɛf, brɛv] (f**brève**) adj, adv short ▷ *Sa lettre était brève.* Her letter was short.; **en bref** in brief ▷ *l'actualité en bref* the news in brief; **Bref, ça s'est bien terminé.** In short, it turned out all right in the end.; **être bref et précis** to be short and to the point

bretelle [brətɛl] nf strap ▷ *La bretelle de son soutien-gorge dépasse.* Her bra strap is showing.; **les bretelles** suspenders ▷ *Il porte des bretelles.* He's wearing suspenders.

brève [brɛv] adj see **bref**

bricolage [brikɔlaʒ] nm do-it-yourself ▷ *Il aime le bricolage.* He loves working on do-it-yourself projects. ▷ *un magasin de bricolage* a store selling do-it-yourself supplies

bricoler [brikɔle] vb to work on do-it-yourself projects ▷ *Il aime bricoler.* He loves working on do-it-yourself projects.

brièvement [brijɛvmɑ̃] adv briefly ▷ *Expliquez-moi brièvement ce qui s'est passé.* Tell me briefly what happened.

brigade [brigad] nf (of police) squad ▷ *la brigade des stups* (informal) the drug squad

brillamment [brijamɑ̃] adv brilliantly ▷ *Il a réussi brillamment à son examen.* He did brilliantly in the exam.

brillant [brijɑ̃, -ɑ̃t] (f**brillante**) adj ❶ brilliant ▷ *une brillante carrière* a brilliant career ❷ shiny ▷ *des cheveux brillants* shiny hair

briller [brije] vb to shine

brin [brɛ̃] nm: **un brin d'herbe** a blade of grass; **un brin de muguet** a sprig of lily of the valley

brindille [brɛ̃dij] nf twig

brioche [brijɔʃ] nf bun

brique [brik] nf brick

briquet [brike] nm lighter

brise [briz] nf breeze

brise-glace [brizglas] (pl **brise-glaces**) nm ice-breaker ▷ *On utilise des brise-glaces pour naviguer dans l'Arctique.* Ice-breakers are used to navigate the Arctic.

se briser [brize] vb to break ▷ *Le vase s'est brisé en mille morceaux.* The vase broke into a thousand pieces.

brisure [brizyr] nf chocolate chip ▷ *un biscuit aux brisures de chocolat* a chocolate chip cookie

broche [brɔʃ] nf brooch ▷ *une broche en argent* a silver brooch; **à la broche** spit-roasted ▷ *un poulet à la broche* a spit-roasted chicken

brochet [brɔʃe] nm pike

brochette [brɔʃet] nf skewer; **les brochettes d'agneau** lamb kebabs

brocheuse [brɔʃøz] nf stapler

brochure [brɔʃyr] nf brochure

broder [brɔde] vb to embroider

broderie [brɔdri] nf embroidery

bronchite [brɔ̃ʃit] nf bronchitis ▷ *avoir une bronchite* to have bronchitis

bronze [brɔ̃z] nm bronze

bronzer [brɔ̃ze] vb to get a tan ▷ *Il est bien bronzé.* He's got a good tan.; **se bronzer** to sunbathe

brosse [brɔs] nf brush; **une brosse à cheveux**

a hairbrush; **une brosse à dents** a toothbrush

brosser [bʀɔse] *vb* to brush; **se brosser les dents** to brush one's teeth ▷ *Je me brosse les dents tous les soirs.* I brush my teeth every night.

brouette [bʀuet] *nf* wheelbarrow

brouillard [bʀujaʀ] *nm* fog ▷ *Il y a du brouillard.* It's foggy.

brouillon [bʀujɔ̃] *nm* first draft ▷ *Ce n'est qu'un brouillon.* It's just a first draft.

broussailles [bʀusaj] *nfpl* undergrowth

brouter [bʀute] *vb* (*animals*) to graze

broyer [bʀwaje] *vb* to crush; **broyer du noir** to be down in the dumps

bruine [bʀɥin] *nf* drizzle ▷ *On prévoit de la bruine aujourd'hui.* They're forecasting drizzle today.

bruiner [bʀɥine] *vb* to drizzle

bruit [bʀɥi] *nm* ❶ noise ▷ *J'ai entendu un bruit.* I heard a noise. ❷ *faire du bruit* to make a noise; **sans bruit** without a sound ❸ rumour ▷ *Des bruits circulent à son sujet.* There are rumours going round about him.

bruitage [bʀɥitaʒ] *nm* sound effects

bruiteur [bʀɥitœʀ] *nm* sound effect specialist

bruiteuse [bʀɥitøz] *nf* sound effect specialist

brûlant [bʀylɑ̃, -ɑ̃t] (*f* **brûlante**) *adj* ❶ blazing ▷ *Un soleil brûlant* a blazing sun ❷ boiling hot ▷ *Elle boit son café brûlant.* She drinks her coffee boiling hot.

brûlé [bʀyle] *nm* smell of burning ▷ *Ça sent le brûlé.* There's a smell of burning.

brûler [bʀyle] *vb* to burn; **se brûler** to burn oneself

brûlure [bʀylyʀ] *nf* burn; **des brûlures d'estomac** heartburn

brume [bʀym] *nf* mist

brumeux [bʀymø, -øz] (*f* **brumeuse**) *adj* misty

brun [bʀœ̃, -yn] (*f* **brune**) *adj* brown; **Elle est brune.** She has dark hair.

brunch [bʀœntʃ] *nm* brunch ▷ *prendre le brunch* to have brunch

brusque [bʀysk(ə)] *adj* abrupt; **d'un ton brusque** brusquely

brusquer [bʀyske] *vb* to rush ▷ *Il ne faut pas la brusquer.* You mustn't rush her.

brut [bʀyt] (*f* **brute**) *adj*: **le champagne brut** dry champagne; **le pétrole brut** crude oil; **son salaire brut** his gross salary

brutaliser [bʀytalize] *vb* to treat roughly ▷ *Il a été brutalisé par la police.* He was treated roughly by the police.

bruyamment [bʀɥijamɑ̃] *adv* noisily

bruyant [bʀɥijɑ̃, -ɑ̃t] (*f* **bruyante**) *adj* noisy

bu [by] *vb see* **boire**

buanderie [bɥɑ̃dʀi] *nf* coin laundry

bûcheron [byʃʀɔ̃] *nm* woodcutter

budget [bydʒe] *nm* budget

buffet [byfe] *nm* ❶ sideboard ▷ *un buffet en chêne* an oak sideboard ❷ buffet ▷ *un buffet froid* a cold buffet; **un buffet à salades** a salad bar

buisson [bɥisɔ̃] *nm* bush

bulle [byl] *nf* bubble ▷ *une bulle de savon* a soap bubble

bulletin [byltɛ̃] *nm* ❶ bulletin; **le bulletin**

d'informations the news bulletin ❷ report card ▷ *Ton bulletin n'est pas fameux.* Your report card isn't very good.; **le bulletin de salaire** pay slip; **le bulletin de vote** the ballot; **le bulletin scolaire** report card

bureau [byʀo] (*pl* **bureaux**) *nm* ❶ desk ▷ *Posez le dossier sur mon bureau.* Put the file on my desk. ❷ office ▷ *Il vous attend dans son bureau.* He's waiting for you in his office.; **le Bureau** (*computer*) the desktop; **un bureau de change** a foreign exchange; **le bureau de poste** the post office; **le bureau de vote** the polling station

bus [bys] *vb see* **boire**
▶ *nm* bus

buste [byst(ə)] *nm* bust

but [by] *vb see* **boire**
▶ *nm* ❶ aim ▷ *Ils n'ont pas de but dans la vie.* They have no aim in life.; **Quel est le but de votre visite?** What's the reason for your visit?; **dans le but de** with the intention of ▷ *Je suis venue dans le but de vous aider.* I came to help you. ❷ goal ▷ *marquer un but* to score a goal

butane [bytan] *nm* butane

butin [bytɛ̃] *nm* loot ▷ *Les cambrioleurs se sont partagé le butin.* The burglars shared the loot.

buvais, buvait *vb see* **boire**

C

c' [s] *pron see* **ce**

ça [sa] *pron* ❶ this ▷ *Est-ce que vous pouvez m'aider avec ça?* Can you help me with this? ❷ that ▷ *Est-ce que tu peux prendre ça, là-bas dans le coin?* Can you bring that from over there in the corner? ❸ it ▷ *Ça ne fait rien.* It doesn't matter.; **Comment ça va?** How are you?; **Ça alors!** Well, well!; **C'est ça.** That's right.; **Ça y est!** That's it!

çà [sa] *adv*: **çà et là** here and there

cabane [kaban] *nf* hut; **la cabane à sucre** sugar shack; **une cabane dans l'arbre** a treehouse

cabine [kabin] *nf* (*on a ship*) cabin; **une cabine d'essayage** a fitting room; **une cabine téléphonique** a phone box

cabinet [kabinɛ] *nm* (*of doctor, of dentist*) consulting room; **un cabinet d'avocats** a law firm

câble [kabl(ə)] *nm* cable; **la télévision par câble** (*television*) cable; **les câbles de démarrage** booster cables

cabosser [kabose] *vb* to dent

cacao [kakao] *nm* cocoa; **le beurre de cacao** cocoa butter

cache-cache [kaʃkaʃ] *nm*: **jouer à cache-cache** to play hide-and-seek

cacher [kaʃe] *vb* to hide ▷ *J'ai caché les cadeaux sous le lit.* I hid the presents under the bed. ▷ *Tu me caches quelque chose!* You're hiding something!; **se cacher** to hide ▷ *Elle s'est cachée sous la table.* She's hiding under the table.

cachet [kaʃe] *nm* ❶ tablet; **un cachet d'aspirine** an aspirin ❷ *(for performer)* fee ▷ *Il a touché un gros cachet pour ce concert.* He got a big fee for the concert.; **le cachet de la poste** the postmark

cachette [kaʃet] *nf* hiding place; **en cachette** on the sly ▷ *Il est sorti en cachette sans réveiller ses parents.* He crept out on the sly without waking his parents.; **jouer à la cachette** to play hide-and-seek

cadavre [kadavʀ(ə)] *nm* corpse

cadeau [kado] *(pl* **cadeaux)** *nm* present ▷ *un cadeau d'anniversaire* a birthday present; **faire un cadeau à quelqu'un** to give somebody a present

cadenas [kadna] *nm* padlock

cadet [kade, -et] *(f* **cadette)** *adj* ❶ *(brother, sister)* younger ▷ *ma sœur cadette* my younger sister ❷ *(son, daughter)* youngest ▷ *son fils cadet* his youngest son
▶ *nm* youngest ▷ *C'est le cadet de la famille.* He's the youngest in the family.

cadette [kadet] *nf* youngest ▷ *C'est la cadette de la famille.* She's the youngest in the family.

cadre [kadʀ(ə)] *nm* ❶ frame ▷ *un cadre en bois* a wooden frame ❷ surroundings ▷ *L'hôtel est situé dans un très beau cadre.* The hotel is located in beautiful surroundings. ❸ executive ▷ *un cadre supérieur* a senior executive

café [kafe] *nm* ❶ coffee ❷ café

cafétéria [kafeteʀja] *nf* cafeteria

cafetière [kaftjɛʀ] *nf* ❶ coffee maker ❷ coffee pot

cage [kaʒ] *nf* cage; **la cage d'escalier** the stairwell

cagoule [kagul] *nf* balaclava

cahier [kaje] *nm* ❶ workbook ❷ notebook

caillou [kaju] *(pl* **cailloux)** *nm* pebble

caisse [kes] *nf* ❶ box ▷ *une caisse à outils* a tool box ❷ cash register; **le ticket de caisse** the sales slip ❸ checkout ▷ *J'ai dû faire la queue à la caisse.* I had to wait in line at the checkout.

caissier [kesje] *nm* cashier

caissière [kesjɛʀ] *nf* cashier

Cajun [kaʒẽ] *(f* **cajun)** *adj, n* Cajun ▷ *la cuisine cajun* Cajun cuisine; **un Cajun** *(man)* a Cajun; **une Cajun** *(woman)* a Cajun

calcul [kalkyl] *nm* ❶ calculation ▷ *Je me suis trompé dans mes calculs.* I made a mistake in my calculations. ❷ arithmetic ▷ *Je ne suis pas très bon en calcul.* I'm not very good at arithmetic.

calculatrice [kalkylatʀis] *nf* calculator

calculer [kalkyle] *vb* to work out ▷ *J'ai calculé combien ça allait coûter.* I worked out how much it was going to cost.

cale [kal] *nf* wedge

caleçon [kalsɔ̃] *nm* ❶ underpants ▷ *un caleçon* a pair of underpants ❷ *(men's)*

calendrier [kalɑ̃dʀije] *nm* calendar

calepin [kalpɛ̃] *nm* notebook

caler [kale] *vb* to stall ▷ *La voiture a calé dans une côte.* The car stalled on a hill.

câlin [kalɛ̃, -in] *(f* **câline)** *adj* cuddly
▶ *nm* cuddle ▷ *faire un câlin à quelqu'un* to give somebody a cuddle

calmant [kalmɑ̃] *nm* tranquilizer

calme [kalm(ə)] *adj* ❶ quiet ▷ *un endroit calme* a quiet place ❷ calm ▷ *Il est resté très calme.* He stayed very calm.
▶ *nm* peace and quiet ▷ *J'ai besoin de calme pour travailler.* I need peace and quiet to work.; **Du calme, s'il vous plaît!** Please stay calm!

calmer [kalme] *vb* to soothe ▷ *Cette pommade calme les démangeaisons.* This ointment soothes itching.; **se calmer** to calm down ▷ *Calme-toi!* Calm down!

calorie [kalɔʀi] *nf* calorie

camarade [kamaʀad] *nmf* friend; **un camarade de classe** a school friend

cambriolage [kɑ̃bʀijɔlaʒ] *nm* burglary

cambrioler [kɑ̃bʀijɔle] *vb* to burgle

cambrioleur [kɑ̃bʀijɔlœʀ] *nm* burglar

cambrioleuse [kɑ̃bʀijɔløz] *nf* burglar

camelot [kamlo] *nmf* paper carrier

camelote [kamlɔt] *nf (informal)* junk ▷ *C'est vraiment de la camelote.* It's absolute junk.

caméra [kameʀa] *nf (movie, TV)* camera; **une caméra numérique** a digital camera

caméscope [kameskɔp] *nm* camcorder

camion [kamjɔ̃] *nm* truck; **un camion citerne** a tanker truck

camionnette [kamjɔnet] *nf* pickup truck

camionneur [kamjɔnœʀ] *nm* truck driver

camionneuse [kamjɔnøz] *nf* truck driver

camisole [kamizɔl] *nf (men's or women's)* undershirt

camomille [kamɔmij] *nf* camomile tea

camp [kɑ̃] *nm* camp ▷ *un camp d'été* a summer camp ▷ *un camp de prisonniers* a prison camp

campagne [kɑ̃paɲ] *nf* ❶ country; **à la campagne** in the country ▷ *Nous passons nos vacances à la campagne.* We spend our holidays in the country. ❷ campaign ▷ *une campagne publicitaire* a marketing campaign

camper [kɑ̃pe] *vb* to camp

campeur [kɑ̃pœʀ] *nm* camper

campeuse [kɑ̃pøz] *nf* camper

camping [kɑ̃piŋ] *nm* camping ▷ *faire du camping* to go camping; **un terrain de camping** a campground; **le camping sauvage** wilderness camping

Canada [kanada] *nm* Canada; **au Canada (1)** in Canada **(2)** to Canada

canadien [kanadjɛ̃, -ɛn] *(f* **canadienne)** *adj, n* Canadian; **un Canadien** *(man)* a Canadian; **une Canadienne** *(woman)* a Canadian

canadien-anglais *(f* **canadienne-anglaise)** *adj* English Canadian

Canadien anglais *(pl* **Canadiens anglais)** *nm (man)* English Canadian

Canadienne anglaise *(pl* **Canadiennes anglaises)** *nf (woman)* English Canadian

canadien-français (f **canadienne-française**) adj French Canadian

Canadien français (pl **Canadiens français**) nm (man) French Canadian

Canadienne française (pl **Canadiennes françaises**), nf (woman) French Canadian

canal [kanal, -o] (pl **canaux**) nm canal

canapé [kanape] nm open-faced sandwich

canard [kanaʀ] nm duck

cancer [kãseʀ] nm cancer ▷ le cancer du poumon lung cancer; **le Cancer** Cancer ▷ Elle est Cancer. She's a Cancer.

candidat [kãdida] nm ❶ (in exam, election) candidate ❷ (for job) applicant

candidate [kãdidat] nf ❶ (in exam, election) candidate ❷ (for job) applicant

candidature [kãdidatyʀ] nf: **poser sa candidature à un poste** to apply for a job ▷ Il a posé sa candidature à des dizaines de postes. He has applied for dozens of jobs.

caneton [kantɔ̃] nm duckling

canette [kanɛt] nf: **une canette de boisson gazeuse** a can of pop

caniche [kaniʃ] nm poodle

canicule [kanikyl] nf heat wave

canif [kanif] nm jackknife

canne [kan] nf walking stick; **une canne à pêche** a fishing rod

canneberge [kanbɛʀʒ] nf cranberry ▷ du jus de canneberge cranberry juice

cannelle [kanɛl] nf cinnamon ▷ une brioche à la cannelle cinnamon roll

canola [kanɔla] nm canola ▷ de l'huile de canola canola oil

canon [kanɔ̃] nm cannon

canot [kano] nm ❶ canoe ❷ dinghy ▷ un canot pneumatique a rubber dinghy; **un canot de sauvetage** a lifeboat

canotage [kanɔtaʒ] nm canoeing ▷ faire du canotage to go canoeing

cantine [kãtin] nf snack bar

caoutchouc [kautʃu] nm rubber; **des bottes en caoutchouc** rubber boots

cap [kap] nm (landform) cape

capable [kapabl(ə)] adj: **Elle est capable de marcher pendant des heures.** She can walk for hours.; **Il est capable de changer d'avis au dernier moment.** He's capable of changing his mind at the last minute.

cape [kap] nf (garment) cape

capitale [kapital] nf capital ▷ la capitale de la Colombie-Britannique the capital of British Columbia

capot [kapo] nm (of car) hood

caprice [kapʀis] nm: **faire des caprices** to make a fuss ▷ Il n'aime pas les enfants qui font des caprices. He doesn't like children who make a fuss.

capricieux [kapʀisjø, -øz] (f **capricieuse**) adj: **un enfant capricieux** a difficult child

Capricorne [kapʀikɔʀn] nm Capricorn ▷ Elle est Capricorne. She's a Capricorn.

captivant [kaptivã, -ãt] (f **captivante**) adj fascinating

captivité [kaptivite] nf captivity ▷ en captivité in captivity

capturer [kaptyʀe] vb to capture

capuche [kapyʃ] nf hood ▷ un manteau à capuche a coat with a hood

capuchon [kapyʃɔ̃] nm (of pen) cap

car [kaʀ] conj because ▷ Nous sommes inquiets car ils ne sont pas encore rentrés. We're worried because they're not back yet.

carabine [kaʀabin] nf rifle

caractère [kaʀaktɛʀ] nm personality ▷ Elle a le même caractère que son père. She has the same personality as her father.; **Il a bon caractère.** He's good-natured.; **Elle a mauvais caractère.** She's bad-tempered.; **Il n'a pas un caractère facile.** He isn't easy to get along with.

caractéristique [kaʀakteʀistik] adj characteristic
▶ nf characteristic

carafe [kaʀaf] nf jug ▷ une carafe d'eau a jug of water

caramel [kaʀamɛl] nm ❶ caramel ▷ la crème caramel crème caramel ❷ toffee

caravane [kaʀavan] nf RV

carbonique [kaʀbɔnik] adj: **le gaz carbonique** carbon dioxide

carburant [kaʀbyʀã] nm fuel

carcajou [kaʀkaʒu] nm wolverine

cardiaque [kaʀdjak] adj: **une crise cardiaque** a heart attack; **Ma tante est cardiaque.** My aunt has heart trouble.

cardiologue [kaʀdjɔlɔg] nmf heart specialist

caresse [kaʀɛs] nf stroke ▷ faire des caresses à un chat to caress a cat

caresser [kaʀese] vb to stroke

caribou [kaʀibu] nm caribou; **la peau de caribou** caribou hide

caricature [kaʀikatyʀ] nf (drawing) cartoon

carie [kaʀi] nf tooth decay ▷ J'ai une carie. I have a cavity.

caritatif [kaʀitatif, -iv] (f **caritative**) adj: **une organisation caritative** a charity

carnaval [kaʀnaval] nm carnival

carnet [kaʀnɛ] nm ❶ notebook ❷ book ▷ un carnet d'adresses an address book ▷ un carnet de chèques a cheque book ▷ un carnet de timbres a book of stamps

carotte [kaʀɔt] nf carrot ▷ les carottes râpées grated carrots

carré [kaʀe] (f **carrée**) adj square; **un mètre carré** a square metre
▶ nm square; **le carré au chocolat** brownie

carreau [kaʀo] (pl **carreaux**) nm ❶ (pattern) check ▷ une chemise à carreaux a checked shirt ❷ (floor, wall) tile ▷ Je viens de laver les carreaux de la cuisine. I've just washed the kitchen floor. ❸ pane ▷ Elle a cassé un carreau. She broke a windowpane. ❹ (cards) diamonds ▷ l'as de carreau the ace of diamonds

carrefour [kaʀfuʀ] nm intersection

carrelage [kaʀlaʒ] nm tiled floor

carrément [kaʀemã] adv ❶ completely ▷ C'est carrément impossible. It's completely impossible. ❷ straight out ▷ Dis-moi carrément ce que tu penses. Tell me straight out what you think.

carrière [kaʀjɛʀ] nf career; **un militaire de**

carrière a professional soldier

carrure [kaʀyʀ] *nf* build ▷ *Il a une carrure d'athlète.* He has an athletic build.

cartable [kaʀtabl(ə)] *nm* binder

carte [kaʀt(ə)] *nf* ❶ card; **une carte d'anniversaire** a birthday card; **une carte postale** a postcard; **une carte de vœux** a Christmas card; **une carte bancaire** a bank card; **une carte de crédit** a credit card; **une carte de fidélité** a frequent customer card; **une carte d'embarquement** a boarding card; **une carte d'identité** an ID card; **une carte de séjour** a residence permit; **une carte téléphonique** a phonecard; **un jeu de cartes (1)** a pack of cards **(2)** a card game ❷ map ▷ *une carte du Manitoba* a map of Manitoba ▷ *une carte routière* a road map; **manger à la carte** to eat à la carte ▷ *Nous allons manger à la carte.* We'll choose from the à la carte menu.

carton [kaʀtɔ̃] *nm* cardboard ▷ *un morceau de carton* a piece of cardboard; **une boîte de carton** a cardboard box ▷ *un carton à chaussures* a shoe box

cartouche [kaʀtuʃ] *nf* cartridge; **une cartouche d'imprimante** a printer cartridge

cas [ka] (*pl* **cas**) *nm* case ▷ *plusieurs cas* several cases; **ne faire aucun cas de** to take no notice of; **en aucun cas** under no circumstances; **en tout cas** at any rate; **au cas où** in case ▷ *Prends un sandwich au cas où la cantine serait fermée.* Take a sandwich in case the snack bar's closed.; **en cas de** in case of ▷ *En cas d'incendie, appelez ce numéro.* In case of fire, call this number.

cascade [kaskad] *nf* waterfall

cascadeur [kaskadœʀ] *nm* stuntman

cascadeuse [kaskadøz] *nf* stuntwoman

case [kaz] *nf* ❶ (*in board game*) square ❷ (*on form*) box; **la case postale** post office box

caserne [kazɛʀn(ə)] *nf* barracks

casier [kazje] *nm* locker

casque [kask(ə)] *nm* helmet; **un casque d'écoute** a pair of headphones

casquette [kaskɛt] *nf* cap

cassant [kasɑ̃, -ɑ̃t] (*f* **cassante**) *adj*: **Il m'a parlé d'un ton cassant.** He spoke to me curtly.

casse-croûte [kaskʀut] (*pl* **casse-croûte**) *nm* snack

casse-noix [kas-] (*pl* **casse-noix**) *nm* nutcracker

casser [kase] *vb* to break ▷ *J'ai cassé un verre.* I've broken a glass.; **se casser** (*bone*) to break ▷ *Il s'est cassé la jambe en faisant du ski.* He broke his leg skiing.; **se casser la tête** (*informal*) to go to a lot of trouble ▷ *Je ne vais pas me casser la tête pour le dîner : je vais ouvrir une boîte de conserve.* I'm not going to go to a whole lot of trouble over dinner: I'll just open a can.

casserole [kasʀɔl] *nf* ❶ saucepan ❷ casserole ▷ *une casserole de thon* a tuna casserole

casse-tête [kastɛt] (*pl* **casse-tête**) *nm*: **C'est un vrai casse-tête!** It's a real headache!

cassette [kasɛt] *nf* cassette

cassis [kasis] *nm* black currant

cassonade [kasɔnad] *nf* brown sugar

castor [kastɔʀ] *nm* beaver

catalogue [katalɔg] *nm* catalogue

catastrophe [katastʀɔf] *nf* disaster

catégorie [kategɔʀi] *nf* category

catégorique [kategɔʀik] *adj* firm ▷ *un refus catégorique* a flat refusal

cathédrale [katedʀal] *nf* cathedral

catholique [katɔlik] *adj* Catholic
▶ *n* Catholic

cauchemar [koʃmaʀ] *nm* nightmare ▷ *faire un cauchemar* to have a nightmare

cause [koz] *nf* cause; **à cause de** because of ▷ *Nous n'avons pas pu sortir à cause du mauvais temps.* We couldn't go out because of the bad weather.

causer [koze] *vb* to cause ▷ *La tempête a causé beaucoup de dégâts.* The storm caused a lot of damage.

cavalier [kavalje] *nm* ❶ rider ❷ (*at dance*) partner

cavalière [kavaljɛʀ] *nf* rider

cave [kav] *nf* cellar

caverne [kavɛʀn(ə)] *nf* cave

CD [sede] (*pl* **CD**) *nm* CD

CD-ROM [sedeʀɔm] (*pl* **CD-ROM**) *nm* CD-ROM

ce [sə, sɛt] (*msg* **cet**, *f* **cette**, *pl* **ces**) *adj* ❶ this ▷ *Tu peux prendre ce livre.* You can take this book. ▷ *cet après-midi* this afternoon ▷ *cet hiver* this winter; **ce livre-ci** this book; **cette voiture-ci** this car ❷ that ▷ *Je n'ai pas du tout aimé ce film.* I didn't like that movie at all.; **ce livre-là** that book; **cette voiture-là** that car
▶ *pron* it ▷ *Ce n'est pas facile.* It's not easy.; **c'est (1)** it is ▷ *C'est vraiment trop cher.* It's really too expensive. ▷ *Ouvre, c'est moi!* Open the door, it's me! **(2)** he is ▷ *C'est un peintre du début du siècle.* He's a painter from the turn of the century. **(3)** she is ▷ *C'est une actrice très célèbre.* She's a very famous actress. **(4)** this is ▷ *C'est inacceptable!* This is unacceptable! **(5)** that is ▷ *C'est bien beau, mais...* That's all very fine, but...; **ce sont** they are ▷ *Ce sont des amis à mes parents.* They're friends of my parents.; **Qui est-ce?** Who is it?; **Qu'est-ce que c'est?** What is it?; **ce qui** what ▷ *C'est ce qui compte.* That's what matters.; **tout ce qui** everything that ▷ *J'ai rangé tout ce qui traînait par terre.* I've tidied up everything that was on the floor.; **ce que** what ▷ *Je vais lui dire ce que je pense.* I'm going to tell her what I think.; **tout ce que** everything ▷ *Tu peux avoir tout ce que tu veux.* You can have everything you want.

ceci [səsi] *pron* this ▷ *Prends ceci, tu en auras besoin.* Take this, you'll need it.

céder [sede] *vb* to give in ▷ *Elle a tellement insisté qu'il a fini par céder.* She was so adamant that he finally gave in.; **céder à** to give in to ▷ *Je ne veux pas céder à ses caprices.* I'm not going to give in to his whims.

cédérom [sedeʀɔm] *nm* CD-ROM

cédille [sedij] *nf* cedilla

cèdre [sɛdʀ(ə)] *nm* cedar; **le bois de cèdre** cedar (wood)

cégep [seʒɛp] *nm* = **collège d'enseignement général et professionnel** (*general and* vocational college) CEGEP

ceinture [sɛtyʀ] nf belt ▷ *une ceinture en cuir* a leather belt; **une ceinture de sauvetage** a lifebelt; **votre ceinture de sécurité** your seatbelt

cela [səla] pron ① it ▷ *Cela dépend.* It depends. ② that ▷ *Je n'aime pas cela.* I don't like that.; **C'est cela.** That's right.; **à part cela** apart from that

célèbre [selɛbʀ(ə)] adj famous

célébrer [selebʀe] vb to celebrate

céleri [sɛlʀi] nm celery; **des branches de céleri** celery stalks

célibataire [selibatɛʀ] adj, n single; **un célibataire** a bachelor; **une célibataire** a single woman

celle [sɛl] pron see **celui**

celles [sɛl] pron see **ceux**

cellule [selyl] nf cell

Celsius [sɛlsjys] (f, pl **Celsius**) adj Celsius ▷ *vingt degrés Celsius* 20 degrees Celsius

celui [səlɥi, sɛl] (f **celle**, mpl **ceux**, fpl **celles**) pron the one ▷ *Prends celui que tu préfères.* Take the one you like best. ▷ *Je n'ai pas d'appareil photo mais je peux emprunter celui de ma sœur.* I don't have a camera but I can borrow my sister's. ▷ *Je n'ai pas de planche à roulettes mais je peux emprunter celle de mon frère.* I don't have a skateboard but I can borrow my brother's.; **celui-ci** this one; **celle-ci** this one; **celui-là** that one; **celle-là** that one

cendre [sɑ̃dʀ(ə)] nf ash

cendrier [sɑ̃dʀije] nm ashtray

censé [sɑ̃se] (f **censée**) adj: **être censé faire quelque chose** to be supposed to do something ▷ *Vous êtes censé arriver à l'heure.* You're supposed to get here on time.

cent [sɑ̃] num a hundred ▷ *cent dollars* a hundred dollars ▷ *trois cents ans* 300 years ▷ *cent deux kilomètres* 102 kilometres ▷ *trois cent cinquante kilomètres* 350 kilometres ▷ *trois cent mille kilomètres* 300 000 kilometres

cent [sɑ̃] nm (currency) cent

centaine [sɑ̃tɛn] nf about a hundred ▷ *Il y avait une centaine de personnes dans la salle.* There were about a hundred people in the hall.; **des centaines de** hundreds of ▷ *Des centaines de réfugiés se sont présentés à l'ambassade.* Hundreds of refugees came to the embassy.

centenaire [sɑ̃tnɛʀ] nm centennial

centième [sɑ̃tjɛm] adj hundredth

centimètre [sɑ̃timɛtʀ(ə)] nm centimetre

central [sɑ̃tʀal, -o] (f **centrale**, mpl **centraux**) adj central

centrale [sɑ̃tʀal] nf power plant ▷ *une centrale nucléaire* a nuclear power plant

centre [sɑ̃tʀ(ə)] nm centre; **un centre commercial** a shopping centre; **un centre communautaire** a community centre; **un centre d'appels** a call centre; **le centre local de services communautaires** (also **CLSC** in Québec) local community service centre; **le centre de jour** drop-in centre; **le centre de villégiature** resort

centre-ville [sɑ̃tʀavil] (pl **centres-villes**) nm town centre

cependant [səpɑ̃dɑ̃] adv however

cercle [sɛʀkl(ə)] nm circle ▷ *Entourez d'un cercle la bonne réponse.* Put a circle round the right answer.; **un cercle vicieux** a vicious circle

cercueil [sɛʀkœj] nm coffin

cereals [sereal] nfpl cereal ▷ *un bol de céréales* a bowl of cereal; **un pain multicéréales** a multigrain loaf

cérémonie [seʀemɔni] nf ceremony

cerf [sɛʀ] nm deer

cerf-volant [sɛʀvɔlɑ̃] (pl **cerfs-volants**) nm kite

cerise [səʀiz] nf cherry

cerisier [səʀizje] nm cherry tree

cerné [sɛʀne] (f **cernée**) adj: **avoir les yeux cernés** to have dark circles under one's eyes ▷ *Elle avait les yeux cernés.* She had dark circles under her eyes.

cerner [sɛʀne] vb: **J'ai du mal à le cerner.** I can't figure him out.

certain [sɛʀtɛ̃, -ɛn] (f **certaine**) adj ① certain ▷ *Je suis certain que je l'ai remis en place.* I'm certain that I put it back. ▷ *Ce n'est pas certain.* It's not certain. ② some ▷ *Certaines personnes n'aiment pas la crème.* Some people don't like cream.; **un certain temps** quite some time ▷ *J'ai mis un certain temps à comprendre ce qu'elle disait.* It took me quite some time to understand what she was saying.

certainement [sɛʀtɛnmɑ̃] adv ① definitely ▷ *C'est certainement le meilleur film que j'ai vu cette année.* It's definitely the best film I've seen this year. ② of course ▷ «*Est-ce que je peux t'emprunter ton stylo?* » — «*Mais certainement!* » "Can I borrow your pen?" — "Of course!"

certains [sɛʀtɛ̃] pron ① some ▷ *certains de ses amis* some of his friends ▷ *certains d'entre vous* some of you ② some people ▷ *Certains pensent que le film est meilleur que le roman.* Some people think that the film is better than the novel.

certes [sɛʀt(ə)] adv certainly ▷ *Nous nous connaissons, certes, mais nous ne sommes pas amis.* We know each other, certainly, but we are not friends.

certificat [sɛʀtifika] nm certificate; **le certificat-cadeau** gift certificate

cerveau [sɛʀvo] (pl **cerveaux**) nm brain

cervelle [sɛʀvɛl] nf brain; **se creuser la cervelle** (informal) to rack one's brains

ces [se] adj ① these ▷ *Tu peux prendre ces photos si tu veux.* You can have these photos if you like.; **ces photos-ci** these photos ② those ▷ *Ces montagnes sont dangereuses en hiver.* Those mountains are dangerous in winter.; **ces livres-là** those books

cesse [sɛs] : **sans cesse** adv continually; **Elle me dérange sans cesse.** She keeps interrupting me.

cesser [sese] vb to stop ▷ *cesser de faire quelque chose* to stop doing something

cessez-le-feu [seselfø] (pl **cessez-le-feu**) nm ceasefire

c'est-à-dire [sɛtadiʀ] adv that is ▷ *Est-ce que tu peux venir lundi prochain, c'est-à-dire le quinze?* Can you come next Monday, that is, the 15th?

cet [sɛt] (f **cette**) adj ① this ▷ *cet après-midi* this afternoon ▷ **cet hiver** this winter ▷ **cette année** this year; **cette semaine-ci** this week ❷ that ▷ *Est-ce que tu peux me passer cette assiette?* Could you pass me that plate?; **cet homme-là** that man; **cette nuit (1)** tonight ▷ *On prévoit de l'orage pour cette nuit.* A storm is forecast for tonight. **(2)** last night ▷ *J'ai très mal dormi cette nuit.* I slept very badly last night.

ceux [sø] (fpl **celles**) pron the ones ▷ *Prends ceux tu préfères.* Take the ones you like best. ▷ *Je n'ai pas de skis mais je peux emprunter ceux de ma sœur.* I don't have any skis but I can borrow my sister's. ▷ *Je n'ai pas de jumelles mais je peux emprunter celles de mon frère.* I don't have any binoculars but I can borrow my brother's.; **ceux-ci** these ones; **celles-ci** these ones; **ceux-là** those ones; **celles-là** those ones

chacun [ʃakœ̃, -yn] pron (f **chacune**) ❶ each ▷ *Il nous a donné un cadeau à chacun.* He gave us each a present. ▷ *Nous avons chacun donné dix dollars.* We each gave 10 dollars. ▷ *Ces verres coûtent cinq dollars chacun.* These glasses cost 5 dollars each. ❷ everyone ▷ *Chacun fait ce qu'il veut.* Everyone does what they like.

chagrin [ʃagrɛ̃] nm: **avoir du chagrin** to be very upset ▷ *Elle a eu beaucoup de chagrin à la mort de son oncle.* She was terribly upset by the death of her uncle.

chahut [ʃay] nm bedlam ▷ *Il y avait du chahut dans la classe.* There was bedlam in the classroom.

chaîne [ʃɛn] nf ❶ chain ▷ *une chaîne en or a* gold chain ❷ (on TV) channel ▷ *Le film passe sur quelle chaîne?* What channel is the film on?; **la chaîne alimentaire** food chain; **une chaîne de montagnes** a mountain range; **une chaîne stéréo** an audio system; **travailler à la chaîne** to work on an assembly line

chair [ʃɛr] nf flesh; **en chair et en os** in the flesh ▷ *Je l'ai vu en chair et en os.* I saw him in the flesh.; **avoir la chair de poule** to have goose pimples

chaise [ʃɛz] nf chair; **une chaise berçante** a rocking chair; **une chaise longue** a lounge chair

chaleur [ʃalœr] nf ❶ heat ❷ warmth

chaleureux [ʃalœrø, -øz] (f **chaleureuse**) adj warm ▷ *un accueil chaleureux* a warm welcome

chaloupe [ʃalup] nf rowboat ▷ *Les enfants sont partis en chaloupe.* The kids left in the rowboat.

se chamailler [ʃamaje] vb (informal) to squabble ▷ *Elle se chamaille sans cesse avec son frère.* She's always squabbling with her brother.

chambre [ʃɑ̃br(ə)] nf room ▷ *C'est la chambre de ma sœur.* This is my sister's room.; **une chambre à coucher** a bedroom; **une chambre d'amis** a spare room; **une chambre à un lit** a single room; **une chambre pour une personne** a single room; **une chambre pour deux personnes** a double room; **la Chambre des communes** House of Commons

chameau [ʃamo] (pl **chameaux**) nm camel

champ [ʃɑ̃] nm field

champignon [ʃɑ̃piɲɔ̃] nm mushroom ▷ *une omelette aux champignons* a mushroom omelette

champion [ʃɑ̃pjɔ̃] nm champion

championnat [ʃɑ̃pjɔna] nm championship ▷ *le championnat du monde* the world championship

championne [ʃɑ̃pjɔn] nf champion

chance [ʃɑ̃s] nf ❶ luck; **Bonne chance!** Good luck!; **par chance** luckily; **avoir de la chance** to be lucky ▷ *Tu as de la chance de partir au soleil!* You're lucky, going off to a sunny place! ❷ chance ▷ *Il n'a aucune chance.* He doesn't have a chance. ▷ *Elle a des chances de réussir.* She has a good chance of passing.

chandail [ʃɑ̃daj] nm sweater ▷ *un chandail de laine* a wool sweater

change [ʃɑ̃ʒ] nm exchange ▷ *le taux de change* the exchange rate

changement [ʃɑ̃ʒmɑ̃] nm change ▷ *Elle n'aime pas le changement.* She doesn't like change.

changer [ʃɑ̃ʒe] vb to change ▷ *Elle n'a pas beaucoup changé.* She hasn't changed much. ▷ *J'ai changé les draps ce matin.* I changed the sheets this morning. ▷ *J'ai changé trois cents dollars.* I changed 300 dollars.; **se changer** to get changed ▷ *Je vais me changer avant de sortir.* I'm going to get changed before I go out.; **changer de** to change ▷ *Je change de chaussures et j'arrive!* I'll change my shoes and then I'll be ready!; **changer d'avis** to change one's mind ▷ *Appelle-moi si tu changes d'avis.* Call me if you change your mind.; **changer de chaîne** to change the channel

chanson [ʃɑ̃sɔ̃] nf song

chant [ʃɑ̃] nm singing ▷ *des cours de chant* singing lessons; **un chant de Noël** a Christmas carol

chantage [ʃɑ̃taʒ] nm blackmail ▷ *faire du chantage à quelqu'un* to blackmail somebody

chanter [ʃɑ̃te] vb to sing

chanteur [ʃɑ̃tœr] nm singer

chanteuse [ʃɑ̃tøz] nf singer

chantier [ʃɑ̃tje] nm building site

Chantilly [ʃɑ̃tiji] nf whipped cream

chantonner [ʃɑ̃tɔne] vb to hum

chapeau [ʃapo] (pl **chapeaux**) nm hat

chapitre [ʃapitr(ə)] nm chapter

chaque [ʃak] adj ❶ every ▷ *chaque année* every year ❷ each ▷ *Donne un livre à chaque élève.* Give a book to each student.

char [ʃar] nm (military) tank

charabia [ʃarabja] nm (informal) gibberish ▷ *Je n'y comprends rien : c'est du charabia.* I don't understand any of it: it's gibberish.

charade [ʃarad] nf ❶ riddle ❷ charade ▷ *jouer aux charades* to play charades

charbon [ʃarbɔ̃] nm coal; **le charbon de bois** charcoal; **être sur des charbons ardents** to be on pins and needles

charcuterie [ʃarkytri] nf ❶ deli ❷ cold cuts

chardon [ʃardɔ̃] nm thistle

charger [ʃarʒe] vb to load; **charger quelqu'un de faire quelque chose** to tell somebody to do something ▷ *Il m'a chargé de vous dire que la clé est sous le paillasson.* He told me to tell you that the key's under the mat.

chariot [ʃarjo] nm shopping cart

charmant [ʃarmɑ̃, -ɑ̃t] (f **charmante**) adj

charming

charme [ʃaʀm(ə)] nm charm

charmer [ʃaʀme] vb to charm

charrue [ʃaʀy] nf plough

chasse [ʃas] nf hunting ▷ *un chien de chasse* a hunting dog ▷ *la chasse au canard* duck hunting; **tirer la chasse d'eau** to flush the toilet

chasse-neige [ʃasnɛʒ] (pl **chasse-neige**) nm snowplow

chasser [ʃase] vb ❶ to hunt ▷ *Mon père chasse le lapin.* My father hunts rabbits. ❷ to chase away ▷ *Ils ont chassé les cambrioleurs.* They chased away the robbers. ❸ to get rid of ▷ *Ouvre donc la fenêtre pour chasser les odeurs de cuisine.* Open the window to get rid of the cooking smells.

chasseur [ʃasœʀ] nm hunter

chasseuse [ʃasøz] nf hunter

chat [ʃa] nm cat

châtain [ʃatɛ̃] (f+pl **châtain**) adj brown ▷ *J'ai les cheveux châtain.* I've got brown hair.

château [ʃato] (pl **châteaux**) nm ❶ castle; **un château fort** a castle ❷ palace ▷ *le château de Versailles* the palace of Versailles

chaton [ʃatɔ̃] nm kitten

chatouiller [ʃatuje] vb to tickle

chatouilleux [ʃatujø, -øz] (f **chatouilleuse**) adj ❶ ticklish ❷ touchy ▷ *Il est un peu chatouilleux sur cette question.* He's a bit touchy on that issue.

chatte [ʃat] nf (female) cat

chaud [ʃo, -od] (f **chaude**) adj ❶ warm ▷ *des vêtements chauds* warm clothes; **avoir chaud** to be warm or hot ▷ *J'ai assez chaud.* I'm warm enough. ❷ hot ▷ *Il fait chaud aujourd'hui.* It's hot today. ▷ *un plat chaud* a hot dish ▷ *Attention, c'est chaud!* Careful, it's hot! ▷ *J'ai trop chaud!* I'm too hot!

chauffage [ʃofaʒ] nm heating ▷ *Le chauffage est en panne.* The heating isn't working. ▷ *Baisse le chauffage.* Turn down the heat.; **le chauffage central** central heating

chauffe-eau [ʃofo] (pl **chauffe-eau**) nm water heater

chauffer [ʃofe] vb to heat ▷ *Je vais mettre de l'eau à chauffer pour faire du thé.* I'm going to put some water on to make tea.

chauffeur [ʃofœʀ] nm driver ▷ *un chauffeur de taxi* a taxi driver

chauffeuse [ʃoføz] nf driver ▷ *une chauffeuse d'autobus* a bus driver

chaussée [ʃose] nf roadway ▷ *Ne fais pas de la planche à roulettes sur la chaussée.* Don't skateboard on the road.

chausser [ʃose] vb: **Vous chaussez du combien?** What size shoe do you take?

chaussette [ʃosɛt] nf sock

chausson [ʃosɔ̃] nm slipper; **un chausson aux pommes** an apple turnover

chaussure [ʃosyʀ] nf shoe; **les chaussures de ski** ski boots

chauve [ʃov] adj bald

chauve-souris [ʃovsuʀi] (pl **chauves-souris**) nf (animal) bat

chef [ʃɛf] nmf ❶ head ▷ *une chef de famille*

monoparentale a single parent; **le chef de l'État** the Head of State; **un chef d'entreprise** the director of a company ❷ chef ▷ *la spécialité de la chef* the chef's specialty; **un chef d'orchestre** a conductor; **le chef de bande** band chief

chef-d'œuvre [ʃe-] (pl **chefs-d'œuvre**) nm masterpiece

chemin [ʃəmɛ̃] nm ❶ path ▷ *Je suis descendu à la plage par un petit chemin.* I took a little path down to the beach. ❷ way ▷ *Quel est le chemin le plus court pour aller à l'aéroport?* What's the quickest way to the airport?; **en chemin** on the way ▷ *Je mangerai mon sandwich en chemin.* I'll eat my sandwich on the way.; **le chemin de fer** the railway

cheminée [ʃəmine] nf ❶ chimney ❷ fireplace

chemise [ʃəmiz] nf ❶ shirt ▷ *une chemise à carreaux* a checked shirt; **une chemise de nuit** a nightgown ❷ folder

chemisier [ʃəmizje] nm blouse

chêne [ʃɛn] nm oak ▷ *une armoire en chêne* an oak wardrobe

chenil [ʃənil] nm kennels

chenille [ʃənij] nf caterpillar

chèque [ʃɛk] nm cheque; **les chèques de voyage** traveller's cheques

chéquier [ʃekje] nm chequebook

cher [ʃɛʀ] (f **chère**) adj, adv ❶ dear ▷ *Chère Madame...* Dear Madam... ❷ expensive ▷ *C'est trop cher.* It's too expensive. ▷ *coûter cher* to be expensive

chercher [ʃɛʀʃe] vb ❶ to look for ▷ *Je cherche mes clés.* I'm looking for my keys. ❷ to look up ▷ *chercher un mot dans le dictionnaire* to look up a word in the dictionary; **aller chercher (1)** to go to get ▷ *Il est allé chercher du pain pour ce midi.* He's gone to get some bread for lunch. **(2)** to pick up ▷ *J'irai te chercher à la bibliothèque.* I'll pick you up at the library.

chercheur [ʃɛʀʃœʀ] nm researcher

chercheuse [ʃɛʀʃøz] nf researcher

chère [ʃɛʀ] adj see **cher**

chéri [ʃeʀi] (f **chérie**) adj darling ▷ *ma petite fille chérie* my darling daughter ▶ nm darling; **mon chéri** darling

chérie [ʃeʀi] nf darling; **ma chérie** darling

cheval [ʃəval, -o] (pl **chevaux**) nm horse ▷ *un cheval de course* a racehorse; **à cheval** on horseback; **faire du cheval** to go riding

chevalier [ʃəvalje] nm knight

chevaux [ʃəvo] nmpl see **cheval**

chevet [ʃəvɛ] nm: **une table de chevet** a bedside table; **une lampe de chevet** a bedside lamp

cheveux [ʃəvø] nmpl hair ▷ *Elle a les cheveux courts.* She has short hair.; **tiré par les cheveux** far-fetched ▷ *Son excuse était complètement tirée par les cheveux.* His excuse was totally far-fetched.

cheville [ʃəvij] nf ankle ▷ *se fouler la cheville* to sprain one's ankle

chèvre [ʃɛvʀ(ə)] nf goat; **le fromage de chèvre** goat cheese

chevreau [ʃəvʀo] (pl **chevreaux**) nm (animal,

leather) kid

chevreuil [ʃəvrœj] nm ❶ deer ❷ venison

chez [ʃe] prep: **chez mon ami (1)** at my friend's house **(2)** to my friend's house; **chez moi (1)** at my house ▷ *Je suis resté chez moi cette fin de semaine.* I stayed home this weekend. **(2)** to my house ▷ *Je vais rentrer chez moi.* I'm going home.; **chez le dentiste (1)** at the dentist's ▷ *J'ai rendez-vous chez le dentiste demain matin.* I've got an appointment at the dentist's tomorrow morning. **(2)** to the dentist's ▷ *Je vais chez le dentiste.* I'm going to the dentist.

chic [ʃik] (f+pl **chic**) adj ❶ smart ▷ *une tenue chic* a smart outfit ❷ nice ▷ *C'est chic de sa part.* (informal) That was nice of her.

chien [ʃjɛ̃] nm dog; **« Attention, chien méchant »** "Beware of dog"

chienne [ʃjɛn] nf (dog) bitch

chiffon [ʃifɔ̃] nm (cleaning, polishing) cloth

chiffonner [ʃifɔne] vb to crease ▷ *Ma robe est toute chiffonnée.* My dress is all creased.

chiffre [ʃifr(ə)] nm figure ▷ *en chiffres ronds* in round figures; **les chiffres romains** Roman numerals

chignon [ʃiɲɔ̃] nm (hair) bun ▷ *Elle s'est fait un chignon.* She put her hair in a bun.

chimie [ʃimi] nf chemistry ▷ *un cours de chimie* a chemistry lesson

chimique [ʃimik] adj chemical ▷ *une réaction chimique* a chemical reaction; **les armes chimiques** chemical weapons; **les produits chimiques** chemicals

Chinook [ʃinuk] nm (warm wind) chinook ▷ *Un coup de chinook peut faire fondre trente centimètres de neige en une heure.* A chinook can melt 30 centimetres of snow in one hour.

chiot [ʃjo] nm puppy

chirurgical [ʃiryʒikal, -o] (f **chirurgicale**, mpl **chirurgicaux**) adj: **une intervention chirurgicale** an operation

chirurgie [ʃiryʒi] nf surgery; **la chirurgie esthétique** plastic surgery

chirurgien [ʃiryʒjɛ̃] nm surgeon

chirurgienne [ʃiryʒjɛn] nf surgeon

choc [ʃɔk] nm shock ▷ *Ça m'a fait un choc de le voir comme ça.* It gave me a shock to see him in that state.; **Elle est encore sous le choc.** She's still in shock.

chocolat [ʃɔkɔla] nm chocolate; **un chocolat chaud** a hot chocolate; **le chocolat noir** dark chocolate

choisir [ʃwazir] vb to choose

choix [ʃwa] nm ❶ choice; **avoir le choix** to have the choice ❷ selection ▷ *Il n'y a pas beaucoup de choix dans ce magasin.* There's not a very wide selection in this store.

chômage [ʃomaʒ] nm unemployment; **être au chômage** to be unemployed

chômeur [ʃomœr] nm unemployed person ▷ *Il est chômeur.* He's unemployed.

chômeuse [ʃomøz] nf unemployed woman ▷ *Elle est chômeuse.* She's unemployed.

choquer [ʃɔke] vb to shock ▷ *Cette remarque m'a choqué.* I was shocked by that remark.

chorale [kɔral] nf choir

chose [ʃoz] nf thing ▷ *J'ai fait des choses*

intéressantes pendant les vacances. I did some interesting things during the holidays.; **C'est peu de chose.** It's nothing really.

chou [ʃu] (pl **choux**) nm cabbage; **les choux de Bruxelles** Brussels sprouts; **un chou à la crème** a cream puff

chouchou [ʃuʃu] nm (informal) teacher's pet

chouchoute [ʃuʃut] nf (informal) teacher's pet

choucroute [ʃukrut] nf (with sausages and ham) sauerkraut

chouette [ʃwet] nf ❶ owl ❷ (to young girl: informal) dear ▷ *Oui, ma chouette!* Yes, my dear!
▸ adj (informal) interesting ▷ *un jeu très chouette* a very interesting game

chou-fleur [ʃuflœr] (pl **choux-fleurs**) nm cauliflower

chrétien [kretjɛ̃, -ɛn] (f **chrétienne**) adj Christian ▷ *Il est chrétien.* He's a Christian.

chronique [krɔnik] adj chronic ▷ *une toux chronique* a chronic cough

chronique [krɔnik] nf column ▷ *Il écrit une chronique pour le journal de l'école.* He writes a column for the school newspaper.

chronologique [krɔnɔlɔʒik] adj chronological

chronomètre [krɔnɔmɛtr(ə)] nm stopwatch

chronométrer [krɔnɔmetre] vb to time

chuchoter [ʃyʃɔte] vb to whisper

chut [ʃyt] excl Shh!

chute [ʃyt] nf fall; **faire une chute** to fall; **les chutes Niagara** Niagara Falls; **une chute d'eau** a waterfall

-ci [si] adv: **ce livre-ci** this book; **ces bottes-ci** these boots

cible [sibl(ə)] nf target

ciboulette [sibulet] nf chives

cicatrice [sikatris] nf scar

se cicatriser [sikatrize] vb to heal up ▷ *Cette plaie s'est vite cicatrisée.* This wound has healed up quickly.

ci-contre [sikɔ̃tr(ə)] adv opposite ▷ *la page ci-contre* the opposite page

ci-dessous [sidəsu] adv below ▷ *la photo ci-dessous* the picture below

ci-dessus [sidəsy] adv above

cidre [sidr(ə)] nm cider

ciel [sjel] nm ❶ sky ▷ *un ciel nuageux* a cloudy sky ❷ heaven ▷ *être au ciel* to be in heaven

cierge [sjerʒ(ə)] nm (in church) candle

cigale [sigal] nf cricket

cigare [sigar] nm cigar ▷ *Il ne fume plus le cigare.* He no longer smokes cigars.

cigarette [sigaret] nf cigarette

ci-joint [siʒwɛ̃] adv enclosed ▷ *Veuillez trouver ci-joint mon curriculum vitæ.* Please find enclosed my résumé.

cil [sil] nm eyelash

ciment [simã] nm cement

cimetière [simtjer] nm cemetery

cinéaste [sineast(ə)] nmf filmmaker

cinéma [sinema] nm movie theatre

cinq [sɛ̃k] num five ▷ *Il est cinq heures du matin.* It's five in the morning. ▷ *Elle a cinq ans.* She's five.; **le cinq février** the fifth of February

cinquantaine [sɛ̃kɑ̃ten] nf about fifty ▷ *Il y avait une cinquantaine de personnes.* There were about fifty people there.; **Il a la cinquantaine.** He's in his fifties.

cinquante [sɛ̃kɑ̃t] *num* fifty ▷ *Elle a cinquante ans.* She's fifty.; **cinquante et un** fifty-one; **cinquante-deux** fifty-two

cinquième [sɛ̃kjɛm] *adj* fifth ▷ *au cinquième étage* on the fifth floor ▷ *Mon frère est en cinquième année.* My brother is in Grade 5.

cintre [sɛ̃tr(ə)] *nm* coat hanger

cirage [siraʒ] *nm* shoe polish

circonflexe [sirkɔ̃flɛks(ə)] *adj*: **un accent circonflexe** a circumflex

circonstance [sirkɔ̃stɑ̃s] *nf* circumstance ▷ *dans les circonstances actuelles* in the present circumstances

circulation [sirkylɑsjɔ̃] *nf* ① traffic ▷ *Il y avait beaucoup de circulation.* There was a lot of traffic. ② circulation ▷ *Elle a des problèmes de circulation.* She has bad circulation.

circuler [sirkyle] *vb* to run ▷ *Il n'y a qu'un autobus sur trois qui circule.* Only one bus in three is running.

cire [sir] *nf* wax

cirer [sire] *vb* (*shoes, floor*) to polish; **papier ciré** waxed paper

cirque [sirk(ə)] *nm* circus

ciseaux [sizo] *nmpl*: **une paire de ciseaux** a pair of scissors

citadin [sitadɛ̃] *nm* city person

citation [sitasjɔ̃] *nf* quotation

cité [site] *nf* town ▷ *une cité industrielle* an industrial town; **une cité universitaire** a university campus; **la cité parlementaire** Parliament buildings (in Québec city)

citer [site] *vb* to quote

citoyen [sitwajɛ̃] *nm* citizen

citoyenne [sitwajɛn] *nf* citizen

citoyenneté [sitwajɛnte] *nf* citizenship

citron [sitrɔ̃] *nm* lemon

citrouille [sitruj] *nf* pumpkin

civière [sivjɛr] *nf* stretcher

civil [sivil] (*f* **civile**) *adj* civilian; **en civil** in civilian clothes

civilisation [sivilizasjɔ̃] *nf* civilization

civique [sivik] *adj* ① civic ▷ *son devoir civique* one's civic duty ② civil ▷ *les droits civiques* civil rights; **avoir le sens civique** to be public-spirited

clair [klɛr] (*f* **claire**) *adj, adv* ① light ▷ *vert clair* light green ▷ *C'est une pièce très claire.* It's a very bright room. ② (*water*) clear; **voir clair** to see clearly; **le clair de lune** moonlight

clairement [klɛrmɑ̃] *adv* clearly

clairière [klɛrjɛr] *nf* clearing

clandestin [klɑ̃dɛstɛ̃, -ɛ̃] (*f* **clandestine**) *adj*: **un passager clandestin** a stowaway

claque [klak] *nf* slap

claquer [klake] *vb* ① to bang ▷ *On entend des volets qui claquent.* You can hear shutters banging. ② to slam ▷ *Elle est partie en claquant la porte.* She left, slamming the door behind her.

claquette [klakɛt] *nf*: **danser la claquette** to tap-dance

clarinette [klarinɛt] *nf* clarinet

classe [klas] *nf* ① class ▷ *C'est le meilleur élève de la classe.* He's the best student in the class. ▷ *voyager en première classe* to travel first class ② classroom

classer [klase] *vb* to arrange ▷ *Les livres sont classés par ordre alphabétique.* The books are arranged in alphabetical order.

classeur [klasœr] *nm* filing cabinet

classique [klasik] *adj* ① classical ▷ *de la musique classique* classical music ② classic ▷ *un style classique* a classic style

clavardage [klavardaʒ] *nm* (*online*) chat

clavarder [klavarde] *vb* (*online*) to chat

clavardoir [klavardwar] *nm* chat room

clavier [klavje] *nm* (*computer, typewriter*) keyboard; **le clavier numérique** keypad

clé [kle] *nf* ① key ▷ *une clé de voiture* a car key ② clef ▷ *la clé de sol* the treble clef ▷ *la clé de fa* the bass clef; **une clé anglaise** a wrench

clef [kle] *nf* = **clé**

clic [klik] *nm* (*computer mouse*) click

client [klijɑ̃] *nm* customer

cliente [klijɑ̃t] *nf* customer

clientèle [klijɑ̃tɛl] *nf* customers

cligner [kliɲe] *vb*: **cligner des yeux** to blink

clignotant [kliɲɔtɑ̃] *nm* turn signal ▷ *Il a mis son clignotant gauche.* He's signalling left.

climat [klima] *nm* climate

climatisation [klimatizasjɔ̃] *nf* air conditioning

climatisé [klimatize] (*f* **climatisée**) *adj* air-conditioned ▷ *L'hôtel est climatisé.* The hotel is air-conditioned.

clin d'œil [klɛ̃-] (*pl* **clins d'œil**) *nm* wink; **en un clin d'œil** in a flash

clinique [klinik] *nf* clinic

clipart [klipart] *nm* clip-art

cliquer [klike] *vb* to click ▷ *cliquer sur une icône* to click on an icon

clochard [klɔʃar] *nm* tramp

cloche [klɔʃ] *nf* bell

clone [klon] *nm* clone

cloner [klone] *vb* to clone

clou [klu] *nm* nail; **un clou de girofle** a clove

clown [klun] *nm* clown

CLSC *nm* = **Centre local de services communautaires**

club [klœb] *nm* club

cobaye [kɔbaj] *nm* guinea pig

cocaïne [kɔkain] *nf* cocaine

coccinelle [kɔksinɛl] *nf* ladybug

cocher [kɔʃe] *vb* to mark with a check ▷ *Cochez la bonne réponse.* Put a check beside the right answer.

cochon [kɔʃɔ̃] *nm* pig; **un cochon d'Inde** a guinea pig

coco [kɔko] *nm*: **une noix de coco** a coconut

cocotte [kɔkɔt] *nf* (*pan*) casserole

code [kɔd] *nm* code; **le code à barres** barcode; **le code postal** the postal code

cœur [kœr] *nm* heart; **avoir bon cœur** to be kind-hearted; **la dame de cœur** the queen of hearts; **avoir mal au cœur** to feel sick; **par cœur** by heart ▷ *apprendre quelque chose par cœur* to learn something by heart

coffre [kɔfr(ə)] *nm* ① (*of car*) trunk ② (*furniture*) chest

coffre-fort [kɔfʀəfɔʀ] (pl **coffres-forts**) nm safe

coffret [kɔfʀɛ] nm: **un coffret à bijoux** a jewellery box

se **cogner** [kɔɲe] vb: **se cogner à quelque chose** to bump into something ▷ *Je me suis cogné à la table.* I bumped into the table. ▷ *Je me suis cogné la tête contre la porte du placard.* I bumped my head on the cupboard door.

coiffé [kwafe] (f **coiffée**) adj: **Tu es bien coiffée.** Your hair looks nice.

coiffer [kwafe] vb: **se coiffer** to do one's hair

coiffeur [kwafœʀ] nm hairdresser

coiffeuse [kwaføz] nf hairdresser

coiffure [kwafyʀ] nf hairstyle ▷ *Cette coiffure te va bien.* That hairstyle suits you.; **un salon de coiffure** a hair salon

coin [kwɛ̃] nm corner; **au coin de la rue** on the corner of the street; **Tu habites dans le coin?** Do you live around here?; **le dépanneur du coin** the local convenience store

coincé [kwɛ̃se] (f **coincée**) adj ❶ stuck ▷ *La clé est coincée dans la serrure.* The key is stuck in the lock. ❷ stuffy ▷ *Il est un peu coincé.* (*informal*) He's a bit stuffy.

coincer [kwɛ̃se] vb to jam ▷ *La porte est coincée.* The door's jammed.

coïncidence [kɔɛ̃sidɑ̃s] nf coincidence

col [kɔl] nm ❶ collar; **un col roulé** a turtleneck ❷ (*mountain*) pass

colère [kɔlɛʀ] nf anger; **Je suis en colère.** I'm angry.; **se mettre en colère** to get angry

colique [kɔlik] nf stomach pain

colis [kɔli] nm parcel

collaborer [kɔlabɔʀe] vb to collaborate

collant [kɔlɑ̃, -ɑ̃t] (f **collante**) adj ❶ sticky ❷ clingy; **Je la trouve un peu collante.** (*informal*) She's always hanging around me. ▶ nm tights ▷ *un collant en laine* woollen tights

collation [kɔlasjɔ̃] nf snack

colle [kɔl] nf glue ▷ *un tube de colle* a tube of glue; **Je n'en sais rien : tu me poses une colle.** (*informal*) I really don't know: you've got me there.

collecte [kɔlɛkt(ə)] nf (*of money*) collection ▷ *On a fait une collecte au profit des victimes.* There was a collection for the victims.; **une collecte de bouteilles vides** a bottle drive

collection [kɔlɛksjɔ̃] nf collection ▷ *une collection de timbres* a stamp collection

collectionner [kɔlɛksjɔne] vb to collect

collège [kɔlɛʒ] nm college; **collège communautaire** community college

collégien [kɔleʒjɛ̃] nm student

collégienne [kɔleʒjɛn] nf student

collègue [kɔlɛg] nmf colleague

coller [kɔle] vb ❶ to stick ▷ *Il y a de la gomme à mâcher collée sous la chaise.* There's a wad of chewing gum stuck under the chair. ❷ to be sticky ▷ *Ce ruban ne colle plus.* This tape is no longer sticky. ❸ to press ▷ *J'ai collé mon oreille au mur pour écouter.* I pressed my ear against the wall to listen.

collier [kɔlje] nm ❶ necklace ▷ *un collier de perles* a pearl necklace ❷ (*of dog, cat*) collar

colline [kɔlin] nf hill; **la Colline du Parlement**

Parliament Hill (in Ottawa)

collision [kɔlizjɔ̃] nf crash

colombe [kɔlɔ̃b] nf dove

Colombie-Britannique nf British Columbia

colonie [kɔlɔni] nf colony ▷ *la colonie de la Nouvelle France* the colony of New France

colonne [kɔlɔn] nf pillar; **la colonne vertébrale** the spine

colorant [kɔlɔʀɑ̃] nm ❶ colouring ❷ dye

coma [kɔma] nm coma ▷ *être dans le coma* to be in a coma

combat [kɔ̃ba] nm fighting ▷ *Les combats ont repris ce matin.* Fighting started again this morning.; **un combat de boxe** a boxing match

combattant [kɔ̃batɑ̃] nm: **un ancien combattant** a war veteran

combattre [kɔ̃batʀ(ə)] vb to fight

combien [kɔ̃bjɛ̃] adv ❶ how much ▷ *Vous en voulez combien? Un kilo?* How much do you want? One kilo?; **C'est combien?** How much is that? ▷ *Combien est-ce que ça coûte?* How much does it cost? ▷ *Combien ça fait?* How much does it come to? ❷ how many ▷ *Tu en veux combien? Deux?* How many do you want? Two?; **combien de (1)** how much ▷ *Combien de purée de pomme de terre est-ce que je vous sers?* How much mashed potato shall I give you? **(2)** how many ▷ *Combien de personnes as-tu invitées?* How many people have you invited?; **combien de temps** how long ▷ *Combien de temps est-ce que tu seras absente?* How long will you be away?; **Il y a combien de temps?** How long ago? ▷ *Il est parti il y a combien de temps?* How long ago did he leave?; **« On est le combien aujourd'hui? »** — **« On est le vingt. »** "What's the date today?" — "It's the 20th."

combinaison [kɔ̃binɛzɔ̃] nf combination ▷ *J'ai changé la combinaison de mon antivol.* I've changed the combination on my bike lock.; **une combinaison de plongée** a wetsuit; **une combinaison de ski** a ski suit

comédie [kɔmedi] nf comedy; **une comédie musicale** a musical

comédien [kɔmedjɛ̃] nm actor

comédienne [kɔmedjɛn] nf actress

comestible [kɔmɛstibl(ə)] adj edible

comique [kɔmik] adj comical ▶ n comedian

comité [kɔmite] nm committee

commandant [kɔmɑ̃dɑ̃] nm (*ship, plane*) captain

commandante [kɔmɑ̃dɑ̃t] nf (*ship, plane*) captain

commande [kɔmɑ̃d] nf order ▷ *un bon de commande* an order form; **être aux commandes** to be at the controls

commander [kɔmɑ̃de] vb ❶ to order ▷ *J'ai commandé une robe par catalogue.* I've ordered a dress from the catalogue. ❷ to give orders ▷ *C'est moi qui commande ici, pas vous!* I give the orders here, not you!; **Elle commande le respect.** She commands respect.

comme [kɔm] conj, adv ❶ like ▷ *Elle est comme son père.* She's like her father. ▷ *Je voudrais un manteau comme celui-là de la photo.* I'd like a coat like the one in the picture. ❷ for ▷ *Qu'est-ce* que tu veux comme dessert? What would you like for dessert? ❷ as ▷ *J'ai travaillé comme serveuse cet été.* I worked as a waitress this summer. ▷ *Faites comme bon vous semble.* Do as you like.; **comme ça** like this ▷ *Ça se plie comme ça.* You fold it like this. ▷ *C'était un poisson grand comme ça.* The fish was this big.; **comme il faut** properly ▷ *Mets le couvert comme il faut!* Set the table properly!; **Comme tu as grandi!** How you've grown!; **Regarde comme c'est beau!** Look, isn't it lovely!; **comme ci comme ça** so-so ▷ *«Comment est-ce que tu as trouvé le film?» — «Comme ci comme ça.»* "What did you think of the film?" — "So-so."

commencement [kɔmɑ̃smɑ̃] *nm* beginning

commencer [kɔmɑ̃se] *vb* to start ▷ *Les cours commencent à huit heures.* Classes start at 8 o'clock. ▷ *Il a commencé à pleuvoir.* It started raining. ▷ *J'ai commencé à réviser pour les examens.* I've started studying for the exams.

comment [kɔmɑ̃] *adv* how ▷ *Comment arrives-tu à travailler dans ce bruit?* How can you possibly work with this noise?; **Comment allez-vous?** How are you?; **Comment dit-on « pomme » en anglais?** How do you say "pomme" in English?; **Comment s'appelle-t-elle?** What's her name?; **Comment?** What did you say?

commentaire [kɔmɑ̃tɛr] *nm* comment

commérages [kɔmeraʒ] *nmpl* gossip

commerçant [kɔmɛrsɑ̃] *nm* storekeeper

commerçante [kɔmɛrsɑ̃t] *nf* storekeeper

commerce [kɔmɛrs(ə)] *nm* ❶ trade ▷ *le commerce extérieur* foreign trade; **le commerce électronique** e-commerce ❷ business ▷ *Il fait des études de commerce.* He's studying business. ▷ *tenir un commerce* to have a business

commercial [kɔmɛrsjal, -o] (*f* **commerciale**, *mpl* **commerciaux**) *adj*: **un centre commercial** a shopping centre

commettre [kɔmɛtr(ə)] *vb* to commit ▷ *Elle a commis un crime grave.* She has committed a serious crime.

commissions [kɔmisjɔ̃] *nfpl* errands ▷ *J'ai quelques commissions à faire.* I've got some errands to run.

commode [kɔmɔd] *adj* handy ▷ *Ce sac est très commode pour les voyages.* This bag is very handy for travelling.; **Son père n'est pas commode.** His father is a difficult character.
▶ *nf* dresser

commun [kɔmœ̃, -yn] (*f* **commune**) *adj* shared ▷ *une salle de bain commune* a shared bathroom ▷ *Nous avons des intérêts communs.* We have interests in common.; **en commun** in common ▷ *Ils n'ont rien en commun.* They have nothing in common.; **les transports en commun** public transport; **mettre quelque chose en commun** to share something ▷ *Nous mettons tous nos livres en commun.* We share all our books.

communauté [kɔmynote] *nf* community

communication [kɔmynikasjɔ̃] *nf* communication; **une communication scientifique** a scientific conference

communiquer [kɔmynike] *vb* to communicate

communiste [kɔmynist(ə)] *adj* communist ▷ *le Parti communiste* the Communist Party

compact [kɔ̃pakt] (*f* **compacte**) *adj* compact; **un disque compact** a compact disc

compagne [kɔ̃paɲ] *nf* ❶ companion ❷ (*living together*) partner

compagnie [kɔ̃paɲi] *nf* company ▷ *J'aime avoir de la compagnie.* I like to have company. ▷ *Je viendrai te tenir compagnie.* I'll come and keep you company.; **une compagnie d'assurances** an insurance company; **une compagnie aérienne** an airline

compagnon [kɔ̃paɲɔ̃] *nm* ❶ companion ❷ (*living together*) partner

comparaison [kɔ̃parɛzɔ̃] *nf* comparison ▷ *en comparaison de* in comparison with

comparer [kɔ̃pare] *vb* to compare

compartiment [kɔ̃partimɑ̃] *nm* compartment

compas [kɔ̃pa] *nm* (*for drawing circles*) compass

compatible [kɔ̃patibl(ə)] *adj* compatible

compétence [kɔ̃petɑ̃s] *nf* ❶ skill ▷ *compétences de vie* life skills ❷ competence

compétent [kɔ̃petɑ̃, -ɑ̃t] (*f* **compétente**) *adj* competent

compétitif [kɔ̃petitif, -iv] (*f* **compétitive**) *adj* competitive

compétition [kɔ̃petisjɔ̃] *nf* competition; **avoir l'esprit de compétition** to be competitive

complet [kɔ̃plɛ, -ɛt] (*f* **complète**) *adj* ❶ complete ▷ *les œuvres complètes de Shakespeare* the complete works of Shakespeare ❷ full ▷ *L'hôtel est complet.* The hotel is full.; **« complet »** "no vacancies"
▶ *nm* (*men's*) suit

complètement [kɔ̃pletmɑ̃] *adv* completely ▷ *J'avais complètement oublié que tu venais.* I'd completely forgotten that you were coming.

compléter [kɔ̃plete] *vb* to complete ▷ *Complétez les phrases suivantes.* Complete the following sentences.

complexe [kɔ̃plɛks(ə)] *adj* complex

complication [kɔ̃plikasjɔ̃] *nf* complication

complice [kɔ̃plis] *nmf* accomplice

compliments [kɔ̃plimɑ̃] *nmpl* compliment; **faire des compliments** to compliment ▷ *Il m'a fait des compliments sur ma robe.* He complimented me on my dress.

compliqué [kɔ̃plike] (*f* **compliquée**) *adj* complicated ▷ *C'est une histoire compliquée.* It's a complicated story.

complot [kɔ̃plo] *nm* (*conspiracy*) plot

comportement [kɔ̃pɔrtəmɑ̃] *nm* behaviour

comporter [kɔ̃pɔrte] *vb* ❶ to consist of ▷ *Le château comporte trois parties.* The castle consists of three parts. ❷ (*as a part*) to have ▷ *Ce modèle comporte un écran couleur.* This model has a colour screen.; **se comporter** to behave ▷ *Elle s'est comportée de façon odieuse.* She behaved atrociously.

composer [kɔ̃poze] *vb* (*music, text*) to compose; **composer un numéro** to dial a number; **se composer de** to consist of

▷ *L'uniforme se compose d'une veste, d'un pantalon et d'une cravate.* The uniform consists of a jacket, pants, and a tie.

compositeur [kɔ̃pozitœʀ] nm composer

composition [kɔ̃pozisjɔ̃] nf (music, writing) composition

compositrice [kɔ̃pozitʀis] nf composer

compostage [kɔ̃pɔstaʒ] nm composting

composter [kɔ̃pɔste] vb to compost

compote [kɔ̃pɔt] nf stewed fruit; **la compote de prunes** stewed plums

compréhensible [kɔ̃pʀeɑ̃sibl(ə)] adj understandable

compréhensif [kɔ̃pʀeɑ̃sif, -iv] (f **compréhensive**) adj understanding

compréhension [kɔ̃pʀeɑ̃sjɔ̃] nf ❶ comprehension ▷ *la compréhension orale* listening comprehension ❷ sympathy; **Elle a fait preuve de beaucoup de compréhension.** She was very sympathetic.

comprendre [kɔ̃pʀɑ̃dʀ(ə)] vb ❶ to understand ▷ *Je ne comprends pas ce que vous dites.* I don't understand what you're saying. ❷ to include ▷ *Le forfait ne comprend pas la location des skis.* The package doesn't include ski rental.

compris [kɔ̃pʀi, -iz] (f **comprise**) adj included ▷ *Le service n'est pas compris.* Service is not included.; **y compris** including ▷ *Ils ont tout vendu, y compris leur voiture.* They sold everything, including their car.; **non compris** excluding ▷ *vingt dollars, frais de livraison non compris* 20 dollars, excluding delivery charges; **cent dollars tout compris** 100 dollars all-inclusive

compromettre [kɔ̃pʀɔmɛtʀ(ə)] vb to compromise

compromis [kɔ̃pʀɔmi] nm compromise ▷ *Ils sont parvenus à un compromis.* They came to a compromise.

comptabilité [kɔ̃tabilite] nf accounting ▷ *un cours de comptabilité* a course in accounting

comptable [kɔ̃tabl(ə)] nmf accountant ▷ *Elle est comptable.* She's an accountant.

comptant [kɔ̃tɑ̃] adv: **payer comptant** to pay cash

compte [kɔ̃t] nm ❶ account ▷ *J'ai déposé le chèque dans mon compte.* I've deposited the cheque into my account. ❷ bill ▷ *le compte d'électricité* electricity bill ▷ *le compte de téléphone* telephone bill; **Le compte est bon.** That's the right amount.; **tenir compte de** **(1)** to take into account ▷ *Ils ont tenu compte de mon expérience.* They took my experience into account. **(2)** to pay attention to ▷ *Il n'a pas tenu compte de mes conseils.* He paid no attention to my advice.; **travailler à son compte** to be self-employed; **en fin de compte** all things considered ▷ *Le voyage ne s'est pas mal passé, en fin de compte.* The trip wasn't bad, all things considered.

compter [kɔ̃te] vb to count

compte rendu [-ʀɑ̃dy] (pl **comptes rendus**) nm report

compteur [kɔ̃tœʀ] nm meter

comptoir [kɔ̃twaʀ] nm counter ▷ *au comptoir* at the counter

se concentrer [kɔ̃sɑ̃tʀe] vb to concentrate ▷ *J'ai du mal à me concentrer.* I'm having trouble concentrating.

conception [kɔ̃sɛpsjɔ̃] nf design

concernant [kɔ̃sɛʀnɑ̃] prep regarding ▷ *Concernant notre nouveau projet, je voudrais ajouter que...* Regarding our new project, I would like to add that...

concerner [kɔ̃sɛʀne] vb to concern ▷ *en ce qui me concerne* as far as I'm concerned; **Je ne me sens pas concerné.** I figure it has nothing to do with me.

concert [kɔ̃sɛʀ] nm concert

concierge [kɔ̃sjɛʀʒ(ə)] nmf caretaker

conclure [kɔ̃klyʀ] vb to conclude

conclusion [kɔ̃klyzjɔ̃] nf conclusion

concombre [kɔ̃kɔ̃bʀ(ə)] nm cucumber

concorder [kɔ̃kɔʀde] vb (agree) to match ▷ *Les dates concordent.* The dates match.

concours [kɔ̃kuʀ] nm ❶ competition ▷ *un concours de chant* a singing competition ❷ contest

concret [kɔ̃kʀɛ, -ɛt] (f **concrète**) adj concrete

conçu [kɔ̃sy] vb designed ▷ *Ces appartements sont très mal conçus.* These apartments are very badly designed.

concurrence [kɔ̃kyʀɑ̃s] nf competition ▷ *La concurrence est vive sur ce marché.* There's a lot of competition in this market.

concurrent [kɔ̃kyʀɑ̃] nm competitor

concurrente [kɔ̃kyʀɑ̃t] nf competitor

condamner [kɔ̃dane] vb ❶ to sentence ▷ *Il a été condamné à deux ans de prison.* He was sentenced to two years in prison. ▷ *condamner à mort* to sentence to death ❷ to condemn ▷ *Le gouvernement a condamné cette décision.* The government condemned this decision.

condition [kɔ̃disjɔ̃] nf condition ▷ *Je le ferai à une condition...* I'll do it, on one condition...; **à condition que** provided that ▷ *Je viendrai à condition qu'elle me le demande.* I'll come provided she asks me to.; **les conditions de vie** living conditions

conditionnel [kɔ̃disjɔnɛl] nm conditional tense

condoléances [kɔ̃dɔleɑ̃s] nfpl sympathy ▷ *Veuillez accepter mes plus sincères condoléances.* Please accept my sincere sympathy.

condom [kɔ̃dɔm] nm condom

conducteur [kɔ̃dyktœʀ] nm driver

conductrice [kɔ̃dyktʀis] nf driver

conduire [kɔ̃dɥiʀ] vb to drive ▷ *Est-ce que tu sais conduire?* Can you drive? ▷ *Je te conduirai chez le docteur.* I'll drive you to the doctor's.; **se conduire** to behave ▷ *Il s'est mal conduit.* He behaved badly.

conduite [kɔ̃dɥit] nf behaviour; **la conduite en état d'ivresse** impaired driving

confédération [kɔ̃fedeʀasjɔ̃] nf confederation ▷ *Le Canada est une confédération.* Canada is a confederation.; **la Confédération** Confederation

conférence [kɔ̃feʀɑ̃s] nf ❶ lecture ▷ *donner une conférence* to give a lecture ❷ conference ▷ *une conférence internationale* an international conference

confetti [kɔ̃feti] nm confetti

confiance [kɔ̃fjɑ̃s] nf ❶ trust; **avoir confiance en quelqu'un** to trust somebody ▷ *Je n'ai pas confiance en lui.* I don't trust him. ❷ confidence; **Tu peux avoir confiance. Il sera à l'heure.** You don't need to worry. He'll be on time.; **confiance en soi** self-confidence ▷ *Elle manque de confiance en elle.* She lacks self-confidence.

confiant [kɔ̃fjɑ̃, -ɑ̃t] (f **confiante**) adj confident

confidences [kɔ̃fidɑ̃s] nfpl: **faire des confidences à quelqu'un** to confide in someone ▷ *Elle me fait quelquefois des confidences.* She sometimes confides in me.

confidentiel [kɔ̃fidɑ̃sjɛl] (f **confidentielle**) adj confidential

confier [kɔ̃fje] vb: **se confier à quelqu'un** to confide in somebody ▷ *Il s'est confié à son meilleur ami.* He confided in his best friend.

confirmer [kɔ̃fiʀme] vb to confirm

confiserie [kɔ̃fizʀi] nf candy store

confisquer [kɔ̃fiske] vb to confiscate

confiture [kɔ̃fityʀ] nf jam ▷ *la confiture de fraises* strawberry jam

conflit [kɔ̃fli] nm conflict

confondre [kɔ̃fɔ̃dʀ(ə)] vb to mix up ▷ *On la confond souvent avec sa sœur.* People often get her mixed up with her sister.

confort [kɔ̃fɔʀ] nm comfort; **tout confort** luxurious ▷ *un appartement tout confort* a luxurious apartment

confortable [kɔ̃fɔʀtabl(ə)] adj comfortable ▷ *des chaussures confortables* comfortable shoes

confus [kɔ̃fy, -yz] (f **confuse**) adj ❶ unclear ▷ *J'ai trouvé ses explications confuses.* I thought his explanation was unclear. ❷ embarrassed ▷ *Il avait l'air confus.* He looked embarrassed.

confusion [kɔ̃fyzjɔ̃] nf ❶ confusion ❷ embarrassment; **rougir de confusion** to blush with embarrassment

congé [kɔ̃ʒe] nm ❶ holiday ▷ *une semaine de congé* a week off; **en congé** on holiday ▷ *Je serai en congé la semaine prochaine.* I'll be on holiday next week. ❷ leave ▷ *être en congé de maladie* to be on sick leave ▷ *congé de maternité* maternity leave

congélateur [kɔ̃ʒelatœʀ] nm freezer

congeler [kɔ̃ʒle] vb to freeze

conjonction [kɔ̃ʒɔ̃ksjɔ̃] nf conjunction

conjugaison [kɔ̃ʒyɡɛzɔ̃] nf conjugation

connaissance [kɔnɛsɑ̃s] nf ❶ knowledge ▷ *Pour approfondir vos connaissances* to increase your knowledge ❷ acquaintance ▷ *Ce n'est pas vraiment une amie, juste une connaissance.* She's not really a friend, just an acquaintance.; **perdre connaissance** to lose consciousness; **faire la connaissance de quelqu'un** to meet somebody ▷ *J'ai fait la connaissance de sa mère.* I met her mother.

connaître [kɔnɛtʀ(ə)] vb to know ▷ *Je ne connais pas du tout cette région.* I don't know this area at all. ▷ *Je le connais de vue.* I know him by sight.; **Ils se sont connus à Sudbury.** They first met in Sudbury.; **s'y connaître en**

quelque chose to know about something ▷ *Je ne m'y connais pas beaucoup en musique classique.* I don't know much about classical music.

se connecter [kɔnɛkte] vb to log on ▷ *Je me suis connecté sur Internet il y a dix minutes.* I logged onto the Internet ten minutes ago.; **être connecté à un serveur** to be connected to a server

connu [kɔny] (f **connue**) adj well-known ▷ *C'est un acteur connu.* He's a well-known actor.

conquérir [kɔ̃keʀiʀ] vb to conquer

consacrer [kɔ̃sakʀe] vb to devote ▷ *Il consacre beaucoup de temps à ses enfants.* He devotes a lot of time to his children. ▷ *Je suis désolé, je n'ai pas beaucoup de temps à y consacrer.* I'm afraid I can't spare much time for it.

conscience [kɔ̃sjɑ̃s] nf conscience ▷ *avoir mauvaise conscience* to have a guilty conscience; **prendre conscience de** to become aware of ▷ *Ils ont fini par prendre conscience de la gravité de la situation.* They eventually became aware of the seriousness of the situation.

consciencieux [kɔ̃sjɑ̃sjø, -øz] (f **consciencieuse**) adj conscientious

conscient [kɔ̃sjɑ̃, -ɑ̃t] (f **consciente**) adj conscious

consécutif [kɔ̃sekytif, -iv] (f **consécutive**) adj consecutive

conseil [kɔ̃sɛj] nm advice ▷ *Est-ce que je peux te demander conseil?* Can I ask you for some advice?; **un conseil** a piece of advice; **un conseil de bande** a band council; **le conseil étudiant** student council; **le conseil municipal** city council

conseiller [kɔ̃seje] vb ❶ to advise ▷ *Je te conseille de ne pas y aller.* I advise you not to go there. ❷ to recommend ▷ *Il m'a conseillé ce livre.* He recommended this book to me.
▶ nm ❶ (political) councillor ▷ *un conseiller municipal* a town councillor ❷ adviser ❸ counsellor; **un conseiller en orientation** a guidance counsellor

conseillère [kɔ̃sejɛʀ] nf ❶ (political) councillor ▷ *une conseillère municipale* a town councillor ❷ adviser ❸ counsellor ▷ *une conseillère familiale* a family counsellor; **une conseillère en orientation** a guidance counsellor

consentement [kɔ̃sɑ̃tmɑ̃] nm consent ▷ *le consentement de tes parents* your parents' consent

consentir [kɔ̃sɑ̃tiʀ] vb to agree ▷ *consentir à quelque chose* to agree to something

conséquence [kɔ̃sekɑ̃s] nf consequence; **en conséquence** consequently

conséquent [kɔ̃sekɑ̃, -ɑ̃t] (f **conséquente**) adj ❶ rational ▷ *un comportement conséquent* rational behaviour ❷ consistent ▷ *de manière conséquente* in a consistent manner; **par conséquent** consequently

conservatoire [kɔ̃sɛʀvatwaʀ] nm school of music ▷ *Elle fait du piano au conservatoire.* She's taking piano at the conservatoire.

conserve [kɔ̃sɛʀv(ə)] nf can ▷ *Je vais ouvrir une conserve.* I'll open a can.; **une boîte de conserve** a can; **les conserves** canned food

▷ Il n'est pas bon de manger des conserves tous les jours. It's not healthy to eat canned food every day.; **en conserve** canned ▷ des petits pois en conserve canned peas

conserver [kɔ̃sɛʀve] vb to keep ▷ J'ai conservé toutes ses lettres. I've kept all her letters.; **se conserver** to keep ▷ Ce pain se conserve plus d'une semaine. This bread will keep for more than a week.

considérable [kɔ̃sideʀabl(ə)] adj considerable ▷ Il a fait des progrès considérables. He's made considerable progress.

considération [kɔ̃sideʀasjɔ̃] nf: **prendre quelque chose en considération** to take something into consideration

considérer [kɔ̃sideʀe] vb to consider ▷ Je la considère compétente. I consider her to be competent.; **considérer que** to believe that ▷ Elle considère que la décision du directeur était juste. She believes that the principal's decision was fair.

consistant [kɔ̃sistɑ̃, -ɑ̃t] (f **consistante**) adj substantial ▷ un petit déjeuner consistant a substantial breakfast

consister [kɔ̃siste] vb: **consister à** to consist of ▷ Mon travail consiste à répondre au téléphone et à recevoir les clients. My job consists of answering the phone and welcoming customers. ▷ En quoi consiste votre travail? What does your job involve?

console de jeu [kɔ̃sɔl-] nf game console

consoler [kɔ̃sɔle] vb to comfort

consommateur [kɔ̃sɔmatœʀ] nm ❶ consumer ❷ (in café) customer

consommation [kɔ̃sɔmasjɔ̃] nf consumption ▷ la consommation d'électricité hydro consumption

consommatrice [kɔ̃sɔmatʀis] nf ❶ consumer ❷ (in café) customer

consommer [kɔ̃sɔme] vb to use ▷ Ces grosses voitures consomment beaucoup d'essence. These big cars use a lot of gas.

consonne [kɔ̃sɔn] nf consonant

constamment [kɔ̃stamɑ̃] adv constantly ▷ Elle se plaint constamment. She's constantly complaining.

constant [kɔ̃stɑ̃, -ɑ̃t] (f **constante**) adj constant

constater [kɔ̃state] vb to notice

constitué [kɔ̃stitɥe] (f **constituée**) adj: **être constitué de** to consist of

constituer [kɔ̃stitɥe] vb to make up ▷ les dix provinces et les trois territoires qui constituent le Canada the ten provinces and three territories that make up Canada

constitution [kɔ̃stitysjɔ̃] nf constitution ▷ la Constitution canadienne the Canadian Constitution

construction [kɔ̃stʀyksjɔ̃] nf building ▷ des matériaux de construction building materials; **une maison en construction** a house being built

construire [kɔ̃stʀɥiʀ] vb to build ▷ Ils font construire une maison neuve. They're having a new house built.

consultation [kɔ̃syltasjɔ̃] nf consultation

consulter [kɔ̃sylte] vb ❶ to consult ▷ Tu devrais consulter un médecin. You should see a doctor. ❷ to see patients ▷ La docteure ne consulte pas le samedi. The doctor doesn't see patients on Saturdays.

contact [kɔ̃takt] nm contact ▷ les contacts humains human contact; **garder le contact avec quelqu'un** to keep in touch with somebody

contacter [kɔ̃takte] vb to get in touch with ▷ Je te contacterai dès que j'aurai des nouvelles. I'll get in touch with you as soon as I have some news.

contagieux [kɔ̃taʒjø, -øz] (f **contagieuse**) adj ❶ infectious ▷ une maladie contagieuse an infectious disease ❷ contagious ▷ Restez chez vous si vous êtes contagieux. Stay at home if you're contagious.

contaminer [kɔ̃tamine] vb to contaminate ▷ de l'eau contaminée contaminated water

conte [kɔ̃t] nm story ▷ un livre de contes a storybook; **un conte de fées** a fairy tale

contempler [kɔ̃tɑ̃ple] vb to gaze at

contemporain [kɔ̃tɑ̃pɔʀɛ̃, -ɛn] (f **contemporaine**) adj contemporary; **un auteur contemporain** a modern writer

contenant [kɔ̃tnɑ̃] nm container ▷ un contenant en plastique a plastic container

contenir [kɔ̃tniʀ] vb to contain ▷ un portefeuille contenant de l'argent a wallet containing money

content [kɔ̃tɑ̃, -ɑ̃t] (f **contente**) adj glad ▷ Je suis content que tu sois venu. I'm glad you came.; **content de** pleased with ▷ Elle m'a dit qu'elle était contente de mon travail. She told me she was pleased with my work.

contenter [kɔ̃tɑ̃te] vb to please ▷ Il est difficile à contenter. He's hard to please.; **Je me contente de peu.** I can make do with very little.

contesté [kɔ̃tɛste] (f **contestée**) adj controversial ▷ Cette décision est très contestée. This is a very controversial decision.

conteur [kɔ̃tœʀ] nm storyteller

conteuse [kɔ̃tøz] nf storyteller

continent [kɔ̃tinɑ̃] nm mainland

continu [kɔ̃tiny] (f **continue**) adj continuous

continuellement [kɔ̃tinɥɛlmɑ̃] adv constantly

continuer [kɔ̃tinɥe] vb to continue ▷ Continuez sans moi! Go on without me! ▷ Il ne veut pas continuer ses études. He doesn't want to continue his studies.; **continuer à faire quelque chose** to go on doing something ▷ Ils ont continué à regarder la télé sans me dire bonjour. They went on watching TV without saying hello to me.; **continuer de faire quelque chose** to go on doing something ▷ Elle continue de fumer malgré son asthme. She continues to smoke despite her asthma.

contourner [kɔ̃tuʀne] vb to go around ▷ La route contourne la ville. The road goes around the town.

contraceptif [kɔ̃tʀasɛptif] nm contraceptive

contraception [kɔ̃tʀasɛpsjɔ̃] nf contraception

contradiction [kɔ̃tradiksjɔ̃] nf contradiction; **par esprit de contradiction** just to be difficult ▷ Il a refusé de venir par esprit de contradiction. He refused to come, just to be difficult.

contraire [kɔ̃tRER] nm opposite ▷ C'est exactement le contraire. It's just the opposite.; **au contraire** on the contrary

contrarier [kɔ̃tRaRje] vb ❶ to annoy ▷ Il avait l'air contrarié. He looked annoyed. ❷ to upset ▷ Est-ce que tu serais contrarié si je ne venais pas? Would you be upset if I didn't come?

contraste [kɔ̃tRast(ə)] nm contrast

contrat [kɔ̃tRa] nm contract

contravention [kɔ̃tRavɑ̃sjɔ̃] nf parking ticket

contre [kɔ̃tR(ə)] prep ❶ against ▷ Ne mets pas ton vélo contre le mur. Don't put your bike against the wall. ▷ Tu es pour ou contre ce projet? Are you for or against this plan? ❷ for ▷ échanger quelque chose contre quelque chose to trade something for something; **par contre** on the other hand

contrebande [kɔ̃tRəbɑ̃d] nf smuggling; **des produits de contrebande** smuggled goods

contrebasse [kɔ̃tRəbas] nf double bass

contrecœur [kɔ̃tRəkœR] : **à contrecœur** adv reluctantly ▷ Elle est venue à contrecœur. She came reluctantly.

contredire [kɔ̃tRədiR] vb to contradict ▷ Il ne supporte pas d'être contredit. He can't stand being contradicted.

contretemps [kɔ̃tRətɑ̃] nm: **Désolé d'être en retard; j'ai eu un contretemps.** Sorry I'm late; I was held up.

contribuer [kɔ̃tRibɥe] vb to contribute ▷ contribuer au succès d'un projet to contribute to the success of a project

contrôle [kɔ̃tRol] nm ❶ control ▷ le contrôle des passeports passport control ❷ check; **un contrôle d'identité** an identity check; **le contrôle des billets** ticket inspection ❸ test ▷ un contrôle antidopage a drug test

contrôler [kɔ̃tRole] vb to check ▷ Personne n'a contrôlé mon billet. Nobody checked my ticket.

controversé [kɔ̃tRoveRse] (f **controversée**) adj controversial

convaincre [kɔ̃vɛ̃kR(ə)] vb ❶ to persuade ▷ Il a essayé de me convaincre de rester. He tried to persuade me to stay. ❷ to convince ▷ Tu n'as pas l'air convaincu. You don't look convinced.

convenable [kɔ̃vnabl(ə)] adj decent ▷ un hôtel convenable a decent hotel; **Ce n'est pas convenable.** It's bad manners.

convenir [kɔ̃vniR] vb: **convenir à** to suit ▷ Est-ce que cette date te convient? Does this date suit you? ▷ J'espère que cela vous conviendra. I hope this will suit you.; **convenir de** to agree on ▷ Nous avons convenu d'une date. We've agreed on a date.

convenu [kɔ̃vny] (f **convenue**) adj agreed ▷ au moment convenu at the agreed time

conversation [kɔ̃veRsasjɔ̃] nf conversation

convivial [kɔ̃vivjal] adj user-friendly ▷ Ce logiciel est très convivial. This program is very user-friendly.

cool [kul] adj (informal) cool

coopératif [kɔɔpeRatif, -iv] (f **coopérative**) adj co-operative ▷ Elle s'est montrée très coopérative. She was very co-operative.

coopération [kɔɔpeRasjɔ̃] nf co-operation

coopérative [kɔɔpeRativ] nf co-op ▷ une coopérative d'habitation a housing co-op

coopérer [kɔɔpeRe] vb to co-operate

coordonnées [kɔɔRdɔne] nfpl contact information ▷ As-tu ses coordonnées? Do you have his contact information?

copain [kɔpɛ̃] nm ❶ (informal) friend ▷ C'est un bon copain. He's a good friend. ❷ boyfriend ▷ Je l'ai vue avec son copain. I saw her with her boyfriend.

copie [kɔpi] nf copy ▷ Ce tableau n'est qu'une copie. This picture is only a copy.

copier [kɔpje] vb to copy; **copier-coller** to copy and paste

copieux [kɔpjø, -øz] (f **copieuse**) adj hearty ▷ un repas copieux a hearty meal

copine [kɔpin] nf ❶ (informal) friend ▷ Je sors avec une copine ce soir. I'm going out with a friend tonight. ❷ girlfriend ▷ Je ne savais pas qu'il avait une copine. I didn't know he had a girlfriend.

copropriété [kɔpRɔpRijete] nf condominium

coq [kɔk] nm rooster

coque [kɔk] nf (of boat) hull; **un œuf à la coque** a soft-boiled egg

coquelicot [kɔkliko] nm poppy

coquerelle [kɔkRɛl] nf cockroach

coquillage [kɔkijaʒ] nm shell ▷ Nous avons ramassé des coquillages sur la plage. We picked up some shells on the beach.

coquille [kɔkij] nf shell; **une coquille d'œuf** an eggshell; **une coquille Saint-Jacques** a scallop

cor [kɔR] nm (instrument) horn ▷ Je joue du cor. I play the horn.

corbeau [kɔRbo] (pl **corbeaux**) nm crow

corbeille [kɔRbɛj] nf basket ▷ une corbeille de fruits a basket of fruit; **une corbeille à papier** a wastepaper basket

corde [kɔRd(ə)] nf ❶ rope ❷ (guitar, tennis racquet) string; **une corde à linge** a clothes line; **une corde élastique** a bungee cord

cordonnerie [kɔRdɔnRi] nf shoe repair shop

corne [kɔRn(ə)] nf (on animal) horn

cornemuse [kɔRnəmyz] nf bagpipes ▷ jouer de la cornemuse to play the bagpipes

cornet [kɔRnɛ] nm: **un cornet de crème glacée** an ice cream cone

cornichon [kɔRniʃɔ̃] nm pickle

corps [kɔR] nm body

correct [kɔRɛkt] (f **correcte**) adj ❶ correct ▷ Ce n'est pas tout à fait correct. That's not quite correct. ❷ acceptable ▷ C'est correct de faire des erreurs quand on apprend. It's OK to make mistakes when you're learning. ▷ Le repas était tout à fait correct. The meal was quite acceptable.

correction [kɔRɛksjɔ̃] nf correction

correspondance [kɔREspɔ̃dɑ̃s] nf ❶ correspondence ▷ La secrétaire s'occupe de toute la correspondance. The secretary takes care of all the correspondence. ❷ (train, plane) connection ▷ Il y a une correspondance pour Montréal à dix heures. There's a connection for Montréal at ten o'clock.

correspondant [kɔrɛspɔ̃dɑ̃] nm penpal

correspondante [kɔrɛspɔ̃dɑ̃t] nf penpal

correspondre [kɔrɛspɔ̃dr(ə)] vb to correspond ▷ Écrivez le numéro qui correspond à votre réponse. Write down the number that corresponds to your answer. ▷ Elle correspond avec sa grand-mère en Inde. She corresponds with her grandmother in India.

corridor [kɔridɔr] nm hallway

corriger [kɔriʒe] vb to mark ▷ Vous pouvez corriger mon test? Can you mark my test?

corvée [kɔrve] nf chore ▷ Quelle corvée! What a drag!

costaud [kɔsto, -od] (f **costaude**) adj well-built

costume [kɔstym] nm ❶ (man's) suit ▷ Tu devrais mettre un costume et une cravate pour l'entrevue. You should wear a suit and tie for the interview. ❷ (theatre) costume ▷ Nous avons fait nous-mêmes tous les costumes pour la pièce. We made all the costumes for the play ourselves.

côte [kot] nf ❶ coastline ▷ La route longe la côte. The road follows the coastline.; **la côte Ouest** the West Coast ❷ hill ▷ J'ai grimpé la côte. I went up the hill. ❸ rib ▷ Il s'est cassé une côte en tombant. He broke a rib when he fell.; **côte à côte** side by side; **les côtes levées** spareribs

côté [kote] nm side; **à côté de (1)** next to ▷ Le café est à côté du sucre. The coffee's next to the sugar. **(2)** next door to ▷ Elle habite à côté de chez moi. She lives next door to me.; **de l'autre côté** on the other side ▷ La pharmacie est de l'autre côté de la rue. The drugstore is on the other side of the street.; **De quel côté sont-ils partis?** Which way did they go?; **mettre quelque chose de côté** to save something ▷ J'ai mis de l'argent de côté. I've saved some money.

côtelette [kotlɛt] nf chop ▷ une côtelette d'agneau a lamb chop

coton [kɔtɔ̃] nm cotton ▷ une chemise en coton a cotton shirt; **le coton hydrophile** cotton wool

cou [ku] nm neck

couchant [kuʃɑ̃] adj: **le soleil couchant** the setting sun

couche [kuʃ] nf ❶ layer ▷ la couche d'ozone the ozone layer ❷ (of paint, varnish) coat ❸ diaper

couché [kuʃe] (f **couchée**) adj ❶ lying down ▷ Il était couché sur le tapis. He was lying on the carpet. ❷ in bed ▷ Il est déjà couché. He's already in bed.

coucher [kuʃe] nm: **un coucher de soleil** a sunset
▶ vb ❶ to go to bed ▷ Je me suis couché tard hier soir. I went to bed late last night. ❷ (sun) to set

couchette [kuʃɛt] nf crib

coude [kud] nm elbow; **donner un coup de coude à quelqu'un** to nudge somebody

coudre [kudr(ə)] vb ❶ to sew ▷ J'aime coudre. I like sewing. ❷ to sew on ▷ Je ne sais même pas coudre un bouton. I can't even sew a button on.

couette [kwɛt] nf duvet

couettes [kwɛt] nfpl pigtails ▷ Quand j'étais petite, ma mère me faisait des couettes. When I was little, my mother put my hair in pigtails.

couler [kule] vb ❶ to run ▷ Ne laissez pas couler les robinets. Don't leave the taps running. ▷ J'ai le nez qui coule. My nose is running. ❷ to flow ▷ La rivière coulait lentement. The river was flowing slowly. ❸ to leak ▷ Mon stylo coule. My pen's leaking. ❹ to sink ▷ Le bateau a coulé. The boat sank.

couleur [kulœr] nf colour ▷ De quelle couleur est leur voiture? What colour is their car? ▷ un film couleur a colour film; **Tu as pris des couleurs.** You've got a tan.

couleuvre [kulœvr(ə)] nf garter snake

coulisses [kulis] nfpl (in theatre) wings; **dans les coulisses** behind the scenes

couloir [kulwar] nm hallway

coup [ku] nm ❶ knock ▷ donner un coup à quelque chose to give something a knock ❷ blow; **Il m'a donné un coup!** He hit me!; **un coup de coude** a nudge; **un coup de pied** a kick; **un coup de poing** a punch ❸ shock ▷ Ça m'a fait un coup de le voir comme ça! (informal) It gave me a shock to see him like that!; **un coup de feu** a shot; **un coup de téléphone** (informal) a call ▷ Je te donnerai un coup de téléphone demain. I'll give you a call tomorrow.; **donner un coup de main à quelqu'un** to give somebody a hand ▷ Je viendrai te donner un coup de main. I'll come and give you a hand.; **un coup d'œil** a quick look ▷ jeter un coup d'œil sur quelque chose to take a quick look at something; **attraper un coup de soleil** to get sunburned; **un coup de tonnerre** a clap of thunder; **après coup** afterwards ▷ Après coup j'ai regretté de m'être mis en colère. Afterwards I was sorry I'd got angry.; **à tous les coups** (informal) every time ▷ Je me trompe de rue à tous les coups. I get the street wrong every time.; **du premier coup** on the first try ▷ Elle a été reçue au permis du premier coup. She passed her driving test on the first try.; **sur le coup** right away ▷ Sur le coup je ne l'ai pas reconnu. I didn't recognize him right away.

coupable [kupabl(ə)] adj guilty
▶ n culprit

coupe [kup] nf (sport) cup ▷ la coupe du monde the World Cup; **une coupe de cheveux** a haircut; **la coupe glacée** sundae

coupe-ongle [kup-] nm nail clippers

couper [kupe] vb ❶ to cut ❷ to turn off ▷ couper le courant to turn off the power ❸ to take a shortcut ▷ On peut couper par la forêt. There's a shortcut through the woods.; **couper l'appétit** to spoil one's appetite; **se couper** to cut oneself ▷ Je me suis coupé le doigt. I cut my finger.; **couper la parole à quelqu'un** to interrupt somebody; **couper les cheveux en quatre** to split hairs

couper-coller vb to cut and paste

coupe-vent [kup-] (pl **coupe-vent**) nm (jacket) windbreaker

couple [kupl(ə)] nm couple

coupure [kupyr] nf cut; **une coupure de courant** a power outage

cour [kur] nf ❶ yard ▷ *la cour de l'école* the school yard ❷ court ▷ *la cour provinciale* the provincial court

courage [kuraʒ] nm courage

courageux [kuraʒø, -øz] (f **courageuse**) adj brave

couramment [kuramã] adv ❶ fluently ▷ *Elle parle couramment japonais.* She speaks Japanese fluently. ❷ commonly ▷ *C'est une expression que l'on emploie couramment.* It's a commonly used phrase.

courant [kurã, -ãt] (f **courante**) adj ❶ common ▷ *C'est une erreur courante.* It's a common mistake. ❷ standard ▷ *C'est un modèle courant.* It's a standard model. ▶ nm ❶ (of river) current; **un courant d'air** a draft ❷ power ▷ *une panne de courant* a power failure; **Je le ferai dans le courant de la semaine.** I'll do it some time during the week.; **être au courant de quelque chose** to know about something ▷ *Je ne suis pas au courant de ses projets pour l'été.* I don't know about her plans for the summer.; **mettre quelqu'un au courant de quelque chose** to tell somebody about something; **Tu es au courant?** Have you heard?; **se tenir au courant de quelque chose** to keep up with something ▷ *J'essaie de me tenir au courant de l'actualité.* I try to keep up with the news.

courbe [kurb(ə)] adj curved ▷ *une surface courbe* a curved surface

courbé [kurbe] adj bent ▷ *des branches courbées sous le poids de la neige* branches bent by the weight of the snow

courbe [kurb(ə)] nf ❶ curve ❷ bend

coureur [kurœr] nm runner; **un coureur à pied** a runner; **un coureur cycliste** a racing cyclist; **un coureur automobile** a race car driver; **coureur des bois** trapper

coureuse [kurøz] nf runner

courgette [kurʒet] nf zucchini

courir [kurir] vb ❶ to run ▷ *Il a traversé la rue en courant.* He ran across the street.; **courir un risque** to run a risk

couronne [kurɔn] nf crown

courons, courez vb see **courir**

courriel [kurjel] nm e-mail ▷ *Envoie-moi un courriel.* Send me an e-mail.

courrier [kurje] nm mail ▷ *Est-ce qu'il y avait du courrier ce matin?* Was there any mail this morning?; **N'oublie pas de poster le courrier.** Don't forget to mail the letters.; **le courrier électronique** e-mail

cours [kur] nm ❶ lesson ▷ *un cours de danse* a dance lesson ▷ *des cours particuliers* private lessons ❷ course ▷ *un cours intensif* a crash course ❸ rate ▷ *le cours du change* the exchange rate; **au cours de** during ▷ *Il a été réveillé trois fois au cours de la nuit.* He was woken up three times during the night.

course [kurs(ə)] nf ❶ running ▷ *la course de fond* long-distance running ❷ race ▷ *une course hippique* a horse race ❸ errand ▷ *J'ai juste une course à faire.* I've just got one errand to do.

court [kur, kurt(ə)] (f **courte**) adj short

court de tennis [kur-] nm tennis court

couru [kury] vb see **courir**

couscous [kuskus] nm couscous

cousin [kuzɛ̃] nm cousin

cousine [kuzin] nf cousin

coussin [kusɛ̃] nm cushion

coût [ku] nm cost ▷ *le coût de la vie* the cost of living; **réduire les coûts** to cut costs

couteau [kuto] (pl **couteaux**) nm knife

coûter [kute] vb to cost ▷ *Est-ce que ça coûte cher?* Does it cost a lot?; **Combien ça coûte?** How much is it?

coûteux [kutø, -øz] (f **coûteuse**) adj expensive

coutume [kutym] nf custom

couture [kutyr] nf ❶ sewing ▷ *Je n'aime pas la couture.* I don't like sewing.; **faire de la couture** to sew ❷ seam ▷ *La couture de mon pantalon s'est défaite.* The seam of my pants has come apart.

couturier [kutyrje] nm fashion designer ▷ *un grand couturier* a top designer

couturière [kutyrjɛr] nf dressmaker

couvercle [kuvɛrkl(ə)] nm ❶ (pot, jar, box, garbage can) lid ❷ (tube, bottle, spray can) cap

couvert [kuver] vb see **couvrir**

couvert [kuver, -ɛrt(ə)] (f **couverte**) adj (sky) overcast; **couvert de** covered with ▷ *Cet arbre est couvert de fleurs au printemps.* This tree is covered with blossoms in spring.

couverts [kuver] nmpl cutlery ▷ *Les couverts sont dans le tiroir de gauche.* The cutlery is in the left-hand drawer.

couverture [kuvɛrtyr] nf ❶ blanket ❷ cover ▷ *la couverture arrière du livre* the back cover of the book; **une page couverture** a cover page ❸ coverage ▷ *la couverture médiatique de l'évènement* media coverage of the event

couvre-lit [kuvrəli] nm bedspread

couvrir [kuvrir] vb to cover ▷ *Le chien est revenu couvert de boue.* The dog came back covered with mud.; **se couvrir (1)** to dress warmly ▷ *Couvre-toi bien : il fait très froid dehors.* Dress warmly: it's very cold outside. **(2)** to cloud over ▷ *Le ciel se couvre.* The sky's clouding over.

crabe [krab] nm crab

cracher [kraʃe] vb to spit

crachin [kraʃɛ̃] nm drizzle

craie [krɛ] nf chalk

craindre [krɛ̃dr(ə)] vb to fear ▷ *Tu n'as rien à craindre.* You have nothing to fear.

crainte [krɛ̃t] nf fear; **de crainte de** for fear of ▷ *Il n'ose rien dire de crainte de la vexer.* He doesn't dare say anything for fear of upsetting her.

craintif [krɛ̃tif, -iv] (f **craintive**) adj timid

crampe [krɑ̃p] nf cramp ▷ *J'ai une crampe au mollet.* I've got a cramp in my calf.

cran [krɑ̃] nm (in belt) hole; **avoir du cran** (informal) to have guts

crâne [krɑn] nm skull

crapaud [krapo] nm toad

craquelin [kraklɛ̃] nm cracker

craquer [krake] vb ❶ to creak ▷ *Le plancher craque.* The floor creaks. ❷ to break ▷ *Les coutures ont craqué sous l'effort.* The seams broke under the strain. ❸ to have a nervous breakdown ▷ *Je vais finir par craquer!* (informal) I'll have a nervous breakdown at this rate!; **Quand j'ai vu cette robe, j'ai craqué!** (informal) When I saw that dress, I couldn't resist it!

crasse [kʀas] *nf* filth

crasseux [kʀasø, øz] (*f* **crasseuse**) *adj* filthy

cravate [kʀavat] *nf* tie

crawl [kʀol] *nm* crawl ▷ *nager le crawl* to do the crawl

crayon [kʀɛjɔ̃] *nm* pencil ▷ *un crayon de couleur* a pencil crayon; **un crayon feutre** a felt pen

création [kʀeasjɔ̃] *nf* creation

crédit [kʀedi] *nm* credit

créer [kʀee] *vb* to create

crème [kʀɛm] *nf* cream; **la crème anglaise** custard; **la crème Chantilly** whipped cream; **la crème fouettée** whipped cream; **la crème glacée** ice cream ▷ *un cornet de crème glacée* an ice cream cone; **une crème caramel** a crème caramel; **une crème au chocolat** a chocolate mousse

crémeux [kʀemø, -øz] (*f* **crémeuse**) *adj* creamy

crêpe [kʀɛp] *nf* crêpe

crêperie [kʀepʀi] *nf* restaurant serving crêpes

crépuscule [kʀepyskyl] *nm* dusk

creuser [kʀøze] *vb* (*a hole*) to dig; **creuser l'appétit** to give an appetite; **se creuser la cervelle** (informal) to rack one's brains

creux [kʀø, -øz] (*f* **creuse**) *adj* hollow

crevaison [kʀəvɛzɔ̃] *nf* flat tire

crevé [kʀəve] (*f* **crevée**) *adj* ❶ (*tire*) flat ❷ bagged ▷ *Je suis complètement crevé!* (informal) I'm bagged!

crever [kʀəve] *vb* ❶ (*balloon*) to burst ❷ (*motorist*) to have a flat tire ▷ *J'ai crevé sur l'autoroute.* I had a flat tire on the highway.; **Je crève de faim!** (informal) I'm starving!; **Je crève de froid!** (informal) I'm freezing!

crevette [kʀəvɛt] *nf* shrimp

cri [kʀi] *nm* ❶ scream ▷ *J'ai entendu un cri.* I heard a scream. ▷ *pousser des cris de douleur* to scream with pain ❷ shout ▷ *des cris de colère* angry shouts ❸ call ▷ *Il sait reconnaître les cris des oiseaux.* He can identify bird calls.; **C'est le dernier cri.** It's the latest style. ▷ *Ce haut est du dernier cri.* This top is the latest style.

criard [kʀijaʀ, -aʀd(ə)] (*f* **criarde**) *adj* (*colours*) garish

cric [kʀik] *nm* (*for car*) jack

crier [kʀije] *vb* to shout; **crier de douleur** to scream with pain

crime [kʀim] *nm* crime ▷ *un crime de guerre* a war crime

criminel [kʀiminɛl] *nm* criminal ▷ *un criminel de guerre* a war criminal

criminelle [kʀiminɛl] *nf* criminal

crinière [kʀinjɛʀ] *nf* mane

crique [kʀik] *nf* creek

criquet [kʀike] *nm* grasshopper

crise [kʀiz] *nf* ❶ crisis; **la crise économique** the recession ❷ attack ▷ *une crise d'asthme* an asthma attack ▷ *une crise cardiaque* a heart attack; **une crise de foie** an upset stomach;

piquer une crise de nerfs to go hysterical; **avoir une crise de fou rire** to have the giggles

cristal [kʀistal, -o] (*pl* **cristaux**) *nm* crystal ▷ *un verre en cristal* a crystal glass

critère [kʀitɛʀ] *nm* criterion

critique [kʀitik] *adj* critical
▶ *nm* critic ▷ *un critique de cinéma* a film critic
▶ *nf* ❶ criticism ▷ *Elle ne supporte pas les critiques.* She can't stand being criticized. ❷ review ▷ *Le film a reçu de bonnes critiques.* The film got good reviews.

critiquer [kʀitike] *vb* to criticize

crochet [kʀoʃe] *nm* ❶ hook ❷ detour ▷ *faire un crochet* to make a detour ❸ crochet ▷ *un chandail au crochet* a crocheted sweater ❹ square bracket

crocodile [kʀokodil] *nm* crocodile

croire [kʀwaʀ] *vb* to believe ▷ *Il croit tout ce qu'on lui raconte.* He believes everything he's told.; **croire que** to think that ▷ *Tu crois qu'il fera meilleur demain?* Do you think the weather will be better tomorrow?; **croire à quelque chose** to believe in something; **croire en Dieu** to believe in God

crois [kʀwa] *vb see* **croire**

croîs [kʀwa] *vb see* **croître**

croisement [kʀwazmɑ̃] *nm* intersection ▷ *Tournez à gauche au croisement.* Turn left at the intersection.

croiser [kʀwaze] *vb*: **J'ai croisé ta sœur dans la rue.** I bumped into your sister in the street.; **croiser les bras** to fold one's arms; **croiser les jambes** to cross one's legs; **se croiser** to pass each other ▷ *Nous nous croisons dans l'escalier tous les matins.* We pass each other on the stairs every morning.

croisière [kʀwazjɛʀ] *nf* cruise

croissance [kʀwasɑ̃s] *nf* growth

croissant [kʀwasɑ̃] *nm* croissant ▷ *un croissant au beurre* a butter croissant; **le Croissant-Rouge** the Red Crescent

croit [kʀwa] *vb see* **croire**

croître [kʀwatʀ(ə)] *vb* to grow

croix [kʀwa] *nf* cross; **la Croix-Rouge** the Red Cross

croque-madame [kʀokmadam] *nm*

croquer [kʀoke] *vb* to munch ▷ *croquer une pomme* to munch on an apple

croquis [kʀoki] *nm* sketch

crosse [kʀos] *nf* lacrosse

crotte [kʀot] *nf*: **une crotte de chien** dog dirt

crottin [kʀotɛ̃] *nm* ❶ manure ▷ *du crottin de cheval* horse manure ❷ small block of goat cheese

croustillant [kʀustijɑ̃, -ɑ̃t] (*f* **croustillante**) *adj* ❶ crisp; **un croustillant aux pommes** an apple crisp ❷ crusty

croustille [kʀustij] *nf* potato chip ▷ *un sac de croustilles* a bag of chips; **des croustilles de maïs** corn chips

croûte [kʀut] *nf* ❶ (*of bread*) crust; **en croûte** in pastry ❷ (*of cheese*) rind ❸ (*on skin*) scab

croûton [kʀutɔ̃] *nm* ❶ (*end of loaf*) crust ❷ crouton ▷ *des croûtons frottés d'ail* garlic croutons

croyons, croyez *vb see* **croire**

cru [kʀy] (f **crue**) vb see **croire**

crû [kʀy] vb see **croître**

cruauté [kʀyote] nf cruelty

cruche [kʀyʃ] nf jug

crudités [kʀydite] nfpl (cut up as hors d'œuvre) raw vegetables

cruel [kʀyɛl] (f **cruelle**) adj cruel

crustacés [kʀystase] nmpl shellfish

cube [kyb] nm cube; **un mètre cube** a cubic metre

cueillette [kœjɛt] nf picking ▷ la cueillette des fraises strawberry picking

cueillir [kœjiʀ] vb (flowers, fruit) to pick

cuiller [kɥijɛʀ] nf spoon; **une cuiller à café** a teaspoon; **une cuiller à soupe** a soup spoon

cuillère [kɥijɛʀ] nf spoon; **une cuillère à café** a teaspoon; **une cuillère à soupe** a soup spoon

cuillerée [kɥijʀe] nf spoonful

cuir [kɥiʀ] nm leather ▷ un sac en cuir a leather bag; **le cuir chevelu** the scalp

cuire [kɥiʀ] vb to cook ▷ cuire quelque chose à feu vif to cook something on high heat; **cuire quelque chose au four** to bake something; **cuire quelque chose à la vapeur** to steam something; **faire cuire** to cook ▷ «Faire cuire pendant une heure» "Cook for one hour"; **bien cuit** well done; **trop cuit** overdone

cuisine [kɥizin] nf ❶ kitchen ❷ cooking ▷ la cuisine française French cooking; **faire la cuisine** to cook

cuisiné [kɥizine] (f **cuisinée**) adj: **un plat cuisiné** a ready-made meal

cuisiner [kɥizine] vb to cook ▷ J'aime beaucoup cuisiner. I love cooking.

cuisinier [kɥizinje] nm cook

cuisinière [kɥizinjɛʀ] nf ❶ cook ❷ stove ▷ une cuisinière à gaz a gas stove

cuisse [kɥis] nf thigh; **une cuisse de poulet** a chicken leg

cuisson [kɥisɔ̃] nf cooking ▷ «une heure de cuisson» "cooking time: one hour"

cuit [kɥi] vb see **cuire**

cuivre [kɥivʀ(ə)] nm copper

culot [kylo] nm (informal: brazenness) nerve ▷ Quel culot! What nerve!

culotte [kylɔt] nf (women's) underpants

cultivateur [kyltivatœʀ] nm farmer

cultivatrice [kyltivatʀis] nf farmer

cultivé [kyltive] (f **cultivée**) adj cultured ▷ Elle est très cultivée. She's very cultured.

cultiver [kyltive] vb to grow ▷ Ils cultivent la vigne. They grow grapes.; **cultiver la terre** to farm the land

culture [kyltyʀ] nf ❶ culture ▷ la culture québécoise Québécois culture ❷ education ▷ Pour cet emploi, on demande une bonne culture générale. For this job, a good general education is needed.; **la culture physique** physical education ❸ farming ▷ les cultures intensives intensive farming

culturisme [kyltyʀism(ə)] nm bodybuilding

cure-dent [kyʀdɑ̃] (pl **cure-dents**) nm toothpick

curieux [kyʀjø, -øz] (f **curieuse**) adj curious

curiosité [kyʀjozite] nf curiosity

curling [kœʀliŋ] nm curling

curriculum vitæ [kyʀikylɔmvite] nm résumé

curseur [kyʀsœʀ] nm cursor

cuvette [kyvɛt] nf bowl ▷ une cuvette en plastique a plastic bowl

CV [seve] nm (= curriculum vitæ) résumé

cybercafé [sibɛʀkafe] nm Internet café

cyclable [siklabl(ə)] adj: **une piste cyclable** a bike path

cycle [sikl(ə)] nm cycle

cyclisme [siklism(ə)] nm cycling

cycliste [siklist(ə)] nmf cyclist

cyclone [siklɔn] nm cyclone

cygne [siɲ] nm swan

cynique [sinik] adj cynical

d

d' [d] prep, art see de

dactylo [daktilo] nf ❶ typist ▷ Elle est dactylo. She's a typist. ❷ typing ▷ Je prends des cours de dactylo. I'm doing typing lessons.

daim [dɛ̃] nm suede ▷ une veste en daim a suede jacket

dame [dam] nf ❶ lady ❷ (in cards, chess) queen

dames [dam] nfpl checkers

danger [dɑ̃ʒe] nm danger; **être en danger** to be in danger; «**Danger de mort**» "Extremely dangerous"

dangereux [dɑ̃ʒʀø, -øz] (f **dangereuse**) adj dangerous

danoise [danwaz] nf (pastry) danish

dans [dɑ̃] prep ❶ in ▷ Je suis dans la cuisine. I'm in the kitchen. ▷ dans deux mois two months from now ❷ into ▷ Il est entré dans mon bureau. He came into my office. ❸ out of ▷ On a bu dans des verres en plastique. We drank out of plastic glasses.

danse [dɑ̃s] nf ❶ dance ▷ la danse moderne modern dance ▷ des danses folkloriques folk dances; **la danse classique** ballet ❷ dancing ▷ des cours de danse dancing lessons

danser [dɑ̃se] vb to dance

danseur [dɑ̃sœʀ] nm dancer

danseuse [dɑ̃søz] nf dancer

date [dat] nf date ▷ votre date de naissance your date of birth ▷ la date limite de vente the best-before date; **un ami de longue date** an old friend

dater [date] vb: **dater de** to date from ▷ Cette coutume date du moyen âge. This custom dates from the Middle Ages.

datte [dat] *nf* (*fruit*) date
dauphin [dofɛ̃] *nm* dolphin
davantage [davɑ̃taʒ] *adv* more ▷ *Le gouvernement doit aider les pauvres davantage.* The government must help poor people more.; **davantage de** more ▷ *Il faudrait davantage de stages de formation.* There should be more training courses.
DC [dese] *nm* (= *disque compact*) CD
de [d(ə)] *prep, art* ❶ of ▷ *le toit de la maison* the roof of the house ▷ *la capitale de Terre-Neuve* the capital of Newfoundland ▷ *la voiture de mes parents* my parents' car ▷ *la population de l'Alberta* the population of Alberta ▷ *deux bouteilles de vin* two bottles of wine ▷ *un litre d'essence* a litre of gas; **un bébé d'un an** a one-year-old baby; **un billet de cinquante dollars** a 50-dollar bill ❷ from ▷ *de Prince George à Whitehorse* from Prince George to Whitehorse ▷ *Je viens de Kingston.* I come from Kingston. ▷ *une lettre de ma sœur* a letter from my sister ❶ by ▷ *augmenter de dix dollars* to increase by ten dollars; **Je voudrais de l'eau.** I'd like some water. ▷ *du pain et de la confiture* bread and jam; **Il n'a pas de famille.** He hasn't got any family.; **Il n'y a plus de biscuits.** There aren't any more cookies.
dé [de] *nm* (*one of a pair of dice*) die; **un dé à coudre** a thimble
débâcle [debɑkl(ə)] *nf* (*ice*) break-up ▷ *La débâcle printanière cause souvent des inondations.* The spring break-up often creates floods.
déballer [debale] *vb* to unpack
débarbouillette [debaʀbujɛt] *nf* washcloth
débardeur [debaʀdœʀ] *nm* tank top
débarquer [debaʀke] *vb* ❶ (*plane, ship*) to disembark ▷ *Nous avons dû débarquer à Halifax.* We had to disembark at Halifax. ❷ (*bus, train*) to get off ▷ *débarquer de l'autobus* to get off the bus; **débarquer chez quelqu'un** (*informal*) to descend on somebody ▷ *Ils ont débarqué chez nous à dix heures du soir.* They descended on us at ten o'clock at night.
débarras [debaʀa] *nm* junk room; **Bon débarras!** Good riddance!
débarrasser [debaʀase] *vb* to clear ▷ *Tu peux débarrasser la table, s'il te plaît?* Can you clear the table please?; **se débarrasser de quelque chose** to get rid of something ▷ *Je me suis débarrassé de mon vieux frigo.* I got rid of my old fridge.
débat [deba] *nm* debate
se débattre [debatʀ(ə)] *vb* to struggle
débile [debil] *adj* crazy ▷ *C'est complètement débile!* (*informal*) That's totally crazy!
débordé [debɔʀde] (*f* **débordée**) *adj:* **être débordé** to be snowed under
déborder [debɔʀde] *vb* (*river*) to overflow; **déborder d'énergie** to be full of energy
déboucher [debuʃe] *vb* ❶ (*sink, pipe*) to unblock ❷ (*bottle*) to open; **déboucher sur** to lead into ▷ *La rue débouche sur une place.* The

street leads into a square.
debout [dəbu] *adv* ❶ standing up ▷ *Il a mangé ses céréales debout.* He ate his cereal standing up. ❷ upright ▷ *Mets les livres debout sur l'étagère.* Put the books upright on the shelf. ❸ up ▷ *Tu es déjà debout? Are you up already?;* **Debout!** Get up!
déboutonner [debutɔne] *vb* to unbutton
débrancher [debʀɑ̃ʃe] *vb* to unplug
débris [debʀi] *nm:* **des débris de verre** bits of glass
débrouillard [debʀujaʀ, -aʀd(ə)] (*f* **débrouillarde**) *adj* resourceful
se débrouiller [debʀuje] *vb* to manage ▷ *C'était difficile, mais je ne me suis pas trop mal débrouillé.* It was difficult, but I managed OK.; **Débrouille-toi tout seul.** Work things out for yourself.
début [deby] *nm* beginning ▷ *au début* at the beginning; **début mai** in early May
débutant [debytɑ̃] *nm* beginner
débutante [debytɑ̃t] *nf* beginner
débuter [debyte] *vb* to start ▷ *Le président a débuté comme concierge.* The president started as a janitor. ▷ *La réunion a débuté par un discours.* The meeting started with a speech.
décaféiné [dekafeine] (*f* **décaféinée**) *adj* decaffeinated
décalage horaire [dekalaʒ-] *nm* (*between time zones*) time difference ▷ *Il y a une heure de décalage horaire entre le Nouveau-Brunswick et l'Ontario.* There's an hour's time difference between New Brunswick and Ontario.
décalquer [dekalke] *vb* to trace
décapotable [dekapɔtabl(ə)] *adj* convertible
décéder [desede] *vb* to die ▷ *Son père est décédé il y a trois ans.* Her father died three years ago.
décembre [desɑ̃bʀ(ə)] *nm* December; **en décembre** in December
décemment [desamɑ̃] *adv* decently
décent [desɑ̃, -ɑ̃t] (*f* **décente**) *adj* decent
déception [desɛpsjɔ̃] *nf* disappointment
décerner [deseʀne] *vb* to award
décès [desɛ] *nm* death
décevant [desvɑ̃, -ɑ̃t] (*f* **décevante**) *adj* disappointing ▷ *Ses résultats sont plutôt décevants.* His results are rather disappointing.
décevoir [desvwaʀ] *vb* to disappoint
décharger [deʃaʀʒe] *vb* to unload
se déchausser [deʃose] *vb* to take off one's shoes
déchets [deʃɛ] *nmpl* waste ▷ *les déchets nucléaires* nuclear waste ▷ *les déchets toxiques* toxic waste ▷ *les déchets dangereux* hazardous waste
déchiffrer [deʃifʀe] *vb* to decipher
déchirant [deʃiʀɑ̃, -ɑ̃t] (*f* **déchirante**) *adj* heart-rending
déchirer [deʃiʀe] *vb* ❶ (*clothes*) to tear ❷ to tear up ▷ *déchirer une lettre* to tear up a letter ❸ to tear out ▷ *déchirer une page d'un livre* to tear a page out of a book; **se déchirer un muscle** to tear a muscle
déchirure [deʃiʀyʀ] *nf* (*rip*) tear; **une déchirure musculaire** a torn muscle
décidé [deside] (*f* **décidée**) *adj* determined;

C'est décidé. It's decided.
décidément [desidemɑ̃] *adv* certainly
▷ *Décidément, je n'ai pas de chance aujourd'hui.* I'm certainly not having much luck today.
décider [deside] *vb* to decide; **décider de faire quelque chose** to decide to do something ▷ *Ils ont décidé de passer leurs vacances en Alberta.* They decided to go to Alberta for their holiday.; **se décider** to make up one's mind ▷ *Elle n'arrive pas à se décider.* She can't make up her mind.
décisif [desizif, -iv] (*f* **décisive**) *adj* decisive
décision [desizjɔ̃] *nf* decision
déclaration [deklaʀɑsjɔ̃] *nf* statement ▷ *Je n'ai aucune déclaration à faire.* I have no statement to make.; **faire une déclaration de vol** to report something as stolen
déclarer [deklaʀe] *vb* to declare ▷ *déclarer la guerre à un pays* to declare war on a country; **se déclarer** to break out ▷ *Un feu s'est déclaré dans le gymnase.* A fire broke out in the gymnasium.
déclencher [deklɑ̃ʃe] *vb* (*alarm, explosion*) to set off; **se déclencher** to go off
déclic [deklik] *nm* click
décoiffé [dekwafe] (*f* **décoiffée**) *adj*: **Elle était toute décoiffée.** Her hair was in a real mess.
décollage [dekɔlaʒ] *nm* (*of plane*) takeoff
décoller [dekɔle] *vb* ❶ (*sticker*) to remove ▷ *décoller une étiquette* to remove a label; **se décoller** to come unstuck ❷ to take off ▷ *L'avion a décollé avec dix minutes de retard.* The plane took off ten minutes late.
décolleté [dekɔlte] (*f* **décolletée**) *adj* low-cut ▷ *nm*: **un décolleté plongeant** a plunging neckline
se décolorer [dekɔlɔʀe] *vb* to fade ▷ *Ce T-shirt s'est décoloré au lavage.* This T-shirt faded in the wash.; **se faire décolorer les cheveux** to get one's hair bleached
décombres [dekɔ̃bʀ(ə)] *nmpl* rubble
se décommander [dekɔmɑ̃de] *vb* to back out ▷ *Il devait venir mais il s'est décommandé à la dernière minute.* He was supposed to come, but he backed out at the last minute.
déconcerté [dekɔ̃sɛʀte] (*f* **déconcertée**) *adj* disconcerted
décongeler [dekɔ̃ʒle] *vb* to thaw
se déconnecter [dekɔnɛkte] *vb* to log out
déconseiller [dekɔ̃seje] *vb*: **déconseiller à quelqu'un de faire quelque chose** to advise somebody not to do something ▷ *Je lui ai déconseillé d'y aller.* I advised her not to go.; **C'est déconseillé.** It's not recommended.
décontenancé [dekɔ̃tnɑ̃se] (*f* **décontenancée**) *adj* disconcerted
décontracté [dekɔ̃tʀakte] (*f* **décontractée**) *adj* relaxed; **des vêtements décontractés** casual clothes
se décontracter [dekɔ̃tʀakte] *vb* to relax ▷ *Il est allé faire du jogging pour se décontracter.* He went jogging to relax.
décor [dekɔʀ] *nm* ❶ décor ❷ scenery ▷ *un décor de montagnes* mountain scenery ❸ (*for movie, play*) set ▷ *un décor de cinéma* the set of a film ▷ *un superbe décor de théâtre* a superb stage set; **faire partie du décor** to be part of the furniture

décorateur [dekɔʀatœʀ] *nm* interior decorator
décoration [dekɔʀɑsjɔ̃] *nf* decoration
décoratrice [dekɔʀatʀis] *nf* interior decorator
décorer [dekɔʀe] *vb* to decorate
décortiquer [dekɔʀtike] *vb* to shell; **des crevettes décortiquées** peeled shrimp
découdre [dekudʀ(ə)] *vb*: **se découdre** to come unstitched
découper [dekupe] *vb* to cut out ▷ *J'ai découpé cet article dans le journal.* I cut this article out of the paper.
décourageant [dekuʀaʒɑ̃, ɑ̃t] (*f* **décourageante**) *adj* discouraging
décourager [dekuʀaʒe] *vb* to discourage; **se décourager** to get discouraged ▷ *Ne te décourage pas!* Don't give up!
décousu [dekuzy] (*f* **décousue**) *adj* unstitched ▷ *L'ourlet est décousu.* The hem's come unstitched.
découvert [dekuvɛʀ] *nm* overdraft
découverte [dekuvɛʀt(ə)] *nf* discovery
découvrir [dekuvʀiʀ] *vb* to discover
décriminaliser [dekʀiminalize] *vb* to decriminalize
décrire [dekʀiʀ] *vb* to describe
décrocher [dekʀɔʃe] *vb* ❶ to take down ▷ *Tu peux m'aider à décrocher les rideaux?* Can you help me take down the curtains? ❷ to pick up the phone ▷ *Il a décroché et a composé le numéro.* He picked up the phone and dialled the number. ❸ (*school*) to drop out ▷ *Il a décroché avant de terminer son secondaire cinq.* He dropped out before finishing Grade 12.; **décrocher le téléphone** to take the phone off the hook
décrocheur [dekʀɔʃœʀ] *nm* dropout
décrocheuse [dekʀɔʃøz] *nf* dropout
déçu [desy] *vb* disappointed
dédaigneux [dedɛɲø, -øz] (*f* **dédaigneuse**) *adj* disdainful ▷ *d'un air dédaigneux* disdainfully
dédain [dedɛ̃] *nm* disdain ▷ *avec dédain* with disdain
dedans [dədɑ̃] *adv* inside ▷ *C'est une jolie boîte : qu'est-ce qu'il y a dedans?* That's a nice box: what's in it?; **là-dedans (1)** in there ▷ *J'ai trouvé les clés là-dedans.* I found the keys in there. **(2)** in that ▷ *Il y a du vrai là-dedans.* There's some truth in that.
dédicacé [dedikase] (*f* **dédicacée**) *adj*: **un exemplaire dédicacé** a signed copy
dédier [dedje] *vb* to dedicate
déduire [deduiʀ] *vb* to deduct ▷ *Tu as déduit les vingt dollars que je te devais?* Did you deduct the twenty dollars I owed you?; **déduire que** to deduce that ▷ *J'en déduis qu'elle m'a menti.* That means she must have been lying.
déesse [dees] *nf* goddess
défaire [defɛʀ] *vb* to undo; **défaire sa valise** to unpack; **se défaire** to come undone
défaite [defɛt] *nf* defeat
défaut [defo] *nm* fault
défavorable [defavɔʀabl(ə)] *adj* unfavourable
défavorisé [defavɔʀize] (*f* **défavorisée**) *adj* underprivileged

défectueux [defɛktɥø, -øz] (f **défectueuse**) adj faulty

défendre [defɑ̃dʀ(ə)] vb ❶ to forbid; **défendre à quelqu'un de faire quelque chose** to forbid somebody to do something ▷ *Sa mère lui a défendu de le revoir.* Her mother forbade her to see him again. ❷ to defend ▷ **défendre ses idées** to defend one's ideas ▷ **défendre quelqu'un** to defend somebody

défendu [defɑ̃dy] (f **défendue**) adj forbidden ▷ *C'est défendu.* It's not allowed.

défense [defɑ̃s] nf defence ▷ *prendre la défense de quelqu'un* to take somebody's side; **« défense de fumer »** "no smoking" ❷ (of elephant) tusk

défi [defi] nm challenge; **d'un air de défi** defiantly; **sur un ton de défi** defiantly

défier [defje] vb ❶ to challenge ▷ *Je te défie de trouver un meilleur exemple.* I challenge you to find a better example. ❷ to dare ▷ *Il m'a défié d'aller à l'école en pyjama.* He dared me to go to school in my pyjamas.

défigurer [defigyʀe] vb to disfigure

défilé [defile] nm ❶ parade; **un défilé de mode** a fashion show ❷ march

défiler [defile] vb to march

définir [definiʀ] vb to define

définitif [definitif, -iv] (f **définitive**) adj final; **en définitive** in the end ▷ *En définitive, ils ont décidé de rester.* In the end, they decided to stay.

définitivement [definitivmɑ̃] adv for good ▷ *Elle s'est définitivement installée en Nouvelle-Écosse en 1980.* She moved to Nova Scotia for good in 1980.

déformer [defɔʀme] vb to stretch ▷ *Ne tire pas sur ton chandail, tu vas le déformer.* Don't pull down on your sweater, you'll stretch it.; **se déformer** to stretch ▷ *Ce T-shirt s'est déformé au lavage.* This T-shirt got stretched in the wash.

se défouler [defule] vb (*relax*) to unwind ▷ *Je fais de l'aérobic pour me défouler.* I do aerobics to unwind.

dégagé [degaʒe] (f **dégagée**) adj: **d'un air dégagé** casually; **sur un ton dégagé** casually

dégager [degaʒe] vb ❶ to free ▷ *Ils ont mis une heure à dégager les victimes.* They took an hour to free the victims. ❷ to clear ▷ *des gouttes qui dégagent le nez* drops to clear your nose; **Ça se dégage.** (*weather*) It's clearing up.

se dégarnir [degaʀniʀ] vb to go bald

dégâts [dega] nmpl damage

dégel [deʒɛl] nm thaw

dégeler [deʒle] vb to thaw ▷ *faire dégeler un poulet congelé* to thaw out a frozen chicken

dégivrer [deʒivʀe] vb ❶ to defrost ❷ to de-ice

dégonfler [degɔ̃fle] vb to let the air out of ▷ *Quelqu'un a dégonflé mes pneus.* Somebody let the air out of my tires.; **se dégonfler** (*informal*) to chicken out

dégouliner [deguline] vb to trickle

dégourdi [deguʀdi] (f **dégourdie**) adj smart ▷ *Il est assez dégourdi.* He's on the ball.

dégourdir [deguʀdiʀ] vb: **se dégourdir les jambes** to stretch one's legs

dégoût [degu] nm disgust ▷ *une expression de*

dégoût a disgusted expression; **avec dégoût** disgustedly

dégoûtant [degutɑ̃, -ɑ̃t] (f **dégoûtante**) adj disgusting

dégoûté [degute] (f **dégoûtée**) adj disgusted; **être dégoûté de tout** to be sick of everything

dégoûter [degute] vb to disgust ▷ *Ce genre de comportement me dégoûte.* That kind of behaviour makes me sick.; **dégoûter quelqu'un de quelque chose** to put somebody off something ▷ *Ça m'a dégoûté de la viande.* That put me off meat.

se dégrader [degʀade] vb to deteriorate

degré [dəgʀe] nm degree; **dix degrés Celsius** 10°C

dégringoler [degʀɛ̃gɔle] vb ❶ to rush down ▷ *Il a dégringolé l'escalier.* He rushed down the stairs. ❷ to collapse ▷ *Elle a fait dégringoler la pile de livres.* She knocked over the stack of books.

dégueulasse [degœlas] adj (*rude*) disgusting

déguisement [degizmɑ̃] nm disguise

déguiser [degize] vb: **se déguiser en quelque chose** to dress up as something ▷ *Elle s'est déguisée en vampire.* She dressed up as a vampire.

déguster [degyste] vb ❶ (*sample*) to taste ❷ to enjoy

dehors [dəɔʀ] adv outside ▷ *Je t'attends dehors.* I'll wait for you outside.; **jeter quelqu'un dehors** to throw somebody out; **en dehors de** apart from ▷ *En dehors de lui, tout le monde était content.* Apart from him, everybody was happy.

déjà [deʒa] adv ❶ already ▷ *J'ai déjà fini.* I'm already finished. ❷ before ▷ *Tu es déjà venu au Canada?* Have you been to Canada before?

déjeuner [deʒœne] vb to have breakfast ▷ nm breakfast

délai [dele] nm ❶ extension ▷ *J'ai demandé un délai d'une semaine.* I asked for a week's extension. ❷ time limit ▷ *être dans les délais* to be within the time limit

délasser [delase] vb to relax ▷ *La lecture délasse.* Reading is relaxing.; **se délasser** to relax ▷ *J'ai pris un bain pour me délasser.* I had a bath to relax.

délavé [delave] (f **délavée**) adj faded ▷ *un jean délavé* a pair of faded jeans

délégué [delege] nm representative ▷ *les délégués de classe* the class representatives

déléguée [delege] nf representative

déléguer [delege] vb to delegate

délibéré [delibeʀe] (f **délibérée**) adj deliberate

délicat [delika, -at] (f **délicate**) adj ❶ delicate ▷ *avoir la peau délicate* to have delicate skin ❷ tricky ▷ *une situation délicate* a tricky situation ❸ tactful ▷ *Il est toujours très délicat.* He's always very tactful. ❹ thoughtful ▷ *C'est une attention délicate de sa part.* That was a kind thought on her part.

délicatement [delikatmɑ̃] adv ❶ gently ❷ tactfully

délice [delis] nm delight ▷ *Vivre ici est un vrai délice.* Living here is a real delight. ▷ *Ce gâteau est un vrai délice.* This cake is a real treat.

délicieux [delisjø, -øz] (f **délicieuse**) *adj* delicious

délinquance [delɛ̃kɑ̃s] *nf* crime ▷ *de nouvelles mesures pour combattre la délinquance juvénile* new measures to fight juvenile delinquency

délinquant [delɛ̃kɑ̃] *nm* criminal

délinquante [delɛ̃kɑ̃t] *nf* criminal

délirer [deliʀe] *vb*: **Mais tu délires!** (*informal*) You're crazy!

délivrer [delivʀe] *vb* (prisoner) to set free

deltaplane [deltaplan] *nm* hang-glider; **faire du deltaplane** to go hang-gliding

demain [dəmɛ̃] *adv* tomorrow; **À demain!** See you tomorrow!

demande [dəmɑ̃d] *nf* request; **une demande en mariage** an offer of marriage; **faire une demande d'emploi** to apply for a job; **« demandes d'emploi »** "employment wanted"

demandé [dəmɑ̃de] (f **demandée**) *adj*: **très demandé** very much in demand

demander [dəmɑ̃de] *vb* ❶ to ask for ▷ *J'ai demandé la permission.* I've asked for permission. ▷ *On a demandé notre chemin à un chauffeur de taxi.* We asked a taxi driver the way. ▷ *Je lui ai demandé de m'aider.* I asked him to help me. ❷ to require ▷ *un travail qui demande beaucoup de temps* a job that requires a lot of time; **se demander** to wonder ▷ *Je me demande à quelle heure elle va venir.* I wonder what time she'll be coming.

demandeur d'emploi [dəmɑ̃dœʀ-] *nm* job applicant

demandeuse d'emploi [dəmɑ̃døz-] *nf* job applicant

démangeaison [demɑ̃ʒɛzɔ̃] *nf* itching

démanger [demɑ̃ʒe] *vb* to itch ▷ *Ça me démange.* It itches.

démaquillant [demakijɑ̃] *nm* make-up remover

démaquiller [demakije] *vb*: **se démaquiller** to remove one's make-up

démarche [demaʀʃ(ə)] *nf* ❶ way of walking ▷ *une drôle de démarche* a funny way of walking ❷ step ▷ *faire les démarches nécessaires* to take the necessary steps

démarrer [demaʀe] *vb* ❶ (*car*) to start ❷ to boot up

démêler [demele] *vb* to untangle

déménagement [demenaʒmɑ̃] *nm* (house) move ▷ *C'était le jour de notre déménagement.* It was the day we moved.; **un camion de déménagement** a moving van

déménager [demenaʒe] *vb* (house) to move

dément [demɑ̃, -ɑ̃t] (f **démente**) *adj* crazy

démentiel [demɑ̃sjɛl] (f **démentielle**) *adj* insane

demeurer [dəmœʀe] *vb* to live

demi [dəmi] (f **demie**) *adj, adv* half ▷ *Il a trois ans et demi.* He's three and a half.; **Il est trois heures et demie.** It's half past three.; **Il est midi et demi.** It's half past twelve.; **à demi endormi** half-asleep

demi-cercle [dəmisɛʀkl(ə)] *nm* semicircle

demi-douzaine [dəmiduzɛn] *nf* half-dozen ▷ *une demi-douzaine d'œufs* half a dozen eggs

demie [dəmi] *nf* half-hour ▷ *L'autobus passe à* la demie. The bus comes on the half-hour.

demi-finale [dəmifinal] *nf* semifinal

demi-frère [dəmifʀɛʀ] *nm* half-brother

demi-heure [dəmijœʀ] *nf* half an hour ▷ *dans une demi-heure* in half an hour ▷ *toutes les demi-heures* every half-hour

demi-litre [dəmilitʀ(ə)] *nm* half litre ▷ *un demi-litre de lait* half a litre of milk

demi-sœur [dəmisœʀ] *nf* half-sister

démission [demisjɔ̃] *nf* resignation; **donner sa démission** to hand in one's resignation

démissionner [demisjɔne] *vb* to resign

demi-tarif [dəmitaʀif] *nm* ❶ half-price ▷ *un billet à demi-tarif* a half-price ticket ❷ half-fare ▷ *voyager à demi-tarif* to travel half-fare

demi-tour [dəmituʀ] *nm*: **faire demi-tour** to turn back ▷ *La nuit commence à tomber; il est temps de faire demi-tour.* It's getting dark; it's time we went back.

démocratie [demɔkʀasi] *nf* democracy

démocratique [demɔkʀatik] *adj* democratic

démodé [demɔde] (f **démodée**) *adj* old-fashioned

demoiselle [dəmwazɛl] *nf* young lady; **une demoiselle d'honneur** a bridesmaid

démolir [demɔliʀ] *vb* to demolish

démon [demɔ̃] *nm* devil

démonter [demɔ̃te] *vb* ❶ (*tent*) to take down ❷ (*machine*) to take apart

démontrer [demɔ̃tʀe] *vb* to show

déneiger [deneʒe] *vb* to clear of snow ▷ *déneiger l'entrée* to shovel the driveway ▷ *déneiger les rues* to plow the streets

déneigeuse [deneʒøz] *nf* ❶ snowplow ❷ snowblower

denim [dənim] *nm* denim ▷ *une veste en denim* a denim jacket

dénoncer [denɔ̃se] *vb* to denounce; **se dénoncer** to give oneself up ▷ *Elle s'est dénoncée à la police.* She gave herself up to the police.

dénouement [denumɑ̃] *nm* outcome

dent [dɑ̃] *nf* tooth ▷ *une dent de lait* a baby tooth ▷ *une dent de sagesse* a wisdom tooth

dentaire [dɑ̃tɛʀ] *adj* dental

dentelle [dɑ̃tɛl] *nf* lace ▷ *un chemisier en dentelle* a lacy blouse

dentier [dɑ̃tje] *nm* denture

dentifrice [dɑ̃tifʀis] *nm* toothpaste

dentiste [dɑ̃tist(ə)] *nmf* dentist

déodorant [deɔdɔʀɑ̃] *nm* deodorant

dépannage [depanaʒ] *nm*: **un service de dépannage** roadside assistance

dépanner [depane] *vb* ❶ to fix ▷ *Elle a dépanné la voiture en cinq minutes.* She fixed the car in five minutes. ❷ to help out ▷ *Il m'a prêté dix dollars pour me dépanner.* (*informal*) He lent me 10 dollars to help me out.

dépanneur [depanœʀ] *nm* convenience store

dépanneuse [depanøz] *nf* tow truck

départ [depaʀ] *nm* departure ▷ *Le départ est à onze heures.* The departure is at 11.; **Je lui téléphonerai la veille de son départ.** I'll phone him the day before he leaves.

département [depaʀtəmɑ̃] *nm* ❶ department ▷ *le département d'anglais à* l'université the English department at the university ▷ *le département des articles ménagers* the appliances department ❷ *(in store)*

dépasser [depase] *vb* ❶ to pass ▷ *Nous avons dépassé Windsor.* We've passed Windsor. ▷ *Il y a une voiture qui essaie de nous dépasser.* There's a car trying to overtake us. ❷ *(sum, limit)* to exceed

dépaysé [depeize] *(f* **dépaysée)** *adj* disoriented

se **dépêcher** [depeʃe] *vb* to hurry ▷ *Dépêche-toi!* Hurry up!

dépendre [depɑ̃dr(ə)] *vb*: **dépendre de** to depend on ▷ *Ça dépend du temps.* It depends on the weather.; **dépendre de quelqu'un** to be dependent on somebody; **Ça dépend.** It depends.

dépenser [depɑ̃se] *vb (money)* to spend

dépensier [depɑ̃sje, -jɛʀ] *(f* **dépensière)** *adj*: **Il est dépensier.** He's a big spender.; **Elle n'est pas dépensière.** She's not exactly extravagant.

dépilatoire [depilatwaʀ] *adj*: **une crème dépilatoire** a depilatory cream

dépit [depi] *nm*: **en dépit de** in spite of ▷ *Il y est allé en dépit de mes conseils.* He went in spite of my advice.

déplacé [deplase] *(f* **déplacée)** *adj* uncalled-for ▷ *C'était une remarque déplacée.* That remark was uncalled-for.

déplacement [deplasmɑ̃] *nm* trip ▷ *Ça vaut le déplacement.* It's worth the trip.

déplacer [deplase] *vb* ❶ to move ▷ *Tu peux m'aider à déplacer la table?* Can you help me move the table? ❷ to put off ▷ *déplacer un rendez-vous* to put off an appointment; **se déplacer (1)** to travel around ▷ *Elle se déplace beaucoup pour son travail.* She travels around a lot for her work. **(2)** to get around ▷ *Elle a du mal à se déplacer.* She has difficulty getting around.; **se déplacer une vertèbre** to slip a disc

déplaire [deplɛʀ] *vb*: **Cela me déplaît.** I dislike this.

déplaisant [deplɛzɑ̃, -ɑ̃t] *(f* **déplaisante)** *adj* unpleasant

dépliant [deplijɑ̃] *nm* brochure ▷ *un dépliant touristique* a tourist brochure; **un dépliant publicitaire** a flyer

déplier [deplije] *vb* to unfold

déposer [depoze] *vb* ❶ to leave ▷ *J'ai déposé mon manteau dans le vestiaire.* I left my coat in the cloakroom. ❷ to put down ▷ *Déposez le paquet sur la table.* Put the parcel down on the table. ❸ to deposit ▷ *J'ai déposé cent dollars dans mon compte.* I deposited 100 dollars into my account.; **déposer quelqu'un** to drop somebody off

dépotoir [depotwaʀ] *nm* dump

dépourvu [depuʀvy] *(f* **dépourvue)** *adj* destitute ▷ *des gens dépourvus* destitute people; **être dépourvu de quelque chose** to lack something ▷ *Elle n'est pas dépourvue de talent.* She has no lack of talent.; **prendre quelqu'un au dépourvu** to take somebody by surprise ▷ *Sa question m'a pris au dépourvu.* His

question took me by surprise.

dépression [depʀesjɔ̃] *nf* depression; **faire de la dépression** to be suffering from depression; **faire une dépression** to have a nervous breakdown

déprimant [depʀimɑ̃, -ɑ̃t] *(f* **déprimante)** *adj* depressing

déprimer [depʀime] *vb* to get depressed ▷ *Il déprime tout le temps.* He gets depressed all the time.; **Ce genre de temps me déprime.** This kind of weather makes me depressed.

depuis [dəpɥi] *prep, adv* ❶ since ▷ *Elle habite Saskatoon depuis 1993.* She's been living in Saskatoon since 1993. ▷ *Je ne lui ai pas parlé depuis.* I haven't spoken to her since.; **depuis que** since ▷ *Il a plu tous les jours depuis qu'elle est arrivée.* It's rained every day since she arrived. ❷ for ▷ *Il habite St. Catharines depuis cinq ans.* He's been living in St. Catharines for five years.; **Depuis combien de temps?** How long? ▷ *Depuis combien de temps est-ce que vous la connaissez?* How long have you known her?; **Depuis quand?** How long? ▷ *Depuis quand est-ce que vous le connaissez?* How long have you known him?

député [depyte] *nm* Member of Parliament; **un député à l'Assemblée législative** a Member of the Legislative Assembly; **un député à l'Assemblée nationale** a Member of the National Assembly; **un député provincial** a Member of Provincial Parliament

députée [depyte] *nf* Member of Parliament; **une députée à l'Assemblée législative** a Member of the Legislative Assembly; **une députée à l'Assemblée nationale** a Member of the National Assembly; **une députée provinciale** a Member of Provincial Parliament

déraciner [deʀasine] *vb* to uproot

dérangement [deʀɑ̃ʒmɑ̃] *nm*: **en dérangement** out of order ▷ *Le téléphone est en dérangement.* The phone's out of order.

déranger [deʀɑ̃ʒe] *vb* ❶ to bother ▷ *Excusez-moi de vous déranger.* I'm sorry to bother you.; **Ne vous dérangez pas, je vais répondre au téléphone.** You stay there, I'll answer the phone. ❷ to disorganize ▷ *Ne dérange pas mes livres, s'il te plaît.* Don't disorganize my books, please.

déraper [deʀape] *vb* to skid

dermatologue [dɛʀmatɔlɔɡ] *nmf* dermatologist ▷ *Elle est dermatologue.* She's a dermatologist.

dernier [dɛʀnje, -jɛʀ] *(f* **dernière)** *adj* ❶ last ▷ *Il est arrivé dernier.* He arrived last. ▷ *la dernière fois* the last time ❷ latest ▷ *leur dernier film* their latest film; **en dernier** last ▷ *Ajoutez le lait en dernier.* Put the milk in last.

dernièrement [dɛʀnjɛʀmɑ̃] *adv* recently

dérouler [deʀule] *vb* ❶ to unroll ❷ to unwind; **se dérouler** to take place ▷ *L'action se déroule dans les années vingt.* The action takes place in the 1920s.; **Tout s'est déroulé comme prévu.** Everything went as planned.

derrière [dɛʀjɛʀ] *adv, prep* behind ▶ *nm* ❶ back ▷ *la porte de derrière* the back door ❷ backside ▷ *un coup de pied dans le derrière* a kick in the backside

DES [deøɛs] nm (= diplôme d'études secondaires) secondary school diploma

des [de] art ❶ some ▷ Tu veux des croustilles? Would you like some chips? ▷ J'ai des cousins en France. I have cousins in France. ▷ pendant des mois for months ❷ any ▷ Tu as des frères? Do you have any brothers? ▷ la fin des vacances the end of the holidays ▷ la voiture des Durand the Durands' car; **Ils arrivent des États-Unis.** They're arriving from the United States.

dès [dɛ] prep as early as ▷ dès le mois de novembre from November; **dès le début** right from the start; **Elle vous appellera dès son retour.** She'll call you as soon as she gets back.; **dès que** as soon as ▷ Il m'a reconnu dès qu'il m'a vu. He recognized me as soon as he saw me.

désabusé [dezabyze] (f **désabusée**) adj disillusioned

désaccord [dezakɔr] nm disagreement

désagréable [dezagreablə)] adj unpleasant

désaltérer [dezaltere] vb: **L'eau gazeuse désaltère bien.** Sparkling water is very thirst-quenching.; **se désaltérer** to quench one's thirst ▷ Nous sommes allés dans un café pour nous désaltérer. We went into a café to have a drink.

désapprobateur [dezaprobatœr, -tris] (f **désapprobatrice**) adj disapproving ▷ un regard désapprobateur a disapproving look

désastre [dezastr(ə)] nm disaster

désavantage [dezavɑ̃taʒ] nm disadvantage

désavantager [dezavɑ̃taʒe] vb: **désavantager quelqu'un** to put somebody at a disadvantage ▷ Cette nouvelle loi va désavantager les femmes. The new law will put women at a disadvantage.

descendre [desɑ̃dr(ə)] vb ❶ to go down ▷ Je suis tombé en descendant l'escalier. I fell as I was going down the stairs. ❷ to come down ▷ Attends, je descends! Wait downstairs; I'm coming down! ❸ to get down ▷ Vous pouvez descendre ma valise, s'il vous plaît? Can you get my suitcase down, please? ❹ to get off ▷ Nous descendons à la prochaine station. We're getting off at the next station.

descente [desɑ̃t] nf way down ▷ Je t'attendrai au bas de la descente. I'll wait for you at the bottom of the hill.; **une descente de police** a police raid

description [dɛskripsjɔ̃] nf description

déséquilibré [dezekilibre] (f **déséquilibrée**) adj unbalanced

déséquilibrer [dezekilibre] vb: **déséquilibrer quelqu'un** to throw somebody off balance ▷ Le coup de poing l'a déséquilibré. The punch threw him off balance.

désert [dezɛr, -ɛrt(ə)] (f **déserte**) adj deserted ▷ Le dimanche, l'école est déserte. On Sundays, the school is deserted.; **une île déserte** a desert island
▶ nm desert

déserter [dezɛrte] vb to desert

désertique [dezɛrtik] adj desert ▷ une région désertique a desert region

désespéré [dezɛspere] (f **désespérée**) adj

desperate

désespérer [dezɛspere] vb to despair ▷ Il ne faut pas désespérer. Don't despair.

désespoir [dezɛspwar] nm despair

déshabiller [dezabije] vb to undress; **se déshabiller** to get undressed

déshériter [dezerite] vb to disinherit; **les déshérités** the underprivileged

déshydraté [dezidrate] (f **déshydratée**) adj dehydrated

désigner [dezine] vb to choose ▷ On l'a désignée pour remettre le prix. She was chosen to present the prize.; **désigner quelque chose du doigt** to point at something

désinfectant [dezɛ̃fɛktɑ̃] nm disinfectant

désinfecter [dezɛ̃fɛkte] vb to disinfect

désintéressé [dezɛ̃terese] (f **désintéressée**) adj ❶ unselfish ▷ un acte désintéressé an unselfish action ❷ impartial ▷ un conseil désintéressé impartial advice

désintéresser [dezɛ̃terese] vb: **se désintéresser de quelque chose** to lose interest in something

désir [dezir] nm ❶ wish ▷ Vos désirs sont des ordres. Your wish is my command. ❷ will ▷ le désir de réussir the will to succeed ❸ desire ▷ Ses yeux brillaient de désir. Her eyes were shining with desire.

désirer [dezire] vb to want ▷ Vous désirez? (in store) What would you like?

désobéir [dezobeir] vb: **désobéir à quelqu'un** to disobey somebody

désobéissant [dezobeisɑ̃, -ɑ̃t] (f **désobéissante**) adj disobedient

désobligeant [dezobliʒɑ̃, -ɑ̃t] (f **désobligeante**) adj unpleasant ▷ faire une remarque désobligeante to make an unpleasant remark

désodorisant [dezodorizɑ̃] nm air freshener

désolé [dezole] (f **désolée**) adj sorry ▷ Je suis vraiment désolé. I'm very sorry.; **Désolé!** Sorry!

désopilant [dezopilɑ̃, -ɑ̃t] (f **désopilante**) adj hilarious

désordonné [dezordone] (f **désordonnée**) adj untidy

désordre [dezordr(ə)] nm messiness; **Quel désordre!** What a mess!; **en désordre** messy ▷ Sa chambre est toujours en désordre. His bedroom is always messy.

désorganisé [dezorganize] adj disorganized

désormais [dezormɛ] adv from now on ▷ Désormais, je travaillerai plus fort. From now on I'll work harder.

desquelles [dekɛl] pron: ▷ des négociations au cours desquelles les patrons ont fait des concessions negotiations during which the employers made concessions

desquels [dekɛl] pron: ▷ les lacs au bord desquels nous avons campé the lakes on the banks of which we camped

dessécher [deseʃe] vb to dry out ▷ Le soleil dessèche la peau. The sun dries your skin out.

desserrer [desere] vb to loosen

dessert [desɛr] nm dessert ▷ Qu'est-ce que vous désirez comme dessert? What would you like for dessert?

dessin [desɛ̃] nm drawing ▷ *C'est un dessin de ma petite sœur.* It's a drawing my little sister did.; **un dessin animé** *(film)* a cartoon; **un dessin humoristique** *(drawing)* a cartoon

dessiner [desine] vb to draw

dessous [dəsu] adv underneath; **en dessous** underneath ▷ *Soulève le pot de fleurs; la clé est en dessous.* Lift the flowerpot; the key's underneath.; **là-dessous** underneath ▷ *Le grillage ne sert à rien; les lapins passent par-dessous.* The fence is useless; the rabbits get in underneath.; **là-dessous** under there ▷ *Elle s'est cachée là-dessous.* She hid under there.; **ci-dessous** below ▷ *Complétez les phrases ci-dessous.* Complete the sentences below.; **au-dessous de** below ▷ *au-dessous de la moyenne* below average
▶ nm underneath; **les voisins du dessous** the downstairs neighbours; **les dessous** underwear ▷ *des dessous en soie* silk underwear

dessus [dəsy] adv on top ▷ *un gâteau avec des bougies dessus* a cake with candles on top; **par-dessus** over ▷ *Nous avons sauté par-dessus la barrière.* We jumped over the gate.; **au-dessus** above ▷ *la taille au-dessus* the size above ▷ *au-dessus du lit* above the bed; **là-dessus** (1) on there ▷ *Tu peux écrire là-dessus.* You can write on there. (2) with that ▷ *« Je démissionne! » Là-dessus, il est parti.* "I resign!" With that, he left.; **ci-dessus** above ▷ *l'exemple ci-dessus* the example above
▶ nm top; **les voisins du dessus** the upstairs neighbours; **avoir le dessus** to have the upper hand

destinataire [dɛstinatɛʀ] nmf addressee

destination [dɛstinasjɔ̃] nf destination; **les passagers à destination de Calgary** passengers travelling to Calgary

destiné [dɛstine] adj intended for ▷ *Ce livre est destiné aux enfants.* This book is intended for children.; **Elle était destinée à faire ce métier.** She was destined to go into that job.

destruction [dɛstʀyksjɔ̃] nf destruction

détachant [detaʃɑ̃] nm stain remover

détacher [detaʃe] vb to undo; **se détacher de quelque chose** to come off something ▷ *La poignée de la porte s'est détachée.* The doorknob came off. ▷ *Un wagon s'est détaché du reste du train.* One car broke away from the rest of the train.

détail [detaj] nm detail; **en détail** in detail

détective [detɛktiv] nmf detective ▷ *un détective privé* a private detective

déteindre [detɛ̃dʀ(ə)] vb *(in wash)* to fade

détendre [detɑ̃dʀ(ə)] vb to relax ▷ *La lecture, ça me détend.* I find reading relaxing.; **se détendre** to relax ▷ *prendre un bain pour se détendre* to take a bath in order to relax

détente [detɑ̃t] nf relaxation

détenu [detny] nm prisoner

détenue [detny] nf prisoner

se détériorer [deteʀjɔʀe] vb to deteriorate

déterminé [detɛʀmine] (f **déterminée**) adj
❶ determined ▷ *C'est un homme déterminé.* He's a determined man. ❷ specific ▷ *un but déterminé* a specific aim

détestable [detɛstabl(ə)] adj horrible

détester [detɛste] vb to hate

détonation [detɔnasjɔ̃] nf bang ▷ *J'ai entendu une détonation.* I heard a bang.

détour [detuʀ] nm detour; **Ça vaut le détour.** It's worth the trip.; **sans détour** to someone's face ▷ *Elle me l'a dit sans détour.* She said it right to my face.

détournement [detuʀnəmɑ̃] nm: **un détournement d'avion** a hijacking

détrempé [detʀɑ̃pe] (f **détrempée**) adj waterlogged

détritus [detʀitys] nmpl litter

détruire [detʀɥiʀ] vb to destroy

dette [dɛt] nf debt

deuil [dœj] nm: **être en deuil** to be in mourning

deux [dø] num two ▷ *Il était deux heures.* It was two o'clock. ▷ *Elle a deux ans.* She's two.; **deux fois** twice; **les deux-points** colon; **tous les deux** both ▷ *Nous y sommes allées toutes les deux.* We both went.; **le deux février** the second of February

deuxième [døzjɛm] adj second ▷ *au deuxième étage* on the second floor

deuxièmement [døzjɛmmɑ̃] adv secondly

devais, devait, devaient vb see **devoir**

dévaliser [devalize] vb to rob

devant [dəvɑ̃] adv, prep ❶ in front ▷ *Il marchait devant.* He was walking in front. ❷ in front of ▷ *Il était assis devant moi.* He was sitting in front of me.; **passer devant** to go past ▷ *Nous sommes passés devant chez toi.* We went past your house.
▶ nm front ▷ *le devant de la maison* the front of the house; **les pattes de devant** the front legs

développement [devlɔpmɑ̃] nm development; **les pays en voie de développement** developing countries

développer [devlɔpe] vb to develop ▷ *donner un film à développer* to take a film to be developed; **se développer** to develop

devenir [dəvniʀ] vb to become

devez [dəve] vb see **devoir**

deviez [dəvje] vb see **devoir**

deviner [dəvine] vb to guess

devinette [dəvinɛt] nf riddle ▷ *poser une devinette à quelqu'un* to ask somebody a riddle

devions [dəvjɔ̃] vb see **devoir**

dévisager [devizaʒe] vb: **dévisager quelqu'un** to stare at somebody

devise [dəviz] nf currency ▷ *les devises étrangères* foreign currency

dévisser [devise] vb to unscrew

dévoiler [devwale] vb to unveil

devoir [dəvwaʀ] vb ❶ to have to ▷ *Je dois partir.* I've got to go. ❷ must ▷ *Tu dois être fatigué.* You must be tired. ❸ to be due to ▷ *Le nouveau centre commercial doit ouvrir en mai.* The new shopping centre is due to open in May.; **devoir quelque chose à quelqu'un** to owe somebody something ▷ *Combien est-ce que je vous dois?* How much do I owe you?
▶ nm ❶ exercise; **les devoirs** homework ❷ duty ▷ *Aller voter fait partie des devoirs du citoyen.* Voting is part of one's duty as a citizen.

devons [dəvɔ̃] *vb see* **devoir**

dévorer [devɔʀe] *vb* to devour

dévoué [devwe] (*f* **dévouée**) *adj* devoted

devra, devrai, devras, devrez, devrons, devront *vb see* **devoir**

diabète [djabɛt] *nm* diabetes

diabétique [djabetik] *adj* diabetic ▷ *Je suis diabétique.* I'm diabetic.

diable [djabl(ə)] *nm* devil

diagonal [djagɔnal, -o] (*f* **diagonale**, *mpl* **diagonaux**) *adj* diagonal

diagonale [djagɔnal] *nf* diagonal; **en diagonale** diagonally

diagramme [djagʀam] *nm* diagram

dialecte [djalɛkt(ə)] *nm* dialect

dialogue [djalɔg] *nm* dialogue

diamant [djamã] *nm* diamond

diamètre [djamɛtʀ(ə)] *nm* diameter

diapo [djapo] *nf* (*informal*) slide; **un film diapo** a slide film

diapositive [djapozitiv] *nf* slide ▷ *projeter des diapositives* to show some slides

diarrhée [djaʀe] *nf* diarrhoea ▷ *avoir la diarrhée* to have diarrhoea

dictateur [diktatœʀ] *nm* dictator

dictatrice [diktatʀis] *nf* dictator

dictature [diktatyʀ] *nf* dictatorship

dictée [dikte] *nf* dictation

dicter [dikte] *vb* to dictate

dictionnaire [diksjɔnɛʀ] *nm* dictionary

diététiste [djetetist] *nmf* dietitian

dieu [djø] (*pl* **dieux**) *nm* god ▷ *Dieu* God ▷ *Mon Dieu!* Oh my God!

différé [difeʀe] *nm:* **une émission en différé** a recording

différence [difeʀɑ̃s] *nf* difference; **la différence d'âge** the age difference; **à la différence de** unlike ▷ *À la différence de certains élèves, j'aime étudier.* Unlike some students, I like to study.

différent [difeʀɑ̃, -ɑ̃t] (*f* **différente**) *adj* ❶ different ▷ *pour des raisons différentes* for different reasons ❷ various ▷ *pour différentes raisons* for various reasons; **différent de** different from ▷ *Son point de vue est différent du mien.* Her point of view is different from mine.

difficile [difisil] *adj* difficult ▷ *C'est difficile à comprendre.* It's difficult to understand.

difficilement [difisilmɑ̃] *adv:* **faire quelque chose difficilement** to have trouble doing something ▷ *Ma grand-mère se déplace difficilement.* My grandmother has trouble getting around. ▷ *Je pouvais difficilement refuser.* It was difficult for me to refuse.

difficulté [difikylte] *nf* difficulty ▷ *avec difficulté* with difficulty; **être en difficulté** to be in difficulties

digérer [diʒeʀe] *vb* to digest

digne [diɲ] *adj:* **digne de** worthy of ▷ *digne de confiance* trustworthy

dignité [diɲite] *nf* dignity

dilemme [dilɛm] *nm* dilemma ▷ *être devant un dilemme* to be faced with a dilemma

diluer [dilɥe] *vb* to dilute

dimanche [dimɑ̃ʃ] *nm* ❶ Sunday ▷ *Aujourd'hui, on est dimanche.* It's Sunday

today. ❷ on Sunday ▷ *Dimanche, nous allons déjeuner chez mes grands-parents.* On Sunday we're having lunch at my grandparents'.; **le dimanche** on Sundays ▷ *Le dimanche, je fais la grasse matinée.* I sleep in on Sundays.; **tous les dimanches** every Sunday; **dimanche dernier** last Sunday; **dimanche prochain** next Sunday

dimension [dimɑ̃sjɔ̃] *nf* ❶ size ▷ *avoir la même dimension* to be the same size ❷ measurement ▷ *Quelles sont les dimensions de cette pièce?* What are the measurements of this room? ❸ scope ▷ *la dimension du projet* the scope of the project

diminuer [diminɥe] *vb* to decrease ▷ *Est-ce que tu peux diminuer le son?* Could you turn down the sound?

diminution [diminysjɔ̃] *nf* ❶ reduction ❷ decrease

dinde [dɛ̃d] *nf* turkey ▷ *la dinde de Noël* the Christmas turkey

dindon [dɛ̃dɔ̃] *nm* turkey

dîner [dine] *nm* lunch
  ▶ *vb* to have lunch

dingue [dɛ̃g] *adj* (*informal*) crazy

diplomate [diplɔmat] *adj* diplomatic
  ▶ *n* diplomat

diplomatie [diplɔmasi] *nf* diplomacy

diplôme [diplom] *nm* diploma

dire [diʀ] *vb* ❶ to say ▷ *Il a dit qu'il ne viendrait pas.* He said he wouldn't come.; **on dit que...** they say that... ▷ *On dit que la nourriture est excellente là-bas.* They say that the food is excellent there. ❷ to tell; **dire quelque chose à quelqu'un** to tell somebody something ▷ *Elle m'a dit la vérité.* She told me the truth. ▷ *Elle nous a dit de regarder cette émission.* She told us to watch this program.; **On dirait qu'il va pleuvoir.** It looks as if it's going to rain.; **se dire quelque chose** ▷ *Quand je l'ai vu, je me suis dit qu'il avait vieilli.* When I saw him, I thought to myself that he'd aged.; **Est-ce que ça se dit?** Can you say that?; **Ça ne me dit rien.** That doesn't appeal to me.

direct [diʀɛkt] (*f* **directe**) *adj* direct; **en direct** live ▷ *une émission en direct* a live broadcast

directement [diʀɛktəmɑ̃] *adv* straight ▷ *Elle est rentrée directement chez elle.* She went straight home.

directeur [diʀɛktœʀ] *nm* ❶ principal ▷ *Il est directeur.* He's a principal. ❷ manager ▷ *Il est directeur du personnel.* He's a personnel manager.

direction [diʀɛksjɔ̃] *nf* ❶ management ▷ *la direction et les ouvriers* management and labour ❷ direction ▷ *dans toutes les directions* in all directions

directrice [diʀɛktʀis] *nf* ❶ principal ▷ *Elle est directrice.* She's a principal. ❷ manager ▷ *Elle est directrice commerciale.* She's a sales manager.

dirent [diʀ] *vb see* **dire**

dirigeant [diʀiʒɑ̃] *nm* leader

dirigeante [diʀiʒɑ̃t] *nf* leader

diriger [diʀiʒe] *vb* to manage ▷ *Il dirige une petite entreprise.* He manages a small company.; **se diriger vers** to head for ▷ *Il se dirigeait vers la* gare. He was heading for the station.

dis [dizε] *vb see* **dire**; **Dis-moi la vérité!** Tell me the truth!; **dis donc** hey ▷ *Elle a drôlement changé, dis donc!* Hey, she's really changed! ▷ *Dis donc, tu te souviens de cette chanson?* Hey, do you remember this song?

disaient, disais, disait *vb see* **dire**

discours [diskuʀ] *nm* speech

discret [diskʀε, -εt] (f **discrète**) *adj* discreet

discrimination [diskʀiminasjɔ̃] *nf* discrimination ▷ *la discrimination raciale* racial discrimination ▷ *la discrimination sexuelle* sex discrimination

discussion [diskysjɔ̃] *nf* discussion

discutable [diskytabl(ə)] *adj* debatable

discuter [diskyte] *vb* ❶ to talk ▷ *Nous avons discuté pendant des heures.* We talked for hours. ❷ to argue ▷ *C'est ce que j'ai décidé, alors ne discutez pas!* That's what I've decided, so don't argue!

disent, disiez, disions *vb see* **dire**

disons [dizɔ̃] *vb see* **dire** let's say ▷ *C'est à, disons, une demi-heure à pied.* It's half an hour's walk, say.

disparaître [dispaʀεtʀ(ə)] *vb* to disappear; **faire disparaître quelque chose (1)** to make something disappear ▷ *Il a fait disparaître le lapin dans son chapeau.* He made the rabbit disappear in his hat. **(2)** to get rid of something ▷ *Ils ont fait disparaître tous les documents compromettants.* They got rid of all the incriminating documents.

disparition [dispaʀisjɔ̃] *nf* disappearance; **une espèce en voie de disparition** an endangered species

disparu [dispaʀy] (f **disparue**) *adj*: **être porté disparu** to be reported missing

dispendieux [dispɑ̃djø, -øz] (f **dispendieuse**) *adj* expensive

dispense [dispɑ̃s] *adj*: **être dispensé de quelque chose** to be excused from something ▷ *Elle est dispensée de gymnastique.* She's excused from gym.

disperser [dispεʀse] *vb* to break up ▷ *La police a dispersé les manifestants.* The police broke up the demonstrators.; **se disperser** to break up ▷ *Une fois l'ambulance partie, la foule s'est dispersée.* Once the ambulance had left, the crowd broke up.

disponible [disponibl(ə)] *adj* ❶ available ▷ *Il y a encore des billets disponibles pour le concert.* Tickets are still available for the concert. ▷ *Ce livre est disponible en librairie.* This book is available in bookstores. ❷ free ▷ *Elle est toujours disponible le vendredi après-midi.* She's always free on Friday afternoons.

disposé [dispoze] (f **disposée**) *adj*: **être disposé à faire quelque chose** to be willing to do something ▷ *Il était disposé à m'aider.* He was willing to help me.

disposer [dispoze] *vb*: **disposer de quelque chose** to have access to something ▷ *Je dispose d'un ordinateur.* I have access to a computer.

disposition [dispozisjɔ̃] *nf*: **prendre ses dispositions** to make arrangements ▷ *Est-ce que vous avez pris vos dispositions pour partir en voyage?* Have you made arrangements for your trip?; **avoir quelque chose à sa disposition** to have something at one's disposal ▷ *J'ai un graveur de DC à ma disposition pour la semaine.* I have a CD burner at my disposal for the week.; **Je suis à votre disposition.** I am at your service.; **Je tiens ces livres à votre disposition.** The books are at your disposal.

dispute [dispyt] *nf* argument

se disputer [dispyte] *vb* to argue

disque [disk(ə)] *nm* record; **un disque compact** a compact disc; **le disque dur** hard disk

disquette [diskεt] *nf* floppy disk

disséminé [disemine] (f **disséminée**) *adj* scattered

disséquer [diseke] *vb* to dissect

dissertation [disεʀtasjɔ̃] *nf* essay

dissimuler [disimyle] *vb* to conceal

se dissiper [disipe] *vb* to lift ▷ *Le brouillard va se dissiper dans l'après-midi.* The fog will lift during the afternoon.

dissolvant [disolvɑ̃, -ɑ̃t] *nm* ❶ solvent ❷ nail polish remover

dissoudre [disudʀ(ə)] *vb* to dissolve; **se dissoudre** to dissolve

dissuader [disɥade] *vb*: **dissuader quelqu'un de faire quelque chose** to dissuade somebody from doing something ▷ *Elle m'a dissuadé d'aller voir ce film.* She dissuaded me from going to see the movie.

distance [distɑ̃s] *nf* distance

distingué [distε̃ge] (f **distinguée**) *adj* distinguished

distinguer [distε̃ge] *vb* to distinguish

distraction [distʀaksjɔ̃] *nf* entertainment ▷ *Il lit beaucoup : c'est sa seule distraction.* He reads a lot: it's his only form of entertainment.

distraire [distʀεʀ] *vb*: **Va voir un film, ça te distraira.** Go see a movie, it'll take your mind off things.

distrait [distʀε, -εt] (f **distraite**) *adj* absent-minded

distribuer [distʀibɥe] *vb* ❶ to give out ▷ *Distribue les livres, s'il te plaît.* Give out the books, please. ❷ (*cards*) to deal

distributrice [distʀibytʀis] *nf* vending machine

dit [di, dit] *vb see* **dire**

dit [di, dit] (f **dite**) *adj* known as ▷ *Toronto, dite Hogtown* Toronto, known as Hogtown

dites [dit] *vb see* **dire**; **Dites-moi ce que vous pensez.** Tell me what you think.; **dites donc** hey ▷ *Dites donc, vous, là-bas!* Hey, you there!

divan [divɑ̃] *nm* sofa; **le divan-lit** sofa bed

divers [divεʀ, -εʀs(ə)] (f **diverse**) *adj* diverse; **pour diverses raisons** for various reasons

se divertir [divεʀtiʀ] *vb* to enjoy oneself

divertissant [divεʀtisɑ̃, -ɑ̃t] (f **divertissante**) *adj* entertaining

divertissements [divεʀtismɑ̃] *nmpl* entertainment ▷ *Le centre touristique offre des sports de plein air, des soirées vidéo et d'autres divertissements.* The resort offers outdoor sports, video nights, and other entertainment.

divin [divɛ̃, -in] (f **divine**) adj divine

diviser [divize] vb to divide ▷ *Quatre divisé par deux égalent deux.* 4 divided by 2 equals 2.

divorcé [divɔʀse] nm divorcee

divorcée [divɔʀse] nf divorcee

divorcer [divɔʀse] vb to get divorced

dix [di, dis, diz] num ten ▷ *Elle a dix ans.* She's ten. ▷ *à dix heures* at ten o'clock; **le dix février** the tenth of February

dix-huit [dizɥit] num: ▷ *Il a dix-huit ans.* He's eighteen. ▷ *à dix-huit heures* at 6 p.m.

dixième [dizjɛm] adj tenth ▷ *au dixième étage* on the tenth floor

dix-neuf [diznœf] num: ▷ *Elle a dix-neuf ans.* She's nineteen. ▷ *à dix-neuf heures* at 7 p.m.

dix-sept [disɛt] num: ▷ *Il a dix-sept ans.* He's seventeen. ▷ *à dix-sept heures* at 5 p.m.

dizaine [dizɛn] nf about ten ▷ *une dizaine de jours* about ten days

do [do] nm ❶ C ▷ *en do majeur* in C major ❷ do ▷ *do, ré, mi…* do, re, mi…

docteur [dɔktœʀ] nm doctor

docteure [dɔktœʀ] nf doctor

document [dɔkymɑ̃] nm document

documentaire [dɔkymɑ̃tɛʀ] nm documentary

documentation [dɔkymɑ̃tasjɔ̃] nf documentation

documenter [dɔkymɑ̃te] vb: **se documenter sur quelque chose** to gather information on something

dodu [dɔdy] (f **dodue**) adj plump

doigt [dwa] nm finger; **les doigts de pied** the toes

dois, doit, doivent vb see **devoir**

domaine [dɔmɛn] nm ❶ estate ▷ *Il possède un immense domaine en Colombie-Britannique.* He owns a huge estate in British Columbia. ❷ field ▷ *La chimie n'est pas son domaine.* Chemistry's not her field.

domestique [dɔmɛstik] adj domestic; **les animaux domestiques** pets

domicile [dɔmisil] nm place of residence; **à domicile** at home ▷ *Il travaille à domicile.* He works at home.

dominer [dɔmine] vb to dominate; **se dominer** to control oneself

dominos [dɔmino] nmpl dominoes ▷ *jouer aux dominos* to play dominoes

dommage [dɔmaʒ] nm ❶ damage ▷ *La tempête a causé d'importants dommages.* The storm has caused a lot of damage.; **C'est dommage.** Too bad. ▷ *C'est dommage que tu ne puisses pas venir.* Too bad you can't come.

dompter [dɔ̃te] vb to tame

dompteur [dɔ̃tœʀ] nm animal tamer

dompteuse [dɔ̃tøz] nf animal tamer

don [dɔ̃] nm ❶ donation ▷ *avoir un don pour quelque chose* to have a gift for something; **Elle a le don de mettre les gens à l'aise.** She's got the knack of putting people at ease.

donc [dɔ̃k] conj so

donjon [dɔ̃ʒɔ̃] nm (of castle) keep

données [dɔne] nfpl data

donner [dɔne] vb ❶ to give; **donner quelque chose à quelqu'un** to give somebody

something ▷ *Elle m'a donné son adresse.* She gave me her address.; **Ça m'a donné faim.** That made me feel hungry. ❷ to give away ▷ *« Tu as toujours ta veste en daim? » « Non, je l'ai donnée. »* "Do you still have your suede jacket?" "No, I gave it away."; **donner sur quelque chose** to overlook something ▷ *une fenêtre qui donne sur la mer* a window overlooking the sea

dont [dɔ̃] pron ❶ of which ▷ *deux livres, dont l'un est en anglais* two books, one of which is in English ▷ *le prix dont il est si fier* the prize he's so proud of ❷ of whom ▷ *dix blessés, dont deux grièvement* ten people injured, two of them seriously ▷ *la fille dont je t'ai parlé* the girl I told you about

doré [dɔʀe] (f **dorée**) adj golden ▷ *une étoile dorée* a golden star; **le pain doré** French toast ▷ nm (fish) walleye

dorénavant [dɔʀenavɑ̃] adv from now on ▷ *Dorénavant, tu feras attention.* From now on, you'll be careful.

dorloter [dɔʀlɔte] vb to pamper

dormir [dɔʀmiʀ] vb ❶ to sleep ▷ *Tu as bien dormi?* Did you sleep well? ❷ to be asleep ▷ *Ne faites pas de bruit, il dort.* Don't make any noise, he's asleep.

dortoir [dɔʀtwaʀ] nm dormitory

dos [do] nm back ▷ *dos à dos* back to back; **faire quelque chose dans le dos de quelqu'un** to do something behind somebody's back ▷ *Elle me critique dans mon dos.* She criticizes me behind my back.; **de dos** from behind; **nager le dos crawlé** to swim the backstroke; **« voir au dos »** "see other side"

dose [doz] nf dose ▷ *Ne pas dépasser la dose prescrite.* Do not exceed the stated dose.

dossier [dosje] nm ❶ file ▷ *une pile de dossiers* a stack of files ❷ record ▷ *un bon dossier scolaire* a good academic record ❸ (computer) folder ❹ (in magazine) feature ❺ (of chair) back

douane [dwan] nf customs

douanier [dwanje] nm customs officer

douanière [dwanjɛʀ] nf customs officer

double [dubl(ə)] adj double; **à double interligne** double-spaced; **le double échec** cross-checking ▷ *faire double échec à un adversaire* to cross-check an opponent ▷ nm: **le double** twice as much ▷ *Il gagne le double.* He earns twice as much. ▷ *le double du prix normal* twice the normal price; **en double** in duplicate ▷ *Garde cette photo, je l'ai en double.* Keep this photo, I've got a copy of it.; **le double messieurs** (tennis) the men's doubles

double-cliquer [dubl(ə)klike] vb to double-click ▷ *double-cliquer sur une icône* to double-click on an icon

doubler [duble] vb ❶ to double ▷ *Le prix a doublé en dix ans.* The price has doubled in 10 years. ❷ (in car) to pass ▷ *Il est dangereux de doubler sur cette route.* It's dangerous to pass on this road.; **un film doublé** a dubbed film

douce [dus] adj see **doux**

doucement [dusmɑ̃] adv ❶ gently ▷ *Elle a frappé doucement à la porte.* She knocked gently at the door. ❷ slowly ▷ *Roulez doucement!* Drive slowly! ▷ *Je ne comprends pas; parle plus* *doucement.* I don't understand; speak more slowly.

douceur [dusœʀ] *nf* ❶ softness ▷ *Cette crème maintient la douceur de votre peau.* This cream keeps your skin soft. ❷ gentleness ▷ *parler avec douceur* to speak gently; **L'avion a atterri en douceur.** The plane made a smooth landing.

douche [duʃ] *nf* shower; **les douches** the shower room; **prendre une douche** to have a shower

se doucher [duʃe] *vb* to take a shower

doué [dwe] (*f* **douée**) *adj* talented; **être doué en quelque chose** to be good at something ▷ *Elle est douée en maths.* She's good at math.

douillet [dujɛ, -ɛt] (*f* **douillette**) *adj* ❶ cozy ▷ *un chandail douillet* a cozy sweater ❷ soft ▷ *Je ne supporte pas la douleur; je suis très douillette.* I can't stand pain; I'm a real softie.

douillette [dujɛt] *nf* comforter

douleur [dulœʀ] *nf* pain

douloureux [duluʀø, -øz] (*f* **douloureuse**) *adj* painful

doute [dut] *nm* doubt; **sans doute** probably

douter [dute] *vb* to doubt; **douter de quelque chose** to doubt something ▷ *Je doute de sa sincérité.* I have my doubts about his sincerity.; **se douter de quelque chose** to suspect something ▷ *Je ne me doutais de rien.* I didn't suspect anything.; **Je m'en doutais.** I thought as much.

douteux [dutø, -øz] (*f* **douteuse**) *adj* ❶ dubious ▷ *une plaisanterie d'un goût douteux* a joke in dubious taste ❷ suspicious-looking ▷ *un individu douteux* a suspicious-looking person

doux [du, dus] (*f* **douce**, *mpl* **doux**) *adj* ❶ soft ▷ *un tissu doux* soft fabric ▷ **les drogues douces** soft drugs ❷ sweet ▷ *du cidre doux* sweet cider ❸ mild ▷ *Il fait doux aujourd'hui.* It's mild out today. ❹ gentle ▷ *C'est quelqu'un de très doux.* He's a very gentle person.; **en douce** on the quiet ▷ *Elle m'a donné cinq dollars en douce.* She slipped me 5 dollars on the quiet.

douzaine [duzɛn] *nf* dozen ▷ *une douzaine d'œufs* a dozen eggs; **une douzaine de personnes** about twelve people

douze [duz] *num* twelve ▷ *Il a douze ans.* He's twelve.; **le douze février** the twelfth of February

douzième [duzjɛm] *adj* twelfth ▷ *au douzième étage* on the twelfth floor

dramatique [dʀamatik] *adj* tragic ▷ *une situation dramatique* a tragic situation; **l'art dramatique** drama

drame [dʀam] *nm* (*incident*) drama; **Ça n'est pas un drame si tu ne viens pas.** It's not the end of the world if you don't come.

drap [dʀa] *nm* (*for bed*) sheet

drapeau [dʀapo] (*pl* **drapeaux**) *nm* flag ▷ *le drapeau canadien* the Canadian flag

dressé [dʀese] (*f* **dressée**) *adj* trained ▷ *un chien bien dressé* a well-trained dog

dresser [dʀese] *vb* ❶ to draw up ▷ *dresser une liste* to draw up a list ❷ to train ▷ *dresser un chien* to train a dog; **dresser l'oreille** to perk up

one's ears ▷ *Quand elle a dit ça, il a dressé l'oreille.* When she said that, he perked up his ears.

drogue [dʀɔg] *nf* drug ▷ *le problème de la drogue* the drug problem ▷ *la lutte contre la drogue* the war against drugs; **les drogues douces** soft drugs; **les drogues dures** hard drugs

drogué [dʀɔge] *nm* drug addict

droguée [dʀɔge] *nf* drug addict

droguer [dʀɔge] *vb*: **droguer quelqu'un** to drug somebody; **se droguer** to take drugs

droit [dʀwa, dʀwat] (*f* **droite**) *adj*, *adv* ❶ right ▷ *le bras droit* the right arm ▷ *le côté droit* the right-hand side ❷ straight ▷ *une ligne droite* a straight line ▷ *Tiens-toi droite!* Stand up straight!; **tout droit** straight ahead

▶ *nm* ❶ right ▷ *les droits de la personne* human rights; **avoir le droit de faire quelque chose** to be allowed to do something ▷ *On n'a pas le droit de fumer à l'école.* We're not allowed to smoke at school. ❷ (*profession*) law ▷ *faire son droit* to study law ▷ *un étudiant en droit* a law student ▷ *pratiquer le droit* to practise law

droite [dʀwat] *nf* right ▷ *sur votre droite* on your right; **à droite (1)** on the right ▷ *la troisième rue à droite* the third street on the right **(2)** to the right ▷ *à droite de la fenêtre* to the right of the window ▷ *Tournez à droite.* Turn right.; **la voie de droite** the right-hand lane; **la droite** (*in politics*) the right ▷ *Il est très à droite.* He's very right-wing.; **une droite** (*math*) a straight line

droitier [dʀwatje, -jɛʀ] (*f* **droitière**) *adj* right-handed ▷ *Elle est droitière.* She's right-handed.

drôle [dʀol] *adj* funny ▷ *Ça n'est pas drôle.* It's not funny.; **un drôle de temps** funny weather

du [dy] *art* ❶ some ▷ *Tu veux du fromage?* Would you like some cheese? ❷ any ▷ *Tu as du chocolat?* Do you have any chocolate? ▷ *la porte du garage* the door of the garage ▷ *le bureau du directeur* the principal's office

dû [dy] *vb* see **devoir**; **Nous avons dû nous arrêter.** We had to stop.

▶ *adj* (*f* **due**, *mpl* **dus**) dû **à** due to ▷ *un retard dû au mauvais temps* a delay due to bad weather

dualité [dɥalite] *nf* duality ▷ *la dualité linguistique du Canada* Canada's linguistic duality

dupe [dyp] *adj*: **Elle me ment mais je ne suis pas dupe.** She lies to me but I'm not taken in.

duplex [dypleks] (*pl* **les duplex**) *nm* duplex

dur [dyʀ] (*f* **dure**) *adj*, *adv* hard ▷ *travailler dur* to work hard ▷ *être dur avec quelqu'un* to be hard on somebody

durant [dyʀã] *prep* ❶ during ▷ *durant la nuit* during the night ❷ for ▷ *durant des années* for years ▷ *des mois durant* for months

durée [dyʀe] *nf* (*time*) length ▷ *Quelle est la durée des études d'ingénieur?* How long does it take to train as an engineer?; **pour une durée de deux semaines** for a period of two weeks; **de courte durée** short ▷ *un séjour de courte durée* a short stay; **de longue durée** long ▷ *une absence de longue durée* a long absence

durement [dyʀmã] *adv* harshly

durer [dyʀe] *vb* to last

dureté [dyʀte] *nf* harshness ▷ *traiter quelqu'un*

avec dureté to treat somebody harshly
DVD [devede] *nm* DVD
dynamique [dinamik] *adj* dynamic
dyslexique [disleksik] *adj* dyslexic

e

eau [o] (*pl* **eaux**) *nf* water; **l'eau minérale** mineral water; **l'eau plate** still water; **tomber à l'eau** to fall through ▷ *Nos projets sont tombés à l'eau.* Our plans have fallen through.
ébahi [ebai] (*f* **ébahie**) *adj* amazed
éblouir [ebluiʀ] *vb* to dazzle
ébouillanter [ebujɑ̃te] *vb* to scald
écaille [ekaj] *nf* (*of fish*) scale
s' écailler [ekaje] *vb* (*paint*) to peel
écart [ekaʀ] *nm* gap; **à l'écart de** away from ▷ *Ils se sont assis à l'écart des autres.* They sat down away from the others.
écarté [ekaʀte] (*f* **écartée**) *adj* remote; **les bras écartés** arms outstretched; **les jambes écartées** legs apart
écarter [ekaʀte] *vb* to spread apart; **écarter les bras** to open one's arms wide; **s'écarter** to move ▷ *Ils se sont écartés pour la laisser passer.* They moved to let her pass.
échafaudage [eʃafodaʒ] *nm* scaffolding
échalote [eʃalɔt] *nf* shallot
échange [eʃɑ̃ʒ] *nm* exchange ▷ *en échange de* in exchange for; **un échange étudiant** a student exchange
échanger [eʃɑ̃ʒe] *vb* to trade ▷ *Je t'échange cette carte de hockey contre celle-là.* I'll trade you this hockey card for that one.
échantillon [eʃɑ̃tijɔ̃] *nm* sample
échapper [eʃape] *vb*: **échapper à** to escape from ▷ *Le prisonnier a réussi à échapper à la police.* The prisoner managed to escape from the police.; **s'échapper** to escape ▷ *Il s'est échappé de prison.* He escaped from prison.; **l'échapper belle** to have a narrow escape ▷ *Nous l'avons échappé belle.* We had a narrow escape.
écharde [eʃaʀd(ə)] *nf* splinter
s' échauffer [eʃofe] *vb* (*before exercise*) to warm up ▷ *Les joueurs se sont échauffés avant le match.* The players warmed up before the game.
échec [eʃɛk] *nm* failure; **subir un échec** to suffer a setback; **voué à l'échec** bound to fail
échecs [eʃɛk] *nmpl* chess ▷ *jouer aux échecs* to play chess
échelle [eʃɛl] *nf* ❶ ladder ❷ (*of map*) scale
écho [eko] *nm* echo
échouer [eʃwe] *vb*: **échouer à un examen** to

fail an exam
éclabousser [eklabuse] *vb* to splash
éclair [eklɛʀ] *nm* ❶ flash of lightning; **un éclair au chocolat** a chocolate éclair; **à la vitesse de l'éclair** with lightning speed; **un éclair de génie** a brainwave
éclairage [eklɛʀaʒ] *nm* lighting
éclaircie [eklɛʀsi] *nf* sunny period
éclairer [eklɛʀe] *vb*: **Cette lampe éclaire bien.** This lamp gives good light.
éclat [ekla] *nm* ❶ (*of glass*) fragment ▷ *Le vase a volé en éclats.* The vase smashed into pieces. ❷ (*of sun, colour*) brightness; **des éclats de rire** roars of laughter
éclatant [eklatɑ̃, -ɑ̃t] (*f* **éclatante**) *adj* brilliant ▷ *un jaune éclatant* a brilliant yellow ▷ *une lumière éclatante* a brilliant light
éclater [eklate] *vb* ❶ (*tire, balloon*) to burst; **éclater de rire** to burst out laughing; **éclater en sanglots** to burst into tears ❷ to break out ▷ *La Seconde Guerre mondiale a éclaté en 1939.* The Second World War broke out in 1939.
éclipse [eklips(ə)] *nf* eclipse
écœurant [ekœʀɑ̃] *adj* sickening
écœurer [ekœʀe] *vb*: **Tous ces mensonges m'écœurent.** All these lies make me sick.
école [ekɔl] *nf* school ▷ *aller à l'école* to go to school ▷ *une école privée* a private school ▷ *une école publique* a public school
écolier [ekɔlje] *nm* schoolboy
écolière [ekɔljɛʀ] *nf* schoolgirl
écologie [ekɔlɔʒi] *nf* ecology
écologique [ekɔlɔʒik] *adj* ecological ▷ *un détergent écologique* an environmentally-friendly detergent
éconergétique [ekɔnɛʀʒetik] *adj* energy-efficient
économie [ekɔnɔmi] *nf* ❶ economy ▷ *l'économie du Canada* the Canadian economy ❷ economics ▷ *un cours d'économie* an economics class
économies [ekɔnɔmi] *nfpl* savings; **faire des économies** to save up ▷ *Je fais des économies pour partir en vacances.* I'm saving up for my holidays.
économique [ekɔnɔmik] *adj* ❶ economic ▷ *une crise économique* an economic crisis ❷ economical ▷ *Il est plus économique d'acheter une grande boîte de détergent.* It's more economical to buy a big box of detergent. ▷ *Cette petite voiture est économique.* This little car is cheap to run.
économiser [ekɔnɔmize] *vb* to save
économiseur d'écran [ekɔnɔmizœʀ-] *nm* screen saver
écorce [ekɔʀs(ə)] *nf* ❶ (*of tree*) bark; **l'écorce de bouleau** birch bark ❷ (*of orange, lemon*) peel
s' écorcher [ekɔʀʃe] *vb*: **Je me suis écorché le genou.** I've grazed my knee.
écosystème [ekɔsistɛm] *nm* ecosystem
s' écouler [ekule] *vb* ❶ (*water*) to flow out ❷ to pass ▷ *Le temps s'écoule trop vite.* Time passes too quickly.
écouter [ekute] *vb* to listen to ▷ *J'aime écouter de la musique.* I like listening to music.; **Écoute-moi!** Listen!

écouteur [ekutœʀ] *nm (of phone)* earpiece

écran [ekʀã] *nm* screen; **le petit écran** television; **l'écran solaire** sunblock

écraser [ekʀɑze] *vb* ❶ to crush ▷ *Écrasez une gousse d'ail.* Crush a clove of garlic. ❷ to run over ▷ *Regarde bien avant de traverser, sinon tu vas te faire écraser.* Look carefully before you cross or you'll get run over.; **s'écraser** to crash ▷ *L'avion s'est écrasé dans le désert.* The plane crashed in the desert.

écrémé [ekʀeme] *(f* **écrémée***) adj*: **le lait écrémé** skim milk

écrevisse [ekʀəvis] *nf* crayfish

écrire [ekʀiʀ] *vb* to write ▷ *Nous nous écrivons régulièrement.* We write to each other regularly.; **Ça s'écrit comment?** How do you spell that?

écrit [ekʀi] *nm* piece of writing ▷ *les écrits de Gabrielle Roy* the writings of Gabrielle Roy; **par écrit** in writing

écriture [ekʀityʀ] *nf* writing ▷ *J'ai du mal à lire son écriture.* I can't read her writing.

écrivain [ekʀivɛ̃] *nm* writer ▷ *Il est écrivain.* He's a writer.

écrivaine [ekʀivɛn] *nf* writer ▷ *Elle est écrivaine.* She's a writer.

écrou [ekʀu] *nm (metal)* nut

s'écrouler [ekʀule] *vb* to collapse

écru [ekʀy] *(f* **écrue***) adj* off-white

écureuil [ekyʀœj] *nm* squirrel

écurie [ekyʀi] *nf* stable

éditer [edite] *vb* ❶ to publish ▷ *On vient d'éditer un nouveau dictionnaire.* A new dictionary has just been published. ❷ *(computer file)* to edit

éditeur [editœʀ] *nm* publisher

édition [edisjɔ̃] *nf* ❶ edition ▷ *une édition de poche* a paperback edition ❷ publishing ▷ *Elle travaille dans l'édition.* She works in publishing.

éducateur [edykatœʀ] *nm (of people with special needs)* teacher

éducatif [edykatif, -iv] *(f* **éducative***) adj* educational ▷ *un jeu éducatif* an educational game

éducation [edykasjɔ̃] *nf* ❶ education; **le cours d'éducation civique** Civics course ▷ *l'éducation physique* physical education ▷ *Il n'a pas beaucoup d'éducation.* He's not very well educated. ❷ upbringing ▷ *Elle a reçu une éducation très stricte.* She had a very strict upbringing.

éducatrice [edykatʀis] *nf (of people with special needs)* teacher

éduquer [edyke] *vb* to educate

effacer [efase] *vb* to erase

effarant [efaʀã, -ãt] *(f* **effarante***) adj* amazing ▷ *Il a mangé une quantité effarante de pain.* He ate an amazing amount of bread.

effectivement [efɛktivmã] *adv* indeed ▷ *Il est effectivement plus rapide de passer par là.* It is indeed quicker to go this way. ▷ *Oui, effectivement.* Yes, indeed.

effectuer [efɛktɥe] *vb* ❶ to make ▷ *Ils ont effectué de nombreux changements.* They have made a lot of changes. ❷ to do ▷ *On vient d'effectuer des travaux dans le bâtiment.* They have

just done some work in the building.

effet [efɛ] *nm* effect; **faire de l'effet** to take effect ▷ *Ce médicament fait rapidement de l'effet.* This medicine takes effect quickly.; **Ça m'a fait un drôle d'effet de le revoir.** It gave me a strange feeling to see him again.; **en effet** yes indeed ▷ *« Je ne me sens pas très bien. » « En effet, tu as l'air pâle. »* "I don't feel very well." "Yes, you do look pale."

efficace [efikas] *adj* ❶ efficient ▷ *C'est une travailleuse efficace.* She's an efficient worker. ❷ effective ▷ *un médicament efficace* an effective medicine

s'effondrer [efɔ̃dʀe] *vb* to collapse

s'efforcer [efɔʀse] *vsb*: **s'efforcer de faire quelque chose** to try hard to do something ▷ *Il s'efforce d'être aimable avec la clientèle.* He tries hard to be polite to the customers.

effort [efɔʀ] *nm* effort ▷ *faire un effort* to make an effort

effrayant [efʀejã, -ãt] *(f* **effrayante***) adj* frightening

effrayer [efʀeje] *vb* to frighten

effronté [efʀɔ̃te] *(f* **effrontée***) adj* mouthy ▷ *Cet enfant est vraiment effronté.* That kid is really mouthy.

effroyable [efʀwajabl(ə)] *adj* horrifying

égal [egal, -o] *(f* **égale**, *mpl* **égaux***) adj* equal ▷ *une quantité égale de farine et de sucre* equal quantities of flour and sugar; **Ça m'est égal.** (1) I have no preference. ▷ *« Tu préfères du riz ou des pâtes? » « Ça m'est égal. »* "Would you rather have rice or pasta?" "Either is fine with me." (2) I don't care. ▷ *Fais ce que tu veux, ça m'est égal.* Do what you like, I don't care.

également [egalmã] *adv* also

égaler [egale] *vb* to equal

égalité [egalite] *nf* equality; **être à égalité** to be tied ▷ *Maintenant les deux joueurs sont à égalité.* The two players are now tied.

égard [egaʀ] *nm*: **à cet égard** in this respect

égarer [egaʀe] *vb* to mislay ▷ *J'ai égaré mes clés.* I've mislaid my keys.; **s'égarer** to get lost ▷ *Ils se sont égarés dans la forêt.* They got lost in the forest.

église [egliz] *nf* church ▷ *aller à l'église* to go to church

égoïsme [egɔism(ə)] *nm* selfishness

égoïste [egɔist(ə)] *adj* selfish

égout [egu] *nm* sewer

égratignure [egʀatiɲyʀ] *nf* scratch

eh [e] *excl* hey!; **eh bien** well

élan [elã] *nm*: **prendre de l'élan** to gather speed

s'élancer [elɑ̃se] *vb* to rush ▷ *Il s'est élancé vers moi.* He rushed towards me.

élargir [elaʀʒiʀ] *vb* ❶ to widen ❷ to expand; **élargir ses horizons** to broaden one's horizons

élastique [elastik] *nm* rubber band

électeur [elɛktœʀ] *nm* voter

élection [elɛksjɔ̃] *nf* election ▷ *une élection provinciale* a provincial election

électrice [elɛktʀis] *nf (woman)* voter

électricien [elɛktʀisjɛ̃] *nm* electrician

électricienne [elɛktʀisjɛn] *nf* electrician

électricité [elɛktʀisite] *nf* ❶ electricity

❷ hydro ▷ *une facture d'électricité* a hydro bill;
allumer l'électricité to turn on the light;
éteindre l'électricité to turn off the light

électrique [elɛktʀik] *adj* electric ▷ *le courant électrique* electric current

électronique [elɛktʀɔnik] *nf* electronics

élégant [elegɑ̃, -ɑ̃t] (*f* **élégante**) *adj* elegant

élémentaire [elemɑ̃tɛʀ] *adj* elementary

éléphant [elefɑ̃] *nm* elephant

élevage [elvaʒ] *nm* cattle farming ▷ *faire de l'élevage* to raise cattle; **un élevage de porcs** a pig farm; **un élevage de poulets** a chicken farm; **le saumon d'élevage** farmed salmon

élevé [elve] (*f* **élevée**) *adj* high ▷ *Le prix est trop élevé.* The price is too high.; **être bien élevé** to be well brought up; **être mal élevé** to be not very well brought up

élève [elɛv] *nmf* (*elementary school*) student

élever [elve] *vb* ❶ to bring up ▷ *Il a été élevé par sa grand-mère.* He was brought up by his grandmother. ❷ to breed ▷ *Son oncle élève des chevaux.* Her uncle breeds horses.; **élever la voix** to raise one's voice; **s'élever à** to come to ▷ *À combien s'élèvent les dégâts?* How much does the damage come to?

éleveur [elvœʀ] *nm* ❶ (*dogs, horses*) breeder ❷ (*cattle, pigs, chickens*) farmer

éliminatoire [eliminatwaʀ] *adj*: **une note éliminatoire** a failing mark; **une épreuve éliminatoire** (*sport*) a qualifying round

éliminatoires [eliminatwaʀ] *nfpl* playoffs ▷ *regarder les éliminatoires de hockey à la télévision* to watch the hockey playoffs on TV

éliminer [elimine] *vb* to eliminate

élire [eliʀ] *vb* to elect

elle [ɛl] *pron* ❶ she ▷ *Elle est institutrice.* She is a primary school teacher. ❷ her ▷ *Vous pouvez avoir confiance en elle.* You can trust her. ❸ it ▷ *Prends cette chaise : elle est plus confortable.* Take this chair: it's more comfortable. ▷ *Elle, elle est toujours en retard!* Oh, SHE's always late!; **elle-même** herself ▷ *Elle l'a choisi elle-même.* She chose it herself.

elles [ɛl] *pron* they ▷ *« Où sont les filles? » « Elles sont allées au cinéma. »* "Where are the girls?" "They've gone to the movies."; **elles-mêmes** themselves

élogieux [elɔʒjø, -øz] (*f* **élogieuse**) *adj* complimentary ▷ *Ton professeur a été très élogieux à propos de ton travail.* Your teacher was very complimentary about your work.

éloigné [elwaɲe] (*f* **éloignée**) *adj* distant

s'éloigner [elwaɲe] *vb* to go far away ▷ *Ne vous éloignez pas : le dîner est bientôt prêt!* Don't go far away: dinner will soon be ready!; **Vous vous éloignez du sujet.** You are getting off the point.

emballage [ɑ̃balaʒ] *nm*: **le papier d'emballage** wrapping paper

emballer [ɑ̃bale] *vb* to wrap; **s'emballer** (*informal*) to get excited ▷ *Elle s'est emballée pour ce projet.* She got really excited about this plan.

embarquement [ɑ̃baʀkəmɑ̃] *nm* boarding ▷ *« embarquement immédiat »* "now boarding" ▷ *L'embarquement des passagers n'a pas encore été annoncé.* Passenger boarding has not been

announced yet.

embarras [ɑ̃baʀa] *nm* embarrassment ▷ *Votre question me met dans l'embarras.* Your question is an awkward one.; **Vous n'avez que l'embarras du choix.** The only problem is choosing.

embarrassant [ɑ̃baʀasɑ̃, -ɑ̃t] (*f* **embarrassante**) *adj* embarrassing

embarrasser [ɑ̃baʀase] *vb* to embarrass ▷ *Cela m'embarrasse de vous demander encore un service.* I'm embarrassed to ask another favour from you.

embaucher [ɑ̃boʃe] *vb* to hire ▷ *L'entreprise vient d'embaucher cinquante ouvriers.* The firm has just hired fifty workers.

embêtant [ɑ̃betɑ̃, -ɑ̃t] (*f* **embêtante**) *adj* annoying

embêtement [ɑ̃betmɑ̃] *nm* trouble ▷ *J'ai eu un embêtement : la voiture est tombée en panne.* I had some trouble: the car broke down.

embêter [ɑ̃bete] *vb* to bother ▷ *Tu m'embêtes avec tes questions.* You're bothering me with your questions.

embouteillage [ɑ̃butejaʒ] *nm* traffic jam

embrasser [ɑ̃bʀase] *vb* to kiss ▷ *Elle m'a embrassé.* She kissed me. ▷ *Ils se sont embrassés.* They kissed.

s'embrouiller [ɑ̃bʀuje] *vb* to get confused ▷ *Il s'embrouille dans ses explications.* He gets confused when he explains things.

émerveiller [emɛʀveje] *vb* to amaze

émeute [emøt] *nf* riot

émigrer [emigʀe] *vb* to emigrate

émission [emisjɔ̃] *nf* ❶ (*radio, TV*) show ▷ *une émission de télévision* a TV show ❷ emission ▷ *les émissions de gaz toxique* toxic gas emissions

emmêler [ɑ̃mele] *vb* ❶ to tangle up ▷ *Mes cheveux sont tout emmêlés.* My hair is all tangled up. ❷ to confuse ▷ *Elle emmêle tout.* She confuses everything.; **s'emmêler** to get tangled up ▷ *Sa ligne de pêche s'est emmêlée dans la mienne.* His fishing line got tangled up with mine.

emménager [ɑ̃menaʒe] *vb* to move in ▷ *Nous venons d'emménager dans une nouvelle maison.* We've just moved into a new house.

emmener [ɑ̃mne] *vb* to take ▷ *Ils m'ont emmené au cinéma pour mon anniversaire.* They took me to the movies for my birthday.

émotif [emotif, -iv] (*f* **émotive**) *adj* emotional ▷ *Il est très émotif.* He's very emotional.

émotion [emosjɔ̃] *nf* emotion

émotionnel [emosjɔnɛl] (*f* **émotionnelle**) *adj* emotional ▷ *un choc émotionnel* an emotional shock

émouvoir [emuvwaʀ] *vb* to move ▷ *Ta lettre l'a beaucoup émue.* She was deeply moved by your letter.

s'emparer [ɑ̃paʀe] *vb*: **s'emparer de** to grab ▷ *Elle s'est emparée de ma valise.* She grabbed my suitcase.

empêchement [ɑ̃pɛʃmɑ̃] *nm*: **Nous avons eu un empêchement de dernière minute.** We were held up at the last minute.

empêcher [ɑ̃peʃe] *vb* to prevent ▷ *Le café le soir m'empêche de dormir.* Coffee at night keeps me awake.; **Il n'a pas pu s'empêcher de rire.** He couldn't help laughing.

empiler [ãpile] *vb* to pile up

empirer [ãpire] *vb* to worsen ▷ *La situation a encore empiré.* The situation got even worse.

emplacement [ãplasmã] *nm* site ▷ *Un panneau indique l'ancien emplacement du château.* A sign shows the former site of the castle.; **un emplacement de camping** a campsite

emploi [ãplwa] *nm* ❶ job ▷ *trouver un emploi* to find a job ❷ use ▷ *prêt à l'emploi* ready for use; **un emploi du temps** a timetable; **le mode d'emploi** directions for use

employé [ãplwaje] *nm* employee; **un employé de bureau** an office worker

employée [ãplwaje] *nf* employee; **une employée de banque** a bank clerk

employer [ãplwaje] *vb* ❶ to use ▷ *Quelle méthode employez-vous?* What method do you use? ❷ to employ ▷ *L'entreprise emploie dix ingénieurs.* The firm employs ten engineers.

employeur [ãplwajœr] *nm* employer

empoisonner [ãpwazɔne] *vb* to poison

emporter [ãpɔrte] *vb* to take ▷ *N'emportez que le strict nécessaire.* Take only the bare minimum.; **mets à emporter** takeout food; **s'emporter** to lose one's temper ▷ *Je m'emporte facilement.* I'm quick to lose my temper.

empreinte [ãprɛ̃t] *nf* : **une empreinte digitale** a fingerprint

s' **empresser** [ãprese] *vb*: **s'empresser de faire quelque chose** to be quick to do something ▷ *Ils se sont empressés de nous annoncer la nouvelle.* They were quick to tell us the news.

emprisonner [ãprizɔne] *vb* to imprison

emprunt [ãprœ̃] *nm* loan

emprunter [ãprœ̃te] *vb* to borrow; **emprunter quelque chose à quelqu'un** to borrow something from somebody ▷ *Je peux t'emprunter dix dollars?* Can I borrow ten dollars from you?

ému [emy] (*f* **émue**) *adj* touched ▷ *J'ai été très ému par sa gentillesse.* I was very touched by her kindness.

en [ã] *prep, pron* ❶ in ▷ *Il habite en Terre-Neuve.* He lives in Newfoundland. ▷ *La mariée est en blanc.* The bride is in white. ▷ *Je le verrai en mai.* I'll see him in May. ❷ to ▷ *Je vais en Saskatchewan cet été.* I'm going to Saskatchewan this summer. ❸ by ▷ *C'est plus rapide en voiture.* It's faster by car. ▷ *On peut apprendre beaucoup en lisant.* You can learn a lot by reading. ❹ made of ▷ *C'est en verre.* It's made of glass. ▷ *un collier en argent* a silver necklace ❺ while ▷ *Il s'est coupé le doigt en ouvrant une boîte de conserve.* He cut his finger while opening a tin.; **Elle est sortie en courant.** She ran out. ▷ *« Est-ce que tu as un dictionnaire? » « Oui, j'en ai un. »* "Have you got a dictionary?" "Yes, I've got one." ▷ *« Combien d'élèves y a-t-il dans ta classe? » « Il y en a trente. »* "How many pupils are there in your class?" "There are 30." ▷ *Si tu as un problème, tu peux m'en parler.* If you have a problem, you can talk to me about it. ▷ *Est-ce que tu peux me rendre ce*

livre? J'en ai besoin. Can you give me back that book? I need it. ▷ *Il a un beau jardin et il en est très fier.* He's got a beautiful garden and is very proud of it.; **J'en ai assez.** I've had enough.

encaisser [ãkese] *vb* (*chèque*) to cash

enceinte [ãsɛ̃t] *adj* pregnant ▷ *Elle est enceinte de six mois.* She's 6 months pregnant.

encercler [ãsɛrkle] *vb* to circle ▷ *Encerclez la bonne réponse.* Circle the right answer.

enchanté [ãʃãte] (*f* **enchantée**) *adj* delighted ▷ *Ma mère est enchantée de sa nouvelle voiture.* My mother's delighted with her new car.; **Enchanté!** Pleased to meet you!

encombrant [ãkɔ̃brã, -ãt] (*f* **encombrante**) *adj* bulky

encombrer [ãkɔ̃bre] *vb* to clutter

encore [ãkɔr] *adv* ❶ again ▷ *Il m'a encore demandé de l'argent.* He asked me for money again. ❷ more ▷ *Mange encore un peu.* Have some more to eat. ❸ still ▷ *Il est encore au travail.* He's still at work. ▷ *Il reste encore deux morceaux de gâteau.* There are two pieces of cake left. ❹ even ▷ *C'est encore mieux.* That's even better.; **encore une fois** once again; **pas encore** not yet ▷ *Je n'ai pas encore fini.* I'm not finished yet.

encourageant [ãkuraʒã, -ãt] (*f* **encourageante**) *adj* encouraging

encourager [ãkuraʒe] *vb* to encourage

encre [ãkr(ə)] *nf* ink

encyclopédie [ãsiklɔpedi] *nf* encyclopedia

endommager [ãdɔmaʒe] *vb* to damage

endormi [ãdɔrmi] (*f* **endormie**) *adj* asleep

endormir [ãdɔrmir] *vb* ❶ to put to sleep ▷ *Il a endormi le bébé en lui chantant une berceuse.* He put the baby to sleep by singing a lullaby. ▷ *Son long discours m'a endormi.* Her long speech put me to sleep. ❷ (*with anesthetic*) to put under ▷ *On l'a endormie pour son opération.* They put her under for the operation.; **s'endormir** to go to sleep

endroit [ãdrwa] *nm* place ▷ *C'est un endroit très tranquille.* It's a very quiet place.; **à l'endroit (1)** right side out ▷ *Remets ton T-shirt à l'endroit.* Put your T-shirt on again right side out. **(2)** the right way up ▷ *Ce tableau est de travers. Il faut le remettre à l'endroit.* This picture is sideways. It must be put the right way up.

endurant [ãdyrã, -ãt] (*f* **endurante**) *adj* (*person*) tough

endurcir [ãdyrsir] *vb* to toughen up ▷ *Ces exercices servent à vous endurcir.* These exercises are to toughen you up.; **s'endurcir** to become hardened

endurer [ãdyre] *vb* to endure

énergie [enɛrʒi] *nf* energy ▷ *Je n'ai pas beaucoup d'énergie ce matin.* I don't have much energy this morning. ❷ power ▷ *l'énergie nucléaire* nuclear power; **avec énergie** vigorously ▷ *Il a protesté avec énergie.* He protested vigorously.

énergique [enɛrʒik] *adj* energetic; **des mesures énergiques** strong measures

énerver [enɛrve] *vb*: **Il m'énerve!** He gets on my nerves!; **Ce bruit m'énerve.** This noise gets on my nerves.; **s'énerver** to get worked up;

Ne t'énerve pas! Take it easy!

enfance [ɑ̃fɑ̃s] nf childhood; **Je la connais depuis l'enfance.** I've known her since I was a child.

enfant [ɑ̃fɑ̃] nmf child

enfer [ɑ̃fɛʀ] nm hell

enfermer [ɑ̃fɛʀme] vb ❶ (in a place) to lock ▷ garder son sac à main enfermé dans son tiroir to keep one's purse locked in a drawer ❷ to shut in ▷ Ne restons pas enfermés par ce beau temps. Let's not stay inside in this lovely weather.; **Il s'est enfermé dans sa chambre.** He shut himself up in his bedroom.

enfiler [ɑ̃file] vb ❶ to put on ▷ J'ai rapidement enfilé un chandail avant de sortir. I quickly put on a sweater before going out. ❷ to thread ▷ J'ai du mal à enfiler cette aiguille. I am having a hard time threading this needle.

enfin [ɑ̃fɛ̃] adv finally ▷ J'ai enfin réussi à la joindre. I have finally managed to contact her.

enfler [ɑ̃fle] vb to swell

enfoncer [ɑ̃fɔ̃se] vb: **Elle marchait, les mains enfoncées dans les poches.** She was walking with her hands thrust into her pockets.; **s'enfoncer** to sink ▷ Les roues de la voiture s'enfonçaient dans la boue. The wheels of the car were sinking into the mud.

s'enfuir [ɑ̃fɥiʀ] vb to run off

engagement [ɑ̃gaʒmɑ̃] nm commitment

engager [ɑ̃gaʒe] vb to hire

s'engager [ɑ̃gaʒe] vb to commit oneself ▷ Le premier ministre s'est engagé à combattre le chômage. The Prime Minister has committed himself to fighting unemployment.; **Elle a décidé de ne pas s'engager dans l'armée.** She decided not to join the army.

engin [ɑ̃ʒɛ̃] nm device

engouement [ɑ̃gumɑ̃] nm fad

engueuler [ɑ̃gœle] vb (informal); **engueuler quelqu'un** to tell somebody off ▷ Tu vas te faire engueuler! You're going to get told off!

énigme [enigm(ə)] nf riddle

s'enivrer [ɑ̃nivre] vb to get drunk

enjambée [ɑ̃ʒɑ̃be] nf stride ▷ monter l'escalier en trois enjambées to go up the stairs in three strides

enjamber [ɑ̃ʒɑ̃be] vb ❶ (by swinging one leg over at a time) to climb over ▷ enjamber une barrière to climb over a fence ❷ to step over ▷ enjamber un fossé to step over a ditch ❸ to straddle

enlèvement [ɑ̃lɛvmɑ̃] nm kidnapping

enlever [ɑ̃lve] vb ❶ to take off ▷ Enlève donc ton manteau! Take off your coat! ❷ to kidnap ▷ Un groupe terroriste a enlevé la femme du ministre. A terrorist group has kidnapped the minister's wife.

enneigé [ɑ̃neʒe] (f **enneigée**) adj snow-covered ▷ Les routes sont encore enneigées. The roads are still covered with snow.

ennemi [ɛnmi] nm enemy

ennemie [ɛnmi] nf enemy

ennui [ɑ̃nɥi] nm ❶ boredom ▷ C'est à mourir d'ennui. It's enough to bore you to death. ❷ problem ▷ avoir des ennuis to have problems

ennuyer [ɑ̃nɥije] vb ❶ to inconvenience

▷ J'espère que cela ne vous ennuie pas trop. I hope it doesn't inconvenience you too much. ❷ to bother ▷ Arrête de m'ennuyer avec tes questions. Stop bothering me with your questions.; **s'ennuyer** to be bored

ennuyeux [ɑ̃nɥijø, -øz] (f **ennuyeuse**) adj ❶ boring ❷ inconvenient ▷ Tu ne peux pas venir plus tôt? C'est bien ennuyeux. You can't come any earlier? That's rather inconvenient.

énorme [enɔʀm(ə)] adj huge

énormément [enɔʀmemɑ̃] adv: **Il a énormément maigri.** He's gotten terribly thin.; **Il y a énormément de neige.** There's an enormous amount of snow.

enquête [ɑ̃kɛt] nf ❶ investigation ▷ La police a ouvert une enquête. The police have launched an investigation. ❷ survey ▷ une enquête parmi les étudiants a montré que... a survey of students has shown that...

enquêter [ɑ̃kɛte] vb to investigate ▷ La police enquête actuellement sur le crime. The police are currently investigating the crime.

enrageant [ɑ̃ʀaʒɑ̃, -ɑ̃t] (f **enrageante**) adj infuriating

enrager [ɑ̃ʀaʒe] vb to be furious ▷ J'enrage de n'avoir pas eu le droit de vous accompagner. I'm furious that I wasn't allowed to go with you.

enregistrement [ɑ̃ʀʒistʀəmɑ̃] nm recording; **l'enregistrement des bagages** baggage check-in

enregistrer [ɑ̃ʀʒistʀe] vb ❶ to record ▷ Ils viennent d'enregistrer un nouvel album. They've just recorded a new album. ▷ J'ai enregistré l'émission sur vidéocassette. I taped the TV show. ❷ (baggage) to check ▷ Vous pouvez enregistrer plusieurs valises. You can check more than one suitcase.

s'enrhumer [ɑ̃ʀyme] vb to catch a cold ▷ Elle s'est enrhumée. She caught a cold.

s'enrichir [ɑ̃ʀiʃiʀ] vb to get rich

enrouler [ɑ̃ʀule] vb to wind ▷ Enroulez le fil autour de la bobine. Wind the thread around the bobbin.

enseignant [ɑ̃seɲɑ̃] nm teacher

enseignante [ɑ̃seɲɑ̃t] nf teacher

enseignement [ɑ̃seɲmɑ̃] nm ❶ education ▷ les réformes de l'enseignement reforms in education ❷ teaching ▷ l'enseignement des langues étrangères the teaching of foreign languages

enseigner [ɑ̃seɲe] vb to teach ▷ Mon père enseigne les maths dans une école secondaire. My father teaches math in a secondary school.

ensemble [ɑ̃sɑ̃bl(ə)] adv together ▷ tous ensemble all together ▷ nm ❶ outfit ▷ Elle portait un ensemble vert. She was wearing a green outfit. ❷ set ▷ un ensemble de couteaux a set of knives; **l'ensemble de** the whole of ▷ L'ensemble du personnel est en grève. The whole staff is on strike.; **aller ensemble** to go together ▷ Le tapis et les meubles ne vont pas ensemble. The carpet and furniture don't go together.; **dans l'ensemble** on the whole

ensoleillé [ɑ̃sɔleje] (f **ensoleillée**) adj sunny

ensuite [ɑ̃sɥit] adv then ▷ Nous sommes allés

au cinéma et ensuite au restaurant. We went to a movie and then to a restaurant.

entamer [ãtame] *vb* to start ▷ *Qui a entamé le gâteau?* Who started on the cake? ▷ *entamer des négociations* to begin negotiations

entasser [ãtase] *vb* to cram ▷ *J'ai tout entassé dans un tiroir.* I crammed everything into a drawer.; **Ils se sont tous entassés dans ma voiture.** They all crammed into my car.

entendre [ãtãdʀ(ə)] *vb* ❶ to hear ▷ *Je ne t'entends pas.* I can't hear you.; **J'ai entendu dire qu'il est dangereux de nager ici.** I've heard that it's dangerous to swim here. ❷ to mean ▷ *Qu'est-ce que tu entends par là?* What do you mean by that?; **s'entendre** to get along ▷ *Il s'entend bien avec sa sœur.* He gets along well with his sister.

entendu [ãtãdy] (*f* **entendue**) *adj*: **C'est entendu!** Agreed! ▷ *Je passerai te prendre à sept heures, c'est entendu.* That's agreed then, I'll pick you up at 7 o'clock.; **bien entendu** of course ▷ *Il est bien entendu que je n'en parlerai à personne.* I won't tell anybody about it, of course.

enterrement [ãtɛʀmã] *nm* (with burial) funeral; **avoir une mine d'enterrement** to look gloomy

enterrer [ãtere] *vb* to bury

entêté [ãtete] (*f* **entêtée**) *adj* stubborn

s'**entêter** [ãtete] *vb* to persist ▷ *Il s'entête à refuser de voir le médecin.* He persists in refusing to go to the doctor.

enthousiasme [ãtuzjasm(ə)] *nm* enthusiasm

s'**enthousiasmer** [ãtuzjasme] *vb* to get enthusiastic ▷ *Elle s'enthousiasme facilement.* She gets very enthusiastic about things.

entier [ãtje, -jɛʀ] *adj* whole ▷ *Il a mangé une quiche entière.* He ate a whole quiche. ▷ *Je n'ai pas lu le livre en entier.* I haven't read the whole book.; **le lait entier** whole milk

entièrement [ãtjɛʀmã] *adv* completely

entorse [ãtɔʀs(ə)] *nf* sprain ▷ *Elle s'est fait une entorse à la cheville.* She sprained her ankle.

entourer [ãtuʀe] *vb* to surround ▷ *Le jardin est entouré d'un mur de pierres.* The garden is surrounded by a stone wall.

entracte [ãtʀakt(ə)] *nm* intermission

entraînement [ãtʀɛnmã] *nm* training

entraîner [ãtʀene] *vb* ❶ to lead ▷ *Il se laisse facilement entraîner par les autres.* He's easily led. ❷ to coach ▷ *Il entraîne l'équipe de soccer depuis cinq ans.* He's been training the soccer team for five years. ❸ to involve ▷ *Un mariage entraîne beaucoup de dépenses.* A wedding involves a lot of expense.; **s'entraîner** to train ▷ *Elle s'entraîne au hockey tous les samedis matins.* She has hockey practice every Saturday morning.

entraîneur [ãtʀɛnœʀ] *nm* coach

entraîneure [ãtʀɛnœʀ] *nf* coach

entre [ãtʀ(ə)] *prep* between ▷ *Il est assis entre son père et sa tante.* He's sitting between his father and his aunt.; **entre eux** among themselves; **l'un d'entre eux** one of them

entrée [ãtʀe] *nf* ❶ entrance ❷ driveway ❸ (of meal) appetizer ▷ *Qu'est-ce que tu prends comme entrée?* What would you like for an

appetizer?; **la touche Entrée** the Enter key

entreposage [ãtʀəpozaʒ] *nm* storage

entreprendre [ãtʀəpʀãdʀ(ə)] *vb* (a process) to start ▷ *Elle a entrepris des travaux de rénovation.* She has started renovations.

entrepreneur [ãtʀəpʀənœʀ] *nm* small business owner

entrepreneure [ãtʀəpʀənœʀ] *nf* small business owner

entreprise [ãtʀəpʀiz] *nf* (company) business

entrer [ãtʀe] *vb* ❶ to come in ▷ *Entrez donc!* Come on in! ❷ to go in ▷ *Ils sont tous entrés dans la maison.* They all went into the house.; **entrer à l'hôpital** to go into the hospital; **entrer des données** to enter data ▷ *J'ai entré toutes les adresses de mes amis sur mon ordinateur.* I've entered the addresses of all my friends into my computer.

entre-temps [ãtʀətã] *adv* meanwhile

entretien [ãtʀətjɛ̃] *nm* ❶ maintenance ▷ *un contrat d'entretien* a maintenance contract ❷ conversation ▷ *un entretien téléphonique* a telephone conversation

entrevue [ãtʀəvy] *nf* ❶ interview ▷ *une entrevue avec le ministre* an interview with the minister ❷ job interview ▷ *mon frère a passé une entrevue pour travailler dans un restaurant.* My brother had a job interview to work in a restaurant.

entrouvert [ãtʀuvɛʀ, -ɛʀt(ə)] (*f* **entrouverte**) *adj* half open ▷ *La porte était entrouverte.* The door was half open.

envahir [ãvaiʀ] *vb* to invade

envahissement [ãvaismã] *nm* invasion

enveloppe [ãvlɔp] *nf* envelope

envelopper [ãvlɔpe] *vb* to wrap

envers [ãvɛʀ] *prep* towards ▷ *Il est très respectueux envers elle.* He's very respectful towards her. ▷ *son attitude envers moi* his attitude to me

▷ *nm*: **à l'envers** (1) inside out ▷ *Je dois repasser ce chemisier à l'envers.* I have to iron this blouse inside out. (2) messy ▷ *Ta chambre est à l'envers.* Your room is messy.

envie [ãvi] *nf*: **avoir envie de faire quelque chose** to feel like doing something ▷ *J'avais envie de pleurer.* I felt like crying.; **Ce gâteau me fait envie.** I wouldn't mind some of that cake.

envier [ãvje] *vb* to envy

environ [ãviʀɔ̃] *adv* about ▷ *C'est à soixante kilomètres environ.* It's about 60 kilometres away.

environnement [ãviʀɔnmã] *nm* environment

environnementaliste [ãviʀɔnmãtalist(ə)] *nmf* environmentalist

environs [ãviʀɔ̃] *nmpl* area ▷ *les environs d'Ottawa* the Ottawa area ▷ *Il y a beaucoup de choses intéressantes à voir dans les environs.* There are a lot of interesting things to see in the area.; **aux environs de dix-neuf heures** around 7 p.m.

envisager [ãvizaʒe] *vb* to consider ▷ *Est-ce que vous envisagez de changer d'école?* Are you considering changing schools?

s'**envoler** [ãvɔle] *vb* ❶ to fly away ▷ *Le papillon*

s'est envolé. The butterfly flew away. ❷ to blow away ▷ *Toutes mes notes de cours se sont envolées.* All my class notes blew away.

envoyer [ɑ̃vwaje] *vb* to send ▷ *Ma tante m'a envoyé une carte pour mon anniversaire.* My aunt sent me a card for my birthday.; **envoyer quelqu'un chercher quelque chose** to send somebody to get something ▷ *Sa mère l'a envoyé chercher du pain.* His mother sent him to get some bread.; **envoyer un courriel à quelqu'un** to send somebody an e-mail

épais [epɛ, -ɛs] (*f* **épaisse**) *adj* thick

épaisseur [epɛsœʀ] *nf* thickness

épargner [epaʀɲe] *vb* (money, energy) to save

épatant [epatɑ̃, -ɑ̃t] (*f* **épatante**) *adj* (informal) great ▷ *C'est un type épatant.* He's a great guy.

épaulard [epolaʀ] *nm* killer whale

épaule [epol] *nf* shoulder

épée [epe] *nf* sword

épeler [eple] *vb* to spell ▷ *Est-ce que vous pouvez épeler votre nom s'il vous plaît?* Could you spell your name please?

épice [epis] *nf* spice

épicé [epise] (*f* **épicée**) *adj* spicy ▷ *Ce n'est pas assez épicé pour moi : je trouve ça trop fade.* It's not spicy enough for me: I think it's too bland.

épicerie [episʀi] *nf* grocery store; **faire l'épicerie** to go grocery shopping

épi de maïs [epi-] *nm* corn on the cob

épidémie [epidemi] *nf* epidemic

épinards [epinaʀ] *nmpl* spinach

épine [epin] *nf* thorn

épinette [epinɛt] *nf* spruce; **la bière d'épinette** rootbeer

épingle [epɛ̃gl(ə)] *nf* pin; **une épingle de sûreté** a safety pin

épisode [epizɔd] *nm* episode

éplucher [eplyʃe] *vb* to peel

épluchette [eplyʃɛt] *nf*

éponge [epɔ̃ʒ] *nf* sponge

époque [epɔk] *nf* time ▷ *à cette époque de l'année* at this time of year; **à l'époque** at that time ▷ *À l'époque, beaucoup de gens n'avaient pas l'eau courante.* At that time a lot of people didn't have running water.

épouse [epuz] *nf* wife

épouser [epuze] *vb* to marry

épouvantable [epuvɑ̃tabl(ə)] *adj* terrible

épouvante [epuvɑ̃t] *nf* terror; **un film d'épouvante** a horror film

épouvanter [epuvɑ̃te] *vb* to terrify

époux [epu] *nm* husband; **les nouveaux époux** the newlyweds

épreuve [epʀœv] *nf* ❶ test ▷ *une épreuve orale* an oral test ▷ *une épreuve écrite* a written test ❷ (sports) event

éprouver [epʀuve] *vb* to feel ▷ *Qu'est-ce que vous avez éprouvé à ce moment-là?* What did you feel at that moment?

épuisé [epɥize] (*f* **épuisée**) *adj* exhausted

épuiser [epɥize] *vb* to wear out ▷ *Ce travail m'a complètement épuisé.* This job has completely worn me out.; **s'épuiser** to wear oneself out ▷ *Il s'épuise à garder un jardin impeccable.* He wears himself out keeping his garden

immaculate.

équateur [ekwatœʀ] *nm* equator

équation [ekwasjɔ̃] *nf* equation

équerre [ekɛʀ] *nf* set square

équilibre [ekilibʀ(ə)] *nm* balance ▷ *J'ai failli perdre l'équilibre.* I nearly lost my balance.

équilibré [ekilibʀe] (*f* **équilibrée**) *adj* well-balanced

équipage [ekipaʒ] *nm* crew

équipe [ekip] *nf* team

équipé [ekipe] (*f* **équipée**) *adj*: **bien équipé** well-equipped

équipement [ekipmɑ̃] *nm* equipment

équipements [ekipmɑ̃] *nmpl* facilities ▷ *les équipements sportifs* sports facilities

équitation [ekitasjɔ̃] *nf* riding ▷ *faire de l'équitation* to go riding

équivalent [ekivalɑ̃] *nm* equivalent

érable [eʀabl(ə)] *nm* maple; **le sirop d'érable** maple syrup

érablière [eʀablijɛʀ] *nf* sugar bush ▷ *Nous irons à une partie de sucre à l'érablière.* We're going to a sugaring-off party in the sugar bush.

erreur [eʀœʀ] *nf* mistake; **faire erreur** to be mistaken

es [ɛ] *vb* see **être**; *Tu es très gentille.* You're very kind.

escabeau [ɛskabo] (*pl* **escabeaux**) *nm* stepladder

escalade [ɛskalad] *nf* rock climbing ▷ *faire de l'escalade* to go rock climbing

escalader [ɛskalade] *vb* to climb

escale [ɛskal] *nf*: **faire escale** to stop off

escalier [ɛskalje] *nm* stairs ▷ *un escalier roulant* an escalator

escargot [ɛskaʀgo] *nm* snail

escarpement [ɛskaʀpəmɑ̃] *nm* escarpment ▷ *l'escarpement de Niagara* the Niagara escarpment

esclavage [ɛsklavaʒ] *nm* slavery

esclave [ɛsklav] *nmf* slave

escrime [ɛskʀim] *nf* fencing

escroc [ɛskʀo] *nm* crook ▷ *Cette femme est un escroc.* That woman is a crook.

espace [ɛspas] *nm* space; **espace de travail** workspace

s'espacer [ɛspase] *vb* to become less frequent ▷ *Ses visites se sont peu à peu espacées.* His visits became less and less frequent.

espadrille [ɛspadʀij] *nf* running shoe

espèce [ɛspɛs] *nf* ❶ sort ▷ *Elle portait une espèce de cape en velours.* She was wearing a sort of velvet cloak. ❷ species ▷ *une espèce en voie de disparition,* an endangered species

espèces [ɛspɛs] *nfpl* cash ▷ *payer en espèces* to pay cash

espérer [ɛspeʀe] *vb* to hope; **J'espère bien.** I hope so. ▷ « *Tu penses avoir réussi?* » « *Oui, j'espère bien.* » "Do you think you passed?" "Yes, I hope so."

espiègle [ɛspjɛgl(ə)] *adj* mischievous

espion [ɛspjɔ̃] *nm* spy

espionnage [ɛspjɔnaʒ] *nm* spying; **un roman d'espionnage** a spy novel

espionne [ɛspjɔn] *nf* spy

espoir [ɛspwaʀ] *nm* hope

esprit [ɛspʀi] nm mind ▷ Ça ne m'est pas venu à l'esprit. It didn't cross my mind.; **avoir de l'esprit** to be witty ▷ Il a beaucoup d'esprit. He's very witty.

essai [esɛ] nm attempt ▷ Ce n'est pas mal pour un coup d'essai. It's not bad for a first attempt.; **prendre quelqu'un à l'essai** to hire somebody for a trial period

essayer [eseje] vb ❶ to try ▷ Essaie de rentrer de bonne heure. Try to come home early. ❷ to try on ▷ Essaie ce chandail : il devrait bien t'aller. Try this sweater on: it ought to look good on you.

essence [esɑ̃s] nf (for car) gas

essentiel [esɑ̃sjɛl] (f **essentielle**) adj essential; **Tu es là : c'est l'essentiel.** You're here: that's the main thing.

s' **essouffler** [esufle] vb to get out of breath

essuie-glace [esɥiglas] nm windshield wiper

essuyer [esɥije] vb to wipe; **essuyer la vaisselle** to dry the dishes; **essuyer un échec** to suffer a setback; **s'essuyer** to dry oneself ▷ Vous pouvez vous essuyer les mains avec cette serviette. You can dry your hands on this towel.

est [ɛst] vb see **être**; **Elle est merveilleuse.** She's marvellous.
▶ adj ❶ east ▷ la côte est du Canada the east coast of Canada ❷ eastern ▷ dans la partie est du pays in the eastern part of the country ▶ nm east ▷ Je vis dans l'est. I live in the East.; **vers l'est** eastward; **à l'est de Rainy River** east of Rainy River; **l'Europe de l'Est** Eastern Europe; **le vent d'est** the east wind

est-ce que [ɛskə] adv: **Est-ce que c'est cher?** Is it expensive?; **Quand est-ce qu'il part?** When is he leaving?

esthéticienne [ɛstetisjɛn] nf beautician

estimation [ɛstimasjɔ̃] nf estimate ▷ Nous avons demandé une estimation avant de faire réparer la voiture. We asked for an estimate before getting the car repaired.

estime [ɛstim] nf: **J'ai beaucoup d'estime pour elle.** I have a lot of respect for her.

estimer [ɛstime] vb: **estimer quelqu'un** to have great respect for somebody ▷ Mon père les estime beaucoup. My father has a lot of respect for them.; **estimer que** to be of the opinion that ▷ J'estime que c'est de sa faute. My opinion is that it's her fault.

estomac [ɛstɔma] nm stomach

estrade [ɛstʀad] nf platform ▷ La ministre a prononcé son discours sur l'estrade. The minister gave her speech from the platform.

et [e] conj and

établir [etabliʀ] vb to establish; **s'établir à son compte** to set up a business

établissement [etablismɑ̃] nm establishment; **un établissement scolaire** a school

étage [etaʒ] nm floor ▷ au premier étage on the first floor; **à l'étage** upstairs

étagère [etaʒɛʀ] nf shelf

étaient [etɛ] vb see **être**

étais, était [etɛ] vb see **être**; **Il était très jeune.** He was very young.

étalage [etalaʒ] nm display

étaler [etale] vb to spread out ▷ Il a étalé la carte sur la table. He spread the map out on the table.

étanche [etɑ̃ʃ] adj ❶ watertight ▷ Le toit n'est pas étanche. The roof isn't watertight. ❷ (watch) waterproof

étang [etɑ̃] nm pond

étant [etɑ̃] vb see **être**; **Mes revenus étant limités...** My income being limited...

étape [etap] nf stage ▷ une étape importante de la vie an important stage in life; **faire étape** to stop off

État [eta] nm (nation) state ▷ un chef d'État a head of state

état [eta] nm ❶ state ▷ dans votre état de santé in your state of health ▷ le chef d'État the head of state ❷ condition ▷ en bon état in good condition ▷ en mauvais état in poor condition; **remettre quelque chose en état** to repair something; **un état d'âme** a frame of mind; **être dans tous ses états** to be beside oneself with anxiety

été [ete] vb see **être**; **Elle a été licenciée.** She's been laid off.
▶ nm summer; **en été** in the summer; **l'été indien** Indian summer

éteindre [etɛ̃dʀ(ə)] vb ❶ (light, TV) to turn off ▷ N'oubliez pas d'éteindre la lumière en sortant. Don't forget to turn off the light when you leave. ❷ (computer) to shut down ▷ Quitte l'application avant d'éteindre l'ordinateur. Exit the application before shutting down the computer. ❸ (cigarette) to put out

étendre [etɑ̃dʀ(ə)] vb to spread ▷ Il a étendu une nappe propre sur la table. He spread a clean cloth on the table.; **étendre le linge** to hang out the wash; **s'étendre** to lie down ▷ Je vais m'étendre cinq minutes. I'm going to lie down for five minutes.

éternité [etɛʀnite] nf: **J'ai attendu une éternité chez le médecin.** I waited for ages at the doctor's.

éternuer [etɛʀnɥe] vb to sneeze

êtes [ɛt] vb see **être**; **Vous êtes en retard.** You're late.

étiez [etje] vb see **être**

étinceler [etɛ̃sle] vb to sparkle

étions [etjɔ̃] vb see **être**

étiquette [etiket] nf label ▷ L'étiquette du pot de confiture s'est décollée. The label has come off the jam jar.

s' **étirer** [etiʀe] vb to stretch ▷ Elle s'est étirée paresseusement. She stretched lazily.

étoile [etwal] nf star; **une étoile de mer** a starfish; **une étoile filante** a shooting star; **dormir à la belle étoile** to sleep under the stars; **le match des étoiles** the all-star game

étonnant [etɔnɑ̃, -ɑ̃t] (f **étonnante**) adj amazing

étonner [etɔne] vb to surprise ▷ Cela m'étonnerait de le voir ici. I'd be surprised to see him here.

étouffer [etufe] vb: **On étouffe ici; ouvre donc les fenêtres.** It's stifling in here; open the windows.; **étouffer un cri** to muffle a cry; **étouffer un incendie** to put out a fire; **s'étouffer** to choke ▷ Ne mange pas si vite : tu *vas t'étouffer!* Don't eat so fast: you'll choke!

étourderie [eturdari] *nf* absent-mindedness; **une erreur d'étourderie** a careless error

étourdi [eturdi] (f**étourdie**) *adj* scatterbrained

étourdissement [eturdismɑ̃] *nm*: **avoir des étourdissements** to feel dizzy

étrange [etrɑ̃ʒ] *adj* strange

étranger [etrɑ̃ʒe, -ɛr] (f**étrangère**) *adj* foreign ▷ *un pays étranger* a foreign country; **une personne étrangère** a stranger
▶ *nm* ❶ foreigner ❷ stranger; **à l'étranger** abroad

étrangère [etrɑ̃ʒɛr] *nf* ❶ foreigner ❷ stranger

étrangler [etrɑ̃gle] *vb* to strangle; **s'étrangler** to choke ▷ *s'étrangler avec quelque chose* to choke on something

être [ɛtr(ə)] *nm*: **un être humain** a human being
▶ *vb* ❶ to be ▷ *Je suis heureux.* I'm happy. ▷ *Mon père est journaliste.* My father's a journalist. ▷ *Il est dix heures.* It's ten o'clock. ❷ to have ▷ *Il n'est pas encore arrivé.* He hasn't arrived yet.

étroit [etrwa, -wat] (f**étroite**) *adj* narrow; **être à l'étroit** to be cramped ▷ *Nous sommes un peu à l'étroit dans cet appartement.* We're a bit cramped in this apartment.

étude [etyd] *nf* study ▷ *une étude de cas* a case study; **faire des études** to be studying ▷ *Elle fait des études de droit.* She's studying law.

étudiant [etydjɑ̃] *nm* (college and university) student

étudiante [etydjɑ̃t] *nf* (college and university) student

étudier [etydje] *vb* to study ▷ *étudier pour un examen* to study for an exam ▷ *étudier une question sous toutes ses coutures* to study a question from every angle

étui [etɥi] *nm* case ▷ *un étui à lunettes* a glasses case

eu [y] *vb see* **avoir**; **J'ai eu une bonne note.** I got a good mark.

euh [ø] *excl* uh ▷ *Euh...je ne m'en souviens pas.* Uh...I can't remember.

euro [øro] *nm* (currency) euro

eux [ø] *pron* them ▷ *Je pense souvent à eux.* I often think of them. ▷ *Elle a accepté l'invitation, mais eux ont refusé.* She accepted the invitation, but THEY refused.

évacuer [evakɥe] *vb* to evacuate

s'évader [evade] *vb* to escape

s'évanouir [evanwir] *vb* to faint

s'évaporer [evapore] *vb* to evaporate

évasif [evazif, -iv] (f**évasive**) *adj* evasive

évasion [evazjɔ̃] *nf* escape ▷ *Ils ont préparé leur évasion pendant des mois.* They spent months planning their escape.

éveillé [eveje] (f**éveillée**) *adj* ❶ awake ▷ *Elle est restée éveillée toute la nuit.* She stayed awake all night. ❷ bright ▷ *C'est un enfant très éveillé.* He's very bright.

s'éveiller [eveje] *vb* to awaken

événement [evenmɑ̃] *nm* event

éventail [evɑ̃taj] *nm* (handheld) fan; **un large**

éventail de prix a wide range of prices

éventualité [evɑ̃tɥalite] *nf*: **dans l'éventualité d'un retard** in the event of a delay

éventuel [evɑ̃tɥɛl] (f**éventuelle**) *adj* possible ▷ *une solution éventuelle* a possible solution ▷ *les conséquences éventuelles* the possible consequences

éventuellement [evɑ̃tɥɛlmɑ̃] *adv* possibly ▷ *Nous pourrions éventuellement avoir besoin de vous.* It's possible we may need you.

évidemment [evidamɑ̃] *adv* ❶ obviously ▷ *Les tomates sont évidemment chères en cette saison.* Tomatoes are obviously expensive at this time of year. ❷ of course ▷ *« Est-ce que je peux utiliser ton téléphone? » « Évidemment, tu n'as pas besoin de demander. »* "Can I use your phone?" "Of course, you don't need to ask."

évidence [evidɑ̃s] *nf*: **C'est une évidence.** It's quite obvious.; **de toute évidence** obviously ▷ *De toute évidence, elle ne veut pas nous voir.* Obviously she doesn't want to see us.; **être en évidence** to be clearly visible ▷ *La lettre était en évidence sur la table.* The letter was clearly visible on the table.; **mettre en évidence** to reveal

évident [evidɑ̃, -ɑ̃t] (f**évidente**) *adj* obvious

évier [evje] *nm* sink

éviter [evite] *vb* to avoid

évolué [evolɥe] (f**évoluée**) *adj* advanced ▷ *une technologie très évoluée* very advanced technology

évoluer [evolɥe] *vb* to progress ▷ *La chirurgie esthétique a beaucoup évolué.* Plastic surgery has progressed a great deal.; **Il a beaucoup évolué.** He has come a long way.

évolution [evolysjɔ̃] *nf* ❶ development ▷ *une évolution rapide* rapid development ❷ evolution ▷ *la théorie de l'évolution* the theory of evolution

évoquer [evoke] *vb* to mention ▷ *Elle a évoqué divers problèmes dans son discours.* She mentioned various problems in her speech.

exact [egzakt] (f**exacte**) *adj* ❶ right ▷ *Avez-vous l'heure exacte?* Have you got the right time? ▷ *« Tu es en secondaire trois, n'est-ce pas? » « C'est exact. »* "You're in grade nine, right?" "Right." ❷ exact ▷ *le prix exact, taxes comprises* the exact price including tax

exactement [egzaktəmɑ̃] *adv* exactly ▷ *C'est exactement ce que je cherchais.* That's exactly what I was looking for.

ex æquo [egzeko] *adj*: **Ils sont arrivés ex æquo.** They finished neck and neck.

exagérer [egzaʒere] *vb* ❶ to exaggerate ▷ *Vous exagérez!* You're exaggerating! ❷ to go too far ▷ *Ça fait trois fois que tu arrives en retard : tu exagères!* That's three times you've been late: you've gone too far!

examen [egzamɛ̃] *nm* exam ▷ *Nous allons passer l'examen d'anglais vendredi matin.* We're doing our English exam on Friday morning. ▷ *un examen de français* a French exam; **un examen médical** a medical

examiner [egzamine] *vb* to examine

exaspérant [egzasperɑ̃, -ɑ̃t] (f**exaspérante**)

adj infuriating

exaspérer [ɛgzaspeʁe] *vb* to infuriate

excédent [ɛksedɑ̃] *nm*: **l' excédent de bagages** excess baggage

excéder [ɛksede] *vb* to exceed ▷ *excéder la limite de vitesse* to exceed the speed limit; **excéder quelqu'un** to drive somebody crazy ▷ *Les cris des enfants l'excédaient.* The noise of the children was driving her crazy.

excellent [ɛksɛlɑ̃, -ɑ̃t] (*f* **excellente**) *adj* excellent

excentrique [ɛksɑ̃tʁik] *adj* eccentric

excepté [ɛksɛpte] *prep* except ▷ *Toutes les chaussures excepté les sandales sont en solde.* All the shoes except sandals are reduced.

exception [ɛksɛpsjɔ̃] *nf* exception; **à l'exception de** except

exceptionnel [ɛksɛpsjɔnɛl] (*f* **exceptionnelle**) *adj* exceptional

excès [ɛksɛ] *nm*: **faire des excès** to overindulge ▷ *On fait souvent des excès aux environs de l'Action de grâce.* People often overindulge around Thanksgiving.; **les excès de vitesse** speeding

excessif [ɛksesif, -iv] (*f* **excessive**) *adj* excessive

excitant [ɛksitɑ̃, -ɑ̃t] (*f* **excitante**) *adj* exciting
▷ *nm* stimulant ▷ *Le thé et le café sont des excitants.* Tea and coffee are stimulants.

excitation [ɛksitasjɔ̃] *nf* excitement

exciter [ɛksite] *vb* to excite ▷ *Il était tout excité à l'idée de revoir ses cousins.* He was all excited about seeing his cousins again.; **s'exciter** (*informal*) to get excited ▷ *Ne t'excite pas trop vite : ça ne va peut-être pas marcher!* Don't get excited too soon: it may not work!

exclamation [ɛksklamasjɔ̃] *nf* exclamation

exclu [ɛkskly] (*f* **exclue**) *adj* excluded ▷ *Elle se sentait exclue du groupe.* She felt excluded from the group.; **Il n'est pas exclu que...** It's not impossible that...

exclusif [ɛksklyzif, -iv] (*f* **exclusive**) *adj* exclusive

excursion [ɛkskyʁsjɔ̃] *nf* ❶ trip ▷ *faire une excursion* to go on a trip ❷ hike ▷ *une excursion dans la montagne* a hike in the hills

excuse [ɛkskyz] *nf* ❶ excuse ▷ *Tu trouves toujours une bonne excuse pour ne pas faire la vaisselle.* You always find a good excuse for not doing the dishes. ❷ apology ▷ *présenter ses excuses* to offer one's apologies; **un mot d'excuse** (*of explanation*) a note ▷ *Vous devez apporter un mot d'excuse signé par vos parents.* You have to bring a note signed by your parents.

excuser [ɛkskyze] *vb* to excuse ▷ *Son retard a été excusé.* His lateness was excused.; **Excusez-moi. (1)** Sorry! ▷ *Excusez-moi, je ne vous avais pas vu.* Sorry, I didn't see you. **(2)** Excuse me. ▷ *Excusez-moi, est-ce que vous avez l'heure?* Excuse me, have you got the time?; **s'excuser** to apologize ▷ *Elle s'est excusée de son retard.* She apologized for being late.

exécuter [ɛgzekyte] *vb* ❶ to execute ▷ *Le prisonnier a été exécuté à l'aube.* The prisoner was executed at dawn. ❷ to perform ▷ *La pianiste*

va maintenant exécuter une valse de Chopin. The pianist will now perform a waltz by Chopin.

exemplaire [ɛgzɑ̃plɛʁ] *nm* copy

exemple [ɛgzɑ̃pl(ə)] *nm* example ▷ *donner l'exemple* to set an example; **par exemple** for example

s'exercer [ɛgzɛʁse] *vb* to practise ▷ *Pour jouer bien, tu devras t'exercer davantage.* To play well, you'll have to practise more. ▷ *s'exercer à parler français* to practise speaking French

exercice [ɛgzɛʁsis] *nm* exercise; **un exercice d'incendie** a fire drill

exhiber [ɛgzibe] *vb* to show off ▷ *Il aime bien exhiber ses décorations.* He likes showing off his medals.; **s'exhiber** to expose oneself

exigeant [ɛgziʒɑ̃, -ɑ̃t] (*f* **exigeante**) *adj*
❶ hard to please ▷ *Elle est vraiment exigeante.* She's really hard to please. ❷ demanding ▷ *un cours très exigeant* a very demanding course

exiger [ɛgziʒe] *vb* ❶ to demand ▷ *Le propriétaire exige d'être payé immédiatement.* The landlord is demanding to be paid immediately. ❷ to require ▷ *Ce travail exige beaucoup de patience.* This job requires a lot of patience.

exil [ɛgzil] *nm* exile

exister [ɛgziste] *vb* to exist ▷ *Ça n'existe pas.* It doesn't exist. ▷ *Ce manteau existe également en rose.* This coat is also available in pink.

exotique [ɛgzɔtik] *adj* exotic ▷ *une plante exotique* an exotic plant ▷ *un yogourt aux fruits exotiques* a tropical fruit yogurt

expédier [ɛkspedje] *vb* to send ▷ *expédier un colis* to send a parcel

expéditeur [ɛkspeditœʁ] *nm* sender

expédition [ɛkspedisjɔ̃] *nf* expedition

expéditrice [ɛkspeditʁis] *nf* sender

expérience [ɛkspeʁjɑ̃s] *nf* ❶ experience ▷ *Elle a plusieurs années d'expérience.* She's got several years of experience. ❷ experiment ▷ *une expérience de chimie* a chemistry experiment

expérimenter [ɛkspeʁimɑ̃te] *vb* to test ▷ *Ces produits de beauté n'ont pas été expérimentés sur des animaux.* These cosmetics have not been tested on animals.

expert [ɛkspɛʁ] *nm* expert

experte [ɛkspɛʁt(ə)] *nf* expert

expirer [ɛkspiʁe] *vb* ❶ (*document, passport*) to expire ❷ (*time allowed*) to run out ❸ (*person*) to breathe out

explication [ɛksplikasjɔ̃] *nf* explanation

expliquer [ɛksplike] *vb* to explain ▷ *Elle m'a expliqué comment faire.* She explained to me how to do it.; **s'expliquer** to explain oneself

exploit [ɛksplwa] *nm* achievement

exploitation [ɛksplwatasjɔ̃] *nf* exploitation ▷ *Cet organisme lutte contre l'exploitation des femmes.* This organization fights against the exploitation of women.; **une exploitation agricole** a farm

exploiter [ɛksplwate] *vb* to exploit ▷ *Il s'est fait exploiter par le patron du restaurant.* He was exploited by the owner of the restaurant.

explorer [ɛksplɔʁe] *vb* to explore

exploser [ɛksploze] *vb* to explode ▷ *La bombe a explosé en pleine rue.* The bomb exploded in the middle of the street.

explosif [ɛksplozif] nm explosive

explosion [ɛksplozjɔ̃] nf explosion

exportation [ɛkspɔrtasjɔ̃] nf export

exporter [ɛkspɔrte] vb to export

exposé [ɛkspoze] nm presentation ▷ un exposé sur l'environnement a presentation on the environment; **un exposé écrit** an essay

exposer [ɛkspoze] vb ❶ to show ▷ Il expose ses peintures dans une galerie d'art. He shows his paintings in a private art gallery. ❷ to expose ▷ N'exposez pas le film à la lumière. Do not expose the film to light. ❸ (explain) to lay out ▷ Elle nous a exposé les raisons de son départ. She laid out the reasons for her departure.; **s'exposer au soleil** to stay out in the sun ▷ Ne vous exposez pas trop longtemps au soleil. Don't stay out in the sun too long.

exposition [ɛkspozisjɔ̃] nf exhibition ▷ une exposition de peinture an exhibition of paintings

exprès [ɛkspres] adv ❶ on purpose ▷ Je suis sûr qu'il l'a fait exprès. I'm sure he did it on purpose. ❷ specially ▷ J'ai fait ce gâteau exprès pour toi. I made this cake specially for you.

express [ɛkspres] nm (bus, train) express ▷ Elle a décidé de prendre l'express de dix heures. She decided to catch the express at 10 o'clock.

expression [ɛkspresjɔ̃] nf ❶ expression ❷ phrase

exprimer [ɛksprime] vb to express; **s'exprimer** to express oneself ▷ Il s'exprime très bien pour un enfant de huit ans. For a child of 8, he expresses himself very well.

exquis [ɛkski, -iz] (f **exquise**) adj exquisite

extérieur [ɛksterjœr] (f **extérieure**) adj outside

▶ nm outside; **à l'extérieur** outside ▷ Prenons le déjeuner à l'extérieur. Let's eat lunch outside.

extincteur [ɛkstɛ̃ktœr] nm fire extinguisher

extra [ɛkstra] (f+pl **extra**) adj excellent ▷ Ce fromage est extra! This cheese is excellent!

extraire [ɛkstrer] vb to extract

extrait [ɛkstre] nm extract

extraordinaire [ɛkstraɔrdiner] adj extraordinary

extra-terrestre [ɛkstraterestr(ə)] nmf alien

extravagant [ɛkstravagɑ̃, -ɑ̃t] (f **extravagante**) adj extravagant

extrême [ɛkstrem] adj extreme ▷ l'extrême droite et l'extrême gauche the far right and the far left

▶ nm extreme; **pousser les choses à l'extrême** to go to extremes

extrêmement [ɛkstrememɑ̃] adv extremely

Extrême-Orient [ɛkstremɔrjɑ̃] nm the Far East

extrémité [ɛkstremite] nf end ▷ La gare est à l'autre extrémité de la ville. The station is at the other end of the town.

f

fa [fa] nm (music) F

fabrication [fabrikasjɔ̃] nf manufacture

fabriquer [fabrike] vb to make ▷ fabriqué au Canada made in Canada

face [fas] nf: **face à face** face to face; **en face de** opposite ▷ L'autobus s'arrête en face de chez moi. The bus stops opposite my house.; **faire face à quelque chose** to face something; **perdre la face** to lose face; **« Pile ou face? »** — **« Face. »** "Heads or tails?" — "Heads."

fâché [faʃe] (f **fâchée**) adj angry; **être fâché contre quelqu'un** to be angry with somebody ▷ Elle est fâchée contre moi. She's angry with me.; **être fâché avec quelqu'un** to be on bad terms with somebody ▷ Elle est fâchée avec sa sœur. She's on bad terms with her sister.

se fâcher [faʃe] vb: **se fâcher contre quelqu'un** to lose one's temper with somebody; **se fâcher avec quelqu'un** to fall out with somebody ▷ Il s'est fâché avec son frère. He had a fight with his brother.

facile [fasil] adj easy; **facile à faire** easy to do

facilement [fasilmɑ̃] adv easily

facilité [fasilite] nf: **un logiciel d'une grande facilité d'utilisation** a very user-friendly piece of software; **Il a de la facilité en langues.** He has a gift for languages.

façon [fasɔ̃] nf way ▷ De quelle façon? In what way?; **de toute façon** anyway

facteur [faktœr] nm letter carrier

factrice [faktris] nf letter carrier

facture [faktyr] nf bill ▷ une facture de gaz a gas bill

facultatif [fakyltatif, -iv] (f **facultative**) adj optional

faculté [fakylte] nf faculty; **avoir une grande faculté de concentration** to have great powers of concentration

fade [fad] adj tasteless ▷ La soupe est un peu fade. The soup is a bit tasteless.

faible [fɛbl(ə)] adj weak ▷ Je me sens encore faible. I still feel a bit weak.; **Il est faible en maths.** He's not very good at math.

faiblesse [fɛbles] nf weakness

faillir [fajir] vb: **J'ai failli tomber.** I nearly fell down.

faillite [fajit] nf bankruptcy; **une entreprise en faillite** a bankrupt business; **faire faillite** to go bankrupt

faim [fɛ̃] nf hunger; **avoir faim** to be hungry

fainéant [feneɑ̃, -ɑ̃t] (f **fainéante**) adj lazy

faire [fer] vb ❶ to make ▷ Je vais faire un gâteau pour ce soir. I'm going to make a cake for tonight. ▷ *Ils font trop de bruit.* They're making too much noise. ▷ *Je voudrais me faire de nouveaux amis.* I'd like to make new friends. ❷ to do ▷ *Qu'est-ce que tu fais?* What are you doing? ▷ *Elle fait de l'italien.* She's doing Italian. ▷ *Qui veut faire la vaisselle?* Who'll do the dishes? ❸ to be ▷ *Qu'est-ce qu'il fait chaud!* Is it ever hot! ▷ *Espérons qu'il fera beau demain.* Let's hope it'll be nice weather tomorrow.; **Ça ne fait rien.** It doesn't matter.; **Ça fait cinquante-trois dollars en tout.** That makes fifty-three dollars in all.; **Ça fait trois ans qu'elle habite à Peterborough.** She's lived in Peterborough for three years.; **faire tomber** to knock over ▷ *Le chat a fait tomber le vase.* The cat knocked over the vase.; **faire faire quelque chose** to get something done ▷ *Je dois faire réparer ma voiture.* I've got to get my car repaired.; **Je vais me faire couper les cheveux.** I'm going to get my hair cut.; **Ne t'en fais pas!** Don't worry!; **se faire des idées** to imagine things

fais, faisaient, faisais, faisait, faisiez, faisions, faisons, fait *vb see* **faire**

fait [fɛ] *nm* fact ▷ *Le fait que...* The fact that...; **un fait divers** a news item; **au fait** by the way ▷ *Au fait, tu as aimé le film d'hier?* By the way, did you enjoy the movie yesterday?; **en fait** actually ▷ *En fait, je n'ai pas beaucoup de temps.* I haven't got much time actually.; **aller au fait** to get to the point

faites [fɛt] *vb see* **faire**

falaise [falɛz] *nf* cliff

falloir [falwaʀ] *vb see* **faut, faudra, faudrait**

famé [fame] (*f* **famée**) *adj* : **un quartier mal famé** a rough area

fameux [famø, -øz] (*f* **fameuse**) *adj* famous ▷ *La Colombie-Britannique est fameuse pour ses montagnes.* British Columbia is famous for its mountains.; **Ce n'est pas fameux.** It's not great.

familial [familjal, -o] (*f* **familiale**, *mpl* **familiaux**) *adj* family ▷ *une atmosphère familiale* a family atmosphere; **les allocations familiales** child benefit

familier [familje, -jɛʀ] (*f* **familière**) *adj* familiar

famille [famij] *nf* ❶ family ▷ *une famille nombreuse* a big family ▷ *Nous fêtons les anniversaires en famille.* We have family birthday celebrations.; **une famille monoparentale** a single-parent family; **une famille nucléaire** a nuclear family; **une famille reconstituée** a blended family ❷ relatives ▷ *J'ai de la famille à Windsor.* I've got relatives in Windsor.

famine [famin] *nf* famine

fanatique [fanatik] *adj* fanatical
▶ *n* fanatic

fanfare [fɑ̃faʀ] *nf* brass band

fanion [fanjɔ̃] *nm* pennant

fantaisie [fɑ̃tezi] *nf* ❶ imagination ▷ *un roman plein de fantaisie* a novel full of imagination ❷ whim ▷ *Ils lui passent toutes ses fantaisies.* They give in to all his whims.; **des bijoux de fantaisie** costume jewellery

fantastique [fɑ̃tastik] *adj* fantastic

fantôme [fɑ̃tom] *nm* ghost

faon [fɑ̃] *nm* fawn

farce [faʀs(ə)] *nf* ❶ (*for chicken, turkey*) stuffing ❷ practical joke ▷ *Elle aime faire des farces.* She likes to play practical jokes.

farci [faʀsi] (*f* **farcie**) *adj* stuffed ▷ *des poivrons verts farcis* stuffed green peppers

farine [faʀin] *nf* flour

fascinant [fasinɑ̃, -ɑ̃t] (*f* **fascinante**) *adj* fascinating

fasciner [fasine] *vb* to fascinate

fascisme [faʃism(ə)] *nm* fascism

fasse, fassent, fasses, fassiez, fassions *vb see* **faire**; **Pourvu qu'il fasse beau demain!** Let's hope it'll be nice out tomorrow!

fatal [fatal] (*f* **fatale**) *adj* fatal; **C'était fatal.** It was bound to happen.

fatalité [fatalite] *nf* fate

fatigant [fatigɑ̃, -ɑ̃t] (*f* **fatigante**) *adj* tiring

fatigue [fatig] *nf* tiredness

fatigué [fatige] (*f* **fatiguée**) *adj* tired

se fatiguer [fatige] *vb* to get tired

fauché [foʃe] (*f* **fauchée**) *adj* (*informal*) hard up

faucon [fokɔ̃] *nm* hawk

faudra [fodʀa] *vb* : **Il faudra qu'on soit plus rapide.** We'll have to be quicker.

faudrait [fodʀɛ] *vb* : **Il faudrait qu'on fasse attention.** We ought to be careful.

se faufiler [fofile] *vb* : **Il s'est faufilé à travers la foule.** He made his way through the crowd.

faune [fon] *nf* wildlife

faunique [fonik] *adj* : **une réserve faunique** a wildlife reserve

fausse [fos] *adj see* **faux**

faut [fo] *vb* : **Il faut faire attention.** You have to be careful.; **Nous n'avons pas le choix, il faut y aller.** We have no choice, we've got to go.; **Il faut que je parte.** I have to go.; **Il faut du courage pour faire ce métier.** It takes courage to do that job.; **Il me faut de l'argent.** I need money.; **s'il le faut** if need be

faute [fot] *nf* ❶ mistake ▷ *faire une faute* to make a mistake ❷ fault ▷ *Ce n'est pas de ma faute.* It's not my fault.; **sans faute** without fail ▷ *Je t'appellerai sans faute.* I'll phone you without fail.

fauteuil [fotœj] *nm* armchair; **un fauteuil roulant** a wheelchair

faux [fo, fos] (*f* **fausse**) *adj, adv* ❶ untrue ▷ *C'est entièrement faux.* It's totally untrue. ❷ forged ▷ *un faux passeport* a forged passport; **faire un faux pas** to trip; **Elle chante faux.** She sings out of tune.; **un faux ami** a false friend
▶ *nm* fake ▷ *Ce tableau est un faux.* This painting is a fake.

faveur [favœʀ] *nf* favour

favori [favɔʀi, -it] (*f* **favorite**) *adj* favourite

favoriser [favɔʀize] *vb* to favour ▷ *Ce système d'examen favorise ceux qui ont de la mémoire.* This exam system favours people with good memories.

fédéral [fedeʀal] *adj* federal ▷ *le gouvernement fédéral* the federal government

fée [fe] *nf* fairy

félicitations [felisitɑsjɔ̃] *nfpl* congratulations

féliciter [felisite] *vb* to congratulate
femelle [fəmɛl] *nf* (animal) female
féminin [feminɛ̃, -in] (*f* **féminine**) *adj*
❶ female ▷ *les personnages féminins du roman* the female characters in the novel ❷ feminine ▷ *Elle est très féminine.* She's very feminine.
❸ women's ▷ *Elle joue dans l'équipe féminine du Canada.* She plays in the Canadian women's team.
féministe [feminist(ə)] *adj* feminist
femme [fam] *nf* ❶ woman ❷ wife ▷ *la femme du directeur* the principal's wife; **une femme au foyer** a housewife; **une femme d'affaires** a businesswoman; **une femme d'État** a stateswoman; **une femme de tête** a strong-minded intelligent woman
se fendre [fɑ̃dʀ(ə)] *vb* to crack
fenêtre [fənɛtʀ(ə)] *nf* window
fente [fɑ̃t] *nf* slot
fer [fɛʀ] *nm* iron; **un fer à cheval** a horseshoe; **un fer à friser** a curling iron; **un fer à repasser** an iron
fera, ferai, feras, ferez *vb see* **faire**
férié [feʀje] (*f* **fériée**) *adj*: **un jour férié** a public holiday
feriez, ferions *vb see* **faire**
ferme [fɛʀm(ə)] *adj* ❶ firm ▷ *Il s'est montré très ferme à mon égard.* He was very firm with me. ▷ *nf* farm
fermé [fɛʀme] (*f* **fermée**) *adj* ❶ closed ▷ *La pharmacie est fermée.* The drugstore is closed. ❷ off ▷ *Est-ce que le gaz est fermé?* Is the gas off?
fermer [fɛʀme] *vb* ❶ to close ▷ *N'oublie pas de fermer la fenêtre.* Don't forget to close the window. ❷ to turn off ▷ *As-tu bien fermé le robinet?* Did you turn the tap off?; **fermer à clef** to lock ▷ *N'oublie pas de fermer la porte à clef!* Don't forget to lock the door!
fermeture [fɛʀmətyʀ] *nf*: **les heures de fermeture** closing times
fermeture éclair® (*pl* **fermetures éclair**) *nf* zipper
fermier [fɛʀmje] *nm* farmer
fermière [fɛʀmjɛʀ] *nf* ❶ (woman) farmer ❷ farmer's wife
féroce [feʀɔs] *adj* fierce
ferons, feront *vb see* **faire**
fesses [fɛs] *nfpl* buttocks
festival [fɛstival] *nm* festival
fête [fɛt] *nf* ❶ party ▷ *On organise une petite fête pour son départ.* We're having a little farewell party for him.; **faire la fête** to party ❷ birthday ▷ *C'est sa fête aujourd'hui.* It's his birthday today.; **une fête foraine** a funfair; **la fête du Canada** Canada Day; **la fête de Dollard** Dollard Day; **la fête du Travail** Labour Day; **la fête de la Reine** Victoria Day; **les fêtes de fin d'année** the festive season
fêter [fete] *vb* to celebrate
feu [fø] (*pl* **feux**) *nm* ❶ fire ▷ *prendre feu* to catch fire ▷ *faire du feu* to make a fire; **Au feu!** Fire!; **un feu de camp** a campfire; **un feu de joie** a bonfire ❷ traffic light ▷ *un feu rouge* a red light ▷ *le feu vert* the green light ▷ *Tournez à gauche aux feux.* Turn left at the lights.; **Avez-vous du feu?** Have you got a light? ❸ heat

▷ *...mijoter à feu doux* ...simmer over low heat; **un feu d'artifice** a firework display; **un feu sauvage** a cold sore
feuillage [fœjaʒ] *nm* leaves
feuille [fœj] *nf* ❶ leaf ▷ *des feuilles mortes* fallen leaves; **la feuille d'érable** (to mean "Canada") the maple leaf ❷ sheet ▷ *une feuille de papier* a sheet of paper; **la feuille de présence** attendance sheet; **une feuille de calcul** (file) a spreadsheet
feuilleté [fœjte] (*f* **feuilletée**) *adj*: **de la pâte feuilletée** flaky pastry
feuilleter [fœjte] *vb* to leaf through
feuilleton [fœjtɔ̃] *nm* serial
feutre [føtʀ(ə)] *nm* felt; **un stylo-feutre** a felt pen
fève [fɛv] *nf* bean ▷ *les fèves vertes* green beans ▷ *les fèves jaunes* wax beans; **les fèves au lard** baked beans ▷ *Il aime ajouter de la mélasse à ses fèves au lard.* He likes to add molasses to his baked beans.
février [fevʀije] *nm* February; **en février** in February
fiable [fjabl(ə)] *adj* reliable
fiançailles [fjɑ̃saj] *nfpl* engagement; **rompre ses fiançailles** to break off one's engagement
fiancé [fjɑ̃se] (*f* **fiancée**) *adj*: **être fiancé à quelqu'un** to be engaged to somebody
se fiancer [fjɑ̃se] *vb* to get engaged
ficelle [fisɛl] *nf* ❶ string ▷ *Passe-moi un bout de ficelle.* Give me a piece of string. ❷ (bread) thin baguette
fiche [fiʃ] *nf* form ▷ *Remplissez cette fiche s'il vous plaît.* Fill in this form, please.
se ficher [fiʃe] *vb* (informal); **Je m'en fiche!** I don't care!; **Fiche-moi la paix!** Leave me alone!; **Quoi, tu n'as fait que ça? Tu te fiches de moi!** You've only done that much? You can't be serious!
fichier [fiʃje] *nm* file; **un fichier joint** (e-mail) an attachment
fichu [fiʃy] (*f* **fichue**) *adj* (informal); **Ce parapluie est fichu.** This umbrella's busted.
fidèle [fidɛl] *adj* faithful
fier [fjɛʀ] (*f* **fière**) *adj* proud
fierté [fjɛʀte] *nf* pride
fièvre [fjɛvʀ(ə)] *nf* fever ▷ *J'ai de la fièvre.* I have a temperature. ▷ *Elle a trente-neuf de fièvre.* She has a temperature of 39°C.
fiévreux [fjevʀø, -øz] (*f* **fiévreuse**) *adj* feverish
figue [fig] *nf* fig
figure [figyʀ] *nf* ❶ face ▷ *Il a reçu le ballon en pleine figure.* The ball hit him smack in the face. ❷ (illustration) figure ▷ *Voir figure 2.1, page 32.* See figure 2.1, page 32.
fil [fil] *nm* ❶ thread ▷ *le fil à coudre* sewing thread ❷ cord ▷ *une souris sans fil* a cordless mouse; **le fil de fer** wire
file [fil] *nf* (of people, objects) line; **une file d'attente** a lineup ▷ *se mettre à la file* to go stand in line; **à la file** one after the other
filer [file] *vb* to speed along ▷ *Les voitures filent sur l'autoroute.* The cars are speeding along the highway.; **File dans ta chambre!** Off to your room with you!
filet [file] *nm* net

fille [fij] nf ❶ girl ▷ *C'est une école de filles.* It's a girls' school. ❷ daughter ▷ *C'est leur fille aînée.* She's their oldest daughter.

fillette [fijɛt] nf little girl

film [film] nm ❶ movie; **un film policier** a thriller; **un film d'aventures** an action movie; **un film d'épouvante** a horror movie ❷ film ▷ *Avec une caméra numérique, on n'a pas besoin de film.* With a digital camera, you don't need film.

fils [fis] nm son

fin [fɛ̃] nf end ▷ *Elle n'a pas regardé la fin du film.* She didn't watch the end of the film.; **« Fin »** "The End"; **À la fin, il a réussi à se décider.** In the end he managed to make up his mind.; **Elle sera en vacances fin juin.** She'll be on holiday at the end of June.; **en fin de journée** at the end of the day; **en fin de compte** ultimately; **sans fin** endless
▶ adj ❶ fine; **des fines herbes** mixed herbs ❷ (informal) nice ▷ *Elle est vraiment fine!* She is so nice!

finale [final] nf (sports) final ▷ *les quarts de finale* the quarter finals

finalement [finalmɑ̃] adv ❶ at last ▷ *Nous sommes finalement arrivés.* At last we arrived. ❷ after all ▷ *Finalement, tu avais raison.* You were right after all.

fin de semaine nf weekend ▷ *Nous avons passé la fin de semaine au chalet.* We spent the weekend at the cottage.

fini [fini] (f **finie**) adj finished

finir [finiʀ] vb to finish ▷ *Le cours finit à onze heures.* The class finishes at 11 o'clock. ▷ *Je viens de finir ce livre.* I've just finished this book.; **Elle a fini par se décider.** She made up her mind in the end.

finissant [finisɑ̃] nm graduating student; **le bal des finissants** graduation party

finissante [finisɑ̃t] nf graduating student

firme [fiʀm(ə)] nf firm

fis [fi] vb see **faire**

fissure [fisyʀ] nf crack

fit [fi] vb see **faire**

fixe [fiks(ə)] adj ❶ steady ▷ *Il n'a pas d'emploi fixe.* He doesn't have a steady job. ❷ set ▷ *Elle mange toujours à heures fixes.* She always eats at set times.; **un menu à prix fixe** a set menu; **une idée fixe** an obsession

fixer [fikse] vb ❶ to hold in place ▷ *Les volets sont fixés avec des crochets.* The shutters are held in place with hooks. ❷ (time) to set ▷ *Nous avons fixé une heure pour nous retrouver.* We set a time to meet. ❸ to stare at ▷ *Ne fixe pas les gens comme ça!* Don't stare at people like that!

flacon [flakɔ̃] nm bottle ▷ *un flacon de parfum* a bottle of perfume

flambé [flɑ̃be] (f **flambée**) adj; **des bananes flambées** flambéed bananas

flamme [flam] nf flame; **en flammes** on fire

flan [flɑ̃] nm baked custard

flâner [flɑne] vb to stroll

flaque [flak] nf (of water) puddle

flash [flaʃ] (pl **flashes**) nm (of camera) flash

flatter [flate] vb to flatter

flèche [flɛʃ] nf arrow

fléchettes [fleʃɛt] nfpl darts ▷ *jouer aux fléchettes* to play darts

flétan [fletɑ̃] nm halibut

fleur [flœʀ] nf flower

fleur de lis [-lis] nf fleur-de-lis

fleurdelisé [flœʀdəlize] nm the Québec flag

fleuri [flœʀi] (f **fleurie**) adj ❶ full of flowers ▷ *Son jardin était très fleuri.* Her garden was full of flowers. ❷ flowery ▷ *un papier peint fleuri* flowery wallpaper

fleurir [flœʀiʀ] vb to flower ▷ *Cette plante fleurit en automne.* This plant flowers in the fall.

fleuriste [flœʀist(ə)] nmf florist

fleuve [flœv] nm river

flirter [flœʀte] vb to flirt

flocon [flɔkɔ̃] nm flake

flotter [flɔte] vb to float

flou [flu] (f **floue**) adj blurry

fluorure [flyɔʀyʀ] nm; **le dentifrice au fluorure** fluoride toothpaste

flûte [flyt] nf flute ▷ *Je joue de la flûte.* I play the flute.; **une flûte à bec** a recorder

foi [fwa] nf faith

foie [fwa] nm liver; **une crise de foie** a stomach upset

foin [fwɛ̃] nm hay; **un rhume des foins** hay fever

foire [fwaʀ] nf fair; **la foire du livre** book fair

fois [fwa] nf time ▷ *la première fois* the first time ▷ *à chaque fois* each time ▷ *À chaque fois que je vais à la bibliothèque, j'oublie ma carte.* Every time I go to the library, I forget my card. ▷ *deux fois deux font quatre* 2 times 2 is 4; **une fois** once; **deux fois** twice ▷ *deux fois plus de gens* twice as many people ▷ *Je vais nager deux fois par semaine.* I go swimming twice a week.; **une fois que** once ▷ *Tu te sentiras mieux une fois que tu auras mangé.* You'll feel better once you've had something to eat.; **à la fois** at once ▷ *Je ne peux pas faire deux choses à la fois.* I can't do two things at once.

folie [fɔli] nf madness ▷ *C'est de la folie pure!* It's absolute madness!; **faire une folie** to be extravagant

folklorique [fɔlklɔʀik] adj folk ▷ *de la musique folklorique* folk music

folle [fɔl] adj see **fou**

foncé [fɔ̃se] (f **foncée**) adj dark ▷ *bleu foncé* dark blue

foncer [fɔ̃se] vb (informal); **Je vais foncer à la boulangerie.** I'm just going to whip over to the bakery.

fonction [fɔ̃ksjɔ̃] nf function; **une voiture de fonction** a company car

fonctionnaire [fɔ̃ksjɔnɛʀ] nmf civil servant

fonctionner [fɔ̃ksjɔne] vb to work

fond [fɔ̃] nm ❶ bottom ▷ *Mon porte-monnaie est au fond de mon sac.* My wallet is at the bottom of my purse. ❷ end ▷ *Les toilettes sont au fond du couloir.* The washrooms are at the end of the hall.; **dans le fond** all things considered ▷ *Dans le fond, ce n'est pas si grave.* All things considered, it's not that bad.

fonder [fɔ̃de] vb to found ▷ *Charles Camsell a fondé la Société géographique royale du Canada.* Charles Camsell founded the Royal Geographical Society of Canada.

fondre [fɔ̃dʀ(ə)] vb to melt ▷ *La tablette de chocolat a fondu dans ma poche.* The bar of chocolate melted in my pocket.; **fondre en larmes** to burst into tears

fondu [fɔ̃dy] (f**fondue**) adj: **du beurre fondu** melted butter

font [fɔ̃] vb see **faire**

fontaine [fɔ̃tɛn] nf fountain

foot [fut] nm (informal) football

football [futbol] nm football ▷ *jouer au football* to play football

force [fɔʀs] nf strength ▷ *Je n'ai pas beaucoup de force dans les bras.* I haven't got much strength in my arms.; **à force de** by ▷ *Il a grossi à force de manger autant.* He got fat by eating so much.; **de force** by force ▷ *Ils lui ont enlevé son pistolet de force.* They took the gun from her by force.; **les forces armées** the armed forces

forcé [fɔʀse] (f**forcée**) adj forced ▷ *un sourire forcé* a forced smile; **C'est forcé.** (informal) It's inevitable.

forcément [fɔʀsemã] adv: **Ça devait forcément arriver.** That was bound to happen.; **pas forcément** not necessarily

foresterie [fɔʀɛstəʀi] nf forestry ▷ *Elle veut étudier en foresterie.* She wants to study forestry.

forêt [fɔʀɛ] nf forest

forfait [fɔʀfɛ] nm package deal; **C'est compris dans le forfait.** It's included in the package.

formalité [fɔʀmalite] nf formality ▷ *Ce n'est qu'une simple formalité.* It's just a formality.

format [fɔʀma] nm size

formatage [fɔʀmataʒ] nm formatting

formater [fɔʀmate] vb to format ▷ *formater un document* to format a document

formation [fɔʀmasjɔ̃] nf training ▷ *la formation professionnelle* vocational training; **Il a une formation d'ingénieur.** He is a trained engineer.

forme [fɔʀm(ə)] nf shape; **être en forme** to be in good shape; **Je ne suis pas en forme aujourd'hui.** I'm not feeling too good today.; **Tu as l'air en forme.** You're looking well.

formellement [fɔʀmɛlmã] adv strictly ▷ *Il est formellement interdit de fumer dans les couloirs.* It is strictly forbidden to smoke in the corridors.

former [fɔʀme] vb to form

formidable [fɔʀmidabl(ə)] adj great

formulaire [fɔʀmylɛʀ] nm (to fill out) form

fort [fɔʀ, fɔʀt(ə)] (f**forte**) adj, adv ❶ strong ▷ *Le café est trop fort.* The coffee's too strong. ❷ good ▷ *Elle est très forte en espagnol.* She's very good at Spanish. ❸ loud ▷ *Est-ce que vous pouvez parler plus fort?* Can you speak louder? ❹ hard ▷ *frapper fort* to hit hard ▷ *travailler fort* to work hard

fortune [fɔʀtyn] nf fortune; **de fortune** makeshift ▷ *Nous avons traversé la rivière sur un radeau de fortune.* We crossed the river on a makeshift raft.

forum de discussion [fɔʀɔm-] nm (Internet) discussion group

fossé [fose] nm ditch

fou [fu, fɔl] (f**folle**) adj mad; **Il y a un monde fou sur la plage!** (informal) There are tons of

people on the beach!; **attraper le fou rire** to get the giggles

foudre [fudʀ(ə)] nf lightning ▷ *Il a été frappé par la foudre.* He was struck by lightning.

foudroyant [fudʀwajã, -ãt] (f**foudroyante**) adj instant ▷ *un succès foudroyant* an instant hit

fouet [fwɛ] nm whisk

fouetter [fwete] vb to whip ▷ *la crème à fouetter* whipping cream

fougère [fuʒɛʀ] nf fern

fouiller [fuje] vb to rummage

fouillis [fuji] nm mess ▷ *Sa chambre est un vrai fouillis.* Her bedroom is a mess.

foulard [fulaʀ] nm scarf ▷ *un foulard en soie* a silk scarf

foule [ful] nf crowd; **une foule de** tons of ▷ *J'ai une foule de choses à faire en fin de semaine.* I have tons of things to do this weekend.

se fouler [fule] vb: **se fouler la cheville** to sprain one's ankle

foulure [fulyʀ] nf sprain

four [fuʀ] nm oven ▷ *un four à micro-ondes* a microwave oven; **un four à céramique** a kiln

fourchette [fuʀʃɛt] nf fork

fourmi [fuʀmi] nf ant; **avoir des fourmis dans les jambes** to have pins and needles

fourneau [fuʀno] (pl **fourneaux**) nm stove

fourni [fuʀni] (f**fournie**) adj (beard, hair) thick

fournir [fuʀniʀ] vb to supply

fournisseur [fuʀnisœʀ] nm supplier; **un fournisseur de services Internet** an Internet service provider

fournitures [fuʀnityʀ] nfpl: **les fournitures scolaires** school supplies

fourré [fuʀe] (f**fourrée**) adj filled ▷ *un gâteau fourré à la confiture* a cake with a jam filling

fourrer [fuʀe] vb (informal) to put ▷ *Où as-tu fourré mon sac?* Where have you put my bag?

fourre-tout [fuʀtu] (pl **fourre-tout**) nm tote bag

fourrure [fuʀyʀ] nf fur ▷ *un manteau de fourrure* a fur coat

foyer [fwaje] nm home ▷ *dans la plupart des foyers canadiens-français* in most French-Canadian homes; **un foyer de jeunes** a youth club

fracture [fʀaktyʀ] nf fracture

fragile [fʀaʒil] adj fragile ▷ *Attention, c'est fragile!* Be careful, it's fragile!

fraîche [fʀɛʃ] adj see **frais**

fraîcheur [fʀeʃœʀ] nf ❶ cool ▷ *la fraîcheur du soir* the cool of the evening ❷ freshness ▷ *Je ne suis pas sûre de la fraîcheur de ce poisson.* I'm not sure about the freshness of this fish.

frais [fʀɛ, fʀɛʃ] (f**fraîche**) adj ❶ fresh ▷ *des œufs frais* fresh eggs ▷ *Cette salade n'est pas très fraîche.* This lettuce isn't very fresh. ❷ chilly ▷ *Il fait un peu frais ce soir.* It's a bit chilly this evening. ❸ cold ▷ *des boissons fraîches* cold drinks; **«servir frais»** "serve chilled"; **garder au frais** to store in a cool place ▶ nmpl expenses

fraise [fʀɛz] nf strawberry ▷ *une fraise des bois* a wild strawberry

framboise [fʀãbwaz] nf raspberry

franc [fʀã, fʀãʃ] (f**franche**) adj frank

français [frɑ̃sɛ, -ɛz] (f **française**) adj, n French ▷ la grammaire française French grammar ▷ Il parle français couramment. He speaks French fluently.

franche [frɑ̃ʃ] adj see **franc**

franchement [frɑ̃ʃmɑ̃] adv ❶ frankly ▷ Elle m'a parlé franchement. She spoke to me frankly. ❷ really ▷ C'est franchement mauvais. It's really bad.

franchir [frɑ̃ʃiʁ] vb to get over ▷ franchir une clôture to get over a fence ▷ Un sourire franchit toutes les barrières linguistiques. A smile crosses all language barriers.

franchise [frɑ̃ʃiz] nf frankness

francophone [frɑ̃kɔfɔn] adj French-speaking ▶ n Francophone ▷ C'est un francophone. He's a Francophone.

francophonie [frɑ̃kɔfɔni] nf the Francophone world

frange [frɑ̃ʒ] nf ❶ fringe ❷ bangs

frangipane [frɑ̃ʒipan] nf almond cream

frapper [frape] vb to strike ▷ Il n'a jamais frappé ses enfants. He has never struck his children. ▷ Son air fatigué m'a frappé. I was struck by how tired she looked.

fredonner [frədɔne] vb to hum

frein [frɛ̃] nm brake; **le frein à main** handbrake

freiner [frene] vb to brake

frêle [frɛl] adj frail

frelon [frəlɔ̃] nm hornet

frémir [fremiʁ] vb to shudder ▷ Cette idée me fait frémir. The idea makes me shudder.

fréquemment [frekamɑ̃] adv frequently

fréquent [frekɑ̃, -ɑ̃t] (f **fréquente**) adj frequent

fréquentée [frekɑ̃te] (f **fréquentée**) adj busy ▷ une rue très fréquentée a very busy street

fréquenter [frekɑ̃te] vb ❶ (person) to see ▷ Je ne le fréquente pas beaucoup. I don't see him often. ❷ (place) to go to ▷ Tu fréquentes les ventes-débarras? Do you go to garage sales?

frère [fʁɛʁ] nm brother

friand [fʁijɑ̃] nm sausage roll

friandises [fʁijɑ̃diz] nfpl sweets

fric [fʁik] nm (informal) cash

frigidaire [fʁiʒidɛʁ] nm refrigerator

frigo [fʁigo] nm (informal) fridge

frileux [fʁilø, -øz] (f **frileuse**) adj: **être frileux** to feel the cold ▷ Je suis très frileuse. I really feel the cold.

fripé [fʁipe] (f **fripée**) adj crumpled

frire [fʁiʁ] vb: **faire frire** to fry ▷ Faites frire les boulettes de viande dans de l'huile très chaude. Fry the meatballs in very hot oil.

frisé [fʁize] (f **frisée**) adj curly ▷ Elle est très frisée. She has very curly hair.

frisson [fʁisɔ̃] nm shiver

frissonner [fʁisɔne] vb to shiver

frit [fʁi, fʁit] (f **frite**) adj fried ▷ du poisson frit fried fish

frites [fʁit] nfpl fries; **poisson et frites** fish and chips

friture [fʁityʁ] nf ❶ fried food ▷ On lui a conseillé d'éviter les fritures. He's been advised to avoid fried food. ❷ fried fish ▷ Nous allons faire une friture ce soir. We're going to have fried fish tonight. ❸ static ▷ Il y a de la friture sur la ligne. There's static on the line.

froid [fʁwa, fʁwad] (f **froide**) adj cold ▷ Ça me laisse froid. It leaves me cold. ▷ de la viande froide cold meat
▶ nm cold; **Il fait froid.** It's cold.; **avoir froid** to be cold ▷ Est-ce que tu as froid? Are you cold?

se froisser [fʁwase] vb ❶ to crease ▷ Ce tissu se froisse très facilement. This material creases very easily. ❷ to take offence ▷ Il se froisse très facilement. He's very quick to take offence.; **se froisser un muscle** to strain a muscle

frôler [fʁole] vb ❶ to brush against ▷ Le chat m'a frôlé au passage. The cat brushed against me as it went past. ❷ to narrowly avoid ▷ Nous avons frôlé la catastrophe. We narrowly avoided disaster.

fromage [fʁɔmaʒ] nm cheese; **le fromage à la crème** cream cheese; **le fromage en grains** cheese curds

fromagerie [fʁɔmaʒʁi] nf cheese shop

froment [fʁɔmɑ̃] nm wheat

froncer [fʁɔ̃se] vb: **froncer les sourcils** to frown

front [fʁɔ̃] nm forehead

frontière [fʁɔ̃tjɛʁ] nf border

frotter [fʁɔte] vb to rub ▷ se frotter les yeux to rub one's eyes; **frotter une allumette** to strike a match

fruit [fʁɥi] nm fruit; **un fruit** a piece of fruit ▷ Est-ce que vous voulez manger un fruit? Would you like some fruit?; **les fruits de mer** seafood

fruité [fʁɥite] (f **fruitée**) adj fruity

frustrer [fʁystʁe] vb to frustrate

fugue [fyg] nf: **faire une fugue** to run away

fuir [fɥiʁ] vb ❶ to flee ▷ fuir devant un danger to flee from danger ❷ to leak ▷ Le robinet fuit. The tap is leaking.

fuite [fɥit] nf ❶ leak ▷ Il y a une fuite de gaz. There is a gas leak. ❷ (escape) flight; **être en fuite** to be on the run

fumé [fyme] (f **fumée**) adj smoked ▷ du saumon fumé smoked salmon

fumée [fyme] nf smoke

fumer [fyme] vb to smoke

fumeur [fymœʁ] nm smoker

fumeuse [fymøz] nf smoker

funérailles [fyneʁaj] nfpl funeral ▷ Les funérailles auront lieu demain. The funeral is tomorrow.

fur [fyʁ]: **au fur et à mesure** adv as you go along ▷ Je vérifie mon travail au fur et à mesure. I check my work as I go along.; **au fur et à mesure que** as ▷ Je réponds à mon courrier au fur et à mesure que je le reçois. I answer my mail as I receive it.

furet [fyʁɛ] nm ferret

fureur [fyʁœʁ] nf fury; **faire fureur** to be all the rage ▷ Ce genre de sac à dos fait fureur actuellement. This sort of backpack is all the rage at the moment.

furieux [fyʁjø, -øz] (f **furieuse**) adj furious

furoncle [fyʁɔ̃kl(ə)] nm (on skin) boil

fus [fy] vb see **être**

fusée [fyze] nf rocket

fusil [fyzi] nm gun

fut [fy] vb see **être**

futé [fyte] (f**futée**) adj crafty

futur [fytyʀ] nm future

futuriste [fytyʀist(ə)] adj futuristic

g

gâcher [gɑʃe] vb to waste ▷ Je n'aime pas gâcher la nourriture. I don't like to waste food.

gâchis [gɑʃi] nm mess ▷ Le chien a fait un beau gâchis sur le tapis. The dog made a real mess on the carpet.

gaffe [gaf] nf: **faire une gaffe** to do something stupid

gageure [gaʒyʀ] nf challenge ▷ J'ai fait la gageure d'apprendre l'espagnol. I took the challenge of learning Spanish. ▷ Réussir ce projet tient de la gageure. To succeed in this project will be a challenge.

gagnant [gaɲɑ̃] nm winner

gagnante [gaɲɑ̃t] nf winner

gagner [gaɲe] vb to win ▷ Qui a gagné? Who won?; **gagner du temps** to gain time; **Il gagne bien sa vie.** He makes a good living.

gai [ge] (f**gaie**) adj cheerful ▷ Elle est très gaie. She's very cheerful.

gaieté [gete] nf cheerfulness

galerie [galʀi] nf gallery ▷ une galerie d'art an art gallery; **une galerie marchande** a shopping arcade

galet [galɛ] nm pebble

galette [galɛt] nf round flat cake ▷ une galette de blé noir a buckwheat pancake

galvaude [galvod] nf

gamin [gamɛ̃] nm (informal) kid

gamine [gamin] nf (informal) kid

gamme [gam] nf (in music) scale ▷ Je dois faire des gammes tous les soirs. I have to do my scales every night.; **une gamme de produits** a range of products; **haut de gamme** top-of-the-line

gammée [game] adj: **la croix gammée** the swastika

gant [gɑ̃] nm glove ▷ des gants en laine woollen gloves

garage [gaʀaʒ] nm garage

garagiste [gaʀaʒist(ə)] nmf ❶ garage owner ❷ mechanic

garantie [gaʀɑ̃ti] nf guarantee

garantir [gaʀɑ̃tiʀ] vb to guarantee

garçon [gaʀsɔ̃] nm boy; **un vieux garçon** a bachelor

garde [gaʀd(ə)] nmf: **un garde de sécurité** a security guard; **un garde du corps** a bodyguard; **un garde forestier** a ranger ▶ nf ❶ guarding ▷ Elle est chargée de la garde des prisonniers. She's responsible for guarding the prisoners. ❷ guard ▷ la relève de la garde the changing of the guard; **être de garde** to be on duty ▷ Mon père est de garde ce soir. My father is on duty tonight.; **la garde des enfants** (in divorce) child custody ▷ Le père a eu la garde des enfants. Child custody was given to the father.; **mettre en garde** to warn ▷ Elle m'a mis en garde contre les voleurs à la tire. She warned me about pickpockets.

garde-côte [gaʀdəkot] (pl **garde-côtes**) nm (boat) coast guard

garder [gaʀde] vb ❶ to keep ▷ Tu as gardé toutes ses lettres? Did you keep all his letters? ❷ to look after ▷ Je garde mon petit cousin samedi après-midi. I'm looking after my little cousin on Saturday afternoon. ❸ to guard ▷ Ils ont pris un gros chien pour garder la maison. They got a big dog to guard the house.; **garder le lit** to stay in bed; **se garder** to keep ▷ Ces crêpes se gardent bien. These pancakes keep well.

garderie [gaʀdəʀi] nf daycare

garde-robe [gaʀdəʀob] nf ❶ (clothes) wardrobe ▷ Elle a une garde-robe bien fournie. She's got an extensive wardrobe. ❷ closet ▷ Son garde-robe est bourré de vêtements de sport. His closet is filled with sportswear.

gardien [gaʀdjɛ̃] nm: **un gardien de but** a goalkeeper; **un gardien de la paix** a peacekeeper; **un gardien d'enfants** a babysitter; **un gardien de prison** a prison guard

gardienne [gaʀdjɛn] nf: **une gardienne de but** a goalkeeper; **une gardienne de la paix** a peacekeeper; **une gardienne d'enfants** a babysitter; **une gardienne de prison** a prison guard

gare [gaʀ] nf station ▷ la gare d'autobus the bus station ▶ excl: **Gare aux serpents!** Watch out for snakes!

garer [gaʀe] vb to park; **se garer** to park ▷ Où t'es-tu garé? Where are you parked?

garni [gaʀni] (f**garnie**) adj: **un plat garni** (vegetables, fries, rice, etc.) a dish served with something on the side; **une pizza garnie** a pizza with everything on it

gars [gɑ] nm (informal) guy

gaspillage [gaspijaʒ] nm waste ▷ Quel gaspillage! What a waste!

gaspiller [gaspije] vb to waste ▷ Je n'aime pas gaspiller la nourriture. I don't like to waste food.

gâteau [gɑto] (pl **gâteaux**) nm cake; **le gâteau des anges** angel food cake

gâter [gɑte] vb to spoil ▷ Il aime gâter ses petits enfants. He likes to spoil his grandchildren.; **se gâter** (1) to go bad ▷ Ces bananes se gâtent. These bananas are going bad. (2) to change for the worse ▷ Le temps va se gâter. The weather's going to change for the worse.

gauche [goʃ] adj left ▷ le bras gauche the left

arm ▷ le côté gauche the left-hand side ▷ nf left ▷ sur votre gauche on your left; à **gauche (1)** on the left ▷ la deuxième rue à gauche the second street on the left **(2)** to the left ▷ à gauche de l'armoire to the left of the cupboard ▷ Tournez à gauche. Turn left.; **la voie de gauche** the left-hand lane; **la gauche** (in politics) the left ▷ Elle est de gauche. She's left-wing.

gaucher [goʃe, -ɛʀ] (f **gauchère**) adj left-handed

gaufre [gofʀ(ə)] nf waffle

gaufrette [gofʀɛt] nf wafer

gaz [gaz] nm gas

gazeux [gazø, -øz] (f **gazeuse**) adj: **une boisson gazeuse** a soft drink; **de l'eau gazeuse** sparkling water

gazon [gazɔ̃] nm lawn

geai bleu [ʒɛ-] nm blue jay

géant [ʒeã] nm giant

gel [ʒɛl] nm ❶ frost ❷ freeze-up ▷ Nous devons aller fermer le chalet avant la saison du gel. We have to go close the cottage before freeze-up.

gelée [ʒəle] nf jelly

geler [ʒəle] vb to freeze ▷ Il a gelé cette nuit. There was a frost last night.

gélule [ʒelyl] nf (containing medicine) capsule

Gémeaux [ʒemo] nmpl Gemini ▷ Je suis Gémeaux. I'm a Gemini.

gémir [ʒemiʀ] vb to moan

gênant [ʒenã, -ãt] (f **gênante**) adj embarrassing ▷ des questions gênantes embarrassing questions ▷ un silence gênant an awkward silence

gencive [ʒãsiv] nf (in mouth) gum

Gendarmerie royale du Canada nf Royal Canadian Mounted Police

gendre [ʒãdʀ(ə)] nm son-in-law

gêné [ʒene] (f **gênée**) adj embarrassed

gêner [ʒene] vb ❶ to bother ▷ Je ne voudrais pas vous gêner. I don't want to bother you. ❷ to embarrass ▷ Son regard la gênait. The way he was looking at her made her feel embarrassed. ❸ to make nervous ▷ Faire un exposé oral me gêne. Giving oral presentations makes me nervous.

général [ʒeneʀal, -o] (f **générale**, mpl **généraux**) adj general; **en général** usually

généralement [ʒeneʀalmã] adv generally

généraliste [ʒeneʀalist(ə)] nmf family doctor

génération [ʒeneʀasjɔ̃] nf generation

généreux [ʒeneʀø, -øz] (f **généreuse**) adj generous

générosité [ʒeneʀozite] nf generosity

génétique [ʒenetik] nf genetics

génétiquement [ʒenetikmã] adv genetically ▷ génétiquement modifié genetically-modified ▷ les aliments génétiquement modifiés GM foods ▷ un organisme génétiquement modifié a genetically-modified organism

génial [ʒenjal, -o] (f **géniale**, mpl **géniaux**) adj (informal) great ▷ Le film d'hier soir était génial. The film last night was great.

genou [ʒnu] (pl **genoux**) nm knee ▷ Je me suis cogné le genou contre la table. I banged my knee

on the table.; **à genoux** on one's knees; **se mettre à genoux** to kneel down

genre [ʒãʀ] nm kind ▷ C'est un genre de gâteau. It's a kind of cake.

gens [ʒã] nmpl people

gentil [ʒãti, -ij] (f **gentille**) adj ❶ nice ▷ Nos voisins sont très gentils. Our neighbours are very nice. ❷ kind ▷ C'était très gentil de votre part. It was very kind of you.

gentillesse [ʒãtijɛs] nf kindness ▷ Je l'ai remerciée de sa gentillesse. I thanked her for her kindness. ▷ C'est un homme d'une grande gentillesse. He is a very nice man.

gentiment [ʒãtimã] adv ❶ nicely ▷ Demande-le lui gentiment. Ask him nicely. ❷ kindly ▷ Ils nous ont gentiment proposé de rester dîner. They kindly invited us to stay for dinner.

géographie [ʒeoɡʀafi] nf geography

géométrie [ʒeometʀi] nf geometry

gérant [ʒeʀã] nm (bank, store) manager

gérante [ʒeʀãt] nf (bank, store) manager

gercé [ʒɛʀse] adj chapped ▷ les lèvres gercées chapped lips

gérer [ʒeʀe] vb to manage ▷ Qui gère cette entreprise? Who's managing this outfit?

germain [ʒɛʀmɛ̃, -ɛn] (f **germaine**) adj: **un cousin germain** a first cousin

geste [ʒɛst(ə)] nm gesture ▷ s'exprimer par des gestes to express oneself using one's hands ▷ un geste de bonne volonté a gesture of goodwill; **Ne faites pas un geste!** Don't move!

gestion [ʒɛstjɔ̃] nf management

gifle [ʒifl(ə)] nf slap on the face

gifler [ʒifle] vb to slap on the face

gigantesque [ʒiɡãtɛsk(ə)] adj gigantic

gigaoctet [ʒiɡaɔktɛ] nm gigabyte ▷ un disque dur de cent vingt gigaoctets a 120-gigabyte hard disk

gilet [ʒilɛ] nm ❶ cardigan ▷ un gilet tricoté à la main a hand-knitted cardigan; **un gilet de sauvetage** a life jacket

gingembre [ʒɛ̃ʒãbʀ(ə)] nm ginger

girafe [ʒiʀaf] nf giraffe

gîte [ʒit] nm: **un gîte du passant** a bed-and-breakfast

glace [ɡlas] nf ❶ ice ▷ L'étang est recouvert de glace. The pond is covered with ice.; **la glace noire** (roads) black ice; **rompre la glace** to break the ice

glacé [ɡlase] (f **glacée**) adj ❶ icy ▷ Il soufflait un vent glacé. An icy wind was blowing. ❷ iced ▷ un thé glacé an iced tea; **la crème glacée** ice cream

glacial [ɡlasjal] (f **glaciale**, mpl **glaciaux**) adj icy

glaçon [ɡlasɔ̃] nm ❶ ice cube ❷ icicle

glissade [ɡlisad] nf ice slide ▷ L'hiver, la ville construit une glissade dans le parc. In winter the city builds an ice slide in the park.

glissant [ɡlisã, -ãt] (f **glissante**) adj slippery

glissement de terrain [ɡlismã-] nm landslide

glisser [ɡlise] vb ❶ to slip ▷ J'ai glissé sur ma peau de banane. I slipped on a banana skin. ❷ to be slippery ▷ Attention, ça glisse! Watch out, it's slippery! **❻** to slide ▷ *descendre la colline en glissant* to slide down the hill **❼** to glide ▷ *glisser sur la neige* to glide over the snow; **glisser-déposer** drag and drop

global [glɔbal, -o] (f **globale**, mpl **globaux**) adj total ▷ *la somme globale* the total amount

gloire [glwaʀ] nf glory

glucide [glysid] nm carbohydrate ▷ *Les pâtes contiennent beaucoup de glucides.* Pasta is high in carbohydrates.

goéland [ɡoelã] nm seagull

golf [gɔlf] nm golf ▷ *Elle joue au golf.* She plays golf.

golfe [gɔlf(ə)] nm gulf ▷ *le golfe du Saint-Laurent* the Gulf of St. Lawrence

gomme [gɔm] nf (for pencil) eraser

gomme à mâcher [gɔm] nf chewing gum ▷ *de la gomme à mâcher à saveur de cannelle* cinnamon-flavoured chewing gum

gommer [ɡɔme] vb (pencil) to erase

gonflé [ɡɔ̃fle] (f **gonflée**) adj **❶** swollen ▷ *Elle a les pieds gonflés.* Her feet are swollen. **❷** inflated ▷ *Le ballon de soccer était mal gonflé.* The soccer ball wasn't properly inflated.

gonfler [ɡɔ̃fle] vb **❶** to blow up ▷ *gonfler un ballon* to blow up a balloon **❷** to pump up ▷ *Tu devrais gonfler ton pneu arrière.* You should pump up your back tire.

gorge [ɡɔʀʒ(ə)] nf **❶** throat ▷ *J'ai mal à la gorge.* I've got a sore throat. **❷** gorge ▷ *la gorge Elora* the Elora Gorge

gorgée [ɡɔʀʒe] nf sip ▷ *une gorgée d'eau* a sip of water

gorille [ɡɔʀij] nm gorilla

goudron [ɡudʀɔ̃] nm tar

gouffre [ɡufʀ(ə)] nm chasm; **Cette voiture est un vrai gouffre!** This car is a money pit!

gourmand [ɡuʀmã, -ãd] (f **gourmande**) adj greedy

gourmandise [ɡuʀmãdiz] nf greed

gourou [ɡuʀu] nm guru

gousse [ɡus] nf: **une gousse d'ail** a clove of garlic

goût [ɡu] nm taste ▷ *Ça n'a pas de goût.* It has no taste. ▷ *Elle a très bon goût.* She has very good taste.; **avoir le goût de** (doing something) to feel like ▷ *J'ai le goût d'aller au cinéma.* I feel like going to the movies.; **de bon goût** in good taste; **de mauvais goût** in bad taste ▷ *Sa blague était de mauvais goût.* His joke was in bad taste.

goûter [ɡute] vb to taste ▷ *Goûte donc ce fromage : tu verras comme il est bon!* Have a taste of this cheese: you'll see how good it is!

goutte [ɡut] nf drop; **C'est la goutte d'eau qui a fait déborder le vase!** That was the last straw!; **C'est une goutte d'eau dans l'océan.** It's a drop in the bucket.

gouvernement [ɡuvɛʀnəmã] nm government

gouverner [ɡuvɛʀne] vb to govern

gouverneur général [ɡuvɛʀnœʀ-] nm Governor General

gouverneure générale [ɡuvɛʀnœʀ-] nf Governor General

grâce [ɡʀɑs] nf: **grâce à** thanks to ▷ *Je suis arrivé à l'heure grâce à toi.* I arrived on time thanks to you.

gracieux [ɡʀasjø, -øz] (f **gracieuse**) adj graceful

gradins [ɡʀadɛ̃] nmpl **❶** (indoor) stands **❷** (outdoor) bleachers

graduel [ɡʀadɥɛl] (f **graduelle**) adj gradual

grain [ɡʀɛ̃] nm grain ▷ *un grain de sable* a grain of sand; **un grain de café** a coffee bean; **un grain de poivre** a peppercorn; **un grain de raisin** a grape

graine [ɡʀɛn] nf seed

graisse [ɡʀɛs] nf fat

grammaire [ɡʀamɛʀ] nf grammar

gramme [ɡʀam] nm gram

grand [ɡʀã, ɡʀãd] (f **grande**) adj, adv **❶** tall ▷ *Il est grand pour son âge.* He's tall for his age. **❷** big ▷ *une grande valise* a big suitcase ▷ *ma grande sœur* my big sister; **une grande personne** a grown-up **❸** long ▷ *un grand voyage* a long journey **❹** great ▷ *C'est un grand ami à moi.* He's a great friend of mine.; **un grand magasin** a department store; **au grand air** out in the open air ▷ *Ça te fera beaucoup de bien d'être au grand air.* It'll be very good for you to be out in the open air.; **grand ouvert** wide open **❺** important ▷ *Le centenaire de la ville a été un grand événement.* The city's 100th anniversary was an important event. ▷ *Je porte cette chemise durant les grandes occasions.* I wear this shirt on important occasions.

grand-chose [ɡʀɑ̃ʃoz] n: **pas grand-chose** not much ▷ *Je n'ai pas acheté grand-chose au marché.* I didn't buy much at the market. ▷ *Voici un petit cadeau : ce n'est pas grand-chose.* Here's a little present: it's nothing much.

grandeur [ɡʀɑ̃dœʀ] nf size

grandir [ɡʀɑ̃diʀ] vb to grow ▷ *Elle a beaucoup grandi.* She's grown a lot.

grand-mère [ɡʀɑ̃mɛʀ] (pl **grands-mères**) nf grandmother

grand-peine [ɡʀɑ̃pɛn]: **à grand-peine** adv with great difficulty

grand-père [ɡʀɑ̃pɛʀ] (pl **grands-pères**) nm grandfather

Grands Lacs nmpl Great lakes

grands-parents [ɡʀɑ̃paʀɑ̃] nmpl grandparents

grange [ɡʀɑ̃ʒ] nf barn

graphique [ɡʀafik] nm **❶** graph ▷ *un graphique à barres* a bar graph **❷** chart ▷ *un graphique circulaire* a pie chart

grappe [ɡʀap] nf: **une grappe de raisin** a bunch of grapes

gras [ɡʀɑ, ɡʀɑs] (f **grasse**) adj **❶** (food) fatty ▷ *Évitez les aliments gras.* Avoid fatty foods. **❷** greasy ▷ *des cheveux gras* greasy hair **❸** oily ▷ *une peau grasse* oily skin; **faire la grasse matinée** to sleep in **❹** (type) bold ▷ *Mets le titre en caractères gras.* Put the title in bold type.

gratte-ciel [ɡʀatsjɛl] (pl **gratte-ciel**) nm skyscraper

gratter [ɡʀate] vb **❶** to scratch ▷ *Ne gratte pas tes piqûres de moustiques.* Don't scratch your mosquito bites. **❷** to be itchy ▷ *C'est épouvantable comme ça gratte!* It's terribly itchy!

gratuit [gʀatɥi, -ɥit] (f **gratuite**) adj free
▷ entrée gratuite entrance free ▷ J'ai deux
places gratuites pour le concert. I've got two
complimentary tickets for the concert.

grave [gʀav] adj ❶ serious ▷ une maladie grave
a serious illness ▷ Elle avait l'air grave. She was
looking serious. ❷ deep ▷ Il a une voix grave.
He's got a deep voice.; Ce n'est pas grave. It
doesn't matter. ▷ J'ai oublié ma clé. » « Ce n'est
pas grave, j'ai la mienne. » "I forgot my key." "It
doesn't matter, I've got mine."

gravement [gʀavmɑ̃] adv seriously ▷ Il a été
gravement blessé. He was seriously injured.

graver [gʀave] vb ❶ (CDs) to burn ❷ to
engrave ▷ Son nom était gravé sur la bague. Her
name was engraved on the ring.

graveur [gʀavœʀ] nm: **un graveur de DC** a
CD burner

grêle [gʀɛl] nf hail

grêler [gʀele] vb: **Il grêle.** It's hailing.

grelotter [gʀɑlɔte] vb to shiver

grenade [gʀɑnad] nf ❶ pomegranate
❷ grenade

grenier [gʀɑnje] nm attic

grenouille [gʀɑnuj] nf frog

grève [gʀɛv] nf ❶ strike; **en grève** on strike
▷ Ils sont en grève depuis dix jours. They have been
on strike for ten days.; **être en grève** to be on
strike; **se mettre en grève** to go on strike; **un
piquet de grève** a picket line ❷ shore ▷ Nous
nous sommes promenés le long de la grève. We
went for a walk along the shore.

gréviste [gʀevist(ə)] nmf striker

grièvement [gʀijevmɑ̃] adv: **grièvement
blessé** seriously injured

griffe [gʀif] nf ❶ claw ▷ Le chat m'a donné un
coup de griffe. The cat scratched me. ❷ label
▷ la griffe d'un grand couturier the label of a top
designer

griffer [gʀife] vb to scratch ▷ Le chat m'a griffé.
The cat scratched me.

grignoter [gʀiɲɔte] vb to nibble

grillade [gʀijad] nf grilled food ▷ une grillade
de légumes grilled vegetables

grille [gʀij] nf ❶ (chain-link) fence ▷ L'usine
est entourée d'une haute grille. The factory is
surrounded by a high fence. ❷ (metal) gate
▷ la grille du jardin the garden gate

grille-pain [gʀijpɛ̃] (pl **grille-pain**) nm
toaster

griller [gʀije] vb ❶ to toast; **du pain grillé**
toast ❷ to grill ▷ des saucisses grillées grilled
sausages

grimace [gʀimas] nf: **faire des grimaces** to
make faces

grimper [gʀɛ̃pe] vb to climb

grincer [gʀɛ̃se] vb to creak

grincheux [gʀɛ̃ʃø, -øz] (f **grincheuse**) adj
grumpy

grippe [gʀip] nf flu; **avoir la grippe** to have
the flu ▷ J'ai eu une mauvaise grippe l'hiver dernier.
I had a bad attack of the flu last winter.

grippé [gʀipe] (f **grippée**) adj: **être grippé** to
have the flu

gris [gʀi, gʀiz] (f **grise**) adj grey

grizzly [gʀizli] nm grizzly bear

grogner [gʀɔɲe] vb to growl ▷ Le chien a grogné
quand je me suis approché de lui. The dog growled
when I went near it.

gronder [gʀɔ̃de] vb ❶ to rumble ▷ J'entends le
tonnerre gronder au loin. I hear thunder rumbling
in the distance. ❷ (animal) to roar; **se faire
gronder** to get told off ▷ Tu vas te faire gronder
par ton père! You're going to get bawled out by
your father!

gros [gʀo, gʀos] (f **grosse**) adj ❶ big ▷ une
grosse pomme a big apple ❷ fat; to roar; **le gros plan**
close-up ▷ Voici un gros plan de mon petit ami.
Here's a close-up of my boyfriend.

groseille [gʀozɛj] nf: **la groseille rouge**
redcurrant; **la groseille à maquereau**
gooseberry

grossesse [gʀosɛs] nf pregnancy

grossier [gʀosje, -jɛʀ] (f **grossière**) adj rude
▷ Ne sois pas si grossier! Don't be so rude!; **une
erreur grossière** a serious mistake

grossir [gʀosiʀ] vb to put on weight ▷ Il a
beaucoup grossi. He's put on a lot of weight.

grosso modo [gʀosomɔdo] adv roughly
▷ Dis-moi grosso modo ce que tu en penses. Give
me a rough idea what you think of it.

grotte [gʀɔt] nf cave

groupe [gʀup] nm group ▷ votre groupe sanguin
your blood group

grouper [gʀupe] vb to group ▷ On nous a
groupés dans différentes classes selon notre niveau.
We were grouped in different classes according
to our level.; **se grouper** to gather ▷ Nous nous
sommes groupés autour du feu. We gathered
round the fire.

gruau [gʀyo] nm porridge

guêpe [gɛp] nf wasp

guérir [geʀiʀ] vb to recover ▷ Elle est
maintenant complètement guérie. She's now
completely recovered.

guérison [geʀizɔ̃] nf recovery; **la guérison
spirituelle** spiritual healing

guerre [gɛʀ] nf war ▷ en guerre at war ▷ une
guerre civile a civil war ▷ la Deuxième Guerre
mondiale the Second World War

guetter [gete] vb to watch for ▷ Elle guette
l'arrivée du facteur tous les matins. She watches
for the letter carrier every morning.

gueule [gœl] nf (rude when used for people)
mouth ▷ Le chat a ramené une souris dans sa
gueule. The cat brought a mouse in its mouth.

gueuler [gœle] vb (informal) to bawl

guichet [giʃɛ] nm (in bank, airport) counter; **le
guichet automatique** bank machine

guide [gid] nm guide

guider [gide] vb to guide

guidon [gidɔ̃] nm handlebars

guillemets [gijmɛ] nmpl quotation marks
▷ entre guillemets in quotes

guimauve [gimov] nf marshmallow; **à la
guimauve** (sentimental) sappy ▷ C'est vraiment
un film à la guimauve. This is a really sappy
movie.

guirlande [giʀlɑ̃d] nf: **des guirlandes** tinsel;
des guirlandes en papier paper chains

guitare [gitaʀ] nf guitar ▷ Sais-tu jouer de la
guitare? Can you play the guitar?

gymnase [ʒimnɑz] nm gym ▷ *L'école a un nouveau gymnase.* The school has a new gym.

gymnastique [ʒimnastik] nf gymnastics ▷ *faire de la gymnastique* to do gymnastics

h

habile [abil] adj skilful ▷ *Elle est très habile de ses mains.* She's very skilled with her hands.

habillé [abije] (f **habillée**) adj ❶ dressed ▷ *Il n'est pas encore habillé.* He's not dressed yet. ❷ smart ▷ *Cette robe fait très habillé.* This dress looks very smart.

s'habiller [abije] vb ❶ to get dressed ▷ *Je me suis rapidement habillé.* I got dressed quickly. ❷ to dress up ▷ *Est-ce qu'il faut s'habiller pour la réception?* Do you have to dress up to go to the party?

l'**habitant** [abitɑ̃] nm inhabitant ▷ *Les habitants du quartier sont contre ce projet.* The local people are against this plan.

l'**habitante** [abitɑ̃t] nf inhabitant

l'**habitat** [abita] nm habitat ▷ *l'habitat naturel du castor* the natural habitat of the beaver ▷ *un habitat menacé* a threatened habitat; **la conservation de l'habitat** habitat conservation

habiter [abite] vb to live ▷ *Il habite à Kitimat.* He lives in Kitimat.

les **habits** [abi] nmpl clothes

l'**habitude** [abityd] nf habit ▷ *une mauvaise habitude* a bad habit; **avoir l'habitude de quelque chose** to be used to something ▷ *Elle a l'habitude des enfants.* She's used to children. ▷ *Je n'ai pas l'habitude de parler en public.* I'm not used to speaking in public.; **d'habitude** usually; **comme d'habitude** as usual

habituel [abityɛl] (f **habituelle**) adj usual

s'habituer [abitɥe] vb: **s'habituer à quelque chose** to get used to something ▷ *Il faudra que tu t'habitues à te lever tôt.* You'll have to get used to getting up early.

la **hache** [aʃ] nf axe; **mettre la hache dans les frais** to cut expenses drastically

hacher [aʃe] vb (meat) to grind; **du bœuf haché** ground beef

la **haie** [ɛ] nf hedge

la **haine** [ɛn] nf hatred

haïr [aiʁ] vb to hate ▷ *Je hais les piqûres de moustique.* I hate mosquito bites.

l'**haleine** [alɛn] nf breath ▷ *avoir mauvaise haleine* to have bad breath ▷ *être hors d'haleine* to be out of breath

le **hall** ['ol] nm (hotel) lobby; **le hall d'exposition** exhibition hall

la **halte** ['alt(ə)] nf stop ▷ *faire halte* to make a stop; **Halte!** Stop!; **une halte routière** a rest stop

l'**haltérophilie** [alteʁɔfili] nf weightlifting

le **hamburger** ['ãbuʁgœʁ] nm hamburger

l'**hameçon** [amsɔ̃] nm fish hook

le **hamster** ['amstɛʁ] nm hamster

la **hanche** ['ãʃ] nf hip

le **handball** ['ãdbal] nm handball ▷ *jouer au handball* to play handball

le **handicapé** ['ãdikape] nm disabled man

la **handicapée** ['ãdikape] nf disabled woman

le **harcèlement** ['aʁsɛlmã] nm harassment ▷ *le harcèlement sexuel* sexual harassment

le **hareng** ['aʁã] nm herring

le **harfang** ['aʁfã] nm snowy owl

le **haricot** ['aʁiko] nm bean; **les haricots au lard** baked beans; **les haricots verts** green beans

le **harpon** ['aʁpɔ̃] nm harpoon

le **hasard** ['azaʁ] nm coincidence ▷ *C'était un pur hasard.* It was pure coincidence.; **au hasard** at random ▷ *Choisis un numéro au hasard.* Choose a number at random.; **par hasard** by chance ▷ *Je l'ai rencontrée tout à fait par hasard au supermarché.* I ran into her completely by chance at the supermarket.; **à tout hasard (1)** just in case ▷ *Prends un parapluie à tout hasard.* Take an umbrella just in case. **(2)** on the off chance ▷ *Je ne sais pas s'il est chez lui, mais je vais l'appeler à tout hasard.* I don't know if he's at home, but I'll phone on the off chance.

la **hâte** ['ɑt] nf: **à la hâte** hurriedly ▷ *Elle s'est habillée à la hâte.* She got dressed hurriedly.; **J'ai hâte de te voir.** I can't wait to see you.

la **hausse** ['os] nf ❶ increase ▷ *la hausse des prix* price increase ❷ rise ▷ *On annonce une légère hausse de température.* They're forecasting a slight rise in temperature.

hausser ['ose] vb: **hausser les épaules** to shrug one's shoulders

haut ['o, 'ot] (f **haute**) adj, adv ❶ high ▷ *une haute montagne* a high mountain ❷ aloud ▷ *penser tout haut* to think aloud ▶ nm: **le haut** top; **un mur de trois mètres de haut** a wall 3 metres high; **en haut (1)** upstairs ▷ *La salle de bain est en haut.* The bathroom is upstairs. **(2)** at the top ▷ *Le nid est tout en haut de l'arbre.* The nest is right at the top of the tree.

le **Haut-Canada** nm Upper Canada

la **hauteur** ['otœʁ] nf height

le **haut-parleur** ['opaʁlœʁ] nm (pl **haut-parleurs**) nm (stereo, computer) speaker

l'**hebdomadaire** [ɛbdɔmadɛʁ] nm (magazine) weekly

l'**hébergement** [ebɛʁʒəmã] nm accommodation

héberger [ebɛʁʒe] vb (guest) to put up ▷ *Mon cousin a dit qu'il nous hébergerait.* My cousin said he would put us up.

hein? ['ɛ̃] excl eh?; **C'était tout un match, hein?** That was quite a game, eh?; **Tu as pris le dernier morceau de tarte, hein?** You took the last piece of pie, eh?; **Hein? Qu'est-ce que tu**

dis? Eh? What did you say?

hélas [ˈelɑs] adv unfortunately ▷ *Hélas, il ne restait plus de billets.* Unfortunately there were no tickets left.

l' **hélicoptère** [elikɔptɛʀ] nm helicopter

l' **herbe** [ɛʀb(ə)] nf grass; **les fines herbes** herbs; **l'herbe à poux** ragweed; **l'herbe à puce** poison ivy

hériter [eʀite] vb to inherit

hermétique [ɛʀmetik] adj airtight

l' **héroïne** [eʀɔin] nf heroine ▷ *l'héroïne du roman* the heroine of the novel

le **héros** [ˈeʀo] nm hero

l' **hésitation** [ezitɑsjɔ̃] nf hesitation

hésiter [ezite] vb to hesitate ▷ *Il n'a pas hésité à nous aider.* He didn't hesitate to help us. ▷ *J'ai hésité entre le chandail vert et la chemise jaune.* I couldn't decide between the green pullover and the yellow shirt. ▷ « *Est-ce que tu viens ce soir?* » « *J'hésite...* » "Are you coming tonight?" "I'm not sure..."; **sans hésiter** without hesitating

l' **heure** [œʀ] nf ❶ hour ▷ *Le trajet dure six heures.* The trip takes six hours. ❷ time ▷ *Vous avez l'heure?* Have you got the time?; **Quelle heure est-il?** What time is it?; **À quelle heure?** What time? ▷ *À quelle heure arrivons-nous?* What time do we arrive?; **deux heures du matin** 2 o'clock in the morning; **être à l'heure** to be on time; **l'heure avancée** daylight-saving time; **l'heure normale** standard time

heureusement [œʀøzmɑ̃] adv luckily ▷ *Heureusement qu'elle n'a pas été blessée.* Luckily she wasn't hurt.

heureux [œʀø, -øz] (f **heureuse**) adj happy

heurter [ˈœʀte] vb to hit ▷ *Je me suis heurté la tête contre la porte.* I hit my head on the door.

hiberner [ibɛʀne] vb to hibernate

le **hibou** [ˈibu] (pl **hiboux**) nm owl

hier [jɛʀ] adv yesterday; **avant-hier** the day before yesterday

hindou [ɛ̃du] ajective Hindu
  ▷ nm Hindu

l' **hindoue** [ɛ̃du] nf Hindu

l' **hippopotame** [ipɔpɔtam] nm hippopotamus

l' **histoire** [istwaʀ] nf ❶ history ▷ *un cours d'histoire* a history lesson ❷ story ▷ *Ce roman raconte l'histoire de deux enfants.* This novel tells the story of two children.; **Ne fais pas d'histoires!** Don't make a fuss!; **une histoire à succès** a success story

historique [istɔʀik] adj ❶ historic ▷ *un monument historique* a historic monument ❷ historical ▷ *un musée historique* a historical museum

l' **hiver** [ivɛʀ] nm winter; **en hiver** in winter

le **hockey** [ˈɔkɛ] nm hockey ▷ *un joueur de hockey* a hockey player ▷ *un bâton de hockey* a hockey stick; **le hockey sur glace** ice hockey

le **homard** [ˈɔmaʀ] nm lobster

l' **hommage** [ɔmaʒ] nm tribute

l' **homme** [ɔm] nm man; **un homme d'affaires** a businessman

homosexuel [ɔmɔsɛksɥɛl] (f **homosexuelle**) adj homosexual

honnête [ɔnɛt] adj honest; **bien honnête (person)** decent

l' **honnêteté** [ɔnɛtte] nf honesty

l' **honneur** [ɔnœʀ] nm honour ▷ *en l'honneur de nos grands-parents* in honour of our grandparents

la **honte** [ˈɔ̃t] nf shame ▷ *avoir honte de quelque chose* to be ashamed of something

l' **hôpital** [ɔpital, -o] (pl **hôpitaux**) nm hospital

le **hoquet** [ˈɔkɛ] nm: **avoir le hoquet** to have hiccups

l' **horaire** [ɔʀɛʀ] nm ❶ timetable ❷ schedule; **l'horaire d'autobus** the bus schedule

l' **horizon** [ɔʀizɔ̃] nm horizon

horizontal [ɔʀizɔ̃tal, -o] (f **horizontale**, mpl **horizontaux**) adj horizontal

l' **horloge** [ɔʀlɔʒ] nf clock

l' **horreur** [ɔʀœʀ] nf horror ▷ *un film d'horreur* a horror movie; **avoir horreur de** to hate ▷ *J'ai horreur du chou.* I hate cabbage.

horrible [ɔʀibl(ə)] adj horrible

hors [ˈɔʀ] prep: **hors de** out of ▷ *Elle est hors de danger maintenant.* She's out of danger now.; **hors taxes** duty-free

le **hors-d'œuvre** (pl **hors-d'œuvre**) nm appetizer

hospitalier [ɔspitalje, -jɛʀ] (f **hospitalière**) adj hospitable ▷ *Ils sont très hospitaliers.* They're very hospitable.; **les services hospitaliers** hospital services

l' **hospitalité** [ɔspitalite] nf hospitality

hostile [ɔstil] adj hostile

le **hot-dog** [ˈɔtdɔg] nm hot dog ▷ *des hot-dogs relish-moutarde* hot dogs with relish and mustard

l' **hôte** [ot] nmf ❶ host ▷ *N'oubliez pas de remercier vos hôtes.* Don't forget to thank your hosts. ❷ guest ▷ *des hôtes payants* paying guests

l' **hôtel** [otɛl] nm hotel; **l'hôtel de ville** the town hall

l' **hôtesse** [otɛs] nf hostess

la **housse** [ˈus] nf cover ▷ *une housse de couette* a quilt cover ▷ *une housse de siège* a seat cover

le **houx** [ˈu] nm holly

le **huard** [ˈɥaʀ] nm ❶ loon ❷ loonie

l' **huile** [ɥil] nf oil; **l'huile solaire** suntan oil

huit [ˈɥi(t)] num eight ▷ *Il est huit heures du matin.* It's eight in the morning. ▷ *Il a huit ans.* He's eight.; **le huit février** the eighth of February; **dans huit jours** in a week's time

la **huitaine** [ˈɥitɛn] nf: **une huitaine de jours** about a week ▷ *Nous serons de retour dans une huitaine de jours.* We'll be back in about a week.

huitième [ˈɥitjɛm] adj eighth ▷ *au huitième étage* on the eighth floor

l' **huître** [ɥitʀ(ə)] nf oyster

humain [ymɛ̃, -ɛn] (f **humaine**) adj human
  ▷ nm: **l'humaine** human being

l' **humeur** [ymœʀ] nf mood ▷ *Il est de bonne humeur.* He's in a good mood. ▷ *Elle était de mauvaise humeur.* She was in a bad mood.

humide [ymid] adj ❶ damp ▷ *L'herbe est humide.* The grass is damp. ▷ *un climat humide* a damp climate ❷ moist ❸ humid

l' **humidex** [ymidɛks] n humidex

humilier [ymilje] vb to humiliate

humoristique [ymɔʀistik] adj humorous; **des dessins humoristiques** cartoons

l' **humour** [ymuʀ] nm humour ▷ *Il n'a pas*

beaucoup d'humour. He doesn't have much sense of humour.

hurler ['yʀle] *vb* to howl

la **hutte** ['yt] *nf* hut

hydratant [idʀatɑ̃, -ɑ̃t] (**f hydratante**) *adj*: **une crème hydratante** a moisturizing cream

l' **hygiène** [iʒjɛn] *nf* hygiene

hygiénique [iʒenik] *adj* hygienic; **une serviette hygiénique** a sanitary napkin; **le papier hygiénique** toilet paper

l' **hymne** [imn(ə)] *nm*: **l'hymne national** the national anthem ▷ *Notre hymne national est Ô Canada.* Our national anthem is O Canada.

l' **hyperlien** [ipɛʀljɛ̃] *nm* hyperlink

hypermétrope [ipɛʀmetʀɔp] *adj* long-sighted

l' **hypothèse** [ipotɛz] *nf* hypothesis

◆

I

iceberg [isbɛʀg] *nm* iceberg; **la pointe de l'iceberg** the tip of the iceberg

ici [isi] *adv* here ▷ *Les assiettes sont ici.* The plates are here.; **La mer monte parfois jusqu'ici.** The tide sometimes comes in as far as this.; **jusqu'ici** so far

icône [ikon] *nf* icon

idéal [ideal, -o] (**f idéale**, *mpl* **idéaux**) *adj* ideal ▷ *C'est l'endroit idéal pour faire un pique-nique.* It's an ideal place to have a picnic.

idée [ide] *nf* idea ▷ *C'est une bonne idée.* It's a good idea.

identifier [idɑ̃tifje] *vb* to identify ▷ *La police a identifié le voleur.* The police have identified the thief.

identique [idɑ̃tik] *adj* identical ▷ *Ils ont obtenu des résultats identiques.* They obtained identical results.

identité [idɑ̃tite] *nf* identity; **une pièce d'identité** a piece of identification ▷ *Avez-vous une pièce d'identité?* Do you have any identification?

idiot [idjo, idjɔt] (**f idiote**) *adj* ❶ stupid ▷ *une plaisanterie idiote* a stupid joke ❷ silly ▷ *Ne sois pas idiot!* Don't be silly!

iglou [iglu] *nm* igloo

ignoble [iɲɔbl(ə)] *adj* horrible ▷ *Il a été ignoble avec elle.* He was horrible to her.

ignorant [iɲɔʀɑ̃, -ɑ̃t] (**f ignorante**) *adj* ignorant

ignorer [iɲɔʀe] *vb* ❶ not to know ▷ *J'ignore son nom.* I don't know his name. ❷ to ignore ▷ *Il m'a complètement ignoré.* He completely

ignored me.

il [il] *pron* ❶ he ▷ *Il est parti ce matin de bonne heure.* He left early this morning. ❷ it ▷ *Méfie-toi de ce chien : il mord.* Be careful of that dog: it bites. ▷ *Il pleut.* It's raining.

île [il] *nf* island; **l'Île du Cap-Breton** Cape Breton Island; **l'Île de Vancouver** Vancouver Island

illégal [ilegal, -o] (**f illégale**, *mpl* **illégaux**) *adj* illegal

illimité [ilimite] (**f illimitée**) *adj* unlimited

illisible [ilizibl(ə)] *adj* illegible ▷ *une écriture illisible* illegible handwriting

illuminer [ilymine] *vb* to floodlight ▷ *Les chutes sont illuminées tous les soirs pendant l'été.* The falls are floodlit every night in the summer.

illusion [ilyzjɔ̃] *nf* illusion; **Tu te fais des illusions!** Don't kid yourself!

illustration [ilystʀasjɔ̃] *nf* illustration

illustré [ilystʀe] (**f illustrée**) *adj* illustrated
  ▶ *nm* comic

illustrer [ilystʀe] *vb* to illustrate ▷ *Vous pouvez illustrer votre rédaction avec des exemples.* You may illustrate your essay with examples.

ils [il] *pron* they ▷ *Ils nous ont appelés hier soir.* They phoned us last night.

image [imaʒ] *nf* picture ▷ *Les films donnent une fausse image de l'Amérique.* Movies give a false picture of America.

imagination [imaʒinasjɔ̃] *nf* imagination
  ▷ *Elle a beaucoup d'imagination.* She has a vivid imagination.

imaginer [imaʒine] *vb* to imagine

imam [imam] *nm* imam

imbécile [ɛ̃besil] *nmf* idiot

imitation [imitasjɔ̃] *nf* imitation

imiter [imite] *vb* to imitate

immatriculation [imatʀikylasjɔ̃] *nf*: **une plaque d'immatriculation** (*of car*) a licence plate

immédiat [imedja] *nm*: **dans l'immédiat** for the moment ▷ *Je n'ai pas besoin de ce livre dans l'immédiat.* I don't need this book for the moment.

immédiatement [imedjatmɑ̃] *adv* immediately

immense [imɑ̃s] *adj* ❶ huge ▷ *une immense fortune* a huge fortune ❷ tremendous ▷ *un immense soulagement* a tremendous relief

immeuble [imœbl(ə)] *nm* building ▷ *un immeuble résidentiel* an apartment building ▷ *un immeuble de bureaux* an office building

immigration [imigʀasjɔ̃] *nf* immigration

immigré [imigʀe] *nm* immigrant

immigrée [imigʀe] *nf* immigrant

immobile [imɔbil] *adj* motionless

immobilier [imɔbilje, -jɛʀ] (**f immobilière**) *adj*: **une agence immobilière** a real estate agency
  ▶ *nm* real estate

immobiliser [imɔbilize] *vb* to immobilize

immunisé [im(m)ynize] (**f immunisée**) *adj* immunized

impact [ɛ̃pakt] *nm* impact

impair [ɛ̃pɛʀ] (**f impaire**) *adj* odd ▷ *un nombre impair* an odd number

impardonnable [ɛ̃pardɔnabl(ə)] *adj*
unforgivable

impasse [ɛ̃pas] *nf* dead end

impatience [ɛ̃pasjɑ̃s] *nf* impatience

impatient [ɛ̃pasjɑ̃, -ɑ̃t] (*f* **impatiente**) *adj*
impatient

impeccable [ɛ̃pekabl(ə)] *adj* ❶ immaculate
▷ *Sa cuisine est toujours impeccable.* Her kitchen
is always immaculate. ❷ perfect ▷ *Il a fait
un travail impeccable.* He's done a perfect job.
▷ *C'est impeccable!* That's perfect!

impératif [ɛ̃peratif] *nm* imperative

imperméable [ɛ̃pɛrmeabl(ə)] *nm* raincoat

impertinent [ɛ̃pɛrtinɑ̃, -ɑ̃t] (*f* **impertinente**)
adj mouthy ▷ *Ne sois pas impertinent!* Don't be
mouthy!

impitoyable [ɛ̃pitwajabl(ə)] *adj* merciless

impliquer [ɛ̃plike] *vb* to mean ▷ *Si tu vas à
l'université, ça implique que tu vas devoir nous
quitter.* If you go to university, that means
you'll have to leave us.; **être impliqué dans** to
be involved in ▷ *Il est impliqué dans un scandale
financier.* He's involved in a financial scandal.

impoli [ɛ̃pɔli] (*f* **impolie**) *adj* rude

importance [ɛ̃pɔrtɑ̃s] *nf* importance ▷ *C'est
sans importance.* It doesn't matter.

important [ɛ̃pɔrtɑ̃, -ɑ̃t] (*f* **importante**) *adj*
❶ important ▷ *un rôle important* an important
role ❷ considerable ▷ *une somme importante* a
considerable sum

importation [ɛ̃pɔrtasjɔ̃] *nf* import ▷ *Les
importations de pétrole ont baissé.* Oil imports
have fallen.

importer [ɛ̃pɔrte] *vb* ❶ (*goods*) to import
❷ to matter ▷ *Peu importe.* It doesn't matter.

imposant [ɛ̃pozɑ̃, -ɑ̃t] (*f* **imposante**) *adj*
imposing

imposer [ɛ̃poze] *vb* to impose; **imposer
quelque chose à quelqu'un** to make
somebody do something

impossible [ɛ̃pɔsibl(ə)] *adj* impossible
▷ *nm*: **Nous ferons l'impossible pour finir à
temps.** We'll do our utmost to finish on time.

imposteur [ɛ̃pɔstœr] *nm* fake ▷ *Cette femme
est un imposteur.* This woman is a fake.

impôt [ɛ̃po] *nm* tax; **une déclaration
d'impôts** an income tax return

imprécis [ɛ̃presi, -iz] (*f* **imprécise**) *adj*
imprecise

impression [ɛ̃presjɔ̃] *nf* impression ▷ *Il a fait
bonne impression à ma mère.* He made a good
impression on my mother.

impressionnant [ɛ̃presjɔnɑ̃, -ɑ̃t] (*f*
impressionnante) *adj* impressive

impressionner [ɛ̃presjɔne] *vb* to impress

imprévisible [ɛ̃previzibl(ə)] *adj*
unpredictable

imprévu [ɛ̃prevy] (*f* **imprévue**) *adj*
unexpected

imprimante [ɛ̃primɑ̃t] *nf* (*for computer*)
printer

imprimé [ɛ̃prime] (*f* **imprimée**) *adj* printed
▷ *un tissu imprimé* a printed fabric ▷ *C'est
imprimé en grandes lettres.* It's printed in large
letters.

imprimer [ɛ̃prime] *vb* to print

improvisation [ɛ̃prɔvizasjɔ̃] *nf* (*theatre*)
improv ▷ *Nous avons fondé une ligue
d'improvisation à l'école.* We started an improv
club at our school.

improviser [ɛ̃prɔvize] *vb* to improvise

improviste [ɛ̃prɔvist(ə)] *adv*: **arriver à
l'improviste** to arrive unexpectedly

imprudence [ɛ̃prydɑ̃s] *nf* carelessness; **Ne
fais pas d'imprudences!** Don't do anything
stupid!

imprudent [ɛ̃prydɑ̃, -ɑ̃t] (*f* **imprudente**)
adj ❶ unwise ▷ *Il serait imprudent de prendre
la voiture aujourd'hui.* It would be unwise to
take the car today. ❷ careless ▷ *un conducteur
imprudent* a careless driver

impuissant [ɛ̃pɥisɑ̃, -ɑ̃t] (*f* **impuissante**)
adj helpless ▷ *Elle se sentait complètement
impuissante.* She felt completely helpless.

impulsif [ɛ̃pylsif, -iv] (*f* **impulsive**) *adj*
impulsive

inabordable [inabɔrdabl(ə)] *adj*
unaffordable ▷ *des prix inabordables*
unaffordable prices

inaccessible [inaksesibl(ə)] *adj* inaccessible
▷ *Cette plage est inaccessible par la route.* This
beach is inaccessible by road.

inachevé [inaʃve] (*f* **inachevée**) *adj*
unfinished

inadmissible [inadmisibl(ə)] *adj*
unacceptable ▷ *Ce type de comportement
est inadmissible!* This sort of behaviour is
unacceptable!

inanimé [inanime] (*f* **inanimée**) *adj*
unconscious ▷ *On l'a retrouvé inanimé sur la
route.* He was found unconscious on the road.

inaperçu [inapɛrsy] (*f* **inaperçue**) *adj*: **passer
inaperçu** to go unnoticed

inattendu [inatɑ̃dy] (*f* **inattendue**) *adj*
unexpected

inattention [inatɑ̃sjɔ̃] *nf*: **une faute
d'inattention** a careless mistake

inaugurer [inɔgyre] *vb* (*an exhibition*) to open

incapable [ɛ̃kapabl(ə)] *adj* incapable ▷ *être
incapable de faire quelque chose* to be incapable
of doing something

incassable [ɛ̃kasabl(ə)] *adj* unbreakable

incendie [ɛ̃sɑ̃di] *nm* fire ▷ *un incendie de forêt*
a forest fire

incertain [ɛ̃sɛrtɛ̃, -ɛn] (*f* **incertaine**) *adj*
❶ uncertain ▷ *Son avenir est encore incertain.*
Her future is still uncertain. ❷ unsettled ▷ *Le
temps est incertain.* The weather is unsettled.

inciter [ɛ̃site] *vb*: **inciter quelqu'un à faire
quelque chose** to encourage somebody to
do something ▷ *J'ai incité mes parents à partir
en voyage.* I encouraged my parents to go on
a trip.

inclure [ɛ̃klyr] *vb* to enclose ▷ *Veuillez inclure
une enveloppe timbrée libellée à votre adresse.*
Please enclose a stamped self-addressed
envelope.; **Les piles sont incluses.** Batteries
are included.

incohérent [ɛ̃kɔerɑ̃, -ɑ̃t] (*f* **incohérente**) *adj*
incoherent

incolore [ɛ̃kɔlɔr] *adj* colourless

incompétent [ɛ̃kɔ̃petɑ̃, -ɑ̃t] (*f*

incompétente) adj incompetent
incompris [ɛ̃kɔ̃pʀi, -iz] (**fincomprise**) adj misunderstood
inconnu [ɛ̃kɔny] nm stranger ▷ Ne parle pas à des inconnus. Don't speak to strangers.; **l'inconnu** the unknown ▷ la peur de l'inconnu the fear of the unknown
inconnue [ɛ̃kɔny] nf stranger
inconsciemment [ɛ̃kɔ̃sjamɑ̃] adv unconsciously
inconscient [ɛ̃kɔ̃sjɑ̃, -ɑ̃t] (**finconsciente**) adj unconscious ▷ Il est resté inconscient quelques minutes. He was unconscious for several minutes.
incontestable [ɛ̃kɔ̃tɛstablə] adj indisputable
incontournable [ɛ̃kɔ̃tuʀnablə] adj essential ▷ Ce livre est incontournable. This book is essential reading.
inconvénient [ɛ̃kɔ̃venjɑ̃] nm disadvantage; **si vous n'y voyez pas d'inconvénient** if you have no objection
incorrect [ɛ̃kɔʀɛkt] (**fincorrecte**) adj ❶ incorrect ▷ une réponse incorrecte an incorrect answer ❷ rude ▷ Il a été incorrect avec la voisine. He was rude to the woman next door.
incroyable [ɛ̃kʀwajablə] adj incredible
inculper [ɛ̃kylpe] vb: **inculper de** to charge with ▷ Elle a été inculpée de fraude. She was charged with fraud.
indécis [ɛ̃desi, -iz] (**findécise**) adj ❶ indecisive ▷ Il est constamment indécis. He's always indecisive. ❷ undecided ▷ Je suis encore indécis. I'm still undecided.
indéfiniment [ɛ̃definimɑ̃] adv indefinitely
indélicat [ɛ̃delika, -at] (**findélicate**) adj tactless
indemne [ɛ̃dɛmnə] adj unharmed ▷ Elle s'en est sortie indemne. She escaped unharmed.
indemniser [ɛ̃dɛmnize] vb to compensate ▷ Les victimes demandent maintenant à être indemnisées. The victims are now demanding compensation.
indépendamment [ɛ̃depɑ̃damɑ̃] adv independently; **indépendamment de** irrespective of ▷ Les allocations familiales devraient être versées indépendamment des revenus. The child tax credit should be given irrespective of income.
indépendance [ɛ̃depɑ̃dɑ̃s] nf independence
indépendant [ɛ̃depɑ̃dɑ̃, -ɑ̃t] (f **indépendante**) adj independent
index [ɛ̃dɛks] nm ❶ index finger ❷ (in book) index
indicatif [ɛ̃dikatif, -iv] (**findicative**) adj: **à titre indicatif** for your information ▶ nm ❶ (of verb) indicative ❷ (of TV show) theme song; **l'indicatif régional** area code
indications [ɛ̃dikasjɔ̃] nfpl instructions ▷ Il suffit de suivre les indications. You just have to follow the instructions.
indice [ɛ̃dis] nm clue ▷ La police cherche des indices. The police are looking for clues.
indifférence [ɛ̃difeʀɑ̃s] nf indifference
indifférent [ɛ̃difeʀɑ̃, -ɑ̃t] (**findifférente**) adj indifferent

indigène [ɛ̃diʒɛn] adj native ▷ les peuples indigènes du Canada the native peoples of Canada ▷ Cette espèce n'est pas indigène au Canada. This species is not native to Canada.
indigeste [ɛ̃diʒɛst(ə)] adj indigestible
indigestion [ɛ̃diʒɛstjɔ̃] nf indigestion
indigne [ɛ̃diɲ] adj unworthy
indigner [ɛ̃diɲe] vb to outrage ▷ Ses propos ont indigné toute l'équipe. Her remarks outraged the whole team.; **s'indigner de quelque chose** to be outraged by something
indiqué [ɛ̃dike] (**findiquée**) adj advisable ▷ Ce n'est pas très indiqué. It's not really advisable.
indiquer [ɛ̃dike] vb to point out ▷ Il m'a indiqué la mairie. He pointed out the town hall to me.
indirect [ɛ̃diʀɛkt] (**findirecte**) adj indirect
indiscipliné [ɛ̃disipline] (**findisciplinée**) adj unruly
indiscret [ɛ̃diskʀe, -ɛt] (**findiscrète**) adj indiscreet
indispensable [ɛ̃dispɑ̃sablə] adj indispensable
individu [ɛ̃dividy] nm individual
individuel [ɛ̃dividɥɛl] (**findividuelle**) adj individual ▷ servi en portions individuelles served in individual portions; **Vous aurez une chambre individuelle.** You'll have a room to yourself.
indolore [ɛ̃dɔlɔʀ] adj painless
indulgent [ɛ̃dylʒɑ̃, -ɑ̃t] (**findulgente**) adj indulgent; **Elle est trop indulgente avec son fils.** She's not firm enough with her son.
industrie [ɛ̃dystʀi] nf industry
industriel [ɛ̃dystʀijɛl] (**findustrielle**) adj industrial
inédit [inedi, -it] (**finédite**) adj unpublished
inefficace [inefikas] adj ❶ (treatment) ineffective ❷ inefficient ▷ un service de transports publics inefficace an inefficient public transit system
inégal [inegal, -o] (**finégale**, mpl **inégaux**) adj ❶ unequal ▷ un combat inégal an unequal struggle ❷ uneven ▷ La qualité est inégale. The quality is uneven.
inévitable [inevitablə] adj unavoidable; **C'était inévitable!** That was bound to happen!
inexact [inegzakt] (**finexacte**) adj inaccurate
infaillible [ɛ̃fajiblə] adj foolproof
infarctus [ɛ̃faʀktys] nm coronary
infatigable [ɛ̃fatigablə] adj tireless ▷ Il est infatigable. He's a tireless worker.
infect [ɛ̃fɛkt] (**finfecte**) adj (meal) revolting
s'infecter [ɛ̃fɛkte] vb to get infected ▷ La plaie s'est infectée. The wound has become infected.
infection [ɛ̃fɛksjɔ̃] nf infection
inférieur [ɛ̃feʀjœʀ] (**finférieure**) adj lower ▷ les membres inférieurs the lower limbs ▷ C'est moins cher, mais de qualité inférieure. It's cheaper but of lower quality.
infernal [ɛ̃fɛʀnal, -o] (**finfernale**, mpl **infernaux**) adj terrible ▷ Ils faisaient un bruit infernal. They were making a terrible noise.
infini [ɛ̃fini] nm infinite; **à l'infini** indefinitely ▷ On pourrait en parler à l'infini. We could discuss this indefinitely.

infinitif [ɛ̃finitif] *nm* infinitive
infirmerie [ɛ̃fiRməRi] *nf* sick room ▷ *Elle est à l'infirmerie.* She's in the sick room.
infirmier [ɛ̃fiRmje] *nm* nurse
infirmière [ɛ̃fiRmjɛR] *nf* nurse
inflammable [ɛ̃flamabl(ə)] *adj* flammable
influence [ɛ̃flyɑ̃s] *nf* influence
influencer [ɛ̃flyɑ̃se] *vb* to influence
infopublicité [ɛ̃fopyblisite] *nf* (TV, radio) infomercial
informaticien [ɛ̃fɔRmatisjɛ̃] *nm* computer scientist
informaticienne [ɛ̃fɔRmatisjɛn] *nf* computer scientist
information [ɛ̃fɔRmasjɔ̃] *nf* information ▷ *Je voudrais de l'information sur la Saskatchewan, s'il vous plaît.* I'd like some information about Saskatchewan, please.; **une information** a piece of information; **les informations** (TV, radio) the news
informatique [ɛ̃fɔRmatik] *nf* computer technology
informer [ɛ̃fɔRme] *vb* to inform; **s'informer** to find out ▷ *Je ne connais pas les heures de fermeture, mais je vais m'informer.* I don't know when they close, but I'm going to find out.
infuser [ɛ̃fyze] *vb* (tea) to steep
infusion [ɛ̃fyzjɔ̃] *nf* herbal tea
ingénieur [ɛ̃ʒenjœR] *nm* engineer
ingénieure [ɛ̃ʒenjœR] *nf* engineer
ingénieux [ɛ̃ʒenjø, -øz] (**f ingénieuse**) *adj* clever ▷ *Quelle solution ingénieuse!* What a clever solution!
ingrat [ɛ̃gRa, -at] (**f ingrate**) *adj* ungrateful
ingrédient [ɛ̃gRedjɑ̃] *nm* ingredient
inhabituel [inabituɛl] (**f inhabituelle**) *adj* unusual
inhumain [inymɛ̃, -ɛn] (**f inhumaine**) *adj* inhuman
ininflammable [inɛ̃flamabl(ə)] *adj* nonflammable
initial [inisjal, -o] (**f initiale, mpl initiaux**) *adj* initial
initiale [inisjal] *nf* initial
initiation [inisjasjɔ̃] *nf* introduction ▷ *un stage d'initiation à la planche à voile* an introductory course in windsurfing
initiative [inisjativ] *nf* initiative ▷ *avoir de l'initiative* to have initiative
injecter [ɛ̃ʒɛkte] *vb* to inject
injection [ɛ̃ʒɛksjɔ̃] *nf* injection
injure [ɛ̃ʒyR] *nf* ❶ insult ▷ *Il a pris ça comme une injure.* He took it as an insult. ❷ abuse ▷ *lancer des injures à quelqu'un* to hurl abuse at somebody
injurier [ɛ̃ʒyRje] *vb* to insult
injurieux [ɛ̃ʒyRjø, -øz] (**f injurieuse**) *adj* (language) abusive
injuste [ɛ̃ʒyst(ə)] *adj* unfair
innocent [inɔsɑ̃, -ɑ̃t] (**f innocente**) *adj* innocent
innombrable [inɔ̃bRabl(ə)] *adj* countless
innover [inɔve] *vb* to break new ground
inoccupé [inɔkype] (**f inoccupée**) *adj* empty ▷ *un appartement inoccupé* an empty apartment
inoffensif [inɔfɑ̃sif, -iv] (**f inoffensive**) *adj* harmless

inondation [inɔ̃dɑsjɔ̃] *nf* flood
inoubliable [inubljabl(ə)] *adj* unforgettable
inoxydable [inɔksidabl(ə)] *adj:* **l'acier inoxydable** stainless steel
inquiet [ɛ̃kjɛ, -ɛt] (**f inquiète**) *adj* worried
inquiétant [ɛ̃kjetɑ̃, -ɑ̃t] (**f inquiétante**) *adj* worrying
inquiéter [ɛ̃kjete] *vb* to worry ▷ *La santé de ma grand-mère inquiète mes parents.* My grandmother's health worries my parents.; **s'inquiéter** (*be worried*) to worry ▷ *Ne t'inquiète pas!* Don't worry!
inquiétude [ɛ̃kjetyd] *nf* anxiety
insatisfait [ɛ̃satisfɛ, -ɛt] (**f insatisfaite**) *adj* dissatisfied
inscription [ɛ̃skRipsjɔ̃] *nf* (for school, course) registration
s'inscrire [ɛ̃skRiR] *vb:* **s'inscrire à** (1) to join ▷ *Je me suis inscrit au club de tennis.* I've joined the tennis club. (2) to register ▷ *N'attends pas trop pour t'inscrire à des cours de natation.* Don't leave it too long to register for swimming lessons.
insecte [ɛ̃sɛkt(ə)] *nm* insect
insensible [ɛ̃sɑ̃sibl(ə)] *adj* insensitive ▷ *Il la trouve insensible.* He thinks she's insensitive.
insérer [ɛ̃seRe] *vb* insert ▷ *Insère le CD dans le lecteur.* Insert the CD in the drive. ▷ *Tu devrais insérer un paragraphe ici pour expliquer.* You should insert a paragraph here, explaining your point.
insigne [ɛ̃siɲ] *nm* badge
insignifiant [ɛ̃siɲifjɑ̃, -ɑ̃t] (**f insignifiante**) *adj* insignificant
insister [ɛ̃siste] *vb* to insist; **N'insiste pas!** Don't keep harping on it!
insolation [ɛ̃sɔlɑsjɔ̃] *nf* sunstroke
insolent [ɛ̃sɔlɑ̃, -ɑ̃t] (**f insolente**) *adj* cheeky
insouciant [ɛ̃susjɑ̃, -ɑ̃t] (**f insouciante**) *adj* carefree
insoutenable [ɛ̃sutnabl(ə)] *adj* unbearable ▷ *une douleur insoutenable* an unbearable pain
inspecter [ɛ̃spɛkte] *vb* to inspect
inspecteur [ɛ̃spɛktœR] *nm* inspector
inspection [ɛ̃spɛksjɔ̃] *nf* inspection
inspectrice [ɛ̃spɛktRis] *nf* inspector
inspirer [ɛ̃spiRe] *vb* ❶ to inspire; **s'inspirer de** to use one's inspiration from ▷ *Le peintre s'est inspiré d'un poème.* The painter took his inspiration from a poem. ❷ to breathe in ▷ *Inspirez! Expirez!* Breathe in! Breathe out!
instable [ɛ̃stabl(ə)] *adj* ❶ (piece of furniture) wobbly ❷ (person) unstable
installations [ɛ̃stalasjɔ̃] *nfpl* facilities ▷ *Cet appartement est pourvu de toutes les installations modernes.* This apartment has all modern facilities.
installer [ɛ̃stale] *vb* to install ▷ *installer un logiciel* to install a computer program ▷ *installer des étagères* to put up some shelves; **s'installer** (be settled in) ▷ *Nous nous sommes installés dans notre nouvel appartement.* We've settled into our new apartment.; **Installez-vous, je vous en prie.** Have a seat, please.
instant [ɛ̃stɑ̃] *nm* moment ▷ *dans un instant*

in a moment ▷ *Le dîner sera prêt dans un instant.* Dinner will be ready in a moment. ▷ *pour l'instant* for the moment

instantané [ɛ̃stɑ̃tane] (f**instantanée**) adj instant ▷ *du café instantané* instant coffee

instinct [ɛ̃stɛ̃] nm instinct

institut [ɛ̃stity] nm institute

institution [ɛ̃stitysjɔ̃] nf institution

instruction [ɛ̃stryksjɔ̃] nf ❶ instruction ▷ *J'ai suivi ses instructions.* I followed her instructions. ❷ education ▷ *Il n'a pas beaucoup d'instruction.* He's not very well-educated.

s'**instruire** [ɛ̃strɥir] vb to educate oneself

instruit [ɛ̃strɥi, -it] (f**instruite**) adj educated

instrument [ɛ̃strymɑ̃] nm instrument ▷ *un instrument de musique* a musical instrument

insuffisant [ɛ̃syfizɑ̃, -ɑ̃t] (f**insuffisante**) adj insufficient ▷ « **travail insuffisant** » (on report card) "must make more effort"

insuline [ɛ̃sylin] nf insulin

insultant [ɛ̃syltɑ̃, -ɑ̃t] (f**insultante**) adj insulting ▷ *Il s'est montré insultant avec elle.* He was insulting towards her.

insulte [ɛ̃sylt(ə)] nf insult

insulter [ɛ̃sylte] vb to insult

insupportable [ɛ̃sypɔrtabl(ə)] adj unbearable

intact [ɛ̃takt] (f**intacte**) adj intact

intégral [ɛ̃tegral, -o] (f**intégrale**, mpl **intégraux**) adj: **le texte intégral** unabridged version; **un remboursement intégral** a full refund

intelligence [ɛ̃teliʒɑ̃s] nf intelligence

intelligent [ɛ̃teliʒɑ̃, -ɑ̃t] (f**intelligente**) adj intelligent

intense [ɛ̃tɑ̃s] adj intense

intensif [ɛ̃tɑ̃sif, -iv] (f**intensive**) adj intensive; **un cours intensif** a crash course

intention [ɛ̃tɑ̃sjɔ̃] nf intention; **avoir l'intention de faire quelque chose** to intend to do something ▷ *J'ai l'intention de lui en parler.* I intend to speak to her about it.

interdiction [ɛ̃tɛrdiksjɔ̃] nf: « **interdiction de stationner** » "no parking"; « **interdiction de fumer** » "no smoking"

interdire [ɛ̃tɛrdir] vb to forbid ▷ *Ses parents lui ont interdit de sortir.* His parents have forbidden him to go out.

interdit [ɛ̃tɛrdi, -it] (f**interdite**) adj ❶ forbidden ▷ *Il est interdit de fumer dans les couloirs.* Smoking in the halls is forbidden. ❷ off-limits ▷ *Cette salle est interdite aux élèves.* This room is off-limits for students.

intéressant [ɛ̃terɛsɑ̃, -ɑ̃t] (f**intéressante**) adj interesting ▷ *un livre intéressant* an interesting book; **On lui a fait une offre intéressante.** They made her an attractive offer.; **On trouve des CD à des prix très intéressants dans ce magasin.** You can get CDs really cheap in this store.

intéresser [ɛ̃terese] vb to interest ▷ *Est-ce que cela t'intéresse?* Does that interest you?; **s'intéresser à** to be interested in ▷ *Est-ce que vous vous intéressez à la politique?* Are you interested in politics?

intérêt [ɛ̃terɛ] nm interest; **avoir intérêt à**

faire quelque chose had better do something ▷ *Tu as intérêt à te dépêcher si tu veux prendre le prochain autobus.* You'd better hurry up if you want to catch the next bus.

intérieur [ɛ̃terjœr] nm inside ▷ *Il fait plus frais à l'intérieur de la maison.* It's cooler inside the house.

interligne [ɛ̃tɛrliɲ] nm: **à double interligne** double-spaced

interlocuteur [ɛ̃tɛrlɔkytœr] nm: **son interlocuteur** the man he's speaking to

interlocutrice [ɛ̃tɛrlɔkytris] nf: **son interlocutrice** the woman he's speaking to

intermédiaire [ɛ̃tɛrmedjɛr] nm intermediary; **par l'intermédiaire de** through ▷ *Je l'ai rencontrée par l'intermédiaire de sa sœur.* I met her through her sister.

international [ɛ̃tɛrnasjɔnal, -o] (f **internationale**, mpl **internationaux**) adj international

internaute [ɛ̃tɛrnot] nmf Internet user

Internet [ɛ̃tɛrnɛt] nm Internet ▷ *sur Internet* on the Internet

interphone [ɛ̃tɛrfɔn] nm intercom

interprète [ɛ̃tɛrprɛt] nmf interpreter

interpréter [ɛ̃tɛrprete] vb to interpret

interrogatif [ɛ̃tɛrɔgatif, -iv] (f **interrogative**) adj interrogative

interrogation [ɛ̃tɛrɔgasjɔ̃] nf ❶ question ▷ test ▷ *une interrogation écrite* a written test

interrogatoire [ɛ̃tɛrɔgatwar] nm questioning; **C'est un interrogatoire ou quoi?** What are you doing, cross-examining me?

interroger [ɛ̃tɛrɔʒe] vb to question

interrompre [ɛ̃tɛrɔ̃pr(ə)] vb to interrupt

interrupteur [ɛ̃tɛryptœr] nm switch

interruption [ɛ̃tɛrypsjɔ̃] nf interruption; **sans interruption** without stopping ▷ *Il a parlé pendant deux heures sans interruption.* He spoke for two hours without stopping.

interurbain [ɛ̃tɛryrbɛ̃] nm long-distance call ▷ *faire un interurbain* to make a long-distance call

intervalle [ɛ̃tɛrval] nm interval; **dans l'intervalle** in the meantime

intervenir [ɛ̃tɛrvənir] vb ❶ to intervene ❷ to take action ▷ *La police est intervenue.* The police took action.

intervention [ɛ̃tɛrvɑ̃sjɔ̃] nf intervention ▷ *une intervention militaire* a military intervention; **une intervention chirurgicale** a surgical operation; **une intervention d'urgence** emergency intervention

interview [ɛ̃tɛrvju] nf (on radio, TV) interview

intestin [ɛ̃tɛstɛ̃] nm intestine

intime [ɛ̃tim] adj intimate; **un journal intime** a diary

intimider [ɛ̃timide] vb to intimidate

intimité [ɛ̃timite] nf: **dans l'intimité** in private ▷ *Dans l'intimité, il est moins guindé.* He's less formal in private.; **Le mariage a eu lieu dans l'intimité.** The wedding ceremony was private.

intitulé [ɛ̃tityle] (f**intitulée**) adj entitled ▷ *un article intitulé « Les jeunes du Canada »* an article entitled "Canada's Youth"

intolérable [ɛ̃tɔlerabl(ə)] *adj* intolerable

intolérance [ɛ̃tɔlerɑ̃s] *nf* intolerance ▷ *une intolérance aux antibiotiques* an antibiotics intolerance ▷ *une attitude d'intolérance envers les autres* an attitude of intolerance towards others

intoxication [ɛ̃tɔksikasjɔ̃] *nf*: **une intoxication alimentaire** food poisoning

intranet *nm* intranet

intransigeant [ɛ̃trɑ̃ziʒɑ̃, -ɑ̃t] (*f* **intransigeante**) *adj* uncompromising

intrigue [ɛ̃trig] *nf* (of book, film) plot

introduction [ɛ̃trɔdyksjɔ̃] *nf* introduction

introduire [ɛ̃trɔdɥir] *vb* to introduce

intuition [ɛ̃tɥisjɔ̃] *nf* intuition

inuit [inɥit] *adj*, *n* Inuit; **un Inuit** (*man*) an Inuk; **une Inuite** (*woman*) an Inuk; **les Inuits** the Inuit

inusable [inyzabl(ə)] *adj* durable

inutile [inytil] *adj* useless

invalide [ɛ̃valid] *nmf* disabled person

invasion [ɛ̃vazjɔ̃] *nf* invasion

inventer [ɛ̃vɑ̃te] *vb* ❶ to invent ❷ to make up ▷ *inventer une excuse* to make up an excuse

inventeur [ɛ̃vɑ̃tœr] *nm* inventor

invention [ɛ̃vɑ̃sjɔ̃] *nf* invention

inventrice [ɛ̃vɑ̃tris] *nf* inventor

inverse [ɛ̃vɛrs(ə)] *adj*: **dans l'ordre inverse** in reverse order; **en sens inverse** in the opposite direction
▶ *nm* reverse; **Tu t'es trompé, c'est l'inverse.** You've got it wrong, it's the other way round.

investissement [ɛ̃vestismɑ̃] *nm* investment

invisible [ɛ̃vizibl(ə)] *adj* invisible

invitation [ɛ̃vitasjɔ̃] *nf* invitation

invité [ɛ̃vite] *nm* guest

invitée [ɛ̃vite] *nf* guest

inviter [ɛ̃vite] *vb* to invite

involontaire [ɛ̃vɔlɔ̃tɛr] *adj* unintentional ▷ *C'était tout à fait involontaire.* It was quite unintentional.

invraisemblable [ɛ̃vrɛsɑ̃blabl(ə)] *adj* unlikely ▷ *une histoire invraisemblable* an unlikely story

ira, irai, iraient, irais *vb see* **aller**; **J'irai demain au supermarché.** I'll go to the supermarket tomorrow.

iras, irez *vb see* **aller**

ironie [irɔni] *nf* irony

ironique [irɔnik] *adj* ironic

irons, iront *vb see* **aller**; **Nous irons à la plage cet après-midi.** We'll go to the beach this afternoon.

irrationnel [irasjɔnɛl] (**f irrationnelle**) *adj* irrational

irréel [ireel] (**f irréelle**) *adj* unreal

irrégulier [iregylje, -jɛr] (**f irrégulière**) *adj* irregular

irrésistible [irezistibl(ə)] *adj* irresistible

irritable [iritabl(ə)] *adj* irritable

irriter [irite] *vb* to irritate

islamique [islamik] *adj* Islamic

isolé [izɔle] (**f isolée**) *adj* isolated ▷ *une ferme isolée* an isolated farm

issue [isy] *nf*: **une voie sans issue** a dead end;

l'issue de secours emergency exit

italique [italik] *nf* italics ▷ *mettre un mot en italique* to put a word in italics

itinéraire [itinerɛr] *nm* route

itinérance [itinerɑ̃s] *nf* homelessness ▷ *Le problème de l'itinérance doit être résolu.* The issue of homelessness needs to be resolved.

itinérant [itinerɑ̃] *nm* homeless man

itinérante [itinerɑ̃t] *nf* homeless woman

ivre [ivr(ə)] *adj* drunk

ivresse [ivrɛs] *nf* drunkenness; **l'ivresse au volant** drunk driving

ivrogne [ivrɔɲ] *nmf* drunk

J

j' [ʒ] *pron see* **je**

jalousie [ʒaluzi] *nf* jealousy

jaloux [ʒalu, -uz] (**f jalouse**) *adj* jealous

jamais [ʒamɛ] *adv* ❶ never ▷ *« Tu vas souvent au cinéma? » « Non, jamais. »* "Do you go to the movies often?" "No, never." ▷ *Il n'écoute jamais la radio.* He never listens to the radio. ❷ ever ▷ *C'est la plus belle chose que j'aie jamais vue.* It's the most beautiful thing I've ever seen.

jambe [ʒɑ̃b] *nf* leg

jambette [ʒɑ̃bɛt] *nf*: **donner une jambette à quelqu'un** to trip somebody up

jambon [ʒɑ̃bɔ̃] *nm* ham

janvier [ʒɑ̃vje] *nm* January; **en janvier** in January

japper [ʒape] *vb* to bark ▷ *Le chien des voisins jappe constamment.* The neighbours' dog is constantly barking.

jardin [ʒardɛ̃] *nm* garden ▷ *un jardin potager* a vegetable garden

jardinage [ʒardinaʒ] *nm* gardening

jardinier [ʒardinje] *nm* gardener

jardinière [ʒardinjɛr] *nf* ❶ gardener ❷ flowerpot

jaser [ʒaze] *vb* to chat ▷ *Ton père jase avec le voisin.* Your father is chatting with the neighbour.; **faire jaser** (*gossip*) to make people talk ▷ *Cela va faire jaser tout le quartier.* That'll set the whole neighbourhood gossiping.

jaune [ʒon] *adj* yellow
▶ *nm* yellow; **un jaune d'œuf** an egg yolk

jaunir [ʒonir] *vb* to turn yellow

Javel [ʒavɛl] *n*: **l'eau de Javel** bleach

jazz [dʒaz] *nm* jazz

J.-C. *abbr* = **Jésus-Christ**; **44 avant J.-C.** 44 BCE; **115 après J.-C.** 115 CE

je [ʒ(ə)] *pron* I ▷ *Je t'appellerai ce soir.* I'll phone you this evening. ▷ *J'arrive!* I'm coming! ▷ *J'hésite.* I'm not sure.

jeans [dʒin] *nmpl* jeans

jet [dʒɛt] *nm* (of water) jet; **un jet d'eau** a fountain

jetable [ʒətabl(ə)] *adj* disposable

jetée [ʒəte] *nf* pier

jeter [ʒəte] *vb* ❶ to throw ▷ *Elle a jeté son sac sur le lit.* She threw her bag onto the bed. ❷ to throw away ▷ *Ils ne jettent jamais rien.* They never throw anything away.; **jeter un coup d'œil sur** to have a look at

jeton [ʒətɔ̃] *nm* (in board game) counter

jeu [ʒø] (*pl* **jeux**) *nm* game ▷ *J'aime les jeux d'adresse.* I like games of skill.; **un jeu d'arcade** a video game; **un jeu de cartes** (1) a pack of cards (2) a card game; **un jeu de hasard** a game of chance; **un jeu de mots** a pun; **un jeu électronique** an electronic game; **un jeu interactif** an interactive game; **les Jeux Olympiques** the Olympic games; **le jeu de rôle** (1) role-play ▷ *Nous avons fait un jeu de rôle sur les restaurants dans le cours de français.* In French class we did a role-play about going to a restaurant. ▷ *Le jeu de rôle est une bonne stratégie d'apprentissage.* Role-play is a good learning strategy. (2) role-playing game; **un jeu de société** (1) a board game (2) a party game; **les jeux vidéo** video games; **en jeu** at stake ▷ *Des vies humaines sont en jeu.* Human lives are at stake.; **hors jeu** (sports) offside

jeudi [ʒødi] *nm* ❶ Thursday ▷ *Aujourd'hui, nous sommes jeudi.* It's Thursday today. ❷ on Thursday ▷ *Il arrivera jeudi matin.* He's arriving on Thursday morning.; **le jeudi** on Thursdays ▷ *Le musée est fermé le jeudi.* The museum is closed on Thursdays.; **tous les jeudis** every Thursday; **jeudi dernier** last Thursday; **jeudi prochain** next Thursday

jeun [ʒɛ̃] *adv* on an empty stomach ▷ *Mange quelque chose.* Il est difficile d'étudier à jeun! Eat something. It's hard to study on an empty stomach!

jeune [ʒœn] *adj* young ▷ *un jeune homme* a young man ▷ *une jeune femme* a young woman; **une jeune fille** a girl
▶ *n* young person ▷ *un concours pour les jeunes* a contest for young people

jeunesse [ʒœnɛs] *nf* youth

job [dʒɔb] *nf* (informal) job

joie [ʒwa] *nf* joy

joindre [ʒwɛ̃dʀ(ə)] *vb* ❶ to put together ▷ *On va joindre les deux tables.* We're going to put the two tables together. ❷ to contact ▷ *Vous pouvez le joindre chez lui.* You can contact him at home.

joint [ʒwɛ̃, -ɛt] (*f* **jointe**) *adj*: **une pièce jointe** (in letter) an enclosure

joli [ʒɔli] (*f* **jolie**) *adj* pretty

jonc [ʒɔ̃] *nm* cattail

jonquille [ʒɔ̃kij] *nf* daffodil

joue [ʒu] *nf* cheek

jouer [ʒwe] *vb* ❶ to play ▷ *Il est allé jouer avec les petits voisins.* He's gone to play with the children next door.; **jouer de** (instrument) to play ▷ *Il joue de la guitare et du piano.* He plays

the guitar and the piano.; **jouer à** (sport, game) to play ▷ *Elle joue au hockey.* She plays hockey. ▷ *jouer aux cartes* to play cards ❷ to act ▷ *Je trouve qu'il joue très bien dans ce film.* I think his acting is very good in this film.; **On joue Hamlet au Théâtre de la Ville.** Hamlet is on at the Théâtre de la Ville.

jouet [ʒwɛ] *nm* toy

joueur [ʒwœʀ] *nm* player; **être mauvais joueur** to be a bad loser

joueuse [ʒwøz] *nf* player

jour [ʒuʀ] *nm* ▷ *J'ai passé trois jours chez mes cousins.* I stayed with my cousins for three days.; **Il fait jour.** It's light out.; **mettre quelque chose à jour** to update something; **le jour de l'An** New Year's Day; **un jour de congé** a day off; **le jour de la marmotte** Groundhog Day; **un jour férié** a public holiday; **dans quinze jours** in two weeks; **de nos jours** nowadays

journal [ʒuʀnal, -o] (*pl* **journaux**) *nm* ❶ newspaper; **le journal télévisé** the news on TV ❷ diary ▷ *Elle tient un journal depuis l'âge de douze ans.* She has been keeping a diary since she was 12. ❸ journal

journalier [ʒuʀnalje, -jɛʀ] (*f* **journalière**) *adj* daily

journalisme [ʒuʀnalism(ə)] *nm* journalism

journaliste [ʒuʀnalist(ə)] *nmf* journalist ▷ *Elle est journaliste.* She's a journalist.

journée [ʒuʀne] *nf* day

joyeux [ʒwajø, -øz] (*f* **joyeuse**) *adj* happy; **Joyeux anniversaire!** Happy birthday!; **Joyeux Noël!** Merry Christmas!

judo [ʒydo] *nm* judo

juge [ʒyʒ] *nmf* judge

juger [ʒyʒe] *vb* to judge

juif [ʒɥif, -iv] (*f* **juive**) *adj* Jewish ▷ *la cuisine juive* Jewish cooking; **un juif** (man) a Jew; **une juive** (woman) a Jew

juillet [ʒɥijɛ] *nm* July; **en juillet** in July

juin [ʒɥɛ̃] *nm* June; **en juin** in June

jumeau [ʒymo] (*pl* **jumeaux**) *nm* twin

jumeler [ʒymle] *vb* to twin ▷ *Thunder Bay est jumelée avec Siderno en Italie.* Thunder Bay is twinned with Siderno, Italy.

jumelle [ʒymɛl] *nf* twin

jumelles [ʒymɛl] *nfpl* binoculars

jument [ʒymɑ̃] *nf* mare

jungle [ʒɔ̃gl(ə)] *nf* jungle

jupe [ʒyp] *nf* skirt

jurer [ʒyʀe] *vb* to swear ▷ *Je jure que c'est vrai!* I swear it's true!

juridique [ʒyʀidik] *adj* (to do with law) legal

jury [ʒyʀi] *nm* jury

jus [ʒy] *nm* juice; **un jus de fruit** a fruit juice

jusqu'à [ʒyska] *prep* ❶ as far as ▷ *Nous avons marché jusqu'au village.* We walked as far as the village. ❷ until ▷ *Il fait généralement chaud jusqu'à la mi-août.* It's usually hot until mid-August.; **jusqu'à ce que** until ▷ *Tu peux rester ici jusqu'à ce qu'il cesse de pleuvoir.* You can stay here until it stops raining.; **jusqu'à présent** so far

jusque [ʒysk(ə)] *prep* as far as ▷ *Je l'ai raccompagnée jusque chez elle.* I went with her as far as her house. ▷ *Jusqu'ici nous n'avons* *pas eu de problèmes.* Up to now we've had no problems. ▷ *Jusqu'où es-tu allé?* How far did you go?

juste [ʒyst(ə)] *adj, adv* ❶ fair ▷ *Elle est sévère, mais juste.* She's strict but fair. ❷ tight ▷ *Ce veston est un peu juste.* This jacket is a bit tight.; **juste assez** just enough; **chanter juste** to sing in tune

justement [ʒystəmɑ̃] *adv* just ▷ *C'est justement pour cela qu'il est parti!* That's just the reason he left!

justesse [ʒystɛs] *nf:* **de justesse** just barely ▷ *Il a eu son permis de justesse.* He just barely passed his driving test.

justice [ʒystis] *nf* justice

justifier [ʒystifje] *vb* to justify

juteux [ʒytø, -øz] (f**juteuse**) *adj* juicy

juvénile [ʒyvenil] *adj* youthful

K

kaki [kaki] *adj* khaki

kangourou [kɑ̃guʀu] *nm* kangaroo

karaté [kaʀate] *nm* karate

kayak [kajak] *nm* kayak ▷ *Ils ont fait une expédition de kayak aux îles de la Reine-Charlotte.* They went on a kayak trip to the Queen Charlotte Islands.; **faire du kayak** to go kayaking

kayakiste [kajakist] *nmf* kayaker

kétaine [ketɛn] *adj* tacky ▷ *un bijou kétaine* a tacky piece of jewellery ▷ *des meubles kétaines* tacky furniture

ketchup [kɛtʃœp] *nm* ketchup

kidnapper [kidnape] *vb* to kidnap

kidnappeur [kidnapœʀ] *nm* kidnapper

kidnappeuse [kidnapøz] *nf* kidnapper

kilo [kilo] *nm* kilo

kilogramme [kilɔgʀam] *nm* kilogram

kilomètre [kilɔmɛtʀ(ə)] *nm* kilometre

kiosque [kjɔsk(ə)] *nm* kiosk; **un kiosque à journaux** a newsstand

kit [kit] *nm:* **en kit** ready to assemble ▷ *Nous avons acheté une étagère en kit.* We bought a bookshelf that you put together yourself.

klaxon [klaksɔn] *nm* (of car) horn

klaxonner [klaksɔne] *vb* to blow the horn

km *abbr* = **kilomètre**; **km/h** kph (= *kilometres per hour*)

l' [l] *art, pron see* **la, le**

la [la] *art, pron* ❶ the ▷ *la maison* the house ▷ *l'actrice* the actress ▷ *l'herbe* the grass ❷ her ▷ *Je la connais depuis longtemps.* I've known her for a long time. ▷ *C'est une femme intelligente : je l'admire beaucoup.* She's an intelligent woman: I admire her very much. ❸ it ▷ *C'est une bonne émission : je la regarde tous les jours.* It's a good program: I watch it every day. ❹ one's; **se mordre la langue** to bite one's tongue ▷ *Je me suis mordu la langue.* I bit my tongue.; **deux dollars la douzaine** two dollars a dozen
▶ *nm* ❶ A ▷ *en la bémol* in A flat ❷ la ▷ *sol, la, si, do* so, la, ti, do

là [la] *adv* ❶ there ▷ *Ton livre est là, sur la table.* Your book's there, on the table. ❷ here ▷ *Elle n'est pas là.* She isn't here.; **C'est là que…** (1) That's where… ▷ *C'est là que je suis né.* That's where I was born. (2) That's when… ▷ *C'est là que j'ai réalisé que je m'étais trompé.* That's when I realized I had made a mistake.

là-bas [labɑ] *adv* over there

laboratoire [labɔʀatwaʀ] *nm* laboratory

labourer [labuʀe] *vb* (fields, soil) to plough

Labrador [labʀadɔʀ] *nm* Labrador

labyrinthe [labiʀɛ̃t] *nm* maze

lac [lak] *nm* lake

lacer [lase] *vb* (shoes) to do up

lacet [lasɛ] *nm* lace; **des chaussures à lacets** lace-up shoes

lâche [lɑʃ] *adj* ❶ loose ▷ *Le nœud est trop lâche.* The knot's too loose. ❷ cowardly; **Il est lâche.** He's a coward.
▶ *nm* coward

lâcher [lɑʃe] *vb* ❶ to let go of ▷ *Elle n'a pas lâché ma main de tout le film.* She didn't let go of my hand through the whole movie. ❷ to drop ▷ *Il a été tellement surpris qu'il a lâché son verre.* He was so surprised that he dropped his glass. ❸ to fail ▷ *Les freins ont lâché.* The brakes failed.

lâcheté [lɑʃte] *nf* cowardice

lacrymogène [lakʀimɔʒɛn] *adj:* **le gaz lacrymogène** tear gas

lacune [lakyn] *nf* gap

là-dedans [ladədɑ̃] *adv* in there ▷ *Qu'est-ce qu'il y a là-dedans?* What's in there?

là-dessous [ladsu] *adv* ❶ under there ▷ *Mon carnet d'adresses est quelque part là-dessous.* My address book is under there somewhere. ❷ behind it ▷ *Il y a quelque chose de louche là-dessous.* There's something fishy behind it.

là-dessus [ladsy] *adv* on there

là-haut [lao] *adv* up there

laid [lɛ, lɛd] *(f* **laide**) *adj* ugly

laideur [lɛdœʀ] *nf* ugliness

laine [lɛn] *nf* wool ▷ *un chandail en laine* a wool sweater; **la laine polaire** *(fabric)* fleece ▷ *une veste en laine polaire* a fleece vest

laïque [laik] *adj*: **une école laïque** a state school

laisse [lɛs] *nf* leash ▷ *Tenez votre chien en laisse.* Keep your dog on a leash.

laisser [lɛse] *vb* ① to leave ▷ *J'ai laissé mon parapluie à la maison.* I've left my umbrella at home. ② to let ▷ *Laisse-le parler.* Let him speak.; **Elle se laisse aller.** She's letting herself go.; **laisser entendre** to imply ▷ *Elle a laissé entendre qu'elle ne venait pas.* She implied that she wasn't coming.; **laisser tomber quelqu'un** to break up with somebody ▷ *Il a laissé tomber sa copine.* He broke up with his girlfriend.

laisser-aller [leseale] *nm* carelessness

lait [lɛ] *nm* milk; **un lait fouetté** a milk shake; **du lait concentré** condensed milk

laitier [letje, -jɛʀ] *(f* **laitière**) *adj* dairy ▷ *une vache laitière* a dairy cow; **les produits laitiers** dairy products

laitue [lety] *nf* lettuce

lambeaux [lãbo] *nmpl*: **en lambeaux** tattered

lame [lam] *nf* blade ▷ *une lame de rasoir* a razor blade

lamelle [lamɛl] *nf* thin strip

lamentable [lamãtabl(ə)] *adj* appalling

se lamenter [lamãte] *vb* to moan

lampadaire [lãpadɛʀ] *nm* ① floor lamp ② street light

lampe [lãp(ə)] *nf* lamp; **une lampe de poche** a flashlight

lance [lãs] *nf* spear

lancement [lãsmã] *nm* launch

lancer [lãse] *vb* ① to throw ▷ *Lance-moi le ballon!* Throw me the ball! ② to launch ▷ *Ils viennent de lancer un nouveau modèle.* They've just launched a new model.; **se lancer** to embark on ▷ *Il s'est lancé là-dedans sans bien réfléchir.* He embarked on it without thinking it through.
▶ *nm*: **le lancer de poids** the shot put; **le lancer frappé** slapshot

lanceur [lãsœʀ] *nm (baseball)* pitcher

lanceuse [lãsøz] *nf (baseball)* pitcher

lancinant [lãsinã, -ãt] *(f* **lancinante**) *adj*: **une douleur lancinante** a shooting pain

langage [lãgaʒ] *nm (other than a specific language)* language ▷ *l'origine du langage* the origin of language ▷ *le langage corporel* body language ▷ *Surveille ton langage!* Watch your language!

langouste [lãgust(ə)] *nf* crayfish

langue [lãg] *nf* ① tongue ▷ *Un petit garçon m'a tiré la langue.* A little boy stuck out his tongue at me.; **sa langue maternelle** her mother tongue ② language ▷ *une langue étrangère* a foreign language ▷ *une langue vivante* a modern language ▷ *les langues officielles du Canada* the official languages of Canada; **la langue non sexiste** inclusive language

lanière [lanjɛʀ] *nf* strap

lanterne [lãtɛʀn(ə)] *nf* lantern

lapin [lapɛ̃] *nm* rabbit

laps [laps] *nm*: **un laps de temps** a space of time

laque [lak] *nf* hair spray

laquelle [lakɛl] *(pl* **lesquelles**) *pron* ① which ▷ *Laquelle de ces photos préfères-tu?* Which of these photos do you prefer? ▷ *À laquelle de tes sœurs ressembles-tu?* Which of your sisters do you look like? ② whom ▷ *la personne à laquelle vous faites référence* the person to whom you are referring ▷ *la personne à laquelle je pense* the person I'm thinking of

lard [laʀ] *nm* fatty pork

large [laʀʒ(ə)] *adj, adv* wide; **voir large** to allow a bit extra ▷ *Achète une autre pain : il vaut mieux voir large.* Buy another loaf of bread: it's better to have a bit extra.
▶ *nm*: **cinq mètres de large** 5 m wide; **le large** the open sea; **au large de** off the coast of ▷ *Le bateau est actuellement au large du Labrador.* The boat is off the coast of Labrador at the moment.

largement [laʀʒəmã] *adv*: **Vous avez largement le temps.** You have plenty of time.; **C'est largement suffisant.** That's plenty.

largeur [laʀʒœʀ] *nf* width

larme [laʀm(ə)] *nf* tear ▷ *être en larmes* to be in tears

laryngite [laʀɛ̃ʒit] *nf* laryngitis

lasagne [lazaɲ] *nf* lasagna

laser [lazɛʀ] *nm* laser; **une imprimante laser** a laser printer

lasser [lase] *vb*: **se lasser de** to get tired of ▷ *Il s'est lassé de la tapisserie à fleurs du salon.* He got tired of the flowery wallpaper in the living room.

Laurentides *nfpl* the Laurentians ▷ *Nous avons fait du camping dans les Laurentides.* We went camping in the Laurentians.

lavable [lavabl(ə)] *adj* washable

lavabo [lavabo] *nm (bathroom)* sink

lavage [lavaʒ] *nm* wash ▷ *Ce chandail a rétréci au lavage.* This sweater shrank in the wash. ▷ *Avez-vous quelque chose à mettre au lavage?* Do you have anything to put in the wash?; **faire le lavage** to do laundry; **le lavage de cerveau** brainwashing

lave-auto [lav-] *(pl* **lave-autos**) *nm* car wash

laver [lave] *vb* to wash; **se laver** to wash ▷ *se laver les mains* to wash one's hands

lavette [lavɛt] *nf* dishcloth

laveuse [lavøz] *nf* washing machine

lave-vaisselle [lavvɛsɛl] *(pl* **lave-vaisselle**) *nm* dishwasher

lavoir [lavwaʀ] *nm* coin laundry

le [l(ə)] *art, pron* ① *le* the book ▷ *l'arbre* the tree ▷ *l'hélicoptère* the helicopter ② him ▷ *C'est un vieil ami : je le connais depuis plus de vingt ans.* He's an old friend: I've known him for over 20 years. ③ it ▷ *Où est mon stylo? Je ne le trouve plus.* Where's my pen? I can't find it. ▷ *« Où est le fromage? » « Je l'ai mis au frigo. »* "Where's the cheese?" "I put it in the fridge." ④ one's; **se laver le visage** to wash one's face

▷ *Évitez de vous laver le visage avec du savon.* Avoid washing your face with soap.; **trois dollars le kilo** 3 dollars a kilo; **Il est arrivé le douze mai.** He arrived on 12 May.

lécher [leʃe] *vb* to lick

leçon [ləsɔ̃] *nf* lesson

lecteur [lɛktœʀ] *nm* ❶ reader ❷ (*computer*) (disk) drive ▷ *Insérer la disquette dans le lecteur A.* Insert the disk in drive A.; **un lecteur de cassettes** a cassette player; **un lecteur de CD** a CD player; **un lecteur de DVD** a DVD player; **un lecteur de MP3** an MP3 player

lectrice [lɛktʀis] *nf* reader

lecture [lɛktyʀ] *nf* reading

légal [legal, -o] (**f légale**, *mpl* **légaux**) *adj* legal

légende [leʒɑ̃d] *nf* ❶ legend ❷ (*of map*) key ❸ (*of picture*) caption

léger [leʒe, -ɛʀ] (**f légère**) *adj* ❶ light ❷ slight ▷ *un léger retard* a slight delay; **à la légère** thoughtlessly ▷ *Elle a agi à la légère.* She acted thoughtlessly.

légèrement [leʒɛʀmɑ̃] *adv* ❶ lightly ▷ *Habille-toi légèrement : il va faire chaud.* Wear light clothes: it's going to be hot. ❷ slightly ▷ *Il est légèrement plus grand que sa sœur.* He's slightly taller than his sister.

légume [legym] *nm* vegetable

lendemain [lɑ̃dmɛ̃] *nm* next day ▷ *le lendemain de son arrivée* the day after she arrived; **le lendemain matin** the next morning; **le lendemain de Noël** Boxing Day

lent [lɑ̃, lɑ̃t] (**f lente**) *adj* slow

lentement [lɑ̃tmɑ̃] *adv* slowly

lenteur [lɑ̃tœʀ] *nf* slowness

lentille [lɑ̃tij] *nf* lentil ▷ *un rôti de porc aux lentilles* roast pork with lentils; **des lentilles cornéennes** contact lenses

léopard [leɔpaʀ] *nm* leopard

lequel [ləkɛl, lakɛl] (**f laquelle**, *mpl* **lesquels**, *fpl* **lesquelles**) *pron* ❶ which ▷ *Lequel de ces deux films as-tu préféré?* Which of these two movies did you prefer? ❷ whom ▷ *l'homme avec lequel elle a été vue pour la dernière fois* the man with whom she was last seen ▷ *le garçon avec lequel elle est sortie* the boy she went out with

les [le] *art, pron* ❶ the ▷ *les arbres* the trees ❷ them ▷ *Elle les a invités à dîner.* She invited them to dinner. ❸ one's; **se brosser les dents** to brush one's teeth ▷ *Elle s'est brossé les dents.* She brushed her teeth.

lesbienne [lɛsbjɛn] *nf* lesbian

lesquels [lekɛl] (**f lesquelles**) *pron* ❶ which ▷ *Lesquelles de ces photos préfères-tu?* Which of these photos do you prefer? ❷ whom ▷ *les personnes avec lesquelles il joue au hockey* the people with whom he plays hockey ▷ *les gens chez lesquels nous avons dîné* the people we had dinner with

lessive [lesiv] *nf* (*laundry*) wash; **faire la lessive** to do the washing

leste [lɛst(ə)] *adj* nimble

lettre [lɛtʀ(ə)] *nf* letter ▷ *écrire une lettre* to write a lettre

leur [lœʀ] *adj, pron* ❶ their ▷ *leur ami* their friend ❷ them ▷ *Je leur ai dit la vérité.* I told

them the truth.; **le leur** theirs ▷ *mon camion et le leur* my truck and theirs ▷ *Ma voiture est rouge, la leur est bleue.* My car's red, theirs is blue.

leurs [lœʀ] *adj, pron* their ▷ *leurs amis* their friends; **les leurs** theirs ▷ *tes livres et les leurs* your books and theirs

levé [ləve] (**f levée**) *adj*: **être levé** to be up ▷ *Est-ce qu'elles sont levées?* Are they up?

levée [ləve] *nf* (*of mail*) collection ▷ *Prochaine levée : 17 heures* Next collection: 5 p.m.; **la levée de fonds** fund-raising

lever [ləve] *vb* to raise ▷ *Levez la main si vous connaissez la réponse.* Raise your hand if you know the answer.; **lever le nez sur quelque chose** to turn something down ▷ *Ils ont levé le nez sur notre offre.* They turned down our offer.; **lever les yeux** to look up; **se lever (1)** to get up ▷ *Elle se lève tous les jours à six heures.* She gets up at 6 o'clock every day. ▷ *Lève-toi!* Get up! **(2)** to rise ▷ *Le soleil se lève plus tard en hiver.* The sun rises later in winter. **(3)** to stand up ▷ *Levez-vous!* Stand up!
▶ *nm*: **le lever du soleil** sunrise

levier [ləvje] *nm* lever

lèvre [lɛvʀ(ə)] *nf* lip

levure [ləvyʀ] *nf* yeast; **la levure chimique** baking powder

lexique [lɛksik] *nm* word list

lézard [lezaʀ] *nm* lizard

liaison [ljɛzɔ̃] *nf* ❶ affair ▷ *Ils ont eu une liaison dans leur jeunesse.* They had an affair when they were younger. ❷ (*in pronunciation*) liaison ▷ *Il faut faire la liaison dans l'expression « les amis ».* You have to make a liaison in the phrase "les amis".

libellule [libelyl] *nf* dragonfly

libérer [libeʀe] *vb* to free ▷ *Les otages ont été libérés hier soir.* The hostages were freed last night.; **se libérer** to find time ▷ *J'essaierai de me libérer cet après-midi.* I'll try to find time this afternoon.

liberté [libɛʀte] *nf* freedom ▷ *la liberté d'expression* freedom of speech; **mettre en liberté** to release ▷ *Il a été mis en liberté au bout d'un an de prison.* He was released after a year in prison.; **en liberté surveillée** on probation

libraire [libʀɛʀ] *nmf* bookseller

librairie [libʀɛʀi] *nf* bookstore

libre [libʀ(ə)] *adj* ❶ free ▷ *Tu es libre de faire ce que tu veux.* You are free to do as you wish. ▷ *Est-ce que cette place est libre?* Is this seat free?; **Avez-vous une chambre de libre?** Have you got a free room? ❷ clear ▷ *La route est libre : vous pouvez traverser.* The road is clear: you can cross.

libre-échange [libʀeʃɑ̃ʒ] *nm* free trade ▷ *un accord de libre-échange* a free-trade agreement

libre-service [libʀəsɛʀvis] (*pl* **libres-services**) *nm* self-serve ▷ *Cette station-service est un libre-service.* This gas station is a self-serve.

licence [lisɑ̃s] *nf* licence ▷ *une licence d'exportation* an export licence ▷ *la licence de logiciel* software licence

licenciement [lisɑ̃simɑ̃] *nm* layoff

licencier [lisɑ̃sje] *vb* to lay off ▷ *Ils viennent*

de licencier sept employés. They've just laid off 7 employees.

liège [ljɛʒ] *nm* cork ▷ *des sous-verres en liège* cork coasters; **un bouchon en liège** (*for bottle*) a cork

lien [ljɛ̃] *nm* ❶ connection ▷ *Il n'y aucun lien entre ces deux événements.* There's no connection between these two events.; **un lien de parenté** a family tie ❷ (*in computing*) link

lier [lje] *vb*: **lier conversation avec quelqu'un** to get into conversation with somebody; **se lier avec quelqu'un** to make friends with somebody ▷ *Je ne me lie pas facilement.* I don't make friends easily.

lierre [ljɛʀ] *nm* ivy

lieu [ljø] (*pl* **lieux**) *nm* place ▷ *votre lieu de travail* your place of work; **avoir lieu** to take place ▷ *La cérémonie a eu lieu dans la salle des fêtes.* The ceremony took place in the community hall.; **au lieu de** instead of ▷ *J'aimerais une pomme au lieu de la crème glacée.* I'd like an apple instead of ice cream.

lieutenant-gouverneur [ljøtnɑ̃guvɛʀnœʀ] *nm* lieutenant-governor

lieutenante-gouverneure [ljøtnɑ̃tguvɛʀnœʀ] *nf* lieutenant-governor

lièvre [ljɛvʀ(ə)] *nm* hare

ligne [liɲ] *nf* ❶ line ▷ *La ligne est occupée.* The line is busy. ▷ *des lignes d'autobus* bus lines ▷ *les lignes électriques* power lines; **en ligne** (*computing*) online; **la ligne d'écoute téléphonique** helpline ❷ figure ▷ *C'est mauvais pour la ligne.* It's bad for your figure.

ligoter [ligote] *vb* to tie up

ligue [lig] *nf* league

lilas [lila] *nm* lilac

limace [limas] *nf* slug

lime [lim] *nf*: **une lime à ongles** a nail file

limitation [limitasjɔ̃] *nf*: **la limitation de vitesse** the speed limit

limite [limit] *nf* ❶ (*of property, sports field*) boundary ❷ limit ▷ *Est-ce qu'il y a une limite d'âge?* Is there an age limit?; **À la limite, on pourrait prendre l'autobus.** At a pinch we could go by bus.; **la date limite** the deadline; **la date limite d'utilisation** the best-before date

limiter [limite] *vb* to limit ▷ *Le nombre de billets est limité à deux par personne.* The number of tickets is limited to two per person.

limonade [limɔnad] *nf* lemonade

lin [lɛ̃] *nm* linen ▷ *un veston en lin* a linen jacket

linge [lɛ̃ʒ] *nm* ❶ linen ▷ *le linge sale* dirty linen ▷ *le linge de maison* household linens ❷ washing ▷ *laver le linge* to do the washing; **le linge à vaisselle** tea towel

lion [ljɔ̃] *nm* lion; **le Lion** Leo ▷ *Il est Lion.* He is a Leo.

lionne [ljɔn] *nf* lioness

liqueur [likœʀ] *nf* (*beverage*) pop

liquide [likid] *adj* liquid
▶ *nm* liquid; **payer quelque chose en liquide** to pay cash for something

lire [liʀ] *vb* to read ▷ *Tu as lu des contes de Roch Carrier?* Have you read any stories by Roch Carrier?

lis, lisent, lisez *vb see* **lire**; **Je lis beaucoup.** I read a lot.

lisible [liziblə] *adj* legible

lisse [lis] *adj* smooth

liste [listə] *nf* list; **faire la liste de** to make a list of ▷ *J'ai fait la liste de tout ce dont j'ai besoin.* I've made a list of all the things I need.

lit [li] *vb see* **lire**

lit [li] *nm* bed ▷ *un grand lit* a double bed ▷ *aller au lit* to go to bed; **faire son lit** to make one's bed ▷ *Je n'ai pas eu le temps de faire mon lit ce matin.* I didn't have time to make my bed this morning.; **un lit de camp** a cot; **un lit d'enfant** a crib

literie [litʀi] *nf* bedding

litière [litjɛʀ] *nf* ❶ (*for cat*) litter ❷ (*of caged pet*) bedding

litre [litʀ(ə)] *nm* litre

littéraire [liteʀɛʀ] *adj* literary; **une œuvre littéraire** a work of literature

littérature [liteʀatyʀ] *nf* literature

littoral [litɔʀal, -o] (*pl* **littoraux**) *nm* coast

livraison [livʀɛzɔ̃] *nf* delivery

livre [livʀ(ə)] *nm* book; **un livre de poche** a paperback
▶ *nf* pound ▷ *une livre de beurre* a pound of butter

livrer [livʀe] *vb* to deliver

livret [livʀɛ] *nm* booklet

livreur [livʀœʀ] *nm* delivery person

livreuse [livʀøz] *nf* delivery person

local [lɔkal, -o] (*f* **locale**, *mpl* **locaux**) *adj* local
▶ *nm* (*pl* **locaux**) venue ▷ *Nous cherchons un local pour les répétitions.* We are looking for a venue to rehearse in.

locataire [lɔkatɛʀ] *nmf* tenant

location [lɔkasjɔ̃] *nf*: **location de voitures** car rental; **location de skis** ski rental

locaux [lɔko] *adj, n see* **local**

locomotive [lɔkɔmɔtiv] *nf* locomotive

loge [lɔʒ] *nf* dressing room

logement [lɔʒmɑ̃] *nm* ❶ housing ❷ accommodation

loger [lɔʒe] *vb* to stay ▷ *Elle loge chez sa cousine.* She's staying with her cousin.; **trouver à se loger** to find somewhere to live ▷ *Ils ont eu du mal à trouver à se loger.* They had difficulty finding somewhere to live.

logiciel [lɔʒisjɛl] *nm* (*computer*) program ▷ *un logiciel de traitement de texte* a word-processing program; **un logiciel antivirus** a piece of antivirus software; **le coût des logiciels pour les écoles** the cost of software for schools

logique [lɔʒik] *adj* logical
▶ *nf* logic

loi [lwa] *nf* law

loin [lwɛ̃] *adv* ❶ far ▷ *Le restaurant n'est pas très loin d'ici.* The restaurant is not very far from here. ❷ far off ▷ *La semaine de relâche n'est plus tellement loin.* March break isn't far off now. ❸ a long time ago ▷ *Les vacances paraissent déjà tellement loin!* The holidays already seem such a long time ago!; **au loin** in the distance ▷ *On aperçoit la mer au loin.* You can see the ocean in the distance.; **de loin (1)** from a long way away

▷ *On voit l'église de loin.* You can see the church from a long way away. **(2)** by far ▷ *C'est de loin l'élève le plus brillant.* He is by far the brightest student.; *C'est plus loin que le cinéma.* It's past the movie theatre.

lointain [lwɛ̃tɛ̃, -ɛn] (f **lointaine**) adj distant ▷ *un pays lointain* a distant country ▷ *C'est un parent lointain de ma mère.* He's a distant relation of my mother.

▶ *nm*: **dans le lointain** in the distance

loir [lwaʀ] *nm*: **dormir comme un loir** to sleep like a log

loisirs [lwaziʀ] *nmpl* ❶ free time ▷ *Qu'est-ce que vous faites pendant vos loisirs?* What do you do in your free time? ❷ hobby ▷ *Le ski et l'équitation sont des loisirs coûteux.* Skiing and riding are expensive hobbies.

long [lɔ̃, lɔ̃g] (f **longue**) adj long; **à l'année longue** all year round

▶ *nm*: **un bateau de trois mètres de long** a boat 3 m long; **tout le long de** all along ▷ *Il y a des sentiers de randonnée tout le long de la côte.* There are hiking trails all along the coast.; **marcher de long en large** to walk up and down

longer [lɔ̃ʒe] *vb*: **La route longe la forêt.** The road runs along the edge of the forest.; **Nous avons longé la rivière Rideau à pied.** We walked along the Rideau.

longtemps [lɔ̃tɑ̃] *adv* a long time ▷ *J'ai attendu longtemps chez le dentiste.* I waited for a long time at the dentist's.; **pendant longtemps** for a long time ▷ *On a cru pendant longtemps que la Terre était plate.* For a long time people thought the Earth was flat.; **mettre longtemps à faire quelque chose** to take a long time to do something ▷ *Il a mis longtemps à répondre à ma lettre.* He took a long time to answer my letter.

longue [lɔ̃g] adj *see* **long**

longue [lɔ̃g] *nf*: **à la longue (1)** in the end ▷ *Elle a fini par convaincre tout le monde à la longue.* In the end she won everybody over. **(2)** over the long term ▷ *À la longue, la malbouffe est mauvaise pour la santé.* Over the long term, junk food is bad for your health.

longuement [lɔ̃gmɑ̃] *adv* at length ▷ *Il m'a longuement parlé de ses projets d'avenir.* He talked to me at length about his future plans.

longueur [lɔ̃gœʀ] *nf* length; **à longueur de journée** all day long ▷ *Elle mâche de la gomme à longueur de journée.* She chews gum all day long.; **dans le sens de la longueur** lengthwise

loques [lɔk] *nfpl*: **être en loques** to be in shreds ▷ *Sa chemise était en loques.* His shirt was torn to shreds.

lors de [lɔʀd(ə)] *prep* during ▷ *Je l'ai rencontrée lors de ma visite à Prince George.* I met her during my stay in Prince George.

lorsque [lɔʀsk(ə)] *conj* when ▷ *J'allais composer ton numéro lorsque tu as appelé.* I was about to dial your number when you called.

lot [lo] *nm* (in draw) prize; **le gros lot** the jackpot

loterie [lɔtʀi] *nf* ❶ lottery ▷ *une loterie nationale* a national lottery ❷ raffle ▷ *J'ai gagné ce baladeur dans une loterie.* I won this personal

CD player in a raffle.

lotion [losjɔ̃] *nf* lotion ▷ *une bouteille de lotion solaire* a bottle of suntan lotion; **une lotion après-rasage** an aftershave; **une lotion démaquillante** facial cleanser

loto [lɔto] *nm* lottery; **un loto sportif** a sports pool

louche [luʃ] *adj* fishy ▷ *une histoire louche* a fishy story

▶ *nf* ladle

loucher [luʃe] *vb* to squint

louer [lwe] *vb* ❶ to rent out ▷ *Ils louent des chambres à des étudiants.* They rent out rooms to students.; **« à louer »** "for rent" ▷ *Ma sœur loue un petit appartement au centre-ville.* My sister rents a little apartment in the centre of town. ❷ to rent ▷ *Nous allons louer une voiture pour le week-end.* We're going to rent a car for the weekend. ❸ to praise ▷ *Les journaux ont loué le courage des pompiers.* The newspapers praised the courage of the firefighters.

loup [lu] *nm* wolf

loupe [lup] *nf* magnifying glass

lourd [luʀ, luʀd(ə)] (f **lourde**) *adj* ❶ heavy ▷ *Mon sac à dos est très lourd.* My backpack is very heavy. ❷ (weather) muggy ▷ *Le temps est lourd aujourd'hui.* It's muggy out today.

loutre [lutʀ(ə)] *nf* otter

louveteau [luvto] *nm* wolf cub

loyal [lwajal, -o] (mpl **loyaux**) *adj* loyal

loyauté [lwajote] *nf* loyalty

loyer [lwaje] *nm* rent

lu [ly] *vb see* **lire**

lucarne [lykaʀn(ə)] *nf* skylight

luge [lyʒ] *nf* sled

lugubre [lygybʀ(ə)] *adj* gloomy

lui [lɥi] *pron* ❶ him ▷ *Il a été très content du cadeau que je lui ai offert.* He was very pleased with the present I gave him. ▷ *C'est bien lui!* It's definitely him! ▷ *J'ai pensé à lui toute la journée.* I thought about him all day long. ❷ to him ▷ *Mon père est d'accord : je lui ai parlé ce matin.* My father said yes: I spoke to him this morning. ❸ her ▷ *Elle a été très contente du cadeau que je lui ai offert.* She was very pleased with the present I gave her. ❹ to her ▷ *Ma mère est d'accord : je lui ai parlé ce matin.* My mother said yes: I spoke to her this morning. ❺ it ▷ *« Qu'est-ce que tu donnes à ton chat? »* « *Je lui donne de la nourriture sèche.* » "What do you give your cat?" "I give it dry food." ▷ *Lui, il est toujours en retard!* Oh him, he's always late!; **lui-même** himself ▷ *Il a construit ce bateau lui-même.* He built this boat himself.

lumière [lymjɛʀ] *nf* light; **la lumière du jour** daylight

lumineux [lyminø, -øz] (f **lumineuse**) *adj*: **une enseigne lumineuse** a neon sign

lunatique [lynatik] *adj* ❶ absent-minded ▷ *Ma sœur est très lunatique.* My sister is very absent-minded. ❷ temperamental ▷ *Il est plutôt lunatique.* He's rather temperamental.

lunch [lœntʃ] *nm* (midday meal) lunch ▷ *Habituellement, j'apporte mon lunch à l'école.* I usually bring my lunch to school.

lundi [lœdi] *nm* ❶ Monday ▷ *Aujourd'hui,*

nous sommes lundi. It's Monday today. ❷ on
Monday ▷ Ils sont arrivés lundi. They arrived on
Monday.; **le lundi** on Mondays ▷ Le lundi, je
vais à la piscine. I go swimming on Mondays.;
tous les lundis every Monday; **lundi dernier**
last Monday; **lundi prochain** next Monday; **le
lundi de Pâques** Easter Monday

lune [lyn] *nf* moon; **la lune de miel**
honeymoon; **être dans la lune** to daydream
▷ Elle ne t'entend pas; elle est dans la lune. She
doesn't hear you; she's daydreaming.

lunettes [lynɛt] *nfpl* glasses; **des lunettes de
soleil** sunglasses; **des lunettes de natation**
swimming goggles

lutte [lyt] *nf* ❶ fight ▷ la lutte contre le racisme
the fight against racism ❷ wrestling ▷ une
épreuve de lutte a wrestling bout

lutter [lyte] *vb* to fight

luxe [lyks(ə)] *nm* luxury; **de luxe** luxury ▷ un
hôtel de luxe a luxury hotel

luxueux [lyksɥø, -øz] (**f luxueuse**) *adj*
luxurious

lynx [lɛ̃ks] *nm* lynx

m

M. *abbr* (= Monsieur) Mr ▷ M. Bernard Mr Bernard

m' [m] *pron see* me

ma [ma] *adj* my ▷ ma mère my mother ▷ ma
montre my watch

macaron [makarɔ̃] *nm* (with slogan, image)
button ▷ Elle portait un macaron qui disait :
«J'aime le français!» She was wearing a button
that said, "I like French!"

macaronis [makarɔni] *nmpl* macaroni

macédoine [masedwan] *nf*: **la macédoine
de fruits** fruit salad; **la macédoine de
légumes** mixed vegetables

mâcher [maʃe] *vb* to chew

machin [maʃɛ̃] *nm* (informal) thingy ▷ Passe-
moi le machin pour râper les carottes. Pass me the
thingy for grating carrots. ▷ Qu'est-ce que c'est
que ce vieux machin? What's this old thing?

machinalement [maʃinalmmã] *adv*: Elle
a regardé sa montre machinalement. She
looked at her watch without thinking.

machine [maʃin] *nf* machine; **une machine
à laver** a washing machine; **une machine à
écrire** a typewriter; **une machine à coudre**
a sewing machine; **une machine à boules** a
pinball machine

machiste [matʃist] *nm* male chauvinist

mâchoire [maʃwar] *nf* jaw

81 | **maintenant**

mâchonner [maʃɔne] *vb* to chew

Madame [madam] (*pl* **Mesdames**) *nf* ❶ Mrs
▷ Madame Legall Mrs Legall ❷ lady ▷ Occupez-
vous de Madame. Could you look after this lady?
❸ Madam ▷ Madame,... Dear Madam,... ❹ (in
letter); **Madame! Vous avez oublié votre
parapluie!** Ma'am, you forgot your umbrella!

Mademoiselle [madmwazɛl] (*pl*
Mesdemoiselles) *nf* Miss ▷ Mademoiselle
Martin Miss Martin

maganer [magane] *vb* (informal) to wreck
▷ La pluie a magané la récolte de fraises. The rain
wrecked the strawberry crop. ▷ J'ai magané
mon baladeur MP3. I wrecked my portable MP3
player.

magasin [magazɛ̃] *nm* store ▷ Les magasins
ouvrent à huit heures. The stores open at 8
o'clock.; **faire les magasins** to go shopping

magasinage [magazinaʒ] *nm* shopping ▷ J'ai
du magasinage à faire. I have some shopping to
do.; **faire du magasinage** to go shopping

magasiner [magazine] *vb* to shop

magasineur [magazinœr] *nm* shopper

magasineuse [magazinøz] *nf* shopper

magazine [magazin] *nm* magazine

magicien [maʒisjɛ̃] *nm* magician

magicienne [maʒisjɛn] *nf* magician

magie [maʒi] *nf* magic ▷ un tour de magie a
magic trick

magique [maʒik] *adj* magic ▷ une baguette
magique a magic wand

magnétique [maɲetik] *adj* magnetic

magnétophone [maɲetɔfɔn] *nm* tape
recorder; **un magnétophone à cassettes** a
cassette recorder

magnétoscope [maɲetɔskɔp] *nm* VCR

magnifique [maɲifik] *adj* superb

mai [mɛ] *nm* May; **en mai** in May

maigre [mɛgr(ə)] *adj* ❶ skinny ▷ Mon père
me trouve trop maigre. My father says I'm too
skinny. ❷ (meat) lean ❸ (cheese, yogurt)
low-fat

maigrir [megrir] *vb* to lose weight ▷ Il fait un
régime pour essayer de maigrir. He's on a diet to
try to lose weight. ▷ Elle a maigri de deux kilos en
un mois. She's lost 2 kilos in a month.

maillot de bain [majo-] *nm* swimsuit

main [mɛ̃] *nf* hand ▷ Donne-moi la main! Give
me your hand!; **serrer la main à quelqu'un**
to shake hands with somebody; **se serrer la
main** to shake hands ▷ Les deux présidents se
sont serré la main. The two presidents shook
hands.; **sous la main** handy ▷ Est-ce que tu
as son adresse sous la main? Have you got his
address handy?

main-d'œuvre [mɛ̃dœvr(ə)] *nf* workforce
▷ la main-d'œuvre canadienne the Canadian
workforce ▷ la main-d'œuvre de l'usine the
factory workers; **les frais de main-d'œuvre**
labour costs

maintenant [mɛ̃tnã] *adv* ❶ now ▷ Qu'est-ce
que tu veux faire maintenant? What do you want
to do now? ▷ C'est maintenant ou jamais. It's
now or never. ❷ nowadays ▷ Maintenant la
plupart des gens font leurs courses au supermarché.
Nowadays most people do their shopping at

the supermarket.

maintenir [mɛ̃tnir] vb to maintain ▷ *Il maintient qu'il n'était pas là le jour du crime.* He maintains he wasn't there on the day of the crime.; **se maintenir** to hold ▷ *Espérons que le beau temps va se maintenir pour la fin de semaine!* Let's hope the good weather will hold over the weekend!

maintien de la paix [mɛ̃tjɛ̃-] nm peacekeeping ▷ *les opérations du maintien de la paix au Rwanda* peacekeeping operations in Rwanda

maire [mɛʀ] nmf mayor

mairie [meʀi] nf town hall

mais [mɛ] conj but ▷ *C'est cher mais de très bonne qualité.* It's expensive, but very good quality.

maïs [mais] nm corn; **du maïs soufflé** popcorn

maison [mezɔ̃] nf house ▷ *Ils habitent dans la maison qui est au bout de la rue.* They live in the house at the end of the street.; **une maison de jeunes** a youth club; **une maison de transition** a halfway house; **des maisons jumelées** semi-detached houses; **des maisons en rangée** townhouses; **à la maison (1)** at home ▷ *Je serai à la maison cet après-midi.* I'll be at home this afternoon. **(2)** home ▷ *Elle est rentrée à la maison.* She's gone home. (f+pl **maison**)
▶ adj homemade ▷ *Je préfère les tartes maison à celles qui sont achetées.* I prefer homemade pies to store-bought ones.

maître [mɛtʀ(ə)] nmf ❶ (*in primary school*) teacher ❷ (*of dog*) master; **un maître d'hôtel** (*in restaurant*) a head waiter; **un maître nageur** a lifeguard; **une maître nageuse** a lifeguard

maîtresse [mɛtʀɛs] nf (*in primary school*) teacher; **la maîtresse de la maison** the lady of the house

maîtrise [mɛtʀiz] nf master's degree ▷ *Elle a une maîtrise d'anglais.* She's got a master's degree in English.; **la maîtrise de soi** self-control

maîtriser [mɛtʀize] vb: **se maîtriser** to control oneself ▷ *Il se met facilement en colère et a du mal à se maîtriser.* He loses his temper easily and finds it hard to control himself.

majestueux [maʒɛstɥø, -øz] (f**majestueuse**) adj majestic

majeur [maʒœʀ] (f**majeure**) adj: **être majeur** to be of age ▷ *Tu feras ce que tu voudras quand tu seras majeure.* You can do what you like once you're of age. ▷ *Elle sera majeure en août.* She comes of age in August.; **la majeure partie** most ▷ *la majeure partie de mon salaire* most of my salary

majorité [maʒɔʀite] nf majority ▷ *dans la majorité des cas* in the majority of cases; **la majorité et l'opposition** the government and the opposition

majuscule [maʒyskyl] nf upper-case letter ▷ *un M majuscule* an upper-case M

mal [mal] (f+pl **mal**) adv, adj ❶ badly ▷ *Ce travail a été mal fait.* The work was badly done.

▷ *Il a mal compris.* He misunderstood. ❷ wrong ▷ *C'est mal de mentir.* It's wrong to tell lies.; **aller mal** to be ill ▷ *Son grand-père va très mal.* Her grandfather is very ill.; **pas mal** quite good ▷ *Je te trouve pas mal sur cette photo.* I think you look quite good in this photo.
▶ nm (pl **maux**) ❶ ache ▷ *J'ai mal à la tête.* I have a headache. ▷ *J'ai mal aux dents.* I have a toothache. ▷ *J'ai mal au dos.* My back hurts. ▷ *Est-ce que vous avez mal à la gorge?* Do you have a sore throat?; **le mal des transports** motion sickness; **Ça fait mal.** It hurts.; **Où est-ce que tu as mal?** Where does it hurt?; **faire mal à quelqu'un** to hurt somebody ▷ *Attention, tu me fais mal!* Be careful, you're hurting me!; **se faire mal** to hurt oneself ▷ *Je me suis fait mal au bras.* I hurt my arm.; **se donner du mal pour faire quelque chose** to go to a lot of trouble to do something ▷ *Il s'est donné beaucoup de mal pour que cette soirée soit réussie.* He went to a lot of trouble to make the party a success.; **avoir le mal de mer** to be seasick; **avoir le mal du pays** to be homesick; **avoir mal au cœur** to feel nauseous ❷ evil ▷ *le bien et le mal* good and evil; **dire du mal de quelqu'un** to speak ill of somebody

malade [malad] adj ill; **tomber malade** to fall ill
▶ n patient

maladie [maladi] nf ❶ illness ❷ disease; **la maladie de la vache folle** mad cow disease

maladif [maladif, -iv] (f**maladive**) adj sickly ▷ *C'est un enfant maladif.* He's a sickly child.

maladresse [maladʀɛs] nf clumsiness

maladroit [maladʀwa, -wat] (f**maladroite**) adj clumsy

malaise [malɛz] nm: **avoir un malaise** to feel faint ▷ *Elle a eu un malaise après le déjeuner.* She felt faint after lunch.; **Son arrivée a créé un malaise parmi les invités.** Her arrival made the guests uncomfortable.

malbouffe [malbuf] nf junk food ▷ *Mes parents sont contre la malbouffe.* My parents are against junk food. ▷ *La malbouffe est devenue un problème dans notre société.* Junk food has become a problem in our society.

malchance [malʃɑ̃s] nf bad luck

mâle [mal] adj male

malédiction [malediksjɔ̃] nf curse

mal en point (f+pl **mal en point**) adj: **Il avait l'air mal en point quand je l'ai vu hier soir.** He didn't look too good when I saw him last night.

malentendu [malɑ̃tɑ̃dy] nm misunderstanding

malfaiteur [malfɛtœʀ] nm criminal

malfaitrice [malfɛtʀis] nf criminal

mal famé (f **mal famée**, f **mal famée**, mpl **mal famés**) adj: **un quartier mal famé** a rough neighbourhood

malgré [malgʀe] prep in spite of ▷ *Il est toujours généreux malgré ses problèmes d'argent.* He's always generous in spite of his financial problems.; **malgré tout** (*nevertheless*) anyway ▷ *Il faisait mauvais mais nous sommes sortis malgré tout.* The weather was bad but we went out anyway.

malheur [malœr] nm tragedy ▷ *Elle a eu beaucoup de malheurs dans sa vie.* She's had a lot of tragedy in her life.; **faire un malheur** (informal) to be a smash hit ▷ *Leur dernier album a fait un malheur.* Their latest album was a smash hit.

malheureusement [malœrøzmã] adv unfortunately

malheureux [malœrø, -øz] (f **malheureuse**) adj miserable ▷ *Qu'est-ce que tu as? Tu as l'air malheureux.* What's wrong with you? You look miserable.

malhonnête [malɔnɛt] adj dishonest

malice [malis] nf mischief ▷ *Son regard était plein de malice.* Her eyes were full of mischief.

malicieux [malisjø, -øz] (f **malicieuse**) adj mischievous

malin [malɛ̃, -iɲ] (f **maligne**) adj ❶ crafty; **C'est malin!** (informal) That's clever! ▷ *Ah c'est malin! Nous voilà enfermés à cause de toi!* That's clever! You've gone and locked us in! ❷ malignant ▷ *une tumeur maligne* a malignant tumor

malodorant [malɔdɔrã, -ãt] (f **malodorante**) adj smelly

malpropre [malprɔpr(ə)] adj dirty

malsain [malsɛ̃, -ɛn] (f **malsaine**) adj unhealthy

maltraiter [maltrete] vb to abuse ▷ *Il maltraite son chien.* He abuses his dog. ▷ *des enfants maltraités* abused children

malveillant [malvejã, -ãt] (f **malveillante**) adj malicious ▷ *des rumeurs malveillantes* malicious rumours

maman [mamã] nf mom

mammifère [mamifɛr] nm mammal

manche [mãʃ] nf ❶ (of clothes) sleeve ❷ (of game) round ▷ *Ils ont gagné la première manche du match.* They won the first round of the match.
▶ nm (of pot, pan) handle

manchette [mãʃɛt] nf headline; **faire la manchette** to make headlines

mandarine [mãdarin] nf mandarin orange

manège [manɛʒ] nm amusement park ride; **Nous avons deviné son manège.** We've seen through his game.

manette [manɛt] nf ❶ lever ❷ joystick

mangeable [mãʒabl(ə)] adj edible ▷ *C'est à peine mangeable!* It's practically inedible!

manger [mãʒe] vb to eat

mangue [mãg] nf mango

maniaque [manjak] adj fussy

manie [mani] nf ❶ obsession; **avoir la manie de** to be obsessive about ▷ *Il a la manie du rangement.* He's obsessive about tidying up. ❷ habit ▷ *J'essaie de respecter ses petites manies.* I try to go along with her little ways.

manier [manje] vb to handle

manière [manjɛr] nf way; **de manière à** so as to ▷ *Nous sommes partis tôt de manière à éviter la circulation.* We left early so as to avoid the traffic.; **de toute manière** in any case ▷ *Je n'aurais pas pu venir de toute manière.* I couldn't have come in any case.

manières [manjɛr] nfpl ❶ manners

▷ **apprendre les bonnes manières** to learn good manners ❷ fuss ▷ *Ne fais pas de manières : mange ta soupe!* Don't make a fuss: eat your soup!

manifestant [manifɛstã] nm demonstrator

manifestante [manifɛstãt] nf demonstrator

manifestation [manifɛstasjõ] nf demonstration ▷ *une manifestation pour la paix* a peace demonstration

manifester [manifɛste] vb to demonstrate

manipuler [manipyle] vb ❶ to handle ▷ *Ce vase doit être manipulé avec soin.* This vase must be handled with care. ❷ to manipulate ▷ *Tous les partis essaient de manipuler l'opinion publique.* All the parties are trying to manipulate public opinion. ❸ to rig ▷ *L'élection a été manipulée.* The election was rigged.

Manitoba nm Manitoba

mannequin [mankɛ̃] nm model ▷ *Elle est mannequin.* She's a model.

manœuvrer [manœvre] vb to manœuvre

manque [mãk] nm ❶ lack ▷ *Le manque de sommeil peut provoquer toutes sortes de troubles.* Lack of sleep can cause all sorts of problems. ❷ withdrawal ▷ *un drogué en état de manque* a drug addict suffering withdrawal symptoms

manqué [mãke] (f **manquée**) adj: **un garçon manqué** a tomboy

manquer [mãke] vb to miss ▷ *Tu n'as rien manqué : le film n'était pas très bon.* You didn't miss anything: the movie wasn't very good. ▷ *Il manque des pages à ce livre.* There are some pages missing from this book.; **Mes parents me manquent.** I miss my parents.; **Ma sœur me manque.** I miss my sister.; **Il manque encore dix dollars.** We are still 10 dollars short.; **manquer de** to lack ▷ *La quiche manque de sel.* The quiche doesn't have enough salt. ▷ *Je trouve qu'il a manqué de tact.* I don't think he was very tactful.; **Il a manqué se tuer.** He nearly got killed.

manteau [mãto] (pl **manteaux**) nm coat

manuel [manɥɛl] (f **manuelle**) adj manual
▶ nm ❶ textbook ❷ handbook

maquereau [makro] (pl **maquereaux**) nm mackerel

maquette [makɛt] nf model ▷ *une maquette de bateau* a model boat

maquillage [makijaʒ] nm make-up

se **maquiller** [makije] vb to put on one's make-up ▷ *Je vais me maquiller en vitesse.* I'll just quickly put on my make-up.

marabout [marabu] (f **marabout**) adj grumpy ▷ *Elles sont marabouts ce matin.* They're grumpy this morning.

marais [marɛ] nm marsh

marbre [marbr(ə)] nm marble ▷ *une statue en marbre* a marble statue

marchand [marʃã] nm ❶ storekeeper
❷ merchant

marchande [marʃãd] nf ❶ storekeeper; **une marchande de fruits et de légumes** a fruit and vegetable seller ❷ merchant

marchander [marʃãde] vb to haggle

marchandise [marʃãdiz] nf goods

marche [marʃ(ə)] nf ❶ step ▷ *Fais attention*

à la marche! Mind the step! ❷ walking ▷ *La marche me fait du bien.* Walking does me good.; **être en état de marche** to be in working order ▷ *Cette voiture est en parfait état de marche.* This car is in perfect running order.; **Ne montez jamais dans un train en marche.** Never try to get into a moving train.; **mettre en marche** to start ▷ *Comment est-ce qu'on met la machine à laver en marche?* How do you start the washing machine?; **la marche arrière** reverse gear; **faire marche arrière** (*vehicle*) to back up ❸ march ▷ *une marche militaire* a military march

marché [maʁʃe] *nm* market; **un marché aux puces** a flea market; **le marché noir** black market; **un marché de producteurs** a farmers' market; **le marché du travail** the labour market

marcher [maʁʃe] *vb* ❶ to walk ▷ *Elle marche cinq kilomètres par jour.* She walks 5 kilometres every day. ❷ to run ▷ *Le métro marche normalement aujourd'hui.* The subway is running normally today. ❸ to work ▷ *Est-ce que l'ascenseur marche?* Is the elevator working? ❹ to go well ▷ *Est-ce que les affaires marchent actuellement?* Is business going well right now?; **Alors les études, ça marche?** (*informal*) How are you doing at school?; **faire marcher quelqu'un** to pull somebody's leg ▷ *Il essaie de te faire marcher.* He's pulling your leg.

marchette [maʁʃɛt] *nf* (*for babies, elderly*) walker

marcheur [maʁʃœʁ] *nm* walker

marcheuse [maʁʃøz] *nf* walker

mardi [maʁdi] *nm* ❶ Tuesday ▷ *Aujourd'hui, nous sommes mardi.* It's Tuesday today. ❷ on Tuesday ▷ *Ils reviennent mardi.* They're coming back on Tuesday.; **le mardi** on Tuesdays ▷ *Le mardi, j'ai mes cours de piano.* I have piano lessons on Tuesdays.; **tous les mardis** every Tuesday; **mardi dernier** last Tuesday; **mardi prochain** next Tuesday

mare [maʁ] *nf* pond

marécage [maʁekaʒ] *nm* marsh

marée [maʁe] *nf* tide ▷ *la marée haute* high tide ▷ *la marée basse* low tide ▷ *La marée monte.* The tide is coming in. ▷ *La marée descend.* The tide is going out.; **une marée noire** an oil slick

margarine [maʁgaʁin] *nf* margarine

marge [maʁʒ(ə)] *nf* margin

mari [maʁi] *nm* husband ▷ *son mari* her husband

mariage [maʁjaʒ] *nm* ❶ marriage ❷ wedding ▷ *un mariage civil* a civil ceremony ▷ *un mariage religieux* a church wedding

marié [maʁje] (*f* **mariée**) *adj* married ▶ *nm* bridegroom; **les mariés** the bride and groom

mariée [maʁje] *nf* bride

se **marier** [maʁje] *vb* to marry ▷ *Elle s'est mariée avec un ami d'enfance.* She married a childhood friend.

marin [maʁɛ̃, -in] (*f* **marine**) *adj* sea ▷ *l'air marin* the sea air ▶ *nm* sailor

marinade [maʁinad] *nf* marinade; **les marinades** pickles

marine [maʁin] (*f+pl* **marine**) *adj*: **bleu marine** navy-blue ▷ *un chandail bleu marine* a navy-blue sweater ▶ *nf* navy ▷ *la marine canadienne* the Canadian navy

maringouin [maʁɛ̃gwɛ̃] *nm* mosquito ▷ *une piqûre de maringouin* a mosquito bite

marionnette [maʁjɔnɛt] *nf* puppet

maritime [maʁitim] *adj* maritime ▷ *les provinces maritimes* the Maritime provinces; **les Maritimes** the Maritimes; **un chantier maritime** a shipyard

marmelade [maʁməlad] *nf*: **la marmelade de pommes** applesauce; **la marmelade d'oranges** marmalade

marmite [maʁmit] *nf* large cooking pot

marmonner [maʁmɔne] *vb* to mumble

marmotte [maʁmɔt] *nf* groundhog; **le jour de la marmotte** Groundhog Day

maroquinerie [maʁɔkinʁi] *nf* leather goods store

marquant [maʁkɑ̃, -ɑ̃t] (*f* **marquante**) *adj* significant ▷ *un événement marquant* a significant event

marque [maʁk(ə)] *nf* ❶ mark ▷ *des marques de doigts* fingermarks ❷ make ▷ *De quelle marque est ta voiture?* What make is your car? ❸ brand ▷ *une grande marque de beurre d'arachide* a well-known brand of peanut butter; **l'image de marque** the public image ▷ *La ministre tient à son image de marque.* The minister cares about her public image.; **une marque déposée** a registered trademark; **A vos marques! prêts! partez!** Ready, set, go!

marquer [maʁke] *vb* ❶ to mark ▷ *Peux-tu marquer sur la carte où se trouve le village?* Can you mark where the village is on the map? ❷ to score ▷ *L'équipe canadienne a marqué dix points.* The Canadian team scored ten points. ❸ to have a lasting effect on ▷ *La guerre a marqué ces enfants.* War has had a lasting effect on these kids. ▷ *Cette peintre a marqué son époque.* This painter had a lasting effect on her time.

marrant [maʁɑ̃, -ɑ̃t] (*f* **marrante**) *adj* (*informal*) funny

marre [maʁ] *adv* (*informal*); **en avoir marre de quelque chose** to be fed up with something ▷ *J'en ai marre de faire la vaisselle.* I'm fed up with doing the dishes.

marron [maʁɔ̃] *nm* chestnut ▷ *les marrons grillés* roasted chestnuts ▶ *adj* (*f+pl* **marron**) brown ▷ *des chaussures marron* brown shoes

marronnier [maʁɔnje] *nm* chestnut tree

mars [maʁs] *nm* March; **en mars** in March

marteau [maʁto] (*pl* **marteaux**) *nm* hammer

martyriser [maʁtiʁize] *vb* to batter ▷ *des enfants martyrisés* battered children

mascotte [maskɔt] *nf* mascot ▷ *La mascotte de notre équipe est le carcajou.* Our team's mascot is a wolverine.

masculin [maskylɛ̃, -in] (*f* **masculine**) *adj* ❶ men's ▷ *la mode masculine* men's fashion ❷ masculine ▷ *« Chat » est un nom masculin.* "Chat" is a masculine noun. ▷ *Elle a une allure* *assez masculine.* She looks rather masculine.

masque [mask(ə)] *nm* mask

massacre [masakʀ(ə)] *nm* massacre

massacrer [masakʀe] *vb* to massacre

massage [masaʒ] *nm* massage

masse [mas] *nf* ① (volume, weight) mass ▷ *la masse musculaire* muscular mass ② majority ▷ *la grande masse des jeunes* the vast majority of young people; **produire en masse** to mass-produce ▷ *Ces jouets sont produits en masse en Chine.* These toys are mass-produced in China.; **venir en masse** to come en masse ▷ *Les gens sont venus en masse pour accueillir Nelson Mandela.* People came en masse to welcome Nelson Mandela.

masser [mase] *vb* to massage; **se masser** to gather ▷ *Les manifestants se sont massés devant l'ambassade.* The demonstrators gathered in front of the embassy.

massif [masif, -iv] (*f* **massive**) *adj* ① (gold, silver, wood) solid ▷ *un bracelet en or massif* a solid gold bracelet ② massive ▷ *une dose massive d'antibiotiques* a massive dose of antibiotics ③ mass ▷ *des départs massifs* a mass exodus

mat [mat] (*f* **mate**) *adj* matte ▷ *blanc mat* matte white ▷ *Je voudrais mes photos en fini mat.* I would like my photos matte.; **être mat** (chess) to be checkmated

match [matʃ] *nm* game ▷ *un match de hockey* a hockey game; **faire match nul** to be tied

matelas [matla] *nm* mattress ▷ *un matelas gonflable* an air mattress

matelot [matlo] *nm* sailor

matériaux [mateʀjo] *nmpl* materials

matériel [mateʀjɛl] *nm* ① equipment ▷ *du matériel de laboratoire* laboratory equipment ② (computer) hardware ▷ *C'est un problème de matériel ou de logiciel?* Is the problem with the hardware or the software? ③ gear ▷ *Il a pris tout son matériel de pêche avec lui.* He took all his fishing gear with him.

maternel [matɛʀnɛl] (*f* **maternelle**) *adj* motherly ▷ *Elle est très maternelle.* She's very motherly.; **ma grand-mère maternelle** my mother's mother; **mon oncle maternel** my mother's brother

maternelle [matɛʀnɛl] *nf* kindergarten

maternité [matɛʀnite] *nf:* **le congé de maternité** maternity leave ▷ *Notre professeur de musique est en congé de maternité.* Our music teacher is on maternity leave.

mathématiques [matematik] *nfpl* mathematics

maths [mat] *nfpl* (informal) math

matière [matjɛʀ] *nf* subject ▷ *Ma matière préférée, c'est le français.* My favourite subject is French.; **sans matières grasses** fat-free; **les matières premières** raw materials

matin [matɛ̃] *nm* morning ▷ *à trois heures du matin* at 3 o'clock in the morning; **du matin au soir** from morning till night; **de bon matin** early in the morning

matinal [matinal, -o] (*f* **matinale**, *mpl* **matinaux**) *adj* morning ▷ *Je fais mes étirements matinaux avant de déjeuner.* I do my morning

stretches before breakfast.; **être matinal** to be up early ▷ *Tu es bien matinal aujourd'hui!* You're up early today!

matinée [matine] *nf* morning ▷ *Je t'appellerai demain dans la matinée.* I'll call you sometime tomorrow morning. ▷ *en début de matinée* early in the morning

matou [matu] *nm* tomcat

maudire [modiʀ] *vb* to curse

maudit [modi, -it] (*f* **maudite**) *adj* (informal) darned ▷ *Où est passé ce maudit parapluie?* Where's that darned umbrella got to?

maussade [mosad] *adj* sulky

mauvais [mɔvɛ, -ɛz] (*f* **mauvaise**) *adj, adv* ① bad ▷ *une mauvaise note* a bad mark ▷ *Tu arrives au mauvais moment.* You've come at a bad time.; **Il fait mauvais.** The weather's bad.; **être mauvais en** to be bad at ▷ *Je suis mauvais en orthographe.* I'm bad at spelling. ② poor ▷ *de mauvaise qualité* of poor quality ▷ *Il est en mauvaise santé.* His health is poor.; **Tu as mauvaise mine.** You don't look well. ③ wrong ▷ *Vous avez fait le mauvais numéro.* You've dialled the wrong number.; **des mauvaises herbes** weeds; **sentir mauvais** to smell

maux [mo] (*sg* **le mal**) *nmpl:* **des maux de dents** toothache; **des maux de ventre** stomachache; **des maux de tête** headache

maximal [maksimal, -o] (*f* **maximale**, *mpl* **maximaux**) *adj* maximum

maximum [maksimɔm] *nm* maximum; **au maximum** (1) as much as one can ▷ *Remplis le seau au maximum.* Fill the pail as full as you can. (2) at the very most ▷ *Ça va vous coûter deux cents dollars au maximum.* It'll cost you 200 dollars at the very most.

mayonnaise [majɔnɛz] *nf* mayonnaise

mazout [mazut] *nm* (furnace) oil

me [m(ə)] *pron* ① me ▷ *Elle me téléphone tous les jours.* She phones me every day. ▷ *Il m'attend depuis une heure.* He's been waiting for me for an hour. ② to me ▷ *Il me parle en français.* He talks to me in French. ▷ *Elle m'a expliqué la situation.* She explained the situation to me. ③ myself ▷ *Je vais me préparer quelque chose à manger.* I'm going to make myself something to eat. ▷ *Je me lève à sept heures tous les matins.* I get up at 7 every morning.

mécanicien [mekanisjɛ̃] *nm* mechanic

mécanicienne [mekanisjɛn] *nf* mechanic

mécanique [mekanik] *nf* ① mechanics ② (of watch, clock) mechanism

mécanisme [mekanism(ə)] *nm* mechanism

méchamment [meʃamɑ̃] *adv* nastily ▷ *Elle lui a répondu méchamment.* She answered her nastily.

méchanceté [meʃɑ̃ste] *nf* meanness

méchant [meʃɑ̃, -ɑ̃t] (*f* **méchante**) *adj* nasty ▷ *C'est un homme méchant.* He's a nasty man.; **Ne sois pas méchant avec ton petit frère.** Don't be mean to your little brother.; **« Attention, chien méchant »** "Beware of the dog"

mèche [mɛʃ] *nf* (of hair) lock

mécontent [mekɔ̃tɑ̃, -ɑ̃t] (*f* **mécontente**) *adj:* **mécontent de** unhappy with ▷ *Elle* *est mécontente de sa coupe de cheveux.* She's unhappy with her haircut.

mécontentement [mekɔ̃tɑ̃tmɑ̃] *nm* displeasure ▷ *Il a exprimé son mécontentement.* He expressed his displeasure.

médaille [medaj] *nf* medal

médecin [medsɛ̃] *nmf* doctor ▷ *aller chez le médecin* to go to the doctor

médecine [medsin] *nf* (*subject*) medicine ▷ *Elle étudie la médecine.* She's studying medicine.

médias [medja] *nmpl* media

médical [medikal, -o] (*f* **médicale**, *mpl* **médicaux**) *adj* medical ▷ *la recherche médicale* medical research; **passer une visite médicale** to have a medical

médicament [medikamɑ̃] *nm* (*drug*) medicine

médiéval [medjeval, -o] (*f* **médiévale**, *mpl* **médiévaux**) *adj* medieval

médiocre [medjɔkʀ(ə)] *adj* poor ▷ *des notes médiocres* poor marks

méduse [medyz] *nf* jellyfish

méfiance [mefjɑ̃s] *nf* mistrust

méfiant [mefjɑ̃, -ɑ̃t] (*f* **méfiante**) *adj* mistrustful

se méfier [mefje] *vb*: **se méfier de quelqu'un** to distrust somebody ▷ *Si j'étais toi, je me méfierais de lui.* I wouldn't trust him if I were you.

mégaoctet [megaɔktɛ] *nm* megabyte

mégarde [megaʀd(ə)] *nf*: **par mégarde** by mistake ▷ *J'ai emporté ton livre par mégarde.* I took your book by mistake.

meilleur [mejœʀ] (*f* **meilleure**) *adj, adv, n* better ▷ *Ce serait meilleur avec du fromage râpé.* It would be better with grated cheese. ▷ *Il paraît que le film est meilleur que le livre.* They say that the film is better than the book.; **le meilleur** the best ▷ *C'est elle qui est la meilleure en sport.* She's the best at sports. ▷ *Je préfère garder le meilleur pour la fin.* I like to keep the best for last.; **le meilleur des deux** the better of the two; **meilleur marché** cheaper ▷ *Les vêtements sont meilleur marché dans ce magasin.* Clothes are cheaper in this store.

mélancolique [melɑ̃kɔlik] *adj* gloomy

mélange [melɑ̃ʒ] *nm* mixture

mélanger [melɑ̃ʒe] *vb* ❶ to mix ▷ *Mélangez le tout.* Mix everything together. ❷ to muddle up ▷ *Tu mélanges tout!* You're muddling everything up!

mélangeur [melɑ̃ʒœʀ] *nm* blender

mêlée [mele] *nf* scuffle

mêler [mele] *vb*: **se mêler** to mix ▷ *Elle ne cherche pas à se mêler aux autres.* She doesn't try to mix with the others.; **Mêle-toi de tes affaires!** (*informal*) Mind your own business!

mélodie [melɔdi] *nf* melody

melon [məlɔ̃] *nm* melon; **le melon d'eau** watermelon

membre [mɑ̃bʀ(ə)] *nm* ❶ limb ❷ member ▷ *un membre de la famille* a member of the family ▷ *les pays membres de l'OTAN* the member countries of NATO

même [mɛm] *adj, adv, pron* ❶ same ▷ *J'ai le même manteau.* I've got the same coat. ▷ *Tiens, c'est curieux, j'ai le même!* That's strange, I've got the same one!; **en même temps** at the same time; **moi-même** myself ▷ *Je l'ai fait moi-même.* I did it myself.; **toi-même** yourself ▷ *Est-ce que tu vas faire les travaux toi-même?* Are you going to do the work yourself?; **eux-mêmes** themselves ❷ even ▷ *Il n'a même pas pleuré.* He didn't even cry.

mémoire [memwaʀ] *nf* memory

menace [mənas] *nf* threat

menacer [mənase] *vb* to threaten

ménage [menaʒ] *nm* housework ▷ *faire le ménage* to do the housework; **une femme de ménage** a cleaning woman

ménager [menaʒe, -ɛʀ] (*f* **ménagère**) *adj*: **les travaux ménagers** housework

mendiant [mɑ̃djɑ̃] *nm* beggar

mendiante [mɑ̃djɑ̃t] *nf* beggar

mendier [mɑ̃dje] *vb* to beg

mener [məne] *vb* to lead ▷ *Cette rue mène directement au parc.* This street leads straight to the park.; **Cela ne vous mènera à rien!** That will get you nowhere!

menottes [mənɔt] *nfpl* handcuffs

mensonge [mɑ̃sɔ̃ʒ] *nm* lie

mensuel [mɑ̃sɥɛl] (*f* **mensuelle**) *adj* monthly

mensurations [mɑ̃syʀasjɔ̃] *nfpl* measurements

menteur [mɑ̃tœʀ] *nm* liar

menteuse [mɑ̃tøz] *nf* liar

menthe [mɑ̃t] *nf* mint

mentionner [mɑ̃sjɔne] *vb* to mention

mentir [mɑ̃tiʀ] *vb* to lie ▷ *Tu mens!* You're lying!

menton [mɑ̃tɔ̃] *nm* chin

menu [məny] *adj, adv* ❶ slim ▷ *Elle est menue.* She's slim. ❷ very fine ▷ *Les oignons doivent être coupés menu.* The onions have to be cut up very fine.
▶ *nm* menu ▷ *le menu du jour* today's menu ▷ *le menu d'aide* the help menu

menuiserie [mənɥizʀi] *nf* woodwork

menuisier [mənɥizje] *nm* carpenter

menuisière [mənɥizjɛʀ] *nf* carpenter

mépris [mepʀi] *nm* contempt ▷ *Il nous a traités avec mépris.* He treated us with contempt.

méprisant [mepʀizɑ̃, -ɑ̃t] (*f* **méprisante**) *adj* contemptuous

mépriser [mepʀize] *vb* to despise

mer [mɛʀ] *nf* ❶ sea ▷ *en mer* at sea; **au bord de la mer** at the seaside ❷ tide ▷ *La mer est basse.* The tide is out. ▷ *La mer sera haute à sept heures.* It'll be high tide at 7 o'clock.

merci [mɛʀsi] *excl* thank you ▷ *Merci de m'avoir raccompagné.* Thank you for taking me home.; **merci beaucoup** thank you very much

mercredi [mɛʀkʀadi] *nm* ❶ Wednesday ▷ *Aujourd'hui, nous sommes mercredi.* It's Wednesday today. ❷ on Wednesday ▷ *Nous comptons partir mercredi.* We plan to leave on Wednesday.; **le mercredi** on Wednesdays ▷ *Le musée est fermé le mercredi.* The museum is shut on Wednesdays.; **tous les mercredis** every Wednesday; **mercredi dernier** last Wednesday; **mercredi prochain** next

Wednesday

mère [mɛʀ] nf mother; **la fête des Mères** Mother's Day

méridional [meʀidjɔnal, -o] (f **méridionale**, mpl **méridionaux**) adj southern ▷ la partie méridionale du Québec the southern part of Québec

meringue [məʀɛ̃g] nf meringue

mériter [meʀite] vb to deserve; **se mériter** to win ▷ Vous pourriez vous mériter un voyage pour deux aux chutes Niagara! You could win a trip for two to Niagara Falls!

merle [mɛʀl(ə)] nm blackbird

merveille [mɛʀvej] nf: **Cet ordinateur est une vraie merveille!** This computer's really wonderful!; **à merveille** wonderfully ▷ Elle joue du violon à merveille. She plays the violin wonderfully.; **les sept merveilles du monde** the seven wonders of the world

merveilleux [mɛʀvejø, -øz] (f **merveilleuse**) adj extraordinary ▷ Elle a un don merveilleux pour l'écriture. She has an extraordinary gift for writing.

mes [me] adj my ▷ mes parents my parents

Mesdames [medam] nf ladies ▷ Bonjour, Mesdames. Good morning, ladies.

Mesdemoiselles [medmwazɛl] nf ladies ▷ Bonjour, Mesdemoiselles. Good morning, ladies.

mesquin [mɛskɛ̃, -in] (f **mesquine**) adj mean

message [mesaʒ] nm message

messagerie [mesaʒʀi] nf: **une messagerie vocale** voice mail; **la messagerie électronique** e-mail; **la messagerie instantanée** instant messaging

messe [mɛs] nf mass ▷ aller à la messe to go to mass

Messieurs [mesjø] nm gentlemen ▷ Que puis-je faire pour vous, Messieurs? What can I do for you, gentlemen?; **Messieurs,...** (in letter) Dear Sirs,

mesure [məzyʀ] nf ❶ measurement ▷ J'ai pris les mesures de la fenêtre. I took the measurements of the window.; **sur mesure** tailor-made ▷ un costume sur mesure a tailor-made suit ❷ measure ▷ L'école a pris des mesures pour lutter contre le vandalisme. The school has taken measures to combat vandalism.; **au fur et à mesure** as one goes along ▷ Quand je cuisine, je préfère faire la vaisselle au fur et à mesure. When I'm cooking, I prefer to wash up as I go along.; **être en mesure de faire quelque chose** to be in a position to do something ▷ Nous ne sommes pas en mesure de vous renseigner. We are not in a position to give you any information.

mesurer [məzyʀe] vb to measure ▷ Mesurez la longueur et la largeur. Measure the length and the width.; **Il mesure un mètre quatre-vingts.** He's 1 m 80 tall.

met [mɛ] vb see **mettre**

métal [metal, -o] (pl **métaux**) nm metal

métallique [metalik] adj metallic

météo [meteo] nf weather forecast ▷ Qu'est-ce que dit la météo pour cet après-midi? What's the weather forecast for this afternoon?

méthode [metɔd] nf method ▷ des méthodes d'enseignement modernes modern teaching methods; **une méthode de guitare** a teach-yourself-guitar book

métier [metje] nm job ▷ Tu aimerais faire quel métier plus tard? What job would you like to do when you're older?

métis [metis] (f **métisse**) adj, n Métis ▷ Les communautés métisses datent de 1690. Métis communities date back to 1690.; **un Métis** (man) a Métis; **une Métisse** (woman) a Métis

mètre [mɛtʀ(ə)] nm metre; **un mètre à ruban** a tape measure

métro [metʀo] nm subway ▷ prendre le métro to take the subway

mets [mɛ] vb see **mettre**

metteur en scène [metœʀ-] (pl **metteurs en scène**) nm ❶ (of play) producer ❷ (of film) director

metteure en scène [metœʀ-] (pl **metteures en scène**) nf ❶ (of play) producer ❷ (of film) director

mettre [mɛtʀ(ə)] vb ❶ to put ▷ Où est-ce que tu as mis les clés? Where did you put the keys? ❷ to put on ▷ Je mets mon manteau et j'arrive. I'll put on my coat and then I'll be ready. ▷ Il fait froid. Je vais mettre le chauffage. It's cold. I'm going to put the heating on. ❸ to wear ▷ Elle ne met pas souvent de jupe. She doesn't often wear a skirt. ▷ Je n'ai rien à me mettre! I've got nothing to wear! ❹ to take ▷ Combien de temps as-tu mis pour aller à Chapleau? How long did it take you to get to Chapleau? ▷ Il met des heures à se préparer. He takes hours to get ready.; **mettre à pied** to lay off; **mettre quelqu'un en échec** to bodycheck somebody; **mettre en marche** to start ▷ Comment met-on la machine à laver en marche? How do you start the washing machine?; **mettre les points sur les i** (make clear) to spell something out; **Vous pouvez vous mettre là.** You can sit there.; **se mettre au lit** to get into bed; **se mettre en maillot de bain** to put on one's swimsuit; **se mettre à** to start ▷ Il s'est mis à la peinture à cinquante ans. He started painting when he was 50. ▷ Il est temps de se mettre au travail. It's time to start work. ▷ Elle s'est mise à pleurer. She started crying.

meuble [mœbl(ə)] nm piece of furniture ▷ Je me suis cogné contre un meuble. I bumped into a piece of furniture. ▷ Ce magasin vend de beaux meubles. This store sells nice furniture.

meublé [mœble] nm furnished apartment

meubler [mœble] vb to furnish

meurtre [mœʀtʀ(ə)] nm murder

meurtrier [mœʀtʀije] nm murderer

meurtrière [mœʀtʀijɛʀ] nf murderess

mi [mi] nm ❶ E ▷ mi bémol E flat ❷ mi ▷ do, ré, mi... do, re, mi...

mi- [mi] prefix ❶ half- ▷ mi-clos half-shut ❷ mid- ▷ à la mi-janvier in mid-January

miauler [mjole] vb to meow

mi-chemin [miʃmɛ̃]: **à mi-chemin** adv halfway

micro [mikʀo] nm microphone

microbe [mikʀɔb] nm germ

micro-ondes nm microwave oven.

microscope [mikʀɔskɔp] nm microscope

midi [midi] nm ① noon ▷ à midi at noon; **midi et demi** 12:30 ② lunchtime ▷ On a bien mangé à midi. We had a good meal at lunchtime.

mie [mi] nf breadcrumbs

miel [mjɛl] nm honey

mien [mjɛ̃] pron: **le mien** mine ▷ Ce vélo-là, c'est le mien. That bike is mine.

mienne [mjɛn] pron: **la mienne** mine ▷ Cette valise-là, c'est la mienne. That suitcase is mine.

miennes [mjɛn] pron: **les miennes** mine ▷ Heureusement que tu as tes clés : j'ai oublié les miennes. It's lucky you've got your keys: I forgot mine.

miens [mjɛ̃] pron: **les miens** mine ▷ Ces CD-là, ce sont les miens. Those CDs are mine.

miette [mjɛt] nf (of bread, cake) crumb

mieux [mjø] adv, adj, ① better ▷ Je la connais mieux que son frère. I know her better than her brother. ② Elle va mieux. She's better. ▷ Les cheveux courts lui vont mieux. She looks better with short hair.; **Il vaut mieux que tu appelles ta mère.** You'd better phone your mother.; **le mieux** the best ▷ C'est la région que je connais le mieux. It's the area I know best.; **faire de son mieux** to do one's best ▷ Essaie de faire de ton mieux. Try to do your best.; **de mieux en mieux** better and better; **au mieux** at best

mignon [miɲɔ̃, -ɔn] (f **mignonne**) adj cute ▷ Qu'est-ce qu'il est mignon! Isn't he cute!

migraine [migʀɛn] nf migraine ▷ J'ai la migraine. I have a migraine.

mijoter [miʒɔte] vb to simmer

milieu [miljø] (pl **milieux**) nm ① middle; **au milieu de** in the middle of ▷ Place le vase au milieu de la table. Put the vase in the middle of the table.; **au beau milieu de** in the middle of ▷ Quelqu'un a sonné à la porte au beau milieu de la nuit. Somebody rang the doorbell in the middle of the night.; ② background ▷ le milieu familial the family background ▷ Il vient d'un milieu modeste. He comes from a modest background.; ③ environment ▷ le milieu marin the marine environment

militaire [militɛʀ] adj military ▷ faire son service militaire to do one's military service ▶ n serviceman, servicewoman; **Son père est militaire.** Her father is in the armed forces.; **un militaire de carrière** a professional soldier

mille [mil] num a thousand ▷ mille dollars a thousand dollars ▷ deux mille personnes two thousand people

millefeuille [milfœj] nm

millénaire [milenɛʀ] nm millennium ▷ le troisième millénaire the third millennium

millénium [milenjɔm] nm millennium

milliard [miljaʀ] nm billion ▷ cinq milliards de dollars five billion dollars

milliardaire [miljaʀdɛʀ] nmf billionaire

millier [milje] nm thousand ▷ des milliers de personnes thousands of people; **par milliers** by the thousand

milligramme [miligʀam] nm milligram

millimètre [milimɛtʀ(ə)] nm millimetre

million [miljɔ̃] nm million ▷ deux millions de personnes two million people

millionnaire [miljɔnɛʀ] nmf millionaire

mime [mim] nmf mime artist

mimer [mime] vb to mimic

mince [mɛ̃s] adj ① thin ▷ une mince tranche de jambon a thin slice of ham ② slim ▷ Il est grand et mince. He's tall and slim.

minceur [mɛ̃sœʀ] nf ① thinness ▷ la minceur des murs the thinness of the walls ② (of person) slimness

mine [min] nf ① (facial) expression; **avoir bonne mine** to look well; **Il a mauvaise mine.** He doesn't look well.; **avoir une mine fatiguée** to look tired ② appearance ▷ Il ne faut pas juger les gens d'après leur mine. You shouldn't judge people by their appearance. ③ (of pencil) lead ④ mine ▷ une mine de charbon a coal mine; **faire mine de faire quelque chose** to pretend to do something ▷ Elle a fait mine de le croire. She pretended to believe him.; **mine de rien** somehow or other ▷ Elle a réussi mine de rien à y entrer. Somehow or other she got in.

minéral [mineʀal, -o] (f **minérale**, mpl **minéraux**) adj mineral ▷ l'eau minérale mineral water

mineur [minœʀ] (f **mineure**) adj minor ▶ nm ① (underage boy) minor; **les mineurs** minors ▷ Il est illégal de vendre les cigarettes aux mineurs. It's illegal to sell cigarettes to minors. ② miner ▷ Mon grand-père était mineur. My grandfather was a miner.

mineure [minœʀ] nf (underage girl) minor

minijupe [miniʒyp] nf miniskirt

minimal [minimal, -o] (f **minimale**, mpl **minimaux**) adj minimum

minimum [minimɔm] nm minimum ▷ Elle en fait le minimum. She does the absolute minimum.; **au minimum** at the very least

ministère [ministɛʀ] nm ministry ▷ le ministère de l'Environnement the Ministry of the Environment

ministre [ministʀ(ə)] nm minister ▷ la ministre de la Santé the Minister of Health

minorité [minɔʀite] nf minority

minuit [minɥi] nm midnight ▷ à minuit et quart at a quarter past midnight

minuscule [minyskyl] adj tiny ▶ nf lower-case letter

minute [minyt] nf minute; **à la minute** just this minute ▷ Je viens de l'appeler à la minute. I just called him this minute.

minutieux [minysjø, -øz] (f **minutieuse**) adj meticulous; **C'est un travail minutieux.** It's a fiddly job.

miracle [miʀakl(ə)] nm miracle

miroir [miʀwaʀ] nm mirror

mis [mi] vb see **mettre**

mis [mi, miz] (f **mise**) adj: **bien mis** well-dressed ▷ Elle est toujours bien mise. She's always well-dressed.

mise [miz] nf: **être de mise** to be appropriate ▷ Ces paroles blessantes ne sont pas de mise. These hurtful remarks are not appropriate.; **une mise à jour** an update; **la mise à pied** layoff; **la mise au jeu** (hockey) face-off; **la mise en**

page (document) layout

miser [mize] vb (informal) to count on ▷ On ne peut pas miser là-dessus. We can't count on it.

misérable [mizerabl(ə)] adj ❶ destitute ▷ une famille misérable a destitute family; **d'aspect misérable** shabby-looking ❷ pitiful ▷ des conditions de vie misérable pitiful living conditions

misère [mizer] nf extreme poverty; **un salaire de misère** starvation wages

missionnaire [misjɔnɛr] nmf missionary

mitaine [miten] nf mitten; **la mitaine à four** oven mitt

mi-temps [mitã] nf ❶ (of game) half ▷ la première mi-temps the first half ▷ la deuxième mi-temps the second half ❷ half-time ▷ Je lui parlerai à la mi-temps. I'll speak to her at half-time.; **travailler à mi-temps** to work part-time

miteux [mitø, -øz] (f **miteuse**) adj ❶ shabby ▷ un imperméable miteux a shabby raincoat ❷ pathetic

mixte [mikst(ə)] adj: **un mariage mixte** a mixed marriage; **une peau mixte** combination skin

Mlle (pl **Mlles**) abbr (= Mademoiselle) Miss ▷ Mlle Renoir Miss Renoir

Mme (pl **Mmes**) abbr (= Madame) Mrs ▷ Mme Leroy Mrs Leroy

mobile [mɔbil] nm motive ▷ Quel était le mobile du crime? What was the motive for the crime?

mobilier [mɔbilje] nm furniture

mocassin [mɔkasɛ̃] nm moccasin

moche [mɔʃ] adj (informal) awful ▷ Cette couleur est vraiment moche. That colour is really awful.; **Il a la grippe. C'est moche pour lui.** He's got the flu. That's a drag for him.

mode [mɔd] nf fashion ▷ être à la mode to be fashionable
▶ nm: **le mode d'emploi** directions for use; **le mode de vie** the way of life

modèle [mɔdɛl] nm ❶ model ▷ Le nouveau modèle sort en septembre. The new model is coming out in September. ❷ (of clothes) style ▷ Est-ce que vous avez le même modèle en plus grand? Have you got the same style in a bigger size?

modéré [mɔdere] (f **modérée**) adj moderate

moderne [mɔdɛrn(ə)] adj modern

moderniser [mɔdɛrnize] vb to modernize

modeste [mɔdɛst(ə)] adj modest ▷ Ne sois pas si modeste! Don't be so modest!

modestie [mɔdɛsti] nf modesty

moelleux [mwalø, -øz] (f **moelleuse**) adj soft ▷ un coussin moelleux a soft cushion

mœurs [mœr] nfpl social attitudes; **l'évolution des mœurs** changing attitudes

moi [mwa] pron me ▷ Coucou, c'est moi! Hello, it's me!; **Moi, je pense que tu as tort.** I personally think you're wrong.; **à moi** mine ▷ Ce livre n'est pas à moi. This book isn't mine. ▷ un ami à moi a friend of mine

moi-même [mwamɛm] pron myself ▷ J'ai tricoté ce chandail moi-même. I knitted this sweater myself.

moindre [mwɛ̃dr(ə)] adj: **le moindre** the slightest ▷ Il ne fait pas le moindre effort. He doesn't make the slightest effort. ▷ Je n'en ai pas la moindre idée. I haven't the slightest idea.

moine [mwan] nm monk

moineau [mwano] (pl **moineaux**) nm sparrow

moins [mwɛ̃] adv, prep ❶ less ▷ Ça coûte moins de deux cents dollars. It costs less than 200 dollars. ❷ fewer ▷ Il y a moins de gens aujourd'hui. There are fewer people today.; **Il est cinq heures moins dix.** It's 10 to 5. ❸ minus ▷ quatre moins trois 4 minus 3 ▷ Il a fait moins cinq la nuit dernière. It was minus 5 last night.; **le moins** the least ▷ C'est le modèle le moins cher. It's the least expensive model. ▷ Ce sont les plages qui sont les moins polluées. These are the least polluted beaches. ▷ C'est l'album que j'aime le moins. This is the album I like least.; **de moins en moins** less and less ▷ Elle vient nous voir de moins en moins. She comes to see us less and less often.; **Tu as trois ans de moins que moi.** You're three years younger than me.; **au moins** at least ▷ Ne te plains pas : au moins il ne pleut pas! Don't complain: at least it's not raining!; **à moins que** unless ▷ Je te retrouverai à dix heures à moins que le train n'ait du retard. I'll meet you at 10 o'clock unless the train is late.

mois [mwa] nm month

moisi [mwazi] nm mould ▷ Il y a du moisi sur le fromage. There is mould on the cheese.; **Ça sent le moisi.** It smells musty.

moisir [mwazir] vb to go mouldy ▷ Le pain a moisi. The bread has gone mouldy.

moisson [mwasɔ̃] nf harvest

moite [mwat] adj sweaty ▷ J'ai toujours les mains moites. My hands are always sweaty.

moitié [mwatje] nf half ▷ Il a mangé la moitié du gâteau à lui seul. He ate half the cake all by himself.; **la moitié du temps** half the time; **à la moitié de** halfway through ▷ Elle est partie à la moitié du film. She left halfway through the movie.; **à moitié** half ▷ Ton verre est encore à moitié plein. Your glass is still half-full. ▷ Ce manteau était à moitié prix. This coat was half-price.; **partager moitié moitié** to split fifty-fifty ▷ On partage moitié moitié, d'accord? We'll split it fifty-fifty, OK?

molaire [mɔlɛr] nf back tooth

molle [mɔl] adj lethargic ▷ Je la trouve un peu molle. I find her a bit lethargic.; see **mou**

mollet [mɔlɛ] nm (of leg) calf
▶ adj: **un œuf mollet** a soft-boiled egg

moment [mɔmã] nm moment; **en ce moment** at the moment ▷ Nous avons beaucoup de travail en ce moment. We have a lot of work at the moment.; **pour le moment** for the moment ▷ Nous restons ici pour le moment. We're staying here for the moment.; **au moment où** just as ▷ Il est arrivé au moment où j'allais partir. He turned up just as I was leaving.; **à ce moment-là (1)** at that point ▷ À ce moment-là, on a vu arriver la police. At that point, we saw the police coming. **(2)** in that case ▷ À ce moment-là, je devrai partir plus tôt. In that case I'll have to leave earlier.; **à tout moment (1)** at any moment ▷ Elle peut arriver à tout moment.

She could arrive at any moment. **(2)** constantly ▷ *Il nous dérange à tout moment pour des riens.* He's constantly bothering us about nothing.; **sur le moment** at the time ▷ *Sur le moment je n'ai rien dit.* At the time I didn't say anything.; **par moments** at times ▷ *Elle se sent seule par moments.* She feels lonely at times.

momentané [mɔmɑ̃tane] (f **momentanée**) *adj* momentary

momie [mɔmi] *nf* (Egyptian) mummy

mon [mɔ̃] (f **ma**, *pl* **mes**) *adj* my ▷ *mon frère* my brother ▷ *mon ami* my friend

monarchie [mɔnaʁʃi] *nf* monarchy

monastère [mɔnastɛʁ] *nm* monastery

monde [mɔ̃d] *nm* ❶ world ▷ *faire le tour du monde* to go around the world ❷ people ▷ *Il y avait beaucoup de monde au concert.* There were a lot of people at the concert. ▷ *peu de monde* not many people; **Il y a du monde.** There are a lot of people.

mondial [mɔ̃djal, -o] (f **mondiale**, *mpl* **mondiaux**) *adj* ❶ world ▷ *la population mondiale* the world population ❷ world-wide ▷ *une crise mondiale* a world-wide crisis

moniteur [mɔnitœʁ] *nm* ❶ instructor ▷ *un moniteur de voile* a sailing instructor ❷ monitor ▷ *le moniteur de mon ordinateur* my computer monitor

monitrice [mɔnitʁis] *nf* instructor ▷ *une monitrice de ski* a ski instructor

monnaie [mɔnɛ] *nf*: **une pièce de monnaie** a coin; **avoir de la monnaie** to have change ▷ *Est-ce que tu as de la monnaie?* Do you have any change? ▷ *Est-ce que vous avez la monnaie de dix dollars?* Do you have change for 10 dollars?; **rendre la monnaie à quelqu'un** to give somebody their change

monopoliser [mɔnɔpolize] *vb* to monopolize ▷ *monopoliser la conversation* to monopolize the conversation ▷ *Tu monopolises le téléphone!* You're monopolizing the phone!

monotone [mɔnɔtɔn] *adj* monotonous

Monsieur [məsjø] (*pl* **Messieurs**) *nm* ❶ Mr ▷ *Monsieur Dupont* Mr Dupont ❷ man ▷ *Il y a un monsieur qui veut te voir.* There's a man to see you. ❸ Sir ▷ *Monsieur,... Dear Sir,...* ❹ (in letter) ▷ *Monsieur! Vous avez oublié votre parapluie!* Sir! You forgot your umbrella!

monstre [mɔ̃stʁ(ə)] *nm* monster ▶ *adj*: **Nous avons un travail monstre.** We have a terrific amount of work.

mont [mɔ̃] *nm* mount; **le mont Logan** Mount Logan

montagne [mɔ̃taɲ] *nf* mountain ▷ *de hautes montagnes* high mountains ▷ *Nous passons nos vacances à la montagne.* We spend our holidays in the mountains.; **les montagnes russes** roller coaster; **se faire une montagne de quelque chose** to blow something out of proportion ▷ *Ils s'en font une montagne.* They're blowing it out of proportion.; **Tu te fais une montagne d'un petit incident de rien.** You're making a mountain out of a molehill.

montagneux [mɔ̃taɲø, -øz] (f **montagneuse**) *adj* mountainous ▷ *une région montagneuse* a mountainous area

montant [mɔ̃tɑ̃, -ɑ̃t] (f **montante**) *adj* ❶ rising ▷ *la marée montante* the rising tide ▷ *une étoile montante* a rising star ❷ high ▷ *un manteau à col montant* a high-necked coat

monter [mɔ̃te] *vb* ❶ to go up ▷ *Elle a du mal à monter les escaliers.* She has difficulty going up stairs. ▷ *Les prix ont encore monté.* Prices have gone up again. ❷ to assemble ▷ *Est-ce que ces étagères sont difficiles à monter?* Are these shelves difficult to assemble?; **monter dans** to board ▷ *Il est temps de monter dans l'avion.* It's time to board the plane.; **monter sur** to climb on ▷ *Tu vas devoir monter sur une chaise pour changer l'ampoule.* You'll have to climb on a chair to change the light bulb.; **monter à cheval** to ride; **se monter à** (total) to amount to ▷ *Ses achats se montaient à quinze dollars.* His purchases amounted to 15 dollars.; **se monter la tête** to get worked up ▷ *Elle s'est montée la tête pour rien.* She got worked up over nothing.

montre [mɔ̃tʁ(ə)] *nf* watch

montrer [mɔ̃tʁe] *vb* to show ▷ *Est-ce que vous pouvez me montrer le musée sur le plan?* Can you show me the museum on the map?

monture [mɔ̃tyʁ] *nf* (of glasses) frames

monument [mɔnymɑ̃] *nm* monument

se moquer [mɔke] *vb*: **se moquer de (1)** to make fun of ▷ *Ils se sont moqués de mes chaussures jaunes.* They made fun of my yellow shoes. **(2)** (informal) not to care about ▷ *Il se moque complètement de la mode.* He couldn't care less about fashion.

moquette [mɔkɛt] *nf* broadloom

moqueur [mɔkœʁ, -øz] (f **moqueuse**) *adj* mocking

moral [mɔʁal, -o] (*mpl* **moraux**) *adj* moral ▷ *une obligation morale* a moral obligation ▶ *nm*: **Elle a le moral.** She's in good spirits.; **J'ai le moral à zéro.** I'm feeling really down.

morale [mɔʁal] *nf* ❶ moral ▷ *La morale de cette histoire est...* The moral of the story is...; **faire la morale à quelqu'un** to lecture somebody ❷ morality ▷ *la morale traditionelle* traditional morality

morceau [mɔʁso] (*pl* **morceaux**) *nm* piece ▷ *un morceau de pain* a piece of bread

mordiller [mɔʁdije] *vb* to nibble ▷ *Ne mordille pas ton crayon.* Don't nibble on your pencil.

mordre [mɔʁdʁ(ə)] *vb* to bite

mordu [mɔʁdy] (f **mordue**) *adj*: **Il est mordu de jazz.** (informal) He's crazy about jazz.

morne [mɔʁn(ə)] *adj* ❶ drab ▷ *un décor morne* a drab décor ❷ (person, weather) gloomy ▷ *Pourquoi as-tu l'air tellement morne?* Why are you looking so gloomy? ▷ *un temps morne* gloomy weather

morse [mɔʁs(ə)] *nm* walrus

morsure [mɔʁsyʁ] *nf* bite

mort [mɔʁ] (f **morte**) *nf* death ▶ *adj* dead ▷ *Nous avons trouvé un oiseau mort.* We found a dead bird. ▷ *Anne Hébert, écrivaine canadienne, est morte en 2000.* Canadian writer Anne Hébert died in 2000.; **Il était mort de peur.** He was scared to death.; **Je suis morte de fatigue.** I'm dead tired.

mortel [mɔʁtɛl] (f **mortelle**) *adj* ❶ deadly

▷ un poison mortel a deadly poison ▷ Ces réunions de famille sont mortelles! (informal) These family gatherings are deadly! ❷ fatal ▷ une chute mortelle a fatal fall

morue [mɔʀy] nf cod

mosquée [mɔske] nf mosque

mot [mo] nm ❶ word ▷ mot à mot word for word; **des mots croisés** a crossword; **le mot de passe** the password ▷ note ▷ Je vais lui écrire un mot pour lui dire qu'on arrive. I'll write her a note to say we're coming.

motard [mɔtaʀ] nm motorcyclist

motarde [mɔtaʀd(ə)] nf motorcyclist

mot-clé [mokle] nm keyword ▷ Entrez le mot-clé dans le moteur de recherche. Enter the keyword in the search engine.

moteur [mɔtœʀ] nm engine; **un bateau à moteur** a motor boat; **un moteur de recherche** a search engine

motif [mɔtif] nm ❶ pattern ▷ des rideaux avec un motif d'oiseaux curtains with a bird pattern; **sans motif** for no reason ▷ Il s'est fâché sans motif. He got angry for no reason.

motivé [mɔtive] (f **motivée**) adj motivated

moto [mɔto] nf motorbike; **la moto tout-terrain** trail bike

motocycliste [mɔtɔsiklist(ə)] nmf motorcyclist

motoneige [mɔtɔnɛʒ] nf snowmobile

motoneigiste [mɔtɔnɛʒist] nmf snowmobiler

mou [mu, mɔl] (f **molle**) adj ❶ soft ▷ Mon matelas est trop mou. My mattress is too soft. ❷ lethargic ▷ Je le trouve un peu mou. I find him a bit lethargic. ❸ limp ▷ devenir mou to go limp

mouche [muʃ] nf ❶ (insect) fly; **la mouche noire** black fly; **prendre la mouche** to get bent out of shape

se moucher [muʃe] vb to blow one's nose

mouchoir [muʃwaʀ] nm handkerchief; **un mouchoir en papier** a tissue

moudre [mudʀ(ə)] vb to grind

moue [mu] nf pout; **faire la moue** to pout

mouette [mwɛt] nf seagull

moufette [mufɛt] nf skunk

mouillé [muje] (f **mouillée**) adj wet

mouiller [muje] vb to get wet ▷ J'ai mouillé les manches de mon chandail. I got the sleeves of my sweater wet.; **se mouiller** to get wet ▷ Attention, tu vas te mouiller! Careful, you'll get wet!

moulant [mulɑ̃, -ɑ̃t] (f **moulante**) adj slinky ▷ une robe moulante a slinky dress

moule [mul] nf mussel

▶ nm: **un moule à gâteaux** a cake tin

moulin [mulɛ̃] nm mill

moulu [muly] vb see **moudre**

mourir [muʀiʀ] vb to die; **mourir de faim** to starve ▷ Des centaines de personnes sont mortes de faim. Hundreds of people starved to death.; **Je meurs de faim!** I'm starving!; **mourir de froid** to die of exposure; **Je meurs de froid!** I'm freezing!; **mourir d'envie de faire quelque chose** to be dying to do something ▷ Je meurs d'envie d'aller me baigner. I'm dying to go for a swim.

mousse [mus] nf ❶ moss ▷ un rocher recouvert de mousse a rock covered with moss ❷ (on soft drink) froth ❸ (of soap, shampoo) lather ❹ mousse ▷ une mousse au chocolat a chocolate mousse ▷ une mousse au saumon a salmon mousse; **la mousse à raser** shaving foam

moustache [mustaʃ] nf moustache; **les moustaches** whiskers

moustiquaire [mustikɛʀ] nmf ❶ (on window) screen ❷ mosquito net

moustique [mustik] nm mosquito

moutarde [mutaʀd(ə)] nf mustard

mouton [mutɔ̃] nm ❶ sheep ▷ une peau de mouton a sheepskin ❷ mutton ▷ un gigot de mouton a leg of mutton

mouvement [muvmɑ̃] nm movement

mouvementé [muvmɑ̃te] (f **mouvementée**) adj eventful ▷ une époque mouvementée de l'histoire du Canada an eventful period in Canada's history

moyen [mwajɛ̃, -ɛn] (f **moyenne**) adj ❶ average ▷ Je suis plutôt moyenne en langues. I'm just average at languages. ❷ medium ▷ Elle est de taille moyenne. She's of medium height.; **le Moyen Âge** the Middle Ages; **le Moyen Orient** the Middle East

▶ nm way ▷ Quel est le meilleur moyen de le convaincre? What's the best way to convince him?; **Je n'en ai pas les moyens.** I can't afford it.; **Ils n'ont pas les moyens de s'acheter une voiture.** They can't afford to buy a car.; **un moyen de transport** a means of transport; **par tous les moyens** by every possible means

moyenne [mwajɛn] nf: **avoir la moyenne** to get a passing grade ▷ J'espère avoir la moyenne en maths. I hope to get a passing grade in math.; **en moyenne** on average; **la moyenne d'âge** the average age

muet [mɥɛ, -ɛt] (f **muette**) adj mute; **un film muet** a silent film

multiculturel [myltikyltyʀɛl] (f **multiculturelle**) adj multicultural

multiple [myltipl(ə)] adj numerous ▷ en de multiples occasions on numerous occasions

multiplier [myltiplije] vb to multiply

municipal [mynisipal, -o] (f **municipale**, mpl **municipaux**) adj: **une élection municipale** a municipal election; **les règlements municipaux** city by-laws; **la bibliothèque municipale** the public library

municipalité [mynisipalite] nf town council

munir [myniʀ] vb: **munir quelqu'un de** to equip someone with; **se munir de** to equip oneself with

munitions [mynisjɔ̃] nfpl ammunition

mur [myʀ] nm wall

mûr [myʀ] (f **mûre**) adj ❶ (fruit) ripe ❷ (person) mature

mûre [myʀ] nf blackberry

mûrir [myʀiʀ] vb ❶ to ripen ▷ Les fraises ont mis du temps à mûrir. The strawberries took a while to ripen. ❷ to make mature ▷ Cette expérience l'a beaucoup mûrie. That experience has made her much more mature.

murmurer [myʀmyʀe] vb to whisper ▷ Il m'a murmuré à l'oreille qu'il allait partir. He whispered in my ear that he was going to go.

muscade [myskad] *nf* nutmeg

muscle [myskl(ə)] *nm* muscle

musclé [myskle] (*f***musclée**) *adj* muscular

museau [myzo] (*pl* **museaux**) *nm* muzzle

musée [myze] *nm* museum

musical [myzikal, -o] (*f***musicale**, *mpl* **musicaux**) *adj* musical; **avoir l'oreille musicale** to be musical

music-hall [myzikol] (*pl* **les music-halls**) *nm* variety ▷ *une chanteuse de music-hall* a variety singer

musicien [myzisjɛ̃] *nm* musician ▷ *Il est musicien de jazz.* He's a jazz musician.

musicienne [myzisjɛn] *nf* musician ▷ *Elle est musicienne de rue.* She's a street musician.

musique [myzik] *nf* music

musulman [myzylmɑ̃, -an] (*f***musulmane**) *adj, n* Muslim; **un musulman** (*man*) a Muslim; **une musulmane** (*woman*) a Muslim

mutation [mytasjɔ̃] *nf* (*job*) transfer ▷ *Il a demandé sa mutation à Winnipeg.* He asked for a transfer to Winnipeg.

mye [mi] *nf* clam ▷ *une chaudrée de myes* clam chowder

myope [mjɔp] *adj* short-sighted

mystère [mistɛʀ] *nm* mystery

mystérieux [misterjø, -øz] (*f***mystérieuse**) *adj* mysterious

mythe [mit] *nm* myth

n

n' [n] *pron see* **ne**

nage [naʒ] *nf*: **traverser une rivière à la nage** to swim across a river; **être en nage** to be sweating profusely

nageoire [naʒwaʀ] *nf* fin

nager [naʒe] *vb* to swim

nageur [naʒœʀ] *nm* swimmer

nageuse [naʒøz] *nf* swimmer

naïf [naif, naiv] (*f***naïve**) *adj* naïve

nain [nɛ̃] *nm* dwarf

naine [nɛn] *nf* dwarf

naissance [nɛsɑ̃s] *nf* birth; **votre date de naissance** your date of birth; **de naissance** from birth ▷ *Il est sourd de naissance.* He was born deaf.

naître [nɛtʀ(ə)] *vb* to be born; **Il est né en 1982.** He was born in 1982.

nappe [nap] *nf* tablecloth

napperon [napʀɔ̃] *nm* placemat

narine [naʀin] *nf* nostril

natal [natal] (*f***natale**, *mpl* **natals**) *adj* native ▷ *mon pays natal* my native country

natation [natasjɔ̃] *nf* swimming ▷ *La natation est mon sport favori.* Swimming is my favourite sport.; **faire de la natation** to go swimming

nation [nasjɔ̃] *nf* nation ▷ *les Nations unies* the United Nations

national [nasjɔnal, -o] (*f***nationale**, *mpl* **nationaux**) *adj* national; **la fête nationale espagnole** the national day of Spain

nationalité [nasjɔnalite] *nf* nationality

nature [natyʀ] *nf* nature (*pl* **nature**)
▶ *adj* plain ▷ *un yogourt nature* a plain yogurt ▷ *des framboises nature* plain strawberries

naturel [natyʀɛl] (*f***naturelle**) *adj* natural

naturellement [natyʀɛlmɑ̃] *adv* of course ▷ *« Vous viendrez à notre fête ? » — « Naturellement ! »* "Are you coming to our party?" — "Of course!" ▷ *Naturellement, elle est encore en retard.* Of course, she's late again.

naufrage [nofʀaʒ] *nm* shipwreck

nausée [noze] *nf* nausea; **avoir la nausée** to feel nauseous; **Cela m'a donné la nausée.** It made me nauseous.

nautique [notik] *adj*: **la sécurité nautique** water safety; **les sports nautiques** water sports; **le ski nautique** water-skiing; **une carte nautique** a nautical chart

navet [navɛ] *nm* turnip

navette [navɛt] *nf* shuttle ▷ *la navette entre l'hôtel et l'aéroport* the shuttle between the hotel and the airport; **faire la navette** to commute ▷ *Je fais la navette entre Guelph et Burlington.* I commute between Guelph and Burlington.

navetteur [navetœʀ] *nm* commuter

navetteuse [navetøz] *nf* commuter

navigateur [navigatœʀ] *nm* (*on computer*) browser ▷ *un navigateur Web* Web browser

navigation [navigasjɔ̃] *nf* ❶ boat traffic ▷ *Il y a beaucoup de navigation sur les Grands Lacs.* There is considerable boat traffic on the Great Lakes.; **La navigation est interdite ici.** Boating is not allowed here. ❷ navigation ▷ *Les récifs rendent la navigation difficile.* Reefs make navigation difficult.; **un système de navigation par écluses** a canal and locks system

naviguer [navige] *vb* ❶ to sail ❷ (*Internet*) to surf ▷ *naviguer sur Internet* to surf the Net

navire [naviʀ] *nm* ship

ne [n(ə)] *adv*: ▷ *Je ne peux pas venir.* I can't come. ▷ *Ils ne regardent jamais la télé.* They never watch TV. ▷ *Je ne connais personne ici.* I don't know anyone here. ▷ *Je n'ai pas d'argent.* I don't have any money. ▷ *Il n'habite plus à Labrador City.* He doesn't live in Labrador City any more. ▷ *C'est plus loin que je ne le croyais.* It's further than I thought.

né [ne] *vb see* **naître** born ▷ *Elle est née en 1980.* She was born in 1980.

néanmoins [neɑ̃mwɛ̃] *adv* nevertheless

nécessaire [neseseʀ] *adj* necessary ▷ *Il est nécessaire de réserver.* It's necessary to make reservations.

négatif [negatif, iv] (*f***négative**) *adj* negative
▶ *nm* (*of photo*) negative

négligé [neglize] (f**négligée**) adj scruffy ▷ *une tenue négligée* scruffy clothes

négliger [neglize] vb to neglect ▷ *Ces derniers temps il a négligé son travail.* He's been neglecting his work recently.

négocier [negosje] vb to negotiate

neige [nɛʒ] nf snow; **la neige fondante** slush; **un bonhomme de neige** a snowman

neiger [neʒe] vb to snow

nénuphar [nenyfar] nm water lily

néon [neɔ̃] nm neon ▷ *une lampe au néon* a neon light ▷ *La cuisine est éclairée au néon.* The kitchen has a neon light.

nerf [nɛʀ] nm nerve; **taper sur les nerfs de quelqu'un** to get on somebody's nerves ▷ *Il me tape sur les nerfs.* He's getting on my nerves.

nerveux [nɛʀvø, -øz] (f**nerveuse**) adj nervous

nervosité [nɛʀvozite] nf nervousness

n'est-ce pas [nɛspa] adv: *C'est le douze aujourd'hui, n'est-ce pas?* It's the 12th today, isn't it? ▷ *Ils sont venus l'an dernier, n'est-ce pas?* They came last year, didn't they? ▷ *Elle aura dix-huit ans en octobre, n'est-ce pas?* She'll be 18 in October, won't she?

net [nɛt] (f**nette**) adj, adv **①** clear ▷ *L'image n'est pas nette.* The picture isn't very clear. **②** net ▷ *Poids net : 500 g.* Net weight: 500 g. **③** flatly ▷ *Il a refusé net de nous aider.* He flatly refused to help us.; **s'arrêter net** to stop dead

nettement [nɛtmɑ̃] adv much ▷ *Ce magasin est nettement plus cher.* This store is much more expensive.

nettoyage [nɛtwajaʒ] nm cleaning; **le nettoyage à sec** dry cleaning

nettoyer [nɛtwaje] vb to clean

nettoyeur [nɛtwajœʀ] nm dry-cleaner ▷ *Je vais porter ce manteau chez le nettoyeur.* I'm going to take this coat to the dry-cleaner's.

neuf [nœf, nœv] num nine ▷ *Elle a neuf ans.* She's nine. ▷ *Il est neuf heures du matin.* It's nine in the morning.; **le neuf février** the ninth of February

▶ adj (f**neuve**) new ▷ *des chaussures neuves* new shoes

neutre [nøtʀ(ə)] adj neutral

neuve [nœv] adj see **neuf**

neuvième [nœvjɛm] adj ninth ▷ *au neuvième étage* on the ninth floor

neveu [nəvø] (pl **neveux**) nm nephew

nez [ne] nm nose; **se trouver nez à nez avec quelqu'un** to come face to face with somebody; *C'était juste sous mon nez.* It was right under my nose.; **mettre le nez dehors** to go outside; **ne pas voir plus loin que le bout de son nez** to lack foresight

ni [ni] conj: **ni...ni...** neither...nor... ▷ *Je n'aime ni les lentilles ni les épinards.* I like neither lentils nor spinach. ▷ *Elles ne sont venues ni l'une ni l'autre.* Neither of them came.

niaiser [njeze] vb **①** (informal: someone) to kid ▷ *Arrête de nous niaiser avec tes histoires incroyables.* Stop kidding us with your unbelievable stories. **②** (waste time) to fool around ▷ *Au bout du compte, on a niaisé tout l'après-midi.* We ended up just fooling around the whole afternoon.

niaiserie [njezʀi] nf (informal) nonsense ▷ *Elle t'a raconté des niaiseries.* What she told you was nonsense. ▷ *Tu dis des niaiseries!* You're talking nonsense!; **faire des niaiseries** to get into trouble ▷ *Il faut surveiller ce petit garçon, sinon il fait des niaiseries.* This little boy needs to be supervised, otherwise he gets into trouble.

niaiseux [njezø, -øz] (f**niaiseuse**) adj (informal) stupid ▷ *J'ai trouvé ce film complètement niaiseux.* I thought that movie was utterly stupid. ▷ *Ne sois pas niaiseuse, fais tes devoirs.* Don't be stupid; do your homework.

niche [niʃ] nf kennel

nid [ni] nm nest

nièce [njɛs] nf niece

nier [nje] vb to deny

n'importe [nɛ̃pɔʀt(ə)] adv: **n'importe quel** any ▷ *N'importe quel stylo fera l'affaire.* Any pen will do.; **n'importe qui** anybody ▷ *N'ouvre pas la porte à n'importe qui.* Don't open the door to just anybody.; **n'importe quoi** anything ▷ *Je ferais n'importe quoi pour lui.* I'd do anything for him.; *Tu dis n'importe quoi.* You're talking nonsense.; **n'importe où** anywhere ▷ *On trouve ces fleurs n'importe où.* You can find these flowers anywhere.; *Ne laisse pas tes affaires n'importe où.* Don't leave your things lying everywhere.; **n'importe quand** any time ▷ *Tu peux venir n'importe quand.* You can come any time.; **n'importe comment** any old way ▷ *Ces livres sont rangés n'importe comment.* These books have been put away any old way.

NIP abbr (= le numéro d'identification personnel) PIN number

niveau [nivo] (pl **niveaux**) nm level ▷ *le niveau de l'eau* the water level ▷ *Ces deux enfants n'ont pas le même niveau.* These two children aren't at the same level.; **le niveau de vie** the standard of living

noble [nɔbl(ə)] adj noble

noblesse [nɔbles] nf nobility

noce [nɔs] nf wedding; **un repas de noce** a wedding reception; **leurs noces d'or** their golden wedding anniversary

nocif [nɔsif, -iv] (f**nocive**) adj harmful ▷ *une substance nocive* a harmful substance

Noël [nɔɛl] nm Christmas; **Joyeux Noël!** Merry Christmas!

nœud nm **①** knot ▷ *Il a fait un nœud à la corde.* He tied a knot in the rope. **②** bow ▷ *La petite fille avait un nœud dans les cheveux.* The little girl had a bow in her hair.; **un nœud papillon** a bow tie; **frapper un nœud** (problem) to hit a snag

noir [nwaʀ] (f**noire**) adj **①** black ▷ *Elle porte une robe noire.* She's wearing a black dress. ▷ *Il est noir.* He's black. **②** dark ▷ *Il fait noir dehors.* It's dark outside.

▶ nm dark ▷ *J'ai peur du noir.* I'm afraid of the dark.; **le travail au noir** moonlighting

Noir nm (man) black; **les Noirs** black people

noirceur [nwaʀsœʀ] nf darkness ▷ *Nous avons perdu notre chemin dans la noirceur.* We lost our way in the darkness.

Noire nf (woman) black

noisette [nwazɛt] nf hazelnut

noix [nwa] (*pl* **noix**) *nf* walnut; **une noix de coco** a coconut; **les noix de cajou** cashews; **une noix de beurre** a dab of butter

nolisé [nɔlize] *adj* charter ▷ *le vol nolisé* charter flight

nom [nɔ̃] *nm* ❶ name ▷ *votre nom* your name; **mon nom de famille** my surname; **son nom de jeune fille** her maiden name ❷ (*in grammar*) noun ▷ *un nom commun* a common noun ▷ *un nom propre* a proper noun; **le nom d'utilisateur** login ID

nombre [nɔ̃bʀ(ə)] *nm* number ▷ *Treize est un nombre impair.* Thirteen is an odd number. ▷ *un grand nombre d'amis* a large number of friends

nombreux [nɔ̃bʀø, -øz] (*f* **nombreuse**) *adj* ❶ many ▷ *Il a gagné de nombreux matchs.* He's won many games. ❷ large ▷ *une famille nombreuse* a large family; **être plus nombreux que** to outnumber; **peu nombreux** few ▷ *Nous étions peu nombreux à la réunion.* There were few of us at the meeting.

nombril [nɔ̃bʀi] *nm* navel

nommer [nɔme] *vb* ❶ to name ▷ *Elle n'a voulu nommer personne.* She didn't want to name anybody. ❷ to appoint ▷ *Elle a été nommée directrice.* She was appointed director.

non [nɔ̃] *adv no* ▷ *« Tu as vu mon frère ? »* — *« Non. »* "Have you seen my brother?" — "No."; **non seulement** not only ▷ *Il est non seulement intelligent, mais aussi très gentil.* Not only is he intelligent, he's also very nice.; **moi non plus** Neither do I. ▷ *« Je n'aime pas les hamburgers. »* — *« Moi non plus. »* "I don't like hamburgers." — "Neither do I." ▷ *Elle n'y est pas allée et moi non plus.* She didn't go and neither did I.

non alcoolisé [nɔ̃nalkɔlize] (*f* **non alcoolisée**) *adj* non-alcoholic ▷ *les boissons non alcoolisées* non-alcoholic drinks

non-fumeur [nɔ̃fymœʀ] *nm* non-smoker ▷ *Je suis un non-fumeur.* I'm a non-smoker.; **la section non-fumeurs** the non-smoking section

non-fumeuse [nɔ̃fymøz] *nf* non-smoker ▷ *Ma sœur est une non-fumeuse.* My sister is a non-smoker.

nord [nɔʀ] *nm* north ▷ *Ils vivent dans le nord de l'île.* They live in the north of the island.; **vers le nord** northwards; **au nord de Jonquière** north of Jonquière; **l'Amérique du Nord** North America; **le vent du nord** the north wind ▶ *adj* ❶ north ▷ *la face nord de la montagne* the north face of the mountain; **le pôle Nord** the North Pole ❷ northern ▷ *Nous avons visité la partie nord de la province.* We visited the northern part of the province.

nord-est [nɔʀɛst] *nm* northeast ▷ *les régions du nord-est* northeastern regions

nord-ouest [nɔʀwɛst] *nm* northwest; **le Passage du Nord-Ouest** The Northwest Passage

normal [nɔʀmal, -o] (*f* **normale**, *mpl* **normaux**) *adj* ❶ normal ▷ *un bébé normal* a normal baby ❷ natural ▷ *C'est tout à fait normal.* It's perfectly natural.; **Vous trouvez que c'est normal ?** Does that seem right to you?

normalement [nɔʀmalmɑ̃] *adv* normally ▷ *Les aéroports fonctionnent tous normalement.* The airports are all operating normally.; **Normalement, elle doit arriver à huit heures.** She's supposed to arrive at 8 o'clock.; *« Tu es libre en fin de semaine ? »* *« Oui, normalement. »* "Are you free this weekend?" "Yes, I should be."

nos [no] *adj* our ▷ *Où sont nos affaires ?* Where's our stuff?

notaire [nɔtɛʀ] *nmf* lawyer ▷ *Sa mère est notaire.* His mother's a lawyer.

note [nɔt] *nf* ❶ note ▷ *J'ai pris des notes pendant la classe.* I took notes in class. ▷ *Il a joué quelques notes au piano.* He played a few notes on the piano. ❷ mark ▷ *Elle a de bonnes notes en maths.* She gets good marks in math.

noter [nɔte] *vb* to make a note of ▷ *Tu as noté leur adresse ?* Did you make a note of their address?

notions [nɔsjɔ̃] *nfpl* basics ▷ *Il faut avoir des notions d'anglais.* You have to have some basic English. ▷ *Elle a des notions de traitement de texte.* She knows the basics of word processing.

notoire [nɔtwaʀ] *adj* notorious ▷ *un criminel notoire* a notorious criminal

notre [nɔtʀ(ə), no] (*pl* **nos**) *adj* our ▷ *Voici notre maison.* Here's our house.

nôtre [notʀ(ə)] *pron* : **le nôtre** ours ▷ *« À qui est ce chien ? » « C'est le nôtre. »* "Whose dog is this?" "It's ours." ▷ *Leur voiture est rouge ; la nôtre est bleue.* Their car is red; ours is blue.

nôtres [notʀ] *pron* : **les nôtres** ours ▷ *Ces places-là sont les nôtres.* Those seats are ours.

nouer [nwe] *vb* to tie

nouilles [nuj] *nfpl* noodles

nounours [nunuʀs] *nm* teddy bear

nourrir [nuʀiʀ] *vb* to feed

nourriture [nuʀityʀ] *nf* food; **la nourriture pour animaux de compagnie** pet food; **une nourriture saine** a healthy diet

nous [nu] *pron* ❶ we ▷ *Nous avons deux enfants.* We have two children. ❷ us ▷ *Viens avec nous.* Come with us.; **nous-mêmes** ourselves

nouveau [nuvo, -ɛl] (*f* **nouvelle**, *mpl* **nouveaux**) *adj* new ▷ *Il me faut un nouveau pantalon.* I need some new pants. ▷ *Ils ont une nouvelle voiture.* They've a new car. ▷ *le nouvel élève dans ma classe* The new boy in my class; **le Nouvel An** New Year's; **le nouvel âge** New Age ▷ *la musique nouvel âge* New Age music ▶ *nm* (*pl* **nouveaux**) new person ▷ *Il y a plusieurs nouveaux dans la classe.* There are several new people in the class.; **de nouveau** again ▷ *Il pleut de nouveau.* It's raining again.

Nouveau-Brunswick [nuvobʀœnswik] *nm* New Brunswick

nouveau-né [nuvone] (*mpl* **les nouveau-nés**, *f* **la nouveau-née**, *fpl* **les nouveau-nées**) *nm* newborn

nouveauté [nuvote] *nf* novelty

nouvel [nuvɛl] *adj see* **nouveau**

nouvelle [nuvɛl] *adj see* **nouveau** ▶ *nf* ❶ (*single item*) news ▷ *Tu connais la nouvelle ? Ma grand-mère a gagné à la loto.* Have you heard the news? My grandmother won the lottery. ▷ *C'est une bonne nouvelle.* That's good news. ❷ short story ▷ *une nouvelle de Janet Lunn* a short story by Janet Lunn; **les nouvelles** the news ▷ *J'ai écouté les nouvelles à la radio.* I listened to the news on the radio.; **avoir des nouvelles de quelqu'un** to hear from somebody ▷ *Je n'ai pas eu de nouvelles de lui.* I haven't heard from him.

Nouvelle-Écosse [nuvɛlekɔs] *nf* Nova Scotia

novembre [nɔvɑ̃bʀ(ə)] *nm* November; **en novembre** in November

noyau [nwajo] (*pl* **noyaux**) *nm* (*of fruit*) stone ▷ *un noyau d'abricot* an apricot stone

se **noyer** [nwaje] *vb* to drown ▷ *Il s'est noyé dans la rivière.* He drowned in the river.

nu [ny] (*f* **nue**) *adj* ❶ naked ▷ *Ils se sont baignés nus.* They went swimming naked. ▷ *tout nus* stark naked ❷ bare ▷ *Elle avait les bras nus.* Her arms were bare. ▷ *Les murs étaient nus.* The walls were bare.

nuage [nɥaʒ] *nm* cloud; **être dans les nuages** to daydream

nuageux [nɥaʒø, -øz] (*f* **nuageuse**) *adj* cloudy

nucléaire [nykleɛʀ] *adj* nuclear ▷ *l'énergie nucléaire* nuclear power ▷ *la famille nucléaire* the nuclear family

nudiste [nydist(ə)] *nmf* nudist

nuit [nɥi] *nf* ❶ night ▷ *Ils ont fait du bruit toute la nuit.* They were noisy all night. ❷ at night ▷ *se promener la nuit* to go for a walk at night; **Il fait nuit.** It's dark out.; **cette nuit** tonight ▷ *Il va rentrer cette nuit.* He'll be back tonight.; **Bonne nuit!** Good night!; **de nuit (1)** by night ▷ *voyager de nuit* to travel by night **(2)** nights ▷ *Il travaille de nuit.* He works nights.; **une nuit blanche** a sleepless night ▷ *J'ai encore passé une nuit blanche.* I had yet another sleepless night.

nul [nyl] (*f* **nulle**) *adj* (*informal*) no good; **être nul** to be no good ▷ *Je suis nul en éducation physique.* I'm no good at phys ed. ▷ *Ce film est nul.* This movie's no good.; **un match nul** (*sports*) a tie ▷ *Ils ont fait match nul.* It was a tie.; **nulle part** nowhere ▷ *Je ne le vois nulle part.* I can't see it anywhere.

numérique [nymeʀik] *adj* digital ▷ *un appareil photo numérique* a digital camera

numéro [nymeʀo] *nm* number ▷ *J'habite au numéro trois.* I live at number 3.; **mon numéro de téléphone** my phone number; **le numéro de compte** the account number; **le numéro d'identification personnel** PIN number; **le numéro confidentiel** unlisted number

Nunavut *nm* Nunavut

nu-pieds [nypje] *adj, adv* barefoot ▷ *Il se promenait nu-pieds.* He was walking barefoot.

nuque [nyk] *nf* nape of the neck

nutriment [nytʀimɑ̃] *nm* nutrient

nutritif [nytʀitif, -iv] (*f* **nutritive**) *adj* ❶ nutritious ▷ *une collation nutritive* a nutritious snack ❷ nutritional ▷ *La malbouffe n'a presque aucune valeur nutritive.* Junk food has almost no nutritional value.

nutrition [nytʀisjɔ̃] *nf* nutrition

nutritionniste [nytʀisjɔnist(ə)] *nmf* nutritionist

nylon [nilɔ̃] *nm* nylon

obéir [ɔbeiʀ] *vb* to obey; **obéir à quelqu'un** to obey somebody ▷ *Elle refuse d'obéir à ses parents.* She refuses to obey her parents.

obéissant [ɔbeisɑ̃, -ɑ̃t] (*f* **obéissante**) *adj* obedient

objet [ɔbʒɛ] *nm* object; **les objets de valeur** valuables; **les objets perdus** the lost-and-found

obligatoire [ɔbligatwaʀ] *adj* compulsory

obliger [ɔbliʒe] *vb*: **obliger quelqu'un à faire quelque chose** to force somebody to do something; **Je suis bien obligé d'accepter.** I can't really refuse.

obscur [ɔpskyʀ] (*f* **obscure**) *adj* dark

obscurité [ɔpskyʀite] *nf* darkness ▷ *dans l'obscurité* in the dark

obséder [ɔpsede] *vb* to obsess ▷ *Il est obsédé par le travail.* He's obsessed by work.

observation [ɔpsɛʀvasjɔ̃] *nf* comment ▷ *J'ai une ou deux observations à faire.* I've got one or two comments to make.

observer [ɔpsɛʀve] *vb* ❶ to watch ▷ *Nous observions nos canards sur le lac.* We watched the ducks on the lake. ❷ (*respect, keep*) to observe ▷ *Ils observent le règlement.* They observe the rules. ▷ *observer une minute de silence pour le Jour du Souvenir* to observe a minute of silence on Remembrance Day

obstacle [ɔpstakl(ə)] *nm* obstacle ▷ *surmonter un obstacle* to overcome an obstacle; **une course d'obstacles** an obstacle race

obstiné [ɔpstine] (*f* **obstinée**) *adj* stubborn

obtenir [ɔptəniʀ] *vb* ❶ to get ▷ *Ils ont obtenu cinquante pour cent des voix.* They got 50% of the votes. ❷ to achieve ▷ *Nous avons obtenu de bons résultats.* We achieved good results.

occasion [ɔkazjɔ̃] *nf* ❶ opportunity ▷ *C'est une occasion à ne pas manquer.* It's an opportunity not to be missed. ❷ occasion ▷ *à l'occasion de sa fête* on the occasion of his birthday ▷ *à plusieurs occasions* on several occasions ❸ bargain ▷ *Cet ordinateur est une bonne occasion.* This computer's a real bargain.; **d'occasion** second-hand ▷ *une voiture d'occasion* a second-hand car

Occident *nm* (*western world*) West; **en Occident** in the West

occidental [ɔksidɑ̃tal, -o] (*f* **occidentale**, *mpl* **occidentaux**) *adj* western; **les pays occidentaux** the West

occupation [ɔkypasjɔ̃] *nf* (*by troops*) occupation ▷ *la France sous l'Occupation* France during the Occupation

occupé [ɔkype] (f **occupée**) adj ❶ busy ▷ *Le directeur est très occupé.* The director's very busy. ▷ *La ligne est occupée.* The line is busy. ❷ taken ▷ *Est-ce que cette place est occupée?* Is this seat taken? ❸ occupied ▷ *Les toilettes sont occupées.* The washroom is occupied.

occuper [ɔkype] vb to occupy ▷ *Les enfants ne sont pas faciles à occuper quand il pleut.* Children aren't easy to keep occupied when it rains.; **s'occuper de quelque chose (1)** to be in charge of something ▷ *Elle s'occupe d'un club de sport.* She's in charge of a sports club. **(2)** to deal with something ▷ *Je vais m'occuper de ce problème tout de suite.* I'm going to deal with this problem right away.

océan [ɔseã] nm ocean ▷ *l'océan Indien* the Indian Ocean

octobre [ɔktɔbʁ(ə)] nm October; **en octobre** in October

odeur [ɔdœʁ] nf smell ▷ *Il y a une drôle d'odeur ici.* There's a funny smell here.

œil [œj, jø] (pl **yeux**) nm eye ▷ *J'ai quelque chose dans l'œil.* I've got something in my eye.; **à l'œil nu** with the naked eye; **un coup d'œil** a glance ▷ *Pourrais-tu jeter un coup d'œil sur ce que j'ai écrit, s'il te plaît?* Could you have a glance at what I've written, please?

œillet [œjɛ] nm carnation

œuf [œf] nm egg; **un œuf à la coque** a soft-boiled egg; **un œuf dur** a hard-boiled egg; **un œuf au plat** a fried egg; **un œuf au miroir** an egg fried sunny side up; **un œuf tourné** an egg fried over easy; **les œufs brouillés** scrambled eggs; **un œuf de Pâques** an Easter egg

œuvre [œvʁ] nf work ▷ *les œuvres complètes de Shakespeare* the complete works of Shakespeare; **une œuvre d'art** a work of art

œuvrer [œvʁe] vb to work ▷ *Elle œuvre auprès des jeunes sans-abri.* She works with homeless youth. ▷ *Toute sa vie, il a œuvré pour la cause de la paix.* He has worked all his life for peace.

offenser [ɔfɑ̃se] vb to offend ▷ *Est-ce que ma plaisanterie t'a offensé?* Did my joke offend you?; **s'offenser de quelque chose** to be offended by something

offert [ɔfɛʁ] vb see **offrir**

office [ɔfis] nm (government agency) office; **un office du tourisme** a tourist office

officiel [ɔfisjɛl] (f **officielle**) adj official

offre [ɔfʁ(ə)] nf offer ▷ *une offre spéciale* a special offer; **« offres d'emploi »** "Employment Opportunities"

offrir [ɔfʁiʁ] vb: **offrir quelque chose (1)** to offer something ▷ *On lui a offert un poste de secrétaire.* They offered him a secretarial post. ▷ *Elle m'a offert à boire.* She offered me a drink. **(2)** to present something ▷ *Il lui a offert des roses.* He presented her with roses.; **s'offrir quelque chose** to treat oneself to something ▷ *Je me suis offert un sous-marin de 12 pouces.* I treated myself to a twelve-inch sub.

oie [wa] nf goose

oignon [ɔɲɔ̃] nm onion

oiseau [wazo] (pl **oiseaux**) nm bird

olive [ɔliv] nf olive ▷ *l'huile d'olive* olive oil

olympique [ɔlɛ̃pik] adj: **les Jeux olympiques** the Olympic Games

ombre [ɔ̃bʁ(ə)] nf ❶ shade ▷ *Je vais me mettre à l'ombre.* I'm going to sit in the shade. ❷ shadow; **l'ombre à paupières** eye shadow

omnipraticien [ɔmnipʁatisjɛ̃] nm general practitioner ▷ *Il est omnipraticien.* He's a general practitioner.

omnipraticienne [ɔmnipʁatisjɛn] nf general practitioner ▷ *Elle est omnipraticienne.* She's a general practitioner.

on [ɔ̃] pron ❶ we ▷ *On va à la plage demain.* We're going to the beach tomorrow. ▷ *On a pensé que ça te ferait plaisir.* We thought you'd be pleased. ❷ someone ▷ *On m'a volé mon sac à main.* Someone has stolen my purse.; **On m'a dit d'attendre.** I was told to wait.; **On vous demande au téléphone.** There's a phone call for you. ❸ you ▷ *On peut visiter le château en été.* You can visit the castle in the summer. ▷ *D'ici on peut voir la tour CN.* From here you can see the CN Tower.

oncle [ɔ̃kl(ə)] nm uncle

onde [ɔ̃d] nf (on radio) wave ▷ *sur les ondes courtes* on shortwave

ongle [ɔ̃gl(ə)] nm nail; **se couper les ongles** to cut one's nails ▷ *Elle s'est coupé les ongles.* She cut her nails.

ont [ɔ̃] vb see **avoir**; **Ils ont beaucoup d'argent.** They have lots of money.; **Elles ont passé de bonnes vacances.** They had a good holiday.

Ontario [ɔ̃taʁjo] nm Ontario

ONU [ɔny] nf (= *Organisation des Nations unies*) UN (= *United Nations*)

onze [ɔ̃z] num eleven ▷ *Il a onze ans.* He's eleven. ▷ *à onze heures* at eleven o'clock; **le onze février** the eleventh of February

onzième [ɔ̃zjɛm] adj eleventh ▷ *au onzième étage* on the eleventh floor

opéra [ɔpeʁa] nm opera

opération [ɔpeʁasjɔ̃] nf operation

opérer [ɔpeʁe] vb to operate on ▷ *Elle a été opérée de l'appendicite.* She was operated on for appendicitis.; **se faire opérer** to have an operation ▷ *Il s'est fait opérer.* He had an operation.

opinion [ɔpinjɔ̃] nf opinion

opposé [ɔpoze] (f **opposée**) adj opposite ▷ *Elle est partie dans la direction opposée.* She went off in the opposite direction.; **être opposé à quelque chose** to be opposed to something ▶ nm the opposite

opposer [ɔpoze] vb: **opposer quelqu'un à quelqu'un** to pit somebody against somebody ▷ *Ce match oppose Edmonton à Toronto.* This match pits Edmonton against Toronto.; **s'opposer** to conflict ▷ *Ces deux points de vue s'opposent.* These two points of view conflict.; **s'opposer à quelque chose** to oppose something ▷ *Son père s'oppose à son mariage.* Her father's against her marriage.

opposition [ɔpozisjɔ̃] nf opposition; **par opposition à** as opposed to ▷ *la littérature contemporaine par opposition à la littérature classique* modern literature, as opposed to classics

opticien [ɔptisjɛ̃] nm optician ▷ *Il est opticien.* He's an optician.

opticienne [ɔptisjɛn] nf optician ▷ *Elle est opticienne.* She's an optician.

optimiste [ɔptimist(ə)] adj optimistic

option [ɔpsjɔ̃] nf option; **une matière à option** an optional subject

or [ɔʁ] nm gold ▷ *un bracelet en or* a gold bracelet
  ▶ *conj* and yet ▷ *Il était sûr de gagner, or il a perdu.* He was sure he would win, and yet he lost.

orage [ɔʁaʒ] nm thunderstorm

orageux [ɔʁaʒø, -øz] (f **orageuse**) adj stormy

oral [ɔʁal, -o] (f **orale**, mpl **oraux**) adj oral; **une présentation orale** an oral presentation; **une épreuve orale** an oral test; **à prendre par voie orale** to be taken orally

orange [ɔʁɑ̃ʒ] nf (fruit) orange
  ▶ *adj* ❶ **orange** (in colour) orange ▷ *des fleurs orange* orange flowers

orchestre [ɔʁkɛstʁ(ə)] nm ❶ orchestra ▷ *un orchestre symphonique* a symphony orchestra ❷ band ▷ *un orchestre de jazz* a jazz band

ordinaire [ɔʁdinɛʁ] adj ordinary ▷ *des gens ordinaires* ordinary people
  ▶ *nm*: **sortir de l'ordinaire** to be out of the ordinary

ordinateur [ɔʁdinatœʁ] nm computer; **un ordinateur portatif** a laptop

ordonnance [ɔʁdɔnɑ̃s] nf prescription

ordonné [ɔʁdɔne] (f **ordonnée**) adj tidy

ordonner [ɔʁdɔne] vb to order ▷ *La prof nous a ordonné de nous taire.* The teacher ordered us to stop talking. ▷ *On a ordonné aux grévistes de retourner au travail.* The strikers were ordered to go back to work.

ordre [ɔʁdʁ(ə)] nm order ▷ *en ordre alphabétique* in alphabetical order; **dans l'ordre** in order ▷ *dans le bon ordre* in the right order; **mettre en ordre** to tidy up; **jusqu'à nouvel ordre** until further notice; **l'ordre publique** law and order

ordures [ɔʁdyʁ] nfpl garbage

oreille [ɔʁɛj] nf ear; **avoir de l'oreille** (for music) to have a good ear; **écouter de toutes ses oreilles** to be all ears; **Je n'écoutais que d'une oreille.** I was only half listening.; **Les oreilles ont dû lui siffler.** Her ears must have been burning.

oreiller [ɔʁeje] nm pillow

oreillons [ɔʁejɔ̃] nmpl mumps

organe [ɔʁgan] nm (in body) organ

organisateur [ɔʁganizatœʁ] nm organizer; **l'organisateur graphique** graphic organizer

organisation [ɔʁganizasjɔ̃] nf organization

organisatrice [ɔʁganizatʁis] nf organizer

organiser [ɔʁganize] vb to organize; **s'organiser** to get organized ▷ *Elle ne sait pas s'organiser.* She can't get organized.

organisme [ɔʁganism(ə)] nm (organization) body

orgue [ɔʁg(ə)] nm organ ▷ *Il joue de l'orgue.* He plays the organ.

orgueilleux [ɔʁgœjø, -øz] (f **orgueilleuse**) adj proud

Orient [ɔʁjɑ̃] nm (eastern world) East; **en Orient** in the East

oriental [ɔʁjɑ̃tal, -o] (f **orientale**, mpl **orientaux**) adj ❶ oriental ▷ *un palais oriental* an oriental palace ❷ eastern ▷ *la frontière orientale de la Saskatchewan* the eastern border of Saskatchewan

orientation [ɔʁjɑ̃tasjɔ̃] nf orientation; **avoir le sens de l'orientation** to have a good sense of direction; **l'orientation professionnelle** career counselling

originaire [ɔʁiʒinɛʁ] adj: **Elle est originaire de Halifax.** She's from Halifax.

original [ɔʁiʒinal, -o] (f **originale**, mpl **originaux**) adj original ▷ *un film en version originale* a film in the original language (pl **originaux**)
  ▶ *nm* original ▷ *L'original est au Musée des beaux-arts de l'Ontario.* The original is in the Art Gallery of Ontario.; **un vieil original** an old eccentric

origine [ɔʁiʒin] nf origin; **à l'origine** originally

orignal [ɔʁiɲal, -o] nm moose

orphelin [ɔʁfəlɛ̃] nm orphan

orpheline [ɔʁfəlin] nf orphan

orteil [ɔʁtɛj] nm toe ▷ *mon gros orteil* my big toe

orthographe [ɔʁtɔgʁaf] nf spelling

os [ɔs] nm bone

oser [oze] vb to dare; **oser faire quelque chose** to dare to do something

otage [ɔtaʒ] nm hostage

ôter [ote] vb ❶ to take off ▷ *Elle a ôté son manteau.* She took off her coat. ❷ to take away

ou [u] conj or; **ou...ou...** either...or... ▷ *Je prendrai ou du lait ou du jus.* I'll have either milk or juice.; **ou bien** or else ▷ *On pourrait aller au cinéma ou bien rentrer directement.* We could go to a movie or else go straight home.

où [u] pron, adv ❶ where ▷ *Où est ton frère?* Where's your brother? ▷ *Où allez-vous?* Where are you going? ▷ *Je sais où il est.* I know where he is. ▷ *C'est la maison où je suis né.* That's the house where I was born. ▷ *la ville d'où je viens* the town I come from ❷ that ▷ *Le jour où il est parti, tout le monde a pleuré.* The day that he left, everyone cried.; **Par où allons-nous passer?** Which way are we going to go?

ouate [wat] nf cotton wool

oublier [ublije] vb ❶ to forget ▷ *N'oublie pas de fermer la porte.* Don't forget to shut the door. ❷ (behind) to leave ▷ *J'ai oublié mon sac à dos dans l'autobus.* I left my backpack on the bus.

ouest [wɛst] nm west ▷ *Elle vit dans l'ouest du Québec.* She lives in the western part of Québec.; **à l'ouest de Saint-Boniface** west of St. Boniface; **vers l'ouest** westwards; **les provinces de l'Ouest** the Western provinces; **le vent d'ouest** the west wind
  ▶ *adj* (f+pl **ouest**) ❶ west ▷ *la côte ouest du Canada* the west coast of Canada ❷ western ▷ *la partie ouest du pays* the western part of the country

ouf [uf] excl phew!

oui [wi] adv yes

ouragan [uʁagɑ̃] nm hurricane

ourlet [uʁlɛ] nm seam

ours [uʁs] nm bear; **un ours en peluche** a teddy bear

ourson [uRsɔ̃] nm bear cub

outarde [utaRd] nf Canada goose

outil [uti] nm tool

outré [utRe] (f **outrée**) adj outraged ▷ Il a été outré de son insolence. He was outraged at her lack of respect.

ouvert [uvɛR] vb see **ouvrir**

ouvert [uvɛR, -ɛRt(ə)] (f **ouverte**) adj ❶ open ▷ Le magasin est ouvert. The store is open. ❷ on ▷ Tu as laissé le robinet ouvert. You left the tap on.; **avoir l'esprit ouvert** to be open-minded

ouverture [uvɛRtyR] nf opening ▷ les heures d'ouverture hours of operation

ouvre-boîte [uvRəbwat] nm can opener

ouvre-bouteille [uvRəbutɛj] (pl **les ouvre-bouteilles**) nm bottle-opener

ouvrier [uvRije] nm worker ▷ Mon père est ouvrier dans une usine. My dad is a factory worker.

ouvrière [uvRijɛR] nf worker

ouvrir [uvRiR] vb to open ▷ Ouvrez! Open up! ▷ Elle a ouvert la porte. She opened the door.; **s'ouvrir** to open ▷ La porte s'est ouverte. The door opened.

ovale [ɔval] adj oval

ovni [ɔvni] nm (= objet volant non identifié) UFO

oxygène [ɔksiʒɛn] nm oxygen

ozone [ozɔn] nm ozone ▷ la couche d'ozone the ozone layer

P

pacane [pakan] nf pecan ▷ la tarte aux pacanes pecan pie

pacifiste [pasifist(ə)] nmf pacifist

pagaie [pagɛ] nf (chiefly kayak) paddle

pagaille [pagaj] nf mess ▷ Quelle pagaille! What a mess!

page [paʒ] nf page ▷ Tournez la page. Turn the page.; **la page d'accueil** the home page

paie [pɛ] nf wages

paiement [pɛmɑ̃] nm payment

paillasson [pajasɔ̃] nm doormat

paille [paj] nf straw

pain [pɛ̃] nm ❶ bread ▷ un morceau de pain a piece of bread ▷ une tranche de pain a slice of bread ❷ loaf ▷ J'ai acheté un pain. I bought a loaf of bread.; **le pain de blé entier** whole grain bread; **le pain d'épice** gingerbread; **le pain aux raisins** raisin bread; **le pain doré** French toast

pair [pɛR] (f **paire**) adj even ▷ un nombre pair an even number

paire [pɛR] nf pair ▷ une paire de chaussures a pair of shoes

paisible [pezibl(ə)] adj peaceful ▷ un village paisible a peaceful village

paix [pɛ] nf peace; **faire la paix (1)** to make peace ▷ Les deux pays ont fait la paix. The two countries have made peace with each other. **(2)** (after quarrel) to make up ▷ Elle a fait la paix avec son frère. She made up with her brother.; **avoir la paix** to have peace and quiet ▷ J'aimerais bien avoir la paix. I'd like to have a bit of peace and quiet.; **Fiche-lui la paix!** (informal) Leave him alone!

palais [palɛ] nm ❶ palace ▷ le palais Montcalm Montcalm Palace; **le palais de justice** court house; **le palais de congrès** convention centre; **le palais des expositions** exhibition hall; **le palais des sports** sports complex ❷ (in mouth) palate

pâle [pɑl] adj pale ▷ bleu pâle pale blue

pâleur [pɑlœR] nf paleness

palier [palje] nm (on stairway) landing ▷ Elle m'attendait sur le palier. She was waiting for me on the landing.

pâlir [pɑliR] vb to go pale

palme [palm(ə)] nf (on animal) flipper

palmé [palme] adj webbed ▷ Les canards ont les pieds palmés. Ducks have webbed feet.

palmier [palmje] nm palm tree

palourde [paluRd(ə)] nf clam

palpitant [palpitɑ̃, -ɑ̃t] (f **palpitante**) adj thrilling ▷ un roman palpitant a thrilling novel

pamplemousse [pɑ̃pləmus] nm grapefruit

pancanadien [pɑ̃kanadjɛ̃, -ɛn] (f **pancanadienne**) adj Canada-wide ▷ une campagne pancanadienne contre le tabac a Canada-wide campaign against tobacco

pancarte [pɑ̃kaRt(ə)] nf sign ▷ Il y a une pancarte dans la vitrine. There's a sign in the window.

pané [pane] (f **panée**) adj breaded ▷ du poisson pané breaded fish

panier [panje] nm basket

panique [panik] nf panic

paniquer [panike] vb to panic.

panne [pan] nf breakdown; **être en panne** to have broken down ▷ L'ascenseur est en panne. The elevator's not working.; **tomber en panne** to break down ▷ Nous sommes tombés en panne sur l'autoroute. We broke down on the highway. ▷ Nous sommes tombés en panne d'essence. We've run out of gas.; **une panne de courant** a power cut

panneau [pano] (pl **panneaux**) nm sign ▷ Ce panneau dit que la maison est à vendre. This sign says that the house is for sale.; **panneau d'affichage** billboard

panorama [panɔrama] nm panorama

pansement [pɑ̃smɑ̃] nm ❶ bandage ❷ bandaid

pantalon [pɑ̃talɔ̃] nm pants ▷ Son pantalon est trop court. His pants are too short.; **un pantalon de ski** a pair of ski pants

panthère [pɑ̃tɛR] nf panther

pantoufle [pɑ̃tufl(ə)] nf slipper

paon [pɑ̃] nm peacock

papa [papa] nm dad

pape [pap] nm pope

papeterie [papetʀi] nf stationery

papier [papje] nm paper ▷ *une feuille de papier* a sheet of paper; **Vos papiers, s'il vous plaît.** Your papers, please.; **les papiers d'identité** (*documents*) identification; **le papier à lettres** writing paper; **le papier hygiénique** toilet paper; **le papier peint** wallpaper

papillon [papijɔ̃] nm butterfly

pâquerette [pakʀɛt] nf daisy

Pâques [pak] nm Easter ▷ *Je viendrai te voir à Pâques.* I'll come and see you at Easter.

paquet [pake] nm ● pack ▷ *Je voudrais un paquet de gomme à mâcher.* I'd like a pack of gum. ● parcel ▷ *Sa mère lui a envoyé un paquet.* His mother sent him a parcel.; **un paquet de** (*informal*) a ton of ▷ *J'ai un paquet de choses à faire.* I've got a ton of things to do. ▷ *Il est tombé un paquet de neige.* A ton of snow has fallen.

paquet-cadeau [pakekado] (*pl* **paquets-cadeaux**) nm gift-wrapped parcel ▷ *La vendeuse m'a fait un paquet-cadeau.* The salesperson gift-wrapped it for me.

par [paʀ] prep ● by ▷ *La lettre a été écrite par son fils.* The letter was written by his son.; **deux par deux** two by two ▷ *Les élèves sont entrés deux par deux.* The pupils went in two by two. ● with ▷ *Son nom commence par un H.* His name begins with H. ● out of ▷ *Elle regardait par la fenêtre.* She was looking out of the window. ● par habitude out of habit ● via ▷ *Nous sommes passés par Windsor pour aller aux États-Unis.* We went via Windsor to the US. ● through ▷ *Il faut passer par la douane avant de prendre l'avion.* You have to go through customs before boarding the plane. ● per ▷ *Prenez trois cachets par jour.* Take three tablets per day. ▷ *Le voyage coûte deux mille dollars par personne.* The trip costs two thousand dollars per person.; **par ici (1)** this way ▷ *Il faut passer par ici pour y arriver.* You have to go this way to get there. **(2)** around here ▷ *Il y a beaucoup de touristes par ici.* There are lots of tourists around here.; **par-ci, par-là** here and there

parachute [paʀaʃyt] nm parachute

parachutiste [paʀaʃytist(ə)] nmf parachutist

paradis [paʀadi] nm heaven

parages [paʀaʒ] nmpl; **dans les parages** in the area ▷ *Il n'y a pas d'hôtel dans les parages.* There are no hotels in the area.

paragraphe [paʀagʀaf] nm paragraph

paraître [paʀɛtʀ(ə)] vb ● to seem ▷ *Ça paraît incroyable.* It seems unbelievable. ● to look ▷ *Elle paraît plus jeune que son frère.* She looks younger than her brother.; **il paraît que** it seems that ▷ *Il paraît que c'est la faute de la direction.* It seems that it's the fault of the management.

parallèle [paʀalɛl] adj parallel ▷ *les barres parallèles* parallel bars
▶ nm parallel ▷ *Il a fait un parallèle entre ces deux événements.* He drew a parallel between the two events.
▶ nf parallel line

paralysé [paʀalize] (*f* **paralysée**) adj paralysed

parapluie [paʀaplɥi] nm umbrella

parascolaire [paʀaskɔlɛʀ] adj extracurricular ▷ *L'école offre plusieurs activités parascolaires.* The school offers several extracurricular activities.

parasol [paʀasɔl] nm parasol

parc [paʀk] nm ● park ▷ *Le dimanche, elle va se promener au parc.* On Sundays she goes for a walk in the park.; **un parc d'attractions** an amusement park ● grounds ▷ *Le château est situé au milieu d'un grand parc.* The castle is surrounded by extensive grounds.; **le parc industriel** industrial park

parce que [paʀsk(ə)] conj because ▷ *Il n'est pas venu parce qu'il n'avait pas de voiture.* He didn't come because he didn't have a car.

parcomètre [paʀkɔmɛtʀ] nm parking meter

parcourir [paʀkuʀiʀ] vb ● *Elle a parcouru cinquante kilomètres à vélo.* She covered 50 kilometres on her bike. ● to glance through ▷ *J'ai parcouru le journal d'aujourd'hui.* I glanced through today's newspaper.

parcours [paʀkuʀ] nm journey

par-dessous [paʀdəsu] adv underneath ▷ *Il portait un chandail et une chemise par-dessous.* He was wearing a sweater with a shirt underneath.

pardessus [paʀdəsy] nm overcoat

par-dessus [paʀdəsy] adv, prep ● on top ▷ *Elle porte un chemisier et un chandail rouge par-dessus.* She's wearing a blouse with a red sweater on top. ● over ▷ *Elle a sauté par-dessus le mur.* She jumped over the wall.; **en avoir par-dessus la tête** to have had enough ▷ *J'en ai par-dessus la tête de tous ces problèmes.* I've had enough of all these problems.

pardon [paʀdɔ̃] nm forgiveness
▶ excl ● sorry! ▷ *Oh, pardon! J'espère que je ne vous ai pas fait mal.* Oh, sorry! I hope I didn't hurt you.; **demander pardon à quelqu'un** to apologize to somebody ▷ *Il leur a demandé pardon.* He apologized to them.; **Je vous demande pardon.** I'm sorry. ● excuse me! ▷ *Pardon, madame! Pouvez-vous me dire où se trouve le bureau de poste?* Excuse me! Could you tell me where the post office is? ● pardon? ▷ *Pardon? Je n'ai pas compris ce que vous avez dit.* Pardon? I didn't understand what you said.

pardonner [paʀdɔne] vb to forgive ▷ *Nous lui avons pardonné de nous avoir menti.* We forgave him for lying to us.

pare-brise [paʀbʀiz] (*pl* **pare-brise**) nm windshield

pare-chocs [paʀʃɔk] nm bumper

pareil [paʀɛj] (*f* **pareille**) adj ● the same ▷ *Ces deux photos ne sont pas pareilles.* These two photos aren't the same. ● like that ▷ *J'aime bien sa montre. J'en veux une pareille.* I like her watch. I want one like that. ● such ▷ *Je refuse d'écouter des bêtises pareilles.* I won't listen to such nonsense.; **sans pareil** unequalled ▷ *un talent sans pareil* unequalled talent

parenthèse [paʀɑ̃tɛz] nf bracket ▷ *entre parenthèses* in brackets

parents [paʀɑ̃] nmpl ● (mother and father)

parents ❷ relatives ▷ *parents et amis* friends and relatives

paresse [parɛs] *nf* laziness

paresseux [parɛsø, -øz] (*f* **paresseuse**) *adj* lazy

parfait [parfɛ, -ɛt] (*f* **parfaite**) *adj* perfect

parfaitement [parfɛtmɑ̃] *adv* perfectly ▷ *Il parle parfaitement l'arabe.* He speaks perfect Arabic.

parfois [parfwa] *adv* sometimes

parfum [parfœ̃] *nm* ❶ perfume ❷ flavour ▷ *« Je voudrais une crème glacée. » « Quel parfum veux-tu ? »* "I'd like an ice cream." "What flavour would you like?"

parfumé [parfyme] (*f* **parfumée**) *adj* ❶ fragrant ▷ *une rose très parfumée* a very fragrant rose ❷ flavoured ▷ *des biscuits parfumés au café* coffee-flavoured cookies

pari [pari] *nm* bet

parier [parje] *vb* to bet

parlement [parləmɑ̃] *nm* parliament; **le Parlement du Canada** the Canadian Parliament

parlementaire [parləmɑ̃tɛr] *adj* parliamentary ▷ *un débat parlementaire* a parliamentary debate; **la Colline parlementaire** Parliament Hill

parler [parle] *vb* ❶ to speak ▷ *Vous parlez français?* Do you speak French? ❷ to talk ▷ *Nous étions en train de parler quand la directrice est entrée.* We were talking when the principal came in.; **parler de quelque chose à quelqu'un** to tell somebody about something ▷ *Il m'a parlé de son nouveau vélo.* He told me about his new bike.

parmi [parmi] *prep* among ▷ *Ils étaient parmi les meilleurs de la classe.* They were among the best in the class.

paroi [parwa] *nf* wall; **une paroi rocheuse** a rock face

paroisse [parwas] *nf* parish

parole [parɔl] *nf* ❶ speech ▷ *l'usage de la parole* the power of speech ❷ word ▷ *Il m'a donné sa parole.* He gave me his word. ▷ *Elle a tenu parole.* She kept her word.; **les paroles** lyrics ▷ *J'aime les paroles de cette chanson.* I like the lyrics of this song.

parquet [parkɛ] *nm* (*wooden*) floor

parrainer [parene] *vb* to sponsor ▷ *Cette entreprise parraine notre équipe de hockey.* This company is sponsoring our hockey team.

pars [par] *vb see* **partir**

part [par] *nf* ❶ share ▷ *Vous n'avez pas eu votre part.* You haven't had your share. ❷ piece ▷ *une part de gâteau* a piece of cake; **prendre part à quelque chose** to take part in something ▷ *Elle va prendre part à la réunion.* She's going to take part in the meeting.; **de la part de** (1) on behalf of ▷ *Je dois vous remercier de la part de mon frère.* I must thank you on behalf of my brother. (2) from ▷ *C'est un cadeau pour toi, de la part de ma sœur.* It's a present for you, from my sister.; **à part** except ▷ *Ils sont tous venus à part lui.* They all came except him.

partager [partaʒe] *vb* ❶ to share ▷ *Ils partagent un appartement.* They share a flat.

❷ to divide ▷ *Nous avons partagé le gâteau en quatre.* We divided the cake into four.

partenaire [partənɛr] *nmf* partner

parti [parti] *nm* party ▷ *le Parti vert* the Green Party

participant [partisipɑ̃] *nm* participant

participante [partisipɑ̃t] *nf* participant

participation [partisipasjɔ̃] *nf* participation

participe [partisip] *nm* participle; **le participe passé** the past participle; **le participe présent** the present participle

participer [partisipe] *vb*: **participer à quelque chose** (1) to take part in something ▷ *Mon frère va participer à la course.* My brother is going to take part in the race. (2) to contribute to something ▷ *Je voudrais participer aux frais.* I would like to contribute to the cost.

particularité [partikylarite] *nf* characteristic

particulier [partikylje, -jɛr] (*f* **particulière**) *adj* ❶ private ▷ *une maison particulière* a private house ❷ distinctive ▷ *Ce fromage a un arôme particulier.* This cheese has a distinctive flavour. ❸ particular ▷ *Dans ce cas particulier, la procédure est différente.* In this particular case, the procedure is different.; **en particulier** (1) particularly ▷ *J'aime les fruits, en particulier les fraises.* I like fruit, particularly strawberries. (2) in private ▷ *Est-ce que je peux vous parler en particulier?* Can I speak to you in private?

particulièrement [partikyljɛrmɑ̃] *adv* particularly

partie [parti] *nf* ❶ part ▷ *Une partie du groupe restera à la ferme.* Part of the group will stay at the farm. ❷ game ▷ *Nous avons fait une partie de badminton.* We played a game of badminton. ▷ *une partie de cartes* a game of cards; **en partie** partly ▷ *Cela explique en partie le problème.* That partly explains the problem.; **en grande partie** largely ▷ *Son histoire est en grande partie vraie.* Her story is largely true.; **faire partie de** to be part of ▷ *Ce tableau fait partie de la collection familiale.* This picture is part of the family collection.

partiel [parsjɛl] (*f* **partielle**) *adj* partial

partir [partir] *vb* to go ▷ *Je t'ai téléphoné mais tu étais déjà parti.* I phoned you but you were already gone.; **partir en vacances** to go on holiday; **partir de** to leave ▷ *Il est parti de Regina à sept heures.* He left Regina at 7.; **à partir de** from ▷ *Je serai chez moi à partir de huit heures.* I'll be at home from eight o'clock onwards.

partition [partisjɔ̃] *nf* (*in music*) score ▷ *une partition de piano* a piano score

partout [partu] *adv* everywhere

party [parti] *nm* party ▷ *un party d'Halloween* a Halloween party

paru [pary] *vb see* **paraître**

parution [parysjɔ̃] *nf* publication ▷ *la parution de son nouveau livre* the publication of her new book; **Ce roman a eu beaucoup de succès dès sa parution.** This novel was a hit from the moment it came out.

parvenir [parvənir] *vb*: **parvenir à faire quelque chose** to manage to do something

▷ *Elle est finalement parvenue à ouvrir la porte.* She finally managed to open the door.; **faire parvenir quelque chose à quelqu'un** to send something to somebody ▷ *Je vous ferai parvenir le colis avant lundi.* I'll send you the parcel before Monday.

pas [pɑ] *adv*: **ne...pas** not ▷ *Il ne pleut pas.* It's not raining. ▷ *Elle n'est pas venue.* She didn't come. ▷ *Ils n'ont pas de voiture.* They don't have a car.; **Vous viendrez à notre soirée, n'est-ce pas?** You're coming to our party, aren't you?; **C'est lui qui a gagné, n'est-ce pas?** He won, didn't he?; **pas moi** not me ▷ *Elle veut aller au cinéma, pas moi.* She wants to go to a movie, but I don't.; **pas du tout** not at all ▷ *Je n'aime pas du tout ça.* I don't like that at all.; **pas mal** not bad ▷ *Ce n'est pas mal pour un début.* That's not bad for a first attempt. ▷ «*Comment allez-vous?*» «*Pas mal.*» "How are you?" "Not bad.";
pas mal de quite a lot of ▷ *Il y avait pas mal de monde au concert.* There were quite a lot of people at the concert.
▶ *nm* ❶ pace ▷ *Il marchait d'un pas rapide.* He walked at a fast pace. ❷ step ▷ *Faites trois pas en avant.* Take three steps forward. ▷ *un pas en arrière* a step backwards ❸ footstep ▷ *J'entends des pas dans l'escalier.* I can hear footsteps on the stairs.; **au pas** at a walk ▷ *Le cheval est parti au pas.* The horse set off at a walk.; **faire les cent pas** to pace up and down ▷ *Il faisait les cent pas dans le corridor.* He was pacing up and down the corridor.

passage [pɑsaʒ] *nm* passage ▷ *J'ai traduit un passage de ce livre.* I translated a passage from this book.; **J'ai été éclaboussé au passage de la voiture.** I was splashed by a passing car.; **de passage** passing through ▷ *Nous sommes de passage à Cornwall.* We're just passing through Cornwall.; **un passage à niveau** a railway crossing; **un passage à piétons** a pedestrian crossing; **un passage souterrain** an underground walkway

passager [pɑsaʒe, -ɛʀ] (*f* **passagère**) *adj* temporary
▶ *nm* passenger; **un passager clandestin** a stowaway

passagère [pɑsaʒɛʀ] *nf* passenger

passant [pɑsɑ̃] *nm* passer-by

passante [pɑsɑ̃t] *nf* passer-by

passé [pɑse] (*f* **passée**) *adj* ❶ last ▷ *Je l'ai vue la semaine passée.* I saw her last week. ❷ past ▷ *Il est minuit passé.* It's past midnight.
▶ *nm* ❶ past ▷ *dans le passé* in the past ❷ past tense ▷ *Mettez ce verbe au passé.* Put this verb into the past tense.; **le passé composé** the perfect tense

passeport [pɑspɔʀ] *nm* passport

passer [pɑse] *vb* ❶ to cross ▷ *Nous avons passé la frontière ontarienne.* We crossed the Ontario border. ❷ to go through ▷ *Il faut passer la douane en sortant.* You have to go through customs on the way out. ❸ to take ▷ *Mon frère a passé ses examens la semaine dernière.* My brother took his exams last week. ❹ to spend ▷ *Elle a passé la journée à ne rien faire.* She spent the day doing nothing. ▷ *Ils passent*

toujours leurs vacances au Québec.* They always spend their holidays in Quebec. ❺ to pass ▷ *Passe-moi le sel, s'il te plaît.* Pass me the salt, please. ❻ to show ▷ *On passe un nouveau film d'animation au cinéma cette semaine.* They're showing a new animated film at the movie theatre this week. ❼ to drop by ▷ *Je passerai chez vous ce soir.* I'll drop by this evening.;
passer à la radio to be on the radio ▷ *Mon père passe à la radio demain soir.* My father's going to be on the radio tomorrow night.; **passer à la télévision** to be on TV ▷ *Mon film préféré passe à la télé ce soir.* My favourite movie is on TV tonight.; **Ne quittez pas, je vous passe la gérante.** Hold on please, I'm putting you through to the manager.; **passer par** to go through ▷ *Ils sont passés par Brandon pour aller à Winnipeg.* They went through Brandon to get to Winnipeg.; **en passant** in passing ▷ *Je lui ai dit en passant que j'allais me marier.* I told her in passing that I was getting married.; **laisser passer** to let through ▷ *Il m'a laissé passer.* He let me through.; **se passer (1)** to take place ▷ *Cette histoire se passe au Moyen Âge.* This story takes place in the Middle Ages. **(2)** to go ▷ *Comment s'est passé le match?* How did the game go? **(3)** to happen ▷ *Que s'est-il passé? Un accident?* What happened? Was there an accident?; **Qu'est-ce qui se passe? Pourquoi est-ce que tu pleures?** What's the matter? Why are you crying?; **se passer de** to do without ▷ *Je me passerai de confiture ce matin.* I'll do without jam this morning.

passerelle [pɑsʀɛl] *nf* ❶ (over river) footbridge ❷ (onto plane, boat) gangway

passe-temps [pɑstɑ̃] *nm* pastime

passif [pɑsif, -iv] (*f* **passive**) *adj* passive
▶ *nm* passive ▷ *Mettez ce verbe au passif.* Put this verb into the passive.

passion [pɑsjɔ̃] *nf* passion

passionnant [pɑsjɔnɑ̃, -ɑ̃t] (*f* **passionnante**) *adj* fascinating

passionné [pɑsjɔne] (*f* **passionnée**) *adj* avid ▷ *Il est un lecteur passionné.* He's an avid reader.; **Elle est passionnée de voile.** She's a sailing fanatic.

passionner [pɑsjɔne] *vb*: **Son travail le passionne.** He's passionate about his work.; **se passionner pour quelque chose** to have a passion for something ▷ *Elle se passionne pour la photographie.* She has a passion for photography.

passoire [pɑswaʀ] *nf* strainer

pastèque [pɑstɛk] *nf* watermelon

pastille [pɑstij] *nf* cough drop

patate [pɑtat] *nf* (informal) potato; **les patates pilées** mashed potatoes; **une patate douce** a sweet potato

pâte [pɑt] *nf* ❶ pastry ❷ dough ❸ cake batter; **la pâte à crêpes** pancake batter; **la pâte à modeler** Plasticine®; **la pâte d'amandes** marzipan; **la pâte dentifrice** toothpaste

pâté [pɑte] *nm* pâté ▷ *Nous avons mangé du pâté en entrée.* We had pâté as an appetizer.; **le pâté chinois** shepherd's pie; **un pâté de**

maisons (of houses) a block

patente [patɑ̃t] nf (imprecise) thing ▷ Pourrais-tu me passer la patente en arrière de la chaise, là? Could you pass me that thing behind the chair?; **les patentes** stuff ▷ Ma mère a laissé tes patentes sur la table. My mom left your stuff on the table. ▷ J'ai plein de patentes à faire en fin de semaine. I have a ton of stuff to do this weekend.

paternel [patɛʀnɛl] (f **paternelle**) adj: **ma grand-mère paternelle** my grandmother on my father's side; **mon oncle paternel** my uncle on my father's side

pâtes [pɑt] nfpl pasta

patience [pasjɑ̃s] nf patience

patient [pasjɑ̃, -ɑ̃t] (f **patiente**) adj patient
▶ nm patient

patiente [pasjɑ̃t] nf patient

patienter [pasjɑ̃te] vb to wait ▷ Veuillez patienter un instant, s'il vous plaît. Please wait a moment.

patin [patɛ̃] nm ❶ skate ▷ Il a enfilé ses patins. He put his skates on. ❷ skating ▷ Ils font du patin tous les mercredis. They go skating every Wednesday.; **accrocher ses patins** to retire; **être vite sur ses patins** to act very fast; **les patins à glace** ice skates; **les patins à roues alignées** inline skates; **les patins à roulettes** roller skates

patinage [patinaʒ] nm skating; **le patinage artistique** figure skating; **le patinage de vitesse** speed skating

patiner [patine] vb to skate

patineur [patinœʀ] nm skater

patineuse [patinøz] nf skater

patinoire [patinwaʀ] nf skating rink

pâtisserie [pɑtisʀi] nf cake shop; **faire de la pâtisserie** to bake ▷ J'adore faire de la pâtisserie. I love baking.; **les pâtisseries** cakes

patrie [patʀi] nf homeland

patron [patʀɔ̃] nm ❶ boss ❷ (for dressmaking) pattern

patronne [patʀɔn] nf boss; **Elle est patronne de café.** She runs a café.

patrouille [patʀuj] nf patrol

patte [pat] nf ❶ (of dog, cat) paw ❷ (of bird, animal) leg

paupière [popjɛʀ] nf eyelid

pause [poz] nf ❶ break ▷ Ils font une pause. They're having a break. ▷ une pause de midi a lunch break ❷ pause ▷ Il y a eu une pause dans la conversation. There was a pause in the conversation.

pauvre [povʀ(ə)] adj poor ▷ Sa famille est pauvre. Her family is poor. ▷ Pauvre lui! Il n'a pas eu de chance! Poor him! He was unlucky!

pauvreté [povʀəte] nf poverty

pavé [pave] (f **pavée**) adj cobbled ▷ Les rues étaient pavées. The streets were cobbled.

pavé numérique nm keypad

payant [pejɑ̃, -ɑ̃t] (f **payante**) adj ❶ paying ▷ Ce sont des hôtes payants. They're paying guests. ❷ profitable; **C'est une profession payante.** It's a highly-paid profession.; **C'est payant.** You have to pay. ▷ L'entrée de la foire est payante. You have to pay to get into the fair.

paye [pɛj] nf wages

payer [peje] vb ❶ to pay for ▷ Combien as-tu payé ta planche à roulettes? How much did you pay for your skateboard?; **J'ai payé ce T-shirt vingt dollars.** I paid 20 dollars for this T-shirt. ❷ to pay ▷ Elle a été payée aujourd'hui. She got paid today. ▷ Son métier paye bien. His job pays well. ▷ Elle est mal payée. She is underpaid.; **faire payer quelque chose à quelqu'un** to charge somebody for something ▷ Il me l'a fait payer dix dollars. He charged me 10 dollars for it.; **payer quelque chose à quelqu'un** to buy somebody something ▷ Allez, je vous paye un café. Come on, I'll buy you a coffee.

pays [pei] nm country

paysage [peizaʒ] nm landscape

paysan [peizɑ̃] nm farmer

paysanne [peizan] nf farmer

PC [pece] nm PC (= personal computer) ▷ Il a tapé le rapport sur son PC. He typed the report on his PC.

péage [peaʒ] nm toll ▷ Nous avons payé cinq dollars de péage. We paid a toll of 5 dollars.

peau [po] (pl **peaux**) nf skin ▷ Tu as la peau douce. You have soft skin.

pêche [pɛʃ] nf ❶ peach ❷ fishing; **aller à la pêche** to go fishing; **la pêche à la ligne** rod fishing; **la pêche sous la glace** ice fishing

péché [peʃe] nm sin

pêcher [peʃe] vb ❶ to fish for ▷ Ils sont partis pêcher la truite. They've gone fishing for trout. ❷ to catch ▷ On a pêché deux saumons. We caught two salmon.

pêcheur [peʃœʀ] nm fisherman ▷ Son père est pêcheur. Her father's a fisherman.

pêcheuse [peʃøz] nf (woman) fisherman ▷ Elle est pêcheuse. She's a fisherman.

pédagogique [pedagɔʒik] adj educational

pédale [pedal] nf pedal

pédestre [pedɛstʀ(ə)] adj: **une randonnée pédestre** a hike

peigne [pɛɲ] nm comb

peigner [peɲe] vb to comb ▷ Elle peigne le bébé. She's combing the baby's hair.; **se peigner** to comb one's hair ▷ Il faut que je me peigne. I must comb my hair.

peignoir [pɛɲwaʀ] nm dressing gown; **un peignoir de bain** a bathrobe

peindre [pɛ̃dʀ(ə)] vb to paint

peine [pɛn] nf trouble; **avoir de la peine à faire quelque chose** to have a hard time doing something ▷ J'ai eu beaucoup de peine à la convaincre. I had a really hard time convincing her.; **se donner de la peine** to go to a lot of trouble ▷ Il s'est donné beaucoup de peine pour obtenir ces renseignements. He went to a lot of trouble to get this information.; **prendre la peine de faire quelque chose** to go to the trouble of doing something ▷ Il a pris la peine de me rapporter ma valise. He went to the trouble of returning my suitcase to me.; **faire de la peine à quelqu'un** to upset somebody ▷ Ça me fait de la peine de te voir pleurer. It upsets me to see you crying.; **ce n'est pas la peine** there's no point ▷ Ce n'est pas la peine de téléphoner. There's no point in phoning.; **à peine (1)** hardly ▷ J'ai à *peine eu le temps de me changer.* I hardly had time to get changed. **(2)** *only just* ▷ *Elle vient à peine de se lever.* She only just got up.

peintre [pɛ̃tʀ(ə)] nmf painter

peinture [pɛ̃tyʀ] nf ❶ painting ▷ *On expose des peintures d'Emily Carr au musée.* There's an exhibition of Emily Carr's paintings at the museum. ❷ paint ▷ *J'ai acheté de la peinture verte.* I bought some green paint.; **« peinture fraîche »** "wet paint"

pêle-mêle [pɛlmɛl] adv higgledy-piggledy

peler [pəle] vb to peel

pelle [pɛl] nf ❶ shovel ▷ *une pelle à neige* a snow shovel ❷ spade

pellicule de plastique nf plastic wrap

pellicules [pelikyl] nfpl dandruff

pelote [pəlɔt] nf ball ▷ *une pelote de laine* a ball of wool

pelouse [pəluz] nf lawn

peluche [pəlyʃ] nf: **un animal en peluche** a stuffed animal

pemmican [pemikã] nm pemmican

penchant [pɑ̃ʃɑ̃] nm: **avoir un penchant pour quelque chose** to have a liking for something

pencher [pɑ̃ʃe] vb to tilt ▷ *Ce tableau penche vers la droite.* The picture is tilted to the right.; **se pencher (1)** to lean over ▷ *Elle s'est penchée sur la table.* She leaned over the table. **(2)** to bend down ▷ *Il s'est penché pour ramasser sa casquette.* He bent down to pick up his cap. **(3)** to lean out ▷ *Ne te penche pas par la fenêtre.* Don't lean out of the window.

pendant [pɑ̃dɑ̃] prep during ▷ *Ça s'est passé pendant l'été.* It happened during the summer.; **pendant que** while ▷ *Il a téléphoné pendant que sa sœur prenait son bain.* He phoned while his sister was having a bath.

pendentif [pɑ̃dɑ̃tif] nm pendant

pendre [pɑ̃dʀ(ə)] vb to hang ▷ *Il a pendu son manteau dans la garde-robe.* He hung his coat in the closet.

pendule [pɑ̃dyl] nf clock

pénétrer [penetʀe] vb ❶ to enter ▷ *Ils ont pénétré dans la maison en passant par le jardin.* They entered the house through the garden. ❷ to penetrate ▷ *Le soleil ne pénètre pas ce feuillage dense.* The sun cannot penetrate this thick foliage.

pénible [penibl(ə)] adj difficult ▷ *une tâche pénible* a difficult task; **Il est vraiment pénible.** He's a real pain.

péniblement [peniblemã] adv with difficulty

pénis [penis] nm penis

pénombre [penɔ̃bʀ(ə)] nf half-light

pensée [pɑ̃se] nf thought ▷ *Il était perdu dans ses pensées.* He was lost in thought.

penser [pɑ̃se] vb to think ▷ *Je pense qu'elle a eu raison de partir.* I think she was right to leave.; **penser à quelque chose** to think about something ▷ *Je pense à mes vacances.* I'm thinking about my holidays. ▷ *Pensez-y.* Think about it.; **faire penser quelqu'un à quelque chose** to remind someone of something ▷ *Cette photo me fait penser à notre voyage.* This photo reminds me of our trip.; **faire penser quelqu'un à faire quelque chose** to remind

someone to do something ▷ *Fais-moi penser à téléphoner à mes parents.* Remind me to phone my parents.; **penser faire quelque chose** to be planning to do something ▷ *Ils pensent partir en Colombie-Britannique en juillet.* They're planning to go to British Columbia in July.

pension [pɑ̃sjɔ̃] nf pension ▷ *Ma grand-mère reçoit sa pension tous les mois.* My grandmother gets her pension every month.

pensionnat [pɑ̃sjɔna] nm boarding school

pente [pɑ̃t] nf slope ▷ *une pente raide* a steep slop; **en pente** sloping ▷ *Le toit de cette maison est en pente.* This house has a sloping roof.

pépin [pepɛ̃] nm (*in fruit*) seed ▷ *Cette orange est pleine de pépins.* This orange is full of seeds.

perçant [pɛʀsɑ̃, -ɑ̃t] (f **perçante**) adj ❶ sharp ▷ *Il a une vue perçante.* He has very sharp eyes. ❷ piercing ▷ *un cri perçant* a piercing cry

percer [pɛʀse] vb to pierce ▷ *Elle s'est fait percer les oreilles.* She got her ears pierced.

percuter [pɛʀkyte] vb to smash into

perdant [pɛʀdɑ̃] nm loser

perdante [pɛʀdɑ̃t] nf loser

perdre [pɛʀdʀ(ə)] vb to lose ▷ *Il a perdu ses clés.* He lost his keys.; **J'ai perdu mon chemin.** I've lost my way.; **perdre un match** to lose a game; **perdre du temps** to waste time ▷ *J'ai perdu beaucoup de temps ce matin.* I've wasted a lot of time this morning. ▷ *Nous avons perdu notre temps à cette réunion.* That meeting was a waste of time.; **se perdre** to get lost ▷ *Je me suis perdu en route.* I got lost on the way here.

perdu [pɛʀdy] vb see **perdre**

père [pɛʀ] nm father

perfectionné [pɛʀfɛksjɔne] (f **perfectionnée**) adj sophisticated

perfectionner [pɛʀfɛksjɔne] vb to improve ▷ *Elle a besoin de perfectionner son anglais.* She needs to improve her English.

pergélisol [pɛʀʒelisɔl] nm permafrost

périmé [peʀime] (f **périmée**) adj out-of-date ▷ *Mon passeport est périmé.* My passport is out of date.; **Ces yogourts sont périmés.** These yogurts are past their best-before date.

période [peʀjɔd] nf period

périodiquement [peʀjɔdikmɑ̃] adv periodically

périphérique [peʀifeʀik] adj outlying ▷ *un quartier périphérique* an outlying district

perle [pɛʀl(ə)] nf pearl

permanence [pɛʀmanɑ̃s] nf: **assurer une permanence** to offer a basic service ▷ *Ma banque assure une permanence le samedi matin.* My bank offers a basic service on Saturday mornings.; **être de permanence** to be on duty ▷ *Elle ne peut pas venir, elle est de permanence ce soir.* She can't come, she's on duty tonight.; **en permanence** permanently ▷ *Il se plaint en permanence.* He's always complaining.

permanent [pɛʀmanɑ̃, -ɑ̃t] (f **permanente**) adj ❶ permanent ▷ *Il a un poste permanent.* He has a permanent job. ❷ continuous ▷ *J'en ai assez de tes critiques permanentes.* I've had enough of your constant criticism.

permanente [pɛʀmanɑ̃t] nf perm

permettre [pɛʀmɛtʀ(ə)] vb to allow;

permettre à quelqu'un de faire quelque chose to allow somebody to do something ▷ *Ses parents lui permettent de sortir le soir.* His parents allow him to go out at night.

permis [pɛrmi] *nm* permit ▷ *Il vous faut un permis pour camper ici.* You need a permit to camp here.; **le permis de conduire** driver's licence; **un permis de pêche** a fishing licence; **un permis de travail** a work permit

permission [pɛrmisjɔ̃] *nf* permission ▷ *Qui t'a donné la permission d'entrer?* Who gave you permission to come in?; **avoir la permission de faire quelque chose** to have permission to do something ▷ *J'ai la permission d'utiliser son baladeur.* I've got his permission to use his personal stereo.; **être en permission** (*from the army*) to be on leave

perpétuel [pɛrpetɥɛl] (*f* **perpétuelle**) *adj* perpetual

perplexe [pɛrplɛks(ə)] *adj* puzzled ▷ *Ma question l'a laissé perplexe.* She was puzzled by my question.

perroquet [pɛrɔkɛ] *nm* parrot

perruche [pɛryʃ] *nf* budgie

perruque [pɛryk] *nf* wig

persil [pɛrsi] *nm* parsley

personnage [pɛrsɔnaʒ] *nm* ❶ figure ▷ *des personnages historiques* historical figures ❷ character ▷ *le personnage principal du film* the main character in the film

personnalité [pɛrsɔnalite] *nf* ❶ personality ▷ *Il a une personnalité forte.* He has a strong personality. ❷ prominent figure ▷ *Il y avait beaucoup de personnalités politiques à ce dîner.* There were lots of prominent political figures at the dinner.

personne [pɛrsɔn] *nf* person ▷ *Il y avait une trentaine de personnes dans la pièce.* There were about 30 people in the room. ▷ *une personne âgée* an elderly person; **en personne** in person ▶ *pron* ❶ nobody ▷ *Il n'y a personne à la maison.* There's nobody at home. ▷ *Personne n'est venu me chercher.* Nobody came to fetch me. ❷ anybody ▷ *Elle ne veut voir personne.* She doesn't want to see anybody.

personnel [pɛrsɔnɛl] (*f* **personnelle**) *adj* personal ▶ *nm* staff ▷ *Il nous faut plus de personnel.* We need more staff.; **le service du personnel** the personnel department

personnellement [pɛrsɔnɛlmɑ̃] *adv* personally ▷ *Personnellement, je ne suis pas d'accord.* Personally, I don't agree.

persuader [pɛrsɥade] *vb* to persuade; **persuader quelqu'un de faire quelque chose** to persuade somebody to do something ▷ *Elle m'a persuadé de l'accompagner au cinéma.* She persuaded me to go to the movie theatre with her.

perte [pɛrt(ə)] *nf* ❶ loss ▷ *la perte de poids* weight loss ▷ *Ça fait huit victoires et deux pertes pour notre équipe.* That's 8 wins and 2 losses for our team. ❷ waste ▷ *Cette réunion a été une perte de temps.* That meeting was a waste of time.

perturber [pɛrtyrbe] *vb* to disrupt ▷ *Le bruit dans le couloir perturbait la classe.* The noise in the hallway was disrupting the class.

pèse-personne [pɛzpɛrsɔn] *nm* bathroom scales

peser [pəze] *vb* to weigh ▷ *Il pèse cinquante kilos.* He weighs 50 kilos.; **peser lourd** to be heavy ▷ *Cette valise pèse lourd.* This suitcase is heavy.

pessimiste [pesimist(ə)] *adj* pessimistic

pétale [petal] *nm* petal

pétard [petar] *nm* firecracker

pétillant [petijɑ̃, -ɑ̃t] (*f* **pétillante**) *adj* sparkling

petit [pəti, -it] (*f* **petite**) *adj* ❶ small ▷ *Nous habitons une petite ville.* We live in a small town. ❷ little ▷ *Elle a une jolie petite maison.* She has a nice little house.; **petit à petit** bit by bit; **un petit ami** a boyfriend; **une petite amie** a girlfriend; **un petit pain** a bread roll; **des petits pois** peas; **les petits** (*of animal*) young ▷ *la lionne et ses petits* the lioness and her young

petite-fille [pətitfij] (*pl* **petites-filles**) *nf* granddaughter

petit-fils [pətifis] (*pl* **petits-fils**) *nm* grandson

petits-enfants [pətizɑ̃fɑ̃] *nmpl* grandchildren

pétoncle [petɔ̃kl] *nm* scallop

pétrole [petrɔl] *nm* oil ▷ *un puits de pétrole* an oil well

peu [pø] *adv, n* not much ▷ *J'ai peu mangé à midi.* I didn't eat much for lunch. ▷ *Il voyage peu.* He doesn't travel much.; **un peu** a bit ▷ *Elle est un peu timide.* She's a bit shy. ▷ *un peu de gâteau* a bit of cake; **un petit peu** a little bit ▷ *un petit peu de crème* a little bit of cream; **peu de (1)** not many ▷ *Il y a peu de bons films au cinéma.* There aren't many good movies playing at the theatre. ▷ *Elle a peu d'amis.* She doesn't have many friends. **(2)** not much ▷ *Il a peu d'espoir de réussir.* He doesn't have much hope of succeeding. ▷ *Il lui reste peu d'argent.* He doesn't have much money left.; **à peu près (1)** more or less ▷ *J'ai à peu près fini.* I've more or less finished. **(2)** about ▷ *Le voyage prend à peu près deux heures.* The journey takes about two hours.; **peu à peu** little by little; **peu avant** shortly before; **peu après** shortly afterwards; **de peu** (*by a narrow margin*) just ▷ *Elle a manqué son train de peu.* She just missed her train.

peuple [pœpl(ə)] *nm* people ▷ *le peuple canadien* the Canadian people

peur [pœr] *nf* fear; **avoir peur de** to be afraid of ▷ *Je n'ai pas peur du noir.* I'm not afraid of the dark.; **avoir peur de faire quelque chose** to be afraid to do something ▷ *Elle a peur d'y aller toute seule.* She's afraid to go on her own.; **faire peur à quelqu'un** to scare somebody ▷ *Cet homme-là me fait peur.* That man scares me.

peureux [pœrø, -øz] (*f* **peureuse**) *adj* fearful

peut [pø] *vb see* **pouvoir**; **Il ne peut pas venir.** He can't come.

peut-être [pøtɛtr(ə)] *adv* maybe ▷ *Je l'ai peut-être oublié à la maison.* Maybe I left it at home.; **peut-être que** it could be that ▷ *Peut-être qu'elles n'ont pas pu téléphoner.* It could be that they weren't able to phone.

peuvent, peux vb see **pouvoir**; Je ne peux pas le faire. I can't do it.

p. ex. abbr (= par exemple) e.g.

phare [faʀ] nm ❶ lighthouse ▷ On voit le phare depuis le pont du bateau. You can see the lighthouse from the ship's deck. ❷ headlight ▷ Il a laissé les phares de sa voiture allumés. He left his headlights on.

pharmacie [faʀmasi] nf drugstore

pharmacien [faʀmasjɛ̃] nm pharmacist

pharmacienne [faʀmasjɛn] nf pharmacist

phénomène [fenɔmɛn] nm phenomenon

philosophie [filɔzɔfi] nf philosophy

phoque [fɔk] nm (animal) seal

photo [fɔto] nf ❶ photo ▷ Elle a fait développer ses photos. She got her photos developed.; **en photo** in pictures ▷ Je n'ai vu les montagnes qu'en photo. I've only ever seen the mountains in pictures.; **prendre quelqu'un en photo** to take a picture of somebody ▷ Maman nous a pris en photo. Mom took a picture of us.; **une photo d'identité** a passport photo

photocopie [fɔtɔkɔpi] nf photocopy

photocopier [fɔtɔkɔpje] vb to photocopy

photocopieuse [fɔtɔkɔpjøz] nf photocopier

photographe [fɔtɔɡʀaf] nf photographer

photographie [fɔtɔɡʀafi] nf ❶ photography ❷ photograph

photographier [fɔtɔɡʀafje] vb to photograph

phrase [fʀɑz] nf sentence

physique [fizik] adj physical
▶ nm: **Il a un physique agréable.** He's quite good-looking.
▶ nf physics ▷ Il est professeur de physique. He's a physics teacher.

pianiste [pjanist(ə)] nmf pianist ▷ Elle est pianiste. She's a pianist.

piano [pjano] nm piano

pic [pik] nm peak ▷ les pics enneigés des Rocheuses the snowy peaks of the Rockies; **à pic** (1) straight down ▷ La falaise tombe à pic dans la mer. The cliff drops straight down into the sea. (2) just at the right time ▷ Tu es arrivé à pic. You arrived just at the right time.

pic-bois nm woodpecker

pièce [pjɛs] nf ❶ room ▷ Mon lit est au centre de la pièce. My bed is in the middle of the room. ❷ play ▷ On joue une pièce de Robert Lepage au théâtre. There's a play by Robert Lepage on at the theatre. ❸ part ▷ Il faut changer une pièce du moteur. There's an engine part that needs changing. ❹ coin ▷ des pièces de un dollar some one-dollar coins; **cinquante dollars pièce** 50 dollars each ▷ J'ai acheté ces T-shirts dix dollars pièce. I bought these T-shirts for ten dollars each.; **un maillot une pièce** a one-piece swimsuit; **un maillot deux-pièces** a two-piece swimsuit; **Avez-vous une pièce d'identité?** Do you have any identification?; **une pièce jointe** an email attachment

pied [pje] nm foot ▷ J'ai mal aux pieds. My feet are hurting.; **à pied** on foot; **avoir pied** to be able to touch bottom ▷ Elle n'aime pas nager là où elle n'a pas pied. She doesn't like swimming where she can't touch bottom.; **avoir les deux pieds dans la même bottine** to be clumsy; **des pieds à la tête** from head to foot; **le pied d'athlète** athlete's foot; **le pied de page** (in document) footer

piège [pjɛʒ] nm trap; **prendre quelqu'un au piège** to trap somebody

piéger [pjeʒe] vb to trap; **un colis piégé** a parcel bomb; **une voiture piégée** a car bomb

pierre [pjɛʀ] nf stone; **une pierre précieuse** a precious stone; **faire d'une pierre deux coups** to kill two birds with one stone

piéton [pjetɔ̃] nm pedestrian

piétonne [pjetɔn] nf pedestrian

piétonnier [pjetɔnje, -jɛʀ] (f **piétonnière**) adj: **une rue piétonnière** a traffic-free street; **un quartier piétonnier** a pedestrian zone

pieuvre [pjœvʀ(ə)] nf octopus

pigeon [piʒɔ̃] nm pigeon

piger [piʒe] vb (informal) to understand

pile [pil] nf ❶ pile ▷ Il y a une pile de disques sur la table. There's a pile of records on the table. ❷ battery ▷ La pile de ma montre est usée. The battery in my watch is dead.
▶ adv: **à deux heures pile** at two on the dot; **jouer à pile ou face** to flip a coin; **Pile ou face?** Heads or tails?

pilote [pilɔt] nmf pilot; **un pilote de course** a race car driver; **un pilote de ligne** an airline pilot

piloter [pilɔte] vb (a plane) to fly

pilule [pilyl] nf pill; **prendre la pilule** to be on the Pill

piment [pimɑ̃] nm chili pepper

pin [pɛ̃] nm pine

pince [pɛ̃s] nf ❶ (tool) pliers ❷ (of crab) pincer; **une pince à épiler** tweezers; **une pince à linge** a clothespin

pinceau [pɛ̃so] (pl **pinceaux**) nm paintbrush

pincée [pɛ̃se] nf: **une pincée de sel** a pinch of salt

pincer [pɛ̃se] vb to pinch ▷ Il m'a pincé le bras. He pinched my arm.

pingouin [pɛ̃ɡwɛ̃] nm penguin

ping-pong [piŋpɔ̃ɡ] nm table tennis ▷ jouer au ping-pong to play table tennis

pion [pjɔ̃] nm ❶ (chess) pawn ❷ (in checkers) piece

pionnier [pjɔnje] nm pioneer

pionnière [pjɔnjɛʀ] nf pioneer

pipe [pip] nf (for smoking) pipe

piquant [pikɑ̃, -ɑ̃t] (f **piquante**) adj ❶ prickly ❷ spicy

pique [pik] nm spades ▷ l'as de pique the ace of spades

pique-nique [piknik] nm picnic

piquer [pike] vb ❶ to bite ▷ Nous avons été piqués par les maringouins. We were bitten by mosquitoes. ❷ to burn ▷ Cette sauce me pique la langue. This sauce is burning my tongue. ❸ to steal ▷ On m'a piqué mon porte-monnaie. (informal) My wallet was stolen.; **se piquer** to prick oneself ▷ Il s'est piqué avec une aiguille. He pricked himself with a needle.

piquet [pike] nm ❶ stake ▷ Le chien est attaché à un piquet. The dog is tied to a stake. ❷ peg ▷ Il nous manque un des piquets de la tente. One of our tent pegs is missing.; **le piquet de grève** the picket line

piqûre [pikyʀ] nf ❶ injection ▷ *Le médecin m'a fait une piqûre.* The doctor gave me an injection. ❷ bite ▷ *une piqûre de maringouin* a mosquito bite ❸ sting ▷ *une piqûre d'abeille* a bee sting

pirate [piʀat] nmf pirate; **un pirate informatique** a hacker

pire [piʀ] adj, n worse ▷ *C'est encore pire qu'avant.* It's even worse than before.; **le pire** the worst ▷ *C'est la pire journée que j'aie jamais passée.* That's the worst day I've ever had. ▷ *Ce gamin est le pire de la bande.* That boy is the worst in the group.; **le pire de** the worst of ▷ *Le pire de tout, c'est qu'on s'ennuie tout le temps.* The worst of it is that we're always bored.

piscine [pisin] nf swimming pool

pistache [pistaʃ] nf pistachio ▷ *une crème glacée à la pistache* a pistachio ice cream

piste [pist(ə)] nf ❶ trail ▷ *La police est sur la piste du criminel.* The police are on the criminal's trail. ❷ runway ▷ *L'avion s'est posé sur la piste.* The plane landed on the runway. ❸ ski run ▷ *La skieuse a descendu la piste.* The skier came down the ski run.; **la piste de danse** the dance floor; **une piste cyclable** a bike path

pistolet [pistɔlɛ] nm pistol

pitié [pitje] nf ❶ pity; **Elle me fait pitié.** I feel sorry for her.; **avoir pitié de quelqu'un** to feel sorry for somebody

pitonner [pitɔne] vb ❶ (TV) to zap ❷ (computer) to key in

pittoresque [pitɔʀɛsk(ə)] adj picturesque

pizza [pidza] nf pizza

placard [plakaʀ] nm cupboard

place [plas] nf ❶ place ▷ *Elle a eu la troisième place au concours.* She got third place in the competition. ▷ *remettre quelque chose en place* to put something back in its place ❷ square ▷ *la place du marché* the market square ❸ (space) room ▷ *Il ne reste plus de place pour se garer.* There's no more room to park. ▷ *Ça prend de la place.* It takes up a lot of room. ❹ seat ▷ *Toutes les places ont été vendues.* All the seats have been sold.; **sur place** on the spot; **à la place** instead ▷ *Il ne reste plus de tarte; désirez-vous quelque chose d'autre à la place?* There's no pie left; would you like something else instead?; **à la place de** instead of

placer [plase] vb ❶ to seat ▷ *Nous étions placés près de la porte.* We were seated near the door. ❷ to invest ▷ *Il a placé ses économies à la Bourse.* He invested his money on the Stock Exchange.

plafond [plafɔ̃] nm ceiling

plage [plaʒ] nf beach

plagiat [plaʒja] nm plagiarism

plaie [plɛ] nf wound

plaindre [plɛ̃dʀ(ə)] vb: **plaindre quelqu'un** to feel sorry for somebody ▷ *Je te plains.* I feel sorry for you.; **se plaindre** to complain ▷ *Il n'arrête pas de se plaindre.* He never stops complaining.; **se plaindre à quelqu'un** to complain to somebody ▷ *Ils se sont plaints à la gérante.* They complained to the manager.; **se plaindre de quelque chose** to complain about something ▷ *Elle s'est plainte du bruit.* She complained

about the noise.

plaine [plɛn] nf (level area) plain

plainte [plɛ̃t] nf complaint; **porter plainte** to lodge a complaint

plaire [plɛʀ] vb: **Ce cadeau me plaît beaucoup.** I like this present a lot.; **Ce film plaît beaucoup aux jeunes.** The film is very popular with young people.; **Ça t'a plu d'aller en Nouvelle-Écosse?** Did you enjoy going to Nova Scotia?; **Elle lui plaît.** He likes her.; **s'il te plaît** please; **s'il vous plaît** please

plaisanter [plezɑ̃te] vb to joke

plaisanterie [plezɑ̃tʀi] nf joke

plaisir [pleziʀ] nm pleasure; **faire plaisir à quelqu'un** to please somebody ▷ *J'y suis allé pour lui faire plaisir.* I went there to please her. ▷ *Ce cadeau me fait très plaisir.* I'm very happy with this present.

plaît [plɛ] vb see **plaire**

plan [plɑ̃] nm ❶ plan ▷ *un plan du centre commercial* a map of the mall; **un plan de la ville** a street map; **au premier plan** in the foreground

planche [plɑ̃ʃ] nf plank; **une planche à neige** a snowboard; **une planche à repasser** an ironing board; **une planche à roulettes** skateboard; **une planche à voile** a sailboard; **une planche de surf** a surfboard

plancher [plɑ̃ʃe] nm floor

planchiste [plɑ̃ʃist(ə)] nmf (skateboarder, snowboarder) boarder

planer [plane] vb to glide ▷ *Un oiseau planait dans l'air.* A bird glided through the air.

planète [planɛt] nf planet

plante [plɑ̃t] nf plant

planter [plɑ̃te] vb ❶ to plant ▷ *Mon père a planté des tomates.* My dad planted some tomatoes. ❷ to hammer in ▷ *Elle a planté un clou dans le mur.* She hammered a nail into the wall. ❸ to pitch ▷ *Les filles ont planté leur tente au bord du lac.* The girls pitched their tent beside the lake. ❹ (computer) to crash ▷ *Mon ordinateur a encore planté.* My computer crashed again.; **Ne reste pas planté là!** Don't just stand there!; **se planter** (informal) to fail ▷ *Je me suis planté en maths.* I failed math.

plaque [plak] nf (metal) plate; **une plaque de verglas** a patch of ice

plaqué [plake] (f **plaquée**) adj: **plaqué or** or gold-plated; **plaqué argent** silver-plated

plastique [plastik] nm plastic

plat [pla, -at] (f **plate**) adj flat; **être à plat ventre** to be lying face down; **l'eau plate** still water
▶ nm ❶ dish ❷ course ▷ *le plat principal* the main course; **un plat cuisiné** a pre-cooked meal; **le plat du jour** the daily special

plateau [plato] (pl **plateaux**) nm ❶ tray; **un plateau de fromages** a selection of cheeses ❷ plateau

platine [platin] nm platinum
▶ nf (of record player) turntable; **une platine laser** a CD player

plâtre [plɑtʀ(ə)] nm plaster ▷ *une statue en plâtre* a plaster statue; **avoir un bras dans le plâtre** to have one's arm in a cast

plein [plɛ̃, -ɛn] (f **pleine**) adj full; **à plein temps** full-time ▷ *Elle travaille à plein temps.* She works full-time.; **plein de** (informal) lots of ▷ *un gâteau avec plein de crème* a cake with lots of cream; **Il y a plein de gens dans la rue.** The street is full of people.; **en plein air** in the open air; **en pleine nuit** in the middle of the night; **en plein jour** in broad daylight
▶ nm: **faire le plein** (gas) to fill it up ▷ *Faites le plein, s'il vous plaît.* Fill it up, please.

pleurer [plœʀe] vb to cry

pleut [plø] vb see **pleuvoir**

pleuvoir [pløvwaʀ] vb to rain ▷ *Il pleut.* It's raining.; **pleuvoir à boire debout** to rain cats and dogs

pli [pli] nm ❶ fold ❷ pleat ▷ *une jupe à plis* a pleated skirt ❸ crease ▷ *Il y a un pli sur la manche de ta chemise.* There's a crease in the sleeve of your shirt.

pliant [plijɑ̃, -ɑ̃t] (f **pliante**) adj folding ▷ *un lit pliant* a folding bed

plier [plije] vb ❶ to fold ▷ *plier une serviette* to fold a towel ❷ to bend ▷ *Il a plié le bras.* He bent his arm.

plomb [plɔ̃] nm lead ▷ *un tuyau en plomb* a lead pipe; **l'essence sans plomb** unleaded gas

plombier [plɔ̃bje] nm plumber; **Il est plombier.** He's a plumber.

plombière [plɔ̃bjɛʀ] nf plumber; **Elle est plombière.** She's a plumber.

plongée [plɔ̃ʒe] nf diving ▷ *faire de la plongée* to go diving

plongeoir [plɔ̃ʒwaʀ] nm diving board

plongeon [plɔ̃ʒɔ̃] nm dive

plonger [plɔ̃ʒe] vb to dive ▷ *Il a plongé dans la piscine.* He dived into the swimming pool.; **J'ai plongé ma main dans l'eau.** I plunged my hand into the water.; **être plongé dans son travail** to be absorbed in one's work; **se plonger dans un livre** to get absorbed in a book

plu [ply] vb see **plaire, pleuvoir**

pluie [plɥi] nf rain ▷ *sous la pluie* in the rain

plume [plym] nf ❶ feather ▷ *une plume d'oiseau* a bird's feather; **un stylo à plume** a fountain pen

plupart [plypaʀ] nf: **la plupart** pron most (of them) ▷ *La plupart ont moins de quinze ans.* Most of them are under 15.; **la plupart de** most of ▷ *La plupart de mes amis sont allés au concert.* Most of my friends went to the concert. ▷ *La plupart des élèves ont fait les devoirs.* Most of the students did the homework.; **la plupart des** most ▷ *La plupart des gens ont déjà vu ce film.* Most people have already seen this film.; **la plupart du temps** most of the time

pluriel [plyʀjɛl] nm plural; **au pluriel** in the plural

plus [plys] adv, prep: **ne…plus** not…anymore ▷ *Il ne travaille plus ici.* He doesn't work here anymore.; **Je n'ai plus de pain.** I have no more bread.; **plus…que** more…than ▷ *Il est plus extraverti que son frère.* He's more outgoing than his brother. ▷ *Elle travaille plus que moi.* She works more than me. ▷ *Elle est plus grande que moi.* She's bigger than me.; **C'est le plus grand de la famille.** He's the tallest in his family.;

plus…plus… the more…the more… ▷ *Plus elle gagne d'argent, plus elle en veut.* The more money she earns, the more she wants.; **plus de** (1) more ▷ *Il nous faut plus de pain.* We need more bread. (2) more than ▷ *Il y avait plus de dix personnes.* There were more than 10 people.; **de plus** more ▷ *Il nous faut un joueur de plus.* We need one more player. ▷ *Le voyage a pris trois heures de plus que prévu.* The journey took 3 more hours than planned.; **en plus** more ▷ *J'ai apporté quelques couvertures en plus.* I brought a few more blankets.; **de plus en plus** more and more ▷ *Il y a de plus en plus de touristes par ici.* There are getting to be more and more tourists around here. ▷ *Il fait de plus en plus chaud.* It's getting hotter and hotter out.; **un peu plus difficile** a bit more difficult ▷ *Il fait un peu plus froid qu'hier.* It's a bit colder than yesterday.; **plus ou moins** more or less; **Quatre plus deux égalent six.** 4 plus 2 is 6.

plusieurs [plyzjœʀ] pron several ▷ *Elle a acheté plusieurs chemises.* She bought several shirts. ▷ *Il y en a plusieurs.* There are several of them.

plus-que-parfait [plyskəpaʀfɛ] nm pluperfect

plutôt [plyto] adv ❶ quite ▷ *Elle est plutôt forte.* She's quite strong. ❷ rather ▷ *La nourriture ici est plutôt chère.* The food here is rather expensive ❸ instead ▷ *Demande-leur plutôt de venir avec toi.* Ask them to come with you instead.; **plutôt que** rather than ▷ *Je prendrai la salade plutôt que les frites avec ça.* I'll have the salad rather than the fries with that.

pluvieux [plyvjø, -øz] (f **pluvieuse**) adj rainy

pneu [pnø] nm tire

pneumonie [pnømɔni] nf pneumonia

poche [pɔʃ] nf pocket; **l'argent de poche** pocket money; **un livre de poche** a paperback; **un ordinateur de poche** a handheld computer

poêle [pwal] nf frying pan; **une poêle à frire** a frying pan

poème [pɔɛm] nm poem

poésie [pɔezi] nf ❶ poetry ❷ poem

poète [pɔɛt] nmf poet

poids [pwa] nm weight ▷ *vendre quelque chose au poids* to sell something by weight; **prendre du poids** to put on weight ▷ *Il a pris du poids.* He's put on weight.; **perdre du poids** to lose weight ▷ *Il a perdu du poids.* He's lost weight.; **un poids lourd** a truck

poignée [pwaɲe] nf ❶ handful ▷ *une poignée de riz* a handful of rice ❷ handle ▷ *la poignée de la porte* the door handle; **une poignée de main** a handshake

poignet [pwaɲɛ] nm ❶ wrist ▷ *Je me suis fait mal au poignet.* I hurt my wrist. ❷ (of shirt) cuff

poil [pwal] nm ❶ hair ▷ *Il y a des poils de chat partout sur la moquette.* There are cat hairs all over the carpet. ❷ fur ▷ *Ton chien a un beau poil.* Your dog has beautiful fur.; **à poil** (informal) stark naked

poilu [pwaly] (f **poilue**) adj hairy

poinçonner [pwɛ̃sɔne] vb to punch ▷ *Le contrôleur a poinçonné les billets.* The conductor punched the tickets.

poing [pwɛ̃] nm fist; **un coup de poing** a punch

point [pwɛ̃] nm ❶ point ▷ *Je ne suis pas d'accord sur ce point.* I don't agree with this point. ▷ *Son point faible, c'est qu'elle est un peu paresseuse.* Her weak point is that she's a bit lazy.; **le point de départ** (*in a race*) the starting line; **point de vue** point of view ❷ (*punctuation*) period ❸ dot ▷ *metter un point sur un « i »* to dot an "i"; **être sur le point de faire quelque chose** to be just about to do something ▷ *J'étais sur le point de te téléphoner.* I was just about to phone you.; **mettre au point** to finalize; **Ce n'est pas encore au point.** It's not finalized yet.; **à point** medium ▷ *« Comment voulez-vous votre steak? » « À point. »* "How would you like your steak?" "Medium."; **un point d'exclamation** an exclamation mark; **un point d'interrogation** a question mark; **un point noir** a blackhead

pointage [pwɛtaʒ] nm (*sports*) score

pointe [pwɛ̃t] nf point ▷ *la pointe d'un couteau* the point of a knife; **être à la pointe du progrès** to be in the forefront of progress; **sur la pointe des pieds** on tiptoe; **les heures de pointe** peak hours

pointillé [pwɛtije] nm dotted line

pointilleux [pwɛtijø, -øz] (*f* **pointilleuse**) adj picky ▷ *Notre prof est pointilleuse sur la grammaire.* Our teacher is picky about grammar.

pointu [pwɛty] (*f* **pointue**) adj pointed ▷ *un chapeau pointu* a pointed hat

pointure [pwɛtyʀ] nf size (*of shoes*) ▷ *Quelle est votre pointure?* What size shoes do you take?

point-virgule [pwɛ̃viʀgyl] (*pl* **points-virgules**) nm semicolon

poire [pwaʀ] nf pear

poireau [pwaʀo] (*pl* **poireaux**) nm leek ▷ *la soupe aux poireaux* leek soup

pois [pwa] nm pea; **les petits pois** peas; **les pois chiches** chickpeas; **à pois** polka-dotted ▷ *une robe à pois* a polka-dotted dress

poison [pwazɔ̃] nm poison

poisson [pwasɔ̃] nm fish ▷ *Je n'aime pas le poisson.* I don't like fish. ▷ *Elle a attrapé deux poissons.* She caught two fish.; **les Poissons** Pisces ▷ *Elle est Poissons.* She's a Pisces.; **Poisson d'avril!** April fool!; **un poisson rouge** a goldfish

poitrine [pwatʀin] nf ❶ chest ▷ *J'ai mal à la poitrine.* I'm having chest pains. ❷ bust ▷ *Quel est votre tour de poitrine?* What's your bust size? ❸ breast ▷ *une poitrine de poulet* a chicken breast

poivre [pwavʀ(ə)] nm (*spice*) pepper

poivron [pwavʀɔ̃] nm (*vegetable*) pepper

pôle [pol] nm pole; **le pôle Nord** the North Pole; **le pôle Sud** the South Pole

poli [pɔli] (*f* **polie**) adj polite

police [pɔlis] nf police ▷ *La police recherche le voleur.* The police are looking for the thief.; **la police de caractères** font; **une police d'assurance** an insurance policy

policier [pɔlisje, -jɛʀ] (*f* **policière**) adj: **un roman policier** a detective novel
▶ nm police officer ▷ *Il est policier.* He's a police officer.

policière [pɔlisjɛʀ] nf police officer ▷ *Elle est policière.* She's a police officer.

politesse [pɔlites] nf politeness

politique [pɔlitik] nf ❶ politics ▷ *La politique ne l'intéresse pas du tout.* He's not at all interested in politics.; **pratiquer la politique de l'autruche** to bury one's head in the sand ❷ policy ▷ *la politique sociale du gouvernement* the government's social policy
▶ adj political ▷ *une question politique* a political issue

politiquement correct [pɔlitikmɑ̃-] adj politically correct

polluer [pɔlɥe] vb to pollute ▷ *Les lacs ont été pollués.* The lakes have been polluted.

pollupostage [pɔlypɔstaʒ] nm spam

polluriel [pɔlyʀjɛl] nm spam message

pollution [pɔlysjɔ̃] nf pollution

polyvalente [pɔlivalɑ̃t] nf

pommade [pɔmad] nf ointment

pomme [pɔm] nf apple; **les pommes de terre** potatoes

pompe [pɔ̃p] nf pump; **une pompe à essence** a gas pump

pompier [pɔ̃pje] nm firefighter

pompière [pɔ̃pjɛʀ] nf firefighter

ponctuel [pɔ̃ktɥɛl] (*f* **ponctuelle**) adj ❶ punctual ▷ *Elle est toujours très ponctuelle.* She's always very punctual. ❷ occasional; **On a rencontré quelques problèmes ponctuels.** We've had the occasional problem.

pondre [pɔ̃dʀ(ə)] vb (*eggs*) to lay

poney [pɔnɛ] nm pony

pont [pɔ̃] nm ❶ bridge ❷ (*of ship*) deck

pop [pɔp] adj (*music*) pop ▷ *des groupes pop* pop bands

populaire [pɔpylɛʀ] adj ❶ popular ▷ *Ce chanteur est très populaire au Québec.* This singer's very popular in Québec. ❷ working-class ▷ *un quartier populaire de la ville* a working-class area of town

population [pɔpylasjɔ̃] nf population; **la population active** the workforce

porc [pɔʀ] nm ❶ pig ▷ *Ils élèvent des porcs.* They breed pigs. ❷ pork ▷ *du rôti de porc* roast pork

porcelaine [pɔʀsəlɛn] nf china ▷ *une tasse en porcelaine* a china cup

porc-épic [pɔʀkepik] (*pl* **porcs-épics**) nm porcupine

port [pɔʀ] nm ❶ harbour ❷ port

portage [pɔʀtaʒ] nm portage ▷ *Cette rivière comporte huit portages.* This river has 8 portages.; **faire du portage** to portage

portager [pɔʀtaʒe] vb to portage

portail [pɔʀtaj] nm (*Web*) portal

portatif [pɔʀtatif, -iv] (*f* **portative**) adj portable

porte [pɔʀt(ə)] nf ❶ door ▷ *Ferme la porte, s'il te plaît.* Close the door, please.; **la porte d'entrée** the front door ❷ gate ▷ *Vol 432 à destination de Calgary : porte numéro trois.* Flight 432 to Calgary: gate 3.; **mettre quelqu'un à la porte** to fire somebody

porte-bagages [pɔʀtbagaʒ] nm luggage rack; **le porte-bagages de toit** roof rack

porte-clés [pɔʀtəkle] nm keychain

portée [pɔʀte] nf: **à portée de la main** within arm's reach; **hors de portée** out of reach

portefeuille [pɔʀtəfœj] nm wallet

portemanteau [pɔʀtmɑ̃to] (pl **portemanteaux**) nm coat rack

porte-monnaie [pɔʀtmɔnɛ] (pl **porte-monnaie**) nm wallet

porte-parole [pɔʀtparɔl] (pl **porte-parole**) nmf spokesperson ▷ **Elle est la porte-parole de notre conseil étudiant.** She's the spokesperson for our student council.

porter [pɔʀte] vb ❶ to carry ▷ **Il portait une valise.** He was carrying a suitcase. ❷ to wear ▷ **Elle porte une robe bleue.** She's wearing a blue dress.; **se porter bien** to be well; **se porter mal** to be unwell

porteur [pɔʀtœʀ] nm porter

portion [pɔʀsjɔ̃] nf portion

portrait [pɔʀtʀɛ] nm portrait

poser [poze] vb ❶ to put down ▷ **J'ai posé la cafetière sur la table.** I put the coffee pot down on the table. ❷ to pose ▷ **Cela pose un problème.** That poses a problem.; **poser une question à quelqu'un** to ask somebody a question; **poser des rideaux** to put up curtains; **poser sa candidature** to apply for a job; **se poser** to land ▷ **L'avion s'est posé à huit heures.** The plane landed at 8 o'clock.

positif [pozitif, -iv] (f **positive**) adj positive

position [pozisjɔ̃] nf position

posséder [posede] vb to own ▷ **Ils possèdent une jolie maison.** They own a lovely home.

possibilité [posibilite] nf possibility

possible [posibl(ə)] adj possible ▷ **Nous leur avons dit que ce n'était pas possible.** We told them it wasn't possible.; **le plus de gens possible** as many people as possible; **le plus tôt possible** as early as possible; **le moins d'argent possible** as little money as possible; **Il travaille le moins possible.** He works as little as possible.; **dès que possible** as soon as possible; **faire son possible** to do all one can ▷ **Je ferai tout mon possible.** I'll do all I can.

poste [pɔst(ə)] nf mail ▷ **Je vais l'envoyer par la poste.** I'm going to send it by mail.; **le bureau de poste** the post office; **mettre une lettre à la poste** to mail a letter
▶ nm ❶ job ▷ **Elle a trouvé un poste de professeure.** She has found a teaching job. ❷ (phone) extension ▷ **Pouvez-vous me passer le poste de M. Salzedo?** Can you put me through to Mr Salzedo's extension? ❸ set ▷ **un poste de radio** a radio set; **le poste de péage** tollbooth; **un poste de police** a police station

poster [pɔste] vb to mail ▷ **Je vais poster ce colis.** I'm going to mail this parcel.
▶ nm poster

pot [po] nm jar ▷ **J'ai fait trois pots de confiture.** I've made three jars of jam.; **un pot de fleurs** a flowerpot

potable [pɔtabl(ə)] adj: **eau potable** drinking water; **« eau non potable »** "not drinking water"

pot-de-vin [podvɛ̃] (pl **pots-de-vin**) nm bribe

poteau [poto] (pl **poteaux**) nm post ▷ **Elle s'est** appuyée contre un poteau. She leaned against a post.; **un poteau indicateur** a signpost

potentiel [pɔtɑ̃sjɛl] (f **potentielle**) adj potential

poterie [pɔtʀi] nf ❶ pottery ▷ **Nous avons fait de la poterie à l'école.** We did pottery at school. ❷ piece of pottery ▷ **J'ai acheté deux poteries.** I bought two pieces of pottery.

potlatch [pɔtlatʃ] nm potlatch

pou [pu] (pl **poux**) nm louse

poubelle [pubɛl] nf garbage can

pouce [pus] nm ❶ thumb ▷ **Je me suis coincé le pouce dans la porte.** I trapped my thumb in the door.; **donner un coup de pouce à quelqu'un** to help out someone; **faire du pouce** to hitchhike ❷ inch

pouding-chômeur [pudiɲʃomœʀ] nm

poudre [pudʀ(ə)] nf ❶ powder ❷ face powder; **le lait en poudre** powdered milk; **le café en poudre** instant coffee

poudrerie [pudʀəʀi] nf blizzard ▷ **Les écoles sont fermées à cause de la poudrerie.** The schools are closed because of the blizzard.

poulain [pulɛ̃] nm foal

poule [pul] nf hen

poulet [pulɛ] nm chicken ▷ **J'adore le poulet.** I love chicken. ▷ **un poulet rôti** a roast chicken

pouls [pu] nm pulse ▷ **Il m'a pris le pouls.** He took my pulse.

poumon [pumɔ̃] nm lung

poupée [pupe] nf doll

pour [puʀ] prep for ▷ **C'est un cadeau pour toi.** It's a present for you. ▷ **Qu'est-ce que tu veux pour ton déjeuner?** What would you like for breakfast?; **pour faire quelque chose** in order to do something ▷ **Je lui ai téléphoné pour l'inviter.** I phoned him in order to invite him.; **Pour aller à Kamloops, s'il vous plaît?** Which way is it to Kamloops, please?; **pour que** so that ▷ **Je lui ai prêté mon chandail pour qu'elle n'ait pas froid.** I lent her my sweater so that she wouldn't be cold.; **pour cent** per cent

pourboire [puʀbwaʀ] nm tip ▷ **Elle a donné un pourboire au garçon.** She gave the waiter a tip.

pourcentage [puʀsɑ̃taʒ] nm percentage

pourquoi [puʀkwa] adv, conj why ▷ **Pourquoi est-ce qu'il ne vient pas avec nous?** Why isn't he coming with us? ▷ **Elle ne m'a pas dit pourquoi.** She didn't tell me why.

pourra, pourrai, pourras, pourrez vb see **pouvoir**

pourri [puʀi] (f **pourrie**) adj rotten

pourrir [puʀiʀ] vb to go bad ▷ **Ces poires ont pourri.** These pears have gone bad.

pourrons, pourront vb see **pouvoir**

poursuite [puʀsɥit] nf chase; **se lancer à la poursuite de quelqu'un** to chase after somebody

poursuivre [puʀsɥivʀ(ə)] vb to carry on with ▷ **Ils ont poursuivi leur travail.** They carried on with their work.; **se poursuivre** to go on ▷ **Le concert s'est poursuivi très tard.** The concert went on very late.

pourtant [puʀtɑ̃] adv however ▷ **Il a raté son examen. Pourtant, il n'est pas bête.** He failed his exam. However, he's not stupid.; **C'est**

pourtant facile! But it's easy!
pourvu [puʀvy] *adj*: **pourvu que... (1)** let's
hope that... ▷ *Pourvu qu'il ne pleuve pas!* Let's
hope it doesn't rain! **(2)** *(on condition that)* as
long as... ▷ *Tu peux y aller, pourvu que tu fasses
tes devoirs avant le souper.* You can go, as long as
you do your homework before supper.
pousser [puse] *vb* ❶ to push ▷ *Elle a pu pousser
la voiture.* She was able to push the car. ❷ to
grow ▷ *Mes cheveux poussent vite.* My hair
grows quickly.; **pousser un cri** to give a cry;
se pousser to move over ▷ *Pousse-toi, je ne vois
rien.* Move over, I can't see a thing.
poussette [puset] *nf* stroller
poussière [pusjɛʀ] *nf* dust ▷ *La table est
couverte de poussière.* The table's covered with
dust.
poussiéreux [pusjeʀø, -øz] (*f* **poussiéreuse**)
adj dusty
poussin [pusɛ̃] *nm* chick
poutine [putin] *nf*
pouvoir [puvwaʀ] *nm* power ▷ *Le premier
ministre a beaucoup de pouvoir.* The prime
minister has a lot of power.
  ▶ *vb* can ▷ *Je peux lui téléphoner si tu veux.* I can
phone her if you want. ▷ *Puis-je venir vous voir
samedi?* May I come and see you on Saturday?
▷ *Je ne pourrai pas venir samedi.* I can't come on
Saturday. ▷ *J'ai fait tout ce que j'ai pu.* I did all I
could.; **Je n'en peux plus.** I'm exhausted.; **Il
se peut que...** It's possible that... ▷ *Il se peut
qu'elle ait déménagé.* It's possible that she's
moved. ▷ *Il se peut que j'y aille.* I might go.
prairie [pʀeʀi] *nf* prairie; **les provinces des
Prairies** the Prairie provinces
pratique [pʀatik] *nf* practice ▷ *Je manque de
pratique.* I'm out of practice.
  ▶ *adj* practical ▷ *Ce sac à main est très pratique.*
This purse is very practical.
pratiquement [pʀatikmã] *adv* practically
▷ *J'ai pratiquement fini.* I've practically finished.
pratiquer [pʀatike] *vb* to practise ▷ *Je dois
pratiquer mon anglais.* I need to practise my
English.; **Pratiquez-vous un sport?** Do you
play any sports?
pré [pʀe] *nm* meadow
précaution [pʀekosjɔ̃] *nf* precaution
▷ *prendre des précautions* to take precautions;
par précaution as a precaution ▷ *Il a pris une
assurance par précaution.* He took out insurance
as a precaution.; **avec précaution** cautiously;
« *à manipuler avec précaution* » "handle
with care"
précédemment [pʀesedamã] *adv* previously
précédent [pʀesedã, -ãt] (*f* **précédente**) *adj*
previous
précieux [pʀesjø, -øz] (*f* **précieuse**) *adj*
precious; **une pierre précieuse** a precious
stone; **de précieux conseils** invaluable advice
précipice [pʀesipis] *nm* ravine ▷ *Leur voiture
est tombée dans un précipice.* Their car fell into
a ravine.
précipitamment [pʀesipitamã] *adv*
hurriedly ▷ *Elle est partie précipitamment.* She
left hurriedly.
précipitation [pʀesipitasjɔ̃] *nf* haste ▷ *Il a*

agi avec précipitation. He acted hastily.
se précipiter [pʀesipite] *vb* to rush
précis [pʀesi, -iz] (*f* **précise**) *adj* precise; **à
huit heures précises** at exactly eight o'clock
précisément [pʀesizemã] *adv* precisely
préciser [pʀesize] *vb* ❶ to be more specific
about ▷ *Pouvez-vous préciser ce que vous voulez
dire?* Can you be more specific about what
you're trying to say? ❷ to specify ▷ *Pouvez-vous
préciser les raisons de ce changement?* Can you
specify the reasons for this change?
précision [pʀesizjɔ̃] *nf* ❶ precision ❷ detail
▷ *Peux-tu me donner quelques précisions?* Can you
give me some details?
prédire [pʀediʀ] *vb* ❶ to predict ▷ *Les
climatologues n'ont pas prédit ce tsunami.*
Climatologists did not predict this tsunami.
❷ to foretell ▷ *Personne ne peut prédire l'avenir.*
No one can foretell the future.
préférable [pʀefeʀabl(ə)] *adj* preferable
préféré [pʀefeʀe] (*f* **préférée**) *adj* favourite
préférence [pʀefeʀãs] *nf* preference ▷ *Je
n'ai pas de préférence.* I have no preference.; **de
préférence** preferably
préférer [pʀefeʀe] *vb* to prefer ▷ *Je préfère la
cuisine de mon père.* I prefer my dad's cooking.
▷ *Je préfère manger à la cafétéria.* I prefer to eat in
the cafeteria.; **je préférerais du thé.** I'd rather
have tea.; **préférer quelque chose à quelque
chose** to prefer something to something ▷ *Je
préfère celui-ci à celui-là.* I prefer this one to
that one.
préhistorique [pʀeistoʀik] *adj* prehistoric
préjugé [pʀeʒyʒe] *nm* prejudice ▷ *avoir des
préjugés contre quelqu'un* to be prejudiced
against somebody
prématernelle [pʀematɛʀnɛl] *nf* junior
kindergarten
premier [pʀəmje, -jɛʀ] (*f* **première**) *adj* first
▷ *au premier étage* on the first floor ▷ *C'est notre
premier jour de vacances.* It's the first day of our
holidays. ▷ *C'est la première fois que je viens ici.*
It's the first time I've been here. ▷ *le premier mai*
the first of May ▷ *Elle est arrivée première.* She
came first.; **le premier ministre (1)** the prime
minister **(2)** *(of province)* the premier
première [pʀəmjɛʀ] *nf* ❶ first class ▷ *Nous
avons voyagé en première.* We travelled first class.
❷ first gear ▷ *Passe en première pour prendre ce
virage.* Change into first to go around this bend.
premièrement [pʀəmjɛʀmã] *adv* firstly
Premières Nations *nfpl* First Nations
▷ *l'Assemblée des Premières Nations* the Assembly
of First Nations
prendre [pʀãdʀ(ə)] *vb* to take ▷ *Prends tes
affaires et viens avec moi.* Take your things and
come with me.; **prendre quelque chose à
quelqu'un** to take something from somebody
▷ *Elle m'a pris mon stylo!* She took my pen!; **Nous
avons pris le vol de huit heures.** We took
the eight o'clock flight.; **Je prends toujours
l'autobus pour aller à l'école.** I always go
to school by bus; **passer prendre** to pick up
▷ *Nous devons passer prendre ma sœur.* We have to
pick up his sister.; **prendre à gauche** to turn
left ▷ *Prenez à gauche en arrivant à la prochaine*

intersection. Turn left at the next intersection.; **Il se prend pour un génie.** He thinks he's a genius.; **s'en prendre à quelqu'un** (verbally) to take it out on somebody ▷ *Il s'en est pris à moi.* He took it out on me.; **s'y prendre** to go about it ▷ *Tu t'y prends mal!* You're going about it the wrong way!; **prendre une décision** to make a decision

prénom [pʀenɔ̃] *nm* first name ▷ *Quel est votre prénom?* What's your first name?

préoccupé [pʀeɔkype] (f **préoccupée**) *adj* worried

préparation [pʀepaʀasjɔ̃] *nf* preparation

préparer [pʀepaʀe] *vb* ❶ to prepare ▷ *Il prépare le dîner.* He's preparing dinner. ❷ to make ▷ *Je vais préparer le café.* I'm going to make the coffee. ❸ to prepare for ▷ *Ma sœur prépare son examen d'économie.* My sister's preparing for her economics exam.; **se préparer** to get ready ▷ *Ils se préparent à partir.* They're getting ready to go.

préposition [pʀepozisjɔ̃] *nf* preposition

près [pʀɛ] *adv*: **tout près** nearby ▷ *J'habite tout près.* I live nearby.; **près de (1)** near (to) ▷ *Est-ce que c'est près d'ici?* Is it near here? **(2)** next to ▷ *Assieds-toi près de moi.* Sit down next to me. **(3)** nearly ▷ *Il y avait près de cinq cents spectateurs.* There were nearly 500 spectators.; **de près** closely ▷ *Elle a regardé la photo de près.* She looked closely at the photo.; **à peu de chose près** more or less

prescription [pʀeskʀipsjɔ̃] *nf* (medical) prescription

présence [pʀezɑ̃s] *nf* ❶ presence ▷ *Sa présence est rassurante.* Her presence is reassuring. ❷ attendance ▷ *La présence aux cours est obligatoire.* Attendance at classes is compulsory.

présent [pʀezɑ̃, -ɑ̃t] (f **présente**) *adj* present ▶ *nm* present tense; **à présent** now

présentation [pʀezɑ̃tasjɔ̃] *nf* presentation; **faire les présentations** to do the introductions

présenter [pʀezɑ̃te] *vb* to present ▷ *Il a présenté son rapport à la classe.* He presented his report to the class.; **présenter quelqu'un à quelqu'un** to introduce somebody to somebody ▷ *Il m'a présenté à sa sœur.* He introduced me to his sister.; **Marc, je te présente Anaïs.** Marc, this is Anaïs.; **se présenter (1)** to introduce oneself ▷ *Elle s'est présentée à ses collègues.* She introduced herself to her colleagues. **(2)** to arise ▷ *Si l'occasion se présente, nous irons au Yukon.* If the chance arises, we'll go to the Yukon. **(3)** to stand ▷ *Elle se présente encore aux élections.* She's standing for election again.

préservatif [pʀezɛʀvatif] *nm* condom

préserver [pʀezɛʀve] *vb* to protect ▷ *préserver du froid* to protect from the cold

président [pʀezidɑ̃] *nm* ❶ president ▷ *le président des États-Unis* the president of the United States ❷ (person) chair ▷ *le président du conseil d'administration* the chair of the board of directors

présidente [pʀezidɑ̃t] *nf* ❶ president

❷ (person) chair ▷ *Elle est présidente du conseil d'administration.* She's the chair of the board of directors.

présider [pʀezide] *vb* ❶ to chair ▷ *Elle a présidé la réunion.* She chaired the meeting. ❷ to be the guest of honour ▷ *Il présidait à table.* He was the guest of honour at the table.

presque [pʀesk(ə)] *adv* nearly ▷ *Il est presque six heures.* It's nearly 6 o'clock. ▷ *Nous sommes presque arrivés.* We're nearly there.; **presque rien** hardly anything ▷ *Elle n'a presque rien mangé.* She's hardly eaten anything.; **presque pas** hardly at all ▷ *Il ne dort presque pas.* He hardly sleeps at all.; **presque pas de** hardly any ▷ *Il n'y a presque pas de place.* There's hardly any room.

presqu'île [pʀeskil] *nf* peninsula

presse [pʀes] *nf* press ▷ *les représentants de la presse* representatives of the press

pressé [pʀese] (f **pressée**) *adj* ❶ in a hurry ▷ *Je ne peux pas rester, je suis pressé.* I can't stay, I'm in a hurry. ❷ urgent ▷ *Ce n'est pas très pressé.* It's not very urgent.

presser [pʀese] *vb* ❶ to squeeze ▷ *presser un citron* to squeeze a lemon ❷ to be urgent ▷ *Est-ce que ça presse?* Is it urgent?; **se presser** to hurry up ▷ *Allez, presse-toi, on va être en retard!* Come on, hurry up, we're going to be late!; **Rien ne presse.** There's no hurry.

pression [pʀesjɔ̃] *nf* pressure; **faire pression sur quelqu'un** to put pressure on somebody; **la pression des pairs** peer pressure

prêt [pʀe, pʀet] (f **prête**) *adj* ready ▷ *Le déjeuner est prêt.* Breakfast is ready. ▷ *Tu es prête?* Are you ready? ▶ *nm* loan

prêt-à-porter [pʀetapɔʀte] *nm* off-the-rack clothing

prétendre [pʀetɑ̃dʀ(ə)] *vb* to claim ▷ *Il prétend qu'on lui a volé son sac à dos.* He claims his knapsack was stolen. ▷ *Elle prétend ne pas le connaître.* She claims she doesn't know him.

prétendu [pʀetɑ̃dy] (f **prétendue**) *adj* so-called ▷ *un prétendu expert* a so-called expert

prétentieux [pʀetɑ̃sjø, -øz] (f **prétentieuse**) *adj* pretentious

prêter [pʀete] *vb*: **prêter quelque chose à quelqu'un** to lend something to someone ▷ *Elle m'a prêté sa calculatrice.* She lent me her calculator.; **prêter attention à quelque chose** to pay attention to something

prétexte [pʀetɛkst(ə)] *nm* excuse ▷ *Il avait un prétexte pour ne pas venir.* He had an excuse for not coming.; **sous aucun prétexte** under no circumstances ▷ *Il ne faut la déranger sous aucun prétexte.* She is not to be disturbed under any circumstances.

prétexter [pʀetɛkste] *vb* to give as an excuse ▷ *Elle a prétexté une réunion.* She gave a meeting as her excuse. ▷ *Il a prétexté qu'il avait un rendez-vous.* He gave the excuse that he had an appointment.

prêtre [pʀetʀ(ə)] *nm* priest

preuve [pʀœv] *nf* ❶ evidence ▷ *Il y a des preuves contre lui.* There's evidence against him. ❷ proof ▷ *Vous n'avez aucune preuve.* You have

no proof.; **faire preuve de courage** to show
courage; **faire ses preuves** to prove oneself
▷ *Pour être embauché ici, il faut faire ses preuves.* To
be employed here, you need to prove yourself.
prévenir [pʀevniʀ] *vb:* **prévenir quelqu'un**
to warn somebody ▷ *Je te préviens, elle est de
mauvaise humeur.* I'm warning you, she's in a
bad mood.
prévention [pʀevɑ̃sjɔ̃] *nf* prevention; **des
mesures de prévention** preventive measures;
la prévention des incendies fire prevention;
la prévention routière road safety
prévision [pʀevizjɔ̃] *nf:* **les prévisions
météorologiques** the weather forecast; **en
prévision de quelque chose** in anticipation
of something
prévoir [pʀevwaʀ] *vb* ❶ to plan ▷ *Nous
prévoyons un pique-nique pour dimanche.* We're
planning to have a picnic on Sunday.; **Le
départ est prévu pour dix heures.** The
departure's scheduled for 10 o'clock. ❷ to
allow ▷ *J'ai prévu assez à manger pour quatre.* I
allowed enough food for four. ❸ to foresee
▷ *J'avais prévu ce problème dès le début.* I had
foreseen this problem from the start.; **Je
prévois qu'il me faudra une heure de plus.** I
figure it'll take me another hour.
prier [pʀije] *vb* to pray ▷ *Les Grecs de l'Antiquité
priaient Dionysos.* The Ancient Greeks prayed to
Dionysos.; **prier quelqu'un de faire quelque
chose** to ask somebody to do something ▷ *Elle
l'a prié de sortir.* She asked him to leave.; **je vous
en prie (1)** please do ▷ *«Je peux m'asseoir?»* —
«Je vous en prie.» "May I sit down?" — "Please do."
(2) please ▷ *Je vous en prie, ne me laissez pas seule.*
Please, don't leave me alone. **(3)** don't mention
it ▷ *«Merci pour votre aide.» —«Je vous en prie.»*
"Thanks for your help." — "Don't mention it."
prière [pʀijɛʀ] *nf* prayer ▷ **faire ses prières**
to say one's prayers; *«prière de ne pas fumer»*
"no smoking please"
primaire [pʀimɛʀ] *nm* elementary school
▷ *Ses enfants sont encore au primaire.* His children
are still in elementary school.; **une école
primaire** an elementary school
prime [pʀim] *nf* ❶ bonus ▷ *Il a eu une prime
de son employeur.* He got a bonus from his
employer. ❷ free gift ▷ *J'ai eu ce stylo en prime
avec l'agenda.* I got this pen as a free gift with
the diary. ❸ premium ▷ *une prime d'assurance*
an insurance premium
prince [pʀɛ̃s] *nm* prince ▷ *le prince de Galles* the
Prince of Wales
princesse [pʀɛ̃sɛs] *nf* princess ▷ *la princesse de
Galles* the Princess of Wales
principal [pʀɛ̃sipal, -o] *(f* **principale**, *mpl*
principaux) *adj* main ▷ *le rôle principal* the
main role
▷ *nm (pl* **principaux)** main thing ▷ *Personne n'a
été blessé; c'est le principal.* Nobody was injured;
that's the main thing.
principe [pʀɛ̃sip] *nm* principle; **pour le
principe** on principle; **en principe (1)** as a rule
▷ *Elle prend son lunch en principe à midi et demi.* As
a rule she has lunch at 12.30. **(2)** in theory ▷ *En
principe le travail doit être assez facile.* In theory,

the work should be fairly easy.
printemps [pʀɛ̃tɑ̃] *nm* spring; **au printemps**
in spring
priorité [pʀijɔʀite] *nf* ❶ priority ▷ *C'est à faire
en priorité.* This needs to be a priority. ❷ right
of way ▷ *Tu n'as pas la priorité.* You don't have
the right of way.
pris [pʀi, pʀiz] *(f* **prise)** *vb* *see* **prendre**
pris [pʀi] *adj* ❶ taken ▷ *Est-ce que cette place
est prise?* Is this seat taken? ❷ busy ▷ *Je serai
très pris la semaine prochaine.* I'll be very busy
next week.; **être pris de panique** to be panic-
stricken
prise [pʀiz] *nf* ❶ plug ❷ socket; **une prise
de courant** an electrical outlet; **une prise de
sang** a blood test
prison [pʀizɔ̃] *nf* prison ▷ *aller en prison* to go
to prison ▷ *être en prison* to be in prison
prisonnier [pʀizɔnje] *nm* prisoner
prisonnière [pʀizɔnjɛʀ] *nf* prisoner
privé [pʀive] *(f* **privée)** *adj* private ▷ *la
propriété privée* private property ▷ *ma vie privée*
my private life; **en privé** in private
priver [pʀive] *vb:* **priver quelqu'un de
quelque chose** to deprive somebody of
something ▷ *Le prisonnier a été privé de
nourriture.* The prisoner was deprived of food.;
Tu seras privé de dessert! You won't get any
dessert!
prix [pʀi] *nm* ❶ price ▷ *Je n'arrive pas à lire le
prix de ce livre.* I can't see the price of this book.
❷ prize ▷ *Elle a eu le prix de la meilleure actrice.*
She got the prize for best actress.; **hors de prix**
exorbitantly priced ▷ *Les repas sont hors de prix
ici!* Meal prices here are exorbitant!; **à aucun
prix** not at any price ▷ *Je n'irai là-bas à aucun
prix.* I'm not going there, not at any price.; **à
tout prix** at all costs ▷ *Je veux à tout prix voir ce
film.* I want to see this movie at all costs.
probable [pʀɔbabl(ə)] *adj* likely ▷ *Il est
probable qu'elle viendra.* It's likely she'll come.;
C'est peu probable. That's unlikely.
probablement [pʀɔbabləmɑ̃] *adv* probably
problème [pʀɔblɛm] *nm* problem
procédé [pʀɔsede] *nm* process
procès [pʀɔsɛ] *nm* trial ▷ *Le procès du
meurtrier commence mardi.* The murder trial
starts on Tuesday.; **Il est en procès avec son
employeur.** He's involved in a lawsuit with his
employer.
prochain [pʀɔʃɛ̃, -ɛn] *(f* **prochaine)** *adj* next
▷ *Nous descendons au prochain arrêt.* We're
getting off at the next stop.; **la prochaine fois**
next time; **la semaine prochaine** next week;
À la prochaine! See you!
prochainement [pʀɔʃɛnmɑ̃] *adv* soon
proche [pʀɔʃ] *adj* ❶ near ▷ *Les magasins
les plus proches étaient à trois kilomètres.* The
nearest stores were 3 kilometres away. ▷ *dans
un proche avenir* in the near future ❷ close ▷ *un
ami proche* a close friend; **proche de** near ▷ *La
cathédrale est proche du château.* The cathedral is
near the castle.
proches [pʀɔʃ] *nmpl* close relatives
proclamer [pʀɔklame] *vb* to proclaim

procurer [pʀɔkyʀe] vb: **procurer quelque chose à quelqu'un** to get something for somebody ▷ *C'est lui qui m'a procuré ce travail.* She got me this job.; **se procurer quelque chose** to get something ▷ *Je me suis procuré leur dernier catalogue.* I got their latest catalogue.

producteur [pʀɔdyktœʀ] nm producer

production [pʀɔdyksjɔ̃] nf production

productrice [pʀɔdyktʀis] nf producer

produire [pʀɔdɥiʀ] vb to produce; **se produire** to take place ▷ *Ces changements se sont produits l'an dernier.* The changes took place last year.

produit [pʀɔdɥi] nm product ▷ *les produits de beauté* beauty products

prof [pʀɔf] nmf (informal) teacher ▷ *Elle est prof de maths.* She's a math teacher.

professeur [pʀɔfesœʀ] nm ❶ teacher ▷ *Il est professeur d'histoire.* He's a history teacher. ❷ professor

professeure [pʀɔfesœʀ] nf ❶ teacher ▷ *Elle est professeure de physique.* She's a physics teacher. ❷ professor ▷ *Elle est professeure agrégée.* She's a full professor.

profession [pʀɔfesjɔ̃] nf profession ▷ *Quelle est votre profession?* What's your profession?

professionnel [pʀɔfesjɔnɛl] (f **professionnelle**) adj professional

profil [pʀɔfil] nm ❶ (of person) profile ▷ *de profil* in profile ❷ (of object) contours

profit [pʀɔfi] nm profit ▷ *La société a fait des profits importants.* The company made significant profits.; **tirer profit de quelque chose** to profit from something; **au profit de** in aid of ▷ *un spectacle au profit d'un organisme de charité local* a show in aid of a local charity

profiter [pʀɔfite] vb: **profiter de quelque chose** to take advantage of something ▷ *Profitez du beau temps pour aller faire du vélo.* Take advantage of the good weather to go biking.; **Profitez-en bien!** Make the most of it!

profond [pʀɔfɔ̃, -ɔ̃d] (f **profonde**) adj deep; **peu profond** shallow

profondeur [pʀɔfɔ̃dœʀ] nf depth

programme [pʀɔgʀam] nm ❶ program ▷ *le programme du festival* the festival program ❷ curriculum ▷ *le programme de maths* the math curriculum ❸ program ▷ *un programme informatique* a computer program

programmer [pʀɔgʀame] vb to program ▷ *Mon ordinateur n'est pas programmé pour ça.* My computer isn't programmed to do that.; **être programmé** to be showing ▷ *Ce film est programmé dimanche soir.* That movie is showing Sunday night.

programmeur [pʀɔgʀamœʀ] nm programmer ▷ *Il est programmeur.* He's a programmer.

programmeuse [pʀɔgʀaməz] nf programmer ▷ *Elle est programmeuse.* She's a programmer.

progrès [pʀɔgʀɛ] nm progress ▷ *faire des progrès* to make progress

progresser [pʀɔgʀese] vb to progress

progressif [pʀɔgʀesif, -iv] (f **progressive**) adj progressive

projecteur [pʀɔʒektœʀ] nm ❶ projector ▷ *un vieux projecteur de diapositives* an old slide projector ❷ spotlight ▷ *sous les projecteurs* in the spotlight

projet [pʀɔʒe] nm plan ▷ *des projets de vacances* holiday plans; **le projet de construction** building plans ▷ *le projet de construction d'un musée* the building plans for a museum; **un projet de loi** (in parliament) a bill

projeter [pʀɔʒte] vb ❶ to plan ▷ *Ils projettent d'acheter une maison.* They're planning to buy a house. ❷ to cast ▷ *L'arbre projetait une ombre sur le mur.* The tree cast a shadow on the wall.; **Elle a été projetée hors de la voiture.** She was thrown out of the car.

prolongation [pʀɔlɔ̃gasjɔ̃] nf (sports) overtime

prolonger [pʀɔlɔ̃ʒe] vb ❶ to prolong ▷ *Ne prolonge pas tes souffrances; va chez le médecin!* Don't prolong the agony; go to the doctor! ❷ to extend ▷ *Je vais prolonger mon abonnement.* I'm going to extend my subscription.; **se prolonger** to go on ▷ *La réunion s'est prolongée tard.* The meeting went on late.

promenade [pʀɔmnad] nf ❶ walk ▷ *Il y a de belles promenades par ici.* There are some nice walks around here.; **faire une promenade** to go for a walk; **faire une promenade en voiture** to go for a drive; **faire une promenade à vélo** to go for a bike ride

promener [pʀɔmne] vb to take for a walk ▷ *Il promène son chien tous les jours.* He takes his dog for a walk every day.; **se promener** to go for a walk ▷ *Elle est partie se promener.* She has gone for a walk.

promesse [pʀɔmɛs] nf promise ▷ *faire une promesse* to make a promise ▷ *tenir sa promesse* to keep one's promise

promettre [pʀɔmɛtʀ(ə)] vb to promise ▷ *On m'a promis un billet gratuit.* They promised me a free ticket. ▷ *Elle m'a promis de me téléphoner.* She promised to phone me.

promotion [pʀɔmɔsjɔ̃] nf promotion ▷ *Il espère avoir bientôt une promotion.* He's hoping to get promotion soon.; **être en promotion** to be on special ▷ *Les côtelettes de porc sont en promotion.* Pork chops are on special.

pronom [pʀɔnɔ̃] nm pronoun

prononcer [pʀɔnɔ̃se] vb ❶ to pronounce ▷ *Ce mot est difficile à prononcer.* That word is difficult to pronounce. ❷ to deliver ▷ *prononcer un discours* to deliver a speech; **se prononcer** to be pronounced ▷ *Le «e» final ne se prononce pas.* The final "e" isn't pronounced.

prononciation [pʀɔnɔ̃sjasjɔ̃] nf pronunciation

propagande [pʀɔpagɑ̃d] nf propaganda

se propager [pʀɔpaʒe] vb to spread ▷ *Le feu s'est propagé rapidement.* The fire spread quickly.

proportion [pʀɔpɔʀsjɔ̃] nf proportion

propos [pʀɔpo] nm: **à propos** by the way ▷ *À propos, quand est-ce que tu viens?* By the way, when are you coming?; **à propos de quelque chose** about something ▷ *C'est à propos de la soirée de vendredi.* It's about the party on Friday.

proposer [pʀɔpoze] vb: **proposer quelque**

chose à quelqu'un (1) to suggest something to somebody ▷ *Nous lui avons proposé une promenade en bateau.* We suggested a boat ride to him. **(2)** to offer somebody something ▷ *Ils m'ont proposé des chocolats.* They offered me some chocolates.

proposition [pʀɔpozisjɔ̃] *nf* offer ▷ *J'accepte ta proposition avec plaisir.* I accept your offer with pleasure.

propre [pʀɔpʀ(ə)] *adj* ❶ clean ▷ *Ce mouchoir n'est pas propre.* This handkerchief isn't clean.; **recopier quelque chose au propre** to make a clean copy of something ❷ own ▷ *Elle l'a fabriqué de ses propres mains.* She made it with her own hands.; **propre à** characteristic of ▷ *C'est une coutume propre à la Gaspésie.* It's a custom you find in the Gaspé region.

proprement [pʀɔpʀəmɑ̃] *adv* properly ▷ *Mange proprement!* Eat properly!; **le village proprement dit** the village itself; **à proprement parler** strictly speaking

propreté [pʀɔpʀəte] *nf* cleanliness

propriétaire [pʀɔpʀijetɛʀ] *nmf* ❶ owner ❷ landlord, landlady

propriété [pʀɔpʀijete] *nf* property ▷ *la propriété privée* private property

prospectus [pʀɔspɛktys] *nm* brochure

prospère [pʀɔspɛʀ] *adj* prosperous

protecteur [pʀɔtɛktœʀ, -tʀis] (*f* **protectrice**) *adj* ❶ protective ▷ *un vernis protecteur* a protective varnish ❷ patronizing ▷ *un ton protecteur* a patronizing tone

protection [pʀɔtɛksjɔ̃] *nf* protection

protéger [pʀɔteʒe] *vb* to protect

protéine [pʀɔtein] *nf* protein

protestant [pʀɔtɛstɑ̃, -ɑ̃t] (*f* **protestante**, *f* **protestante**) *adj* Protestant ▷ *une église protestante* a Protestant church

protestation [pʀɔtɛstasjɔ̃] *nf* protest

protester [pʀɔtɛste] *vb* to protest ▷ *Ils protestent contre leurs mauvaises conditions de travail.* They're protesting their poor working conditions.

prouver [pʀuve] *vb* to prove

provenance [pʀɔvnɑ̃s] *nf* origin; **un avion en provenance de Winnipeg** a plane arriving from Winnipeg

provenir [pʀɔvniʀ] *vb*: **provenir de (1)** to come from ▷ *Ces pêches proviennent de la région du Niagara.* These peaches come from the Niagara region. **(2)** to be the result of ▷ *Cela provient d'un manque d'organisation.* This is the result of a lack of organization.

proverbe [pʀɔvɛʀb(ə)] *nm* proverb

province [pʀɔvɛ̃s] *nf* province

provincial [pʀɔvɛ̃sjal, -o] (*mpl* **provinciaux**) *adj* provincial ▷ *le gouvernement provincial* the provincial government

provision [pʀɔvizjɔ̃] *nf* supply ▷ *une provision de pommes de terre* a supply of potatoes

provisions [pʀɔvizjɔ̃] *nfpl* food ▷ *Nous n'avons plus beaucoup de provisions.* We don't have much food left.; **faire les provisions** to go grocery shopping

provisoire [pʀɔvizwaʀ] *adj* temporary ▷ *un emploi provisoire* a temporary job

provoquer [pʀɔvɔke] *vb* ❶ to provoke ▷ *Il l'a provoquée en la traitant d'imbécile.* He provoked her by calling her stupid. ❷ to cause ▷ *Cet accident a provoqué la mort de quarante personnes.* The accident caused the death of 40 people.

proximité [pʀɔksimite] *nf* proximity; **à proximité** nearby ▷ *Elle habite à proximité.* She lives nearby.

prudemment [pʀydamɑ̃] *adv* ❶ carefully ▷ *Conduisez prudemment!* Drive carefully! ❷ wisely ▷ *Prudemment, il a fait des économies.* He wisely saved some money. ❸ cautiously ▷ *Le gouvernement a réagi prudemment.* The government reacted cautiously.

prudence [pʀydɑ̃s] *nf* caution; **avec prudence** carefully ▷ *Ils ont conduit avec prudence.* They drove carefully.

prudent [pʀydɑ̃, -ɑ̃t] (*f* **prudente**) *adj* ❶ careful ▷ *Soyez prudents!* Be careful! ❷ wise ▷ *Laisse ton passeport à la maison, c'est plus prudent.* It would be wiser to leave your passport at home.

prune [pʀyn] *nf* plum

pruneau [pʀyno] (*pl* **pruneaux**) *nm* prune

psychiatre [psikjatʀ(ə)] *nmf* psychiatrist

psychologie [psikɔlɔʒi] *nf* psychology

psychologique [psikɔlɔʒik] *adj* psychological

psychologue [psikɔlɔg] *nmf* psychologist

pu [py] *vb see* **pouvoir**; **Je n'ai pas pu venir.** I couldn't come.

pub [pyb] *nf* ❶ (*informal*) advertising ▷ *C'est de l'excellente pub.* That's excellent advertising. ❷ ad ▷ *des pub percutantes* powerful ads

public [pyblik] (*f* **publique**) *adj* public ▷ *le transport public* public transport ▷ *une école publique* a public school ▷ *nm* ❶ public ▷ *Ce parc est ouvert au public.* This park is open to the public. ❷ audience ▷ *Le public a applaudi le chanteur.* The audience applauded the singer.; **en public** in public ▷ *Je déteste parler en public.* I hate speaking in public.

publicitaire [pyblisitɛʀ] *adj*: **une agence publicitaire** an advertising agency; **une campagne publicitaire** a publicity campaign

publicité [pyblisite] *nf* ❶ advertising ▷ *Elle travaille dans la publicité.* She works in advertising. ❷ ad ▷ *Il y a trop de publicités dans ce journal.* There are too many ads in this newspaper.; **faire de la publicité pour quelque chose** to publicize something

publier [pyblije] *vb* to publish ▷ *Il vient de publier son nouveau roman.* He has just published his new novel.

publique [pyblik] *adj see* **public**

puce [pys] *nf* ❶ flea ▷ *Ce chien a des puces.* This dog has fleas.; **un marché aux puces** a flea market ❷ chip ▷ *une puce électronique* a microchip; **une carte à puce** a smart card

puer [pɥe] *vb* to stink ▷ *Ça pue le tabac ici!* It stinks of tobacco here!

puis [pɥi] *vb see* **pouvoir**; **Puis-je venir vous voir samedi?** May I come and see you on Saturday?
▷ *adv* then ▷ *Faites dorer le poulet, puis ajoutez la sauce au miel et à l'ail.* Fry the chicken till golden,

then add the honey garlic sauce.

puisque [pɥisk(ə)] conj since ▷ *Puisque c'est si cher, nous irons manger ailleurs.* Since it's so expensive, we'll eat elsewhere.

puissance [pɥisɑ̃s] nf power ▷ *la puissance de l'imagination* the power of imagination ▷ *Ce pays est une puissance nucléaire.* This country is a nuclear power.

puissant [pɥisɑ̃, -ɑ̃t] (f **puissante**) adj powerful

puits [pɥi] nm well ▷ *Il a un puits dans son jardin.* He has a well in his garden.; **un puits de pétrole** an oil well

pulvérisateur [pylverizatœr] nm spray ▷ *un pulvérisateur de parfum* a perfume spray

pulvériser [pylverize] vb ❶ to pulverize ▷ *L'explosion a pulvérisé le bâtiment.* The explosion pulverized the building. ❷ to spray ▷ *Elle ne pulvérise jamais d'insecticide sur ses plantes.* She never sprays insecticide on her plants.

punaise [pynɛz] nf thumbtack

punir [pynir] vb to punish ▷ *Il a été puni pour avoir menti.* He was punished for lying.

punition [pynisjɔ̃] nf ❶ punishment ❷ (sports) penalty; **le banc de punition** the penalty box

pupitre [pypitr(ə)] nm (for student) desk

pur [pyr] (f **pure**) adj. pure ▷ *L'eau de cette source est très pure.* The water from this spring is very pure.; **c'est de la folie pure** it's sheer madness

purée [pyre] nf purée; **la purée de pommes de terre** mashed potatoes

puzzle [pœzl(ə)] nm jigsaw puzzle

pyjama [piʒama] nm pyjamas

pyramide [piramid] nf pyramid

q

QI [kyi] nm (= quotient intellectuel) IQ

quai [ke] nm ❶ dock; **Le navire est à quai.** The ship has docked. ❷ platform ▷ *Le train partira du quai numéro quatre.* The train will leave from platform 4.

qualifié [kalifje] (f **qualifiée**) adj qualified

qualifier [kalifje] vb: **se qualifier** to qualify ▷ *Il s'est qualifié pour la demi-finale.* He has qualified for the semifinal.

qualité [kalite] nf quality ▷ *Ces outils sont de très bonne qualité.* These are very good quality tools.

quand [kɑ̃] conj, adv when ▷ *Quand est-ce que tu pars en vacances?* When are you going

on vacation? ▷ *Quand je serai riche, j'achèterai une belle maison.* When I'm rich, I'll buy a nice house.; **quand même** anyway ▷ *Je ne voulais pas finir mes devoirs, mais je les ai faits quand même.* I didn't want to finish my homework, but I did it anyway.

quant à prep regarding ▷ *Quant au problème de chauffage...* Regarding the heating problem... ▷ *Quant à moi, je n'arriverai qu'à dix heures.* As for me, I won't be arriving till 10 o'clock.

quantité [kɑ̃tite] nf amount; **des quantités de** a great deal of

quarantaine [karɑ̃tɛn] nf about forty ▷ *une quarantaine de personnes* about forty people; **Elle a la quarantaine.** She's in her forties.

quarante [karɑ̃t] num forty ▷ *Elle a quarante ans.* She's forty.; **quarante et un** forty-one; **quarante-deux** forty-two

quart [kar] nm quarter; **le quart de** a quarter of ▷ *Il a mangé le quart du gâteau.* He ate a quarter of the cake.; **trois quarts** three quarters; **un quart d'heure** a quarter of an hour; **deux heures et quart** a quarter after two; **dix heures moins le quart** a quarter to ten

quartier [kartje] nm (of town) area ▷ *un quartier tranquille* a quiet area; **un cinéma de quartier** a local movie theatre

quartz [kwarts] nm: **une montre à quartz** a quartz watch

quasi [kazi] adv nearly ▷ *La quasi-totalité des récoltes a été détruite.* Nearly all of the crop was destroyed.

quasiment [kazimɑ̃] adv nearly ▷ *Le film est quasiment fini.* The movie's nearly over.; **quasiment jamais** hardly ever ▷ *Ils ne vont quasiment jamais au cinéma.* They hardly ever go to the movies.

quatorze [katɔrz(ə)] num fourteen ▷ *Mon frère a quatorze ans.* My brother's fourteen. ▷ *à quatorze heures* at 2 p.m.; **le quatorze février** the fourteenth of February

quatre [katr(ə)] num four ▷ *Il est quatre heures du matin.* It's four in the morning. ▷ *Elle a quatre ans.* She's four.; **le quatre février** the fourth of February

quatre-vingts [katrəvɛ̃] num eighty ▷ *quatre-vingts élèves* eighty students ▷ *Elle a quatre-vingt-deux ans.* She's eighty-two.; **quatre-vingt-dix** ninety; **quatre-vingt-onze** ninety-one; **quatre-vingt-quinze** ninety-five; **quatre-vingt-dix-huit** ninety-eight

quatrième [katrijɛm] adj fourth ▷ *au quatrième étage* on the fourth floor ▷ *Il est en quatrième année.* He's in Grade 4.

que [kə] conj, pron, adv ❶ that ▷ *Il sait que tu es là.* He knows that you're here. ▷ *la dame que j'ai rencontrée hier* the lady I met yesterday ▷ *Le gâteau qu'elle a fait est délicieux.* The cake she made is delicious.; **Je veux que tu viennes.** I want you to come. ❷ what ▷ *Que fais-tu?* What are you doing? ▷ *Que vas-tu lui dire?* What are you going to tell her? **Qu'est-ce que...?** What...? ▷ *Qu'est-ce que tu fais?* What are you doing? ▷ *Qu'est-ce que c'est?* What's that?; **plus...que** more...than ▷ *C'est plus difficile que* je ne le pensais. It's more difficult than I thought. ▷ *Il est plus grand que moi.* He's bigger than me.; **aussi…que** as…as ▷ *Elle est aussi intelligente que toi.* She's as smart as you are. ▷ *Le train est aussi cher que l'avion.* The train is as expensive as the plane.; **ne…que** only ▷ *Il ne boit que de l'eau.* He only drinks water. ▷ *Je ne l'ai vu qu'une fois.* I've only seen him once.; **Que tu es bête!** You're so silly!

Québec [kebɛk] nm Québec

québécois [kebekwa, -waz] adj, n Québec ▷ *la culture québécoise* Québec culture; **un Québécois** (man) a Quebecker; **une Québécoise** (woman) a Quebecker

quel [kɛl] (f **quelle**) adj ① what ▷ *Quelle est ta couleur préférée?* What's your favourite colour? ② which ▷ *Quel groupe préfères-tu?* Which band do you like best? ③ who ▷ *Quel est ton chanteur préféré?* Who's your favourite singer? ▷ *Quelle heure est-il?* What time is it? ▷ *Quelle bonne surprise!* What a surprise!; **quel que soit (1)** whatever ▷ *quel que soit votre avis* whatever your opinion **(2)** whoever ▷ *quel que soit le coupable* whoever is the guilty one

quelle [kɛl] adj see **quel**

quelque [kɛlkə] adj, adv ① some ▷ *Il a quelques amis à Victoria.* He has some friends in Victoria. ▷ *J'ai acheté quelques disques.* I bought some records. ② a few ▷ *Il reste quelques pointes de pizza.* There are a few pizza slices left. ③ few ▷ *Ils ont fini les quelques sandwichs qui restaient.* They finished the few sandwiches that were left.; **quelque chose (1)** something ▷ *J'ai quelque chose pour toi.* I've got something for you. ▷ *Je voudrais quelque chose de moins cher.* I'd like something cheaper. **(2)** anything ▷ *Avez-vous quelque chose à déclarer?* Have you got anything to declare? ▷ *Tu as pensé à quelque chose d'autre?* Did you think of anything else?; **quelque part (1)** somewhere ▷ *J'ai oublié mes lunettes quelque part.* I've left my glasses somewhere. **(2)** anywhere ▷ *Vous allez quelque part en fin de semaine?* Are you going anywhere this weekend?

quelquefois [kɛlkəfwa] adv sometimes

quelques-uns [kɛlkəzœ̃ -yn] (f **quelques-unes**) pron some ▷ *As-tu vu ses films? J'en ai vu quelques-uns.* Have you seen her films? I've seen some of them.

quelqu'un [kɛlkœ̃] pron ① somebody ▷ *Quelqu'un t'a appelé.* Somebody phoned you. ▷ *Il y a quelqu'un à la porte.* There's somebody at the door. ② anybody ▷ *Est-ce que quelqu'un a vu mon parapluie?* Has anybody seen my umbrella? ▷ *Il y a quelqu'un?* Is there anybody there?

quenouille [kənuj] nf cattail

qu'est-ce que [kɛskə]; see **que**

qu'est-ce qui [kɛski]; see **que**

question [kɛstjɔ̃] nf ① question ▷ *Je t'ai posé une question.* I asked you a question. ② matter ▷ *Ils se sont disputés pour des questions d'argent.* They argued over money matters. ③ issue ▷ *une importante question politique* an important political issue; **Il n'en est pas question.** There's no question about it. ▷ *Il n'est pas question que je paye.* There's no question of me

paying.; **De quoi est-il question?** What's it about?; **Il est question de l'organisation du concert.** It's about organizing the concert.; **hors de question** out of the question ▷ *Il est hors de question que nous restions ici.* It's out of the question that we stay here.

questionnaire [kɛstjɔnɛr] nm questionnaire

questionner [kɛstjɔne] vb to question

quétaine [ketɛn] adj tacky ▷ *des meubles quétaines* tacky furniture ▷ *un bijou quétaine* a tacky piece of jewellery

queue [kø] nf ① tail ▷ *Le chien a agité la queue.* The dog wagged its tail.; **faire la queue** to line up; **une queue de cheval** a ponytail ② rear ▷ *en queue du train* at the rear of the train ③ bottom ▷ *en queue de liste* at the bottom of the list ④ (of fruit, leaf) stem ▷ *la queue d'une cerise* a cherry stem

qui [ki] pron ① who ▷ *Qui a téléphoné?* Who phoned? ② whom ▷ *C'est la personne à qui j'ai parlé hier.* It's the person to whom I spoke yesterday. ③ that ▷ *Donne-moi le manteau qui est sur la chaise.* Give me the jacket that's on the chair.; **Qui est-ce qui…?** Who…? ▷ *Qui est-ce qui t'emmène au spectacle?* Who's taking you to the show?; **Qui est-ce que…?** Whom…? ▷ *Qui est-ce que tu as vu à cette soirée?* Whom did you see at the party?; **Qu'est-ce qui…?** What…? ▷ *Qu'est-ce qui est sur la table?* What's on the table? ▷ *Qu'est-ce qui te prend?* What's the matter with you?; **À qui est le sac à dos?** Whose knapsack is this?; **À qui parlais-tu?** Who were you talking to?

quille [kij] nf bowling pin; **jouer aux quilles** to go bowling

quincaillerie [kɛ̃kajʀi] nf hardware store

quinzaine [kɛ̃zɛn] nf about fifteen ▷ *Il y avait une quinzaine de personnes.* There were about fifteen people there.; **une quinzaine de jours** two weeks

quinze [kɛ̃z] num fifteen ▷ *Elle a quinze ans.* She's fifteen. ▷ *à quinze heures* at 3 p.m.; **le quinze février** the fifteenth of February; **dans quinze jours** two weeks from now

quitter [kite] vb ① to leave ▷ *J'ai quitté la maison à huit heures.* I left the house at 8 o'clock.; **se quitter** to part ▷ *Les deux amis se sont quittés devant le café.* The two friends parted in front of the café.; **Ne quittez pas.** (on telephone) Hold the line. ▷ *Ne quittez pas, je vous passe la directrice.* Hold on please, I'll put you through to the director.

quoi [kwa] pron what? ▷ *À quoi penses-tu?* What are you thinking about? ▷ *C'est quoi, ce truc?* What's this thing?; **Quoi de neuf?** What's new?; **As-tu quoi écrire?** Have you got anything to write with?; **Quoi qu'il arrive.** Whatever happens.; **Il n'y a pas de quoi.** Don't mention it.; **Il n'y a pas de quoi s'énerver.** There's no reason to get worked up.; **En quoi puis-je vous aider?** How may I help you?

quoique [kwak(ə)] conj even though ▷ *Il va l'acheter quoique ce soit cher.* He's going to buy it even though it's expensive.

quotidien [kɔtidjɛ̃, -ɛn] (f **quotidienne**) adj daily ▷ *Il est parti faire sa promenade*

quotidienne. He's gone for his daily walk.; **la vie quotidienne** everyday life
▶ *nm* daily paper ▷ *Le Globe and Mail est un quotidien.* The Globe and Mail is a daily paper.

r

rabais [Rabε] *nm (in price)* reduction ▷ *25 pour cent de rabais* 25 percent off; **au rabais** at a discount
rabbin [Rabε̃] *nm* rabbi
raccompagner [Rakɔ̃paɲe] *vb* to take home ▷ *Peux-tu me raccompagner?* Can you take me home?
raccourci [Rakursi] *nm (also computer)* shortcut
raccrocher [Rakrɔʃe] *vb* to hang up *(telephone)*
race [Ras] *nf* ❶ race ▷ *la race humaine* the human race ❷ breed ▷ *De quelle race est ton chat?* What breed is your cat?
racheter [Raʃte] *vb* ❶ to buy another ▷ *J'ai racheté un portefeuille.* I bought another wallet. ▷ *racheter du lait* to buy more milk ❷ to buy ▷ *Il m'a racheté mon vélo.* He bought my bike from me.
racine [Rasin] *nf* root
racinette [Rasinεt] *nf* root beer
racisme [Rasism(ə)] *nm* racism
raciste [Rasist(ə)] *adj* racist
raconter [Rakɔ̃te] *vb* to tell ▷ *Raconte-moi ce qui s'est passé.* Tell me what happened. ▷ *Raconte-moi une histoire.* Tell me a story.; **Qu'est-ce que tu racontes?** What are you talking about?
radar [Radar] *nm* radar
radiateur [Radjatœr] *nm* radiator; **un radiateur électrique** an electric heater
radio [Radjo] *nf* ❶ radio ▷ *à la radio* on the radio ❷ X-ray; **passer une radio** to have an X-ray ▷ *Elle a passé une radio des poumons.* She had a chest X-ray.
radio-réveil [Radjorevεj] *(pl* **radios-réveils)** *nm* clock radio
radis [Radi] *nm* radish
raffoler [Rafɔle] *vb:* **raffoler de** to be crazy about ▷ *Elle raffole de la tarte aux pommes.* She really loves apple pie.
rafraîchir [Rafreʃir] *vb* to cool down; **se rafraîchir (1)** to get cooler ▷ *Le temps se rafraîchit.* The weather's getting cooler. **(2)** to freshen up ▷ *Il a pris une douche pour se rafraîchir.* He had a shower to freshen up.

rafraîchissant [Rafreʃisã, -ãt] *(f* **rafraîchissante)** *adj* refreshing
rage [Raʒ] *nf* rabies; **une rage de dents** a raging toothache; **la rage au volant** road rage
ragoût [Ragu] *nm* stew
raide [Rεd] *adj* ❶ steep ▷ *Cette pente est raide.* This is a steep slope. ❷ straight ▷ *Elle a les cheveux raides.* She has straight hair. ❸ stiff ▷ *Son bras est encore raide.* His arm's still stiff.
raie [Rε] *nf* ❶ *(in hair)* parting ❷ *(fish)* ray
rail [Raj] *nm* rail ▷ *par rail* by rail
raisin [Rεzε̃] *nm* grapes ▷ *le raisin blanc* green grapes ▷ *J'ai mangé du raisin.* I ate some grapes.; **un grain de raisin** a grape; **des raisins secs** raisins
raison [Rεzɔ̃] *nf* reason ▷ *sans raison* for no reason ▷ *Raison de plus pour y aller.* All the more reason for going.; **Ce n'est pas une raison.** That's no excuse.; **avoir raison** to be right ▷ *Tu as raison.* You're right.; **en raison de** because of ▷ *en raison d'une grève* because of a strike
raisonnable [Rεzɔnabl(ə)] *adj* sensible ▷ *Elle est très raisonnable pour son âge.* She's very sensible for her age.
raisonnement [Rεzɔnmã] *nm* reasoning ▷ *J'ai du mal à suivre son raisonnement.* I have a hard time following his reasoning.
rajouter [Raʒute] *vb (more)* to add ▷ *Ne rajoute pas de sel, j'en ai déjà mis.* Don't add more salt, I already put some in.; **en rajouter** to exaggerate ▷ *Elle en rajoute toujours.* She always exaggerates.
ralentir [Ralãtir] *vb* to slow down
ramassage [Ramasaʒ] *nm:* **le ramassage scolaire** the school bus service
ramasser [Ramase] *vb* ❶ to pick up ▷ *Il a ramassé son crayon.* He picked up his pencil. ❷ to collect ▷ *Il a ramassé les copies.* He collected the exam papers.
rame [Ram] *nf* ❶ *(of boat)* oar ❷ subway train
rameau [Ramo] *(pl* **rameaux)** *nm* branch
ramener [Ramne] *vb* ❶ to bring back ▷ *Je t'ai ramené un souvenir de Jonquière.* I brought you back a souvenir from Jonquière. ❷ to take home ▷ *Peux-tu me ramener à la maison?* Will you take me home?
ramer [Rame] *vb* to row ▷ *C'est ma sœur qui ramait.* My sister was rowing.
rampe [Rãp] *nf* banister
ramper [Rãpe] *vb* to crawl
rancune [Rãkyn] *nf:* **garder rancune à quelqu'un** to hold a grudge against somebody; **Sans rancune!** No hard feelings!
rancunier [Rãkynje, -jεr] *(f* **rancunière)** *adj:* **Elle est un peu rancunière.** She tends to hold grudges.
randonnée [Rãdɔne] *nf:* **une randonnée à vélo** a bike ride; **une randonnée pédestre** a hike; **faire de la randonnée** to go hiking
randonneur [Rãdɔnœr] *nm* hiker
randonneuse [Rãdɔnøz] *nf* hiker
rang [Rã] *nm (line)* row ▷ *au premier rang* in the front row ▷ *se mettre en rangs* to form rows
rangée [Rãʒe] *nf (line)* row ▷ *une rangée de chaises* a row of chairs
ranger [Rãʒe] *vb* ❶ to put away ▷ *J'ai rangé*

tes affaires. I put your things away. ❷ to tidy up ▷ *Va ranger ta chambre.* Go and tidy up your room.

rap [Rap] nm rap ▷ *un chanteur de rap* a rap singer

râpe à fromage [Rɑp-] nf cheese grater

râper [Rɑpe] vb to grate ▷ *le fromage râpé* grated cheese

rapide [Rapid] adj ❶ fast ▷ *Cette voiture est très rapide.* This is a very fast car. ❷ quick ▷ *J'ai jeté un coup d'œil rapide sur ton travail.* I had a quick glance at your work.
▶ nm rapids ▷ *Ils ont descendu les rapides en canot.* They went down the rapids in a canoe. ▷ *Ce rapide est très difficile à naviguer.* This set of rapids is very difficult to navigate.

rapidement [Rapidmɑ̃] adv quickly

rappel [Rapɛl] nm ❶ (vaccination) booster ❷ curtain call

rappeler [Raple] vb to call back ▷ *Je te rappelle dans cinq minutes.* I'll call you back in 5 minutes.; **rappeler quelque chose à quelqu'un** to remind somebody of something ▷ *Cette odeur me rappelle mon enfance.* This smell reminds me of my childhood.; **rappeler à quelqu'un de faire quelque chose** to remind somebody to do something ▷ *Rappelle-moi d'acheter des billets.* Remind me to get tickets.; **se rappeler** to remember ▷ *Il s'est rappelé qu'il avait une course à faire.* He remembered he had an errand to run.

rapport [RapɔR] nm ❶ report ▷ *Elle a écrit un rapport.* She wrote a report. ❷ connection ▷ *Je ne vois pas le rapport.* I can't see the connection.; **par rapport à** in comparison with

rapporter [RapɔRte] vb to bring back ▷ *Je leur ai rapporté un cadeau.* I brought them back a present.

rapporteur [RapɔRtœR] nm tattletale

rapporteuse [RapɔRtøz] nf tattletale

rapports [RapɔR] nmpl relations ▷ *Leurs rapports avec leurs voisins se sont améliorés.* Their relations with their neighbours have improved.; **les rapports sexuels** sexual intercourse

rapprocher [RapRɔʃe] vb ❶ to bring together ▷ *Cet accident a rapproché les deux frères.* The accident brought the two brothers together. ❷ to bring closer ▷ *Elle a rapproché le fauteuil de la télé.* She brought the armchair closer to the TV.; **se rapprocher** to come closer ▷ *Rapproche-toi, tu verras mieux.* Come closer, you'll see better.

raquette [Rakɛt] nf ❶ (tennis) racquet ❷ (table tennis) paddle

rare [RaR] adj rare ▷ *une plante rare* a rare plant

rarement [RaRmɑ̃] adv rarely

ras [Rɑ, Rɑz] (f rase) adj, adv short ▷ *un chien à poil ras* a short-haired dog; **à ras bords** to the brim ▷ *Elle a rempli son verre à ras bords.* She filled her glass to the brim.; **un chandail ras du cou** a crew-neck sweater

raser [Rɑze] vb to shave off ▷ *Mon père a rasé sa barbe.* My dad has shaved off his beard.; **se raser** to shave

rasoir [RɑzwaR] nm razor

rassembler [Rasɑ̃ble] vb to gather together ▷ *Il a rassemblé les enfants dans la cour.* He gathered the children together in the playground.; **se rassembler** to gather ▷ *Les passagers se sont rassemblés près de l'autobus.* The passengers gathered near the bus.

rassurer [RasyRe] vb to reassure; **Je suis rassuré.** I don't need to worry any more.; **se rassurer** to be reassured ▷ *Rassure-toi!* Don't worry!

rat [Ra] nm rat

raté [Rate] (f ratée) adj unsuccessful; **Le gâteau est raté.** The cake didn't turn out.

râteau [Rɑto] (pl râteaux) nm rake

rater [Rate] vb ❶ to miss ▷ *Elle a raté son train.* She missed her train. ❷ to fail ▷ *J'ai raté mon examen de maths.* I failed my math exam. ❸ *Elle a raté sa pizza.* Her pizza didn't turn out right.

raton laveur [Ratɔ̃lavœR] nm raccoon

rattacher [Rataʃe] vb to tie again ▷ *rattacher ses lacets* to tie one's laces

rattrapage [RatRapaʒ] nm catching up ▷ *À cause de mon absence, j'ai beaucoup de rattrapage scolaire.* I have a lot of catching up to do at school because I was away.; **le cours de rattrapage** remedial class

rattraper [RatRape] vb ❶ to recapture ▷ *La police a rattrapé le voleur.* The police recaptured the thief. ❷ to catch up with ▷ *Je vais la rattraper.* I'll catch up with her. ▷ *Je dois rattraper mon retard à l'école.* I have to catch up at school. ❸ to make up for ▷ *Il faut rattraper le temps perdu.* We must make up for lost time. ▷ *J'ai des heures à rattraper.* I have some hours to make up.; **se rattraper** to make up for it ▷ *Je n'ai pas le temps de sortir, mais je me rattraperai après les examens.* I don't have time to go out, but I'll make up for it after the exams.

rature [RatyR] nf correction ▷ *un texte sans ratures* a text with no corrections

ravi [Ravi] (f ravie) adj: **être ravi** to be delighted ▷ *Ils étaient ravis de nous voir.* They were delighted to see us. ▷ *Je suis ravi que vous puissiez venir.* I'm delighted that you can come.

se raviser [Ravize] vb to change your mind ▷ *Il allait accepter, mais il s'est ravisé.* He was going to accept, but he changed his mind.

ravissant [Ravisɑ̃, -ɑ̃t] (f ravissante) adj lovely

rayé [Reje] (f rayée) adj striped ▷ *une chemise rayée* a striped shirt

rayer [Reje] vb ❶ to scratch ▷ *Il a rayé la peinture de sa voiture.* He scratched the paint on his car. ❷ to cross off ▷ *Son nom a été rayé de la liste.* Her name has been crossed off the list.

rayon [Rejɔ̃] nm ❶ ray ▷ *un rayon de soleil* a ray of sunshine ❷ radius ▷ *le rayon d'un cercle* the radius of a circle ❸ shelf ▷ *les rayons d'une bibliothèque* the shelves of a bookcase ❹ department ▷ *le rayon des chaussures* the shoe department; **les rayons X** X-rays

rayure [RejyR] nf stripe

ré [Re] nm ❶ D ▷ *en ré majeur* in D major ❷ re ▷ *do, ré, mi...* do, re, mi...

réaction [Reaksjɔ̃] nf reaction

réagir [ReaʒiR] vb to react

réalisateur [ʀealizatœʀ] *nm* director (of film) ▷ *Atom Egoyan est réalisateur.* Atom Egoyan is a film director.

réalisation [ʀealizasjɔ̃] *nf* ❶ achievement ▷ *Elle compte de nombreuses réalisations à son actif.* She has several achievements to her credit. ❷ fulfilment ▷ *la réalisation d'un grand rêve* the fulfillment of a great dream

réalisatrice [ʀealizatʀis] *nf* director (of film) ▷ *Patricia Rozema est réalisatrice.* Patricia Rozema is a film director.

réaliser [ʀealize] *vb* ❶ to carry out ▷ *Ils ont réalisé leur projet.* They carried out their plan. ❷ to fulfill ▷ *Il a réalisé son rêve.* He has fulfilled his dream. ❸ to realize ▷ *Réalises-tu ce que tu dis?* Do you realize what you're saying? ❹ to make ▷ *réaliser un film* to make a movie; **se réaliser** to come true ▷ *Mon rêve s'est réalisé.* My dream has come true.

réaliste [ʀealist(ə)] *adj* realistic

réalité [ʀealite] *nf* reality; **en réalité** in fact

rebelle [ʀəbɛl] *nmf* rebel

rebondir [ʀəbɔ̃diʀ] *vb* to bounce

rebord [ʀəbɔʀ] *nm* edge ▷ *le rebord du lavabo* the edge of the sink; **le rebord de la fenêtre** the window ledge

récemment [ʀesamɑ̃] *adv* recently

récent [ʀesɑ̃, -ɑ̃t] (*f* **récente**) *adj* recent

récepteur [ʀesɛptœʀ] *nm* receiver

réception [ʀesɛpsjɔ̃] *nf* (in office) reception

réceptionniste [ʀesɛpsjɔnist(ə)] *nmf* receptionist ▷ *Il est réceptionniste.* He's a receptionist.

recette [ʀəsɛt] *nf* recipe

recevoir [ʀəsəvwaʀ] *vb* ❶ to receive ▷ *J'ai reçu une lettre.* I received a letter. ❷ to see ▷ *Elle a déjà reçu trois clients.* She's already seen three clients. ❸ to have over ▷ *Je reçois des amis à dîner.* I'm having friends over for dinner.

rechange [ʀəʃɑ̃ʒ] *nm*: **de rechange** (battery, bulb) spare ▷ *des vêtements de rechange* a change of clothes

recharge [ʀəʃaʀʒ(ə)] *nf* refill

réchaud [ʀeʃo] *nm* (portable) stove

réchauffer [ʀeʃofe] *vb* ❶ to reheat ▷ *Je vais réchauffer les légumes.* I'll reheat the vegetables. ❷ to warm up ▷ *Un bon chocolat chaud va te réchauffer.* A nice cup of hot chocolate will warm you up.; **se réchauffer** to warm oneself ▷ *Je vais me réchauffer près du feu.* I'm going to warm up by the fire.

recherche [ʀəʃɛʀʃ(ə)] *nf* research ▷ *Je voudrais faire de la recherche.* I'd like to do some research.; **être à la recherche de quelque chose** to be looking for something ▷ *Je suis à la recherche d'un emploi.* I'm looking for a job.; **les recherches** search ▷ *La police a interrompu les recherches.* The police called off the search.

recherché [ʀəʃɛʀʃe] (*recherchée*) *adj* ❶ (book, painting, speaker) much sought-after ❷ (criminal) wanted

rechercher [ʀəʃɛʀʃe] *vb* to look for ▷ *La police recherche l'assassin.* The police are looking for the killer.

rechute [ʀəʃyt] *nf* relapse

récipient [ʀesipjɑ̃] *nm* container

récit [ʀesi] *nm* story

réciter [ʀesite] *vb* to recite

réclamation [ʀeklamasjɔ̃] *nf* complaint ▷ *J'ai une réclamation à faire.* I want to make a complaint.; **les réclamations** the complaints department

réclamer [ʀeklame] *vb* ❶ to demand ▷ *Nous réclamons la semaine de trente heures.* We demand a 30-hour week. ❷ to complain ▷ *Elles sont toujours en train de réclamer.* They're always complaining about something.

reçois [ʀəswa] *vb see* **recevoir**

récolte [ʀekɔlt(ə)] *nf* harvest

récolter [ʀekɔlte] *vb* ❶ to harvest ▷ *Ils ont récolté le blé.* They harvested the wheat. ❷ to collect ▷ *Ils ont récolté deux cents dollars.* They collected 200 dollars. ❸ to get ▷ *Elle a récolté une amende.* (informal) She got a fine.

recommandé [ʀəkɔmɑ̃de] *nm*: **en recommandé** by registered mail ▷ *Je voudrais envoyer ce paquet en recommandé.* I'd like to register this parcel.

recommander [ʀəkɔmɑ̃de] *vb* to recommend ▷ *Je vous recommande ce restaurant.* I recommend this restaurant.

recommencer [ʀəkɔmɑ̃se] *vb* ❶ to start again ▷ *Il a recommencé à pleuvoir.* It's started raining again. ❷ to do again ▷ *S'il n'est pas puni, il va recommencer.* If he's not punished, he'll do it again.

récompense [ʀekɔ̃pɑ̃s] *nf* reward

récompenser [ʀekɔ̃pɑ̃se] *vb* to reward ▷ *Il m'a récompensée de mes efforts.* He rewarded me for my efforts.

réconcilier [ʀekɔ̃silje] *vb*: **se réconcilier avec quelqu'un** to make up with somebody ▷ *Il s'est réconcilié avec sa sœur.* He has made up with his sister.

reconnaissant [ʀəkɔnɛsɑ̃, -ɑ̃t] (*f* **reconnaissante**) *adj* grateful

reconnaître [ʀəkɔnɛtʀ(ə)] *vb* ❶ to recognize ▷ *Je ne l'ai pas reconnu.* I didn't recognize him. ❷ to admit ▷ *Je reconnais que j'ai eu tort.* I admit I was wrong.

reconstruire [ʀəkɔ̃stʀɥiʀ] *vb* to rebuild

record [ʀəkɔʀ] *nm* record ▷ *battre un record* to break a record

recouvrir [ʀəkuvʀiʀ] *vb* to cover ▷ *La neige recouvre le sol.* Snow covers the ground.

récréation [ʀekʀeasjɔ̃] *nf* recess ▷ *Les élèves sont en récréation.* The students are having recess.; **la cour de récréation** the playground (of school)

rectangle [ʀɛktɑ̃gl(ə)] *nm* rectangle

rectangulaire [ʀɛktɑ̃gylɛʀ] *adj* rectangular

rectifier [ʀɛktifje] *vb* to correct

rectitude politique [ʀɛktityd-] *nf* political correctness

reçu [ʀəsy] *nm* receipt ▷ *vb see* **recevoir**; **J'ai reçu un colis ce matin.** I received a parcel this morning.

reculer [ʀəkyle] *vb* ❶ to step back ▷ *Il a reculé pour la laisser entrer.* He stepped back to let her in. ❷ (vehicle) to back up ▷ *J'ai reculé pour laisser passer le camion.* I backed up to let the truck past. ❸ to postpone ▷ *Ils ont reculé la date du* *spectacle*. They postponed the show.

reculons [ʀəkylɔ̃]: **à reculons** adv backwards ▷ *Elle est entrée à reculons.* She came in backwards.

récupérer [ʀekypeʀe] vb ❶ to get back ▷ *Je vais essayer de récupérer mon argent.* I'm going to try to get my money back. ❷ to recover ▷ *J'ai besoin de récupérer.* I need to recover. ❸ (data, files) to retrieve

recycler [ʀəsikle] vb to recycle; **se recycler** to retrain ▷ *Il a décidé de se recycler en informatique.* He decided to retrain as a computer programmer.

rédaction [ʀedaksjɔ̃] nf ❶ writing ▷ *Voici des exercices pour améliorer vos aptitudes en rédaction.* Here are some exercises to improve your writing skills. ❷ essay ▷ *Il faut remettre la rédaction sur notre future carrière demain.* We have to hand in the essay on our future career tomorrow.

redemander [ʀədmɑ̃de] vb ❶ to ask again for ▷ *Je vais lui redemander son adresse.* I'll ask her for her address again. ❷ to ask for more ▷ *Je vais redemander des carottes.* I'm going to ask for more carrots.

redémarrer [ʀədemaʀe] vb ❶ to reboot ▷ *J'ai redémarré l'ordinateur.* I rebooted the computer. ❷ to start up again ▷ *La voiture a redémarré.* The car started up again.

redescendre [ʀədesɑ̃dʀ(ə)] vb to go back down ▷ *Il est redescendu au premier étage.* He went back down to the first floor. ▷ *Elle a redescendu l'escalier.* She went back down the stairs.

rediffusion [ʀədifyzjɔ̃] nf rerun; **en rediffusion** ▷ *Le téléjournal sera en rediffusion à onze heures.* The news will be rebroadcast at 11.

redoubler [ʀəduble] vb to repeat a year ▷ *Il a raté son examen et doit redoubler.* He failed his exam and will have to repeat the year.

réduction [ʀedyksjɔ̃] nf ❶ reduction ▷ *une réduction du nombre des touristes* a reduction in the number of tourists ❷ discount ▷ *une réduction de vingt dollars* a 20 dollar discount

réduire [ʀedɥiʀ] vb to cut ▷ *Ils ont réduit leurs prix.* They've cut their prices. ▷ *Elle a réduit de moitié ses dépenses.* She has cut her spending by half. ▷ **Réduire, réutiliser, recycler.** Reduce, reuse, recycle.

réel [ʀeel] (f **réelle**) adj real

réellement [ʀeelmɑ̃] adv really

refaire [ʀəfɛʀ] vb ❶ to do again ▷ *Je dois refaire ce rapport.* I've got to do this report again. ❷ to take up again ▷ *Je voudrais refaire du ski.* I'd like to take up skiing again.

référence [ʀefeʀɑ̃s] nf reference; **faire référence à quelque chose** to refer to something; **Ce n'est pas une référence!** That's no recommendation!

réfléchi [ʀefleʃi] (f **réfléchie**) adj (verb) reflexive; **C'est tout réfléchi.** My mind's made up.

réfléchir [ʀefleʃiʀ] vb to think ▷ *Il est en train de réfléchir.* He's thinking.; **réfléchir à quelque chose** to think about something ▷ *Je vais réfléchir à ta proposition.* I'll think about your

suggestion.

reflet [ʀəflɛ] nm reflection ▷ *les reflets du soleil sur la mer* the reflection of the sun on the sea

refléter [ʀəflete] vb to reflect

réflexe [ʀeflɛks(ə)] nm reflex ▷ *avoir de bons réflexes* to have good reflexes

réflexion [ʀeflɛksjɔ̃] nf ❶ thought ▷ *Elle est en pleine réflexion.* She's deep in thought. ❷ remark ▷ *faire des réflexions désagréables* to make nasty remarks; **réflexion faite** on reflection

refrain [ʀəfʀɛ̃] nm chorus (of song)

réfrigérateur [ʀefʀiʒeʀatœʀ] nm refrigerator

refroidir [ʀəfʀwadiʀ] vb to cool ▷ *Laissez le gâteau refroidir.* Leave the cake to cool.; **se refroidir** to get colder ▷ *Le temps se refroidit.* It's getting colder out.

refroidissement éolien [ʀəfʀwadismɑ̃eɔljɛ̃] nm wind chill ▷ *Le facteur de refroidissement éolien est de moins dix degrés aujourd'hui.* The wind chill factor is -10 today.

se réfugier [ʀefyʒje] vb to take shelter ▷ *Je me suis réfugié sous un arbre.* I took shelter under a tree.

refus [ʀəfy] nm refusal; **Ce n'est pas de refus.** I wouldn't say no. ▷ *« Voulez-vous du thé glacé? »* — *« Ce n'est pas de refus. »* "Would you like some iced tea?" — "I wouldn't say no."

refuser [ʀəfyze] vb to refuse ▷ *Il a refusé de payer sa part.* He refused to pay his share. ▷ *On lui a refusé la permission.* She was refused permission.; **Je refuse qu'on me parle ainsi!** I won't let anybody talk to me like that!

se régaler [ʀegale] vb: **Merci beaucoup: je me suis régalé!** Thank you very much: it was absolutely delicious!

regard [ʀəgaʀ] nm look ▷ *Il nous a jeté un regard méfiant.* He gave us a mistrustful look. ▷ *On voyait à son regard qu'elle était contrariée.* You could tell from the look in her eyes that she was upset.; **Tous les regards se sont tournés vers lui.** All eyes turned towards him.

regarder [ʀəgaʀde] vb ❶ to look at ▷ *Il regardait ses photos de vacances.* He was looking at his vacation photos. ▷ *Regarde! J'ai presque fini.* Look! I'm almost finished. ❷ to watch ▷ *Je regarde la télévision.* I'm watching television. ▷ *Regarde où tu mets les pieds!* Watch where you put your feet! ❸ to concern ▷ *Ça ne nous regarde pas.* It doesn't concern us.; **ne pas regarder à la dépense** to spare no expense

régime [ʀeʒim] nm ❶ régime (of a country) ❷ diet ▷ *un régime sans sel* a salt-free diet ▷ *se mettre au régime* to go on a diet ▷ *suivre un régime* to be on a diet; **un régime de bananes** a bunch of bananas

région [ʀeʒjɔ̃] nf region; **la région des Barrens** the Barrens

régional [ʀeʒjɔnal, -o] (f **régionale**, mpl **régionaux**) adj regional

registre [ʀaʒistʀ(ə)] nm (record book) register ▷ *Veuillez signer le registre.* Please sign the register.

règle [ʀɛgl(ə)] nf ❶ ruler ▷ *Elle a souligné son nom avec une règle.* She underlined her name with a ruler. ❷ rule ▷ *C'est la règle.* That's the rule. ▷ *en règle générale* as a general rule; **être en règle** to be in order ▷ *Est-ce que tout est en règle pour votre voyage?* Is everything in order for your trip?; **les règles** (*menstruation*) period

règlement [ʀɛɡləmɑ̃] *nm* rules ▷ *Le règlement est affiché à l'entrée.* The rules are posted by the entrance.

régler [ʀeɡle] *vb* ❶ to adjust ▷ *Il faut que je règle mon rétroviseur.* I have to adjust my rearview mirror. ❷ to set ▷ *J'ai réglé le thermostat à vingt degrés.* I've set the thermostat to 20 degrees. ❸ to solve ▷ *Le problème est réglé.* The problem is solved. ❹ (*pay up*) to settle ▷ *Elle a réglé sa facture.* She settled her bill.

réglisse [ʀeɡlis] *nf* licorice

règne [ʀɛɲ] *nm* reign ▷ *sous le règne de Henri IV* in the reign of Henry IV

régner [ʀeɲe] *vb* to reign

regret [ʀəɡʀɛ] *nm* regret; **à regret** reluctantly

regretter [ʀəɡʀɛte] *vb* ❶ to regret ▷ *Elle regrette ce qu'elle a dit.* She regrets what she said.; **Je regrette.** I'm sorry. ▷ *Je ne peux pas vous aider.* I'm sorry, I can't help you. ❷ to miss ▷ *Je regrette mon ancienne école.* I miss my old school.

regrouper [ʀəɡʀupe] *vb* to group together ▷ *Nous avons regroupé les enfants selon leur âge.* We grouped the children together according to age.; **se regrouper** to join together ▷ *Les agriculteurs se sont regroupés pour constituer un syndicat.* The farmers joined together to form a union.

régulier [ʀeɡylje, -jɛʀ] (*f* **régulière**) *adj* ❶ regular ▷ *des livraisons régulières* regular deliveries ▷ *des autobus réguliers* a regular bus service ❷ steady ▷ *à un rythme régulier* at a steady rate ❸ scheduled ▷ *des vols réguliers pour Whitehorse* scheduled flights to Whitehorse

régulièrement [ʀeɡyljɛʀmɑ̃] *adv* regularly

rein [ʀɛ̃] *nm* kidney; **les reins** (*of body*) back ▷ *J'ai mal aux reins.* My back hurts.

reine [ʀɛn] *nf* queen

rejoindre [ʀəʒwɛ̃dʀ(ə)] *vb* to go back to ▷ *J'ai rejoint mes amis.* I went back to my friends.; **Je te rejoins au café.** I'll see you at the café.; **se rejoindre** to meet up ▷ *Elles se sont rejointes une heure après.* They met up an hour later.

relâcher [ʀəlɑʃe] *vb* (*prisoner, animal*) to release; **se relâcher** to get slack ▷ *Il se relâche dans son travail.* He's slacking off in his work.

relais [ʀəlɛ] *nm* relay race ▷ *le relais quatre fois cent mètres* the 4 x 100 metre relay; **prendre le relais** to take over; **le relais routier** truck stop

relation [ʀəlɑsjɔ̃] *nf* relationship; **les relations entre le Canada et les États-Unis** Canada-US relations; **les relations publiques** public relations

se relaxer [ʀəlakse] *vb* to relax

se relayer [ʀəleje] *vb*: **se relayer pour faire quelque chose** to take turns doing something

relevé [ʀəlve] *nm*: **un relevé de compte** a bank statement

relever [ʀəlve] *vb* ❶ to find ▷ *J'ai relevé six erreurs dans ton devoir.* I found six mistakes in your homework. ❷ to react to ▷ *Je n'ai pas relevé sa réflexion.* I didn't react to his remark.; **relever la tête** to look up; **se relever** to get up ▷ *Il est tombé mais s'est relevé aussitôt.* He fell, but got up immediately.

religieuse [ʀəliʒjøz] *nf* nun

religieux [ʀəliʒjø, -øz] (*f* **religieuse**) *adj* religious

religion [ʀəliʒjɔ̃] *nf* religion

relire [ʀəliʀ] *vb* ❶ to read over ▷ *Elle a relu son examen avant de le rendre.* She read her exam paper over before handing it in. ❷ to read again ▷ *Je voudrais relire ce roman.* I'd like to read this novel again.

remarquable [ʀəmaʀkabl(ə)] *adj* remarkable

remarque [ʀəmaʀk(ə)] *nf* ❶ remark ▷ *une remarque désagréable* a nasty remark ❷ comment ▷ *Avez-vous des remarques à faire?* Do you have any comments?

remarquer [ʀəmaʀke] *vb* to notice ▷ *J'ai remarqué qu'elle avait l'air triste.* I noticed she was looking sad.; **faire remarquer quelque chose à quelqu'un** to point something out to somebody ▷ *Je lui ai fait remarquer que c'était un peu cher.* I pointed out to him that it was a bit expensive.; **Remarquez, elle n'est pas si bête que ça.** Mind you, she's not as stupid as all that.; **se remarquer** to be noticeable ▷ *Il ne s'est pas rasé ce matin. Ça se remarque.* It's obvious he didn't shave this morning.; **se faire remarquer** to call attention to oneself

remboursement [ʀɑ̃buʀsəmɑ̃] *nm* refund

rembourser [ʀɑ̃buʀse] *vb* ❶ to pay back ▷ *Il m'a remboursé l'argent qu'il me devait.* He paid me back the money he owed me. ❷ to refund ▷ *Le vol a été annulé et on m'a remboursé mon billet.* The flight was cancelled and they refunded my ticket.

remède [ʀəmɛd] *nm* ❶ medicine ❷ cure

remercier [ʀəmɛʀsje] *vb* to thank ▷ *Je te remercie pour ton cadeau.* Thank you for your present.; **remercier quelqu'un d'avoir fait quelque chose** to thank somebody for doing something ▷ *Je vous remercie de m'avoir invité.* Thank you for inviting me.

remettre [ʀəmɛtʀ(ə)] *vb* ❶ to put back on ▷ *Elle a remis son chandail.* She put her sweater back on. ❷ to put back ▷ *Il a remis son manteau dans le garde-robe.* He put his coat back in the closet. ❸ to put off ▷ *J'ai dû remettre mon rendez-vous.* I had to put off my appointment.; **se remettre** (*from illness*) to recover ▷ *Ma tante s'est bien remise de son opération.* My aunt has fully recovered from her operation.; **« Satisfaction garantie ou argent remis »** "Satisfaction guaranteed or your money back"

remonte-pente [ʀəmɔ̃tpɑ̃t] *nm* ski lift

remonter [ʀəmɔ̃te] *vb* ❶ to go back up ▷ *Il est remonté à sa chambre.* He's gone back up to his room. ❷ to go up ▷ *Ils ont remonté la pente.* They went up the hill. ❸ to comfort ▷ *Cette nouvelle m'a un peu remonté.* The news comforted me a bit.; **remonter le moral à quelqu'un** to lift somebody's spirits

remords [ʀəmɔʀ] *nm*: **avoir des remords** to

feel remorse

remorque [Rəmɔʀk(ə)] *nf* (*of car*) trailer

remparts [Rɑ̃paʀ] *nmpl* city walls

remplaçant [Rɑ̃plasɑ̃] *nm* supply teacher

remplaçante [Rɑ̃plasɑ̃t] *nf* supply teacher

remplacer [Rɑ̃plase] *vb* to replace ▷ *Il faut remplacer cette ampoule.* We need to replace this bulb. ▷ *Il remplace le prof de maths.* He's replacing the math teacher.; **remplacer par** to replace with

rempli [Rɑ̃pli] (*f* **remplie**) *adj* full ▷ *une journée bien remplie* a very full day; **rempli de** full of ▷ *La salle était remplie de monde.* The room was full of people.

remplir [Rɑ̃pliʀ] *vb* ❶ to fill up ▷ *Elle a rempli son verre d'eau.* She filled her glass with water. ❷ to fill out ▷ *Tu as rempli ton formulaire?* Have you filled out your form?; **se remplir** to fill up ▷ *La salle s'est remplie de monde.* The room filled up with people.

remue-méninges [Rəmymenɛʒ] (*pl* **remue-méninges**) *nm* brainstorming ▷ *une séance de remue-méninges* a brainstorming session

remuer [Rəmɥe] *vb* ❶ to move ▷ *Elle a remué le bras.* She moved her arm. ❷ to stir ▷ *Remuez la sauce pendant deux minutes.* Stir the sauce for two minutes.

renard [Rənaʀ] *nm* fox

renardeau [Rənaʀdo] (*pl* **renardeaux**) *nm* fox cub

rencontre [Rɑ̃kɔ̃tʀ(ə)] *nf*: **faire la rencontre de quelqu'un** to meet somebody ▷ *J'ai fait la rencontre de personnes intéressantes ce soir.* I met some interesting people this evening.; **aller à la rencontre de quelqu'un** to go and meet somebody ▷ *Je viendrai à ta rencontre.* I'll come and meet you.

rencontrer [Rɑ̃kɔ̃tʀe] *vb* to meet; **se rencontrer** to meet ▷ *Ils se sont rencontrés il y a deux ans.* They met two years ago.

rendez-vous [Rɑ̃devu] *nm* ❶ appointment ▷ *J'ai rendez-vous chez le coiffeur.* I've got an appointment at the hairdresser's. ▷ *prendre rendez-vous avec quelqu'un* to make an appointment with somebody ▷ *Je sors ce soir?* » — « *Oui, j'ai un rendez-vous.* » "Are you going out tonight?" — "Yes, I've got a date."; **donner rendez-vous à quelqu'un** to arrange to meet somebody

rendre [Rɑ̃dʀ(ə)] *vb* ❶ to give back ▷ *J'ai rendu ses disques à ta sœur.* I've given your sister her records back. ❷ to take back ▷ *J'ai rendu mes livres à la bibliothèque.* I've taken my books back to the library.; **rendre quelqu'un célèbre** to make somebody famous; **se rendre** to give oneself up ▷ *Le voleur s'est rendu à la police.* The robber gave himself up to the police.; **se rendre compte de quelque chose** to realize something

renfermé [Rɑ̃fɛʀme] *nm*: **sentir le renfermé** to smell stuffy

renifler [Rənifle] *vb* to sniff

renne [Rɛn] *nm* reindeer

renommé [R(ə)nɔme] (*f* **renommée**) *adj* renowned ▷ *La baie de Fundy est renommée pour ses marées.* The Bay of Fundy is renowned for

its tides.

renoncer [Rənɔ̃se] *vb*: **renoncer à** to give up ▷ *Ils ont renoncé à leur projet.* They've given up their plan.; **renoncer à faire quelque chose** to give up the idea of doing something

renouvelable [R(ə)nuvlabl(ə)] *adj* renewable; **les ressources non renouvelables** non-renewable resources

renouveler [Rənuvle] *vb* (*passport, contract*) to renew; **se renouveler** to happen again ▷ *J'espère que ça ne se renouvellera pas.* I hope that won't happen again.

renseignement [Rɑ̃sɛɲmɑ̃] *nm* piece of information ▷ *Il me manque un renseignement.* There's one piece of information I still need.; **les renseignements** (1) information ▷ *Il m'a donné des renseignements.* He gave me some information. (2) information desk

renseigner [Rɑ̃seɲe] *vb*: **renseigner quelqu'un sur quelque chose** to give somebody information about something; **se renseigner** to inquire ▷ *Nous nous sommes renseignés sur l'horaire.* We inquired about the schedule.

rentable [Rɑ̃tabl(ə)] *adj* profitable

rentrée [Rɑ̃tʀe] *nf*: **la rentrée (des classes)** the start of the new school year; **la vente de la rentrée** back-to-school sale

rentrer [Rɑ̃tʀe] *vb* ❶ to come in ▷ *Rentre, tu vas prendre froid.* Come in, you'll catch cold. ❷ to go in ▷ *Elle est rentrée dans le magasin.* She went into the store. ❸ to get home ▷ *Je suis rentré à sept heures hier soir.* I got home at 7 o'clock last night. ❹ to bring in ▷ *As-tu rentré ton vélo?* Did you bring your bike in?; **rentrer dans** to crash into ▷ *Sa voiture est rentrée dans un arbre.* He crashed into a tree.; **rentrer dans l'ordre** to get back to normal

renverse [Rɑ̃vɛʀs(ə)] *nf*: **tomber à la renverse** to fall backwards

renverser [Rɑ̃vɛʀse] *vb* ❶ to knock over ▷ *J'ai renversé mon verre.* I knocked over my glass. ❷ to run over ▷ *Elle a été renversée par une voiture.* She was run over by a car. ❸ to spill ▷ *Il a renversé de l'eau partout.* He has spilled water everywhere.; **se renverser** (*glass, vase*) to fall over

renvoyer [Rɑ̃vwaje] *vb* ❶ to send back ▷ *Il a renvoyé les documents.* He sent back the documents. ❷ to fire ▷ *On a renvoyé deux employés.* Two employees have been fired.

répandu [Repɑ̃dy] (*f* **répandue**) *adj* widespread ▷ *C'est une croyance très répandue.* It's a very widespread belief.; **du jus répandu sur la table** juice spilled on the table; **des papiers répandus sur le sol** papers scattered over the floor

réparateur [Repaʀatœʀ] *nm* repairman

réparation [Repaʀasjɔ̃] *nf* repair

réparatrice [Repaʀatʀis] *nf* repairwoman

réparer [Repaʀe] *vb* to repair

repartir [Rəpaʀtiʀ] *vb* to set off again ▷ *Il s'est arrêté pour manger avant de repartir.* He stopped to eat before setting off again. ▷ *Il était là tout à l'heure, mais il est reparti.* He was here a moment ago, but he's gone again.; **repartir à zéro** to start from scratch again

repas [Rəpɑ] nm meal; **le repas de midi** lunch; **le repas du soir** supper

repassage [Rəpɑsaʒ] nm ironing ▷ *Je déteste le repassage.* I hate ironing.

repasser [Rəpɑse] vb ❶ to come back ▷ *Je repasserai demain.* I'll come back tomorrow. ❷ to go back ▷ *Je dois repasser au magasin.* I've got to go back to the store. ❸ to iron ▷ *J'ai repassé ma chemise.* I ironed my shirt. ❹ to resit ▷ *Elle doit repasser son examen.* She has to rewrite her exam.

repérer [Rəpere] vb to spot ▷ *J'ai repéré deux fautes.* I spotted two mistakes.; **se repérer** to find one's way around ▷ *J'ai du mal à me repérer de nuit.* I have a hard time finding my way at night.

répertoire [RepeRtwaR] nm directory

répéter [Repete] vb ❶ to repeat ▷ *Elle répète toujours la même chose.* She keeps repeating the same thing. ❷ to rehearse ▷ *Les acteurs répètent une scène.* The actors are rehearsing a scene.; **se répéter** to happen again ▷ *J'espère que cela ne se répétera pas!* I hope this won't happen again!

répétition [Repetisjɔ̃] nf ❶ repetition ▷ *Il y a beaucoup de répétitions dans ce texte.* There's a lot of repetition in this text.; **des grèves à répétition** repeated strikes ❷ rehearsal ▷ *Ils ont une répétition cet après-midi.* They have a rehearsal this afternoon.; **la répétition générale** the dress rehearsal

répondeur [Repɔ̃dœR] nm answering machine

répondre [Repɔ̃dR(ə)] vb to answer ▷ *répondre à quelqu'un* to answer somebody

réponse [Repɔ̃s] nf answer ▷ *C'est la bonne réponse.* That's the right answer.

reportage [RəpɔRtaʒ] nm ❶ report ▷ *J'ai vu ce reportage aux informations.* I saw that report on the news. ❷ story ▷ *J'ai lu ce reportage dans La Gazette.* I read that story in the *Gazette*.

repos [Rəpo] nm rest

reposer [Rəpoze] vb to put back down ▷ *Elle a reposé son verre sur la table.* She put her glass back down on the table.; **se reposer** to rest ▷ *Tu pourras te reposer demain.* You'll be able to rest tomorrow.; **se reposer sur quelqu'un** to rely on somebody

repousser [Rəpuse] vb ❶ to grow again ▷ *Ses cheveux ont repoussé.* Her hair has grown again. ❷ to postpone ▷ *Le voyage est repoussé.* The trip's been postponed.

reprendre [RəpRɑ̃dR(ə)] vb ❶ to take back ▷ *Il a repris son livre.* He took back his book. ❷ to go back to ▷ *Elle a repris le travail.* She went back to work. ❸ to start again ▷ *La réunion reprendra à deux heures.* The meeting will start again at 2 o'clock.; **reprendre du pain** to take more bread; **reprendre la route** to set off again; **reprendre son souffle** to catch one's breath

représentant [RəpRezɑ̃tɑ̃] nm rep ▷ *Il est représentant chez une grande maison d'édition.* He's a rep for a major publisher.

représentante [RəpRezɑ̃tɑ̃t] nf rep ▷ *Elle est représentante pour une grande société d'informatique.* She's a sales rep for a big software company.

représentation [RəpRezɑ̃tasjɔ̃] nf performance ▷ *la dernière représentation d'une pièce* the final performance of a play

représenter [RəpRezɑ̃te] vb ❶ to show ▷ *Le tableau représente un enfant et un chat.* The picture shows a child with a cat. ❷ to represent; **se représenter** to come up again ▷ *Cette occasion ne se représentera pas.* This opportunity won't come up again.

reprise [RəpRiz] nf ❶ rerun ▷ *La série Le Canada : une histoire populaire est en reprise ce soir à la télé.* There is a rerun of the series *Canada: A People's History* on TV tonight. ❷ recovery ▷ *la reprise économique* economic recovery; **à plusieurs reprises** repeatedly

reproche [RəpRɔʃ] nm: **faire des reproches à quelqu'un** to reproach somebody

reprocher [RəpRɔʃe] vb: **reprocher quelque chose à quelqu'un** to reproach somebody for something ▷ *Il m'a reproché mon retard.* He reproached me for being late.; **Qu'est-ce que tu lui reproches?** What have you got against her?

reproduction [RəpRɔdyksjɔ̃] nf reproduction

reproduire [RəpRɔduiR] vb reproduce; **se reproduire** to happen again ▷ *Je te promets que ça ne se reproduira pas!* I promise it won't happen again!

république [Repyblik] nf republic ▷ *Le Canada n'est pas une république, c'est une confédération.* Canada is not a republic, it's a confederation.

répugnant [Repynɑ̃, -ɑ̃t] (f **répugnante**) adj repulsive

réputation [Repytasjɔ̃] nf reputation

requin [Rəkɛ̃] nm shark

réseau [Rezo] (pl **réseaux**) nm network

réseautage [Rezotaʒ] nm networking ▷ *De bonnes techniques de réseautage* good networking techniques ▷ *Il est spécialiste du réseautage.* He's a networking specialist.

réservation [RezeRvasjɔ̃] nf reservation ▷ *J'ai fait des réservations pour un groupe de six personnes.* I made reservations for a group of six.

réserve [RezeRv(ə)] nf supply ▷ *une réserve énorme d'énergie* an enormous supply of energy; **avoir quelque chose en réserve** to have something in stock; **mettre quelque chose en réserve** to put something aside; **la réserve indienne** First Nations reserve

réserver [RezeRve] vb ❶ to reserve ▷ *Cette table est réservée.* This table is reserved. ❷ to book ▷ *Nous avons réservé une chambre.* We've booked a room.

réservoir [RezeRvwaR] nm gas tank

résidence [Rezidɑ̃s] nf residence ▷ *une résidence pour personnes âgées* a seniors' residence; **en résidence surveillée** under house arrest; **le lieu de résidence** place of residence; **une résidence secondaire** a second home

résistant [Rezistɑ̃, -ɑ̃t] (f **résistante**) adj ❶ durable ▷ *Ce tissu est résistant.* This fabric is durable. ❷ (strong) tough ▷ *Il faut être résistant* *pour faire ce travail.* You have to be tough to do this work. ▷ *Elle est rarement malade; elle est très résistante.* She's hardly ever sick; she's very tough.

résister [Reziste] *vb* to resist

résolu [Rezɔly] *adj:* **Le problème est résolu.** The problem's solved.

résoudre [Rezudʀ(ə)] *vb* to solve

respect [Rɛspɛ] *nm* respect; **manquer de respect** to be disrespectful

respecter [Rɛspɛkte] *vb* to respect

respiration [Rɛspiʀasjɔ̃] *nf* breathing

respirer [Rɛspiʀe] *vb* to breathe

responsabilité [Rɛspɔ̃sabilite] *nf* responsibility

responsable [Rɛspɔ̃sabl(ə)] *adj* responsible ▷ *être responsable de quelque chose* to be responsible for something
▶ *n* ❶ person in charge ▷ *Je voudrais parler au responsable.* I'd like to speak to the person in charge. ❷ person responsible ▷ *Il faut punir les responsables.* Those responsible must be punished.

ressembler [Rəsɑ̃ble] *vb:* **ressembler à (1)** to look like ▷ *Elle ne ressemble pas à sa sœur.* She doesn't look like her sister. **(2)** to be like ▷ *Ça ressemble à un conte de fées.* It's like a fairy tale.; **se ressembler (1)** to look alike ▷ *Les deux frères ne se ressemblent pas.* The two brothers don't look alike. **(2)** to be very similar ▷ *Ces deux jeux vidéo se ressemblent.* These two video games are quite similar.

ressort [Rəsɔʀ] *nm* (metal) spring ▷ *Le ressort est cassé.* The spring is broken.

ressortir [Rəsɔʀtiʀ] *vb* to go out again

restaurant [Rɛstɔʀɑ̃] *nm* restaurant

restauroute [Rɛstɔʀut] *nm* roadside restaurant ▷ *Nous avons mangé au restauroute.* We ate at the roadside restaurant.

reste [Rɛst(ə)] *nm* rest; **un reste de poulet** some leftover chicken; **les restes** the leftovers

rester [Rɛste] *vb* ❶ to stay ▷ *Je reste à la maison en fin de semaine.* I'm staying home this weekend. ❷ to be left ▷ *Il reste du pain.* There's some bread left. ▷ *Il me reste assez de temps.* I still have enough time.; **Il me reste plus qu'à…** I just have to… ▷ *Il ne me reste plus qu'à ranger mes affaires.* I just have to put my things away.; **Restons-en là.** Let's leave it at that.

résultat [Rezylta] *nm* result ▷ *le résultat des examens* the exam results

résumé [Rezyme] *nm* summary

résumer [Rezyme] *vb* to summarize

se rétablir [Retabliʀ] *vb* to get well

retard [RətaʀR] *nm* delay ▷ *un retard de livraison* a delay in delivery; **avoir du retard** to be late; **être en retard de deux heures** to be two hours late; **prendre du retard** to be delayed

retarder [Rətaʀde] *vb* ❶ to be slow ▷ *Ma montre retarde.* My watch is slow. ❷ to put back ▷ *Je dois retarder l'horloge d'une heure.* I have to put the clock back an hour.; **être retardé** to be delayed ▷ *J'ai été retardé par un coup de téléphone.* I was held up by a phone call.

retenir [Rətniʀ] *vb* ❶ to remember ▷ *Tu as retenu leur adresse?* Do you remember their

address? ❷ to book ▷ *J'ai retenu une chambre à l'hôtel.* I've booked a room at the hotel.; **retenir son souffle** to hold one's breath

retenu [Rətny] **(f retenue)** *adj* ❶ reserved ▷ *Cette place est retenue.* This seat is reserved. ❷ held up ▷ *J'ai été retenu par un coup de téléphone.* I was held up by a phone call.

retenue [Rətny] *nf* detention ▷ *Il est en retenue.* He has a detention.

retirer [Rətiʀe] *vb* ❶ to withdraw ▷ *Elle a retiré de l'argent.* She withdrew some money. ❷ to take off ▷ *Il a retiré son chandail.* He took off his sweater.

retour [RətuʀR] *nm* return; **être de retour** to be back ▷ *Je serai de retour la semaine prochaine.* I'll be back next week.

retourner [Rətuʀne] *vb* ❶ to go back ▷ *Est-ce que tu es retourné à Whitehorse?* Have you been back to Whitehorse? ❷ to turn over ▷ *Elle a retourné la crêpe.* She flipped the pancake over. ▷ *Il a retourné la poubelle.* He turned the garbage can upside down.; **se retourner (1)** to turn around ▷ *Elle s'est retournée.* She turned around. **(2)** to turn over ▷ *La voiture s'est retournée.* The car turned over.

retraite [RətʀɛtR] *nf:* **être à la retraite** to be retired; **prendre sa retraite** to retire

retraité [Rətʀete] **(f retraitée)** *adj* retired ▷ *Mon oncle est maintenant retraité.* My uncle is now retired.
▶ *nm* retiree

retraitée [Rətʀete] *nf* retiree

rétrécir [Retʀesiʀ] *vb* to shrink ▷ *Mon chandail a rétréci au lavage.* My sweater shrank in the wash.; **se rétrécir** to get narrower ▷ *La rue se rétrécit.* The street gets narrower.

retrouver [RətʀuveR] *vb* ❶ (something lost) to find ▷ *J'ai retrouvé mon portefeuille.* I found my wallet. ❷ to meet up with ▷ *Je te retrouve au café à trois heures.* I'll meet you at the coffee shop at 3 o'clock.; **se retrouver (1)** to meet up ▷ *Ils se sont retrouvés devant le cinéma.* They met up in front of the movie theatre. **(2)** to find one's way around ▷ *Je n'arrive pas à me retrouver.* I can't find my way around.

rétroviseur [Retʀovizœʀ] *nm* rearview mirror

réunion [Reynjɔ̃] *nf* meeting

se réunir [Reyniʀ] *vb* to meet ▷ *Ils se sont réunis à cinq heures.* They met at 5 o'clock.

réussi [Reysi] **(f réussie)** *adj* successful ▷ *une soirée très réussie* a very successful party; **être réussi** to be a success ▷ *Le repas était très réussi.* The meal was a hit.

réussir [Reysiʀ] *vb* to be successful ▷ *Tous ses enfants ont très bien réussi.* All her children are very successful.; **réussir à faire quelque chose** to succeed in doing something; **réussir à un examen** to pass an exam

réussite [Reysit] *nf* success

réutiliser [Reytilize] *vb* to reuse ▷ *Les trois R sont « réduire, réutiliser et recycler ».* The 3 Rs are "reduce, reuse, recycle".

revanche [Rəvɑ̃ʃ] *nf* ❶ revenge ❷ return game; **prendre sa revanche** to get even ▷ *Il a pris sa revanche en refusant de lui prêter son vélo.* He got even by refusing to lend her his bike.; **en revanche** on the other hand ▷ *C'est cher mais en revanche c'est de la bonne qualité.* It's expensive but on the other hand it's good quality.

rêve [ʀɛv] *nm* dream; **des vacances de rêve** a dream vacation

réveil [ʀevɛj] *nm* alarm clock; **mettre le réveil à huit heures** to set the alarm for eight o'clock

réveille-matin [ʀevɛjmatɛ̃] *(pl* **réveille-matin)** *nm* alarm clock

réveiller [ʀeveje] *vb* to wake up ▷ *réveiller quelqu'un* to wake somebody up; **se réveiller** to wake up

réveillon [ʀevɛjɔ̃] *nm*: **le réveillon du Jour de l'An** New Year's Eve celebrations; **le réveillon de Noël** Christmas Eve celebrations

réveillonner [ʀevɛjɔne] *vb* ❶ to celebrate New Year's Eve ❷ to celebrate Christmas Eve

revenir [ʀəvniʀ] *vb* to come back ▷ *Reviens vite!* Come back soon! ▷ *Son nom m'est revenu cinq minutes après.* His name came back to me five minutes later.; **Ça revient au même.** It comes to the same thing.; **Ça revient cher.** It costs a lot.; **Je n'en reviens pas!** I can't get over it!; **revenir sur ses pas** to retrace one's steps

revenu [ʀəvny] *nm* income

rêver [ʀeve] *vb* to dream; **rêver de quelque chose** to dream of something ▷ *J'ai rêvé de mes vacances cette nuit.* I dreamed about my holidays last night.

réverbère [ʀeveʀbɛʀ] *nm* streetlight

revers [ʀəvɛʀ] *nm* ❶ backhand ▷ *Tu as un excellent revers.* You have an excellent backhand. ❷ *(of jacket)* lapel; **le revers de la médaille** the other side of the coin

revient [ʀəvjɛ̃] *vb see* **revenir**

réviser [ʀevize] *vb* ❶ to study ▷ *Je dois réviser mon français.* I have to study my French. ❷ to review ▷ *La prof a révisé l'unité avec nous.* The teacher reviewed the unit with us. ❸ to revise ▷ *l'édition révisée* the revised edition ❹ to service ▷ *Je dois faire réviser ma voiture.* I must get my car serviced.

révision [ʀevizjɔ̃] *nf* ❶ studying ▷ *Malgré deux heures de révision, il a raté l'examen.* Despite two hours of studying, he failed the exam. ❷ review ▷ *une révision complète* a thorough review

revoir [ʀəvwaʀ] *vb* ❶ to see again ▷ *Je l'ai revue hier soir.* I saw her again last night. ❷ to study ▷ *Il est en train de revoir sa géographie.* He's studying his geography.; **au revoir** goodbye

révolution [ʀevɔlysjɔ̃] *nf* revolution ▷ *la révolution tranquille* the Quiet Revolution

revue [ʀəvy] *nf* magazine

rez-de-chaussée [ʀedʃose] *(pl* **rez-de-chaussée)** *nm* ground floor ▷ *au rez-de-chaussée* on the ground floor

rhinocéros [ʀinɔseʀɔs] *nm* rhinoceros

rhubarbe [ʀybaʀb(ə)] *nf* rhubarb

rhume [ʀym] *nm* cold ▷ *J'ai attrapé un rhume.* I've caught a cold.; **un rhume de cerveau** a head cold; **le rhume des foins** hay fever

ri [ʀi] *vb see* **rire**; **Nous avons bien ri.** We had a good laugh.

riche [ʀiʃ] *adj* rich ▷ *Sa famille est très riche.* His family's very rich. ▷ *riche en vitamines* rich in vitamins

rideau [ʀido] *(pl* **rideaux)** *nm* curtain ▷ *tirer les rideaux* to draw the curtains; **grimper dans les rideaux** to climb the walls ▷ *Cela l'a fait grimper dans les rideaux quand je suis en retard.* It drives her up the wall when I'm late.

ridicule [ʀidikyl] *adj* ridiculous ▷ *Je trouve ça complètement ridicule.* I think that's absolutely ridiculous.

rien [ʀjɛ̃] *pron* ❶ nothing ▷ «*Qu'est-ce que tu as acheté?» « Rien.* "What have you bought?" "Nothing." ▷ *Il a fait tout ce travail pour rien.* He did all this work for nothing.; **Ça n'a rien à voir.** It has nothing to do with it.; **rien d'intéressant** nothing interesting; **rien d'autre** nothing else; **rien du tout** nothing at all ❷ anything ▷ *Il n'a rien dit.* He didn't say anything.; **rien que (1)** just ▷ *rien que pour lui faire plaisir* just to please her ▷ *Rien que la voiture coûte soixante mille dollars.* The car alone costs sixty thousand dollars. **(2)** nothing but ▷ *rien que la vérité* nothing but the truth; **De rien!** You're welcome! ▷ « *Merci beaucoup!» « De rien!* » "Thank you very much!" "You're welcome!"
  ▶ *nm*: **pour un rien** at the slightest thing ▷ *Elle se met en colère pour un rien.* She loses her temper over the slightest thing.; **en un rien de temps** in no time at all

rigoler [ʀigɔle] *vb* ❶ *(informal)* to laugh ▷ *Elle a rigolé durant tout le film.* She laughed all the way through the movie. ❷ to have fun ▷ *On a bien rigolé hier soir.* We had a lot of fun last night. ❸ to be joking ▷ *Ne te fâche pas, je rigolais.* Don't get upset, I was only joking.; **pour rigoler** for a laugh

rigolo [ʀigɔlo, -ɔt] *(f* **rigolote)** *adj* *(informal)* funny

rincer [ʀɛ̃se] *vb* to rinse

rire [ʀiʀ] *vb* to laugh ▷ *Ce film m'a vraiment fait rire.* That movie really made me laugh. ▷ *Nous avons bien ri.* We had a good laugh.; **pour rire** for a laugh; **Oups, c'était juste pour rire.** Oops, that was just a joke.
  ▶ *nm* laughter ▷ *Il a un rire bruyant.* He has a loud laugh.

risque [ʀisk(ə)] *nm* ❶ risk ▷ *prendre des risques* to take risks ▷ *à tes risques et périls* at your own risk ❷ danger ▷ *Il n'y a pas de risque qu'il l'apprenne.* There's no danger of him finding out.

risqué [ʀiske] *(f* **risquée)** *adj* risky

risquer [ʀiske] *vb* to risk; **Ça ne risque rien.** It's quite safe. ▷ *Elle risque de se tuer.* She could get herself killed.; **C'est ce qui risque de se passer.** That's what might well happen.

rivage [ʀivaʒ] *nm* shore

rivière [ʀivjɛʀ] *nf* river

riz [ʀi] *nm* rice

robe [ʀɔb] *nf* dress; **une robe de soirée** an evening gown; **une robe de mariée** a wedding dress; **une robe de chambre** a dressing gown

robinet [ʀɔbinɛ] *nm* tap

robot [ʀɔbo] *nm* robot; **le robot culinaire** food processor

roche [ʀɔʃ] *nf* *(stone)* rock

rocher [ʀɔʃe] *nm* rock

rock [ʀɔkɛnʀɔl] *nm* (*music*) rock ▷ *un chanteur de rock* a rock singer

rôder [ʀode] *vb* to lurk

rognons [ʀɔɲɔ̃] *nmpl* (*in cooking*) kidneys

roi [ʀwa] *nm* king

rôle [ʀol] *nm* role

romain [ʀɔmɛ̃, -ɛn] (*f* **romaine**) *adj* Roman ▷ *des ruines romaines* Roman ruins

roman [ʀɔmã] *nm* novel; **un roman policier** a detective novel; **un roman d'espionnage** a spy novel

romancier [ʀɔmãsje] *nm* novelist

romancière [ʀɔmãsjɛʀ] *nf* novelist

romantique [ʀɔmãtik] *adj* romantic

rompre [ʀɔ̃pʀ(ə)] *vb* ❶ to split up ▷ *Mon frère et sa petite amie ont rompu.* My brother and his girlfriend have split up ❷ to break off ▷ *Ils ont rompu leurs fiançailles.* They've broken off their engagement.; **rompre la glace** to break the ice

ronces [ʀɔ̃s] *nfpl* thornbushes

ronchonner [ʀɔ̃ʃɔne] *vb* (*informal*) to gripe

rond [ʀɔ̃, ʀɔ̃d] (*f* **ronde**) *adj* ❶ round ▷ *La Terre est ronde.* The earth is round.; **ouvrir des yeux ronds** to stare in amazement ❷ chubby ▷ *Il a les joues rondes.* He has chubby cheeks.
▶ *nm* circle ▷ *Elle a dessiné un rond sur le sable.* She drew a circle in the sand.; **en rond** in a circle ▷ *Ils se sont assis en rond.* They sat down in a circle.; **tourner en rond** to go around in circles

rondelle [ʀɔ̃dɛl] *nf* ❶ puck ❷ (*of something round*) slice ▷ *une rondelle de citron* a slice of lemon

ronfler [ʀɔ̃fle] *vb* to snore

ronronner [ʀɔ̃ʀɔne] *vb* to purr

rosbif [ʀɔsbif] *nm* roast beef

rose [ʀoz] *nf* rose
▶ *adj* pink

rosier [ʀozje] *nm* rosebush

rôti [ʀoti] *nm* roast meat; **un rôti de bœuf** a roast of beef

rôtir [ʀotiʀ] *vb* to roast ▷ *faire rôtir quelque chose* to roast something

roue [ʀu] *nf* wheel ▷ *les roues arrière d'une voiture* the rear wheels of a vehicle

rouge [ʀuʒ] *adj* red; **brûler un feu rouge** to go through a red light ▷ *Il a brûlé un feu rouge.* He went through a red light.
▶ *nm* red ▷ *Le rouge est ma couleur préférée.* Red is my favourite colour.; **passer au rouge** to change to red ▷ *Le feu est passé au rouge.* The light changed to red.; **le rouge à lèvres** lipstick

rougeole [ʀuʒɔl] *nf* measles

rougir [ʀuʒiʀ] *vb* ❶ to blush ▷ *Il a rougi en me voyant.* He blushed when he saw me. ❷ to turn red ▷ *Elle a rougi de colère.* She turned red with anger.

rouille [ʀuj] *nf* rust

rouillé [ʀuje] (*f* **rouillée**) *adj* rusty

rouiller [ʀuje] *vb* to rust

roulant [ʀulã, -ãt] (*f* **roulante**) *adj*: **un fauteuil roulant** a wheelchair; **une table roulante** a serving cart; **un tapis roulant** (1) a treadmill (2) a moving sidewalk

rouleau [ʀulo] (*pl* **rouleaux**) *nm* roll ▷ *un rouleau de tapisserie* a roll of wallpaper; **rouleau du printemps** a spring roll; **un rouleau à pâtisserie** a rolling pin

rouler [ʀule] *vb* ❶ to go ▷ *Le train roulait à 250 km/h.* The train was going at 250 km an hour. ❷ to drive ▷ *Il a roulé sans s'arrêter.* He drove without stopping. ❸ to roll ▷ *Elle a roulé le ballon vers moi.* She rolled the ball towards me. ❹ to roll up ▷ *Il a roulé le tapis.* He rolled up the carpet. ❺ to con ▷ *Ils se sont fait rouler.* (*informal*) They were conned.

rousse [ʀus] *adj* *see* **roux**

rousse [ʀus] *nf* redhead

route [ʀut] *nf* ❶ road ▷ *au bord de la route* at the roadside ❷ way ▷ *Je ne connais pas la route.* I don't know the way.; **Il y a trois heures de route.** It's a 3-hour journey.; **en route** on the way ▷ *Ils se sont arrêtés en route.* They stopped on the way.; **mettre en route** to start up ▷ *Elle a mis le moteur en route.* She started up the engine.; **se mettre en route** to set off ▷ *Nous nous sommes mis en route à cinq heures.* We set off at 5 o'clock.

routier [ʀutje] *nm* truck driver ▷ *Mon père est routier.* My father's a truck driver.

routière [ʀutjɛʀ] *nf* truck driver

routine [ʀutin] *nf* routine

roux [ʀu, ʀus] (*f* **rousse**) *adj* ❶ red ▷ *Il a les cheveux roux.* He has red hair. ❷ red-haired ▷ *la petite fille rousse* the little red-haired girl
▶ *nm* redhead

royal [ʀwajal, -o] (*f* **royale**, *mpl* **royaux**) *adj* royal

royaume [ʀwajom] *nm* kingdom

ruban [ʀybã] *nm* ribbon; **le ruban adhésif** adhesive tape

ruban-cache [-kaʃ] *nm* masking tape

rubéole [ʀybeɔl] *nf* German measles

ruche [ʀyʃ] *nf* hive

rue [ʀy] *nf* street

ruelle [ʀɥɛl] *nf* alley

rugueux [ʀygø, -øz] (*f* **rugueuse**) *adj* rough

ruine [ʀɥin] *nf* ruin ▷ *les ruines de la cathédrale* the ruins of the cathedral

ruiner [ʀɥine] *vb* to ruin

ruisseau [ʀɥiso] (*pl* **ruisseaux**) *nm* stream

rumeur [ʀymœʀ] *nf* rumour

rupture [ʀyptyʀ] *nf* break-up

ruse [ʀyz] *nf* trickery ▷ *une ruse* a trick

rusé [ʀyze] (*f* **rusée**) *adj* cunning

rythme [ʀitm(ə)] *nm* ❶ rhythm ▷ *J'aime le rythme de cette musique.* I like the beat of this music. ❷ pace ▷ *Elle marche à un bon rythme.* She walks at a good pace.

S

s' [s] pron see **se**

sa [sa] adj ❶ his ▷ Il est allé voir sa grand-mère. He's gone to see his grandmother. ❷ her ▷ Elle a embrassé sa mère. She kissed her mother.

sable [sabl(ə)] nm sand; **les sables bitumineux** tar sands; **des sables mouvants** quicksand

sablé [sable] nm shortbread cookie

sabot [sabo] nm ❶ clog ❷ (of horse) hoof

sac [sak] nm bag; **un sac de voyage** a travel bag; **un sac de couchage** a sleeping bag; **un sac à main** a purse; **un sac à dos** a knapsack; **un sac gonflable** an airbag; **voyager avec son sac au dos** to go backpacking

sachet [saʃe] nm (of sugar, coffee) packet; **du potage en sachet** instant soup

sacoche [sakɔʃ] nf ❶ (for mail, newspapers) bag ❷ (bicycle) pannier; **une sacoche de bicyclette** (for bike) a seat pack

sacre [sakr(ə)] nm swearword

sacré [sakre] (f**sacrée**) adj sacred

sacrer [sakre] vb to swear

sage [saʒ] adj ❶ (well-behaved) good ▷ Sois sage. Be good. ❷ (sensible) wise ▷ Il serait plus sage d'attendre. It would be wiser to wait.

sagesse [saʒes] nf wisdom ▷ Il a eu la sagesse de ne pas y aller. He wisely didn't go.; **une dent de sagesse** a wisdom tooth

Sagittaire [saʒiter] nm Sagittarius ▷ Il est Sagittaire. He's a Sagittarius.

saignant [seɲɑ̃, -ɑ̃t] (f**saignante**) adj (meat) rare

saigner [seɲe] vb to bleed; **saigner du nez** to have a nosebleed

sain [sɛ̃, sɛn] (f**saine**) adj healthy; **sain et sauf** safe and sound

saint [sɛ̃, sɛ̃t] (f**sainte**) adj holy; **la Saint-Jean-Baptiste** Saint-Jean-Baptiste Day ▶ nm saint

sainte [sɛ̃t] nf saint

sais [se] vb see **savoir**; Je ne sais pas. I don't know.

saisir [sezir] vb to take hold of; **saisir l'occasion de faire quelque chose** to seize the opportunity to do something

saison [sezɔ̃] nf season ▷ Ce n'est pas la saison des fraises. Strawberries are out of season.; **la belle saison** summer

sait [se] vb see **savoir**; Il sait que... He knows that...; On ne sait jamais! You never know!

salade [salad] nf ❶ lettuce ❷ salad ▷ une salade composée a mixed salad ▷ une salade de fruits a fruit salad ▷ une salade César a Caesar salad; **la salade de chou** cole slaw

saladier [saladje] nm salad bowl

salaire [saler] nm salary

salami [salami] nm salami

sale [sal] adj dirty

salé [sale] (f**salée**) adj salty ▷ La soupe est trop salée. The soup is too salty.

saler [sale] vb to put salt in ▷ J'ai oublié de saler la soupe. I forgot to put salt in the soup.

saleté [salte] nf dirt ▷ J'ai horreur de la saleté. I hate dirt. ▷ Il y a une saleté sur ta chemise. There's some dirt on your shirt.

salir [salir] vb: **salir quelque chose** to get something dirty; **se salir** to get oneself dirty ▷ Mets un tablier, sinon tu vas te salir. Put on an apron or you'll get yourself dirty.

salle [sal] nf ❶ room ❷ audience ▷ Toute la salle l'a applaudi. The whole audience applauded him. ❸ (in hospital) ward ▷ Elle est à la salle douze. She's in Ward 12.; **la salle à manger** the dining room; **la salle de lavage** the laundry room; **la salle de bains** the bathroom; **la salle d'attente** the waiting room; **une salle de classe** a classroom; **une salle de concert** a concert hall

salon [salɔ̃] nm living room; **le salon des professeurs** (in school) staff room; **le salon funéraire** funeral parlour; **un salon de coiffure** a hair salon; **un salon de beauté** a beauty salon

salopette [salɔpet] nf overalls

saluer [salɥe] vb: **saluer quelqu'un (1)** to say hello to somebody ▷ Je l'ai croisé dans la rue et il m'a salué. I met him in the street and he said hello. **(2)** to say goodbye to somebody ▷ Elle nous a salués et elle est partie. She said goodbye and left.

salut [saly] excl (informal) Hi!

salutation [salytasjɔ̃] nf greeting

samedi [samdi] nm ❶ Saturday ▷ Aujourd'hui, nous sommes samedi. It's Saturday today. ❷ on Saturday ▷ Nous sommes allés au cinéma samedi. We went to the movies on Saturday.; **le samedi** on Saturdays ▷ Le magasin ferme à dix-huit heures le samedi. The store closes at 6 p.m. on Saturdays.; **tous les samedis** every Saturday; **samedi dernier** last Saturday; **samedi prochain** next Saturday

sandale [sɑ̃dal] nf sandal

sandwich [sɑ̃dwitʃ] nm sandwich; **un sandwich au smoked meat** a smoked meat sandwich

sang [sɑ̃] nm blood; **en sang** covered with blood

sang-froid [sɑ̃frwa] nm: **garder son sang-froid** to keep calm; **perdre son sang-froid** to lose one's cool; **faire quelque chose de sang-froid** to do something in cold blood

sangle [sɑ̃gl(ə)] nf (on sandal, backpack) strap

sanglot [sɑ̃glo] nm: **éclater en sanglots** to burst into tears

sans [sɑ̃] prep without ▷ Elle est venue sans son frère. She came without her brother.; **un haut sans manches** a sleeveless top

sans-abri [sɑ̃zabri] (pl**sans-abri**) nmf homeless person ▷ les sans-abri the homeless

sans-gêne [sãʒɛn] *adj* inconsiderate
santé [sãte] *nf* health ▷ *en bonne santé* in good health
sapin [sapɛ̃] *nm* fir tree; **un sapin de Noël** a Christmas tree
sardine [sardin] *nf* sardine
Saskatchewan [saskatʃɛwan] Saskatchewan
satellite [satelit] *nm* satellite ▷ *la télévision par satellite* satellite TV
satisfaire [satisfɛr] *vb* to satisfy
satisfaisant [satisfəzɑ̃, -ɑ̃t] (*f* **satisfaisante**) *adj* satisfactory
satisfait [satisfɛ, -ɛt] (*f* **satisfaite**) *adj* satisfied ▷ *être satisfait de quelque chose* to be satisfied with something
sauce [sos] *nf* ❶ sauce ❷ gravy
saucisse [sosis] *nf* sausage
saucisson [sosisɔ̃] *nm* (eaten sliced, cold) sausage
sauf [sof] *prep* except ▷ *Tout le monde est venu sauf elle.* Everyone came except her.; **sauf si** unless ▷ *On ira se promener, sauf s'il fait mauvais.* We'll go for a walk, unless the weather's bad.; **sauf que** except that ▷ *Tout s'est bien passé, sauf que nous sommes arrivés en retard.* Everything went OK, except that we arrived late.
saule à chaton [sol-] *nm* pussy willow
saumon [somɔ̃] *nm* salmon; **le saumon atlantique** Atlantic salmon; **le saumon quinnat** Chinook salmon; **le saumon rouge** Sockeye salmon
saut [so] *nm* jump; **le saut en longueur** the long jump; **le saut en hauteur** the high jump; **le saut à la perche** the pole vault; **le saut à l'élastique** bungee jumping; **un saut périlleux** a somersault
sauter [sote] *vb* to jump ▷ *Nous avons sauté par-dessus la barrière.* We jumped over the gate.; **sauter à la corde** to skip (*with a rope*); **faire sauter quelque chose** to blow something up ▷ *On a fait sauter le poste de police la nuit dernière.* The police station was blown up last night.; **faire sauter** (*food*) to stir-fry ▷ *J'ai fait sauter les légumes.* I stir-fried the vegetables.
sauterelle [sotrɛl] *nf* grasshopper
sauvage [sovaʒ] *adj* ❶ wild ▷ *des animaux sauvages* wild animals ▷ *le camping sauvage* wilderness camping; **une région sauvage** a wilderness area ❷ shy ▷ *Il est sauvage.* He's shy.
sauvegarder [sovgarde] *vb* (file on computer) to save
sauver [sove] *vb* to save; **se sauver (1)** to run away ▷ *Elle s'est sauvée à toutes jambes.* She ran away as fast as she could. **(2)** (*informal*) to be off ▷ *Allez, je me sauve!* Right, I'm off.
sauvetage [sovtaʒ] *nm* rescue
sauveteur [sovtœr] *nm* ❶ rescuer ❷ lifeguard
sauveteure [sovtœr] *nf* ❶ rescuer ❷ lifeguard
savais, savait *vb see* **savoir**; *Je ne savais pas qu'il devait venir.* I didn't know he was going to come.
savent *vb see* **savoir**; *Ils ne savent pas ce qu'ils veulent.* They don't know what they want.

saveur [savœr] *nf* flavour
savez *vb see* **savoir**; *Est-ce que vous savez où elle habite?* Do you know where she lives?
savoir [savwar] *vb* to know ▷ *Je ne sais pas où elle est allée.* I don't know where she's gone. ▷ *Nous ne savons pas s'il est bien arrivé.* We don't know if he's arrived safely. ▷ *Savais-tu que Winnipeg était la capitale du Manitoba?* Did you know Winnipeg was the capital of Manitoba? ▷ *Il ne sait pas ce qu'il va faire ce week-end.* He doesn't know what he's going to do this weekend.; **Tu sais nager?** Can you swim?
savon [savɔ̃] *nm* ❶ soap ❷ bar of soap
savons [savɔ̃] *vb see* **savoir**
savoureux [savurø, -øz] (*f* **savoureuse**) *adj* tasty
saxophone [saksofon] *nm* sax
saxophoniste [saksɔfɔnist(ə)] *nmf* sax player
scandale [skɑ̃dal] *nm* scandal; **faire scandale** to cause a scandal ▷ *Ce film a fait scandale.* The film caused a scandal.
scandaleux [skɑ̃dalø, -øz] (*f* **scandaleuse**) *adj* outrageous
scarabée [skarabe] *nm* beetle
scène [sɛn] *nf* ❶ scene ▷ *une scène d'amour* a love scene ▷ *la scène du crime* the scene of the crime ▷ *Il m'a fait une scène.* He made a scene.; **une scène de ménage** a domestic quarrel ❷ stage ▷ *Elle fait ses débuts sur la scène.* It is her stage debut.; **les arts de la scène** performing arts
sceptique [sɛptik] *adj* sceptical
schéma [ʃema] *nm* diagram
schématique [ʃematik] *adj* oversimplified ▷ *Cette interprétation est un peu trop schématique.* This interpretation is a bit oversimplified.
scie [si] *nf* saw
science [sjɑ̃s] *nf* science; *Elle est forte en sciences.* She is good at science.; **les sciences physiques** the physical sciences; **les sciences naturelles** the natural sciences; **les sciences économiques** economics; **les sciences politiques** political science ▷ *Il a un diplôme de sciences politiques.* He has a degree in political science.
science-fiction [sjɑ̃sfiksjɔ̃] *nf* science fiction
scientifique [sjɑ̃tifik] *adj* scientific
▶ *n* scientist
scier [sje] *vb* to saw
scolaire [skɔlɛr] *adj* school ▷ *l'année scolaire* the school year ▷ *les vacances scolaires* the school holidays ▷ *le transport scolaire* school transportation; **l'abandon scolaire** dropping out of school
Scorpion [skɔrpjɔ̃] *nm* Scorpio ▷ *Elle est Scorpion.* She's a Scorpio.
scrupule [skrypyl] *nm* scruple
sculpter [skylte] *vb* to sculpt
sculpteur [skyltœr] *nm* sculptor
sculpteure [skyltœr] *nf* sculptor
sculpture [skyltyr] *nf* sculpture
se [s(ə)] *pron* ❶ himself ▷ *Il se regarde dans le miroir.* He's looking at himself in the mirror. ❷ herself ▷ *Elle se regarde dans le miroir.* She's looking at herself in the mirror. ❸ itself ▷ *Le chien s'est fait mal.* The dog hurt itself.

① oneself ▷ *se regarder dans un miroir* to look at oneself in a mirror **②** themselves ▷ *Ils se sont regardés dans le miroir.* They looked at themselves in the mirror. ▷ *Elle s'admire dans sa nouvelle robe.* She's admiring herself in her new dress. **③** each other ▷ *Ils s'aiment.* They love each other.

séance [seɑ̃s] nf session ▷ *une séance de physiothérapie* a physiotherapy session

seau [so] (pl **seaux**) nm bucket

sec [sɛk, sɛʃ] (f **sèche**) adj **①** dry ▷ *un shampooing pour les cheveux secs* shampoo for dry hair ▷ *Mes mitaines sont sèches.* My mitts are dry. **②** dried ▷ *des figues sèches* dried figs

séchage [seʃaʒ] nm drying ▷ *Voulez-vous un séchage à la brosse?* Would you like a blow-dry? ▷ *Le séchage à la machine n'est pas recommandé pour ce chandail.* Machine drying is not recommended for this sweater.

sèche-cheveux [sɛʃəvø] (pl **sèche-cheveux**) nm hair dryer

sécher [seʃe] vb to dry ▷ *Faire sécher à plat.* Lay flat to dry.; **sécher à la brosse** to blow-dry; **se sécher** to dry oneself ▷ *Sèche-toi avec cette serviette.* Dry yourself with this towel.

sécheresse [sɛʃʀɛs] nf drought ▷ *une terrible sécheresse* a terrible drought

sécheuse [seʃøz] nf dryer

séchoir [seʃwaʀ] nm dryer

second [səgɔ̃, -ɔ̃d] (f **seconde**) adj second ▷ *Il est arrivé second.* He came second.

secondaire [səgɔ̃dɛʀ] adj secondary ▷ *l'école secondaire* secondary school; **des effets secondaires** side effects
▶ nm (level) high school ▷ *les enseignants et les élèves du secondaire* high school teachers and students ▷ *Elle est en secondaire cinq.* She's in Grade 12.

seconde [səgɔ̃d] nf second ▷ *Attends une seconde!* Wait a second!

secouer [səkwe] vb to shake ▷ *secouer la tête* to shake one's head ▷ *L'accident l'a beaucoup secouée.* The accident has really shaken her.

secourir [səkuʀiʀ] vb to rescue

secourisme [səkuʀism(ə)] nm first aid ▷ *J'ai un brevet de secourisme.* I have a first aid certificate.

secours [səkuʀ] nm help ▷ *Elle est allée chercher du secours.* She went to get help. ▷ *Au secours!* Help!; **les premiers secours** first aid; **une sortie de secours** an emergency exit; **le pneu de secours** the spare tire

secret [səkʀɛ, -ɛt] nm secret
▶ adj (f **secrète**) secret

secrétaire [səkʀetɛʀ] nmf secretary

secrétariat [s(ə)kʀetaʀja] nm secretary's office

secteur [sɛktœʀ] nm sector ▷ *le secteur public* the public sector ▷ *le secteur privé* the private sector

section [sɛksjɔ̃] nf (of school) section

sécuritaire [sekyʀitɛʀ] adj safe ▷ *un milieu de travail sécuritaire* a safe working environment

sécurité [sekyʀite] nf **①** safety; **être en sécurité** to be safe ▷ *On ne se sent pas en sécurité dans ce quartier.* You don't feel safe in this neighbourhood.; **la sécurité routière** road safety; **une ceinture de sécurité** a seatbelt **②** security ▷ *par mesure de sécurité* as a security measure; **la sécurité de l'emploi** job security

séduisant [sedɥizɑ̃, -ɑ̃t] (f **séduisante**) adj attractive

seigle [sɛgl(ə)] nm rye ▷ *un pain de seigle* a loaf of rye bread

Seigneur [sɛɲœʀ] nm (God) the Lord

sein [sɛ̃] nm breast; **au sein de** within ▷ *le statut des autochtones au sein du Canada* the status of Aboriginals within Canada

seize [sɛz] num sixteen ▷ *Elle a seize ans.* She's sixteen. ▷ *à seize heures* at 4 p.m.; **le seize février** the sixteenth of February

seizième [sɛzjɛm] adj sixteenth

séjour [seʒuʀ] nm stay ▷ *J'ai fait un séjour d'une semaine en Alberta.* I stayed in Alberta for a week.

sel [sɛl] nm salt

sélectionner [selɛksjɔne] vb to select

selle [sɛl] nf saddle

selon [səlɔ̃] prep according to ▷ *selon lui* according to him ▷ *selon mon humeur* according to what mood I'm in ▷ *Ils sont répartis selon leur âge.* They're divided up according to age.

semaine [səmɛn] nf week; **en semaine** on weekdays; **la semaine de relâche** March Break; **la fin de semaine** the weekend

semblable [sɑ̃blabl(ə)] adj similar

semblant [sɑ̃blɑ̃] nm: **faire semblant de faire quelque chose** to pretend to do something ▷ *Elle fait semblant de dormir.* She's pretending to be asleep.

sembler [sɑ̃ble] vb to seem ▷ *Le temps semble s'améliorer.* The weather seems to be improving. ▷ *Il me semble inutile de s'en inquiéter.* It seems pointless to me to worry about it.

semelle [səmɛl] nf **①** sole **②** insole

Sénat [sena] nm Senate

sens [sɑ̃s] nm **①** sense ▷ *avoir le sens de l'humour* to have a sense of humour ▷ *Je n'ai pas le sens de l'orientation.* I have no sense of direction. ▷ *avoir le sens du rythme* to have a sense of rhythm ▷ *Ça n'a pas de sens.* It doesn't make sense.; **le bon sens** common sense; **sans bon sens** unreasonably ▷ *Elle conduit vite sans bons sens.* She drives unreasonably fast. **②** direction ▷ *Tu tournes la poignée dans le mauvais sens.* You're turning the handle in the wrong direction.; **sens dessus dessous** upside down; **un sens interdit** a one-way street ▷ *J'ai failli prendre un sens interdit.* I nearly went the wrong way down a one-way street.; **un sens unique** a one-way street

sensation [sɑ̃sasjɔ̃] nf feeling

sensationnel [sɑ̃sasjɔnɛl] (f **sensationnelle**) adj sensational

sensé [sɑ̃se] (f **sensée**) adj sensible

sensible [sɑ̃sibl(ə)] adj **①** sensitive ▷ *Elle est très sensible.* She's very sensitive. ▷ *Ce film est déconseillé aux personnes sensibles.* This film contains scenes which some viewers may find disturbing. **②** noticeable ▷ *une amélioration sensible* a noticeable improvement

sensiblement [sɑ̃sibləmɑ̃] adv **①** noticeably

▷ *Elle a sensiblement progressé.* She has noticeably progressed. ❷ approximately ▷ *Elles sont sensiblement de la même taille.* They are approximately the same height.

sentence [sɑ̃tɑ̃s] *nf* (judgement) sentence

sentier [sɑ̃tje] *nm* path

sentiment [sɑ̃timɑ̃] *nm* feeling

sentimental [sɑ̃timɑ̃tal, -o] (*f* **sentimentale**, *mpl* **sentimentaux**) *adj* sentimental

sentir [sɑ̃tir] *vb* ❶ to smell ▷ *Ça sent bon.* That smells good. ▷ *Ça sent mauvais.* It smells bad. ❷ to smell of ▷ *Ça sent les frites ici.* It smells like fries in here. ❸ to taste ▷ *Tu sens l'ail dans le rôti?* Can you taste the garlic in the roast? ❹ to feel ▷ *«Ça t'a fait mal?» «Non, je n'ai rien senti.»* "Did it hurt?" "No, I didn't feel a thing." ▷ *Je ne me sens pas bien.* I don't feel well.; **Il ne peut pas la sentir.** (informal) He can't stand her.

séparation [separasjɔ̃] *nf* separation

séparatisme [separatism(ə)] *nm* separatism

séparé [separe] (*f* **séparée**) *adj* separated ▷ *Mes parents sont séparés.* My parents are separated.

séparément [separemɑ̃] *adv* separately

séparer [separe] *vb* to separate ▷ *Séparez le blanc du jaune.* Separate the yolk from the white.; **se séparer** to separate ▷ *Mes parents se sont séparés l'année dernière.* My parents separated last year.

sept [sɛt] *num* seven ▷ *Il est arrivé à sept heures.* He arrived at seven o'clock. ▷ *Il a sept ans.* He's seven.; **le sept février** the seventh of February; **ouvert sept jours sur sept** open 7 days a week

septembre [sɛptɑ̃br(ə)] *nm* September; **en septembre** in September

septième [sɛtjɛm] *adj* seventh ▷ *au septième étage* on the seventh floor

sera, serai, seras, serez *vb see* **être**; **Je serai de retour à dix heures.** I'll be back at 10 o'clock.

série [seri] *nf* series

sérieusement [serjøzmɑ̃] *adv* seriously

sérieux [serjø, -øz] (*f* **sérieuse**) *adj* ❶ serious ▷ *«Il plaisantait?» «Non, il était sérieux.»* "Was he joking?" "No, he was serious." ❷ responsible ▷ *C'est une employée très sérieuse.* She's a very responsible employee.

▶ *nm:* **garder son sérieux** to keep a straight face ▷ *J'ai eu du mal à garder mon sérieux.* I had trouble keeping a straight face.; **prendre quelque chose au sérieux** to take something seriously; **prendre quelqu'un au sérieux** to take somebody seriously; **Il manque un peu de sérieux.** He's not very responsible.

seringue [sərɛ̃g] *nf* syringe

séronégatif [seronegatif, -iv] (*f* **séronégative**) *adj* HIV-negative

serons, seront *vb see* **être**

séropositif [seropozitif, -iv] (*f* **séropositive**) *adj* HIV-positive

serpent [sɛrpɑ̃] *nm* snake

serre [sɛr] *nf* greenhouse; **l'effet de serre** the greenhouse effect

serré [sere] (*f* **serrée**) *adj* ❶ tight ▷ *Mon pantalon est trop serré.* My pants are too tight.

❷ (competition) close ▷ *Ça a été un match serré.* It was a close game.

serrer [sere] *vb:* **Ce pantalon me serre trop.** These pants are too tight for me.; **serrer la main à quelqu'un** to shake hands with somebody; **se serrer** to make yourself compact ▷ *Serrez-vous un peu pour que je puisse m'asseoir.* Squeeze over a bit so I can sit down.; **serrer quelqu'un dans ses bras** to hug somebody

serrure [seryr] *nf* lock

sers, sert *vb see* **servir**

serveur [sɛrvœr] *nm* ❶ (in café) waiter ❷ (computer) server

serveuse [sɛrvøz] *nf* waitress

serviable [sɛrvjabl(ə)] *adj* helpful

service [sɛrvis] *nm* ❶ (in restaurant) service ▷ *Le service est compris.* Service is included.; **être de service** to be on duty; **hors service** out of order; **faire le service** (at table) to serve ▷ *Tu peux faire le service s'il te plaît?* Could you serve, please?; **le service d'assistance téléphonique** directory assistance ❷ favour ▷ *rendre service à quelqu'un* to do somebody a favour ▷ *Est-ce que je peux te demander un service?* Can I ask you a favour? ❸ (sports) serve ▷ *Il a un bon service.* He has a good serve.; **un service commémoratif** a memorial service; **le service militaire** military service; **les services sociaux** social services; **les services secrets** the secret service

serviette [sɛrvjɛt] *nf* ❶ towel ▷ *une serviette de bain* a bath towel; **une serviette hygiénique** a sanitary napkin ❷ (napkin) serviette ❸ briefcase

servir [sɛrvir] *vb* to serve ▷ *Est-ce qu'on vous a servi?* Have you been served?; **À toi de servir.** (tennis) It's your serve.; **se servir** to help oneself ▷ *Servez-vous.* Help yourself.; **se servir de** to use ▷ *Tu te sers souvent de ton vélo?* Do you use your bike a lot?; **servir à quelqu'un** to be of use to somebody ▷ *Ça m'a beaucoup servi.* It was very useful.; **À quoi ça sert?** What's it for?; **Ça ne sert à rien.** It's no use. ▷ *Ça ne sert à rien d'insister.* It's no use insisting.

ses [se] *adj* ❶ his ▷ *Il est parti voir ses grands-parents.* He's gone to see his grandparents. ❷ her ▷ *Elle a oublié ses livres.* She forgot her books. ❸ its ▷ *la ville et ses alentours* the town and its surroundings

seuil [sœj] *nm* doorstep

seul [sœl] (*f* **seule**) *adj, adv* ❶ alone ▷ *vivre seul* to live alone ❷ by oneself ▷ *Elle est venue seule.* She came by herself.; **faire quelque chose tout seul** to do something by oneself ▷ *Elle a fait ça toute seule?* Did she do it by herself?; **se sentir seul** to feel lonely; **un seul livre** one book only ▷ *Vous avez droit à un seul livre.* You're entitled to one book only.; **Il reste une seule nectarine.** There's only one nectarine left.; **le seul livre que... the** only book ▷ *C'est le seul Troon Harrison que je n'ai pas lu.* That's the only Troon Harrison I haven't read.; **le seul** the only one ▷ *C'est le seul que je ne connaisse pas.* He's the only one I don't know.

seulement [sœlmɑ̃] *adv* only; **non**

seulement…mais not only…but ▷ *Non seulement il a plu, mais en plus il a fait froid.* Not only did it rain, but it was cold as well.

sévère [sevɛʀ] *adj* strict ▷ *Mon prof de maths est très sévère.* My math teacher is very strict.

sexe [sɛks(ə)] *nm* sex

sexuel [sɛksɥɛl] (*f* **sexuelle**) *adj* sexual ▷ *l'éducation sexuelle* sex education ▷ *l'orientation sexuelle* sexual orientation

shampooing [ʃɑ̃pwɛ̃] *nm* shampoo; **se faire un shampooing** to wash one's hair

short [ʃɔʀt] *nm* shorts ▷ *Il était en short.* He was wearing shorts.

si [si] *nm* ❶ B ▷ **en si bémol** in B flat ▷ *ti* ▷ *la, si, ti, do*
▶ *conj, adv* ❶ if ▷ *si tu veux* if you like ▷ *Je me demande si elle va venir.* I wonder if she'll come. ▷ **si seulement** if only ❷ so ▷ *Elle est si gentille.* She's so kind. ▷ *Tout s'est passé si vite.* Everything happened so fast.

sida [sida] *nm* AIDS ▷ *Il a le sida.* He has AIDS.

siècle [sjɛkl(ə)] *nm* century ▷ *le vingtième siècle* the twentieth century

siège [sjɛʒ] *nm* (*in vehicle*) seat; **un siège pliant** a folding chair; **le siège social** head office

sien [sjɛ̃] *pron*: **le sien (1)** his ▷ *« Est-ce que c'est le vélo de ton frère ? » — « Oui, c'est le sien. »* "Is this your brother's bike?" —"Yes, it's his." **(2)** hers ▷ *« Est-ce que c'est le vélo de ta sœur ? » — « Oui, c'est le sien. »* "Is this your sister's bike?" —"Yes, it's hers."

sienne [sjɛn] *pron*: **la sienne (1)** his ▷ *« Est-ce que c'est la montre de ton père ? » — « Oui, c'est la sienne. »* "Is this your father's watch?" — "Yes, it's his." **(2)** hers ▷ *« Est-ce que c'est la montre de ta mère ? » — « Oui, c'est la sienne. »* "Is this your mother's watch?" — "Yes, it's hers."

siennes [sjɛn] *pron*: **les siennes (1)** his ▷ *« Est-ce que ce sont les bottes de ton frère ? »* — *« Oui, ce sont les siennes. »* "Are these your brother's boots?" —"Yes, they're his." **(2)** hers ▷ *« Est-ce que ce sont les lunettes de ta tante ? »* — *« Oui, ce sont les siennes. »* "Are these your aunt's glasses?" — "Yes, they're hers."

siens [sjɛ̃] *pron*: **les siens (1)** his ▷ *« Est-ce que ce sont les sandwichs de ton frère ? » — « Oui, ce sont les siens. »* "Are these your brother's sandwiches?" — "Yes, they're his." **(2)** hers ▷ *« Est-ce que ce sont les sandwichs de ta sœur ? »* — *« Oui, ce sont les siens. »* "Are these your sister's sandwiches?" — "Yes, they're hers."

sieste [sjɛst(ə)] *nf* nap ▷ **faire la sieste** to have a nap

siffler [sifle] *vb* to whistle

sifflet [siflɛ] *nm* whistle

siffleux [sifløe] *nm* marmot

sigle [sigl(ə)] *nm* acronym

signal [sinal, -o] (*pl* **signaux**) *nm* signal

signature [sinatyʀ] *nf* signature

signe [siɲ] *nm* sign; **faire un signe de la main** to wave; **faire signe à quelqu'un d'entrer** to motion to somebody to come in; **les signes du zodiaque** the signs of the zodiac

signer [siɲe] *vb* to sign

signet [siɲɛ] *nm* bookmark; **mettre un signet à un site Web** to bookmark a website

signification [siɲifikasjɔ̃] *nf* meaning

signifier [siɲifje] *vb* to mean ▷ *Que signifie ce mot ? What* does this word mean?

silence [silɑ̃s] *nm* silence; **Silence!** Be quiet!

silencieux [silɑ̃sjø, -øz] (*f* **silencieuse**) *adj* ❶ silent ▷ *Elle est restée silencieuse.* She remained silent. ❷ quiet ▷ *C'est très silencieux ici.* It's very quiet here.

silhouette [silwɛt] *nf* figure ▷ *J'ai vu une silhouette dans le brouillard.* I saw a figure in the mist.

similaire [similɛʀ] *adj* similar

simple [sɛ̃pl(ə)] *nm* (*tennis*) singles ▷ *le simple messieurs* the men's singles ▷ *le simple dames* the women's singles
▶ *adj* simple

simplement [sɛ̃pləmɑ̃] *adv* simply ▷ *C'est tout simplement inadmissible.* It's simply unacceptable.

simuler [simyle] *vb* to simulate

simultané [simyltane] (*f* **simultanée**) *adj* simultaneous

sincère [sɛ̃sɛʀ] *adj* sincere

sincèrement [sɛ̃sɛʀmɑ̃] *adv* sincerely

sincérité [sɛ̃seʀite] *nf* sincerity

singe [sɛ̃ʒ] *nm* monkey

singulier [sɛ̃gylje] *nm* singular ▷ *au féminin singulier* in the feminine singular

sinistre [sinistʀ(ə)] *adj* sinister

sinon [sinɔ̃] *conj* otherwise ▷ *Dépêche-toi, sinon je pars sans toi.* Hurry up, otherwise I'll leave without you.

sinusite [sinyzit] *nf* sinusitis ▷ *avoir de la sinusite* to have sinusitis

sirène [siʀɛn] *nf* mermaid; **la sirène d'alarme** the fire alarm

sirop [siʀo] *nm* syrup; **le sirop contre la toux** cough syrup; **le sirop d'érable** maple syrup

site [sit] *nm* setting ▷ *un site très sauvage* a wilderness setting ▷ *un site d'enfouissement* a landfill site; **un site pittoresque** a scenic attraction; **un site touristique** a tourist attraction; **un site archéologique** an archaeological site; **un site Web** a website

sitôt [sito] *adv*: **sitôt dit, sitôt fait** no sooner said than done; **pas de sitôt** not for a long time ▷ *On ne le reverra pas de sitôt.* We won't see him again for a long time.

situation [sitɥasjɔ̃] *nf* ❶ situation; **la situation de famille** marital status ❷ job ▷ *Il a une belle situation.* He's got a good job.; **la situation économique** economic conditions

se situer [sitɥe] *vb* to be situated ▷ *Sudbury se situe à l'ouest de North Bay.* Sudbury is situated to the west of North Bay.; **bien situé** well situated

six [sis] *num* six ▷ *Elle est rentrée à six heures.* She got back at six o'clock. ▷ *Il a six ans.* He's six.; **le six février** the sixth of February

sixième [sizjɛm] *adj* sixth ▷ *au sixième étage* on the sixth floor

ski [ski] *nm* ❶ ski ▷ *J'ai loué des skis.* I rented skis. ❷ skiing ▷ *J'adore le ski.* I love skiing. ▷ *faire du ski* to go skiing; **le ski de fond** cross-country skiing; **le ski nautique** water-skiing; **le ski alpin** downhill skiing; **le ski de randonnée** cross-country skiing

skier [skje] vb to ski
skieur [skjœʀ] nm skier
skieuse [skjøz] nf skier
sloche [slɔʃ] nf slush
snob [snɔb] (f **snob**) adj snobbish
snorkel [snɔʀkɛl] nm snorkel; **faire du snorkel** to go snorkelling
sobre [sɔbʀ(ə)] adj ❶ sober ❷ plain ▷ C'est une veste très sobre. It's a very plain jacket.
sociable [sɔsjabl(ə)] adj sociable
social [sɔsjal, -o] (f **sociale**, mpl **sociaux**) adj social
socialiste [sɔsjalist(ə)] nmf socialist
société [sɔsjete] nf ❶ society; **la société distincte** distinct society ❷ company ▷ une société financière a finance company
sociologie [sɔsjɔlɔʒi] nf sociology
sœur [sœʀ] nf sister; **une bonne sœur** (informal) a nun
soi [swa] pron oneself ▷ avoir confiance en soi to have confidence in oneself; **rester chez soi** to stay at home; **Ça va de soi.** It goes without saying.
soi-disant [swadizɑ̃] adv, adj supposedly ▷ Il était soi-disant parti à Moncton. He had supposedly left for Moncton.; **un soi-disant poète** a so-called poet
soie [swa] nf silk
soif [swaf] nf thirst; **avoir soif** to be thirsty
soigner [swaɲe] vb (ill person, animal) to look after ▷ Soigne-toi bien en fin de semaine! Take care of yourself this weekend!
soigneux [swaɲø, -øz] (f **soigneuse**) adj careful ▷ Tu devrais être plus soigneux avec tes livres. You should be more careful with your books.
soi-même [swamɛm] pron oneself ▷ Il vaut mieux le faire soi-même. It's better to do it oneself.
soin [swɛ̃] nm care; **prendre soin de quelque chose** to take care of something ▷ Prends bien soin de ce livre. Take good care of this book.
soins [swɛ̃] nmpl treatment; **les premiers soins** first aid
soir [swaʀ] nm evening ▷ ce soir this evening; **à sept heures du soir** at 7 p.m.; **demain soir** tomorrow night; **hier soir** last night
soirée [swaʀe] nf evening ▷ en tenue de soirée in evening dress
sois vb see **être**; **Sois tranquille!** Be quiet!
soit [swa] conj: **soit..., soit...** (1) either...or... ▷ soit lundi, soit mardi either Monday or Tuesday (2) whether...or... ▷ Je les ferai, mes devoirs, soit aujourd'hui, soit demain. I'll do my homework eventually, whether today or tomorrow.
soixantaine [swasɑ̃tɛn] nf about sixty ▷ une soixantaine de personnes about sixty people; **Elle a la soixantaine.** She's in her sixties.
soixante [swasɑ̃t] num sixty ▷ Il a soixante ans. He's sixty. ▷ soixante et un sixty-one ▷ soixante-deux sixty-two; **soixante et onze** seventy-one; **soixante-quinze** seventy-five
soixante-dix [swasɑ̃tdis] num seventy ▷ Il a soixante-dix ans. He's seventy.
sol [sɔl] nm ❶ floor ▷ un sol carrelé a tiled floor; **à même le sol** on the floor ❷ soil ▷ sur le sol

canadien on Canadian soil ❸ G ▷ **sol dièse** G sharp ❹ so ▷ do, ré, mi, fa, sol... do, re, mi, fa, so...
solaire [sɔlɛʀ] adj solar ▷ le système solaire the solar system; **la crème solaire** sun cream
soldat [sɔlda] nm soldier
soldate [sɔldat] nf soldier
solde [sɔld(ə)] nm: **être en solde** to be on sale ▷ Les chemisiers sont en solde. The blouses are on sale.; **les soldes** the sales ▷ les soldes de janvier the January sales
soldé [sɔlde] (f **soldée**) adj: **être soldé** to be on sale ▷ un article soldé à dix dollars an item on sale for 10 dollars
sole [sɔl] nf (fish) sole
soleil [sɔlɛj] nm sun ▷ au soleil in the sun; **Il fait soleil.** It's sunny out.; **le coup de soleil** sunburn; **le coucher de soleil** sunset
solfège [sɔlfɛʒ] nm musical theory ▷ Elle joue du violon sans connaître le solfège. She plays the violin but she can't read music.
solidaire [sɔlidɛʀ] adj: **être solidaire de quelqu'un** to back somebody up
solide [sɔlid] adj ❶ (person) strong ❷ (object) solid
solitaire [sɔlitɛʀ] adj solitary
  ▶ n loner
solitude [sɔlityd] nf loneliness
solution [sɔlysjɔ̃] nf solution; **une solution de facilité** an easy way out
sombre [sɔ̃bʀ(ə)] adj dark
sommaire [sɔmɛʀ] nm summary
somme [sɔm] nm sum
  ▶ nm nap ▷ faire un somme to take a nap
sommeil [sɔmɛj] nm sleep; **avoir sommeil** to be sleepy
sommes [sɔm] vb see **être**; **Nous sommes en vacances.** We're on vacation.
sommet [sɔmɛ] nm summit
somnifère [sɔmnifɛʀ] nm sleeping pill
somptueux [sɔ̃ptɥø, -øz] (f **somptueuse**) adj sumptuous
son [sɔ̃] (f **sa**, pl **ses**) adj ❶ his ▷ son père his father ▷ Il a perdu son portefeuille. He lost his wallet. ❷ her ▷ son père her father ▷ Elle a perdu son manteau. She lost her coat.
  ▶ nm ❶ sound ▷ Le son n'est pas très bon. The sound is not very good. ▷ baisser le son to turn down the sound ❷ bran; **le pain de son** bran bread
sondage [sɔ̃daʒ] nm survey; **un sondage d'opinion** an opinion poll
sonder [sɔ̃de] vb to poll ▷ Nous avons sondé l'opinion des élèves pour savoir quelle station de radio est la plus populaire. We polled the students to find out which radio station was most popular.
sonner [sɔne] vb to ring ▷ On a sonné. Somebody rang the doorbell. ▷ Le téléphone a sonné. The phone rang.
sonnerie [sɔnʀi] nf (electric) bell ▷ La sonnerie du téléphone l'a réveillée. She was woken by the phone ringing.
sonnette [sɔnɛt] nf bell ▷ la sonnette d'alarme the alarm bell
sont [sɔ̃] vb see **être**; **Ils sont en vacances.**

They're on holiday.

sophistiqué [sɔfistike] (f **sophistiquée**) adj sophisticated

sorcier [sɔʀsje] nm wizard

sorcière [sɔʀsjɛʀ] nf witch

sort [sɔʀ] nm ● spell ▷ jeter un sort à quelqu'un to cast a spell on somebody; **un mauvais sort** a curse; **jeter un sort à quelque chose** to put a jinx on something ● fate ▷ abandonner quelqu'un à son triste sort to leave somebody to their fate; **tirer au sort** to draw lots

sorte [sɔʀt(ə)] nf sort ▷ C'est une sorte de gâteau. It's a sort of cake. ▷ toutes sortes de choses all sorts of things

sortie [sɔʀti] nf way out ▷ Où est la sortie? Where's the way out?; **la sortie de secours** the emergency exit; **une sortie éducative** a field trip

sortir [sɔʀtiʀ] vb ● to go out ▷ Elle est sortie sans rien dire. She went out without saying a word. ▷ Il est sorti acheter un journal. He's gone out to buy a newspaper. ▷ J'aime sortir. I like going out. ● to come out ▷ Elle sort de l'hôpital demain. She's coming out of the hospital tomorrow. ▷ Je l'ai rencontré en sortant de la pharmacie. I met him coming out of the drugstore. ▷ Ce modèle vient juste de sortir. This model has just come out. ● to take out ▷ Elle a sorti son porte-monnaie de son sac. She took her wallet out of her purse. ▷ Je vais sortir la voiture du garage. I'll get the car out of the garage.; **sortir avec quelqu'un** to be going out with somebody ▷ Tu sors avec lui? Are you going out with him?; **s'en sortir** to manage ▷ Ne t'en fais pas, tu t'en sortiras. Don't worry, you'll manage OK.

sottise [sɔtiz] nf: **Ne fais pas de sottises.** Don't do anything silly.; **Ne dis pas de sottises.** Don't talk nonsense.

sou [su] nm (informal) cent ▷ Les tranches de pizza ne coûtent que quatre-vingt-neuf sous aujourd'hui. Pizza slices are only 89 cents today.; **Je n'ai pas un sou sur moi.** I haven't got a penny on me.; **être près de ses sous** (informal) to be tight-fisted

souci [susi] nm worry; **se faire du souci** to worry

soucieux [susjø, -øz] (f **soucieuse**) adj worried ▷ Tu as l'air soucieux. You look worried.

soucoupe [sukup] nf saucer; **une soucoupe volante** a flying saucer

soudain [sudɛ̃, -ɛn] (f **soudaine**) adj, adv ● sudden ▷ une douleur soudaine a sudden pain ● suddenly ▷ Soudain, il s'est fâché. Suddenly he got angry.

souffle [sufl(ə)] nm breath; **à bout de souffle** out of breath

soufflé [sufle] nm soufflé ▷ un soufflé au fromage a cheese soufflé

souffler [sufle] vb ● to blow ▷ Le vent soufflait fort. The wind was blowing hard. ● to blow out ▷ Souffle les bougies! Blow out the candles!

souffleuse [sufløz] nf snowblower ▷ Mon père a passé la souffleuse pour déneiger l'entrée. My father used the snowblower to clear the driveway.

souffrance [sufʀɑ̃s] nf suffering

souffrant [sufʀɑ̃, -ɑ̃t] (f **souffrante**) adj unwell

souffrir [sufʀiʀ] vb to be in pain ▷ Elle souffre beaucoup. She's in a lot of pain.

souhait [swɛ] nm wish ▷ faire un souhait to make a wish ▷ Tous nos souhaits de réussite. All our best wishes for your success. ▷ les souhaits de bonne année New Year's wishes; **« Atchoum! »** **« À tes souhaits! »** "Atchoo!" "Bless you!"

souhaiter [swete] vb to wish ▷ Je souhaite aller à l'université. I wish to go to university. ▷ Nous vous souhaitons une bonne année. We wish you a happy New Year.

soûl [su, sul] (f **soûle**) adj (informal) drunk

soulager [sulaʒe] vb to relieve

soulever [sulve] vb ● to lift ▷ Je n'arrive pas à soulever cette valise. I can't lift this suitcase. ● to raise ▷ Il faudra soulever la question lors de la réunion. We'll have to raise the matter at the meeting.; **soulever un bon point** to make a good point

soulier [sulje] nm shoe

souligner [suliɲe] vb to underline

soupçon [supsɔ̃] nm suspicion; **un soupçon de** a dash of ▷ Ajoutez un soupçon de crème. Add a dash of cream.

soupçonner [supsɔne] vb to suspect

soupe [sup] nf soup ▷ la soupe au poulet et aux nouilles chicken noodle soup

souper [supe] nm supper ▷ Qu'est-ce qu'il y a pour souper? What's for supper?
▶ vb to have supper

soupir [supiʀ] nm sigh

soupirer [supiʀe] vb to sigh

souple [supl(ə)] adj flexible

source [suʀs(ə)] nf spring ▷ l'eau de source spring water

sourcil [suʀsij] nm eyebrow

sourd [suʀ, suʀd(ə)] (f **sourde**) adj deaf

souriant [suʀjɑ̃, -ɑ̃t] (f **souriante**) adj cheerful

sourire [suʀiʀ] nm smile; **avoir le sourire fendu jusqu'aux oreilles** to grin from ear to ear
▶ vb to smile ▷ sourire à quelqu'un to smile at somebody

souris [suʀi] nf (also computer) mouse

sournois [suʀnwa, -waz] (f **sournoise**) adj sly

sous [su] prep under; **sous terre** underground; **sous la pluie** in the rain

sous-entendu [suzɑ̃tɑ̃dy] (f **sous-entendue**) adj implied
▶ nm insinuation

sous-marin [sumaʀɛ̃, -in] (f **sous-marine**) adj underwater
▶ nm ● submarine ▷ un sous-marin nucléaire a nuclear submarine ● (sandwich) sub ▷ un sous-marin bacon, laitue et tomates a BLT sub

sous-produit [supʀɔdɥi] nm by-product

sous-sol [susɔl] nm basement

sous-titre [sutitʀ(ə)] nm subtitle

sous-titré [sutitʀe] (f **sous-titrée**) adj with subtitles

soustraction [sustʀaksjɔ̃] nf subtraction

soustraire [sustʀɛʀ] vb to subtract

sous-vêtements [suvɛtmã] *nmpl* underwear

soutenir [sutniʀ] *vb* to support ▷ *Il m'a toujours soutenu.* He's always supported me.; **soutenir que** to maintain that ▷ *Elle soutenait que c'était impossible.* She maintained that it was impossible.; **soutenir l'allure** to keep up ▷ *Elle marchait trop vite et je n'arrivais pas à soutenir l'allure.* She was walking too fast and I couldn't keep up.

souterrain [sutɛʀɛ̃, -ɛn] (*f* **souterraine**) *adj* underground
  ▶ *nm* underground passage

soutien [sutjɛ̃] *nm* support

soutien-gorge [sutjɛ̃gɔʀʒ(ə)] (*pl* **soutiens-gorge**) *nm* bra

souvenir [suvniʀ] *nm* ❶ memory ▷ *garder un bon souvenir de quelque chose* to have happy memories of something ❷ souvenir; **Garde ce livre en souvenir de moi.** Keep this book to remember me by.; **le jour du Souvenir** Remembrance Day
  ▶ *vb*: **se souvenir de quelque chose** to remember something ▷ *Je ne me souviens pas de son adresse.* I can't remember his address.; **se souvenir que** to remember that ▷ *Je me souviens qu'il neigeait.* I remember it was snowing.

souvent [suvã] *adv* often

souveraineté [suvʀɛnte] *nf* sovereignty ▷ *Êtes-vous en faveur de la souveraineté du Québec?* Are you in favour of Québec sovereignty?

souverainiste [suvʀɛnist] *nmf* sovereigntist

soya [soja] *nm* soya; **des germes de soya** bean sprouts; **du lait de soya** soy milk

soyez, soyons *vb see* **être**

spacieux [spasjø, -øz] (*f* **spacieuse**) *adj* spacious

spaghettis [spageti] *nmpl* spaghetti

spécial [spesjal, -o] (*f* **spéciale**, *mpl* **spéciaux**) *adj* ❶ special ▷ « *Qu'est-ce que tu fais en fin de semaine?* » « *Rien de spécial.* » "What are you doing this weekend?" "Nothing special."; **les effets spéciaux** special effects ❷ peculiar ▷ *Elle a des goûts un peu spéciaux.* She has rather peculiar tastes.

spécialement [spesjalmã] *adv* ❶ specially ▷ *Il est venu spécialement pour te parler.* He came specially to speak to you. ❷ particularly ▷ *Ce n'est pas spécialement difficile.* It's not particularly difficult.

se spécialiser [spesjalize] *vb*: **se spécialiser dans quelque chose** to specialize in something ▷ *Je vais me spécialiser dans biologie marine.* I'm going to specialize in marine biology.

spécialiste [spesjalist(ə)] *nmf* specialist

spécialité [spesjalite] *nf* specialty

spécifier [spesifje] *vb* to specify

spectacle [spɛktakl(ə)] *nm* show

spectaculaire [spɛktakylɛʀ] *adj* spectacular

spectateur [spɛktatœʀ] *nm* ❶ member of the audience ❷ spectator

spectatrice [spɛktatʀis] *nf* ❶ member of the audience ❷ spectator

spermophile [spɛʀmɔfil] *nm* gopher

spirituel [spiʀitɥɛl] (*f* **spirituelle**) *adj* ❶ spiritual ❷ witty

splendide [splãdid] *adj* magnificent

spontané [spɔ̃tane] (*f* **spontanée**) *adj* spontaneous

sport [spɔʀ] *nm* sport ▷ *faire du sport* to do sports; **les sports d'hiver** winter sports; **le sport extrême** extreme sport (*f+pl* **sport**)
  ▶ *adj* casual ▷ *une veste sport* a casual jacket

sportif [spɔʀtif, -iv] (*f* **sportive**) *adj* ❶ athletic ▷ *Elle est très sportive.* She's very athletic. ❷ sports ▷ *un club sportif* a sports club
  ▶ *nm* sportsman

sportive [spɔʀtiv] *nf* sportswoman

squelette [skəlɛt] *nm* skeleton

SRAS [sʀas] *nm* = **syndrome respiratoire aigu sévère** SARS

stable [stabl(ə)] *adj* stable; **un emploi stable** a steady job

stade [stad] *nm* stadium

stage [staʒ] *nm* ❶ training course ▷ *faire un stage de formation professionnelle* to take a vocational training course ❷ co-op placement ▷ *Il a fait un stage dans une bibliothèque.* He did a co-op placement in a library.; **faire un stage en entreprise** to do a work placement

stagiaire [staʒjɛʀ] *nmf* trainee

stampede [stampid] *nm*: **le Stampede de Calgary** Calgary Stampede

stand [stãd] *nm* ❶ (*at exhibition*) booth ❷ (*at fair*) stall

standardiste [stãdaʀdist(ə)] *nmf* operator

station [stasjɔ̃] *nf*: **une station de métro** a subway station; **une station de taxis** a taxi stand; **une station de ski** a ski resort

stationnement [stasjɔnmã] *nm* ❶ parking ❷ parking lot; « **stationnement interdit** » "no parking"

stationner [stasjɔne] *vb* to park ▷ *J'ai stationné la voiture dans la rue.* I parked the car on the street.; **se stationner** to park ▷ *Elle s'est stationnée dans la rue.* She's parked on the street.

station-service [stasjɔ̃sɛʀvis] (*pl* **stations-service**) *nf* service station

statistique [statistik] *nf* ❶ statistic ▷ *Voici des statistiques sur les exportations canadiennes.* Here are some statistics on Canadian exports. ❷ (*the science*) statistics

steak [stɛk] *nm* steak; **un steak haché** a hamburger patty; **le steak haché** hamburger meat ▷ *J'ai acheté du steak haché.* I bought some hamburger meat.

stérile [steʀil] *adj* sterile

stimulant [stimylã, -ãt] (*f* **stimulante**) *adj* stimulating

stimuler [stimyle] *vb* to stimulate

stopper [stɔpe] *vb* to stop

store [stɔʀ] *nm* (*on window*) blind ▷ *un store horizontal* horizontal blinds ▷ *Toutes les fenêtres ont des stores verticaux.* All the windows have vertical blinds.

stratégie [stʀateʒi] *nf* strategy

stratégique [stʀateʒik] *adj* strategic

stressant [stʀesã, -ãt] (*f* **stressante**) *adj*

stressful

stressé [stʁese] (f **stressée**) adj stressed out

strict [stʁikt(ə)] (f **stricte**) adj ❶ (person) strict ▷ Mon prof de français est très strict. My French teacher's very strict. ❷ (clothes) plain ▷ une tenue très stricte a very plain outfit; **le strict minimum** the bare minimum

strophe [stʁɔf] nf stanza

studieux [stydjø, -øz] (f **studieuse**) adj studious

studio [stydjo] nm ❶ studio apartment ▷ studio ▷ un studio de télévision a television studio ▷ un studio de peintre a painter's studio

stupéfait [stypefε, -εt] (f **stupéfaite**) adj astonished

stupéfiants [stypefjɑ̃] nmpl narcotics

stupéfier [stypefje] vb to astonish ▷ Sa réponse m'a stupéfié. I was astonished by his answer.

stupide [stypid] adj stupid

style [stil] nm style

styliste [stilist(ə)] nmf designer

stylo [stilo] nm pen; **un stylo plume** a fountain pen; **un stylo à bille** a ballpoint pen; **un stylo-feutre** a felt pen

su [sy] vb see **savoir**; Si j'avais su... If I'd known...

subir [sybiʁ] vb (defeat) to suffer; **subir une opération** to have an operation

subit [sybi, -it] (f **subite**) adj sudden

subitement [sybitmɑ̃] adv suddenly

subjectif [sybʒεktif, -iv] (f **subjective**) adj subjective

subjonctif [sybʒɔ̃ktif] nm subjunctive

substituer [sypstitɥe] vb to substitute ▷ substituer un mot à un autre to substitute one word for another

subtil [syptil] (f **subtile**) adj subtle

subvention [sybvɑ̃sjɔ̃] nf subsidy

subventionner [sybvɑ̃sjɔne] vb to subsidize

succès [syksε] nm success ▷ avoir du succès to be successful

successeur [syksesœʁ] nm successor

successeure [syksesœʁ] nf successor

succursale [sykyʁsal] nf (of company) branch

sucer [syse] vb to suck

suçon [sysɔ̃] nm lollipop

sucre [sykʁ(ə)] nm sugar ▷ « Combien de sucre dans votre café? » « Deux sucres, s'il vous plaît. » "How many sugars do you take in your coffee?" "Two, please."; **le sucre brun** brown sugar; **le sucre d'érable** maple sugar; **du sucre en cubes** sugar cubes; **un sucre d'orge** a barley sugar; **du sucre à glacer** icing sugar

sucré [sykʁe] (f **sucrée**) adj ❶ sweet ▷ Ce gâteau est un peu trop sucré. This cake is a bit too sweet. ❷ sweetened ▷ du lait concentré sucré sweetened condensed milk

sucrer [sykʁe] vb to add sugar ▷ J'ai sucré mon café. I added sugar to my coffee.; **se sucrer le bec** to eat sweets ▷ Elle adore se sucrer le bec. She loves sweets.

sucreries [sykʁəʁi] nfpl sweets

sucrier [sykʁije] nm sugar bowl

sud [syd] nm south ▷ Ils vivent dans le sud de la Colombie-Britannique. They live in the south of British Columbia.; **vers le sud** southwards; **au sud d'Edmonton** south of Edmonton; **l'Amérique du Sud** South America; **le vent du sud** the south wind

▶ adj ❶ south ▷ la côte sud de Terre-Neuve the south coast of Newfoundland; **le pôle sud** the South Pole ❷ southern ▷ Nous avons visité la partie sud du pays. We visited the southern part of the country.

sud-est [sydεst] nm southeast ▷ au sud-est in the southeast

sud-ouest [sydwεst] nm southwest ▷ au sud-ouest in the southwest

suer [sɥe] vb to sweat

sueur [sɥœʁ] nf sweat; **en sueur** sweating

suffire [syfiʁ] vb to be enough ▷ Tiens, voilà dix dollars. Ça te suffit? Here's 10 dollars. Is that enough for you?; **Ça suffit!** That's enough!

suffisamment [syfizamɑ̃] adv enough ▷ Ça n'est pas suffisamment grand. It's not big enough. ▷ Il n'y a pas suffisamment de chaises. There aren't enough chairs.

suffisant [syfizɑ̃, -ɑ̃t] (f **suffisante**) adj ❶ good enough ▷ Ça n'est pas une raison suffisante. That's not a good enough reason. ❷ smug ▷ Il est un peu trop suffisant. He's a bit too smug.

suffoquer [syfɔke] vb to suffocate

suggérer [sygʒeʁe] vb to suggest

se suicider [sɥiside] vb to commit suicide

suis [sɥi] vb see **être**; **suivre**; **Je suis rapide.** I'm fast.; **Suis-moi.** Follow me.

suisse [sɥis] nm chipmunk

suite [sɥit] nf ❶ rest ▷ Je vous raconterai la suite de l'histoire demain. I'll tell you the rest of the story tomorrow. ❷ (to book, film) sequel; **tout de suite** right away ▷ J'y vais tout de suite. I'll go right away.; **de suite** in a row ▷ Il a commis la même erreur trois fois de suite. He made the same mistake three times in a row.; **par la suite** later ▷ Elle s'est avérée par la suite qu'elle était coupable. She later turned out to be guilty.

suivant [sɥivɑ̃, -ɑ̃t] (f **suivante**) adj following ▷ le jour suivant the following day ▷ l'exercice suivant the following exercise; **Au suivant!** Next!

suivre [sɥivʁ(ə)] vb ❶ to follow ▷ Il m'a suivie jusque chez moi. He followed me home. ▷ Vous me suivez ou est-ce que je parle trop vite? Are you following me, or am I talking too fast? ❷ (course) to take ▷ Elle suit un cours d'anglais au collège. She's taking an English course at college. ❸ to keep up ▷ Il n'arrive pas à suivre en maths. He can't keep up in math. ▷ J'aime suivre l'actualité. I like to keep up with the news.; **« à suivre »** "to be continued"; **suivre un régime** to be on a diet

sujet [syʒε, -εt] (f **sujette**) adj: **être sujet à** to be prone to ▷ Il est sujet au vertige. He suffers from fear of heights.

▶ nm subject; **au sujet de** about ▷ « C'est à quel sujet? » « C'est au sujet de l'annonce parue dans le Globe and Mail d'aujourd'hui. » "What's it about?" "It's about the advertisement in today's Globe and Mail."; **un sujet de conversation** a topic of conversation; **un**

sujet d'examen an examination question; **un sujet de plaisanterie** something to joke about

super [sypɛʀ] *adj* great ▷ *C'est super que tu puisses venir avec nous!* It's great that you can come with us!

superficiel [sypɛʀfisjɛl] (*f* **superficielle**) *adj* superficial

superflu [sypɛʀfly] (*f* **superflue**) *adj* superfluous

supérieur [ŝypeʀjœʀ] (*f* **supérieure**) *adj* ● upper ▷ *la lèvre supérieure* the upper lip ● superior ▷ *qualité supérieure* superior quality ▷ *Ne me parle pas sur ce ton supérieur.* Don't talk to me in that superior tone of voice.; **supérieur à** greater than ▷ *Choisissez un nombre supérieur à cent.* Choose a number greater than 100.

supermarché [sypɛʀmaʀʃe] *nm* supermarket

superposé [sypɛʀpoze] (*f* **superposée**) *adj*: **des lits superposés** bunk beds

superstitieux [sypɛʀstisjø, -øz] (*f* **superstitieuse**) *adj* superstitious

suppléant [sypleã] *nm* substitute teacher

suppléante [sypleãt] *nf* substitute teacher

supplément [syplemã] *nm*: **payer un supplément** to pay an additional charge; **Le toit ouvrant est en supplément.** The sunroof is extra.; **un supplément de travail** extra work

supplémentaire [syplemãtɛʀ] *adj* additional ▷ *Voici quelques exercices supplémentaires.* Here are some additional exercises.; **faire des heures supplémentaires** to work some overtime

supplice [syplis] *nm* torture ▷ *C'était un supplice.* It was torture.

supplier [syplije] *vb*: **supplier quelqu'un de faire quelque chose** to beg somebody to do something ▷ *Je t'en supplie!* I'm begging you!

supportable [sypɔʀtabl(ə)] *adj* bearable

supporter [sypɔʀte] *vb* (tolerate) to stand ▷ *Je ne supporte pas l'hypocrisie.* I can't stand hypocrisy. ▷ *Elle ne supporte pas qu'on la critique.* She can't stand being criticized. ▷ *Je ne peux pas la supporter.* I can't stand her. ▷ *Je ne supporte mal la chaleur.* I can't stand hot weather.

supposer [sypoze] *vb* to suppose

supprimer [sypʀime] *vb* ● to cut ▷ *Deux mille emplois ont été supprimés.* Two thousand jobs have been cut. ● to cancel ▷ *L'autobus de Nelson a été supprimé.* The bus to Nelson has been cancelled. ● to get rid of ▷ *Ils ont supprimé les témoins de l'enlèvement.* They got rid of the witnesses to the kidnapping. ● to delete ▷ *Elle a supprimé quelques vieux fichiers.* She deleted some old files.

suprême [sypʀɛm] *adj* supreme ▷ *la Cour suprême* the Supreme Court

sur [syʀ] *prep* ● on ▷ *Pose-le sur la table.* Put it on the table. ● *Vous verrez l'hôpital sur votre droite.* You'll see the hospital on your right. ▷ *une conférence sur l'écologie* a lecture on ecology ● in ▷ *une personne sur dix* 1 person in 10 ● out of ▷ *J'ai eu neuf sur dix en maths.* I got 9 out of 10 in math. ● by ▷ *quatre mètres sur deux* 4 metres by 2

sûr [syʀ] (*f* **sûre**) *adj* ● sure ▷ *Tu es sûr?* Are you sure?; **sûr et certain** absolutely certain ● reliable ▷ *C'est quelqu'un de très sûr.* He's a very reliable person. ● safe ▷ *Ce quartier n'est pas très sûr la nuit.* This neighbourhood isn't very safe at night.; **sûr de soi** self-confident ▷ *Elle est très sûre d'elle.* She's very self-confident.

surdose [syʀdoz] *nf* overdose

sûrement [syʀmã] *adv* certainly ▷ *Sûrement pas!* Certainly not! ▷ *Il est sûrement déjà parti.* He's sure to have already left.

sûreté [syʀte] *nf*: **mettre quelque chose en sûreté** to put something in a safe place

surf [sœʀf] *nm* surfing; **le surf des neiges** snow surfing

surface [syʀfas] *nf* surface; **les grandes surfaces** the supermarkets

surfaceuse [syʀfasøz] *nf* Zamboni®

surfer [sœʀfe] *vb* to go surfing; **surfer sur Internet** to surf the Net

surgelé [syʀʒale] (*f* **surgelée**) *adj* frozen ▷ *des frites surgelées* frozen fries

surgelés [syʀʒale] *nmpl* frozen foods

surhumain [syʀymɛ̃, -ɛn] (*f* **surhumaine**) *adj* superhuman

surintendant [syʀɛ̃tãdã] *nm* superintendent ▷ *Son père est surintendant de police.* Her father is a police superintendent.

surintendante [syʀɛ̃tãdãt] *nf* superintendent ▷ *Sa mère est surintendante scolaire.* His mother is a school superintendent.

sur-le-champ [syʀlaʃã] *adv* immediately

surlendemain [syʀlãdmɛ̃] *nm*: **le surlendemain de son arrivée** two days after she arrived; **le surlendemain dans la matinée** two days later, in the morning

se surmener [syʀmane] *vb* to work too hard ▷ *Ne te surmène pas trop pendant la fin de semaine.* Don't work too hard over the weekend.

surmonter [syʀmõte] *vb* to overcome ▷ *Il nous reste de nombreux obstacles à surmonter.* We still have many obstacles to overcome.

surnaturel [syʀnatyʀɛl] (*f* **surnaturelle**) *adj* supernatural

surnom [syʀnõ] *nm* nickname

surnommer [syʀnɔme] *vb* to nickname ▷ *On l'a surnommé « la bolle des maths ».* We nicknamed him "the math whiz".

surpeuplé [syʀpœple] (*f* **surpeuplée**) *adj* overpopulated

surprenant [syʀpʀanã, -ãt] (*f* **surprenante**) *adj* surprising

surprendre [syʀpʀãdʀ(ə)] *vb* to surprise ▷ *Ça me surprendrait beaucoup qu'elle arrive à l'heure.* I'd be very surprised if she arrived on time.; **surprendre quelqu'un en train de faire quelque chose** to catch somebody doing something ▷ *Je l'ai surpris en train de fouiller dans mon casier.* I caught him rummaging in my locker.

surpris [syʀpʀi, -iz] (*f* **surprise**) *adj* surprised ▷ *Elle était surprise de me voir.* She was surprised to see me.

surprise [syʀpʀiz] *nf* surprise ▷ *faire une surprise à quelqu'un* to give somebody a surprise

sursauter [syʀsote] *vb* to jump ▷ *J'ai sursauté en entendant mon nom.* I jumped when I heard my name.

surtout [syʀtu] *adv* ❶ especially ▷ *Il est assez timide, surtout avec les filles.* He's rather shy, especially with girls. ❷ above all ▷ *Ce manteau est bon marché, pratique et, surtout, paraît bien.* This coat is reasonably priced, practical, and above all great-looking. ▷ *Surtout, ne répète pas ce que je t'ai dit!* Whatever you do, don't repeat what I told you!

surveiller [syʀveje] *vb* ❶ to keep an eye on ▷ *Tu peux surveiller mes bagages?* Can you keep an eye on my luggage? ❷ to keep a watch on ▷ *La police a surveillé la maison pendant une semaine.* The police kept the house under surveillance for a week. ❸ to supervise ▷ *Nous sommes toujours surveillés pendant la récréation.* We're always supervised during recess.; **surveiller sa ligne** to watch one's figure

survêtement [syʀvɛtmɑ̃] *nm* track suit ▷ *un haut de survêtement* a track top ▷ *un pantalon de survêtement* track pants

survie [syʀvi] *nf* survival

survivant [syʀvivɑ̃] *nm* survivor

survivante [syʀvivɑ̃t] *nf* survivor

survivre [syʀvivʀ(ə)] *vb* to survive ▷ *survivre à un accident* to survive an accident

survoler [syʀvɔle] *vb* to fly over

sus [sy] *adv*: **en sus** in addition

susceptible [syseptibl(ə)] *adj* touchy

suspect [syspɛ(kt), -ɛkt(ə)] (*f* **suspecte**) *adj* suspicious ▷ *dans des circonstances suspectes* under suspicious circumstances

suspecter [syspɛkte] *vb* to suspect

suspense [syspɑ̃s] *nm* suspense; **un film à suspense** a thriller

suture [sytyʀ] *nf*: **un point de suture** a stitch

svelte [svɛlt(ə)] *adj* slender

SVP *abbr* (= *s'il vous plaît*) please

syllabe [silab] *nf* syllable

symbole [sɛ̃bɔl] *nm* symbol

symbolique [sɛ̃bɔlik] *adj* symbolic

symboliser [sɛ̃bɔlize] *vb* to symbolize

symétrique [simetʀik] *adj* symmetrical

sympathie [sɛ̃pati] *nf*: *J'ai beaucoup de sympathie pour lui.* I like him a lot.

sympathique [sɛ̃patik] *adj* nice ▷ *Ce sont des gens très sympathiques.* They're very nice people.

sympathiser [sɛ̃patize] *vb* to get along well ▷ *Nous avons immédiatement sympathisé avec nos voisins.* We hit it off with our neighbours right away.

symptôme [sɛ̃ptom] *nm* symptom

synagogue [sinagɔg] *nf* synagogue

syndicat [sɛ̃dika] *nm* trade union

syndrome [sɛ̃dʀom] *nm* syndrome; **le syndrome de Down** Down syndrome; **le syndrome respiratoire aigu sévère** Severe Acute Respiratory Syndrome

synonyme [sinɔnim] *adj* synonymous ▷ *être synonyme de* to be synonymous with ▷ *nm* synonym

synthétique [sɛ̃tetik] *adj* synthetic

syntoniser [sɛ̃tɔnize] *vb* (*radio*) to tune ▷ *J'ai syntonisé la radio sur Radio-Canada.* I tuned the radio to CBC.

systématique [sistematik] *adj* systematic

système [sistɛm] *nm* system; **le système d'exploitation** DOS (disk operating system)

t

t' [t(ə)] *pron see* **te**

ta [ta] *adj* your ▷ *J'ai vu ta sœur hier.* I saw your sister yesterday.

tabac [taba] *nm* ❶ tobacco ▷ *Le tabac est originaire d'Amérique.* Tobacco is native to America. ❷ smoking ▷ *Le tabac est mauvais pour la santé.* Smoking is bad for you.

table [tabl(ə)] *nf* table; **mettre la table** to set the table; **se mettre à table** to sit down to eat; **À table!** Dinner's ready!; **une table de jeu** card table; **une table de nuit** a night table; **table des matières** table of contents

tableau [tablo] (*pl* **tableaux**) *nm* ❶ painting ▷ *un tableau de Monet* a painting by Monet; **le tableau d'affichage** the notice board; **le tableau noir** the chalkboard ❷ chart

tablette [tablɛt] *nf*: **une tablette de chocolat** a bar of chocolate

tableur [tablœʀ] *nm* spreadsheet

tablier [tablije] *nm* apron

tabloïd [tablɔid] *nm* tabloid

tabouret [tabuʀɛ] *nm* stool

tache [taʃ] *nf* (*stain*) mark; **des taches de rousseur** freckles

tâche [taʃ] *nf* task

tacher [taʃe] *vb* to leave a stain

tâcher [taʃe] *vb*: **tâcher de faire quelque chose** to try to do something ▷ *Tâche d'être à l'heure!* Try to be on time!

tactique [taktik] *nf* tactics; **changer de tactique** to try something different

taie [tɛ] *nf*: **une taie d'oreiller** a pillowcase

taille [taj] *nf* ❶ waist ▷ *avoir la taille fine* to have a slim waist ❷ height ▷ *Ils sont de la même taille.* They are the same height. ❸ size ▷ *Avez-vous ma taille?* Have you got my size?

taille-crayon [tajkʀɛjɔ̃] *nm* pencil sharpener

tailleur [tajœʀ] *nm* ❶ tailor ❷ (*women's*) suit; **Il est assis en tailleur.** He's sitting cross-legged.

se taire [tɛʀ] *vb* to stop talking; **Taisez-vous!** Be quiet!

talent [talɑ̃] *nm* talent ▷ *Elle a le talent de mettre les gens à l'aise.* She has a talent for putting people at ease.; **avoir du talent** to have talent

talentueux [talɑ̃tɥø, -øz] (f **talentueuse**) adj talented

talle [tal] nf patch of shrubs or berries ▷ *une talle de bleuets* a patch of blueberries

talon [talɔ̃] nm heel; **les talons hauts** high heels

tambour [tɑ̃buʀ] nm drum

tampon [tɑ̃pɔ̃] nm pad ▷ *un tampon à récurer* a scouring pad; **un tampon hygiénique** a tampon

tandis que [tɑ̃di-] conj while ▷ *Elle a toujours de bonnes notes, tandis que les miennes sont mauvaises.* She always gets good marks, while mine are poor.

tant [tɑ̃] adv so much ▷ *Je l'aime tant!* I love him so much!; **tant de (1)** so much ▷ *tant de nourriture* so much food **(2)** so many ▷ *tant de livres* so many books; **tant pis (1)** never mind **(2)** too bad; **tant que (1)** until ▷ *Tu ne sortiras pas tant que tu n'auras pas fini tes devoirs.* You're not going out until you've finished your homework. **(2)** while ▷ *Profites-en tant que tu peux.* Make the most of it while you can.; **tant mieux** so much the better; **tant pis** never mind

tante [tɑ̃t] nf aunt

tantôt [tɑ̃to] adv sometimes ▷ *Nous venons tantôt à pied, tantôt en autobus.* Sometimes we walk, sometimes we come by bus.

tapage [tapaʒ] nm ❶ racket ▷ *Ils ont fait du tapage toute la nuit.* They made a racket all night long. ❷ fuss ▷ *On a fait beaucoup de tapage autour de cette affaire.* There was a lot of fuss about that business.

taper [tape] vb ❶ to beat down ▷ *Le soleil tape.* The sun's really beating down.; **taper quelqu'un** to hit somebody ▷ *Maman, elle m'a tapé dessus!* Mom, she hit me!; **taper sur quelque chose** to bang on something; **taper des pieds** to stamp one's feet; **taper des mains** to clap one's hands ❷ to type ▷ *Tapez votre mot de passe.* Type your password.

tapis [tapi] nm carpet; **le tapis roulant (1)** the moving sidewalk **(2)** (*in factory*) the conveyor belt; **un tapis de souris** a mouse pad

tapisser [tapise] vb to paper

tapisserie [tapisʀi] nf ❶ wallpaper ▷ *Tu aimes la tapisserie de ma chambre?* Do you like the wallpaper in my bedroom? ❷ tapestry

tapoter [tapɔte] vb ❶ to pat ▷ *Elle lui a tapoté l'épaule affectueusement.* She patted his shoulder affectionately. ❷ to tap ▷ *Il tapotait impatiemment sur la table.* He was tapping impatiently on the table.

taquiner [takine] vb to tease

tard [taʀ] adv late ▷ *Il est tard.* It's late.; **plus tard** later on; **au plus tard** at the latest

tardif [taʀdif, -iv] (f **tardive**) adj late ▷ *un petit lunch tardif* a late breakfast

tarif [taʀif] nm: **payer plein tarif** to pay full price; **payer le tarif étudiant** to pay the student rate; **le tarif horaire** hourly rate

tarte [taʀt(ə)] nf pie; **tarte au sucre** sugar pie

tartelette [taʀtəlɛt] nf tart ▷ *une tartelette aux raisins secs* butter tart

tartine [taʀtin] nf slice of bread ▷ *une tartine de confiture* a slice of bread and jam

tartiner [taʀtine] vb to spread; **le fromage à tartiner** cheese spread

tas [tɑ] nm heap ▷ *un tas de sable* a heap of sand; **un tas de** (*informal*) a ton of ▷ *J'ai lu un tas de livres pendant les vacances.* I read a ton of books on the holidays.

tasse [tɑs] nf cup

taureau [tɔʀo] (pl **taureaux**) nm bull; **le Taureau** Taurus ▷ *Ils sont tous les deux Taureau.* They are both Tauruses.

taux [to] nm rate ▷ *le taux de change* the exchange rate

taxe [taks(ə)] nf tax

taxi [taksi] nm taxi; **la station de taxi** taxi stand

te [t(ə)] pron ❶ you ▷ *Je te vois.* I can see you. ▷ *Elle t'a vu?* Did she see you? ❷ to you ▷ *Est-ce qu'il te parle en français?* Does he talk to you in French? ▷ *Elle t'a parlé?* Did she speak to you? ❸ yourself ▷ *Tu vas te rendre malade.* You'll make yourself sick. ▷ *Comment tu t'appelles?* What's your name?

technicien [tɛknisjɛ̃] nm technician

technicienne [tɛknisjɛn] nf technician

technique [tɛknik] adj technical
▶ nf technique

techno [tɛkno] nf techno music

technologie [tɛknɔlɔʒi] nf technology

teindre [tɛ̃dʀ(ə)] vb to dye; **se teindre les cheveux** to dye one's hair

teint [tɛ̃] nm complexion ▷ *avoir le teint clair* to have a clear complexion

teinte [tɛ̃t] nf (*colour*) shade

teinté [tɛ̃te] adj tinted ▷ *des lunettes teintées* tinted glasses

tel [tɛl] (f **telle**) adj: **Il a un tel enthousiasme!** He's got such enthusiasm!; **rien de tel** nothing like ▷ *Il n'y a rien de tel qu'une bonne nuit de sommeil.* There's nothing like a good night's sleep.; **J'ai tout laissé tel quel.** I left everything as it was.; **tel que** such as

télé [tele] nf TV ▷ *à la télé* on TV

téléavertisseur [teleavɛʀtisœʀ] nm pager

télécarte [telekaʀt(ə)] nf phonecard

téléchargement [teleʃaʀʒəmɑ̃] nm download/downloading; **un téléchargement vers le serveur** an upload

télécharger [teleʃaʀʒe] vb to download; **télécharger vers le serveur** to upload

télécommande [telekɔmɑ̃d] nf remote control

téléconférence [telekɔ̃feʀɑ̃s] nf video conference

télécopie [telekɔpi] nf fax

télécopier [telekɔpje] vb to fax

télécopieur [telekɔpjœʀ] nm fax machine

téléphérique [telefeʀik] nm cable car

téléphone [telefɔn] nm telephone ▷ *Elle est au téléphone.* She's on the phone.; **un téléphone cellulaire** cellphone

téléphoner [telefɔne] vb to phone ▷ *Je vais lui téléphoner.* I'll phone her. ▷ *Je peux téléphoner?* Can I make a phone call?

téléphonique [telefɔnik] adj: **une carte**

téléphonique prépayée a prepaid phone card; **un appel téléphonique** a phone call

téléphoniste [telefɔnist(ə)] nmf (telephone) operator

téléroman [teleʀɔmã] nm soap opera

télésiège [telesjɛʒ] nm chairlift

téléski [teleski] nm ski lift

téléspectateur [telespɛktatœʀ] nm (TV) viewer

téléspectatrice [telespɛktatʀis] nf (TV) viewer

téléviseur [televizœʀ] nm television set

télévision [televizjɔ̃] nf television ▷ **à la télévision** on television; **la télévision à haute définition** HDTV (high-definition TV); **la télévision numérique** digital TV

telle [tɛl] adj: **Je n'ai jamais eu une telle peur.** I've never been so scared.; **telle que** such as

tellement [tɛlmã] adv ❶ so ▷ **Il est tellement gentil.** He's so nice. ▷ **Il travaille tellement.** He works so hard. ❷ so much ▷ **J'ai tellement mangé que…** I ate so much that… ❸ so many ▷ **Il y avait tellement de monde.** There were so many people.

telles [tɛl] adj such ▷ **Je n'ai jamais entendu de telles niaiseries!** I've never heard such nonsense!

tels [tɛl] adj such ▷ **Nous n'avons pas de tels orages chez nous.** We don't have such storms back home.

témoignage [temwaɲaʒ] nm testimony

témoigner [temwaɲe] vb to testify

témoin [temwɛ̃] nmf witness

température [tãpeʀatyʀ] nf temperature ▷ **avoir de la température** to have a temperature

tempête [tãpɛt] nf storm

temple [tãpl(ə)] nm ❶ (Protestant) church ❷ (Hindu, Sikh, Buddhist) temple

temporaire [tãpɔʀɛʀ] adj temporary

temps [tã] nm ❶ weather ▷ **Quel temps fait-il?** What's the weather like? ❷ time ▷ **Je n'ai pas le temps.** I don't have time. ▷ **Prends ton temps.** Take your time. ▷ **Il est temps de partir.** It's time to go.; **juste le temps** just in time; **de temps en temps** from time to time; **en même temps** at the same time; **à temps** in time ▷ **Nous sommes arrivés à temps pour le match.** We arrived in time for the game.; **à plein temps** full time ▷ **Elle travaille à plein temps.** She works full time.; **à temps complet** full time; **à temps partiel** part time ▷ **le travail à temps partiel** part-time work; **dans le temps** at one time ▷ **Dans le temps, on pouvait circuler en vélo sans danger.** At one time, it was safe to go around by bike. ❸ (of verb) tense

tenais, tenait vb see **tenir**

tendance [tãdãs] nf: **avoir tendance à faire quelque chose** to tend to do something ▷ **Elle a tendance à exagérer.** She tends to exaggerate.

tendre [tãdʀ(ə)] adj tender ▶ vb to stretch out ▷ **Ils ont tendu une corde entre deux arbres.** They stretched a rope between two trees.; **tendre quelque chose à quelqu'un** to hold something out to somebody ▷ **Il lui a tendu les clés.** He held out the keys to her.; **tendre la main** to hold out one's hand; **tendre le bras** to reach out; **tendre un piège à**

quelqu'un to set a trap for someone

tendresse [tãdʀɛs] nf tenderness

tendu [tãdy] (f **tendue**) adj tense ▷ **Il était très tendu aujourd'hui.** He was very tense today.

tenir [təniʀ] vb to hold ▷ **Tu peux tenir la lampe de poche, s'il te plaît?** Can you hold the flashlight, please? ▷ **Elle tenait un enfant par la main.** She was holding a child by the hand.; **Tenez votre chien en laisse.** Keep your dog on the leash.; **tenir à quelqu'un** to be attached to somebody ▷ **Il tient beaucoup à elle.** He's very attached to her.; **tenir à faire quelque chose** to be determined to do something ▷ **Il tient à aller.** He's determined to go.; **tenir de quelqu'un** to take after somebody ▷ **Il tient de son père.** He takes after his father.; **Tiens, voilà un stylo.** Here's a pen.; **Tiens, c'est ta sœur là-bas!** Look, that's your sister over there!; **Tiens?** Really?; **se tenir (1)** to stand ▷ **Elle se tenait près de la porte.** She was standing by the door. **(2)** to be held ▷ **Le festival va se tenir au centre communautaire.** The festival will be held at the community centre.; **se tenir droit (1)** to stand up straight ▷ **Tiens-toi droit!** Stand up straight! **(2)** to sit up straight ▷ **Arrête de manger le nez dans ton assiette, tiens-toi droit.** Don't slouch while you're eating, sit up straight.; **se tenir mal** to have bad posture; **Tiens-toi bien!** Behave yourself!

tennis [tenis] nm ❶ tennis ▷ **Elle joue au tennis.** She plays tennis.; **le tennis de table** table tennis ❷ tennis court ▷ **Il est au tennis.** He's at the tennis court.

tentant [tãtã, -ãt] (f **tentante**) adj tempting

tentation [tãtasjɔ̃] nf temptation

tentative [tãtativ] nf attempt

tente [tãt] nf tent

tenter [tãte] vb to tempt ▷ **J'ai été tenté de tout abandonner.** I was tempted to give up. ▷ **Ça ne me tente vraiment pas d'aller à la piscine.** I don't really feel like going to the swimming pool.; **tenter de faire quelque chose** to try to do something ▷ **Il a tenté plusieurs fois de s'évader.** He tried several times to escape.

tenu [təny] vb see **tenir**

tenue [təny] nf clothes

terme [tɛʀm(ə)] nm: **à court terme** short-term; **à long terme** long-term

terminaison [tɛʀminɛzɔ̃] nf (on a word) ending ▷ **une terminaison féminine** a feminine ending

terminer [tɛʀmine] vb to finish; **se terminer** to end ▷ **Les vacances se terminent demain.** The holidays end tomorrow.

terrain [tɛʀɛ̃] nm land ▷ **Elle veut acheter un terrain en Ontario.** She wants to buy some land in Ontario.; **un terrain de camping** a campground; **un terrain de football** a football field; **un terrain de golf** a golf course; **un terrain de jeu** a playground

terrasse [tɛʀas] nf terrace ▷ **Si on s'asseyait à la terrasse?** (at café) Shall we sit outside?

terre [tɛʀ] nf earth; **la Terre** the Earth; **Elle s'est assise par terre.** She sat on the floor.; **Il est tombé par terre.** He fell down.; **la terre cuite** terracotta ▷ **un pot en terre cuite a**

terracotta pot; **la terre glaise** clay

Terre-Neuve [tɛʀnœv] *nf* Newfoundland
▷ *un voyage à Terre-Neuve* a trip to
Newfoundland ▷ *La capitale de Terre-Neuve est
St. John's.* The capital of Newfoundland is St.
John's.

terreur [tɛʀœʀ] *nf* terror ▷ *un régime de terreur*
a reign of terror

terrible [tɛʀibl(ə)] *adj* terrible ▷ *Quelque chose
de terrible est arrivé.* Something terrible has
happened.

territoire [tɛʀitwaʀ] *nm* territory

Territoires du Nord-Ouest *nmpl* Northwest
Territories ▷ *J'habite aux Territoires du Nord-
Ouest.* I live in the Northwest Territories.

terrorisé [tɛʀɔʀize] (*f* **terrorisée**) *adj* terrified

terrorisme [tɛʀɔʀism(ə)] *nm* terrorism

terroriste [tɛʀɔʀist(ə)] *nmf* terrorist

tes [te] *adj* your ▷ *J'aime bien tes chaussures de
course.* I like your running shoes.

test [tɛst] *nm* test

testament [tɛstamɑ̃] *nm* will ▷ *Il est mort sans
testament.* He died without leaving a will.

tester [tɛste] *vb* to test

tétanos [tetanos] *nm* tetanus

têtard [tɛtaʀ] *nm* tadpole

tête [tɛt] *nf* head ▷ *de la tête aux pieds* from
head to foot; **se laver la tête** to wash one's
hair; **la tête la première** headfirst; **tenir tête
à quelqu'un** to stand up to somebody; **en
avoir par-dessus la tête** to be fed up; **avoir la
tête sur les épaules** to be level-headed; **avoir
mal à la tête** to have a headache; **prendre la
tête** to take the lead

têtu [tety] (*f* **têtue**) *adj* stubborn ▷ *Elle est trop
têtue pour changer d'opinion.* She is too stubborn
to change her opinion.

texte [tɛkst(ə)] *nm* text

thé [te] *nm* tea ▷ *Je vous offre un thé?* Would you
like a cup of tea?

théâtre [teatʀ(ə)] *nm* theatre; **faire du
théâtre** to act ▷ *Est-ce que tu as déjà fait du
théâtre?* Have you ever acted?

théière [tejɛʀ] *nf* teapot

thème [tɛm] *nm* subject ▷ *Quel est le thème de
l'émission?* What's the program about?

théorie [teɔʀi] *nf* theory

thermomètre [tɛʀmɔmɛtʀ(ə)] *nm*
thermometer

thon [tɔ̃] *nm* tuna; **la salade de thon** tuna
salad

tibia [tibja] *nm* ❶ shinbone ▷ *une fracture du
tibia* a broken shinbone ❷ shin ▷ *Elle m'a donné
un coup de pied dans le tibia.* She kicked me in
the shin.

tic [tik] *nm* nervous twitch

ticket [tikɛ] *nm* ticket ▷ *un ticket de métro* a
subway ticket; **le ticket de caisse** the cash
register receipt

tiède [tjɛd] *adj* ❶ (water, air) warm ❷ (food,
drink) lukewarm

tien [tjɛ̃] *pron*: **le tien** yours ▷ *J'ai oublié mon
stylo. Tu peux me prêter le tien?* I forgot my pen.
Can you lend me yours?

tienne [tjɛn] *pron*: **la tienne** yours ▷ *Ce n'est
pas ma raquette, c'est la tienne.* It's not my

racquet, it's yours.

tiennes [tjɛn] *pron*: **les tiennes** yours ▷ *J'ai
pris mes lunettes de soleil, mais j'ai oublié les
tiennes.* I brought my sunglasses, but I forgot
yours.

tiens [tjɛ̃] *pron*: **les tiens** yours ▷ *Je ne trouve
pas mes feutres. Je peux utiliser les tiens?* I can't
find my markers. Can I use yours?

tiens, tient *vb see* **tenir**

tiers [tjɛʀ] *nm* third ▷ *Un tiers de la classe était
pour.* A third of the class were in favour.

tige [tiʒ] *nf* stem

tigre [tigʀ(ə)] *nm* tiger

timbre [tɛ̃bʀ(ə)] *nm* stamp

timide [timid] *adj* shy

timidement [timidmɑ̃] *adv* shyly

timidité [timidite] *nf* shyness

tirage [tiʀaʒ] *nm*: **par tirage au sort** by
drawing lots ▷ *Les prix seront attribués par tirage
au sort.* The prizes will be awarded by drawing
lots.

tire [tiʀ] *nf* taffy; **la tire d'érable** maple taffy

tire-bouchon [tiʀbuʃɔ̃] *nm* corkscrew

tirer [tiʀe] *vb* ❶ to pull ▷ *Elle a tiré un mouchoir
de son sac à main.* She pulled a handkerchief out
of her purse. ▷ *Il m'a tiré les cheveux.* He pulled
my hair. ▷ *«Tirer» "Pull"* ❷ to draw ▷ *tirer les
rideaux* to draw the curtains ▷ *tirer un trait*
to draw a line ▷ *tirer des conclusions* to draw
conclusions; **tirer au sort** to draw lots ❸ to
fire ▷ *Il a tiré plusieurs coups de feu.* He fired
several shots. ▷ *Elle a tiré sur les policiers.* She
fired at the police.

tiret [tiʀe] *nm* (hyphen) dash

tiroir [tiʀwaʀ] *nm* drawer

tisane [tizan] *nf* herbal tea

tisser [tise] *vb* to weave

tissu [tisy] *nm* material

titre [titʀ(ə)] *nm* title; **les gros titres** the
headlines

tituber [titybe] *vb* to stagger

toast [tost] *nm* piece of toast

toi [twa] *pron* you ▷ *«Ça va?» «Oui, et toi?»*
"How are you?" "Fine, and you?" ▷ *J'ai faim, pas
toi?* I'm hungry, aren't you?; **Assieds-toi.** Sit
down.; **C'est à toi de jouer.** It's your turn to
play.; **Est-ce que ce stylo est à toi?** Is this pen
yours?

toile [twal] *nf*: **un pantalon de toile** cotton
pants; **un sac de toile** a canvas bag; **une toile
d'araignée** a spiderweb

toilette [twalɛt] *nf*: **faire sa toilette** to wash
oneself; **une toilette élégante** an elegant
outfit

toilettes [twalɛt] *nfpl* washroom; **les
toilettes extérieures** outhouse

toi-même [twamɛm] *pron* yourself ▷ *Tu as fait
ça toi-même?* Did you do it yourself?

toit [twa] *nm* roof; **un toit ouvrant** a sunroof

tolérant [tɔleʀɑ̃, -ɑ̃t] (*f* **tolérante**) *adj*
tolerant

tolérer [tɔleʀe] *vb* to tolerate

tomate [tɔmat] *nf* tomato; **être rouge
comme une tomate** to be beet red

tombe [tɔ̃b] *nf* grave

tombeau [tɔ̃bo] (*pl* **tombeaux**) *nm* tomb

tombée [tɔ̃be] nf: **à la tombée de la nuit** at nightfall

tomber [tɔ̃be] vb to fall ▷ Attention, tu vas tomber! Be careful, you'll fall!; **laisser tomber (1)** to drop ▷ Elle a laissé tomber son stylo. She dropped her pen. **(2)** to give up ▷ Elle a laissé tomber le piano. She quit piano. **(3)** to let down ▷ Il ne laisse jamais tomber ses amis. He never lets his friends down.; **tomber sur quelqu'un** to bump into someone ▷ Je suis tombé sur lui en sortant du restaurant. I bumped into him coming out of the restaurant.; **Ça tombe bien.** That's lucky.; **Il tombe de sommeil.** He's asleep on his feet.

ton [tɔ̃] (f **ta**, pl **tes**) adj your ▷ C'est ton stylo? Is this your pen?
▶ nm ❶ tone of voice ▷ Ne me parle pas sur ce ton. Don't speak to me in that tone of voice. ❷ colour ▷ J'adore les tons pastel. I love pastel colours.

tonalité [tɔnalite] nf dial tone

tondeuse [tɔ̃døz] nf lawnmower

tondre [tɔ̃dʀ(ə)] vb to mow

tonique [tɔnik] adj energizing

tonne [tɔn] nf tonne

tonneau [tɔno] (pl **tonneaux**) nm barrel

tonnerre [tɔnɛʀ] nm thunder

tonus [tɔnys] nm: **avoir du tonus** to be energetic

torchon [tɔʀʃɔ̃] nm tea towel

tordre [tɔʀdʀ(ə)] vb: **se tordre la cheville** to twist one's ankle

tordu [tɔʀdy] (f **tordue**) adj ❶ bent ▷ Ce clou est un peu tordu. This nail's a bit bent. ❷ crazy ▷ une histoire complètement tordue a crazy story

tornade [tɔʀnad] nf tornado

torrent [tɔʀɑ̃] nm mountain stream

torse [tɔʀs(ə)] nm chest ▷ Il était torse nu. He was bare-chested.

tort [tɔʀ] nm: **avoir tort** to be wrong; **donner tort à quelqu'un** to lay the blame on somebody

torticolis [tɔʀtikɔli] nm stiff neck ▷ J'ai le torticolis. I've got a stiff neck.

tortue [tɔʀty] nf tortoise

torture [tɔʀtyʀ] nf torture

torturer [tɔʀtyʀe] vb to torture

tôt [to] adv early; **au plus tôt** at the earliest; **tôt ou tard** sooner or later

total [tɔtal, -o] (f **totale**, mpl **totaux**) adj total
▶ nm (pl **totaux**) total ▷ faire le total to add up the total; **au total** in total

totalement [tɔtalmɑ̃] adv totally

totaliser [tɔtalize] n to add up ▷ Totalise ces chiffres. Add up these numbers.

totalité [tɔtalite] nf: **la totalité des profs** all the teachers; **la totalité du personnel** the entire staff

touchant [tuʃɑ̃, -ɑ̃t] (f **touchante**) adj touching

toucher [tuʃe] vb ❶ to touch ▷ Ne touche pas à mes livres! Don't touch my books!; **Nos deux jardins se touchent.** Our gardens are next to each other. ❷ to feel ▷ Ce chandail a l'air doux. Je peux toucher? That sweater looks soft. Can I feel it? ❸ to hit ▷ La rondelle l'a touché en pleine poitrine. The puck hit him right in the chest. ❹ to affect ▷ Ces nouvelles réformes ne nous touchent pas. The new reforms don't affect us. ❺ to receive ▷ Elle a touché une grosse somme d'argent. She received a large sum of money.

toujours [tuʒuʀ] adv ❶ always ▷ Il est toujours très gentil. He's always very nice.; **pour toujours** forever ❷ still ▷ Quand on est revenus, maman était toujours là. When we got back Mom was still there.

toundra [tundʀa] nf tundra

toupet [tupɛ] nm (informal); **avoir du toupet** to have a nerve

tour [tuʀ] nf ❶ tower ▷ la Tour CN the CN Tower ❷ high-rise; **une tour à bureaux** an office tower; **une tour d'habitation** an apartment high-rise
▶ nm turn ▷ C'est ton tour de jouer. It's your turn to play.; **faire un tour** to go for a walk ▷ Allons faire un tour dans le parc. Let's go for a walk in the park.; **faire un tour en voiture** to go for a drive; **faire un tour à vélo** to go for a ride ▷ Tu veux aller faire un tour à vélo? Do you want to go for a bike ride?; **faire le tour du monde** to travel around the world; **à tour de rôle** alternately; **un tour de magie** magic trick ▷ faire des tours de magie to do magic tricks; **le tour du chapeau** (sports) hat trick

tourbillon [tuʀbijɔ̃] nm whirlpool

tourisme [tuʀism(ə)] nm tourism

touriste [tuʀist(ə)] nmf tourist

touristique [tuʀistik] adj tourist

se tourmenter [tuʀmɑ̃te] vb to fret ▷ Ne te tourmente pas, ça s'arrangera. Don't fret about it, it'll be all right.

tournant [tuʀnɑ̃] nm ❶ bend ▷ Il y a beaucoup de tournants dangereux sur cette route. There are a lot of dangerous bends in this road. ❷ turning point ▷ Ça a été un tournant dans sa vie. It was a turning point in his life.

tournée [tuʀne] nf ❶ round ▷ Le facteur commence sa tournée à sept heures du matin. The letter carrier starts his round at 7 o'clock in the morning. ❷ tour ▷ Elle est en tournée aux T.N.-O. She's on tour in the NWT.

tourner [tuʀne] vb ❶ to turn ▷ Tournez à droite au prochain feu. Turn right at the next lights. ▷ Tourne-toi un peu plus vers moi, et souris! Turn towards me a bit more, and smile! ❷ to go sour ▷ Le lait a tourné. The milk has gone sour.; **mal tourner** to go wrong ▷ Ça a mal tourné. It all went wrong.; **tourner le dos à quelqu'un** to have one's back to somebody; **tourner un film** to shoot a movie

tournesol [tuʀnəsɔl] nm sunflower

tournevis [tuʀnəvis] nm screwdriver

tournoi [tuʀnwa] nm tournament

tourtière [tuʀtjɛʀ] nf

tous [tus] adj, pron see **tout**

tousser [tuse] vb to cough

tout [tu, tut] (mpl **tous**, fpl **toutes**) adj, adv, pron ❶ all ▷ tout le lait all the milk ▷ toute la nuit all night ▷ tous les livres all the books ▷ toutes les filles all the girls ▷ toute la journée all day ▷ tout le temps all the time ▷ C'est tout. That's all. ▷ Je les connais tous. I know them all. ▷ *Nous y sommes toutes allées.* We all went. ▷ *Ça fait combien en tout?* How much is that all together?; **Elle est toute seule.** She's all alone.; **pas du tout** not at all; **tout de même** all the same ❷ every ▷ *tous les jours* every day ▷ *tous les deux jours* every two days; **tout le monde** everybody; **tous les deux** both ▷ *Nous y sommes allés tous les deux.* We both went.; **tous les trois** all three ▷ *Je les ai invités tous les trois.* I invited all three of them. ❸ everything ▷ *Il a tout organisé.* He organized everything. ❹ very ▷ *J'habite tout près.* I live very close by.; **tout en haut** right at the top; **tout droit** straight ahead; **tout d'abord** first of all; **tout à coup** suddenly; **tout à fait** absolutely ❺ quite; **tout à l'heure (1)** just now ▷ *Je l'ai vu tout à l'heure.* I saw him just now. **(2)** in a moment ▷ *Je finirai ça tout à l'heure.* I'll finish it in a moment.; **À tout à l'heure!** See you later!; **tout de suite** right away; **Nous avons fait notre travail tout en chantant.** We sang as we worked.

tout-aller *adj* casual ▷ *des chaussures tout-aller* casual shoes ▷ *un manteau tout-aller* casual coat

toutefois [tutfwa] *adv* however

toutes [tut] *adj, pron see* **tout**

toux [tu] *nf* cough

toxicomane [tɔksikɔman] *nmf* drug addict

toxicomanie [tɔksikɔmani] *nf* drug addiction

toxique [tɔksik] *adj* toxic; **les déchets toxiques** toxic waste

TPS [tepees] *nf* GST ▷ *Est-ce qu'il faut payer la TPS sur les livres?* Do you have to pay GST on books?

trac [tʀak] *nm*: **avoir le trac** to be feeling nervous

tracasser [tʀakase] *vb* to worry ▷ *La santé de ma mère me tracasse.* My mom's health worries me.; **se tracasser** to worry ▷ *Arrête de te tracasser pour rien!* Stop worrying about nothing!

trace [tʀas] *nf* ❶ trace ▷ *Le voleur n'a pas laissé de traces.* The thief left no traces. ❷ mark ▷ *des traces de doigts* finger marks; **des traces de pas** footprints

tracer [tʀase] *vb* to draw ▷ *tracer un trait* to draw a line

tracteur [tʀaktœʀ] *nm* tractor

tradition [tʀadisjɔ̃] *nf* tradition

traditionnel [tʀadisjɔnɛl] *(f* **traditionnelle***) adj* traditional

traducteur [tʀadyktœʀ] *nm* translator

traduction [tʀadyksjɔ̃] *nf* translation

traductrice [tʀadyktʀis] *nf* translator

traduire [tʀadɥiʀ] *vb* to translate

trafic [tʀafik] *nm* ❶ traffic ▷ *le trafic aérien* air traffic; **le trafic de drogue** drug trafficking

trafiquant [tʀafikɑ̃] *nm*: **un trafiquant de drogue** a drug trafficker

tragique [tʀaʒik] *adj* tragic

trahir [tʀaiʀ] *vb* to betray

trahison [tʀaizɔ̃] *nf* betrayal

train [tʀɛ̃] *nm* train; **un train électrique** a train set; **Elle est en train de manger.** She's

eating.; **le train de banlieue** commuter train

traîneau [tʀɛno] *(pl* **traîneaux***) nm* sled

traîner [tʀene] *vb* ❶ to wander around ▷ *J'ai vu des jeunes qui traînaient en ville.* I saw some young people wandering around town. ❷ to dawdle ▷ *Dépêche-toi, ne traîne pas!* Hurry up, don't dawdle! ❸ to drag on ▷ *La réunion a traîné jusqu'à midi.* The meeting dragged on till 12 o'clock.; **traîner des pieds** to drag sth along the ground; **laisser traîner qch** to leave sth lying around ▷ *Ne laisse pas traîner tes affaires.* Don't leave your things lying around.

traîne sauvage [tɛn-] *nf* toboggan; **faire de la traîne sauvage** to go tobogganing

train-train [tʀɛ̃tʀɛ̃] *nm* daily routine

traire [tʀɛʀ] *vb* to milk

trait [tʀɛ] *nm* ❶ line ▷ *Tracez un trait.* Draw a line. ❷ feature ▷ *avoir les traits réguliers* to have regular features ❸ characteristic ▷ *un de tes plus beaux traits* one of the nicest things about you; **un trait de personnalité** personality trait; **boire quelque chose d'un trait** to drink something down in one gulp; **un trait d'union** a hyphen

traité [tʀete] *nm* treaty

traitement [tʀɛtmɑ̃] *nm* treatment; **le traitement de texte** word processing; **le traitement de données** data processing

traiter [tʀete] *vb* to treat ▷ *Elle le traite bien.* She treats him well.; **Il m'a traité d'imbécile.** He called me an idiot.; **traiter de** to be about ▷ *Cet article traite des sans-abri.* This article is about the homeless.

traiteur [tʀetœʀ] *nm* caterer

trajet [tʀaʒɛ] *nm* ❶ journey ▷ *Ils n'ont pas arrêté de parler pendant tout le trajet.* They talked for the whole journey. ▷ *J'ai une heure de trajet pour aller au travail.* My journey to work takes an hour. ❷ route ▷ *C'est le trajet le plus court.* It's the shortest route.

tramway [tʀamwɛ] *nm* streetcar

tranchant [tʀɑ̃ʃɑ̃, -ɑ̃t] *(f* **tranchante***) adj* (knife) sharp

tranche [tʀɑ̃ʃ] *nf* slice

tranquille [tʀɑ̃kil] *adj* quiet ▷ *Cette rue est très tranquille.* This is a very quiet street.; **Sois tranquille, il ne va rien lui arriver.** Don't worry, nothing will happen to him.; **Tiens-toi tranquille!** Be quiet!; **Laisse-moi tranquille.** Leave me alone.; **Laisse ça tranquille.** Leave it alone.

tranquillement [tʀɑ̃kilmɑ̃] *adv* quietly ▷ *Nous étions tranquillement installés dans le salon.* We were just sitting quietly in the living room.; **Je peux travailler tranquillement cinq minutes?** Can I have five minutes to work in peace?

tranquillité [tʀɑ̃kilite] *nf* peace and quiet

Transcanadienne [tʀɑ̃skanadjɛn] *nf* Trans-Canada Highway

transférer [tʀɑ̃sfeʀe] *vb* to transfer

transformer [tʀɑ̃sfɔʀme] *vb* ❶ to transform ▷ *Son séjour en Saskatchewan l'a transformé.* His stay in Saskatchewan has transformed him. ❷ to convert ▷ *Ils ont transformé la grange en garage.* They've converted the barn into a garage.; **se transformer en** to turn into ▷ *La chenille se transforme en papillon.* The caterpillar turns into a butterfly.

transfusion [trɑ̃sfyzjɔ̃] *nf*: **une transfusion sanguine** a blood transfusion

transiger [trɑ̃ziʒe] *vb* to compromise

transmettre [trɑ̃smetr(ə)] *vb* to broadcast ▷ *On a transmis le discours du premier ministre à la radio.* They broadcast the prime minister's speech on the radio.; **transmettre quelque chose à quelqu'un** to pass something on to somebody

transparent [trɑ̃sparɑ̃] *nm* transparency ▷ *Mets le transparent dans le rétroprojecteur.* Put the transparency on the overhead projector.

transpercer [trɑ̃sperse] *vb* to go through ▷ *La pluie a transpercé mes vêtements.* The rain went through my clothes.

transpiration [trɑ̃spirasjɔ̃] *nf* perspiration

transpirer [trɑ̃spire] *vb* to perspire

transport [trɑ̃spɔr] *nm* transport; **les transports en commun** public transport

transporter [trɑ̃spɔrte] *vb* ❶ to carry ▷ *Le train transportait des marchandises.* The train was carrying freight. ❷ to move ▷ *Je ne sais pas comment je vais transporter mes affaires.* I don't know how I'm going to move my stuff.

traumatiser [tromatize] *vb* to traumatize

travail [travaj, -o] (*pl* **travaux**) *nm* ❶ work ▷ *J'ai beaucoup de travail.* I've got a lot of work. ❷ job ▷ *Il a un travail intéressant.* He's got an interesting job.; **Il est sans travail depuis un an.** He has been out of work for a year.; **le travail au noir** moonlighting

travailler [travaje] *vb* to work

travailleur [travajœr, -øz] (*f* **travailleuse**) *adj* hard-working
▶ *nm* worker

travailleuse [travajøz] *nf* worker

travaillistes [travajist] *nmpl* the Labour Party

travaux [travo] *nmpl* ❶ work ▷ *des travaux de construction* building work ❷ roadworks ▷ *Il y a beaucoup de bruit à cause des travaux dans la rue.* There's a lot of noise from the roadworks.; **être en travaux** to be undergoing alterations; **les travaux dirigés** supervised practical work; **les travaux manuels** handicrafts; **les travaux ménagers** housework; **les travaux pratiques** practical work

travers [traver] *nm*: **en travers de** across ▷ *Il y avait un arbre en travers de la route.* There was a tree lying across the road.; **de travers** crooked ▷ *Son chapeau était de travers.* His hat was crooked.; **comprendre de travers** to misunderstand ▷ *Elle comprend toujours tout de travers.* She always gets the wrong idea.; **J'ai avalé de travers.** Something went down the wrong way.; **à travers** through ▷ *Cette vitre est tellement sale qu'on ne voit rien à travers.* This window is so dirty you can't see anything through it.

traversée [traverse] *nf* crossing

traverser [traverse] *vb* ❶ to cross ▷ *Traversez la rue.* Cross the street. ❷ to go through ▷ *Nous avons traversé l'Alberta pour aller en*

Colombie-Britannique. We went through Alberta on the way to British Columbia. ▷ *La pluie a traversé mon manteau.* The rain went through my coat.

traversier [traversje] *nm* ferry

trébucher [trebyʃe] *vb* (*trip*) to stumble

trèfle [trefl(ə)] *nm* ❶ clover ❷ clubs ❸ (*at cards*) ▷ *le roi de trèfle* the king of clubs

treize [trez] *num* thirteen ▷ *Il a treize ans.* He's thirteen. ▷ *à treize heures* at 1 p.m.; **le treize février** the thirteenth of February

treizième [trezjem] *adj* thirteenth

tremblement de terre [trɑ̃bləmɑ̃-] *nm* earthquake

trembler [trɑ̃ble] *vb* to tremble ▷ *trembler de peur* to tremble with fear; **trembler de froid** to shiver

trempé [trɑ̃pe] (*f* **trempée**) *adj* soaking wet; **trempé jusqu'aux os** soaked to the skin

tremper [trɑ̃pe] *vb* to soak; **tremper sa main dans l'eau** to dip one's hand in the water

trempette [trɑ̃pet] *nf* dip ▷ *une trempette à l'ail* a garlic dip

tremplin [trɑ̃plɛ̃] *nm* ❶ diving board ❷ ski jump

trentaine [trɑ̃ten] *nf* about thirty ▷ *une trentaine de personnes* about thirty people; **Il a la trentaine.** He's in his thirties.

trente [trɑ̃t] *num* thirty ▷ *Elle a trente ans.* She's thirty.; **le trente janvier** the thirtieth of January; **trente et un** thirty-one; **trente-deux** thirty-two

trentième [trɑ̃tjem] *adj* thirtieth

très [tre] *adv* very

trésor [trezɔr] *nm* treasure

tresse [tres] *nf* braid; **les tresses rasta** dreadlocks

tresser [trese] *vb* to braid

triangle [trijɑ̃gl(ə)] *nm* triangle

tribunal [tribynal, -o] (*pl* **tribunaux**) *nm* court

tribune téléphonique [tribyn-] *nf* (*phone-in show*) hotline

tricher [triʃe] *vb* to cheat

tricot [triko] *nm* knitting ▷ *Ma grand-mère aime faire du tricot.* My grandmother enjoys knitting.

tricoter [trikɔte] *vb* to knit

trier [trije] *vb* to sort out ▷ *Je vais trier mes papiers avant de partir en vacances.* I'm going to sort out my papers before I go on holiday.

trimestre [trimestr(ə)] *nm* term

triomphe [trijɔ̃f] *nm* triumph

triompher [trijɔ̃fe] *vb* to triumph

triple [tripl(ə)] *nm*: **Ça m'a coûté le triple.** It cost me three times as much.; **Il gagne le triple de mon salaire.** He earns three times my salary.

triplées [triple] *nfpl* triplets

tripler [triple] *vb* to treble

triplés [triple] *nmpl* triplets

triste [trist(ə)] *adj* sad

tristesse [tristes] *nf* sadness

trognon [trɔɲɔ̃] *nm* core ▷ *un trognon de pomme* an apple core

trois [trwɑ] *num* three ▷ *à trois heures du matin*

at three in the morning ▷ *Elle a trois ans.* She's three. ▷ *trois fois* three times; **le trois février** the third of February

troisième [tʀwazjɛm] *adj* third ▷ *au troisième étage* on the third floor

trois-quarts *nmpl* three-quarters ▷ *les trois-quarts de la classe* three-quarters of the class

trombone [tʀɔbɔn] *nm* ❶ trombone ▷ *Il joue du trombone.* He plays the trombone. ❷ paper clip

trompe [tʀɔp] *nf* trunk ▷ *la trompe d'un éléphant* an elephant's trunk

tromper [tʀɔpe] *vb* to deceive; **se tromper** to make a mistake ▷ *Tout le monde peut se tromper.* Anyone can make a mistake.; **se tromper de jour** to get the wrong day; **Vous vous êtes trompé de numéro.** You've got the wrong number.

trompette [tʀɔpɛt] *nf* trumpet ▷ *Elle joue de la trompette.* She plays the trumpet.; **Elle a le nez en trompette.** She has a turned-up nose.

tronc [tʀɔ] *nm* trunk ▷ *un tronc d'arbre* a tree trunk

trop [tʀo] *adv* ❶ too ▷ *Il conduit trop vite.* He drives too fast. ❷ too much ▷ *J'ai trop mangé.* I've eaten too much.; **trop de (1)** too much ▷ *J'ai acheté trop de pain.* I bought too much bread. ▷ *trois dollars de trop* 3 dollars too much **(2)** too many ▷ *Nous avons apporté trop de vêtements.* We brought too many clothes.; **trois personnes de trop** 3 people too many

tropique [tʀɔpik] *nm* tropic

trottoir [tʀɔtwaʀ] *nm* sidewalk

trou [tʀu] *nm* hole; **J'ai eu un trou de mémoire.** My mind went blank.; **le trou noir** black hole

trouble [tʀublə)] *adj, adv* cloudy ▷ *L'eau est trouble.* The water's cloudy.

trouble [tʀublə)] *nm*: **une période de troubles politiques** a period of political instability; **le trouble alimentaire** eating disorder

trouer [tʀue] *vb* to make a hole in

trouille [tʀuj] *nf*: **avoir la trouille** (*informal*) to be scared to death

troupe [tʀup] *nf* troop; **une troupe de théâtre** a theatre company

troupeau [tʀupo] (*pl* **troupeaux**) *nm*: **un troupeau de moutons** a flock of sheep; **un troupeau de vaches** a herd of cows

trousse [tʀus] *nf* kit ▷ *une trousse de secours* a first-aid kit; **une trousse de maquillage** a make-up bag

trouver [tʀuve] *vb* ❶ to find ▷ *Je ne trouve pas mes lunettes.* I can't find my glasses. ❷ to think ▷ *Je trouve que c'est bête.* I think it's stupid.; **se trouver** to be ▷ *Où se trouve le bureau de poste?* Where's the post office? ▷ *Hull se trouve au Québec.* Hull is in Québec.; **se trouver mal** to pass out

truc [tʀyk] *nm* ❶ (*informal*) thing ▷ *un truc en plastique* a plastic thing ❷ trick ▷ *Je vais te montrer un truc qui réussit à tous les coups.* I'll show you a trick that never fails.

truite [tʀɥit] *nf* trout

T-shirt [tiʃœʀt] *nm* T-shirt

tu [ty] *pron* you ▷ *Est-ce que tu as un animal domestique?* Have you got a pet?

tuba [tyba] *nm* ❶ tuba ▷ *Je joue du tuba.* I play the tuba. ❷ snorkel

tube [tyb] *nm* tube ▷ *un tube de dentifrice* a tube of toothpaste; **un tube de rouge à lèvres** a lipstick

tuer [tɥe] *vb* to kill; **se tuer** to get killed ▷ *Elle s'est tuée dans un accident de voiture.* She got killed in a car accident.

tuile [tɥil] *nf* tile

tunique [tynik] *nf* tunic

tunnel [tynɛl] *nm* tunnel ▷ *Empruntez le tunnel qui passe sous le fleuve Fraser.* Take the tunnel under the Fraser River.

turbulent [tyʀbylɑ̃, -ɑ̃t] (*f* **turbulente**) *adj* boisterous

tutoyer [tytwaje] *vb*: **tutoyer quelqu'un** to address somebody as "tu"; **On se tutoie?** Shall we use "tu" to each other?

tuyau [tɥijo] (*pl* **tuyaux**) *nm* pipe; **un tuyau d'arrosage** a hose

tympan [tɛ̃pɑ̃] *nm* eardrum

type [tip] *nm* (*kind*) type ▷ *Il y a plusieurs types de vélo de montagne.* There are many types of mountain bike.

typique [tipik] *adj* typical

tyran [tiʀɑ̃] *nm* tyrant ▷ *C'est un vrai tyran.* He's a real tyrant.

u

un [œ̃] *art, pron, adj* ❶ a ▷ *un garçon* a boy, an ▷ *un œuf* an egg ❷ one ▷ *l'un des meilleurs* one of the best ▷ *un citron et deux oranges* one lemon and two oranges ▷ *« Combien de timbres? »* — *« Un. »* "How many stamps?" — "One." ▷ *Elle a un an.* She's one year old.; **l'un..., l'autre...** one..., the other... ▷ *L'un est grand, l'autre est petit.* One is tall, the other is short.; **les uns..., les autres...** some..., others... ▷ *Les uns marchaient, les autres couraient.* Some were walking, others were running.; **l'un ou l'autre** either of them ▷ *Prends l'un ou l'autre, ça m'est égal.* Take either of them, I don't mind.; **un par un** one by one ▷ *Ils entraient un par un.* They went in one by one.

unanime [ynanim] *adj* unanimous

unanimité [ynanimite] *nf*: **à l'unanimité** unanimously

une [yn] *art, pron, adj* ❶ a ▷ *une fille* a girl, an ▷ *une pomme* an apple ❷ one ▷ *une pomme et deux bananes* one apple and two bananas

▷ «Combien de cartes postales?» — «Une.»
"How many postcards?" — "One." ▷ à une heure
du matin at one in the morning ▷ l'une des
meilleures one of the best; l'une..., l'autre...
one..., the other... ▷ L'une est grande, l'autre
est petite. One is tall, the other is short.; les
unes..., les autres... some..., others... ▷ Les
unes marchaient, les autres couraient. Some
were walking, others were running.; l'une ou
l'autre either of them ▷ Prends l'une ou l'autre,
ça m'est égal. Take either of them, I don't mind.;
une par une one by one ▷ Elles entraient une par
une. They went in one by one.

uni [yni] (f **unie**) adj ❶ plain ▷ un tissu uni a
plain fabric ❷ close-knit ▷ une famille unie a
close-knit family

unifolié [ynifɔlje] nm the Canadian flag

uniforme [ynifɔrm(ə)] nm uniform

unilingue [ynilɛ̃g] adj unilingual

union [ynjɔ̃] nf union

unique [ynik] adj unique ▷ Tout individu a des
empreintes uniques. Everyone's fingerprints are
unique. ▷ C'est une occasion unique. It's a unique
opportunity.; Il est fils unique. He's an only
child.; Elle est fille unique. She's an only child.

uniquement [ynikmɑ̃] adv only

unité [ynite] nf ❶ unity ▷ l'unité nationale
national unity ❷ unit ▷ une unité de mesure a
unit of measurement

univers [yniver] nm universe

universitaire [yniversiter] adj university
▷ un diplôme universitaire a university degree
▷ le campus universitaire university campus;
faire des études universitaires to study at
university

université [yniversite] nf university ▷ aller à
l'université to go to university

urgence [yrʒɑ̃s] nf: C'est une urgence. It's
urgent.; Il n'y a pas urgence. It's not urgent.;
le service des urgences the emergency
department; Il a été transporté d'urgence
à l'hôpital. He was rushed to hospital.;
Téléphonez d'urgence. Phone as soon as
possible.

urgent [yrʒɑ̃, -ɑ̃t] (f **urgente**) adj urgent

urine [yrin] nf urine

usage [yzaʒ] nm use ▷ à usage interne for
internal use ▷ à usage externe for external use
only; hors d'usage out of service ▷ Cet appareil
est hors d'usage. That machine's out of service.

usagé [yzaʒe] (f **usagée**) adj ❶ old ▷ un
manteau usagé an old coat ❷ used ▷ une
seringue usagée a used syringe

usager [yzaʒe] nm user ▷ les usagers de la route
road users

usagère [yzaʒer] nf user ▷ une usagère des
transports publics a public transit user

usé [yze] (f **usée**) adj worn ▷ Mes jeans sont un
peu usés. My jeans are a bit worn.

s' **user** [yze] vb to wear out ▷ Mes pantoufles se
sont usées en quinze jours. My slippers wore out
in two weeks.

usine [yzin] nf factory ▷ une usine de meubles a
furniture factory

ustensile [ystɑ̃sil] nm: un ustensile de
cuisine a kitchen utensil; les ustensiles
cutlery

usuel [yzɥɛl] (f **usuelle**) adj everyday ▷ la
langue usuelle everyday language

utile [ytil] adj useful

utilisateur [ytilizatœr] nm (technology) user
▷ un utilisateur d'Internet an Internet user

utilisation [ytilizasjɔ̃] nf use ▷ L'utilisation des
calculatrices est interdite. It is forbidden to use
calculators.

utilisatrice [ytilizatris] nf (technology) user
▷ une utilisatrice d'Internet an Internet user

utiliser [ytilize] vb to use

utilité [ytilite] nf (usefulness) use ▷ Cet objet
n'est pas d'une grande utilité. This object isn't
much use.

V

va [va] vb see **aller**

vacances [vakɑ̃s] nfpl ❶ vacation ▷ aller en
vacances to go on vacation ▷ être en vacances
to be on vacation ❷ holidays ▷ les vacances de
Noël the Christmas holidays ▷ les vacances de
Pâques the Easter holidays ▷ les vacances d'été
the summer holidays

vacarme [vakarm(ə)] nm racket ▷ Qu'est-ce
que c'est que ce vacarme? What's all this racket?

vaccin [vaksɛ̃] nm vaccination

vaccination [vaksinasjɔ̃] nf vaccination
▷ La vaccination est obligatoire. Vaccination is
compulsory.

vacciner [vaksine] vb to vaccinate ▷ se faire
vacciner contre la rubéole to be vaccinated
against German measles

vache [vaʃ] nf cow
▶ adj (informal) mean ▷ C'est vraiment vache, ce
qu'il a dit. What he said was really mean.

vadrouille [vadruj] nf mop ▷ J'ai passé la
vadrouille sur le plancher. I mopped the floor.

vagabond [vagabɔ̃] nm transient

vagabonde [vagabɔ̃d] nf transient

vagin [vaʒɛ̃] nm vagina

vague [vag] nf (in sea) wave; une vague de
chaleur a heat wave
▶ adj vague ▷ J'ai un vague souvenir d'elle. I
vaguely remember her.

vain [vɛ̃, vɛn] (f **vaine**) adj: en vain in vain

vaincre [vɛ̃kr(ə)] vb ❶ to defeat ▷ L'armée
a été vaincue. The army was defeated. ❷ to
overcome ▷ Il a réussi à vaincre sa timidité. He
managed to overcome his shyness.

vainqueur [vɛ̃kœr] nm winner

vais [vɛ] vb see **aller**; Je vais écrire à mes

cousins. I'm going to write to my cousins.

vaisseau [vɛso] (pl **vaisseaux**) nm: **un vaisseau spatial** a spaceship; **un vaisseau sanguin** a blood vessel

vaisselle [vɛsɛl] nf dishes ▷ Je vais faire la vaisselle. I'll do the dishes. ▷ Peux-tu ranger la vaisselle s'il te plaît? Can you put the dishes away please?

valable [valabl(ə)] adj valid ▷ Ce billet d'avion est valable un an. This plane ticket is valid for one year.

valentin [valɑ̃tɛ̃] nm (person) valentine ▷ Seras-tu mon valentin? Will you be my valentine?

valentine [valɑ̃tin] nf (person) valentine ▷ Seras-tu ma valentine? Will you be my valentine?

valet [valɛ] nm (in card games) jack ▷ le valet de carreau the jack of diamonds

valeur [valœr] nf value ▷ sans valeur of no value; **des objets de valeur** valuables ▷ Ne laissez pas d'objets de valeur dans votre chambre. Don't leave any valuables in your room.

valider [valide] vb to stamp ▷ Vous devez faire valider votre billet avant votre départ. You must get your ticket stamped before you leave.

valise [valiz] nf suitcase; **faire sa valise** to pack

vallée [vale] nf valley; **la vallée du Bas-Fraser** the Lower Mainland

valoir [valwar] vb to be worth ▷ Ça vaut combien? How much is it worth? ▷ Cette voiture vaut très cher. This car's worth a lot of money.; **Ça vaut mieux.** That would be better. ▷ Il vaut mieux ne rien dire. It would be better to say nothing.; **valoir la peine** to be worth it ▷ Ça vaudrait la peine d'essayer. It would be worth a try.

vampire [vɑ̃pir] nmf vampire

vandale [vɑ̃dal] nmf vandal

vandaliser [vɑ̃dalize] vb to vandalize

vandalisme [vɑ̃dalism(ə)] nm vandalism

vanille [vanij] nf vanilla ▷ une crème glacée à la vanille a vanilla ice cream

vanité [vanite] nf vanity

vaniteux [vanitø, -øz] (f **vaniteuse**) adj conceited

se **vanter** [vɑ̃te] vb to brag

vapeur [vapœr] nf steam ▷ des légumes cuits à la vapeur steamed vegetables

variable [varjabl(ə)] adj (weather) changeable

varicelle [varisɛl] nf chickenpox ▷ Elle a la varicelle. She has chickenpox.

varié [varje] (f **variée**) adj varied ▷ Son travail est très varié. His job is very varied.

varier [varje] vb to vary; **Le menu varie tous les jours.** The menu changes every day.

variété [varjete] nf variety ▷ Il n'y a pas beaucoup de variété. There isn't much variety.; **une émission de variétés** (television) a variety show

vas [vazi] vb see **aller**

vase [vɑz] nm vase
▷ nf mud

vaste [vast(ə)] adj vast

vaudrait, vaut vb see **valoir**

vautour [votur] nm vulture

veau [vo] (pl **veaux**) nm ❶ (animal) calf ❷ (meat) veal

vécu [veky] vb see **vivre**; Elle a vécu à Laval pendant dix ans. She lived in Laval for ten years.

vedette [vədɛt] nf ❶ star ▷ une vedette de cinéma a movie star ❷ motorboat

végétal [veʒetal, -o] (f **végétale**, mpl **végétaux**) adj vegetable ▷ l'huile végétale vegetable oil

végétalien [veʒetaljɛ̃, -ɛn] (f **végétalienne**) adj vegan

végétarien [veʒetarjɛ̃, -ɛn] (f **végétarienne**) adj vegetarian ▷ Je suis végétarien. I'm a vegetarian.

végétation [veʒetasjɔ̃] nf vegetation

véhicule [veikyl] nm vehicle ▷ le véhicule utilitaire sport sport utility vehicule

veille [vɛj] nf the day before ▷ la veille de son départ the day before he left ▷ la veille au soir the previous evening; **la veille de Noël** Christmas Eve; **la veille du jour de l'An** New Year's Eve; **la mode Veille** (computing) standby mode

veiller [veje] vb to stay up; **veiller sur quelqu'un** to watch over somebody

veine [vɛn] nf vein; **avoir de la veine** (informal) to be lucky

véliplanchiste [veliplɑ̃ʃist(ə)] nmf windsurfer

vélo [velo] nm bike ▷ faire du vélo to go biking; **un vélo de montagne** a mountain bike; **un vélo d'exercice** an exercise bike

vélomoteur [velomotœr] nm moped

velours [vəlur] nm velvet ▷ une robe en velours a velvet dress; **le velours côtelé** corduroy ▷ un pantalon en velours côtelé corduroy pants

vendeur [vɑ̃dœr] nm (in store) salesperson

vendeuse [vɑ̃døz] nf (in store) salesperson

vendre [vɑ̃dr(ə)] vb to sell; **vendre quelque chose à quelqu'un** to sell somebody something ▷ Elle m'a vendu son vélo. She sold me her bike.; **« à vendre »** "for sale"

vendredi [vɑ̃drədi] nm ❶ Friday ▷ Aujourd'hui, nous sommes vendredi. It's Friday today. ❷ on Friday ▷ Il est venu vendredi. He came on Friday.; **le vendredi** on Fridays ▷ Je joue au hockey le vendredi. I play hockey on Fridays.; **tous les vendredis** every Friday; **vendredi dernier** last Friday; **vendredi prochain** next Friday; **le Vendredi saint** Good Friday

vénéneux [venenø, -øz] (f **vénéneuse**) adj (plant) poisonous ▷ un champignon vénéneux a poisonous mushroom

vengeance [vɑ̃ʒɑ̃s] nf revenge

se **venger** [vɑ̃ʒe] vb to get revenge

venimeux [venimø, -øz] (f **venimeuse**) adj (animal) poisonous ▷ un serpent venimeux a poisonous snake

venin [vənɛ̃] nm poison

venir [vənir] vb to come ▷ Il viendra demain. He'll come tomorrow. ▷ Elle est venue nous voir. She came to see us.; **venir de** to have just ▷ Je viens de la voir. I've just seen her. ▷ Je viens de lui téléphoner. I've just phoned her.; **faire venir**

quelqu'un to send for somebody ▷ *faire venir le plombier* to send for the plumber

vent [vã] *nm* wind ▷ *Il y a du vent.* It's windy.

vente [vãt] *nf* sale; **en vente** on sale ▷ *Ce modèle est en vente dans les grands magasins.* This model is on sale in department stores.; **la vente par téléphone** telemarketing; **une vente aux enchères** an auction; **une vente de garage** a garage sale

ventilateur [vãtilatœr] *nm* (*for cooling*) fan

ventre [vãtr(ə)] *nm* stomach ▷ *avoir mal au ventre* to have a stomachache

venu [vəny] *vb see* **venir**

ver [ver] *nm* worm; **un ver de terre** an earthworm

verbe [verb(ə)] *nm* verb

verbomoteur [verbomotœr] *nm* talkative person

verbomotrice [verbomotris] *nf* talkative person ▷ *Cette politicienne est plutôt verbomotrice.* This politician is quite a talkative person.

verger [verʒe] *nm* orchard

verglacé [verglase] (*f* **verglacée**) *adj* icy ▷ *La route était verglacée.* The road was icy.

verglas [vergla] *nm* black ice; **la tempête de verglas** ice storm

véridique [veridik] *adj* truthful

vérification [verifikasjɔ̃] *nf* check ▷ *une vérification d'identité* an identity check

vérifier [verifje] *vb* to check

véritable [veritabl(ə)] *adj* real ▷ *C'était un véritable cauchemar.* It was a real nightmare.; **en cuir véritable** made of real leather

vérité [verite] *nf* truth ▷ *dire la vérité* to tell the truth

verni [verni] (*f* **vernie**) *adj* varnished

vernir [vernir] *vb* to varnish

vernis [verni] *nm* varnish; **le vernis à ongles** nail polish

verra, verrai, verras *vb see* **voir**; **on verra...** we'll see...

verre [ver] *nm* ❶ glass ▷ *un bibelot en verre* a glass ornament ▷ *un verre d'eau* a glass of water ❷ (*of spectacles*) lens ▷ *des verres de contact* contact lenses

verrez, verrons, verront *vb see* **voir**

verrou [veru] *nm* (*on door*) bolt

verrouiller [veruje] *vb* to bolt ▷ *N'oublie pas de verrouiller la porte du garage.* Don't forget to bolt the garage door.

verrue [very] *nf* wart

vers [ver] *nm* (*of poetry*) line ▷ *au troisième vers* in the third line
▷ *prep* ❶ towards ▷ *Il allait vers l'école.* He was going towards the school. ❷ *at* about ▷ *Nous sommes rentrés chez nous vers cinq heures.* We went home at about 5 o'clock.

verse [vers(ə)] **: à verse** *adv* ▷ *Il pleut à verse.* It's pouring rain.

Verseau [verso] *nm* Aquarius ▷ *Il est Verseau.* He's an Aquarius.

versement [versəmã] *nm* instalment ▷ *en cinq versements* in 5 instalments

verser [verse] *vb* to pour ▷ *Est-ce que tu peux me verser un verre d'eau?* Could you pour me a

glass of water?

version [versjɔ̃] *nf* ❶ version ❷ (*from the foreign language*) translation; **un film en version originale** a film in the original language

verso [verso] *nm* (*of sheet of paper*) back; **voir au verso** see other side

vert [ver, vert(ə)] (*f* **verte**) *adj* green

vertèbre [vertebr(ə)] *nf* vertebra

vertical [vertikal, -o] (*f* **verticale**, *mpl* **verticaux**) *adj* vertical

vertige [vertiʒ] *nm* fear of heights ▷ *avoir le vertige* to be afraid of heights

veste [vest(ə)] *nf* ❶ jacket ❷ (*sleeveless*) vest ▷ *une veste en polaire* a polar fleece vest

vestiaire [vestjer] *nm* ❶ (*in theatre, museum*) cloakroom ❷ (*at school, sports complex*) changing room

vestibule [vestibyl] *nm* hall

vêtement [vetmã] *nm* article of clothing; **les vêtements** clothes

vétérinaire [veteriner] *nmf* vet ▷ *Elle est vétérinaire.* She's a vet.

veuf [vœf] *nm* widower ▷ *Il est veuf.* He's a widower.

veuille, veuillez, veuillons, veulent, veut *vb see* **vouloir**; **Veuillez fermer la porte en sortant.** Please shut the door when you go out.

veuve [vœv] *nf* widow ▷ *Elle est veuve.* She's a widow.

veux [vø] *vb see* **vouloir**

vexer [vekse] *vb* **: vexer quelqu'un** to hurt somebody's feelings; **se vexer** to be offended

viande [vjãd] *nf* meat; **la viande hachée** hamburger meat

vibrer [vibre] *vb* to vibrate

vice [vis] *nm* vise

victime [viktim] *nf* victim

victoire [viktwar] *nf* victory

vidanges [vidãʒ] *nfpl* garbage ▷ *As-tu mis les vidanges dehors?* Did you put the garbage out?; **le camion de vidanges** garbage truck; **le sac de vidanges** garbage bag

vide [vid] *adj* empty
▷ *nm* vacuum ▷ *emballé sous vide* vacuum-packed; **avoir peur du vide** to be afraid of heights

vidéo [video] *nf* video
▷ *adj* (*f+pl* **vidéo**) video ▷ *des jeux vidéo* video games ▷ *une caméra vidéo* a video camera

vidéocassette [videokaset] *nf* videocassette

vidéoclip [videoklip] *nm* music video

vidéoclub [videoklœb] *nm* video rental store

vidéoconférence [videokɔ̃fe] *nf* videoconference

vider [vide] *vb* to empty

vie [vi] *nf* life; **être en vie** to be alive

vieil [vjej] *adj see* **vieux**

vieillard [vjejar] *nm* old man

vieille [vjej] *adj see* **vieux**
▷ *nf* old woman; **Eh bien, ma vieille...** (*informal*) Well, my dear...

vieillesse [vjejes] *nf* old age

vieillir [vjejir] *vb* to age ▷ *Il a beaucoup vieilli depuis la dernière fois que je l'ai vu.* He's aged a lot since I last saw him.

viendrai, vienne, viens vb see **venir**; **Je viendrai dès que possible.** I'll come as soon as possible.; **Je voudrais que tu viennes.** I'd like you to come.; **Viens ici!** Come here!

Vierge [vjɛʀʒ(ə)] nf Virgo ▷ Elle est Vierge. She's a Virgo.

vierge [vjɛʀʒ(ə)] adj ❶ virgin ▷ Il est vierge. He's a virgin. ❷ blank ▷ une cassette vierge a blank cassette

vieux [vjø, vjɛj] (f **vieille**) adj old ▷ un vieux livre an old book ▷ une vieille dame an old lady ▷ un vieil arbre an old tree ▷ Il fait plus vieux que son âge. He looks older than he is.
▶ nm old man ▷ Eh bien, mon vieux… (informal) Well, old friend…

vieux jeu (f+pl **vieux jeu**) adj old-fashioned ▷ Elle est un peu vieux jeu. She's a bit old-fashioned.

vif [vif, viv] (f **vive**) adj ❶ (mentally) sharp ▷ Elle est très vive. She's very sharp.; **avoir l'esprit vif** to be quick-witted ❷ crisp ▷ L'air est plus vif à la campagne qu'en ville. The air is crisper in the country than in the city. ❸ (colour) bright ▷ un bleu vif a bright blue

vigne [viɲ] nf vine

vignoble [viɲɔbl(ə)] nm vineyard

vilain [vilɛ̃, -ɛn] (f **vilaine**) adj naughty ▷ C'est très vilain de dire des mensonges. It's very naughty to tell lies.

village [vilaʒ] nm village

villageois [vilaʒwa] nm villager

villageoise [vilaʒwaz] nf villager

ville [vil] nf town ▷ Je vais en ville. I'm going into town.; **une grande ville** a city

vinaigre [vinɛgʀ(ə)] nm vinegar

vinaigrette [vinɛgʀɛt] nf salad dressing

vingt [vɛ̃] num twenty ▷ Elle a vingt ans. She's twenty. ▷ à vingt heures at 8 p.m.; **le vingt février** the twentieth of February; **vingt et un** twenty-one; **vingt-deux** twenty-two

vingtaine [vɛ̃tɛn] nf about twenty ▷ une vingtaine de personnes about twenty people; **Il a une vingtaine d'années.** He's about twenty.

vingtième [vɛ̃tjɛm] adj twentieth

viol [vjɔl] nm rape

violemment [vjɔlamɑ̃] adv violently

violence [vjɔlɑ̃s] nf violence; **la violence familiale** family violence

violent [vjɔlɑ̃, -ɑ̃t] (f **violente**) adj violent

violer [vjɔle] vb to rape

violet [vjɔlɛ, -ɛt] (f **violette**) adj purple

violon [vjɔlɔ̃] nm violin ▷ Je joue du violon. I play the violin.

violoncelle [vjɔlɔ̃sɛl] nm cello ▷ Elle joue du violoncelle. She plays the cello.

violoniste [vjɔlɔnist(ə)] nmf violinist

vipère [vipɛʀ] nf viper

virage [viʀaʒ] nm bend ▷ une route pleine de virages dangereux a road full of dangerous turns

virgule [viʀgyl] nf ❶ comma ❷ decimal point ▷ trois virgule cinq three point five

virus [viʀys] nm (also computing) virus

vis [vis] vb see **vivre**
▶ nf screw

visa [viza] nm visa

visage [vizaʒ] nm face ▷ Elle a le visage rond. She's got a round face.

vis-à-vis de [vizavi-] prep (informal) with regard to ▷ Ce n'est pas très juste vis-à-vis de lui. It's not very fair to him.

viser [vize] vb to aim at ▷ Il faut viser la cible. You have to aim at the target.

visibilité [vizibilite] nf visibility

visible [vizibl(ə)] adj visible

visière [vizjɛʀ] nf (of cap) visor

visite [vizit] nf visit; **rendre visite à quelqu'un** to visit somebody ▷ Je vais rendre visite à mon grand-père. I'm going to visit my grandfather.; **avoir de la visite** to have visitors ▷ Nous avons de la visite aujourd'hui. We have visitors today.; **une visite guidée** a guided tour; **une visite médicale** a medical examination

visiter [vizite] vb to visit

visiteur [vizitœʀ] nm visitor

visiteuse [vizitøz] nf visitor

visou [vizu] nm (skill at aiming) aim ▷ Ça prend du visou pour jouer au billard. You have to have good aim to play pool.

vit [vi] vb see **vivre**; **Il vit chez ses parents.** He lives with his parents.

vital [vital, -o] (f **vitale**, mpl **vitaux**) adj vital ▷ C'est une question vitale. It's of vital importance.; **les signes vitaux** vital signs

vitamine [vitamin] nf vitamin

vite [vit] adv ❶ quick ▷ Vite, ils arrivent! Quick, they're coming! ❷ « Je peux aller dire au revoir à ma mère? » « Oui, mais fais ça vite! » "Can I go and say goodbye to my mom?" "Yes, but be quick! ▷ Prenons la voiture, ça va aller plus vite. Let's take the car, it'll be quicker.; **Le temps passe vite.** Time flies. ❷ fast ▷ Elle roule trop vite. She drives too fast. ❸ soon ▷ Il va vite oublier. He'll soon forget.

vitesse [vitɛs] nf ❶ speed ▷ à toute vitesse at top speed ▷ Nous sommes rentrés à toute vitesse. We rushed back home. ❷ gear ▷ en première vitesse in first gear

vitrail [vitʀaj, -o] (pl **vitraux**) nm stained-glass window

vitre [vitʀ(ə)] nf window ▷ Il a cassé une vitre. He broke a window.

vitrine [vitʀin] nf store window

vivant [vivɑ̃, -ɑ̃t] (f **vivante**) adj ❶ living ▷ les êtres vivants living creatures ▷ les expériences sur les animaux vivants experiments on live animals ❷ lively ▷ Elle est très vivante. She's very lively.

vive [viv] (msg **vif**) adj ❶ (mentally) sharp ▷ Elle est très vive. She's very sharp. ❷ (colour) bright ▷ Lavez les couleurs vives à l'eau froide. Wash bright colours in cold water.; **à vive allure** at a brisk pace; **de vive voix** in person ▷ Je te le dirai de vive voix. I'll tell you about it when I see you.
▶ excl : **Vive la reine!** Long live the queen!

vivement [vivmɑ̃] adv ❶ quickly ▷ Elle a réagi vivement. She reacted quickly. ❷ brightly ▷ des tissus vivement colorés brightly coloured fabrics

vivre [vivʀ(ə)] vb to live ▷ J'aimerais vivre à l'étranger. I'd like to live abroad. ▷ Et ta grand-mère? Elle vit encore en bonne santé? What about your grandmother? Is she still in good health?

vocabulaire [vɔkabylɛʀ] nm vocabulary
vocation [vɔkasjɔ̃] nf vocation
vœu [vø] (pl **vœux**) nm wish ▷ *faire un vœu* to make a wish ; **Le voici!** Here he is! ▷ *Tu veux tes clés? Tiens, les voici!* You want your keys? Here you are!
vogue [vɔg] nf fashion ▷ *C'est très en vogue en ce moment.* It's very fashionable at the moment.
voici [vwasi] prep ❶ this is ▷ *Voici mon frère et voilà ma sœur.* This is my brother and that's my sister. ❷ here is ▷ *Tu as perdu ton stylo? Tiens, en voici un autre.* Have you lost your pen? Here's another one. ; **Le voici!** Here he is! ▷ *Tu veux tes clés? Tiens, les voici!* You want your keys? Here you are!
voie [vwa] nf lane ▷ *une route à trois voies* a 3-lane road; **par voie buccale** orally ▷ *à prendre par voie buccale* to be taken orally; **la voie ferrée** the railway track; **la voie maritime du Saint-Laurent** the Saint Lawrence Seaway
voilà [vwala] prep ❶ there is ▷ *Tiens! Voilà ton frère.* Look! There's your brother. ▷ *Tu as perdu ton stylo, en voilà un autre.* Have you lost your pen? There's another one. ; **Les voilà!** There they are! ❷ that is ▷ *Voilà ma sœur.* That's my sister. ; **Et voilà!** That's it!
voile [vwal] nm veil ▷ *un voile de mariée* a wedding veil ; **un voile blanc** a whiteout ▷ nf ❶ sail ❷ sailing ▷ *faire de la voile* to go sailing; **un bateau à voiles** a sailboat
voilier [vwalje] nm sailboat
voir [vwaʀ] vb to see ▷ *Venez me voir quand vous serez à Edmonton.* Come and see me when you're in Edmonton. ▷ *Je ne vois pas pourquoi il a fait ça.* I can't see why he did that. ; **faire voir quelque chose à quelqu'un** to show somebody something ▷ *Il m'a fait voir sa collection de timbres.* He showed me his stamp collection. ; **se voir** to be obvious ▷ *Est-ce que cette tache se voit?* Does that stain show? ▷ « *Ça fait des années qu'elle n'a pas joué au soccer* » « *Oui, ça se voit!* » "She hasn't played soccer for years" "Yes, you can tell!"; **avoir quelque chose à voir avec** to have something to do with ▷ *Ça n'a rien à voir avec lui, c'est entre toi et moi.* It's nothing to do with him, it's between you and me.
voisin [vwazɛ̃] nm neighbour
voisinage [vwazinaʒ] nm: **dans le voisinage** in the neighbourhood
voisine [vwazin] nf neighbour
voiture [vwatyʀ] nf car ▷ *une voiture de sport* a sports car
voix [vwa] (pl **voix**) nf ❶ voice ▷ *à voix basse* in a low voice; **à haute voix** aloud ❷ vote ▷ *Il a obtenu cinquante pour cent des voix.* He got 50% of the votes.
vol [vɔl] nm ❶ flight; **à vol d'oiseau** as the crow flies ❷ theft ▷ *un vol à main armée* an armed robbery
volaille [vɔlaj] nf poultry
volant [vɔlɑ̃] nm ❶ steering wheel ❷ (badminton) birdie
volcan [vɔlkɑ̃] nm volcano
volée [vɔle] nf (in tennis) volley; **rattraper une balle à la volée** to catch a ball in mid-air
voler [vɔle] vb ❶ to fly ▷ *J'aimerais savoir voler.* I'd like to be able to fly. ❷ to steal ▷ *On a volé*

mon appareil photo. My camera's been stolen. ; **voler quelque chose à quelqu'un** to steal something from somebody ▷ *Ça n'est pas son stylo, il me l'a volé.* That's not his pen, he stole it from me. ; **voler quelqu'un** to rob somebody
volet [vɔlɛ] nm shutter
voleur [vɔlœʀ] nm thief; **Au voleur!** Stop thief!
voleuse [vɔløz] nf thief
volley-ball [vɔlɛbol] nm volleyball ▷ *jouer au volley-ball* to play volleyball
volontaire [vɔlɔ̃tɛʀ] nmf volunteer
volonté [vɔlɔ̃te] nf willpower ▷ *Elle a beaucoup de volonté.* She has a lot of willpower. ; **la bonne volonté** goodwill; **la mauvaise volonté** lack of goodwill
volontiers [vɔlɔ̃tje] adv gladly ▷ *Je l'aiderais volontiers si elle me le demandais.* I'd gladly help her if she asked me.
volume [vɔlym] nm volume ▷ *un dictionnaire en deux volumes* a two-volume dictionary
volumineux [vɔlyminø, -øz] (f **volumineuse**) adj bulky
vomir [vɔmiʀ] vb to vomit ▷ *Il a vomi toute la nuit.* He was vomiting all night.
vont [vɔ̃] vb see **aller**
vos [vo] adj your ▷ *Rangez vos jouets, les enfants!* Children, put your toys away! ▷ *Merci pour vos fleurs.* Thanks for your flowers.
vote [vɔt] nm vote
voter [vɔte] vb to vote
votre [vɔtʀ] (pl **vos**) adj your ▷ *C'est votre manteau?* Is this your coat?
vôtre [votʀ(ə)] pron: **le vôtre** yours ▷ *J'aime bien notre prof de maths, mais la vôtre est plus patiente.* I like our math teacher, but yours is more patient. ▷ *À qui est ce foulard? C'est le vôtre?* Whose scarf is this? Is it yours?
vôtres [votʀ(ə)] pron: **les vôtres** yours ▷ *J'ai oublié mes lunettes de soleil. Vous avez apporté les vôtres?* I forgot my sunglasses. Did you bring yours?
voudra, voudrai, voudrais, voudras, voudrez, voudrons, voudront vb see **vouloir**; **Je voudrais…** I'd like… ▷ *Je voudrais deux litres de lait, s'il vous plaît.* I'd like two litres of milk, please.
vouloir [vulwaʀ] vb to want ▷ *Elle veut un vélo pour sa fête.* She wants a bike for her birthday. ▷ *Je ne veux pas de dessert.* I don't want any dessert. ▷ *Il ne veut pas venir.* He doesn't want to come. ▷ « *On va au cinéma?* » « *Si tu veux.* » "Shall we go to the movies?" "If you like."; **Je veux bien.** I'll be happy to. ▷ *Je veux bien le faire à ta place si ça t'arrange.* I don't mind doing it for you if you prefer.; **sans le vouloir** without meaning to ▷ *Je l'ai vexé sans le vouloir.* I upset him without meaning to.; **en vouloir à quelqu'un** to be angry at somebody ▷ *Il m'en veut de ne pas l'avoir invité à ma fête.* He's angry at me for not inviting him to my birthday party.; **vouloir dire** to mean ▷ *Qu'est-ce que ça veut dire?* What does that mean?
voulu [vuly] vb see **vouloir**
vous [vu] pron ❶ you ▷ *Vous aimez la pizza?* Do you like pizza? ❷ to you ▷ *Je vous écrirai bientôt.*

I'll write to you soon. ❶ yourself ▷ *Vous vous êtes fait mal?* Have you hurt yourself?; **vous-même** yourself ▷ *Vous l'avez fait vous-même?* Did you do it yourself?

vouvoyer [vuvwaje] *vb:* **vouvoyer quelqu'un** to address somebody as "vous"; **Est-ce que je dois vouvoyer ta sœur?** Should I use "vous" to your sister?

voyage [vwajaʒ] *nm* journey ▷ *Avez-vous fait bon voyage?* Did you have a good journey?; **Bon voyage!** Have a good trip!

voyager [vwajaʒe] *vb* to travel

voyageur [vwajaʒœr] *nm* passenger

voyageuse [vwajaʒøz] *nf* passenger

voyaient, voyais, voyait *vb see* **voir**

voyelle [vwajɛl] *nf* vowel

voyez, voyiez, voyions *vb see* **voir**

voyons [vwajɔ̃] *vb see* **voir** ❶ let's see ▷ *Voyons ce qu'on peut faire.* Let's see what we can do. ❷ come on ▷ *Voyons, sois raisonnable!* Come on, be reasonable!

voyou [vwaju] *nmf* thug

vrac [vrak] *en vrac adv* loose ▷ *du thé en vrac* loose tea ▷ *des épices en vrac* loose spices

vrai [vre] (*f* **vraie**) *adj* true ▷ *une histoire vraie* a true story ▷ *C'est vrai?* Is that true?; **à vrai dire** to tell the truth

vraiment [vremɑ̃] *adv* really

vraisemblable [vresɑ̃blabl(ə)] *adj* likely ▷ *C'est peu vraisemblable.* That's not very likely. ▷ *Il va falloir trouver une excuse vraisemblable.* We'll have to find a convincing excuse.

vu [vy] *prep* given ▷ *vu la situation* given the circumstances; **vu que** in view of the fact that ▷ *vu qu'il est toujours en retard* in view of the fact that he's always late

vue [vy] *nf* ❶ eyesight ▷ *J'ai une mauvaise vue.* I've got bad eyesight. ❷ view ▷ *Il y a une belle vue d'ici.* There's a lovely view from here.; **à vue d'œil** visibly ▷ *Elle grandit à vue d'œil.* Every time you see her, she's taller.

vulgaire [vylger] *adj* vulgar ▷ *Ne dit pas ça, c'est très vulgaire.* Don't say that, it's very vulgar.

browse the Web

webmestre [webmɛstr] *nmf* webmaster

webographie [webɔgrafi] *nf* webography

webzine [webzin] *nm* webzine

western [wɛstɛrn] *nm* (*film*) western

wok [wɔk] *nm* wok

xénophobe [gzenɔfɔb] *adj* prejudiced against foreigners

xénophobie [gzenɔfɔbi] *nf* prejudice against foreigners

xylophone [ksilɔfɔn] *nm* xylophone ▷ *Elle joue du xylophone.* She plays the xylophone.

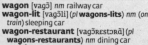

wagon [vagɔ̃] *nm* railway car

wagon-lit [vagɔ̃li] (*pl* **wagons-lits**) *nm* (*on train*) sleeping car

wagon-restaurant [vagɔ̃restɔrɑ̃] (*pl* **wagons-restaurants**) *nm* dining car

wapiti [wapiti] *nm* elk

Web [web] *nm* Web; **naviguer sur le Web** to

y [i] *pron* there ▷ *Nous y sommes allés l'été dernier.* We went there last summer. ▷ *Regarde dans le tiroir : je pense que les clés y sont.* Look in the drawer: I think the keys are in there.; « *Je pensais à l'examen.* » « *Mais arrête d'y penser!* » "I was thinking about the exam." "Well, stop thinking about it!"; « *Je ne m'attendais pas à ça.* » « *Moi, je m'y attendais.* » "I wasn't expecting that." "I was expecting it."

yeux [jø] (*sg* **œil**) *nmpl* eyes ▷ *Elle a les yeux bleus.* She has blue eyes.; **regarder quelqu'un dans les yeux** to look someone in the eye

yoga [jɔga] *nm* yoga

yogourt [jɔgurt] *nm* yogurt ▷ *un yogourt nature* a plain yogurt ▷ *un yogourt aux bleuets* a blueberry yogurt

youpi [jupi] *excl* Yippee!

yoyo [jojo] (*pl* **yoyo**) *nm* yo-yo

Yukon *nm* Yukon

Z

zapper [zape] *vb* to channel hop
zappette [zapɛt] *nf* (*for TV*) remote control
zappeur [zapœʀ] *nm* (*for TV*) remote control
zèbre [zɛbʀ(ə)] *nm* zebra
zéro [zeʀo] *nm* zero; **Ils ont gagné trois à zéro.** They won three-nothing.
zézayer [zezeje] *vb* to lisp ▷ *Il zézaie.* He's got a lisp.
zigonner [zigone] *vb* to fiddle ▷ *Comme la serrure était gelée, j'ai zigonné avec la clef.* Since the lock was frozen, I tried fiddling with the key.
zigzag [zigzag] *nm*: **faire des zigzags** to zigzag
zone [zon] *nf* zone; **la zone de but** (*sports*) crease; **une zone piétonne** a pedestrian zone
zoo [zoo] *nm* zoo
zoologique [zɔɔlɔʒik] *adj* zoological ▷ *un jardin zoologique* zoological gardens
zut [zyt] *excl* Oh heck!

a

a [eɪ, ə] *art* un *m*, une *f* ▷ *a book* un livre ▷ *a year ago* il y a un an ▷ *an apple* une pomme ▷ *a car* une auto ▷ *He's a butcher.* Il est boucher. ▷ *She's a doctor.* Elle est médecin.; **once a week** une fois par semaine; **10 km an hour** dix kilomètres à l'heure; **3 dollars a kilo** trois dollars le kilo; **a hundred times** cent fois

abandon [əˈbændən] *vb* abandonner

abbreviation [əbriːvɪˈeɪʃən] *n* abréviation *f*

ability [əˈbɪlɪtɪ] *n*: **to have the ability to do something** être capable de faire quelque chose

able [ˈeɪbl] *adj*: **to be able to do something** être capable de faire quelque chose

aboiteau [ˈæbətəʊ] *n* aboiteau *m* (*pl* aboiteaux) ▷ *Aboiteaus open as the tide comes in and close as it goes out.* Les aboiteaux ouvrent à marée montante et ferment à marée descendante.

abolish [əˈbɒlɪʃ] *vb* abolir

Aboriginal [æbəˈrɪdʒɪnəl] *adj* autochtone ▷ *Aboriginal languages* les langues autochtones ▷ *Aboriginal rights* les droits des autochtones ▷ *the Aboriginal peoples of Canada* les autochtones du Canada

abortion [əˈbɔːʃən] *n* avortement *m*

about [əˈbaʊt] *prep, adv* ❶ (*concerning*) à propos de ▷ *I'm phoning you about tomorrow's meeting.* Je vous appelle à propos de la réunion de demain. ❷ (*approximately*) environ ▷ *It takes about 10 hours.* Ça prend dix heures environ.; **about a hundred pages** une centaine de pages; **at about 11 o'clock** vers onze heures ❸ (*around*) dans ▷ *to walk around town* se promener dans la ville ❹ sur ▷ *a book about Manitoba* un livre sur Manitoba; **to be about to do something** être sur le point de faire quelque chose ▷ *I was about to go out.* J'étais sur le point de sortir.; **to talk about something** parler de quelque chose; **What's it about?** De quoi s'agit-il?; **How about going to the movies?** Et si nous allions au cinéma?

above [əˈbʌv] *prep, adv* ❶ (*higher than*) au-dessus de ▷ *He put his hands above his head.* Il a mis ses mains au-dessus de sa tête.; **the floor above** l'étage du dessus; **mentioned above** mentionné ci-dessus; **above all** par-dessus tout ❷ (*more than*) plus de ▷ *above 40 degrees* plus de quarante degrés

abroad [əˈbrɔːd] *adv* à l'étranger ▷ *to go abroad* partir à l'étranger

abrupt [əˈbrʌpt] *adj* brusque ▷ *He was a bit abrupt with me.* Il s'est montré un peu brusque avec moi.

absence [ˈæbsəns] *n* absence *f*

absent [ˈæbsənt] *adj* absent

absent-minded [ˈæbsəntˈmaɪndɪd] *adj* distrait ▷ *She's a bit absent-minded.* Elle est un peu distraite.

absolutely [æbsəˈluːtlɪ] *adv* ❶ (*completely*) tout à fait ▷ *You're absolutely right.* Tu as tout à fait raison. ❷ absolument ▷ *"Do you think it's a good idea?" — "Absolutely!"* « Tu trouves que c'est une bonne idée? » — « Absolument! »

absorbed [əbˈsɔːbd] *adj*: **to be absorbed in something** être absorbé par quelque chose; **to be absorbed in a book** être plongé dans un livre

absurd [əbˈsɜːd] *adj* absurde ▷ *That's absurd!* C'est absurde!

abuse [əˈbjuːz] *n* (*misuse*) abus *m*; **to shout abuse at somebody** insulter quelqu'un; **the issue of child abuse** la question des enfants maltraités; **the problem of drug abuse** le problème de la drogue
▶ *vb* ❶ maltraiter ▷ *abused children* les enfants maltraités; **to be abused** (*child, woman*) être maltraité ❷ (*insult*) injurier; **to abuse drugs** se droguer ❸ abuser de ▷ *to abuse a privilege* abuser d'un privilège

abusive [əˈbjuːsɪv] *adj* (*insulting*) insultant ▷ *abusive behaviour* un comportement insultant; **When I refused, he became abusive.** Quand j'ai refusé, il s'est mis à m'injurier.; **children with abusive parents** les enfants maltraités par leurs parents

academic [ækəˈdɛmɪk] *adj* scolaire ▷ *the academic year* l'année scolaire

academy [əˈkædəmɪ] *n* collège *m* ▷ *a military academy* un collège militaire

Acadia [əˈkeɪdɪə] *n* Acadie *f* ▷ *My ancestors were from Acadia.* Mes ancêtres étaient originaires de l'Acadie.

Acadian [əˈkeɪdɪən] *adj* acadien *m* (*f* acadienne) ▷ *the Acadian flag* le drapeau acadien ▷ *Acadian poutine* la poutine acadienne
▶ *n* Acadien *m*, Acadienne *f* ▷ *He's an Acadian.* C'est un Acadien. ▷ *She's an Acadian.* C'est une Acadienne.

accelerate [ækˈsɛləreɪt] *vb* accélérer

accelerator [ækˈsɛləreɪtəʳ] *n* accélérateur *m*

accent [ˈæksɛnt] *n* accent *m* ▷ *She's got a French accent.* Elle a l'accent français.

accept [əkˈsɛpt] *vb* accepter

acceptable [əkˈsɛptəbl] *adj* acceptable

access [ˈæksɛs] *n* ❶ accès *m* ▷ *He has access to confidential information.* Il a accès à des renseignements confidentiels. ❷ droit de visite *m* ▷ *Her ex-husband has access to the children.* Son ex-mari a le droit de visite.

accessible [ækˈsɛsəbl] *adj* accessible

accessory [ækˈsɛsərɪ] *n* accessoire *m* ▷ *fashion accessories* les accessoires de mode

accident [ˈæksɪdənt] *n* accident *m* ▷ *to have an accident* avoir un accident; **by accident** (1) (*by mistake*) accidentellement ▷ *I hit her with my elbow by accident.* Je l'ai heurtée accidentellement du coude. (2) (*by chance*) par hasard ▷ *She met him by accident.* Elle l'a rencontré par hasard.

accidental [æksɪˈdɛntl] *adj* accidentel (*f* accidentelle)

accommodate [əˈkɒmədeɪt] *vb* recevoir ▷ *The hotel can accommodate 50 people.* L'hôtel peut recevoir cinquante personnes.

accommodation [əkɒməˈdeɪʃən] *n* logement *m*

accompany [əˈkʌmpənɪ] *vb* accompagner

accord [əˈkɔːd] *n*: **of one's own accord** de son plein gré ▷ *She left of her own accord.* Elle est partie de son plein gré.

accordingly [əˈkɔːdɪŋlɪ] *adv* en conséquence

according to [əˈkɔːdɪən] *prep* selon ▷ *according to him* selon lui

accordion [əˈkɔːdɪən] *n* accordéon *m*

account [əˈkaunt] *n* ❶ compte *m* ▷ *a bank account* un compte en banque; **to do the accounts** tenir la comptabilité. ❷ (*report*) compte rendu *m* (*pl* comptes rendus) ▷ *He gave a detailed account of what happened.* Il a donné un compte rendu détaillé des événements.; **to take something into account** tenir compte de quelque chose; **on account of** à cause de ▷ *We couldn't go out on account of the bad weather.* Nous n'avons pas pu sortir à cause du mauvais temps.

account for *vb* expliquer ▷ *If she was ill, that would account for her poor results.* Si elle était malade, cela expliquerait ses résultats médiocres.

accountable [əˈkauntəbl] *adj*: **to be accountable to someone for something** être responsable de quelque chose devant quelqu'un

accountancy [əˈkauntənsɪ] *n* comptabilité *f*

accountant [əˈkauntənt] *n* comptable ▷ *She's an accountant.* Elle est comptable.

accuracy [ˈækjurəsɪ] *n* exactitude *f*

accurate [ˈækjurɪt] *adj* précis ▷ *accurate information* des renseignements précis *m*

accurately [ˈækjurɪtlɪ] *adv* avec précision

accusation [ækjuˈzeɪʃən] *n* accusation *f*

accuse [əˈkjuːz] *vb*: **to accuse somebody of something** accuser quelqu'un de quelque chose ▷ *Her parents accused her of being lazy.* Ses parents l'ont accusée d'être paresseuse.

ace [eɪs] *n* as *m* ▷ *the ace of hearts* l'as de cœur

ache [eɪk] *n* douleur *f*
▶ *vb*: **My leg aches.** J'ai mal à la jambe.

achieve [əˈtʃiːv] *vb* ❶ (*an aim*) atteindre ❷ (*victory*) remporter

achievement [əˈtʃiːvmənt] *n* exploit *m* ▷ *That was quite an achievement.* C'était un véritable exploit.

acid [ˈæsɪd] *n* acide *m*

acid rain *n* pluies *fpl* acides

acne [ˈæknɪ] *n* acné *f*

acre [ˈeɪkəʳ] *n* demi-hectare *m*

acrobat [ˈækrəbæt] *n* acrobate *mf* ▷ *He's an acrobat.* Il est acrobate.

acrobatics [ækrəˈbætɪks] *n* acrobatie *f*

across [əˈkrɒs] *prep*, *adv* de l'autre côté de ▷ *the house across the road* la maison de l'autre côté de la rue; **to walk across the road** traverser la rue; **to run across the road** traverser la rue

en courant; **across from** (*opposite*) en face de ▷ *He sat down across from us.* Il s'est assis en face de nous.

act [ækt] *vb* ❶ (*in play, film*) jouer ▷ *He acts really well.* Il joue vraiment bien. ▷ *She's acting the part of Juliet.* Elle joue le rôle de Juliette. ❷ (*take action*) agir ▷ *The police acted quickly.* La police a agi rapidement.; **She acts as his interpreter.** Elle lui sert d'interprète.; **to act like an idiot** se comporter comme un imbécile ▶ *n* (*in play*) acte *m* ▷ *in the first act* au premier acte

action [ˈækʃən] *n* action *f* ▷ *The film was full of action.* Il y avait beaucoup d'action dans le film.; **to take firm action against** prendre des mesures énergiques contre

active [ˈæktɪv] *adj* actif (*f* active) ▷ *He's very active.* Il est très actif.; **an active volcano** un volcan en activité

activity [ækˈtɪvɪtɪ] *n* activité *f* ▷ *outdoor activities* les activités de plein air

actor [ˈæktəʳ] *n* acteur *m*

actress [ˈæktrɪs] *n* actrice *f*

actual [ˈæktjuəl] *adj* réel (*f* réelle) ▷ *The film is based on actual events.* Le film repose sur des faits réels.; **What's the actual amount?** Quel est le montant exact?

actually [ˈæktjuəlɪ] *adv* ❶ (*really*) vraiment ▷ *Did it actually happen?* Est-ce que c'est vraiment arrivé? ❷ (*in fact*) en fait ▷ *Actually, I don't know her at all.* En fait, je ne la connais pas du tout.

acupuncture [ˈækjupʌŋktʃəʳ] *n* acuponcture *f*

ad [æd] *n* ❶ (*in paper*) annonce *f* ❷ (*on TV, radio*) pub *f*

AD *abbr* [eɪˈdiː] *ap. J.-C.* (= *après Jésus-Christ*) ▷ *in 800 AD* en huit cents après Jésus-Christ

adapt [əˈdæpt] *vb* adapter ▷ *Her novel was adapted for television.* Son roman a été adapté pour la télévision.; **to adapt to something** (*get used to*) s'adapter à quelque chose ▷ *He adapted to his new school very quickly.* Il s'est adapté très vite à sa nouvelle école.

adaptation [ædæpˈteɪʃən] *n* adaptation *f* ▷ *a TV adaptation of a novel* une adaptation télévisée d'un roman

adapter [əˈdæptəʳ] *n* adaptateur *m*

add [æd] *vb* ajouter ▷ *Add two eggs to the mixture.* Ajoutez deux œufs au mélange.; **to add up** additionner ▷ *Add up the figures.* Additionnez les chiffres.

addict [ˈædɪkt] *n* (*drug addict*) drogué *m*, droguée *f*; **She's a football addict.** C'est une mordue de football.

addicted [əˈdɪktɪd] *adj*: **to be addicted to** (*drug*) s'adonner à; **He's addicted to soap operas.** C'est un mordu des téléromans.; **I'm addicted to chocolate.** Je ne peux résister au chocolat.

addition [əˈdɪʃən] *n*: **in addition** en plus ▷ *He's broken his leg and, in addition, he's caught a cold.* Il s'est cassé la jambe et en plus, il a attrapé un rhume.; **in addition to** en plus de ▷ *In addition to the price of the cassette, there's a charge for postage.* En plus du prix de la cassette, il y a des

frais de port.
address [ə'drɛs] n adresse f ▷ *What's your address?* Quelle est votre adresse?
adjective ['adʒɛktɪv] n adjectif m
adjust [ə'dʒʌst] vb régler ▷ *You can adjust the height of the chair.* Tu peux régler la hauteur de la chaise.; **to adjust to something** (*get used to*) s'adapter à quelque chose ▷ *He adjusted to his new school very quickly.* Il s'est adapté très vite à sa nouvelle école.
adjustable [ə'dʒʌstəbl] adj réglable
administration [ədmɪnɪs'treɪʃən] n administration f
admire [əd'maɪə'] vb admirer
admission [əd'mɪʃən] n entrée f ▷ *"free admission"* « entrée gratuite »
admit [əd'mɪt] vb ❶ (*agree*) admettre ▷ *I must admit that...* Je dois admettre que... ❷ (*confess*) reconnaître ▷ *She admitted that she'd done it.* Elle a reconnu qu'elle l'avait fait.
admittance [əd'mɪtəns] n: **"no admittance"** « accès interdit »
adolescence [ædəu'lɛsns] n adolescence f
adolescent [ædəu'lɛsnt] n adolescent m, adolescente f
adopt [ə'dɔpt] vb adopter ▷ *I was adopted.* J'ai été adopté.
adopted [ə'dɔptɪd] adj adoptif (f adoptive) ▷ *an adopted son* un fils adoptif
adoption [ə'dɔpʃən] n adoption f
adore [ə'dɔː'] vb adorer
adult ['ædʌlt] n adulte mf; **adult education** l'éducation f des adultes
advance [əd'vɑːns] vb ❶ (*move forward*) avancer ▷ *The troops are advancing.* Les troupes avancent. ❷ (*progress*) progresser ▷ *Technology has advanced a lot.* La technologie a beaucoup progressé.
▷ n: **in advance** à l'avance ▷ *They bought the tickets in advance.* Ils ont acheté les billets à l'avance.
advanced [əd'vɑːnst] adj avancé
advantage [əd'vɑːntɪdʒ] n avantage m ▷ *Going to university has many advantages.* Aller à l'université présente de nombreux avantages.; **to take advantage of something** profiter de quelque chose ▷ *He took advantage of the good weather to go for a walk.* Il a profité du beau temps pour faire une promenade.; **to take advantage of somebody** exploiter quelqu'un ▷ *The company was taking advantage of its employees.* La société exploitait ses employés.
adventure [əd'vɛntʃə'] n aventure f
adventurer [əd'vɛntʃərə'] n aventurier m, aventurière f
adventurous [əd'vɛntʃərəs] adj aventureux (f aventureuse)
adverb ['ædvəːb] n adverbe m
advertise ['ædvətaɪz] vb faire de la publicité pour ▷ *They're advertising the new model.* Ils font de la publicité pour leur nouveau modèle.; **Jobs are advertised in the paper.** Le journal publie des annonces d'emplois.
advertisement [əd'vəːtɪsmənt] n ❶ (*on TV*) publicité f ❷ (*in newspaper*) annonce f
advertising ['ædvətaɪzɪŋ] n publicité f

advice [əd'vaɪs] n conseils mpl ▷ *to give somebody advice* donner des conseils à quelqu'un; **a piece of advice** un conseil ▷ *She gave me a good piece of advice.* Elle m'a donné un bon conseil.
advise [əd'vaɪz] vb conseiller ▷ *They advised me to wait.* Ils m'ont conseillé d'attendre. ▷ *I advise you not to go there.* Je te conseille de ne pas y aller.
aerial ['ɛərɪəl] n antenne f
aerobics [ɛə'rəubɪks] npl aérobic f ▷ *I'm going to aerobics tonight.* Je vais au cours d'aérobic ce soir.
affair [ə'fɛə'] n ❶ (*romantic*) aventure f ▷ *to have an affair with somebody* avoir une aventure avec quelqu'un ❷ (*event*) affaire f
affect [ə'fɛkt] vb ❶ concerner ▷ *It affects all of us.* Cela nous concerne tous. ❷ avoir des conséquences pour ▷ *If you smoke, it will affect the people around you.* Si tu fumes, cela aura des conséquences pour les gens autour de toi. ❸ décourager ▷ *We mustn't let it affect us.* Nous ne devons pas nous laisser décourager par cela.
affectionate [ə'fɛkʃənɪt] adj affectueux (f affectueuse)
afford [ə'fɔːd] vb avoir les moyens d'acheter ▷ *I can't afford a new pair of jeans.* Je n'ai pas les moyens d'acheter un nouveau jean.; **We can't afford to go on a holiday.** Nous n'avons pas les moyens de partir en vacances.
afraid [ə'freɪd] adj: **to be afraid of something** avoir peur de quelque chose ▷ *I'm afraid of spiders.* J'ai peur des araignées.; **I'm afraid I can't come.** Je crains de ne pouvoir venir.; **I'm afraid so.** Hélas oui.; **I'm afraid not.** Hélas non.
after ['ɑːftə'] prep, adv, conj après ▷ *after dinner* après le dîner ▷ *He ran after me.* Il a couru après moi. ▷ *soon after* peu après; **after I've had a rest** après m'être reposé; **after having asked** après avoir demandé; **after all** après tout
afternoon ['ɑːftə'nuːn] n après-midi mf ▷ *3 o'clock in the afternoon* trois heures de l'après-midi ▷ *this afternoon* cet après-midi ▷ *on Saturday afternoon* samedi après-midi
afterwards ['ɑːftəwəd] adv après ▷ *She left not long afterwards.* Elle est partie peu de temps après.
again [ə'gɛn] adv ❶ (*one more time*) encore une fois ▷ *Can you tell me again?* Tu peux me le dire encore une fois? ❷ (*once more*) de nouveau ▷ *They're friends again.* Ils sont de nouveau amis.; **not... again** ne... plus ▷ *I won't go there again.* Je n'y retournerai plus.; **Do it again!** Refais-le!; **again and again** à plusieurs reprises
against [ə'gɛnst] prep contre ▷ *He leaned against the wall.* Il s'est appuyé contre le mur. ▷ *I'm against nuclear testing.* Je suis contre les essais nucléaires.
age [eɪdʒ] n âge m ▷ *at the age of 16* à l'âge de seize ans ▷ *an age limit* une limite d'âge; **I haven't been to the movies in ages.** Ça fait une éternité que je ne suis pas allé au cinéma.
aged ['eɪdʒɪd] adj: **aged 10** âgé de dix ans;

their aged parents leurs parents âgés

agency ['eɪdʒənsɪ] n agence f ▷ a travel agency une agence de voyages ▷ a real estate agency une agence immobilière

agenda [ə'dʒendə] n ❶ ordre m du jour ▷ on the agenda à l'ordre du jour ▷ the agenda for today's meeting l'ordre du jour de la réunion d'aujourd'hui ❷ agenda (daybook) m ▷ I wrote it in my agenda. Je l'ai écrit dans mon agenda.

agent ['eɪdʒənt] n agent m, agente f; a real estate agent un agent immobilier; She's a travel agent. Elle est agente de voyage.

aggressive [ə'ɡrɛsɪv] adj agressif (f agressive)

ago [ə'ɡəʊ] adv: **two days ago** il y a deux jours; **two years ago** il y a deux ans; **not long ago** il n'y a pas longtemps; **How long ago did it happen?** Il y a combien de temps que c'est arrivé?

agony ['æɡənɪ] n: **to be in agony** souffrir le martyre ▷ I was in agony. Je souffrais le martyre.

agree [ə'ɡriː] vb: **to agree with** être d'accord avec ▷ I agree with her. Je suis d'accord avec elle.; **to agree to do something** accepter de faire quelque chose ▷ He agreed to go and pick her up. Il a accepté d'aller la chercher.; **to agree that...** admettre que... ▷ I agree that it's difficult. J'admets que c'est difficile.; **Garlic doesn't agree with me.** Je ne supporte pas l'ail.

agreed [ə'ɡriːd] adj convenu ▷ at the agreed time au moment convenu

agreement [ə'ɡriːmənt] n accord m; **to be in agreement** être d'accord ▷ Everybody was in agreement with me. Tout le monde était d'accord avec moi.

agricultural [æɡrɪ'kʌltʃərəl] adj agricole

agriculture ['æɡrɪkʌltʃər] n agriculture f

ahead [ə'hed] adv ❶ devant ▷ She looked straight ahead. Elle regardait droit devant elle.; **ahead of time** en avance; **to plan ahead** organiser à l'avance; **Our team is 5 points ahead.** Notre équipe a cinq points d'avance.; **Go ahead!** Allez-y!

aid [eɪd] n: **in aid of charity** au profit d'associations caritatives

AIDS [eɪdz] n sida m

aim [eɪm] vb ❶ pointer ▷ He aimed his flashlight at me. Il a pointé sa lampe de poche sur moi. ❷ viser ▷ Aim at the target. Vise la cible. ❸ avoir l'intention de ▷ We aim to leave at 5 o'clock. Nous avons l'intention de partir à cinq heures.; **The film is aimed at children.** Le film est destiné aux enfants.
▶ n objectif m ▷ The aim of the festival is to raise money. L'objectif du festival est de collecter des fonds.; **My aim is bad.** Je vise mal.

air [ɛər] n air m ▷ to get some fresh air prendre l'air; **by air** en avion ▷ I prefer to travel by air. Je préfère voyager en avion.

air bag n sac gonflable m

air-conditioned ['eəkən'dɪʃənd] adj climatisé

air conditioning [-kən'dɪʃnɪŋ] n climatisation f

Air Force n armée f de l'air

airline ['eəlaɪn] n compagnie aérienne f

airmail ['eəmeɪl] n: **by airmail** par avion

airplane ['eəpleɪn] n avion m

airport ['eəpɔːt] n aéroport m

aisle [aɪl] n ❶ (theatre, supermarket) allée f ❷ (airplane) couloir m

alarm [ə'lɑːm] n (warning) alarme f; **a fire alarm** un avertisseur d'incendie

alarm clock n réveil m

Alberta [æl'bɜːtə] Alberta f

album ['ælbəm] n album m

alcohol ['ælkəhɒl] n alcool m

alcoholic [ælkə'hɒlɪk] n alcoolique mf ▷ a clinic for alcoholics une clinique pour les alcooliques
▶ adj alcoolisé ▷ alcoholic drinks des boissons alcoolisées

alert [ə'lɜːt] adj ❶ (bright) vif (f vive) ▷ a very alert baby un bébé très vif ❷ (paying attention) vigilant ▷ We must stay alert. Nous devons rester vigilants.

alibi ['ælɪbaɪ] n alibi m

alien ['eɪlɪən] n (from outer space) extra-terrestre mf

alike [ə'laɪk] adv: **to look alike** se ressembler ▷ The two sisters look alike. Les deux sœurs se ressemblent.

alive [ə'laɪv] adj vivant

all [ɔːl] adj, pron, adv tout (mpl tous) ▷ all the time tout le temps ▷ I ate all of it. J'ai tout mangé. ▷ all day toute la journée ▷ all the books tous les livres ▷ all the girls toutes les filles; **All of us went.** Nous y sommes tous allés.; **after all** après tout ▷ After all, nobody can make us go. Après tout, personne ne peut nous obliger à y aller.; **all alone** tout seul ▷ She's all alone. Elle est toute seule.; **not at all** pas du tout ▷ I'm not tired at all. Je ne suis pas du tout fatigué.; **The score is 5 all.** Le score est de cinq partout.

allergic [ə'lɜːdʒɪk] adj allergique; **to be allergic to something** être allergique à quelque chose ▷ I'm allergic to cat hair. Je suis allergique aux poils de chat.

allergy ['ælədʒɪ] n allergie f ▷ I have allergies. J'ai des allergies.; **a food allergy** une allergie alimentaire

alley ['ælɪ] n ruelle f

allophone ['æləfəʊn] adj allophone mf
▶ n allophone mf ▷ Allophones speak neither French nor English as their first language. La langue maternelle des allophones n'est ni le français ni l'anglais.

allow [ə'laʊ] vb: **to be allowed to do something** être autorisé à faire quelque chose ▷ He's not allowed to go out at night. Il n'est pas autorisé à sortir le soir.; **to allow somebody to do something** permettre à quelqu'un de faire quelque chose ▷ His mom allowed him to go out. Sa mère lui a permis de sortir.

allowance [ə'laʊəns] n argent m de poche ▷ Do you get a weekly allowance? Est-ce que tu reçois de l'argent de poche chaque semaine?

all right adv ❶ (okay) bien ▷ Everything turned out all right. Tout s'est bien terminé.; **Are you all right?** Ça va? ❷ (not bad) pas mal ▷ The film was all right. Le film n'était pas mal. ❸ (when agreeing) d'accord ▷ "We'll talk about it later." —"All right." « On en reparlera plus tard. » —

« D'accord. »; **Is that all right with you?** Tu es d'accord?

almond ['ɑːmənd] n amande f

almost ['ɔːlməʊst] adv presque ▷ I'm almost finished. J'ai presque fini.

alone [ə'ləʊn] adj, adv seul ▷ He lives alone. Il habite seul.; **to leave somebody alone** laisser quelqu'un tranquille ▷ Leave me alone! Laissemoi tranquille!; **to leave something alone** ne pas toucher à quelque chose ▷ Leave my things alone! Ne touche pas à mes affaires!

along [ə'lɒŋ] prep, adv le long de ▷ I was walking along the beach. Je me promenais le long de la plage.; **all along** depuis le début ▷ He was lying to me all along. Il m'a menti depuis le début.

aloud [ə'laʊd] adv à haute voix ▷ He read the poem aloud. Il a lu le poème à haute voix.

alphabet ['ælfəbɛt] n alphabet m

alphabetical [ælfə'bɛtɪkl] adj alphabétique ▷ in alphabetical order en ordre alphabétique

already [ɔːl'rɛdɪ] adv déjà ▷ She had already gone. Elle était déjà partie.

also ['ɔːlsəʊ] adv aussi

altar ['ɔːltər] n autel m

alter ['ɔːltər] vb changer

alternate ['ɔːltəneɪt] adj: **on alternate days** tous les deux jours

alternative [ɔːl'tɜːnətɪv] n choix m ▷ You have no alternative. Tu n'as pas le choix.; **Fruit is a healthy alternative to chocolate.** Les fruits sont plus sains que le chocolat.; **There are several alternatives.** Il y a plusieurs possibilités.
▶ adj autre ▷ They made alternative plans. Ils ont pris d'autres dispositions.; **an alternative solution** une solution de rechange; **alternative medicine** la médecine douce

alternatively [ɔːl'tɜːnətɪvlɪ] adv: **Alternatively, we could just stay at home.** On pourrait aussi rester à la maison.

although [ɔːl'ðəʊ] conj bien que ▷ Although she was tired, she stayed up late. Bien qu'elle soit fatiguée, elle s'est couchée tard.

altogether [ɔːltə'gɛðər] adv ❶ (in total) en tout ▷ You owe me $20 altogether. Tu me dois vingt dollars en tout. ❷ (completely) tout à fait ▷ I'm not altogether happy with your work. Je ne suis pas tout à fait satisfait de votre travail.

aluminum [ə'luːmɪnəm] n aluminium m

always ['ɔːlweɪz] adv toujours ▷ He's always grumbling. Il est toujours en train de ronchonner.

am [æm] vb see **be**

a.m. [eɪ'ɛm] abbr du matin ▷ at 4 a.m. à quatre heures du matin

amateur ['æmətər] n amateur m; **amateur sports** le sport amateur

amazed [ə'meɪzd] adj stupéfait ▷ their amazed parents leurs parents stupéfaits ▷ I was amazed that I managed to do it. J'étais stupéfait d'avoir réussi.

amazing [ə'meɪzɪŋ] adj ❶ (surprising) stupéfiant ▷ That's amazing news! C'est une nouvelle stupéfiante! ❷ (excellent) exceptionnel (f exceptionnelle) ▷ My dad's an amazing cook. Mon père est un cuisinier exceptionnel.

ambassador [æm'bæsədər] n ambassadeur m, ambassadrice f

ambition [æm'bɪʃən] n ambition f

ambitious [æm'bɪʃəs] adj ambitieux (f ambitieuse) ▷ She's very ambitious. Elle est très ambitieuse.

ambulance ['æmbjʊləns] n ambulance f

amenities [ə'miːnɪtɪz] npl aménagements mpl; **The hotel has very good amenities.** L'hôtel est très bien aménagé.

among [ə'mʌŋ] prep parmi ▷ There were six children among them. Il y avait six enfants parmi eux.; **We were among friends.** Nous étions entre amis.; **among other things** entre autres

amount [ə'maʊnt] n ❶ somme f ▷ a large amount of money une grosse somme d'argent ❷ quantité f; **a huge amount of rice** une énorme quantité de riz

amp ['æmpeər] n ❶ (of electricity) ampère m ❷ (amplifier) amplificateur m

amplifier ['æmplɪfaɪər] n (for hi-fi) amplificateur m

amuse [ə'mjuːz] vb amuser ▷ She was not amused by their rude jokes. Leurs blagues grossières ne l'ont pas amusée.

amusement arcade [ə'mjuːzməntɑːˈkeɪd] n salle de jeux électroniques

an [æn, ən, n] art see **a**

analysis [ə'næləsɪs] n analyse f

analyze ['ænəlaɪz] vb analyser

ancestor ['ænsɪstər] n ancêtre mf

anchor ['æŋkər] n ancre f

ancient ['eɪnʃənt] adj ❶ (civilization) antique ▷ ancient Greece la Grèce antique ❷ (custom, building) ancien (f ancienne) ▷ an ancient monument un monument ancien

and [ænd] conj et ▷ you and me toi et moi ▷ 2 and 2 are 4 deux et deux font quatre; **Please try and come!** Essaie de venir!; **He talked and talked.** Il n'a pas arrêté de parler.; **better and better** de mieux en mieux

angel ['eɪndʒəl] n ange m

anger ['æŋgər] n colère f

angle ['æŋgl] n angle m

Anglophone ['æŋgləfəʊn] n anglophone mf ▷ A lot of Anglophones live in Montréal. Beaucoup d'anglophones habitent à Montréal.
▶ adj anglophone ▷ an Anglophone community une communauté anglophone

angry ['æŋgrɪ] adj en colère ▷ Dad looks very angry. Papa a l'air très en colère.; **to be angry with somebody** être furieux contre quelqu'un ▷ Mom's really angry with you. Maman est vraiment furieuse contre toi.; **to get angry** se fâcher

animal ['ænɪməl] n animal m (pl animaux)

animation [ænɪ'meɪʃən] n ❶ film d'animation m ▷ We went to see the new 3D animation. Nous sommes allés voir le nouveau film d'animation 3D. ❷ animation f ▷ She's studying animation. Elle étudie l'animation.; **computer animation** l'animatique f

ankle ['æŋkl] n cheville f

anniversary [ænɪ'vɜːsərɪ] n anniversaire m ▷ a wedding anniversary un anniversaire de mariage

announce [ə'naʊns] vb annoncer

announcement [ə'naʊnsmənt] n annonce f

annoy [ə'nɔɪ] vb agacer ▷ He's really annoying me. Il m'agace vraiment.; **to get annoyed** se fâcher ▷ Don't get so annoyed! Ne vous fâchez pas!

annoying [ə'nɔɪɪŋ] adj agaçant ▷ It's really annoying. C'est vraiment agaçant.

annual ['ænjʊəl] adj annuel (f annuelle) ▷ an annual meeting une réunion annuelle

anorexia [ænə'rɛksɪə] n anorexie f

another [ə'nʌðə'] adj un autre, une autre ▷ Would you like another piece of cake? Tu veux un autre morceau de gâteau? ▷ Have you got another skirt? Tu as une autre jupe?

answer ['ɑːnsə'] vb répondre à ▷ Can you answer my question? Peux-tu répondre à ma question? ▷ to answer the phone répondre au téléphone; **to answer the door** aller ouvrir ▷ Can you answer the door please? Tu peux aller ouvrir s'il te plaît?
  ▷ n ❶ (to question) réponse f ❷ (to problem) solution f

answering machine ['ɑːnsərɪŋ-] n répondeur m

ant [ænt] n fourmi f

antagonize [æn'tægənaɪz] vb contrarier ▷ He didn't want to antagonize her. Il ne voulait pas la contrarier.

Antarctic [ænt'ɑːktɪk] n Antarctique f

anthem ['ænθəm] n: **the national anthem** l'hymne m national ▷ Our national anthem is "O Canada". Notre hymne national est « Ô Canada ».

antibiotic ['æntɪbaɪ'ɔtɪk] n antibiotique m

antifreeze ['æntɪfriːz] n antigel m

antique [æn'tiːk] n antiquité f; **an antique dealer** un marchand d'antiquités

antique shop n magasin d'antiquités m

antivirus software [æntɪ'vaɪərəs'sɔftweə'] n logiciel antivirus m ▷ to download free antivirus software télécharger un logiciel antivirus gratuit

antlers ['æntləz] npl bois mpl ▷ The moose sheds its antlers every year. Les bois de l'orignal tombent chaque année.

anxious ['æŋkʃəs] adj anxieux (f anxieuse) ▷ He's a little anxious about the test. Il est un peu anxieux à propos du test.; **to be anxious to do something** avoir hâte de faire quelque chose

any ['ɛnɪ] adj, pron, adv ❶ du ▷ Do you want any bread? Tu veux du pain? ❷ de la ▷ Is there any ice cream? Est-ce qu'il y a de la crème glacée? ❸ de l' ▷ Have you got any mineral water? Avez-vous de l'eau minérale? ❹ des ▷ Do you have any CDs? Avez-vous des DC? ❺ de, d' ▷ I don't have any books. Je n'ai pas de livres. ▷ I don't have any money. Je n'ai pas d'argent. ❻ en ▷ Sorry, I don't have any. Désolé, je n'en ai pas.; **any more** **(1)** (additional) encore de ▷ Would you like any more coffee? Est-ce que tu veux encore du café? **(2)** (no longer) ne... plus ▷ I don't see her any more. Je ne la vois plus.

anybody ['ɛnɪbɒdɪ] pron ❶ (in question) quelqu'un ▷ Does anybody have a pen? Est-ce

que quelqu'un a un stylo? ❷ (no matter who) n'importe qui ▷ Anybody can learn to swim. N'importe qui peut apprendre à nager. ❸ ne... personne ▷ I can't see anybody. Je ne vois personne.

anyone ['ɛnɪwʌn] pron ❶ (in question) quelqu'un ▷ Has anyone got a pen? Est-ce que quelqu'un a un stylo? ❷ (no matter who) n'importe qui ▷ Anyone can learn to swim. N'importe qui peut apprendre à nager. ❸ ne... personne ▷ I can't see anyone. Je ne vois personne.

anything ['ɛnɪθɪŋ] pron ❶ (in question) quelque chose ▷ Would you like anything to eat? Tu veux manger quelque chose? ❷ (no matter what) n'importe quoi ▷ Anything could happen. Il pourrait arriver n'importe quoi. ❸ ne... rien ▷ I can't hear anything. Je n'entends rien.

anyway ['ɛnɪweɪ] adv de toute façon ▷ He doesn't want to go out, and anyway he's not allowed. Il ne veut pas sortir et de toute façon il n'y est pas autorisé.

anywhere ['ɛnɪwɛə'] adv ❶ (in question) quelque part ▷ Have you seen my coat anywhere? Est-ce tu as vu mon manteau quelque part? ❷ n'importe où ▷ You can buy stamps almost anywhere. On peut acheter des timbres presque n'importe où. ❸ ne... nulle part ▷ I can't find it anywhere. Je ne le trouve nulle part.

apart [ə'pɑːt] adv: **The two towns are 10 kilometres apart.** Les deux villes sont à dix kilomètres l'une de l'autre.; **apart from** à part ▷ Apart from that, everything's fine. À part ça, tout va bien.

apartment [ə'pɑːtmənt] n appartement m

apologize [ə'pɒlədʒaɪz] vb s'excuser ▷ He apologized for being late. Il s'est excusé de son retard.; **I apologize!** Je m'excuse!

apology [ə'pɒlədʒɪ] n excuses fpl

apostrophe [ə'pɒstrəfɪ] n apostrophe f

apparatus [æpə'reɪtəs] n ❶ (in lab) matériel m ❷ (in gym) agrès mpl

apparent [ə'pærənt] adj apparent

apparently [ə'pærəntlɪ] adv apparemment

appeal [ə'piːl] vb lancer un appel ▷ They appealed for help. Ils ont lancé un appel au secours.; **Greece doesn't appeal to me.** Ça ne me tente pas la Grèce.; **Does that appeal to you?** Ça te tente?
  ▷ n appel m ▷ They have launched an appeal. Ils ont lancé un appel.

appear [ə'pɪə'] vb ❶ (come into view) apparaître ▷ The bus appeared around the corner. L'autobus est apparu au coin de la rue.; **to appear on TV** passer à la télé ❷ (seem) paraître ▷ She appeared to be asleep. Elle paraissait dormir.

appearance [ə'pɪərəns] n (looks) apparence f ▷ He takes great care over his appearance. Il prend grand soin de son apparence.

appendicitis [əpɛndɪ'saɪtɪs] n appendicite f

appetite ['æpɪtaɪt] n appétit m

applaud [ə'plɔːd] vb applaudir

applause [ə'plɔːz] n applaudissements mpl

apple ['æpl] n pomme f; **an apple tree** un pommier

applicant ['æplɪkənt] n candidat m, candidate f ▷ There were a hundred applicants for the job. Il y avait cent candidats pour ce poste.

application [æplɪ'keɪʃən] n application (computer) f ▷ to open an application lancer une application; **a job application** une demande d'emploi

application form n ❶ (for job) dossier de candidature m ❷ (college or university) demande d'admission f

apply [ə'plaɪ] vb: **to apply for a job** poser sa candidature à un poste; **to apply to** (be relevant) s'appliquer à ▷ This rule doesn't apply to us. Ce règlement ne s'applique pas à nous.

appointment [ə'pɔɪntmənt] n rendez-vous m ▷ I have a dental appointment. J'ai rendez-vous chez le dentiste.

appreciate [ə'pri:ʃɪeɪt] vb être reconnaissant de ▷ I really appreciate your help. Je vous suis extrêmement reconnaissant de votre aide.

apprentice [ə'prɛntɪs] n apprenti m, apprentie f

approach [ə'prəʊtʃ] vb ❶ (get nearer to) s'approcher de ▷ She approached the house. Elle s'est approchée de la maison. ❷ (tackle) aborder ▷ to approach a problem aborder un problème

appropriate [ə'prəʊprɪeɪt] adj approprié ▷ That dress isn't very appropriate for an interview. Cette robe n'est pas très appropriée pour une entrevue.

approval [ə'pru:vəl] n approbation f

approve [ə'pru:v] vb: **to approve of** approuver ▷ I don't approve of your choice. Je n'approuve pas ton choix.; **They didn't approve of his girlfriend.** Sa copine ne leur a pas plu.

approximate [ə'prɒksɪmɪt] adj approximatif (f approximative)

apricot ['eɪprɪkɒt] n abricot m

April ['eɪprəl] n avril m; **in April** en avril; **April Fool's Day** le premier avril

apron ['eɪprən] n tablier m

Aquarius [ə'kwɛərɪəs] n Verseau m ▷ I'm Aquarius. Je suis Verseau.

Arabic ['ærəbɪk] n arabe m

arch [ɑ:tʃ] n arc m

archaeologist [ɑ:kɪ'ɒlədʒɪst] n archéologue mf ▷ He's an archaeologist. Il est archéologue.

archaeology [ɑ:kɪ'ɒlədʒɪ] n archéologie f

architect ['ɑ:kɪtɛkt] n architecte mf ▷ She's an architect. Elle est architecte.

architecture ['ɑ:kɪtɛktʃə] n architecture f

Arctic ['ɑ:ktɪk] n Arctique m

are [ɑ:] vb see **be**

area ['ɛərɪə] n ❶ région f ▷ I live in the Kingston area. J'habite dans la région de Kingston. ❷ quartier m ▷ This is my favourite area of Montréal. C'est le quartier de Montréal que je préfère. ❸ superficie f ▷ The field has an area of 1500 m². Le champ a une superficie de mille cinq cent mètres carrés.

area code n indicatif m régional

arena [ə'ri:nə] n aréna m ▷ They're building a new arena in Timmins. On construit un nouvel aréna à Timmins.

argue ['ɑ:gju:] vb se disputer ▷ They never stop arguing. Ils n'arrêtent pas de se disputer.

argument ['ɑ:gjumənt] n: **to have an argument** se disputer ▷ They had an argument. Ils se sont disputés.

Aries ['ɛəri:z] n Bélier m ▷ I'm Aries. Je suis Bélier.

arm [ɑ:m] n bras m

armchair ['ɑ:mtʃɛə] n fauteuil m

armour ['ɑ:mə] n armure f

army ['ɑ:mɪ] n armée f

around [ə'raʊnd] prep, adv ❶ autour de ▷ She wore a scarf around her neck. Elle portait une écharpe autour du cou. ❷ (approximately) environ ▷ It costs around $100. Cela coûte environ cent dollars. ❸ (date, time) vers ▷ Let's meet at around 8 p.m. Retrouvons-nous vers vingt heures.; **around here (1)** (nearby) près d'ici ▷ Is there a drugstore around here? Est-ce qu'il y a une pharmacie près d'ici? **(2)** (in this area) dans les parages ▷ He lives around here. Il habite dans les parages.

arrange [ə'reɪndʒ] vb: **to arrange to do something** prévoir de faire quelque chose ▷ They arranged to go out together on Friday. Ils ont prévu de sortir ensemble vendredi.; **to arrange a meeting** convenir d'un rendez-vous ▷ Can we arrange a meeting?; **to arrange a party** organiser une fête

arrangement [ə'reɪndʒmənt] n (plan) arrangement m; **They made arrangements to go out on Friday night.** Ils ont organisé une sortie vendredi soir.

arrest [ə'rɛst] vb arrêter ▷ The police have arrested 5 people. La police a arrêté cinq personnes.
▶ n arrestation f ▷ You're under arrest! Vous êtes en état d'arrestation!

arrival [ə'raɪvl] n arrivée f; **to welcome the new arrivals** accueillir les nouveaux venus

arrive [ə'raɪv] vb arriver ▷ I arrived at 5 o'clock. Je suis arrivé à cinq heures.

arrogant ['ærəgənt] adj arrogant

arrow ['ærəʊ] n flèche f

art [ɑ:t] n art m

artery ['ɑ:tərɪ] n artère f

art gallery n galerie d'art f

article ['ɑ:tɪkl] n article m ▷ a newspaper article un article de journal

artificial [ɑ:tɪ'fɪʃl] adj artificiel (f artificielle)

artist ['ɑ:tɪst] n artiste mf ▷ She's an artist. C'est une artiste.

artistic [ɑ:'tɪstɪk] adj artistique

as [æz] conj, adv ❶ (while) au moment où ▷ He came in as I was leaving. Il est arrivé au moment où je partais. ❷ (since) puisque ▷ As it's a holiday, you can sleep in. Tu peux faire la grasse matinée, puisque c'est un jour de congé.; **as... as** aussi... que ▷ I'm as tall as he is. Je suis aussi grand que lui.; **twice as... as** deux fois plus... que ▷ Her coat cost twice as much as mine. Son manteau a coûté deux fois plus cher que le mien.; **as much... as** autant... que ▷ I don't have as much money as you. Je n'ai pas autant d'argent que toi.; **as soon as possible** dès que possible ▷ I'll do it as soon as possible. Je le ferai dès que possible.; **as of tomorrow** à partir de demain ▷ *As of tomorrow, the store will stay open until 10 p.m.* À partir de demain, le magasin restera ouvert jusqu'à vingt-deux heures.; **as though** comme si ▷ *She acted as though she hadn't seen me.* Elle a fait comme si elle ne m'avait pas vu.; **as if** comme si; **He works as a waiter.** Il travaille comme serveur.

ASAP [eɪeɪ'piː] *abbr* (= *as soon as possible*) dès que possible

ashamed [ə'ʃeɪmd] *adj*: **to be ashamed** avoir honte ▷ *I was ashamed of my rude behaviour.* J'avais honte d'avoir été si impoli.

ashtray ['æʃtreɪ] *n* cendrier *m*

ask [ɑːsk] *vb* ❶ (*inquire, request*) demander ▷ *"Are you finished?" she asked.* « Tu as fini? » a-t-elle demandé.; **to ask somebody something** demander quelque chose à quelqu'un ▷ *He asked her how old she was.* Il lui a demandé quel âge elle avait.; **to ask for something** demander quelque chose ▷ *He asked for a cup of tea.* Il a demandé une tasse de thé.; **to ask somebody to do something** demander à quelqu'un de faire quelque chose ▷ *She asked him to do the shopping.* Elle lui a demandé de faire les courses.; **to ask about something** se renseigner sur quelque chose ▷ *I asked about tourist attractions.* Je me suis renseigné sur les attractions touristiques.; **to ask somebody a question** poser une question à quelqu'un ❷ inviter ▷ *Have you asked him to the party?* Est-ce que tu l'as invité à la fête?; **He asked her out.** (*on a date*) Il lui a demandé de sortir avec lui.

asleep [ə'sliːp] *adj*: **to be asleep** dormir ▷ *She's asleep.* Elle dort.; **to fall asleep** s'endormir ▷ *I fell asleep in front of the TV.* Je me suis endormi devant la télé.

asparagus [əs'pærəgəs] *n* asperges *fpl*

aspect ['æspekt] *n* aspect *m*

aspirin ['æsprɪn] *n* aspirine *f*

assemble [ə'sɛmbl] *vb* ❶ assembler ▷ *You have to assemble the bookshelf yourself.* Tu dois assembler l'étagère toi-même. ❷ se réunir ▷ *The students assembled in the gym.* Les élèves se sont réunis dans le gymnase.

assembly [ə'sɛmblɪ] *n* réunion d'école *f* (*school*) ▷ *The winner was announced in the assembly on Friday.* Le nom du gagnant a été annoncé durant la réunion d'école vendredi.

Assembly of First Nations *n* Assemblée *f* des Premières Nations

asset ['æsɛt] *n* atout *m* ▷ *Her experience will be an asset to the firm.* Son expérience sera un atout pour l'entreprise.

assignment [ə'saɪnmənt] *n* (*in school*) devoir *m*

assistance [ə'sɪstəns] *n* aide *f*

assistant [ə'sɪstənt] *n* ❶ (*in store*) vendeur *m*, vendeuse *f* ❷ (*helper*) assistant *m*, assistante *f*

association [əsəʊsɪ'eɪʃən] *n* association *f*

assorted [ə'sɔːtɪd] *adj* assorti ▷ *assorted chocolates* des chocolats assortis

assortment [ə'sɔːtmənt] *n* assortiment *m*

assume [ə'ʃuːm] *vb* supposer ▷ *I assume you won't be coming.* Je suppose que tu ne viendras

pas.

assure [ə'ʃuə^r] *vb* assurer ▷ *He assured me he was coming.* Il m'a assuré qu'il viendrait.

asthma ['æsmə] *n* asthme *m* ▷ *I have asthma.* J'ai de l'asthme.

astonish [ə'stɒnɪʃ] *vb* étonner

astonishing [ə'stɒnɪʃɪŋ] *adj* étonnant

astrology [əs'trɒlədʒɪ] *n* astrologie *f*

astronaut ['æstrənɔːt] *n* astronaute *mf*

astronomer [əs'trɒnəmə^r] *n* astronome *mf*

astronomy [əs'trɒnəmɪ] *n* astronomie *f*

asylum seeker [-sɪ:kə^r] *n* demandeur d'asile *m*, demandeuse d'asile *f*

at [æt] *prep* ❶ ▷ *at 4 o'clock* à quatre heures ▷ *at Christmas* à Noël ▷ *at 50 km/h* à cinquante km/h ▷ *at home* à la maison ▷ *two at a time* deux à la fois ▷ *at school* à l'école, au ▷ *at the office* au bureau, aux ▷ *at the races* aux courses; **at night** la nuit

ate [eɪt] *vb see* **eat**

athlete ['æθliːt] *n* athlète *mf*; **athlete's foot** pied d'athlète

athletic [æθ'lɛtɪk] *adj* athlétique

Atlantic Provinces [ət'læntɪk'prɒvɪnsəz] *npl* provinces *fpl* atlantiques

atlas ['ætləs] *n* atlas *m*

atmosphere ['ætməsfɪə^r] *n* ❶ atmosphère *f* ❷ ambiance *f* ▷ *J'aime l'ambiance de ce café.* I like the atmosphere in this café.

atom ['ætəm] *n* atome *m*

atomic [ə'tɒmɪk] *adj* atomique

attach [ə'tætʃ] *vb* fixer ▷ *He attached a rope to the car.* Il a fixé une corde à la voiture.; **Please find attached…** Veuillez trouver ci-joint…

attached [ə'tætʃt] *adj*: **to be attached to** être attaché à ▷ *He's very attached to his family.* Il est très attaché à sa famille.

attachment [ə'tætʃmənt] *n* (*email*) pièce jointe *f*

attack [ə'tæk] *vb* attaquer ▷ *The dog attacked her.* Le chien l'a attaquée.
▶ *n* attaque *f*

attempt [ə'tɛmpt] *n* tentative *f* ▷ *She gave up after several attempts.* Elle y a renoncé après plusieurs tentatives.
▶ *vb*: **to attempt to do something** essayer de faire quelque chose ▷ *I attempted to write a song.* J'ai essayé d'écrire une chanson.

attend [ə'tɛnd] *vb* assister à ▷ *to attend a meeting* assister à une réunion

attendance [ə'tɛndəns] *n*: **to take attendance** prendre les présences

attention [ə'tɛnʃən] *n* attention *f*; **to pay attention to** faire attention à ▷ *He didn't pay attention to what I was saying.* Il ne faisait pas attention à ce que je disais.

attic ['ætɪk] *n* grenier *m*

attitude ['ætɪtjuːd] *n* (*way of thinking*) attitude *f* ▷ *I really don't like your attitude!* Je n'aime pas du tout ton attitude!

attract [ə'trækt] *vb* attirer ▷ *Niagara Falls attracts lots of tourists.* Les chutes Niagara attirent de nombreux touristes.

attraction [ə'trækʃən] *n* attraction *f* ▷ *a tourist attraction* une attraction touristique

attractive [ə'træktɪv] *adj* séduisant ▷ *She's*

very attractive. Elle est très séduisante.

uction ['ɔːkʃən] n vente aux enchères f

udience ['ɔːdɪəns] n (in theatre) spectateurs mpl

udio ['ɔːdɪəu] adj audio (f+pl audio) ▷ audio files des fichiers audio ▷ an audio clip un audioclip ▷ audio equipment le matériel audio

udition [ɔːˈdɪʃən] n audition f
▷ vb auditionner

ugust ['ɔːgəst] n août m; **in August** en août

unt, aunty [ɑːnt, 'ɑːntɪ] n tante f ▷ my aunt ma tante

uthor ['ɔːθər] n auteur m, auteure f

utobiography [ɔːtəbaɪˈɒɡrəfɪ] n autobiographie f

utograph ['ɔːtəɡrɑːf] n autographe m

utomatic [ɔːtəˈmætɪk] adj automatique ▷ an automatic door une porte automatique

utumn ['ɔːtəm] n automne m; **in autumn** en automne

vailable [əˈveɪləbl] adj disponible ▷ Free brochures are available on request. Des brochures gratuites sont disponibles sur demande. ▷ Is he available today? Est-ce qu'il est disponible aujourd'hui?

valanche ['ævəlɑːnʃ] n avalanche f

venue ['ævənjuː] n avenue f

verage ['ævərɪdʒ] n moyenne f ▷ on average en moyenne
▷ adj moyen (f moyenne) ▷ the average price le prix moyen

vocado [ævəˈkɑːdəu] n avocat m

void [əˈvɔɪd] vb éviter ▷ We avoid him when he's in a bad mood. Nous l'évitons lorsqu'il est de mauvaise humeur.; **to avoid doing something** éviter de faire quelque chose ▷ Avoid going out on your own at night. Évite de sortir seul le soir.

wake [əˈweɪk] adj: **to be awake** être réveillé ▷ Is she awake? Elle est réveillée?; **He was still awake.** Il ne dormait pas encore.

ward [əˈwɔːd] n prix m ▷ She won an award. Elle a remporté un prix. ▷ the award for the best actor le prix du meilleur acteur

ware [əˈweər] adj: **to be aware of something** être conscient de quelque chose

way adj, adv (not here) absent ▷ She's away today. Elle est absente aujourd'hui.; **He's away for a week.** Il est parti pour une semaine.; **The town's 2 kilometres away.** La ville est à deux kilomètres d'ici.; **The coast is 2 hours away by car.** La côte est à deux heures de route.; **Go away!** Va-t'en!; **to put something away** ranger quelque chose ▷ He put the dishes away in the cupboard. Il a rangé la vaisselle dans le placard.

way game n match à l'extérieur m (pl matchs à l'extérieur)

wful ['ɔːfəl] adj affreux (f affreuse) ▷ That's awful! C'est affreux!; **an awful lot of...** énormément de...

wkward ['ɔːkwəd] adj ① (difficult to deal with) délicat ▷ an awkward situation une situation délicate ② (embarrassing) gênant ▷ an awkward question une question gênante;

It's a bit awkward for me to come today. Ce n'est pas très pratique pour moi de venir aujourd'hui.

awoke, awoken [əˈwəuk, əˈwəukn] vb see **awake**

axe [æks] n hache f

BA [biːˈeɪ] n baccalauréat m; **a BA in French** un baccalauréat en français

baby ['beɪbɪ] n bébé m

babysit ['beɪbɪsɪt] vb garder des enfants

babysitter ['beɪbɪsɪtə] n gardien d'enfants m, gardienne d'enfants f

babysitting ['beɪbɪsɪtɪŋ] n garde d'enfants f

bachelor ['bætʃələ] n célibataire m ▷ He's a bachelor. Il est célibataire.

back [bæk] n ① (of person, horse, book) dos m ② (of car, house) arrière m ▷ in the back à l'arrière ③ (of page) verso m ▷ on the back au verso ④ (of room, garden) fond m ▷ at the back au fond
▷ adj, adv arrière (f+pl arrière) ▷ the back seat le siège arrière ▷ the back wheel of my bike la roue arrière de mon vélo; **the back door** la porte de derrière; **to get back** rentrer ▷ What time did you get back? À quelle heure est-ce que tu es rentré?; **We went there by bus and walked back.** Nous y sommes allés en autobus et nous sommes rentrés à pied.; **She's not back yet.** Elle n'est pas encore rentrée.; **to call somebody back** rappeler quelqu'un ▷ I'll call back later. Je rappellerai plus tard.
▷ vb (support) soutenir ▷ I'm backing the other candidate. Je soutiens l'autre candidat.; **to back out** se désister ▷ They promised to help and then backed out. Ils avaient promis de nous aider et ils se sont désistés.; **to back somebody up** soutenir quelqu'un

backache ['bækeɪk] n mal au dos m ▷ to have backache avoir mal au dos

backfire [bækˈfaɪə] vb avoir l'effet inverse ▷ Her tactics could backfire on her. Sa stratégie pourrait avoir l'effet inverse.

background ['bækɡraund] n ① (of picture) arrière-plan m ▷ a house in the background une maison à l'arrière-plan; **background noise** les m bruits de fond ② milieu m (pl milieux) ▷ his family background son milieu familial

backhand ['bækhænd] n revers m

backing ['bækɪŋ] n (support) soutien m

backpack ['bækpæk] n sac à dos m

backpacker ['bækpækə] n ① (globetrotter)

routard *m*, routarde *f* ❷ (*hiker*) randonneur *m*, randonneuse *f*

backpacking ['bækpækɪŋ] *n*: **to go backpacking** voyager sac au dos

back pain *n* mal au dos *m* ▷ **to have back pain** avoir mal au dos

backside ['bæksaɪd] *n* derrière *m*

backslash ['bækslæʃ] *n* barre oblique inverse *f*

backstroke ['bækstrəuk] *n* dos crawlé *m*

backup ['bækʌp] *n* (*support*) soutien *m*; **a backup file** une sauvegarde

backwards ['bækwədz] *adv* en arrière ▷ **to take a step backwards** faire un pas en arrière; **to fall backwards** tomber à la renverse

backyard [bæk'jɑːd] *n* cour *f*

bacon ['beɪkən] *n* ❶ (*British type*) bacon *m* ▷ **bacon and eggs** des œufs au bacon ❷ (*French type*) lard *m*

bad [bæd] *adj* ❶ *mauvais* ▷ **a bad film** un mauvais film ▷ **the bad weather** le mauvais temps ▷ **to be in a bad mood** être de mauvaise humeur; **to be bad at something** être mauvais en quelque chose ▷ **I'm really bad at math.** Je suis vraiment mauvais en maths. ❷ (*serious*) grave ▷ **a bad accident** un accident grave ❸ (*naughty*) vilain ▷ **bad words** vilains mots; **to go bad** (*food*) se gâter; **I feel bad about it.** Ça m'ennuie.; **not bad** pas mal ▷ **That's not bad at all.** Ce n'est pas mal du tout.

badge [bædʒ] *n* badge *m*

badly ['bædlɪ] *adv* mal ▷ **badly paid** mal payé; **badly wounded** grièvement blessé; **He badly needs a rest.** Il a sérieusement besoin de se reposer.

badminton ['bædmɪntən] *n* badminton *m* ▷ **to play badminton** jouer au badminton

bad-tempered ['bæd'tempəd] *adj*: **to be bad-tempered (1)** (*by nature*) avoir mauvais caractère ▷ **She's a really bad-tempered person.** Elle a vraiment mauvais caractère. **(2)** (*temporarily*) être de mauvaise humeur ▷ **He was really bad-tempered yesterday.** Il était vraiment de mauvaise humeur hier.

Baffin Island ['bæfɪn'aɪlənd] *n* île *f* de Baffin

baffled ['bæfld] *adj* déconcerté

bag [bæg] *n* sac *m*

bagel ['beɪgl] *n* baguel *m* ▷ **a toasted bagel** un baguel grillé

baggage ['bægɪdʒ] *n* bagages *mpl*

baggy ['bægɪ] *adj* ample

bagpipes ['bægpaɪps] *npl* cornemuse *f* ▷ **She plays the bagpipes.** Elle joue de la cornemuse.

bake [beɪk] *vb*: **to bake a cake** faire un gâteau

baked [beɪkt] *adj* cuit au four ▷ **baked potatoes** les pommes de terre cuites au four *f*; **baked beans** les haricots *mpl* au lard

baker ['beɪkə^r^] *n* boulanger *m*, boulangère *f* ▷ **She's a baker.** Elle est boulangère.

bakery ['beɪkərɪ] *n* boulangerie *f*

baking ['beɪkɪŋ] *adj*: **It's baking in here!** Il fait une chaleur torride ici!

balance ['bæləns] *n* équilibre *m* ▷ **to lose one's balance** perdre l'équilibre

balanced ['bælənst] *adj* équilibré

balcony ['bælkənɪ] *n* balcon *m*

bald [bɔːld] *adj* chauve

ball [bɔːl] *n* ❶ (*tennis, golf, baseball*) balle *f* ❷ (*football, soccer*) ballon *m*

ballet ['bæleɪ] *n* ballet *m* ▷ **We went to a ballet.** Nous sommes allés voir un ballet.; **ballet lessons** les cours de danse classique

ballet dancer *n* danseur classique *m*, danseuse classique *f*

ballet shoes *npl* chaussons *mpl* de danse

balloon [bə'luːn] *n* (*for parties*) ballon *m*; **a hot-air balloon** une montgolfière

ballpoint pen ['bɔːlpɔɪnt'pen] *n* stylo à bille *m*

ban [bæn] *n* interdiction *f*; **a ban on video games** une interdiction de jeux vidéo ▶ *vb* interdire

banana [bə'nɑːnə] *n* banane *f* ▷ **a banana peel** une peau de banane

band [bænd] *n* ❶ (*rock band*) groupe *m* ❷ (*brass band*) fanfare *f* ❸ (*First Nations*) bande *f*; **a band chief** un chef de bande

bandage ['bændɪdʒ] *n* bandage *m* ▶ *vb* mettre un bandage à ▷ **The nurse bandaged my arm.** L'infirmière m'a mis un bandage au bras.

bandaid ['bændeɪd] *n* pansement adhésif *m*

band council *n* conseil de bande *m*

bandit ['bændɪt] *n* bandit *m*

bang [bæŋ] *n* ❶ détonation *f* ▷ **I heard a loud bang.** J'ai entendu une forte détonation. ❷ coup *m* ▷ **a bang on the head** un coup sur la tête; **Bang!** Pan! ▶ *vb* (*part of body*) se cogner ▷ **I banged my head.** Je me suis cogné la tête.; **to bang the door** claquer la porte; **to bang on the door** cogner à la porte

bangs [bæŋz] *npl* frange *f* ▷ **short bangs** une frange courte

bank [bæŋk] *n* ❶ (*financial*) banque *f* ❷ (*of river, lake*) bord *m*

bank account *n* compte en banque *m*

banker ['bæŋkə^r^] *n* banquier *m*

banned [bænd] *adj* interdit

bannock ['bænək] *n* banique *f*

banquet ['bæŋkwɪt] *n* banquet *m* ▷ **the graduation banquet** le banquet des finissants

bar [bɑː^r^] *n* (*metal*) barre *f*; **a chocolate bar** une tablette de chocolat; **a bar of soap** une savonnette

barbaric [bɑː'bærɪk] *adj* barbare

barbecue ['bɑːbɪkjuː] *n* barbecue *m*; **barbecue sauce** la sauce barbecue ▶ *vb* griller au barbecue ▷ **to barbecue chicken** griller du poulet au barbecue; **barbecued pork chops** des côtelettes de porc grillées au barbecue

barber ['bɑːbə^r^] *n* coiffeur pour hommes *m*

bare [beə^r^] *adj* nu

barefoot ['beəfut] *adj, adv* nu-pieds (*f+pl* nu-pieds) ▷ **The children go around barefoot.** Les enfants se promènent nu-pieds.; **to be barefoot** avoir les pieds nus ▷ **She was barefoot.** Elle avait les pieds nus.

barely ['beəlɪ] *adv* à peine ▷ **I could barely hear what they were saying.** J'entendais à peine ce qu'ils disaient.

bargain ['bɑːgɪn] *n* affaire *f* ▷ **It was a bargain!** C'était une affaire!

bark [bɑːk] n (tree) écorce f
▶ vb aboyer

barn [bɑːn] n grange f

barrel ['bærəl] n tonneau m (pl tonneaux)

Barrens ['bærənz] npl région des Barrens f

barrier ['bæriə'] n barrière f

base [beɪs] n base f

baseball ['beɪsbɔːl] n baseball m; **a baseball cap** une casquette de baseball

based [beɪst] adj: **based on** fondé sur

basement ['beɪsmənt] n sous-sol m

basic ['beɪsɪk] adj ❶ de base ▷ It's a basic model. C'est un modèle de base. ❷ rudimentaire ▷ The accommodation is pretty basic. Le logement est plutôt rudimentaire.

basically ['beɪsɪklɪ] adv tout simplement ▷ Basically, I just don't like him. Tout simplement, je ne l'aime pas.

basics ['beɪsɪks] npl rudiments mpl

basin ['beɪsn] n (washbasin) lavabo m

basis ['beɪsɪs] n: **on a daily basis** quotidiennement; **on a regular basis** régulièrement

basket ['bɑːskɪt] n panier m

basketball ['bɑːskɪtbɔːl] n basket m

bass [beɪs] n ❶ (guitar, singer) basse f ▷ She plays the bass. Elle joue de la basse. ▷ He's a bass. Il est basse.; **a bass guitar** une guitare basse; **a double bass** une contrebasse ❷ (on stereo) graves mpl ❸ (fish) achigan m

bass drum n grosse caisse f

bassoon [bə'suːn] n basson m ▷ I play the bassoon. Je joue du basson.

bat [bæt] n ❶ (for baseball) batte f; **Who's up to bat?** Qui est à la batte? ❷ (for table tennis) raquette f ❸ (animal) chauve-souris f (pl chauves-souris)

bath [bɑːθ] n ❶ bain m ▷ to have a bath prendre un bain; **a hot bath** un bain chaud ❷ (bathtub) baignoire f ▷ There's a spider in the bath. Il y a une araignée dans la baignoire.

bathe [beɪð] vb se baigner

bathing suit ['beɪðɪŋ suːt] n maillot de bain m

bathroom ['bɑːθrʊm] n salle de bains f

batter ['bætə'] n ❶ pâte f ▷ cake batter la pâte à gâteau ❷ (baseball) batteur m

battery ['bætərɪ] n ❶ (for flashlight, toy) pile f ❷ (of car) batterie f

battle ['bætl] n bataille f ▷ the Battle of the Plains of Abraham la bataille des Plaines d'Abraham; **It was a battle, but we succeeded in the end.** Il a fallu se battre, mais on a fini par y arriver.

bay [beɪ] n baie f

bazaar [bə'zɑː'] n bazar m ▷ Our school holds a bazaar every spring. Notre école tient un bazar tous les printemps.

BC ['biː'siː] abbr (= before Christ) av. J.-C. (= avant Jésus-Christ) ▷ in 200 BC en deux cents avant Jésus-Christ

BCE [biːsiː'iː] abbr (= before the Common Era) av. J.-C. (= avant Jésus-Christ) ▷ in 200 BCE en deux cents avant Jésus-Christ

be [biː] vb être ▷ I'm tired. Je suis fatigué. ▷ You're late. Tu es en retard. ▷ She's English. Elle est anglaise. ▷ Iqaluit is in Nunavut. Iqaluit est

au Nunavut. ▷ It's 4 o'clock. Il est quatre heures. ▷ We are all happy. Nous sommes tous heureux. ▷ They are in Moncton at the moment. Ils sont à Moncton en ce moment. ▷ I've been ill. J'ai été malade.; **It's the 28th of October today.** Nous sommes le vingt-huit octobre.; **Have you been to Greece before?** Est-ce que tu es déjà allé en Grèce?; **I've never been to Chicoutimi.** Je ne suis jamais allé à Chicoutimi.; **to be killed** être tué ▷ She's a doctor. Elle est médecin. ▷ He's a student. Il est étudiant.; **I'm cold.** J'ai froid.; **I'm hungry.** J'ai faim.; **I'm fourteen.** J'ai quatorze ans.; **How old are you?** Quel âge as-tu?; **It's cold.** Il fait froid.; **It's too hot.** Il fait trop chaud.; **It's a nice day.** Il fait beau.

beach [biːtʃ] n plage f

bead [biːd] n perle f

beak [biːk] n bec m

beam [biːm] n ❶ (of light) rayon m ❷ (wooden) poutre f

beans [biːnz] n ❶ haricots mpl ❷ (baked beans) haricots mpl au lard ▷ I had beans on toast. J'ai mangé des haricots au lard sur du pain grillé.; **green beans** les m haricots verts; **kidney beans** les m haricots rouges

bear [beə'] n ours m.; **a bear cub** un ourson ▶ vb supporter; **I can't bear it!** C'est insupportable!; **to bear up** tenir le coup; **Bear up!** Tiens bon!

beard [bɪəd] n barbe f; **He has a beard.** Il est barbu.; **a man with a beard** un barbu

bearded ['bɪədɪd] adj barbu

beat [biːt] n rythme m
▶ vb battre ▷ We beat them 3-0. On les a battus trois à zéro.

beautiful ['bjuːtɪfʊl] adj beau (f belle, mpl beaux) ▷ a beautiful smile un beau sourire ▷ a beautiful afternoon un bel après-midi

beautifully ['bjuːtɪflɪ] adv admirablement

beauty ['bjuːtɪ] n beauté f

beaver ['biːvə'] n castor m

became [bɪ'keɪm] vb see **become**

because [bɪ'kɒz] conj parce que ▷ I did it because... Je l'ai fait parce que...; **because of** à cause de ▷ because of the weather à cause du temps

become [bɪ'kʌm] vb devenir ▷ She became a famous writer. Elle est devenue un grand écrivain.

bed [bɛd] n lit m ▷ in bed au lit; **to go to bed** aller se coucher

bed and breakfast n chambre d'hôte f ▷ We stayed in a bed and breakfast. Nous avons logé dans une chambre d'hôte.; **How much is it for bed and breakfast?** C'est combien pour la chambre et le petit déjeuner?

bedding ['bɛdɪŋ] n literie f

bedroom ['bɛdrʊm] n chambre f

bedspread ['bɛdsprɛd] n dessus-de-lit m (pl dessus-de-lit)

bedtime ['bɛdtaɪm] n: **Ten o'clock is my usual bedtime.** Je me couche généralement à dix heures.; **Bedtime!** Au lit!

bee [biː] n abeille f

beef [biːf] n bœuf m; **roast beef (1)** (served rare) le rosbif **(2)** (served well done) le rôti de bœuf

been [bi:n] *vb see* **be**

beep [bi:p] *n* bip *m* ▷ *Leave your message after the beep.* Laissez votre message après le bip.

beet [bi:t] *n* betterave rouge *f*

beetle ['bi:tl] *n* scarabée *m*

before [bɪ'fɔːʳ] *prep, conj, adv* ❶ avant ▷ *before Tuesday* avant mardi ❷ avant de ▷ *before going avant de partir* ▷ *Before opening the box, read the instructions.* Avant d'ouvrir la boîte, lisez le mode d'emploi. ▷ *I'll phone before I leave.* J'appellerai avant de partir. ❸ *(already)* déjà ▷ *I've seen this film before.* J'ai déjà vu ce film. ▷ *Have you been to Alberta before?* Vous êtes déjà venu en Alberta?; **the day before** la veille; **the week before** la semaine précédente

beforehand [bɪ'fɔːhænd] *adv* à l'avance

beg [bɛg] *vb* ❶ *(for money)* mendier ❷ supplier ▷ *I beg you to stop.* Je te supplie d'arrêter.

began [bɪ'gæn] *vb see* **begin**

beggar ['bɛgəʳ] *n* mendiant *m*, mendiante *f*

begin [bɪ'gɪn] *vb* commencer; **to begin doing something** commencer à faire quelque chose

beginner [bɪ'gɪnəʳ] *n* débutant *m*, débutante *f* ▷ *I'm just a beginner.* Je ne suis qu'un débutant.

beginning [bɪ'gɪnɪŋ] *n* début *m* ▷ *in the beginning* au début

begun [bɪ'gʌn] *vb see* **begin**

behalf [bɪ'hɑːf] *n*: **on behalf of somebody** pour quelqu'un

behave [bɪ'heɪv] *vb* se comporter ▷ *He behaved like an idiot.* Il s'est comporté comme un idiot. ▷ *She behaved very badly.* Elle s'est très mal comportée.; **to behave oneself** être sage ▷ *Did the children behave themselves?* Est-ce que les enfants ont été sages?; **Behave!** Sois sage!

behaviour [bɪ'heɪvjəʳ] *n* comportement *m*

behind [bɪ'haɪnd] *prep, adv* derrière *m* ▷ *behind the television* derrière la télévision; **to be behind** *(late)* avoir du retard ▷ *I'm behind with my homework.* J'ai du retard dans mes devoirs.
▶ *n* derrière *m*

beige [beɪʒ] *adj* beige

believe [bɪ'li:v] *vb* croire ▷ *I don't believe you.* Je ne te crois pas.; **to believe in something** croire à quelque chose ▷ *Do you believe in ghosts?* Tu crois aux fantômes?; **to believe in God** croire en Dieu

bell [bɛl] *n* ❶ *(doorbell)* sonnette *f*; **to ring the bell** sonner à la porte ❷ *(in church)* cloche *f* ❸ *(in school)* sonnerie *f* ❹ clochette *f* ▷ *Our cat has a bell around its neck.* Notre chat a une clochette sur son collier.

belly ['bɛlɪ] *n* ventre *m*

belong [bɪ'lɔŋ] *vb*: **to belong to somebody** être à quelqu'un ▷ *Who does it belong to?* C'est à qui? ▷ *That belongs to me.* C'est à moi.; **Do you belong to any clubs?** Est-ce que tu es membre d'un club?; **Where does this belong?** Où est-ce que ça va?

belongings [bɪ'lɔŋɪŋz] *npl* affaires *fpl*

below [bɪ'ləʊ] *prep, adv* ❶ au-dessous de ▷ *below sea level* au-dessous du niveau de la mer ❷ en dessous ▷ *on the floor below* à l'étage en dessous; **10 degrees below freezing** moins dix

belt [bɛlt] *n* ceinture *f*

bench [bɛntʃ] *n* ❶ *(seat)* banc *m* ❷ *(workbench)* établi *m*

bend [bɛnd] *n* ❶ *(in road)* virage *m* ❷ *(in river)* coude *m*
▶ *vb* ❶ *(one's back)* courber ❷ *(leg, arm)* plier ▷ *I can't bend my arm.* Je n'arrive pas à plier le bras.; **"do not bend"** « ne pas plier » ❸ *(road)* tourner ▷ *The road bends to the right.* La route tourne vers la droite. ❹ *(object)* tordre ▷ *You've bent it.* Tu l'as tordu.; **to bend** se tordre ▷ *It bends easily.* Ça se tord facilement.; **to bend down** se baisser; **to bend over** se pencher

beneath [bɪ'ni:θ] *prep* sous

benefit ['bɛnɪfɪt] *n* ❶ *(advantage)* avantage *m*; **unemployment benefit** les allocations de chômage
▶ *vb*: **He'll benefit from the change.** Le changement lui fera du bien.

bent [bɛnt] *vb see* **bend**
▶ *adj* tordu ▷ *a bent fork* une fourchette tordue

beret ['bɛreɪ] *n* béret *m*

berry ['bɛrɪ] *n* baie *f*

berserk [bə'zɜːk] *adj*: **to go berserk** devenir fou furieux ▷ *She went berserk.* Elle est devenue folle furieuse.

beside [bɪ'saɪd] *prep* à côté de ▷ *beside the television* à côté de la télévision; **He was beside himself.** Il était hors de lui.; **That's beside the point.** Cela n'a rien à voir.

besides [bɪ'saɪdz] *adv* en plus ▷ *Besides, it's too expensive.* En plus, c'est trop cher.

best [bɛst] *adj, adv* ❶ meilleur ▷ *He's the best player on the team.* Il est le meilleur joueur de l'équipe. ▷ *She's the best at math.* Elle est la meilleure en maths. ❷ le mieux ▷ *She sings best.* C'est elle qui chante le mieux. ▷ *That's the best I can do.* Je ne peux pas faire mieux.; **to do one's best** faire de son mieux ▷ *It's not perfect, but I did my best.* Ça n'est pas parfait, mais j'ai fait de mon mieux.; **to make the best of it** s'en contenter ▷ *We'll have to make the best of it.* Il va falloir nous en contenter.

best man *n* garçon d'honneur *m*

bet [bɛt] *n* pari *m* ▷ *to make a bet* faire un pari
▶ *vb* parier ▷ *I bet you he won't come.* Je te parie qu'il ne viendra pas. ▷ *I bet she forgot.* Je parie qu'elle a oublié.

betray [bɪ'treɪ] *vb* trahir

betrayal [bɪ'treɪəl] *n* trahison *f*

better ['bɛtəʳ] *adj, adv* ❶ meilleur ▷ *This one's better than that one.* Celui-ci est meilleur que celui-là. ▷ *a better way to do it* une meilleure façon de le faire ❷ mieux ▷ *That's better!* C'est mieux comme ça. ▷ *This pen writes better.* Ce stylo-ci écrit mieux.; **better still** encore mieux ▷ *Go and see her tomorrow, or better still, go today.* Va la voir demain, ou encore mieux, vas-y aujourd'hui.; **to get better (1)** *(improve)* s'améliorer ▷ *I hope the weather gets better soon.* J'espère que le temps va s'améliorer bientôt. ▷ *My French is getting better.* Mon français s'améliore. **(2)** *(from illness)* se remettre ▷ *I hope you get better soon.* J'espère que tu vas vite te remettre.; **to feel better** se sentir mieux ▷ *Are you feeling better now?* Tu te sens mieux maintenant?; **You'd better do it right away.** Vous feriez mieux de le faire immédiatement.;

I'd better go home. Je ferais mieux de rentrer.

between [bɪ'twiːn] *prep* entre ▷ *Moose Jaw is between Swift Current and Regina.* Moose Jaw est entre Swift Current et Regina. ▷ *between 15 and 20 minutes* entre quinze et vingt minutes

beware [bɪ'weəʳ] *vb* se méfier ▷ *Beware of strangers.* Méfie-toi des inconnus.; **"Beware of dog"** «Attention, chien méchant»

bewildered [bɪ'wɪldəd] *adj:* **He looked bewildered.** Il avait l'air perplexe.

beyond [bɪ'jɒnd] *prep* au-delà de ▷ *There was a lake beyond the mountain.* Il y avait un lac au-delà de la montagne.; **beyond belief** incroyable; **beyond repair** irréparable

biased ['baɪəst] *adj* partial

bibliography [bɪblɪ'ɒɡrəfɪ] *n* bibliographie *f*

bicycle ['baɪsɪkl] *n* vélo *m*

big [bɪɡ] *adj* ❶ grand ▷ *a big house* une grande maison ▷ *her big sister* sa grande sœur; **He's a big guy.** C'est un grand gaillard. ❷ (*car, animal, book, package*) gros (*f* grosse) ▷ *a big car* une grosse voiture

bike [baɪk] *n* vélo *m* ▷ *by bike* en vélo

bikini [bɪ'kiːnɪ] *n* bikini *m*

bilingual [baɪ'lɪŋɡwəl] *adj* bilingue

bilingualism [baɪ'lɪŋɡwəlɪzəm] *n* bilinguisme *m*

bill [bɪl] *n* ❶ (*in restaurant*) addition *f* ▷ *Can we have the bill, please?* L'addition, s'il vous plaît. ❷ (*for gas, electricity*) facture *f* ❸ billet *m* ▷ *a five-dollar bill* un billet de cinq dollars

billion ['bɪljən] *n* milliard *m* ▷ *two billion people* deux milliards de gens

binder ['baɪndəʳ] *n* reliure *f*

bingo ['bɪŋɡəu] *n* bingo *m*

binoculars [bɪˈnɒkjuləʳ] *npl* jumelles *fpl*; **a pair of binoculars** des jumelles

biochemistry [baɪə'kemɪstrɪ] *n* biochimie *f*

biodegradable ['baɪəudɪ'ɡreɪdəbl] *adj* biodégradable

biography [baɪ'ɒɡrəfɪ] *n* biographie *f*

biology [baɪ'ɒlədʒɪ] *n* biologie *f*

birch [bəːtʃ] *n* bouleau *m* (*pl* bouleaux); **birch bark** l'écorce *f* de bouleau

bird [bəːd] *n* oiseau *m* (*pl* oiseaux)

birth [bəːθ] *n* naissance *f* ▷ *date of birth* la date de naissance

birth certificate *n* acte *m* de naissance

birth control *n* contraception *f*

birthday ['bəːθdeɪ] *n* anniversaire *m* ▷ *When's your birthday?* Quelle est la date de ton anniversaire?; **a birthday cake** un gâteau d'anniversaire; **a birthday card** une carte d'anniversaire; **I'm going to have a birthday party.** Je vais faire une fête pour mon anniversaire.

bison ['baɪsən] *n* bison *m*

bit [bɪt] *vb see* **bite**
▶ *n:* **a bit** un peu ▷ *I'm a bit tired.* Je suis un peu fatigué. ▷ *a bit too hot* un peu trop chaud ▷ *Stay a bit longer.* Reste un peu plus longtemps. ▷ *"Do you play soccer?" —"A bit."* «Tu joues au soccer?» — «Un peu.»; **a bit of** un peu de ▷ *a bit of music* un peu de musique; **It's a bit of a nuisance.** C'est ennuyeux.; **bit by bit** petit à petit

bite [baɪt] *vb* ❶ (*person, dog*) mordre ❷ (*insect*) piquer ▷ *I got bitten by mosquitoes.* Je me suis fait piquer par des moustiques.; **to bite one's nails** se ronger les ongles
▶ *n* ❶ (*insect bite*) piqûre *f* ❷ (*animal bite*) morsure *f*; **to have a bite to eat** manger un morceau

bitten ['bɪtn] *vb see* **bite**

bitter ['bɪtəʳ] *adj* ❶ amer (*f* amère) ❷ (*weather, wind*) glacial (*mpl* glaciaux) ▷ *It's bitter out today.* Il fait un froid glacial aujourd'hui.

bizarre [bɪ'zɑːʳ] *adj* bizarre ▷ *a bizarre dream* un rêve bizarre

black [blæk] *adj* noir ▷ *a black jacket* une veste noire ▷ *She's black.* Elle est noire.

blackberry ['blækbərɪ] *n* mûre *f*

black currant ['blæk'kʌrnt] *n* cassis *m*

black fly *n* mouche noire *f*

black hole *n* trou noir *m*

blackmail ['blækmeɪl] *n* chantage *m* ▷ *That's blackmail!* C'est du chantage!
▶ *vb:* **to blackmail somebody** faire chanter quelqu'un ▷ *He blackmailed them.* Il les a fait chanter.

blackout ['blækaut] *n* (*power cut*) panne d'électricité *f*

blade [bleɪd] *n* lame *f*

blame [bleɪm] *vb:* **Don't blame me!** Ça n'est pas ma faute!; **I blame the police.** À mon avis, c'est la faute de la police.; **He blamed it on my sister.** Il a dit que c'était la faute de ma sœur.

blank [blæŋk] *adj* ❶ (*paper*) blanc *m* (*f* blanche) ❷ (*cassette, video, page*) vierge; **My mind went blank.** J'ai eu un trou.
▶ *n* blanc *m* ▷ *Fill in the blanks.* Remplissez les blancs.

blank cheque *n* chèque en blanc *m*

blanket ['blæŋkɪt] *n* couverture *f*

blast [blɑːst] *n:* **a bomb blast** une explosion

blatant ['bleɪtənt] *adj* flagrant

blaze [bleɪz] *n* incendie *m*

blazer ['bleɪzəʳ] *n* blazer *m*

bleach [bliːtʃ] *n* eau *f* de Javel
▶ *vb* décolorer ▷ *She bleached her hair.* Elle a décoloré ses cheveux.; **bleached jeans** jeans délavés

bleachers ['bliːtʃəz] *npl* gradins *mpl* ▷ *a seat in the bleachers* un siège dans les gradins

bleak [bliːk] *adj* (*place*) désolé; **The future looks bleak.** L'avenir semble peu prometteur.

bleed [bliːd] *vb* saigner ▷ *My nose is bleeding.* Je saigne du nez.

blender ['blendəʳ] *n* mélangeur *m*

bless [bles] *vb* (*religiously*) bénir; **Bless you!** (*after sneezing*) À tes souhaits!

blew [bluː] *vb see* **blow**

blind [blaɪnd] *adj* aveugle
▶ *n* (*for window*) store *m*

blindfold ['blaɪndfəuld] *n* bandeau *m* (*pl* bandeaux)
▶ *vb:* **to blindfold somebody** bander les yeux à quelqu'un

blink [blɪŋk] *vb* cligner des yeux

bliss [blɪs] *n:* **It was bliss!** C'était merveilleux!

blister ['blɪstəʳ] *n* ampoule *f*

blizzard ['blɪzəd] *n* tempête de neige *f*

blob [blɒb] *n* goutte *f* ▷ *a blob of glue* une

goutte de colle

block [blɒk] n ➊ (wood) bille f ➋ (stone) bloc m; **They live on our block.** Ils habitent notre quartier.; **It's two blocks away.** C'est à deux coins de rue.; **to go around the block** faire le tour du pâté de maisons
▶ vb bloquer

blockage ['blɒkɪdʒ] n obstruction f

blog [blɒg] n blogue m

blond [blɒnd] adj blond ▷ **She has blond hair.** Elle a les cheveux blonds.

blood [blʌd] n sang m

blood pressure n: **to have high blood pressure** faire de la tension

blood test n prise de sang f

blouse [blauz] n chemisier m

blow [bləʊ] n coup m
▶ vb (wind, person) souffler; **to blow one's nose** se moucher; **to blow a whistle** siffler; **to blow out a candle** éteindre une bougie; **to blow up (1)** faire sauter ▷ **They blew up the old bridge and built a new one.** Ils ont fait sauter le vieux pont et en ont bâti un nouveau. **(2)** gonfler ▷ **to blow up a balloon** gonfler un ballon; **The house blew up.** La maison a sauté.

blow-dry ['bləʊdraɪ] n séchage à la brosse m; **A cut and blow-dry, please.** Une coupe et un séchage à la brosse, s'il vous plaît.
▶ vb sécher à la brosse ▷ **I blow-dry my hair.** Je me sèche les cheveux à la brosse.

blown [bləʊn] vb see **blow**

blue [bluː] adj bleu m ▷ **a blue dress** une robe bleue; **It came out of the blue.** C'était complètement inattendu.

blueberry ['bluːbəri] n bleuet m ▷ **blueberry pie** la tarte aux bleuets

blue jay ['bluːdʒeɪ] n geai bleu m

blues [bluːz] npl blues m ▷ **I like blues (music).** J'aime le blues.; **to have the blues** avoir le cafard

bluff [blʌf] vb bluffer
▶ n bluff m ▷ **It's just a bluff.** C'est du bluff.

blunder ['blʌndər] n gaffe f

blunt [blʌnt] adj ➊ (person) brusque ➋ (knife) émoussé

blurry ['blʌri] adj flou

blush [blʌʃ] vb rougir

board [bɔːd] n ➊ (wooden) planche f ➋ (skateboard) planche à roulettes f ➌ (snowboard) planche à neige f ➍ (chalkboard) tableau m (pl tableaux) ▷ **on the board** au tableau ➎ (notice board) panneau m (pl panneaux) ➏ (for board games) jeu m (pl jeux) ➐ (for chess) échiquier m; **on board** à bord

boarder ['bɔːdər] n interne mf

board game n jeu de société m (pl jeux de société)

boarding ['bɔːdɪŋ] n ➊ (skateboarding) planche à roulettes f ▷ **He loves boarding.** Il adore la planche à roulettes. ➋ (snowboarding) planche à neige f ▷ **She's great at boarding.** Elle est formidable à la planche à neige. ▷ **Want to go boarding?** Si on faisait de la planche à neige?

boarding card ['bɔːdɪŋ-] n carte d'embarquement f

boarding school ['bɔːdɪŋ-] n pensionnat m; **I**

go to boarding school. Je suis pensionnaire.

boards [bɔːdz] npl (hockey) bande f ▷ **The other player shoved me into the boards.** L'autre joueur m'a poussé dans la bande.

boat [bəʊt] n bateau m (pl bateaux)

body ['bɒdi] n corps m

bodybuilding ['bɒdɪbɪldɪŋ] n culturisme m

bodycheck ['bɒdɪtʃɛk] vb mettre en échec ▷ **You bodychecked him.** Tu l'as mis en échec.

bodyguard ['bɒdɪɡɑːd] n garde du corps m

bog [bɒg] n (marsh) tourbière f

boil [bɔɪl] n furoncle m
▶ vb ➊ faire bouillir ▷ **to boil some water** faire bouillir de l'eau; **to boil an egg** faire cuire un œuf ➋ bouillir ▷ **The water's boiling.** L'eau bout ▷ **The water's boiled.** L'eau a bouilli.; **to boil over** déborder

boiled [bɔɪld] adj ➊ à l'eau ▷ **boiled potatoes** des pommes de terre à l'eau ➋ bouilli ▷ **boiled water** eau bouillie; **a boiled egg** un œuf à la coque

boiling ['bɔɪlɪŋ] adj: **It's boiling in here!** Il fait une chaleur torride ici!; **boiling hot** torride ▷ **a boiling hot day** une journée torride

bolt [bəʊlt] n ➊ (on door) verrou m ➋ (with nut) boulon m

bomb [bɒm] n bombe f
▶ vb bombarder

bomber ['bɒmər] n bombardier m

bombing ['bɒmɪŋ] n attentat m à la bombe

bond [bɒnd] n lien m

bone [bəʊn] n ➊ (of human, animal) os m ➋ (of fish) arête f

bone dry adj complètement sec (f complètement sèche)

bonfire ['bɒnfaɪər] n feu de joie m (pl feux de joie)

bonus ['bəʊnəs] n ➊ (extra payment) prime f ➋ (added advantage) plus m

book [buk] n livre m
▶ vb réserver ▷ **We haven't booked.** Nous n'avons pas réservé.

bookcase ['bukkeɪs] n bibliothèque f

booklet ['buklɪt] n brochure f

bookmark ['bukmɑːk] n (also computing) signet m
▶ vb mettre un signet à ▷ **I'm going to bookmark this Web site.** Je mets un signet à ce site Web.

bookshelf ['bukʃelf] n étagère f à livres

bookstore ['bukstɔːr] n librairie f

boost [buːst] vb stimuler ▷ **to boost the economy** stimuler l'économie; **The win boosted the team's morale.** La victoire a remonté le moral de l'équipe.

boot [buːt] n ➊ (fashion boot) botte f ➋ (for hiking) chaussure de marche f

boot up vb démarrer

border ['bɔːdər] n frontière f

bore [bɔːr] vb see **bear**

bored [bɔːd] adj: **to be bored** s'ennuyer ▷ **I was bored.** Je m'ennuyais.; **to get bored** s'ennuyer

boredom ['bɔːdəm] n ennui m

boring ['bɔːrɪŋ] adj ennuyeux (f ennuyeuse)

born [bɔːn] adj: **to be born** naître ▷ **I was born in 1994.** Je suis né en mille neuf cent quatre-vingt-quatorze.

borrow ['bɒrəʊ] vb emprunter ▷ Can I borrow your pen? Je peux emprunter ton stylo?; **to borrow something from somebody** emprunter quelque chose à quelqu'un ▷ I borrowed some money from a friend. J'ai emprunté de l'argent à un ami.

boss [bɒs] n patron m, patronne f

boss around vb: **to boss somebody around** donner des ordres à quelqu'un

bossy ['bɒsɪ] adj autoritaire

both [bəʊθ] adj, pron tous m les deux, toutes f les deux ▷ We both went. Nous y sommes allés tous les deux. ▷ Emma and Jane both went. Emma et Jane y sont allées toutes les deux. ▷ Both of your answers are wrong. Vos réponses sont toutes les deux mauvaises. ▷ Both of them have left. Ils sont partis tous les deux. ▷ Both of us went. Nous y sommes allés tous les deux. ▷ Both Maggie and John are against it. Maggie et John sont tous les deux contre.; **He speaks both German and Italian.** Il parle allemand et italien.

bother ['bɒðə'] vb ❶ (worry) tracasser ▷ What's bothering you? Qu'est-ce qui te tracasse? ❷ (disturb) déranger ▷ I'm sorry to bother you. Je suis désolé de vous déranger.; **no bother** aucun problème; **Don't bother!** Ça n'est pas la peine!; **to bother to do something** prendre la peine de faire quelque chose ▷ He didn't bother to tell me about it. Il n'a pas pris la peine de m'en parler.

bottle ['bɒtl] n bouteille f

bottle-opener ['bɒtləʊpnə'] n ouvre-bouteille m

bottom ['bɒtəm] n ❶ (of container, bag, sea) fond m ❷ (of page, list) bas m ▷ adj inférieur ▷ the bottom shelf l'étagère inférieure; **the bottom sheet** le drap de dessous

bought [bɔːt] vb see **buy**

bounce [baʊns] vb rebondir

bouncer ['baʊnsə'] n videur m

bound [baʊnd] adj: **He's bound to win.** Il va sûrement gagner.

boundary ['baʊndrɪ] n frontière f

bounds [baʊndz] npl: **out of bounds** (1) interdit ▷ The creek is out of bounds for students. Le ruisseau est interdit aux élèves. (2) à l'extérieur du terrain ▷ The ball landed out of bounds. Le ballon est tombé à l'extérieur du terrain.

bow [n bəʊ, vb baʊ] n ❶ (knot) nœud m ▷ to tie a bow faire un nœud ❷ arc m ▷ a bow and arrows un arc et des flèches ▷ vb faire une révérence

bowl [bəʊl] n (for soup, cereal) bol m

bowling ['bəʊlɪŋ] n jeu de quilles m; **to go bowling** jouer aux quilles; **a bowling alley** une salle de quilles

bow tie [bəʊ-] n nœud papillon m

box [bɒks] n boîte f ▷ a box of matches une boîte d'allumettes; **a cardboard box** un carton

boxer ['bɒksə'] n boxeur m

boxer shorts ['bɒksəʃɔːts] npl caleçon m ▷ a pair of boxer shorts un caleçon

boxing ['bɒksɪŋ] n boxe f

Boxing Day n lendemain de Noël m ▷ on Boxing Day le lendemain de Noël

boy [bɔɪ] n garçon m

boycott ['bɔɪkɒt] vb boycotter

boyfriend ['bɔɪfrɛnd] n copain m ▷ Do you have a boyfriend? Est-ce que tu as un copain?

bra [brɑː] n soutien-gorge m (pl soutiens-gorge)

brace [breɪs] n appareil m orthopédique ▷ He wears a leg brace. Il porte un appareil orthopédique pour sa jambe.

bracelet ['breɪslɪt] n bracelet m

braces ['breɪsɪz] n (on teeth) appareil m orthodontique ▷ She wears braces. Elle a un appareil orthodontique.

brackets ['brækɪts] npl: **in brackets** entre parenthèses

brag [bræg] vb se vanter ▷ Stop bragging! Arrête de te vanter!; **to brag about something** se vanter de quelque chose

braid [breɪd] n (hair) tresse f ▷ vb tresser ▷ to braid one's hair se tresser les cheveux

brain [breɪn] n cerveau m (pl cerveaux)

brainstorm ['breɪnstɔːm] vb faire un remue-méninges; **a brainstorming session** une session de remue-méninges

brainteaser ['breɪntiːzə'] n casse-tête m

brake [breɪk] n frein m ▷ vb freiner

branch [brɑːntʃ] n ❶ (of tree) branche f ❷ (of bank) succursale f

brand [brænd] n marque f ▷ a well-known brand of cereal une marque de céréales bien connue

brand name n marque f

brand-new ['brænd'njuː] adj tout neuf (f toute neuve)

brass [brɑːs] n cuivre m; **the brass section** les cuivres

brass band n fanfare f

brave [breɪv] adj courageux (f courageuse)

bread [brɛd] n pain m ▷ brown bread le pain de blé entier ▷ white bread le pain blanc; **bread and butter** les tartines de pain beurrées

break [breɪk] n ❶ (rest) pause f ▷ to take a break faire une pause ❷ (at school) récréation f ▷ during morning break pendant la récréation du matin; **the Christmas break** les vacances de Noël; **Give me a break!** Laisse-moi tranquille!; **to give somebody a break** donner sa chance à quelqu'un ▷ vb ❶ casser ▷ Careful, you'll break something! Attention, tu vas casser quelque chose! ❷ (get broken) se casser ▷ Careful, it'll break! Attention, ça va se casser!; **to break one's leg** se casser la jambe ▷ I broke my leg. Je me suis cassé la jambe.; **She broke her arm.** Elle s'est cassé le bras.; **to break a promise** rompre une promesse; **to break a record** battre un record; **to break the law** violer la loi

break down vb tomber en panne ▷ The car broke down. La voiture est tombée en panne.

break in vb entrer par effraction

break off vb ❶ casser ▷ He broke off a piece of chocolate. Il a cassé un bout de chocolat. ❷ se casser ▷ *The branch broke off.* La branche s'est cassée.; *She broke off the engagement.* Elle a rompu ses fiançailles.

break open vb *(door, cupboard)* forcer

break out vb ❶ *(fire)* se déclarer ❷ *(war)* éclater ❸ *(prisoner)* s'évader; **to break out in a rash** être couvert de boutons

break up vb ❶ *(couple)* se séparer; **He broke up with his girlfriend.** Il a rompu avec sa petite amie. ❷ *(crowd)* se disperser ❸ *(meeting, party)* se terminer ❹ *(divide)* répartir ▷ *Break up into groups.* Répartissez-vous en groupes.; **to break up a fight** mettre fin à une bagarre

breakdown ['breɪkdaʊn] n ❶ *(in vehicle)* panne f ▷ *to have a breakdown* tomber en panne ❷ *(mental)* dépression f ▷ *to have a breakdown* faire une dépression

breakfast ['brekfəst] n déjeuner m ▷ *What would you like for breakfast?* Qu'est-ce vous voulez pour le déjeuner?

break-in ['breɪkɪn] n cambriolage m

break-up ['breɪkʌp] n ❶ *(friendship)* rupture f ❷ *(ice)* débâcle f ▷ *After spring break-up you often get floods.* Après la débâcle printanière, on a souvent des inondations.

breast [brest] n *(of woman)* sein m; **chicken breast** la poitrine de poulet

breath [brεθ] n haleine f ▷ *to have bad breath* avoir mauvaise haleine; **to be out of breath** être essoufflé; **to catch one's breath** reprendre son souffle

breathe [briːð] vb respirer

breathe in vb inspirer

breathe out vb expirer

breed [briːd] vb *(reproduce)* se reproduire; **to breed dogs** faire de l'élevage de chiens ▶ n race f

breeze [briːz] n brise f

bribe [braɪb] vb soudoyer

brick [brɪk] n brique f; **a brick wall** un mur en brique

bricklayer ['brɪkleɪə'] n maçon m

bride [braɪd] n mariée f

bridegroom ['braɪdgruːm] n marié m

bridesmaid ['braɪdzmeɪd] n demoiselle d'honneur f

bridge [brɪdʒ] n ❶ pont m ▷ *a suspension bridge* un pont suspendu ❷ bridge m ▷ *to play bridge* jouer au bridge

brief [briːf] adj bref *(f* brève)

briefcase ['briːfkeɪs] n serviette f

briefly ['briːflɪ] adv brièvement

briefs [briːfs] npl ❶ *(women's)* culotte f ❷ *(men's)* caleçon m

bright [braɪt] adj ❶ *(colour, light)* vif *(f* vive) ▷ *a bright colour* une couleur vive; **bright blue** bleu vif ▷ *a bright blue car* une voiture bleu vif ❷ *intelligent* ▷ *He's very bright.* Il est très intelligent.

brilliant ['brɪljənt] adj ❶ *(clever)* brillant ▷ *a brilliant scientist* un savant brillant ❷ *(colour, light)* éclatant

bring [brɪŋ] vb ❶ apporter ▷ *Bring warm clothes.* Apportez des vêtements chauds. ▷ *Could you bring me my mitts?* Tu peux

m'apporter mes mitaines? ❷ *(person)* amener ▷ *Can I bring a friend?* Est-ce que je peux amener un ami?

bring about vb provoquer ▷ *The war brought about a change in people's attitudes.* La guerre a provoqué un changement dans l'attitude des gens.

bring back vb rapporter

bring up vb ❶ mentionner ▷ *You've brought up an interesting point.* Tu as mentionné un fait intéressant. ❷ élever ▷ *She brought up the children on her own.* Elle a élevé les enfants toute seule.

British Columbia ['brɪtɪʃkə'lʌmbɪə] n Colombie-Britannique f

broad [brɔːd] adj *(wide)* large; **in broad daylight** en plein jour

broadcast ['brɔːdkɑːst] n émission f ▶ vb diffuser ▷ *The interview was broadcast all over the world.* L'entrevue a été diffusée dans le monde entier.; **to broadcast live** retransmettre en direct

broad-minded ['brɔːd'maɪndɪd] adj large d'esprit

broccoli ['brɔkəlɪ] n brocoli m

brochure ['brəʊʃuə'] n brochure f

broil [brɔɪl] vb faire griller; **broiled fish** le poisson grillé

broke [brəʊk] vb see **break** ▶ adj: **to be broke** *(without money)* être fauché

broken ['brəʊkn] adj cassé ▷ *It's broken.* C'est cassé. ▷ *a broken leg* une jambe cassée ▷ *She's got a broken arm.* Elle a le bras cassé.

bronchitis [brɔŋ'kaɪtɪs] n bronchite f

bronze [brɔnz] n bronze m ▷ *the bronze medal* la médaille de bronze

brooch [brəʊtʃ] n broche f

broom [brum] n balai m

brother ['brʌðə'] n frère m ▷ *my brother* mon frère ▷ *my big brother* mon grand frère

brother-in-law ['brʌðərɪn'lɔː'] n beau-frère m *(pl* beaux-frères)

brought [brɔːt] vb see **bring**

brown [braʊn] adj ❶ *(clothes)* marron *(f+pl* marron) ❷ *(hair)* brun ❸ *(tanned)* bronzé; **brown bread** le pain de blé entier; **brown sugar** la cassonade

brownie ['braʊnɪ] n carré au chocolat m

browse [braʊz] vb ❶ naviguer sur Internet; **Browse button** bouton Naviguer ❷ *(magazine, book)* feuilleter ❸ *(store)* regarder

browser ['braʊzə'] n *(for internet)* navigateur m

bruise [bruːz] n bleu m

brunch [brʌntʃ] n brunch m ▷ *to have brunch* prendre le brunch

brush [brʌʃ] n ❶ brosse f ❷ *(paintbrush)* pinceau m *(pl* pinceaux) ▶ vb brosser; **to brush one's hair** se brosser les cheveux ▷ *I brushed my hair.* Je me suis brossé les cheveux.; **to brush one's teeth** se brosser les dents ▷ *I brush my teeth every night.* Je me brosse les dents tous les soirs.

Brussels sprout [-spraut] n chou m de Bruxelles *(pl* choux de Bruxelles)

brutal ['bruːtl] adj brutal *(mpl* brutaux)

BSc [biː'ɛs'siː] n (= *Bachelor of Science*)

baccalauréat ès sciences m; **a BSc in biology** un baccalauréat en biologie

bubble ['bʌbl] n bulle f

bubble bath n bain moussant m

bubble gum n gomme à mâcher f

bucket ['bʌkɪt] n seau m (pl seaux)

buckle ['bʌkl] n (on belt, watch, shoe) boucle f

Buddhist ['budɪst] adj bouddhiste
▶ n bouddhiste

buddy ['bʌdɪ] n copain m, copine f

budget ['bʌdʒɪt] n budget m

budgie ['bʌdʒɪ] n perruche f

buffet ['bʌfɪt] n buffet m

bug [bʌg] n ❶ (insect) insecte m ❷ (infection) microbe m ▷ There's a bug going round. Il y a un microbe qui traîne. ❸ (in computer) bogue m

bugged [bʌgd] adj sur écoute ▷ The room was bugged. La pièce était sur écoute.

build [bɪld] vb construire ▷ We're building a garage. Nous construisons un garage.; **to build up** (increase) s'accumuler

builder ['bɪldə^r] n ❶ (owner of firm) entrepreneur m ❷ (worker) maçon m

building ['bɪldɪŋ] n bâtiment m

built [bɪlt] vb see **build**

bulb [bʌlb] n (electric) ampoule f

bulimia [bə'lɪmɪə] n boulimie f

bull [bul] n taureau m (pl taureaux)

bullet ['bulɪt] n balle f

bulletin board ['bulətɪnbɔːd] n tableau d'affichage

bully ['bulɪ] n intimidateur m ▷ He's a bully. C'est un intimidateur. ▷ She's a bully. Elle fait de l'intimidation.
▶ vb intimider

bullying ['bulɪŋ] n intimidation f ▷ a workshop about bullying un atelier sur l'intimidation ▷ The school has a policy on bullying. L'école a adopté une politique sur l'intimidation.

bum [bʌm] n (bottom) derrière

bump [bʌmp] n (lump) bosse f
▶ vb: **to bump into something** rentrer dans quelque chose ▷ We bumped into her car. Nous sommes rentrés dans sa voiture.; **to bump into somebody (1)** (literally) rentrer dans quelqu'un ▷ He stopped suddenly and I bumped into him. Il s'est arrêté subitement et je lui suis rentré dedans. **(2)** (meet by chance) rencontrer par hasard ▷ I bumped into your sister in the supermarket. J'ai rencontré ta sœur par hasard au supermarché.

bumper ['bʌmpə^r] n pare-chocs m (pl pare-chocs)

bumpy ['bʌmpɪ] adj cahoteux (f cahoteuse)

bun [bʌn] n petit pain

bunch [bʌntʃ] n: **a bunch of flowers** un bouquet de fleurs; **a bunch of grapes** une grappe de raisin; **a bunch of keys** un trousseau de clés; **A bunch of students are going.** Un groupe d'élèves y vont.

bungalow ['bʌŋgələu] n bungalow m

bungee cord ['bʌndʒiːkɔːd] n corde élastique f

bungee jumping ['bʌndʒiː'dʒʌmpɪŋ] n saut à l'élastique m

bunk [bʌŋk] n couchette f; **bunk beds** les lits superposés

buoy [bɔɪ] n (swimming) bouée f

burger ['bəːgə^r] n hamburger m

burglar ['bəːglə^r] n cambrioleur m, cambrioleuse f

burglarize ['bəːgləraɪz] vb cambrioler

burglary ['bəːglərɪ] n cambriolage m

burn [bəːn] n ❶ brûlure f ❷ (sunburn) coup de soleil m
▶ vb ❶ brûler ❷ (food) faire brûler ▷ I burned the cake. J'ai fait brûler le gâteau.; **to burn oneself** se brûler ▷ I burned myself on the oven door. Je me suis brûlé sur la porte du four.; **I've burned my hand.** Je me suis brûlé la main.; **to burn down** brûler ▷ The factory burned down. L'usine a brûlé. ❸ (CD) graver

burst [bəːst] vb éclater ▷ The balloon burst. Le ballon a éclaté.; **to burst a balloon** faire éclater un ballon; **to burst out laughing** éclater de rire; **to burst into flames** prendre feu; **to burst into tears** fondre en larmes

bury ['berɪ] vb enterrer

bus [bʌs] n autobus m ▷ a bus stop un arrêt d'autobus; **the school bus** l'autobus scolaire; **a bus station** une gare routière; **a bus ticket** un ticket d'autobus

bush [buʃ] n ❶ (shrub) buisson m ❷ (forest) bois mpl; **a sugar bush** une érablière

business ['bɪznɪs] n ❶ (firm) entreprise f ▷ He's got his own business. Il a sa propre entreprise. ❷ (commerce) affaires f ▷ She's away on business. Elle est en voyage d'affaires.; **a business trip** un voyage d'affaires; **It's none of my business.** Ça ne me regarde pas.

businessman ['bɪznɪsmən] n homme m d'affaires

businesswoman ['bɪznɪswumən] n femme f d'affaires

bust [bʌst] n (chest) poitrine f

busy ['bɪzɪ] adj ❶ (person, phone line) occupé ❷ (day, schedule) chargé ❸ (store, street) très fréquenté

busy signal n tonalité « occupé »

but [bʌt] conj mais ▷ I'd like to come, but I'm busy. J'aimerais venir mais je suis occupé.

butcher ['butʃə^r] n boucher m ▷ He's a butcher. Il est boucher.

butcher shop n boucherie f

butter ['bʌtə^r] n beurre m

butterfly ['bʌtəflaɪ] n papillon m

buttocks ['bʌtəks] npl fesses fpl

button ['bʌtn] n bouton m

buy [baɪ] vb acheter ▷ She bought me an ice cream. Elle m'a acheté une crème glacée. ▷ I bought her an ice cream. Je lui ai acheté une crème glacée.; **to buy something from somebody** acheter quelque chose à quelqu'un ▷ I bought a watch from him. Je lui ai acheté une montre.
▶ n: **It was a good buy.** C'était une bonne affaire.

buzz [bʌz] vb ❶ (insect) bourdonner ❷ (intercom) appeler par interphone

buzzer ['bʌzə^r] n sonnerie f

by [baɪ] prep ❶ par ▷ The thieves were caught by the police. Les voleurs ont été arrêtés par la police. **②** de ▷ *a painting by Emily Carr* un tableau d'Emily Carr ▷ *a book by Kenneth Oppel* un livre de Kenneth Oppel **③** en **③** *by car* en voiture **③** *by train* en train **③** *by bus* en autobus **④** *(close to)* à côté de ▷ *"Where's the bank?" — "It's by the post office."* « Où est la banque ? » — « Elle est à côté de la poste. » **③** *(not later than)* avant ▷ *We have to be there by 4 o'clock.* Nous devons y être avant quatre heures.; **by the time...** quand... ▷ *By the time I got there it was too late.* Quand je suis arrivé il était déjà trop tard. ▷ *It'll be ready by the time you get back.* Ça sera prêt quand vous reviendrez.; **That's fine by me.** Ça me va.; **all by himself** tout seul; **all by herself** toute seule; **I did it all by myself.** Je l'ai fait tout seul.; **the way** au fait

bye ['baɪbaɪ] *excl* salut!

by-product ['baɪprɒdʌkt] *n* sous-produit *m*

C

cab [kæb] *n* taxi *m*
cabbage ['kæbɪdʒ] *n* chou *m* (*pl* choux)
cabin ['kæbɪn] *n (cottage)* chalet *m*; **a log cabin** un chalet en bois rond
cabinet ['kæbɪnɪt] *n*: **a medicine cabinet** une armoire de salle de bain
cable ['keɪbl] *n* câble *m*
cable car ['keɪblkɑː*] *n* téléphérique *m*
cable television *n* télévision par câble *f*
cactus ['kæktəs] *n* cactus *m*
café ['kæfeɪ] *n* café *m*
cafeteria [kæfɪ'tɪərɪə] *n* cafétéria *f*
cage [keɪdʒ] *n* cage *f*
Cajun ['keɪdʒən] *adj* cajun (*f+pl* cajun) ▷ *Cajun cuisine* la cuisine cajun
  ▷ *n* Cajun
cake [keɪk] *n* gâteau *m* (*pl* gâteaux)
calculate ['kælkjuleɪt] *vb* calculer
calculation [kælkju'leɪʃən] *n* calcul *m*
calculator ['kælkjuleɪtə*] *n* calculatrice *f*
calendar ['kælɪndə*] *n* calendrier *m*
calf [kɑːf] *n* **①** *(of cow)* veau *m* (*pl* veaux) **②** *(of leg)* mollet *m*
call [kɔːl] *n* **①** *(by phone)* appel *m* ▷ *Thanks for your call.* Merci de votre appel.; **a phone call** un coup de téléphone; **to be on call** *(doctor)* être de permanence ▷ *She's on call this evening.* Elle est de permanence ce soir.
  ▷ *vb* appeler ▷ *I'll tell him you called.* Je lui dirai que vous avez appelé. ▷ *This is the number to call.* C'est le numéro à appeler. ▷ *We called the police.* Nous avons appelé la police. ▷ *Everyone calls her Marie.* Tout le monde l'appelle Marie.; **to be called** s'appeler ▷ *The game is called Drago.* Le jeu s'appelle Drago. ▷ *What's this dish called?* Comment s'appelle ce plat?; **to call somebody names** insulter quelqu'un; **He called me an idiot.** Il m'a traité d'imbécile.
call back *vb (phone again)* rappeler ▷ *I'll call back at 6 o'clock.* Je rappellerai à six heures.
call for *vb* ▷ *I'll call for you at 2:30.* Je passerai te prendre à deux heures et demie.; **This calls for a celebration!** Il faut fêter ça!
call off *vb* annuler ▷ *The game was called off.* Le match a été annulé.
calm [kɑːm] *adj* calme
calm down *vb* se calmer ▷ *Calm down!* Calme-toi!
calorie ['kælərɪ] *n* calorie *f*
calves [kɑːvz] *npl see* **calf**
camcorder ['kæmkɔːdə*] *n* caméscope *m*
came [keɪm] *vb see* **come**
camel ['kæməl] *n* chameau *m* (*pl* chameaux)
camera ['kæmərə] *n* **①** *(for photos)* appareil *m* photo (*pl* appareils photo) **②** *(movie, TV)* caméra *f*
cameraman ['kæmərəmæn] *n* cadreur *m*, cadreuse *f*
camp [kæmp] *vb* camper
  ▷ *n* camp *m*; **a camp stove** un réchaud de camping; **to break camp** lever le camp; **to set up camp** installer son camp ▷ *We set up camp by the river.* Nous avons installé notre camp à côté de la rivière.
campaign [kæm'peɪn] *n* campagne *f*
camper ['kæmpə*] *n* **①** *(person)* campeur *m*, campeuse *f* **②** *(van)* caravane *f*
campfire ['kæmpfaɪə*] *n* feu de camp *m*
campground ['kæmpgraʊnd] *n* terrain de camping *m*
camping ['kæmpɪŋ] *n* camping *m*; **to go camping** faire du camping ▷ *We went camping in the Yukon.* Nous avons fait du camping au Yukon.
campsite ['kæmpsaɪt] *n* emplacement *m* (de camping)
campus ['kæmpəs] *n* campus *m*
can [kæn] *n* **①** *(food)* boîte *f* ▷ *a can of corn* une boîte de maïs **②** *(drink)* canette *f* ▷ *a can of pop* une canette de boisson gazeuse
  ▷ *vb* **①** *(be able to, be allowed to)* pouvoir ▷ *I can't come.* Je ne peux pas venir. ▷ *Can I help you?* Est-ce que je peux vous aider? ▷ *Can I use your phone?* Est-ce que je peux me servir de votre téléphone? ▷ *You could rent a bike.* Tu pourrais louer un vélo. ▷ *I couldn't sleep because of the noise.* Je ne pouvais pas dormir à cause du bruit. ▷ *I can't hear you.* Je ne t'entends pas. ▷ *I can't remember.* Je ne m'en souviens pas. ▷ *Can you speak French?* Parlez-vous français? **②** *(know how to)* savoir ▷ *I can swim.* Je sais nager. ▷ *He can't drive.* Il ne sait pas conduire.; **That can't be true!** Ce n'est pas possible!; **You could be right.** Vous avez peut-être raison.
Canada ['kænədə] *n* Canada *m*; **in Canada** au Canada; **to Canada** au Canada
Canada Day *n* Fête du Canada *f*

Canada goose n outarde f
Canadian [kə'neɪdɪən] adj canadien (f canadienne)
▸ n Canadien m, Canadienne f
Canadian Shield n Bouclier canadien m
canal [kə'næl] n canal m (pl canaux)
canary [kə'nɛərɪ] n canari m
cancel ['kænsəl] vb annuler ▷ The game was cancelled. Le match a été annulé.
cancellation [kænsə'leɪʃən] n annulation f
cancer ['kænsəʳ] n ① cancer m ▷ She's got cancer. Elle a le cancer. ② Cancer m ▷ I'm a Cancer. Je suis Cancer.
candidate ['kændɪdeɪt] n candidat m, candidate f
candle ['kændl] n bougie f
candy ['kændɪ] n bonbons mpl; **a candy** un bonbon
canned ['kænd] adj (food) en conserve
cannot ['kænɒt] vb see **can**
canoe [kə'nuː] n canot m
canoeing [kə'nuːɪŋ] n canotage m; **to go canoeing** faire du canotage ▷ We went canoeing. Nous avons fait du canotage.
canola [kə'nəʊlə] n canola m ▷ canola oil l'huile de canola f
can opener ['-əʊpnəʳ] n ouvre-boîte m
can't [kɑːnt] vb see **can**
canvas ['kænvəs] n toile f
cap [kæp] n ① (hat) casquette f ② (of bottle, tube) bouchon m
capable ['keɪpəbl] adj capable
capital ['kæpɪtl] n ① capitale f ▷ Toronto is the capital of Ontario. Toronto est la capitale de l'Ontario. ② (letter) majuscule f ▷ Write your address in capitals. Écris ton adresse en majuscules.
capital punishment n peine capitale f
Capricorn ['kæprɪkɔːn] n Capricorne m ▷ I'm a Capricorn. Je suis Capricorne.
capsize [kæp'saɪz] vb chavirer ▷ The boat capsized. Le bateau a chaviré. ② faire chavirer ▷ Careful, you'll capsize the boat. Attention, tu vas faire chavirer le bateau.
captain ['kæptɪn] n capitaine m ▷ She's captain of the hockey team. Elle est capitaine de l'équipe de hockey.
caption ['kæpʃən] n légende f
capture ['kæptʃəʳ] vb capturer
car [kɑːʳ] n voiture f; **to go by car** aller en voiture ▷ We went by car. Nous sommes allés en voiture.; **a car accident** un accident de voiture
caramel ['kærəməl] n caramel m
carbohydrate [kɑːbəʊ'haɪdreɪt] n glucide m ▷ Pasta is high in carbohydrates. Les pâtes contiennent beaucoup de glucides.
card [kɑːd] n carte f; **a card game** un jeu de cartes
cardboard ['kɑːdbɔːd] n carton m
cardigan ['kɑːdɪgən] n cardigan m
care [kɛəʳ] n soin m ▷ with care avec soin; **to take care of** s'occuper de ▷ I take care of the children on Saturdays. Le samedi, je m'occupe des enfants.; **Take care!** **(1)** (Be careful!) Fais attention! **(2)** (Look after yourself!) Prends bien

soin de toi!
▸ vb: **to care about** se soucier de ▷ They don't care about their image. Ils se soucient peu de leur image.; **I don't care!** Ça m'est égal! ▷ He doesn't care. Ça lui est égal.; **to care for somebody** (patients, elderly people) s'occuper de quelqu'un
career [kə'rɪəʳ] n carrière f; **Career day** la journée d'orientation; **Career Studies** (course) Choix de carrières
careful ['kɛəful] adj: **Be careful!** Fais attention!
carefully ['kɛəfəlɪ] adv ① soigneusement ▷ He carefully avoided talking about it. Il évitait soigneusement d'en parler. ② (safely) prudemment ▷ Drive carefully! Conduisez prudemment!; **Think carefully!** Réfléchis bien!
caregiver ['kɛəgɪvəʳ] n ① (for children) gardien m, gardienne f ② (for sick person) soignant m, soignante f
careless ['kɛəlɪs] adj ① (work) peu soigné; **a careless mistake** une faute d'inattention ② (person) peu soigneux (f peu soigneuse) ▷ She's very careless. Elle est bien peu soigneuse. ③ imprudent ▷ a careless driver un conducteur imprudent
caribou ['kærɪbuː] n caribou m; **caribou hide** la peau de caribou
caring ['kɛərɪŋ] adj: **She's a very caring teacher.** C'est un professeur qui se préoccupe du bien-être de ses élèves.; **She has very caring parents.** Ses parents sont très affectueux.
carnation [kɑː'neɪʃən] n œillet m
carnival [kɑː'nɪvl] n carnaval m
carol ['kærəl] n: **a Christmas carol** une cantique de Noël
carpenter ['kɑːpɪntəʳ] n menuisier m, menuisière f ▷ He's a carpenter. Il est menuisier.
carpentry ['kɑːpɪntrɪ] n menuiserie f
carpet ['kɑːpɪt] n ① tapis m ▷ a Persian carpet un tapis persan ② (broadloom) moquette f
car rental n location de voitures f
carrot ['kærət] n carotte f
carry ['kærɪ] vb ① porter ▷ I'll carry your bag. Je vais porter ton sac. ② transporter ▷ a plane carrying 100 passengers un avion transportant cent passagers
carry on vb ① soutenir ▷ How can you carry on a conversation with all this noise? Comment peut-on soutenir une conversation avec tout ce bruit? ② continuer ▷ Carry on! Continue! ▷ She carried on with her life as before. Elle a continué sa vie comme auparavant.
carry out vb (orders) exécuter
cart [kɑːt] n charrette f
carton ['kɑːtən] n (milk, cream) carton m
cartoon [kɑː'tuːn] n ① (film) dessin animé m ② (in newspaper) caricature f
cartridge ['kɑːtrɪdʒ] n cartouche f; **printer cartridge** une cartouche d'imprimante
carve [kɑːv] vb ① sculpter ▷ He carved a little boat out of wood. Il a sculpté un petit bateau en bois. ② graver ▷ We carved our initials into the bench. Nous avons gravé nos initiales sur

le banc.

car wash *n* lave-auto *m* (*pl* lave-autos)

case [keɪs] *n* ❶ étui *m* ▷ *a violin case* un étui de violon ❷ cas *m* (*pl* cas) ▷ *in some cases* dans certains cas; **in that case** dans ce cas ▷ *"I don't want it." — "In that case, I'll take it."* « Je n'en veux pas. » — « Dans ce cas, je le prends. »; **in case** au cas où ▷ *in case it rains* au cas où il pleuvrait; **just in case** à tout hasard ▷ *Take some money, just in case.* Prends de l'argent à tout hasard.

cash [kæʃ] *n* argent *m* ▷ *I'm a bit short of cash.* Je suis un peu à court d'argent.; **in cash** en liquide ▷ *$200 in cash* deux cent dollars en liquide; **to pay cash** payer comptant; **a cash card** une carte de retrait; **the cash desk** la caisse; **a cash dispenser** un guichet automatique; **a cash register** une caisse

cashew [kæˈʃuː] *n* noix de cajou *f*

cashier [kæˈʃɪər] *n* caissier *m*, caissière *f*

cashmere [ˈkæʃmɪər] *n* cachemire *m* ▷ *a cashmere sweater* un chandail en cachemire

casino [kəˈsiːnəʊ] *n* casino *m*

casserole [ˈkæsərəʊl] *n* casserole *f* ▷ *a tuna casserole* une casserole de thon; **a casserole dish** une cocotte

cassette [kæˈset] *n* cassette *f*; **a cassette player** un lecteur de cassettes; **a cassette recorder** un magnétophone

cast [kɑːst] *n* ❶ acteurs *mpl* ▷ *After the play, we met the cast.* Après la représentation, nous avons rencontré les acteurs. ❷ (*for broken bone*) plâtre *m*

castle [ˈkɑːsl] *n* château *m* (*pl* châteaux)

casual [ˈkæʒjʊl] *adj* ❶ décontracté ▷ *casual clothes* les vêtements décontractés ❷ désinvolte ▷ *a casual attitude* une attitude désinvolte ❸ en passant ▷ *It was just a casual remark.* C'était juste une remarque en passant.

casually [ˈkæʒjʊlɪ] *adv* **to dress casually** s'habiller de façon décontractée

cat [kæt] *n* chat *m*, chatte *f*

catalogue [ˈkætəlɒg] *n* catalogue *m*

catastrophe [kəˈtæstrəfɪ] *n* catastrophe *f*

catch [kætʃ] *vb* ❶ attraper ▷ *to catch a thief* attraper un voleur ▷ *My cat catches birds.* Mon chat attrape des oiseaux.; **to catch somebody doing something** attraper quelqu'un en train de faire quelque chose ▷ *if they catch you cheating* s'ils t'attrapent en train de tricher; **to catch a cold** attraper un rhume ❷ (*bus, train*) prendre ▷ *We caught the last bus.* On a pris le dernier autobus. ❸ (*hear*) saisir ▷ *I didn't catch his name.* Je n'ai pas saisi son nom.; **to catch up** rattraper son retard ▷ *I have to catch up: I was away last week.* Je dois rattraper mon retard : j'étais absent la semaine dernière.; **to catch up with somebody** rattraper quelqu'un; **to get caught up in something** être pris dans quelque chose

category [ˈkætɪgərɪ] *n* catégorie *f*

cathedral [kəˈθiːdrəl] *n* cathédrale *f*

Catholic [ˈkæθəlɪk] *adj* catholique ▷ *n* catholique *m* ▷ *I'm a Catholic.* Je suis catholique.

cattle [ˈkætl] *npl* bétail *m*

caught [kɔːt] *vb see* catch

cauliflower [ˈkɒlɪflaʊər] *n* chou-fleur *m* (*pl* choux-fleurs)

cause [kɔːz] *n* cause *f* ▷ *vb* provoquer ▷ *to cause an accident* provoquer un accident

caution [ˈkɔːʃən] *interjection* Attention!

cautious [ˈkɔːʃəs] *adj* prudent

cautiously [ˈkɔːʃəslɪ] *adv* avec précaution ▷ *She cautiously opened the door.* Elle a ouvert la porte avec précaution.; **He reacted cautiously.** Il a réagi prudemment.

cave [keɪv] *n* grotte *f*

cavity [ˈkævɪtɪ] *n* (*in tooth*) carie *f* ▷ *I have cavities.* J'ai des caries.

CCTV = **closed-circuit television** *n* télévision en circuit fermé *f*

CD *n* (*abbreviation for disque compact*) DC *m* (*pl* DC)

CD burner [-bɜːnər] *n* graveur de DC *m*

CD player *n* lecteur de DC *m*

CD-ROM [siːdiːˈrɒm] *n* CD-ROM *m* (*pl* CD-ROM)

CE *abbr* (= *Common Era*) ap. J.-C. (= *après Jésus-Christ*) ▷ *in 800 CE* en huit cents après Jésus-Christ

ceasefire [ˈsiːsfaɪər] *n* cessez-le-feu *m* (*pl* cessez-le-feu)

cedar [ˈsiːdər] *n* cèdre *m*

ceiling [ˈsiːlɪŋ] *n* plafond *m*

celebrate [ˈselɪbreɪt] *vb* fêter

celebrity [sɪˈlebrɪtɪ] *n* célébrité *f*

celery [ˈselərɪ] *n* céleri *m*

cell [sel] *n* cellule *f*

cellar [ˈselər] *n* cave *f*

cello [ˈtʃeləʊ] *n* violoncelle *m* ▷ *I play the cello.* Je joue du violoncelle.

cellphone [ˈselfəʊn] *n* téléphone cellulaire *f*

Celsius [ˈselsɪəs] *adj* Celsius ▷ *20 degrees Celsius* vingt degrés Celsius

cement [səˈment] *n* ciment *m*

cemetery [ˈsemɪtrɪ] *n* cimetière *m*

cent [sent] *n* cent *m* ▷ *twenty cents* vingt cents

centennial [senˈtenɪəl] *n* centenaire *m*

centimetre [ˈsentɪmiːtər] *n* centimètre *m*

central [ˈsentrəl] *adj* central (*mpl* centraux)

central heating *n* chauffage central *m*

centre [ˈsentər] *n* centre *m* ▷ *a sports centre* un centre sportif

century [ˈsentjʊrɪ] *n* siècle *m* ▷ *the 20th century* le vingtième siècle ▷ *the 21st century* le vingt et unième siècle

cereal [ˈsɪərɪəl] *n* céréales *fpl* ▷ *I have cereal for breakfast.* Je prends des céréales au petit déjeuner.

ceremony [ˈserɪmənɪ] *n* cérémonie *f*

certain [ˈsɜːtən] *adj* certain ▷ *a certain person* une certaine personne ▷ *I'm absolutely certain it was him.* Je suis absolument certain que c'était lui.; **I don't know for certain.** Je n'en suis pas certain.; **to make certain** s'assurer ▷ *I made certain the door was locked.* Je me suis assuré que la porte était fermée à clé.

certainly [ˈsɜːtənlɪ] *adv* vraiment ▷ *I certainly expected something better.* Je m'attendais vraiment à quelque chose de mieux.; **Certainly not!** Certainement pas!; "*So it was* a surprise?" — "It certainly was!" « C'était donc une surprise ? » — « Ça oui alors ! »

certificate [sə'tıfıkıt] n certificat m

CFCs npl CFC mpl

chain [tʃeɪn] n chaîne f

chair [tʃɛəʳ] n ❶ chaise f ▷ a table and 4 chairs une table et quatre chaises ❷ (armchair) fauteuil m

chairlift ['tʃɛəlıft] n télésiège m

chairperson ['tʃɛəpə:sn] n président m, présidente f

chalet ['ʃæleı] n chalet m

chalk [tʃɔ:k] n craie f

chalkboard ['tʃɔ:kbɔ:d] n tableau m

challenge ['tʃælındʒ] n défi m
▶ vb ❶ défier ▷ to challenge authority défier l'autorité; **She challenged me to a race.** Elle m'a proposé de faire la course avec elle. ❷ contester ▷ to challenge somebody's opinion contester l'avis de quelqu'un

challenging ['tʃælındʒıŋ] adj stimulant ▷ a challenging job un travail stimulant

champion ['tʃæmpıən] n champion m, championne f

championship ['tʃæmpıənʃıp] n championnat m

chance [tʃɑ:ns] n ❶ chance f ▷ Do you think I've got a chance? Tu crois que j'ai une chance? ▷ Their chances of winning are very good. Ils ont de fortes chances de gagner.; **Not a chance!** Pas question! ❷ occasion f ▷ I'd like to have a chance to travel. J'aimerais avoir l'occasion de voyager.; **I'll write when I get the chance.** J'écrirai quand j'aurai un moment.; **by chance** par hasard ▷ We met by chance. Nous nous sommes rencontrés par hasard.; **to take a chance** prendre un risque ▷ I'm taking no chances! Je ne veux prendre aucun risque!

change [tʃeındʒ] vb ❶ changer ▷ The town has changed a lot. La ville a beaucoup changé. ▷ I'd like to change $50. Je voudrais changer cinquante dollars. ❷ changer de ▷ You have to change planes in Edmonton. Il faut changer d'avion à Edmonton. ▷ I'm going to change my shoes. Je vais changer de chaussures. ▷ He wants to change his job. Il veut changer d'emploi.; **to change one's mind** changer d'avis ▷ I've changed my mind. J'ai changé d'avis.; **to change gears** changer de vitesse ❸ se changer ▷ She's changing to go out. Elle est en train de se changer pour sortir.; **to get changed** se changer ▷ I'm going to get changed. Je vais me changer. ❹ (exchange) échanger ▷ Can I change this sweater? It's too small. Est-ce que je peux échanger ce chandail? Il est trop petit.
▶ n ❶ changement m ▷ There's been a change of plan. Il y a eu un changement de programme. ❷ (money) monnaie f ▷ I haven't got any change. Je n'ai pas de monnaie.; **a change of clothes** des vêtements de rechange; **for a change** pour changer ▷ Let's play tennis for a change. Si on jouait au tennis pour changer?

changeable ['tʃeındʒəbl] adj variable

change room n ❶ (in store) salon d'essayage m ❷ (for sport) vestiaire m

channel ['tʃænl] n (TV) chaîne f ▷ There's hockey on the other channel. Il y a du hockey sur l'autre chaîne.

chaos ['keıɒs] n chaos m

chapel ['tʃæpl] n (part of church) chapelle f

chapped [tʃæpt] adj gercé ▷ I have chapped lips. J'ai les lèvres gercées.

chapter ['tʃæptəʳ] n chapitre m

character ['kærıktəʳ] n ❶ caractère m ▷ Give me some idea of his character. Décris-moi un peu son caractère.; **She's quite a character.** C'est un drôle de numéro. ❷ (in play, film) personnage m ▷ The character played by Donald Sutherland… Le personnage joué par Donald Sutherland…

characteristic ['kærıktə'rıstık] n caractéristique f

charcoal ['tʃɑ:kəʊl] n charbon de bois m

charge [tʃɑ:dʒ] n ❶ frais mpl ▷ Is there a charge for delivery? Est-ce qu'il y a des frais de livraison?; **an extra charge** un supplément; **free of charge** gratuit; **to reverse the charges** appeler à frais virés ▷ I'd like to reverse the charges. Je voudrais appeler à frais virés.; **to be in charge** être responsable ▷ She was in charge of the group. Elle était responsable du groupe.
▶ vb ❶ (money) prendre ▷ How much did she charge you? Combien est-ce qu'elle vous a demandé? ▷ They charge $10 an hour. Ils demandent dix dollars de l'heure. ❷ (with crime) inculper ▷ The police have charged him with fraud. La police l'a inculpé de fraude.

charity ['tʃærıtı] n association f caritative ▷ They gave the money to charity. Ils ont donné l'argent à une association caritative.

charm [tʃɑ:m] n charme m ▷ He's got a lot of charm. Il a beaucoup de charme.

charming ['tʃɑ:mıŋ] adj charmant

chart [tʃɑ:t] n tableau m (pl tableaux) ▷ The chart shows the increase in unemployment. Le tableau indique la progression du chômage.; **the charts** le palmarès ▷ This album is number one in the charts. Cet album est numéro un au palmarès.

chase [tʃeıs] vb pourchasser
▶ n poursuite f ▷ a car chase une poursuite en voiture

chat [tʃæt] n ❶ bavardage m ▷ Enough chat; let's get to work. Assez de bavardage; mettons-nous au travail. ❷ (online) clavardage m; **to have a chat** bavarder
▶ vb ❶ bavarder ❷ (online) clavarder

chat room n clavardoir m

chauvinist ['ʃəʊvınıst] n: **a male chauvinist** un machiste

cheap [tʃi:p] adj bon marché (f+pl bon marché) ▷ a cheap T-shirt un T-shirt bon marché

cheaper ['tʃi:pəʳ] adj moins cher (f moins chère) ▷ It's cheaper by bus. C'est moins cher en autobus.

cheat [tʃi:t] vb tricher ▷ You're cheating! Tu triches!

cheater ['tʃi:təʳ] n tricheur m, tricheuse f

check [tʃɛk] n ❶ contrôle m ▷ a security check un contrôle de sécurité ❷ (mark) coche f ❸ (square in pattern) carreau m

▶ vb vérifier ▷ I'll check the time of the flight. Je vais vérifier l'heure du vol. ▷ Could you check the oil, please? Pourriez-vous vérifier le niveau d'huile, s'il vous plaît?; **to check in (1)** (at airport) se présenter à l'enregistrement ▷ What time do I have to check in? À quelle heure est-ce que je dois me présenter à l'enregistrement? **(2)** (in hotel) se présenter à la réception; **to check on** jeter un coup d'œil sur ▷ Check on the baby. Jette un coup d'œil sur le bébé.; **to check out** (from hotel) régler sa note

checked ['tʃɛkt] adj (fabric) à carreaux
checkers ['tʃɛkəz] n dames fpl ▷ to play checkers jouer aux dames
check-in ['tʃɛkin] n enregistrement m
checkout ['tʃɛkaut] n caisse
checkup ['tʃɛkʌp] n examen m de santé
cheek [tʃiːk] n joue f ▷ He kissed her on the cheek. Il l'a embrassée sur la joue.
cheer [tʃiəʳ] n hourras mpl; **to give a cheer** pousser des hourras; **Cheers! (1)** (good health) À la vôtre! **(2)** (goodbye) Salut
▶ vb applaudir; **to cheer somebody up** remonter le moral à quelqu'un ▷ I was trying to cheer them up. J'essayais de leur remonter le moral.; **Cheer up!** Ne te laisse pas abattre!
cheerful ['tʃiəfʊl] adj gai
cheese [tʃiːz] n fromage m; **cheese curds** du fromage en grains
chef [ʃɛf] n chef m
chemical ['kɛmɪkl] adj chimique ▷ a chemical reaction une réaction chimique ▷ chemical weapons les armes chimiques f
▶ n produit chimique m
chemist ['kɛmɪst] n chimiste m
chemistry ['kɛmɪstrɪ] n chimie f ▷ the chemistry lab le laboratoire de chimie
cheque [tʃɛk] n chèque m ▷ to write a cheque faire un chèque ▷ to pay by cheque payer par chèque
cherry ['tʃɛrɪ] n cerise f; **a cherry tree** un cerisier
chess [tʃɛs] n échecs mpl ▷ to play chess jouer aux échecs
chessboard ['tʃɛsbɔːd] n échiquier m
chest [tʃɛst] n (of person) poitrine f ▷ his chest measurement son tour de poitrine; **a chest of drawers** une commode
chestnut ['tʃɛsnʌt] n marron m ▷ roasted chestnuts les marrons grillés
chew [tʃuː] vb mâcher
chewing gum ['tʃuː-ɪŋ-] n gomme à mâcher f
chick [tʃɪk] n poussin m ▷ a hen and her chicks une poule et ses poussins
chicken ['tʃɪkɪn] n ❶ (meat) poulet m ❷ (live bird) poule f ▷ to raise chickens élever des poules
chicken pox [-pɒks] n varicelle f
chick peas n pois mpl chiches
chief [tʃiːf] n chef m ▷ the chief of security le chef de la sécurité; **band chief** un chef de bande
▶ adj principal ▷ Canada's chief exports les articles d'exportation principaux du Canada
child [tʃaɪld] n enfant mf ▷ all the children tous les enfants
childish ['tʃaɪldɪʃ] adj puéril
children ['tʃɪldrən] npl see **child**

chili ['tʃaɪlɪ] n ❶ (pepper) piment m ❷ (dish) chili m
chill [tʃɪl] vb mettre au frais ▷ Put the wine in the fridge to chill. Mets le vin au frais au réfrigérateur.
chilly ['tʃɪlɪ] adj froid m
chimney ['tʃɪmnɪ] n cheminée f
chin [tʃɪn] n menton m
china ['tʃaɪnə] n porcelaine f ▷ a china plate une assiette en porcelaine
chinook [tʃɪ'nuːk] n (wind) chinook m
chip [tʃɪp] n ❶ (potato chip) croustille f ▷ a bag of chips un sac de croustilles ❷ (fry) frite f ▷ fish and chips poisson et frites ❸ (chocolate) brisure f ❹ (in computer) puce f; **This plate has a chip in it.** Cette assiette est ébréchée.
chipmunk ['tʃɪpmʌŋk] n suisse m
chives ['tʃaɪvz] npl ciboulette f
chocolate ['tʃɔklɪt] n chocolat m ▷ a chocolate cake un gâteau au chocolat; **hot chocolate** le chocolat chaud
chocolate chip n brisure de chocolat f; **a chocolate chip cookie** un biscuit aux brisures de chocolat
choice [tʃɔɪs] n choix m ▷ I had no choice. Je n'avais pas le choix.
choir ['kwaɪəʳ] n chorale f ▷ I sing in the school choir. Je chante dans la chorale de l'école.
choke [tʃəuk] vb s'étrangler; **He choked on a fishbone.** Il s'est étranglé avec une arête de poisson.
choose [tʃuːz] vb choisir ▷ It's difficult to choose. C'est difficile de choisir. ▷ I chose to stay home. J'ai décidé de rester chez moi.
chop [tʃɒp] vb ❶ émincer ▷ Chop the onions. Émincez les oignons. ❷ (wood) couper; **to chop down a tree** abattre un arbre
▶ n côtelette f ▷ a pork chop une côtelette de porc
chopsticks ['tʃɒpstɪks] npl baguettes fpl
chose, chosen ['tʃəuz, 'tʃəuzn] vb see **choose**
Christian ['krɪstɪən] n chrétien m, chrétienne f
▶ adj chrétien m (f chrétienne)
Christmas ['krɪsməs] n Noël m ▷ Merry Christmas! Joyeux Noël!; **Christmas Day** le jour de Noël; **Christmas Eve** la veille de Noël
chronic ['krɒnɪk] adj chronique f ▷ a chronic cough une toux chronique
chunk [tʃʌŋk] n gros morceau m (pl gros morceaux) ▷ Cut the meat into chunks. Coupez la viande en gros morceaux.
church [tʃɜːtʃ] n église f
cider ['saɪdəʳ] n cidre m
cigarette [sɪgə'rɛt] n cigarette f
cinema ['sɪnəmə] n cinéma m
cinnamon ['sɪnəmən] n cannelle f
circle ['sɜːkl] n cercle m ▷ to stand in a circle faire cercle ▷ to draw a circle tracer un cercle ▷ to go around in circles tourner en rond
▶ vb encercler ▷ Circle the correct answer. Encerclez la bonne réponse.
circular ['sɜːkjuləʳ] adj circulaire
circulation [sɜːkju'leɪʃən] n ❶ (of blood) circulation f ❷ (of newspaper) tirage m
circumflex ['sɜːkəmflɛks] n accent m circonflexe

circumstances ['sə:kəmstənsɪz] *npl* circonstances *fpl*

circus ['sə:kəs] *n* cirque *m*

citizen ['sɪtɪzn] *n* citoyen *m*, citoyenne *f* ▷ *a Canadian citizen* un citoyen canadien

citizenship ['sɪtɪznʃɪp] *n* citoyenneté *f*

city ['sɪtɪ] *n* ville *f*; **the city centre** le centre-ville ▷ *It's in the city centre.* C'est au centre-ville.

city hall *n* hôtel *m* de ville

civilization [sɪvɪlaɪ'zeɪʃən] *n* civilisation *f*

civil servant *n* fonctionnaire

civil war *n* guerre civile *f*

claim [kleɪm] *vb* ❶ prétendre ▷ *He claims to have found the money.* Il prétend avoir trouvé l'argent. ❷ réclamer ▷ *No one has claimed this jacket.* Personne n'a réclamé cette veste.
▶ *n* (on insurance policy) demande d'indemnité *f* ▷ *to make a claim* faire une demande d'indemnité

clam [klæm] *n* palourde *f*

clap [klæp] *vb* (applaud) applaudir; **to clap one's hands** frapper dans ses mains ▷ *I've trained my dog to sit when I clap my hands.* J'ai dressé mon chien à s'asseoir quand je frappe dans mes mains.

clarinet [klærɪ'nɛt] *n* clarinette *f* ▷ *I play the clarinet.* Je joue de la clarinette.

clash [klæʃ] *vb* ❶ (colours) jurer ▷ *These two colours clash.* Ces deux couleurs jurent. ❷ (events) tomber en même temps ▷ *The concert clashes with my party.* Le concert tombe en même temps que ma soirée.

clasp [klɑ:sp] *n* (of necklace) fermoir *m*

class [klɑ:s] *n* ❶ (group) classe *f* ▷ *We're in the same class.* Nous sommes dans la même classe. ❷ (lesson) cours *m* ▷ *I go to dancing classes.* Je vais à des cours de danse.

classic ['klæsɪk] *adj* classique *m* ▷ *a classic example* un cas classique
▶ *n* (book, film) classique *m*

classical ['klæsɪkl] *adj* classique ▷ *I like classical music.* J'aime la musique classique.

classmate ['klɑ:smeɪt] *n* camarade de classe

classroom ['klɑ:srum] *n* classe *f*

claw [klɔ:] *n* ❶ (of cat, dog) griffe *f* ❷ (of bird) serre *f* ❸ (of crab, lobster) pince *f*

clay [kleɪ] *n* argile *f*

clean [kli:n] *adj* propre ▷ *a clean shirt* une chemise propre
▶ *vb* nettoyer

cleaner ['kli:nə'] *n* (of building) préposé au ménage *m*, préposée au ménage *f*

cleaners ['kli:nəz] *n* teinturerie *f*

clear [klɪə'] *adj* ❶ clair ▷ *a clear explanation* une explication claire ▷ *It's clear you don't believe me.* Il est clair que tu ne me crois pas. ❷ transparent ▷ *clear plastic* du plastique transparent ❸ (distinct) net ▷ *clear handwriting* une écriture nette ❹ (road, way) libre ▷ *The road's clear now.* La route est libre maintenant.
▶ *vb* ❶ dégager ▷ *The police are clearing the road after the accident.* La police dégage la route après l'accident. ❷ (fog, mist) se dissiper ▷ *The mist cleared.* La brume s'est dissipée.; **to clear the table** débarrasser la table ▷ *I'll clear the table.* Je vais débarrasser la table.; **to clear up**

résoudre ▷ *We've cleared up the problem.* Nous avons résolu le problème.; **I think it's going to clear up.** (weather) Je pense que le temps va se lever.

clearing ['klɪərɪŋ] *n* clairière *f* ▷ *a clearing in the forest* une clairière dans la forêt

clearly ['klɪəlɪ] *adv* ❶ clairement ▷ *She explained it very clearly.* Elle l'a expliqué très clairement. ❷ nettement ▷ *The Labrador coast was clearly visible.* On distinguait nettement la côte du Labrador. ❸ distinctement ▷ *to speak clearly* parler distinctement

clementine ['klɛməntaɪn] *n* clémentine *f*

clever ['klɛvə'] *adj* astucieux (*f* astucieuse) ▷ *a clever system* un système astucieux; **What a clever idea!** Quelle bonne idée!

click [klɪk] *n* (of door, camera) petit bruit sec *m*
▶ *vb* (with mouse) cliquer; **to click on an icon** cliquer sur une icône; **The lid clicked shut.** Le couvercle s'est fermé avec un petit bruit sec.

client ['klaɪənt] *n* client *m*, cliente *f*

cliff [klɪf] *n* falaise

climate ['klaɪmɪt] *n* climat *m*

climb [klaɪm] *vb* ❶ escalader ▷ *We're going to climb the Niagara Escarpment.* Nous allons escalader l'escarpement du Niagara. ❷ (stairs) monter ❸ (tree) grimper dans

clinic ['klɪnɪk] *n* clinique *f*

clip [klɪp] *n* ❶ (for hair) barrette *f* ❷ (film) court extrait *m* ▷ *some clips from his latest film* quelques courts extraits de son dernier film
▶ *vb* ❶ attacher ▷ *Clip these pages together.* Attache ces pages. ❷ couper ▷ *She clipped my bangs.* Elle m'a coupé la frange.; **to clip an article out of the newspaper** découper un article dans le journal

clip-art ['klɪpɑ:t] *n* clipart *m*

clippers ['klɪpəz] *npl*: **nail clippers** le coupe-ongle *m* (*pl* les coupe-ongles)

cloakroom ['kləʊkrum] *n* (for coats) vestiaire *m*

clock [klɒk] *n* ❶ horloge *f* ▷ *the church clock* l'horloge de l'église ❷ (smaller) pendule *f*; **an alarm clock** un réveil; **a clock-radio** un radio-réveil

clockwork ['klɒkwə:k] *n*: **Everything went like clockwork.** Tout a marché comme sur des roulettes.

clog [klɒg] *vb* boucher ▷ *The drain is clogged.* L'égout est bouché.

clone [kləʊn] *n* (animal, plant) clone *m*
▶ *vb* cloner ▷ *a cloned sheep* un mouton cloné

close [kləʊz] *adj, adv* ❶ (near) près ▷ *The mall is very close.* Le centre commercial est tout près.; **close to** près de ▷ *The youth hostel is close to the station.* L'auberge de jeunesse est près de la gare.; **Come closer.** Rapproche-toi.; **to look at something close up** regarder quelque chose de près ❷ (in relationship) proche ▷ *We're just inviting close relations.* Nous n'invitons que les parents proches. ▷ *She's a close friend of mine.* C'est une amie proche. ▷ *I'm very close to my brother.* Je suis très proche de mon frère. ❸ (contest) serré ▷ *It's going to be very close.* Ça va être très serré.
▶ *vb* ❶ fermer ▷ *What time does the pool close?*

La piscine ferme à quelle heure? ▷ *The stores close at 5.30.* Les magasins ferment à cinq heures et demie. ▷ *Please close the door.* Fermez la porte, s'il vous plaît. ❷ *se fermer* ▷ *The doors close automatically.* Les portes se ferment automatiquement.

closed [kləʊzd] *adj* fermé ▷ *The bank's closed.* La banque est fermée.

closely ['kləʊslɪ] *adv* (look, examine) de près

closet ['klɒzɪt] *n* garde-robe *m* ▷ *She hung her coat in the closet.* Elle a pendu son manteau dans le garde-robe.

close-up ['kləʊsʌp] *n* gros plan *m* ▷ *Here's a close-up of my boyfriend.* Voici un gros plan de mon petit ami.

cloth [klɒθ] *n* (material) tissu *m*; **a cloth** un chiffon ▷ *Wipe it with a damp cloth.* Nettoyez-le avec un chiffon humide.

clothes [kləʊðz] *npl* vêtements *mpl* ▷ *new clothes* des vêtements neufs; **a clothes line** un fil à linge; **a clothes peg** une pince à linge

cloud [klaʊd] *n* nuage *m*

cloudy ['klaʊdɪ] *adj* nuageux (*f* nuageuse)

clove [kləʊv] *n*: **a clove of garlic** une gousse d'ail

clown [klaʊn] *n* clown

club [klʌb] *n* club *m* ▷ *a golf club* (society and for playing golf) un club de golf; **the youth club** le club de jeunes; **clubs** (in cards) le trèfle ▷ *the ace of clubs* l'as de trèfle

clue [kluː] *n* indice *m* ▷ *an important clue* un indice important; **I haven't a clue.** Je n'en ai pas la moindre idée.

clumsy ['klʌmzɪ] *adj* maladroit

clutch [klʌtʃ] *n* (of car) pédale d'embrayage *f*

clutter ['klʌtər] *n* désordre *m* ▷ *There's too much clutter in here.* Il y a trop de désordre ici.
▶ *vb* encombrer ▷ *Don't clutter up the hallway.* N'encombrez pas le couloir. ▷ *a desk cluttered with papers and books* un bureau encombré de papiers et de livres

coach [kəʊtʃ] *n* entraîneur *m*, entraîneuse *f* ▷ *the hockey coach* l'entraîneur de l'équipe de hockey

coal [kəʊl] *n* charbon *m*; **a coal mine** une mine de charbon; **a coal miner** un mineur

coarse [kɔːs] *adj* ❶ (surface, fabric) rugueux (*f* rugueuse) ▷ *The bag was made of coarse cloth.* Le sac était fait d'un tissu rugueux. ❷ (vulgar) grossier (*f* grossière) ▷ *coarse language* un langage grossier

coast [kəʊst] *n* côte *f* ▷ *It's on the west coast of Canada.* C'est sur la côte ouest du Canada.

coast guard *n* (boat) garde-côte *m* (pl garde-côtes)

coat [kəʊt] *n* manteau *m* (pl manteaux) ▷ *a warm coat* un manteau chaud; **a coat of paint** une couche de peinture

coat hanger *n* cintre *m*

cobweb ['kɒbwɛb] *n* toile d'araignée *f*

cocoa ['kəʊkəʊ] *n* cacao *m* ▷ *a cup of cocoa* une tasse de cacao

coconut ['kəʊkənʌt] *n* noix de coco *f*

code [kəʊd] *n* code *m*

coffee ['kɒfɪ] *n* café *m*; **A cup of coffee,**

please. Un café, s'il vous plaît.

coffeepot ['kɒfɪpɒt] *n* cafetière *f*

coffee table *n* table basse *f*

coffin ['kɒfɪn] *n* cercueil *m*

coin [kɔɪn] *n* pièce de monnaie *f*

coincidence [kəʊ'ɪnsɪdəns] *n* coïncidence *f*

colander ['kɒləndər] *n* passoire *f*

cold [kəʊld] *adj* froid *m* ▷ *The water's cold.* L'eau est froide.; **cold cuts** l'assiette anglaise; **it's cold today.** Il fait froid aujourd'hui.; **to be cold** (person) avoir froid ▷ *I'm cold.* J'ai froid. ▷ *Are you cold?* Est-ce que tu as froid?
▶ *n* ❶ froid ▷ *I can't stand the cold.* Je ne supporte pas le froid. ❷ rhume *m* ▷ *to catch a cold* attraper un rhume; **to have a cold** avoir un rhume ▷ *I've got a bad cold.* J'ai un gros rhume.; **a cold sore** un bouton de fièvre

coleslaw ['kəʊlslɔː] *n* salade de chou

collapse [kə'læps] *vb* s'effondrer ▷ *He collapsed.* Il s'est effondré.

collar ['kɒlər] *n* ❶ (of coat, shirt) col *m* ❷ (for animal) collier *m*

collarbone ['kɒləbəʊn] *n* clavicule *f* ▷ *I broke my collarbone.* Je me suis cassé la clavicule.

colleague ['kɒliːg] *n* collègue

collect [kə'lɛkt] *vb* ❶ ramasser ▷ *The teacher collected the homework.* Le professeur a ramassé les travaux. ❷ faire collection de ▷ *I collect stamps.* Je fais collection de timbres. ❸ faire une collecte ▷ *They're collecting for charity.* Ils font une collecte pour une association caritative.
▶ *adv*: **to call collect** téléphoner à frais virés

collect call *n* appel *m* à frais virés

collection [kə'lɛkʃən] *n* ❶ collection *f* ▷ *my CD collection* ma collection de DC ❷ collecte *f* ▷ *a collection for charity* une collecte pour une association caritative

collector [kə'lɛktər] *n* collectionneur *m*, collectionneuse *f*

college ['kɒlɪdʒ] *n* collège *m* ▷ *a technical college* un collège d'enseignement technique

collide [kə'laɪd] *vb* entrer en collision

collision [kə'lɪʒən] *n* collision *f*

colon ['kəʊlən] *n* (punctuation mark) deux-points *m* (pl les deux-points)

colony ['kɒlənɪ] *n* colonie *f* ▷ *the colony of New France* la colonie de la Nouvelle France

colour ['kʌlər] *n* couleur *f* ▷ *What colour is it?* C'est de quelle couleur?; **a colour printer** une imprimante couleur; **a colour scheme** une combinaison de couleurs

colourful ['kʌləful] *adj* aux couleurs vives ▷ *a colourful skirt* une jupe aux couleurs vives

colouring ['kʌlərɪŋ] *n* (for food) colorant *m*

column ['kɒləm] *n* ❶ colonne *f* ▷ *to format text in columns* disposer un texte en colonnes ❷ chronique *f* ▷ *He writes a column for the school newspaper.* Il écrit une chronique pour le journal de l'école.

coma ['kəʊmə] *n* coma *m* ▷ *to be in a coma* être dans le coma

comb [kəʊm] *n* peigne *m*
▶ *vb*: **to comb one's hair** se peigner ▷ *You haven't combed your hair.* Tu ne t'es pas peigné.

combination [kɒmbɪ'neɪʃən] *n* combinaison *f*

combine ['kɒmbaɪn] vb ❶ allier ▷ *The film combines humour with suspense.* Le film allie l'humour au suspense. ❷ concilier ▷ *It's difficult to combine a career with family.* Il est difficile de concilier carrière et vie de famille.

come [kʌm] vb ❶ venir ▷ *Can I come too?* Est-ce que je peux venir aussi? ▷ *Some friends came to see us.* Quelques amis sont venus nous voir. ▷ *I'll come with you.* Je viens avec toi. ❷ *(arrive)* arriver ▷ *I'm coming!* J'arrive! ▷ *They came late.* Ils sont arrivés en retard. ▷ *The letter came this morning.* La lettre est arrivée ce matin.; **to come back** revenir ▷ *Come back!* Reviens!; **to come down (1)** *(person, elevator)* descendre **(2)** *(prices)* baisser; **to come from** venir de ▷ *Where do you come from?* Tu viens d'où?; **to come in** entrer ▷ *Come in!* Entrez!; **Come on!** Allez!; **to come out** sortir ▷ *when we came out of the movie theatre* quand nous sommes sortis du cinéma ▷ *It's just come out on video.* Ça vient de sortir en vidéo.; **None of my photos came out.** Mes photos n'ont rien donné.; **to come around** *(after faint, operation)* reprendre connaissance; **to come up** monter ▷ *Come up here!* Monte!; **to come up to somebody (1)** s'approcher de quelqu'un ▷ *She came up to me and kissed me.* Elle s'est approchée de moi et m'a embrassée. **(2)** *(to speak to them)* aborder quelqu'un ▷ *A man came up to me and said...* Un homme m'a abordé et m'a dit...

comedian [kə'miːdɪən] n comique

comedy ['kɒmɪdɪ] n comédie f

comfort ['kʌmfət] vb consoler ▷ *He tried to comfort her.* Il a essayé de la consoler.

comfortable ['kʌmfətəbl] adj ❶ *(bed, chair)* confortable ❷ *(person)* à l'aise ▷ *I'm very comfortable, thanks.* Je suis parfaitement à l'aise, merci.

comic ['kɒmɪk] n *(magazine)* illustré m

comic strip n bande dessinée f

coming ['kʌmɪŋ] adj prochain ▷ *in the coming months* au cours des prochains mois ▷ *this coming Thursday* jeudi prochain

comma ['kɒmə] n virgule f

command [kə'mɑːnd] n ordre m; **a good command of English** ▷ *une bonne maîtrise de l'anglais*
▶ vb ordonner ▷ *He commanded us to leave.* Il nous a ordonné de partir.; **She commands respect.** Elle commande le respect.

comment ['kɒment] n commentaire m ▷ *He made no comment.* Il n'a fait aucun commentaire.; **No comment!** Je n'ai rien à dire!
▶ vb: **to comment on something** faire des commentaires sur quelque chose

commentary ['kɒməntərɪ] n *(on TV, radio)* reportage m en direct m

commentator ['kɒmənteɪtər] n commentateur sportif m, commentatrice sportive f

commercial [kə'mɜːʃəl] n annonce f publicitaire

commission [kə'mɪʃən] n commission f ▷ *Salesmen work on commission.* Les représentants travaillent à la commission.

commit [kə'mɪt] vb: **to commit a crime** commettre un crime; **to commit oneself** s'engager ▷ *I don't want to commit myself.* Je ne veux pas m'engager.; **to commit suicide** se suicider ▷ *She committed suicide.* Elle s'est suicidée.

committee [kə'mɪtɪ] n comité m

common ['kɒmən] adj courant m ▷ *a common expression* une expression courante; **in common** en commun ▷ *We have a lot in common.* Nous avons beaucoup de choses en commun.

Commons ['kɒmənz] npl: **the House of Commons** la Chambre des communes

common sense n bon sens m ▷ *Use your common sense!* Sers-toi de ton bon sens!

communicate [kə'mjuːnɪkeɪt] vb communiquer

communication [kəmjuːnɪ'keɪʃən] n communication

communism ['kɒmjunɪzəm] n communisme m

communist ['kɒmjunɪst] n communiste
▶ adj communiste

community [kə'mjuːnɪtɪ] n communauté f

community centre n centre communautaire m

community college n collège communautaire m

commute [kə'mjuːt] vb faire la navette ▷ *She commutes between Kitchener and Toronto.* Elle fait la navette entre Kitchener et Toronto.

commuter [kə'mjuːtər] n navetteur m, navetteuse f; **a commuter train** un train de banlieue

compact disc n disque compact m; **a compact disc player** un lecteur de DC

companion [kəm'pænjən] n compagnon m, compagne f

company ['kʌmpənɪ] n ❶ société f ▷ *She works for a big company.* Elle travaille pour une grosse société. ❷ compagnie f ▷ *an insurance company* une compagnie d'assurance ▷ *a theatre company* une compagnie théâtrale; **to keep somebody company** tenir compagnie à quelqu'un ▷ *I'll keep you company.* Je vais te tenir compagnie.

comparatively [kəm'pærətɪvlɪ] adv relativement

compare [kəm'pɛər] vb comparer ▷ *People always compare him with his brother.* On le compare toujours à son frère.; **compared with** en comparaison de ▷ *Victoria is small compared with Vancouver.* Victoria est une petite ville en comparaison de Vancouver.

comparison [kəm'pærɪsən] n comparaison f

compartment [kəm'pɑːtmənt] n compartiment m

compass ['kʌmpəs] n ❶ *(for directions)* boussole f ❷ *(math instrument)* compas m

compatible [kəm'pætɪbl] adj compatible

compelling [kəm'pelɪŋ] adj *(gripping)* fascinant ▷ *It's a compelling film.* C'est un film fascinant.

compensation [kɒmpən'seɪʃən] n indemnité f ▷ *They got $2000 compensation.* Ils ont reçu une indemnité de deux mille dollars.

compete [kəm'pi:t] vb participer ▷ I'm competing in the marathon. Je participe au marathon.; **to compete with someone** (sports) concourir avec quelqu'un; **to compete with someone** (general) rivaliser avec quelqu'un; **to compete for something** se disputer quelque chose ▷ There are 50 students competing for 6 places. Ils sont cinquante élèves à se disputer six places.

competent ['kɒmpɪtənt] adj compétent

competition [kɒmpɪ'tɪʃən] n concours m ▷ a singing competition un concours de chant

competitive [kəm'petɪtɪv] adj compétitif (f compétitive) ▷ a very competitive price un prix très compétitif; **to be competitive** (person) avoir l'esprit de compétition ▷ He's a very competitive person. Il a vraiment l'esprit de compétition.

competitor [kəm'petɪtər] n concurrent m, concurrente f

complain [kəm'pleɪn] vb se plaindre ▷ I'm going to complain to the manager. Je vais me plaindre à la directrice. ▷ We complained about the noise. Nous nous sommes plaints du bruit.

complaint [kəm'pleɪnt] n plainte f ▷ There were lots of complaints about the food. Il y a eu beaucoup de plaintes à propos de la nourriture.

complete [kəm'pli:t] adj complet (f complète)

completely [kəm'pli:tlɪ] adv complètement

complex ['kɒmpleks] adj complexe

complexion [kəm'plekʃən] n teint m

complicated ['kɒmplɪkeɪtɪd] adj compliqué

compliment ['kɒmplɪmənt] n compliment m ▶ vb complimenter ▷ They complimented me on my French. Ils m'ont complimenté sur mon français.

complimentary [kɒmplɪ'mentərɪ] adj ① (flattering) élogieux (f élogieuse) ▷ He was very complimentary about my poem. Il a été très élogieux à propos de mon poème. ② (free) gratuit; **I have two complimentary tickets for tonight.** J'ai deux places gratuites pour ce soir.

composer [kəm'pəʊzər] n compositeur m, compositrice f

compost ['kɒmpɒst] n compost m; **a compost heap** un tas de compost

comprehension [kɒmprɪ'henʃən] n compréhension f

comprehensive [kɒmprɪ'hensɪv] adj complet (f complète) ▷ a comprehensive guide un guide complet

compromise ['kɒmprəmaɪz] n compromis m ▷ We reached a compromise. Nous sommes parvenus à un compromis. ▶ vb: **Let's compromise.** Essayons de trouver un compromis.

compulsory [kəm'pʌlsərɪ] adj obligatoire

computer [kəm'pju:tər] n ordinateur m

computer game n jeu électronique (pl jeux électroniques)

computer programmer n programmeur m, programmeuse f ▷ She's a computer programmer. Elle est programmeuse.

computer room n salle d'informatique f

computer science n informatique f

computing [kəm'pju:tɪŋ] n informatique f

concentrate ['kɒnsəntreɪt] vb se concentrer ▷ I couldn't concentrate. Je n'arrivais pas à me concentrer.

concentration [kɒnsən'treɪʃən] n concentration f

concern [kən'sɜ:n] n (worry) inquiétude f ▷ They expressed concern about the school's image. Ils ont exprimé leur inquiétude concernant l'image de l'école.; **That's none of your concern.** Ce n'est pas ton affaire.

concerned [kən'sɜ:nd] adj: **to be concerned** s'inquiéter ▷ His mother is concerned about him. Sa mère s'inquiète à son sujet.; **as far as I'm concerned** en ce qui me concerne

concerning [kən'sɜ:nɪŋ] prep concernant

concert ['kɒnsət] n concert m

conclusion [kən'klu:ʒən] n conclusion f ▷ Your essay should have an introduction and a conclusion. Votre dissertation devrait avoir une introduction et une conclusion.; **I came to the conclusion that...** J'ai conclu que...; **in conclusion** en conclusion

concrete ['kɒŋkri:t] n béton m

condemn [kən'dem] vb condamner ▷ The government has condemned the decision. Le gouvernement a condamné cette décision.

condition [kən'dɪʃən] n ① condition f ▷ I'll do it, on one condition... Je veux bien le faire, à une condition... ② état m ▷ in bad condition en mauvais état ▷ in good condition en bon état

conditional [kən'dɪʃənl] n conditionnel m

conditioner [kən'dɪʃənər] n (for hair) revitalisant m

condom ['kɒndəm] n condom m

condominium [kɒndə'mɪnɪəm] n copropriété f ▷ We live in a condominium. Nous habitons dans une copropriété.

conduct [kən'dʌkt] vb (orchestra) diriger

conductor [kən'dʌktər] n chef d'orchestre m

cone [kəʊn] n cornet m ▷ an ice cream cone un cornet de crème glacée

Confederation [kənfedə'reɪʃən] n Confédération f ▷ fifty years after Confederation cinquante ans après la Confédération

conference ['kɒnfərəns] n conférence f

confess [kən'fes] vb avouer ▷ He finally confessed. Il a fini par avouer. ▷ He confessed to the crime. Il a avoué avoir commis le crime.

confession [kən'feʃən] n confession f

confetti [kən'fetɪ] n confettis mpl

confidence ['kɒnfɪdns] n ① confiance f ▷ I have confidence in you. J'ai confiance en toi. ② assurance f ▷ She lacks confidence. Elle manque d'assurance.

confident ['kɒnfɪdənt] adj sûr ▷ I'm confident everything will be okay. Je suis sûr que tout ira bien.; **She's seems quite confident.** Elle a l'air sûre d'elle.

confidential [kɒnfɪ'denʃəl] adj confidentiel (f confidentielle)

confirm [kən'fɜ:m] vb (booking) confirmer

confirmation [kɒnfə'meɪʃən] n confirmation f

conflict ['kɒnflɪkt] *n* conflit *m*

confuse [kən'fjuːz] *vb*: **to confuse somebody** embrouiller les idées de quelqu'un ▷ *Don't confuse me!* Ne m'embrouille pas les idées!

confused [kən'fjuːzd] *adj* désorienté

confusing [kən'fjuːzɪŋ] *adj* déroutant ▷ *It was confusing at first.* C'était déroutant au début.; **The traffic signs are confusing.** Les panneaux de signalisation ne sont pas clairs.

confusion [kən'fjuːʒən] *n* confusion *f*

congratulate [kən'grætjuleɪt] *vb* féliciter ▷ *My friends congratulated me on passing the test.* Mes amis m'ont félicité d'avoir réussi à l'examen.

congratulations [kəngrætjuˈleɪʃənz] *npl* félicitations *fpl* ▷ *Congratulations on your new job!* Félicitations pour votre nouveau poste!

conjunction [kən'dʒʌŋkʃən] *n* conjonction *f*

connect [kə'nɛkt] *vb* ❶ (*plug in*) brancher ▷ *You have to connect the printer.* Tu dois brancher l'imprimante. ❷ connecter ▷ *to be connected to the Internet* être connecté à l'Internet ❸ associer ▷ *I connect summer with camping.* J'associe l'été au camping.

connection [kə'nɛkʃən] *n* ❶ rapport *m* ▷ *There's no connection between the two events.* Il n'y a aucun rapport entre les deux événements. ❷ (*electrical*) contact *m* ▷ *There's a loose connection.* Il y a un mauvais contact. ❸ (*of trains, planes, buses*) correspondance *f* ▷ *We missed our connection.* Nous avons raté la correspondance.

conquer ['kɒŋkəʳ] *vb* conquérir

conscience ['kɒnʃəns] *n* conscience *f*

conscientious [kɒnʃɪˈɛnʃəs] *adj* consciencieux (*f* consciencieuse)

conscious ['kɒnʃəs] *adj* conscient

consciousness ['kɒnʃəsnɪs] *n* connaissance *f*; **to lose consciousness** perdre connaissance ▷ *I lost consciousness.* J'ai perdu connaissance.

consequence ['kɒnsɪkwəns] *n* conséquence *f* ▷ *What are the consequences for the environment?* Quelles sont les conséquences pour l'environnement?; **as a consequence** en conséquence; **to suffer the consequences** accepter les conséquences

consequently ['kɒnsɪkwəntlɪ] *adv* par conséquent

conservation [kɒnsəˈveɪʃən] *n* protection *f*

conservative [kən'səːvətɪv] *adj* conservateur (*f* conservatrice)

consider [kən'sɪdəʳ] *vb* ❶ considérer ▷ *He considers it a waste of time.* Il considère que c'est une perte de temps. ❷ envisager ▷ *We considered cancelling our holiday.* Nous avons envisagé d'annuler nos vacances.; **I'm considering the idea.** J'y songe.

considerate [kən'sɪdərɪt] *adj* délicat

considering [kən'sɪdərɪŋ] *prep* ❶ étant donné ▷ *Considering we were there for a month…* Étant donné que nous étions là pour un mois… ❷ tout compte fait ▷ *I got a good mark, considering.* J'ai eu une bonne note, tout compte fait.

consist [kən'sɪst] *vb*: **to consist of** être composé de ▷ *The band consists of three*

guitarists and a drummer. Le groupe est composé de trois guitaristes et une batteuse.

consonant ['kɒnsənənt] *n* consonne *f*

constant ['kɒnstənt] *adj* constant

constantly ['kɒnstəntlɪ] *adv* constamment

constitution [kɒnstɪˈtjuːʃən] *n* constitution *f* ▷ *the Canadian constitution* la Constitution canadienne

construct [kən'strʌkt] *vb* construire

construction [kən'strʌkʃən] *n* construction *f*

consult [kən'sʌlt] *vb* consulter

consumer [kən'sjuːməʳ] *n* consommateur *m*, consommatrice *f*

contact ['kɒntækt] *n* contact *m* ▷ *I'm in contact with her.* Je suis en contact avec elle. ▶ *vb* joindre ▷ *Where can we contact you?* Où pouvons-nous vous joindre?

contact lenses [-'lɛnzɪz] *npl* verres *mpl* de contact

contagious [kən'teɪdʒəs] *adj* contagieux (*f* contagieuse) ▷ *It's not contagious.* Ce n'est pas contagieux.

contain [kən'teɪn] *vb* contenir

container [kən'teɪnəʳ] *n* contenant *m* ▷ *a plastic container* un contenant en plastique

contaminated [kən'tæmɪneɪtɪd] *adj* contaminé ▷ *contaminated water* de l'eau contaminée

contempt [kən'tɛmpt] *n* mépris *m*

contents ['kɒntɛnts] *npl* ❶ (*of container*) contenu *m* ❷ (*of book*) table *f* des matières

contest [kən'tɛst] *n* concours *m*

contestant [kən'tɛstənt] *n* concurrent *m*, concurrente *f*

context ['kɒntɛkst] *n* contexte *m*

continent ['kɒntɪnənt] *n* continent *m* ▷ *How many continents are there?* Combien y a-t-il de continents?

continental breakfast [kɒntɪˈnɛntl-] *n* déjeuner continental *m*

continue [kən'tɪnjuː] *vb* ❶ continuer ▷ *She continued talking.* Elle a continué à parler. ❷ (*after interruption*) reprendre ▷ *We continued working after lunch.* Nous avons repris le travail après le déjeuner.

continuous [kən'tɪnjuəs] *adj* continu

contraceptive [kɒntrə'sɛptɪv] *n* contraceptif *m*

contract [kən'trækt] *n* contrat *m*

contradict [kɒntrə'dɪkt] *vb* contredire

contrary [kən'trɛərɪ] *n*: **on the contrary** au contraire

contrast [kən'trɑːst] *n* contraste *m*

contribute [kən'trɪbjuːt] *vb* ❶ (*to success, achievement*) contribuer ▷ *The treaty will contribute to world peace.* Le traité va contribuer à la paix dans le monde. ❷ (*share in*) participer ▷ *They didn't contribute to the discussion.* Ils n'ont pas participé à la discussion. ❸ (*give*) donner ▷ *She contributed $10.* Elle a donné dix dollars.

contribution [kɒntrɪˈbjuːʃən] *n* contribution *f*

control [kən'trəʊl] *n* contrôle *m*; **to lose control** (*of vehicle*) perdre le contrôle ▷ *He lost control of the car.* Il a perdu le contrôle de son véhicule.; **the controls** (*of machine*) les

f commandes; **to be in control** être maître de la situation; **to keep control** (of people) se faire obéir ▷ He can't keep control of the class. Il n'arrive pas à se faire obéir de sa classe.; **out of control** (child, class) déchaîné
▶ vb ❷ (country, organization) diriger ▷ She can't control the class. Elle n'arrive pas à se faire obéir de sa classe. ❸ maîtriser ▷ I couldn't control the horse. Je ne suis pas arrivé à maîtriser le cheval. ❹ (temperature, speed) régler; **to control oneself** se contrôler

controversial [kɒntrə'vɜːʃl] adj controversé ▷ a controversial book un livre controversé

convenience store [kən'viːniəns-] n dépanneur m

convenient [kən'viːniənt] adj: **The hotel is in a convenient location.** L'hôtel est bien situé.; **It's not a convenient time for me.** C'est une heure qui ne m'arrange pas.; **Would Monday be convenient for you?** Est-ce que lundi vous conviendrait?

conventional [kən'vɛnʃənl] adj conventionnel (f conventionnelle)

conversation [kɒnvə'seɪʃən] n conversation f ▷ a French conversation class un cours de conversation française

convert ['kɒnvɜːt] vb transformer ▷ We've converted the loft into a spare room. Nous avons transformé le grenier en chambre d'amis.

convict ['kɒnvɪkt] vb reconnaître coupable ▷ She was convicted of the crime. Elle a été reconnue coupable du crime.

convince [kən'vɪns] vb persuader ▷ I'm not convinced. Je n'en suis pas persuadé.

cook [kuk] vb ❶ faire la cuisine ▷ I can't cook. Je ne sais pas faire la cuisine. ❷ préparer ▷ He's cooking supper. Il est en train de préparer le souper. ❸ faire cuire ▷ Cook the pasta for 10 minutes. Faites cuire les pâtes pendant dix minutes.; **to be cooked** être cuit ▷ When the potatoes are cooked... Lorsque les pommes de terre sont cuites...
▶ n cuisinier m, cuisinière f ▷ Matthew's an excellent cook. Matthew est un excellent cuisinier.

cookbook ['kukbuk] n livre de cuisine m

cookie ['kukɪ] n biscuit m

cooking ['kukɪŋ] n cuisine f ▷ I like cooking. J'aime bien faire la cuisine.

cool [kuːl] adj ❶ frais (f fraîche) ▷ a cool place un endroit frais ❷ (trendy, OK) cool ▷ Your website is cool! Ton site Web est super! ❸ (excellent) génial ▷ You're coming along? Cool! Tu viens aussi? C'est génial!; **to stay cool** (keep calm) garder son calme ▷ She stayed cool. Elle a gardé son calme.; **keep cool!** du calme!

co-operation [kəʊɒpə'reɪʃn] n coopération f

co-operative [kəʊ'ɒprətɪv] adj coopératif (f coopérative) ▷ She was very co-operative. Elle s'est montrée très coopérative.

cop [kɒp] n (informal) flic m

cope [kəʊp] vb se débrouiller ▷ It was hard, but we coped. C'était dur, mais nous nous sommes débrouillés.; **to cope with** faire face à ▷ She has a lot of problems to cope with. Elle doit faire face à de nombreux problèmes.

copper ['kɒpə'] n cuivre m ▷ a copper bracelet un bracelet en cuivre

copy ['kɒpɪ] n ❶ (of letter, document) copie f ❷ (of book) exemplaire m
▶ vb copier ▷ The teacher accused him of copying. Le professeur l'a accusé d'avoir copié.; **to copy and paste** copier-coller

cord [kɔːd] n fil m ▷ The cord isn't long enough. Le fil n'est pas assez long.

cordless ['kɔːdlɪs] adj sans fil ▷ a cordless mouse une souris sans fil

core [kɔːʳ] n (of fruit) trognon m ▷ an apple core un trognon de pomme

cork [kɔːk] n (of bottle) bouchon m

corkscrew ['kɔːkskruː] n tire-bouchon m

corn [kɔːn] n maïs m; **corn on the cob** l'épi m de maïs

corner ['kɔːnə'] n coin m ▷ in a corner of the room dans un coin de la pièce; **the shop on the corner** la boutique au coin de la rue; **He lives just around the corner.** Il habite tout près d'ici.

corn starch [-stɑːtʃ] n amidon m de maïs

corporal punishment ['kɔːpərəl-] n châtiment corporel m

corpse [kɔːps] n cadavre m

correct [kə'rɛkt] adj exact ▷ That's correct. C'est exact.; **the correct choice** le bon choix; **the correct answer** la bonne réponse
▶ vb corriger

correction [kə'rɛkʃən] n correction f

correctly [kə'rɛktlɪ] adv correctement

correspond [kɒrɪs'pɒnd] vb (match, agree) correspondre ▷ Write down the letter that corresponds to the correct answer. Écris la lettre qui correspond à la bonne réponse.; **She corresponds with her aunt in India.** Elle correspond avec sa tante en Inde.

corridor ['kɒrɪdɔː'] n couloir m

corruption [kə'rʌpʃən] n corruption f

cosmetics [kəz'mɛtɪks] npl produits mpl de beauté

cosmetic surgery [kəz'mɛtɪk'sə:dʒərɪ] n chirurgie esthétique f

cost [kɒst] vb coûter ▷ The meal costs a hundred dollars. Le repas coûte cent dollars. ▷ How much does it cost? Combien est-ce que ça coûte? ▷ It costs too much. Ça coûte trop cher.
▶ n coût m; **the cost of living** le coût de la vie; **at all costs** à tout prix; **to cut costs** réduire les coûts

costume ['kɒstjuːm] n costume m

cot [kɒt] n lit de camp m

cottage ['kɒtɪdʒ] n chalet m

cottage cheese n fromage cottage

cotton ['kɒtn] n coton m ▷ a cotton shirt une chemise en coton; **a cotton ball** une boule de coton; **cotton candy** la barbe à papa

couch [kautʃ] n canapé m

cough [kɒf] vb tousser
▶ n toux f ▷ a bad cough une mauvaise toux; **I've got a cough.** Je tousse.; **a cough drop** une pastille

could [kud] vb see **can**

coulee ['kuːlɪ] n ravine f ▷ The coulee is usually dry in summer. La ravine est normalement sans eau en été.

council ['kaʊnsl] n conseil; **He's on the city council.** Il fait partie du conseil municipal.; **She's on the student council.** Elle fait partie du conseil étudiant.

councillor ['kaʊnslə'] n conseiller municipal m, conseillère municipale f

counsellor ['kaʊnslə'] n ❶ conseiller m, conseillère f; **a guidance counsellor** une conseillère en orientation ❷ (camp) animateur m, animatrice f

count [kaʊnt] vb compter; **to count on** compter sur ▷ You can count on me. Tu peux compter sur moi.

counter ['kaʊntə'] n ❶ (in store) comptoir m ❷ (in post office, bank) guichet m ❸ (in game) jeton m

counterfeit ['kaʊntəfɪt] adj faux (f fausse) ▷ a counterfeit bill un faux billet ▷ counterfeit money la fausse monnaie

country ['kʌntrɪ] n ❶ pays m ▷ the border between the two countries la frontière entre les deux pays ❷ campagne f ▷ I live in the country. J'habite à la campagne.; **country music** la musique country; **a country road** une route de campagne

countryside ['kʌntrɪsaɪd] n campagne f

county ['kaʊntɪ] n comté m

couple ['kʌpl] n couple m ▷ the couple who live next door le couple qui habite à côté; **a couple** deux ▷ a couple of hours deux heures; **Could you wait a couple of minutes?** Pourriez-vous attendre quelques minutes?

coupon ['ku:pɒn] n bon de réduction m ▷ I have a coupon for 10% off. J'ai un bon de réduction de dix pour cent.

courage ['kʌrɪdʒ] n courage m

courageous [kə'reɪdʒəs] adj courageux (f courageuse)

courier ['kʊrɪə'] n messageries fpl ▷ They sent it by courier. Ils l'ont envoyé par messageries.

course [kɔ:s] n ❶ cours m ▷ a French course un cours de français ▷ to take a course suivre un cours ❷ plat m ▷ the main course le plat principal; **the first course** l'entrée ❸ terrain m ▷ a golf course un terrain de golf; **of course** bien sûr ▷ "Do you understand?" — "Of course I do!" «Tu comprends?» — «Bien sûr que oui!»

court [kɔ:t] n ❶ (of law) tribunal m (pl tribunaux) ▷ He was in court last week. Il est passé devant le tribunal la semaine dernière. ❷ (tennis) court m ▷ There are tennis and squash courts. Il y a des courts de tennis et de squash.

courtyard ['kɔ:tjɑ:d] n cour f

cousin ['kʌzn] n cousin m, cousine f

cover ['kʌvə'] n ❶ (book cover, blanket) couverture f ❷ (duvet, computer) housse f; **a cover page** une page couverture; **blow someone's cover** démasquer quelqu'un ▶ vb ❶ couvrir ▷ My face was covered with mosquito bites. J'avais le visage couvert de piqûres de moustique. ❷ prendre en charge ▷ Our insurance didn't cover it. Notre assurance ne l'a pas pris en charge.; **to cover up a scandal** étouffer un scandale

coverage ['kʌvərɪdʒ] n couverture f ▷ media

coverage la couverture médiatique

cow [kaʊ] n vache f

coward ['kaʊəd] n lâche ▷ She's a coward. Elle est lâche.

cowardly ['kaʊədlɪ] adj lâche

cowhand ['kaʊhænd] n vacher m, vachère f

coyote [kɔɪ'əʊtɪ] n coyote m

cozy ['kəʊzɪ] adj douillet (f douillette)

crab [kræb] n crabe m

crack [kræk] n ❶ (in wall) fissure f ❷ (in cup, window) fêlure f; **I'll have a crack at it.** Je vais tenter le coup.
▶ vb (nut, egg) casser; **to crack a joke** sortir une blague

crack down on vb être ferme avec ▷ The police are cracking down on motorists who drive too fast. La police va être ferme avec les automobilistes qui roulent trop vite.

cracked [krækt] adj (cup, window) fêlé

cracker ['krækə'] n (biscuit) craquelin m

cradle ['kreɪdl] n berceau m (pl berceaux)

crafter ['krɑ:ftə'] n artisan m, artisane f

crafts [krɑ:fts] n artisanat m ▷ to do crafts faire de l'artisanat; **a craft shop** une boutique d'artisanat

cram [kræm] vb ❶ entasser ▷ We crammed our stuff into the trunk. Nous avons entassé nos affaires dans le coffre. ❷ préparer un examen

crammed [kræmd] adj: **crammed with** bourré de ▷ Her pack was crammed with books. Son sac à dos était bourré de livres.

cranberry ['krænbərɪ] n canneberge f ▷ turkey with cranberry sauce de la dinde aux canneberges

crane [kreɪn] n (machine) grue f

crash [kræʃ] vb ❶ entrer en collision ▷ The two cars crashed. Les deux autos sont entrées en collision.; **to crash into something** rentrer dans quelque chose; **The dishes crashed to the floor.** La vaisselle s'est fracassée sur le plancher.; **The plane crashed.** L'avion s'est écrasé. ❷ (computer) se planter ▷ My computer crashed. Mon ordinateur s'est planté.
▶ n ❶ (of car) collision f ❷ (of plane) accident m ❸ (sound) fracas m; **a computer crash** un plantage d'ordinateur; **a crash helmet** un casque; **a crash course** un cours intensif

crawl [krɔ:l] vb (baby) marcher à quatre pattes; **A spider crawled across the floor.** Une araignée avançait le long du plancher.
▶ n crawl m ▷ to do the crawl nager le crawl

crazy ['kreɪzɪ] adj fou (f folle)

cream [kri:m] n ❶ crème f ▷ strawberries and cream les fraises à la crème; **cream cheese** le fromage à la crème; **a cream puff** un chou à la crème

crease [kri:s] n ❶ pli m ❷ (hockey) zone de but f

creased [kri:st] adj froissé

create [kri:'eɪt] vb créer

creation [kri:'eɪʃən] n création f

creative [kri:'eɪtɪv] adj créatif (f créative)

creature ['kri:tʃə'] n créature f

credit ['krɛdɪt] n crédit m ▷ on credit à crédit

credit card n carte de crédit f

creek [kri:k] n ruisseau m

creeps [kri:ps] *npl*: **It gives me the creeps.** Ça me donne la chair de poule.

creep up [kri:p'ʌp] *vb* s'approcher à pas de loup; **to creep up on somebody** s'approcher de quelqu'un à pas de loup

crept [krɛpt] *vb see* **creep up**

crew [kru:] *n* (*of ship, plane*) équipage *m*, équipe *f* ▷ *a film crew* une équipe de tournage

crib [krɪb] *n* lit d'enfant *m*

cricket ['krɪkɪt] *n* grillon *m*

crime [kraɪm] *n* ❶ crime ▷ *Murder is a crime.* Le meurtre est un crime. ❷ (*lawlessness*) criminalité *f*; **to reduce crime** réduire la criminalité

criminal ['krɪmɪnl] *n* criminel, criminelle *f*
▶ *adj* criminel (*f* criminelle) ▷ *It's criminal!* C'est criminel!; **It's a criminal offence.** C'est un crime puni par la loi.; **to have a criminal record** avoir un casier judiciaire

crisis ['kraɪsɪs] *n* crise *f*

crisp [krɪsp] *adj* (*food*) croustillant

criterion [kraɪ'tɪərɪən] *n* critère *m*

critic ['krɪtɪk] *n* critique

critical ['krɪtɪkl] *adj* critique; **a critical remark** une critique

criticism ['krɪtɪsɪzəm] *n* critique

criticize ['krɪtɪsaɪz] *vb* critiquer

crochet ['krəʊʃeɪ] *vb* faire du crochet

crocodile ['krɔkədaɪl] *n* crocodile *m*

crook [kruk] *n* (*criminal*) escroc *m* ▷ *That woman is a crook.* Cette femme est un escroc.

crooked [krukɪd] *adj* ❶ (*bent*) tordu *f* *a crooked line* une ligne tordue ❷ (*on an angle*) de travers ▷ *Your tie's crooked.* Ta cravate est de travers.

crop [krɔp] *n* ❶ récolte *f* ▷ *a good crop of apples* une bonne récolte de pommes ❷ culture *f* ▷ *Wheat is one of Canada's main crops.* Le blé est l'une des cultures les plus importantes du Canada.

cross [krɔs] *n* croix *f*
▶ *vb* (*street, bridge*) traverser; **to cross out** barrer; **to cross over** traverser

cross-check ['krɔstʃɛk] *vb* faire double échec à ▷ *He cross-checked his opponent.* Il a fait double échec à son adversaire.

cross-checking ['krɔstʃɛkɪŋ] *n* double échec *m* ▷ *a penalty for cross-checking* une punition pour double-échec

cross-country ['krɔs'kʌntrɪ] *n* (*race*) cross *m*; **cross-country skiing** le ski de fond

crossroads ['krɔsrəudz] *n* carrefour *m*

crosswalk ['krɔswɔːk] *n* passage à piétons *m*

crossword ['krɔswəːd] *n* mots *mpl* croisés ▷ *I like doing crosswords.* J'aime faire les mots croisés.

crouch down *vb* s'accroupir

crow [krəu] *n* corbeau *m* (*pl* corbeaux)

crowd [kraud] *n* foule *f*; **the crowd** (*spectators*) les spectateurs

crowded ['kraudɪd] *adj* bondé

crown [kraun] *n* couronne *f*

crude [kru:d] *adj* (*vulgar*) grossier (*f* grossière)

cruel ['kru:əl] *adj* cruel (*f* cruelle)

cruise [kru:z] *n* croisière *f* ▷ *to go on a cruise* faire une croisière

crumb [krʌm] *n* miette *f*

crunchy ['krʌntʃɪ] *adj* ❶ (*cookie*) croustillant ❷ (*carrot, apple*) croquant

crush [krʌʃ] *vb* écraser

crust [krʌst] *n* croûte *f*

crutch [krʌtʃ] *n* béquille *f*

cry [kraɪ] *n* cri *m* ▷ *He gave a cry of surprise.* Il a poussé un cri de surprise.; **Go on, have a good cry!** Vas-y, pleure un bon coup!
▶ *vb* pleurer ▷ *The baby's crying.* Le bébé pleure.

crystal ['krɪstl] *n* cristal *m* (*pl* cristaux)

cub [kʌb] *n* ❶ (*bear*) ourson *m* ❷ (*wolf*) louveteau *m* (*pl* louveteaux) ❸ (*lion*) lionceau *m* (*pl* lionceaux) ❹ (*fox*) renardeau *m* (*pl* renardeaux)

cube [kju:b] *n* cube *m*

cubic ['kju:bɪk] *adj*: **a cubic metre** un mètre cube

cucumber ['kju:kʌmbər] *n* concombre *m*

cuddly ['kʌdlɪ] *adj* câlin

cue [kju:] *n* ❶ signal *m* ❷ (*for snooker, pool*) queue de billard *f*

culprit ['kʌlprɪt] *n* coupable

culture ['kʌltʃər] *n* culture *f*

cup [kʌp] *n* ❶ tasse *f* ▷ *a china cup* une tasse en porcelaine; **a cup of coffee** un café ❷ (*trophy*) coupe *f*

cupboard ['kʌbəd] *n* placard *m*

cure [kjuər] *vb* guérir
▶ *n* remède *m*

curious ['kjuərɪəs] *adj* curieux (*f* curieuse)

curl [kəːl] *n* (*in hair*) boucle *f*
▶ *vb* ❶ boucler ▷ *to curl one's hair* boucler ses cheveux ❷ (*sport*) jouer au curling

curling ['kəːlɪŋ] *n* curling *m* ▷ *a curling league* une ligue de curling

curling iron *n* fer à friser *m*

curly ['kəːlɪ] *adj* (*loosely curled*) bouclé ❷ (*tightly curled*) frisé

currency ['kʌrnsɪ] *n* devise *f* ▷ *foreign currency* les devises étrangères

current ['kʌrnt] *n* courant *m* ▷ *The current is very strong.* Le courant est très fort.
▶ *adj* actuel (*f* actuelle); **current events** l'actualité

curriculum [kə'rɪkjuləm] *n* programme d'études *m*

curry ['kʌrɪ] *n* curry *m*

curse [kəːs] *n* (*spell*) malédiction *f*

cursor ['kəːsər] *n* curseur *m*

curtain ['kəːtn] *n* rideau *m* (*pl* rideaux); **to draw the curtains** tirer les rideaux

curved [kəːvd] *adj* courbe ▷ *a curved surface* une surface courbe; **a curved line** une courbe

cushion ['kuʃən] *n* coussin *m*

custard ['kʌstəd] *n* crème anglaise *f*

custody ['kʌstədɪ] *n* (*of child*) garde *f*

custom ['kʌstəm] *n* coutume *f* ▷ *It's an old custom.* C'est une ancienne coutume.

customer ['kʌstəmər] *n* client *m*, cliente *f*

customs ['kʌstəmz] *npl* douane *f*

customs officer *n* douanier *m*, douanière *f*

cut [kʌt] *n* ❶ coupure *f* ▷ *He's got a cut on his forehead.* Il a une coupure au front. ❷ (*hairstyle*) ▷ *a cut and blow-dry* une coupe et un séchage à la brosse ❸ (*in price, spending*) réduction *f*

▶ vb ❶ couper ▷ *I'll cut some bread.* Je vais couper du pain.; **to cut oneself** se couper ▷ *I cut my foot on a piece of glass.* Je me suis coupé au pied avec un morceau de verre.; **to cut and paste** couper-coller ❷ (*price, spending*) réduire; **to cut down** (*tree*) abattre; **to cut off** couper ▷ *The power was cut off.* L'électricité a été coupée.; **to cut up** (*vegetables, meat*) hacher

cutback ['kʌtbæk] n réduction f ▷ *staff cutbacks* des réductions de personnel

cute [kjuːt] adj mignon (f mignonne)

cutlery ['kʌtləri] n couverts mpl

cybercafé ['saɪbəkæfeɪ] n cybercafé m

cycle ['saɪkl] n cycle m; **a vicious cycle** un cycle infernal

cycling ['saɪklɪŋ] n cyclisme m

cyclist ['saɪklɪst] n cycliste

cylinder ['sɪlɪndə'] n cylindre m

cynical ['sɪnɪkl] adj cynique

d

dad [dæd] n ❶ père m ▷ *my dad* mon père ▷ *his dad* son père ❷ papa m; **Dad!** Papa! ▷ *I'll ask Dad.* Je vais demander à papa.

daffodil ['dæfədɪl] n jonquille f

daily ['deɪlɪ] adj, adv ❶ quotidien (f quotidienne) ▷ *It's part of my daily routine.* Ça fait partie de mes occupations quotidiennes. ❷ tous les jours ▷ *The pool is open daily from 9 a.m. to 6 p.m.* La piscine est ouverte tous les jours de neuf heures à dix-huit heures.

dairy products ['dɛərɪ-] npl produits mpl laitiers

daisy ['deɪzɪ] n pâquerette f

dam [dæm] n barrage m

damage ['dæmɪdʒ] n dégâts mpl ▷ *The storm did a lot of damage.* La tempête a fait beaucoup de dégâts.
▶ vb endommager

damp [dæmp] adj humide

dance [dɑːns] n ❶ danse f ▷ *The last dance was a waltz.* La dernière danse était une valse. ❷ bal m ▷ *Are you going to the dance tonight?* Tu vas au bal ce soir?
▶ vb danser; **to go dancing** aller danser ▷ *Let's go dancing!* Si on allait danser?

dancer ['dɑːnsə'] n danseur m, danseuse f

dandruff ['dændrəf] n pellicules fpl

danger ['deɪndʒə'] n danger m; **in danger** en danger ▷ *His life is in danger.* Sa vie est en danger.; **to be in danger of** risquer de ▷ *We were in danger of missing the plane.* Nous

risquions de rater l'avion.

dangerous ['deɪndʒrəs] adj dangereux (f dangereuse)

danish ['deɪnɪʃ] n (*pastry*) danoise f

dare [dɛə'] vb oser; **to dare to do something** oser faire quelque chose ▷ *I didn't dare tell my parents.* Je n'ai pas osé le dire à mes parents.; **to dare someone to do something** défier quelqu'un de faire quelque chose

daring ['dɛərɪŋ] adj audacieux (f audacieuse)

dark [dɑːk] adj ❶ (*room*) sombre ▷ *It's dark.* (*inside*) Il fait sombre.; **It's dark outside.** Il fait nuit dehors.; **It's getting dark.** La nuit tombe. ❷ (*colour*) foncé ▷ *She's got dark hair.* Elle a les cheveux foncés. ▷ *a dark green sweater* un chandail vert foncé
▶ n noir m ▷ *I'm afraid of the dark.* J'ai peur du noir.; **after dark** après la tombée de la nuit

darkness ['dɑːknɪs] n obscurité f ▷ *The room was in darkness.* La chambre était dans l'obscurité.

darling ['dɑːlɪŋ] n chéri m, chérie f ▷ *Thank you, darling!* Merci, chéri!

dart [dɑːt] n fléchette f ▷ *to play darts* jouer aux fléchettes

dash [dæʃ] vb se précipiter ▷ *Everyone dashed to the window to look.* Tout le monde s'est précipité vers la fenêtre pour regarder.
▶ n (*punctuation mark*) tiret m

data ['deɪtə] npl données fpl

database ['deɪtəbeɪs] n (*on computer*) base de données f

date [deɪt] n ❶ date f ▷ *my date of birth* ma date de naissance; **to have a date with somebody** sortir avec quelqu'un ▷ *She's got a date with her boyfriend tonight.* Elle sort avec son petit ami ce soir.; **out of date** (1) (*passport*) périmé (2) (*technology*) dépassé (3) (*clothes*) démodé ❷ (*fruit*) datte f
▶ vb sortir ensemble ▷ *They're dating.* Ils sortent ensemble. ▷ *He's dating my sister.* Il sort avec ma sœur.

daughter ['dɔːtə'] n fille f

daughter-in-law ['dɔːtərɪnlɔː] n belle-fille f (pl belles-filles)

dawn [dɔːn] n aube f ▷ *at dawn* à l'aube

day [deɪ] n ❶ jour m ▷ *We stayed in St. John's for three days.* Nous sommes restés trois jours à St. John's.; **every day** tous les jours ❷ journée f ▷ *during the day* dans la journée ▷ *I stayed at home all day.* Je suis resté à la maison toute la journée.; **the day before** la veille ▷ *the day before my birthday* la veille de mon anniversaire; **the day after** le lendemain; **the day after tomorrow** après-demain ▷ *We're leaving the day after tomorrow.* Nous partons après-demain.; **the day before yesterday** avant-hier ▷ *He arrived the day before yesterday.* Il est arrivé avant-hier.

daycare ['deɪkɛə'] n (*place*) garderie f

daylight-saving time [deɪlaɪt'seɪvɪŋ-] n heure f avancée

dead [dɛd] adj, adv ❶ mort f ▷ *He was already dead when the doctor came.* Il était déjà mort quand le docteur est arrivé.; **She was shot dead.** Elle a été abattue. ❷ (*totally*) absolument ▷ *You're dead right!* Tu as absolument raison!

dead end n impasse f

deadline ['dɛdlaɪn] n date limite f ▷ *The deadline for entries is May 2nd.* La date limite d'inscription est le deux mai.

deaf [dɛf] adj sourd

deafening ['dɛfnɪŋ] adj assourdissant

deal [diːl] n marché m; **It's a deal!** Marché conclu!; **to make a deal with someone** conclure un marché avec quelqu'un; **a great deal** beaucoup ▷ *a great deal of money* beaucoup d'argent
▶ vb (cards) donner ▷ *It's your turn to deal.* C'est à toi de donner.; **to deal with something** s'occuper de quelque chose ▷ *She promised to deal with it immediately.* Elle a promis de s'en occuper immédiatement.

dealer ['diːlər] n marchand m, marchande f

dealt [dɛlt] vb see **deal**

dear [dɪər] adj cher (f chère) ▷ *Dear Mrs Duval* Chère Madame Duval; **Dear Sir/Madam** (in a circular) Madame, Monsieur

death [dɛθ] n mort f ▷ *after his death* après sa mort; **I was bored to death.** Je me suis ennuyé à mourir.

debate [dɪ'beɪt] n débat m
▶ vb débattre

debt [dɛt] n dette f ▷ *He's got a lot of debts.* Il a beaucoup de dettes.; **to be in debt** avoir des dettes

decade ['dɛkeɪd] n décennie f

decaffeinated [di'kæfɪneɪtɪd] adj décaféiné

decay [dɪ'keɪ] vb ❶ (vegetation, wood) pourrir ❷ (teeth) se carier ❸ (building) se délabrer ▷ *a decaying mansion* un manoir qui se délabre
▶ n (tooth) carie f

deceive [dɪ'siːv] vb tromper

December [dɪ'sɛmbər] n décembre m; **in December** en décembre

decent ['diːsənt] adj convenable ▷ *a decent education* une éducation convenable; **He's a decent person.** Il est bien honnête.

decide [dɪ'saɪd] vb ❶ décider ▷ *I decided to write to her.* J'ai décidé de lui écrire. ▷ *I decided not to go.* J'ai décidé de ne pas y aller. ❷ se décider ▷ *I can't decide.* Je n'arrive pas à me décider. ▷ *Haven't you decided yet?* Tu ne t'es pas encore décidé?; **to decide on something** (together) se mettre d'accord sur quelque chose ▷ *They haven't decided on a name yet.* Ils ne se sont pas encore mis d'accord sur un nom.

decimal ['dɛsɪməl] adj décimal ▷ *the decimal system* le système décimal

decipher [dɪ'saɪfər] vb déchiffrer ▷ *I can't decipher his handwriting.* Je ne déchiffre pas son écriture.

decision [dɪ'sɪʒən] n décision f; **to make a decision** prendre une décision

decisive [dɪ'saɪsɪv] adj (person) décidé

deck [dɛk] n ❶ (on house) terrasse f ❷ (of ship) pont; **on deck** sur le pont ❸ (of cards) jeu m (pl jeux)

declare [dɪ'klɛər] vb déclarer

decorate ['dɛkəreɪt] vb ❶ décorer ▷ *I decorated the cake with chocolate sprinkles.* J'ai

décoré le gâteau avec du chocolat granulé. ❷ (paint) peindre ❸ (wallpaper) tapisser

decrease [di'kriːs] n diminution f ▷ *a decrease in the number of unemployed people* une diminution du nombre de chômeurs
▶ vb diminuer

decriminalize [diː'krɪmɪnəlaɪz] vb décriminaliser

dedicated ['dɛdɪkeɪtɪd] adj dévoué ▷ *a very dedicated teacher* un professeur très dévoué; **dedicated to** (1) consacré à ▷ *a museum dedicated to First Nations history* un musée consacré à l'histoire des autochtones (2) dédicacé à ▷ *The book is dedicated "to Emma, with love from Mike".* Le livre est dédicacé « à Emma, avec tout mon amour, Mike ».

dedication [dɛdɪ'keɪʃən] n ❶ (commitment) dévouement m ❷ (in book, on radio) dédicace f

deduct [dɪ'dʌkt] vb déduire

deep [diːp] adj ❶ (water, hole, cut) profond ▷ *Is it deep?* Est-ce que c'est profond?; **How deep is the lake?** Quelle est la profondeur du lac?; **a hole 4 metres deep** un trou de quatre mètres de profondeur ❷ (snow) épais (f épaisse) ▷ *The snow was really deep.* Il y avait une épaisse couche de neige.; **He's got a deep voice.** Il a la voix grave.; **to take a deep breath** respirer à fond

deeply ['diːplɪ] adv profondément

deer [dɪər] n chevreuil m

defeat [dɪ'fiːt] n défaite f
▶ vb battre

defect [dɪ'fɛkt] n défaut m

defence [dɪ'fɛns] n défense f

defend [dɪ'fɛnd] vb défendre

define [dɪ'faɪn] vb définir

definite ['dɛfɪnɪt] adj ❶ précis ▷ *I don't have any definite plans.* Je n'ai pas de projets précis. ❷ net (f nette) ▷ *It's a definite improvement.* Cela constitue une nette amélioration. ❸ sûr ▷ *Perhaps we'll go to the Northwest Territories, but it's not definite.* Nous irons peut-être aux Territoires du Nord-Ouest, mais ce n'est pas sûr.; **She was definite about it.** Elle a été catégorique.

definitely ['dɛfɪnɪtlɪ] adv vraiment ▷ *He's definitely the best player.* C'est vraiment lui le meilleur joueur.; **"She's the best player."** — **"Definitely!"** « C'est la meilleure joueuse. » — « Certainement! »; **I definitely think they'll come.** Je suis sûr qu'ils vont venir.

definition [dɛfɪ'nɪʃən] n définition f

degree [dɪ'griː] n ❶ degré m ▷ *a temperature of 30 degrees* une température de trente degrés ❷ baccalauréat m ▷ *a degree in music* un baccalauréat en musique

dehydrated [diːhaɪ'dreɪtɪd] adj déshydraté

delay [dɪ'leɪ] vb ❶ retarder ▷ *We decided to delay our departure.* Nous avons décidé de retarder notre départ. ❷ tarder ▷ *Don't delay!* Ne tarde pas!; **to be delayed** être retardé ▷ *Our flight was delayed.* Notre vol a été retardé.
▶ n retard m ▷ *There will be delays on most flights.* Il y aura des retards sur la plupart des vols.

delete [dɪ'liːt] vb ❶ (on computer, tape) effacer ❷ (cross out) rayer

deli ['delɪ] n charcuterie f
deliberate [dɪ'lɪbərɪt] adj délibéré
deliberately [dɪ'lɪbərɪtlɪ] adv exprès ▷ She did it deliberately. Elle l'a fait exprès.
delicate ['delɪkɪt] adj délicat
delicious [dɪ'lɪʃəs] adj délicieux (f délicieuse)
delight [dɪ'laɪt] n: **to her delight** à sa plus grande joie
delighted [dɪ'laɪtɪd] adj ravi ▷ He'll be delighted to see you. Il sera ravi de vous voir.
delightful [dɪ'laɪtful] adj (meal, evening) délicieux (f délicieuse)
deliver [dɪ'lɪvəʳ] vb ❶ livrer ▷ I deliver newspapers. Je livre les journaux. ❷ (mail) distribuer
delivery [dɪ'lɪvərɪ] n livraison f
demand [dɪ'mɑ:nd] vb exiger
  ▷ n (for product) demande f
demanding [dɪ'mɑ:ndɪŋ] adj exigeant ▷ She's a very demanding teacher. C'est une professeure très exigeante.; **it's a very demanding job.** C'est un travail très astreignant.
demo ['deməu] n ❶ (product) modèle de démonstration m ❷ (software) version démo f ❸ (recording) CD de démonstration m
democracy [dɪ'mɒkrəsɪ] n démocratie f
democratic [deməˈkrætɪk] adj démocratique
demolish [dɪ'mɒlɪʃ] vb démolir
demonstrate ['demənstreɪt] vb ❶ (show) faire une démonstration de ▷ She demonstrated the technique. Elle a fait une démonstration de la technique. ❷ (protest) manifester; **to demonstrate against something** manifester contre quelque chose
demonstration [demən'streɪʃən] n ❶ (of method, technique) démonstration f ❷ (protest) manifestation f
demonstrator ['demənstreɪtəʳ] n (protester) manifestant m, manifestante f
denim ['denɪm] n (fabric) denim m ▷ a denim jacket une veste en denim
dense [dens] adj ❶ (crowd, fog) dense ❷ (smoke) épais (f épaisse)
dent [dent] n bosse f
  ▷ vb cabosser
dental ['dentl] adj dentaire; **dental floss** le fil dentaire
dentist ['dentɪst] n dentiste ▷ He is a dentist. Il est dentiste.
deny [dɪ'naɪ] vb nier ▷ She denied everything. Elle a tout nié.
deodorant [di:'əudərənt] n déodorant m
depart [dɪ'pɑ:t] vb partir
department [dɪ'pɑ:tmənt] n département m ▷ the English department le département d'anglais ▷ the shoe department le département des chaussures
department store n grand magasin m
departure [dɪ'pɑ:tʃəʳ] n départ m
departure lounge n salle d'embarquement f
depend [dɪ'pend] vb: **to depend on** dépendre de ▷ The price depends on the quality. Le prix dépend de la qualité.; **depending on the weather** selon le temps; **It depends.** Ça dépend.
deport [dɪ'pɔ:t] vb expulser

deposit [dɪ'pɒzɪt] n ❶ (bank) dépôt m ▷ a deposit of 30 dollars un dépôt de trente dollars ❷ (when renting something) caution f ▷ You get the deposit back when you return the bike. On vous remboursera la caution quand vous ramènerez le vélo.; **to put down a deposit** (as prepayment) verser un acompte ❸ (on bottle) consigne f
  ▷ vb déposer ▷ I deposited 100 dollars into my account. J'ai déposé cent dollars dans mon compte.
depressed [dɪ'prest] adj déprimé ▷ I'm feeling depressed. Je suis déprimé.
depressing [dɪ'presɪŋ] adj déprimant
depth [depθ] n profondeur f
descend [dɪ'send] vb descendre
describe [dɪs'kraɪb] vb décrire
description [dɪs'krɪpʃən] n description f
desert [dɪ'zə:t] n désert m
desert island n île f déserte
deserve [dɪ'zə:v] vb mériter
design [dɪ'zaɪn] n ❶ conception f ▷ It's a completely new design. C'est une conception entièrement nouvelle. ❷ motif m ▷ a geometric design un motif géométrique; **fashion design** le stylisme
  ▷ vb (clothes, furniture) dessiner; **designed for young people** conçu pour les jeunes
designer [dɪ'zaɪnəʳ] n (of clothes) styliste; **designer clothes** les vêtements griffés
desire [dɪ'zaɪəʳ] n désir m
  ▷ vb désirer
desk [desk] n ❶ (in office) bureau m (pl bureaux) ❷ (for student) pupitre m ❸ (in hotel) réception f ❹ (at airport) comptoir m
desktop ['desktɒp] n (on computer) bureau m ▷ Save the file to the desktop. Enregistre le fichier sur le bureau.
despair [dɪs'peəʳ] n désespoir m; **I was in despair.** J'étais désespéré.
desperate ['despərɪt] adj désespéré ▷ a desperate situation une situation désespérée; **to get desperate** désespérer ▷ I was getting desperate. Je commençais à désespérer.
desperately ['despərɪtlɪ] adv ❶ terriblement ▷ We're desperately worried. Nous sommes terriblement inquiets. ❷ désespérément ▷ He was desperately trying to persuade her. Il essayait désespérément de la persuader.
despise [dɪs'paɪz] vb mépriser
despite [dɪs'paɪt] prep malgré
dessert [dɪ'zə:t] n dessert m ▷ for dessert comme dessert
destination [destɪ'neɪʃən] n destination f
destitute ['destɪtju:t] adj dépourvu ▷ a destitute family une famille dépourvue
destroy [dɪs'trɔɪ] vb détruire
destruction [dɪs'trʌkʃən] n destruction f
detail ['di:teɪl] n détail m ▷ in detail en détail
detailed ['di:teɪld] adj détaillé
detective [dɪ'tektɪv] n enquêteur m, enquêteuse f; **a private detective** un détective privé; **a detective story** un roman policier
detention [dɪ'tenʃən] n: **to get a detention** être en retenue
detergent [dɪ'tə:dʒənt] n détergent m

deteriorate [dɪˈtɪərɪəreɪt] vb se détériorer
determined [dɪˈtɜːmɪnd] adj déterminé;
to be determined to do something être
déterminé à faire quelque chose ▷ *She's
determined to succeed.* Elle est déterminée à
réussir.
detour [ˈdiːtuəʳ] n détour m
devastated [ˈdɛvəsteɪtɪd] adj anéanti ▷ *I was
devastated.* J'étais anéanti.
devastating [ˈdɛvəsteɪtɪŋ] adj ❶ (upsetting)
accablant ❷ (flood, storm) dévastateur (f
dévastatrice)
develop [dɪˈvɛləp] vb ❶ développer ▷ *to get
a film developed* faire développer un film ❷ se
développer ▷ *Girls develop faster than boys.*
Les filles se développent plus vite que les
garçons.; **to develop into** se transformer en
▷ *The argument developed into a fight.* La dispute
s'est transformée en bagarre.; **a developing
country** un pays en voie de développement
development [dɪˈvɛləpmənt] n
développement m ▷ *the latest developments* les
derniers développements
device [dɪˈvaɪs] n appareil m
devil [ˈdɛvl] n diable m; **Poor devil!** Pauvre
diable!
devise [dɪˈvaɪz] vb concevoir ▷ *We devised a
plan.* Nous avons conçu un plan.
devoted [dɪˈvəʊtɪd] adj dévoué ▷ *He's
completely devoted to her.* Il lui est très dévoué.
diabetes [daɪəˈbiːtiːz] n diabète m
diabetic [daɪəˈbɛtɪk] n diabétique ▷ *I'm a
diabetic.* Je suis diabétique.
diagonal [daɪˈægənl] adj diagonal (mpl
diagonaux)
diagram [ˈdaɪəgræm] n diagramme m
dial [ˈdaɪəl] vb (number) composer
dialogue [ˈdaɪəlɒg] n dialogue m
dial tone n tonalité f
diamond [ˈdaɪəmənd] n diamant m ▷ *a
diamond ring* une bague en diamant;
diamonds (cards) le carreau m
diaper [ˈdaɪəpəʳ] n couche f
diarrhea [daɪəˈrɪə] n diarrhée f
diary [ˈdaɪərɪ] n journal m (pl journaux) ▷ *I keep
a diary.* Je tiens un journal.
dice [daɪs] npl dés
dictation [dɪkˈteɪʃən] n dictée f
dictator [dɪkˈteɪtəʳ] n dictateur m, dictatrice f
dictionary [ˈdɪkʃənrɪ] n dictionnaire m
did [dɪd] vb see **do**
die [daɪ] vb mourir ▷ *He died last year.* Il est
mort l'année dernière.; **to be dying to do
something** mourir d'envie de faire quelque
chose ▷ *I'm dying to see you.* Je meurs d'envie
de te voir.
diesel [ˈdiːzl] n ❶ (fuel) carburant diesel ▷ *30
litres of diesel* trente litres de carburant diesel
❷ (car) voiture diesel f ▷ *Our car is a diesel.* Nous
avons une voiture diesel.
diet [ˈdaɪət] n ❶ alimentation f ▷ *a healthy diet*
une alimentation saine ❷ (weight loss) régime
m ▷ *I'm on a diet.* Je suis au régime.
▶ vb faire un régime ▷ *I've been dieting for two
months.* Je fais un régime depuis deux mois.
dietitian [daɪəˈtɪʃn] n diététiste ▷ *He's a*

dietitian. Il est diététiste.
difference [ˈdɪfrəns] n différence f ▷ *There's
not much difference in age between us.* Il n'y a pas
une grande différence d'âge entre nous.; **It
makes no difference.** Ça revient au même.
different [ˈdɪfrənt] adj différent ▷ *We are
very different.* Nous sommes très différents.
▷ *Victoria is different from Vancouver.* Victoria est
différent de Vancouver.
difficult [ˈdɪfɪkəlt] adj difficile ▷ *It's difficult to
choose.* C'est difficile de choisir.
difficulty [ˈdɪfɪkəltɪ] n difficulté f ▷ *without
difficulty* sans difficulté; **to have difficulty
doing something** avoir du mal à faire quelque
chose
dig [dɪg] vb ❶ (hole) creuser ❷ (garden) bêcher;
to dig something up déterrer quelque chose
digestion [dɪˈdʒɛstʃən] n digestion f
digital [ˈdɪdʒɪtl] adj numérique ▷ *a digital
camera* un appareil photo numérique ▷ *a digital
recording* un enregistrement audionumérique;
a digital watch une montre à affichage
numérique
dim [dɪm] adj (light) faible
dime [daɪm] n pièce de dix cents f; **They're a
dime a dozen.** Il y en a à la pelle.
dimension [daɪˈmɛnʃən] n dimension f
diminish [dɪˈmɪnɪʃ] vb diminuer
diner [ˈdaɪnəʳ] n petit restaurant m
dinghy [ˈdɪŋɪ] n: **a rubber dinghy** un canot
pneumatique
dining room [ˈdaɪnɪŋ-] n salle à manger f
dinner [ˈdɪnəʳ] n ❶ (at midday) dîner m
❷ (evening) souper m
dinnertime [ˈdɪnətaɪm] n ❶ (midday) heure
f du dîner ❷ (midday) heure f du déjeuner
❸ (evening) heure f du souper ❹ (evening)
heure f du dîner
dinosaur [ˈdaɪnəsɔːʳ] n dinosaure m
dip [dɪp] n (decrease) baisse f ▷ *a dip in prices* une
baisse de prix; **to go for a dip** aller se baigner
▶ vb tremper ▷ *She dipped a cookie into her coffee.*
Elle a trempé un biscuit dans son café.
diploma [dɪˈpləʊmə] n diplôme m ▷ *a
high school diploma* un diplôme en études
secondaires
diplomat [ˈdɪpləmæt] n diplomate m
diplomatic [dɪpləˈmætɪk] adj diplomatique
direct [daɪˈrɛkt] adj, adv direct ▷ *the most direct
route* le chemin le plus direct ▷ *You can fly direct
from Hamilton to Ottawa.* Il y a un vol direct de
Hamilton à Ottawa.
▶ vb ❶ (film, program) réaliser ❷ (play, show)
mettre en scène
direction [dɪˈrɛkʃən] n direction f ▷ *We're
going in the wrong direction.* Nous allons dans
la mauvaise direction.; **to ask somebody for
directions** demander son chemin à quelqu'un
directly [dɪˈrɛktlɪ] adv directement; **directly
across from** juste en face de; **to be directly
related** avoir un rapport direct
director [dɪˈrɛktəʳ] n ❶ (of company) directeur
m, directrice f ❷ (of play) metteur en scène m
(pl metteurs en scène), metteuse en scène f (pl
metteuses en scène) ❸ (of film, programme)
réalisateur m, réalisatrice f

directory [dɪˈrɛktərɪ] n ❶ (*phone book*) annuaire m ❷ (*computing*) répertoire m

dirt [dɜ:t] n saleté f

dirt bike n moto tout-terrain f (pl les motos tout-terrains)

dirty [ˈdɜ:tɪ] adj sale; **to get dirty** se salir; **to get something dirty** salir quelque chose

disabled [dɪsˈeɪbld] adj handicapé

disadvantage [dɪsədˈvɑ:ntɪdʒ] n désavantage m

disagree [dɪsəˈgri:] vb: **We always disagree.** Nous ne sommes jamais d'accord.; **I disagree!** Je ne suis pas d'accord!; **He disagrees with me.** Il n'est pas d'accord avec moi.

disagreement [dɪsəˈgri:mənt] n désaccord m

disappear [dɪsəˈpɪəʳ] vb disparaître

disappearance [dɪsəˈpɪərəns] n disparition f

disappointed [dɪsəˈpɔɪntɪd] adj déçu

disappointing [dɪsəˈpɔɪntɪŋ] adj décevant

disappointment [dɪsəˈpɔɪntmənt] n déception f

disaster [dɪˈzɑ:stəʳ] n désastre m

disastrous [dɪˈzɑ:strəs] adj désastreux (f désastreuse)

disc [dɪsk] n disque m

discipline [ˈdɪsɪplɪn] n discipline f

disc jockey [-dʒɒkɪ] n disc-jockey m

disconnect [dɪskəˈnɛkt] vb ❶ (*unplug*) débrancher ❷ (*log off*) se déconnecter ❸ (*telephone, water supply*) couper

discount [ˈdɪskaʊnt] n réduction f ▷ *a discount for students* une réduction pour les étudiants

discourage [dɪsˈkʌrɪdʒ] vb décourager; **to get discouraged** se décourager ▷ *Don't get discouraged!* Ne te décourage pas!

discover [dɪsˈkʌvəʳ] vb découvrir

discrimination [dɪskrɪmɪˈneɪʃən] n discrimination f ▷ *racial discrimination* la discrimination raciale

discuss [dɪˈskʌs] vb ❶ discuter ▷ *This trip has been discussed at length with my parents.* Ce voyage a été longuement discuté avec mes parents. ❷ discuter de ▷ *We discussed the problem of pollution.* Nous avons discuté du problème de la pollution. ▷ *We discussed it.* Nous en avons discuté.

discussion [dɪˈskʌʃən] n discussion f

disease [dɪˈzi:z] n maladie f

disgraceful [dɪsˈgreɪsfʊl] adj scandaleux (f scandaleuse)

disguise [dɪsˈgaɪz] vb déguiser ▷ *He was disguised as a policeman.* Il était déguisé en policier.

disgusted [dɪsˈgʌstɪd] adj dégoûté ▷ *I was absolutely disgusted.* J'étais complètement dégoûté.

disgusting [dɪsˈgʌstɪŋ] adj ❶ (*food, smell*) dégoûtant ▷ *It looks disgusting.* Ça a l'air dégoûtant. ❷ (*disgraceful*) honteux ▷ *That's disgusting!* C'est honteux!

dish [dɪʃ] n plat m ▷ *a china dish* un plat en porcelaine ▷ *a vegetarian dish* un plat végétarien; **to do the dishes** faire la vaisselle ▷ *She never does the dishes.* Elle ne fait jamais la vaisselle.

dishcloth [ˈdɪʃklɒθ] n lavette f

dish detergent n savon à vaisselle m

dishonest [dɪsˈɒnɪst] adj malhonnête

dishtowel [ˈdɪʃtaʊəl] n linge à vaisselle m

dishwasher [ˈdɪʃwɒʃəʳ] n lave-vaisselle m (pl lave-vaisselle)

disinfectant [dɪsɪnˈfɛktənt] n désinfectant m

disk [dɪsk] n disque m; **a floppy disk** une disquette; **the hard disk** le disque dur

diskette [dɪsˈkɛt] n disquette f

dislike [dɪsˈlaɪk] vb ne pas aimer ▷ *I really dislike cabbage.* Je n'aime vraiment pas le chou. ▶ n: **my likes and dislikes** ce que j'aime et ce que je n'aime pas

dismal [ˈdɪzml] adj lugubre

dismiss [dɪsˈmɪs] vb (*employee*) renvoyer

disobey [dɪsəˈbeɪ] vb désobéir ▷ *to disobey one's parents* désobéir à ses parents; **to disobey a rule** violer une règle

disorganized [dɪsˈɔ:gənaɪzd] adj désorganisé

disoriented [dɪsˈɔ:rɪəntɪd] adj dépaysé

display [dɪsˈpleɪ] n étalage m ▷ *There was a lovely display of fruit in the window.* Il y avait un superbe étalage de fruits en vitrine.; **to be on display** être exposé ▷ *Her best paintings were on display.* Ses meilleurs tableaux étaient exposés. ▶ vb ❶ montrer ▷ *She proudly displayed her medal.* Elle a montré sa médaille avec fierté. ❷ (*in store window*) exposer

disposable [dɪsˈpəʊzəbl] adj jetable

disqualify [dɪsˈkwɒlɪfaɪ] vb disqualifier; **to be disqualified** être disqualifié ▷ *He was disqualified.* Il a été disqualifié.

disrespectful [dɪsrɪˈspɛktfʊl] adj: ▷ **to be disrespectful towards someone** manquer de respect envers quelqu'un

disrupt [dɪsˈrʌpt] vb perturber ▷ *Protesters disrupted the meeting.* Des manifestants ont perturbé la réunion. ▷ *Bus service is being disrupted by the strike.* Les horaires d'autobus sont perturbés par la grève.

dissatisfied [dɪsˈsætɪsfaɪd] adj: **We were dissatisfied with the service.** Nous n'étions pas satisfaits du service.

dissolve [dɪˈzɒlv] vb dissoudre

distance [ˈdɪstns] n distance f ▷ *a distance of 40 kilometres* une distance de quarante kilomètres; **It's within walking distance.** On peut y aller à pied.; **in the distance** au loin

distant [ˈdɪstnt] adj lointain ▷ *in the distant future* dans un avenir lointain

distinction [dɪsˈtɪŋkʃən] n distinction f ▷ **to make a distinction between…** faire la distinction entre…

distinctive [dɪsˈtɪŋktɪv] adj distinctif (f distinctive)

distinct society [dɪsˈtɪŋkt-] n société distincte f ▷ *Quebec considers itself a distinct society within Canada.* Le Québec se considère comme une société distincte au sein du Canada.

distract [dɪsˈtrækt] vb distraire

distribute [dɪsˈtrɪbju:t] vb distribuer

district [ˈdɪstrɪkt] n ❶ (*of town*) quartier m ❷ (*of country*) région f

disturb [dɪsˈtɜ:b] vb déranger ▷ *I'm sorry to disturb you.* Je suis désolé de vous déranger.

ditch [dɪtʃ] n fossé m
  ▷ vb (informal) plaquer ▷ Let's ditch that idea. Laissons tomber cette idée.

dive [daɪv] n plongeon m
  ▷ vb plonger

diver ['daɪvər] n plongeur m, plongeuse f

divide [dɪ'vaɪd] vb ❶ diviser ▷ Divide the chocolate bar in half. Divisez la barre de chocolat en deux. ▷ 12 divided by 3 is 4. Douze divisé par trois égalent quatre. ❷ se diviser ▷ We divided into two groups. Nous nous sommes divisés en deux groupes.

diving ['daɪvɪŋ] n plongée f; **a diving board** un tremplin

division [dɪ'vɪʒən] n division f

divorce [dɪ'vɔ:s] n divorce m

divorced [dɪ'vɔ:st] adj divorcé ▷ My parents are divorced. Mes parents sont divorcés.

dizzy ['dɪzɪ] adj: **to feel dizzy** avoir la tête qui tourne ▷ I feel dizzy. J'ai la tête qui tourne.

DJ n disc-jockey m

do [du:] vb ❶ faire ▷ What are you doing this evening? Qu'est-ce que tu fais ce soir? ▷ I do a lot of biking. Je fais beaucoup de vélo. ▷ I haven't done my homework. Je n'ai pas fait mes devoirs. ▷ She did it by herself. Elle l'a fait toute seule. ▷ I'll do my best. Je ferai de mon mieux.; **to do well** (1) marcher bien ▷ The firm is doing well. L'entreprise marche bien. ▷ She's doing well at school. Ses études marchent bien. (2) être sur la bonne voie ▷ The patient is doing well. La malade est sur la bonne voie. ❷ (be enough) aller ▷ It's not very good, but it'll do. Ce n'est pas très bon, mais ça ira.; **That'll do, thanks.** Ça ira, merci. ▷ Do you like French food? Est-ce que vous aimez la cuisine française? ▷ Where does he live? Où est-ce qu'il habite? ▷ Do you speak English? Parlez-vous anglais? ▷ I don't understand. Je ne comprends pas. ▷ Why didn't you come? Pourquoi n'êtes-vous pas venus? ▷ "I hate math." — "So do I." « Je déteste les maths. » — « Moi aussi. » ▷ "I didn't like the film." — "Neither did I." « Je n'ai pas aimé le film. » — « Moi non plus. » ▷ "Do you like horses?" — "No I don't." « Est-ce que tu aimes les chevaux? » — « Non. » ▷ You go swimming on Fridays, don't you? Tu fais de la natation le vendredi, n'est-ce pas?; **to do away with** (1) (law, practice) abolir (2) (kill) tuer; **to do up** (1) (shoes) lacer ▷ Do up your shoes! Lace tes chaussures! (2) (shirt, cardigan) boutonner; **to do up one's fly** fermer sa braguette; **to do without** se passer de ▷ I couldn't do without my computer. Je ne pourrais pas me passer de mon ordinateur.; **That has nothing to do with it.** Cela n'a rien à voir.

dock [dɔk] n (for ships) dock m

doctor ['dɔktər] n médecin ▷ She's a doctor. Elle est médecin.

document ['dɔkjumənt] n document m

documentary [dɔkju'mɛntərɪ] n documentaire m

dodge [dɔdʒ] vb (attacker) échapper à

dodgeball ['dɔdʒbɔ:l] n ballon chasseur m

does [dʌz] vb see do

doesn't ['dʌznt] = does not

dog [dɔg] n ❶ chien m ❷ (female) chienne f

dogsled ['dɔgslɛd] n traîneau à chiens m ▷ by dogsled en traîneau à chiens.

dole out [dəul-] vb distribuer

doll [dɔl] n poupée f

dollar ['dɔlər] n dollar m

dolphin ['dɔlfɪn] n dauphin m

domestic [də'mɛstɪk] adj: **a domestic flight** un vol intérieur; **domestic violence** la violence familiale

dominoes ['dɔmɪnəuz] npl: **to have a game of dominoes** jouer une partie de dominos

donate [də'neɪt] vb donner

done [dʌn] vb see do

donkey ['dɔŋkɪ] n âne m

donor ['dəunər] n ❶ (to charity) donateur m, donatrice f ❷ (of blood, organ for transplant) donneur m, donneuse f

don't [dəunt]; = do not

door [dɔ:r] n ❶ porte f ▷ the first door on the right la première porte à droite ❷ (of car, bus) portière f

doorbell ['dɔ:bɛl] n sonnette f; **to ring the doorbell** sonner; **Suddenly the doorbell rang.** Soudain, on a sonné.

doorman ['dɔ:mən] n portier m

doorstep ['dɔ:stɛp] n pas de la porte m

dormitory ['dɔ:mɪtrɪ] n dortoir m

dose [dəus] n dose f

dot [dɔt] n (on letter "i", in e-mail address) point m; **on the dot** à l'heure pile ▷ He arrived at 9 o'clock on the dot. Il est arrivé à neuf heures pile.

double ['dʌbl] vb doubler ▷ The number of overweight children has doubled. Le nombre d'enfants obèses a doublé.
  ▷ adj, adv double m ▷ a double helping une double portion; **to cost double** coûter le double ▷ First-class tickets cost double. Les billets de première classe coûtent le double.; **a double bed** un grand lit; **a double room** une chambre pour deux personnes

double bass n contrebasse f ▷ I play the double bass. Je joue de la contrebasse.

double-click ['dʌbl'klɪk] vb double-cliquer ▷ to double-click on an icon double-cliquer sur une icône

doubles ['dʌblz] npl (in tennis) double m ▷ to play mixed doubles jouer en double mixte

double-spaced [dʌbl'speɪst] adj à double interligne

doubt [daut] n doute m ▷ I have my doubts. J'ai des doutes.
  ▷ vb douter de; **I doubt it.** J'en doute.; **to doubt that** douter que ▷ I doubt he'll agree. Je doute qu'il soit d'accord.

doubtful ['dautful] adj: **to be doubtful about doing something** hésiter à faire quelque chose ▷ I'm doubtful about going by myself. J'hésite à y aller tout seul.; **It's doubtful.** Ce n'est pas sûr.; **You sound doubtful.** Tu n'as pas l'air sûr.

dough [dəu] n pâte f

doughnut ['dəunʌt] n beigne m ▷ a jam doughnut un beigne à la confiture

down [daun] adv, adj, prep ❶ (below) en bas ▷ Her office is down on the first floor. Son bureau est en bas, au premier étage. ▷ It's down there. C'est là-bas. ❷ (to the ground) à terre ▷ *He threw down his racquet.* Il a jeté sa raquette à terre.; **They live just down the road.** Ils habitent tout à côté.; **to come down** descendre ▷ *Come down here.* Descends.; **to go down** descendre ▷ *The rabbit went down the hole.* Le lapin est descendu dans le terrier.; **to sit down** s'asseoir ▷ *Please sit down.* Asseyez-vous, s'il vous plaît.; **to feel down** se sentir déprimé ▷ *I'm feeling a bit down.* Je me sens un peu déprimée.; **The computer's down.** L'ordinateur est en panne.

ownhill skiing ['daʊnhɪl-] *n* ski alpin *m*
ownload ['daʊnləʊd] *vb* télécharger ▷ *to download a file* télécharger un fichier
ownpour ['daʊnpɔː] *n* pluie torrentielle *f* ▷ *a sudden downpour* une pluie soudaine et torrentielle
ownstairs ['daʊn'stɛəz] *adv, adj* ❶ au rez-de-chaussée ▷ *The bathroom's downstairs.* La salle de bain est au rez-de-chaussée. ❷ du rez-de-chaussée ▷ *the downstairs bathroom* la salle de bain du rez-de-chaussée; **the people downstairs** les voisins du dessous
owntown ['daʊn'taʊn] *adv* dans le centre-ville
oze [dəʊz] *vb* sommeiller; **to doze off** s'assoupir
ozen ['dʌzn] *n* douzaine *f* ▷ *two dozen* deux douzaines ▷ *a dozen eggs* une douzaine d'œufs; **I've told you that dozens of times.** Je te l'ai dit ça des dizaines de fois.
rab [dræb] *adj* ❶ morne ❷ (*clothes*) terne
raft [drɑːft] *n* courant d'air *m*
rag [dræg] *vb* (*thing, person*) traîner ▷ *n*: **It's a real drag!** (*informal*) Quelle corvée!
ragon ['drægən] *n* dragon *m*
ragonfly ['drægənflaɪ] *n* libellule *f*
rain [dreɪn] *n* égout *m* ▷ *The drains are blocked.* Les égouts sont bouchés.
▷ *vb* (*vegetables, pasta*) égoutter
rainboard ['dreɪnbɔːd] *n* égouttoir *m*
rainpipe ['dreɪnpaɪp] *n* tuyau d'écoulement *m*
rama ['drɑːmə] *n* art *m* dramatique ▷ *Drama is my favourite subject.* L'art dramatique est ma matière préférée.; **drama school** l'école d'art dramatique ▷ *I'd like to go to drama school.* J'aimerais entrer dans une école d'art dramatique.; **Greek drama** le théâtre grec
ramatic [drə'mætɪk] *adj* ❶ spectaculaire ▷ *It was really dramatic!* C'était vraiment spectaculaire! ▷ *a dramatic improvement* une amélioration spectaculaire ❷ théâtral ▷ *a dramatic entrance* une entrée théâtrale
rank [dræŋk] *vb see* **drink**
rapes [dreɪps] *npl* rideaux *mpl*
rastic ['dræstɪk] *adj* (*change*) radical (*mpl* radicaux); **to take drastic action** prendre des mesures énergiques
raw [drɔː] *vb* dessiner ▷ *She's good at drawing.* Elle dessine bien.; **to draw a picture** faire un dessin; **to draw a picture of somebody** faire le portrait de quelqu'un; **to draw the curtains** tirer les rideaux; **to draw lots** tirer au sort
▷ *n* ❶ (*sport*) match nul *m* ▷ *The game ended*

in a draw. La partie s'est soldée par un match nul. ❷ (*in lottery*) tirage au sort ▷ *The draw takes place on Saturday.* Le tirage au sort a lieu samedi.
drawback ['drɔːbæk] *n* inconvénient *m*
drawer ['drɔːə] *n* tiroir *m*
drawing ['drɔːɪŋ] *n* dessin *m*
drawn [drɔːn] *vb see* **draw**
dreadful ['drɛdfʊl] *adj* ❶ terrible ▷ *a dreadful mistake* une terrible erreur ❷ affreux (*f* affreuse) ▷ *The weather was dreadful.* Il a fait un temps affreux.
dreadlocks ['drɛdlɒks] *npl* tresses *fpl* rasta
dream [driːm] *vb* rêver ▷ *I dreamed I was in Nunavut.* J'ai rêvé que j'étais au Nunavut.
▷ *n* rêve *m* ▷ *It was just a dream.* Ce n'était qu'un rêve.; **a bad dream** un cauchemar
drench [drɛntʃ] *vb*: **to get drenched** se faire tremper ▷ *We got drenched.* Nous nous sommes fait tremper.
dress [drɛs] *n* ❶ robe *f* ❷ tenue *f* ▷ *in traditional dress* en tenue traditionnelle; **a dress rehearsal** une répétition générale
▷ *vb* s'habiller ▷ *I got up, dressed, and went downstairs.* Je me suis levé, je me suis habillé et je suis descendu.; **to dress somebody** habiller quelqu'un ▷ *She dressed the children.* Elle a habillé les enfants.; **to get dressed** s'habiller ▷ *I got dressed quickly.* Je me suis habillé rapidement.; **to dress up** se déguiser ▷ *I dressed up as a ghost.* Je me suis déguisé en fantôme.
dressed [drɛst] *adj* habillé ▷ *I'm not dressed yet.* Je ne suis pas encore habillé.; **He was dressed in a green sweater and jeans.** Il portait un chandail vert et un jean.
dresser ['drɛsə] *n* (*furniture*) commode *f*
dressing gown ['drɛsɪŋgaʊn] *n* robe de chambre *f*
drew [druː] *vb see* **draw**
dried [draɪd] *vb see* **dry**
drift [drɪft] *n*: **a snow drift** une congère
▷ *vb* ❶ (*boat*) aller à la dérive ❷ (*snow*) s'amonceler
drill [drɪl] *n* perceuse *f*
▷ *vb* percer ▷ *to drill a hole* percer un trou
drink [drɪŋk] *n* boisson *f* ▷ *a cold drink* une boisson fraîche ▷ *a hot drink* une boisson chaude; **Would you like a drink?** Voulez-vous quelque chose à boire?
▷ *vb* boire ▷ *What would you like to drink?* Qu'est-ce que vous voulez boire? ▷ *She drank three cups of tea.* Elle a bu trois tasses de thé.; **Don't drink and drive.** Pas d'alcool au volant.; **I don't drink.** Je ne bois pas d'alcool.
drinking water ['drɪŋkɪŋ-] *n* eau *f* potable
drip [drɪp] *vb* (*tap*) goutter; **dripping wet** complètement trempé
drive [draɪv] *n* tour en voiture *m*; **to go for a drive** aller faire un tour en voiture ▷ *We went for a drive in the country.* Nous sommes allés faire un tour à la campagne.; **We've got a long drive tomorrow.** Nous avons une longue route à faire demain.
▷ *vb* ❶ (*a car*) conduire ▷ *He's learning to drive.* Il apprend à conduire. ▷ *Can you drive?* Tu sais

conduire? ❷ (*go by car*) aller en voiture ▷ *"Did you fly?" — "No, we drove."* « Vous êtes partis en avion? » — « Non, nous y sommes allés en voiture. » ❸ emmener en voiture ▷ *My mother drives me to school.* Ma mère m'emmène à l'école en voiture.; **to drive somebody home** raccompagner quelqu'un ▷ *He offered to drive me home.* Il m'a proposé de me raccompagner.; **to drive somebody crazy** rendre quelqu'un fou ▷ *He drives me crazy.* Il me rend folle.

driven ['drɪvn]; *see* **drive**

driver ['draɪvə'] *n* ❶ conducteur *m*, conductrice *f* ▷ *She's an excellent driver.* C'est une excellente conductrice. ❷ (*of taxi, bus*) chauffeur *m* ▷ *He's a bus driver.* Il est chauffeur d'autobus.

driver's licence ['draɪvəz-] *n* permis de conduire *m*

driveway ['draɪvweɪ] *n* entrée *f*

driving lesson ['draɪvɪŋ-] *n* leçon de conduite *f*

driving school *n* auto-école *f*

driving test *n*: **to take one's driving test** passer son examen de conduite automobile ▷ *He's taking his driving test tomorrow.* Il passe son examen de conduite demain.; **She's just passed her driving test.** Elle vient d'avoir son permis.

drizzle ['drɪzl] *vb* bruiner

drop [drɒp] *n* ❶ goutte *f* ▷ *a drop of water* une goutte d'eau ❷ (*decrease*) baisse *f* ▷ *a drop in temperature* une baisse de température
▶ *vb* ❶ laisser tomber ▷ *I dropped the glass and it broke.* J'ai laissé tomber le verre et il s'est cassé. ▷ *I'm going to drop chemistry.* Je vais laisser tomber la chimie.; **to drop out of school** décrocher ▷ *He dropped out before finishing Grade 12.* Il a décroché avant de terminer son secondaire cinq. ❷ déposer ▷ *Could you drop me at the station?* Pouvez-vous me déposer à la gare?

drop-in centre ['drɒpɪn-] *n* centre de jour *m*

dropout ['drɒpaʊt] *n* décrocheur *m*, décrocheuse *f*

drought [draʊt] *n* sécheresse *f*

drove [drəʊv] *vb see* **drive**

drown [draʊn] *vb* se noyer ▷ *A boy drowned here yesterday.* Un jeune garçon s'est noyé ici hier.

drug [drʌg] *n* ❶ (*medicine*) médicament *m* ▷ *They need food and drugs.* Ils ont besoin de nourriture et de médicaments. ❷ (*illegal*) drogue *f* ▷ *hard drugs* les drogues dures ▷ *soft drugs* les drogues douces; **to take drugs** se droguer; **a drug addict** un drogué ▷ *She's a drug addict.* C'est une droguée.

drugstore ['drʌgstɔːr'] *n* pharmacie *f*

drum [drʌm] *n* tambour *m* ▷ *an African drum* un tambour africain; **a set of drums** une batterie; **drums** la batterie *f* ▷ *I play drums.* Je joue de la batterie.

drummer ['drʌmə'] *n* (*in rock group*) batteur *m*, batteuse *f*

drunk [drʌŋk] *adj* ivre ▷ *He was drunk.* Il était ivre.; **drunk driving** la conduite en état d'ivresse

▶ *n* ivrogne *mf*

dry [draɪ] *adj* ❶ sec (*f* sèche) ▷ *The paint isn't dry yet.* La peinture n'est pas encore sèche. ❷ (*weather*) sans pluie ▷ *a long dry period* une longue période sans pluie
▶ *vb* ❶ sécher ▷ *The wash will dry quickly in the sun.* Le linge va sécher vite au soleil. ▷ *some dried flowers* des fleurs séchées; **to dry one's hair** se sécher les cheveux ▷ *I haven't dried my hair yet.* Je ne me suis pas encore séché les cheveux. ❷ (*clothes*) faire sécher ▷ *There's nowhere to dry clothes here.* Il n'y a pas d'endroit où faire sécher les vêtements ici.; **to dry the dishes** essuyer la vaisselle

dry cleaners *n* nettoyeur *m*

dryer ['draɪə'] *n* ❶ (*machine*) sécheuse *f* ❷ (*rack*) séchoir; **a hair dryer** un sèche-cheveux

dubbed [dʌbd] *adj* doublé ▷ *The film was dubbed into French.* Le film était doublé en français.

dubious ['djuːbɪəs] *adj* ❶ réticent ▷ *My parents were a bit dubious about it.* Mes parents étaient un peu réticents à ce sujet. ❷ douteux ▷ *a dubious reputation* une réputation douteuse

duck [dʌk] *n* canard *m*

duckling ['dʌklɪŋ] *n* caneton *m*

due [djuː] *adj, adv*: **The essay is due on Friday.** La rédaction doit être rendue vendredi.; **The plane's due in half an hour.** L'avion doit arriver dans une demi-heure.; **When's the baby due?** Le bébé est prévu pour quand?; **due to** (1) à cause de ▷ *The trip was cancelled due to bad weather.* Le voyage a été annulé à cause du mauvais temps. (2) ▷ *The fire was due to an electrical problem.* L'incendie est dû à un problème électrique.; **to be due to do something** devoir faire quelque chose ▷ *He's due to arrive tomorrow.* Il doit arriver demain.

dug [dʌg] *vb see* **dig**

dull [dʌl] *adj* ❶ ennuyeux (*f* ennuyeuse) ▷ *He's nice, but a bit dull.* Il est sympathique, mais un peu ennuyeux. ❷ (*weather, day*) maussade

dumb [dʌm] *adj* bête ▷ *That was a really dumb thing I did!* C'était vraiment bête de ma part!

dump [dʌmp] *n* dépotoir *m*; **It's a real dump!** C'est un endroit miteux!
▶ *vb* déposer ▷ *"no dumping"* « défense de déposer des ordures » ▷ *Just dump your things on the sofa.* Tu peux déposer tes affaires sur le sofa.

duplex ['djuːpleks] *n* duplex *m* (*pl* les duplex)

duration [djuə'reɪʃən] *n* durée *f*

during ['djuərɪŋ] *prep* pendant ▷ *during the day* pendant la journée

dusk [dʌsk] *n* crépuscule *m* ▷ *at dusk* au crépuscule

dust [dʌst] *n* poussière *f*
▶ *vb* épousseter ▷ *I dusted the shelves.* J'ai épousseté les étagères.

dusty ['dʌstɪ] *adj* poussiéreux (*f* poussiéreuse)

duty ['djuːtɪ] *n* devoir *m* ▷ *It was his duty to tell the police.* C'était son devoir de prévenir la police.; **to be on duty** (1) (*policeman*) être de service (2) (*doctor, nurse*) être de garde

duty-free ['djuːtɪ'friː] *adj* hors *f* + *pl* taxes; **the duty-free shop** la boutique hors taxes

duvet ['du:veɪ] n couette f
DVD n DVD m (pl DVD) ▷ I've got that movie on DVD. J'ai ce film en DVD.
DVD player n lecteur de DVD m
dwarf [dwɔ:f] n nain m, naine f
dye [daɪ] vb teindre ▷ to dye one's hair se teindre les cheveux ▷ I dyed my T-shirt green. J'ai teint mon T-shirt en vert.
dying ['daɪɪŋ] vb see **die**
dynamic [daɪ'næmɪk] adj dynamique
dyslexia [dɪs'lɛksɪə] n dyslexie f

e

each [i:tʃ] adj, pron ❶ chaque ▷ each day chaque jour ▷ Each house in our street has its own garden. Chaque maison dans notre rue a son propre jardin. ❷ chacun (f chacune) ▷ The girls each have their own bedroom. Les filles ont chacune leur chambre. ▷ They have 10 points each. Ils ont dix points chacun. ▷ The plates cost $5 each. Les assiettes coûtent cinq dollars chacune. ▷ He gave each of us $10. Il nous a donné dix dollars à chacun.; **They hate each other.** Ils se détestent.; **We wrote to each other.** Nous nous sommes écrit.; **They don't know each other.** Ils ne se connaissent pas.
eager ['i:gəʳ] adj: **to be eager to do something** être impatient de faire quelque chose
eagle ['i:gl] n aigle m
ear [ɪəʳ] n oreille f; **to perk up one's ears** dresser les oreilles
earache ['ɪəreɪk] n: **to have earache** avoir mal aux oreilles
earlier ['ɜ:lɪəʳ] adv ❶ tout à l'heure ▷ I saw him earlier. Je l'ai vu tout à l'heure. ❷ (in the day) plus tôt ▷ I ought to get up earlier. Je devrais me lever plus tôt.; **earlier than** avant
early ['ɜ:lɪ] adv, adj ❶ (early in the day) tôt ▷ I have to get up early. Je dois me lever tôt.; **to have an early night** se coucher tôt ❷ (ahead of time) d'avance ▷ I came early to get a good seat. Je suis venu d'avance pour avoir une bonne place.
earn [ɜ:n] vb gagner ▷ She earns $4 an hour for babysitting. Elle gagne quatre dollars de l'heure quand elle garde des enfants.
earnings ['ɜ:nɪŋz] npl salaire m
earring ['ɪərɪŋ] n boucle d'oreille f
earth [ɜ:θ] n terre f
earthquake ['ɜ:θkweɪk] n tremblement de terre m
easily ['i:zɪlɪ] adv facilement

east [i:st] adj, adv ❶ est (f+pl est) ▷ the east coast la côte est; **an east wind** un vent d'est; **east of** à l'est de ▷ It's east of Red Deer. C'est à l'est de Red Deer. ❷ vers l'est ▷ We were travelling east. Nous allions vers l'est.
▶ n est m ▷ in the east dans l'est
eastbound ['i:stbaund] adj: **The car was eastbound on the highway.** La voiture se trouvait sur l'autoroute en direction de l'est.; **Eastbound traffic is moving very slowly.** La circulation vers l'est avance très lentement.
Easter ['i:stəʳ] n Pâques f ▷ at Easter à Pâques ▷ We went to my grandparents' for Easter. Nous sommes allés chez mes grands-parents à Pâques.
eastern ['i:stən] adj: **the eastern part of the island** la partie est de l'île; **Eastern Europe** l'Europe de l'Est
easy ['i:zɪ] adj facile
easy chair n fauteuil m
easy-going ['i:zɪ'gəuɪŋ] adj facile à vivre (pl faciles à vivre) ▷ She's very easy-going. Elle est très facile à vivre.
eat [i:t] vb manger; **Would you like something to eat?** Est-ce que tu veux manger quelque chose?
eaten ['i:tn] vb see **eat**
eccentric [ɪk'sentrɪk] adj excentrique
echo ['ɛkəu] n écho m
▶ vb retentir ▷ Their shouts echoed across the lake. Leurs cris ont retenti jusqu'au bout du lac.
eclipse [ɪ'klɪps] n éclipse f ▷ a partial eclipse une éclipse partielle
eco-friendly [i:kəu'frɛndlɪ] adj respectueux de l'environnement (f respectueuse de l'environnement)
ecological [i:kə'lɒdʒɪkəl] adj écologique
ecology [ɪ'kɒlədʒɪ] n écologie f
e-commerce [i:kɒmɜ:s] n commerce électronique m
economic [i:kə'nɒmɪk] adj économique ▷ economic conditions les conditions économiques
economical [i:kə'nɒmɪkl] adj ❶ (person) économe ❷ (purchase, car) économique
economics [i:kə'nɒmɪks] n économie f ▷ He's studying economics. Il étudie les sciences économiques.
economize [ɪ'kɒnəmaɪz] vb faire des économies ▷ to economize on something faire des économies sur quelque chose
economy [ɪ'kɒnəmɪ] n économie f
ecosystem ['i:kəusɪstəm] n écosystème m
eczema ['ɛksɪmə] n eczéma m
edge [ɛdʒ] n ❶ bord m; **on edge** tendu ❷ (advantage) avantage m
edgy ['ɛdʒɪ] adj tendu
edible ['ɛdɪbl] adj comestible
edit ['ɛdɪt] vb (text) éditer ▷ I have to edit my web page. Je dois éditer ma page Web.
editor ['ɛdɪtəʳ] n (of newspaper) rédacteur en chef m, rédactrice en chef f
educated ['ɛdjukeɪtɪd] adj cultivé
education [ɛdju'keɪʃən] n ❶ éducation f ▷ There should be more investment in education. On devrait investir plus dans l'éducation.

❷ (teaching) enseignement m ▷ She works in education. Elle travaille dans l'enseignement.

educational [ɛdjuˈkeɪʃənl] adj (experience, toy) éducatif (f éducative) ▷ It was very educational. C'était très éducatif.

effect [ɪˈfɛkt] n effet m ▷ special effects les effets spéciaux

effective [ɪˈfɛktɪv] adj efficace

effectively [ɪˈfɛktɪvlɪ] adv efficacement

efficient [ɪˈfɪʃənt] adj efficace

effort [ˈɛfət] n effort m

e.g. abbr p. ex. (= par exemple)

egg [ɛg] n œuf m ▷ a hard-boiled egg un œuf dur ▷ a soft-boiled egg un œuf à la coque ▷ a fried egg un œuf sur le plat; **scrambled eggs** les œufs brouillés

eh [eɪ] interjection hein ▷ C'était tout un match, hein? That was quite a match, eh?

eight [eɪt] num huit ▷ She's eight. Elle a huit ans.

eighteen [eɪˈtiːn] num dix-huit ▷ He's eighteen. Il a dix-huit ans.

eighteenth [eɪˈtiːnθ] adj dix-huitième ▷ your eighteenth birthday ton dix-huitième anniversaire ▷ the eighteenth floor le dix-huitième étage; **the eighteenth of August** le dix-huit août

eighth [eɪtθ] adj huitième ▷ the eighth floor le huitième étage; **the eighth of August** le huit août

eighty [ˈeɪtɪ] num quatre-vingts

either [ˈaɪðər] adv, conj, pron non plus ▷ I don't like milk, and I don't like eggs either. Je n'aime pas le lait, et je n'aime pas les œufs non plus. ▷ "I've never been to Spain." – "I haven't either." « Je ne suis jamais allé en Espagne. » — « Moi non plus. »; **either...or** soit...soit ▷ You can have either ice cream or yogurt. Tu peux prendre soit une crème glacée soit un yogourt.; **either of them** l'un ou l'autre ▷ Take either of them. Prends l'un ou l'autre.; **I don't like either of them.** Je n'aime ni l'un ni l'autre.

elastic [ɪˈlæstɪk] n élastique m

elbow [ˈɛlbəʊ] n coude m

elder [ˈɛldər] adj aîné ▷ my elder sister ma sœur aînée

elderly [ˈɛldəlɪ] adj âgé; **the elderly** les personnes âgées

eldest [ˈɛldɪst] adj aîné ▷ my eldest sister ma sœur aînée ▷ He's the eldest. C'est l'aîné.

elect [ɪˈlɛkt] vb élire

election [ɪˈlɛkʃən] n élection f

electric [ɪˈlɛktrɪk] adj électrique ▷ an electric guitar une guitare électrique; **an electric blanket** une couverture chauffante

electrical [ɪˈlɛktrɪkl] adj électrique; **an electrical engineer** un ingénieur électricien

electrician [ɪlɛkˈtrɪʃən] n électricien m, électricienne f ▷ He's an electrician. Il est électricien.

electricity [ɪlɛkˈtrɪsɪtɪ] n électricité f

electronic [ɪlɛkˈtrɒnɪk] adj électronique

electronics [ɪlɛkˈtrɒnɪks] n électronique f ▷ My hobby is electronics. Ma passion, c'est l'électronique.

elegant [ˈɛlɪgənt] adj élégant

elementary school [ɛlɪˈmɛntərɪ-] n école f primaire

elephant [ˈɛlɪfənt] n éléphant m

elevator [ˈɛlɪveɪtər] n ascenseur m

eleven [ɪˈlɛvn] num onze ▷ She's eleven. Elle a onze ans.

eleventh [ɪˈlɛvnθ] adj onzième ▷ the eleventh floor le onzième étage ▷ the eleventh of August le onze août

else [ɛls] adv d'autre ▷ somebody else quelqu'un d'autre ▷ nobody else personne d'autre ▷ nothing else rien d'autre; **something else** autre chose; **anything else** autre chose ▷ Would you like anything else? Désirez-vous autre chose?; **I don't want anything else.** Je ne veux rien d'autre.; **somewhere else** ailleurs; **anywhere else** n'importe où ailleurs; **or else (1)** (otherwise) sinon ▷ Study well or else you'll fail. Étudie bien, sinon tu vas échouer. **(2)** (alternatively) ou bien ▷ You can call me, or else I can drop by your place after school. Tu peux me téléphoner, ou bien je peux passer chez toi après l'école.

e-mail [ˈiːmeɪl] n courriel m; **e-mail address** l'adresse f de courriel ▷ My e-mail address is... Mon adresse de courriel, c'est...
▶ vb: **to e-mail somebody** envoyer un courriel à quelqu'un

embarrassed [ɪmˈbærəst] adj gêné ▷ I was really embarrassed. J'étais vraiment gêné.

embarrassing [ɪmˈbærəsɪŋ] adj gênant ▷ It was so embarrassing. C'était tellement gênant.

emergency [ɪˈmɜːdʒənsɪ] n urgence f ▷ This is an emergency! C'est une urgence!; **an emergency exit** une sortie de secours; **an emergency landing** un atterrissage forcé; **the emergency services** les services d'urgence

emigrate [ˈɛmɪgreɪt] vb émigrer

emission control [ɪˈmɪʃn-] n lutte contre les émissions f

emotion [ɪˈməʊʃən] n émotion f

emotional [ɪˈməʊʃənl] adj ❶ (person) émotif (f émotive) ❷ plein d'émotion ▷ an emotional farewell un adieu plein d'émotion ❸ émotionnel ▷ an emotional shock un choc émotionnel; **an emotional issue** une question qui soulève les passions; **to be on an emotional roller coaster** être pris dans un tourbillon d'émotions; **to become emotional** être ému

emphasize [ˈɛmfəsaɪz] vb: **to emphasize something** insister sur quelque chose; **to emphasize that...** souligner que...

empire [ˈɛmpaɪər] n empire m

employ [ɪmˈplɔɪ] vb employer ▷ The factory employs 600 people. L'usine emploie six cents personnes.

employee [ɪmplɔɪˈiː] n employé m, employée f

employer [ɪmˈplɔɪər] n employeur m, employeuse f

employment [ɪmˈplɔɪmənt] n emploi m

empty [ˈɛmptɪ] adj vide
▶ vb vider; **to empty something out** vider quelque chose

encourage [ɪnˈkʌrɪdʒ] vb encourager; **to**

encourage somebody to do something encourager quelqu'un à faire quelque chose
encouragement [ɪnˈkʌrɪdʒmənt] n encouragement m
encouraging [ɪnˈsaɪkləˈpiːdiə] adj encourageant
encyclopedia [ɪnsaɪkləˈpiːdiə] n encyclopédie f
end [end] n ❶ fin f ▷ the end of the movie la fin du film ▷ the end of the holidays la fin des vacances; **in the end** en fin de compte ▷ In the end I decided to stay home. En fin de compte, j'ai décidé de rester à la maison.; **It turned out all right in the end.** Ça s'est bien terminé. ❷ bout m ▷ at the end of the street au bout de la rue ▷ at the other end of the table à l'autre bout de la table; **for hours on end** des heures entières ▶ vb finir ▷ What time does the movie end? À quelle heure est-ce que le film finit?; **to end up doing something** finir par faire quelque chose ▷ I ended up walking home. J'ai fini par rentrer chez moi à pied.
ending [ˈendɪŋ] n fin f ▷ It was an exciting movie, especially the ending. C'était un film passionnant, surtout la fin.
endless [ˈendlɪs] adj interminable ▷ The journey seemed endless. Le voyage a paru interminable.
enemy [ˈenəmɪ] n ennemi m, ennemie f
energetic [enəˈdʒetɪk] adj (person) énergique
energy [ˈenədʒɪ] n énergie f
energy-efficient [ˈenədʒɪˈfɪʃənt] adj éconergétique
enforce [ɪnˈfɔːs] vb faire respecter ▷ to enforce a rule faire respecter un règlement
engaged [ɪnˈɡeɪdʒd] adj fiancé ▷ She's engaged to my cousin. Elle est fiancée à mon cousin.; **to get engaged** se fiancer
engagement [ɪnˈɡeɪdʒmənt] n fiançailles fpl ▷ an engagement ring une bague de fiançailles ▷ to break off one's engagement rompre ses fiançailles
engine [ˈendʒɪn] n moteur m
engineer [endʒɪˈnɪə] n ingénieur m, ingénieure f ▷ She's an engineer. Elle est ingénieure.
engineering [endʒɪˈnɪərɪŋ] n ingénierie f
English [ˈɪŋɡlɪʃ] adj anglais ▷ English grammar la grammaire anglaise ▶ n anglais m ▷ Do you speak English? Est-ce que vous parlez anglais?
English-Canadian [ˈɪŋɡlɪʃkəˈneɪdiən] adj canadien-anglais (f canadienne-anglaise) ▷ an English-Canadian family une famille canadienne-anglaise ▶ n Canadien anglais m, Canadienne anglaise f ▷ She married an English-Canadian. Elle a épousé un Canadien anglais.
engrossed [ɪnˈɡrəʊst] adj absorbé ▷ She was so engrossed by her book that she didn't hear me. Elle était si absorbée par son livre qu'elle ne m'a pas entendu.
enjoy [ɪnˈdʒɔɪ] vb ❶ aimer ▷ Did you enjoy the film? Est-ce que vous avez aimé le film?; **to enjoy oneself** s'amuser ▷ I really enjoyed myself. Je me suis vraiment bien amusé. ▷ Did you enjoy yourselves at the party? Est-ce que vous

vous êtes bien amusés à la fête? ❷ (benefit from) jouir de ▷ My grandfather still enjoys good health. Mon grand-père jouit encore d'une bonne santé.
enjoyable [ɪnˈdʒɔɪəbl] adj agréable
enlarge [ɪnˈlɑːdʒ] vb agrandir ▷ to enlarge an image agrandir une image
enormous [ɪˈnɔːməs] adj énorme
enough [ɪˈnʌf] pron, adj assez de ▷ enough time assez de temps ▷ I didn't have enough money. Je n'avais pas assez d'argent. ▷ Do you have enough? Tu en as assez? ▷ I've had enough! J'en ai assez!; **big enough** suffisamment grand; **warm enough** suffisamment chaud; **That's enough.** Ça suffit.
enter [ˈentə] vb entrer ▷ She entered the room. Elle est entrée dans la salle. ▷ to enter text in a file entrer du texte dans un fichier; **to enter a competition** s'inscrire à une compétition; **the Enter key** la touche Entrée
entertain [entəˈteɪn] vb (guests) recevoir
entertainer [entəˈteɪnə] n artiste mf de variétés
entertaining [entəˈteɪnɪŋ] adj divertissant
entertainment [entəˈteɪnmənt] n divertissement m ▷ The resort offers outdoor sports, video nights, and other entertainment. Le centre de villégiature offre des sports de plein air, des soirées vidéo et d'autres divertissements.
enthusiasm [ɪnˈθuːzɪæzəm] n enthousiasme m
enthusiastic [ɪnθuːzɪˈæstɪk] adj enthousiaste
entire [ɪnˈtaɪə] adj entier (f entière) ▷ the entire world le monde entier
entirely [ɪnˈtaɪəlɪ] adv entièrement
entrance [ˈentrəns] n entrée f; **an entrance exam** un examen d'admission; **entrance fee** le prix d'entrée
entry [ˈentrɪ] n entrée f; **"no entry"** (1) (on door) « défense d'entrer » (2) (on road sign) « sens interdit »; **an entry form** une feuille d'inscription
envelope [ˈenvələʊp] n enveloppe f
envious [ˈenvɪəs] adj envieux (f envieuse)
environment [ɪnˈvaɪərnmənt] n environnement m
environmental [ɪnvaɪərnˈmentl] adj écologique
environmentalist [ɪnvaɪərnˈmentlɪst] n environnementaliste mf
environment-friendly [ɪnˈvaɪərənmənt-frendlɪ] adj écologique
envy [ˈenvɪ] n envie f ▶ vb envier ▷ I don't envy you! Je ne t'envie pas!
epidemic [epɪˈdemɪk] n épidémie f ▷ a flu epidemic une épidémie de grippe
epilepsy [ˈepɪlepsɪ] n épilepsie f
episode [ˈepɪsəʊd] n (of TV series, story) épisode m
equal [ˈiːkwl] adj égal (mpl égaux) ▶ vb égaler
equality [iːˈkwɒlɪtɪ] n égalité f
equator [ɪˈkweɪtə] n équateur m
equipment [ɪˈkwɪpmənt] n équipement

m ▷ *fishing equipment* l'équipement de pêche ▷ *skiing equipment* l'équipement de ski

equipped [ɪ'kwɪpt] *adj*: **equipped with** équipé de; **to be well equipped** être bien équipé

equivalent [ɪ'kwɪvələnt] *n* équivalent *m*; **equivalent to** équivalent à

erase [ɪ'reɪz] *vb* effacer

eraser [ɪ'reɪzə*ʳ*] *n* gomme *f*

errand ['ɛrnd] *n* course *f* ▷ *I have to run a few errands for my mother.* J'ai quelques courses à faire pour ma mère.

error ['ɛrə*ʳ*] *n* erreur *f*

escalator ['ɛskəleɪtə*ʳ*] *n* escalier *m* roulant

escape [ɪ'skeɪp] *n* (*from prison*) évasion *f* ▷ *vb* s'échapper ▷ *A lion has escaped.* Un lion s'est échappé.; **to escape from prison** s'évader de prison

escarpment [ɪs'kɑːpmənt] *n* escarpement *m* ▷ *The Niagara escarpment* l'escarpement de Niagara

especially [ɪ'spɛʃlɪ] *adv* surtout ▷ *It's very hot there, especially in the summer.* Il fait très chaud là-bas, surtout en été.

essay ['eseɪ] *n* dissertation *f* ▷ *a history essay* une dissertation d'histoire

essential [ɪ'sɛnʃl] *adj* essentiel (*f* essentielle) ▷ *It's essential to bring warm clothes.* Il est essentiel d'apporter des vêtements chauds.

estate [ɪ'steɪt] *n* propriété *f*

estimate ['estɪmeɪt] *vb* estimer ▷ *They estimated it would take three weeks.* Ils ont estimé que cela prendrait trois semaines.
▶ *n* estimation *f* ▷ *We asked for an estimate before getting the car repaired.* Nous avons demandé une estimation avant de faire réparer la voiture.

etc. *abbr* (= *et cetera*) etc.

ethnic ['ɛθnɪk] *adj* ethnique ▷ *an ethnic minority* une minorité ethnique

euro ['juərəʊ] *n* euro *m* ▷ *50 euros* 50 euros

evacuate [ɪ'vækjueɪt] *vb* évacuer

evaporate [ɪ'væpəreɪt] *vb* s'évaporer; **evaporated milk** le lait condensé

eve [iːv] *n*: **Christmas Eve** la veille de Noël; **New Year's Eve** la veille du Jour de l'An

even ['iːvn] *adv* même ▷ *I like all animals, even snakes.* J'aime tous les animaux, même les serpents.; **even if** même si ▷ *I'd never do that, even if you asked me to.* Je ne ferais jamais ça, même si tu me le demandais.; **not even** même pas ▷ *He never stops working, not even on the weekend.* Il n'arrête jamais de travailler, même pas la fin de semaine.; **even though** bien que ▷ *She never has any money, even though her parents are quite rich.* Elle n'a jamais d'argent, bien que ses parents soient assez riches.; **even more** encore plus ▷ *I liked the book even more than the movie.* J'ai encore plus aimé le livre que le film. ▶ *adj* régulier (*f* régulière) ▷ *an even layer of snow* une couche régulière de neige ❷ plat ▷ *an even surface* une surface plate; **an even number** un nombre pair; **to get even with somebody** prendre sa revanche sur quelqu'un ▷ *He wanted to get even with her.* Il voulait prendre sa revanche sur elle.; **The score is**

even. On est à égalité.

evening ['iːvnɪŋ] *n* soir *m* ▷ *in the evening* le soir ▷ *yesterday evening* hier soir ▷ *tomorrow evening* demain soir; **all evening** toute la soirée; **Good evening!** Bonsoir!

event [ɪ'vɛnt] *n* événement *m*; **a sporting event** une épreuve sportive

eventful [ɪ'vɛntful] *adj* mouvementé

eventually [ɪ'vɛntʃuəlɪ] *adv* finalement

ever ['ɛvə*ʳ*] *adv*: **Have you ever been to Prince Edward Island?** Est-ce que tu es déjà allé à l'Île-du-Prince-Édouard?; **more than ever** plus que jamais ▷ *happier than ever* plus heureux que jamais; **Have you ever seen her?** Vous l'avez déjà vue?; **I haven't ever done that.** Je ne l'ai jamais fait.; **the best I've ever seen** le meilleur que j'aie jamais vu; **for the first time ever** pour la première fois; **ever since** depuis que ▷ *ever since I met him* depuis que je l'ai rencontré; **ever since then** depuis ce moment-là

every ['ɛvrɪ] *adj* chaque ▷ *every student* chaque élève; **every time** chaque fois ▷ *Every time I see him he's depressed.* Chaque fois que je le vois, il est déprimé.; **every day** tous les jours; **every week** toutes les semaines; **every now and then** de temps en temps; **every other Friday** un vendredi sur deux; **every three days** tous les trois jours

everybody ['ɛvrɪbɒdɪ] *pron* tout le monde ▷ *Everybody had a good time.* Tout le monde s'est bien amusé. ▷ *Everybody makes mistakes.* Tout le monde peut se tromper.

everyday ['ɛvrɪdeɪ] *adj* ❶ (*ordinary*) de tous les jours ▷ *everyday clothes* les vêtements de tous les jours ❷ (*daily*) quotidien (*f* quotidienne) ▷ *everyday activities* les activités quotidiennes; **an everyday situation** une situation courante

everyone ['ɛvrɪwʌn] *pron* tout le monde ▷ *Everyone opened their presents.* Tout le monde a ouvert ses cadeaux. ▷ *Everyone should have a hobby.* Tout le monde devrait avoir un passe-temps.

everything ['ɛvrɪθɪŋ] *pron* tout ▷ *You've thought of everything!* Tu as pensé à tout!; **Have you remembered everything?** Est-ce que tu n'as rien oublié?; **Money isn't everything.** L'argent ne fait pas le bonheur.

everywhere ['ɛvrɪwɛə*ʳ*] *adv* partout ▷ *I looked everywhere, but I couldn't find it.* J'ai regardé partout, mais je n'ai pas pu le trouver. ▷ *There were policemen everywhere.* Il y avait des policiers partout.

evil ['iːvl] *adj* mauvais
▶ *n* mal *m* (*pl* les maux)

ex- [ɛks] *prefix* ex- ▷ *his ex-wife* son ex-femme

exact [ɪg'zækt] *adj* exact

exactly [ɪg'zæktlɪ] *adv* exactement ▷ *exactly the same* exactement le même ▷ *not exactly.* pas exactement.; **It's exactly 10 o'clock.** Il est dix heures précises.

exaggerate [ɪg'zædʒəreɪt] *vb* exagérer

exaggeration [ɪgzædʒə'reɪʃən] *n* exagération *f*

exam [ɪg'zæm] *n* examen *m* ▷ *a French exam* un examen de français ▷ *the exam results* les résultats des examens m

examination [ɪgˌzæmɪˈneɪʃən] n examen m

examine [ɪgˈzæmɪn] vb examiner ▷ He examined her passport. Il a examiné son passeport. ▷ The doctor examined him. Le docteur l'a examiné.

example [ɪgˈzɑːmpl] n exemple m; **for example** par exemple

excellent [ˈɛksələnt] adj excellent ▷ Her results were excellent. Elle a eu d'excellents résultats.; **You can come? Excellent!** Tu peux venir? C'est super!

except [ɪkˈsɛpt] prep sauf ▷ everyone except me tout le monde sauf moi; **except for** sauf; **except that** sauf que ▷ The weather was great, except that it was a bit cold. Il a fait un temps superbe, sauf qu'il a fait un peu froid.

exception [ɪkˈsɛpʃən] n exception f; **to make an exception** faire une exception

exceptional [ɪkˈsɛpʃənl] adj exceptionnel (f exceptionnelle)

exchange [ɪksˈtʃeɪndʒ] vb échanger ▷ I exchanged the book for a video. J'ai échangé le livre contre une vidéo.

exchange rate n taux de change m

excited [ɪkˈsaɪtəd] adj excité

exciting [ɪkˈsaɪtɪŋ] adj passionnant

exclamation mark [ɛkskləˈmeɪʃən-] n point d'exclamation m

excuse [n ɪksˈkjuːs, vb ɪkˈskjuːz] n excuse f
▶ vb ❶ excuser ▷ Your lateness is excused. Ton retard a été excusé. ▷ She excused him from class. Elle lui a permis de s'absenter de la classe. ❷ dispenser ▷ He was excused from writing the exam. On l'a dispensé de passer l'examen.; **Excuse me!** Pardon!; **to excuse oneself** s'excuser

execute [ˈɛksɪkjuːt] vb exécuter

execution [ɛksɪˈkjuːʃən] n exécution f

executive [ɪgˈzɛkjʊtɪv] n (in business) cadre m ▷ He's an executive. Il est cadre.

exercise [ˈɛksəsaɪz] n exercice m; **an exercise bike** un vélo d'appartement; **an exercise book** un cahier

exhausted [ɪgˈzɔːstɪd] adj épuisé

exhaust fumes [ɪgˈzɔːst-] npl gaz mpl d'échappement

exhaust pipe [ɪgˈzɔːst-] n tuyau d'échappement m

exhibition [ɛksɪˈbɪʃən] n exposition f

exist [ɪgˈzɪst] vb exister

exit [ˈɛksɪt] n sortie f
▶ vb ❶ sortir ▷ Exit via the rear door. Sortez par la porte arrière. ❷ (from vehicle) descendre

exotic [ɪgˈzɒtɪk] adj exotique

expand [ɪkˈspænd] vb ❶ (increase) élargir ▷ to expand one's knowledge élargir ses connaissances ❷ (develop) développer ▷ to expand an idea développer une idée

expect [ɪkˈspɛkt] vb ❶ attendre ▷ I'm expecting her for dinner. Je l'attends pour dîner. ▷ She's expecting a baby. Elle attend un enfant. ❷ s'attendre à ▷ I was expecting the worst. Je m'attendais au pire. ❸ supposer ▷ I expect it's a mistake. Je suppose qu'il s'agit d'une erreur.

expedition [ɛkspəˈdɪʃən] n expédition f

expel [ɪkˈspɛl] vb: **to get expelled** (from school) se faire renvoyer

expenses [ɪkˈspɛnsɪz] npl frais mpl

expensive [ɪkˈspɛnsɪv] adj ❶ cher (f chère) ❷ dispendieux (f dispendieuse)

experience [ɪkˈspɪərɪəns] n expérience f

experienced [ɪkˈspɪərɪənst] adj expérimenté

experiment [ɪkˈspɛrɪmənt] n expérience f

expert [ˈɛkspɜːt] n spécialiste f ▷ She's a computer expert. C'est une spécialiste en informatique.; **He's an expert cook.** Il cuisine très bien.

expire [ɪkˈspaɪəˀ] vb expirer

explain [ɪkˈspleɪn] vb expliquer

explanation [ɛkspləˈneɪʃən] n explication f

explode [ɪkˈspləʊd] vb exploser

exploit [ɪkˈsplɔɪt] vb exploiter

exploitation [ɛksplɔɪˈteɪʃən] n exploitation f

explore [ɪkˈsplɔːˀ] vb ❶ (place) explorer ❷ (issue, possibilities) étudier

explorer [ɪkˈsplɔːrəˀ] n explorateur m, exploratrice f

explosion [ɪkˈspləʊʒən] n explosion f

explosive [ɪkˈspləʊsɪv] adj explosif (f explosive)
▶ n explosif m

expose [ɪkˈspəʊz] vb ❶ découvrir ❷ (to sun, radiation) exposer

express [ɪkˈsprɛs] vb exprimer; **to express oneself** s'exprimer ▷ It's not easy to express oneself in a foreign language. Ce n'est pas facile de s'exprimer dans une langue étrangère.

expression [ɪkˈsprɛʃən] n expression f ▷ It's an English expression. C'est une expression anglaise.

expressway [ɪkˈsprɛsweɪ] n autoroute f urbaine

extension [ɪkˈstɛnʃən] n ❶ (of building) annexe f ❷ (telephone) poste m; **Extension 3137, please.** Poste trente et un trente-sept, s'il vous plaît.

extensive [ɪkˈstɛnsɪv] adj ❶ (knowledge, range) vaste ▷ an extensive property une vaste propriété ▷ extensive knowledge of Canadian history une vaste connaissance de l'histoire canadienne ❷ (damage, alterations) considérable ▷ The earthquake caused extensive damage. Le tremblement de terre a causé des dommages considérables. ❸ approfondi ▷ extensive research des recherches approfondies; **extensive surgery** plusieurs interventions chirurgicales

extensively [ɪkˈstɛnsɪvlɪ] adv: **He has travelled extensively in Europe.** Il a beaucoup voyagé en Europe.; **The building was extensively renovated last year.** Le bâtiment a été entièrement rénové l'année dernière.

extent [ɪkˈstɛnt] n: **to some extent** dans une certaine mesure; **to the extent that** au point que

exterior [ɛkˈstɪərɪəˀ] adj extérieur

extinct [ɪkˈstɪŋkt] adj: **to become extinct** disparaître; **to be extinct** avoir disparu ▷ The species is almost extinct. Cette espèce a presque disparu.

extinguisher [ɪkˈstɪŋgwɪʃəʳ] n (fire extinguisher) extincteur m

extra [ˈekstrə] adj, adv supplémentaire ▷ an extra blanket une couverture supplémentaire; **to pay extra** payer un supplément; **Breakfast is extra.** Il y a un supplément pour le petit déjeuner.; **Do you have an extra pen?** As-tu un stylo à me passer?; **It costs extra.** Il y a un supplément.

extracurricular [ˈekstrəkəˈrɪkjuləʳ] adj parascolaire

extraordinary [ɪkˈstrɔːdɪnrɪ] adj extraordinaire

extravagant [ɪkˈstrævəgənt] adj ❶ (person) dépensier (f dépensière) ❷ (gift, wedding) somptueux (f somptueuse)

extreme [ɪkˈstriːm] adj extrême

extremist [ɪkˈstriːmɪst] n extrémiste mf

eye [aɪ] n œil m (pl yeux) ▷ I have green eyes. J'ai les yeux verts.; **to keep an eye on something** surveiller quelque chose

eyebrow [ˈaɪbraʊ] n sourcil m

eyelash [ˈaɪlæʃ] n cil m

eyelid [ˈaɪlɪd] n paupière f

eyeliner [ˈaɪlaɪnəʳ] n ligneur m

eye shadow [ˈaɪʃædəʊ] n fard à paupières m

eyesight [ˈaɪsaɪt] n vue f ▷ poor eyesight une vue faible

f

fabric [ˈfæbrɪk] n tissu m

fabulous [ˈfæbjuləs] adj formidable ▷ The show was fabulous. Le spectacle était formidable.

face [feɪs] n ❶ (of person) visage m ❷ (of clock) cadran m ❸ (of cliff) paroi f; **on the face of it** à première vue; **in the face of these difficulties** face à ces difficultés; **face to face** face à face; **to someone's face** sans détour ▷ She said it right to my face. Elle m'a dit sans détour.
▶ vb (place, problem) faire face à; **to face up to something** faire face à quelque chose ▷ You must face up to your responsibilities. Vous devez faire face à vos responsabilités.

facecloth [ˈfeɪsklɒθ] n débarbouillette f

face-off [ˈfeɪsɒf] n mise au jeu f

facilities [fəˈsɪlɪtɪz] npl équipement m ▷ This school has excellent facilities. Cette école dispose d'excellents équipements.; **toilet facilities** les f toilettes

fact [fækt] n fait m; **in fact** en fait

factory [ˈfæktərɪ] n usine f

fad [fæd] n engouement m

fade [feɪd] vb ❶ (colour) passer ▷ The colour has faded in the sun. La couleur a passé au soleil.; **My jeans have faded.** Mon jean est délavé. ❷ baisser ▷ The light was fading fast. La lumière baissait rapidement. ❸ diminuer ▷ The noise gradually faded. Le bruit a diminué peu à peu.

fail [feɪl] vb ❶ rater ▷ I failed the history exam. J'ai raté l'examen d'histoire. ❷ échouer ▷ In our class, no one failed. Dans notre classe, personne n'a échoué. ❸ Our efforts failed. Nos efforts ont échoué. ❹ lâcher ▷ My brakes failed. Mes freins ont lâché. ❺ tomber en panne ▷ The engine failed. Le moteur est tombé en panne. ❻ faiblir ▷ His eyesight is failing. Sa vue faiblit.; **to fail to do something** ne pas faire quelque chose ▷ She failed to return her library books. Elle n'a pas rendu ses livres à la bibliothèque.
▶ n: **without fail** sans faute

failure [ˈfeɪljəʳ] n ❶ échec m ▷ feelings of failure un sentiment d'échec ❷ raté m, ratée f ▷ You are not a failure. Tu n'es pas un raté. ❸ défaillance f ▷ a mechanical failure une défaillance mécanique

faint [feɪnt] adj faible ▷ His voice was very faint. Sa voix était très faible.; **to feel faint** se trouver mal
▶ vb s'évanouir ▷ All of a sudden she fainted. Tout à coup elle s'est évanouie.

fair [fɛəʳ] adj ❶ juste ▷ That's not fair. Ce n'est pas juste. ❷ (skin) clair ▷ people with fair skin les gens qui ont la peau claire ❸ (weather) beau (f belle) ▷ The weather was fair. Il faisait beau. ❹ (good enough) assez bon (f assez bonne) ▷ I have a fair chance of winning. J'ai d'assez bonnes chances de gagner. ❺ (sizeable) considérable ▷ That's a fair distance. Ça représente une distance considérable.
▶ n foire f ▷ They went to the fair. Ils sont allés à la foire.; **a trade fair** une foire commerciale; **a book fair** une foire du livre

fairground [ˈfɛəgraʊnd] n champ de foire m

fairly [ˈfɛəlɪ] adv ❶ équitablement ▷ The cake was divided fairly. Le gâteau a été partagé équitablement. ❷ (quite) assez ▷ That's fairly good. C'est assez bien.

fairness [ˈfɛənɪs] n justice f

fairy [ˈfɛərɪ] n fée f

fairy tale n conte de fées m (pl contes de fées)

faith [feɪθ] n ❶ foi f ▷ The Catholic faith la foi catholique ❷ confiance f ▷ People have lost faith in the government. Les gens ont perdu confiance dans le gouvernement.

faithful [ˈfeɪθful] adj fidèle

faithfully [ˈfeɪθfəlɪ] adv: **Yours faithfully...** (in letter) Veuillez agréer mes salutations distinguées...

fake [feɪk] n faux m ▷ The painting was a fake. Le tableau était un faux.
▶ adj faux m (f fausse) ▷ She wore fake fur. Elle portait une fausse fourrure.
▶ vb ❶ (signature) imiter ❷ (photo, event) truquer; **He faked a headache.** Il a fait semblant d'avoir mal à la tête.; **She's faking it.** Elle fait semblant.

fall [fɔːl] n ❶ chute f ▷ a fall of snow une chute

de neige ▷ *She had a nasty fall.* Elle a fait une mauvaise chute.; **the Niagara Falls** les chutes du Niagara ❷ automne *m*; **fall fair** la foire d'automne
▶ *vb* ❶ tomber ▷ *He tripped and fell.* Il a trébuché et il est tombé. ❷ baisser ▷ *Prices are falling.* Les prix baissent.; **to fall apart** tomber en morceaux; **Their marriage is falling apart.** Leur mariage s'effond.; **to fall behind** rester en arrière; **to fall down (1)** (*person*) tomber ▷ *She's fallen down.* Elle est tombée. **(2)** (*building*) s'écrouler ▷ *The house is slowly falling down.* La maison est en train de s'écrouler.; **to fall for (1)** se laisser prendre à ▷ *They fell for it.* Ils s'y sont laissé prendre. **(2)** tomber amoureux de ▷ *She's falling for him.* Elle est en train de tomber amoureuse de lui.; **to fall off** tomber de ▷ *The book fell off the shelf.* Le livre est tombé de l'étagère.; **to fall through** tomber à l'eau ▷ *Our plans have fallen through.* Nos projets sont tombés à l'eau.
fallen [ˈfɔːlən] *vb see* **fall**
false [fɔːls] *adj* faux (*f* fausse); **a false alarm** une fausse alerte; **false teeth** le dentier
fame [feɪm] *n* renommée *f*
familiar [fəˈmɪljər] *adj* familier (*f* familière) ▷ *a familiar face* un visage familier; **to be familiar with something** bien connaître quelque chose ▷ *I'm familiar with his work.* Je connais bien ses œuvres.
family [ˈfæmɪlɪ] *n* famille *f*; **the Cooke family** la famille Cooke
famine [ˈfæmɪn] *n* famine *f*
famous [ˈfeɪməs] *adj* célèbre
fan [fæn] *n* ❶ (*handheld*) éventail *m* ❷ (*electric*) ventilateur *m* ❸ fan *f* ▷ *I'm a fan of Jann Arden.* Je suis un fan de Jann Arden. ▷ *hockey fans* les fans de hockey
fanatic [fəˈnætɪk] *n* fanatique
fancy [ˈfænsɪ] *adj* élaboré
fantastic [fænˈtæstɪk] *adj* fantastique
far [fɑːʳ] *adj, adv* loin ▷ *Is it far?* Est-ce que c'est loin? ▷ *far from* loin de ▷ *It's not far from London.* Ce n'est pas loin de London. ▷ *It's far from easy.* C'est loin d'être facile.; **How far is it?** C'est à quelle distance?; **How far is it to Hull?** Combien y a-t-il jusqu'à Hull?; **How far are you?** (*with a task*) Où en êtes-vous?; **at the far end** à l'autre bout ▷ *at the far end of the room* à l'autre bout de la pièce; **far better** beaucoup mieux; **as far as I know** pour autant que je sache
fare [fɛəʳ] *n* ❶ (*trains, buses*) prix du billet *m* ❷ (*taxi*) prix de la course *m*; **half fare** le demi-tarif; **full fare** le plein tarif
Far East *n* Extrême-Orient *m*; **in the Far East** en Extrême-Orient
far-fetched [ˈfɑːˈfɛtʃt] *adj* tiré par les cheveux
farm [fɑːm] *n* ferme *f*
farmer [ˈfɑːməʳ] *n* ❶ agriculteur *m*, agricultrice *f* ▷ *He's a farmer.* Il est agriculteur. ❷ fermier *m*, fermière *f*
farmhouse [ˈfɑːmhaus] *n* ferme *f*
farming [ˈfɑːmɪŋ] *n* agriculture *f*; **dairy farming** l'industrie laitière
fascinating [ˈfæsɪneɪtɪŋ] *adj* fascinant

fashion [ˈfæʃən] *n* mode *f* ▷ *a fashion show* un défilé de mode; **in fashion** à la mode
fashionable [ˈfæʃnəbl] *adj* à la mode ▷ *She wears very fashionable clothes.* Elle porte des vêtements très à la mode. ▷ *a fashionable restaurant* un restaurant à la mode
fast [fɑːst] *adj, adv* ❶ vite ▷ *He can run fast.* Il sait courir vite. ❷ rapide ▷ *a fast car* une voiture rapide; **fast food** la bouffe-minute; **fast forward** l'avance *f* rapide; **That clock's fast.** Cette pendule avance.; **She's fast asleep.** Elle est profondément endormie.
fat [fæt] *adj* gros (*f* grosse)
▶ *n* ❶ (*on meat, in food*) gras *m* ▷ *It's very high in fat.* C'est très gras. ▷ *to cut down on fat* couper le gras ❷ (*for cooking*) matière grasse *f*; **body fat** le tissu adipeux
fatal [ˈfeɪtl] *adj* ❶ (*causing death*) mortel (*f* mortelle) ▷ *a fatal accident* un accident mortel ❷ (*disastrous*) fatal ▷ *He made a fatal mistake.* Il a fait une erreur fatale.
father [ˈfɑːðəʳ] *n* père *m* ▷ *my father* mon père
father-in-law [ˈfɑːðərənlɔː] *n* beau-père *m* (*pl* beaux-pères)
fault [fɔːlt] *n* ❶ (*mistake*) faute *f* ▷ *It's my fault.* C'est de ma faute. ❷ (*defect*) défaut *m* ▷ *in spite of all her faults* malgré tous ses défauts; **a mechanical fault** une défaillance mécanique
faulty [ˈfɔːltɪ] *adj* défectueux (*f* défectueuse) ▷ *This machine is faulty.* Cette machine est défectueuse.
favour [ˈfeɪvəʳ] *n* service *m*; **to do somebody a favour** rendre service à quelqu'un ▷ *Could you do me a favour?* Tu peux me rendre service?; **to be in favour of something** être pour quelque chose ▷ *I'm in favour of nuclear disarmament.* Je suis pour le désarmement nucléaire.
favourite [ˈfeɪvrɪt] *adj* favori *m* (*f* favorite) ▷ *Blue is my favourite colour.* Le bleu est ma couleur favorite.
▶ *n* favori *m*, favorite *f* ▷ *The Canadian is the favourite to win gold in speed skating.* La Canadienne est la favorite pour gagner l'or en patinage de vitesse. ▷ *The next song is my favourite.* La prochaine chanson est ma favorite.
fawn [fɔːn] *n* faon *m*
fax [fæks] *n* ❶ (*document*) télécopie *f*; **to send somebody a fax** envoyer une télécopie à quelqu'un ❷ (*machine*) télécopieur *m*
▶ *vb* télécopier ▷ *Can you fax me your document?* Peux-tu me télécopier ton document?
fear [fɪəʳ] *n* peur *f*
▶ *vb* craindre ▷ *You have nothing to fear.* Vous n'avez rien à craindre.
feather [ˈfɛðəʳ] *n* plume *f*
feature [ˈfiːtʃəʳ] *n* (*of person, object*) caractéristique *f* ▷ *an important feature* une caractéristique essentielle; **a feature film** un long métrage
February [ˈfɛbruərɪ] *n* février *m*; **in February** en février
fed [fɛd] *vb see* **feed**
federal [ˈfɛdərəl] *adj* fédéral ▷ *the federal government* le gouvernement fédéral
fed up [fɛdˈʌp] *adj*: **to be fed up with**

something en avoir marre de quelque chose ▷ *I'm fed up with waiting for him.* J'en ai marre de l'attendre.

feed [fi:d] *vb* donner à manger à ▷ *Have you fed the cat?* Est-ce que tu as donné à manger au chat?; **She worked hard to feed her family.** Elle travaillait dur pour nourrir sa famille.

feedback ['fi:dbæk] *n* rétroaction *f* ▷ *I need your feedback on my story.* J'ai besoin de ta rétroaction sur ma composition.

feel [fi:l] *vb* ❶ se sentir ▷ *I don't feel well.* Je ne me sens pas bien. ▷ *I feel a bit lonely.* Je me sens un peu seul. ❷ sentir ▷ *I didn't feel much pain.* Je n'ai presque rien senti. ❸ toucher ▷ *The doctor felt my forehead.* Le docteur m'a touché le front.; **I was feeling hungry.** J'avais faim.; **I was feeling cold, so I went inside.** J'avais froid, alors je suis rentré.; **to feel like... (want)** J'ai envie de... ▷ *Do you feel like an ice cream?* Tu as envie d'une crème glacée?

feeling ['fi:lɪŋ] *n* ❶ (*physical*) sensation *f* ▷ *a burning feeling* une sensation de brûlure ❷ (*emotional*) sentiment *m* ▷ *a feeling of satisfaction* un sentiment de satisfaction

feet [fi:t] *npl see* **foot**

fell [fɛl] *vb see* **fall**

felt [fɛlt] *vb see* **feel**

felt pen *n* stylo-feutre *m*

female ['fi:meɪl] *adj* ❶ femelle *f* ▷ *a female animal* un animal femelle ❷ féminin ▷ *the female sex* le sexe féminin
  ▶ *n* (*animal*) femelle *f*

feminine ['fɛmɪnɪn] *adj* féminin

feminist ['fɛmɪnɪst] *n* féministe

fence [fɛns] *n* barrière *f*

fern [fɜːn] *n* fougère *f*

ferret ['fɛrɪt] *n* furet *m*

ferry ['fɛrɪ] *n* traversier *m*

fertile ['fɜːtaɪl] *adj* fertile

fertilizer ['fɜːtɪlaɪzə'] *n* engrais *m*

festival ['fɛstɪvəl] *n* festival *m* ▷ *a jazz festival* un festival de jazz

fetch [fɛtʃ] *vb* ❶ aller chercher ▷ *Fetch the bucket.* Va chercher le seau. ❷ (*sell for*) se vendre ▷ *His painting fetched $5000.* Son tableau s'est vendu cinq mille dollars.

fever ['fi:və'] *n* (*temperature*) fièvre *f*

few [fju:] *adj, pron* (*not many*) peu de ▷ *few books* peu de livres; **a few** (1) quelques ▷ *a few hours* quelques heures (2) quelques-uns ▷ *"How many apples do you want?" — "A few."* «Tu veux combien de pommes?» — «Quelques-unes.»; **quite a few people** pas mal de monde

fewer ['fju:ə'] *adj* moins de ▷ *There are fewer people than there were yesterday.* Il y a moins de monde qu'hier. ▷ *There are fewer students in this class.* Il y a moins d'élèves dans cette classe.

fiancé [fɪ'ɑ̃:nseɪ] *n* fiancé *m*

fiancée [fɪ'ɑ̃:nseɪ] *n* fiancée *f*

fiction ['fɪkʃən] *n* (*novels*) romans *mpl*

field [fi:ld] *n* ❶ (*in countryside*) champ *m* ▷ *a field of wheat* un champ de blé ❷ (*for sport*) terrain *m* ▷ *a soccer field* un terrain de soccer ❸ (*subject*) domaine *m* ▷ *He's an expert in his field.* C'est un expert dans son domaine.; **a field trip** une sortie éducative

fierce [fɪəs] *adj* ❶ féroce ▷ *The dog looked very fierce.* Le chien avait l'air très féroce. ❷ violent ▷ *The wind was very fierce.* Le vent était très violent. ▷ *a fierce attack* une attaque violente

fifteen [fɪf'ti:n] *num* quinze ▷ *I'm fifteen.* J'ai quinze ans.

fifteenth [fɪf'ti:nθ] *adj* quinzième ▷ *the fifteenth floor* le quinzième étage; **the fifteenth of August** le quinze août

fifth [fɪfθ] *adj* cinquième ▷ *the fifth floor* le cinquième étage; **the fifth of August** le cinq août

fifty ['fɪftɪ] *num* cinquante ▷ *She's fifty.* Elle a cinquante ans.

fifty-fifty ['fɪftɪ'fɪftɪ] *adj, adv* moitié-moitié ▷ *They split the prize money fifty-fifty.* Ils ont partagé l'argent du prix moitié-moitié.; **a fifty-fifty chance** une chance sur deux

fight [faɪt] *n* ❶ bagarre *f* ▷ *There was a fight in the hallway.* Il y a eu une bagarre dans le couloir. ❷ lutte *f* ▷ *the fight against cancer* la lutte contre le cancer
  ▶ *vb* ❶ se battre ▷ *They were fighting.* Ils se battaient. ❷ lutter contre ▷ *The doctors tried to fight the disease.* Les médecins ont essayé de lutter contre la maladie. ▷ *He fought against the urge to smoke.* Il a lutté contre son envie de fumer.

fighting ['faɪtɪŋ] *n* bagarres *fpl* ▷ *Fighting broke out in the schoolyard.* Des bagarres ont éclaté dans la cour de l'école.

figure ['fɪgə'] *n* ❶ (*number*) chiffre *m* ▷ *Can you give me the exact figures?* Pouvez-vous me donner les chiffres exacts? ❷ (*outline of person*) silhouette *f* ▷ *I saw the figure of a man on the bridge.* J'ai vu la silhouette d'un homme sur le pont.; **I have to watch my figure.** Je dois faire attention à ma ligne. ❸ (*personality*) personnage *m* ▷ *She's an important political figure.* C'est un personnage politique important.

figure out *vb* ❶ calculer ▷ *I'll try to figure out how much it'll cost.* Je vais essayer de calculer combien ça va coûter. ❷ voir ▷ *I couldn't figure out what it meant.* Je n'arrivais pas à voir ce que ça voulait dire. ❸ cerner ▷ *I can't figure him out at all.* Je n'arrive pas du tout à le cerner.

figure skating *n* patinage artistique *m*

file [faɪl] *n* ❶ (*document*) dossier *m* ▷ *Have we got a file on the suspect?* Est-ce que nous avons un dossier sur le suspect? ❷ (*on computer*) fichier *m* ❸ (*for nails, metal*) lime *f*; **a file folder** une chemise
  ▶ *vb* ❶ (*papers*) classer ❷ (*nails, metal*) limer ▷ *to file one's nails* se limer les ongles

fill [fɪl] *vb* remplir ▷ *She filled the glass with water.* Elle a rempli le verre d'eau.; **to fill in** boucher ▷ *He filled the hole in with soil.* Il a bouché le trou avec de la terre.; **to fill in for somebody** remplacer quelqu'un; **to fill out** remplir ▷ *Can you fill out this form, please?* Est-ce que vous pouvez remplir ce formulaire, s'il vous plaît?; **to fill up** remplir ▷ *She filled the cup up to the brim.* Elle a rempli la tasse à ras bords.; **Fill it up, please.** (*at gas station*) Le plein, s'il vous plaît.

film [film] *n* film *m*

filmmaker ['filmmeikə^r] *n* cinéaste

filthy ['filθi] *adj* crasseux (*f* crasseuse)

final ['faɪnl] *adj* ❶ (*last*) dernier (*f* dernière) ▷ *our final farewells* nos derniers adieux ❷ (*definite*) définitif (*f* définitive) ▷ *a final decision* une décision définitive; **I'm not going and that's final.** Je n'y vais pas, un point c'est tout.
▷ *n* finale *f* ▷ *She's playing in the final.* Elle va disputer la finale.

finally ['faɪnəli] *adv* ❶ (*lastly*) enfin ▷ *Finally, I would like to say...* Enfin, je voudrais dire... ❷ (*eventually*) finalement ▷ *They finally decided to leave on Saturday instead of Friday.* Ils ont finalement décidé de partir samedi au lieu de vendredi.

find [faɪnd] *vb* ❶ trouver ▷ *I can't find the exit.* Je ne trouve pas la sortie. ❷ (*something lost*) retrouver ▷ *Did you find your pen?* Est-ce que tu as retrouvé ton crayon?; **to find something out** découvrir quelque chose ▷ *I'm determined to find out the truth.* Je suis décidé à découvrir la vérité.; **to find out about (1)** (*make enquiries*) se renseigner sur ▷ *Try to find out about the price.* Essaye de te renseigner sur le prix. **(2)** (*by chance*) apprendre ▷ *I found out about their secret plan.* J'ai appris leur projet secret.

fine [faɪn] *adj, adv* ❶ (*very good*) excellent ▷ *He's a fine musician.* C'est un excellent musicien.; **to be fine** aller bien ▷ *"How are you?" — "I'm fine."* « Comment ça va? » — « Ça va bien. »; **I feel fine.** Je me sens bien.; **The weather is fine today.** Il fait beau aujourd'hui. ❷ (*not coarse*) fin ▷ *She has very fine hair.* Elle a les cheveux très fins.
▷ *n* ❶ amende *f* ▷ *She got a $50 fine.* Elle a eu une amende de cinquante dollars. ❷ (*for traffic offence*) contravention *f* ▷ *I got a fine for driving through a red light.* J'ai eu une contravention pour avoir grillé un feu rouge.

finger ['fɪŋɡə^r] *n* doigt *m*; **my little finger** mon petit doigt

fingernail ['fɪŋɡəneɪl] *n* ongle *m*

fingerprint ['fɪŋɡəprɪnt] *n* empreinte *f* digitale

finish ['fɪnɪʃ] *n* (*of race*) arrivée *f* ▷ *We saw the finish of the marathon.* Nous avons vu l'arrivée du marathon.; **the finish line** la ligne d'arrivée; **a fight to the finish** un combat sans merci; **from start to finish** du début à la fin
▷ *vb* ❶ finir ▷ *I've finished!* J'ai fini!; **to finish doing something** finir de faire quelque chose ❷ terminer ▷ *I've finished the book.* J'ai terminé ce livre. ▷ *The film has finished.* Le film est terminé.

fir [fə:^r] *n* sapin *m*; **Douglas fir** le douglas vert

fire [faɪə^r] *n* ❶ feu *m* (*pl* feux) ▷ *He made a fire to warm himself.* Il a fait du feu pour se réchauffer.; **to be on fire** être en feu ❷ (*accidental*) incendie *m* ▷ *The house was destroyed by fire.* La maison a été détruite par un incendie.; **the fire department** les *m* pompiers; **a fire alarm** un avertisseur d'incendie; **a fire drill** un exercice d'incendie; **a fire engine** un camion d'incendie; **a fire escape** un escalier de secours; **a fire**

extinguisher un extincteur; **a fire hydrant** une borne-fontaine (*pl* les bornes-fontaines); **a fire station** un poste de pompiers
▷ *vb* (*shoot*) tirer ▷ *She fired twice.* Elle a tiré deux fois.; **to fire at somebody** tirer sur quelqu'un ▷ *The terrorist fired at the crowd.* Le terroriste a tiré sur la foule.; **to fire a gun** tirer un coup de feu; **to fire somebody** mettre quelqu'un à la porte ▷ *He was fired from his job.* Il a été mis à la porte.

firefighter ['faɪəfaɪtə^r] *n* pompier *m*, pompière *f* ▷ *She's a firefighter.* Elle est pompière.

fireplace ['faɪəpleɪs] *n* cheminée *f*

fireworks ['faɪəwə:ks] *npl* feu *m* d'artifice ▷ *Are you going to see the fireworks?* Est-ce que tu vas voir le feu d'artifice?

firm [fə:m] *adj* ferme ▷ *to be firm with somebody* se montrer ferme avec quelqu'un
▷ *n* entreprise *f* ▷ *She works for a large firm in Kitchener.* Elle travaille pour une grande entreprise à Kitchener.

first [fə:st] *adj, adv* ❶ premier *m* (*f* première) ▷ *the first of September* le premier septembre ▷ *the first time* la première fois; **to come first** (*in exam, race*) arriver premier ▷ *Who came first?* Qui est arrivé premier? ❷ *adv* ▷ *I want to get a job, but first I have to finish school.* Je veux trouver du travail, mais d'abord je dois finir mes études.; **first of all** tout d'abord
▷ *n* premier *m*, première *f* ▷ *She was the first to arrive.* Elle est arrivée la première.; **at first** au début

first aid *n* premiers *mpl* soins; **a first aid kit** une trousse de premiers soins

first-class ['fə:st'klɑ:s] *adj* ❶ de première classe ▷ *He has booked a first-class ticket.* Il a réservé un billet de première classe. ❷ excellent ▷ *a first-class meal* un excellent repas

firstly ['fə:stli] *adv* premièrement ▷ *Firstly, let's see what the book is about.* Premièrement, voyons de quoi parle ce livre.

First Ministers *npl* premiers *mpl* ministres ▷ *a First Ministers' conference* une conférence des premiers ministres

First Nations *npl* Premières *fpl* Nations ▷ *the Assembly of First Nations* l'Assemblée des Premières Nations

fish [fɪʃ] *n* poisson *m* ▷ *I caught three fish.* J'ai pêché trois poissons. ▷ *I don't like fish.* Je n'aime pas le poisson.; **fish bone** l'arête *f*; **fish sticks** les *m* bâtonnets de poisson
▷ *vb* pêcher ▷ *to fish for trout* pêcher la truite; **to go fishing** aller à la pêche ▷ *We went fishing in the Miramichi River.* Nous sommes allés à la pêche sur la rivière Miramichi.

fisherman ['fɪʃəmən] *n* pêcheur *m*, pêcheuse *f* ▷ *She's a fisherman.* Elle est pêcheuse.

fishing ['fɪʃɪŋ] *n* pêche *f* ▷ *My hobby is fishing.* La pêche est mon passe-temps favori.

fishing boat ['fɪʃɪŋ-] *n* bateau de pêche *m*

fishing rod ['fɪʃɪŋ-] *n* canne à pêche *f*

fishing tackle ['fɪʃɪŋ-] *n* matériel de pêche *m*

fist [fɪst] *n* poing *m*

fit [fɪt] *vb* ❶ (*be the right size*) être la bonne

taille ▷ *Does it fit?* Est-ce que c'est la bonne taille?; **These pants don't fit me. (1)** (*too big*) Ce pantalon est trop grand pour moi. **(2)** (*too small*) Ce pantalon est trop petit pour moi. ❷ (*match*) correspondre ▷ *That story doesn't fit with what he told us.* Cette histoire ne correspond pas à ce qu'il nous a dit. ❸ adapter ▷ *She fitted a plug to the hair dryer.* Elle a adapté une prise au sèche-cheveux.; **to fit in** s'adapter ▷ *She fits in well at her new school.* Elle s'est bien adaptée à sa nouvelle école.
▶ *adj* (*in condition*) en forme ▷ *He felt relaxed and fit after his holiday.* Il se sentait détendu et en forme après ses vacances.
▶ *n*: **to have a fit** (*be upset*) piquer une crise de nerfs ▷ *My mom will have a fit when she sees the carpet!* Ma mère va piquer une crise de nerfs quand elle va voir la moquette!; **a fit of coughing** une quinte de toux; **to be in fits of laughter** se tordre de rire

fitting room ['fɪtɪŋ-] *n* cabine d'essayage *f*

five [faɪv] *num* cinq ▷ *He's five.* Il a cinq ans.

fix [fɪks] *vb* ❶ (*mend*) réparer ▷ *Can you fix my bike?* Est-ce que tu peux réparer mon vélo? ❷ préparer ▷ *He fixed us a snack.* Il nous a préparé une collation.

fixed [fɪkst] *adj* fixe ▷ *at a fixed time* à une heure fixe ▷ *at a fixed price* à un prix fixe ▷ *a fixed-price menu* un menu à prix fixe; **My parents have very fixed ideas.** Mes parents ont des idées très arrêtées.

flabby ['flæbi] *adj* flasque

flag [flæg] *n* drapeau *m* (*pl* drapeaux)

flame [fleɪm] *n* flamme *f*

flap [flæp] *vb* ❶ (*wings*) battre de ▷ *The bird flapped its wings.* L'oiseau battait des ailes. ❷ (*noisily*) claquer ▷ *The flags were flapping in the wind.* Les drapeaux claquaient dans le vent.

flash [flæʃ] *n* flash *m* (*pl* flashes) ▷ *Has your camera got a flash?* Est-ce que ton appareil photo a un flash?; **a flash of lightning** un éclair; **in a flash** en un clin d'œil
▶ *vb* ❶ clignoter ▷ *The police car's blue light was flashing.* Le gyrophare de la voiture de police clignotait. ❷ projeter ▷ *They flashed a light in his face.* Ils lui ont projeté la lumière d'une lampe de poche en plein visage.; **She flashed her headlights.** Elle a fait un appel de phares.

flashlight ['flæʃlaɪt] *n* lampe de poche *f*

flat [flæt] *adj, adv* ❶ plat ▷ *a flat roof* un toit plat ▷ *flat shoes* des chaussures plates ❷ (*tire*) crevé ▷ *I've got a flat tire.* J'ai un pneu crevé. ❸ (*music*) faux ▷ *We went flat in that last song.* Nous avons chanté faux dans cette dernière chanson.; **B flat** si bémol

flatter ['flætər] *vb* flatter

flavour ['fleɪvər] *n* ❶ (*taste*) goût *m* ▷ *It has a very strong flavour.* Ça a un goût très fort. ❷ (*variety*) saveur *f* ▷ *Which flavour of ice cream would you like?* Quelle saveur de crème glacée est-ce que tu veux?

flavouring ['fleɪvərɪŋ] *n* arôme *m*

flea [fliː] *n* puce *f*; **a flea market** un marché aux puces

flew [fluː] *vb see* **fly**

flexible ['flɛksəbl] *adj* flexible ▷ *flexible working hours* les horaires flexibles

flicker ['flɪkər] *vb* trembloter ▷ *The light flickered.* La lumière a trembloté.

flight [flaɪt] *n* vol *m* ▷ *What time is the flight to Sault Ste. Marie?* À quelle heure est le vol pour Sault Ste. Marie?; **a flight of stairs** un escalier

flight attendant [-ə'tɛndənt] *n* agent *m* de bord, agente *f* de bord

flip [flɪp] *vb*: **to flip a coin** tirer à pile ou face; **to flip through a book** feuilleter un livre; **Flip the card over.** Retourne la carte.

flippers ['flɪpəz] *n* ❶ (*for people*) palmes *fpl* ❷ (*on animals*) nageoires *fpl*

float [fləʊt] *vb* flotter ▷ *A leaf was floating on the water.* Une feuille flottait sur l'eau.

flock [flɒk] *n*: **a flock of sheep** un troupeau de moutons; **a flock of birds** un vol d'oiseaux

flood [flʌd] *n* ❶ inondation *f* ▷ *The rain has caused many floods.* La pluie a provoqué de nombreuses inondations. ❷ flot *m* ▷ *He received a flood of letters.* Il a reçu un flot de lettres.
▶ *vb* ❶ déborder ▷ *The river has flooded.* La rivière a débordé. ❷ inonder ▷ *The river has flooded the village.* La rivière a inondé le village.

flooding ['flʌdɪŋ] *n* inondations *fpl*

floor [flɔːr] *n* ❶ plancher *m* ▷ *a hardwood floor* un plancher de bois franc; **on the floor** par terre ❷ (*storey*) étage *m* ▷ *the fourth floor* le quatrième étage; **the ground floor** le premier étage; **on the third floor** au troisième étage

flop [flɒp] *n* fiasco *m* ▷ *The movie was a flop.* Le film a été un fiasco.

floppy disk ['flɒpɪ-] *n* disquette *f*

florist ['flɒrɪst] *n* fleuriste

flour ['flaʊər] *n* farine *f*

flow [fləʊ] *vb* ❶ (*river*) couler ❷ (*flow out*) s'écouler ▷ *Water was flowing from the pipe.* De l'eau s'écoulait du tuyau.

flower ['flaʊər] *n* fleur *f*

flown [fləʊn] *vb see* **fly**

flu [fluː] *n* grippe *f* ▷ *She has the flu.* Elle a la grippe.

fluent ['fluːənt] *adj*: **She speaks fluent French.** Elle parle couramment le français.

flung [flʌŋ] *vb see* **fling**

flush [flʌʃ] *vb*: **to flush the toilet** tirer la chasse

flute [fluːt] *n* flûte *f* ▷ *I play the flute.* Je joue de la flûte.

fly [flaɪ] *n* ❶ (*insect*) mouche *f* ❷ (*on pants*) braguette *f* ❸ (*on tent*) double toit *m*
▶ *vb* ❶ voler ▷ *The plane flies at a speed of 400 km per hour.* L'avion vole à quatre cents kilomètres à l'heure. ❷ (*passenger*) aller en avion ▷ *He flew from Goose Bay to Charlottetown.* Il est allé de Goose Bay à Charlottetown en avion.; **to fly away** s'envoler ▷ *The bird flew away.* L'oiseau s'est envolé.

foal [fəʊl] *n* poulain *m*

focus ['fəʊkəs] *n*: **to be out of focus** être flou ▷ *The house is out of focus in this photo.* La maison est floue sur cette photo.
▶ *vb* mettre au point ▷ *Try to focus the binoculars.* Essaye de mettre les jumelles au point.; **to focus on something (1)** (*with lens*) régler la mise au point sur quelque

chose ▷ *The photographer focused on the bird.*
La photographe a réglé la mise au point sur
l'oiseau. **(2)** *(concentrate)* se concentrer sur
quelque chose ▷ *Let's focus on the plot of the play.*
Concentrons-nous sur l'intrigue de la pièce.

fog [fɒg] n brouillard m

foggy ['fɒgɪ] adj: **It's foggy.** Il y a du brouillard.;
a foggy day un jour de brouillard

foil [fɔɪl] n *(kitchen foil)* papier d'aluminium m
▷ *She wrapped the meat in foil.* Elle a enveloppé la
viande dans du papier d'aluminium.

fold [fəʊld] n pli m
▶ vb plier ▷ *He folded the newspaper in half.* Il a
plié le journal en deux.; **to fold something up**
plier quelque chose; **to fold one's arms** croiser
ses bras ▷ *She folded her arms.* Elle a croisé les
bras.

folder ['fəʊldə'] n **①** chemise f ▷ *She kept all her
letters in a folder.* Elle gardait toutes ses lettres
dans une chemise. **②** *(computer)* dossier m

folding ['fəʊldɪŋ] adj: **a folding chair** une
chaise pliante; **a folding bed** un lit pliant

follow ['fɒləʊ] vb suivre ▷ *She followed him.* Elle
l'a suivi. ▷ *You go first and I'll follow.* Va devant,
je te suis.

following ['fɒləʊɪŋ] adj suivant ▷ *the following
day* le jour suivant

fond [fɒnd] adj: **to be fond of somebody**
aimer beaucoup quelqu'un ▷ *I'm very fond of
him.* Je l'aime beaucoup.

font [fɒnt] n police de caractères f

food [fu:d] n nourriture f; **We need to buy
some food.** Nous devons acheter à manger.;
cat food la nourriture pour chat; **dog food**
la nourriture pour chien; **a food bank** une
banque alimentaire; **the food chain** la chaîne
alimentaire; **food poisoning** l'intoxication f
alimentaire

food processor [-'prəʊsesə'] n robot m

fool [fu:l] n **①** idiot m, idiote f
▶ vb **①** *(tease)* plaisanter ▷ *I'm only fooling.* Je ne
fais que plaisanter. **②** *(trick)* duper ▷ *You can't
fool me.* Tu ne me duperas pas.; **to fool around**
(1) *(waste time)* perdre son temps ▷ *Stop fooling
around and get to work.* Arrêtez de perdre votre
temps et mettez-vous au travail. **(2)** *(do silly
things)* faire des bêtises **(3)** *(with something)*
toucher à ▷ *Don't fool around with drugs.* Ne
touche pas à la drogue.

foolproof ['fu:lpru:f] adj infaillible

foosball ['fu:zbɔ:l] n baby-foot m

foot [fʊt] n **①** *(of person)* pied m ▷ *My feet are
aching.* J'ai mal aux pieds. **②** *(of animal)* patte f
▷ *The dog's foot was injured.* Le chien était blessé
à la patte.; **on foot** à pied **③** *(12 inches)* pied
m; **My dad is 6 feet tall.** Mon père mesure un
mètre quatre-vingt.

football ['fʊtbɔ:l] n **①** *(game)* football m ▷ *I
like playing football.* J'aime jouer au football.
② *(ball)* ballon m ▷ *I threw the football over the
fence.* J'ai envoyé le ballon par dessus la clôture.

footer ['fʊtə'] n *(word processing)* pied de
page m

footprint ['fʊtprɪnt] n trace de pas f ▷ *He saw
some footprints in the snow.* Il a vu des traces de
pas sur la neige.

footstep ['fʊtstɛp] n pas m ▷ *I can hear
footsteps on the stairs.* J'entends des pas dans
l'escalier.

for [fɔ:'] prep **①** pour ▷ *a present for me* un
cadeau pour moi ▷ *the bus for Sherbrooke*
l'autobus pour Sherbrooke ▷ *He works for the
government.* Il travaille pour le gouvernement.
▷ *I'll do it for you.* Je vais le faire pour toi. ▷ *Can
you do it for tomorrow?* Est-ce que vous pouvez
le faire pour demain? ▷ *Are you for or against
the idea?* Êtes-vous pour ou contre cette idée?
▷ *The Bay of Fundy is famous for its high tides.* La
baie de Fundy est célèbre pour la hauteur de
ses marées. **②** pendant ▷ *He worked in France
for two years.* Il a travaillé en France pendant
deux ans. ▷ *She will be away for a month.* Elle
sera absente pendant un mois. **③** depuis ▷ *I've
been learning French for two years.* J'apprends le
français depuis deux ans. ▷ *She's been away for a
month.* Elle est absente depuis un mois. ▷ *I sold
it for 50 dollars.* Je l'ai vendu cinquante dollars.
▷ *He paid five dollars for his ticket.* Il a payé son
billet cinq dollars.; **What's the French for
"lion"?** Comment dit-on "lion" en français?;
It's time for lunch. C'est l'heure du déjeuner.;
What for? Pour quoi faire? ▷ *"Give me some
money!" — "What for?"* « Donne-moi de l'argent! »
— « Pour quoi faire? »; **What's it for?** Ça sert à
quoi?; **for sale** à vendre ▷ *Their house is for sale.*
Leur maison est à vendre.

forbid [fə'bɪd] vb défendre; **to forbid
somebody to do something** défendre à
quelqu'un de faire quelque chose ▷ *I forbid you
to go out tonight!* Je te défends de sortir ce soir.

forbidden [fə'bɪdn] adj défendu ▷ *Smoking
is strictly forbidden.* Il est strictement défendu
de fumer.

force [fɔ:s] n force f ▷ *the force of the explosion* la
force de l'explosion; **in force** en vigueur ▷ *No-
smoking rules are now in force.* Un règlement qui
interdit de fumer est maintenant en vigueur.
▶ vb forcer ▷ *They forced her to open the safe.* Ils
l'ont obligée à ouvrir le coffre-fort.

forecast ['fɔ:kɑ:st] n: **the weather forecast**
la météo

foreground ['fɔ:graʊnd] n premier plan m
▷ *in the foreground* au premier plan

forehead ['fɒrɪd] n front m

foreign ['fɒrɪn] adj étranger (f étrangère)

foresee [fɔ:'si:] vb prévoir ▷ *She had foreseen the
problem.* Elle avait prévu le problème.

forest ['fɒrɪst] n forêt f

forestry ['fɒrɪstrɪ] n foresterie f ▷ *He wants to
study forestry.* Il veut étudier en foresterie.

forever [fə'rɛvə'] adv **①** pour toujours
▷ *He's gone forever.* Il est parti pour toujours.
② *(always)* toujours ▷ *You're forever complaining.*
Tu es toujours en train de te plaindre.

forgave, forgiven [fə'geɪv, fə'gɪvn] vb see
forgive

forge [fɔ:dʒ] vb contrefaire ▷ *She tried to forge
his signature.* Elle a essayé de contrefaire sa
signature.

forged [fɔ:dʒd] adj faux (f fausse) ▷ *forged
banknotes* des faux billets

forget [fə'gɛt] vb oublier ▷ *I've forgotten*

his name. J'ai oublié son nom. ▷ *I'm sorry, I completely forgot!* Je suis désolé, j'ai complètement oublié!

forgive [fə'gɪv] *vb*: **to forgive somebody** pardonner à quelqu'un ▷ *I forgive you.* Je te pardonne.; **to forgive somebody for doing something** pardonner à quelqu'un d'avoir fait quelque chose ▷ *He forgave her for forgetting his birthday.* Il lui a pardonné d'avoir oublié son anniversaire.

forgot, forgotten [fə'gɒt, fə'gɒtn] *vb see* **forget**

fork [fɔːk] *n* ① (*for eating*) fourchette *f* ② (*for gardening*) fourche *f* ③ (*in road*) bifurcation *f*

form [fɔːm] *n* ① (*paper*) formulaire *m* ▷ **to fill in a form** remplir un formulaire ② (*type*) forme *f* ▷ *I'm against hunting in any form.* Je suis contre la chasse sous toutes ses formes.; **in top form** en pleine forme

formal ['fɔːməl] *adj* ① (*occasion*) officiel (*f* officielle) ▷ *a formal dinner* un dîner officiel ② (*person*) guindé ③ (*language*) soutenu ▷ *In English, "residence" is a formal term.* En anglais, "residence" est un terme soutenu.; **formal clothes** une tenue habillée; **She has no formal education.** Elle n'a pas fait beaucoup d'études.

format ['fɔːmæt] *vb* formater ▷ **to format a document** formater un document

formatting ['fɔːmætɪŋ] *n* formatage *m*

former ['fɔːmə'] *adj* ancien (*f* ancienne) ▷ *a former student* un ancien élève ▷ *the former Prime Minister* l'ancien Premier ministre

formerly ['fɔːməlɪ] *adv* autrefois

fort [fɔːt] *n* fort *m*

forth [fɔːθ] *adv*: **to go back and forth** aller et venir; **and so forth** et ainsi de suite

fortunate ['fɔːtʃənɪt] *adj*: **to be fortunate** avoir de la chance ▷ *He was extremely fortunate to survive.* Il a eu énormément de chance de survivre.; **It's fortunate that I remembered the map.** C'est une chance que j'aie pris la carte.

fortunately ['fɔːtʃənɪtlɪ] *adv* heureusement ▷ *Fortunately, it didn't rain.* Heureusement, il n'a pas plu.

fortune ['fɔːtʃən] *n* fortune *f* ▷ *She earns a fortune!* Elle gagne une fortune!; **to tell somebody's fortune** dire la bonne aventure à quelqu'un

forty ['fɔːtɪ] *num* quarante ▷ *He's forty.* Il a quarante ans.

forward ['fɔːwəd] *adv*: **to move forward** avancer
▶ *vb* faire suivre ▷ *He forwarded all my letters.* Il a fait suivre toutes mes lettres.

forward slash [-slæʃ] *n* barre oblique *f*

foster ['fɒstə'] *vb*: **She has fostered more than fifteen children.** Plus de quinze enfants ont été placés chez elle.

foster child *n* enfant *m* placé en foyer nourricier, enfant *f* placée en foyer nourricier

fought [fɔːt] *vb see* **fight**

foul [faul] *adj* infect ▷ *The weather was foul.* Le temps était infect. ▷ *What a foul smell!* Quelle odeur infecte!
▶ *n* faute *f* ▷ *Their goalie committed a foul.* Leur gardienne de but a fait une faute.

found [faund] *vb see* **find**
▶ *vb* fonder ▷ *John Graves Simcoe founded the town of York.* John Graves Simcoe a fondé la ville de York.

foundations [faun'deɪʃəns] *npl* fondations *fpl*

fountain ['fauntɪn] *n* fontaine *f*

four [fɔː'] *num* quatre ▷ *She's four.* Elle a quatre ans.

fourteen ['fɔː'tiːn] *num* quatorze ▷ *I'm fourteen.* J'ai quatorze ans.

fourteenth ['fɔː'tiːnθ] *adj* quatorzième ▷ *the fourteenth floor* le quatorzième étage; **the fourteenth of August** le quatorze août

fourth ['fɔːθ] *adj* quatrième ▷ *the fourth floor* le quatrième étage

fox [fɒks] *n* renard *m*; **a fox cub** un renardeau

fragile ['frædʒaɪl] *adj* fragile

frame [freɪm] *n* (*for picture*) cadre *m*; **glasses frames** la monture de lunettes

Francophone ['fræŋkəfəun] *adj* francophone ▷ *a Francophone community* une communauté francophone
▶ *n* francophone ▷ *She's a Francophone.* C'est une francophone.

frankly ['fræŋklɪ] *adv* franchement ▷ *He spoke to me frankly.* Il m'a parlé franchement.

frantic ['fræntɪk] *adj*: **I was going frantic.** J'étais dans tous mes états.; **to be frantic with worry** être folle d'inquiétude; **a frantic attempt** un essai désespéré

fraud [frɔːd] *n* ① (*crime*) fraude *f* ▷ *He was jailed for fraud.* On l'a mis en prison pour fraude. ② (*person*) imposteur *m* ▷ *He's not a real doctor, he's a fraud.* Ce n'est pas un vrai médecin, c'est un imposteur.

freckles ['freklz] *npl* taches *fpl* de rousseur

free [friː] *adj* ① (*free of charge*) gratuit ▷ *a free brochure* une brochure gratuite ② (*not busy, not taken*) libre ▷ *Is this seat free?* Est-ce que cette place est libre? ▷ *Are you free after school?* Tu es libre après l'école?
▶ *vb* libérer

freedom ['friːdəm] *n* liberté *f*

free trade *n* libre-échange *m*

freeware ['friːweə'] *n* gratuiciel *m*

freeze [friːz] *vb* ① geler ▷ *The water had frozen.* L'eau avait gelé. ② (*food*) congeler ▷ *We froze the rest of the raspberries.* Nous avons congelé le reste des framboises. ③ (*stop moving*) se figer; **Freeze!** Pas un geste!

freezer ['friːzə'] *n* congélateur *m*

freeze-up ['friːzʌp] *n* saison du gel *f* ▷ *We have to go close the cottage before freeze-up.* Nous devons aller fermer le chalet avant la saison du gel.

freezing ['friːzɪŋ] *adj*: **It's freezing!** Il fait un froid de canard! (*informal*); **I'm freezing!** (*informal*) Je suis gelé!; **3 degrees below freezing** moins trois

freight [freɪt] *n* (*goods*) cargaison *f*; **a freight train** un train de marchandises

French [frentʃ] *adj* français *m* ▷ *a French song* une chanson en français
▶ *n* (*language*) français *m* ▷ *Do you speak French?*

Est-ce que tu parles français?; **the French** (*people*) les Français

French-Canadian [ˈfrɛntʃkəˈneɪdɪən] *adj* canadien-français (*f* canadienne-française) ▷ *a French-Canadian family* une famille canadienne-française
▶ *n* Canadien français *m*, Canadienne française *f* ▷ *She married a French-Canadian.* Elle a épousé un Canadien français.

French fries *npl* frites *fpl*

French horn *n* cor (d'harmonie) *m* ▷ *I play the French horn.* Je joue du cor.

French stick *n* baguette *f*

French toast *n* pain doré *m*

French windows *npl* porte-fenêtre *f* (*pl* portes-fenêtres)

frequent [ˈfriːkwənt] *adj* fréquent ▷ *frequent showers* des averses fréquentes; **There are frequent buses to the town centre.** Il y a beaucoup d'autobus pour le centre-ville; **He's a frequent visitor here.** C'est un habitué ici.

fresh [frɛʃ] *adj* frais (*f* fraîche); **I need some fresh air.** J'ai besoin de prendre l'air.

fret [frɛt] *vb* se tracasser ▷ *He was fretting about his exams.* Il se tracassait au sujet de ses examens.

Friday [ˈfraɪdɪ] *n* vendredi *m* ▷ *on Friday* vendredi ▷ *on Fridays* le vendredi ▷ *every Friday* tous les vendredis ▷ *last Friday* vendredi dernier ▷ *next Friday* vendredi prochain

fridge [frɪdʒ] *n* frigo *m*

fried [fraɪd] *adj* frit ▷ *fried mushrooms* des champignons frits; **a fried egg** un œuf sur le plat

friend [frɛnd] *n* ami *m*, amie *f*

friendly [ˈfrɛndlɪ] *adj* ❶ gentil (*f* gentille) ▷ *She's really friendly.* Elle est vraiment gentille. ❷ accueillant ▷ *Kitchener is a very friendly city.* Kitchener est une ville très accueillante.

friendship [ˈfrɛndʃɪp] *n* amitié *f*

fries [fraɪz] *npl* frites *f*

fright [fraɪt] *n* peur *f* ▷ *I got a terrible fright!* Ça m'a fait une peur terrible!

frighten [ˈfraɪtn] *vb* faire peur à ▷ *Horror films frighten him.* Les films d'horreur lui font peur.

frightening [ˈfraɪtnɪŋ] *adj* effrayant

fringe [frɪndʒ] *n* (*on rug, clothing*) frange *f*

Frisbee® [ˈfrɪzbɪ] *n* Frisbee® *m* ▷ *to play Frisbee* jouer au Frisbee

fro [frəu] *adv*: **to go to and fro** aller et venir

frog [frɔg] *n* grenouille *f*

from [frɔm] *prep* de ▷ *Where do you come from? D'où venez-vous?* ▷ *I come from Cape Breton Island.* Je viens de l'île du Cap-Breton. ▷ *a letter from my sister* une lettre de ma sœur ▷ *The hotel is one kilometre from the beach.* L'hôtel est à un kilomètre de la plage.; **from ... to ...** de ... à ... ▷ *He drove from Lethbridge to Swift Current.* Il a conduit de Lethbridge à Swift Current. ▷ *from 1 o'clock to 2* d'une heure à deux heures ▷ *The price was reduced from $10 to $5.* Ils ont réduit le prix de dix dollars à cinq.; **from ... onwards** à partir de... ▷ *We'll be at home from 7 o'clock onwards.* Nous serons chez nous à partir de sept heures.

front [frʌnt] *n* ❶ devant *m* ▷ *the front of the house* le devant de la maison.; **in front** devant

m ▷ *a house with a car in front* une maison avec une voiture devant ▷ *the car in front* la voiture de devant; **in front of** devant ▷ *in front of the house* devant la maison ▷ *the car in front of us* la voiture devant nous; **in the front** (*of car*) à l'avant ▷ *I was sitting in the front.* J'étais assis à l'avant.; **at the front of the class** à l'avant de la classe ❷ (*of body*) ventre *m* ▷ *to lie on one's front* se coucher sur le ventre
▶ *adj* ❶ de devant ▷ *the front row* la rangée de devant ❷ avant ▷ *the front seats of the car* les sièges avant de la voiture; **the front door** la porte d'entrée

frontier [ˈfrʌntɪə*r*] *n* frontière *f*

frost [frɔst] *n* gel *m*

frosting [ˈfrɔstɪŋ] *n* glaçage *m*

frosty [ˈfrɔstɪ] *adj*: **It's frosty today.** Il gèle aujourd'hui.

frown [fraun] *vb* froncer les sourcils ▷ *He frowned.* Il a froncé les sourcils.

froze [frəuz] *vb see* **freeze**

frozen [ˈfrəuzn] *adj* ❶ gelé ▷ *the frozen pond* l'étang gelé ❷ (*food*) congelé ▷ *frozen vegetables* des légumes congelés

fruit [fruːt] *n* fruit *m*; **fruit juice** le jus de fruits; **a fruit salad** une salade de fruits

frustrated [frʌsˈtreɪtɪd] *adj* frustré

fry [fraɪ] *vb* faire frire ▷ *Fry the onions for 5 minutes.* Faites frire les oignons pendant cinq minutes.

frying pan [ˈfraɪɪŋ-] *n* poêle *f*

fudge [fʌdʒ] *n* fudge *m*

fuel [fjuəl] *n* (*for car, plane*) carburant *m* ▷ *to run out of fuel* avoir une panne de carburant

fuel-efficient [fjuəlɪˈfɪʃənt] *adj* économique

fulfill [fulˈfɪl] *vb* réaliser ▷ *He fulfilled his dream to visit China.* Il a réalisé son rêve de visiter la Chine.

full [ful] *adj, adv* ❶ plein ▷ *The tank's full.* Le réservoir est plein. ❷ complet (*f* complète) ▷ *She asked for full information on the job.* Elle a demandé des renseignements complets sur le poste.; **your full name** vos nom et prénoms ▷ *My full name is Ian John Marr.* Je m'appelle Ian John Marr.; **I'm full.** (*after meal*) J'ai bien mangé.; **at full speed** à toute vitesse ▷ *She drove at full speed.* Elle conduisait à toute vitesse.; **There was a full moon.** C'était la pleine lune.; **a full house** (*for performance*) une salle comble

full-time [ˈfulˈtaɪm] *adj, adv* à plein temps ▷ *She has a full-time job.* Elle a un travail à plein temps. ▷ *She works full-time.* Elle travaille à plein temps.

fully [ˈfulɪ] *adv* complètement ▷ *He hasn't fully recovered from his illness.* Il n'est pas complètement remis de sa maladie.

fumes [fjuːmz] *npl* fumées *fpl* ▷ *The factory gave out dangerous fumes.* L'usine rejetait des fumées dangereuses.; **exhaust fumes** les gaz d'échappement

fun [fʌn] *adj* amusant ▷ *This is a fun book.* Ce livre est très amusant.; **She's a fun person.** On s'amuse bien avec elle.
▶ *n*: **to have fun** s'amuser ▷ *We had a lot of fun playing in the snow.* Nous nous sommes

bien amusés à jouer dans la neige.; **for fun** pour rire ▷ *He entered the competition just for fun.* Il a participé à la compétition juste pour rire.; **to make fun of somebody** se moquer de quelqu'un ▷ *They made fun of her.* Ils se sont moqués d'elle.; **It's fun!** C'est amusant!; **Have fun!** Amuse-toi bien!

funds [fʌndz] *npl* fonds *mpl* ▷ *to raise funds* collecter des fonds

funeral ['fjuːnərəl] *n* funérailles *fpl*; **funeral home** le salon funéraire

funny ['fʌnɪ] *adj* ❶ *(amusing)* drôle ▷ *It was really funny.* C'était vraiment drôle. ❷ *(strange)* bizarre ▷ *There's something funny about him.* Il est un peu bizarre.; **to taste funny** avoir un drôle de goût

fur [fɜːʳ] *n* ❶ fourrure *f* ▷ *a fur coat* un manteau de fourrure ❷ poil *m* ▷ *the dog's fur* le poil du chien

furious ['fjuərɪəs] *adj* furieux *(f* furieuse*)* ▷ *Dad was furious with me.* Papa était furieux contre moi.

furniture ['fɜːnɪtʃəʳ] *n* meubles *mpl* ▷ *a piece of furniture* un meuble; **to be part of the furniture** faire parti du décor

further ['fɜːðəʳ] *adv, adj* plus loin ▷ *Moncton is further from Halifax than Truro is.* Moncton est plus loin de Halifax que Truro.; **How much further is it?** C'est encore loin?

fuse [fjuːz] *n* fusible *m* ▷ *The fuse has blown.* Le fusible a sauté.

fuss [fʌs] *n* agitation *f* ▷ *What's all the fuss about?* Qu'est-ce que c'est que toute cette agitation?; **to make a fuss** faire des histoires ▷ *He's always making a fuss about nothing.* Il fait toujours des histoires pour rien.

fussy ['fʌsɪ] *adj* difficile ▷ *She is very fussy about her food.* Elle est très difficile sur la nourriture.

future ['fjuːtʃəʳ] *n* ❶ avenir *m* ▷ *What are your plans for the future?* Quels sont vos projets pour l'avenir?; **in future** à l'avenir ▷ *Be more careful in future.* Sois plus prudent à l'avenir. ❷ *(in grammar)* futur *m* ▷ *Put this sentence into the future.* Mettez cette phrase au futur.

futuristic [fjuːtʃə'rɪstɪk] *adj* futuriste

g

gadget ['gædʒɪt] *n* gadget *m* ▷ *electronic gadgets* les gadgets électroniques

gain [geɪn] *vb* gagner; **to gain weight** prendre du poids; **to gain speed** prendre de la vitesse

gallery ['gælərɪ] *n* musée *m* ▷ *an art gallery* un musée d'art

gallop ['gæləp] *vb* galoper

gamble ['gæmbl] *vb* jouer ▷ *He gambled $100 at the casino.* Il a joué cent dollars au casino.

gambler ['gæmbləʳ] *n* joueur *m*, joueuse *f*

game [geɪm] *n* ❶ jeu *m (pl* jeux*)* ▷ *The children were playing a game.* Les enfants jouaient à un jeu. ❷ match *m* ▷ *a game of football* un match de football; **a game of cards** une partie de cartes

gang [gæŋ] *n* bande *f*

gangster ['gæŋstəʳ] *n* gangster *m*

gap [gæp] *n* ❶ trou *m* ▷ *There's a gap in the hedge.* Il y a un trou dans la haie. ❷ intervalle *m* ▷ *a gap of four years* un intervalle de quatre ans

garage ['gærɑːʒ] *n* garage *m*; **a garage sale** une vente-débarras

garbage ['gɑːbɪdʒ] *n* ordures *fpl*; **garbage can** la poubelle

garden ['gɑːdn] *n* jardin *m*

gardener ['gɑːdnəʳ] *n* jardinier *m*, jardinière *f* ▷ *He's a gardener.* Il est jardinier.

gardening ['gɑːdnɪŋ] *n* jardinage *m* ▷ *She loves gardening.* Elle aime le jardinage.

garlic ['gɑːlɪk] *n* ail *m*

garment ['gɑːmənt] *n* vêtement *m*

gas [gæs] *n* ❶ gaz *m*; **a gas stove** une cuisinière à gaz; **a gas leak** une fuite de gaz ❷ *(gasoline)* essence *f*; **to be out of gas** avoir une panne d'essence

gasoline ['gæsəliːn] *n* essence *f*

gas station *n* station-service *f*

gate [geɪt] *n* ❶ *(of garden)* grille *f* ❷ *(of field)* barrière *f* ❸ *(at airport)* porte *f*

gather ['gæðəʳ] *vb* ❶ *(assemble)* se rassembler ▷ *People gathered on Parliament Hill.* Les gens se sont rassemblés sur la Colline du Parlement. ❷ *(things)* ramasser ▷ *to gather wood for a fire* ramasser du bois à brûler ▷ *He gathered up his things and left.* Il a ramassé ses affaires et est parti.; **I gather she isn't coming.** Je crois comprendre qu'elle ne viendra pas.; **to gather dust** prendre la poussière; **to gather speed** prendre de la vitesse ▷ *The train gathered speed.* Le train a pris de la vitesse.

gave [geɪv] *vb* see **give**

gay [geɪ] *adj* homosexuel *(f* homosexuelle*)*

gaze [geɪz] *vb*: **to gaze at something** fixer quelque chose du regard ▷ *He gazed at her.* Il l'a fixée du regard.

gear [gɪəʳ] *n* ❶ *(car, bike)* vitesse *f* ▷ *in first gear* en première vitesse ▷ *to change gear* changer de vitesse ❷ matériel *m* ▷ *camping gear* le matériel de camping

gearshift ['gɪəʃɪft] *n* levier de vitesse *m*

geese [giːs] *npl* see **goose**

gel [dʒel] *n* gel *m*; **hair gel** le gel pour les cheveux

gem [dʒem] *n* pierre précieuse *f*

Gemini ['dʒemɪnaɪ] *n* Gémeaux *mpl* ▷ *I'm a Gemini.* Je suis Gémeaux.

gender ['dʒendəʳ] *n* ❶ *(of person)* sexe *m* ❷ *(of noun)* genre *m*

gene [dʒiːn] *n* gène *m*

general ['dʒenərəl] *adj* général *(mpl* généraux*)*; **in general** en général

general election n élection f générale

general knowledge n connaissances fpl générales

generally ['dʒɛnrəlɪ] adv généralement
▷ I generally go shopping on Saturday. Généralement, je fais mon magasinage le samedi.

generation [dʒɛnə'reɪʃən] n génération f
▷ the younger generation la nouvelle génération

generator ['dʒɛnəreɪtə'] n générateur m

generous ['dʒɛnərəs] adj généreux (f généreuse) ▷ That's very generous of you. C'est très généreux de votre part.

genetic [dʒɪ'nɛtɪk] adj génétique f

genetically-modified [dʒɪ'nɛtɪklɪ'mɔdɪfaɪd] adj génétiquement modifié

genetics [dʒɪ'nɛtɪks] n génétique f

genius ['dʒiːnɪəs] n génie m ▷ She's a genius! C'est un génie!

gentle ['dʒɛntl] adj doux (f douce)

gentleman ['dʒɛntlmən] n monsieur m (pl messieurs) ▷ Good morning, gentlemen. Bonjour messieurs.

gently ['dʒɛntlɪ] adv doucement

genuine ['dʒɛnjuɪn] adj ❶ (real) véritable ▷ These are genuine diamonds. Ce sont de véritables diamants. ❷ (sincere) sincère ▷ She's a very genuine person. C'est quelqu'un de très sincère.

geography [dʒɪ'ɔgrəfɪ] n géographie f

gerbil ['dʒɜːbɪl] n gerbille f

germ [dʒəːm] n microbe m

gesture ['dʒɛstʃə'] n geste m
▶ vb: She gestured towards the door. Elle a désigné la porte d'un geste.; He gestured to us to stand up. Il nous a fait signe de nous lever.

get [gɛt] vb ❶ (have, receive) avoir ▷ I got lots of presents. J'ai eu beaucoup de cadeaux. ▷ He got first prize. Il a eu le premier prix. ▷ She got good exam results. Elle a eu de bons résultats aux examens. ▷ How many have you got? Combien en avez-vous? ❷ (fetch) aller chercher ▷ Quick, get help! Allez vite chercher de l'aide! ❸ (catch) attraper ▷ They've got the thief. Ils ont attrapé le voleur. ❹ (train, bus) prendre ▷ I'm getting the bus into town. Je prends l'autobus pour aller en ville. ❺ (understand) comprendre ▷ I don't get it. Je ne comprends pas. ❻ (go) aller ▷ How do you get to the library? Comment est-ce qu'on va à la bibliothèque? ❼ (arrive) arriver ▷ He should get here soon. Il devrait arriver bientôt. ❽ (become) devenir ▷ to get old devenir vieux; **to get along with somebody** s'entendre avec quelqu'un ▷ He doesn't get along with his parents. Il ne s'entend pas avec ses parents. ▷ We got along really well. Nous nous sommes très bien entendus.; **to get at** (1) (reach) atteindre (2) (touch) toucher à; **to get away with something** faire quelque chose impunément ▷ He got away with skipping class. Il a fait l'école buissonnière impunément.; **to get something done** faire faire quelque chose ▷ to get one's hair cut se faire couper les cheveux; **to get something for somebody** trouver quelque chose pour quelqu'un ▷ The librarian got the book for me. Le bibliothécaire m'a trouvé le livre.; **to have got to do something** devoir faire quelque chose ▷ I've got to tell him. Je dois le lui dire.; **to get away** s'échapper ▷ One of the burglars got away. L'un des cambrioleurs s'est échappé.; **to get back** (1) rentrer ▷ What time did you get back? Tu es rentrée à quelle heure? (2) récupérer ▷ He got his money back. Il a récupéré son argent.; **to get in** rentrer ▷ What time did you get in last night? Tu es rentré à quelle heure hier soir?; **to get into** monter dans ▷ She got into the car. Elle est montée dans la voiture.; **to get off** (vehicle, bike) descendre de ▷ I got off the train. Je suis descendu du train.; **to get on** (1) (vehicle) monter dans ▷ She got on the bus. Elle est montée dans l'autobus. (2) (bike) enfourcher ▷ He got on his bike. Il a enfourché son vélo.; **to get out** sortir ▷ She got out of the car. Elle est sortie de la voiture. ▷ Get out! Sortez!; **to get something out** sortir quelque chose ▷ She got the map out. Elle a sorti la carte.; **to get over** (1) se remettre ▷ It took her a long time to get over the illness. Il lui a fallu longtemps pour se remettre de sa maladie. (2) surmonter ▷ He managed to get over the problem. Il a réussi à résoudre le problème.; **to get through to someone** réussir à communiquer avec quelqu'un ▷ I tried to phone her but couldn't get through. J'ai essayé de lui téléphoner, mais je n'ai pas réussi à la joindre.; **to get together** se retrouver ▷ Could we get together this evening? Pourrait-on se retrouver ce soir?; **to get up** se lever ▷ What time do you get up? Tu te lèves à quelle heure?

ghost [gəust] n fantôme m

giant ['dʒaɪənt] adj énorme ▷ They ate a giant meal. Ils ont mangé un énorme repas.
▶ n géant m, géante f

gift [gɪft] n ❶ (present) cadeau m (pl cadeaux); **a gift certificate** un chèque-cadeau ❷ (talent) don m; **to have a gift for something** être doué pour quelque chose ▷ My brother has a gift for painting. Mon frère est doué pour la peinture.

gifted ['gɪftɪd] adj doué ▷ She is a gifted dancer. Elle est douée pour la danse.

gift shop n boutique f de cadeaux

gigabyte ['dʒɪgəbaɪt] n gigaoctet m

gigantic [dʒaɪ'gæntɪk] adj gigantesque

giggle ['gɪgl] vb avoir le fou rire ▷ Every time I look at her, she giggles. Chaque fois que je la regarde, elle a le fou rire.

ginger ['dʒɪndʒə'] n gingembre m ▷ Add a teaspoon of ginger. Ajoutez une cuillère à café de gingembre.

giraffe [dʒɪ'rɑːf] n girafe f

girl [gəːl] n ❶ fille f ▷ They have a girl and two boys. Ils ont une fille et deux garçons. ❷ (young) petite fille f ▷ a five-year-old girl une petite fille de cinq ans ❸ (older) jeune fille f ▷ a sixteen-year-old girl une jeune fille de seize ans ▷ a Canadian girl une jeune Canadienne

girlfriend ['gəːlfrɛnd] n ❶ (romantic) copine f ▷ His girlfriend's name is Justine. Sa copine s'appelle Justine. ❷ (friend) amie f ▷ She often went out with her girlfriends. Elle sortait souvent avec ses amies.

give [gɪv] vb donner; **to give something to somebody** donner quelque chose à quelqu'un ▷ He gave me $10. Il m'a donné dix dollars.; **to give something back to somebody** rendre quelque chose à quelqu'un ▷ I gave the book back to her. Je lui ai rendu le livre.; **to give something out** distribuer quelque chose ▷ The teacher gave out the books. Le professeur a distribué les livres.; **to give in** céder ▷ Her Mom gave in and let her go out. Sa mère a cédé et l'a laissée sortir.; **to give out** distribuer ▷ He gave out the exam papers. Il a distribué les feuilles d'examen.; **to give up** laisser tomber ▷ I couldn't do it, so I gave up. Je n'arrivais pas à le faire, alors j'ai laissé tomber.; **to give up doing something** arrêter de faire quelque chose ▷ She gave up smoking. Elle a arrêté de fumer.; **to give oneself up** se rendre ▷ The thief gave himself up. Le voleur s'est rendu.; **to give way** s'effondrer ▷ The floor gave way under our feet. Le plancher s'est effondré sous nos pieds.

glacier ['glæsɪə^r] n glacier m

glad [glæd] adj content ▷ She's glad she did it. Elle est contente de l'avoir fait.

glamorous ['glæmərəs] adj ❶ (person) glamour ▷ She's very glamorous. Elle est très glamour. ❷ (job) prestigieux (f prestigieuse); **to have a glamorous lifestyle** vivre comme une star

glance [glɑːns] vb: **to glance at something** jeter un coup d'œil à quelque chose ▷ She glanced at her watch. Elle a jeté un coup d'œil à sa montre.
▷ n coup d'œil m ▷ **at first glance** au premier coup d'œil

glare [glɛə^r] vb: **to glare at somebody** lancer un regard furieux à quelqu'un ▷ He glared at me. Il m'a lancé un regard furieux.

glaring ['glɛərɪŋ] adj: **a glaring mistake** une erreur qui saute aux yeux

glass [glɑːs] n verre m ▷ **a glass of milk** un verre de lait

glasses ['glɑːsɪz] npl lunettes fpl ▷ My dad wears glasses. Mon père porte des lunettes.

glide [glaɪd] vb ❶ glisser ▷ The sled glided across the snow. Le traîneau glissait sur la neige. ❷ planer ▷ A bird glided through the air. Un oiseau planait dans l'air.

glider ['glaɪdə^r] n planeur m

gliding ['glaɪdɪŋ] n vol à voile m ▷ My hobby is gliding. Je fais du vol à voile.

global ['gləʊbl] adj mondial (mpl mondiaux); **on a global scale** à l'échelle mondiale

global warming [-'wɔːmɪŋ] n réchauffement de la planète m

globe [gləʊb] n globe m

gloomy ['gluːmɪ] adj ❶ morose ▷ She's been feeling very gloomy recently. Elle se sent très morose ces derniers temps. ❷ lugubre ▷ They live in a small gloomy apartment. Ils habitent un petit appartement lugubre.

glorious ['glɔːrɪəs] adj magnifique

glove [glʌv] n gant m

glove compartment n boîte à gants f

glue [gluː] n colle f
▷ vb coller

GM adj (= genetically modified) génétiquement modifié ▷ GM foods les aliments génétiquement modifiés m

GMO abbr (= genetially-modified organism) OGM m (= l'organisme génétiquement modifié)

go [gəʊ] vb ❶ aller ▷ I'm going to the movies tonight. Je vais au cinéma ce soir. ❷ (leave) partir ▷ "Where's your friend?" — "He's gone." « Où est ton ami? » — « Il est parti. » ❸ (go away) s'en aller ▷ I'm going now. Je m'en vais. ❹ (vehicle) marcher ▷ My car won't go. Ma voiture ne marche pas.; **a hamburger to go** un hamburger à emporter; **how to go about something** comment s'y prendre pour faire quelque chose ▷ I don't know how to go about it. Je ne sais pas m'y prendre.; **to go home** rentrer à la maison ▷ I go home at about 4 o'clock. Je rentre à la maison vers quatre heures.; **to go for a walk** aller se promener ▷ Shall we go for a walk? Si on allait se promener?; **to go through with something** mettre quelque chose à exécution; **to let go of something** lâcher quelque chose; **How did it go?** Comment est-ce que ça s'est passé?; **I'm going to do it tomorrow.** Je vais le faire demain.; **It's going to be difficult.** Ça va être difficile.

go after vb suivre ▷ Quick, go after them! Vite, suivez-les!

go ahead vb: **The play will go ahead as planned.** La pièce aura bien lieu comme prévu.; **Let's go ahead with your plan.** Mettons votre projet à exécution.; **Go ahead!** Vas-y!

go around vb ❶ (turn) tourner ▷ Do the wheels really go around? Est-ce que les roues tournent vraiment? ❷ tourner autour de ▷ The earth goes around the sun. La terre tourne autour du soleil.; **to go around a corner** prendre un tournant; **to go around the shops** faire les boutiques; **There's a bug going around.** Il y a un microbe qui circule.

go away vb s'en aller ▷ Go away! Allez-vous-en!

go back vb ❶ retourner ▷ We went back to the same place. Nous sommes retournés au même endroit. ❷ rentrer ▷ "Is she still here?" — "No, she's gone back home." « Est-ce qu'elle est encore là? » — « Non, elle est rentrée chez elle. »

go by vb passer ▷ Two police officers went by. Deux policiers sont passés.

go down vb ❶ (person) descendre ▷ to go down the stairs descendre l'escalier ❷ (decrease) baisser ▷ The price of computers has gone down. Le prix des ordinateurs a baissé. ❸ (deflate) se dégonfler ▷ My airbed kept going down. Mon matelas gonflant se dégonflait constamment.

go for vb (attack) attaquer ▷ Suddenly the dog went for me. Soudain, le chien m'a attaqué.; **Go for it!** (go on!) Vas-y, fonce!

go in vb entrer ▷ She knocked on the door and went in. Elle a frappé à la porte et elle est entrée.

go off vb ❶ (bomb) exploser ▷ The bomb went off. La bombe a explosé. ❷ (alarm, gun) se déclencher ▷ The fire alarm went off. L'avertisseur d'incendie s'est déclenché.

❸ (alarm clock) sonner ▷ My alarm clock goes off at seven every morning. Mon réveil sonne à sept heures tous les matins. ❹ (food) surir ▷ The milk's gone off. Le lait a suri. ❺ (go away) partir ▷ He went off in a huff. Il est parti de mauvaise humeur.

go on vb ❶ (happen) se passer ▷ What's going on? Qu'est-ce qui se passe? ❷ (carry on) continuer ▷ The concert went on until 11 o'clock at night. Le concert a continué jusqu'à onze heures du soir. ❸ Go on to the next question. Passe à la prochaine question.; **to go on doing something** continuer à faire quelque chose ▷ She went on reading. Elle a continué à lire.; **Go on!** Allez! ▷ Go on, tell me what the problem is! Allez, dis-moi quel est le problème!

go out vb ❶ (person) sortir ▷ Are you going out tonight? Tu sors ce soir?; **to go out with somebody** sortir avec quelqu'un ▷ Are you going out with him? Est-ce que tu sors avec lui? ❷ (light, fire, candle) s'éteindre ▷ Suddenly the lights went out. Soudain, les lumières se sont éteintes.

go past vb: **to go past something** passer devant quelque chose ▷ He went past the store. Il est passé devant le magasin.

go through vb traverser ▷ We went through Manitoba to get to Saskatchewan. Nous avons traversé Manitoba pour aller à Saskatchewan.

go up vb ❶ (person) monter ▷ to go up the stairs monter l'escalier ❷ (increase) augmenter ▷ The price has gone up. Le prix a augmenté.; **to go up in flames** s'embraser ▷ The whole factory went up in flames. L'usine toute entière s'est embrasée.

go with vb aller avec ▷ Does this blouse go with that skirt? Est-ce que ce chemisier va avec cette jupe?

goal [goul] n but m ▷ to score a goal marquer un but ▷ His goal is to become the world champion. Son but est de devenir champion du monde.

goalkeeper ['goulki:pəʳ] n gardien de but m, gardienne de but f

goat [gəut] n chèvre f; **goat cheese** le fromage de chèvre

god [gɔd] n dieu m (pl dieux) ▷ I believe in God. Je crois en Dieu.

goddess ['gɔdɪs] n déesse f

goggles ['gɔglz] npl ❶ (of welder, mechanic etc) lunettes fpl de protection ❷ (of swimmer) lunettes fpl de natation

gold [gəuld] n or m ▷ They found some gold. Ils ont trouvé de l'or. ▷ a gold necklace un collier en or

goldfish ['gəuldfɪʃ] n poisson rouge m ▷ I've got five goldfish. J'ai cinq poissons rouges.

gold-plated ['gəuld'pleɪtɪd] adj plaqué or (f plaquée or)

golf [gɔlf] n golf m ▷ My mom plays golf. Ma mère joue au golf.; a golf club un club de golf; **a golf course** un terrain de golf

gone [gɔn] vb see **go**

good [gud] adj ❶ bon (f bonne) ▷ It's a very good movie. C'est un très bon film. ▷ Vegetables are good for you. Les légumes sont bons pour la santé.; **to be good at something** être bon

en quelque chose ▷ Jane's very good at soccer. Jane est très bonne en soccer. ❷ (kind) gentil (f gentille) ▷ They were very good to me. Ils ont été très gentils avec moi. ▷ That's very good of you. C'est très gentil de votre part. ❸ (not naughty) sage ▷ Be good! Sois sage!; **for good** pour de bon ▷ One day he left for good. Un jour il est parti pour de bon.; **Good morning!** Bonjour!; **Good afternoon!** Bonjour!; **Good evening!** Bonsoir!; **Good night!** Bonne nuit!; **It's no good complaining.** Cela ne sert à rien de se plaindre.

goodbye [gud'baɪ] excl au revoir!

Good Friday n Vendredi saint m

good-looking ['gud'lukɪŋ] adj beau (also bel, f belle, mpl beaux) ▷ He's very good-looking. Il est très beau. ▷ Who's your good-looking friend? Qui est ton bel ami?

good-natured ['gud'neɪtʃəd] adj (person) facile à vivre

goods [gudz] npl (in store) marchandises fpl

goose [gu:s] n oie f

gooseberry ['guzbəri] n groseille à maquereau f

gopher ['gəufəʳ] n spermophile m

gorgeous ['gɔ:dʒəs] adj ❶ superbe ▷ She's gorgeous! Elle est superbe! ❷ splendide ▷ The weather was gorgeous. Il a fait un temps splendide.

gorilla [gə'rɪlə] n gorille m

gospel ['gɔspl] n (music) gospel m

gossip ['gɔsɪp] n ❶ (rumours) cancans mpl ▷ Tell me the gossip! Raconte-moi les cancans! ❷ (woman) commère f ▷ She's such a gossip! C'est une vraie commère! ❸ (man) bavard m ▷ What a gossip! Quel bavard!
▶ vb ❶ (chat) bavarder ▷ They were always gossiping. Ils étaient tout le temps en train de bavarder. ❷ (about somebody) faire des commérages ▷ They gossiped about him. Elles faisaient des commérages à son sujet.

got [gɔt] vb see **get**

gotten ['gɔtn] vb see **get**

government ['gʌvnmənt] n gouvernement m

Governor General ['gʌvənəʳ-] n gouverneur général m, gouverneure générale f

GP n (= General Practitioner) omnipraticien m, omnipraticienne f

grab [græb] vb saisir

graceful ['greɪsful] adj élégant

grade [greɪd] n (at school) note f ▷ I got good grades this year. J'ai eu de bonnes notes cette année.

grade school n école f élémentaire

gradual ['grædjuəl] adj progressif (f progressive)

gradually ['grædjuəli] adv peu à peu ▷ We gradually got used to it. Nous nous y sommes habitués peu à peu.

graduate ['grædjuert] n ❶ (from university) diplômé m, diplômée f ❷ (from high school) finissant m, finissante f
▶ vb ❶ (from high school) obtenir son diplôme ❷ (from university) obtenir son baccalauréat

graduation party [grædju'eɪʃən-] n bal des

finissants *m*

graffiti [grəˈfiːtɪ] *npl* graffiti *mpl*

grain [greɪn] *n* ❶ (*of salt, sand*) grain *m* ❸ céréales *fpl* ▷ *wheat and other grains* le blé et d'autres céréales ▷ *Grains are essential to a healthy diet.* Les céréales sont essentielles pour une alimentation saine.

gram [græm] *n* gramme *m*

grammar [ˈgræmər] *n* grammaire *f*

grammatical [grəˈmætɪkl] *adj* grammatical (*mpl* grammaticaux)

grand [grænd] *adj* somptueux (*f* somptueuse) ▷ *She lives in a very grand house.* Elle habite une maison somptueuse.; **a grand piano** un piano à queue

grandchild [ˈgræntʃaɪld] *n* petit-fils *m*, petite-fille *f*; **my grandchildren** mes *m* petits-enfants

granddaughter [ˈgrændɔːtər] *n* petite-fille *f* (*pl* petites-filles)

grandfather [ˈgrændfɑːðər] *n* grand-père *m* (*pl* grands-pères) ▷ *my grandfather* mon grand-père

grandmother [ˈgrænmʌðər] *n* grand-mère *f* (*pl* grands-mères) ▷ *my grandmother* ma grand-mère

grandparents [ˈgrændpɛərənts] *npl* grands-parents *mpl* ▷ *my grandparents* mes grands-parents

grandson [ˈgrænsʌn] *n* petit-fils *m* (*pl* petits-fils)

grant [grɑːnt] *vb* ❶ (*give*) accorder ▷ *to grant political asylum* accorder l'asile politique ❷ (*say yes to*) accepter ▷ *They granted our request.* Ils ont accepté notre requête.

grape [greɪp] *n* (*single grape*) grain de raisin *m*; **grapes** le raisin ▷ *a bunch of grapes* une grappe de raisin ▷ *I ate some grapes.* J'ai mangé du raisin.; **grape-flavoured** à saveur du raisin

grapefruit [ˈgreɪpfruːt] *n* pamplemousse *m*

graph [grɑːf] *n* graphique *m*

graphic organizer [ˈgræfɪkˈɔːɡənaɪzər] *n* organisateur *m* graphique

graphics [ˈgræfɪks] *npl* images *fpl* de synthèse ▷ *I designed the graphics and she wrote the text.* J'ai conçu les images de synthèse et elle a écrit le texte.; **He works in computer graphics.** Il fait de l'infographie.

grasp [grɑːsp] *vb* saisir

grass [grɑːs] *n* herbe *f* ▷ *The grass is long.* L'herbe est haute.; **to cut the grass** tondre le gazon

grasshopper [ˈgrɑːshɔpər] *n* sauterelle *f*

grate [greɪt] *vb* râper ▷ *to grate some cheese* râper du fromage

grateful [ˈgreɪtful] *adj* reconnaissant ▷ *We are grateful for your help.* Nous sommes reconnaissants de votre aide.

grater [ˈgreɪtər] *n* râpe *f* ▷ *a cheese grater* une râpe à fromage

grave [greɪv] *n* tombe *f*

gravel [ˈgrævl] *n* gravier *m*

graveyard [ˈgreɪvjɑːd] *n* cimetière *m*

gravy [ˈgreɪvɪ] *n* sauce *f*

grease [griːs] *n* ❶ (*cooking*) graisse *f* ❸ (*engine*) lubrifiant *m*

greasy [ˈgriːsɪ] *adj* gras (*f* grasse) ▷ *I have*

greasy hair. J'ai les cheveux gras. ▷ *The food was very greasy.* La nourriture était très grasse.

great [greɪt] *adj* ❶ génial (*mpl* géniaux) ▷ *That's great!* C'est génial! ❷ grand ▷ *a great event* un grand événement; **Greater Vancouver** l'agglomération *f* de Vancouver

great-grandfather [greɪtˈgrænfɑːðər] *n* arrière-grand-père *m* (*pl* arrière-grands-pères)

great-grandmother [greɪtˈgrænmʌðər] *n* arrière-grand-mère *f* (*pl* arrière-grands-mères)

Great Lakes *n* Grands *mpl* Lacs

greedy [ˈgriːdɪ] *adj* ❶ (*for food*) gourmand ▷ *"I want some more cake." — "Don't be so greedy!"* « Je veux encore du gâteau. » — « Ne sois pas si gourmand! » ❷ (*for money*) avide

green [griːn] *adj* ❶ vert *m* ▷ *a green car* une voiture verte ▷ *a green light* un feu vert ▷ *a green salad* une salade verte ❷ (*movement, candidate*) écologiste ▷ *the Green Party* le parti écologiste ▶ *n* vert *m* ▷ *a dark green* un vert foncé; **greens** (*vegetables*) les légumes verts

greenhouse [ˈgriːnhaus] *n* serre *f*; **the greenhouse effect** l'effet *m* de serre

greet [griːt] *vb* accueillir ▷ *He greeted me with a kiss.* Il m'a accueilli en me donnant un baiser.

greeting [ˈgriːtɪŋ] *n*: **Greetings from Bangor!** Bonjour de Bangor!; **"Season's greetings"** "Meilleurs vœux pour les fêtes de fin d'année"

greeting card *n* carte de vœux *f*

grew [gruː] *vb see* **grow**

grey [greɪ] *adj* gris ▷ *She has grey hair.* Elle a les cheveux gris.; **He's going grey.** Il grisonne.

grey-haired [greɪˈhɛəd] *adj* grisonnant

grief [griːf] *n* chagrin *m*

grill [grɪl] *n* (*for food*) gril *m*; **a mixed grill** les *f* grillades ▶ *vb*: **to grill something** faire griller quelque chose; **grilled chicken** du poulet grillé

grim [grɪm] *adj* sinistre

grin [grɪn] *vb* sourire ▷ *He grinned at me.* Il m'a souri. ▶ *n* large sourire *m*

grind [graɪnd] *vb* (*coffee, pepper*) moudre

grip [grɪp] *vb* saisir

gripping [ˈgrɪpɪŋ] *adj* (*exciting*) palpitant

grizzly bear [ˈgrɪzlɪ-] *n* grizzly *m*

groan [grəun] *vb* gémir ▷ *She groaned with pain.* Elle a gémi sous l'effet de la douleur. ▶ *n* (*of pain*) gémissement *m*

groceries [ˈgrəusərɪz] *npl* épicerie *f* ▷ *Would you put the groceries in the cupboard, please?* Pourrais-tu ranger l'épicerie dans l'armoire, s'il te plaît?

grocery store [ˈgrəusərɪ-] *n* épicerie *f*

groom [gruːm] *n* (*bridegroom*) marié *m* ▷ *the groom and his best man* le marié et son témoin

grope [grəup] *vb*: **to grope for something** chercher quelque chose à tâtons ▷ *She groped for the light switch.* Elle a cherché à tâtons l'interrupteur.

gross [grəus] *adj* (*revolting*) dégoûtant ▷ *It was really gross!* C'était vraiment dégoûtant!

grossly [ˈgrəuslɪ] *adv* largement ▷ *They're grossly underpaid.* Ils sont largement sous-payés.

ground [graund] *n* ❶ (*earth*) sol *m* ▷ *The*

ground's wet. Le sol est mouillé. ❷ *(reason)*
raison f ▷ *We have grounds for complaint.* Nous
avons des raisons de nous plaindre.; **on the
ground** par terre ▷ *We sat on the ground.* Nous
nous sommes assis par terre.
▶ *vb see* **grind; ground coffee** le café moulu

ground floor n premier étage m; **on the
ground floor** au rez-de-chaussée

groundhog ['graʊndhɒg] n marmotte
commune f ▷ *Groundhog Day* le jour de la
marmotte

group [gruːp] n groupe m; **a group home** un
foyer de groupe

grow [grəʊ] vb ❶ *(plant)* pousser ▷ *Grass grows
quickly.* L'herbe pousse vite. ❷ *(person, animal)*
grandir ▷ *Haven't you grown!* Comme tu as
grandi! ❸ *(increase)* augmenter ▷ *The number
of unemployed people has grown.* Le nombre de
chômeurs a augmenté. ❹ *(cultivate)* faire
pousser ▷ *My mom grows tomatoes.* Ma mère
fait pousser des tomates.; **to grow a beard** se
laisser pousser la barbe; **to grow up** grandir
▷ *Oh, grow up!* Ne fais pas l'enfant!; **She's
grown out of her jacket.** Sa veste est devenue
trop petite pour elle.

growl [graʊl] vb grogner

grown [grəʊn] vb see **grow**

growth [grəʊθ] n croissance f ▷ *economic
growth* la croissance économique

grudge [grʌdʒ] n rancune f; **to bear a
grudge against somebody** garder rancune à
quelqu'un

gruesome ['gruːsəm] adj horrible

grumpy ['grʌmpɪ] adj ❶ marabout
m, f ▷ *They're grumpy this morning.* Elles
sont marabouts ce matin. ❷ grognon (f
grognonne)

GST n TPS f (= *taxe sur les produits et services*)

guarantee [gærən'tiː] n garantie f; **a five-
year guarantee** une garantie de cinq ans
▶ vb garantir ▷ *I can't guarantee he'll come.* Je ne
peux pas garantir qu'il viendra.

guard [gɑːd] vb garder ▷ *They guarded the
prisoner.* Ils gardaient le prisonnier.; **to guard
against something** protéger contre quelque
chose
▶ n *(person)* garde m; **to catch somebody
off guard** prendre quelqu'un au dépourvu; **a
guard dog** un chien de garde

guardian ['gɑːdɪən] n *(legal)* tuteur m, tuteur
f ▷ *The form must be signed by your parent or
guardian.* La feuille doit être signée par ton
parent ou tuteur.; **the guardians of freedom**
les gardiens de la liberté

guess [gɛs] vb deviner ▷ *Can you guess what
it is?* Devine ce que c'est!; **to guess wrong**
se tromper ▷ *She guessed wrong.* Elle s'est
trompée.
▶ n supposition f ▷ *It's just a guess.* C'est une
simple supposition.; **Take a guess!** Devine!

guest [gɛst] n ❶ invité m, invitée f ▷ *We have
guests staying with us.* Nous avons des invités.
❷ *(of hotel)* client m, cliente f

guide [gaɪd] n *(book, person)* guide m ▷ *We
bought a guide to Paris.* Nous avons acheté un
guide sur Paris. ▷ *The guide showed us around the*

museum. Le guide nous a fait visiter le musée.
▶ vb guider ▷ *She guided us through the caves.*
Elle nous a guidés à travers les cavernes. ▷ *The
guide showed us round the museum.* Le guide
nous a fait visiter le musée.

guidebook ['gaɪdbʊk] n guide m

guide dog n chien d'aveugle m

guideline ['gaɪdlaɪn] n directive f ▷ *Here
are some guidelines for your research projects.*
Voici quelques directives générales pour vos
projets de recherche.; **a rough guideline** une
indication générale

guilty ['gɪltɪ] adj coupable ▷ *to feel guilty* se
sentir coupable ▷ *She was found guilty.* Elle a été
reconnue coupable.

guinea pig ['gɪnɪ-] n cobaye m

guitar [gɪ'tɑːʳ] n guitare f ▷ *I play the guitar.* Je
joue de la guitare.

gullible ['gʌlɪbl] adj crédule

gum [gʌm] n gomme à mâcher f; **gums** (in
mouth) les gencives f

gun [gʌn] n ❶ *(small)* pistolet m ❷ *(rifle)*
fusil m

guru ['gʊruː] n gourou m

gust [gʌst] n: **a gust of wind** une rafale de vent

guy [gaɪ] n type m ▷ *Who's that guy?* C'est qui ce
type? ▷ *He's a nice guy.* C'est un type sympa.

gym [dʒɪm] n ❶ gymnase m ▷ *She goes to the
gym every day.* Elle va tous les jours au gymnase.
❷ éducation f physique

gymnast ['dʒɪmnæst] n gymnaste ▷ *She's a
gymnast.* Elle est gymnaste.

gymnastics [dʒɪm'næstɪks] n gymnastique f
▷ *to do gymnastics* faire de la gymnastique

h

habit ['hæbɪt] n habitude f ▷ *a bad habit* une
mauvaise habitude

hack [hæk] vb: **to hack into a system**
s'introduire dans un système

hacker ['hækəʳ] n pirate informatique

had [hæd] vb see **have**

hadn't ['hædnt]; = **had not**

hail [heɪl] n grêle f
▶ vb grêler ▷ *It's hailing.* Il grêle.

hair [hɛəʳ] n cheveux mpl ▷ *She has long hair.*
Elle a les cheveux longs. ▷ *He has black hair.* Il a
les cheveux noirs. ▷ *He's losing his hair.* Il perd
ses cheveux.; **to brush one's hair** se brosser
les cheveux ▷ *I'm brushing my hair.* Je me brosse
les cheveux.; **to wash one's hair** se laver les
cheveux ▷ *I need to wash my hair.* Il faut que je

me lave les cheveux.; **to have one's hair cut** se faire couper les cheveux ▷ *I've just had my hair cut.* Je viens de me faire couper les cheveux.; **a hair (1)** *(from head)* un cheveu **(2)** *(from body)* un poil **③** *(fur of animal)* pelage *m*

hairbrush ['hɛəbrʌʃ] *n* brosse à cheveux *f*

hair clip *n* la pince à cheveux

haircut ['hɛəkʌt] *n* coupe de cheveux *f*; **to have a haircut** se faire couper les cheveux ▷ *I've just had a haircut.* Je viens de me faire couper les cheveux.

hairdresser ['hɛədrɛsə'] *n* coiffeur *m*, coiffeuse *f* ▷ *She's a hairdresser.* Elle est coiffeuse. ▷ *at the hairdresser's* chez le coiffeur

hair gel *n* gel pour les cheveux *m*

hair spray *n* laque *f*

hairstyle ['hɛəstaɪl] *n* coiffure *f*

hairy ['hɛərɪ] *adj* poilu ▷ *hairy legs* les jambes poilues

half [hɑːf] *n* moitié *f* ▷ *half of the cake* la moitié du gâteau; **two and a half** deux et demi; **half an hour** une demi-heure; **half past ten** dix heures et demie; **half a kilo** cinq cents grammes; **to cut something in half** couper quelque chose en deux
▶ *adj, adv* **①** demi ▷ *a half chicken* un demi-poulet **②** à moitié ▷ *He was half asleep.* Il était à moitié endormi.

half-brother ['hɑːfbrʌðə'] *n* demi-frère *m*

half-hour ['hɑːf'aʊə'] *n* demi-heure *f*

half-price ['hɑːf'praɪs] *adj, adv*: **at half-price** à moitié prix

half-sister ['hɑːf'sɪstə'] *n* demi-sœur *f*

half-time ['hɑːf'taɪm] *n* mi-temps *f* ▷ *The score at half-time was 6-4.* Le pointage à mi-temps était 6-4.

halfway ['hɑːf'weɪ] *adv* **①** à mi-chemin ▷ *halfway between Sudbury and Kenora* à mi-chemin entre Sudbury et Kenora; **a halfway house** une maison de transition **②** à la moitié ▷ *halfway through the chapter* à la moitié du chapitre

hall [hɔːl] *n* **①** *(hallway)* couloir *m* **②** *(large room)* salle *f* ▷ *the community hall* la salle communautaire

Halloween [hæləʊ'iːn] *n* Halloween *f*

hallway ['hɔːlweɪ] *n* vestibule *m*

ham [hæm] *n* jambon *m*; **a ham sandwich** un sandwich au jambon

hamburger ['hæmbɜːgə'] *n* **①** hamburger *m* **②** *(meat)* le bœuf haché

hammer ['hæmə'] *n* marteau *m* *(pl* marteaux*)*

hamster ['hæmstə'] *n* hamster *m*

hand [hænd] *n* **①** *(of person)* main *f*; **by hand** à la main; **to give somebody a hand (1)** *(help)* donner un coup de main à quelqu'un ▷ *Can you give me a hand?* Tu peux me donner un coup de main? **(2)** *(applaud)* applaudir quelqu'un; **on the one hand..., on the other hand...** d'une part..., d'autre part... **②** *(of clock)* aiguille *f*
▶ *vb* passer ▷ *He handed me the book.* Il m'a passé le livre.; **to hand something in** rendre quelque chose ▷ *She handed her exam paper in.* Elle a rendu sa copie d'examen.; **to hand something out** distribuer quelque chose ▷ *The teacher handed out the books.* Le professeur a

distribué les livres.; **to hand something over** remettre quelque chose ▷ *She handed the keys over to me.* Elle m'a remis les clés.

handball ['hændbɔːl] *n* **①** *(game)* handball *m*; **to play handball** jouer au handball

handbook ['hændbʊk] *n* manuel *m*

handcuffs ['hændkʌfs] *npl* menottes *f*

handful ['hændfʊl] *n* la poignée ▷ *a handful of popcorn* une poignée de maïs soufflé

handheld ['hædhɛld] *adj* de poche ▷ *a handheld computer* un ordinateur de poche

handkerchief ['hæŋkətʃɪf] *n* mouchoir *m*

handle ['hændl] *n* **①** *(of door)* poignée *f* **②** *(of cup)* anse *f* **③** *(of knife)* manche *m* **④** *(of saucepan)* queue *f*
▶ *vb* **①** *(use, control)* manœuvrer ▷ *to handle a canoe* manœuvrer un canot **②** *(touch)* toucher à ▷ *Don't handle the fruit.* Ne touche pas aux fruits.; **He handled it well.** Il s'en est bien tiré.; **The teacher handled the travel arrangements.** La professeure s'est occupée de l'organisation du voyage.; **She knows how to handle children.** Elle sait bien s'y prendre avec les enfants.

handlebars ['hændlbɑːz] *npl* guidon *m*

handmade ['hænd'meɪd] *adj* fait à la main

hands-free [hændz'friː] *adj* mains libres *(f+pl* mains libres*)* ▷ *a hands-free phone* un téléphone mains libres

handsome ['hænsəm] *adj* beau *(f* belle*)* ▷ *He's handsome.* Il est beau. ▷ *a handsome man* un bel homme

handwriting ['hændraɪtɪŋ] *n* écriture *f*

handy ['hændɪ] *adj* **①** pratique ▷ *This knife's very handy.* Ce couteau est très pratique. **②** sous la main ▷ *Have you got a pen handy?* Est-ce que tu as un stylo sous la main?

hang [hæŋ] *vb* **①** accrocher ▷ *I hung the painting on the wall.* J'ai accroché le tableau au mur. **②** pendre ▷ *They hanged the criminal.* Ils ont pendu le criminel.; **to hang around** traîner ▷ *Let's go hang around in the park for a while.* Si on allait traîner dans le parc quelque temps?; **to hang in** ne pas lâcher ▷ *Hang in there, you're almost done!* Ne lâche pas, tu as presque fini!; **to hang on** patienter ▷ *Hang on a minute please.* Patientez une minute s'il vous plaît.; **to hang up (1)** *(clothes)* accrocher ▷ *Hang your jacket up on the hook.* Accrochez votre manteau au portemanteau. **(2)** *(phone)* raccrocher ▷ *I tried to phone her but she hung up on me.* J'ai essayé de l'appeler, mais elle m'a raccroché au nez.

hanger ['hæŋə'] *n* *(coat hanger)* cintre *m*

hang-gliding ['hæŋglaɪdɪŋ] *n* deltaplane *m*; **to go hang-gliding** faire du deltaplane

happen ['hæpən] *vb* se passer ▷ *What happened?* Qu'est-ce qui s'est passé?; **as it happens** justement ▷ *As it happens, I don't want to go.* Justement, je ne veux pas y aller.; **I happened to find 5 dollars lying in the street.** Il m'est arrivé de trouver cinq dollars dans la rue.; **Do you happen to know this neighbour?** Connaîtrais-tu ce voisin, par hasard?

happily ['hæpɪlɪ] *adv* **①** joyeusement ▷ *"Don't worry!" he said happily.* « Ne te fais pas de souci!» dit-il joyeusement. ❷ (fortunately) heureusement ▷ Happily, everything went well. Heureusement, tout s'est bien passé.

happiness ['hæpɪnəs] n bonheur m

happy ['hæpɪ] adj heureux (f heureuse) ▷ She looks happy. Elle a l'air heureuse.; **I'm very happy with your work.** Je suis très satisfait de ton travail.; **Happy birthday!** Bonne fête!

harassment ['hærəsmənt] n harcèlement m ▷ sexual harassment le harcèlement sexuel

harbour ['hɑːbər] n port m

hard [hɑːd] adj, adv ❶ dur ▷ This cheese is very hard. Ce fromage est très dur. ▷ He worked very hard. Il a travaillé très dur. ❷ difficile ▷ This question is too hard for me. Cette question est trop difficile pour moi.; **hard copy** la copie papier; **to be hard of hearing** être dur d'oreille

hard-boiled [hɑːd'bɔɪld] adj dur

hard disk n (of computer) disque dur m

hardly ['hɑːdlɪ] adv: **I've hardly got any money.** Je n'ai presque pas d'argent.; **I hardly know you.** Je te connais à peine.; **hardly ever** presque jamais

hardware ['hɑːdwɛər] n ❶ (computing) matériel m ❷ (bolts, hinges) quincaillerie f; **a hardware store** une quincaillerie

hare [hɛər] n lièvre m

harm [hɑːm] vb: **to harm somebody** faire du mal à quelqu'un ▷ I didn't mean to harm you. Je ne voulais pas te faire de mal.; **to harm something** nuire à quelque chose ▷ Chemicals harm the environment. Les produits chimiques nuisent à l'environnement.

harmful ['hɑːmful] adj nuisible ▷ harmful chemicals des produits chimiques nuisibles

harmless ['hɑːmlɪs] adj inoffensif (f inoffensive) ▷ Most spiders are harmless. La plupart des araignées sont inoffensives.

harpoon [hɑː'puːn] n harpon m

harsh [hɑːʃ] adj dur

has [hæz] vb see have

hasn't ['hæznt] = has not

hassle ['hæsl] n: **It's such a hassle.** C'est toute une affaire.; **It isn't worth the hassle.** Ça n'en vaut pas la peine.

hat [hæt] n chapeau m (pl chapeaux)

hate [heɪt] vb détester ▷ I hate math. Je déteste les maths.

hatred ['heɪtrɪd] n haine f

hat trick n tour de chapeau m

haunted ['hɔːntɪd] adj hanté; **a haunted house** une maison hantée

have [hæv] vb ❶ avoir ▷ Do you have a sister? Tu as une sœur? ▷ He has blue eyes. Il a les yeux bleus. ▷ I have a cold. J'ai un rhume. ▷ He's done it, hasn't he? Il l'a fait, non? ▷ "Have you got any money?" — "No, I haven't!" « Est-ce que tu as de l'argent? » — « Non, je n'en ai pas! » ❷ être ▷ They have arrived. Ils sont arrivés. ▷ Has she gone? Est-ce qu'elle est partie? ❸ prendre ▷ He had his breakfast. Il a pris son petit déjeuner. ▷ to have a shower prendre une douche; **to have to do something** devoir faire quelque chose ▷ She has to do it. Elle doit le faire.; **to have a party** faire une fête; **to have one's hair cut** se faire couper les cheveux; **I've had it!** J'en

ai assez!

haven't ['hævnt] = have not

hawk [hɔːk] n faucon m

hay [heɪ] n foin m

hay fever n rhume des foins m ▷ Do you get hay fever? Est-ce que vous êtes sujet au rhume des foins?

hazardous waste ['hæzədəs-] n déchets mpl dangereux

hazelnut ['heɪzlnʌt] n noisette f

he [hiː] pron il ▷ He loves dogs. Il aime les chiens.

head [hɛd] n ❶ (of person) tête f ▷ All the praise went to her head. Tous les compliments lui sont montés à la tête. ▷ I bumped my head. Je me suis cogné la tête. ❷ (leader) chef m ▷ a head of state un chef d'État ▷ She's the head of the organization. Elle est la chef de l'organisation.; **from head to toe** de la tête aux pieds; **head first** la tête la première; **Get it into your head that…** Mets-toi dans la tête que…; **to be head over heels in love with someone** être follement amoureux de quelqu'un; **to have a head for figures** être doué pour les chiffres; **"Heads or tails?" — "Heads."** « Pile ou face? » — « Face. »
▷ vb: **to head for something** se diriger vers quelque chose ▷ They headed for the church. Ils se sont dirigés vers l'église.; **Who's heading up the project?** Qui est à la tête du projet?

headache ['hɛdeɪk] n: **I've got a headache.** J'ai mal à la tête.

headlight ['hɛdlaɪt] n phare m

headline ['hɛdlaɪn] n titre m

headphones ['hɛdfəunz] npl écouteurs mpl

headquarters ['hɛdkwɔːtəz] npl (of organization) siège m

heal [hiːl] vb ❶ (person) guérir ▷ He was healed. Il a été guéri. ❷ cicatriser ▷ The wound soon healed. La blessure a vite cicatrisé.

health [hɛlθ] n santé f; **health care** les m soins de santé ▷ the Canadian health care system le système de soins canadien

healthy ['hɛlθɪ] adj ❶ (person) en bonne santé ▷ She's a healthy person. Elle est en bonne santé. ❷ (climate, food) sain ▷ a healthy diet une alimentation saine

heap [hiːp] n tas m ▷ a heap of snow un tas de neige

hear [hɪər] vb ❶ entendre ▷ He heard the dog bark. Il a entendu le chien aboyer. ▷ She can't hear very well. Elle entend mal. ▷ I heard that she was ill. J'ai entendu dire qu'elle était malade.; **to hear about something** entendre parler de quelque chose ▷ (news) apprendre ▷ Did you hear the good news? Est-ce que tu as appris la bonne nouvelle?; **to hear from somebody** avoir des nouvelles de quelqu'un ▷ I haven't heard from him recently. Je n'ai pas eu de ses nouvelles récemment.

heart [hɑːt] n cœur m; **in his heart of hearts** au fond de lui-même; **to break someone's heart** briser le cœur de quelqu'un; **to learn something by heart** apprendre quelque chose par cœur; **the ace of hearts** l'as de cœur; **with all my heart** de tout mon cœur

heart attack n crise cardiaque f

heartbroken ['hɑːtbrəukən] adj: **to be heartbroken** avoir le cœur brisé

heat [hiːt] n chaleur f
▶ vb faire chauffer ▷ Heat gently for 5 minutes. Faire chauffer à feu doux pendant cinq minutes.; **to heat up (1)** (cooked food) faire réchauffer ▷ He heated the soup up. Il a fait réchauffer la soupe. **(2)** (water, oven) chauffer ▷ The water is heating up. L'eau chauffe.

heater ['hiːtəʳ] n (car, office) chaufferette f

heating ['hiːtɪŋ] n chauffage m

heaven ['hɛvn] n paradis m

heavily ['hɛvɪlɪ] adv lourdement ▷ The car was heavily loaded. La voiture était lourdement chargée.; **heavily armed** fortement armé; **heavily made up** très maquillé; **She's heavily into jazz.** Elle est très mordue de jazz.

heavy ['hɛvɪ] adj ① lourd ▷ This bag is very heavy. Ce sac est très lourd.; **heavy rain** une grosse averse ② (busy) chargé ▷ I've got a very heavy week ahead. Je vais avoir une semaine très chargée. ③ dense ▷ heavy traffic une circulation dense ④ gros ▷ a heavy sigh un gros soupir ▷ to do the heavy work faire le gros travail

he'd [hiːd] = **he would**; **he had**

hedge [hɛdʒ] n haie f

heel [hiːl] n talon m

height [haɪt] n ① (of person) taille f ② (of object) hauteur f ③ (of mountain) altitude f; **fear of heights** le vertige

held [hɛld] vb see **hold**

helicopter ['hɛlɪkɒptəʳ] n hélicoptère m

hell [hɛl] n enfer m

he'll [hiːl] = **he will**; **he shall**

hello [hə'ləu] excl ① bonjour! ② (on phone) allô

helmet ['hɛlmɪt] n casque m

help [hɛlp] vb aider ▷ Can you help me? Est-ce que vous pouvez m'aider?; **Help!** Au secours!; **Help yourself!** Servez-vous!; **He can't help it.** Il n'y peut rien.
▶ n aide f ▷ Do you need any help? Vous avez besoin d'aide?

helpful ['hɛlpful] adj serviable ▷ She was very helpful. Elle a été très serviable.

helpline ['hɛlplaɪn] n ligne d'écoute téléphonique f

hen [hɛn] n poule f

her [həːʳ] adj son m, sa f, ses pl ▷ her father son père ▷ her mother sa mère ▷ her parents ses parents; **her friend (1)** (male) son ami **(2)** (female) son amie ▷ She's going to wash her hair. Elle va se laver les cheveux. ▷ She's brushing her teeth. Elle se brosse les dents. ▷ She hurt her foot. Elle s'est fait mal au pied.
▶ pron ① la ▷ I can see her. Je la vois. ▷ Look at her! Regarde-la! ▷ I saw her. Je l'ai vue. ② lui ▷ I gave her a book. Je lui ai donné un livre. ▷ I told her the truth. Je lui ai dit la vérité. ③ elle ▷ I'm going with her. Je vais avec elle. ▷ He sat next to her. Il s'est assis à côté d'elle. ▷ I'm older than her. Je suis plus âgé qu'elle.

herb [həːb] n herbe; **herbs** les f fines herbes ▷ What herbs do you use in this sauce? Quelles fines herbes utilise-t-on pour cette sauce?

here [hɪəʳ] adv ici ▷ I live here. J'habite ici.; **here is...** voici... ▷ Here's Mom. Voici maman. ▷ Here

he is! Le voici!; **here are...** voici... ▷ Here are the books. Voici les livres.

heritage ['hɛrɪtɪdʒ] n patrimoine m; **Heritage Day** la fête du Patrimoine

hero ['hɪərəu] n héros m ▷ He's a real hero! C'est un véritable héros!

heroine ['hɛrəuɪn] n héroïne f ▷ the heroine of the novel l'héroïne du roman

hers [həːz] pron le + m sien, la + f sienne, les + m siens, les + f siennes ▷ "Is this her coat?" — "No, hers is black." « C'est son manteau? » — « Non, le sien est noir. » ▷ "Is this her car?" — "No, hers is white." « C'est sa voiture? » — « Non, la sienne est blanche. » ▷ my parents and hers mes parents et les siens ▷ my reasons and hers mes raisons et les siennes; **Is this hers?** C'est à elle? ▷ This book is hers. Ce livre est à elle. ▷ "Whose is this?" — "It's hers." « C'est à qui? » — « À elle. »

herself [həː'sɛlf] pron ① se ▷ She's hurt herself. Elle s'est blessée. ② (after preposition) elle ▷ She talked mainly about herself. Elle a surtout parlé d'elle. ③ elle-même ▷ She did it herself. Elle l'a fait elle-même.; **by herself** toute seule ▷ She doesn't like travelling by herself. Elle n'aime pas voyager toute seule.

he's [hiːz] = **he is**; **he has**

hesitate ['hɛzɪteɪt] vb hésiter

heterosexual ['hɛtərəu'sɛksjuəl] adj hétérosexuel (hétérosexuelle)

hi [haɪ] excl salut!

hibernate ['haɪbəneɪt] vb hiberner

hiccups ['hɪkʌps] npl: **to have hiccups** avoir le hoquet

hide [haɪd] vb se cacher ▷ He hid behind a bush. Il s'est caché derrière un buisson.; **to hide something** cacher quelque chose ▷ We hid the present. Nous avons caché le cadeau.

hide-and-seek ['haɪdən'siːk] n: **to play hide-and-seek** jouer à la cachette

hideous ['hɪdɪəs] adj hideux (hideuse)

high [haɪ] adj, adv ① haut ▷ It's too high. C'est trop haut.; **How high is the wall?** Quelle est la hauteur du mur?; **The wall is 2 metres high.** Le mur fait deux mètres de haut. ② élevé ▷ a high price un prix élevé ▷ a high temperature une température élevée; **at high speed** à grande vitesse; **It's very high in fat.** C'est très gras.; **She's got a very high voice.** Elle a la voix très aiguë.

higher education ['haɪə-] n enseignement m supérieur

high heels npl chaussures f pl à talons hauts

high jump n (sport) saut en hauteur m

highlight ['haɪlaɪt] n ① clou m ▷ the highlight of the evening le clou de la soirée
▶ vb ① (emphasize) souligner ② (with highlighter pen) surligner

highlighter ['haɪlaɪtəʳ] n surligneur m

high-rise ['haɪraɪz] n tour f ▷ I live in a high-rise. Je demeure dans une tour d'habitation.

high school n école f secondaire

highsticking ['haɪstɪkɪŋ] n bâton m élevé ▷ to get a penalty for highsticking recevoir une punition pour bâton élevé

highway ['haɪweɪ] n autoroute f

hijack ['haɪdʒæk] vb détourner

hijacker ['haɪdʒækə'] n pirate de l'air
hike [haɪk] n randonnée pédestre f
hiking ['haɪkɪŋ] n: **to go hiking** faire une randonnée pédestre; **hiking boots** les f chaussures de randonnée pédestre
hilarious [hɪ'lɛərɪəs] adj hilarant ▷ It was hilarious! C'était hilarant!
hill [hɪl] n colline f ▷ She walked up the hill. Elle a gravi la colline.
him [hɪm] pron ❶ le, l' ▷ I can see him. Je le vois. ▷ Look at him! Regarde-le! ▷ I saw him. Je l'ai vu. ❷ lui ▷ I gave him a book. Je lui ai donné un livre. ▷ I told him the truth. Je lui ai dit la vérité. ▷ I'm going with him. Je vais avec lui. ▷ She sat next to him. Elle s'est assise à côté de lui. ▷ I'm older than him. Je suis plus âgé que lui.
himself [hɪm'sɛlf] pron ❶ se ▷ He hurt himself. Il s'est blessé. ❷ lui ▷ He talked mainly about himself. Il a surtout parlé de lui. ❸ lui-même ▷ He did it himself. Il l'a fait lui-même.; **by himself** tout seul ▷ He was travelling by himself. Il voyageait tout seul.
Hindu ['hɪnduː] adj hindou ▷ a Hindu temple un temple hindou
▷ n hindou m, hindoue f
hint [hɪnt] n allusion f
▷ vb laisser entendre ▷ He hinted that he was getting me a present. Il m'a laissé entendre qu'il allait me donner un cadeau.; **What are you hinting at?** Qu'est-ce que vous voulez dire par là?
hip [hɪp] n hanche f
hippie ['hɪpɪ] n hippie
hippo ['hɪpəʊ] n hippopotame m
hire ['haɪə'] vb engager ▷ They hired a receptionist. Ils ont engagé une réceptionniste.
his [hɪz] adj son m, sa f, ses pl ▷ his father son père ▷ his mother sa mère ▷ his parents ses parents; **his friend (1)** (male) son ami **(2)** (female) son amie ▷ He's going to wash his hair. Il va se laver les cheveux. ▷ He's brushing his teeth. Il se brosse les dents. ▷ He hurt his foot. Il s'est fait mal au pied.
▷ pron le + m sien, la + f sienne, les + m siens, + f siennes "Is this his coat?" — "No, his is black." « C'est son manteau? » — « Non, le sien est noir. » ▷ "Is this his car?" — "No, his is white." « C'est sa voiture? » — « Non, la sienne est blanche. » ▷ my parents and his mes parents et les siens ▷ my reasons and his mes raisons et les siennes; **Is this his?** C'est à lui? ▷ This book is his. Ce livre est à lui. ▷ "Whose is this?" — "It's his." « C'est à qui? » — « À lui. »
history ['hɪstərɪ] n histoire f
hit [hɪt] vb ❶ frapper ▷ She hit the ball on the first try. Elle a frappé la balle du premier coup. ❷ renverser ▷ He was hit by a car. Il a été renversé par une voiture. ❸ toucher ▷ The arrow hit the target. La flèche a touché la cible.; **I hit my head on the table.** Je me suis cogné la tête contre la table.; **It suddenly hit me that...** Je me suis soudain rendu compte que...; **to hit it off with somebody** bien s'entendre avec quelqu'un ▷ She hit it off with his parents. Elle s'est bien entendue avec ses parents.
▷ n ❶ (song) tube m ▷ the band's latest hit le

dernier tube de la bande ❷ (success) succès m ▷ The film was a huge hit. Le film a eu un immense succès.
hitch [hɪtʃ] n contretemps m ▷ There's been a slight hitch. Il y a eu un léger contretemps.
hitchhike ['hɪtʃhaɪk] vb ❶ faire du pouce ▷ She hitchhiked into town Elle a fait du pouce jusqu'en ville. ❷ faire de l'auto-stop ▷ They hitchhiked to Summerside. Ils ont fait de l'auto-stop jusqu'à Summerside.
hitchhiker ['hɪtʃhaɪkə'] n auto-stoppeur m, auto-stoppeuse f
hitchhiking ['hɪtʃhaɪkɪŋ] n auto-stop m ▷ Hitchhiking can be dangerous. Il peut être dangereux de faire de l'auto-stop.
HIV-negative ['eɪtʃaɪviː'nɛgətɪv] adj séronégatif (f séronégative)
HIV-positive ['eɪtʃaɪviː'pozɪtɪv] adj séropositif (f séropositive)
hobby ['hɒbɪ] n passe-temps favori m ▷ What are your hobbies? Quels sont tes passe-temps favoris?
hockey ['hɒkɪ] n hockey m ▷ I play hockey. Je joue au hockey.; **a hockey stick** un bâton de hockey
hold [həʊld] n: **on hold** (on phone) en attente; **to get hold of someone** (reach) contacter quelqu'un; **to get hold of something** (obtain) trouver quelque chose ▷ Where did you get hold of that book? Où as-tu trouvé ce livre?
▷ vb ❶ (hold on to) tenir ▷ He held the baby. Il tenait le bébé. ❷ (contain) contenir ▷ This bottle holds one litre. Cette bouteille contient un litre.; **to hold a meeting** avoir une réunion; **Hold the line!** (on telephone) Ne quittez pas!; **Hold it!** (wait) Attends!; **to hold one's breath** retenir son souffle.
hold back vb ❶ (tears) retenir ❷ se retenir ▷ I wanted to say something but I held back. J'ai voulu dire quelque chose, mais je me suis retenu.
hold on vb ❶ (keep hold) tenir bon ▷ The cliff was slippery but she managed to hold on. La falaise était glissante, mais elle est parvenue à tenir bon.; **to hold on to something** se cramponner à quelque chose ▷ He held on to the chair. Il se cramponnait à la chaise. ❷ (wait) attendre ▷ Hold on, I'm coming! Attends, je viens!; **Hold on!** (on telephone) Ne quittez pas!
hold up vb ❶ **to hold somebody up** (delay) retenir quelqu'un ▷ I was held up at the office. J'ai été retenu au bureau.; **to hold up a bank** (rob) cambrioler une banque (informal)
holdup ['həʊldʌp] n ❶ (at bank) vol à main armée m ❷ (delay) retard m ❸ (traffic jam) bouchon m
hole [həʊl] n trou m
holiday ['hɒlədɪ] n ❶ vacances fpl ▷ Did you have a good holiday? Tu as passé de bonnes vacances? ▷ our holidays in Newfoundland nos vacances à Terre-Neuve; **on holiday** en vacances ▷ to go on holiday partir en vacances ▷ We are on holiday. Nous sommes en vacances.; **the school holidays** les vacances scolaires ❷ (public holiday) jour férié m ▷ Next Wednesday is a holiday. Mercredi prochain est un jour férié. ❸ (day off) jour de congé m ▷ He took a day's

holiday. Il a pris un jour de congé.; **a holiday resort** un centre villégiature

hollow ['hɔləu] *adj* creux (*f* creuse)

holly ['hɔlɪ] *n* houx *m* ▷ *a sprig of holly* un brin de houx

holy ['həulɪ] *adj* saint

home [həum] *n* maison *f*; **at home** à la maison; **Make yourself at home.** Faites comme chez vous.
▶ *adv* à la maison ▷ *I'll be home at 5 o'clock.* Je serai à la maison à cinq heures.; **to get home** rentrer ▷ *What time did she get home?* Elle est rentrée à quelle heure?

home game *n* match à domicile *m*

homeland ['həumlænd] *n* patrie *f*

homeless ['həumlɪs] *adj* itinérant ▷ *a shelter for homeless youth* un refuge pour les jeunes itinérants; **a homeless man** un itinérant; **a homeless woman** une itinérante

homelessness ['həumlɪsnɪs] *n* itinérance *f*

home page *n* page d'accueil *f*

homesick ['həumsɪk] *adj*: **to be homesick** avoir le mal du pays

homework ['həumwɜːk] *n* devoirs *mpl* ▷ *Have you done your homework?* Est-ce que tu as fait tes devoirs? ▷ *my geography homework* mes devoirs de géographie

homosexual [hɔməu'sɛksjuəl] *adj* homosexuel (*f* homosexuelle)
▶ *n* homosexuel *m*, homosexuelle *f*

honest ['ɔnɪst] *adj* ❶ (*trustworthy*) honnête ▷ *She's a very honest person.* Elle est très honnête. ❷ (*sincere*) franc (*f* franche) ▷ *He was very honest with her.* Il a été très franc avec elle.

honestly ['ɔnɪstlɪ] *adv* franchement ▷ *I honestly don't know.* Franchement, je n'en sais rien.

honesty ['ɔnɪstɪ] *n* honnêteté *f*

honey ['hʌnɪ] *n* miel *m*

honeymoon ['hʌnɪmuːn] *n* lune de miel *f*

honour ['ɔnə^r] *n* honneur *m* ▷ *in honour of our grandparents* en l'honneur de nos grands-parents; **the honour roll** le tableau d'honneur

hood [hud] *n* ❶ (*on coat*) capuchon *m* ❷ (*of car*) capot *m*

hook [huk] *n* crochet *m* ▷ *He hung the painting on the hook.* Il a suspendu le tableau au crochet.; **to take the phone off the hook** décrocher le téléphone; **a fish-hook** un hameçon

hope [həup] *vb* espérer ▷ *I hope he comes.* J'espère qu'il va venir. ▷ *I'm hoping for good results.* J'espère avoir de bons résultats.; **I hope so.** Je l'espère.; **I hope not.** J'espère que non.
▶ *n* espoir *m*; **to give up hope** perdre espoir ▷ *Don't give up hope!* Ne perds pas espoir!

hopeful ['həupful] *adj* ❶ plein d'espoir ▷ *I'm hopeful.* Je suis plein d'espoir.; **She's hopeful of winning.** Elle a bon espoir de gagner. ❷ (*situation*) prometteur (*f* prometteuse) ▷ *The prospects look hopeful.* Les perspectives semblent prometteuses.

hopefully ['həupfulɪ] *adv* avec un peu de chance ▷ *Hopefully he'll make it in time.* Avec un peu de chance, il arrivera à temps.

hopeless ['həuplɪs] *adj* ❶ désespéré

▷ *The situation is hopeless.* La situation est désespérée. ❷ nul (*f* nulle) ▷ *I'm hopeless at math.* Je suis nul en maths. ; **It's hopeless, I can't do it!** C'est désespérant, je n'arrive pas à le faire!

horizon [hə'raɪzn] *n* horizon *m*

horizontal [hɔrɪ'zɔntl] *adj* horizontal (*mpl* horizontaux)

horn [hɔːn] *n* ❶ (*of car*) klaxon *m* ▷ *He blew his horn.* Il a klaxonné. ❷ cor *m* ▷ *I play the horn.* Je joue du cor. ❸ (*of animal*) corne *f*

horoscope ['hɔrəskəup] *n* horoscope *m*

horrible ['hɔrɪbl] *adj* horrible ▷ *What a horrible dress!* Quelle robe horrible!

horrifying ['hɔrɪfaɪɪŋ] *adj* effrayant

horror ['hɔrə^r] *n* horreur *f* ▷ *a horror movie* un film d'horreur

horse [hɔːs] *n* cheval *m* (*pl* chevaux)

horse-racing ['hɔːsreɪsɪŋ] *n* courses *fpl* de chevaux

horseshoe ['hɔːsʃuː] *n* fer à cheval *m*

hose [həuz] *n* tuyau *m* (*pl* tuyaux) ▷ *a garden hose* un tuyau d'arrosage

hospital ['hɔspɪtl] *n* hôpital *m* (*pl* hôpitaux) ▷ *Take me to the hospital!* Emmenez-moi à l'hôpital! ▷ *in the hospital* à l'hôpital

hospitality [hɔspɪ'tælɪtɪ] *n* hospitalité *f*

host [həust] *n* hôte *m*, hôtesse *f*

hostage ['hɔstɪdʒ] *n* otage *m*; **to take somebody hostage** prendre quelqu'un en otage

hostel ['hɔstl] *n* (*for refugees, homeless people*) refuge *m*; **a youth hostel** une auberge de jeunesse

hostile ['hɔstaɪl] *adj* hostile

hot [hɔt] *adj* ❶ (*warm*) chaud ▷ *a hot bath* un bain chaud ▷ *a hot country* un pays chaud ▷ *I'm hot.* J'ai chaud. ▷ *I'm too hot.* J'ai trop chaud. ▷ *It's hot.* Il fait chaud. ▷ *It's very hot today.* Il fait très chaud aujourd'hui. ❷ (*spicy*) épicé ▷ *a very hot curry* un curry très épicé

hot dog *n* hot-dog *m*

hotel [həu'tɛl] *n* hôtel *m* ▷ *We stayed in a hotel.* Nous avons logé à l'hôtel.

hotline ['hɔtlaɪn] *n* ❶ (*for info, advice*) service d'assistance téléphonique *m* ❷ (*for help in crisis*) ligne d'écoute téléphonique *f* ❸ (*for phone-in show*) ligne ouverte

hour ['auə^r] *n* heure *f* ▷ *He always takes hours to get ready.* Il passe toujours des heures à se préparer.; **a quarter of an hour** un quart d'heure; **half an hour** une demi-heure; **two and a half hours** deux heures et demie

hourly ['auəlɪ] *adj, adv* toutes les heures ▷ *There are hourly buses.* Il y a des autobus toutes les heures.; **to be paid hourly** être payé à l'heure

house [haus] *n* maison *f*; **at his house** chez lui; **We stayed at their house.** Nous sommes restés chez eux.; **House of Assembly** (*Nfld*) la Chambre d'assemblée; **House of Commons** la Chambre des communes

housework ['hauswɜːk] *n* ménage *m*; **to do the housework** faire le ménage

how [hau] *adv* comment ▷ *How are you?* Comment allez-vous?; **How many?** Combien?;

How many...? Combien de...? ▷ *How many students are there in the class?* Combien d'élèves y a-t-il dans la classe?; **How much?** Combien?; **How much...?** Combien de...? ▷ *How much sugar do you want?* Combien de sucre voulez-vous?; **How old are you?** Quel âge as-tu?; **How far is it to Rimouski?** Combien y a-t-il de kilomètres d'ici à Rimouski?; **How long have you been here?** Depuis combien de temps êtes-vous là?; **How do you say "apple" in French?** Comment dit-on « apple » en français?

however [haʊˈevər] *conj* pourtant ▷ *This, however, isn't true.* Pourtant, ce n'est pas vrai.

howl [haʊl] *vb* hurler

HTML *n* langage HTML *m* ▷ *an HTML document* un document en langage HTML

Hudson Bay [ˈhʌdsən-] *n* baie d'Hudson *f*

hug [hʌg] *vb* serrer dans ses bras ▷ *He hugged her.* Il a serré dans ses bras.
  ▷ *n*: **to give somebody a hug** serrer quelqu'un dans ses bras ▷ *She gave them a hug.* Elle les a serrés dans ses bras.

huge [hjuːdʒ] *adj* immense

hum [hʌm] *vb* fredonner

human [ˈhjuːmən] *adj* humain ▷ *the human body* le corps humain; **human rights** les droits de la personne ▷ *a human rights issue* une question relative aux droits de la personne; **human resources** *(available people)* les ressources humaines ▷ *We have both the human resources and the funds to carry out this project.* Nous avons les ressources humaines et financières pour réaliser ce projet.

human being [-ˈbiːɪŋ] *n* être *m* humain

humankind [hjuːmənˈkaɪnd] *n* humanité *f*

humble [ˈhʌmbl] *adj* humble

humidex [ˈhjuːmɪdɛks] *n* humidex *m*

humour [ˈhjuːməʳ] *n* humour *m*; **to have a sense of humour** avoir le sens de l'humour

hundred [ˈhʌndrəd] *num*: **a hundred** cent ▷ *a hundred dollars* cent dollars; **five hundred** cinq cents; **five hundred and one** cinq cent un; **hundreds of people** des centaines de personnes

hung [hʌŋ] *vb see* hang

hunger [ˈhʌŋgəʳ] *n* faim *f*

hungry [ˈhʌŋgrɪ] *adj*: **to be hungry** avoir faim ▷ *I'm hungry.* J'ai faim.

hunt [hʌnt] *vb* ① *(animal)* chasser; **to go hunting** aller à la chasse ② *(criminal)* pourchasser ▷ *The police are hunting the criminal.* La police pourchasse le criminel.; **to hunt for something** *(search)* chercher quelque chose partout ▷ *I hunted everywhere for that book.* J'ai cherché ce livre partout.

hunting [ˈhʌntɪŋ] *n* chasse *f*

hurdle [ˈhəːdl] *n* obstacle *m*

hurricane [ˈhʌrɪkən] *n* ouragan *m*

hurry [ˈhʌrɪ] *vb* se dépêcher ▷ *She hurried back home.* Elle s'est dépêchée de rentrer chez elle.; **Hurry up!** Dépêche-toi!
  ▷ *n*: **to be in a hurry** être pressé; **to do something in a hurry** faire quelque chose en vitesse; **There's no hurry.** Rien ne presse.

hurt [həːt] *vb*: **to hurt somebody** (1) *(physically)* faire mal à quelqu'un ▷ *You're hurting me!* Tu me fais mal! (2) *(emotionally)* blesser quelqu'un ▷ *His remarks really hurt me.* Ses remarques m'ont vraiment blessé.; **to hurt oneself** se faire mal ▷ *I fell and hurt myself.* Je me suis fait mal en tombant.; **That hurts.** Ça fait mal. ▷ *It hurts to have a tooth out.* Ça fait mal de se faire arracher une dent.; **My leg hurts.** J'ai mal à la jambe.
  ▷ *adj* blessé ▷ *Were you badly hurt?* Est-ce que tu as été grièvement blessé? ▷ *He was hurt in the leg.* Il a été blessé à la jambe. ▷ *I was hurt by what she said.* J'ai été blessé par ce qu'elle a dit.; **Luckily, nobody got hurt.** Heureusement, il n'y a pas eu de blessés.

husband [ˈhʌzbənd] *n* mari *m*

hut [hʌt] *n* hutte *f*

hydro [ˈhaɪdrəʊ] *n* électricité *f* ▷ *Hydro costs a lot.* L'électricité coûte cher.

hyperlink [ˈhaɪpəlɪŋk] *n* hyperlien *m*

hyphen [ˈhaɪfn] *n* trait d'union *m*

hypothesis [haɪˈpɒθɪsɪs] *n* hypothèse *f*

◆

I

I [aɪ] *pron* ① je ▷ *I speak French.* Je parle français. ▷ *I love cats.* J'aime les chats. ② moi ▷ *my sister and I* ma sœur et moi

ice [aɪs] *n* ① glace *f* ▷ *There was ice on the lake.* Il y avait de la glace sur le lac. ② *(on road)* verglas; **to break the ice** rompre la glace

iceberg [ˈaɪsbəːg] *n* iceberg *m*; **the tip of the iceberg** la pointe de l'iceberg

icebreaker [ˈaɪsbreɪkəʳ] *n* brise-glace *m (pl* les brise-glaces) ▷ *Icebreakers are used to navigate the Arctic.* On utilise des brise-glaces pour naviguer dans l'Arctique.

ice cream *n* crème glacée *f* ▷ *vanilla ice cream* la crème glacée à la vanille

ice cube *n* glaçon *m*

ice fishing *n* pêche sous la glace *f* ▷ *to go ice fishing* faire de la pêche sous la glace

ice hockey *n* hockey sur glace *m*

ice rink *n* patinoire *f*

ice skating [ˈaɪsskeɪtɪŋ] *n* patinage sur glace *m*; **to go ice skating** faire du patin à glace

ice slide *n* glissade *f* ▷ *In winter the city builds an ice slide in the park.* L'hiver, la ville construit une glissade dans le parc.

ice storm *n* tempête de verglas *f*

icicle [ˈaɪsɪkl] *n* glaçon *m*

icing [ˈaɪsɪŋ] *n (on cake)* glaçage *m*; **icing sugar** le sucre glace

icon [ˈaɪkɒn] *n* icône *f*

icy ['aɪsɪ] adj glacial (mpl glaciaux) ▷ There was an icy wind. Il y avait un vent glacial.; **The roads are icy.** Il y a du verglas sur les routes.

I'd [aɪd]; = **I had**; = **I would**

ID card n carte d'identité f

idea [aɪ'dɪə] n idée f ▷ Good idea! Bonne idée!

ideal [aɪ'dɪəl] adj idéal (mpl idéaux)

identical [aɪ'dentɪkl] adj identique

identification [aɪdentɪfɪ'keɪʃən] n identification f

identify [aɪ'dentɪfaɪ] vb identifier

i.e. [aɪ'iː] abbr c.-à-d. (= c'est-à-dire)

if [ɪf] conj si ▷ You can have it if you like. Tu peux le prendre si tu veux. ▷ Do you know if he's there? Savez-vous s'il est là?; **if only** si seulement ▷ If only I had more money! Si seulement j'avais plus d'argent!; **if not** sinon ▷ Are you coming? If not, I'll go with my brother. Est-ce que tu viens? Sinon, j'irai avec mon frère.

igloo ['ɪgluː] n igloo m

ignorant ['ɪgnərənt] adj ignorant

ignore [ɪg'nɔːʳ] vb: **to ignore something** ne tenir aucun compte de quelque chose ▷ She ignored my advice. Elle n'a tenu aucun compte de mes conseils.; **to ignore somebody** ignorer quelqu'un ▷ She saw me, but she ignored me. Elle m'a vu, mais elle m'a ignoré.; **Just ignore him!** Ne fais pas attention à lui!

ill [ɪl] adj (sick) malade

I'll [aɪl]; = **I will**

illegal [ɪ'liːgl] adj illégal (mpl illégaux)

illegible [ɪ'ledʒɪbl] adj illisible

illness ['ɪlnɪs] n maladie f

illusion [ɪ'luːʒən] n illusion f

illustration [ɪlə'streɪʃən] n illustration f

image ['ɪmɪdʒ] n image f ▷ The company has changed its image. La société a changé d'image.

imagination [ɪmædʒɪ'neɪʃən] n imagination f

imagine [ɪ'mædʒɪn] vb imaginer ▷ You can imagine how I felt! Tu peux imaginer ce que j'ai ressenti! ▷ "Is he angry?" — "I imagine so." « Est-ce qu'il est en colère? » — « J'imagine que oui. »

imam [ɪ'mɑːm] n imam m

imitate ['ɪmɪteɪt] vb imiter

imitation [ɪmɪ'teɪʃən] n imitation f

immediate [ɪ'miːdɪət] adj immédiat ▷ her immediate family sa famille immédiate

immediately [ɪ'miːdɪətlɪ] adv immédiatement ▷ I'll do it immediately. Je vais le faire immédiatement.

immigrant ['ɪmɪgrənt] n immigré m, immigrée f

immigration [ɪmɪ'greɪʃən] n immigration f

immoral [ɪ'mɔrəl] adj immoral (mpl immoraux)

impartial [ɪm'pɑːʃl] adj impartial (mpl impartiaux)

impatience [ɪm'peɪʃəns] n impatience f

impatient [ɪm'peɪʃənt] adj impatient; **to get impatient** s'impatienter ▷ People are getting impatient. Les gens commencent à s'impatienter.

impatiently [ɪm'peɪʃəntlɪ] adv avec impatience ▷ We waited impatiently. Nous avons attendu avec impatience.

impersonal [ɪm'pɜːsənl] adj impersonnel (f impersonnelle)

imply [ɪm'plaɪ] vb laisser entendre ▷ She implied that she wasn't coming. Elle a laissé entendre qu'elle ne venait pas.

importance [ɪm'pɔːtns] n importance f

important [ɪm'pɔːtnt] adj important

impossible [ɪm'pɒsɪbl] adj impossible

impress [ɪm'pres] vb impressionner ▷ She's trying to impress you. Elle essaie de t'impressionner.

impressed [ɪm'prest] adj impressionné ▷ I'm very impressed! Je suis très impressionné!

impression [ɪm'preʃən] n impression f ▷ I was under the impression that... J'avais l'impression que...

impressive [ɪm'presɪv] adj impressionnant

improv ['ɪmprɒv] n improvisation f ▷ We started an improv club in our school. Nous avons fondé une ligue d'improvisation à l'école.

improve [ɪm'pruːv] vb **①** (make better) améliorer ▷ They have improved the service. Ils ont amélioré le service. **②** (get better) s'améliorer ▷ The weather is improving. Le temps s'améliore. ▷ My French has improved. Mon français s'est amélioré.

improvement [ɪm'pruːvmənt] n **①** (of condition) amélioration f ▷ It's a great improvement. C'est une nette amélioration. **②** (of learner) progrès m ▷ There's been an improvement in your French. Tu as fait des progrès en français.

improvise ['ɪmprəvaɪz] vb improviser

in [ɪn] prep, adv **①** dans ▷ in the house dans la maison ▷ in my backpack dans mon sac à dos ▷ I'll see you in three weeks. Je te verrai dans trois semaines. **②** à ▷ in the country à la campagne ▷ in school à l'école ▷ in hospital à l'hôpital ▷ in Steinbach à Steinbach ▷ in spring au printemps ▷ in the sun au soleil ▷ in the shade à l'ombre ▷ in a loud voice à voix haute ▷ the boy in the blue shirt le garçon à la chemise bleue ▷ It was written in pencil. C'était écrit au crayon. ▷ in the month of May au mois de mai **③** en ▷ in French en français ▷ in summer en été ▷ in May en mai ▷ in 1996 en dix-neuf cent quatre-vingt seize ▷ I did it in 3 hours. Je l'ai fait en trois heures. ▷ in town en ville ▷ in prison en prison ▷ in tears en larmes ▷ in good condition en bon état ▷ in France en France ▷ in Portugal au Portugal ▷ in the United States aux États-Unis **④** de ▷ the best team in the world la meilleure équipe du monde ▷ the tallest person in the family le plus grand de la famille ▷ at 4 o'clock in the afternoon à quatre heures de l'après-midi ▷ at 6 in the morning à six heures du matin; **In the afternoon I work at the store.** L'après-midi, je travaille au magasin.; **You look good in that dress.** Tu es jolie avec cette robe.; **in time** à temps ▷ We arrived in time for dinner. Nous sommes arrivés à temps pour le dîner.; **in here** ici ▷ It's hot in here. Il fait chaud ici.; **in the rain** sous la pluie; **in the sixties** durant les années soixante; **one person in ten** une personne sur dix; **to be in** (at home, work) être là ▷ She wasn't in. Elle n'était pas là.; **to ask somebody in** inviter quelqu'un à entrer

inaccurate [ɪn'ækjurət] adj inexact

inadequate [ɪnˈædɪkwət] adj (measures, resources) inadéquat; **I felt completely inadequate.** Je ne me sentais absolument pas à la hauteur.

incentive [ɪnˈsɛntɪv] n: **There is no incentive to work.** Il n'y a rien qui incite à travailler.

inch [ɪntʃ] n pouce m; **6 inches** quinze centimètres

incident [ˈɪnsɪdnt] n incident m

inclined [ɪnˈklaɪnd] adj: **to be inclined to do something** avoir tendance à faire quelque chose ▷ **He's inclined to arrive late.** Il a tendance à arriver en retard.

include [ɪnˈkluːd] vb comprendre ▷ Service is not included. Le service n'est pas compris.

including [ɪnˈkluːdɪŋ] prep compris ▷ It will be 200 dollars, including tax. Ça coûtera deux cents dollars, taxes comprises.

inclusive [ɪnˈkluːsɪv] adj compris ▷ The inclusive price is 200 dollars. Ça coûte deux cents dollars tout compris.; **pages 9 to 12 inclusive** de la page neuf à la page douze inclusivement; **inclusive language** la langue non sexiste

income [ˈɪnkʌm] n revenu m

income tax n impôt m sur le revenu

incompetent [ɪnˈkɒmpɪtnt] adj incompétent

incomplete [ɪnkəmˈpliːt] adj incomplet (f incomplète)

inconsistent [ɪnkənˈsɪstnt] adj ❶ (behaviour) changeant ❷ (work, quality) inégal ❸ (statements) contradictoire; **Her actions are inconsistent with what she says.** Ses actes ne concordent pas avec ce qu'elle dit.

inconvenience [ɪnkənˈviːnjəns] n: **I don't want to cause any inconvenience.** Je ne veux pas vous déranger.

inconvenient [ɪnkənˈviːnjənt] adj inopportun ▷ at an inconvenient time à un moment inopportun; **That's very inconvenient for me.** Ça ne m'arrange pas du tout.

incorrect [ɪnkəˈrɛkt] adj incorrect

increase n [ˈɪnkriːs] n augmentation f ▷ an increase in traffic accidents une augmentation des accidents de la route
▶ vb augmenter

incredible [ɪnˈkrɛdɪbl] adj incroyable

indecisive [ɪndɪˈsaɪsɪv] adj (person) indécis

independence [ɪndɪˈpɛndns] n indépendance f

independent [ɪndɪˈpɛndnt] adj indépendant; **an independent school** une école privée

index [ˈɪndɛks] n (in book) index m

index finger n index m

Indian summer [ˈɪndɪən-] n été m indien

indicate [ˈɪndɪkeɪt] vb indiquer

indigestion [ɪndɪˈdʒɛstʃən] n indigestion f; **I have indigestion.** J'ai une indigestion.

individual [ɪndɪˈvɪdjuəl] adj individuel (f individuelle)
▶ n ❶ individu m ▷ the rights of the individual les droits de l'individu ❷ personne f ▷ a rather strange individual une personne un peu étrange; **She's a real individual.** Elle est vraiment unique.

indoor [ˈɪndɔːʳ] adj d'intérieur ▷ indoor activities les activités d'intérieur ▷ indoor shoes les chaussures d'intérieur ▷ indoor sports les sports d'intérieur; **an indoor swimming pool** une piscine intérieure

indoors [ɪnˈdɔːz] adv à l'intérieur ▷ They're indoors. Ils sont à l'intérieur.; **to go indoors** rentrer ▷ We'd better go indoors. Nous ferions mieux de rentrer.

industrial [ɪnˈdʌstrɪəl] adj industriel (f industrielle)

industry [ˈɪndəstrɪ] n industrie f ▷ the tourist industry l'industrie du tourisme ▷ the oil industry l'industrie pétrolière ▷ I'd like to work in industry. J'aimerais travailler dans l'industrie.

inefficient [ɪnɪˈfɪʃənt] adj inefficace

inevitable [ɪnˈɛvɪtəbl] adj inévitable

inexpensive [ɪnɪkˈspɛnsɪv] adj bon marché (f+pl bon marché) ▷ an inexpensive hotel un hôtel bon marché ▷ inexpensive holidays des vacances bon marché

inexperienced [ɪnɪkˈspɪərɪənst] adj inexpérimenté

infection [ɪnˈfɛkʃən] n infection f ▷ an ear infection une infection de l'oreille; **a throat infection** un mal de gorge

infectious [ɪnˈfɛkʃəs] adj contagieux (f contagieuse) ▷ It's not infectious. Ce n'est pas contagieux.

infinite [ˈɪnfɪnɪt] adj ❶ infini ▷ an infinite variety une variété infinie ❷ illimité ▷ The possibilities are infinite. Les possibilités sont illimitées.

infinitive [ɪnˈfɪnɪtɪv] n infinitif m

inflatable [ɪnˈfleɪtəbl] adj (mattress, dinghy) gonflable

inflation [ɪnˈfleɪʃən] n inflation f

influence [ˈɪnfluəns] n influence f ▷ He's a bad influence on her. Il a mauvaise influence sur elle.
▶ vb influencer

infomercial [ˈɪnfəʊmɜːʃl] n infopublicité f

inform [ɪnˈfɔːm] vb informer; **to inform somebody of something** informer quelqu'un de quelque chose ▷ Nobody informed me of the new plan. Personne ne m'a informé de ce nouveau projet.

informal [ɪnˈfɔːml] adj ❶ (person, party) décontracté ▷ "informal dress" « tenue décontractée » ❷ (language) familier (f familière) ▷ informal language le langage familier; **an informal visit from the principal** une visite non officielle du directeur

information [ɪnfəˈmeɪʃən] n ❶ renseignements mpl ▷ important information les renseignements importants; **a piece of information** un renseignement; **Could you give me some information about the Quebec Carnival?** Pourriez-vous me renseigner sur le Carnaval de Québec?; **for your information** à titre de renseignement ❷ information f ▷ I found some information for my project on pollution. J'ai trouvé de l'information pour mon projet sur la pollution.

information desk n bureau de renseignements m

infuriating [ɪnˈfjʊərɪeɪtɪŋ] adj exaspérant

ingenious [ɪnˈdʒiːnjəs] adj ingénieux (f

ingénieuse)

ingredient [ɪnˈgriːdɪənt] n ingrédient m

inhabitant [ɪnˈhæbɪtnt] n habitant m, habitante f

inherit [ɪnˈherɪt] vb hériter de ▷ She inherited her father's house. Elle a hérité de la maison de son père.

initials [ɪˈnɪʃəlz] npl initiales fpl ▷ My initials are CDT. Mes initiales sont CDT.

initiative [ɪˈnɪʃətɪv] n initiative f

inject [ɪnˈdʒekt] vb (drug) injecter

injection [ɪnˈdʒekʃən] n piqûre

injure [ˈɪndʒəʳ] vb blesser

injury [ˈɪndʒərɪ] n blessure f

injustice [ɪnˈdʒʌstɪs] n injustice f

ink [ɪŋk] n encre f

in-laws [ˈɪnlɔːz] npl beaux-parents mpl

inn [ɪn] n auberge f

inner [ˈɪnəʳ] adj intérieur; **the inner city** les quartiers déshérités du centre ville

inner tube n chambre à air f

innocent [ˈɪnəsnt] adj innocent

inquest [ˈɪnkwest] n enquête f

inquire [ɪnˈkwaɪəʳ] vb: **to inquire about something** se renseigner sur quelque chose ▷ I'm going to inquire about show times. Je vais me renseigner sur les horaires de cinéma.

inquiry [ɪnˈkwaɪərɪ] n: **to make inquiries about something** faire des demandes de renseignement ▷ "inquiries" « renseignements »

inquisitive [ɪnˈkwɪzɪtɪv] adj curieux (f curieuse)

insane [ɪnˈseɪn] adj fou (f folle)

inscription [ɪnˈskrɪpʃən] n inscription f

insect [ˈɪnsekt] n insecte m

insect repellent n antimoustiques m

insensitive [ɪnˈsensɪtɪv] adj indélicat ▷ That was a bit insensitive of you. C'était un peu indélicat de ta part.

insert [ɪnˈsəːt] vb insérer ▷ Insert the CD in the drive. Insère le CD dans le lecteur. ▷ You should insert a paragraph here, explaining your point. Tu devrais insérer un paragraphe ici pour expliquer.

inside [ˈɪnˈsaɪd] n intérieur m
▶ adv, prep à l'intérieur ▷ They're inside. Ils sont à l'intérieur. ▷ inside the house à l'intérieur de la maison; **to go inside** rentrer; **Come inside!** Rentrez!

insincere [ɪnsɪnˈsɪəʳ] adj peu sincère

insist [ɪnˈsɪst] vb insister ▷ I didn't want to, but he insisted. Je ne voulais pas, mais il a insisté.; **to insist on doing something** insister pour faire quelque chose ▷ She insisted on paying. Elle a insisté pour payer.; **He insisted he was innocent.** Il affirmait qu'il était innocent.

inspect [ɪnˈspekt] vb inspecter

inspector [ɪnˈspektəʳ] n inspecteur m, inspectrice f

install [ɪnˈstɔːl] vb: **to install a piece of software** installer un logiciel ▷ We've just installed new kitchen cupboards. Nous venons d'installer de nouvelles armoires de cuisine.

instalment [ɪnˈstɔːlmənt] n ❶ (payment) versement m ▷ to pay in instalments payer en plusieurs versements ❷ (episode) épisode m

instance [ˈɪnstəns] n: **for instance** par exemple

instant [ˈɪnstənt] adj ❶ immédiat ▷ It was an instant success. Ça a été un succès immédiat. ❷ (coffee, foods) instantané ▷ instant pudding le pouding instantané; **instant messaging** la messagerie instantanée

instantly [ˈɪnstəntlɪ] adv tout de suite

instead [ɪnˈsted] adv: **instead of** (1) (followed by noun) à la place de ▷ He went instead of his brother. Il y est allé à la place de son frère. (2) (followed by verb) au lieu de ▷ We played tennis instead of going swimming. Nous avons joué au tennis au lieu d'aller nager.; **The pool was closed, so we played tennis instead.** La piscine était fermée, alors nous avons joué au tennis.

instinct [ˈɪnstɪŋkt] n instinct m

institute [ˈɪnstɪtjuːt] n institut m

institution [ɪnstɪˈtjuːʃən] n institution f

instruct [ɪnˈstrʌkt] vb: **to instruct somebody to do something** donner l'ordre à quelqu'un de faire quelque chose ▷ She instructed us to wait outside. Elle nous a donné l'ordre d'attendre dehors.

instructions [ɪnˈstrʌkʃənz] npl
❶ instructions fpl ▷ Follow the instructions carefully. Suivez soigneusement les instructions. ❷ (for product) mode m d'emploi ▷ Where are the instructions? Où sont le mode d'emploi?

instructor [ɪnˈstrʌktəʳ] n moniteur m, monitrice f ▷ a ski instructor un moniteur de ski ▷ a driving instructor un moniteur d'auto-école

instrument [ˈɪnstrumənt] n instrument m ▷ Do you play an instrument? Est-ce que tu joues d'un instrument?

insufficient [ɪnsəˈfɪʃənt] adj insuffisant

insulin [ˈɪnsjulɪn] n insuline f

insult [ˈɪnsʌlt] n insulte f
▶ vb insulter

insurance [ɪnˈʃuərəns] n assurance f ▷ her car insurance son assurance automobile; **an insurance policy** une police d'assurance

intelligent [ɪnˈtelɪdʒənt] adj intelligent

intend [ɪnˈtend] vb: **to intend to do something** avoir l'intention de faire quelque chose ▷ I intend to do French at university. J'ai l'intention d'étudier le français à l'université.

intense [ɪnˈtens] adj intense

intensive [ɪnˈtensɪv] adj intensif (f intensive)

intention [ɪnˈtenʃən] n intention f

intercom [ˈɪntəkɒm] n interphone m

interest [ˈɪntrɪst] n intérêt m ▷ to show an interest in something manifester de l'intérêt pour quelque chose; **What interests do you have?** Quels sont tes centres d'intérêt?; **My main interest is music.** Ce qui m'intéresse le plus c'est la musique.; **an interest group** un groupe d'intérêt; **interest rate** (bank account) le taux d'intérêt
▶ vb intéresser ▷ It doesn't interest me. Ça ne m'intéresse pas.; **to be interested in something** s'intéresser à quelque chose ▷ I'm not interested in politics. Je ne m'intéresse pas à la politique.

interesting ['ɪntrɪstɪŋ] adj intéressant
interfere [ɪntə'fɪəʳ] vb: **Stop interfering in my social life.** Arrête de te mêler dans ma vie sociale.; **The weather interfered with our plans.** Le mauvais temps a contrarié nos projets.
interior [ɪn'tɪərɪəʳ] n intérieur m
interior designer n décorateur d'intérieur m, décoratrice d'intérieur f
intermediate [ɪntə'miːdɪət] adj (course, level) moyen (f moyenne)
intermission [ɪntə'mɪʃən] n entracte m
internal [ɪn'tɜːnl] adj interne
international [ɪntə'næʃənl] adj international (mpl internationaux)
Internet ['ɪntənet] n Internet m ▷ **on the Internet** sur Internet
Internet café n cybercafé
Internet user n internaute mf
interpret [ɪn'tɜːprɪt] vb ❶ servir d'interprète ▷ **He couldn't speak French, so his friend interpreted.** Comme il ne savait pas le français, son ami a servi d'interprète. ❷ interpréter ▷ **I don't know how to interpret her response.** Je ne sais pas comment interpréter sa réaction.
interpreter [ɪn'tɜːprɪtəʳ] n interprète mf
interrupt [ɪntə'rʌpt] vb interrompre
interruption [ɪntə'rʌpʃən] n interruption f
intersection [ɪntə'sekʃən] n intersection f ▷ **What's the nearest intersection?** Quelle est l'intersection la plus proche? ▷ **Turn left at the next intersection.** Tourne à gauche à la prochaine intersection.
interview ['ɪntəvjuː] n ❶ (on TV, radio) interview f ❷ (for job) entretien m ▶ vb (on TV, radio) interviewer ▷ **I was interviewed on the radio.** J'ai été interviewé à la radio.
interviewer ['ɪntəvjuəʳ] n (on TV, radio) intervieweur m, intervieweuse f
intimate ['ɪntɪmət] adj intime
into ['ɪntu] prep ❶ dans ▷ **He got into the car.** Il est monté dans la voiture. ❷ en ▷ **I'm going into town.** Je vais en ville. ▷ **Translate it into French.** Traduisez ça en français. ▷ **Divide into two groups.** Répartissez-vous en deux groupes.
intolerant [ɪn'tɒlərnt] adj intolérant; **She's lactose-intolerant.** Elle est intolérante au lactose.
intramurals [ɪntrə'mjuərəlz] npl les f activités intramurales ▷ **Did you sign up for intramurals?** Tu t'es inscrit aux activités intramurales?
introduce [ɪntrə'djuːs] vb présenter ▷ **I'd like to introduce my grandmother.** Je vous présente ma grand-mère. ▷ **He introduced me to his parents.** Il m'a présentée à ses parents.
introduction [ɪntrə'dʌkʃən] n (in book) introduction f
intruder [ɪn'truːdəʳ] n intrus m, intruse f
intuition [ɪntjuː'ɪʃən] n intuition f
Inuit ['ɪnuɪt] npl Inuits mpl ▶ adj inuit ▷ **traditional Inuit culture** la culture inuite traditionnelle
Inuk ['ɪnuk] n Inuit m, Inuite f
invade [ɪn'veɪd] vb envahir; **to invade**

someone's privacy s'ingérer dans la vie privée de quelqu'un
invasion [ɪn'veɪʒən] n envahissement m
invent [ɪn'vent] vb inventer
invention [ɪn'venʃən] n invention f
inventor [ɪn'ventəʳ] n inventeur m, inventrice f
investigation [ɪnvestɪ'geɪʃən] n (police) enquête f
investment [ɪn'vestmənt] n investissement m ▷ **Education is an investment in your future.** L'éducation, c'est un investissement dans ton avenir.
invincible [ɪn'vɪnsɪbl] adj invincible ▷ **He thinks he's invincible.** Il se croit invincible.
invisible [ɪn'vɪzɪbl] adj invisible
invitation [ɪnvɪ'teɪʃən] n invitation f
invite [ɪn'vaɪt] vb inviter ▷ **You're all invited.** Vous êtes tous invités.; **to invite somebody to a party** inviter quelqu'un à une fête
involve [ɪn'vɒlv] vb nécessiter ▷ **This job involves a lot of travelling.** Ce travail nécessite de nombreux déplacements.; **to be involved in something** (crime, drugs) être impliqué dans quelque chose; **to be involved with somebody** (in relationship) avoir une relation avec quelqu'un
IQ n (= intelligence quotient) Q. I. m (= quotient intellectuel)
iron ['aɪən] n ❶ (metal) fer m ❷ (for clothes) fer à repasser m ▶ vb repasser
ironic [aɪ'rɒnɪk] adj ironique
ironing ['aɪənɪŋ] n repassage m ▷ **to do the ironing** faire le repassage
ironing board n planche à repasser f
irregular [ɪ'regjuləʳ] adj irrégulier (f irrégulière) ▷ **an irregular verb** un verbe irrégulier
irrelevant [ɪ'reləvnt] adj hors de propos ▷ **That's irrelevant.** C'est hors de propos.
irresistible [ɪrɪ'zɪstɪbl] adj irrésistible ▷ **irresistible desserts** des desserts irrésistibles ▷ **an irresistible urge** une envie irrésistible
irresponsible [ɪrɪ'spɒnsɪbl] adj (person) irresponsable ▷ **That was irresponsible of them.** C'était irresponsable de leur part.
irritating ['ɪrɪteɪtɪŋ] adj irritant
is [ɪz] vb see **be**
Islamic [ɪz'lɑːmɪk] adj islamique ▷ **Islamic law** la loi islamique
island ['aɪlənd] n île f
isolated ['aɪsəleɪtɪd] adj isolé
ISP n (= Internet service provider) fournisseur de services Internet m
issue ['ɪʃuː] n ❶ (matter) question f ▷ **a controversial issue** une question controversée ❷ (of magazine) numéro m ▶ vb (equipment, supplies) distribuer
it [ɪt] pron ❶ il, elle ▷ **"Where's my book?" — "It's on the table."** « Où est mon livre? » — « Il est sur la table. » ▷ **"When does the pool close?" — "It closes at 8."** « La piscine ferme à quelle heure? » — « Elle ferme à vingt heures. » ❷ le, la, l' ▷ **There's a croissant left. Do you want it?** Il reste un croissant. Tu le veux? ▷ **It's a good film. Did**

you see it? C'est un bon film. L'as-tu vu ? ▷ *I don't want this apple. Take it.* Je ne veux pas de cette pomme. Prends-la. ▷ *"He's got a new car." — "Yes, I saw it."* « Il a une nouvelle voiture. » — « Oui, je l'ai vue. »; *It's raining.* Il pleut.; *It's 6 o'clock.* Il est six heures.; *It's Friday tomorrow.* Demain, c'est vendredi.; **"Who is it?" — "It's me."** « Qui est-ce ? » — « C'est moi. »; *It's expensive.* C'est cher.

italics [ɪˈtælɪks] *n* italique *f* ▷ *to put a word in italics* mettre un mot en italique

itch [ɪtʃ] *vb*: *It itches.* Ça me démange.; *My head's itching.* J'ai des démangeaisons à la tête.

itchy [ˈɪtʃɪ] *adj*: *My arm is itchy.* J'ai le bras qui démange.

it'd [ˈɪtɪd]; = **it had**; **it would**

item [ˈaɪtəm] *n* (*object*) article *m*

itinerary [aɪˈtɪnərəri] *n* itinéraire *m*

it'll [ˈɪtl]; = **it will**

its [ɪts] *adj* son *m*, sa *f*, ses *pl* ▷ *What's its name?* Quel est son nom ? ▷ *Everything in its place.* Chaque chose à sa place. ▷ *The dog is losing its hair.* Le chien perd ses poils.

it's [ɪts]; = **it is**; **it has**

itself [ɪtˈsɛlf] *pron* se ▷ *The bear was trying to defend itself.* L'ours essayait de se défendre.

I've [aɪv]; = **I have**

j

jab [dʒæb] *vb* planter ▷ *He jabbed his fork into the potato.* Il a planté sa fourchette dans la pomme de terre.; *She jabbed me with her elbow.* Elle m'a donné un coup de coude.

jack [dʒæk] *n* ❶ (*for car*) cric *m* ❷ (*playing card*) valet *m*

jacket [ˈdʒækɪt] *n* veston *m*

jackknife [ˈdʒæknaɪf] *n* canif *m*

jackpot [ˈdʒækpɔt] *n* gros lot *m*; *to win the jackpot* gagner le gros lot

jail [dʒeɪl] *n* prison *f*; *to go to jail* aller en prison; *to put someone in jail* emprisonner quelqu'un

jam [dʒæm] *n* confiture *f* ▷ *strawberry jam* la confiture de fraises; *a traffic jam* un embouteillage; *to be in a jam* être dans le pétrin; *to get somebody out of a jam* sortir quelqu'un du pétrin

jam jar *n* pot à confiture *m*

jammed [dʒæmd] *adj* coincé ▷ *The window's jammed.* La fenêtre est coincée.

jam-packed [dʒæmˈpækt] *adj* bondé ▷ *The room was jam-packed.* La salle était bondée.

janitor [ˈdʒænɪtər] *n* concierge ▷ *He's a janitor.* Il est concierge.

January [ˈdʒænjuəri] *n* janvier *m*; *in January* en janvier

jar [dʒɑːr] *n* bocal *m* (*pl* bocaux) ▷ *an empty jar* un bocal vide; *a jar of honey* un pot de miel

javelin [ˈdʒævlɪn] *n* javelot *m*

jaw [dʒɔː] *n* mâchoire *f*

jazz [dʒæz] *n* jazz *m*

jealous [ˈdʒɛləs] *adj* jaloux (*f* jalouse)

jeans [dʒiːnz] *npl* jeans *mpl*

Jehovah's Witness [dʒɪˈhəʊvəz-] *n* témoin de Jéhovah ▷ *She's a Jehovah's Witness.* Elle est témoin de Jéhovah.

Jello® [ˈdʒɛləʊ] *n* gelée *f*

jelly [ˈdʒɛlɪ] *n* gelée *f*

jelly bean *n* bonbon haricot *m*

jellyfish [ˈdʒɛlɪfɪʃ] *n* méduse *f*

jersey [ˈdʒəːzɪ] *n* (*pullover*) maillot *m*

jet [dʒɛt] *n* ❶ (*plane*) avion *m* à réaction ❷ jet *m* ▷ *a jet of water* un jet d'eau

jetlag [ˈdʒɛtlæg] *n*: *to be suffering from jetlag* subir les effets du décalage horaire

Jew [dʒuː] *n* juif *m*, juive *f*

jewel [ˈdʒuːəl] *n* bijou *m* (*pl* bijoux)

jeweller [ˈdʒuːələr] *n* bijoutier *m*, bijoutière *f* ▷ *He's a jeweller.* Il est bijoutier.

jewellery [ˈdʒuːəlri] *n* bijoux *mpl*

jewellery store *n* bijouterie *f*

Jewish [ˈdʒuːɪʃ] *adj* juif (*f* juive)

jigsaw [ˈdʒɪgsɔː] *n* puzzle *m*

jingle [ˈdʒɪŋgl] *vb* (*bells*) tinter ❷ (*coins*) cliqueter

jinx [dʒɪŋks] *n* sort *m* ▷ *to put a jinx on something* jeter un sort à quelque chose

job [dʒɔb] *n* ❶ emploi *m* ▷ *He lost his job.* Il a perdu son emploi.; *I have a Saturday job.* Je travaille le samedi. ❷ (*chore, task*) travail *m* (*pl* travaux) ▷ *That was a difficult job.* C'était un travail difficile.

job centre [ˈdʒɔbsɛntər] *n* centre d'emploi *m*

jobless [ˈdʒɔblɪs] *adj* sans emploi

jog [dʒɔg] *vb* faire du jogging

jogging [ˈdʒɔgɪn] *n* jogging *m*; *to go jogging* faire du jogging

join [dʒɔɪn] *vb* ❶ (*become member of*) s'inscrire à ▷ *I'm going to join the ski club.* Je vais m'inscrire au club de ski. ❷ se joindre à ▷ *Do you mind if I join you?* Puis-je me joindre à vous ?

joint [dʒɔɪnt] *n* ❶ (*in body*) articulation *f* ❷ (*of meat*) rôti *m*

joke [dʒəʊk] *n* plaisanterie *f*; *to tell a joke* raconter une plaisanterie; *He can't take a joke.* Il prend mal la plaisanterie.; *It's a joke.* (*waste of time*) C'est de la blague. ; *to play a joke on somebody* jouer un tour à quelqu'un ▷ *I'm only joking.* Je plaisante.

jolly [ˈdʒɔlɪ] *adj* jovial (*mpl* joviaux)

jot down *vb* noter

journal [ˈdʒəːnl] *n* journal *m* ▷ *She keeps a journal of her experiences.* Elle note ses expériences dans un journal.

journalism [ˈdʒəːnəlɪzəm] *n* journalisme *m*

journalist [ˈdʒəːnəlɪst] *n* journaliste *f* ▷ *She's a journalist.* Elle est journaliste.

journey ['dʒɜːnɪ] n ① voyage m ▷ I don't like long journeys. Je n'aime pas les longs voyages.; **to go on a journey** faire un voyage ② (to school, work) trajet m ▷ The journey to school takes about half an hour. Il y a une demi-heure de trajet pour aller à l'école.; **a bus journey** un trajet en autobus

joy [dʒɔɪ] n joie f

joystick ['dʒɔɪstɪk] n (for computer game) manette de jeu f

judge [dʒʌdʒ] n juge ▷ She's a judge. Elle est juge.
▷ vb juger

judo ['dʒuːdəʊ] n judo m ▷ My hobby is judo. Je fais du judo.

jug [dʒʌg] n cruche f

juggler ['dʒʌglə'] n jongleur m, jongleuse f

juice [dʒuːs] n jus m ▷ orange juice le jus d'orange

July [dʒuːˈlaɪ] n juillet m; **in July** en juillet

jumble ['dʒʌmbl] n fouillis m ▷ a jumble of information un fouillis de renseignements; **a jumble of ideas** des pensées confuses; **a jumble of papers** des papiers en vrac; **Her thoughts were all in a jumble.** Ses pensées étaient toutes confuses.

jump [dʒʌmp] vb sauter; **to jump over something** sauter par-dessus quelque chose; **to jump out of the window** sauter par la fenêtre; **to jump off the roof** sauter du toit; **to jump to conclusions** sauter aux conclusions

jumper ['dʒʌmpə'] n robe chasuble f

June [dʒuːn] n juin m; **in June** en juin

jungle ['dʒʌŋgl] n jungle f

junior ['dʒuːnɪə'] adj ① (sports) junior (f+pl junior) ▷ the junior leagues les ligues junior ② (work) subalterne ▷ a junior employee un employé subalterne ③ (in name) fils ▷ Bill Smith, Jr. Bill Smith, fils; **in junior high school** à l'école secondaire de premier cycle; **junior kindergarten** la prématernelle; **She's three years my junior.** Elle a trois ans de moins que moi.

junk [dʒʌŋk] n ① (old things) bric-à-brac no pl ▷ The attic's full of junk. Le grenier est rempli de bric-à-brac. ② (worthless stuff) camelote f ▷ Don't read that, it's junk. Ne lis pas ça, c'est de la camelote.; **a junk shop** un magasin d'objets usagés; **junk mail** la publicité-rebut; **junk e-mail** le pourriel

junk food n (in general) malbouffe f ▷ My parents are against junk food. Mes parents sont contre la malbouffe. ▷ Junk food is becoming a problem in our society. La malbouffe est devenue un problème dans notre société. ② (specific food) aliment m vide ▷ Potato chips are junk food. Les croustilles sont un aliment vide. ▷ I ate junk food for lunch. J'ai mangé des aliments vides pour le dîner.

jury ['dʒʊərɪ] n jury m

just [dʒʌst] adv, adj juste ▷ just after Christmas juste après Noël ▷ We had just enough money. Nous avions juste assez d'argent. ▷ just in time juste à temps ▷ a just policy une politique juste; **They're just jealous.** Ils sont simplement jaloux.; **I'm rather busy just now.** Je suis assez occupé en ce moment.; **I did it just now.** Je viens de le faire.; **He's just arrived.** Il vient d'arriver.; **I'm just coming!** J'arrive!; **It's just a suggestion.** Ce n'est qu'une suggestion.; **just for you** spécialement pour toi; **to be just about to do something** être sur le point de faire quelque chose

justice ['dʒʌstɪs] n justice f

justify ['dʒʌstɪfaɪ] vb justifier

kangaroo [kæŋgəˈruː] n kangourou m

karaoke [kɑːrəˈəʊkɪ] n karaoké m

karate [kəˈrɑːtɪ] n karaté m

kayak ['kaɪæk] n kayak m

kebab [kəˈbæb] n brochette f

keen [kiːn] adj ① (enthusiastic) enthousiaste ▷ He doesn't seem very keen. Il n'a pas l'air très enthousiaste.; **She's a keen student.** C'est une étudiante assidue.; **to be keen on something** aimer quelque chose ▷ I'm not very keen on that band. Je n'aime pas trop cette bande.; **to be keen on doing something** avoir très envie de faire quelque chose ▷ I'm not very keen on going. Je n'ai pas très envie d'y aller.

keep [kiːp] vb ① (retain) garder ▷ You can keep it. Tu peux le garder. ② (remain) rester ▷ Keep still! Reste tranquille!; **Keep quiet!** Tais-toi!; **I keep forgetting my keys.** J'oublie tout le temps mes clés.; **to keep on doing something** (1) (continuously) continuer à faire quelque chose ▷ He kept on reading. Il a continué à lire. (2) (repeatedly) ne pas arrêter de faire quelque chose ▷ The car keeps on breaking down. La voiture n'arrête pas de tomber en panne.; **"keep out"** « défense d'entrer »

keep up vb (someone) suivre ▷ She walks so fast I can't keep up. Elle marche tellement vite que je n'arrive pas à la suivre. ▷ I can't keep up with the rest of the class. Je n'arrive pas à suivre le reste de la classe.; **You should keep up your guitar lessons.** Tu devrais continuer tes cours de guitare.; **Keep it up!** Continue!

kennel ['kɛnl] n niche f

kept [kɛpt] vb see **keep**

kerosene ['kɛrəsiːn] n pétrole m

ketchup ['kɛtʃəp] n ketchup m

kettle ['kɛtl] n bouilloire f

key [kiː] n ① clé f; **key word** le mot clé; **key card** la carte magnétique ② (on keyboard) touche f ③ (music) ton m ▷ to change key changer de ton; **in the key of C** en do; **to**

sing off key chanter faux; **key signature** l'armature *f*

keyboard ['ki:bɔ:d] *n* clavier *m* ▷ *The musician on keyboards is...* Le musicien aux claviers est... ▷ *a computer keyboard* un clavier d'ordinateur

keychain ['ki:tʃeɪn] *n* porte-clés *m*

key in *vb* entrer ▷ *to key in data* entrer des données ▷ *Key in your password.* Entre ton mot de passe.

keypad ['ki:pæd] *n* pavé numérique *m*

kick [kɪk] *n* coup de pied *m*
▷ *vb*: **to kick somebody** donner un coup de pied à quelqu'un ▷ *He kicked me.* Il m'a donné un coup de pied. ▷ *She kicked the ball hard.* Elle a donné un bon coup de pied dans le ballon.; **to kick off** (football, soccer) donner le coup d'envoi

kick-off ['kɪkɔf] *n* coup d'envoi *m* ▷ *The kick-off is at 10 o'clock.* Le coup d'envoi sera donné à dix heures.

kid [kɪd] *n* (child) jeune
▷ *vb* plaisanter ▷ *I'm just kidding.* Je plaisante.; **You're kidding!** Sans blague!

kidnap ['kɪdnæp] *vb* kidnapper

kidnapper ['kɪdnæpər] *n* kidnappeur *m*, kidnappeuse *f*

kidnapping ['kɪdnæpɪŋ] *n* enlèvement *m*

kidney ['kɪdnɪ] *n* ❶ (human) rein *m* ▷ *He's got kidney trouble.* Il a des problèmes de reins. ❷ (to eat) rognon *m* ▷ *I don't like kidneys.* Je n'aime pas les rognons.

kill [kɪl] *vb* tuer ▷ *She was killed in a car accident.* Elle a été tuée dans un accident de voiture.; **Luckily, nobody was killed.** Il n'y a heureusement pas eu de victimes.; **Six people were killed in the accident.** L'accident a fait six morts.; **to kill oneself** se suicider

killer ['kɪlər] *n* (murderer) meurtrier *m*, meurtrière *f*; **Meningitis can be a killer.** La méningite peut être mortelle.; **That math test was a killer.** Ce test de maths était tuant.; **killer whale** l'épaulard *m*

kiln [kɪln] *n* four à céramique *m*

kilo ['ki:ləu] *n* kilo *m* ▷ *2 dollars a kilo* deux dollars le kilo

kilometre ['kɪləmi:tər] *n* kilomètre *m*

kilt [kɪlt] *n* kilt *m*

kind [kaɪnd] *adj* gentil (*f* gentille); **to be kind to somebody** être gentil avec quelqu'un; **Thank you for being so kind.** Merci pour votre gentillesse.
▷ *n* sorte ▷ *It's a kind of sausage.* C'est une sorte de saucisse.

kindergarten ['kɪndəgɑ:tn] *n* maternelle *f*

kindly ['kaɪndlɪ] *adv* gentiment ▷ *"Don't worry," she said kindly.* « Ne t'en fais pas », m'a-t-elle dit gentiment.; **Kindly refrain from smoking.** Veuillez vous abstenir de fumer.

kindness ['kaɪndnɪs] *n* gentillesse *f*

king [kɪŋ] *n* roi *m*

kingdom ['kɪŋdəm] *n* royaume *m*

kiosk ['ki:ɔsk] *n* kiosque *m*

kipper ['kɪpər] *n* hareng fumé *m*

kiss [kɪs] *n* baiser *m* ▷ *a passionate kiss* un baiser passionné
▷ *vb* ❶ embrasser ▷ *He kissed her passionately.* Il l'a embrassée passionnément. ❷ s'embrasser

▷ *They kissed.* Ils se sont embrassés.

kit [kɪt] *n* trousse *f* ▷ *a tool kit* une trousse à outils ▷ *a first aid kit* une trousse de secours ▷ *a tire repair kit* une trousse de réparations; **a sewing kit** un nécessaire à couture

kitchen ['kɪtʃɪn] *n* cuisine *f*; **a kitchen knife** un couteau de cuisine

kite [kaɪt] *n* cerf-volant *m* (*pl* cerfs-volants)

kitten ['kɪtn] *n* chaton *m*

knapsack ['næpsæk] *n* sac à dos *m*

knee [ni:] *n* genou *m* (*pl* genoux); **He was on his knees.** Il était à genoux.

kneel (down) [ni:l-] *vb* s'agenouiller

knew [nju:] *vb see* **know**

knife [naɪf] *n* couteau *m* (*pl* couteaux); **a kitchen knife** un couteau de cuisine; **a hunting knife** un couteau de chasse

knit [nɪt] *vb* tricoter

knitting ['nɪtɪŋ] *n* tricot *m* ▷ *I like knitting.* J'aime faire du tricot.

knives [naɪvz] *npl see* **knife**

knob [nɔb] *n* (on door, radio, TV, radiator) bouton *m*

knock [nɔk] *vb* frapper ▷ *Someone's knocking at the door.* Quelqu'un frappe à la porte.; **to knock somebody down** renverser quelqu'un; **to knock something over** renverser quelque chose ▷ *She knocked over a glass.* Elle a renversé un verre.; **to knock somebody out** (stun) assommer ▷ *They knocked out the watchman.* Ils ont assommé le gardien.
▷ *n* coup *m*

knot [nɔt] *n* nœud *m*; **to tie a knot in something** faire un nœud à quelque chose

know [nəu] *vb* ❶ savoir ▷ *"It's a long way."* — *"Yes, I know."* « C'est loin. » — « Oui, je sais. » ▷ *I don't know.* Je ne sais pas. ▷ *I don't know what to do.* Je ne sais pas quoi faire. ▷ *I don't know how to do it.* Je ne sais pas comment faire. ❷ connaître ▷ *I know her.* Je la connais. ▷ *I know Halifax well.* Je connais bien Halifax.; **I don't know any German.** Je ne parle pas du tout allemand.; **to know that...** savoir que... ▷ *I know that you like chocolate.* Je sais que tu aimes le chocolat. ▷ *I didn't know that your dad was a policeman.* Je ne savais pas que ton père était policier.; **to know about something** **(1)** (be aware of) être au courant de quelque chose ▷ *Do you know about the meeting this afternoon?* Tu es au courant de la réunion de cet après-midi? **(2)** (be knowledgeable about) s'y connaître en quelque chose ▷ *She knows a lot about cars.* Elle s'y connaît en voitures. ▷ *I don't know much about computers.* Je ne m'y connais pas bien en informatique.; **to know how to do something** savoir faire quelque chose ▷ *He knows how to swim.* Il sait nager.; **to get to know somebody** apprendre à connaître quelqu'un; **I'll let you know tomorrow.** Je te le ferai savoir demain.; **Let me know if you need any help.** Si tu as besoin d'aide, dis-le moi.; **How should I know?** (I don't know!) Comment veux-tu que je le sache?; **You never know!** On ne sait jamais!

know-how ['nəuhau] *n* savoir-faire *m*

know-it-all ['nəuɪtɔ:l] *n* je-sais-tout *m* ▷ *He's*

such a know-it-all! C'est Monsieur je-sais-tout!

knowledge ['nɒlɪdʒ] *n* connaissance *f*

knowledgeable ['nɒlɪdʒəbl] *adj*: **to be knowledgeable about something** s'y connaître en quelque chose ▷ *She's very knowledgeable about computers.* Elle s'y connaît bien en informatique.

known [nəʊn] *vb see* **know**

lab [læb] *n* (= *laboratory*) labo *m*; **a lab technician** un laborantin

label ['leɪbl] *n* étiquette *f*

laboratory [lə'bɒrətərɪ] *n* laboratoire *m*

labour ['leɪbər] *n*: **to be in labour** être en train d'accoucher; **the labour market** le marché du travail; **a labour union** un syndicat

Labour Day *n* fête du Travail *f*

labourer ['leɪbərə'] *n* manœuvre *m* ▷ *He got the job despite his lack of experience.* Il a obtenu le poste en dépit de son manque d'expérience.; **a farm labourer** un ouvrier agricole

Labrador ['læbrədɔ:'] *n* Labrador *m*

lace [leɪs] *n* (*of shoe*) lacet *m* dentelle *f* ▷ *a lace collar* un col en dentelle

lack [læk] *n* manque *m* ▷ *He got the job despite his lack of experience.* Il a obtenu le poste en dépit de son manque d'expérience.; **There was no lack of volunteers.** Les volontaires ne manquaient pas.

lacquer ['lækə'] *n* laque *f*

lacrosse [lə'krɒs] *n* crosse *f* ▷ *a lacrosse stick* une crosse

ladder ['lædə'] *n* échelle *f*

lady ['leɪdɪ] *n* dame *f*; **a young lady** une jeune fille; **Ladies and gentlemen...** Mesdames, Messieurs...; **the ladies' room** les toilettes *fpl* pour dames

ladybug ['leɪdɪbʌg] *n* coccinelle *f*

lag behind [læg-] *vb* rester en arrière

laid [leɪd] *vb see* **lay**

laid-back [leɪd'bæk] *adj* relax ▷ *Ma mère est très relax.* My mom is very laid-back.

lain [leɪn] *vb see* **lie**

lake [leɪk] *n* lac *m*; **Lake Superior** le lac Supérieur; **Lake Erie** le lac Érié

lamb [læm] *n* agneau *m* (*pl* agneaux); **a lamb chop** une côtelette d'agneau

lame [leɪm] *adj*: **to be lame** boîter ▷ *My pony is lame.* Mon poney boîte.; **a lame excuse** une piètre excuse

lamp [læmp] *n* lampe *f*

lampshade ['læmpʃeɪd] *n* abat-jour *m* (*pl* abat-jour)

land [lænd] *n* terre *f*; **a piece of land** un terrain (*country*) pays *m* ▷ *vb* (*plane, passenger*) atterrir

landfill site ['lændfɪl-] *n* site d'enfouissement *m*

landing ['lændɪŋ] *n* (*of plane*) atterrissage *m* (*of staircase*) palier *m*

landlady ['lændleɪdɪ] *n* propriétaire

landlord ['lændlɔ:d] *n* propriétaire

landmark ['lændmɑ:k] *n* (*for finding your way*) point de repère *m*; **The CN Tower is one of Toronto's most famous landmarks.** La tour CN est l'un des sites les plus célèbres du paysage torontois.

landowner ['lændəʊnə'] *n* propriétaire terrien *m*

landscape ['lænskeɪp] *n* paysage *m*

landslide ['lændslaɪd] *n* glissement de terrain *m*

lane [leɪn] *n* (*leading to country house*) entrée *f* (*on highway*) voie *f* (*small road in city*) ruelle *f*

language ['læŋgwɪdʒ] *n* langue *f* ▷ *French isn't a difficult language.* Le français n'est pas une langue difficile. langage *m* ▷ *the origin of language* l'origine du langage ▷ *Watch your language!* Surveille ton langage! ▷ *body language* le langage corporel; **to use bad language** dire des grossièretés

lantern ['læntn] *n* lanterne *f*

lap [læp] *n* (*sport*) tour de piste *m* ▷ *I ran 10 laps.* J'ai fait dix tours de piste en courant. (*pool*) longueur *f* ▷ *I swam 30 laps.* J'ai fait trente longueurs.; **on my lap** sur mes genoux

laptop ['læptɒp] *n* (*computer*) portable *m*

large [lɑ:dʒ] *adj* grand ▷ *a large house* une grande maison (*person, animal*) gros (*f* grosse) ▷ *a large dog* un gros chien

largely ['lɑ:dʒlɪ] *adv* en grande partie ▷ *It's largely the fault of the government.* C'est en grande partie la faute du gouvernement.

laryngitis [lærɪn'dʒaɪtɪs] *n* laryngite *f*

lasagna [lə'zænjə] *n* lasagne *f*

laser ['leɪzə'] *n* laser *m*; **a laser printer** une imprimante laser

last [lɑ:st] *adj, adv* dernier (*f* dernière) ▷ *last Friday* vendredi dernier ▷ *last week* la semaine dernière ▷ *last summer* l'été dernier en dernier ▷ *She arrived last.* Elle est arrivée en dernier.; **"I lost my wallet." — "When did you see it last?"** «J'ai perdu mon portefeuille.» — «Quand est-ce que tu l'as vu pour la dernière fois?»; **When I last saw him, he was wearing a blue shirt.** La dernière fois que je l'ai vu, il portait une chemise bleue.; **the last time** la dernière fois ▷ *the last time I saw her* la dernière fois que je l'ai vue ▷ *That's the last time I take your advice!* C'est la dernière fois que je suis tes conseils!; **last night** (*evening*) hier soir ▷ *I got home at midnight last night.* Je suis rentré à minuit hier soir. (2) (*sleeping hours*) la nuit dernière ▷ *I couldn't sleep last night.* J'ai eu du mal à dormir la nuit dernière.; **at last** enfin ▷ *vb* durer ▷ *The concert lasts two hours.* Le concert dure deux heures.

lastly ['lɑ:stlɪ] *adv* finalement ▷ *Lastly, what*

time do you arrive? Finalement, à quelle heure arrives-tu?

late [leɪt] adj, adv **①** en retard ▷ Hurry up or you'll be late! Dépêche-toi, sinon tu vas être en retard! ▷ I'm often late for school. J'arrive souvent en retard à l'école.; **to arrive late** arriver en retard ▷ She arrived late. Elle est arrivée en retard. **②** tard ▷ I went to bed late. Je me suis couché tard.; **in the late afternoon** en fin d'après-midi; **in late May** fin mai

lately ['leɪtlɪ] adv ces derniers temps ▷ I haven't seen him lately. Je ne l'ai pas vus ces derniers temps.

later ['leɪtər] adv plus tard ▷ I'll do it later. Je ferai ça plus tard.; **See you later!** À tout à l'heure!

latest ['leɪtɪst] adj dernier (f dernière) ▷ their latest album leur dernier album; **at the latest** au plus tard ▷ by 10 o'clock at the latest à dix heures au plus tard

latter ['lætər] n second m, seconde f; **the former..., the latter...** le premier..., le second... ▷ The former lives in Saskatchewan, the latter in New Brunswick. Le premier habite en Saskatchewan, le second au Nouveau-Brunswick.; **The latter is the more expensive of the two systems.** Ce dernier système est le plus coûteux des deux.

laugh [lɑːf] n rire m; **It was a good laugh.** (it was funny) C'était bien amusant.
▶ vb rire m; **to laugh at something** (make fun of) se moquer de quelque chose ▷ They laughed at her. Ils se sont moqués d'elle.

launch [lɔːntʃ] vb (product, rocket, boat) lancer ▷ They're going to launch a new model. Ils vont lancer un nouveau modèle.

laundromat® ['lɔːndrəmæt] n lavoir m

laundry ['lɔːndrɪ] n **①** (clothes) linge m **②** (task) lavage m ▷ to do the laundry faire le lavage **③** (public, with machines) lavoir m ▷ Does this campground have a laundry? Ce terrain de camping a un lavoir?; **laundry room** la salle de lavage; **coin laundry** le lavoir

Laurentians [lɔːˈrɛnʃənz] npl Laurentides fpl ▷ We went camping in the Laurentians. Nous avons fait du camping dans les Laurentides.

law [lɔː] n **①** loi f ▷ The laws are very strict. Les lois sont très sévères.; **It's against the law.** C'est illégal. **②** (subject) droit m ▷ My brother is studying law. Mon frère fait des études de droit.; **law and order** l'ordre m public; **law school** la faculté de droit

lawn [lɔːn] n pelouse f

lawnmower ['lɔːnməʊər] n tondeuse à gazon f

lawyer ['lɔːjər] n avocat m, avocate f ▷ My mother's a lawyer. Ma mère est avocate.

lay [leɪ] vb mettre ▷ He laid the baby in her crib. Il a mis le bébé dans son lit.

lay off vb mettre à pied ▷ My father has been laid off. Mon père a été mis à pied.

layer ['leɪər] n couche f ▷ the ozone layer la couche d'ozone

layout ['leɪaʊt] n **①** (publishing) mise en page f **②** (of house, buildings) disposition f ▷ It took me some time to get familiar with the layout

of the school. J'ai mis un certain temps à me familiariser avec la disposition de l'école.

lazy ['leɪzɪ] adj paresseux (f paresseuse)

lead [n lɛd, vb liːd] n (metal) plomb m; **to be in the lead** être en tête ▷ Our team is in the lead. Notre équipe est en tête.; **to have a two-point lead** avoir deux points d'avance; **to take the lead (1)** (sports) prendre la tête **(2)** (act first) prendre l'initiative
▶ vb mener **①** (of street) the street that leads to the arena la rue qui mène à l'aréna; **to lead the way** montrer le chemin; **to lead somebody away** emmener quelqu'un ▷ The police led the man away. La police a emmené l'homme.

leader ['liːdər] n **①** (of expedition, gang, political party) chef ▷ She's the party leader. C'est la chef du parti politique. **②** (of organization, company) dirigeant m, dirigeante f

lead singer [liːd-] n chanteur principal m, chanteuse principale f

leaf [liːf] n feuille f

leaflet ['liːflɪt] n brochure f

league [liːg] n ligue f ▷ They are at the top of the league. Ils sont en tête de la ligue.; **a minor league** une ligue mineure; **a major league** une ligue majeure

leak [liːk] n fuite f ▷ a gas leak une fuite de gaz
▶ vb (pipe, water, gas) fuir

lean [liːn] adj maigre ▷ lean meat la viande maigre
▶ vb **①** (support oneself) s'appuyer ▷ He leaned against the wall. Il s'est appuyé contre le mur. **②** (support an object) appuyer ▷ She leaned her bike against the railing. Elle a appuyé son vélo contre la rampe.; **The ladder was leaning against the wall.** L'échelle était appuyée contre le mur. **③** (bend) se pencher ▷ Don't lean over too far. Ne te penche pas trop. ▷ She leaned out of the window. Elle s'est penchée par la fenêtre. ▷ to lean forward se pencher en avant

leap [liːp] vb sauter ▷ They leapt over the stream. Ils ont sauté pour traverser la rivière.; **He leapt out of his chair when his team scored.** Il s'est levé d'un bond lorsque son équipe a marqué.

leap year n année f bissextile

learn [lɜːn] vb apprendre ▷ I'm learning to ski. J'apprends à skier.

learner ['lɜːnər] n: **She's a quick learner.** Elle apprend vite.; **second language learners** ceux qui apprennent une langue seconde

learnt [lɜːnt] vb see **learn**

leash [liːʃ] n laisse f ▷ Keep your dog on a leash. Tenez votre chien en laisse.

least [liːst] adv, adj, pron: **the least (1)** (followed by noun) le moins de ▷ It takes the least time. C'est ce qui prend le moins de temps. **(2)** (after a verb) le moins ▷ Music is the subject I like the least. La musique est la matière que j'aime le moins.; **the least... (1)** le moins... ▷ the least expensive hotel l'hôtel le moins cher **(2)** le moins... ▷ the least expensive seat la place la moins chère **(3)** les moins... ▷ the least expensive hotels les hôtels les moins chers ▷ the least expensive seats les places les moins chères; **It's the least I can do.** C'est le moins que je puisse faire.; **at least (1)** au moins ▷ *It'll cost at least $200.* Ça va coûter au moins deux cents dollars. **(2)** du moins ▷ *...but at least nobody was hurt.* ...mais du moins personne n'a été blessé. ▷ *"It's totally unfair" — "at least, that's my opinion."* « C'est vraiment injuste » — « du moins c'est ce que je pense. »

leather ['lɛðəʳ] *n* cuir *m* ▷ *a black leather jacket* un manteau de cuir noir

leave [liːv] *n* ❶ *(from job)* congé *m* ▷ *sick leave* le congé de maladie ▷ *maternity leave* le congé de maternité ❷ *(from army)* permission *f* ▷ *My brother is on leave for a week.* Mon frère est en permission pendant une semaine.
▷ *vb* ❶ *(deliberately)* laisser ▷ *Don't leave your camera in the car.* Ne laisse pas ton appareil-photo dans la voiture. ❷ *(by mistake)* oublier ▷ *I left my book at home.* J'ai oublié mon livre à la maison. ▷ *Make sure you haven't left anything behind.* Vérifiez bien que vous n'avez rien oublié. ❸ *(go)* partir ▷ *The bus leaves at 8.* L'autobus part à huit heures. ▷ *She just left.* Elle vient de partir. ❹ *(go away from)* quitter ▷ *We leave London at six o'clock.* Nous quittons London à six heures. ▷ *My sister left home last year.* Ma sœur a quitté la maison l'an dernier.; **to leave somebody alone** laisser quelqu'un tranquille ▷ *Leave me alone!* Laisse-moi tranquille!

leave out *vb* ❶ *(person)* mettre à l'écart ▷ *Not knowing the language, I felt really left out.* Comme je ne connaissais pas la langue, je me suis vraiment senti à l'écart. ❷ *(word, sentence)* omettre ▷ *You left out a word there.* Tu as omis un mot là.

leaves [liːvz] *npl see* **leaf**

lecture ['lɛktʃəʳ] *n* ❶ *(public)* conférence *f* ❷ *(at university)* cours magistral *m* (*pl* cours magistraux) ▷ *(scolding)* sermon *m* ▷ *a lecture on table manners* un sermon sur les bonnes manières à table
▷ *vb* ❶ enseigner ▷ *He lectures at the technical college.* Il enseigne au collège technique. ❷ faire la morale ▷ *He's always lecturing us.* Il n'arrête pas de nous faire la morale.

led [lɛd] *vb see* **lead**

leek [liːk] *n* poireau *m* (*pl* poireaux)

left [lɛft] *vb see* **leave**
▷ *adj, adv* ❶ gauche *f* ▷ *my left hand* ma main gauche ▷ *on the left side of the road* sur le côté gauche de la route ❷ à gauche ▷ *Turn left at the traffic lights.* Tournez à gauche aux prochains feux.; **I have no money left.** Il ne me reste plus d'argent.
▷ *n* gauche *f*; **on the left** à gauche ▷ *Our house is on the left.* Notre maison est à gauche.

left-hand ['lɛfthænd] *adj*: **the left-hand side** la gauche ▷ *It's on the left-hand side.* C'est à gauche.

left-handed [lɛft'hændɪd] *adj* gaucher (*f* gauchère)

leg [lɛg] *n* jambe *f* ▷ *She's broken her leg.* Elle s'est cassé la jambe.; **a chicken leg** une cuisse de poulet; **a leg of lamb** un gigot d'agneau

legal ['liːgl] *adj* (*mpl* légaux) *m* ▷ *the legal driving age* l'âge légal pour conduire ▷ *Is it legal to copy this CD?* Est-il légal de faire une

copie de ce CD? ❷ juridique ▷ *the legal system* le système juridique ▷ *legal aid* l'aide juridique *f* ▷ *legal action* une poursuite juridique

legend ['lɛdʒənd] *n* légende *f*

leggings ['lɛgɪŋz] *n* collant *m*

legible ['lɛdʒəbl] *adj* lisible

Legislative Assembly ['lɛdʒɪslətɪv-] *n* Assemblée f législative

leisure ['lɛʒəʳ] *n* loisirs *mpl* ▷ *What do you do in your leisure time?* Qu'est-ce que tu fais pendant tes loisirs?

leisure centre *n* centre de loisirs *m*

lemon ['lɛmən] *n* citron *m*

lemonade [lɛmə'neɪd] *n* limonade *f*

lend [lɛnd] *vb* ▷ *I can lend you some money.* Je peux te prêter de l'argent.

length [lɛŋθ] *n* longueur *f*; **It's about a metre in length.** Ça fait environ un mètre de long.

lengthwise ['lɛŋθwaɪz] *adv* dans le sens de la longueur

lens [lɛnz] *n* ❶ *(contact lens)* lentille cornéenne *f* ❷ *(of spectacles)* verre *m* ❸ *(of camera)* objectif *m*

lent [lɛnt] *vb see* **lend**

lentil ['lɛntl] *n* lentille *f*

Leo ['liːəu] *n* Lion *m* ▷ *I'm a Leo.* Je suis Lion.

leotard ['liːətɑːd] *n* léotard *m*

lesbian ['lɛzbɪən] *n* lesbienne *f*

less [lɛs] *pron, adv, adj* ❶ moins ▷ *He's less athletic than her.* Il est moins athlétique qu'elle. ▷ *A bit less, please.* Un peu moins, s'il vous plaît. ❷ moins de ▷ *I've got less time for hobbies now.* J'ai moins de temps pour les loisirs maintenant.; **less than (1)** *(with amounts)* moins de ▷ *It's less than a kilometre from here.* C'est à moins d'un kilomètre d'ici. ▷ *It costs less than 100 dollars.* Ça coûte moins de cent dollars. ▷ *less than half* moins de la moitié **(2)** *(in comparisons)* moins que ▷ *He spent less than me.* Il a dépensé moins que moi. ▷ *I've got less than you.* J'en ai moins que toi. ▷ *It cost less than we thought.* Ça a coûté moins cher que nous ne le pensions.

lesson ['lɛsn] *n* ❶ leçon *f* ▷ *a French lesson* une leçon de français ▷ *"Lesson Sixteen" (in textbook)* "Leçon seize" ❷ cours *m* ▷ *dancing lessons* cours de danse ▷ *Each lesson lasts 40 minutes.* Chaque cours dure quarante minutes.

let [lɛt] *vb (allow)* laisser; **to let somebody do something** laisser quelqu'un faire quelque chose ▷ *Let me have a look.* Laisse-moi voir. ▷ *My parents won't let me stay out that late.* Mes parents ne me laissent pas sortir aussi tard.; **to let somebody know** faire savoir à quelqu'un ▷ *I'll let you know as soon as possible.* Je vous le ferai savoir dès que possible.; **to let down** décevoir ▷ *I won't let you down.* Je ne vous décevrai pas.; **to let go** lâcher ▷ *Let me go!* Lâche-moi! ▷ *Let go of the rope.* Lâche la corde. ▷ *Let go! Lâche prise!*; **to let in** laisser entrer ▷ *They wouldn't let me in because I was under 18.* Ils ne m'ont pas laissé entrer parce que j'avais moins de dix-huit ans.; **to let out** laisser sortir ▷ *Don't let the cat out.* Ne laisse pas sortir le chat.; **to let up** *(rain)* diminuer ▷ *Let's go to a movie!* Si on allait au cinéma?; **Let's go!**

Allons-y!

letter ['lɛtə'] n lettre f

lettuce ['lɛtɪs] n salade f

leukemia [lu:'ki:mɪə] n leucémie f

level ['lɛvl] adj plan ▷ A pool table must be perfectly level. Une table de billard doit être parfaitement plane.
▶ n niveau m (pl niveaux) ▷ The water level is rising. Le niveau d'eau monte.

lever ['li:və'] n levier m

liable ['laɪəbl] adj: **He's liable to lose his temper.** Il se met facilement en colère.; **It's liable to snow tonight.** Il risque de neiger ce soir.

liar ['laɪə'] n menteur m, menteuse f

liberal ['lɪbərəl] adj (opinions) libéral (mpl libéraux)

liberation [lɪbə'reɪʃən] n libération f

liberty ['lɪbətɪ] n liberté f

Libra ['li:brə] n Balance f ▷ I'm a Libra. Je suis Balance.

librarian [laɪ'brɛərɪən] n bibliothécaire ▷ She's a librarian. Elle est bibliothécaire.

library ['laɪbrərɪ] n bibliothèque f

licence ['laɪsns] n permis m; **a driver's licence** un permis de conduire; **fishing licence** le permis de pêche; **licence plate** la plaque d'immatriculation; **licence number** le numéro d'immatriculation

lick [lɪk] vb lécher

licorice ['lɪkərɪs] n réglisse f

lid [lɪd] n couvercle m

lie [laɪ] vb (not tell the truth) mentir ▷ I know she's lying. Je sais qu'elle ment.; **to lie down** s'allonger; **to be lying down** être allongé; **He was lying on the sofa.** Il était allongé sur le sofa. ▷ When I'm on holiday I lie on the beach all day. Quand je suis en vacances, je reste allongé sur la plage toute la journée.
▶ n mensonge m; **to tell a lie** mentir; **That's a lie!** Ce n'est pas vrai!

lieutenant-governor [lɛf'tɛnənt-] n lieutenant-gouverneur m, lieutenante-gouverneure f

life [laɪf] n vie f

lifeboat ['laɪfbəut] n canot de sauvetage m

lifeguard ['laɪfɡɑ:d] n sauveteur m, sauveteure f

life jacket n gilet de sauvetage m

lifesaving ['laɪfseɪvɪŋ] n sauvetage m ▷ I've done a course in lifesaving. J'ai pris des cours de sauvetage.

lifestyle ['laɪfstaɪl] n style de vie m

lift [lɪft] vb soulever ▷ It's too heavy. I can't lift it. C'est trop lourd. Je ne peux pas le soulever.
▶ n: **He gave me a lift to the movie theatre.** Il m'a emmené au cinéma en voiture.; **Would you like a lift?** Est-ce que je peux vous déposer quelque part?

light [laɪt] adj (not heavy) léger (f légère) ▷ a light jacket un veston léger ▷ a light meal un repas léger (colour) clair ▷ a light blue sweater un chandail bleu clair
▶ n lumière f ▷ to switch on the light allumer la lumière ▷ to switch off the light éteindre la lumière lampe f ▷ There's a light by my bed. Il y

a une lampe près de mon lit.; **the traffic lights** les m feux; **Have you got a light?** (match, lighter) Avez-vous du feu?
▶ vb (candle, fire) allumer

light bulb n ampoule f

lighter ['laɪtə'] n briquet m

lighthouse ['laɪthaus] n phare m

lightning ['laɪtnɪŋ] n éclairs mpl; **a flash of lightning** un éclair

like [laɪk] vb ❶ aimer ▷ I don't like mustard. Je n'aime pas la moutarde. ▷ I like riding. J'aime monter à cheval. ❷ aimer bien ▷ I like him, but I don't want to go out with him. Je l'aime bien, mais je ne veux pas sortir avec lui.; **I'd like…** Je voudrais… ▷ I'd like an orange juice, please. Je voudrais un jus d'orange, s'il vous plaît. ▷ Would you like some coffee? Voulez-vous du café?; **I'd like to…** J'aimerais… ▷ I'd like to go to Russia one day. J'aimerais aller en Russie un jour. ▷ I'd like to wash my hands. J'aimerais me laver les mains.; **Would you like to go for a walk?** Tu veux aller faire une promenade?; **…if you like** …si tu veux
▶ prep comme ▷ It's fine like that. C'est bien comme ça. ▷ Do it like this. Fais-le comme ça. ▷ a city like St. John's une ville comme St. John's ▷ It's a bit like salmon. C'est un peu comme du saumon.; **What's the weather like?** Quel temps fait-il?; **to look like somebody** ressembler à quelqu'un ▷ You look like my brother. Tu ressembles à mon frère.

likely ['laɪklɪ] adj probable ▷ That's not very likely. C'est peu probable.; **She's likely to come.** Elle viendra probablement.; **She's not likely to come.** Elle ne viendra probablement pas.

lime [laɪm] n (fruit) lime f

limit ['lɪmɪt] n limite f ▷ The speed limit is 100 km/h. La vitesse limite est de cent kilomètres à l'heure.

limousine ['lɪməzi:n] n limousine f

limp [lɪmp] vb boiter

line [laɪn] n ❶ ligne f ▷ a straight line une ligne droite ▷ a bus line une ligne d'autobus ▷ There's static on the line. Il y a de la friture sur la ligne. ❷ (to divide, cancel) trait m ▷ Draw a line under each answer. Tirez un trait sous chaque réponse. ❸ (lineup) queue f ▷ We had to stand in line. Nous avons dû faire la queue. ❹ rangée f ▷ a line of trees une rangée d'arbres; **Hold the line, please.** Ne quittez pas.; **online** (computing) en ligne

linen ['lɪnɪn] n lin m ▷ a linen jacket un veston en lin

linguist ['lɪŋɡwɪst] n: **to be a good linguist** être doué pour les langues ▷ She's a good linguist. Elle est douée pour les langues.

lining ['laɪnɪŋ] n (of jacket, skirt etc) doublure f

link [lɪŋk] n ❶ rapport m ▷ The link between smoking and cancer le rapport entre le tabagisme et le cancer ❷ (computing) lien m
▶ vb relier

linoleum [lɪ'nəulɪəm] n linoléum m

lion [laɪən] n lion m

lioness ['laɪənɪs] n lionne f

lip [lɪp] n lèvre f

lip-read ['lɪpriːd] vb lire sur les lèvres

lip salve [-sælv] n pommade pour les lèvres f

lipstick ['lɪpstɪk] n rouge à lèvres m

liquid ['lɪkwɪd] adj liquide m
▷ n liquide m

list [lɪst] n liste f
▷ vb faire une liste de ▷ List your hobbies. Fais une liste de tes passe-temps.

listen ['lɪsn] vb écouter ▷ Listen to this! Écoutez ceci! ▷ Listen to me! Écoutez-moi!

listener ['lɪsnə'] n auditeur m, auditrice f

lit [lɪt] vb see **light**

literally ['lɪtrəlɪ] adv (completely) vraiment ▷ It was literally impossible to find a seat. Il était vraiment impossible de trouver une place.; **to translate literally** faire une traduction littérale

literature ['lɪtrɪtʃə'] n littérature f ▷ Canadian literature la littérature canadienne

litre ['liːtə'] n litre m

litter ['lɪtə'] n ordures fpl

little ['lɪtl] adj petit ▷ a little boy un petit garçon; **a little** un peu ▷ "How much would you like?" — "Just a little." « Combien en voulez-vous? » — « Juste un peu. »; **very little** très peu ▷ We have very little time. Nous avons très peu de temps.; **little by little** petit à petit

live [adj laɪv, vb lɪv] adj ❶ (animal) vivant ❷ (broadcast) en direct; **There's live music on Fridays.** Il y a des musiciens qui jouent le vendredi.
▷ vb ❶ vivre ▷ I live with my grandmother. Je vis avec ma grand-mère.; **to live on something** vivre de quelque chose ▷ He lives on a small salary. Il vit d'un modeste salaire. ❷ (reside) habiter ▷ Where do you live? Où est-ce que tu habites? ▷ I live in Moncton. J'habite à Moncton.; **to live together** (1) (as roommates) partager un appartement ▷ She's living with two other students. Elle partage un appartement avec deux autres étudiantes. (2) vivre ensemble ▷ My parents aren't living together any more. Mes parents ne vivent plus ensemble.; **They're not married, they're living together.** Ils ne sont pas mariés, ils vivent en union libre.

lively ['laɪvlɪ] adj animé ▷ It was a lively party. C'était une soirée animée.; **He has a lively personality.** Il est plein de vitalité.

liver ['lɪvə'] n foie m

lives [laɪvz] npl vies fpl

livestock ['laɪvstɔk] n animaux mpl d'élevage

living ['lɪvɪŋ] n: **to make a living** gagner sa vie; **What does she do for a living?** Qu'est-ce qu'elle fait dans la vie?

living room n salle de séjour f

lizard ['lɪzəd] n lézard m

load [ləud] n: **loads of** un tas de ▷ loads of money un tas d'argent; **That's a load of rubbish!** Tu ne dis que des niaiseries!
▷ vb charger ▷ a trolley loaded with luggage un chariot chargé de bagages

loaf [ləuf] n pain m; **a loaf of bread** un pain
▷ vb traîner ▷ Are you going to loaf around all day? Tu vas traîner toute la journée?

loan [ləun] n prêt m ▷ a bank loan un prêt

bancaire ▷ to pay back a loan payer un prêt
▷ vb prêter

loathe [ləuð] vb détester ▷ I loathe country music. Je déteste la musique country.

loaves [ləuvz] npl see **loaf**

lobby ['lɔbɪ] n hall m ▷ in the hotel lobby dans le hall de l'hôtel

lobster ['lɔbstə'] n homard m

local ['ləukl] adj local (mpl locaux) ▷ the local paper le journal local ▷ a local call un appel local

location [ləu'keɪʃən] n endroit m ▷ a hotel set in a beautiful location un hôtel situé dans un endroit magnifique

lock [lɔk] n serrure f ▷ The lock is broken. La serrure est cassée.
▷ vb fermer à clé ▷ Make sure you lock your door. N'oubliez pas de fermer votre porte à clé.

lock out vb: **The door slammed and I was locked out.** La porte a claqué et je me suis retrouvé à la porte.

locker ['lɔkə'] n casier m; **the locker room** le vestiaire; **storage lockers** (airport, mall) la consigne automatique

locket ['lɔkɪt] n médaillon m

loft [lɔft] n grenier m

log [lɔg] n (of wood) bûche f

log in vb se connecter

log off vb se déconnecter

log on vb se connecter

log out vb se déconnecter

logical ['lɔdʒɪkl] adj logique

login ['lɔgɪn] n ❶ (action) ouverture f de session ❷ (ID) nom d'utilisateur m

logo ['ləugəu] n logo m

lollipop ['lɔlɪpɔp] n suçon m

loneliness ['ləunlɪnɪs] n solitude f

lonely ['ləunlɪ] adj seul; **to feel lonely** se sentir seul ▷ He feels a bit lonely. Il se sent un peu seul.

lonesome ['ləunsəm] adj: **to feel lonesome** se sentir seul

long [lɔŋ] adj, adv long (f longue) ▷ She has long hair. Elle a les cheveux longs. ▷ The room is 6 metres long. La pièce fait six mètres de long.; **how long?** (time) combien de temps? ▷ How long did you stay there? Combien de temps êtes-vous resté là-bas? ▷ How long have you been here? Depuis combien de temps êtes-vous ici? ▷ How long is the flight? Combien de temps dure le vol?; **I've been waiting a long time.** J'attends depuis longtemps.; **It takes a long time.** Ça prend du temps.; **as long as** si ▷ I'll come as long as it's not too expensive. Je viendrai si ce n'est pas trop cher.
▷ vb: **to long to do something** attendre avec impatience de faire quelque chose; **I'm longing to see my dad again.** J'attends avec impatience de revoir mon père.

long-distance [lɔŋ'dɪstəns] adj: **a long-distance call** un appel interurbain; **to call long distance** faire un appel interurbain

longer ['lɔŋgə'] adv: **They're no longer going out together.** Ils ne sortent plus ensemble.; **I can't stand it any longer.** Je ne peux plus le supporter.

long jump n saut en longueur m

look [luk] n: **to take a look** regarder ▷ *Take a look at this!* Regardez cecil; **I don't like the look of it.** Ça ne me dit rien qui vaille.

▷ vb ❶ regarder ▷ *Look!* Regardez!; **to look at something** regarder quelque chose ▷ *Look at this picture.* Regarde cette image. ❷ (seem) avoir l'air ▷ *She looks surprised.* Elle a l'air surprise. ▷ *That cake looks delicious.* Ce gâteau a l'air délicieux. ▷ *It looks fine.* Ça a l'air bien.; **to look like somebody** ressembler à quelqu'un ▷ *He looks like his brother.* Il ressemble à son frère.; **What does he look like?** Comment est-il physiquement?; **Look out!** Attention!; **to look after** s'occuper de ▷ *I look after my little sister.* Je m'occupe de ma petite sœur.; **to look for** chercher ▷ *I'm looking for my passport.* Je cherche mon passeport.; **to look forward to something** attendre quelque chose avec impatience ▷ *I'm looking forward to the holidays.* J'attends les vacances avec impatience.; **Looking forward to hearing from you...** J'espère avoir bientôt de tes nouvelles...; **to look around (1)** (look behind) se retourner ▷ *I shouted and he looked around.* J'ai crié et il s'est retourné. **(2)** (have a look) jeter un coup d'œil ▷ *I'm just looking around.* Je jette simplement un coup d'œil.; **I like looking around the stores.** J'aime faire les magasins.; **to look up** (word, name) chercher ▷ *If you don't know a word, look it up in the dictionary.* Si tu ne connaissez pas un mot, cherchez-le dans le dictionnaire.

lookout ['lukaut] n (scenic) belvédère m
loon [luːn] n huard m
loonie ['luːnɪ] n huard m
loop [luːp] n boucle f ▷ *Make a loop in the ribbon.* Fais une boucle au ruban.; **to be in the loop** être au courant ▷ *Keep me in the loop.* Tiens-moi au courant.
loose [luːs] adj (clothes) ample; **loose change** la petite monnaie; **a loose sheet of paper** une feuille volante; **A tiger got loose.** Un tigre s'est échappé.; **This screw is loose.** Cette vis s'est desserrée.
lopsided [lɒp'saɪdɪd] adj de travers ▷ *Your sculpture looks a bit lopsided.* Ta sculpture semble un peu de travers.
lose [luːz] vb perdre ▷ *I lost my purse.* J'ai perdu mon sac à main.; **to get lost** se perdre ▷ *I was afraid of getting lost.* J'avais peur de me perdre.
loser ['luːzəʳ] n perdant m, perdante f; **to be a bad loser** être mauvais perdant
loss [lɒs] n perte f
lost [lɒst] vb see **lose**
▷ adj perdu
lost-and-found [lɒstən'faund] n objets mpl perdus
lot [lɒt] n: **a lot** beaucoup; **a lot of** beaucoup de ▷ *a lot of work* beaucoup de travail ▷ *We saw a lot of interesting things.* Nous avons vu beaucoup de choses intéressantes.; **lots of** (informal) un tas de ▷ *She has lots of money.* Elle a un tas d'argent. ▷ *He has lots of friends.* Il a un tas d'amis.; **"What did you do on the weekend?" — "Not a lot."** « Qu'as-tu fait en fin de semaine? » — « Pas grand-chose. »; **"Do you like baseball?" — "Not a lot."** « Tu aimes

le baseball? » — « Pas tellement. »; **That's the lot.** C'est tout.
lottery ['lɒtərɪ] n loterie f; **to win the lottery** gagner à la loterie
loud [laud] adj fort ▷ *The television is too loud.* La télévision est trop forte.
loudly ['laudlɪ] adv fort
lounge [laundʒ] n salon m
lousy ['lauzɪ] adj infect ▷ *The food in the cafeteria is lousy.* La nourriture de la cafétéria est infecte.; **I feel lousy.** Je ne me sens pas bien.
love [lʌv] n amour m; **to be in love** être amoureux ▷ *She's in love with him.* Elle est amoureuse de lui.; **to make love** faire l'amour; **Give your sister my love.** Embrasse ta sœur pour moi.; **Love, Rosemary.** Amitiés, Rosemary.
▷ vb ❶ (be in love with) aimer ▷ *I love you.* Je t'aime. ❷ (like a lot) aimer beaucoup ▷ *Everybody loves her.* Tout le monde l'aime beaucoup. ▷ *I'd love to come.* J'aimerais beaucoup venir. ❸ (things) adorer ▷ *I love chocolate.* J'adore le chocolat. ▷ *I love skiing.* J'adore le ski.
lovely ['lʌvlɪ] adj charmant ▷ *What a lovely surprise!* Quelle charmante surprise! ▷ *She's a lovely person.* Elle est charmante.; **It's a lovely day.** Il fait très beau aujourd'hui.; **a lovely meal** un repas délicieux; **They've got a lovely house.** Ils ont une très belle maison.; **Have a lovely time!** Amusez-vous bien!
lover ['lʌvəʳ] n ❶ (in relationship) amant m, maîtresse f ❷ (of hobby, wine) amateur m ▷ *an art lover* un amateur d'art ▷ *He is a lover of good food.* Il est amateur de bonne cuisine.
low [ləu] adj, adv (price, level) bas (f basse) ▷ *That plane is flying very low.* Cet avion vole très bas. ▷ *in the low season* en basse saison
low-carb ['ləukɑːb] adj faible en glucides ▷ *a low-carb snack* une collation faible en glucides
lower ['ləuəʳ] adj inférieur ▷ *on the lower floor* à l'étage inférieur; **Lower Canada** le Bas-Canada
▷ vb baisser
low-fat ['ləu'fæt] adj allégé ▷ *a low-fat yogurt* un yogourt allégé
loyal ['lɔɪəl] adj loyal
Loyalist ['lɔɪəlɪst] n Loyaliste m
loyalty ['lɔɪəltɪ] n fidélité f
lozenge ['lɒzɪndʒ] n pastille f
luck [lʌk] n chance f ▷ *She hasn't had much luck.* Elle n'a pas eu beaucoup de chance.; **Good luck!** Bonne chance!; **Bad luck!** Pas de chance!
luckily ['lʌkɪlɪ] adv heureusement
lucky ['lʌkɪ] adj: **to be lucky (1)** (be fortunate) avoir de la chance ▷ *He's lucky. He has a job.* Il a de la chance. Il a un emploi. ▷ *"He wasn't hurt." — "That was lucky!"* « Il n'a pas été blessé. » — « C'est une chance! » **(2)** (bring luck) porter bonheur ▷ *Four-leaf clovers are lucky.* Les trèfles à quatre feuilles portent bonheur.; **a lucky charm** un porte-bonheur
luggage ['lʌgɪdʒ] n bagages mpl
lukewarm ['luːkwɔːm] adj (water, food) tiède; **Their response was lukewarm.** Leur réaction a été peu enthousiaste.

lump [lʌmp] n ❶ morceau m (pl morceaux)
▷ a lump of butter un morceau de beurre
❷ (swelling) bosse f ▷ He's got a lump on his
forehead. Il a une bosse sur le front.

lunatic ['luːnətɪk] n ❶ cinglé m, cinglée f ▷ He's
an absolute lunatic. Il est complètement cinglé.

lunch [lʌntʃ] n lunch m; **to have lunch** dîner
▷ We have lunch at 12:30. Nous dînons à midi et
demie.

lung [lʌŋ] n poumon m; **lung cancer** le cancer
du poumon

lurk [lɜːk] vb ❶ rôder ▷ The criminal is still
lurking in the neighbourhood. Le malfaiteur
rôde encore dans le quartier. ❷ (on Internet)
badauder ▷ She just lurks on that discussion
group. Elle ne fait que badauder dans ce groupe
de discussion.

luscious ['lʌʃəs] adj délicieux (f délicieuse)

lush [lʌʃ] adj luxuriant

luxurious [lʌg'zjʊərɪəs] adj luxueux (f
luxueuse)

luxury ['lʌkʃərɪ] n luxe m ▷ It was luxury! C'était
un vrai luxe!; **a luxury hotel** un hôtel de luxe

lying ['laɪɪŋ] vb see **lie**

lynx [lɪŋks] n lynx m

lyrics ['lɪrɪks] npl (of song) paroles fpl

m

macaroni [mækə'rəʊnɪ] n macaronis mpl

machine [mə'ʃiːn] n machine f

machinery [mə'ʃiːnərɪ] n machines fpl

mackerel ['mækrl] n maquereau m (pl
maquereaux)

mad [mæd] adj ❶ (angry) furieux (f furieuse)
▷ She'll be mad when she finds out. Elle sera
furieuse quand elle va s'en apercevoir.
❷ (insane) fou m (f folle) ▷ You're mad! Tu es fou!;
to get mad at somebody se fâcher contre
quelqu'un; **like mad** comme un fou ▷ I worked
like mad. J'ai travaillé comme un fou.; **mad cow
disease** la maladie de la vache folle

madam ['mædəm] n madame f ▷ Would you
like to order, Madam? Désirez-vous commander,
Madame?

made [meɪd] vb see **make**

madly ['mædlɪ] adv: **They're madly in love.** Ils
sont éperdument amoureux.

madness ['mædnɪs] n folie f ▷ It's absolute
madness. C'est de la pure folie.

magazine [mægə'ziːn] n magazine m

magic ['mædʒɪk] adj magique ▷ a magic wand
une baguette magique; **a magic trick** un tour

de magie.
▷ n magie f; **My hobby is magic.** Je fais des
tours de magie.

magician [mə'dʒɪʃən] n (conjurer)
prestidigitateur m, prestidigitatrice f

magnet ['mægnɪt] n aimant m

magnificent [mæg'nɪfɪsnt] adj magnifique
▷ a magnificent view une vue magnifique

magnifying glass ['mægnɪfaɪɪŋ-] n loupe f

maiden name ['meɪdən-] n nom de jeune
fille m

mail [meɪl] n courrier m ▷ Here's your mail. Voici
ton courrier.; **e-mail** (electronic mail) le courriel;
by mail par la poste
▷ vb poster

mailbox ['meɪlbɒks] n boîte aux lettres f

mailing list ['meɪlɪŋ-] n liste d'adresses f

main [meɪn] adj principal (mpl principaux)
▷ the main problem le principal problème; **main
road** la grande route ▷ I don't like biking on main
roads. Je n'aime pas faire du vélo sur les grandes
routes.; **the main thing is to...** l'essentiel
est de...

mainland ['meɪnlənd] n continent m ▷ A ferry
travels between Newfoundland and the mainland.
Un traversier circule entre Terre-Neuve et le
continent.; **the Lower Mainland** la vallée du
Bas-Fraser

mainly ['meɪnlɪ] adv principalement

maintain [meɪn'teɪn] vb ❶ (machine, building)
entretenir ❷ (insist) maintenir ▷ He maintains
that he told the truth. Il maintient qu'il a dit la
vérité.

maintenance ['meɪntənəns] n (of machine,
building) entretien m

majesty ['mædʒɪstɪ] n majesté f; **Your
Majesty** Votre Majesté

major ['meɪdʒər] adj majeur ▷ a major problem
un problème majeur; **in C major** en do majeur

majority [mə'dʒɒrɪtɪ] n majorité f

make [meɪk] n marque f ▷ What make is that
car? De quelle marque est cette voiture?
▷ vb ❶ faire ▷ I'm going to make a cake. Je vais
faire un gâteau. ▷ He made it himself. Il l'a fait
lui-même. ▷ I make my bed every morning. Je fais
mon lit tous les matins. ▷ 2 and 2 make 4. Deux
et deux font quatre. ❷ (manufacture) fabriquer
▷ made in Canada fabriqué au Canada ❸ (earn)
gagner ▷ She makes a lot of money. Elle gagne
beaucoup d'argent.; **to make somebody do
something** obliger quelqu'un à faire quelque
chose ▷ My parents make me do my homework.
Mes parents m'obligent à faire mes devoirs.;
to make lunch préparer le repas ▷ He's making
supper. Il prépare le souper.; **to make a phone
call** donner un coup de téléphone ▷ I'd like to
make a phone call. J'aimerais donner un coup
de téléphone.; **to make fun of somebody** se
moquer de quelqu'un ▷ They made fun of me. Ils
se sont moqués de moi.

make it vb ❶ arriver ▷ We finally made it to
Calgary. Nous sommes enfin arrivés à Calgary.;
We made it to the finals. Nous sommes allés
en finale. ❷ venir ▷ I'm sorry, I can't make it
tonight. Désolé, je ne peux pas venir ce soir.
❸ réussir ▷ Way to go! You made it! Bravo! Tu

as réussi!

make out vb ❶ (*read*) déchiffrer ▷ *I can't make out the address on the label.* Je n'arrive pas à déchiffrer l'adresse sur l'étiquette. ❷ (*understand*) comprendre ▷ *I can't make out what she's trying to say.* Je n'arrive pas du tout à comprendre ce qu'elle veut dire. ❸ (*claim, pretend*) prétendre ▷ *They're making out it was my fault.* Ils prétendent que c'était ma faute.; **to make a cheque out to somebody** libeller un chèque à l'ordre de quelqu'un

make up vb ❶ (*invent*) inventer ▷ *He made up the whole story.* Il a inventé cette histoire de toutes pièces. ❷ (*after argument*) se réconcilier ▷ *They had a quarrel, but soon made up.* Ils se sont disputés, mais se sont vite réconciliés.

maker ['meɪkə'] n fabriquant m ▷ *Europe's biggest car maker* le plus grand fabriquant de voitures d'Europe

make-up ['meɪkʌp] n maquillage m

male [meɪl] adj ❶ (*animals, plants*) mâle ▷ *a male ostrich* une autruche mâle ▷ *a male kitten* un chaton ❷ (*person, on official forms*) masculin ▷ *Sex: male.* Sexe: masculin.; **Most football players are male.** La plupart des joueurs de football sont des hommes.; **a male chauvinist** un macho; **a male nurse** un infirmier

malicious [mə'lɪʃəs] adj malveillant ▷ *a malicious rumour* une rumeur malveillante

mall [mɔːl] n centre commercial m

mammoth ['mæməθ] n mammouth m
▶ adj monstre m ▷ *a mammoth task* un travail monstre

man [mæn] n homme m ▷ *an old man* un vieil homme

manage ['mænɪdʒ] vb ❶ (*be in charge of*) diriger ▷ *She manages a big store.* Elle dirige un grand magasin. ▷ *Who manages your soccer team?* Qui dirige votre équipe de soccer? ❷ (*get by*) se débrouiller ▷ *We haven't got much money, but we manage.* Nous n'avons pas beaucoup d'argent, mais nous nous débrouillons. ▷ *It's okay, I can manage.* Ça va, je me débrouille.; **Can you manage okay?** Tu y arrives?; **to manage to do something** réussir à faire quelque chose ▷ *Luckily I managed to pass the exam.* J'ai heureusement réussi à avoir mon examen.; **I can't manage all that.** (*food*) C'est trop pour moi.

manageable ['mænɪdʒəbl] adj (*task*) faisable

management ['mænɪdʒmənt] n ❶ (*work of managing*) gestion f ▷ *He's responsible for the management of the company.* Il est responsable de la gestion de la société. ❷ (*people in charge*) direction f ▷ *"under new management"* « changement de direction »

manager ['mænɪdʒə'] n ❶ (*of company*) directeur m, directrice f ❷ (*of store, restaurant*) gérant m, gérante f ❸ (*of sports team*) gérant d'équipe m, gérante d'équipe f ❹ (*of performer*) imprésario m

mandarin ['mændərɪn] n (*fruit*) mandarine f

mango ['mæŋɡəʊ] n mangue f

mania ['meɪnɪə] n manie f

maniac ['meɪnɪæk] n fou m, folle f ▷ *She drives like a maniac.* Elle conduit comme une folle.

manipulate [mə'nɪpjʊleɪt] vb manipuler

Manitoba [mænɪ'təʊbə] n Manitoba m

manner ['mænə'] n façon f; **They were behaving in an odd manner.** Ils se comportaient de façon étrange.; **He has a confident manner.** Il a de l'assurance.

manners npl manières fpl ▷ *good manners* les bonnes manières ▷ *Her manners are appalling.* Elle a de très mauvaises manières.; **It's bad manners to speak with your mouth full.** Ce n'est pas poli de parler la bouche pleine.

manoeuvre [mə'nuːvə'] vb manœuvrer

mansion ['mænʃən] n manoir m

mantelpiece ['mæntlpiːs] n cheminée f

manual ['mænjʊəl] n manuel m
▶ adj: **manual labour** la main-d'œuvre; **manual controls** les commandes manuelles

manufacture [mænjʊ'fæktʃə'] vb fabriquer

manufacturer [mænjʊ'fæktʃərə'] n fabricant m

manure [mə'njʊə'] n fumier m

manuscript ['mænjʊskrɪpt] n manuscrit m

many ['mɛnɪ] adj, pron beaucoup de ▷ *The film has many special effects.* Le film a beaucoup d'effets spéciaux. ▷ *He doesn't have many friends.* Il n'a pas beaucoup d'amis. ▷ *Were there many people at the concert?* Est-ce qu'il y avait beaucoup de gens au concert?; **very many** beaucoup de ▷ *I don't have very many CDs.* Je n'ai pas beaucoup de CD.; **Not many.** Pas beaucoup.; **How many?** Combien? ▷ *How many do you want?* Combien en veux-tu?; **how many...?** combien de...? ▷ *How many euros do you get for a dollar?* Combien d'euros a-t-on pour un dollar?; **too many** trop ▷ *That's too many.* C'est trop.; **too many...** trop de... ▷ *She makes too many mistakes.* Elle fait trop d'erreurs.; **so many** autant ▷ *I didn't know there would be so many.* Je ne pensais pas qu'il y en aurait autant.; **so many...** autant de... ▷ *I've never seen so many books.* Je n'ai jamais vu autant de livres.

map [mæp] n ❶ (*of country, area*) carte f ❷ (*of town*) plan m

maple ['meɪpl] n érable m ▷ *maple syrup* le sirop d'érable ▷ *a maple leaf* une feuille d'érable

marathon ['mærəθən] n marathon m ▷ *the Terry Fox Marathon of Hope* le marathon d'espoir de Terry Fox

marble ['mɑːbl] n marbre m ▷ *a marble statue* une statue en marbre; **to play marbles** jouer aux billes

March [mɑːtʃ] n mars m; **in March** en mars; **March Break** la semaine de relâche

march [mɑːtʃ] n (*demonstration*) manifestation f ▷ *a peace march* une manifestation pour la paix
▶ vb ❶ (*soldiers*) marcher au pas ❷ (*protesters*) défiler

mare [mɛə'] n jument f

margarine [mɑːdʒə'riːn] n margarine f

margin ['mɑːdʒɪn] n marge f ▷ *Write notes in the margin.* Écrivez vos notes dans la marge.

marijuana [mærɪ'wɑːnə] n marijuana f

marina [mə'riːnə] n marina f

maritime ['mærɪtaɪm] adj maritime ▷ *the Maritime provinces* les provinces maritimes f;

the Maritimes les Maritimes

mark [ma:k] n ❶ (in school) note f ▷ I get good marks in French. J'ai de bonnes notes en français. ❷ (stain) tache f ▷ You've got a mark on your skirt. Tu as une tache sur ta jupe.
▷ vb corriger ▷ The teacher hasn't marked my homework yet. Le professeur n'a pas encore corrigé mon devoir.; **to mark up the price of something** majorer le prix de quelque chose

marker ['ma:kə'] n (pen) marqueur m

market ['ma:kɪt] n marché m

marketing ['ma:kɪtɪŋ] n marketing

marketplace ['ma:kɪtpleɪs] n place du marché f

marmalade ['ma:məleɪd] n confiture d'oranges f

maroon [mə'ru:n] adj (colour) bourgogne

marriage ['mærɪdʒ] n mariage m

married ['mærɪd] adj marié ▷ They are not married. Ils ne sont pas mariés. ▷ They have been married for 15 years. Ils sont mariés depuis quinze ans. ▷ a married couple un couple marié

marrow ['mærəu] n: **bone marrow** la moelle

marry ['mærɪ] vb épouser ▷ He wants to marry her. Il veut l'épouser.; **to get married** se marier ▷ My sister's getting married in June. Ma sœur se marie en juin.

marsh [ma:ʃ] n marais m

marshmallow ['ma:ʃˌmæləu] n guimauve f ▷ to roast marshmallows rôtir des guimauves

martial ['ma:ʃl] adj: **martial arts** les arts martiaux; **martial law** la loi martiale

marvellous ['ma:vləs] adj ❶ excellent ▷ He's a marvellous cook. C'est un excellent cuisinier. ❷ superbe ▷ The weather was marvellous. Il a fait un temps superbe.

marzipan ['ma:zɪpæn] n pâte d'amandes f

mascara [mæs'ka:rə] n mascara m

mascot ['mæskət] n mascotte f ▷ The team's mascot is a wolverine. La mascotte de l'équipe est le carcajou.

masculine ['mæskjulɪn] adj masculin

mashed potatoes [mæʃt-] npl purée de pommes de terre f ▷ sausages and mashed potatoes des saucisses avec de la purée de pommes de terre

mask [ma:sk] n masque m

masking tape ['ma:skɪŋ-] ruban-cache m

mass [mæs] n ❶ multitude ▷ a mass of books and papers une multitude de livres et de papiers ❷ (scientific) masse f ❸ (in church) messe f ▷ to go to mass aller à la messe; **the mass media** les médias

massage ['mæsa:ʒ] n massage m

massive ['mæsɪv] adj énorme

mass-produce ['mæsprə'dju:s] vb fabriquer en série

master ['ma:stə'] vb maîtriser

masterpiece ['ma:stəpi:s] n chef-d'œuvre m (pl chefs-d'œuvre)

mat [mæt] n ❶ (small rug) tapis m ❷ (doormat) paillasson m; **a bath mat** un tapis de baignoire; **an exercise mat** un tapis d'exercice

match [mætʃ] n ❶ allumette f ▷ a box of matches une boîte d'allumettes ❷ (sport) match m (pl matchs) ▷ a tennis match un match de tennis; **He's no match for you.** Il n'est pas de taille à lutter contre toi.; **They're a good match.** Ils sont bien assortis.
▷ vb être assorti à ▷ The jacket matches the pants. La veste est assortie au pantalon.; **These colours don't match.** Ces couleurs ne vont pas ensemble.

matching ['mætʃɪŋ] adj assorti ▷ My bedroom has matching wallpaper and curtains. Ma chambre a un papier peint et des rideaux assortis.

material [mə'tɪərɪəl] n ❶ (cloth) tissu m ❷ (information, data) documentation f ▷ I'm collecting material for my project. Je rassemble une documentation pour mon dossier.; **raw materials** les f matières premières

math [mæθ] n maths fpl

mathematics [mæθə'mætɪks] n mathématiques fpl

matter ['mætə'] n question f ▷ It's a matter of life and death. C'est une question de vie ou de mort.; **What's the matter?** Qu'est-ce qui ne va pas?; **as a matter of fact** en fait; **for that matter** d'ailleurs; **no matter what** quelles que soient les circonstances; **no matter what they say** quoi qu'ils disent; **no matter where** où que ce soit
▷ vb: **it doesn't matter** (1) (I don't mind) ça ne fait rien ▷ "I can't give you the money today." — "It doesn't matter." « Je ne peux pas te donner l'argent aujourd'hui. » — « Ça ne fait rien. » (2) (it makes no difference) ça n'a pas d'importance ▷ "Shall I phone today or tomorrow?" — "Whenever, it doesn't matter." « Est-ce que j'appelle aujourd'hui ou demain? » — « Quand tu veux, ça n'a pas d'importance. »; **It matters a lot to me.** C'est très important pour moi.

mattress ['mætrɪs] n matelas m

mature [mə'tjuə'] adj mûr ▷ She's quite mature for her age. Elle est très mûre pour son âge.

maximum ['mæksɪmə] n maximum m
▷ adj maximum m (f+pl maximum) ▷ The maximum speed is 100 km/h. La vitesse maximum autorisée est de cent kilomètres à l'heure.; **the maximum amount** le maximum

May [meɪ] n mai m; **in May** en mai

may [meɪ] vb: **He may come.** Il va peut-être venir. ▷ It may rain. Il va peut-être pleuvoir.; **"Are you going to the party?" — "I don't know. I may."** « Est-ce que tu vas à la soirée? » — « Je ne sais pas. Peut-être. »; **May I come along?** Est-ce que je peux vous accompagner?

maybe ['meɪbɪ] adv peut-être ▷ maybe not peut-être pas ▷ a bit boring, maybe peut-être un peu ennuyeux ▷ Maybe she's at home. Elle est peut-être chez elle. ▷ Maybe he'll change his mind. Il va peut-être changer d'avis.

mayonnaise [meɪə'neɪz] n mayonnaise f

mayor [mɛə'] n maire m

maze [meɪz] n labyrinthe m

me [mi:] pron ❶ me, m' ▷ Could you lend me your pen? Est-ce que tu peux me prêter ton stylo? ▷ Can you tell me the way to the community centre? Est-ce que vous pouvez m'indiquer le chemin du centre communautaire? ▷ Can you help me? Est-ce que tu peux m'aider? ▷ They

heard me. Ils m'ont entendu. ❷ moi ▷ *Me too!*
Moi aussi! ▷ *Excuse me!* Excusez-moi! ▷ *Look at
me!* Regarde-moi! ▷ *Wait for me!* Attends-moi!
▷ *Come with me!* Suivez-moi! ▷ *You're after me.*
Tu es après moi. ▷ *Is it for me?* C'est pour moi?
▷ *She's older than me.* Elle est plus âgée que moi.
meal [miːl] *n* repas *m*
mealtime ['miːltaɪm] *n*: **at mealtimes** aux
heures de repas
mean [miːn] *vb* vouloir dire ▷ *What does
"complet" mean?* Qu'est-ce que « complet » veut
dire? ▷ *I don't know what it means.* Je ne sais pas
ce que ça veut dire. ▷ *What do you mean?* Qu'est
que vous voulez dire? ▷ *That's not what I meant.*
Ce n'est pas ce que je voulais dire.; **Which one
do you mean?** Duquel veux-tu parler?; **Do you
really mean it?** Tu es sérieux?; **to mean to do
something** avoir l'intention de faire quelque
chose ▷ *I didn't mean to offend you.* Je n'avais pas
l'intention de vous blesser.
▶ *adj* (unkind) méchant ▷ *You're being mean to
me.* Tu es méchant avec moi.; **That's a really
mean thing to say!** Ce n'est vraiment pas
gentil de dire ça!
meaning ['miːnɪŋ] *n* sens *m*
means [miːnz] *n* moyen *m* ▷ *She'll do it by any
possible means.* Elle le fera par tous les moyens.
▷ *a means of transport* un moyen de transport;
by means of au moyen de ▷ *He got in by means
of a stolen key.* Il est entré au moyen d'une clé
volée.; **by all means** bien sûr ▷ *"Can I come?"
— "By all means!"* « Est-ce que je peux venir? » —
« Bien sûr! »
meant [ment] *vb see* **mean**
meanwhile ['miːnwaɪl] *adv* pendant ce
temps
measles ['miːzlz] *n* rougeole
measure ['meʒəʳ] *vb* ❶ mesurer ▷ *I measured
the desk.* J'ai mesuré le bureau. ❷ faire ▷ *The
room measures 3 metres by 4.* La pièce fait trois
mètres sur quatre.
measurements ['meʒəmənts] *npl*
❶ (of object) dimensions *fpl* ▷ *What are
the measurements of the room?* Quelles
sont les dimensions de la pièce? ❷ (of
body) mensurations *fpl* ▷ *What are your
measurements?* Quelles sont tes mensurations?;
my waist measurement mon tour de taille;
What's your neck measurement? Quel est
votre tour de cou?
meat [miːt] *n* viande *f* ▷ *I don't eat meat.* Je ne
mange pas de viande.
mechanic [mɪ'kænɪk] *n* mécanicien *m*,
mécanicienne *f* ▷ *He's a mechanic.* Il est
mécanicien.
mechanical [mɪ'kænɪkl] *adj* mécanique
medal ['medl] *n* médaille *f*; **the gold medal** la
médaille d'or
medallion [mɪ'dælɪən] *n* médaillon *m*
media ['miːdɪə] *npl* médias *mpl*
median strip ['miːdɪən-] *n* terre-plein
central *m*
medical ['medɪkl] *adj* médical (*mpl* médicaux)
▷ *medical treatment* les soins médicaux;
medical insurance l'assurance maladie; **a
medical centre** un centre médical; **to have**

medical problems avoir des problèmes de
santé; **She's a medical student.** Elle est
étudiante en médecine.
▶ *n*: **to have a medical** passer un examen
médical
medicine ['medsɪn] *n* ❶ (subject) médecine
f ▷ *I want to study medicine.* Je veux étudier la
médecine.; **alternative medicine** la médecine
douce ❷ (medication) médicament *m* ▷ *I need
some medicine.* J'ai besoin d'un médicament.
medieval [medɪ'iːvl] *adj* ❶ médiéval (*mpl*
médiévaux) ▷ *a medieval town* une ville
médiévale ▷ *in medieval times* à l'époque
médiévale ❷ (person) du Moyen Âge ▷ *a
medieval knight* un chevalier du Moyen Âge
mediocre [miːdɪ'əukəʳ] *adj* médiocre ▷ *I think
they're a mediocre band.* À mon avis, c'est un
groupe musical médiocre.
medium ['miːdɪəm] *adj* moyen *m* (*f* moyenne)
▷ *a man of medium height* un homme de taille
moyenne
medium-sized ['miːdɪəm'saɪzd] *adj* de taille
moyenne ▷ *a medium-sized town* une ville de
taille moyenne
meet [miːt] *vb* ❶ (by chance) rencontrer ▷ *I
met your sister in the street.* J'ai rencontré ta
sœur dans la rue. ▷ *Have you met her before?*
Tu l'as déjà rencontrée? ❷ se rencontrer
▷ *We met by chance in the shopping centre.*
Nous nous sommes rencontrés par hasard
au centre commercial. ❸ (by arrangement)
retrouver ▷ *I'm going to meet my friends.* Je vais
retrouver mes amis. ❹ se retrouver ▷ *Let's
meet in front of the tourist office.* Retrouvons-
nous devant le bureau de tourisme.; **I like
meeting new people.** J'aime faire de nouvelles
connaissances. ❺ (pick up) chercher
▷ *I'll meet you at the airport.* J'irai te chercher à
l'aéroport.; **to meet up** se retrouver ▷ *What
time shall we meet up?* On se retrouve à quelle
heure?
meeting ['miːtɪŋ] *n* ❶ (gathering) réunion
f ▷ *a business meeting* une réunion d'affaires
❷ (encounter) rencontre *f* ▷ *their first meeting*
leur première rencontre
mega ['megə] *adj*: **He's mega rich.** (informal) Il
est hyper riche.
megabyte ['megəbaɪt] *n* mégaoctet *m*
melody ['melədɪ] *n* mélodie *f*
melon ['melən] *n* melon *m*
melt [melt] *vb* fondre ▷ *The snow is melting.* La
neige est en train de fondre.
member ['membəʳ] *n* membre *m* ▷ *Are you a
member of the Student Council?* Es-tu membre
du Conseil des élèves?; **We're all members
of society.** Nous faisons tous partie de la
société.; **a Member of Parliament** un député;
a Member of the Legislative Assembly un
député à l'Assemblée législative; **a Member
of the National Assembly** un député
de l'Assemblée nationale; **a Member of
Provincial Parliament** un député provincial
membership ['membəʃɪp] *n* (of party, union)
adhésion *f* ▷ *to apply for membership* faire une
demande d'adhésion
membership card *n* carte de membre *f*

memento [məˈmɛntəu] n souvenir m

memorial [mɪˈmɔːrɪəl] n monument m ▷ a war memorial un monument aux morts; **a memorial service** un service commémoratif

memorize [ˈmɛməraɪz] vb apprendre par cœur

memory [ˈmɛmərɪ] n ❶ (also for computer) mémoire f ▷ I don't have a good memory. Je n'ai pas bonne mémoire. ▷ Your computer needs more memory. Ton ordinateur a besoin de plus de mémoire. ❷ (recollection) souvenir m ▷ to bring back memories rappeler des souvenirs

men [mɛn] npl see **man** hommes mpl

mend [mɛnd] vb réparer

meningitis [mɛnɪnˈdʒaɪtɪs] n méningite f

mental [ˈmɛntl] adj mental (mpl mentaux) ▷ a mental illness une maladie mentale; **a mental hospital** un hôpital psychiatrique

mentality [mɛnˈtælɪtɪ] n mentalité f

mention [ˈmɛnʃən] vb mentionner; **"Thank you!" — "Don't mention it!"** « Merci! » — « Il n'y a pas de quoi! »

menu [ˈmɛnjuː] n menu m ▷ Could I have the menu please? Est-ce que je pourrais avoir le menu s'il vous plaît?

meow [mɪˈau] vb miauler

mercy [ˈmɜːsɪ] n pitié f

mere [mɪəʳ] adj: **a mere 5 percent** à peine cinq pour cent; **It's a mere formality.** C'est une simple formalité.; **the merest hint of criticism** la moindre petite critique

meringue [məˈræŋ] n meringue f

merry [ˈmɛrɪ] adj: **Merry Christmas!** Joyeux Noël!

mess [mɛs] n ❶ fouillis ▷ My bedroom's usually a mess. Il y a du fouillis dans ma chambre. ❷ gâchis m ▷ We'd better clean up this mess. Nous devrions nettoyer ce gâchis.; **in a mess** en désordre

mess around vb: **to mess around with something** (interfere with) tripoter quelque chose ▷ Stop messing around with my computer! Arrête de tripoter mon ordinateur!; **Don't mess around with my things!** Ne touche pas à mes affaires!

mess up vb: **to mess something up** mettre la pagaille dans quelque chose ▷ My little brother has messed up my CDs. Mon petit frère a mis la pagaille dans mes CD.; **I'm sorry, I really messed up.** Je regrette, j'ai tout gâché.

message [ˈmɛsɪdʒ] n message m

messenger [ˈmɛsɪndʒəʳ] n messager m, messagère f

messy [ˈmɛsɪ] adj ❶ (dirty) salissant ▷ a messy job un travail salissant ❷ (untidy) en désordre ▷ Your desk is really messy. Ton bureau est vraiment en désordre. ❸ (person) désordonnée ▷ She's so messy! Elle est tellement désordonnée!; **My writing is terribly messy.** J'ai une écriture de cochon.

met [mɛt] vb see **meet**

metal [ˈmɛtl] n métal m (pl métaux)

meter [ˈmiːtəʳ] n ❶ (for gas, hydro, taxi) compteur m ❷ (parking meter) parcomètre m

method [ˈmɛθəd] n méthode f

Métis [meɪˈtiːs] n Métis m, Métisse f

▷ adj métis (f métisse)

metre [ˈmiːtəʳ] n mètre m

metric [ˈmɛtrɪk] adj métrique

mice [maɪs] npl see **mouse**

microchip [ˈmaɪkrəutʃɪp] n puce f

microphone [ˈmaɪkrəfəun] n microphone m

microscope [ˈmaɪkrəskəup] n microscope m

microwave oven [ˈmaɪkrəweɪv-] n four à micro-ondes m

mid [mɪd] adj: **in mid May** à la mi-mai

midday [mɪdˈdeɪ] n midi m; **at midday** à midi

middle [ˈmɪdl] n milieu m ▷ in the middle of the road au milieu de la route ▷ in the middle of the night au milieu de la nuit ▷ the middle seat la place du milieu; **the Middle Ages** le Moyen Âge; **the Middle East** le Moyen-Orient

middle-aged [mɪdlˈeɪdʒd] adj d'âge moyen ▷ a middle-aged man un homme d'âge moyen; **to be middle-aged** avoir la cinquantaine; **She's middle-aged.** Elle a la cinquantaine.

middle-class [mɪdlˈklɑːs] adj de la classe moyenne ▷ a middle-class family une famille de la classe moyenne

middle name n deuxième prénom m

midnight [ˈmɪdnaɪt] n minuit m; **at midnight** à minuit

midwife [ˈmɪdwaɪf] n sage-femme f (pl sages-femmes) ▷ She's a midwife. Elle est sage-femme.

might [maɪt] vb: ▷ He might come later. Il va peut-être venir plus tard. ▷ We might go to the Yukon next year. Nous irons peut-être au Yukon l'an prochain. ▷ She might not have understood. Elle n'a peut-être pas compris.

migraine [ˈmiːgreɪn] n migraine f ▷ I have a migraine. J'ai la migraine.

mike [maɪk] n micro m

mild [maɪld] adj doux (f douce) ▷ The winters are quite mild. Les hivers sont assez doux.

mile [maɪl] n mille m ▷ It's five miles from here. C'est à huit kilomètres d'ici.; **We walked miles!** Nous avons marché plusieurs kilomètres!

military [ˈmɪlɪtərɪ] adj militaire

milk [mɪlk] n lait m ▷ tea with milk du thé au lait ▷ vb traire

milk chocolate n chocolat au lait m

milkshake [ˈmɪlkʃeɪk] n lait fouetté m

mill [mɪl] n moulin m ▷ a pepper mill un moulin à poivre

millennium [mɪˈlɛnɪəm] n millénaire m ▷ the third millennium le troisième millénaire; **the millennium** le millénium

millimetre [ˈmɪlɪmiːtəʳ] n millimètre m

million [ˈmɪljən] n million m

millionaire [mɪljəˈnɛəʳ] n millionnaire m

mimic [ˈmɪmɪk] vb imiter

mincemeat pie [ˈmɪnsmiːt-] n tarte au mincemeat f

mind [maɪnd] vb: Do you mind if I open the window? Est-ce que ça vous dérange si j'ouvre la fenêtre?; **I don't mind.** Ça ne me dérange pas. ▷ I don't mind the noise. Le bruit ne me dérange pas.; **Never mind!** Ça ne fait rien!; **Mind the step!** Attention à la marche!

▷ n esprit ▷ a logical mind un esprit logique ▷ Great minds think alike. Les grands esprits se

rencontrent. ▷ *to come to mind* venir à l'esprit;
to make up one's mind se décider ▷ *I haven't
made up my mind yet.* Je ne me suis pas encore
décidé.; **to change one's mind** changer d'avis
▷ *He changed his mind.* Il a changé d'avis.; **Are
you out of your mind?** Tu as perdu la tête?;
What's on your mind? À quoi penses-tu?; **to
read somebody's mind** lire dans les pensées
de quelqu'un; **Put it out of your mind.** N'y
pense plus.

mine [maɪn] *pron* le + mien, la + f mienne, les
+ m miens, les + f miennes ▷ *"Is this your coat?"
— "No, mine's black."* « C'est ton manteau? » —
« Non, la mien est noir. » ▷ *"Is this your car?"* —
"No, mine's green." « C'est ta voiture? » —
« Non, la mienne est verte. » ▷ *her parents and
mine* ses parents et les miens ▷ *Your hands are
dirty. Mine are clean.* Tes mains sont sales. Les
miennes sont propres.; **It's mine.** C'est à moi.
▷ *This book is mine.* Le livre est à moi. ▷ *"Whose is
this?" — "It's mine."* « C'est à qui? » — « À moi. »
▶ *n* mine f ▷ *a diamond mine* une mine de
diamants ▷ *a land mine* une mine terrestre

miner ['maɪnər] *n* mineur m, mineuse f

mineral ['mɪnərəl] *n* minéral m (*pl* les
minéraux)

mineral water *n* eau f minérale

miniature ['mɪnətʃər] *adj* miniature f ▷ *a
miniature version* une version miniature
▶ *n* miniature f

Minidisc® ['mɪnɪdɪsk] *n* minidisque m

minimum ['mɪnɪməm] *n* minimum m
▶ *adj* minimum m (*f+pl* minimum) ▷ *the
minimum wage* le salaire minimum ▷ *The
minimum age for driving is 16.* L'âge minimum
pour conduire est seize ans.; **the minimum
amount** le minimum

miniskirt ['mɪnɪskɜːt] *n* minijupe f

minister ['mɪnɪstər] *n* ❶ (*in government*)
ministre m ❷ (*of church*) pasteur m

ministry ['mɪnɪstri] *n* (*in government*)
ministère m ▷ *the Ministry of the Environment* le
ministère de l'Environnement

mink [mɪŋk] *n* vison m

minor ['maɪnər] *adj* mineur m ▷ *a minor
problem* un problème mineur; **in D minor** en
ré mineur; **a minor operation** une opération
bénigne

minority [maɪ'nɒrɪti] *n* minorité f

mint [mɪnt] *n* ❶ (*plant*) menthe f ▷ *mint ice
cream* la crème glacée à la menthe ❷ (*candy*)
bonbon à la menthe m

minus ['maɪnəs] *prep* moins ▷ *16 minus 3 is 13.*
Seize moins trois égale treize. ▷ *It's minus two
outside.* Il fait moins deux dehors. ▷ *I got a B
minus.* J'ai eu un B moins.

minute [maɪ'njuːt] *n* minute f ▷ *Wait a minute!*
Attends une minute! ▷ *I'll do it right this minute.*
Je le ferai tout de suite.
▶ *adj* minuscule ▷ *minute details* des détails
minuscules

miracle ['mɪrəkl] *n* miracle m

mirror ['mɪrər] *n* ❶ (*on wall*) miroir m ❷ (*in
car*) rétroviseur m

misbehave [mɪsbɪ'heɪv] *vb* se conduire mal

miscellaneous [mɪsɪ'leɪnɪəs] *adj* divers

mischief ['mɪstʃɪf] *n* bêtises fpl ▷ *My little
sister's always up to mischief.* Ma petite sœur fait
constamment des bêtises.

mischievous ['mɪstʃɪvəs] *adj* espiègle

miser ['maɪzər] *n* avare mf

miserable ['mɪzərəbl] *adj* ❶ (*person*)
malheureux m (*f* malheureuse) ▷ *You look
miserable.* Tu as l'air malheureux. ❷ (*weather*)
épouvantable ▷ *The weather was miserable.*
Il faisait un temps épouvantable.; **to feel
miserable** ne pas avoir le moral ▷ *I'm feeling
miserable.* Je n'ai pas le moral.

misery ['mɪzəri] *n* (*unhappiness*) tristesse f
▷ *All that money brought nothing but misery.* Tout
cet argent n'a apporté que de la tristesse.

misfortune [mɪs'fɔːtʃən] *n* malheur m

mishap ['mɪshæp] *n* mésaventure f

misjudge [mɪs'dʒʌdʒ] *vb* (*person*) mal juger
▷ *I've misjudged him.* Je l'ai mal jugé.; **He
misjudged the turn.** Il a mal pris le virage.

misleading [mɪs'liːdɪŋ] *adj* trompeur (*f*
trompeuse)

misplace [mɪs'pleɪs] *vb* égarer ▷ *I've misplaced
my passport.* J'ai égaré mon passeport.

Miss [mɪs] *n* ❶ Mademoiselle (*pl
Mesdemoiselles*) ❷ (*in address*) Mlle (*pl* Mlles)

miss [mɪs] *vb* ❶ rater ▷ *Hurry or you'll miss the
bus.* Dépêche-toi ou tu vas rater l'autobus.
▷ *He missed the target.* Il a raté la cible.
❷ manquer ▷ *to miss an opportunity* manquer
une occasion; **I miss you.** Tu me manques.
▷ *I'm missing my family.* Ma famille me manque.

missing ['mɪsɪŋ] *adj* manquant ▷ *the missing
piece* la pièce manquante; **to be missing** avoir
disparu ▷ *My backpack is missing.* Mon sac à
dos a disparu. ▷ *Two members of the group are
missing.* Deux membres du groupe ont disparu.

missionary ['mɪʃənri] *n* missionnaire

mist [mɪst] *n* brume f

mistake [mɪs'teɪk] *n* ❶ (*slip*) faute f ▷ *a
spelling mistake* une faute d'orthographe; **to
make a mistake** (1) (*in writing, speaking*) faire
une faute (2) (*be mistaken*) se tromper ▷ *I'm
sorry, I made a mistake.* Je suis désolé, je me suis
trompé. ❷ (*misjudgement*) erreur f ▷ *It was a
mistake to buy those yellow shoes.* J'ai fait une
erreur en achetant ces chaussures jaunes.; **by
mistake** par erreur ▷ *I took her bag by mistake.*
J'ai pris son sac par erreur.
▶ *vb*: **He mistook me for my sister.** Il m'a prise
pour ma sœur.

mistaken [mɪs'teɪkən] *adj*: **to be mistaken**
se tromper ▷ *If you think I'm going to get up at six
o'clock, you're mistaken.* Si tu penses que je vais
me lever à six heures, tu te trompes.

mistook [mɪs'tʊk] *vb see* **mistake**

mistrust [mɪs'trʌst] *vb* se méfier de

misty ['mɪsti] *adj* brumeux (*f* brumeuse) ▷ *a
misty morning* un matin brumeux

misunderstand [mɪsʌndə'stænd] *vb* mal
comprendre ▷ *Sorry, I misunderstood you.* Je suis
désolé, je t'avais mal compris.

misunderstanding ['mɪsʌndə'stændɪŋ] *n*
malentendu m

mitten ['mɪtn] *n* mitaine f

mix [mɪks] *n* mélange m ▷ *It's a mix of science*

fiction and comedy. C'est un mélange de science-fiction et de comédie.; **a cake mix** une préparation pour gâteau
▶ vb ① mélanger ▷ *Mix the flour with the sugar.* Mélangez la farine au sucre. ② combiner ▷ *He's mixing business with pleasure.* Il combine les affaires et le plaisir.; **He doesn't mix with other people.** Il se tient à l'écart.; **to mix up** (*people*) confondre ▷ *She always mixes me up with my brother.* Elle confond toujours avec mon frère.; **The travel agent mixed up the bookings.** L'agente de voyage s'est embrouillée dans les réservations.; **I'm getting mixed up.** Je ne m'y retrouve plus.
mixed [mɪkst] *adj*: **a mixed salad** une salade composée; **a mixed family** une famille mixte; **a mixed grill** un assortiment de grillades
mixture ['mɪkstʃər] *n* mélange *m* ▷ *a mixture of spices* un mélange d'épices
mix-up ['mɪksʌp] *n* confusion *f*
moan [məʊn] *vb* gémir ▷ *He was moaning with pain.* Il gémissait de douleur.
mobile home ['məʊbaɪl-] *n* maison mobile
mobile phone ['məʊbaɪl-] *n* téléphone cellulaire *m*
moccasin ['mɒkəsɪn] *n* mocassin *m*
mock [mɒk] *vb* ridiculiser
▶ *adj*: **a mock trial** une simulation de procès; **a mock parliamentary debate** une simulation de débat parlementaire
model ['mɒdl] *n* ① (*type*) modèle *m* ▷ *His car is the latest model.* Sa voiture est le tout dernier modèle. ② (*mock-up*) maquette *f* ▷ *a model of the castle* une maquette du château ③ (*fashion*) mannequin *m* ▷ *She's a famous model.* C'est un mannequin célèbre.
▶ *adj*: **a model plane** un modèle réduit d'avion; **a model railway** un modèle réduit de voie ferrée; **He's a model student.** C'est un élève modèle.
▶ *vb*: **She was modelling an Alfred Sung outfit.** Elle présentait une tenue de la collection Alfred Sung.
modem ['məʊdɛm] *n* modem *m*
moderate ['mɒdərɪt] *adj* modéré ▷ *Her views are quite moderate.* Ses opinions sont assez modérées.; **a moderate amount of** un peu de; **a moderate price** un prix raisonnable
modern ['mɒdən] *adj* moderne
modernize ['mɒdənaɪz] *vb* moderniser
modest ['mɒdɪst] *adj* modeste
modify ['mɒdɪfaɪ] *vb* modifier
moist [mɔɪst] *adj* (*skin, soil*) humide ▷ *Make sure the soil is moist.* Assurez-vous que la terre est humide.
moisture ['mɔɪstʃər] *n* humidité *f*
moisturizer ['mɔɪstʃəraɪzər] *n* ① (*cream*) crème hydratante *f* ② (*lotion*) lait hydratant *m*
mom [mɒm] *n* ① mère *f* ▷ *my mom* ma mère ▷ *her mom* sa mère ② maman *f* ▷ *Mom!* Maman! ▷ *I'll ask Mom.* Je vais demander à maman.
moment ['məʊmənt] *n* instant *m* ▷ *Could you wait a moment?* Pouvez-vous attendre un instant? ▷ *in a moment* dans un instant ▷ *Just a moment!* Un instant!; **at the moment** en ce

moment; **any moment now** d'un moment à l'autre ▷ *They'll be arriving any moment now.* Ils vont arriver d'un moment à l'autre.
momentous [məʊ'mɛntəs] *adj* (*event*) capital
monarch ['mɒnək] *n* monarque *m*
monarchy ['mɒnəkɪ] *n* monarchie *f*
monastery ['mɒnəstərɪ] *n* monastère *m*
Monday ['mʌndɪ] *n* lundi *m* ▷ *on Monday* lundi ▷ *on Mondays* le lundi ▷ *every Monday* tous les lundis ▷ *last Monday* lundi dernier ▷ *next Monday* lundi prochain
money ['mʌnɪ] *n* argent *m* ▷ *I need to change some money.* J'ai besoin de changer de l'argent.; **to make money** gagner de l'argent
monitor ['mɒnɪtər] *n* (*of computer*) moniteur *m*
monk [mʌŋk] *n* moine *m*
monkey ['mʌŋkɪ] *n* singe *m*
monopolize [mə'nɒpəlaɪz] *vb* monopoliser ▷ *to monopolize the conversation* monopoliser la conversation ▷ *You're monopolizing the phone!* Tu monopolises le téléphone!
monotonous [mə'nɒtənəs] *adj* monotone
monster ['mɒnstər] *n* monstre *m*
month [mʌnθ] *n* mois *m* ▷ *this month* ce mois-ci ▷ *next month* le mois prochain ▷ *last month* le mois dernier ▷ *every month* tous les mois ▷ *at the end of the month* à la fin du mois
monthly ['mʌnθlɪ] *adj* mensuel (*f* mensuelle)
monument ['mɒnjumənt] *n* monument *m*
mood [muːd] *n* humeur *f*; **to be in a bad mood** être de mauvaise humeur; **to be in a good mood** être de bonne humeur
moody ['muːdɪ] *adj* ① (*temperamental*) lunatique ② (*in a bad mood*) maussade
moon [muːn] *n* lune *f* ▷ *There's a full moon tonight.* Il y a pleine lune ce soir.; **to be over the moon** (*happy*) être aux anges
moonlight ['muːnlaɪt] *n* clair de lune *m* ▷ *in the moonlight* au clair de lune
moor [muər] *vb* (*boat*) amarrer
moose [muːs] *n* orignal *m*
mop [mɒp] *n* (*for floor*) vadrouille *f*
moped ['məʊpɛd] *n* cyclomoteur *m*
moral ['mɒrl] *adj* moral (*mpl* moraux)
▶ *n* morale *f* ▷ *the moral of the story* la morale de l'histoire; **morals** la moralité
morale [mɒ'rɑːl] *n* moral *m* ▷ *Their morale is very low.* Leur moral est très bas.
more [mɔːr] *adj, pron, adv* ① plus ▷ *Fruit is more expensive in Britain.* Les fruits sont plus chers en Grande-Bretagne. ▷ *Could you speak more slowly?* Est-ce que vous pourriez parler plus lentement? ▷ *a bit more* un peu plus ▷ *There isn't any more.* Il n'y en a plus.; **more...than** plus...que ▷ *He's more athletic than me.* Il est plus sportif que moi. ▷ *She practises more than I do.* Elle s'entraîne plus que moi. ▷ *More boys play hockey than girls.* Il y a plus de garçons que de filles qui jouent au hockey. ② (*followed by noun*) plus de ▷ *There are more girls in the class.* Il y a plus de filles dans la classe. ▷ *I get more homework than you do.* J'ai plus de devoirs que toi. ▷ *I spent more than 500 dollars.* J'ai dépensé plus de cinq cents dollars. ③ encore ▷ *Is there any more?* Est-ce qu'il y en a encore? ▷ *Would you like some more?* Vous en voulez encore?

▷ *It'll take a few more days.* Ça prendra encore quelques jours. ❸ *(followed by noun)* encore de ▷ *Could I have some more fries?* Est-ce que je pourrais avoir encore des frites? ▷ *Do you want some more tea?* Voulez-vous encore du thé?; **more or less** plus ou moins; **more than ever** plus que jamais

moreover ['mɔː'rəʊvə'] *adv* en outre

morning ['mɔːnɪŋ] *n* matin *m* ▷ *this morning* ce matin ▷ *tomorrow morning* demain matin ▷ *every morning* tous les matins; **in the morning** le matin ▷ *at 7 o'clock in the morning* à sept heures du matin; **a morning paper** un journal du matin

mosque [mɒsk] *n* mosquée *f*

mosquito [mɒs'kiːtəʊ] *n* moustique *m*; **a mosquito bite** une piqûre de moustique

most [məʊst] *adv, adj, pron* ❶ la plupart de ▷ *most of my friends* la plupart de mes amis ▷ *most people* la plupart des gens ▷ *Most cats are affectionate.* La plupart des chats sont affectueux.; **most of them** la plupart d'entre eux; **most of the time** la plupart du temps ❷ la majeure partie de ▷ *most of the work* la majeure partie du travail ▷ *most of the class* la majeure partie de la classe ▷ *most of the night* la majeure partie de la nuit; **the most** le plus ▷ *He's the one who talks the most.* C'est lui qui parle le plus.; **the most... (1)** le plus... ▷ *the most expensive restaurant* le restaurant le plus cher **(2)** la plus... ▷ *the most expensive seat* la place la plus chère **(3)** les plus... ▷ *the most expensive restaurants* les restaurants les plus chers ▷ *the most expensive seats* les places les plus chères; **for the most part** pour la plupart ▷ *The students seem to like French, for the most part.* Les élèves semblent aimer le français, pour la plupart.; **to make the most of something** profiter au maximum de quelque chose; **at the most** au maximum ▷ *Two hours at the most.* Deux heures au maximum.

mostly ['məʊstlɪ] *adv*: **I went mostly because my friends were going.** J'y suis allé surtout parce que mes amis y allaient.; **The teachers are mostly quite nice.** La plupart des professeurs sont assez gentils.; **We mostly do the shopping on Saturdays.** *(usually)* D'habitude, nous magasinons le samedi.

motel [məʊ'tɛl] *n* motel *m*

moth [mɒθ] *n* papillon de nuit *m*

mother ['mʌðə'] *n* mère *f* ▷ *my mother* ma mère; **mother tongue** la langue maternelle

mother-in-law ['mʌðərɪnlɔː] *n* belle-mère *f* *(pl* belles-mères*)*

Mother's Day *n* fête des Mères *f*

motion ['məʊʃən] *n* ❶ mouvement *m* ▷ *the motion of the train* le mouvement du train ❷ geste *m* ▷ *He made a motion towards the door.* Il a fait un geste vers la porte.; **in motion** en marche; **motion sickness** le mal des transports; **We were just going through the motions.** Nous le faisions tout à fait machinalement.

motionless ['məʊʃənlɪs] *adj* immobile

motivated ['məʊtɪveɪtɪd] *adj* motivé ▷ *She is*

highly motivated. Elle est très motivée.

motivation [məʊtɪ'veɪʃən] *n* motivation *f*

motive ['məʊtɪv] *n* mobile *m* ▷ *the motive for the crime* le mobile du crime

motor ['məʊtə'] *n* moteur *m* ▷ *The boat has a motor.* Le bateau a un moteur.

motorbike ['məʊtəbaɪk] *n* moto *f*

motorboat ['məʊtəbəʊt] *n* bateau à moteur *m*

motorcycle ['məʊtəsaɪkl] *n* motocyclette *f*

motorcyclist ['məʊtəsaɪklɪst] *n* motard *m*, motarde *f*

motorist ['məʊtərɪst] *n* automobiliste *mf*

mouldy ['məʊldɪ] *adj* moisi

mount [maʊnt] *vb* ❶ monter ▷ *He mounted his horse and rode off.* Il est monté à son cheval et est parti. ▷ *to mount a bicycle* monter sur un vélo ▷ *They're mounting a publicity campaign.* Ils montent une campagne publicitaire. ❷ augmenter ▷ *Tension is mounting.* La tension augmente.

mount up *vb* ❶ s'accumuler ▷ *The mail had mounted up during our holidays.* Les lettres s'étaient accumulées pendant nos vacances. ❷ augmenter ▷ *My savings are mounting up gradually.* Mes économies augmentent progressivement.

mountain ['maʊntɪn] *n* montagne *f*; **a mountain bike** un vélo de montagne; **a mountain range** une chaîne de montagnes

mountainous ['maʊntɪnəs] *adj* montagneux *(f* montagneuse*)*

Mountie ['maʊntɪ] *n* agent *m* de la GRC, agente *f* de la GRC

mouse [maʊs] *n (also for computer)* souris *f* ▷ *white mice* des souris blanches

mouse pad *n* tapis de souris *m*

mousse [muːs] *n* ❶ *(food)* mousse *f* ▷ *chocolate mousse* la mousse au chocolat ❷ *(for hair)* mousse coiffante *f*

moustache [məs'tɑːʃ] *n* moustache *f* ▷ *He has a moustache.* Il a une moustache.; **a man with a moustache** un moustachu

mouth [maʊθ] *n* bouche *f*

mouthful ['maʊθfʊl] *n* bouchée *f*

mouth organ *n* musique à bouche *f* ▷ *I play the mouth organ.* Je joue de la musique à bouche.

mouthwash ['maʊθwɒʃ] *n* bain de bouche *m*

move [muːv] *n* ❶ tour *m* ▷ *It's your move.* C'est ton tour. ❷ déménagement *m* ▷ *Our move from Edmundston to Pugwash...* Notre déménagement d'Edmundston à Pugwash...; **to get a move on** se remuer ▷ *Get a move on!* Remue-toi!

▷ *vb* ❶ bouger ▷ *Don't move!* Ne bouge pas! ▷ *Could you move your stuff please?* Est-ce que tu peux bouger tes affaires s'il te plaît? ❷ avancer ▷ *The car was moving very slowly.* La voiture avançait très lentement. ❸ émouvoir ▷ *I was very moved by the film.* J'ai été très émue par ce film. ❹ déménager ▷ *We're moving in July.* Nous allons déménager en juillet.; **to move forward** avancer; **to move in** emménager ▷ *They're moving in next week.* Ils emménagent la semaine prochaine.; **to move over** se pousser ▷ *Could you move over a bit?* Est-ce que vous pouvez vous

pousser un peu?
movement ['muːvmənt] n mouvement m
movie ['muːvɪ] n film m; **the movies** le cinéma ▷ Let's go to the movies! Si on allait au cinéma?; **a movie star** une vedette de cinéma
moving ['muːvɪŋ] adj ❶ (not stationary) en marche ▷ a moving bus un bus en marche ❷ (touching) touchant ▷ a moving story une histoire touchante; **a moving van** un camion de déménagement
mow [məʊ] vb tondre; **to mow the lawn** tondre le gazon
mower ['məʊə'] n tondeuse à gazon f
mown [məʊn] vb see **mow**
MP n député m ▷ She's an MP. Elle est député.
MP3 adj MP3 ▷ an MP3 file un fichier MP3 ▷ an MP3 player un lecteur MP3
Mr ['mɪstə'] n ❶ Monsieur (pl Messieurs) ❷ (in address) M. (pl MM.)
Mrs ['mɪsɪz] n ❶ Madame (pl Mesdames) ❷ (in address) Mme (pl Mmes)
MS n (= multiple sclerosis) sclérose en plaques f ▷ He has MS. Il a la sclérose en plaques.
Ms [mɪz] n ❶ Madame (pl Mesdames) ❷ (in address) Mme (pl Mmes)
much [mʌtʃ] adj, adv, pron ❶ (with verb, adjective, adverb) beaucoup ▷ Do you go out much? Tu sors beaucoup? ▷ I don't like sports much. Je n'aime pas beaucoup le sport. ▷ I feel much better now. Je me sens beaucoup mieux maintenant. ❷ (followed by noun) beaucoup de ▷ I haven't got much money. Je n'ai pas beaucoup d'argent. ▷ I don't want much rice. Je ne veux pas beaucoup de riz.; **very much** beaucoup ▷ I enjoyed the film very much. J'ai beaucoup apprécié le film. ▷ Thank you very much. Merci beaucoup. ▷ I don't have very much money. Je n'ai pas beaucoup d'argent.; **not much** (1) pas beaucoup ▷ "Do you have a lot of luggage?" — "No, not much." « As-tu beaucoup de bagages? » — « Non, pas beaucoup. » (2) pas grand-chose ▷ "What's on TV?" — "Not much." « Qu'est-ce qu'il y a à la télé? » — « Pas grand-chose. » ▷ "What did you think of it?" — "Not much." « Qu'est-ce que tu en as pensé? » — « Pas grand-chose. »; **How much?** Combien? ▷ How much do you want? Tu en veux combien? ▷ How much time do you have? Tu as combien de temps? ▷ How much is it? (cost) Combien est-ce que ça coûte?; **too much** trop ▷ That's too much! C'est trop! ▷ It costs too much. Ça coûte trop cher. ▷ They give us too much homework. Ils nous donnent trop de devoirs.; **so much** autant ▷ I didn't think it would cost so much. Je ne pensais pas que ça coûterait autant. ▷ I've never seen so much traffic. Je n'ai jamais vu autant de circulation.
mud [mʌd] n boue f
muddle up ['mʌdl-] vb (people) confondre ▷ He muddles me up with my sister. Il me confond avec ma sœur.; **to get muddled up** s'embrouiller ▷ I'm getting muddled up. Je m'embrouille.
muddy ['mʌdɪ] adj boueux (f boueuse)
muesli ['mjuːzlɪ] n muesli m
muffin ['mʌfɪn] n muffin m
muffle ['mʌfl] vb ❸ (voice) étouffer ▷ a muffled

cry un cri étouffé ▷ in a muffled voice d'une voix étouffée ❷ (other sounds) assourdir ▷ to muffle the noise of traffic assourdir le bruit de la circulation
muffler ['mʌflə'] n silencieux m
mug [mʌg] n grande tasse f ▷ Do you want a cup or a mug? Est-ce que vous voulez une tasse normale ou une grande tasse?; **mug shot** la photo d'identité judiciaire
▷ vb agresser ▷ He was mugged in the city centre. Il s'est fait agresser au centre ville.
mugger ['mʌgə'] n agresseur m ▷ The mugger was a woman. L'agresseur était une femme.
mugging ['mʌgɪŋ] n agression f
muggy ['mʌgɪ] adj lourd ▷ It's muggy out today. Le temps est lourd aujourd'hui.
multicultural ['mʌltɪ'kʌltʃərəl] adj multiculturel (f multiculturelle)
multimedia ['mʌltɪ'miːdɪə] adj multimédia ▷ a multimedia presentation une présentation multimédia
multiple choice test ['mʌltɪpl-] n test à choix multiple m
multiple sclerosis [-sklɪ'rəʊsɪs] n sclérose en plaques f ▷ She has multiple sclerosis. Elle a la sclérose en plaques.
multiplication [mʌltɪplɪ'keɪʃən] n multiplication f
multiply ['mʌltɪplaɪ] vb multiplier ▷ to multiply 6 by 3 multiplier six par trois
multi-storey ['mʌltɪ'stɔːrɪ] adj à plusieurs étages ▷ a multi-storey parking garage un stationnement à plusieurs étages
mummy ['mʌmɪ] n (Egyptian) momie f
mumps [mʌmps] n oreillons mpl
municipal [mjuː'nɪsɪpl] adj municipal (mpl municipaux) ▷ municipal government le gouvernement municipal
mural ['mjʊərl] n murale f ▷ The Grade 8s painted a mural in the gym. Les élèves de huitième année ont peint une murale dans le gymnase.
murder ['mɜːdə'] n meurtre m
▷ vb assassiner
murderer ['mɜːdərə'] n assassin m, assassine f
muscle ['mʌsl] n muscle m
muscular ['mʌskjʊlə'] adj musclé
museum [mjuː'zɪəm] n musée m
mushroom ['mʌʃrʊm] n champignon m ▷ mushroom omelette l'omelette aux champignons
music ['mjuːzɪk] n musique f
musical ['mjuːzɪkl] adj doué pour la musique ▷ I'm not musical. Je ne suis pas doué pour la musique.; **a musical instrument** un instrument de musique
▷ n comédie musicale f
musician [mjuː'zɪʃən] n musicien m, musicienne f
muskeg ['mʌskeg] n muskeg m
Muslim ['mʌzlɪm] n musulman m, musulmane f ▷ He's a Muslim. Il est musulman.
▷ adj musulman m
mussel ['mʌsl] n moule f
must [mʌst] vb ❶ devoir ▷ You must be tired. Tu dois être fatigué. ▷ There must be some problem.

Il doit y avoir un problème. ▷ *I must clean up my room.* Je dois nettoyer ma chambre. ▷ *We must win this game.* Nous devons gagner ce match. ❷ *(want)* **My mum wants me to buy some presents.** Il faut que j'achète des cadeaux. ▷ *I really must go now.* Il faut que j'y aille.; **You must not lie.** Il ne faut pas mentir.; **Students must not operate this machine.** Les élèves n'ont pas le droit d'utiliser cet appareil.; **You mustn't forget to send her a card.** N'oublie surtout pas de lui envoyer une carte.; **You must come and see us.** *(invitation)* Venez donc nous voir.

mustard ['mʌstəd] *n* moutarde *f*
mustn't ['mʌsnt] *vb* = **must not**
mute [mjuːt] *adj* muet *(f* muette*)*
mutter ['mʌtə'] *vb* marmonner
my [maɪ] *adj* mon *m,* ma *f,* mes *pl* ▷ *my father* mon père ▷ *my aunt* ma tante ▷ *my parents* mes parents; **my friend (1)** *(male)* mon ami **(2)** *(female)* mon amie ▷ *I want to wash my hair.* Je voudrais me laver les cheveux. ▷ *I'm going to brush my teeth.* Je vais me brosser les dents. ▷ *I've hurt my foot.* Je me suis fait mal au pied.
myself [maɪ'sɛlf] *pron* ❶ me ▷ *I've hurt myself.* Je me suis fait mal. ▷ *I really enjoyed myself.* Je me suis vraiment bien amusé. ▷ *...when I look at myself in the mirror.* ...quand je me regarde dans le miroir. ❷ moi ▷ *I don't like talking about myself.* Je n'aime pas parler de moi. ❸ moi-même ▷ *I made it myself.* Je l'ai fait moi-même.; **by myself** tout seul ▷ *I don't like travelling by myself.* Je n'aime pas voyager tout seul.
mysterious [mɪs'tɪərɪəs] *adj* mystérieux *(f* mystérieuse*)*
mystery ['mɪstərɪ] *n* mystère *m;* **a murder mystery** *(novel)* un roman policier
myth [mɪθ] *n* ❶ *(legend)* mythe *m* ▷ *a Greek myth* un mythe grec ❷ *(untrue idea)* idée reçue *f* ▷ *That's a myth.* C'est une idée reçue.
mythology [mɪ'θɒlədʒɪ] *n* mythologie *f*

n

nag [næg] *vb (scold)* harceler ▷ *They're always nagging me.* Ils me harcèlent constamment.
nail [neɪl] *n* ❶ *(on finger, toe)* ongle *m* ▷ *Don't bite your nails!* Ne te ronge pas les ongles! ❷ *(made of metal)* clou *m*
nail brush *n* brosse à ongles *f*
nail clippers *npl* coupe-ongles *m (pl* coupe-ongles*)*
nail file *n* lime à ongles *f*
nail polish *n* vernis à ongles *m;* **nail polish**

remover le dissolvant
naked ['neɪkɪd] *adj* nu
name [neɪm] *n* nom *m;* **What's your name?** Comment vous appelez-vous?; **to call somebody names** traiter quelqu'un de tous les noms
▶ *vb* ❶ *(call)* appeler ▷ *They named the baby Petra.* Ils ont appelé le bébé Petra.; **I was named after my uncle.** J'ai reçu le nom de mon oncle. ❷ nommer ▷ *Name the provinces.* Nomme les provinces. ▷ *She was named Artist of the Year.* Elle a été nommée Artiste de l'année.
nanny ['nænɪ] *n* bonne d'enfants *f* ▷ *She's a nanny.* C'est une bonne d'enfants.
nap [næp] *n* petit somme *m;* **to have a nap** faire un petit somme
napkin ['næpkɪn] *n* serviette *f*
narrow ['nærəʊ] *adj* étroit
narrow-minded [nærəʊ'maɪndɪd] *adj* borné
nasty ['nɑːstɪ] *adj* ❶ *(bad)* mauvais ▷ *a nasty cold* un mauvais rhume ▷ *a nasty smell* une mauvaise odeur ❷ *(unfriendly)* méchant ▷ *He gave me a nasty look.* Il m'a regardé d'un air méchant.
nation ['neɪʃən] *n* nation *f*
national ['næʃənl] *adj* national *(mpl* nationaux*)* ▷ *He's the national champion.* C'est le champion national.; **the National Assembly** l'Assemblée nationale
national anthem *n* hymne *m* national ▷ *Our national anthem is "O Canada".* Notre hymne national est « Ô Canada ».
nationalism ['næʃnəlɪzəm] *n* nationalisme *m* ▷ *Québec nationalism* le nationalisme québécois
nationalist ['næʃnəlɪst] *n* nationaliste
nationality [næʃə'nælɪtɪ] *n* nationalité *f*
national park *n* parc national *m (pl* parcs nationaux*)*
native ['neɪtɪv] *adj* natal ▷ *my native country* mon pays natal; **native language** la langue maternelle ▷ *English is not their native language.* L'anglais n'est pas leur langue maternelle.; **Native Peoples** les *m* peuples autochtones
natural ['nætʃrəl] *adj* naturel *(f* naturelle*)*; **natural resources** les *f* ressources naturelles
naturalist ['nætʃrəlɪst] *n* naturaliste
naturally ['nætʃrəlɪ] *adv* naturellement ▷ *Naturally, we were very disappointed.* Nous avons naturellement été très déçus.
nature ['neɪtʃə'] *n* nature *f*
naughty ['nɔːtɪ] *adj* vilain ▷ *Naughty dog!* Vilain chien! ▷ *Don't be naughty!* Ne fais pas le vilain!
nauseous ['nɔːsɪəs] *adj*: **to feel nauseous** avoir la nausée; **It made me nauseous.** Cela m'a donné la nausée.; **a nauseous smell** une odeur écœurante
navel ['neɪvl] *n* nombril *m*
navy ['neɪvɪ] *n* marine *f* ▷ *He's in the navy.* Il est dans la marine.
navy blue *adj* bleu marine *(f+pl* bleu marine*)* ▷ *a navy blue skirt* une jupe bleu marine
Nazi ['nɑːtsɪ] *n* nazi *m,* nazie *f* ▷ *the Nazis* les nazis
near [nɪə'] *adj* proche ▷ *It's fairly near.* C'est assez proche.; **It's near enough to walk.** On

peut facilement y aller à pied.; **the nearest** le plus proche ▷ *Where's the nearest service station?* Où est la station-service la plus proche? ▷ *The nearest stores were three kilometres away.* Les magasins les plus proches étaient à trois kilomètres.

▶ *prep, adv* près de ▷ *I live near Fredericton.* J'habite près de Fredericton. ▷ *near my house* près de chez moi; **near here** près d'ici ▷ *Is there a bank near here?* Est-ce qu'il y a une banque près d'ici?

nearby ['nɪə'baɪ] *adv* à proximité ▷ *There's a supermarket nearby.* Il y a un supermarché à proximité.

▶ *adj* ① (*close*) proche ▷ *a nearby convenience store* un dépanneur proche ② (*neighbouring*) voisin *m* ▷ *We went to the nearby village of St. Jacob's.* Nous sommes allés à St. Jacob's, le village voisin.

nearly ['nɪəlɪ] *adv* presque ▷ *Dinner's nearly ready.* Le dîner est presque prêt. ▷ *I'm nearly 15.* J'ai presque quinze ans. ▷ **I nearly missed the bus.** J'ai failli rater l'autobus.

neat [niːt] *adj* soigné ▷ *She has very neat writing.* Elle a une écriture très soignée.

neatly ['niːtlɪ] *adv* soigneusement ▷ *neatly folded* soigneusement plié; **neatly dressed** impeccable

necessarily ['nɛsɪsrɪlɪ] *adv*: **not necessarily** pas forcément

necessary ['nɛsɪsrɪ] *adj* nécessaire

necessity [nɪˈsɛsɪtɪ] *n* nécessité *f* ▷ *A car is a necessity, not a luxury.* Une voiture est une nécessité et non pas un luxe.

neck [nɛk] *n* ① (*of body*) cou *m*; **a stiff neck** un torticolis ② (*of garment*) encolure *f* ▷ *a V-neck sweater* un chandail avec une encolure en V

necklace ['nɛklɪs] *n* collier *m*

nectarine ['nɛktərɪn] *n* nectarine *f*

need [niːd] *vb* avoir besoin de ▷ *I need a bigger size.* J'ai besoin d'une plus grande taille.; **to need to do something** avoir besoin de faire quelque chose ▷ *I need to use the phone.* J'ai besoin d'utiliser le téléphone.

▶ *n*: **There's no need to make reservations.** Il n'est pas nécessaire de réserver.

needle ['niːdl] *n* aiguille *f*

negative ['nɛgətɪv] *n* (*photo*) négatif *m*

▶ *adj* négatif *m* (*f* négative) ▷ *He's got a very negative attitude.* Il a une attitude très négative.

neglected [nɪˈglɛktɪd] *adj* (*untidy*) mal tenu ▷ *The garden is neglected.* Le jardin est mal tenu.

negotiate [nɪˈgəʊʃɪeɪt] *vb* négocier

negotiations [nɪgəʊʃɪˈeɪʃənz] *npl* négociations *fpl*

neighbour ['neɪbər] *n* voisin *m*, voisine *f* ▷ *the neighbours' garden* le jardin des voisins

neighbourhood ['neɪbəhʊd] *n* quartier *m*

neither ['naɪðər] *pron, conj, adv* aucun des deux, aucune des deux ▷ *"Carrots or peas?" —"Neither, thanks."* « Des carottes ou des petits pois? » — « Aucun des deux merci. » ▷ *Neither of them is coming.* Aucun des deux ne vient.; **neither...nor...** ni...ni... ▷ *Neither my mom nor my dad is coming to the school play.* Ni ma mère ni mon père ne viennent à la pièce de l'école.;

---

239 | **Newfoundland**

Neither do I. Moi non plus. ▷ *"I don't like him." —"Neither do I!"* « Je ne l'aime pas. » — « Moi non plus! »; **Neither have I.** Moi non plus. ▷ *"I've never been to the Northwest Territories." —"Neither have I."* « Je ne suis jamais allé aux Territoires du Nord-Ouest. » — « Moi non plus. »

neon ['niːɒn] *n* néon *m*; **a neon light** une lampe au néon

nephew ['nɛvjuː] *n* neveu *m* (*pl* neveux) ▷ *my nephew* mon neveu

nerve [nɜːv] *n* ① nerf *m* ▷ *She sometimes gets on my nerves.* Elle me tape quelquefois sur les nerfs. ② (*boldness*) toupet *m* ▷ *He's got some nerve!* Il a du toupet! ; **It's only nerves.** C'est de la nervosité.; **to have an attack of nerves** avoir le trac

nerve-racking ['nɜːˈrækɪŋ] *adj* angoissant

nervous ['nɜːvəs] *adj* (*tense*) nerveux (*f* nerveuse) ▷ *I bite my nails when I'm nervous.* Je me ronge les ongles quand je suis nerveux.; **to be nervous about something** craindre quelque chose ▷ *I'm nervous about my piano exam.* Je crains mon examen de piano.; **to be nervous about doing something** craindre de faire quelque chose ▷ *I'm a bit nervous about flying to Newfoundland by myself.* Je crains un peu d'aller toute seule en avion à Terre-Neuve.

nest [nɛst] *n* nid *m*

Net [nɛt] *n* Internet *m* ▷ *to surf the Net* naviguer sur Internet

net [nɛt] *n* filet *m* ▷ *a volleyball net* un filet de volleyball

network ['nɛtwɜːk] *n* réseau *m* (*pl* réseaux)

neurotic [njʊəˈrɒtɪk] *adj* névrosé

neutral ['njuːtrəl] *adj* neutre ▷ *neutral colours* des couleurs neutres ▷ *a neutral country* un pays neutre ▷ *I don't want to take sides; I'm staying neutral.* Je ne veux pas prendre parti; je vais rester neutre.

never ['nɛvər] *adv* ① jamais ▷ *"Have you ever been to the West Coast?" —"No, never."* « Est-ce que tu es déjà allé jusqu'à la côte Ouest? » — « Non, jamais. » ▷ *"When are you going to phone him?" —"Never!"* « Quand est-ce que tu vas l'appeler? » — « Jamais! » ② ne...jamais ▷ *I never watch soap operas.* Je ne regarde jamais les téléromans. ▷ *I have never been camping.* Je n'ai jamais fait de camping. ▷ *Never leave valuables in your car.* Ne laissez jamais d'objets de valeur dans votre voiture.; **Never again!** Plus jamais!; **Never mind.** Ça ne fait rien.

new [njuː] *adj* ① nouveau (*f* nouvelle, *mpl* nouveaux) ▷ *her new bike* son nouveau vélo ▷ *I need a new dress.* J'ai besoin d'une nouvelle robe. ▷ *his new friend* son nouvel ami; **New Age** nouvel âge ▷ *New Age music* la musique nouvel âge ② (*brand new*) neuf (*f* neuve) ▷ *They've got a new car.* Ils ont une voiture neuve.

newborn ['njuːbɔːn] *n* nouveau-né *m* (*pl* nouveau-nés), nouveau-née *f* (*pl* nouveau-nées); **a newborn baby** un nouveau-né

New Brunswick [-'brʌnzwɪk] *n* Nouveau-Brunswick *m*

newcomer ['njuːkʌmər] *n* nouveau venu *m* (*pl* nouveaux venus), nouvelle venue *f*

Newfoundland ['njuːfənlənd] *n* Terre-Neuve

news [nju:z] n ❶ nouvelles fpl ▷ good news
de bonnes nouvelles ▷ I've had some bad news.
J'ai reçu de mauvaises nouvelles. ▷ It was nice
to get your news. J'ai été content d'avoir de tes
nouvelles. ❷ (single piece of news) nouvelle f
▷ That's wonderful news! Quelle bonne nouvelle!
❸ (on TV) journal télévisé m ▷ I watch the news
every evening. Je regarde le journal télévisé
tous les soirs. ❹ (on radio) informations fpl
▷ I listen to the news every morning. J'écoute les
informations tous les matins.
newspaper ['nju:zpeipə'] n journal m (pl
journaux) ▷ I deliver newspapers. Je distribue
des journaux.
newsstand ['nju:zstænd] n kiosque à
journaux m
New Year's n Nouvel An m ▷ to celebrate New
Year's fêter le Nouvel An; **Happy New Year!**
Bonne Année!; **New Year's Day** le jour de l'An;
New Year's Eve la veille du jour de l'An ▷ a New
Year's Eve party un réveillon du jour de l'An
next [nekst] adj, adv, prep ❶ (in time) prochain
▷ next Saturday samedi prochain ▷ next
year l'année prochaine ▷ next summer l'été
prochain ❷ (in sequence) suivant ▷ the next
train le train suivant ▷ Next please! Au suivant!
❸ (afterwards) ensuite ▷ What shall I do next?
Qu'est-ce que je fais ensuite? ▷ What happened
next? Qu'est-ce qui s'est passé ensuite?; **next
to** à côté de ▷ next to the bank à côté de la
banque; **the next day** le lendemain ▷ The next
day we visited Windsor. Le lendemain nous avons
visité Windsor.; **the next time** la prochaine
fois ▷ the next time you see her la prochaine fois
que tu la verras; **next door** à côté ▷ They live
next door. Ils habitent à côté. ❹ the people next
door les gens d'à côté; **the next room** la pièce
d'à côté
nibble ['nibl] vb ❶ (food) grignoter ▷ to nibble
on a cookie grignoter un biscuit ❷ mordiller
▷ Don't nibble on your pencil. Ne mordille pas ton
crayon.; **nibble food** les m amuse-gueules
nice [nais] adj ❶ (kind) gentil (f gentille)
▷ Your parents are very nice. Tes parents sont
très gentils. ▷ It was nice of you to remember my
birthday. C'était gentil de ta part de te souvenir
de ma fête.; **to be nice to somebody** être
gentil avec quelqu'un ❷ (pretty) joli ▷ That's a
nice dress! Qu'est-ce qu'elle est jolie, cette robe!
▷ Banff is a nice town. Banff est une jolie ville.
❸ (general term of approval) bon (f bonne) ▷ a
nice cup of coffee une bonne tasse de café; **Have
a nice time!** Amuse-toi bien!; **nice weather** le
beau temps; **It's a nice day.** Il fait beau.
nickel ['nikl] n ❶ (coin) pièce de cinq cents f
❷ (mineral) nickel m
nickname ['nikneim] n surnom m
niece [ni:s] n nièce f ▷ my niece ma nièce
night [nait] n ❶ nuit f ▷ I want a single room for
two nights. Je veux une chambre individuelle
pour deux nuits.; **My mother works nights.**
Ma mère travaille la nuit; **at night** la nuit;
Good night! Bonne nuit!; **a night club** une
boîte de nuit ❷ (evening) soir m ▷ tomorrow
night demain soir; **last night (1)** hier soir ▷ We
watched a video last night. Nous avons regardé

un vidéo hier soir. **(2)** la nuit dernière ▷ Last
night I had a bad dream. La nuit dernière, j'ai fait
un mauvais rêve.
nightgown ['naitgaun] n chemise de nuit f
nightmare ['naitmɛə'] n cauchemar m
▷ It was a real nightmare! Ça a été un vrai
cauchemar!; **to have a nightmare** faire un
cauchemar
nightshirt ['naitʃə:t] n chemise de nuit f
nine [nain] num neuf ▷ He's nine. Il a neuf ans.
nineteen [nain'ti:n] num dix-neuf ▷ She's
nineteen. Elle a dix-neuf ans.
nineteenth [nain'ti:nθ] adj dix-neuvième
▷ the nineteenth day of our holidays la dix-
neuvième journée de nos vacances ▷ the
nineteenth floor le dix-neuvième étage; **the
nineteenth of August** le dix-neuf août
ninety ['nainti] num quatre-vingt-dix
ninth [nainθ] adj neuvième ▷ the ninth floor
le neuvième étage; **the ninth of August** le
neuf août
no [nəu] adv, adj ❶ non ▷ "Are you coming?"
— "No." « Est-ce que vous venez? » — « Non. »
▷ "Would you like some more?" — "No thank you."
« Vous en voulez encore? » — « Non merci. »
❷ (not any) pas de ▷ There's no hot water. Il n'y a
pas d'eau chaude. ▷ There's no mail on Sundays. Il
n'y a pas de courrier le dimanche. ▷ No problem.
Pas de problème.; **I have no idea.** Je n'en ai
aucune idée.; **No way!** Pas question!; **"no
smoking"** « Défense de fumer »; **No kidding!**
Sans blague!
nobody ['nəubədi] pron ❶ personne
▷ "Who's going with you?" — "Nobody." « Qui
t'accompagne? » — « Personne. » ❷ ne...
personne ▷ There was nobody in the office. Il
n'y avait personne au bureau.; **Nobody likes
this new rule.** Personne n'aime ce nouveau
règlement.
nod [nɒd] vb (in agreement) acquiescer d'un
signe de tête; **to nod to somebody** (as
greeting) saluer quelqu'un d'un signe de tête
noise [nɔiz] n bruit m ▷ Please make less noise.
Faites moins de bruit, s'il vous plaît.
noisy ['nɔizi] adj bruyant
nominate ['nɒmineit] vb (propose) proposer
▷ I nominate Ian Alexander as president of the
society. Je propose Ian Alexander comme
président de la société.; **He was nominated
for a Governor General's Award.** Il a été
nominé pour un Prix du Gouverneur général.
none [nʌn] pron ❶ aucun, aucune f ▷ "How
many sisters do you have?" — "None." « Tu as
combien de sœurs? » — « Aucune. » ❷ "What
sports do you play?" — "None." « Qu'est-ce que tu
fais comme sport? » — « Je n'en fais aucun. »
❸ aucun...ne ▷ None of my friends wanted to
come. Aucun de mes amis n'a voulu venir.;
There's none left. Il n'y en a plus.; **There are
none left.** Il n'y en a plus.
non-renewable ['nɒnri'nju:əbl] adj non
renouvelable ▷ non-renewable resources les
ressources non renouvelables
nonsense ['nɒnsəns] n niaiseries fpl ▷ She
talks a lot of nonsense. Elle dit beaucoup de
niaiseries. ▷ Nonsense! Arrête tes niaiseries!

non-smoker ['nɒn'sməukə^r] *n* non-fumeur *m*, non-fumeuse *f* ▷ *I'm a non-smoker.* Je suis non-fumeur.

non-smoking ['nɒn'sməukɪŋ] *adj* non-fumeur *m* ▷ *a non-smoking section* une section non-fumeurs

non-stop ['nɒn'stɒp] *adj, adv* ❶ direct ▷ *a non-stop flight* un vol direct ▷ *We flew non-stop.* Nous avons pris un vol direct. ❷ sans arrêt ▷ *He talks non-stop.* Il parle sans arrêt.

noodles ['nu:dlz] *npl* nouilles *fpl*

noon [nu:n] *n* midi *m* ▷ *at noon* à midi ▷ *before noon* avant midi

no one *pron* ❶ personne ▷ *"Who's going with you?" — "No one."* « Qui t'accompagne? » — « Personne. » ❷ ne...personne ▷ *There was no one in the office.* Il n'y avait personne au bureau.; **No one likes homework.** Personne n'aime les devoirs.

nor [nɔː^r] *conj*: **neither...nor** ni...ni ▷ *neither the mall nor the pool* ni le centre commercial, ni la piscine; **Nor do I.** Moi non plus. ▷ *"I didn't like the movie." — "Nor did I."* « Je n'ai pas aimé le film. » — « Moi non plus. »; **Nor have I.** Moi non plus. ▷ *"I haven't seen her." — "Nor have I."* « Je ne l'ai pas vue. » — « Moi non plus. »

normal ['nɔːml] *adj* ❶ (*usual*) habituel (*f* habituelle) ▷ *at the normal time* à l'heure habituelle ❷ (*standard*) normal (*mpl* normaux) ▷ *a normal car* une voiture normale

normally ['nɔːməlɪ] *adv* ❶ (*usually*) généralement ▷ *I normally arrive at nine o'clock.* J'arrive généralement à neuf heures. ❷ (*as normal*) normalement ▷ *In spite of the strike, the airports are operating normally.* Malgré la grève, les aéroports fonctionnent normalement.

north [nɔːθ] *adj, adv* nord *m* (*f+pl* nord) ▷ *the north shore* la rive nord; **a north wind** un vent du nord ❷ vers le nord ▷ *We were travelling north.* Nous allions vers le nord.; **north of** au nord de ▷ *It's north of Cobourg.* C'est au nord de Cobourg.
▷ *n* nord *m* ▷ *in the north* dans le nord

North America *n* Amérique *f* du Nord

northbound ['nɔːθbaund] *adj*: ▷ *The truck was northbound on Hwy 400.* Le camion se trouvait sur l'autoroute 400 en direction du nord.; **Northbound traffic is moving very slowly.** La circulation vers le nord avance très lentement.

northeast [nɔːθ'iːst] *n* nord-est *m* ▷ *in the northeast* au nord-est

northern ['nɔːðən] *adj*: **the northern part of the province** la partie nord de la province; **Northern Québec** le Nord du Québec; **the northern lights** l'aurore *f* boréale

North Pole *n* pôle Nord *m*

northwest [nɔːθ'west] *n* nord-ouest *m* ▷ *in the northwest* au nord-ouest

Northwest Territories *n* Territoires *mpl* du Nord-Ouest

nose [nəuz] *n* nez *m* (*pl* nez); **to look down one's nose at someone** prendre quelqu'un de haut; **to turn up one's nose at something** faire le dégoûté devant quelque chose; **It was right under my nose.** C'était là juste sous mon nez.

nosebleed ['nəuzbliːd] *n*: **to have a nosebleed** saigner du nez ▷ *I often get nosebleeds.* Je saigne souvent du nez.

nosy ['nəuzɪ] *adj* fouineur (*f* fouineuse)

not [nɒt] *adv* ❶ pas ▷ *Are you coming or not?* Est-ce que tu viens ou pas?; **not really** pas vraiment; **not at all** pas du tout; **not yet** pas encore ▷ *"Are you finished?" — "Not yet."* « As-tu fini? » — « Pas encore. » ❷ ne...pas ▷ *I'm not sure.* Je ne suis pas sûr. ▷ *It's not raining.* Il ne pleut pas. ▷ *You shouldn't do that.* Tu ne devrais pas faire ça. ▷ *They haven't arrived yet.* Ils ne sont pas encore arrivés. ❸ non ▷ *I hope not.* J'espère que non. ▷ *"Can you lend me $10?" — "I'm afraid not."* « Est-ce que tu peux me prêter dix dollars? » — « Non, désolé. »

note [nəut] *n* ❶ note *f* ▷ *to take notes* prendre des notes ❷ (*letter*) mot *m* ▷ *I'll write her a note.* Je vais lui écrire un mot.

notebook ['nəutbʊk] *n* ❶ carnet *m* ❷ ordinateur *m* bloc-notes

note down *vb* noter

notepad ['nəutpæd] *n* bloc-notes *m* (*pl* blocs-notes)

nothing ['nʌθɪŋ] *n* ❶ rien ▷ *"What's wrong?" — "Nothing."* « Qu'est-ce qui ne va pas? » — « Rien. » ▷ *nothing special* rien de particulier ❷ ne...rien ▷ *He does nothing.* Il ne fait rien. ▷ *He ate nothing for breakfast.* Il n'a rien mangé au déjeuner.; **Nothing is open on Christmas Day.** Rien n'est ouvert le jour de Noël.

notice ['nəutɪs] *n* (*sign*) panneau *m* (*pl* panneaux); **to put up a notice** mettre un panneau; **a warning notice** un avertissement; **Don't take any notice of her!** Ne fais pas attention à elle!
▷ *vb* remarquer

notorious [nəu'tɔːrɪəs] *adj* notoire ▷ *a notorious criminal* un criminel notoire ▷ *His pranks are notorious.* Ses mauvais tours sont notoires.

noun [naun] *n* nom *m*

Nova Scotia ['nəuvə'skəuʃə] *n* Nouvelle-Écosse *f*

novel ['nɒvl] *n* roman *m*

novelist ['nɒvəlɪst] *n* romancier *m*, romancière *f*

November [nəu'vɛmbə^r] *n* novembre *m*; **in November** en novembre

now [nau] *adv, conj* maintenant ▷ *What are you doing now?* Qu'est-ce que tu fais maintenant?; **just now** en ce moment ▷ *I'm rather busy just now.* Je suis très occupé en ce moment.; **I did it just now.** Je viens de le faire.; **He should be there by now.** Il doit être arrivé à l'heure qu'il est.; **It should be ready by now.** Ça devrait être déjà prêt.; **now and then** de temps en temps; **now that you're here...** maintenant que tu es là...

nowadays ['nauədeɪz] *adv* de nos jours ▷ *Nowadays we have better medical care.* De nos jours, on a de meilleurs soins de santé.

nowhere ['nəuwɛə^r] *adv* nulle part ▷ *nowhere else* nulle part ailleurs

nuclear ['njuːklɪə^r] *adj* nucléaire ▷ *nuclear power* l'énergie nucléaire ▷ *a nuclear power* *station* une centrale nucléaire ▷ *the nuclear family* la famille nucléaire

nude [njuːd] *adj* nu; **to sunbathe nude** faire du bronzage intégral

nudge [nʌdʒ] *vb:* **She nudged me when she saw him.** Elle m'a donné un coup de coude quand elle l'a vu.

nudist ['njuːdɪst] *n* nudiste

nuisance ['njuːsns] *n:* **It's a nuisance.** C'est très embêtant.; **Sorry to be a nuisance.** Désolé de vous déranger.

numb [nʌm] *adj* engourdi ▷ *My leg's gone numb.* J'ai les jambes engourdies.; **numb with cold** engourdi par le froid

number ['nʌmbə'] *n* ❶ (*total amount*) nombre *m* ▷ *a large number of people* un grand nombre de gens ❷ (*of house, telephone, bank account*) numéro *m* ▷ *They live at number 5.* Ils habitent au numéro cinq. ▷ *What's your phone number?* Quel est votre numéro de téléphone? ▷ *You've got the wrong number.* Vous vous êtes trompé de numéro. ❸ (*figure, digit*) chiffre *m* ▷ *I can't read the second number.* Je n'arrive pas à lire le deuxième chiffre.

nun [nʌn] *n* religieuse *f* ▷ *She's a nun.* Elle est religieuse.

Nunavut ['nʌnəvət] *n* Nunavut *m*

nurse [nəːs] *n* infirmier *m*, infirmière *f* ▷ *She's a nurse.* Elle est infirmière.

nursery ['nəːsəri] *n* (*for plants*) pépinière *f*

nursery school *n* jardin d'enfants *m*

nut [nʌt] *n* ❶ (*edible*) noix *f* (*pl* noix) ❷ (*made of metal*) écrou *m*; **You're a nut!** Tu es dingue!

nutmeg ['nʌtmeg] *n* noix de muscade *f*

nutrient ['njuːtriənt] *n* nutriment *m*

nutrition [njuː'trɪʃən] *n* nutrition *f*

nutritional [njuː'trɪʃənl] *adj* nutritif (*f* nutritive) ▷ *Junk food has almost no nutritional value.* La malbouffe n'a presque aucune valeur nutritive.

nutritionist [njuː'trɪʃənɪst] *n* nutritionniste

nutritious [njuː'trɪʃəs] *adj* nutritif (*f* nutritive) ▷ *a nutritious snack* une collation nutritive

nuts [nʌts] *adj:* **He's nuts.** Il est dingue.

nylon ['naɪlən] *n* nylon *m*

O

oak [əuk] *n* chêne *m* ▷ *an oak table* une table en chêne

oar [ɔː'] *n* aviron *m*

oatmeal ['əutmiːl] *n* gruau *m*

obedient [ə'biːdɪənt] *adj* obéissant

obey [ə'beɪ] *vb:* **to obey the rules** respecter le règlement; **to obey one's parents** obéir à ses parents

object [əb'dʒekt] *n* objet *m* ▷ *a familiar object* un objet familier

objection [əb'dʒekʃən] *n* objection *f*

objective [əb'dʒektɪv] *n* objectif *m*

oboe ['əubəu] *n* hautbois *m* ▷ *I play the oboe.* Je joue du hautbois.

obscene [əb'siːn] *adj* obscène

observant [əb'zəːvnt] *adj* observateur (*f* observatrice)

observe [əb'zəːv] *vb* observer

obsessed [əb'sest] *adj* obsédé ▷ *He's obsessed with trains.* Il est obsédé par les trains.

obsession [əb'seʃən] *n* obsession *f* ▷ *It's getting to be an obsession with you.* Ça devient une obsession chez toi.; **Hockey is an obsession of mine.** Le hockey est une de mes passions.

obsolete ['ɔbsəliːt] *adj* dépassé

obstacle ['ɔbstəkl] *n* obstacle *m*

obstruct [əb'strʌkt] *vb* bloquer ▷ *A truck was obstructing the traffic.* Un camion bloquait la circulation.

obtain [əb'teɪn] *vb* obtenir

obvious ['ɔbvɪəs] *adj* évident

obviously ['ɔbvɪəslɪ] *adv* ❶ (*of course*) évidemment ▷ *"Do you want to pass the exam?" — "Obviously!"* « Tu veux réussir à l'examen? » — « Évidemment! »; **Obviously not!** Bien sûr que non! ❷ (*visibly*) manifestement ▷ *She was obviously exhausted.* Elle était manifestement épuisée.

occasion [ə'keɪʒən] *n* occasion *f* ▷ *a special occasion* une occasion spéciale; **on several occasions** à plusieurs reprises

occasionally [ə'keɪʒənəlɪ] *adv* de temps en temps

occupation [ɔkjuː'peɪʃən] *n* profession *f*

occupy ['ɔkjupaɪ] *vb* occuper ▷ *That seat is occupied.* Cette place est occupée.

occur [ə'kəː'] *vb* (*happen*) avoir lieu ▷ *The accident occurred yesterday.* L'accident a eu lieu hier.; **It suddenly occurred to me that...** Il m'est soudain venu à l'esprit que...

ocean ['əuʃən] *n* océan *m*

o'clock [ə'klɔk] *adv:* **at four o'clock** à quatre heures; **It's five o'clock.** Il est cinq heures.

October [ɔk'təubə'] *n* octobre *m*; **in October** en octobre

octopus ['ɔktəpəs] *n* pieuvre *f*

odd [ɔd] *adj* ❶ bizarre ▷ *That's odd!* C'est bizarre! ❷ impair ▷ *an odd number* un chiffre impair

of [ɔv, əv] *prep* ❶ de, d', du, des ▷ *some photos of my holiday* des photos de mes vacances ▷ *a boy of ten* un garçon de dix ans ▷ *a kilo of oranges* un kilo d'oranges ▷ *the end of the movie* la fin du film ▷ *the end of the holidays* la fin des vacances ❷ (*with quantity, amount*) en ▷ *He has four sisters.* I've met two of them. Il a quatre sœurs. J'en ai rencontré deux. ▷ *Can I have half of that?* Je peux en avoir la moitié?; **three of us** trois d'entre nous; **a friend of mine** un de mes amis; **the 14th of September** le quatorze septembre; **That's very kind of you.** C'est très gentil de votre part.; **It's made of wood.** C'est en bois.

off [ɔf] *adv, prep, adj* ❶ *(heater, light, TV)* éteint ▷ *All the lights are off.* Toutes les lumières sont éteintes. ❷ *(tap, gas)* fermé ▷ *Are you sure the tap is off?* Tu es sûr que le robinet est fermé? ❸ *(cancelled)* annulé ▷ *The game is off.* Le match est annulé.; **to be off sick** être malade; **a day off** un jour de congé ▷ *to take a day off work* prendre un jour de congé; **She's off school today.** Elle n'est pas à l'école aujourd'hui.; **I must be off now.** Je dois m'en aller maintenant.; **I'm off.** Je m'en vais.

offence [əˈfɛns] *n (crime)* délit; **No offence, but...** Sans vouloir t'offenser,...; **to take offence at something** s'offenser de quelque chose

offend [əˈfɛnd] *vb* offenser ▷ *Did my joke offend you?* Est-ce que ma plaisanterie t'a offensé?; **to be offended by something** s'offenser de quelque chose

offensive [əˈfɛnsɪv] *adj* choquant

offer [ˈɔfəʳ] *n* proposition *f* ▷ *a good offer* une proposition intéressante ▷ *Make me an offer.* Faites-moi une proposition.; **$30 or best offer** 30 dollars ou offre la plus intéressante ▶ *vb* ❶ offrir ▷ *He offered me a cookie.* Il m'a offert un biscuit. ❷ proposer ▷ *He offered to help me.* Il m'a proposé de m'aider. ▷ *I offered to go with them.* Je leur ai proposé de les accompagner.

office [ˈɔfɪs] *n* bureau *m (pl* bureaux*)* ▷ *She works in an office.* Elle travaille dans un bureau.

officer [ˈɔfɪsəʳ] *n* ❶ *(police)* agent *m* de police, agente *f* de police ❷ *(other)* officier *m*, officière *f*

official [əˈfɪʃl] *adj* officiel *(f* officielle*)*

off-season [ˈɔfˈsiːzn] *n:* **It's cheaper during the off-season.** C'est moins cher hors saison.

offside [ˈɔfˈsaɪd] *adj (sports)* hors jeu

often [ˈɔfn] *adv* souvent ▷ *It often rains.* Il pleut souvent. ▷ *How often do you go to the movies?* Tu vas souvent au cinéma? ▷ *I'd like to go skiing more often.* J'aimerais aller skier plus souvent.

oil [ɔɪl] *n* ❶ *(for lubrication, cooking)* huile *f*; **an oil painting** une peinture à l'huile ❷ *(crude oil)* pétrole *m* ▷ *oil from the Alberta tar sands* le pétrole des sables bitumineux de l'Alberta ▶ *vb* graisser

oil rig *n* plateforme pétrolière *f* ▷ *She works on an oil rig.* Elle travaille sur une plateforme pétrolière.

oil slick *n* marée noire

oil well *n* puits de pétrole *m*

ointment [ˈɔɪntmənt] *n* onguent *m*

okay [ˈəuˈkeɪ] *excl, adj (agreed)* d'accord ▷ *"Could you call back later?" — "Okay!"* «Tu peux rappeler plus tard?» — «D'accord!» ▷ *I'll meet you at six o'clock, okay?* Je te retrouve à six heures, d'accord? ▷ *Is that okay?* C'est d'accord?; **I'll do it tomorrow, if that's okay with you.** Je le ferai demain, si tu es d'accord.; **Are you okay?** Ça va?; **"How was your holiday?" — "It was okay."** «C'était comment tes vacances?» — «Pas mal.»; **"What's your teacher like?"**

— **"He's okay."** «Il est comment ton prof?» — «Il est sympathique. *(informal)*»

old [əuld] *adj* ❶ vieux *(f* vieille*)* ▷ *an old dog* un vieux chien ▷ *an old house* une vieille maison ▷ *an old man* un vieil homme ❷ âgé ▷ *old people* les personnes âgées ❸ *(former)* ancien *(f* ancienne*)* ▷ *my old school* mon ancienne école; **How old are you?** Quel âge as-tu?; **He's ten years old.** Il a dix ans.; **my older brother** mon frère aîné ▷ *my older sister* ma sœur aînée; **She's two years older than me.** Elle a deux ans de plus que moi.; **I'm the oldest in the family.** Je suis l'aîné de la famille.

old-fashioned [ˈəuldˈfæʃnd] *adj* ❶ démodé ▷ *She wears old-fashioned clothes.* Elle porte des vêtements démodés. ❷ *(person)* vieux jeu *(f+pl* vieux jeu*)* ▷ *My parents are rather old-fashioned.* Mes parents sont plutôt vieux jeu.

olive [ˈɔlɪv] *n* olive *f*; **olive oil** l'huile d'olive

Olympic [əuˈlɪmpɪk] *adj* olympique; **the Olympics** les *m* Jeux olympiques

omelette [ˈɔmlɪt] *n* omelette *f*

on [ɔn] *prep, adv* ❶ sur ▷ *on the table* sur la table ▷ *on an island* sur une île ❷ à ▷ *on the left* à gauche ▷ *on the 2nd floor* au deuxième étage ▷ *I go to school on my bike.* Je vais à l'école à vélo.; **on TV** à la télé ▷ *What's on TV?* Qu'est-ce qu'il y a à la télé?; **on the radio** à la radio ▷ *I heard it on the radio.* Je l'ai entendu à la radio.; **on the bus (1)** *(by bus)* en autobus ▷ *I go into town on the bus.* Je vais en ville en autobus. **(2)** *(inside)* dans l'autobus ▷ *There were no empty seats on the bus.* Il n'y avait pas de places libres dans l'autobus.; **on holiday** en vacances ▷ *They're on holiday.* Ils sont en vacances.; **on strike** en grève ▷ *on Friday* vendredi ▷ *on Fridays* le vendredi ▷ *on Christmas Day* le jour de Noël ▷ *on June 20th* le vingt juin ▷ *on my birthday* le jour de mon anniversaire ▶ *adj* ❶ *(heater, light, TV)* allumé ▷ *I think I left the light on.* Je crois que j'ai laissé la lumière allumée. ❷ *(tap, gas)* ouvert ▷ *You left the tap on.* Tu as laissé le robinet ouvert. ❸ *(machine)* en marche ▷ *Is the dishwasher on?* Est-ce que le lave-vaisselle est en marche?; **What's on at the movie theatre?** Qu'est-ce qui passe au cinéma?

once [wʌns] *adv* une fois ▷ *once a week* une fois par semaine ▷ *once more* encore une fois ▷ *I've been to Nunavut once before.* J'y ai déjà été une fois au Nunavut.; **Once upon a time...** Il était une fois...; **at once** tout de suite; **all at once** *(suddenly)* tout à coup; **once in a while** de temps en temps

one [wʌn] *num, pron* ❶ un ▷ *one day* un jour ▷ *"Do you need a stamp?" — "No thanks, I've got one."* «Est-ce que tu as besoin d'un timbre?» — «Non merci, j'en ai un.» ❷ *(feminine)* une ▷ *one minute* une minute ▷ *I have one brother and one sister.* J'ai un frère et une sœur. ❸ *(impersonal)* on ▷ *One never knows.* On ne sait jamais.; **one by one** un à un; **one after the other** l'un après l'autre; **this one (1)** *(masculine)* celui-ci ▷ *"Which foot is hurting?" — "This one."* «Quel pied te fait mal?» — «Celui-ci.» **(2)** *(feminine)* celle-ci ▷ *"Which is the best photo? — "This one."*

« Quelle est la meilleure photo? » — « Celle-ci. »; **that one (1)** *(masculine)* celui-là ▷ *Which bag is yours?" — "That one."* « Lequel est ton sac? » — « Celui-là. »; **(2)** *(feminine)* celle-là ▷ *"Which seat do you want?" — "That one."* « Quelle place voulez-vous? » — « Celle-là. »

oneself [wʌn'sɛlf] *pron* ❶ se ▷ *to hurt oneself* se faire mal ❷ soi-même ▷ *It's quicker to do it oneself.* C'est plus rapide de le faire soi-même.

one-way [wʌn'weɪ] *adj*: **a one-way street** une impasse

onion [ˈʌnjən] *n* oignon *m* ▷ *onion soup* la soupe à l'oignon

online [ˈɒnlaɪn] *adj* en ligne

only [ˈəʊnlɪ] *adv, adj, conj* ❶ seul ▷ *Monday is the only day I'm free.* Le lundi est le seul jour où je suis libre. ▷ *French is the only subject I like.* Le français est la seule matière que j'aime. ❷ seulement ▷ *"How much was it?" — "Only $10."* « Combien c'était? » — « Seulement dix dollars. » ▷ *Not only is she intelligent, she's also very nice.* Elle est non seulement intelligente, mais aussi très gentille. ❸ ne...que ▷ *We only want to stay for one night.* Nous ne voulons rester qu'une nuit. ▷ *These cassettes are only $5.* Ces cassettes ne coûtent que cinq dollars. ❹ mais ▷ *I'd like the same sweater, only in black.* Je voudrais le même chandail, mais en noir.; **an only child** un enfant unique

Ontario [ɒnˈtɛərɪəʊ] *n* l'Ontario *m*

onwards [ˈɒnwədz] *adv* à partir de ▷ *from July onwards* à partir de juillet

open [ˈəʊpn] *adj* ❶ ouvert ▷ *The bakery is open on Sunday morning.* La boulangerie est ouverte le dimanche matin. ▷ *I'm open to suggestions.* Je suis ouvert aux suggestions. ❷ franc *(f* franche) ▷ *She was very open with me.* Elle a été tout à fait franche avec moi. ❸ vacant ▷ *Is the position still open?* Est-ce que le poste est encore vacant?; **in the open air** en plein air; **to have an open mind** avoir l'esprit ouvert ▷ *vb* ❶ ouvrir ▷ *Can I open the window?* Est-ce que je peux ouvrir la fenêtre? ▷ *What time do the stores open?* Les magasins ouvrent à quelle heure? ❷ s'ouvrir ▷ *The door opens automatically.* La porte s'ouvre automatiquement. ▷ *The door opened and in came the teacher.* La porte s'est ouverte et la professeure est entrée.

opening [ˈəʊpnɪŋ] *n* ❶ ouverture *f* ▷ *the opening of Parliament* l'ouverture de la session parlementaire ▷ *an opening in the wall* une ouverture dans le mur ❷ *(to cave, tunnel)* entrée *f* ❸ *(in clouds)* éclaircie *f* ❹ *(for specific job)* poste vacant *m* ▷ *We have an opening for a receptionist.* Nous avons un poste vacant de réceptionniste. ❺ *(potential job opportunity)* débouché *m* ▷ *There are a lot of openings in the computer industry.* Il y a beaucoup de débouchés dans l'informatique.

opera [ˈɒpərə] *n* opéra *m*

operate [ˈɒpəreɪt] *vb* ❶ fonctionner ▷ *I don't know how the legal system operates in Québec.* Je ne sais pas comment fonctionne le système judiciaire au Québec. ❷ faire fonctionner ▷ *How do you operate the VCR?* Comment fait-on

fonctionner le magnétoscope? ❸ *(medically)* opérer ▷ *to operate on someone* opérer quelqu'un

operation [ɒpəˈreɪʃən] *n* opération *f* ▷ *a major operation* une grave opération; **to have an operation** se faire opérer ▷ *I have never had an operation.* Je ne me suis jamais fait opérer.

operator [ˈɒpəreɪtəʳ] *n* *(on telephone)* standardiste

opinion [əˈpɪnjən] *n* avis *m* ▷ *in my opinion* à mon avis ▷ *He asked me my opinion.* Il m'a demandé mon avis.; **What's your opinion?** Qu'est-ce que vous en pensez?

opinion poll *n* sondage *m*

opponent [əˈpəʊnənt] *n* adversaire *mf*

opportunity [ɒpəˈtjuːnɪtɪ] *n* occasion *f*; **to have the opportunity to do something** avoir l'occasion de faire quelque chose ▷ *I've never had the opportunity to go to the Northwest Territories.* Je n'ai jamais eu l'occasion d'aller aux Territoires du Nord-Ouest.

opposed [əˈpəʊzd] *adj*: ▷ *I've always been opposed to violence.* J'ai toujours été contre la violence.; **as opposed to** par opposition à

opposing [əˈpəʊzɪŋ] *adj* *(team)* opposé

opposite [ˈɒpəzɪt] *adj, prep* ❶ opposé ▷ *It's in the opposite direction.* C'est dans la direction opposée. ❷ en face de ▷ *the girl sitting opposite me* la fille assise en face de moi; **the opposite sex** l'autre sexe

opposition [ɒpəˈzɪʃən] *n* opposition *f* ▷ *the leader of the Opposition* le chef de l'opposition ▷ *We ran into a lot of opposition.* Nous avons rencontré beaucoup d'opposition.

optimist [ˈɒptɪmɪst] *n* optimiste *mf*

optimistic [ɒptɪˈmɪstɪk] *adj* optimiste

option [ˈɒpʃən] *n* *(choice)* choix *m* ▷ *Our only option is to take the bus.* Notre seul choix est de prendre de l'autobus.

optional [ˈɒpʃənl] *adj* facultatif *(f* facultative)

optometrist [ɒpˈtɒmətrɪst] *n* optométriste *mf* ▷ *I picked up my new glasses at the optometrist's.* J'ai passé prendre mes nouvelles lunettes chez l'optométriste.

or [ɔːʳ] *conj* ❶ ou ▷ *Would you like tea or coffee?* Est-ce que tu veux du thé ou du café? ▷ *I don't eat meat or fish.* Je ne mange ni viande ni poisson. ❷ *(otherwise)* sinon ▷ *Hurry up or you'll miss the bus.* Dépêche-toi, sinon tu vas rater l'autobus.; **Give me the money, or else!** Donne-moi l'argent, sinon tu vas le regretter!

oral [ˈɔːrəl] *adj* oral *(mpl* oraux); **an oral presentation** une présentation orale

orange [ˈɒrɪndʒ] *n* orange *f*; **an orange juice** un jus d'orange ▷ *adj* orange *(f+pl* orange)

orchard [ˈɔːtʃəd] *n* verger *m*

orchestra [ˈɔːkɪstrə] *n* orchestre *m* ▷ *I play in the school orchestra.* Je joue dans l'orchestre de l'école.

order [ˈɔːdəʳ] *n* ❶ *(sequence)* ordre *m* ▷ *in alphabetical order* en ordre alphabétique ❷ *(instruction)* commande *f* ▷ *The waiter took our order.* Le serveur a pris notre commande.; **in order to** pour ▷ *She mows lawns in order to earn money.* Elle tond les gazons pour gagner de

l'argent.; **"out of order"** «en panne»
▶ *vb* commander ▷ *I ordered a hamburger and fries.* J'ai commandé un hamburger et des frites. ▷ *Are you ready to order?* Vous êtes prêt à commander?; **to order somebody around** donner des ordres à quelqu'un ▷ *She was fed up with being ordered around.* Elle en avait assez de toujours se faire donner des ordres.

ordinary ['ɔːdnrɪ] *adj* ❶ ordinaire ▷ *an ordinary day* une journée ordinaire ❷ *(people)* comme les autres ▷ *an ordinary family* une famille comme les autres ▷ *He's just an ordinary guy.* C'est un type comme les autres.

organ ['ɔːgən] *n* ❶ *(instrument)* orgue *m* ▷ *I play the organ.* Je joue de l'orgue. ❷ *(in body)* organe *m*

organic [ɔː'gænɪk] *adj (vegetables, fruit)* biologique

organization [ˌɔːgənaɪ'zeɪʃən] *n* organisation *f*

organize ['ɔːgənaɪz] *vb* organiser

origin ['ɒrɪdʒɪn] *n* origine *f*

original [ə'rɪdʒɪnl] *adj* original *(mpl* originaux*)* ▷ *It's a very original idea.* C'est une idée très originale. ▷ *Our original plan was to go camping.* Au départ, nous avions l'intention de faire du camping.

originally [ə'rɪdʒɪnəlɪ] *adv* au départ

ornament ['ɔːnəmənt] *n* bibelot *m*

orphan ['ɔːfn] *n* orphelin *m*, orpheline *f*

orthodontist [ɔːθə'dɒntɪst] *n* orthodontiste *mf* ▷ *I have to go to the orthodontist this afternoon.* Il faut que j'aille chez l'orthodontiste cet après-midi.

ostrich ['ɒstrɪtʃ] *n* autruche *f*

other ['ʌðə'] *adj, pron* autre ▷ *Have you got these jeans in other colours?* Est-ce que vous avez ces jeans dans d'autres couleurs? ▷ *on the other side of the street* de l'autre côté de la rue ▷ *the other day* l'autre jour; **the other one** l'autre ▷ *"This one?" — "No, the other one."* « Celui-ci? » — « Non, l'autre. »; **the others** les autres ▷ *The others are going but I'm not.* Les autres y vont mais pas moi.; **every other day** tous les deux jours; **other than** autre chose ▷ part ça

otherwise ['ʌðəwaɪz] *adv, conj* ❶ *(if not)* sinon ▷ *Write down the number, otherwise you'll forget it.* Note le numéro, sinon tu vas l'oublier. ▷ *Put some sunscreen on; you'll get burned otherwise.* Mets une crème solaire, sinon tu vas attraper des coups de soleil. ❷ *(in other ways)* ▷ *"I'm tired, but otherwise I'm fine.* Je suis fatigué, mais à part ça, ça va.

otter ['ɒtə'] *n* loutre *f*

ought [ɔːt] *vb*: ▷ *I ought to phone my parents.* Je devrais appeler mes parents. ▷ *He ought to win.* Il devrait gagner.

our ['auə'] *adj* ❶ notre ▷ *Our house is quite big.* Notre maison est plutôt grande. ❷ *(with plural)* nos ▷ *Our neighbours are very nice.* Nos voisins sont très gentils.

ours [auəz] *pron* ❶ le + *m* nôtre ▷ *Your garden is very big. Ours is much smaller.* Votre jardin est très grand. Le nôtre est beaucoup plus petit. ❷ *(with feminine)* la nôtre ▷ *Your school is very different from ours.* Votre école est très

différente de la nôtre. ❸ *(with plural)*, les nôtres ▷ *"Our teachers are strict." — "Ours are too."* « Nos professeurs sont sévères. » — « Les nôtres aussi. »; **Is this ours?** C'est à nous? ▷ *This car is ours.* Cette voiture est à nous. ▷ *"Whose is this?" — "It's ours."* « C'est à qui? » — « À nous. »

ourselves [auə'selvz] *pron* ❶ nous ▷ *We really enjoyed ourselves.* Nous nous sommes vraiment bien amusés. ❷ nous-mêmes ▷ *We built our garage ourselves.* Nous avons construit notre garage nous-mêmes.

out [aut] *adv* ❶ *(outside)* dehors ▷ *It's cold out.* Il fait froid dehors. ❷ *(light, fire)* éteint ▷ *All the lights are out.* Toutes les lumières sont éteintes.; **She's out.** Elle est sortie.; **He's out shopping.** Il est sorti faire des courses.; **She's out for the afternoon.** Elle ne sera pas là de tout l'après-midi.; **out there** dehors ▷ *It's cold out there.* Il fait froid dehors.; **to go out** sortir ▷ *I'm going out tonight.* Je sors ce soir.; **to go out with somebody** sortir avec quelqu'un ▷ *She's been going out with him for two months.* Elle sort avec lui depuis deux mois.; **out of** (1) dans ▷ *to drink out of a glass* boire dans un verre (2) sur ▷ *in 9 cases out of 10* dans neuf cas sur dix (3) en dehors de ▷ *He lives out of town.* Il habite en dehors de la ville.; **3 km out of town** à trois kilomètres de la ville; **out of curiosity** par curiosité; **out of date** (1) *(expired)* périmé (2) *(outmoded)* démodé, qui n'est plus en emploi; **That's out of the question.** C'est hors de question.; **You're out!** *(in game)* Tu es éliminé!

outbreak ['autbreɪk] *n* ❶ *(of disease)* épidémie *f* ▷ *an outbreak of the flu* une épidémie de grippe ❷ début *m* ▷ *the outbreak of war* le début de la guerre

outcome ['autkʌm] *n* issue *f* ▷ *What was the outcome of the negotiations?* Quelle a été l'issue des négociations?

outdoor [aut'dɔː'] *adj* en plein air ▷ *an outdoor swimming pool* une piscine en plein air; **outdoor activities** les activités de plein air

outdoors [aut'dɔːz] *adv* au grand air

outer ['autə'] *adj* extérieur ▷ *the outer surface* la surface extérieure; **the outer door** la porte extérieure; **outer space** l'espace *m*; **outer clothing** les *m* vêtements d'extérieur

outfit ['autfɪt] *n* tenue *f* ▷ *She bought a new outfit for the wedding.* Elle a acheté une nouvelle tenue pour le mariage.; **a cowboy outfit** un costume de cowboy

outgoing ['autgəuɪŋ] *adj* extraverti ▷ *He's very outgoing.* Il est très extraverti.

outhouse ['authaus] *n* toilettes *fpl* extérieures

outing ['autɪŋ] *n* sortie *f* ▷ *to go on an outing* faire une sortie

outline ['autlaɪn] *n* ❶ *(summary)* grandes *fpl* lignes ▷ *This is an outline of the plan.* Voici les grandes lignes du projet. ❷ *(shape)* contours *mpl* ▷ *We could see the outline of the mountain in the mist.* Nous distinguions les contours de la montagne dans la brume.

outlook ['autluk] *n* ❶ *(attitude)* attitude *f* ▷ *my outlook on life* mon attitude face à la vie

❷ (prospects) perspectives fpl ▷ the economic outlook les perspectives économiques; **The outlook is poor.** Les choses s'annoncent mal.

outnumber [aut'nʌmbə'] vb: **We're outnumbered.** Ils sont plus nombreux que nous.; **Girls outnumber boys three to one here.** Les filles sont trois fois plus nombreuses que les garçons ici.

outrageous [aut'reɪdʒəs] adj ❶ (behaviour) scandaleux (f scandaleuse) ❷ (price) exorbitant

outside [aut'saɪd] n extérieur m ▷ adj, adv, prep ❶ extérieur ▷ the outside walls les murs extérieurs ❷ dehors ▷ It's very cold outside. Il fait très froid dehors. ❸ en dehors de ▷ outside the school en dehors de l'école ▷ outside school hours en dehors des heures de cours

outskirts ['autskɜːts] npl banlieue f ▷ on the outskirts of the town dans les banlieues de la ville

outstanding [aut'stændɪŋ] adj remarquable

oval ['əuvl] adj ovale

oven ['ʌvn] n four m

over ['əuvə'] prep, adv, adj ❶ par-dessus ▷ The ball went over the wall. Le ballon est passé par-dessus le mur. ❷ au-dessus de ▷ There's a mirror over the washbasin. Il y a un miroir au-dessus du lavabo. ❸ (more than) plus de ▷ It's over twenty kilos. Ça pèse plus de vingt kilos. ▷ The temperature was over thirty degrees. Il faisait une température de plus de trente degrés. ❹ (during) pendant ▷ over the holidays pendant les vacances ▷ over Christmas pendant les fêtes de Noël ❺ (finished) terminé ▷ I'll be happy when the exams are over. Je serai content quand les examens seront terminés.; **over here**; **over there** là-bas; **all over the province** dans toute la province; **I spilled coffee over my shirt.** J'ai renversé du café sur ma chemise.

overall [əuvə'rɔːl] adv (generally) dans l'ensemble ▷ My marks were pretty good overall. Mes notes étaient assez bonnes dans l'ensemble.

overalls ['əuvərɔːlz] npl vêtements mpl de travail

overcast ['əuvəkɑːst] adj couvert ▷ The sky was overcast. Le ciel était couvert.

overcharge [əuvə'tʃɑːdʒ] vb: **He overcharged me.** Il m'a fait payer trop cher.; **They overcharged us for the meal.** Ils nous ont fait payer trop cher pour le repas.

overcoat ['əuvəkəut] n pardessus m

overdone [əuvə'dʌn] adj (food) trop cuit

overdose ['əuvədəus] n (of drugs) surdose f ▷ He died of an overdose. Il a succombé à une surdose.

overdue [əuvə'djuː] adj: **This book is overdue.** Je suis en retard pour rendre ce livre.

overestimate [əuvər'estɪmeɪt] vb surestimer

overflow [əuvə'fləu] vb déborder ▷ to overflow with enthusiasm déborder d'enthousiasme ▷ The toilet is overflowing. La toilette déborde. ▷ The river has overflowed its banks. La rivière a débordé de son lit.

overhead projector ['əuvəhed-] n

rétroprojecteur m

overlap ['əuvəlæp] vb se chevaucher ▷ The boards overlap. Les planches se chevauchent. ▷ Your job overlaps with mine. Ton travail et le mien se chevauchent.

overlook [əuvə'luk] vb ❶ (have view of) donner sur ▷ The hotel overlooks the beach. L'hôtel donne sur la plage. ❷ (forget about) négliger ▷ She had overlooked one important problem. Elle avait négligé un problème important.

overreact [əuvəri:'ækt] vb réagir de façon exagérée ▷ I may have overreacted. J'ai peut-être réagi de façon exagérée.; **You're always overreacting.** Tu dramatises toujours tout.

overseas [əuvə'siːz] adv à l'étranger ▷ I'd like to work overseas. J'aimerais travailler à l'étranger.

oversight ['əuvəsaɪt] n oubli m

oversleep [əuvə'sliːp] vb se réveiller en retard ▷ I overslept this morning. Je me suis réveillé en retard ce matin.

overtime ['əuvətaɪm] n ❶ heures fpl supplémentaires ▷ to work overtime faire des heures supplémentaires ❷ (sports) prolongation f ▷ thirty minutes of overtime trente minutes de prolongation ▷ The game went into overtime. Le match est allé en prolongation.

overweight [əuvə'weɪt] adj trop gros (f trop grosse)

overwhelm [əuvə'welm] vb ❶ accabler ▷ overwhelmed with work accablé de travail ▷ overwhelmed with sadness accablé de tristesse ❷ inonder ▷ We've been overwhelmed with offers of help. Nous sommes inondés d'offres d'aide. ❸ bouleverser ▷ The experience overwhelmed me. L'expérience m'a bouleversée.; **overwhelming support** un soutien enthousiaste; **Her kindness has been overwhelming.** Sa gentillesse m'a comblé.

owe [əu] vb devoir; **to owe somebody something** devoir quelque chose à quelqu'un ▷ I owe you $50. Je te dois cinquante dollars.

owl [aul] n hibou m (pl hiboux)

own [əun] adj propre ▷ I have my own cell phone. J'ai mon propre téléphone cellulaire.; **I'd like a room of my own.** J'aimerais avoir une chambre à moi.; **on his own** tout seul ▷ on her own toute seule ▷ on our own tout seuls ▷ vb posséder

own up vb avouer; **to own up to something** admettre quelque chose

owner ['əunə'] n propriétaire

oxygen ['ɔksɪdʒən] n oxygène m

oyster ['ɔɪstə'] n huître f

ozone ['əuzəun] n ozone f; **the ozone layer** la couche d'ozone

p

PA *n*: **the PA system** (*public address*) les *m* haut-parleurs

pace [peɪs] *n* (*speed*) allure *f* ▷ *He was walking at a brisk pace.* Il marchait à vive allure.

pacifier ['pæsɪfaɪər] *n* sucette *f*

pack [pæk] ▣ *vb* faire ses bagages ❷ *I'll help you pack.* Je vais t'aider à faire tes bagages.; **I've already packed my suitcase.** J'ai déjà fait ma valise.
▶ *n* ❶ (*packet*) paquet *m* ▷ *a pack of gum* un paquet de gomme à mâcher ❷ (*backpack*) sac à dos ▷ *Carry it home in your pack.* Rapporte-le chez toi dans ton sac à dos.; **a pack of cards** un jeu de cartes

package ['pækɪdʒ] *n* paquet *m*; **a package holiday** un voyage organisé

packed [pækt] *adj* (*crowded*) plein ▷ *The movie theatre was packed.* Le cinéma était plein.

packet ['pækɪt] *n* paquet *f* ▷ *a packet of sunflower seeds* un paquet de graines de tournesol

pad [pæd] *n* (*notepad*) bloc-notes *m* (*pl* blocs-notes)

paddle ['pædl] *vb* ❶ (*canoe*) pagayer ❷ (*play in water*) faire trempette
▶ *n* ❶ (*canoe*) aviron *m* ❷ (*chiefly kayak*) pagaie *f*

padlock ['pædlɒk] *n* cadenas *m*

page [peɪdʒ] *n* ❶ (*of book*) page *f* ❷ (*in Parliament*) page *f* ▷ *In Grade 6 I was a parliamentary page in Ottawa.* En sixième année, j'ai été page parlementaire à Ottawa.
▶ *vb*: **to page somebody** faire appeler quelqu'un

pager ['peɪdʒər] *n* téléavertisseur *m*

paid [peɪd] *vb see* **pay**
▶ *adj* ❷ (*work*) rémunéré ❷ payé ▷ *3 weeks' paid holiday* trois semaines de congés payés

pail [peɪl] *n* seau *m* (*pl* seaux)

pain [peɪn] *n* douleur *f* ▷ *a terrible pain* une douleur insupportable; **I have a pain in my stomach.** J'ai mal à l'estomac.; **to be in pain** souffrir ▷ *She's in a lot of pain.* Elle souffre beaucoup.; **He's a real pain.** Il est vraiment pénible.

painful ['peɪnful] *adj* douloureux (*f* douloureuse) ▷ *a painful injury* une blessure douloureuse; **a painful experience** une expérience pénible; **Is it painful?** Ça te fait mal?

painkiller ['peɪnkɪlər] *n* analgésique *m*

paint [peɪnt] *n* peinture *f*
▶ *vb* peindre ▷ *to paint something green* peindre

quelque chose en vert

paintbrush ['peɪntbrʌʃ] *n* pinceau *m* (*pl* pinceaux)

painter ['peɪntər] *n* peintre *m*

painting ['peɪntɪŋ] *n* ❶ peinture *f* ▷ *My hobby is painting.* Je fais de la peinture. ❷ (*picture*) tableau *m* (*pl* tableaux) ▷ *a painting by Jean Paul Lemieux* un tableau de Jean Paul Lemieux

pair [peər] *n* paire *f* ▷ *a pair of shoes* une paire de chaussures ▷ *a pair of scissors* une paire de ciseaux; **a pair of pants** un pantalon; **a pair of jeans** une paire de jeans; **a pair of underpants** (1) (*briefs*) une culotte (2) (*boxer shorts*) un caleçon; **in pairs** deux par deux ▷ *We work in pairs.* On travaille deux par deux.

pal [pæl] *n* copain *m*, copine *f*

palace ['pæləs] *n* palais *m*

pale [peɪl] *adj* pâle ▷ *a pale blue shirt* une chemise bleu pâle

palm [pɑːm] *n* (*of hand*) paume *f*; **a palm tree** un palmier

pamphlet ['pæmflət] *n* brochure *f*

pan [pæn] *n* ❶ (*saucepan*) casserole *f* ❷ (*frying pan*) poêle *f* ❸ (*baking*) moule *m* ▷ *a cake pan* un moule à gâteau

pancake ['pænkeɪk] *n* crêpe *f*

panic ['pænɪk] *n* panique *f*
▶ *vb* s'affoler; **Don't panic!** Pas de panique!

panther ['pænθər] *n* panthère *f*

panties ['pæntɪz] *npl* culotte *f*

pantomime ['pæntəmaɪm] *n* pantomime *f*

pants [pænts] *npl* pantalon *m* ▷ *a pair of pants* un pantalon

pantyhose ['pæntɪhəʊz] *npl* bas-culotte *m* (*pl* bas-culottes)

paper ['peɪpər] *n* ❶ papier *m* ▷ *a piece of paper* un morceau de papier ▷ *a paper towel* une serviette en papier ❷ (*newspaper*) journal *m* (*pl* journaux) ▷ *I saw an ad in the paper.* J'ai vu une annonce dans le journal.; **an exam paper** un examen écrit

paperback ['peɪpəbæk] *n* livre de poche *m*

paperboy ['peɪpəbɔɪ] *n* livreur de journaux *m*

paper clip *n* trombone *m*

papergirl ['peɪpəgɜːl] *n* livreuse de journaux *f*

paper route *n* tournée de distribution de journaux *f*

paperwork ['peɪpəwɜːk] *n* paperasse *f* ▷ *She had a lot of paperwork to do.* Elle avait beaucoup de paperasse à faire.

parachute ['pærəʃuːt] *n* parachute *m*

parade [pə'reɪd] *n* défilé *m*

paradise ['pærədaɪs] *n* paradis *m* ▷ *a skiers' paradise* un paradis pour les skieurs

paragraph ['pærəgrɑːf] *n* paragraphe *m*

parallel ['pærəlɛl] *adj* parallèle

paralysed ['pærəlaɪzd] *adj* paralysé

paramedic [pærə'mɛdɪk] *n* ambulancier *m* paramédical, ambulancière *f* paramédicale

parcel ['pɑːsl] *n* colis *m*

pardon ['pɑːdn] *n*: **Pardon?** Pardon?

parent ['peərənt] *n* ❶ (*father*) père *m* ❷ (*mother*) mère *f*; **my parents** mes parents *mpl*

park [pɑːk] *n* parc *m*; **a national park** un parc national; **a theme park** un parc d'attractions

▶ vb ❶ stationner ▷ *Where can I park my car?* Où est-ce que je peux stationner ma voiture? ❷ se garer ▷ *We couldn't find anywhere to park.* Nous avons eu du mal à nous garer.

parking ['pɑːkɪŋ] *n* stationnement *m* ▷ *"no parking"* « stationnement interdit »

parking lot *n* stationnement *m*

parking meter *n* parcomètre *m*

parking ticket *n* contravention de stationnement *f*

parliament ['pɑːləmənt] *n* parlement *m*

parole [pə'rəʊl] *n*: **on parole** en liberté conditionnelle

parrot ['pærət] *n* perroquet *m*

parsley ['pɑːslɪ] *n* persil *m*

part [pɑːt] *n* ❶ (*section*) partie *f* ▷ *The first part of the movie was boring.* La première partie du film était ennuyeuse. ❷ (*component*) pièce *f* ▷ *spare parts* les pièces de rechange ❸ (*in play, film*) rôle *m*; **for the most part** pour la plupart ▷ *They were co-operative for the most part.* Ils se sont montrés coopératifs pour la plupart.; **to do one's part** fournir sa part ▷ *We each have to do our part.* Nous devons chacun fournir notre part.; **to take part in something** participer à quelque chose ▷ *A lot of people took part in the demonstration.* Beaucoup de gens ont participé à la manifestation.

part with *vb*: **to part with something** se défaire de quelque chose

participate [pɑː'tɪsɪpeɪt] *vb* participer ▷ *The whole class participated in the discussion.* Toute la classe a participé à la discussion.

particular [pə'tɪkjʊlər] *adj* particulier (*f* particulière) ▷ *Are you looking for anything particular?* Est-ce que vous voulez quelque chose de particulier?; **nothing in particular** rien de particulier

particularly [pə'tɪkjʊlərlɪ] *adv* particulièrement

parting ['pɑːtɪŋ] *n* (*in hair*) raie *f*

partly ['pɑːtlɪ] *adv* en partie

partner ['pɑːtnər] *n* ❶ (*in game*) partenaire ❷ (*in business*) associé *m*, associée *f* ❸ (*in dance*) cavalier *m*, cavalière *f* ❹ (*boyfriend, girlfriend*) compagnon *m*, compagne *f*

part-time ['pɑːt'taɪm] *adj, adv* à temps partiel ▷ *a part-time job* un travail à temps partiel ▷ *She works part-time.* Elle travaille à temps partiel.

party ['pɑːtɪ] *n* ❶ fête *f* ▷ *a birthday party* une fête d'anniversaire ▷ *a New Year's party* une fête du Nouvel An ❷ party *m* ▷ *a Halloween party* un party d'Halloween ❸ (*more formal*) soirée *f* ▷ *I'm going to a party on Saturday.* Je vais à une soirée samedi. ❹ (*political*) parti *m* ▷ *the Conservative Party* le Parti conservateur ❺ (*group*) groupe *m* ▷ *reservations for a party of four* une réservation pour un groupe de quatre

pass [pɑːs] *n* ❶ (*in mountains*) col *m* ▷ *The pass was blocked with snow.* Le col était enneigé. ❷ (*in football*) passe *f* ❸ laissez-passer *m* ▷ *You can't get in without a pass.* Tu ne peux pas entrer sans laissez-passer.

▶ *vb* ❶ (*exam*) réussir ▷ *to pass an exam* réussir à un examen ▷ *I hope I pass the exam.* J'espère que je réussirai à l'examen. ▷ *Did you pass?* Tu

as réussi? ❷ passer ▷ *Could you pass me the salt, please?* Est-ce que vous pourriez me passer le sel, s'il vous plaît? ▷ *The time has passed quickly.* Le temps a passé rapidement. ❸ passer devant ▷ *I pass his house on my way to school.* Je passe devant chez lui en allant à l'école. ❹ (*legislation*) adopter ▷ *The bill was passed.* On a adopté le projet de loi.; **to pass for** se faire passer pour ▷ *You could easily pass for 16.* Tu pourrais te faire passer pour un jeune de seize ans.; **to pass up an opportunity** laisser passer une occasion

pass out *vb* ❶ (*faint*) s'évanouir ❷ (*hand out*) distribuer ▷ *Pass out the workbooks, please.* Distribue les cahiers, s'il te plaît.

passage ['pæsɪdʒ] *n* ❶ (*piece of writing*) passage *m* ▷ *Read the passage carefully.* Lisez attentivement le passage. ❷ (*corridor*) couloir *m*

passenger ['pæsɪndʒər] *n* passager *m*, passagère *f*

passerby [pɑːsə'baɪ] *n* passant *m*, passante *f* ▷ *We asked a passerby for the time.* Nous avons demandé l'heure à un passant.

passion ['pæʃən] *n* passion *f*

passive ['pæsɪv] *adj* passif (*f* passive); **passive smoking** le tabagisme passif

passport ['pɑːspɔːt] *n* passeport *m* ▷ *passport control* le contrôle des passeports

password ['pɑːswɑːd] *n* mot de passe *m*

past [pɑːst] *adv, prep* (*beyond*) après ▷ *It's on the right, just past the station.* C'est sur la droite, juste après la gare.; **to go past (1)** passer ▷ *The bus went past without stopping.* Le bus est passé sans s'arrêter. **(2)** passer devant ▷ *The bus goes past our house.* Le bus passe devant notre maison.; **It's half past ten.** Il est dix heures et demie.; **It's quarter past nine.** Il est neuf heures et quart.; **It's past eight.** Il est huit heures dix.; **It's past midnight.** Il est minuit passé.

▶ *n* passé *m* ▷ *She lives in the past.* Elle vit dans le passé.; **He had a difficult past.** Il a eu un passé difficile.; **in the past** (*previously*) autrefois ▷ *This was common in the past.* C'était courant autrefois.

pasta ['pæstə] *n* pâtes *fpl* ▷ *Pasta is easy to cook.* Les pâtes sont faciles à préparer.

paste [peɪst] *n* (*glue*) colle *f*

pastel ['pæstl] *n* crayon pastel *m*; **pastel colours** des tons pastels *mpl*

pastime ['pɑːstaɪm] *n* passe-temps *m* (*pl* passe-temps) ▷ *Her favourite pastime is biking.* Son passe-temps favori est le cyclisme.

pastry ['peɪstrɪ] *n* ❶ (*dough*) pâte *f* ▷ *pie pastry* la pâte à tarte ❷ (*baked dessert*) pâtisserie *f* ▷ *a plate of pastries* une assiette de pâtisseries

pat [pæt] *vb*: **She patted my cheek.** Elle m'a tapoté la joue.; **to pat someone on the back (1)** (*literally*) donner une petite tape à quelqu'un dans le dos **(2)** (*compliment*) congratuler quelqu'un

patch [pætʃ] *n* ❶ pièce *f* ▷ *a patch of material* une pièce de tissu ❷ (*for flat tire*) rustine *f* ❸ (*colour*) tache *f* ▷ *a patch of blue* une tache de bleu; **a patch of ice** une plaque de glace; **He's**

got a bald patch. Il a le crâne dégarni.
patched [pætʃt] *adj* rapiécé ▷ *a pair of patched jeans* des jeans rapiécés
pâté ['pæteɪ] *n* pâté *m*
path [pɑ:θ] *n* ❶ *(footpath)* chemin ❷ *(paved)* allée *f*
pathetic [pə'θetɪk] *adj* lamentable ▷ *Our team was pathetic.* Notre équipe a été lamentable.
patience ['peɪʃns] *n* patience *f* ▷ *He doesn't have much patience.* Il n'a pas beaucoup de patience.
patient ['peɪʃnt] *n* patient, patiente *f*
▶ *adj* patient
patio ['pætɪəʊ] *n* patio *m*
patriotic [pætrɪ'ɒtɪk] *adj* patriote
patrol [pə'trəʊl] *n* patrouille *f*; **patrol car** la voiture de police
pattern ['pætən] *n* motif *m* ▷ *a geometric pattern* un motif géométrique; **a sewing pattern** un patron
pause [pɔ:z] *n* pause
pavement ['peɪvmənt] *n* ❶ *(roadway)* chaussée *f* ❷ *(elsewhere)* asphalte *m*
paw [pɔ:] *n* patte *f*
pay [peɪ] *n* salaire *m*
▶ *vb* ❶ payer ▷ *They pay her more on Sundays.* Elle est payée davantage le dimanche. ❷ régler ▷ *to pay by cheque* régler par chèque ▷ *to pay by credit card* régler par carte de crédit; **to pay for something** payer quelque chose ▷ *I paid for my ticket.* J'ai payé mon billet. ▷ *I paid 50 dollars for it.* Je l'ai payé cinquante dollars.; **to pay extra for something** payer un supplément pour quelque chose ▷ *You have to pay extra for parking.* Il faut payer un supplément pour le stationnement.; **to pay attention** faire attention ▷ *Don't pay any attention to him!* Ne fais pas attention à lui!; **to pay somebody a visit** rendre visite à quelqu'un ▷ *They paid us a visit last night.* Ils nous ont rendu visite hier soir.; **to pay somebody back** rembourser quelqu'un ▷ *I'll pay you back tomorrow.* Je te rembourserai demain.
payable ['peɪəbl] *adj:* **Make the cheque payable to "ABC Ltd".** Libellez le chèque à l'ordre de « ABC Ltd ».
payment ['peɪmənt] *n* paiement *m*
pay phone *n* téléphone public *m*
PC *n* (= *personal computer*) PC *m* ▷ *She typed the report on her PC.* Elle a tapé le rapport sur son PC.
PE *n* éducation *f* physique ▷ *We have PE twice a week.* Nous avons l'éducation physique deux fois par semaine.
pea [pi:] *n* petit pois *m*
peace [pi:s] *n* ❶ *(after war)* paix *f* ❷ *(quietness)* calme
peaceful ['pi:sful] *adj* ❶ *(calm)* paisible ▷ *a peaceful afternoon* un après-midi paisible ❷ *(not violent)* pacifique ▷ *a peaceful protest* une manifestation pacifique
peacekeeper ['pi:ski:pər] *n* gardien de la paix *m*, gardienne de la paix *f*
peacekeeping ['pi:ski:pɪŋ] *n* maintien de la paix *m*
peach [pi:tʃ] *n* pêche *f*

peacock ['pi:kɒk] *n* paon *m*
peak [pi:k] *n* *(of mountain)* cime *f*; **the peak rate** le plein tarif ▷ *You pay the peak rate for calls at this time of day.* On paie le plein tarif quand on appelle à cette heure-ci.; **in peak season** en haute saison
▶ *vb:* **The temperature peaked at 34 degrees.** La température a atteint trente-quatre degrés à son plus haut niveau.
peanut ['pi:nʌt] *n* arachide *f* ▷ *a packet of peanuts* un paquet d'arachides
peanut butter *n* beurre d'arachide *m* ▷ *a peanut-butter sandwich* un sandwich au beurre d'arachide
pear [pɛər] *n* poire *f*
pearl [pɜ:l] *n* perle *f*
pebble ['pebl] *n* galet *m* ▷ *a pebble beach* une plage de galets
pecan ['pi:kæn] *n* pacane *f* ▷ *a pecan pie* une tarte aux pacanes
peculiar [pɪ'kju:lɪər] *adj* bizarre ▷ *He's a bit peculiar.* Il est un peu bizarre.
pedal ['pedl] *n* pédale *f*
▶ *vb* pédaler
pedestrian [pɪ'destrɪən] *n* piéton *m*, piétonne *f*
pedestrian crossing [-'krɒsɪn] *n* passage à piétons *m*
peek [pi:k] *n:* **to have a peek at something** jeter un coup d'œil à quelque chose; **No peeking!** On ne regarde pas!
peel [pi:l] *n* ❶ *(orange)* écorce *f* ❷ *(banana)* peau *f* ❸ *(apple, potato)* épluchure *f*
▶ *vb* ❶ éplucher ▷ *Shall I peel the potatoes?* J'épluche les pommes de terre? ❷ peler ▷ *My nose is peeling.* Mon nez pèle.
peer pressure ['pɪər-] *n* pression des pairs *f*
peg [peg] *n* ❶ *(for coats)* portemanteau *m* (*pl* portemanteaux) ❷ *(clothes peg)* pince à linge *f* ❸ *(tent peg)* piquet *m*
pellet ['pelɪt] *n* boulette *f*
pemmican ['pemɪkən] *n* pemmican *m*
pen [pen] *n* stylo *m*
penalize ['pi:nəlaɪz] *vb* pénaliser
penalty ['penltɪ] *n* ❶ *(punishment)* peine *f*; **the death penalty** la peine de mort ❷ *(sports)* punition *f* ▷ *a penalty for body-checking* une punition pour mise en échec corporelle; **a penalty shot** un lancer de pénalité; **penalty box** le banc de punition; **a penalty kick** un coup de pied de pénalité
pencil ['pensl] *n* crayon *m*; **in pencil** au crayon; **pencil crayons** les crayons de couleur
pencil case *n* trousse *f*
pencil sharpener [-'ʃɑ:pnər] *n* taille-crayon *m*
pendant ['pendnt] *n* pendentif *m*
penguin ['pengwɪn] *n* pingouin *m*
penicillin [penɪ'sɪlɪn] *n* pénicilline *f*
peninsula [pə'nɪnsjʊlə] *n* presqu'île *f*
penis ['pi:nɪs] *n* pénis *m*
penknife ['pennaɪf] *n* canif *m*
pennant ['penənt] *n* fanion *m* ▷ *Our school won the soccer pennant last year.* Notre école a gagné le fanion en soccer l'année dernière.
penny ['penɪ] *n* cent *m*
penpal ['penpæl] *n* correspondant *m*,

correspondante f
pension ['pɛnʃən] n retraite f
pensioner ['pɛnʃənər] n retraité m, retraitée f
pentathlon [pɛn'tæθlən] n pentathlon m
people ['pi:pl] npl ❶ gens mpl ▷ *The people were nice.* Les gens étaient sympathiques.
❶ *(individuals)* personnes fpl ▷ *six people* six personnes ▷ *several people* plusieurs personnes
❶ *(nation)* peuple m ▷ *Canada's native peoples* les peuples autochtones du Canada ▷ *to give more power to the people* donner plus de pouvoir au peuple; **How many people are there in your family?** Vous êtes combien dans votre famille? **French people** les Français; **black people** les Noirs; **People say that...** On dit que...
pepper ['pɛpər] n ❶ *(spice)* poivre m ▷ *Pass the pepper, please.* Passez-moi le poivre, s'il vous plaît. ❶ *(vegetable)* poivron m ▷ *a green pepper* un poivron vert ❶ *(chili)* piment m ▷ *hot peppers* les piments piquants
peppermint ['pɛpəmɪnt] n ❶ *(candy)* pastille de menthe f ❶ *(flavour)* menthe f ▷ *I don't like chocolate and mint together.* Je n'aime pas le chocolat et la menthe ensemble.; **peppermint chewing gum** la gomme à mâcher à la menthe
pepperoni [pɛpə'rəʊni] n pepperoni m
per [pə:r] prep par ▷ *per day* par jour ▷ *per week* par semaine; **30 miles per hour** trente miles à l'heure
percent [pə'sɛnt] adv pour cent ▷ *fifty percent* cinquante pour cent
percentage [pə'sɛntɪdʒ] n pourcentage m
percussion [pə'kʌʃən] n percussion f ▷ *I play percussion.* Je joue des percussions.
perfect [pə'fɛkt] adj parfait ▷ *She speaks perfect English.* Elle parle un anglais parfait.
perfectly ['pə:fɪktlɪ] adv parfaitement
perform [pə'fɔ:m] vb *(act, play)* jouer
performance [pə'fɔ:məns] n ❶ *(show)* spectacle m ▷ *The performance lasts two hours.* Le spectacle dure deux heures. ❶ *(acting)* interprétation f ▷ *his performance as Hamlet* son interprétation d'Hamlet ❶ *(results)* performance f ▷ *the team's poor performance* la médiocre performance de l'équipe
performing arts [pə'fɔ:mɪŋ] npl arts mpl de la scène
perfume ['pə:fju:m] n parfum m
perhaps [pə'hæps] adv peut-être ▷ *A bit boring, perhaps* peut-être un peu ennuyeux ▷ *Perhaps he's sick.* Il est peut-être malade.; **perhaps not** peut-être pas
period ['pɪərɪəd] n ❶ période f ▷ *for a limited period* pour une période limitée ❶ *(in history)* époque f ▷ *the Victorian period* l'époque victorienne ❶ *(punctuation)* point m ▷ *You need a period at the end of a sentence.* Il faut un point à la fin de la phrase. ❶ *(menstruation)* règles fpl ▷ *I'm having my period.* J'ai mes règles. ❶ *(lesson time)* cours m ▷ *Each period lasts forty minutes.* Chaque cours dure quarante minutes.
perm [pə:m] n permanente f ▷ *She has a perm.* Elle a une permanente.; **to get a perm** se faire faire une permanente
permafrost ['pə:məfrɔst] n pergélisol m

permanent ['pə:mənənt] adj permanent
permission [pə'mɪʃən] n permission f ▷ *Could I have permission to leave early?* Pourrais-je avoir la permission de partir plus tôt?
permit [pə'mɪt] n permis m ▷ *a fishing permit* un permis de pêche
persecute ['pə:sɪkju:t] vb persécuter
persistent [pə'sɪstənt] adj *(person)* tenace
person ['pə:sn] n personne f ▷ *She's a very nice person.* C'est une personne très sympathique.; **in person** en personne
personal ['pə:snl] adj personnel m (f personnelle); **personals column** les annonces personnelles fpl
personality [pə:sə'nælɪtɪ] n personnalité f
personally ['pə:snlɪ] adv personnellement ▷ *I don't know him personally.* Je ne le connais pas personnellement. ▷ *Personally I don't agree.* Personnellement, je ne suis pas d'accord.
personal stereo n baladeur m
personnel [pə:sə'nɛl] n personnel m
perspiration [pə:spɪ'reɪʃən] n transpiration f
persuade [pə'sweɪd] vb persuader; **to persuade somebody to do something** persuader quelqu'un de faire quelque chose ▷ *She persuaded me to go with her.* Elle m'a persuadé de l'accompagner.
pessimist ['pɛsɪmɪst] n pessimiste ▷ *I'm a pessimist.* Je suis pessimiste.
pessimistic [pɛsɪ'mɪstɪk] adj pessimiste
pest [pɛst] n enquiquineur m, enquiquineuse f
pester ['pɛstər] vb importuner
pesticide ['pɛstɪsaɪd] n pesticide m
pet [pɛt] n animal m de compagnie ▷ *Have you got a pet?* Est-ce que tu as un animal de compagnie?; **a pet shop** une animalerie
petition [pə'tɪʃən] n pétition f
petrified ['pɛtrɪfaɪd] adj pétrifié
petroleum [pə'trəʊlɪəm] n pétrole m
phantom ['fæntəm] n fantôme m
pharmacy ['fɑ:məsɪ] n pharmacie f
philosophy [fɪ'lɔsəfɪ] n philosophie f
phobia ['fəʊbjə] n phobie f
phone [fəʊn] n téléphone m ▷ *Where's the phone?* Où est le téléphone? ▷ *Is there a phone here?* Est-ce qu'il y a un téléphone ici?; **by phone** par téléphone; **to be on the phone** être au téléphone ▷ *She's on the phone at the moment.* Elle est au téléphone en ce moment.; **Can I use the phone, please?** Est-ce que je peux téléphoner, s'il vous plaît?
▶ vb ❶ appeler ▷ *I'll phone the library.* Je vais appeler la bibliothèque. ❶ téléphoner ▷ *Are you going to phone him, or send an e-mail?* Tu vas lui téléphoner, ou envoyer un courriel?
phone bill n compte de téléphone m
phone book n annuaire m
phone booth n cabine téléphonique f
phone call n appel m ▷ *There's a phone call for you.* Il y a un appel pour vous.; **to make a phone call** ▷ *Can I make a phone call?* Est-ce que je peux téléphoner?
phone card n carte téléphonique f
phone number n numéro de téléphone m
photo ['fəʊtəʊ] n photo f; **to take a photo** prendre une photo; **to take a photo of**

somebody prendre quelqu'un en photo
photocopier ['fəʊtəʊkɒpɪə'] n
photocopieuse f
photocopy ['fəʊtəʊkɒpɪ] n photocopie f
▶ vb photocopier
photograph ['fəʊtəgræf] n photo f; **to take
a photograph** prendre une photo; **to take a
photograph of somebody** prendre quelqu'un
en photo
▶ vb photographier
photographer [fə'tɒgrəfə'] n photographe
▷ She's a photographer. Elle est photographe.
photography [fə'tɒgrəfɪ] n photo f ▷ My hobby
is photography. Je fais de la photo.
phrase [freɪz] n expression f
phrase book n guide de conversation m
phys ed ['fɪz'ed] n éducation f physique
▶ n examen m médical
physical ['fɪzɪkl] adj physique f
physicist ['fɪzɪsɪst] n physicien m, physicienne
f ▷ He's a physicist. Il est physicien.
physics ['fɪzɪks] n physique f ▷ She teaches
physics. Elle enseigne la physique.
physiotherapist [fɪzɪəʊ'θerəpɪst] n
physiothérapeute
physiotherapy [fɪzɪəʊ'θerəpɪ] n
physiothérapie f
pianist ['pi:ənɪst] n pianiste
piano [pɪ'ænəʊ] n piano m ▷ I play the piano. Je
joue du piano. ▷ I take piano lessons. Je prends
des leçons de piano.
pick [pɪk] n (guitar) médiator m; **The youngest
gets first pick.** Le plus jeune choisit en
premier.; **Take your pick!** Faites votre choix!
▶ vb ❶ (choose) choisir ▷ I picked the biggest
piece. J'ai choisi le plus gros morceau. ❷ (for
team) sélectionner ▷ I've been picked for the
team. J'ai été sélectionné pour faire partie de
l'équipe. ❸ (fruit, flowers) cueillir; **to pick on
somebody** harceler quelqu'un ▷ He's always
picking on me. Il me harcèle constamment.;
to pick out (1) choisir ▷ I like them all – it's
difficult to pick one out. Ils me plaisent tous
– c'est difficile d'en choisir un. **(2)** (distinguish)
repérer ▷ I can pick out her voice on the recording.
Je peux repérer sa voix sur l'enregistrement.
(3) (recognize) reconnaître ▷ Can you pick me out
in this picture? Peux-tu me reconnaître sur cette
photo?; **to pick up (1)** (collect) venir chercher
▷ We'll come to the airport to pick you up. Nous
irons vous chercher à l'aéroport. **(2)** (from floor)
ramasser ▷ Could you help me pick up the toys? Tu
peux m'aider à ramasser les jouets? **(3)** (learn)
apprendre ▷ I picked up some Spanish during my
holiday. J'ai appris quelque mots d'espagnol
pendant mes vacances.
picket ['pɪkɪt] vb piqueter ▷ The workers
picketed the factory. Les ouvriers ont piqueté
l'usine.; **a picket line** une ligne de piquetage
pickle ['pɪkl] n cornichon m ▷ dill pickles les
cornichons à l'aneth
pickpocket ['pɪkpɒkɪt] n voleur à la tire m,
voleuse à la tire f
pickup truck ['pɪkʌp-] n camionnette f
picky ['pɪkɪ] adj pointilleux (f pointilleuse)
▷ Our teacher is picky about grammar. Notre prof

est pointilleux sur la grammaire.
picnic ['pɪknɪk] n pique-nique m; **to have a
picnic** pique-niquer ▷ We had a picnic on the
beach. Nous avons pique-niqué sur la plage.
picture ['pɪktʃə'] n ❶ illustration f ▷ Children's
books have lots of pictures. Il y a beaucoup
d'illustrations dans les livres pour enfants.
❷ photo f ▷ My picture was in the paper. Ma
photo était dans le journal. ❸ (painting)
tableau m (pl tableaux) ▷ a famous picture
un tableau célèbre; **to paint a picture
of something** peindre quelque chose
❹ (drawing) dessin m; **to draw a picture of
something** dessiner quelque chose
picturesque [pɪktʃə'resk] adj pittoresque
pie [paɪ] n tarte f ▷ an apple pie une tarte aux
pommes; **a pie chart** un graphique circulaire
piece [pi:s] n morceau m (pl morceaux) ▷ A
small piece, please. Un petit morceau, s'il vous
plaît.; **a piece of furniture** un meuble; **a piece
of advice** un conseil
pier [pɪə'] n jetée f
pierce [pɪəs] vb percer ▷ She's going to get her
ears pierced. Elle va se faire percer les oreilles. ▷ I
have pierced ears. J'ai les oreilles percées.
piercing ['pɪəsɪŋ] adj perçant ▷ a piercing cry
un cri perçant
pig [pɪg] n cochon m
pigeon ['pɪdʒən] n pigeon m.
piggyback ['pɪgɪbæk] n: **to give somebody a
piggyback** ▷ I can't give you a piggyback, you're
too heavy. Je ne peux pas te porter sur mon dos,
tu es trop lourd.
pigtail ['pɪgteɪl] n couette f
pike [paɪk] n brochet m ▷ a northern pike un
grand brochet
pile [paɪl] n ❶ (untidy heap) tas m ❷ (tidy
stack) pile f
▶ vb ❶ (stack) empiler ▷ I piled the books on
the table. J'ai empilé les livres sur la table.
❷ (heap) entasser ▷ She piles her dirty clothes
on the floor. Elle entasse ses vêtements sales
sur le plancher.; **to pile up** s'accumuler
▷ My homework is piling up. Mes devoirs
s'accumulent.
pile-up ['paɪlʌp] n carambolage m
pill [pɪl] n pilule f; **to be on the Pill** prendre
la pilule
pillar ['pɪlə'] n pilier m
pillow ['pɪləʊ] n oreiller m
pilot ['paɪlət] n pilote ▷ She's a pilot. Elle est
pilote.
pimple ['pɪmpl] n bouton m
pin [pɪn] n épingle f; **I have pins and needles
in my foot.** J'ai des fourmis dans le pied.; **to
be on pins and needles** être sur des charbons
ardents
PIN [pɪn] n (= personal identification number)
NIP m
pinball ['pɪnbɔ:l] n machine à boules f ▷ to play
pinball jouer à la machine à boules
pinch [pɪntʃ] vb pincer ▷ He pinched me! Il m'a
pincé!
pine [paɪn] n pin m ▷ a pine table une table en
pin; **a pine cone** un cône de pin
pineapple ['paɪnæpl] n ananas m

pink [pɪŋk] adj rose
pioneer [paɪə'nɪəʳ] n pionnier m, pionnière f
pipe [paɪp] n ⓵ (for water, gas) tuyau m (pl tuyaux) ▷ The pipes froze. Les tuyaux d'eau ont gelé. ⓶ (for smoking) pipe f; **the pipes** (bagpipes) la cornemuse ▷ He plays the pipes. Il joue de la cornemuse.
pirate ['paɪərət] n pirate
pirated ['paɪərətɪd] adj pirate ▷ a pirated video une vidéo pirate
Pisces ['paɪsi:z] n Poissons mpl ▷ I'm a Pisces. Je suis Poissons.
pistol ['pɪstl] n pistolet m
pit [pɪt] n ⓵ (deep hole) fosse f ⓶ (in fruit) noyau m ▷ a peach pit un noyau de pêche
pitch [pɪtʃ] n ⓵ (baseball) lancer m ▷ That was a fast pitch. C'était un lancer rapide. ⓶ (musical note) hauteur f; **Excitement was at fever pitch.** L'excitation était à son comble.
▶ vb ⓵ (tent) planter ▷ We pitched our tent near the beach. Nous avons planté notre tente près de la plage. ⓶ (baseball) lancer m ▷ Who's pitching? Qui est-ce qui lance?
pitcher ['pɪtʃəʳ] n ⓵ (baseball) lanceur m, lanceuse f ⓶ (jug) cruche f ▷ a pitcher of lemonade une cruche de limonade
pity ['pɪtɪ] n pitié f; **What a pity!** Quel dommage!
▶ vb plaindre
pizza ['pi:tsə] n pizza f
place [pleɪs] n ⓵ (location) endroit m ▷ It's a quiet place. C'est un endroit tranquille. ▷ There are a lot of interesting places to visit. Il y a beaucoup d'endroits intéressants à visiter. ⓶ (space) place f ▷ a parking place une place de stationnement ▷ She was not in her usual place. Elle n'était pas à sa place habituelle. ▷ There were six places at the table. Il y avait six places à table.; **to take someone's place** prendre la place de quelqu'un; **to change places** changer de place ▷ I'll change places with you. Je changerai de place avec toi.; **to take place** avoir lieu; **at your place** chez toi ▷ Shall we meet at your place? On se retrouve chez toi?; **to my place** chez moi ▷ Do you want to come to my place? Tu veux venir chez moi?; **I feel out of place here.** Je ne me sens pas à ma place ici.
▶ vb ⓵ poser ▷ He placed his hand on the keyboard. Il a posé la main sur le clavier. ⓶ (in competition, exam) place
placemat ['pleɪsmæt] n napperon m
plagiarism ['pleɪdʒərɪzəm] n plagiat m
plaid [plæd] adj écossais ▷ a plaid shirt une chemise écossaise
plain [pleɪn] n plaine f
▶ adj, adv ⓵ (not patterned) uni ▷ a plain carpet un tapis uni ⓶ (not fancy) simple ▷ a plain white blouse un chemisier blanc simple
plan [plæn] n ⓵ projet m ▷ What are your plans for the holidays? Quels sont tes projets pour les vacances? ▷ to make plans faire des projets; **Everything went according to plan.** Tout s'est passé comme prévu. ⓶ (map) plan m ▷ a floor plan of the new house un plan à niveau de la nouvelle maison
▶ vb ⓵ (make plans for) préparer ▷ We're

planning a trip to Alberta. Nous préparons un voyage en Alberta. ⓶ (make schedule for) planifier ▷ Plan your day carefully. Planifiez votre journée avec soin.; **to plan to do something** avoir l'intention de faire quelque chose ▷ I'm planning to go to university. J'ai l'intention d'aller à l'université.
plane [pleɪn] n avion m ▷ by plane en avion
planet ['plænɪt] n planète f
planning ['plænɪŋ] n préparation f ▷ The trip needs careful planning. Le voyage nécessite une préparation méticuleuse.; **family planning** la planification familiale
plant [plɑːnt] n ⓵ plante f ▷ to water the plants arroser les plantes ⓶ (factory) usine f
▶ vb planter
plaque [plæk] n ⓵ (on wall) plaque f ⓶ (on teeth) plaque dentaire f
plaster ['plɑːstəʳ] n plâtre m; **a plaster cast** un plâtre
plastic ['plæstɪk] n plastique m ▷ It's made of plastic. C'est en plastique.
▶ adj en plastique ▷ a plastic bag un sac en plastique ▷ a plastic raincoat un imperméable en plastique; **plastic surgery** la chirurgie esthétique; **plastic wrap** la pellicule de plastique
plate [pleɪt] n (for food) assiette f
platform ['plætfɔːm] n ⓵ (for performers) estrade f ⓶ (at station) quai m ▷ on platform 7 sur le quai numéro sept
play [pleɪ] n pièce f ▷ a play by Rick Salutin une pièce de Rick Salutin; **to put on a play** monter une pièce
▶ vb ⓵ jouer ▷ He's playing with his friends. Il joue avec ses amis. ▷ What sort of music do they play? Quel genre de musique jouent-ils? ⓶ (against person, team) jouer contre ▷ Montreal will play Edmonton tomorrow night. Montréal jouera contre Edmonton demain soir. ⓷ (sport, game) jouer à ▷ I play hockey. Je joue au hockey. ▷ Can you play chess? Tu sais jouer aux échecs? ⓸ (instrument) jouer de ▷ I play the guitar. Je joue de la guitare. ⓹ (record, cassette, music) écouter ▷ She's always playing that CD. Elle écoute tout le temps ce CD.
play down vb dédramatiser ▷ He tried to play down his illness. Il a essayé de dédramatiser sa maladie.
player ['pleɪəʳ] n (of sport) joueur m, joueuse f ▷ a hockey player un joueur de hockey; **a piano player** un pianiste; **a bass player** un bassiste
playful ['pleɪful] adj espiègle
playground ['pleɪɡraund] n ⓵ (at school) cour de récréation f ⓶ (in park) aire f de jeux
playing card ['pleɪɪŋ-] n carte à jouer f (pl cartes à jouer)
playing field ['pleɪɪŋ-] n terrain de sport m
playoffs ['pleɪɔfs] npl éliminatoires fpl
playtime ['pleɪtaɪm] n récréation f
playwright ['pleɪraɪt] n dramaturge
plead [pli:d] vb: **to plead guilty** plaider coupable; **I pleaded with them to stop.** Je les ai suppliés d'arrêter.
pleasant ['plɛznt] adj agréable
please [pli:z] excl ⓵ (polite form) s'il vous plaît

▷ *Two coffees, please.* Deux cafés, s'il vous plaît. ❸ *(familiar form)* s'il te plaît ▷ *Please write back soon.* Réponds vite, s'il te plaît.

pleased ['pli:zd] *adj* content ▷ *My mother's not going to be very pleased.* Ma mère ne va pas être contente du tout. ▷ *It's beautiful: she'll be pleased with it.* C'est beau : elle va être contente.; **Pleased to meet you!** Enchanté!

pleasure ['plɛʒəʳ] *n* plaisir *m* ▷ *I read for pleasure.* Je lis pour le plaisir.

plenty ['plɛntɪ] *n* largement assez ▷ *I've got plenty.* J'en ai largement assez. ▷ *That's plenty, thanks.* Ça suffit largement, merci.; **plenty of (1)** *(a lot)* beaucoup de ▷ *I have plenty to do.* J'ai beaucoup de choses à faire. **(2)** *(enough)* largement assez de ▷ *I have plenty of money.* J'ai largement assez d'argent. ▷ *We've got plenty of time.* Nous avons largement le temps.

pliers ['plaɪəz] *npl* pince *f*; **a pair of pliers** une pince

plot [plɒt] *n* ❶ *(of story, play)* intrigue *f* ❷ *(against somebody)* conspiration *f* ▷ *a plot against the president* une conspiration contre le président ❸ *(of land)* carré *m* ▷ *a vegetable plot* un carré de légumes
▶ *vb* comploter ▷ *They were plotting to kill him.* Ils complotaient de le tuer.

plough [plaʊ] *n* charrue *f*
▶ *vb* labourer

plow [plaʊ] *n* *(snow)* déneigeuse *f*
▶ *vb* ▷ *Have they plowed the roads yet?* Est-ce qu'on a déjà déneigé les rues?

plug [plʌɡ] *n* ❶ *(electrical)* prise de courant *f* ▷ *The plug is faulty.* La prise est défectueuse. ❷ *(for sink)* bouchon *m*

plug in *vb* brancher ▷ *Is it plugged in?* Est-ce que c'est branché?

plum [plʌm] *n* prune *f* ▷ *plum jam* la confiture de prunes

plumber ['plʌməʳ] *n* plombier *m*, plombière *f* ▷ *He's a plumber.* Il est plombier.

plumbing ['plʌmɪŋ] *n* plomberie *f* ▷ *Our cottage doesn't have indoor plumbing.* Notre chalet n'a pas de plomberie intérieure.

plump [plʌmp] *adj* dodu

plunge [plʌndʒ] *vb* plonger

plural ['plʊərl] *n* pluriel *m* ▷ *in the plural* au pluriel

plus [plʌs] *prep, adj* plus ▷ *4 plus 3 equals 7.* Quatre plus trois égalent sept. ▷ *three children plus a dog* trois enfants plus un chien; **I got a B plus.** J'ai eu B plus.

p.m. *abbr*: **at 8 p.m.** à huit heures du soir; **at 2 p.m.** à quatorze heures

pneumonia [njuː'məʊnɪə] *n* pneumonie *f*

poached [pəʊtʃt] *adj* poché ▷ *a poached egg* un œuf poché

pocket ['pɒkɪt] *n* poche *f*; **pocket money** l'argent *m* de poche ▷ *$10 a week pocket money* dix dollars d'argent de poche par semaine

pocketknife ['pɒkɪtnaɪf] *n* canif *m*

poem ['pəʊɪm] *n* poème *m*

poet ['pəʊɪt] *n* poète *m*

poetry ['pəʊɪtrɪ] *n* poésie *f*

point [pɔɪnt] *n* ❶ *(spot, score)* point *m* ▷ *a point on the horizon* un point à l'horizon ▷ *They*

scored 5 points. Ils ont marqué cinq points. ❷ *(comment)* remarque *f* ▷ *He made some interesting points.* Il a fait quelque remarques intéressantes. ❸ *(tip)* pointe *f* ▷ *a pencil with a sharp point* un crayon à la pointe aiguisée ❹ *(in time)* moment *m* ▷ *At that point, we decided to leave.* À ce moment-là, nous avons décidé de partir.; **a point of view** un point de vue; **to get the point** comprendre ▷ *Sorry, I don't get the point.* Désolé, je ne comprends pas.; **That's beside the point.** Cela n'a rien à voir.; **to the point** précis ▷ *His answer was short and to the point.* Sa réponse était brève et précise.; **That's a good point!** C'est vrai; **There's no point.** Cela ne sert à rien. ▷ *There's no point in waiting.* Cela ne sert à rien d'attendre.; **What's the point?** À quoi bon? ▷ *What's the point of leaving so early?* À quoi bon partir si tôt?; **Punctuality isn't my strong point.** La ponctualité n'est pas mon fort.; **two point five (2.5)** deux virgule cinq (2,5)
▶ *vb* montrer du doigt ▷ *Don't point!* Ne montre pas du doigt!; **to point at somebody** montrer quelqu'un du doigt ▷ *She pointed at her friend.* Elle a montré son ami du doigt.; **to point a gun at somebody** braquer un revolver sur quelqu'un; **to point something out (1)** *(show)* montrer quelque chose ▷ *The guide pointed out Sainte-Anne-de-Beaupré to us.* Le guide nous a montré Sainte-Anne-de-Beaupré. **(2)** *(mention)* signaler quelque chose ▷ *I should point out that…* Je dois vous signaler que…

pointless ['pɔɪntlɪs] *adj* inutile ▷ *It's pointless to argue.* Il est inutile de discuter.

poison ['pɔɪzn] *n* poison *m*
▶ *vb* empoisonner

poison ivy [-'aɪvɪ] *n* herbe *f* à puce

poisonous ['pɔɪznəs] *adj* ❶ *(snake)* venimeux (venimeuse *f*) ❷ *(plant, mushroom)* vénéneux (*f* vénéneuse) ❸ *(gas)* toxique

poke [pəʊk] *vb*: **He poked the ground with his stick.** Il tapotait le sol avec sa canne.; **She poked me in the ribs.** Elle m'a enfoncé le doigt dans les côtes.

poker ['pəʊkəʳ] *n* poker *m* ▷ *I play poker.* Je joue au poker.

polar bear ['pəʊləʳ-] *n* ours *m* blanc

pole [pəʊl] *n* poteau *m* (*pl* poteaux) ▷ *a telephone pole* un poteau de téléphone; **a tent pole** un montant de tente; **a ski pole** un bâton de ski; **the North Pole** le pôle Nord; **the South Pole** le pôle Sud

pole vault ['pəʊlvɔːlt] *n* saut à la perche *m*

police [pə'liːs] *npl* police *f* ▷ *We called the police.* Nous avons appelé la police.; **a police car** une voiture de police; **a police dog** un chien policier; **a police station** un commissariat de police

police officer *n* policier *m*, policière *f* ▷ *She's a police officer.* Elle est policière.

policy ['pɒlɪsɪ] *n* politique *f* ▷ *the new immigration policy* la nouvelle politique d'immigration

polish ['pɒlɪʃ] *n* ❶ *(for shoes)* cirage *m* ❷ *(for furniture)* cire *f*
▶ *vb* ❶ *(shoes, furniture)* cirer ❷ *(glass)* faire

briller

polite [pəˈlaɪt] *adj* poli

politely [pəˈlaɪtlɪ] *adv* poliment

politeness [pəˈlaɪtnɪs] *n* politesse *f*

political [pəˈlɪtɪkl] *adj* politique *f*; **political correctness** la rectitude politique

politically [pəˈlɪtɪklɪ] *adv*: **politically correct** politiquement correct

politician [ˌpɒlɪˈtɪʃən] *n* politicien *m*, politicienne *f*

politics [ˈpɒlɪtɪks] *npl* politique *f* ▷ *I'm not interested in politics*. La politique ne m'intéresse pas.

polka dots [ˈpɒlkə-] *npl* pois *mpl* ▷ *a skirt with polka dots* une jupe à pois

poll [pəʊl] ❶ *n* sondage *m* ▷ *A recent poll revealed that…* Un sondage récent a révélé que… ❷ (*place to vote*) bureau de vote *m* ▷ *The polls close at 9 p.m.* Les bureaux de vote ferment à neuf heures du soir.; **to go to the polls** aller voter
▶ *vb*: **We polled all the students to find out which radio station was most popular.** Nous avons sondé l'opinion de tous les élèves pour savoir quelle station de radio est la plus populaire.

pollen [ˈpɒlən] *n* pollen *m*

pollute [pəˈluːt] *vb* polluer ▷ *We have polluted the rivers.* Nous avons pollué les rivières.

pollution [pəˈluːʃən] *n* pollution *f*

polo shirt [ˈpəʊləʊ-] *n* polo *m*

pond [pɒnd] ❶ *n* ❶ (*big*) étang *m* ❷ (*smaller*) mare *f* ❸ bassin *m* ▷ *We've got a pond in our garden.* Nous avons un bassin dans notre jardin.

pony [ˈpəʊnɪ] *n* poney *m*

ponytail [ˈpəʊnɪteɪl] *n* queue de cheval *f* ▷ *He's got a ponytail.* Il a une queue de cheval.

poodle [ˈpuːdl] *n* caniche *m*

pool [puːl] *n* ❶ (*for swimming*) piscine *f* ❷ (*pond*) étang *m* ❸ (*puddle*) flaque *f* ❹ (*game*) billard américain *m* ▷ *Let's have a game of pool.* Jouons au billard américain.

poor [pʊə] *adj* ❶ pauvre ▷ *a poor family* une famille pauvre ▷ *Your poor sister, she's very unlucky!* Ta pauvre sœur, elle n'a vraiment pas de chance!; **the poor** les *m* pauvres ❷ (*bad*) médiocre ▷ *a poor mark* une note médiocre

poorly [ˈpʊəlɪ] *adv* mal ▷ *poorly designed* mal conçu

pop [pɒp] *adj* pop ▷ *pop music* la musique pop ▷ *a pop star* une vedette pop ▷ *a pop group* un groupe pop ▷ *a pop song* une chanson pop
▶ *n* boisson gazeuse *f* ▷ *Do you want a can of pop?* Tu veux une canette de boisson gazeuse?

popcorn [ˈpɒpkɔːn] *n* ❶ (*popped*) maïs soufflé *m* ❷ (*unpopped*) maïs à éclater *m*

pope [pəʊp] *n* pape *m*

poppy [ˈpɒpɪ] *n* coquelicot *m*

Popsicle® [ˈpɒpsɪkl] *n* sucette glacée *f*

popular [ˈpɒpjʊlə] *adj* populaire ▷ *She's a very popular girl.* C'est une fille très populaire. ▷ *This is a very popular style.* C'est un style très populaire.

population [ˌpɒpjuˈleɪʃən] *n* population *f*

pop-up [ˈpɒpʌp] *adj* contextuel (*f*

contextuelle) ▷ *a pop-up menu* un menu contextuel

porch [pɔːtʃ] *n* porche *m*

porcupine [ˈpɔːkjʊpaɪn] *n* porc-épic *m* (*pl* porcs-épics) ▷ *a porcupine quill* un piquant de porc-épic

pork [pɔːk] *n* porc *m* ▷ *a pork chop* une côtelette de porc ▷ *I don't eat pork.* Je ne mange pas de porc.

pornographic [ˌpɔːnəˈɡræfɪk] *adj* pornographique ▷ *a pornographic magazine* un magazine pornographique

pornography [pɔːˈnɒɡrəfɪ] *n* pornographie *f*

porridge [ˈpɒrɪdʒ] *n* gruau *m*

port [pɔːt] *n* (*harbour*) port *m*

portable [ˈpɔːtəbl] *adj* portable ▷ *a portable TV* un téléviseur portable

portion [ˈpɔːʃən] *n* portion *f* ▷ *a large portion of fries* une grosse portion de frites

portrait [ˈpɔːtreɪt] *n* portrait *m*

posh [pɒʃ] *adj* chic (*f+pl* chic) ▷ *a posh hotel* un hôtel chic

position [pəˈzɪʃən] *n* position *f* ▷ *an uncomfortable position* une position inconfortable

positive [ˈpɒzɪtɪv] *adj* ❶ (*good*) positif (*f* positive) ▷ *a positive attitude* une attitude positive ❷ (*sure*) certain ▷ *I'm positive.* J'en suis certain.

possess [pəˈzɛs] *vb* posséder

possession [pəˈzɛʃən] *n*: **Have you got all your possessions?** Est-ce tu as toutes tes affaires?

possibility [ˌpɒsɪˈbɪlɪtɪ] *n*: **It's a possibility.** C'est possible.

possible [ˈpɒsɪbl] *adj* possible ▷ *as soon as possible* aussitôt que possible

possibly [ˈpɒsɪblɪ] *adv* (*perhaps*) peut-être ▷ *"Are you coming to the party?" —"Possibly."* « Est-ce que tu viens à la soirée? » — « Peut-être. »; **…if you possibly can.** …si cela vous est possible.; **I can't possibly come.** Je ne peux vraiment pas venir.

post [pəʊst] *n* ❶ (*on lists*) article *m* de forum ▷ *Did you read that last post?* Tu as lu ce dernier article de forum? ❷ (*pole*) poteau *m* (*pl* poteaux) ▷ *The ball hit the post.* Le ballon a heurté le poteau.
▶ *vb* poster ▷ *I just posted a reply on the listserv.* Je viens de poster une réponse sur la liste de diffusion.

postage [ˈpəʊstɪdʒ] *n* affranchissement *m*

postal code [ˈpəʊstəl-] *n* code postal *m*

postcard [ˈpəʊstkɑːd] *n* carte postale *f*

poster [ˈpəʊstəʳ] *n* affiche *f* ▷ *I have posters on my bedroom walls.* J'ai des affiches sur les murs de ma chambre. ▷ *There are posters all over town.* Il y a des affiches dans toute la ville.

postmark [ˈpəʊstmɑːk] *n* cachet de la poste *m*

post office *n* bureau de poste *m* ▷ *Where's the post office, please?* Où est le bureau de poste, s'il vous plaît? ▷ *She works for the post office.* Elle travaille au bureau de poste.

postpone [pəsˈpəʊn] *vb* remettre à plus tard ▷ *The match has been postponed.* Le match a été

remis à plus tard.
postscript ['pəʊstskrɪpt] n post-scriptum m
posture ['pɒstʃə^r] n posture f ▷ *Good posture is important when working at the computer.* La bonne posture est très importante quand on travaille à l'ordinateur.; **to have poor posture** se tenir mal
pot [pɒt] n ❶ (*for cooking*) casserole f ▷ *a pot of soup* une casserole de soupe ❷ (*teapot*) théière f ❸ (*coffeepot*) cafetière f; **the pots and pans** les casseroles
potato [pə'teɪtəʊ] n pomme de terre f ▷ *potato salad* la salade de pommes de terre; **mashed potatoes** la purée de pommes de terre; **boiled potatoes** les pommes de terre bouillies; **a baked potato** une pomme de terre en robe des champs
potential [pə'tenʃl] n: **He has great potential.** Il a de l'avenir.
▶ adj possible ▷ *a potential problem* un problème possible
pothole ['pɒthəʊl] n (*in road*) nid de poule m
potlatch ['pɒtlætʃ] n potlatch m
potted plant ['pɒtɪd-] n plante en pot f
pottery ['pɒtərɪ] n poterie f
pound [paʊnd] n
▶ vb battre ▷ *My heart was pounding.* J'avais le cœur qui battait.
pour [pɔː^r] vb ❶ (*liquid*) verser ▷ *She poured some water into the pan.* Elle a versé de l'eau dans la casserole.; **He poured her a drink.** Il lui a servi à boire.; **Shall I pour you a cup of tea?** Je vous sers une tasse de thé? ❷ (*rain*) pleuvoir à verse ▷ *It's pouring.* Il pleut à verse.; **in the pouring rain** sous une pluie torrentielle
pout [paʊt] vb faire la moue ▷ *Don't pout.* Ne fais pas la moue.
poverty ['pɒvətɪ] n pauvreté f
powder ['paʊdə^r] n poudre f
power ['paʊə^r] n ❶ (*electricity*) courant m ▷ *The power's off.* Le courant est coupé.; **a power cut** une coupure de courant; **a power plant** une centrale électrique ❷ (*energy*) énergie f ▷ *nuclear power* l'énergie nucléaire ▷ *solar power* l'énergie solaire ❸ (*authority*) pouvoir m ▷ **to be in power** être au pouvoir ❹ (*nation*) puissance f ▷ *the nuclear powers* les puissances nucléaires ▷ *a world power* une puissance mondiale
powerful ['paʊəful] adj puissant
power play n attaque f à cinq
practical ['præktɪkl] adj pratique ▷ *a practical suggestion* un conseil pratique; **She's very practical.** Elle a l'esprit pratique.; **a practical joke** une farce; **a practical joker** un farceur ▷ *She's a real practical joker!* Elle est une vraie farceuse!
practically ['præktɪklɪ] adv pratiquement ▷ *It's practically impossible.* C'est pratiquement impossible.
practice ['præktɪs] n (*for sport*) entraînement m ▷ *soccer practice* l'entraînement de soccer; **It's common practice in our school.** C'est ce qui se fait dans notre école.; **in practice** en pratique; **a medical practice** un cabinet médical; **out of practice** rouillé

practise ['præktɪs] vb ❶ pratiquer ▷ *I practised my French when we were in Quebec.* J'ai pratiqué mon français quand nous étions au Québec. ▷ *I have to practise the piano.* Je dois pratiquer le piano. ❷ s'exercer ▷ *She loves basketball and practises dribbling every day.* Elle adore le basket-ball et s'exerce à dribbler tous les jours. ▷ *I should practise more.* Je devrais m'exercer davantage. ❸ s'entraîner ▷ *The team practises on Thursdays.* L'équipe s'entraîne le jeudi.
prairie ['preərɪ] n prairie f ▷ *the Prairie provinces* les provinces des Prairies; **a prairie dog** un chien-de-prairie
praise [preɪz] vb faire l'éloge de ▷ *Everyone praises his cooking.* Tout le monde fait l'éloge de sa cuisine. ▷ *The teachers praised our work.* Les professeurs ont fait l'éloge de notre travail.
prank [præŋk] n farce f ▷ *to play a prank on somebody* faire une farce à quelqu'un
prawn [prɔːn] n crevette f
pray [preɪ] vb prier ▷ *to pray for something* prier pour quelque chose ▷ *to pray to God* prier Dieu
prayer [preə^r] n prière f
precaution [prɪ'kɔːʃən] n précaution f; **to take precautions** prendre ses précautions
preceding [prɪ'siːdɪŋ] adj précédent
precious ['preʃəs] adj précieux (f précieuse)
precise [prɪ'saɪs] adj précis ▷ *at that precise moment* à cet instant précis
precisely [prɪ'saɪslɪ] adv précisément ▷ *Precisely!* Précisément!; **at 10 a.m. precisely** à dix heures précises
predict [prɪ'dɪkt] vb prédire
predictable [prɪ'dɪktəbl] adj prévisible ▷ *The movie had a very predictable plot.* Le film avait une intrigue très prévisible.; **She's so predictable.** Ses réactions sont tellement prévisibles.
prefer [prɪ'fɜː^r] vb préférer ▷ *Which would you prefer?* Lequel préfères-tu? ▷ *I prefer French to phys ed.* Je préfère le français à l'éducation physique.
preferably ['prefrəblɪ] adv de préférence ▷ *Save me a seat, preferably near the door.* Garde-moi une place, de préférence près de la porte.
preference ['prefrəns] n préférence f
pregnancy ['pregnənsɪ] n grossesse f
pregnant ['pregnənt] adj enceinte ▷ *She's six months pregnant.* Elle est enceinte de six mois.
prehistoric ['priːhɪs'tɒrɪk] adj préhistorique
prejudice ['predʒʊdɪs] n ❶ préjugé m ▷ *That's just a prejudice.* C'est un préjugé. ❷ préjugés mpl ▷ *There's a lot of racial prejudice.* Il y a beaucoup de préjugés raciaux.
prejudiced ['predʒʊdɪst] adj: **to be prejudiced against somebody** avoir des préjugés contre quelqu'un
premature ['premətʃʊə^r] adj prématuré; **a premature baby** un prématuré
premier ['premɪə^r] n premier ministre m, première ministre f ▷ *the premier of Manitoba* le premier ministre de Manitoba
premises ['premɪsɪz] npl lieux mpl ▷ *to vacate the premises* vider les lieux ▷ *Smoking is not allowed on the premises.* Il est interdit de fumer sur les lieux.

preoccupied [pri:'ɔkjupaɪd] *adj* préoccupé

preparation [prepə'reɪʃən] *n* préparation f

prepare [prɪ'pɛəʳ] *vb* préparer ▷ *to prepare a meal* préparer un repas ▷ *He has to prepare his valedictory address.* Il doit préparer son discours d'adieu.; **to prepare for something** se préparer pour quelque chose ▷ *We're preparing for our skiing holiday.* Nous nous préparons pour nos vacances de ski.

prepared [prɪ'pɛəd] *adj*: **to be prepared to do something** être prêt à faire quelque chose ▷ *I'm prepared to help you.* Je suis prêt à t'aider.

preschool [pri:'sku:l] *n* école f maternelle ▷ *My little brother goes to preschool.* Mon petit frère va à l'école maternelle.; **a preschool child** un enfant d'âge préscolaire

prescribe [prɪ'skraɪb] *vb* prescrire

prescription [prɪ'skrɪpʃən] *n* ordonnance f ▷ *You can't get it without a prescription.* On ne peut pas se le procurer sans ordonnance.; **a prescription drug** un médicament d'ordonnance

presence ['prɛzns] *n* présence f; **presence of mind** présence d'esprit

present [*adj, n* 'prɛznt, *vb* prɪ'zɛnt] *adj* ❶ (*in attendance*) présent ▷ *He wasn't present at the meeting.* Il n'était pas présent à la réunion. ❷ (*current*) actuel (f actuelle) ▷ *the present situation* la situation actuelle; **the present tense** le présent
▶ *n* ❶ (*gift*) cadeau *m* (pl cadeaux) ▷ *I'm going to buy presents.* Je vais acheter des cadeaux.; **to give somebody a present** offrir un cadeau à quelqu'un ❷ (*time*) présent *m* ▷ *up to the present* jusqu'à présent; **for the present** pour l'instant; **at present** en ce moment
▶ *vb* ❶ (*play, concert*) donner ❷ (*information*) présenter; **to present somebody with something** (1) (*prize, medal*) remettre quelque chose à quelqu'un (2) (*gift*) offrir quelque chose à quelqu'un; **She presented herself very well.** Elle s'est très bien présentée.

presently ['prɛzntlɪ] *adv* (*at present*) actuellement ▷ *They're presently on tour.* Ils sont actuellement en tournée.

president ['prɛzɪdənt] *n* président *m*, présidente f

press [prɛs] *n* presse; **a press conference** une conférence de presse
▶ *vb* ❶ appuyer ▷ *Don't press too hard!* N'appuie pas trop fort! ❷ appuyer sur ▷ *He pressed the button.* Il a appuyé sur le bouton.

pressed [prɛst] *adj*: **We are pressed for time.** Le temps nous manque.

pressure ['prɛʃəʳ] *n* pression ▷ *She's under a lot of pressure at work.* Elle est sous pression au travail.; **a pressure group** un groupe de pression
▶ *vb* faire pression sur ▷ *My parents are pressuring me.* Mes parents font pression sur moi.

pressurize ['prɛʃəraɪz] *vb* pressuriser ▷ *a pressurized spacesuit* une combinaison spatiale pressurisée

prestige [prɛs'ti:ʒ] *n* prestige *m*

prestigious [prɛs'tɪdʒəs] *adj* prestigieux (f prestigieuse)

presumably [prɪ'zju:məblɪ] *adv* vraisemblablement

presume [prɪ'zju:m] *vb* supposer ▷ *I presume so.* Je suppose que oui.

pretend [prɪ'tɛnd] *vb*: **to pretend to do something** faire semblant de faire quelque chose ▷ *He pretended to be asleep.* Il faisait semblant de dormir.

pretty ['prɪtɪ] *adj, adv* ❶ joli ▷ *She's very pretty.* Elle est très jolie. ❷ (*rather*) plutôt ▷ *That film was pretty bad.* Ce film était plutôt mauvais.; **The weather was pretty awful.** Il faisait très mauvais temps.; **It's pretty much the same.** C'est pratiquement la même chose.

pretzel ['prɛtsəl] *n* bretzel *m*

prevent [prɪ'vɛnt] *vb* ❶ empêcher ▷ *They tried to prevent us from leaving.* Ils ont essayé de nous empêcher de partir. ❷ (*disease*) prévenir ▷ *in order to prevent AIDS* pour prévenir le sida ❸ (*accident, war, fire*) éviter

preventive [prɪ'vɛntɪv] *adj* préventif (f préventive) ▷ *preventive medicine* la médecine préventive; **preventive measures** des mesures de prévention

preview ['pri:vju:] *n* (*of movie*) bande-annonce f

previous ['pri:vɪəs] *adj* précédent

previously ['pri:vɪəslɪ] *adv* auparavant

prey [preɪ] *n* proie f ▷ *a bird of prey* un oiseau de proie

price [praɪs] *n* prix *m* ▷ *a high price* un prix élevé ▷ *the price list* la liste de prix

prick [prɪk] *vb* piquer ▷ *I pricked my finger.* Je me suis piqué le doigt.

prickly ['prɪklɪ] *adj* épineux (f épineuse) ▷ *a prickly plant* une plante épineuse

pride [praɪd] *n* ❶ (*positive*) fierté f ▷ *She's her parents' pride and joy.* Elle est la fierté de ses parents.; **to take pride in something** être fier de quelque chose ❷ (*arrogance*) orgueil *m* ▷ *Pride prevented him from apologizing.* L'orgueil l'a empêché de demander pardon.

priest [pri:st] *n* prêtre *m* ▷ *He's a priest.* Il est prêtre.

primarily ['praɪmərɪlɪ] *adv* principalement

primary ['praɪmərɪ] *adj* ❶ (*main*) principal (mpl principaux) ▷ *our primary purpose* notre but principal ❷ (*first*) primaire ▷ *books for the primary grade level* des livres pour le niveau primaire

prime minister [praɪm-] *n* premier ministre *m*, première ministre f

primitive ['prɪmɪtɪv] *adj* primitif (f primitive)

prince [prɪns] *n* prince *m* ▷ *the Prince of Wales* le prince de Galles

Prince Edward Island [-ɛdwəd-] *n* Île-du-Prince-Édouard f

princess [prɪn'sɛs] *n* princesse f ▷ *Princess Anne* la princesse Anne

principal ['prɪnsɪpl] *n* directeur *m*, directrice f

principle ['prɪnsɪpl] *n* principe *m*; **on principle** par principe

print [prɪnt] *n* ❶ (*photo*) tirage *m* ▷ *colour prints* des tirages en couleur ❷ (*letters*) caractères mpl ▷ *in small print* en petits

caractères ❸ (*fingerprint*) empreinte *f* digitale ❹ (*picture*) gravure *f* ▷ *a framed print* une gravure encadrée
▶ *vb* (*print out, publish*) imprimer ▷ *Click on the icon to print the file.* Clique sur l'icône pour imprimer le fichier.

printer ['prɪntər] *n* (*machine*) imprimante *f*

printout ['prɪntaut] *n* sortie d'imprimante *f*

priority [praɪ'ɒrɪtɪ] *n* priorité *f*

prison ['prɪzn] *n* prison *f*; **in prison** en prison

prisoner ['prɪznər] *n* prisonnier *m*, prisonnière *f*

prison guard *n* gardien de prison *m*, gardienne de prison *f*

privacy ['prɪvəsɪ] *n* intimité *f*

private ['praɪvɪt] *adj* privé ▷ *a private school* une école privée; **private property** la propriété privée; **"private"** (*on envelope*) «personnel»; **a private bathroom** une salle de bain individuelle; **I take private lessons.** Je prends des cours particuliers.

privatize ['praɪvɪtaɪz] *vb* privatiser

privilege ['prɪvɪlɪdʒ] *n* privilège *m*

prize [praɪz] *n* prix *m* ▷ *to win a prize* gagner un prix

prizewinner ['praɪzwɪnər] *n* gagnant *m*, gagnante *f*

prize-winning ['praɪzwɪnɪŋ] *adj* primé ▷ *a prize-winning documentary* un film documentaire primé

pro [prəu] *n* (*athlete*) pro; **You're a real pro at making crêpes!** Tu es une vraie pro des crêpes!; **the pros and cons** le pour et le contre ▷ *We weighed the pros and cons.* Nous avons pesé le pour et le contre.

probability [prɒbə'bɪlɪtɪ] *n* probabilité *f*

probable ['prɒbəbl] *adj* probable

probably ['prɒbəblɪ] *adv* probablement ▷ *probably not* probablement pas

probation [prə'beɪʃən] *n*: **on probation** en liberté surveillée

problem ['prɒbləm] *n* problème *m* ▷ *No problem!* Pas de problème!

proceeds ['prəusi:dz] *npl* bénéfices *mpl*

process ['prəusɛs] *n* processus *m* ▷ *the peace process* le processus de paix; **to be in the process of doing something** être en train de faire quelque chose ▷ *We're in the process of painting the kitchen.* Nous sommes en train de peindre la cuisine.

procession [prə'sɛʃən] *n* défilé *m*

procrastinate [prəu'kræstɪneɪt] *vb*: **I tend to procrastinate.** J'ai tendance à tout remettre au lendemain.

produce [prə'dju:s] *vb* ❶ (*create, manufacture*) produire ❷ (*play, show*) monter

producer [prə'dju:sər] *n* ❶ (*of play, show*) metteur en scène *m*, metteuse en scène *f* ❷ (*business*) producteur *m*, productrice *f* ▷ *Canada is the world's greatest producer of hydroelectric power.* Le Canada est le plus grand producteur d'hydro-électricité au monde.

product ['prɒdʌkt] *n* produit *m*

production [prə'dʌkʃən] *n* ❶ production *f* ▷ *world coffee production* la production mondiale de café ❷ (*play, show*) mise en scène

f ▷ *a production of "Hamlet"* une mise en scène de «Hamlet»

profession [prə'fɛʃən] *n* profession *f*

professional [prə'fɛʃənl] *n* professionnel *m*, professionnelle *f*
▶ *adj* (*player*) professionnel *m* (*f* professionnelle) ▷ *a professional musician* un musicien professionnel; **a very professional piece of work** un vrai travail de professionnel

professor [prə'fɛsər] *n* professeur d'université *m*, professeure d'université *f*

profit ['prɒfɪt] *n* bénéfice *m*

profitable ['prɒfɪtəbl] *adj* rentable

program ['prəugræm] *n* ❶ programme *m* ▷ *a computer program* un programme informatique ❷ (*on TV, radio*) émission *f* ▷ *a TV program* une émission de télé ❸ (*of events*) programme *m*
▶ *vb* (*computer*) programmer

programmer ['prəugræmər] *n* programmeur *m*, programmeuse *f* ▷ *She's a programmer.* Elle est programmeuse.

programming ['prəugræmɪŋ] *n* programmation *f*

progress [prə'grɛs] *n* progrès *m* ▷ *You're making progress!* Vous faites des progrès!

prohibit [prə'hɪbɪt] *vb* interdire ▷ *Smoking is prohibited.* Il est interdit de fumer.

project [prə'dʒɛkt] *n* projet *m* ▷ *a development project* un projet de développement ▷ *I'm doing a project on the rain forest.* Je travaille à un projet de recherche sur la forêt pluviale.

projector [prə'dʒɛktər] *n* projecteur *m*

promise ['prɒmɪs] *n* promesse *f* ▷ *He made me a promise.* Il m'a fait une promesse.; **That's a promise!** C'est promis!
▶ *vb* promettre ▷ *He promised to write.* Il a promis d'écrire. ▷ *I'll write, I promise!* J'écrirai, c'est promis!

promising ['prɒmɪsɪŋ] *adj* prometteur (*f* prometteuse) ▷ *a promising player* un joueur prometteur

promote [prə'məut] *vb* promouvoir ▷ *Our school tries to promote recycling.* Notre école essaie de promouvoir le recyclage. ▷ *We made posters to promote the school play.* Nous avons fait des affiches pour promouvoir la pièce de théâtre de l'école.; **to be promoted** être promu ▷ *She was promoted after six months.* Elle a été promue au bout de six mois.

promotion [prə'məuʃən] *n* promotion *f*

prompt [prɒmpt] *adj, adv* rapide ▷ *a prompt reply* une réponse rapide

promptly ['prɒmptlɪ] *adv*: **We left promptly at seven.** Nous sommes partis à sept heures précises.

pronoun ['prəunaun] *n* pronom *m*

pronounce [prə'nauns] *vb* prononcer ▷ *How do you pronounce that word?* Comment est-ce qu'on prononce ce mot?

pronunciation [prənʌnsɪ'eɪʃən] *n* prononciation *f*

proof [pru:f] *n* preuve *f*

proofread ['pru:fri:d] *vb* relire et corriger ▷ *Don't forget to proofread your book report.* N'oublie pas de relire et de corriger ton compte-rendu de livre.

prop [prɒp] n (for play) accessoire m
propaganda [prɒpə'gændə] n propagande f
propane ['prəupeɪn] n propane m ▷ a propane
cylinder (for camping) une bonbonne de propane
▷ a propane stove un réchaud au propane
proper ['prɒpər] adj ❶ (genuine) vrai ▷ proper
French bread du vrai pain français ▷ We didn't
have a proper lunch, just sandwiches. Nous
n'avons pas pris de vrai lunch, juste des
sandwichs.; **It's difficult to get a proper job.**
Il est difficile de trouver un travail correct.
❷ adéquat ▷ You have to have the proper
equipment. Il faut avoir l'équipement adéquat.
▷ We need proper training. Il nous faut une
formation adéquate.; **If you had come at the
proper time…** Si tu étais venu à l'heure dite…
properly ['prɒpəlɪ] adv ❶ (correctly) comme
il faut ▷ You're not doing it properly. Tu ne t'y
prends pas comme il faut. ❷ (appropriately)
convenablement ▷ Dress properly for your
interview. Habille-toi convenablement pour
ton entrevue.
property ['prɒpətɪ] n propriété f; **"private
property"** « propriété privée »; **stolen
property** les objets volés
proportional [prə'pɔːʃənt] adj proportionnel
(f proportionnelle) ▷ proportional representation
la représentation proportionnelle
proposal [prə'pəuzl] n (suggestion)
proposition f
propose [prə'pəuz] vb ❶ proposer ▷ I propose
a new plan. Je propose un changement de
programme.; **to propose to do something**
avoir l'intention de faire quelque chose ▷ What
do you propose to do? Qu'est-ce que tu as
l'intention de faire?; **to propose to somebody**
(for marriage) demander quelqu'un en mariage
▷ He proposed to her at the restaurant. Il l'a
demandée en mariage au restaurant.
prosecute ['prɒsɪkjuːt] vb poursuivre en
justice ▷ They were prosecuted for murder. Ils
ont été poursuivis en justice pour meurtre.;
"Trespassers will be prosecuted" « Défense
d'entrer sous peine de poursuites »
prospect ['prɒspɛkt] n perspective f ▷ It'll
improve my career prospects. Ça va améliorer mes
perspectives d'avenir.
protect [prə'tɛkt] vb protéger
protection [prə'tɛkʃən] n protection f
protein ['prəutiːn] n protéine f
protest n ['prəutɛst] n protestation f ▷ He ignored
their protests. Il a ignoré leurs protestations.; **a
protest march** une manifestation
▶ vb protester
Protestant ['prɒtɪstənt] n protestant m,
protestante f
▶ adj protestant m ▷ a Protestant church une
église protestante
protester [prə'tɛstər] n manifestant m,
manifestante f
proud [praud] adj fier (f fière) ▷ Her parents are
proud of her. Ses parents sont fiers d'elle.
prove [pruːv] vb prouver ▷ The police couldn't
prove it. La police n'a pas pu le prouver.
proverb ['prɒvɜːb] n proverbe m
provide [prə'vaɪd] vb fournir; **to provide

somebody with something** fournir quelque
chose à quelqu'un ▷ They provided us with maps.
Ils nous ont fourni des cartes.
provide for vb subvenir aux besoins de ▷ She
can now provide for her family. Maintenant elle
peut subvenir aux besoins de sa famille.
provided [prə'vaɪdɪd] conj à condition que
▷ He'll play in the next match provided he comes to
the practice. Il jouera dans le prochain match, à
condition qu'il vienne à l'entraînement.
province ['prɒvɪns] n province f
provincial [prə'vɪnʃəl] adj provincial (mpl
provinciaux) ▷ the provincial capital la capitale
provinciale
prowler ['praulər] n rôdeur m, rôdeuse f
prune [pruːn] n (pl pruneaux)
pry [praɪ] vb: **to pry into other people's
affairs** mettre son nez dans les affaires des
autres
pseudonym ['sjuːdənɪm] n pseudonyme m
psychiatrist [saɪ'kaɪətrɪst] n psychiatre
▷ She's a psychiatrist. Elle est psychiatre.
psychological [saɪkə'lɒdʒɪkl] adj
psychologique
psychologist [saɪ'kɒlədʒɪst] n psychologue
▷ He's a psychologist. Il est psychologue.
psychology [saɪ'kɒlədʒɪ] n psychologie f
public ['pʌblɪk] n public m ▷ open to the public
ouvert au public; **in public** en public
▶ adj public m (f publique); **a public holiday** un
jour férié; **public opinion** l'opinion f publique;
the public address system les haut-parleurs;
a public school une école publique; **public
transport** les transports m en commun;
public relations les relations publiques
publicity [pʌb'lɪsɪtɪ] n publicité f
publish ['pʌblɪʃ] vb publier
publisher ['pʌblɪʃər] n (company) maison
d'édition f
puck [pʌk] n rondelle f
pudding ['pudɪŋ] n pouding m ▷ instant vanilla
pudding du pouding instantané à la vanille;
rice pudding le riz au lait
puddle ['pʌdl] n flaque f
puffin ['pʌfɪn] n macareux m
puff pastry [pʌf-] n pâte feuilletée f
pull [pul] vb ❶ tirer ▷ Pull! Tirez! ❷ (tooth,
weed) arracher; **to pull the trigger** appuyer
sur la gâchette; **to pull a muscle** se froisser un
muscle ▷ I pulled a muscle when I was training.
Je me suis froissé un muscle à l'entraînement.;
You're pulling my leg! Tu me fais marcher!;
to pull off the road arrêter la voiture sur le
bord de la route; **to pull out (1)** (from driveway,
parking space) sortir ❷ (in traffic) sortir de la file
▷ The car pulled out to pass. La voiture est sortie
de la file pour doubler. **(3)** (withdraw) se retirer
▷ He pulled out of the tournament. Il s'est retiré du
tournoi.; **The police pulled us over.** La police
nous a fait nous arrêter.; **to pull through** s'en
sortir ▷ They think he'll pull through. Ils pensent
qu'il va s'en sortir.; **to pull up** (car) s'arrêter ▷ A
black car pulled up beside me. Une voiture noire
s'est arrêtée à côté de moi.
pullover ['puləuvər] n chandail m
pulse [pʌls] n pouls ▷ The nurse felt my pulse.

L'infirmière a pris mon pouls.

pump [pʌmp] n pompe f ▷ a bicycle pump une pompe à vélo ▷ a gas pump une pompe à essence
▶ vb pomper; **to pump up** (tire) gonfler

pumpkin ['pʌmpkɪn] n citrouille f

punch [pʌntʃ] n ❶ (blow) coup de poing m ❷ (drink) punch m ❸ (tool) perforateur m ▷ Use the three-hole punch on the teacher's desk. Utilise le perforateur à trois trous sur le bureau de la prof.
▶ vb ❶ (hit) donner un coup de poing à ▷ She punched me! Elle m'a donné un coup de poing! ❷ (papers) perforer ▷ The pages are already punched. Les feuilles sont déjà perforées. ❸ (ticket) poinçonner ▷ He forgot to punch my ticket. Il a oublié de poinçonner mon billet.

punctual ['pʌŋktjuəl] adj ponctuel (f ponctuelle)

punctuation [pʌŋktjuˈeɪʃən] n ponctuation f

puncture ['pʌŋktʃəʳ] n (tire, balloon) crever

punish ['pʌnɪʃ] vb punir; **to punish somebody for something** punir quelqu'un de quelque chose; **to punish somebody for doing something** punir quelqu'un d'avoir fait quelque chose

punishment ['pʌnɪʃmənt] n punition f

punk [pʌŋk] n (person) punk; **a punk rock band** un groupe de punk rock

puppet ['pʌpɪt] n marionnette f

puppy ['pʌpɪ] n chiot m

purchase ['pəːtʃɪs] vb acheter

pure [pjuəʳ] adj pur ▷ pure orange juice du pur jus d'orange ▷ the pure sciences les sciences pures

purple ['pəːpl] adj violet (f violette)

purpose ['pəːpəs] n but m ▷ What is the purpose of these changes? Quel est le but de ces changements? ▷ his purpose in life son but dans la vie; **on purpose** exprès ▷ She did it on purpose. Elle l'a fait exprès.

purr [pəːʳ] vb ronronner

purse [pəːs] n ❶ sac à main m (pl sacs à main) ❷ (for coins) porte-monnaie m (pl porte-monnaie)

pursue [pəˈsjuː] vb poursuivre

pursuit [pəˈsjuːt] n: **in pursuit of adventure** à la recherche de l'aventure; **She escaped with her brother in hot pursuit.** Elle s'est échappée avec son frère à ses trousses.

push [puʃ] n: **to give somebody a push** pousser quelqu'un ▷ He gave me a push. Il m'a poussé.; **a push for more affordable housing** une campagne pour des logements à loyer modéré
▶ vb ❶ pousser ▷ Don't push! Arrêtez de pousser! ❷ (button) appuyer sur; **to push somebody to do something** pousser quelqu'un à faire quelque chose ▷ My parents are pushing me to take piano. Mes parents me poussent à prendre des cours de piano.; **to push drugs** revendre de la drogue

push around vb bousculer ▷ Stop pushing people around. Arrête de bousculer les gens.

push through vb se frayer un passage ▷ The paramedics pushed through the crowd. Les ambulanciers se sont frayé un passage dans la foule.; **I pushed my way through.** Je me suis frayé un passage.

pusher ['puʃəʳ] n (of drugs) revendeur m, revendeuse f

push-up ['puʃʌp] n pompe f; **to do push-ups** faire des pompes

pussy willow ['pusɪ'wɪləu] n saule à chatons m

put [put] vb ❶ (place) mettre ▷ Where shall I put my things? Où est-ce que je peux mettre mes affaires? ▷ He's putting the baby to bed. Il met le bébé au lit. ❷ (write) écrire ▷ Don't forget to put your name on the paper. N'oubliez pas d'écrire votre nom sur la feuille.

put aside vb mettre de côté ▷ Can you put this aside for me till tomorrow? Est-ce que vous pouvez mettre ça de côté pour moi jusqu'à demain?

put away vb ranger ▷ Can you put away the dishes, please? Tu peux ranger la vaisselle, s'il te plaît?

put back vb (replace) remettre en place ▷ Put it back when you've finished with it. Remets-le en place une fois que tu auras fini.

put down vb ❶ poser ▷ I'll put these bags down for a minute. Je vais poser ces sacs une minute. ❷ (in writing) noter ▷ I've put down a few ideas. J'ai noté quelques idées. ❸ (belittle) rabaisser ▷ I don't like jokes that put other people down. Je n'aime pas les plaisanteries qui rabaissent les autres. ▷ Stop putting yourself down. Arrête de te rabaisser.; **to have an animal put down** faire piquer un animal ▷ We had to have our old dog put down. Nous avons dû faire piquer notre vieux chien.

put forward vb ❶ (clock) avancer ▷ Next week it'll be time to put the clocks forward an hour. La semaine prochaine, il sera temps d'avancer les montres d'une heure. ❷ (idea, argument) proposer ▷ to put forward a suggestion proposer une suggestion

put in vb (install) installer ▷ We're going to get new cupboards put in. Nous allons faire installer de nouvelles armoires.; **She has put in a lot of work on this project.** Elle a fourni beaucoup de travail pour ce projet.

put off vb ❶ (postpone) remettre à plus tard ▷ I keep putting it off. Je n'arrête pas de remettre ça à plus tard. ❷ (discourage) décourager ▷ He's not easily put off. Il ne se laisse pas facilement décourager.

put on vb ❶ (clothes, lipstick, record) mettre ▷ I'll put my coat on. Je vais mettre mon manteau. ❷ (play, show) monter ▷ We're putting on "Bon Voyage, Charlie Brown". Nous sommes en train de monter « Bon voyage, Charlie Brown ». ❸ mettre à cuire ▷ I'll put the potatoes on. Je vais mettre les pommes de terre à cuire.; **to put on weight** grossir ▷ He's put on a bit of weight. Il a un peu grossi. ▷ to put on two kilos gagner deux kilos

put out vb (light, cigarette, fire) éteindre ▷ It took them five hours to put out the fire. Ils ont mis cinq heures à éteindre l'incendie.

put through vb ❶ passer ▷ Can you put me

through to the manager? Est-ce que vous pouvez me passer le directeur?; **I'm putting you through.** Je vous passe la communication. ❷ soumettre ▷ *The new drug was put through a series of tests.* On a soumis le nouveau médicament à une série d'épreuves.

put up *vb* ❶ *(pin up)* mettre ▷ *The poster's great. I'll put it up on my wall.* L'affiche est super. Je vais le mettre au mur. ❷ *(tent)* monter ▷ *We put up our tent in a field.* Nous avons monté la tente dans un champ. ❸ *(price)* augmenter ▷ *They've put up the price.* Ils ont augmenté les prix. ❹ *(accommodate)* héberger ▷ *My friends will put me up for the night.* Mes amis vont m'héberger pour la nuit.; **to put one's hand up** lever la main ▷ *If you have any questions, put up your hand.* Si vous avez une question, levez la main.; **to put up with something** supporter quelque chose ▷ *I'm not going to put up with it any longer.* Je ne vais pas supporter ça plus longtemps.

puzzle ['pʌzl] *n (jigsaw)* puzzle *m*
puzzled ['pʌzld] *adj* perplexe ▷ *You look puzzled!* Tu as l'air perplexe!
puzzling ['pʌzlɪŋ] *adj* déconcertant
pyjamas [pɪ'dʒɑːməz] *npl* pyjama *m* ▷ *my pyjamas* mon pyjama; **a pair of pyjamas** un pyjama; **a pyjama top** un haut de pyjama
pyramid ['pɪrəmɪd] *n* pyramide *f*

q

quaint [kweɪnt] *adj (house, village)* pittoresque
qualifications [kwɔlɪfɪ'keɪʃənz] *npl* qualifications *fpl* ▷ *What are your qualifications?* Quelles sont vos qualifications professionnelles?
qualified ['kwɔlɪfaɪd] *adj* ❶ *(trained)* qualifié ▷ *a qualified driving instructor* un moniteur d'auto-école qualifié ❷ *(nurse, teacher)* diplômé ▷ *a qualified nurse* une infirmière diplômée
qualify ['kwɔlɪfaɪ] *vb (in competition)* se qualifier ▷ *Our team didn't qualify.* Notre équipe ne s'est pas qualifiée.; **to qualify for a job** avoir les compétences requises pour un poste; **to qualify for unemployment benefits** avoir droit aux allocations d'assurance-emploi; **That hardly qualifies as art.** Cela ne mérite guère le nom d'art.
quality ['kwɔlɪtɪ] *n* qualité *f* ▷ *good quality of life* une bonne qualité de vie ▷ *good quality ingredients* des ingrédients de bonne qualité ▷ *She has lots of good qualities.* Elle a beaucoup

de qualités.
quantity ['kwɔntɪtɪ] *n* quantité *f*
quarantine ['kwɔrəntiːn] *n* quarantaine *f* ▷ *in quarantine* en quarantaine
quarrel ['kwɔrəl] *n* dispute *f*
▷ *vb* se disputer
quarry ['kwɔrɪ] *n (for stone)* carrière *f*
quarter ['kwɔːtər] *n* quart *m*; **three quarters** trois quarts; **a quarter of an hour** un quart d'heure ▷ *three quarters of an hour* trois quarts d'heure; **a quarter after ten** dix heures et quart; **a quarter to eleven** onze heures moins le quart
quarterfinal ['kwɔːtə'faɪnl] *n* quart de finale *m*
quartet [kwɔː'tɛt] *n* quatuor *m* ▷ *a string quartet* un quatuor à cordes
queasy ['kwiːzɪ] *adj:* **to feel queasy** avoir mal au cœur ▷ *I'm feeling queasy.* J'ai mal au cœur.
Québec [kwɪ'bɛk] *n* Québec *m*
queen [kwiːn] *n* ❶ reine *f* ▷ *Queen Elizabeth* la reine Élisabeth ❷ *(playing card)* dame *f* ▷ *the queen of hearts* la dame de cœur; **the Queen Mother** la reine mère; **beauty queen** la reine de beauté; **a queen-sized bed** un grand lit
query ['kwɪərɪ] *n* question *f*
▷ *vb* mettre en question ▷ *No one queried my decision.* Personne n'a mis en question ma décision.
question ['kwɛstʃən] *n* question *f* ▷ *Can I ask a question?* Est-ce que je peux poser une question? ▷ *That's a difficult question.* C'est une question difficile.; **It's out of the question.** C'est hors de question.; **There's no question he's going to win.** Il est certain qu'il va gagner.; **There's no question of you paying!** Il n'est pas question que tu payes!
▷ *vb* interroger ▷ *He was questioned by the police.* Il a été interrogé par la police.
questionable ['kwɛstʃənəbl] *adj* douteux *(f* douteuse*)* ▷ *questionable behaviour* une conduite douteuse
question mark *n* point d'interrogation *m*
questionnaire [kwɛstʃə'nɛər] *n* questionnaire *m*
quick [kwɪk] *adj, adv* rapide ▷ *a quick lunch* un déjeuner rapide ▷ *It's quicker by train.* C'est plus rapide en train.; **Be quick!** Dépêche-toi!; **She's a quick learner.** Elle apprend vite.; **Quick, phone the police!** Téléphonez vite à la police!
quickly ['kwɪklɪ] *adv* vite ▷ *It was all over very quickly.* Ça s'est passé très vite.
quicksand ['kwɪksænd] *n* sable mouvant *m*
quiet ['kwaɪət] *adj* ❶ *(not talkative or noisy)* silencieux ▷ *You're very quiet today.* Tu es bien silencieux aujourd'hui. ▷ *The engine is very quiet.* Le moteur est très silencieux. ❷ *(peaceful)* tranquille ▷ *a quiet little town* une petite ville tranquille ▷ *a quiet weekend* une fin de semaine tranquille; **Be quiet!** Tais-toi!; **Quiet!** Silence!
quietly ['kwaɪətlɪ] *adv* ❶ *(speak)* doucement ▷ *"She's very sick," he said quietly.* « Elle est très malade », déclara-t-il doucement. ❷ *(move)* silencieusement ▷ *He quietly opened the door.* Il a ouvert la porte sans faire de bruit.

quilt [kwɪlt] n ● (*pieced, with special stitching*) courtepointe f ● (*comforter*) douillette f

quit [kwɪt] vb (*place, premises, job*) quitter ▷ She's decided to quit her job. Elle a décidé de quitter son emploi.; **I quit!** J'abandonne!

quite [kwaɪt] adv ● (*rather*) assez ▷ It's quite warm today. Il fait assez chaud aujourd'hui. ● (*entirely*) tout à fait ▷ I'm not quite sure. Je n'en suis pas tout à fait sûr. ▷ It's not quite the same. Ce n'est pas tout à fait la même chose.; **quite good** pas mal; **I've been there quite a few times.** J'y suis allé pas mal de fois.; **quite a lot of money** pas mal d'argent; **It costs quite a lot to go to Europe.** Ça coûte assez cher d'aller en Europe.; **It's quite a long way.** C'est assez loin.; **It was quite a shock.** Ça a été tout un choc.; **There were quite a few people there.** Il y avait pas mal de gens.

quiz [kwɪz] n ● (*in school*) interrogation f ● (*in magazine*) questionnaire m; **a quiz show** un jeu-questionnaire

quota ['kwəʊtə] n quota m

quotation [kwəʊ'teɪʃən] n citation f ▷ a quotation from a book une citation d'un livre

quote [kwəʊt] n citation f ▷ a quote from Pierre Trudeau une citation de Pierre Trudeau; **quotes** (*quotation marks*) les m guillemets ▷ in quotes entre guillemets
▶ vb citer ▷ He's always quoting famous people. Il n'arrête pas de citer des gens célèbres.

r

rabbi ['ræbaɪ] n rabbin m

rabbit ['ræbɪt] n lapin m; **a rabbit hutch** un clapier

rabies ['reɪbiːz] n rage f; **a dog with rabies** un chien enragé

raccoon [rə'kuːn] n raton laveur m

race [reɪs] n ● (*sport*) course f ▷ a bike race une course cycliste ● (*species*) race f ▷ the human race la race humaine; **race relations** les f relations interraciales
▶ vb ● (*have a race*) faire la course; **I'll race you!** On fait la course! ● courir ▷ We raced to catch the bus. Nous avons couru pour attraper l'autobus.

race car n voiture de course f

race car driver n pilote de course

racecourse ['reɪskɔːs] n champ de courses m

racehorse ['reɪshɔːs] n cheval de course m (pl chevaux de course)

racer ['reɪsər] n (*bike*) vélo de course

racetrack ['reɪstræk] n piste f

racial ['reɪʃl] adj racial (mpl raciaux) ▷ racial discrimination la discrimination raciale

racism ['reɪsɪzəm] n racisme m

racist ['reɪsɪst] adj raciste
▶ n raciste

rack [ræk] n ● (*for luggage*) porte-bagages m (pl porte-bagages) ● (*for coats*) portemanteau m (pl portemanteaux) ● (*for dishes*) égouttoir m

racket ['rækɪt] n ● (*noise*) tapage m ▷ They're making a terrible racket. Ils font un tapage de tous les diables. ● (*informal*)

racquet ['rækɪt] n raquette f

radar ['reɪdɑːr] n radar m

radiation [reɪdɪ'eɪʃən] n radiation f

radiator ['reɪdɪeɪtər] n radiateur m

radio ['reɪdɪəʊ] n radio f; **on the radio** à la radio; **a radio station** une station de radio

radioactive ['reɪdɪəʊ'æktɪv] adj radioactif (f radioactive)

radio-controlled ['reɪdɪəʊkən'trəʊld] adj (*model plane, car*) téléguidé

radish ['rædɪʃ] n radis

raffle ['ræfl] n tombola f ▷ a raffle ticket un billet de tombola

raft [rɑːft] n radeau m (pl radeaux)

rag [ræg] n chiffon m; **dressed in rags** en haillons

rage [reɪdʒ] n rage f; **to be in a rage** être furieux ▷ She was in a rage. Elle était furieuse.; **It's all the rage.** Ça fait fureur.

raid [reɪd] n ● incursion f ▷ a raid by enemy soldiers une incursion de soldats ennemis ● descente f ▷ a police raid une descente de police
▶ vb ● (*military*) faire une incursion dans ● (*police*) faire une descente dans ▷ The police raided the club. La police a fait une descente dans le club.

rail [reɪl] n (*on railway line*) rail m; **by rail** en train

railing ['reɪlɪŋz] n ● (*on stairs*) rampe f ● (*on bridge, balcony*) balustrade f ▷ Don't lean over the railing! Ne vous penchez pas sur la balustrade!

railway ['reɪlweɪ] n chemin de fer m ▷ the privatization of the railways la privatisation des chemins de fer; **a railway crossing** une traverse; **a railway line** une ligne de chemin de fer; **a railway station** une gare

rain [reɪn] n pluie f ▷ in the rain sous la pluie
▶ vb pleuvoir ▷ It rains a lot here. Il pleut beaucoup par ici.; **It's raining.** Il pleut.

rainbow ['reɪnbəʊ] n arc-en-ciel m (pl arcs-en-ciel)

raincoat ['reɪnkəʊt] n imperméable m

rainforest ['reɪnfɒrɪst] n forêt tropicale humide f

rainy ['reɪnɪ] adj pluvieux (f pluvieuse)

raise [reɪz] vb ● (*lift*) lever ▷ He raised his hand. Il a levé la main. ● (*children, animals*) élever ▷ We raise pigs. Nous élevons des porcs. ▷ They've raised three children. Ils ont élevé trois enfants. ● (*improve*) améliorer ▷ They want to raise standards in schools. Ils veulent améliorer le niveau dans les écoles.; **to raise money**

collecter des fonds ▷ *The school is raising money for a new gym.* L'école collecte des fonds pour un nouveau gymnase.

raisin ['reɪzn] *n* raisin sec *m*

rake [reɪk] *n* râteau *m* (pl râteaux)

rally ['rælɪ] *n* ❶ (*of people*) rassemblement *m* ❷ (*sport*) rallye *m* ▷ *a rally driver* un pilote de rallye

ram [ræm] *n* (*sheep*) bélier *m*
▶ *vb* (*vehicle*) emboutir ▷ *The thieves rammed a police car.* Les voleurs ont embouti une voiture de police.

ramp [ræmp] *n* ❶ (*for wheelchairs*) rampe d'accès *f* ❷ (*on highway*) bretelle *f*

ran [ræn] *vb see* **run**

ranch [rɑːntʃ] *n* ranch *m*

random ['rændəm] *adj*: **a random selection** une sélection effectuée au hasard; **at random** au hasard ▷ *We picked the number at random.* Nous avons choisi le numéro au hasard.

rang [ræŋ] *vb see* **ring**

range [reɪndʒ] *n* ❶ choix *m* ▷ *a wide range of colours* un grand choix de coloris; **a range of subjects** diverses matières ▷ *We study a range of subjects.* Nous étudions diverses matières.; **a mountain range** une chaîne de montagnes
▶ *vb*: **to range from...** se situer entre... et ▷ *Temperatures in summer range from 18 to 33 degrees.* Les températures estivales se situent entre dix-huit et trente-trois degrés.; **Tickets range from $5 to $40.** Les billets coûtent entre cinq et quarante dollars.

ranger ['reɪndʒəʳ] *n* garde forestier *m*, garde forestière *f*

rank [ræŋk] *vb*: **She ranks third in Canada in speed skating.** Elle est classée troisième au Canada pour le patinage de vitesse.

ransom ['rænsəm] *n* rançon *f*

rap [ræp] *n* (*music*) rap *m* ▷ *a rap singer* un chanteur de rap

rapids ['ræpɪdz] *npl* rapides *mpl*

rare [rɛəʳ] *adj* ❶ (*unusual*) rare ▷ *I've got a rare plant* une plante rare ❷ (*steak*) saignant

rash [ræʃ] *n* éruption *f* de boutons ▷ *I've got a rash on my chest.* J'ai une éruption de boutons sur la poitrine.

raspberry ['rɑːzbərɪ] *n* framboise *f* ▷ *raspberry jam* la confiture de framboises

rat [ræt] *n* rat *m*

rate [reɪt] *n* ❶ (*price*) tarif *m* ▷ *There are reduced rates for students.* Il y a des tarifs réduits pour les étudiants. ❷ (*level*) taux *m* ▷ *the birth rate* le taux de naissances ▷ *a high rate of interest* un taux d'intérêt élevé
▶ *vb*: **He is rated the best.** Il est considéré comme le meilleur.; **How do you rate this film?** Qu'est-ce que vous pensez de ce film?; **This rates a 9 out of 10.** Cela mérite un 9 sur 10.

rather ['rɑːðəʳ] *adv* plutôt ▷ *I was rather disappointed.* J'étais plutôt déçu.; **rather than** plutôt que ▷ *We decided to camp rather than stay at a hotel.* Nous avons décidé de camper plutôt que d'aller à l'hôtel.; **I'd rather...** j'aimerais mieux... ▷ *I'd rather stay in tonight.* J'aimerais mieux rester à la maison ce soir. ▷ *"Would you*

like a candy?" — "I'd rather have an apple." « Tu veux un bonbon? » — « J'aimerais mieux une pomme. »

rattle ['rætl] *n* (*for baby*) hochet *m*

rattlesnake ['rætlsneɪk] *n* serpent à sonnette *m*

rave [reɪv] *vb* s'extasier ▷ *They raved about the movie.* Ils se sont extasiés sur le film.
▶ *n* (*party*) rave *m*; **rave music** la musique rave

ravenous ['rævənəs] *adj*: **to be ravenous** avoir une faim de loup ▷ *I'm ravenous!* J'ai une faim de loup!

raw [rɔː] *adj* (*food*) cru; **raw materials** les *f* matières premières

razor ['reɪzəʳ] *n* rasoir *m* ▷ *some disposable razors* des rasoirs jetables; **a razor blade** une lame de rasoir

RCMP *n* GRC *f*

reach [riːtʃ] *n*: **out of reach** hors de portée ▷ *The light switch was out of reach.* L'interrupteur était hors de portée. ▷ **within easy reach of** à proximité de ▷ *The hotel is within easy reach of the town centre.* L'hôtel se trouve à proximité du centre-ville.
▶ *vb* ❶ arriver à ▷ *We reached the hotel at 7 p.m.* Nous sommes arrivés à l'hôtel à sept heures du soir. ▷ *Have you reached a decision?* Tu es arrivé à une décision? ❷ (*decision*) parvenir à ▷ *Eventually they reached a decision.* Ils sont finalement parvenus à une décision.; **He reached for his flashlight.** Il a tendu la main pour prendre sa lampe de poche.

react [riːˈækt] *vb* réagir

reaction [riːˈækʃən] *n* réaction *f*

reactor [riːˈæktəʳ] *n* réacteur *m* ▷ *a nuclear reactor* un réacteur nucléaire

read [riːd] *vb* lire ▷ *I don't read much.* Je ne lis pas beaucoup. ▷ *Have you read this book?* Est-ce que tu as lu ce livre? ▷ *Read the text out loud.* Lis le texte à haute voix.

reader ['riːdəʳ] *n* (*person*) lecteur *m*, lectrice *f*

readily ['rɛdɪlɪ] *adv* volontiers ▷ *She readily agreed.* Elle a accepté volontiers.

reading ['riːdɪŋ] *n* lecture *f* ▷ *Reading is one of my hobbies.* La lecture est l'une de mes activités favorites.

ready ['rɛdɪ] *adj* prêt ▷ *She's nearly ready.* Elle est presque prête. ▷ *He's always ready to help.* Il est toujours prêt à rendre service.; **to get ready** se préparer ▷ *She's getting ready to go out.* Elle est en train de se préparer pour sortir.; **to get something ready** préparer quelque chose ▷ *He's getting dinner ready.* Il est en train de préparer le dîner.

ready-made ['rɛdɪ'meɪd] *adj* ❶ tout fait ▷ *ready-made curtains* des rideaux tous faits ▷ *a ready-made solution* une solution toute faite ❷ (*food*) cuisiné ▷ *a ready-made meal* un plat cuisiné

real [rɪəl] *adj* ❶ vrai ▷ *He wasn't a real policeman.* Ce n'était pas un vrai policier. ▷ *Her real name is Cordelia.* Son vrai nom est Cordelia. ❷ véritable ▷ *It's real leather.* C'est du cuir véritable. ▷ *It was a real nightmare.* C'était un véritable cauchemar.; **in real life** dans la réalité

real estate n immobilier m ▷ *He works in real estate.* Il travaille dans l'immobilier.; **a real estate agency** une agence immobilière; **a real estate agent** un agent immobilier

realistic [rɪəˈlɪstɪk] adj réaliste

reality [riːˈælɪtɪ] n réalité f

realize [ˈrɪəlaɪz] vb: **to realize that...** se rendre compte que... ▷ *We realized that something was wrong.* Nous nous sommes rendu compte que quelque chose n'allait pas.

really [ˈrɪəlɪ] adv vraiment ▷ *She's really nice.* Elle est vraiment sympathique. ▷ *"Do you want to go?" — "Not really."* « Tu veux y aller? » — « Pas vraiment. »; **"I'm learning to ride."** — **"Really?"** « J'apprends à monter à cheval. » — « Ah bon? »; **Do you really think so?** Tu es sûr?

rear [rɪəʳ] adj arrière (f+pl arrière) ▷ *a rear wheel* une roue arrière
▶ n arrière m ▷ *at the rear of the train* à l'arrière du train

reason [ˈriːzn] n raison f ▷ *There's no reason to think that...* Il n'y a aucune raison de penser que...; **for security reasons** pour des raisons de sécurité; **That was the main reason I went.** C'est surtout pour ça que j'y suis allé.

reasonable [ˈriːznəbl] adj ⓐ (sensible) raisonnable ▷ *Be reasonable!* Sois raisonnable! ⓑ (not bad) convenable ▷ *He wrote a reasonable essay.* Sa dissertation était convenable.

reasonably [ˈriːznəblɪ] adv raisonnablement ▷ *The team played reasonably well.* L'équipe a joué raisonnablement bien.; **reasonably priced accommodation** un logement à un prix raisonnable

reassure [riːəˈʃʊəʳ] vb rassurer

reassuring [riːəˈʃʊərɪŋ] adj rassurant

rebellious [rɪˈbeljəs] adj rebelle

reboot [riːˈbuːt] vb redémarrer ▷ *I rebooted the computer.* J'ai redémarré l'ordinateur.

receipt [rɪˈsiːt] n reçu m

receive [rɪˈsiːv] vb recevoir

receiver [rɪˈsiːvəʳ] n (of phone) combiné m; **to pick up the receiver** décrocher

recent [ˈriːsnt] adj récent

recently [ˈriːsntlɪ] adv ces derniers temps ▷ *I've been doing a lot of biking recently.* J'ai fait beaucoup de cyclisme ces derniers temps.

reception [rɪˈsepʃən] n réception f ▷ *Please leave your key at reception.* Merci de laisser votre clé à la réception. ▷ *The reception will be at a big hotel.* La réception aura lieu dans un grand hôtel.

receptionist [rɪˈsepʃənɪst] n réceptionniste

recession [rɪˈseʃən] n récession f

recipe [ˈresɪpɪ] n recette f

reclining [rɪˈklaɪnɪŋ] adj: **a reclining armchair** un fauteuil inclinable; **a reclining seat** (in plane, car) un siège inclinable

recognizable [ˈrekəgnaɪzəbl] adj reconnaissable

recognize [ˈrekəgnaɪz] vb reconnaître ▷ *You'll recognize me by my red hair.* Vous me reconnaîtrez à mes cheveux roux.

recommend [rekəˈmend] vb recommander ▷ *What do you recommend?* Qu'est-ce que vous

me recommandez?

reconsider [riːkənˈsɪdəʳ] vb reconsidérer

record [n ˈrekəd, vb rɪˈkɔːd] n ⓐ (recording) disque m ▷ *my favourite record* mon disque préféré ⓑ (sport) record m ▷ *the world record* le record du monde; **in record time** en un temps record ▷ *She finished the job in record time.* Elle a terminé le travail en un temps record.; **a criminal record** un casier judiciaire ▷ *She's got a criminal record.* Elle a un casier judiciaire.; **records** (of police, hospital) les archives f ▷ *I'll check the records.* Je vais vérifier dans les archives.; **There is no record of your booking.** Il n'y a aucune trace de votre réservation.
▶ vb (on film, tape) enregistrer ▷ *They've just recorded their new album.* Ils viennent d'enregistrer leur nouveau disque.

recorder [rɪˈkɔːdəʳ] n (instrument) flûte à bec f ▷ *She plays the recorder.* Elle joue de la flûte à bec.; **a cassette recorder** un magnétophone à cassettes; **a video recorder** un magnétoscope

recording [rɪˈkɔːdɪŋ] n enregistrement m

record player n tourne-disque m

recover [rɪˈkʌvəʳ] vb se remettre ▷ *He's recovering from a knee injury.* Il se remet d'une blessure au genou.

recovery [rɪˈkʌvərɪ] n rétablissement m; **Best wishes for a speedy recovery!** Meilleurs vœux de prompt rétablissement!

recreational vehicle [rekrɪˈeɪʃənl-] n caravane f

rec room [ˈrek-] n salle de jeux f

rectangle [ˈrektæŋgl] n rectangle m

rectangular [rekˈtæŋgjuləʳ] adj rectangulaire

recycle [riːˈsaɪkl] vb recycler

recycling [riːˈsaɪklɪŋ] n recyclage m

red [red] adj ⓐ rouge ▷ *a red rose* une rose rouge ▷ *red meat* la viande rouge; **a red light** (traffic light) un feu rouge ▷ *to go through a red light* brûler un feu rouge ⓑ (hair) roux m (f rousse) ▷ *He's got red hair.* Il a les cheveux roux.

Red Crescent [-ˈkresnt] n Croissant-Rouge

Red Cross n Croix-Rouge

redecorate [riːˈdekəreɪt] vb redécorer

red-haired [redˈheəʳd] adj roux m (f rousse)

red-handed [redˈhændɪd] adj: **to catch somebody red-handed** prendre quelqu'un la main dans le sac ▷ *We were caught red-handed.* Nous avons été pris la main dans le sac.

redhead [ˈredhed] n roux, rousse f

redo [riːˈduː] vb refaire

reduce [rɪˈdjuːs] vb réduire ▷ *at a reduced price* à prix réduit; **Reduce, reuse, recycle.** Réduire, réutiliser, recycler.

reduction [rɪˈdʌkʃən] n réduction f ▷ *a 5% reduction* une réduction de cinq pour cent

redwood [ˈredwʊd] n séquoia m

reed [riːd] n (plant) roseau m (pl roseaux)

reel [riːl] n (on fishing rod) moulinet m

reel in vb ramener ▷ *I reeled in a huge trout.* J'ai ramené une truite énorme.

refer [rɪˈfəːʳ] vb: **to refer to** faire allusion à ▷ *What are you referring to?* À quoi faites-vous allusion?

referee [refəˈriː] n arbitre m

reference [ˈrefrəns] n ⓐ allusion f ▷ *He*

made no reference to the incident. Il n'a fait aucune allusion à l'incident. **②** *(for job application)* références fpl ▷ *Would you please give me a reference?* Pouvez-vous me fournir des références?; **a reference book** un ouvrage de référence

refill ['riːfɪl] *vb* remplir à nouveau ▷ *She refilled my glass.* Elle a rempli mon verre à nouveau.

refinery [rɪ'faɪnərɪ] *n* raffinerie f

reflect [rɪ'flɛkt] *vb* (light, image) refléter

reflection [rɪ'flɛkʃən] *n* (in mirror) reflet m

reflex ['riːflɛks] *n* réflexe m

reflexive [rɪ'flɛksɪv] *adj* réfléchi ▷ *a reflexive verb* un verbe réfléchi

refresher course [rɪ'frɛʃə-] *n* cours de recyclage m

refreshing [rɪ'frɛʃɪŋ] *adj* rafraîchissant

refreshments [rɪ'frɛʃmənts] *npl* rafraîchissements mpl

refrigerator [rɪ'frɪdʒəreɪtə⁰] *n* réfrigérateur m

refuel [riː'fjuəl] *vb* se ravitailler en carburant ▷ *The plane stops in Montréal to refuel.* L'avion s'arrête à Montréal pour se ravitailler en carburant.

refuge ['rɛfjuːdʒ] *n* refuge m

refugee [rɛfju'dʒiː] *n* réfugié m, réfugiée f

refund [rɪ'fʌnd] *n* remboursement m
▸ *vb* rembourser

refusal [rɪ'fjuːzəl] *n* refus m

refuse [rɪ'fjuːz] *vb* refuser

regain [rɪ'geɪn] *vb*: **to regain consciousness** reprendre connaissance

regard [rɪ'gɑːd] *n*: **Give my regards to your mom.** Transmettez mon bon souvenir à ta mère.; **My parents send their regards.** Vous avez le bonjour de mes parents.; **with regard to** quant à ▷ *with regard to the new rule…* quant au nouveau règlement…
▸ *vb*: **to regard something as** considérer quelque chose comme; **as regards…** concernant…

regarding [rɪ'gɑːdɪŋ] *prep* relatif à (f relative à) ▷ *the laws regarding the export of animals* les lois relatives à l'exportation des animaux; **Regarding your oral presentations,…** Quant à vos présentations orales,…

regardless [rɪ'gɑːdlɪs] *adv* (nevertheless) quand même ▷ *We will go regardless.* Nous irons quand même.; **regardless of the weather** peu importe le temps; **regardless of the consequences** peu importent les conséquences

regiment ['rɛdʒɪmənt] *n* régiment m

region ['riːdʒən] *n* région f

regional ['riːdʒənl] *adj* régional (pl régionaux)

register ['rɛdʒɪstə⁰] *vb* (sign up, enroll) s'inscrire

registered ['rɛdʒɪstəd] *adj*: **a registered letter** une lettre recommandée

registration [rɛdʒɪs'treɪʃən] *n* inscription f ▷ *The deadline for registration is March 6.* La date limite pour l'inscription est le 6 mars.

regret [rɪ'grɛt] *n* regret m; **I have no regrets.** Je ne regrette rien.
▸ *vb* regretter ▷ *Give me the money or you'll regret it!* Donne-moi l'argent, sinon tu vas le regretter!; **to regret doing something**

made no reference to the incident. Il n'a fait aucune allusion à l'incident.

regretter d'avoir fait quelque chose ▷ *I regret saying that.* Je regrette d'avoir dit ça.

regular ['rɛgjulə⁰] *adj* **①** régulier (f régulière) ▷ *at regular intervals* à intervalles réguliers ▷ *a regular verb* un verbe régulier **②** (standard) normal (pl normaux) ▷ *a regular portion of fries* une portion de frites normale

regularly ['rɛgjuləlɪ] *adv* régulièrement ▷ *to exercise regularly* faire de l'exercice régulièrement

regulation [rɛgju'leɪʃən] *n* règlement m

rehearsal [rɪ'hɜːsəl] *n* répétition f

rehearse [rɪ'hɜːs] *vb* répéter

rein [reɪn] *n* rêne f ▷ *the reins* les rênes

reindeer ['reɪndɪə⁰] *n* renne m

reject [rɪ'dʒɛkt] *vb* (idea, suggestion) rejeter ▷ *We rejected that idea right away.* Nous avons immédiatement rejeté cette idée.; **I auditioned for the part but they rejected me.** J'ai auditionné pour le rôle, mais ils m'ont rejeté.

relapse [rɪ'læps] *n* rechute f ▷ *to have a relapse* faire une rechute

related [rɪ'leɪtɪd] *adj* (people) apparenté ▷ *We're related.* Nous sommes apparentés.; **The two events were not related.** Il n'y avait aucun rapport entre les deux événements.

relation [rɪ'leɪʃən] *n* **①** (connection) rapport m ▷ *It has no relation to reality.* Cela n'a aucun rapport avec la réalité.; **in relation to** par rapport à **②** (person) parent m, parente f ▷ *He's a distant relation.* C'est un parent éloigné.

relationship [rɪ'leɪʃənʃɪp] *n* relations fpl ▷ *We have a good relationship.* Nous avons de bonnes relations.; **I'm not in a relationship at the moment.** Je ne sors avec personne en ce moment.

relative ['rɛlətɪv] *n* parent m, parente f ▷ *my close relatives* mes proches parents; **all her relatives** toute sa famille

relatively ['rɛlətɪvlɪ] *adv* relativement

relax [rɪ'læks] *vb* se détendre ▷ *I listen to music to relax.* J'écoute de la musique pour me détendre.; **Relax! Everything's fine.** Ne t'en fais pas! Tout va bien.

relaxation [riːlæk'seɪʃən] *n* détente f ▷ *I don't have much time for relaxation.* Je n'ai pas beaucoup de moments de détente.

relaxed [rɪ'lækst] *adj* détendu

relaxing [rɪ'læksɪŋ] *adj* reposant; **I find cooking relaxing.** Cela me détend de faire la cuisine.

relay ['riːleɪ] *n*: **a relay race** une course de relais

release [rɪ'liːs] *vb* **①** (prisoner) libérer **②** (report, news) divulguer **③** (record, video) sortir
▸ *n* **①** (from prison) libération f ▷ *the release of the hostages* la libération des otages; **the band's latest release** le dernier disque du groupe; **a press release** un communiqué

relevant ['rɛləvənt] *adj* (documents) approprié; **That's not relevant.** Ça n'a aucun rapport.; **to be relevant to something** être en rapport avec quelque chose ▷ *Education should be relevant to real life.* L'enseignement devrait être en rapport avec la réalité.

reliable [rɪˈlaɪəbl] *adj* fiable ▷ *a reliable car* une voiture fiable ▷ *He's not very reliable.* Il n'est pas très fiable.

relief [rɪˈliːf] *n* soulagement *m* ▷ *That's a relief!* Quel soulagement!

relieve [rɪˈliːv] *vb* soulager ▷ *This injection will relieve the pain.* Cette piqûre va soulager la douleur. ▷ *I was relieved to hear...* J'ai été soulagé d'apprendre...

religion [rɪˈlɪdʒən] *n* religion *f*

religious [rɪˈlɪdʒəs] *adj* ❶ religieux (*f* religieuse) ▷ *my religious beliefs* mes croyances religieuses ❷ croyant ▷ *Are you religious?* Tu es croyant?

reluctant [rɪˈlʌktənt] *adj*: **to be reluctant to do something** être peu disposé à faire quelque chose ▷ *They were reluctant to help us.* Ils étaient peu disposés à nous aider.

reluctantly [rɪˈlʌktəntlɪ] *adv* à contrecœur ▷ *She reluctantly accepted.* Elle a accepté à contrecœur.

rely on [rɪˈlaɪ-] *vb* compter sur ▷ *I'm relying on you.* Je compte sur toi.

remain [rɪˈmeɪn] *vb* rester; **to remain silent** garder le silence

remaining [rɪˈmeɪnɪŋ] *adj*: **the remaining ingredients** le reste des ingrédients; **my one remaining friend** le seul ami qui me reste

remains [rɪˈmeɪnz] *npl* restes *mpl* ▷ *the remains of the picnic* les restes du pique-nique ▷ *human remains* des restes humains

remake [ˈriːmeɪk] *n* (*of film*) nouvelle version *f*

remark [rɪˈmɑːk] *n* remarque *f*

remarkable [rɪˈmɑːkəbl] *adj* remarquable

remarkably [rɪˈmɑːkəblɪ] *adv* remarquablement

remarry [riːˈmærɪ] *vb* se remarier ▷ *She remarried three years ago.* Elle s'est remariée il y a trois ans.

rematch [ˈriːmætʃ] *n*: **There will be a rematch on Friday.** Le match sera rejoué vendredi.

remedy [ˈrɛmədɪ] *n* remède *m* ▷ *a good remedy for sore throat* un bon remède contre le mal de gorge

remember [rɪˈmɛmbər] *vb* se souvenir de ▷ *I can't remember his name.* Je ne me souviens pas de son nom. ▷ *I don't remember.* Je ne m'en souviens pas. ▷ *Remember your passport!* N'oublie pas ton passeport! ▷ *Remember to write your name on the form.* N'oubliez pas d'écrire votre nom sur le formulaire.

Remembrance Day [rɪˈmɛmbrəns-] *n* jour *m* du Souvenir ▷ *on Remembrance Day* le jour du Souvenir

remind [rɪˈmaɪnd] *vb* rappeler ▷ *It reminds me of Newfoundland.* Cela me rappelle Terre-Neuve. ▷ *I'll remind you tomorrow.* Je te le rappellerai demain. ▷ *Remind me to speak to the principal.* Rappelle-moi de parler au directeur.

remorse [rɪˈmɔːs] *n* remords *m* ▷ *He showed no remorse.* Il n'a manifesté aucun remords.

remote [rɪˈməut] *adj* isolé ▷ *a remote village* un village isolé

remote control *n* télécommande *f*

remotely [rɪˈməutlɪ] *adv*: **I'm not remotely interested.** Je ne suis absolument pas intéressé.; **Do you think it would be remotely possible?** Pensez-vous que cela serait éventuellement possible?

removable [rɪˈmuːvəbl] *adj* amovible

remove [rɪˈmuːv] *vb* ❶ enlever ▷ *Please remove your bag from my seat.* Est-ce que vous pouvez enlever votre sac de mon siège? ▷ *She removed her coat.* Elle a enlevé son manteau. ❷ (*stain*) faire partir ▷ *Did you remove the stain?* Est-ce que tu as fait partir la tache?

rendezvous [ˈrɔndɪvuː] *n* rendez-vous *m* (*pl* rendez-vous)

renew [rɪˈnjuː] *vb* (*passport, licence*) renouveler

renewable [rɪˈnjuːəbl] *adj* (*energy, resource*) renouvelable

renovate [ˈrɛnəveɪt] *vb* rénover ▷ *The building's been renovated.* Le bâtiment a été rénové.

renowned [rɪˈnaund] *adj* renommé

rent [rɛnt] *n* loyer *m*
▶ *vb* louer ▷ *We rented a car.* Nous avons loué une voiture.

rental [ˈrɛntl] *n* location *f* ▷ *Car rental is included in the price.* Le prix comprend la location d'une voiture.

rental car *n* voiture de location

reorganize [riːˈɔːgənaɪz] *vb* réorganiser

rep [rɛp] *n* (= *representative*) représentant *m*, représentante *f*

repaid [riːˈpeɪd] *vb see* **repay**

repair [rɪˈpɛər] *vb* réparer; **to get something repaired** faire réparer quelque chose ▷ *We got the washing machine repaired.* Nous avons fait réparer la laveuse.
▶ *n* réparation *f*

repay [riːˈpeɪ] *vb* (*money*) rembourser

repayment [riːˈpeɪmənt] *n* remboursement *m*

repeat [rɪˈpiːt] *vb* répéter
▶ *n* répétition *f* ▷ *This lesson was just a repeat of the last one.* Cette leçon n'était qu'une répétition de la précédente.

repeatedly [rɪˈpiːtɪdlɪ] *adv* à plusieurs reprises

repellent [rɪˈpɛlənt] *n*: **insect repellent** l'insectifuge *m*; **mosquito repellent** la lotion antimoustiques

repetitive [rɪˈpɛtɪtɪv] *adj* ❶ (*movement, work*) répétitif (*f* répétitive) ❷ (*writing, speech*) plein de redites

replace [rɪˈpleɪs] *vb* remplacer

replay [ˈriːpleɪ] *n* reproduction *f* ▷ *an instant replay* une reproduction instantanée

replica [ˈrɛplɪkə] *n* réplique *f*

reply [rɪˈplaɪ] *n* réponse *f*
▶ *vb* répondre

report [rɪˈpɔːt] *n* ❶ (*of event*) compte rendu *m* (*pl* comptes rendus) ❷ (*news report*) reportage *m* ▷ *a report in the paper* un reportage dans le journal ❸ (*at school*) bulletin scolaire *m* ▷ *I got a good report this term.* J'ai un bon bulletin scolaire ce trimestre.; **report card** le bulletin scolaire
▶ *vb* ❶ signaler ▷ *I reported the theft to the*

police. J'ai signalé le vol à la police. ❷ se présenter ▷ *Report to reception when you arrive.* Présentez-vous à la réception à votre arrivée.; **to report on something** rendre compte de quelque chose

reporter [rɪ'pɔːtəʳ] n reporter ▷ *She is a reporter.* Elle est reporter.

represent [reprɪ'zent] vb représenter

representative [reprɪ'zentətɪv] adj représentatif (f représentative)

reproduction [riːprə'dʌkʃən] n reproduction f

reptile ['reptaɪl] n reptile m

republic [rɪ'pʌblɪk] n république f

repulsive [rɪ'pʌlsɪv] adj repoussant

reputable ['repjutəbl] adj de bonne réputation

reputation [repju'teɪʃən] n réputation f

request [rɪ'kwest] n demande f
▶ vb demander

require [rɪ'kwaɪəʳ] vb exiger ▷ *The job requires a good knowledge of classical music.* Cet emploi exige une bonne connaissance de la musique classique.; **a required course** une matière obligatoire

requirement [rɪ'kwaɪəmənt] n condition requise f ▷ *to meet the requirements* remplir les conditions requises; **to meet somebody's requirements** (please verify) satisfaire aux exigences de quelqu'un; **entry requirements** (for university) les critères d'entrée

rerun ['riːrʌn] n rediffusion f ▷ *There's nothing but reruns on TV tonight.* Il n'y a que des rediffusions à la télé ce soir.

rescue ['reskjuː] vb sauver
▶ n ❶ sauvetage m ▷ *a rescue operation* une opération de sauvetage ▷ *a rescue team* une équipe de sauvetage ❷ secours ▷ *rescue services* les services de secours; **to come to somebody's rescue** venir au secours de quelqu'un ▷ *He came to my rescue.* Il est venu à mon secours.

research [rɪ'sɜːtʃ] n ❶ (experimental) recherche f ▷ *He's doing research.* Il fait de la recherche. ❷ (theoretical) recherches fpl ▷ *She's doing some research in the library.* Elle fait des recherches à la bibliothèque.

resemblance [rɪ'zembləns] n ressemblance f ▷ *a strong family resemblance* une grande ressemblance de famille

resent [rɪ'zent] vb être contrarié par ▷ *I really resented your criticism.* J'ai été vraiment contrarié par tes critiques.

resentful [rɪ'zentful] adj plein de ressentiment; **to feel resentful towards somebody** en vouloir à quelqu'un

reservation [rezə'veɪʃən] n (booking) réservation f ▷ *I'd like to make a reservation for this evening.* J'aimerais faire une réservation pour ce soir.

reserve [rɪ'zɜːv] n réserve f ▷ *a First Nations reserve* une réserve indienne ▷ *a nature reserve* une réserve naturelle; **oil reserves** des réserves de pétrole; **to hold something in reserve** tenir quelque chose en réserve
▶ vb réserver ▷ *I'd like to reserve a table for*

tomorrow evening. J'aimerais réserver une table pour demain soir.

reserved [rɪ'zɜːvd] adj réservé ▷ *a reserved seat* une place réservée

reservoir ['rezəvwaːʳ] n réservoir m

resident ['rezɪdənt] n résident m, résidente f

residential [rezɪ'denʃəl] adj résidentiel (f résidentielle) ▷ *a residential area* un quartier résidentiel

resign [rɪ'zaɪn] vb donner sa démission

resist [rɪ'zɪst] vb résister à ▷ *to resist authority* résister à l'autorité; **Sorry, I couldn't resist!** Pardon, je n'ai pas pu résister!; **I couldn't resist having another biscuit.** Je n'ai pas pu m'empêcher de prendre encore un biscuit.

resolution [rezə'luːʃən] n résolution f; **Have you made any New Year's resolutions?** Tu as pris de bonnes résolutions pour l'année nouvelle?

resort [rɪ'zɔːt] n centre de villégiature m; **a ski resort** une station de ski; **a seaside resort** une station balnéaire; **as a last resort** en dernier recours

resource [rɪ'sɔːs] n ressource f

resourceful [rɪ'sɔːsful] adj débrouillard

respect [rɪs'pekt] n respect m
▶ vb respecter

respectable [rɪs'pektəbl] adj ❶ respectable ❷ (standard, marks) correct

respectively [rɪs'pektɪvlɪ] adv respectivement

responsibility [rɪsponsɪ'bɪlɪtɪ] n responsabilité f

responsible [rɪs'ponsɪbl] adj ❶ responsable ▷ *He's responsible for booking the tickets.* Il est responsable de la réservation des billets. ▷ *Humans are responsible for the destruction of animal habitats.* Les humains sont responsables de la destruction des habitats des animaux.; **to hold somebody responsible for something** tenir quelqu'un responsable de quelque chose; **Who is responsible for this mess?** Qui a fait ce gâchis?; **She is responsible for our success.** Nous lui devons notre succès.; **It's a responsible job.** C'est un poste à responsabilités. ❷ (mature) sérieux (f sérieuse) ▷ *You should be more responsible.* Tu devrais être un peu plus sérieux.

rest [rest] n ❶ (relaxation) repos m ▷ *five minutes' rest* cinq minutes de repos; **to have a rest** se reposer ▷ *We stopped to have a rest.* Nous nous sommes arrêtés pour nous reposer. ❷ (remainder) reste m ▷ *I'll do the rest.* Je ferai le reste. ▷ *the rest of the money* le reste de l'argent; **the rest of them** les autres ▷ *The rest of them went swimming.* Les autres sont allés nager.
▶ vb ❶ (relax) se reposer ▷ *She's resting in her room.* Elle se repose dans sa chambre. ❷ (not overstrain) ménager ▷ *He has to rest his knee.* Il doit ménager son genou. ❸ (lean) appuyer ▷ *I rested my bike against the wall.* J'ai appuyé mon vélo contre le mur.

restaurant ['restərɔŋ] n restaurant m ▷ *We don't often go to restaurants.* Nous n'allons pas souvent au restaurant.; **a restaurant car** (on train) un wagon-restaurant

restful ['restful] adj reposant

restless ['restlis] adj agité

restoration [restə'reiʃən] n restauration f

restore [ri'stɔː'] vb (building, picture) restaurer

restrict [ris'trikt] vb limiter

rest stop n ⓐ halte routière f ▷ We ate our sandwiches at the rest stop. Nous avons mangé nos sandwichs à la halte routière. ⓑ (with restaurant, gas station) restauroute m

result [ri'zʌlt] n résultat m ▷ my exam results mes résultats d'examen ▷ "What was the result?" — "One-nothing." « Quel a été le résultat? » — « Un à zéro. »; **as a result of** à la suite de
▶ vb: **to result in** entraîner; **to result from** résulter de

resume [ri'zjuːm] vb reprendre ▷ They've resumed work. Ils ont repris le travail.

résumé ['reizjuː.mei] n curriculum vitæ m

retire [ri'taiə'] vb prendre sa retraite ▷ He retired last year. Il a pris sa retraite l'an dernier.

retired [ri'taiəd] adj retraité ▷ She's retired. Elle est retraitée.; **a retired teacher** un professeur à la retraite

retirement [ri'taiəmənt] n retraite f

retrace [riː'treis] vb: **to retrace one's steps** revenir sur ses pas ▷ I retraced my steps. Je suis revenu sur mes pas.

return [ri'təːn] n retour m ▷ after our return à notre retour; **the return trip** le voyage de retour; **a return match** un match retour; **a return ticket** un aller et retour ▷ A return ticket to Winnipeg, please. Un aller et retour pour Winnipeg, s'il vous plaît.; **It costs $500 return.** L'aller et retour coûte cinq cent dollars.; **in return** en échange ▷ ...and I help her in return ...et je l'aide en échange; **in return for** en échange de; **Many happy returns!** Bonne fête!
▶ vb ⓐ (come back) revenir ▷ I've just returned from vacation. Je viens de revenir de vacances.; **to return home** rentrer à la maison ⓑ (go back) retourner ▷ He returned to Inuvik the following year. Il est retourné à Inuvik l'année suivante. ⓒ (give back) rendre ▷ She borrows my things and doesn't return them. Elle m'emprunte mes affaires et ne me les rend pas.

reunion [riː'juːniən] n réunion f

reuse [riː'juːz] vb réutiliser

reveal [ri'viːl] vb révéler

revenge [ri'vendʒ] n vengeance f ▷ in revenge par vengeance; **to take revenge (1)** se venger ▷ They planned to take revenge on him. Ils voulaient se venger de lui. **(2)** (sports) prendre sa revanche ▷ The player who was defeated yesterday will be able to take revenge in tomorrow's game. La joueuse battue hier pourra prendre sa revanche au match de demain.

reverse [ri'vəːs] vb inverser ▷ She reversed the two numbers by mistake. Elle a inversé les deux chiffres par erreur.; **to reverse the charges** (telephone) virer les frais; **a call with charges reversed** un appel à frais virés
▶ n: **in reverse** dans l'ordre inverse ▷ Now do the whole thing in reverse. Maintenant fais tout dans l'ordre inverse.; **This is the reverse of what happened yesterday.** C'est le contraire de ce qui est arrivé hier.
▶ adj inverse ▷ in reverse order dans l'ordre inverse; **in reverse gear** en marche arrière

review [ri'vjuː] n ⓐ révision f ▷ We will have a thorough review before the test. Nous ferons une révision complète avant l'épreuve. ⓑ (of book, film, programme) critique f ▷ The book had good reviews. Ce livre a eu de bonnes critiques.
▶ vb ⓐ réviser ▷ The class reviewed the last chapter together. La classe a révisé le dernier chapitre ensemble. ⓑ faire la critique de ▷ She reviewed the concert for the school newspaper. Elle a fait la critique du concert pour le journal de l'école.

revise [ri'vaiz] vb réviser ▷ They revise the dictionary every five years. On révise le dictionnaire tous les cinq ans. ▷ the revised edition l'édition révisée; **I've revised my opinion.** J'ai changé d'opinion.

revive [ri'vaiv] vb ranimer ▷ The nurses tried to revive him. Les infirmières ont essayé de le ranimer.

revolting [ri'vəultiŋ] adj dégoûtant

revolution [revə'luːʃən] n révolution f; **the Quiet Revolution** la révolution tranquille

revolutionary [revə'luːʃənri] adj révolutionnaire

revolve [ri'vɒlv] vb tourner ▷ The earth revolves around the sun. La terre tourne autour du soleil.

reward [ri'wɔːd] n récompense f; **a rewards card** (at store) une carte de fidélité

rewarding [ri'wɔːdiŋ] adj gratifiant ▷ a rewarding job un travail gratifiant

rewind [riː'waind] vb rembobiner ▷ to rewind a cassette rembobiner une cassette

rheumatism ['ruː.mətizəm] n rhumatisme m

rhinoceros [rai'nɒsərəs] n rhinocéros m

rhubarb ['ruː.bɑː.b] n rhubarbe f ▷ a rhubarb pie une tarte à la rhubarbe

rhyme [raim] vb rimer

rhythm ['riðm] n rythme m

rib [rib] n côte f

ribbon ['ribən] n ruban m

rice [rais] n riz m; **rice pudding** le pudding au riz

rich [ritʃ] adj riche; **the rich** les m riches

rid [rid] vb: **to get rid of** se débarrasser de ▷ I want to get rid of some old clothes. Je veux me débarrasser de vieux vêtements.

ridden ['ridn] vb see ride

ride [raid] n: **to go for a ride (1)** (on horse) monter à cheval **(2)** (on bike) faire un tour en vélo ▷ We went for a bike ride. Nous sommes allés faire un tour en vélo.; **Can you give me a ride to the mall?** Tu peux m'emmener au centre commercial dans ta voiture?; **It's a short bus ride to the town centre.** Ce n'est pas loin du centre-ville en autobus.; **I had three rides on the roller coaster.** J'ai fait trois tours de montagnes russes.
▶ vb (on horse) monter à cheval ▷ I'm learning to ride. J'apprends à monter à cheval.; **to ride a bike** faire du vélo ▷ Can you ride a bike? Est-ce que tu sais faire du vélo?; **We rode into town on the bus.** Nous avons pris l'autobus pour aller en ville.

rider ['raɪdər] n ● (on horse) cavalier m, cavalière f ▷ She's a good rider. C'est une bonne cavalière. ● (on bike) cycliste

ridiculous [rɪ'dɪkjʊləs] adj ridicule ▷ Don't be ridiculous! Ne sois pas ridicule!

riding ['raɪdɪŋ] n ● (for voting) circonscription électorale f ● équitation f; **to go riding** faire de l'équitation; **a riding school** une école d'équitation

rifle ['raɪfl] n fusil ▷ a hunting rifle un fusil de chasse

rig [rɪg] vb truquer ▷ The election was rigged. L'élection a été truquée.

right [raɪt] adj, adv ● (factually correct, suitable) bon (f bonne) ▷ the right answer la bonne réponse ▷ It isn't the right size. Ce n'est pas la bonne taille. ▷ We're on the right train. Nous sommes dans le bon train.; **Is this the right road for Peterborough?** Est-ce que c'est bien la route pour aller à Peterborough?; **to be right (1)** (person) avoir raison ▷ You were right! Tu avais raison! (2) (statement, opinion) être vrai ▷ That's right! C'est vrai! ● (correctly) correctement ▷ Am I pronouncing it right? Est-ce que je prononce ça correctement? ● (accurate) juste ▷ Do you have the right time? Est-ce que vous avez l'heure juste? ● (morally correct) bien ▷ It's not right to behave like that. Ce n'est pas bien d'agir comme ça.; **I think you did the right thing.** Je pense que tu as bien fait. ● (not left) droit m ▷ my right hand ma main droite ● (turn, look) à droite ▷ Turn right at the traffic lights. Tournez à droite aux prochains feux.; **Right! Let's get started.** Bon! On commence.; **right away** tout de suite ▷ I'll do it right away. Je vais le faire tout de suite.; **right side out** à l'endroit ▷ Put your T-shirt with the right side out. Remets ton T-shirt à l'endroit.; **right way up** à l'endroit ▷ This picture is sideways. It must be put the right way up. Ce tableau est de travers. Il faut le remettre à l'endroit. ▷ n ● droit m; **You have no right to do that.** Vous n'avez pas le droit de faire ça. ● (not left) droite f; **on the right** à droite ▷ Our house is on the right. Notre maison est à droite.; **right of way** la priorité ▷ It was our right of way. Nous avions la priorité.

right-hand ['raɪthænd] adj: **the right-hand side** la droite ▷ It's on the right-hand side. C'est à droite.; **the right-hand drawer** le tiroir de droite

right-handed [raɪt'hændɪd] adj droitier (f droitière)

rightly ['raɪtlɪ] adv avec raison ▷ He rightly decided not to go. Il a décidé, avec raison, de ne pas y aller.; **if I remember rightly** si je me souviens bien

rim [rɪm] n ● (edge) bord m ● monture f ▷ glasses with wire rims des lunettes avec une monture métallique

ring [rɪŋ] n ● anneau m (pl anneaux) ▷ a gold ring un anneau en or ● (with stones) bague f ▷ a diamond ring une bague de diamants; **a wedding ring** une alliance ● (circle) cercle m ▷ to stand in a ring se mettre en cercle ● (of bell) coup de sonnette m ▷ I was woken by a ring at the door. J'ai été réveillé par un coup de sonnette. ▷ vb sonner ▷ The phone's ringing. Le téléphone sonne.; **to ring the bell** (doorbell) sonner à la porte ▷ I rang the bell three times. J'ai sonné trois fois à la porte.

rink [rɪŋk] n ● (for ice-skating) patinoire f ● (for roller-skating) piste f

rinse [rɪns] vb rincer

riot ['raɪət] n émeute f ▷ vb faire une émeute

rip [rɪp] vb ● déchirer ▷ I've ripped my jeans. J'ai déchiré mes jeans. ● se déchirer ▷ My skirt ripped. Ma jupe s'est déchirée.

rip off vb ● (cheat) escroquer ▷ The hotel ripped us off. L'hôtel nous a escroqués. ● copier ▷ He ripped off that idea from a movie. Il a copié cette idée d'un film.

rip up vb déchirer ▷ He read the note and then ripped it up. Il a lu le mot, puis l'a déchiré.

ripe [raɪp] adj mûr

rip-off ['rɪpɔf] n: **It's a rip-off!** (informal) C'est du vol!; **Those shoes are just a rip-off of the other brand.** Ces souliers ne sont qu'une imitation de l'autre marque.

rise [raɪz] n (in prices, temperature) hausse f ▷ a sudden rise in temperature une hausse subite de température ▷ vb ● (increase) augmenter ▷ Prices are rising. Les prix augmentent. ● se lever ▷ The sun rises early in June. Le soleil se lève tôt en juin.

riser ['raɪzər] n: **to be an early riser** être matinal

risk [rɪsk] n risque m; **to take risks** prendre des risques; **It's at your own risk.** C'est à vos risques et périls. ▷ vb risquer ▷ You risk getting a fine. Vous risquez de recevoir une amende.; **I wouldn't risk it if I were you.** À votre place, je ne prendrais pas ce risque.

risky ['rɪskɪ] adj risqué

rival ['raɪvl] n rival m (pl rivaux), rivale f ▷ adj ● rival m ▷ a rival gang une bande rivale ● concurrent ▷ a rival company une société concurrente

rivalry ['raɪvlrɪ] n (between towns, schools) rivalité f

river ['rɪvər] n ● rivière f ▷ The river runs alongside the canal. La rivière longe le canal. ● (major) fleuve m ▷ the Fraser River le fleuve Fraser

road [rəʊd] n ● route f ▷ There's a lot of traffic on the roads. Il y a beaucoup de circulation sur les routes. ● (street) rue f ▷ They live across the road. Ils habitent de l'autre côté de la rue.

road map n carte routière f

road rage n rage au volant f

road sign ['rəʊdsaɪn] n panneau de signalisation m (pl panneaux de signalisation)

roast [rəʊst] adj rôti ▷ roast chicken le poulet rôti ▷ roast potatoes les pommes de terre rôties; **roast pork** le rôti de porc; **roast beef** le rôti de bœuf

rob [rɒb] vb: **to rob somebody** voler quelqu'un ▷ I've been robbed. On m'a volé.; **to rob somebody of something** voler quelque chose à quelqu'un ▷ He was robbed of his wallet. Il lui a volé son portefeuille.; **to rob a bank** dévaliser une banque

robber ['rɒbə'] n voleur m; **a bank robber** un cambrioleur de banques

robbery ['rɒbərɪ] n vol m; **a bank robbery** un cambriolage de banque; **armed robbery** le vol à main armée

robin ['rɒbɪn] n rouge-gorge m

robot ['rəʊbɒt] n robot m

rock [rɒk] n ❶ (substance) roche f ▷ They tunnelled through the rock. Ils ont creusé un tunnel dans la roche. ❷ (boulder) rocher m ▷ I sat on a rock. Je me suis assis sur un rocher. ❸ (stone) pierre f ▷ The crowd started to throw rocks. La foule s'est mise à lancer des pierres. ❹ (music) rock m ▷ a rock concert un concert de rock ▷ She's a rock star. C'est une vedette de rock.; **rock and roll** le rock and roll
▶ vb ❶ bercer ▷ He rocked the baby in his arms. Il berçait le bébé dans les bras. ▷ The little boat was gently rocked by the waves. Le petit bateau était doucement bercé par les vagues. ❷ (shake) ébranler ▷ The explosion rocked the building. L'explosion a ébranlé le bâtiment.

rocket ['rɒkɪt] n (firework, spacecraft) fusée f

rock garden n rocaille f

rocking chair ['rɒkɪŋ-] n chaise berçante f

rocky ['rɒkɪ] adj rocheux (f rocheuse); **the Rocky Mountains** les montagnes Rocheuses

rod [rɒd] n (for fishing) canne à pêche

rode [rəʊd] vb see **ride**

rodeo ['rəʊdɪəʊ] n rodéo ▷ The Calgary Stampede is a famous rodeo. Le Stampede de Calgary est un rodéo célèbre.

role [rəʊl] n rôle m

role play n jeu de rôle m (pl jeux de rôles) ▷ to do a role play faire un jeu de rôle

roll [rəʊl] n ❶ rouleau m (pl rouleaux) ▷ a roll of tape un rouleau de ruban adhésif ▷ a roll of toilet paper un rouleau de papier hygiénique; **to be on a roll** avoir le vent en poupe ❷ (bread) petit pain m
▶ vb rouler; **to roll out pastry** abaisser la pâte

roller ['rəʊlə'] n rouleau m (pl rouleaux)

Rollerblade® ['rəʊləbleɪd] n patin à roues alignées m ▷ a pair of Rollerblades une paire de patins à roues alignées

roller coaster [-kəʊstə'] n montagnes fpl russes

roller skates npl patins mpl à roulettes

roller skating n patinage à roulettes m; **to go roller skating** faire du patinage à roulettes

rolling pin ['rəʊlɪŋ-] n rouleau à pâtisserie m

romance [rə'mæns] n ❶ (novels) romans mpl d'amour ▷ I read a lot of romance. Je lis beaucoup de romans d'amour. ❷ (glamour) charme m ▷ the romance of a walk in the moonlight le charme d'une promenade au clair de lune; **a holiday romance** une idylle de vacances

romantic [rə'mæntɪk] adj romantique

roof [ru:f] n toit m

roof rack n porte-bagages de toit m

room [ru:m] n ❶ pièce f ▷ the biggest room in the house la plus grande pièce de la maison ❷ (bedroom) chambre f ▷ She's in her room. Elle est dans sa chambre.; **a single room**

une chambre pour une personne; **a double room** une chambre pour deux personnes ❸ (in school) salle f ▷ the music room la salle de musique ❹ (space) place f ▷ There's no room for that box. Il n'y a pas de place pour cette boîte.

roommate ['ru:mmeɪt] n ❶ (in apartment) colocataire ▷ My sister gets along very well with her roommates. Ma sœur s'entend à merveille avec ses colocataires. ❷ (at boarding school) camarade de chambre

rooster ['ru:stə'] n coq m

root [ru:t] n racine f

root out vb traquer ▷ They are determined to root out corruption. Ils sont déterminés à traquer la corruption.

root beer n bière d'épinette f

rope [rəʊp] n corde f

rope in vb ❶ enrôler ▷ I was roped in to help with the refreshments. J'ai été enrôlé pour servir les rafraîchissements. ❷ se faire embarquer ▷ She was roped into another insane project. Elle s'est encore fait embarquer dans un projet de fous.

rose [rəʊz] vb see **rise**
▶ n (flower) rose f

rot [rɒt] vb pourrir

rotten ['rɒtn] adj ❶ (decayed) pourri ▷ a rotten apple une pomme pourrie; **rotten weather** un temps pourri; **That's a rotten thing to do.** Ce n'est vraiment pas gentil.; **to feel rotten** filer un mauvais coton (informal)

rough [rʌf] adj ❶ (surface) rugueux (f rugueuse) ▷ My hands are rough. J'ai les mains rugueuses. ❷ (game) violent ▷ Hockey's a rough sport. Le hockey est un sport violent. ❸ (area) difficile ▷ It's a rough area. C'est un quartier difficile. ❹ (water) houleux (f houleuse) ▷ The sea was rough. La mer était houleuse. ❺ approximatif (f approximative); **I've got a rough idea.** J'en ai une idée approximative.

roughly ['rʌflɪ] adv à peu près ▷ It weighs roughly 20 kilos. Ça pèse à peu près vingt kilos.

round [raʊnd] adj rond ▷ a round table une table ronde; **all year round** toute l'année
▶ n ❶ (of tournament) manche f ❷ (of boxing match) round m; **a round of golf** une partie de golf

round off vb ❶ (figure) arrondir ▷ Round each figure off to the nearest hundred. Arrondissez chaque chiffre à la centaine près. ❷ terminer ▷ They rounded off the meal with lemon sherbet. Ils ont terminé le repas par du sorbet au citron.

round up vb ❶ (sheep, cattle, suspects) rassembler ❷ (figure) arrondir

round trip n aller m et retour; **a round-trip ticket** un billet aller et retour

route [ru:t] n ❶ itinéraire m ▷ We're planning our route. Nous établissons notre itinéraire. ❷ (of bus) parcours m

routine [ru:'ti:n] n: **my daily routine** ma routine quotidienne

row [n raʊ, vb rəʊ] n ❶ rangée f ▷ a row of houses une rangée de maisons ❷ (of seats) rang m ▷ Our seats are in the front row. Nos places se trouvent au premier rang.; **five times in a row** cinq fois d'affilée
▶ vb ❶ ramer ▷ We took turns rowing. Nous

avons ramé à tour de rôle. ❷ (as sport) faire de l'aviron

rowboat ['rəubəut] n chaloupe f

rowing ['rəuɪŋ] n (sport) aviron m ▷ My hobby is rowing. Je fais de l'aviron.

royal ['rɔɪəl] adj royal (mpl royaux); **the royal family** la famille royale

Royal Canadian Mounted Police n Gendarmerie royale du Canada f

rub [rʌb] vb ❶ (stain) frotter ❷ (part of body) se frotter ▷ Don't rub your eyes! Ne te frotte pas les yeux!; **to rub something out** effacer quelque chose

rubber ['rʌbər] n ❶ caoutchouc m ▷ rubber soles des semelles en caoutchouc ❷ (eraser) gomme à effacer f ▷ Can I borrow your rubber? Je peux emprunter ta gomme à effacer?; **a rubber band** un élastique

rubbish ['rʌbɪʃ] n ❶ (refuse) ordures fpl ▷ When do they collect the rubbish? Quand est-ce qu'ils ramassent les ordures? ❷ (nonsense) niaiserie f ▷ Don't talk rubbish! Ne dis pas de niaiseries!; **That's a load of rubbish!** (informal) C'est vraiment n'importe quoi!

rude [ruːd] adj ❶ (impolite) impoli ▷ It's rude to interrupt. C'est impoli de couper la parole aux gens. ❷ (offensive) grossier (f grossière) ▷ a rude joke une plaisanterie grossière ▷ He was very rude to me. Il a été très grossier avec moi.; **a rude word** un gros mot

rug [rʌg] n tapis m ▷ a Persian rug un tapis persan

ruin ['ruːɪn] n ruine f ▷ the ruins of the castle les ruines du château; **in ruin** en ruine ▶ vb ❶ abîmer ▷ You'll ruin your shoes. Tu vas abîmer tes chaussures. ❷ gâcher ▷ It ruined our holiday. Ça a gâché nos vacances. ❸ (financially) ruiner

rule [ruːl] n ❶ règle f ▷ the rules of grammar les règles de grammaire; **as a rule** en règle générale ❷ (regulation) règlement m ▷ It's against the rules. C'est contre le règlement.

rule out vb (possibility) écarter ▷ I'm not ruling anything out. Je n'écarte aucune possibilité.

ruler ['ruːlər] n règle f ▷ Can I borrow your ruler? Je peux emprunter ta règle?

rummage ['rʌmɪdʒ] vb fouiller ▷ She rummaged in her purse for some change. Elle a fouillé dans son sac à main pour trouver de la monnaie.

rummage sale n vente de charité f

rumour ['ruːmər] n rumeur f ▷ It's just a rumour. Ce n'est qu'une rumeur.

run [rʌn] n ❶ (baseball) coup de circuit m ▷ to hit a home run frapper un coup de circuit ❷ (in nylons) échelle f; **to go for a run** courir ▷ I go for a run every morning. Je cours tous les matins.; **I did a ten-kilometre run.** J'ai couru dix kilomètres.; **on the run** en fuite ▷ The criminals are still on the run. Les criminels sont toujours en fuite.; **in the long run** à long terme ▶ vb ❶ courir ▷ I ran five kilometres. J'ai couru cinq kilomètres.; **to run a marathon** participer à un marathon ❷ (manage) diriger ▷ She runs a large company. Elle dirige une grosse société. ❸ (organize) organiser ▷ They

run music courses in the holidays. Ils organisent des cours de musique pendant les vacances. ❹ (water) couler ▷ Don't leave the tap running. Ne laisse pas couler le robinet.; **to run a bath** faire couler un bain ❺ (by car) conduire ▷ I can run you to the station. Je peux te conduire à la gare.; **to run away** s'enfuir ▷ They ran away before the police came. Ils se sont enfuis avant l'arrivée de la police.; **Time is running out.** Il ne reste plus beaucoup de temps.; **to run out of something** se trouver à court de quelque chose ▷ We ran out of money. Nous nous sommes trouvés à court d'argent.; **to run somebody over** écraser quelqu'un; **to get run over** se faire écraser ▷ Be careful, or you'll get run over! Fais attention, sinon tu vas te faire écraser!

rung [rʌŋ] vb see **ring**

runner ['rʌnər] n coureur m, coureuse f

runner-up [rʌnər'ʌp] n second m, seconde f

running ['rʌnɪŋ] n course f ▷ Running is my favourite sport. La course est mon sport préféré.

running shoe n chaussure de sport f

runway ['rʌnweɪ] n piste f

rural ['ruərəl] adj rural (mpl ruraux)

rush [rʌʃ] n hâte f; **in a rush** à la hâte ▶ vb ❶ (run) se précipiter ▷ Everyone rushed outside. Tout le monde s'est précipité dehors. ❷ (hurry) se dépêcher ▷ There's no need to rush. Ce n'est pas la peine de se dépêcher.

rush hour n heure f de pointe ▷ in the rush hour à l'heure de pointe

rust [rʌst] n rouille f ▶ vb rouiller ▷ Your bike will rust if you leave it out in the rain. Ton vélo va rouiller si tu le laisses sous la pluie.

rusty ['rʌstɪ] adj rouillé ▷ a rusty bike un vélo rouillé ▷ My French is very rusty. Mon français est très rouillé.

ruthless ['ruːθlɪs] adj sans pitié

RV n caravane f

rye [raɪ] n seigle m; **rye bread** le pain de seigle

S

sack [sæk] n sac m; **to get the sack** être mis à la porte ▶ vb: **to sack somebody** mettre quelqu'un à la porte ▷ She was sacked. On l'a mise à la porte.

sacred ['seɪkrɪd] adj sacré

sacrifice ['sækrɪfaɪs] n sacrifice m

sad [sæd] adj triste

saddle ['sædl] n selle f

saddlebag ['sædlbæg] n sacoche f

sadly ['sædlɪ] adv ❶ tristement ▷ "She's gone," he said sadly. « Elle est partie, » a-t-il dit tristement. ❷ (unfortunately) malheureusement ▷ Sadly, it was too late. Malheureusement, il était trop tard.

safe [seɪf] n coffre-fort m (pl coffres-forts) ▷ He put the money in the safe. Il a mis l'argent dans le coffre-fort.
▶ adj ❶ sans danger ▷ Don't worry, it's perfectly safe. Ne vous inquiétez pas, c'est absolument sans danger.; **Is it safe?** Ça n'est pas dangereux? ❷ (machine, ladder) sécuritaire ▷ This car isn't safe. Cette voiture n'est pas sécuritaire. ❸ (out of danger) en sécurité ▷ You're safe now. Vous êtes en sécurité maintenant.; **to feel safe** se sentir en sécurité; **safe sex** le sexe sans risques

safety ['seɪftɪ] n sécurité f; **a safety belt** une ceinture de sécurité; **a safety pin** une épingle de sûreté

Sagittarius [sædʒɪ'tɛərɪəs] n Sagittaire ▷ I'm a Sagittarius. Je suis Sagittaire.

said [sɛd] vb see **say**

sail [seɪl] n voile f
▶ vb ❶ (as skill, sport) faire de la voile ▷ Do you know how to sail? Est-ce que tu sais faire de la voile? ❷ (travel) naviguer ❸ (set off) prendre la mer ▷ The boat sails at eight o'clock. Le bateau prend la mer à huit heures.

sailboat ['seɪlbəʊt] n voilier m

sailing ['seɪlɪŋ] n voile f ▷ Her hobby is sailing. Son passe-temps, c'est la voile.; **to go sailing** faire de la voile; **a sailing ship** un grand voilier

sailor ['seɪlər] n matelot ▷ He's a sailor. Il est matelot.; **I'm not much of a sailor.** Je n'ai pas le pied très marin.

saint [seɪnt] n saint m, sainte f

sake [seɪk] n: **for the sake of** dans l'intérêt de

salad ['sæləd] n salade f ▷ a fruit salad une salade de fruits ▷ a Caesar salad une salade César; **salad dressing** la vinaigrette

salami [sə'lɑːmɪ] n salami m

salary ['sælərɪ] n salaire m

sale [seɪl] n (reductions) soldes mpl ▷ Spring sales will start soon. Les soldes du printemps commenceront bientôt.; **on sale** en vente; **The factory's for sale.** L'usine est en vente.; **"for sale"** « à vendre »

sales assistant [seɪlz-] n vendeur m, vendeuse f ▷ She's a sales assistant. Elle est vendeuse.

sales rep [seɪlz-] n représentant m, représentante f

salmon ['sæmən] n saumon m

salon ['sælɔn] n salon m ▷ a hair salon un salon de coiffure ▷ a beauty salon un salon de beauté

salt [sɔːlt] n sel m

salty ['sɔːltɪ] adj salé

salute [sə'luːt] vb saluer

same [seɪm] adj même ▷ the same model le même modèle ▷ at the same time en même temps; **They're exactly the same.** Ils sont exactement pareils.; **It's not the same.** Ça n'est pas pareil.

sample ['sɑːmpl] n échantillon m

sand [sænd] n sable m

sandal ['sændl] n sandale f ▷ a pair of sandals une paire de sandales

sand castle ['sændkɑːsl] n château de sable m (pl châteaux de sable)

sandwich ['sændwɪtʃ] n sandwich m ▷ a cheese sandwich un sandwich au fromage

sang [sæŋ] vb see **sing**

sanitary napkin ['sænɪtrɪ] n serviette hygiénique f

sank [sæŋk] vb see **sink**

sarcastic [sɑː'kæstɪk] adj sarcastique

sardine [sɑː'diːn] n sardine f

SARS [sɑːz] abbr (= Severe Acute Respiratory Syndrome) SRAS m (= syndrome respiratoire aigu sévère)

Saskatchewan [sə'skætʃəwən] n Saskatchewan f

sat [sæt] vb see **sit**

satellite ['sætəlaɪt] n satellite m ▷ satellite television la télévision par satellite; **a satellite dish** une antenne parabolique

satisfactory [sætɪs'fæktərɪ] adj satisfaisant

satisfied ['sætɪsfaɪd] adj satisfait

Saturday ['sætədɪ] n samedi m ▷ on Saturday samedi ▷ on Saturdays le samedi ▷ every Saturday tous les samedis ▷ last Saturday samedi dernier ▷ next Saturday samedi prochain; **I've got a Saturday job.** Je travaille le samedi.

sauce [sɔːs] n sauce f

saucepan ['sɔːspən] n casserole f

saucer ['sɔːsər] n soucoupe f

sauna ['sɔːnə] n sauna m

sausage ['sɒsɪdʒ] n ❶ saucisse f ❷ (sliced, served cold) saucisson m; **a sausage roll** un friand

save [seɪv] vb ❶ (save up money) mettre de côté ▷ I've saved 50 dollars already. J'ai déjà mis cinquante dollars de côté. ❷ (spend less) économiser ▷ I saved 20 dollars by waiting for the sale. J'ai économisé vingt dollars en attendant les soldes.; **to save time** gagner du temps ▷ We took a taxi to save time. Nous avons pris un taxi pour gagner du temps. ▷ It saved us time. Ça nous a fait gagner du temps. ❸ (rescue) sauver ▷ Luckily, all the passengers were saved. Heureusement, tous les passagers ont été sauvés. ❹ (on computer) sauvegarder ▷ I saved the file onto a diskette. J'ai sauvegardé le fichier sur disquette.; **to save up** mettre de l'argent de côté ▷ I'm saving up for a new bike. Je mets de l'argent de côté pour un nouveau vélo.

savings ['seɪvɪŋz] npl économies fpl ▷ She spent all her savings on a computer. Elle a dépensé toutes ses économies en achetant un ordinateur.

saw [sɔː] vb see **see**
▶ n scie f

sax [sæks] n sax m (informal) ▷ I play the sax. Je joue du sax.

saxophone ['sæksəfəʊn] n saxophone m ▷ I play the saxophone. Je joue du saxophone.

say [seɪ] vb dire ▷ What did he say? Qu'est-ce qu'il a dit? ▷ Did you hear what she said? Tu as entendu ce qu'elle a dit?; **Could you say that**

again? Pourriez-vous répéter, s'il vous plaît?;
That goes without saying. Cela va sans dire.

saying ['seɪɪŋ] n dicton m ▷ It's just a saying.
C'est juste un dicton.

scale [skeɪl] n ① (of map) échelle f ▷ a large-
scale map une carte à grande échelle ② (size,
extent) ampleur f ▷ a disaster on a massive scale
un désastre d'une ampleur incroyable ③ (in
music) gamme f

scales [skeɪlz] npl balance f

scandal ['skændl] n ① (outrage) scandale
m ▷ It caused a scandal. Ça a fait scandale.
② (gossip) commérages mpl ▷ It's just scandal.
Ce ne sont que des commérages.

scar [skɑːʳ] n cicatrice f

scarce [skɛəs] adj limité ▷ scarce resources des
ressources limitées; **Jobs are scarce these
days.** Il y a peu de travail ces temps-ci.

scarcely ['skɛəslɪ] adv à peine ▷ I scarcely knew
her. Je la connaissais à peine.

scare [skɛəʳ] n to scare somebody faire peur
à quelqu'un ▷ He scares me. Il me fait peur.

scarecrow ['skɛəkrəʊ] n épouvantail m

scared [skɛəd] adj: **to be scared** avoir peur ▷ I
was scared stiff. J'avais terriblement peur.; **to be
scared of** avoir peur de ▷ Are you scared of her?
Est-ce que tu as peur d'elle?

scarf [skɑːf] n foulard m

scary ['skɛərɪ] adj effrayant ▷ It was really scary.
C'était vraiment effrayant.

scene [siːn] n ① (place) lieux mpl ▷ The police
were soon on the scene. La police est vite arrivée
sur les lieux. ▷ the scene of the crime les lieux du
crime ② (event, sight) spectacle m ▷ It was an
amazing scene. C'était un spectacle étonnant.;
to make a scene faire une scène

scenery ['siːnərɪ] n (landscape) paysage m

scent [sɛnt] n (perfume) parfum m

schedule ['ʃɛdjuːl] n programme m ▷ a busy
schedule un programme chargé; **on schedule**
comme prévu; **to be behind schedule** avoir
du retard

scheduled flight ['ʃɛdjuːld-] n vol
régulier m

scheme [skiːm] n ① (idea) truc m ▷ a crazy
scheme he dreamed up un truc farfelu qu'il a
inventé ② (project) projet m ▷ the town's
road-widening scheme le projet municipal
d'élargissement des routes

scholarship ['skɒləʃɪp] n bourse f

school [skuːl] n école f; **to go to school** aller à
l'école; **a school of fish** un banc de poissons

schoolbag ['skuːlbæg] n sac d'école m

schoolbook ['skuːlbʊk] n manuel scolaire m

school bus n autobus m scolaire

schoolyard ['skuːljɑːd] n cour d'école f

science ['saɪəns] n science f

science fiction n science-fiction f

scientific [saɪən'tɪfɪk] adj scientifique

scientist ['saɪəntɪst] n ① (academic)
scientifique ② (doing research) chercheur m,
chercheure f

scissors ['sɪzəz] npl ciseaux mpl ▷ a pair of
scissors une paire de ciseaux

scoff [skɒf] vb se moquer ▷ They scoffed at my
idea. Ils se sont moqués de mon idée.

scooter ['skuːtəʳ] n trottinette f

scope [skəʊp] n dimension f ▷ the scope of the
project la dimension du projet

score [skɔːʳ] n pointage m ▷ The score was three
nothing. Le pointage était trois à zéro.
▶ vb (goal, point) marquer ▷ to score a goal
marquer un but; **to score 6 out of 10** obtenir
un pointage de six sur dix; **He shoots, he
scores!** Il lance et compte!

Scorpio ['skɔːpɪəʊ] n Scorpion m ▷ I'm a
Scorpio. Je suis Scorpion.

scrambled eggs ['skræmbld-] npl œufs mpl
brouillés

scrap [skræp] n ① bout m ▷ a scrap of paper un
bout de papier; **They feed their dog scraps.**
Ils nourrissent leur chien avec des restants.
② (fight) bagarre f; **scrap iron** la ferraille
▶ vb (plan) abandonner ▷ The idea was scrapped.
L'idée a été abandonnée.

scrapbook ['skræpbʊk] n album m

scratch [skrætʃ] vb ① gratter ▷ Can you
scratch my back, please? Peux-tu me gratter le
dos, s'il te plaît? ▷ Don't scratch your mosquito
bites. Ne gratte pas tes piqûres de maringouin.
② (oneself) se gratter ▷ He scratched until it bled.
Il s'est gratté jusqu'au sang. ▷ She scratched
her head. Elle s'est gratté la tête.; **The cat
scratched me.** Le chat m'a donné des coups
de griffe.
▶ n (on skin) égratignure f; **to start from
scratch** partir de zéro

scream [skriːm] n hurlement m
▶ vb hurler

screen [skriːn] n écran m

screen saver [-seɪvəʳ] n économiseur m
d'écran

screw [skruː] n vis f

screwdriver ['skruːdraɪvəʳ] n tournevis m

scribble ['skrɪbl] vb griffonner

scrub [skrʌb] vb récurer ▷ to scrub a pan récurer
une casserole

sculpture ['skʌlptʃəʳ] n sculpture f

sea [siː] n mer f

seafood ['siːfuːd] n fruits mpl de mer ▷ I don't
like seafood. Je n'aime pas les fruits de mer.

seagull ['siːgʌl] n mouette f

seal [siːl] n (animal) phoque m
▶ vb (letter) coller

search [sɜːtʃ] vb fouiller ▷ They searched the
woods for her. Ils ont fouillé les bois pour la
trouver.; **to search for something** chercher
quelque chose ▷ He searched for evidence. Il
cherchait des preuves.
▶ n fouille f

search engine n moteur de recherche m

search party n expédition f de secours

seashore ['siːʃɔːʳ] n bord de la mer m ▷ on the
seashore au bord de la mer

seasick ['siːsɪk] adj: **to be seasick** avoir le mal
de mer

season ['siːzn] n saison f ▷ What's your favourite
season? Quelle est ta saison préférée?; **in the
off season** hors saison ▷ It's cheaper to go there
in the off season. C'est moins cher d'y aller hors
saison.; **during the holiday season** en période
de vacances; **out of season** hors saison

▷ *Cherries are out of season.* Les cerises sont hors saison.; **a season ticket** un abonnement

seat [siːt] *n* siège *m*

seat belt *n* ceinture de sécurité *f*

seaweed ['siːwiːd] *n* algues *fpl*

second [sɪˈkɒnd] *adj* deuxième ▷ *on the second page* à la deuxième page; **to come second** (*in race*) arriver deuxième; **the second of March** le deux mars

▶ *n* seconde *f* ▷ *It'll only take a second.* Ça va prendre juste une seconde.

secondary school ['sɛkəndərɪ-] *n* école *f* secondaire

second-class ['sɛkəndˈklɑːs] *adj*: **a second-class citizen** un citoyen de deuxième ordre

second-hand ['sɛkəndˈhænd] *adj* usagé ▷ *a secondhand car* une voiture usagée

secondly ['sɛkəndlɪ] *adv* deuxièmement; **firstly...secondly...** premièrement... deuxièmement... ▷ *Firstly, it's too expensive. Secondly, it wouldn't work anyway.* Premièrement, c'est trop cher. Deuxièmement, ça ne marcherait quand même pas.

secret ['siːkrɪt] *adj* secret *m* (*f* secrète) ▷ *a secret mission* une mission secrète

▶ *n* secret *m* ▷ *It's a secret.* C'est un secret. ▷ *Can you keep a secret?* Tu sais garder un secret?; **in secret** en secret

secretary ['sɛkrətrɪ] *n* secrétaire ▷ *She's a secretary.* Elle est secrétaire.

secretly ['siːkrɪtlɪ] *n* secrètement

section ['sɛkʃən] *n* section *f*

security [sɪˈkjʊərɪtɪ] *n* ❶ sécurité *f* ▷ *a feeling of security* un sentiment de sécurité ▷ *a campaign to improve airport security* une campagne visant à améliorer la sécurité dans les aéroports; **job security** la sécurité de l'emploi; **a security guard** (*on guard*) un garde chargé de la sécurité ❷ (*transporting money*) un convoyeur de fonds

security guard *n* ❶ agent *m* de sécurité, agente *f* de sécurité ❷ (*with armoured car*) garde de voiture blindée

see [siː] *vb* voir ▷ *I can't see.* Je ne vois rien. ▷ *I saw him yesterday.* Je l'ai vu hier. ▷ *Have you seen him?* Est-ce que tu l'as vu?; **See you!** Salut!; **See you soon!** À bientôt!; **to see to something** s'occuper de quelque chose ▷ *The window's stuck again. Can you see to it, please?* La fenêtre est encore coincée. Peux-tu t'en occuper, s'il te plaît?

seed [siːd] *n* graine *f* ▷ *sunflower seeds* des graines de tournesol

seek [siːk] *vb* chercher; **to seek help** chercher de l'aide

seem [siːm] *vb* avoir l'air ▷ *She seems tired.* Elle a l'air fatiguée. ▷ *The store seemed to be closed.* Le magasin avait l'air d'être fermé.; **That seems like a good idea.** Ce n'est pas une mauvaise idée.; **It seems that...** Il paraît que... ▷ *It seems they're getting married.* Il paraît qu'ils vont se marier.; **There seems to be a problem.** Il semble y avoir un problème.

seen [siːn] *vb* see **see**

seesaw ['siːsɔː] *n* balançoire à bascule *f*

see-through ['siːθruː] *adj* transparent

seldom ['sɛldəm] *adv* rarement

select [sɪˈlɛkt] *vb* sélectionner

selection [sɪˈlɛkʃən] *n* sélection *f*

self-assured [sɛlfəˈʃʊəd] *adj* sûr de soi ▷ *She's very self-assured.* Elle est très sûre d'elle.

self-centred [sɛlfˈsɛntəd] *adj* égocentrique

self-confidence [sɛlfˈkɒnfɪdns] *n* confiance en soi *f* ▷ *He hasn't got much self-confidence.* Il n'a pas très confiance en lui.

self-conscious [sɛlfˈkɒnʃəs] *adj*: **to be self-conscious** (1) (*embarrassed*) être mal à l'aise ▷ *She was really self-conscious at first.* Elle était vraiment mal à l'aise au début. (2) (*shy*) manquer d'assurance ▷ *He's always been rather self-conscious.* Il a toujours manqué un peu d'assurance.

self-control [sɛlfkənˈtrəʊl] *n* sang-froid *m*

self-defence [sɛlfdɪˈfɛns] *n* autodéfense *f* ▷ *self-defence classes* les cours d'autodéfense; **She killed the dog in self-defence.** Elle a tué le chien en légitime défense.

self-discipline [sɛlfˈdɪsɪplɪn] *n* autodiscipline *f*

self-disciplined [sɛlfˈdɪsɪplɪnd] *adj*: **He is self-disciplined.** Il fait preuve d'autodiscipline.

self-employed [sɛlfɪmˈplɔɪd] *adj*: **to be self-employed** travailler à son compte ▷ *He's self-employed.* Il travaille à son compte.; **the self-employed** les travailleurs autonomes

selfish ['sɛlfɪʃ] *adj* égoïste ▷ *Don't be so selfish.* Ne sois pas si égoïste.

self-respect [sɛlfrɪsˈpɛkt] *n* amour-propre *m*

self-serve [sɛlfˈsəːv] *n* libre-service *m* ▷ *This gas station is a self-serve.* Cette station-service est un libre-service.

sell [sɛl] *vb* vendre ▷ *She sold it to me.* Elle me l'a vendu.; **to sell off** liquider; **The tickets are all sold out.** Il ne reste plus de billets.; **The tickets sold out in three hours.** Tous les billets ont été vendus en trois heures.

sell out *vb* ❶ se vendre ▷ *The tickets sold out in three hours.* Les billets se sont tous vendus en trois heures. ❷ (*compromise one's standards*) se prostituer ▷ *The artist refused to sell out.* L'artiste a refusé de se prostituer.

selling price ['sɛlɪŋ-] *n* prix de vente *m*

semicircle ['sɛmɪsɜːkl] *n* demi-cercle *m*

semicolon [sɛmɪˈkəʊlən] *n* point-virgule *m*

semi-detached house [sɛmɪdɪˈtætʃt-] *n* maison jumelée *f* ▷ *We live in a semi-detached house.* Nous habitons dans une maison jumelée.

semi-final [sɛmɪˈfaɪnl] *n* demi-finale *f*

Senate ['sɛnɪt] *n* Sénat *m*

send [sɛnd] *vb* envoyer ▷ *She sent me a birthday card.* Elle m'a envoyé une carte de fête.; **to send back** renvoyer; **to send away for something** (*free*) se faire envoyer quelque chose ▷ *I've sent away for a brochure.* Je me suis fait envoyer une brochure.; **to send out** envoyer ▷ *My mom sent me out to buy milk.* Ma mère m'a envoyé acheter du lait.

sender ['sɛndər] *n* expéditeur *m*, expéditrice *f*

senior ['siːnɪər] *adj* principal ▷ *senior accountant* la comptable principale ▷ *senior architect* l'architecte principal; **senior citizen** la personne âgée; **senior management** la haute direction; **senior manager** le cadre supérieur

sensational [sɛn'seɪʃənl] adj sensationnel (f sensationnelle)

sense [sɛns] n **❶** (wisdom) bon sens m ▷ Use your common sense! Un peu de bon sens, voyons!; **It makes sense.** C'est logique.; **It doesn't make sense.** Ça n'a pas de sens. **❷** (faculty) sens m ▷ the five senses les cinq sens; **the sense of touch** le toucher; **the sense of smell** l'odorat m; **the sixth sense** le sixième sens; **sense of humour** le sens de l'humour ▷ He has no sense of humour. Il n'a aucun sens de l'humour.
▶ vb sentir ▷ I sensed that she was afraid. J'ai senti qu'elle avait peur.

senseless ['sɛnslɪs] adj insensé

sensible ['sɛnsɪbl] adj raisonnable ▷ Be sensible! Sois raisonnable!

sensitive ['sɛnsɪtɪv] adj sensible ▷ She's very sensitive. Elle est très sensible.

sensuous ['sɛnsjuəs] adj sensuel (f sensuelle)

sent [sɛnt] vb see **send**

sentence ['sɛntəns] n **❶** phrase f ▷ What does this sentence mean? Que veut dire cette phrase? **❷** (judgment) condamnation f **❸** (punishment) peine f ▷ the death sentence la peine de mort; **He got a life sentence.** Il a été condamné à la réclusion à perpétuité.
▶ vb: **to sentence somebody to life imprisonment** condamner quelqu'un à la réclusion à perpétuité; **to sentence somebody to death** condamner quelqu'un à mort

sentimental [sɛntɪ'mɛntl] adj sentimental (mpl sentimentaux)

separate ['sɛprət] adj séparé ▷ I wrote it on a separate sheet. Je l'ai écrit sur une feuille séparée.; **The children have separate rooms.** Les enfants ont chacun leur chambre.; **on separate occasions** à différentes reprises
▶ vb **❶** séparer **❷** (married couple) se séparer

separately ['sɛprɪtlɪ] adv séparément

separation [sɛpə'reɪʃən] n séparation f

separatism ['sɛprətɪzəm] n séparatisme m

separatist ['sɛprətɪst] n séparatiste

September [sɛp'tɛmbə'] n septembre m; **in September** en septembre

sequel ['si:kwl] n (book, film) suite f

sequence ['si:kwəns] n **❶** ordre m; **in sequence** en ordre; **a sequence of events** une succession d'événements **❷** (in film) séquence f

series ['sɪərɪz] n **❶** série f ▷ a TV series une série télévisée **❷** (of numbers, events) suite f

serious ['sɪərɪəs] adj **❶** sérieux (f sérieuse) ▷ You look very serious. Tu as l'air sérieux.; **Are you serious?** Sérieusement? **❷** (illness, mistake) grave

seriously ['sɪərɪəslɪ] adv sérieusement ▷ No, but seriously... Non, mais sérieusement...; **to take somebody seriously** prendre quelqu'un au sérieux; **seriously injured** gravement blessé; **Seriously?** Vraiment?

sermon ['sə:mən] n sermon m

serve [sə:v] vb **❶** servir ▷ Dinner is served. Le

souper est servi. ▷ It's his turn to serve. C'est à son tour de servir. **❷** (prison sentence) purger; **to serve time** être en prison; **It serves you right.** C'est bien fait pour toi.
▶ n (tennis) service m; **It's your serve.** C'est à toi de servir.

server [sə:və'] n (computing) serveur m

service ['sə:vɪs] vb (car, washing machine) réviser
▶ n **❶** service m ▷ Service is included. Le service est compris. **❷** (of car) révision f; **a memorial service** un service commémoratif; **a funeral service** un service funèbre

service area n aire f de service

service charge n service ▷ There's no service charge. Le service est compris.

service station n station-service f (pl stations-service)

serviette [sə:vɪ'ɛt] n serviette f

session ['sɛʃən] n séance f

set [sɛt] n **❶** jeu m (pl jeux) ▷ a set of keys un jeu de clés ▷ a chess set un jeu d'échecs; **a set of drums** une batterie; **a train set** un train électrique **❷** (in tennis) manche f
▶ vb **❶** mettre ▷ I set the alarm for 7 o'clock. J'ai mis le réveil à sept heures. ▷ Set the plants on the floor. Mets les plantes sur le plancher. **❷** (record) établir ▷ The world record was set last year. Le record du monde a été établi l'année dernière. **❸** (sun) se coucher ▷ The sun was setting. Le soleil se couchait.; **The film is set in Manitoba.** L'action du film se déroule au Manitoba.; **to set off** partir ▷ We set off for Tadoussac at 9 o'clock. Nous sommes partis pour Tadoussac à neuf heures.; **to set out** partir ▷ We set out for Saint John at 9 o'clock. Nous sommes partis pour Saint John à neuf heures.; **to set sail** prendre la mer; **to set the table** mettre la table

settle ['sɛtl] vb **❶** (problem) résoudre **❷** (argument, account) régler; **to settle down** (calm down) se calmer; **Settle down!** Du calme!; **to settle in** s'installer; **to settle on something** opter pour quelque chose

seven ['sɛvn] num sept ▷ She's seven. Elle a sept ans.

seventeen [sɛvn'ti:n] num dix-sept ▷ He's seventeen. Il a dix-sept ans.

seventeenth [sɛvn'ti:nθ] adj dix-septième ▷ his seventeenth birthday son dix-septième anniversaire de naissance ▷ the seventeenth floor le dix-septième étage; **the seventeenth of August** le dix-sept août

seventh ['sɛvnθ] adj septième ▷ the seventh floor le septième étage; **the seventh of August** le sept août

seventy ['sɛvntɪ] num soixante-dix

several ['sɛvrəl] adj, pron plusieurs ▷ several schools plusieurs écoles; **several of them** plusieurs ▷ I've seen several of them. J'en ai vu plusieurs.

sew [səʊ] vb coudre; **to sew up** (tear) recoudre

sewing ['səʊɪŋ] n couture f ▷ I like sewing. J'aime faire de la couture.; **a sewing machine** une machine à coudre

sewn [səʊn] vb see **sew**

sex [sɛks] n sexe m; **to have sex with somebody** coucher avec quelqu'un; **sex education** l'éducation f sexuelle

sexism ['sɛksɪzəm] n sexisme m

sexist ['sɛksɪst] adj sexiste

sexual ['sɛksjuəl] adj sexuel (f sexuelle) ▷ *sexual discrimination* la discrimination sexuelle ▷ *sexual harassment* le harcèlement sexuel

sexuality [sɛksjuˈælɪtɪ] n sexualité f

sexy ['sɛksɪ] adj sexy (f+pl sexy)

shabby ['ʃæbɪ] adj miteux (f miteuse)

shade [ʃeɪd] n ❶ ombre f, **in the shade** à l'ombre ▷ *It was 35 degrees in the shade.* Il faisait trente-cinq à l'ombre. ❷ (colour) nuance f ▷ *a shade of blue* une nuance de bleu

shadow ['ʃædəu] n ombre f

shake ['ʃeɪk] vb ❶ secouer ▷ *She shook the rug.* Elle a secoué le tapis. ❷ (tremble) trembler ▷ *He was shaking with cold.* Il tremblait de froid.; **to shake one's head** (in refusal) faire non de la tête; **to shake hands with somebody** serrer la main à quelqu'un ▷ *They shook hands.* Ils se sont serré la main.

shaken ['ʃeɪkən] adj secoué ▷ *I was feeling a bit shaken.* J'étais un peu secoué.

shaky ['ʃeɪkɪ] adj (hand, voice) tremblant

shall [ʃæl] vb: **Shall I shut the window?** Vous voulez que je ferme la fenêtre?; **Shall we ask them to come with us?** Si on leur demandait de venir avec nous?

shallow ['ʃæləu] adj (water, pool) peu profond

shambles ['ʃæmblz] n pagaille f ▷ *It's a complete shambles.* C'est la pagaille complète.

shame [ʃeɪm] n honte f ▷ *The shame of it!* Quelle honte!; **What a shame!** Quel dommage!; **It's a shame that...** c'est dommage que... ▷ *It's a shame he isn't here.* C'est dommage qu'il ne soit pas ici.

shampoo [ʃæmˈpuː] n shampooing m ▷ *a bottle of shampoo* une bouteille de shampooing

shape [ʃeɪp] n forme f

share [ʃɛəʳ] n ❶ part f ▷ *Everybody pays their share.* Tout le monde paie sa part. ❷ (in company) action f ▷ *They have shares in several Canadian companies.* Ils ont des actions de plusieurs compagnies canadiennes.
▶ vb partager ▷ *to share a room with somebody* partager une chambre avec quelqu'un; **to share out** distribuer ▷ *They shared the sweets out among the children.* Ils ont distribué les bonbons aux enfants.

shark [ʃɑːk] n requin m

sharp [ʃɑːp] adj ❶ (razor, knife) tranchant ❷ (spike, point) pointu ❸ (clever) intelligent ▷ *She's very sharp.* Elle est très intelligente. ❹ (elegant) chic (f chic) ▷ *Those boots are really sharp!* Ces bottes sont vraiment chics!; **at two o'clock sharp** à deux heures pile

shave [ʃeɪv] vb (oneself) se raser; **to shave one's legs** se raser les jambes

shaver ['ʃeɪvəʳ] n: **an electric shaver** un rasoir électrique

shaving cream ['ʃeɪvɪŋ-] n crème à raser f

shaving foam ['ʃeɪvɪŋfəum] n mousse à raser f

she [ʃiː] pron elle ▷ *She's very nice.* Elle est très gentille.

shed [ʃɛd] n remise f

she'd [ʃiːd]; = **she had**; **she would**

sheep [ʃiːp] n mouton m

sheer [ʃɪəʳ] adj pur ▷ *It's sheer greed.* C'est de l'avidité pure.

sheet [ʃiːt] n ❶ (on bed) drap m; **a sheet of paper** une feuille de papier

shelf [ʃɛlf] n ❶ (in house) étagère f ❷ (in store) rayon m

shell [ʃɛl] n ❶ (on beach) coquillage m ❷ (of egg, nut) coquille f ❸ (explosive) obus m

she'll [ʃiːl]; = **she will**

shellfish ['ʃɛlfɪʃ] n fruits m de mer

shell suit n survêtement m

shelter ['ʃɛltəʳ] n: **to take shelter** se mettre à l'abri; **a bus shelter** un arrêt d'autobus

shelves ['ʃɛlvz] npl see **shelf**

shepherd ['ʃɛpəd] n berger m

sheriff ['ʃɛrɪf] n shérif m

she's [ʃiːz]; = **she is**; **she has**

shield [ʃiːld] n bouclier m

shift [ʃɪft] n poste m ▷ *Her shift starts at 8 o'clock.* Son poste commence à huit heures. ▷ *the night shift* le poste de nuit
▶ vb ❶ changer ▷ *His position on the issue continues to shift.* Sa position sur cette question continue de changer. ▷ *The meaning of this word has shifted.* Le sens de ce mot a changé. ❷ (wind) tourner ▷ *The wind has shifted a little.* Le vent a tourné un peu. ❸ (eyes, gaze) détourner ▷ *He shifted his gaze so as not to embarrass her.* Il a détourné son regard pour ne pas l'embarrasser. ❹ (gears) passer ▷ *She shifted into reverse.* Elle a passé la marche arrière. ▷ *to shift into second* passer en seconde; **to shift gears** changer de vitesse

shifty ['ʃɪftɪ] adj ❶ (person) louche ▷ *He looked shifty.* Il avait l'air louche. ❷ (eyes) fuyant

shin [ʃɪn] n tibia m

shine [ʃaɪn] vb briller ▷ *The sun was shining.* Le soleil brillait.

shiny ['ʃaɪnɪ] adj brillant

ship [ʃɪp] n ❶ bateau m (pl bateaux) ❷ (ocean-going) navire m

shipbuilding ['ʃɪpbɪldɪŋ] n construction navale f

shipwreck ['ʃɪprɛk] n naufrage m

shipwrecked ['ʃɪprɛkt] adj: **to be shipwrecked** faire naufrage

shipyard ['ʃɪpjɑːd] n chantier naval m

shirt [ʃəːt] n ❶ (man's) chemise f ❷ (woman's) chemisier m

shiver ['ʃɪvəʳ] vb frissonner

shock [ʃɔk] n choc m; **to get a shock** (1) (surprise) avoir un choc (2) (electric) recevoir un choc électrique; **an electric shock** un choc électrique
▶ vb ❶ (upset) bouleverser ▷ *They were shocked by the tragedy.* Ils ont été bouleversés par la tragédie. ❷ (scandalize) choquer ▷ *I was rather shocked by her attitude.* J'ai été assez choqué par son attitude.

shocking ['ʃɔkɪŋ] adj ❶ (scandalous) choquant ▷ *It's shocking!* C'est choquant! ❷ (upsetting) bouleversant ▷ *That's a shocking piece of news.* C'est une nouvelle bouleversante. ❸ (*appalling*) épouvantable ▷ *a shocking waste* un gaspillage épouvantable

shoe [ʃuː] n ❶ soulier m ❷ chaussure f

shoelace ['ʃuːleɪs] n lacet m

shoe polish n cirage m

shoe store n magasin de chaussures m

shone [ʃɒn] vb see **shine**

shook [ʃʊk] vb see **shake**

shoot [ʃuːt] vb ❶ (*kill*) abattre ▷ *He was shot by a sniper.* Il a été abattu par un tireur d'élite. ❷ (*execute*) fusiller ▷ *He was shot at dawn.* Il a été fusillé à l'aube. ❸ (*gun*) tirer ▷ *Don't shoot!* Ne tirez pas!; **to shoot at somebody** tirer sur quelqu'un; **She was shot in the leg.** Elle a reçu une balle dans la jambe.; **to shoot an arrow** envoyer une flèche ❹ (*film*) tourner ▷ *The film was shot in Toronto.* Le film a été tourné à Toronto.

shooting ['ʃuːtɪŋ] n coups mpl de feu ▷ *They heard shooting.* Ils ont entendu des coups de feu.; **a shooting** une fusillade; **a drive-by shooting** un mitraillage à partir d'un véhicule

shop [ʃɒp] n ❶ boutique f ▷ *a gift shop* une boutique de cadeaux ▷ *a souvenir shop* une boutique de souvenirs; **a doughnut shop** une beignerie ❷ (*workshop*) atelier m ▷ *He has a shop in his basement.* Il a un atelier au sous-sol. ❸ (*school subject*) menuiserie f ▷ *I made a bookshelf in shop class.* J'ai fait une étagère en menuiserie.

shoplifting ['ʃɒplɪftɪŋ] n vol à l'étalage m

shopping ['ʃɒpɪŋ] n ❶ (*purchases*) achats mpl ▷ *Can you get the shopping from the car?* Tu peux aller chercher mes achats dans la voiture? ❷ magasinage m ▷ *I love shopping.* J'adore faire du magasinage.; **to go shopping (1)** (*for food*) faire l'épicerie **(2)** (*for pleasure*) faire du magasinage; **a shopping bag** un sac à provisions; **a shopping centre** un centre commercial

shore [ʃɔːr] n rivage m; **on shore** à terre

short [ʃɔːt] adj ❶ court ▷ *a short skirt* une jupe courte ▷ *short hair* les cheveux courts; **too short** trop court ▷ *It was a great holiday, but too short.* C'étaient des vacances super, mais trop courtes. ❷ (*person, period of time*) petit ▷ *She's quite short.* Elle est assez petite. ▷ *a short break* une petite pause ▷ *a short walk* une petite promenade; **to be short of something** être à court de quelque chose ▷ *I'm short of money.* Je suis à court d'argent.; **at short notice** au dernier moment; **In short, the answer's no.** Bref, la réponse est non.

shortage ['ʃɔːtɪdʒ] n pénurie f ▷ *a water shortage* une pénurie d'eau

shortcut ['ʃɔːtkʌt] n raccourci m ▷ *I took a shortcut.* J'ai pris un raccourci.

shortly ['ʃɔːtlɪ] adv bientôt

shorts [ʃɔːts] npl short m; **a pair of shorts** un short

short-sighted [ʃɔːt'saɪtɪd] adj myope

short story n nouvelle f

shot [ʃɒt] vb see **shoot**
▶ n ❶ (*gunshot*) coup de feu m (pl coups de feu) ❷ (*photo*) photo f ▷ *a shot of the Château Frontenac* une photo du château Frontenac ❸ (*vaccination*) vaccin m ▷ *flu shot* le vaccin contre la grippe

should [ʃʊd] vb devoir ▷ *You should take more exercise.* Vous devriez faire plus d'exercice. ▷ *He should be there by now.* Il devrait être arrivé maintenant. ▷ *That shouldn't be too hard.* Ça ne devrait pas être trop difficile.; **should have** avoir dû ▷ *I should have told you before.* J'aurais dû te le dire avant.; **I should be so lucky!** Ça serait trop beau!

shoulder ['ʃəʊldər] n épaule f; **a shoulder bag** un sac à bandoulière

shouldn't ['ʃʊdnt] = **should not**

shout [ʃaʊt] vb crier ▷ *Don't shout!* Ne criez pas! ▷ *"Go away!" he shouted.* «Allez-vous-en!» a-t-il crié.
▶ n cri m

shovel ['ʃʌvl] n pelle f
▶ vb pelleter ▷ *After the snowstorm I shovelled the driveway.* Après la tempête de neige, j'ai pelleté l'entrée. ▷ *We shovelled the dirt into the hole.* Nous avons pelleté la terre dans le trou.

show [ʃəʊ] n ❶ (*performance*) spectacle m ❷ (*TV*) émission f ❸ (*exhibition*) salon m
▶ vb ❶ montrer; **to show somebody something** montrer quelque chose à quelqu'un ▷ *Have I shown you my new DVD?* Est-ce que je t'ai montré mon nouveau DVD? ▷ *She showed me how to set up a blog.* Elle m'a montré comment monter un blogue. ❷ faire preuve de ▷ *She showed great courage.* Elle a fait preuve de beaucoup de courage. ❸ (*movie*) projeter ▷ *What's showing at the movie theatre tonight?* Qu'est-ce qui est projeté au cinéma ce soir?; **it shows.** Ça se voit. ▷ *"I've never been riding before." — "It shows."* «Je n'ai jamais fait de cheval.» — «Ça se voit.»; **to show off** se vanter (*informal*); **to show up (1)** (*arrive*) se pointer ▷ *He showed up late as usual.* Il s'est pointé en retard comme d'habitude. **(2)** (*be noticeable*) ▷ *The yellow font doesn't show up well on the screen.* Les caractères jaunes ne se voient pas sur l'écran.; **to show somebody around** faire faire le tour à quelqu'un ▷ *She showed us around.* Elle nous a fait faire le tour.; **Your slip is showing.** On voit ton jupon.

shower ['ʃaʊər] n ❶ douche f; **to have a shower** prendre une douche ❷ (*of rain*) averse f

showing ['ʃəʊɪŋ] n (*of film*) projection f

shown [ʃəʊn] vb see **show**

show-off ['ʃəʊɒf] n vantard m, vantarde f

shrank [ʃræŋk] vb see **shrink**

shriek [ʃriːk] vb hurler

shrimp [ʃrɪmp] n crevette f ▷ *I like shrimp.* J'aime les crevettes.

shrink [ʃrɪŋk] vb (*clothes, fabric*) rétrécir

shrug [ʃrʌg] vb **to shrug one's shoulders** hausser les épaules

shrunk [ʃrʌŋk] vb see **shrink**

shudder ['ʃʌdər] vb frissonner

shuffle ['ʃʌfl] vb: **to shuffle the cards** battre les cartes; **I put the CD on shuffle mode.** J'ai mis le CD en lecture aléatoire.

shut [ʃʌt] vb fermer ▷ *Shut the door.* Ferme la porte. ▷ *The door doesn't shut properly.* La porte ferme mal.; ▷ *The door slammed shut.* La porte a claqué.; **to shut down** fermer ▷ *The movie theatre shut down last year.* Le cinéma a fermé l'année dernière. ▷ *Did you shut down the computer?* As-tu fermé l'ordinateur?

shutters [ˈʃʌtəz] n volets mpl

shuttle [ˈʃʌtl] n navette f

shuttlecock [ˈʃʌtlkɔk] n (*badminton*) volant m

shy [ʃaɪ] adj timide

sick [sɪk] adj **❶** (*ill*) malade ▷ *He was sick for four days.* Il a été malade pendant quatre jours. **❷** (*joke, humour*) de mauvais goût ▷ *That's really sick!* C'est vraiment de mauvais goût!; **to be sick** (*vomit*) vomir ▷ *I feel sick.* J'ai envie de vomir.; **to be sick of something** en avoir assez de quelque chose ▷ *I'm sick of your jokes.* J'en ai assez de tes plaisanteries.

sickening [ˈsɪknɪŋ] adj écœurant

sickness [ˈsɪknɪs] n maladie f

sick note n **❶** (*from parents*) mot d'absence m **❷** (*from doctor*) certificat médical m

side [saɪd] n **❶** (*of object, building, car*) côté m ▷ *She was driving on the wrong side of the road.* Elle roulait du mauvais côté de la route. ▷ *She had the telephone by her side.* Le téléphone était à côté d'elle. **❷** (*of pool, river, road*) bord m ▷ *by the side of the lake* au bord du lac **❸** (*of hill*) flanc m; **He's on my side.** (1) (*on my team*) Il est dans mon équipe. (2) (*supporting me*) Il est de mon côté.; **side by side** côte à côte; **the side entrance** l'entrée latérale; **to take sides** ▷ *She always takes his side.* Elle prend toujours son parti.

side-effect [ˈsaɪdɪfɛkt] n effet m secondaire

side street n petite rue transversale f

sidewalk [ˈsaɪdwɔːk] n trottoir m

sideways [ˈsaɪdweɪz] adv **❶** (*look, be facing*) de côté **❷** (*move*) de travers

sieve [sɪv] n passoire f

sigh [saɪ] n soupir m
▷ vb soupirer

sight [saɪt] n **❶** vue f ▷ *Stay within sight of the group.* Restez à portée de vue du groupe. ▷ *At the sight of the police, he took off.* À la vue de la police, il s'est enfui.; **to know somebody by sight** connaître quelqu'un de vue **❷** spectacle ▷ *It was an amazing sight.* C'était un spectacle époustouflant.; **in sight** hors de vue; **out of sight** hors de vue; **the sights** (*tourist spots*) les attractions touristiques; **to see the sights of London** visiter Londres

sightseeing [ˈsaɪtsiːɪŋ] n tourisme m; **to go sightseeing** faire du tourisme

sign [saɪn] n **❶** (*notice*) panneau m (pl panneaux) ▷ *There was a big sign saying "private".* Il y avait un grand panneau indiquant « privé ».; **a road sign** un panneau routier **❷** (*gesture, indication*) signe m ▷ *There's no sign of improvement.* Il n'y a aucun signe d'amélioration.; **What sign are you?** (*star sign*) Tu es de quel signe?
▷ vb signer; **to sign up** s'inscrire ▷ *She signed up for volleyball.* Elle s'est inscrite au volley-ball.

signal [ˈsɪgnl] n signal m (pl signaux)

▷ vb: **to signal to somebody** faire un signe à quelqu'un

signature [ˈsɪgnətʃəʳ] n signature f

significance [sɪgˈnɪfɪkəns] n importance f

significant [sɪgˈnɪfɪkənt] adj important

sign language n langage des signes m

signpost [ˈsaɪnpəʊst] n poteau indicateur m

Sikh [siːk] n sikh m, sikhe f
▷ adj sikh m

silence [ˈsaɪlns] n silence m

silent [ˈsaɪlnt] adj silencieux (f silencieuse)

silk [sɪlk] n soie f
▷ adj en soie ▷ *a silk scarf* un foulard en soie

silky [ˈsɪlkɪ] adj soyeux (f soyeuse)

silly [ˈsɪlɪ] adj bête

silver [ˈsɪlvəʳ] n argent m ▷ *a silver medal* une médaille d'argent; **a silver van** une fourgonnette de couleur argent

similar [ˈsɪmɪləʳ] adj semblable; **similar to** semblable à

simple [ˈsɪmpl] adj simple m ▷ *It's very simple.* C'est très simple.

simply [ˈsɪmplɪ] adv simplement ▷ *It's simply not possible.* Ça n'est tout simplement pas possible.

simultaneous [sɪməlˈteɪnɪəs] adj simultané

sin [sɪn] n péché m
▷ vb pécher

since [sɪns] prep, adv, conj **❶** depuis ▷ *since yesterday* depuis hier ▷ *since then* depuis ce moment-là ▷ *I haven't seen him since.* Je ne l'ai pas vu depuis.; **ever since** depuis ce moment-là **❷** depuis que ▷ *I haven't seen her since she left.* Je ne l'ai pas vue depuis qu'elle est partie. **❸** (*because*) puisque ▷ *Since you're tired, let's stay at home.* Puisque tu es fatigué, restons à la maison.

sincere [sɪnˈsɪəʳ] adj sincère

sincerely [sɪnˈsɪəlɪ] adv: **Yours sincerely…** (1) (*in business letter*) Veuillez agréer l'expression de mes sentiments les meilleurs… (2) (*in personal letter*) Cordialement…

sing [sɪŋ] vb chanter ▷ *He sang out of tune.* Il chantait faux. ▷ *Have you ever sung this tune before?* Vous avez déjà chanté cet air-là?

singer [ˈsɪŋəʳ] n chanteur m, chanteuse f

singing [ˈsɪŋɪŋ] n chant m ▷ *singing lessons* des cours de chant

single [ˈsɪŋgl] adj (*unmarried*) célibataire; **a single room** une chambre pour une personne; **not a single thing** rien du tout
▷ n: **a CD single** un CD simple

single parent n: **She's a single parent.** Elle est parent unique.; **a single-parent family** une famille monoparentale

singles [ˈsɪŋglz] npl (*in tennis*) simple m ▷ *the women's singles* le simple dames

singular [ˈsɪŋgjuləʳ] n singulier m ▷ *in the singular* au singulier

sinister [ˈsɪnɪstəʳ] adj sinistre

sink [sɪŋk] n évier m
▷ vb couler

sir [səʳ] n monsieur m; **Yes, sir.** Oui, Monsieur.

siren [ˈsaɪərn] n sirène f

sister [ˈsɪstəʳ] n sœur f ▷ *my little sister* ma petite sœur

sister-in-law ['sɪstərɪnlɔː] n belle-sœur f (pl belles-sœurs)

sit [sɪt] vb s'asseoir ▷ She sat on the chair. Elle s'est assise sur la chaise.; **to sit down** s'asseoir ▷ Sit down, please. Asseyez-vous, s'il vous plaît.; **to be sitting** être assis

sitcom ['sɪtkɒm] n comédie de situation f (pl comédies de situation)

site [saɪt] n ❶ site m ▷ an archaeological site un site archéologique; **the site of the accident** le lieu de l'accident ❷ (campsite) emplacement m de camping; **a building site** un chantier de construction

sitting room ['sɪtɪŋ-] n salon

situated ['sɪtjueɪtɪd] adj: **to be situated** être situé ▷ The village is situated on a hill. Le village est situé sur une colline.

situation [sɪtjuˈeɪʃən] n situation f

six [sɪks] num six ▷ He's six. Il a six ans.

sixteen [sɪksˈtiːn] num seize ▷ He's sixteen. Il a seize ans.

sixteenth [sɪksˈtiːnθ] adj seizième ▷ the sixteenth floor le seizième étage; **the sixteenth of August** le seize août

sixth ['sɪksθ] adj sixième ▷ the sixth floor le sixième étage; **the sixth of August** le six août

sixty ['sɪkstɪ] num soixante

size [saɪz] n ❶ (of object, clothing) taille f ▷ What size do you take? Quelle taille est-ce que vous portez?; **I'm a size ten.** Je porte du dix ans. ❷ (of shoes) pointure f, **I take size six.** Je porte du six.

skate [skeɪt] vb ❶ (ice-skate) faire du patin à glace ❷ (roller-skate) faire du patin à roulettes

skateboard ['skeɪtbɔːd] n planche à roulettes f

skateboarder ['skeɪtbɔːdəʳ] n le/la planchiste

skateboarding ['skeɪtbɔːdɪŋ] n planche à roulettes f ▷ to go skateboarding faire de la planche à roulettes. ▷ She's a skateboarding champ. C'est une vraie championne de la planche à roulettes. ▷ My brother loves skateboarding. Mon frère adore la planche à roulettes.

skater ['skeɪtəʳ] n patineur m, patineuse f

skates [skeɪts] npl patins mpl

skating ['skeɪtɪŋ] n patin à glace m ▷ to go skating faire du patin à glace; **a skating rink** une patinoire

skeleton ['skɛlɪtn] n squelette m

sketch [skɛtʃ] n (drawing) croquis m
▶ vb: **to sketch something** faire un croquis de quelque chose

ski [skiː] n ❶ ski m; **ski boots** les f chaussures de ski; **a ski lift** un remonte-pente; **ski pants** le pantalon m de ski; **a ski pole** un bâton de ski; **a ski slope** une piste de ski; **a ski suit** une combinaison de ski
▶ vb skier ▷ Can you ski? Tu sais skier?

skid [skɪd] vb déraper

skier ['skiːəʳ] n skieur m, skieuse f

skiing ['skiːɪŋ] n ski m ▷ to go skiing faire du ski; **to go on a skiing holiday** aller aux sports d'hiver

skilful ['skɪlful] adj adroit

skill [skɪl] n talent m ▷ He played with great skill. Il a joué avec beaucoup de talent.

skilled [skɪld] adj: **a skilled worker** un ouvrier spécialisé

skim milk [skɪm-] n lait écrémé m

skimpy ['skɪmpɪ] adj ❶ (clothes) minuscule ❷ (meal) maigre

skin [skɪn] n peau f (pl peaux); **skin cancer** le cancer de la peau

skinhead ['skɪnhɛd] n skinhead

skinny ['skɪnɪ] adj maigre

skin-tight ['skɪntaɪt] adj collant

skip [skɪp] vb ▷ to skip a meal sauter un repas; **to skip a class** sécher un cours

skirt [skəːt] n jupe f

skull [skʌl] n crâne m

sky [skaɪ] n ciel m

skyscraper ['skaɪskreɪpəʳ] n gratte-ciel m (pl gratte-ciel)

slack [slæk] adj ❶ (rope) lâche ❷ (person) négligent

slam [slæm] vb claquer ▷ The door slammed. La porte a claqué. ▷ She slammed the door. Elle a claqué la porte.

slang [slæŋ] n argot m

slap [slæp] n claque f
▶ vb: **to slap somebody** donner une claque à quelqu'un

slapshot ['slæpʃɒt] n lancer frappé m

sled [slɛd] n traîneau m

sledding ['slɛdɪŋ] n: **to go sledding** faire du traîneau

sleep [sliːp] n sommeil m; **I need some sleep.** J'ai besoin de dormir.; **to go to sleep** s'endormir
▶ vb dormir ▷ I couldn't sleep last night. J'ai mal dormi la nuit dernière.; **to sleep with somebody** coucher avec quelqu'un; **to sleep together** coucher ensemble

sleep in vb ❶ (accidentally) ne pas se réveiller ▷ I'm sorry I'm late, I slept in. Désolé d'être en retard : je ne me suis pas réveillé. ❷ (on purpose) faire la grasse matinée

sleeping bag ['sliːpɪŋ-] n sac de couchage m (pl sacs de couchage)

sleeping pill ['sliːpɪŋ-] n somnifère m

sleepy ['sliːpɪ] adj: **to feel sleepy** avoir sommeil ▷ I was feeling sleepy. J'avais sommeil.; **a sleepy little village** un petit village tranquille

sleet [sliːt] n neige fondante f
▶ vb: **It's sleeting.** Il tombe de la neige fondante.

sleeve [sliːv] n ❶ manche f ▷ long sleeves les manches longues ▷ short sleeves les manches courtes ❷ (record sleeve) pochette f

sleigh [sleɪ] n traîneau m (pl traîneaux)

slept [slɛpt] vb see **sleep**

slice [slaɪs] n tranche f
▶ vb couper en tranches

slick [slɪk] n: **an oil slick** une marée noire

slide [slaɪd] n ❶ (in playground) glissoire f ❷ (photo) diapositive f
▶ vb glisser

slight [slaɪt] adj léger (f légère) ▷ a slight problem un léger problème ▷ a slight

improvement une légère amélioration
slightly ['slaɪtlɪ] *adv* légèrement
slim [slɪm] *adj* mince
sling [slɪŋ] *n* écharpe f ▷ *She had her arm in a sling.* Elle avait le bras en écharpe.
slip [slɪp] *n* ❶ (*mistake*) erreur f ❷ (*underskirt*) jupon m; **a slip of paper** un bout de papier; **a slip of the tongue** un lapsus
▶ *vb* glisser ▷ *I slipped on the ice.* J'ai glissé sur le verglas.; **to slip up** (*make a mistake*) faire une erreur
slipper ['slɪpə'] *n* pantoufle f; **a pair of slippers** des pantoufles
slippery ['slɪpərɪ] *adj* glissant
slip-up ['slɪpʌp] *n* erreur f
slope [sləup] *n* pente f
sloppy ['slɔpɪ] *adj* ❶ (*work*) bâclé ❷ (*person, appearance*) négligé
slot [slɔt] *n* fente f
slot machine *n* (*for gambling*) machine à sous f
slough [sluː] *n* bourbier m
slow [sləu] *adj, adv* ❶ lent ▷ *He's a bit slow.* Il est un peu lent. ❷ lentement ▷ *To go slow* (*person, car*) aller lentement ▷ *Drive slower!* Conduisez plus lentement!; **My watch is slow.** Ma montre retarde.
slow down *vb* ralentir
slowly ['sləulɪ] *adv* lentement
slug [slʌg] *n* limace f
slum [slʌm] *n* (*area*) quartier insalubre m
slush [slʌʃ] *n* neige fondante f
sly [slaɪ] *adj* (*person*) rusé; **a sly smile** un sourire sournois
smack [smæk] *n* tape f
▶ *vb*: **to smack somebody** donner une tape à quelqu'un
small [smɔːl] *adj* petit; **small change** la petite monnaie
smart [smɑːt] *adj* ❶ (*clever*) intelligent; **a smart idea** une idée astucieuse ❷ (*elegant*) chic (*f* chic)
smash [smæʃ] *vb* ❶ (*break*) casser ▷ *I've smashed my watch.* J'ai cassé ma montre. ❷ (*get broken*) se briser ▷ *The glass smashed into tiny pieces.* Le verre s'est brisé en mille morceaux.
smell [smɛl] *n* odeur f, **the sense of smell** l'odorat m
▶ *vb* ❶ sentir mauvais ▷ *That old dog really smells!* Ce vieux chien sent vraiment mauvais! **to smell something** sentir quelque chose ▷ *It smells like gas.* Ça sent l'essence. ❷ (*detect*) sentir ▷ *I can't smell anything.* Je ne sens rien.
smelly ['smɛlɪ] *adj* qui sent mauvais ▷ *He's got smelly feet.* Il a les pieds qui sentent mauvais.
smile [smaɪl] *n* sourire m
▶ *vb* sourire m
smiley ['smaɪlɪ] *n* binette f
smoke [sməuk] *n* fumée f
▶ *vb* fumer ▷ *I don't smoke.* Je ne fume pas.
smoked meat sandwich [sməukt-] *n* sandwich au smoked meat m
smoker ['sməukə'] *n* fumeur m, fumeuse f
smoking ['sməukɪŋ] *n*: **to give up smoking** arrêter de fumer; **Smoking is bad for you.** Le tabac, est mauvais pour la santé.; "**no smoking**" « défense de fumer »

smooth [smuːð] *adj* ❶ (*surface*) lisse ❷ (*person*) mielleux (*f* mielleuse)
smudge [smʌdʒ] *n* bavure f
smug [smʌg] *adj* suffisant
smuggle ['smʌgl] *vb* ❶ (*goods*) passer en fraude ▷ *to smuggle cigarettes into a country* faire passer des cigarettes en fraude dans un pays ❷ (*people*) faire passer clandestinement; **They managed to smuggle her out of prison.** Ils ont réussi à la faire sortir de prison clandestinement.
smuggler ['smʌglə'] *n* contrebandier m, contrebandière f
smuggling ['smʌglɪŋ] *n* contrebande f
snack [snæk] *n* collation f; **to have a snack** manger une collation
snack bar *n* casse-croûte m (*pl* casse-croûte)
snail [sneɪl] *n* escargot m
snake [sneɪk] *n* serpent m
snap [snæp] *vb* (*break*) casser net ▷ *The branch snapped.* La branche a cassé net.; **to snap one's fingers** faire claquer ses doigts
snap fastener [-fɑːsnə'] *n* bouton-pression m (*pl* boutons-pression)
snapshot ['snæpʃɔt] *n* photo f
snarl [snɑːl] *vb* (*animal*) gronder
snatch [snætʃ] *vb*: **to snatch something from somebody** arracher quelque chose à quelqu'un ▷ *He snatched the keys from my hand.* Il m'a arraché les clés des mains.; **My purse was snatched.** On m'a arraché mon sac à main.
sneak [sniːk] *vb*: **to sneak in** entrer furtivement; **to sneak out** sortir furtivement; **to sneak up on somebody** s'approcher de quelqu'un sans faire de bruit
sneakers ['sniːkəz] *npl* chaussures *fpl* de sport
sneeze [sniːz] *vb* éternuer
sniff [snɪf] *vb* ❶ renifler ▷ *Stop sniffing!* Arrête de renifler! ❷ flairer ▷ *The dog sniffed my hand.* Le chien m'a flairé la main.
snob [snɔb] *n* snob
snooker ['snuːkə'] *n* billard m ▷ *to play snooker* jouer au billard
snooze [snuːz] *n* petit somme m ▷ *to have a snooze* faire un petit somme
snore [snɔː'] *vb* ronfler
snorkel ['snɔːkl] *n* snorkel m
▶ *vb* faire du snorkel ▷ *We went snorkelling.* Nous sommes allés faire du snorkel.
snow [snəu] *n* neige f ▷ *snow sports* les sports d'hiver
▶ *vb* neiger ▷ *It's snowing.* Il neige.
snowball ['snəubɔːl] *n* boule de neige f (*pl* boules de neige)
snowbank ['snəubæŋk] *n* banc de neige (*pl* bancs de neige)
snow blindness [-blaɪndnɪs] *n* cécité des neiges f
snowblower ['snəubləuə'] *n* souffleuse f ▷ *My father used the snowblower to clear the driveway.* Mon père a passé la souffleuse pour déneiger l'entrée.
snowboard ['snəubɔːd] *n* planche à neige f
snowboarder ['snəubɔːdə'] *n* planchiste m
snowboarding ['snəubɔːdɪŋ] *n* planche à neige f ▷ *to go snowboarding* faire de la planche

à neige

snowflake ['snəʊfleɪk] n flocon de neige m (pl flocons de neige)

snowman ['snəʊmæn] n bonhomme de neige m (pl bonshommes de neige) ▷ to build a snowman faire un bonhomme de neige

snowmobile ['snəʊməʊbiːl] n motoneige f

snowmobiler ['snəʊməʊbiːləʳ] n motoneigiste

snowplow ['snəʊplaʊ] n déneigeuse f

snowstorm ['snəʊstɔːm] n tempête de neige f (pl tempêtes de neige)

snowy owl ['snəʊ-] n harfang m

so [səʊ] conj, adv ❶ alors ▷ The store was closed, so I went home. Le magasin était fermé, alors je suis rentré chez moi. ▷ So, have you always lived in Repentigny? Alors, vous avez toujours vécu à Repentigny?; **So what?** Et alors? ❷ (so that) donc ▷ It rained, so I got wet. Il pleuvait, donc j'ai été mouillé. ❸ (very) tellement ▷ It was so heavy! C'était tellement lourd! ▷ She was talking so fast I couldn't understand. Elle parlait tellement vite que je ne comprenais pas.; **It's not so heavy!** Ça n'est pas si lourd que ça!; **"How's your father?" — "Not so good."** « Comment va ton père? » — « Pas très bien. »; **so much** (a lot) tellement ▷ I love you so much. Je t'aime tellement.; **so much..., so many...** tellement de... ▷ I have so much work. J'ai tellement de travail. ▷ I have so many things to do today. J'ai tellement de choses à faire aujourd'hui. ❹ (in comparisons) aussi ▷ He's like his sister but not so outgoing. Il est comme sa sœur mais pas aussi extraverti.; **so do I** moi aussi ▷ "I love horses." — "So do I." « J'aime les chevaux. » — « Moi aussi. »; **so have we** nous aussi ▷ "I've been to Prince Edward Island twice." — "So have we." « Je suis allé à l'Île-du-Prince-Édouard deux fois. » — « Nous aussi. »; **I think so.** Je crois. ▷ **I hope so.** J'espère bien. ▷ **That's not so.** Ça n'est pas le cas.; **so far** jusqu'à présent ▷ It's been easy so far. Ça a été facile jusqu'à présent.; **so far so good** jusqu'ici ça va; **ten or so people** environ dix personnes; **at five o'clock or so** à environ cinq heures

soak [səʊk] vb tremper; **soaking wet** trempé

soaked adj trempé ▷ By the time we got back we were soaked. Nous sommes rentrés trempés.

soap [səʊp] n savon m

soap opera n téléroman m

sob [sɒb] vb sangloter ▷ She was sobbing. Elle sanglotait.

sober ['səʊbəʳ] adj sobre

sober up vb dessoûler

soccer ['sɒkəʳ] n soccer m ▷ We play soccer twice a week. Nous jouons au soccer deux fois par semaine. ▷ He's the best soccer player on the team. C'est le meilleur joueur de soccer de l'équipe.

social ['səʊʃl] adj social (mpl sociaux) ▷ a social class une classe sociale; **I have a good social life.** Je vois beaucoup de monde.

social assistance n (money) aide f sociale; **to be on social assistance** recevoir de l'aide sociale

socialism ['səʊʃəlɪzəm] n socialisme m

socialist ['səʊʃəlɪst] adj socialiste ▶ n socialiste

social worker n travailleur social m (pl travailleurs sociaux), travailleuse sociale f ▷ He's a social worker. Il est travailleur social. ▷ She's a social worker. Elle est travailleuse sociale.

society [sə'saɪətɪ] n société f ▷ We live in a multicultural society. Nous vivons dans une société multiculturelle.

sociology [səʊsɪ'ɒlədʒɪ] n sociologie f

sock [sɒk] n chaussette f

socket ['sɒkɪt] n prise de courant f (pl prises de courant)

soda ['səʊdə] n (soda water) soda m

sofa ['səʊfə] n divan m; **a sofa bed** un divan-lit

soft [sɒft] adj ❶ (fabric, texture) doux (f douce) ❷ (pillow, bed) mou (f molle); **soft cheeses** les fromages à pâte molle ❸ (hair) fin; **to be soft on somebody** (be kind to) être indulgent avec quelqu'un; **a soft drink** une boisson gazeuse

software ['sɒftwɛəʳ] n logiciels mpl ▷ Have you installed all the software? As-tu installé tous les logiciels? ▷ a piece of software un logiciel ▷ a piece of antivirus software un logiciel antivirus

soggy ['sɒgɪ] adj ❶ (soaked) trempé ▷ a soggy tissue un mouchoir de papier trempé ❷ (not crisp) mou (f molle) ▷ soggy fries des frites molles

soil [sɔɪl] n terre f

solar ['səʊləʳ] adj solaire; **solar panel** le panneau solaire

solar power n énergie f solaire

sold [səʊld] vb see **sell**

soldier ['səʊldʒəʳ] n soldat m, soldate f ▷ She's a soldier. Elle est soldate.

solid ['sɒlɪd] adj ❶ (not hollow) massif (f massive) ▷ solid gold l'or massif ❷ solide ▷ a solid wall un mur solide; **for three hours solid** pendant trois heures entières

solo ['səʊləʊ] n solo m ▷ a guitar solo un solo de guitare

solution [sə'luːʃən] n solution f

solve [sɒlv] vb résoudre

some [sʌm] adj, pron ❶ du ▷ Would you like some bread? Voulez-vous du pain?, de la ▷ Would you like some jam? Voulez-vous de la confiture?, de l' ▷ I would like some mineral water. Je voudrais de l'eau minérale., des ▷ I have some detective novels. J'ai des romans policiers.; **Some people say that...** Il y a des gens qui disent que...; **some day** un de ces jours; **some day next week** un jour la semaine prochaine ❷ (some but not all) certains ▷ "Are these mushrooms poisonous?" — "Only some." « Est-ce que ces champignons sont vénéneux? » — « Certains le sont. »; **some of them** quelques-uns ▷ I only sold some of them. J'en ai seulement vendu quelques-uns.; **I only took some of it.** J'en ai seulement pris un peu.; **I'm going to buy some stamps. Do you want some too?** Je vais acheter des timbres. Est-ce que tu en veux aussi?; **"Would you like some coffee?" — "No thanks, I've got some."** « Tu veux du café? » — « Non merci, j'en ai déjà. »

somebody ['sʌmbədɪ] pron quelqu'un

▷ *Somebody stole my personal stereo.* Quelqu'un a volé mon baladeur.

somehow ['sʌmhaʊ] *adv:* **I'll do it somehow.** Je trouverai le moyen de le faire.; **Somehow I don't think he believed me.** Quelque chose me dit qu'il ne m'a pas cru.

someone ['sʌmwʌn] *pron* quelqu'un ▷ *Someone stole my wallet.* Quelqu'un a volé mon porte-monnaie.

something ['sʌmθɪŋ] *pron* quelque chose ▷ *something special* quelque chose de spécial ▷ *Wear something warm.* Mets quelque chose de chaud. ▷ *That's really something!* C'est vraiment quelque chose! ▷ *It cost 100 dollars, or something like that.* Ça a coûté cent dollars, ou quelque chose comme ça.

sometime ['sʌmtaɪm] *adv* un de ces jours ▷ *You must come and see us sometime.* Passez donc nous voir un de ces jours.; **sometime last month** dans le courant du mois dernier

sometimes ['sʌmtaɪmz] *adv* quelquefois ▷ *Sometimes I think she hates me.* Quelquefois j'ai l'impression qu'elle me déteste.

somewhere ['sʌmwɛəʳ] *adv* quelque part ▷ *I left my keys somewhere.* J'ai laissé mes clés quelque part. ▷ *I'd like to go somewhere sunny.* J'aimerais aller quelque part où il fait du soleil.

son [sʌn] *n* fils *m*

song [sɒŋ] *n* chanson *f*

son-in-law ['sʌnɪnlɔː] *n* gendre *m*

soon [suːn] *adv* bientôt ▷ *very soon* très bientôt; **soon afterwards** peu après; **as soon as possible** aussitôt que possible

sooner ['suːnəʳ] *adv* plus tôt ▷ *Can't you come a bit sooner?* Tu ne peux pas venir un peu plus tôt?; **sooner or later** tôt ou tard

soot [sʊt] *n* suie *f*

sorcerer ['sɔːsərəʳ] *n* sorcier *m*

sore [sɔːʳ] *adj:* **My feet are sore.** J'ai mal aux pieds.; **It's sore.** Ça fait mal.; **That's a sore point.** C'est un point sensible.
▶ *n* plaie *f*

sorry ['sɒrɪ] *adj* désolé ▷ *I'm really sorry.* Je suis vraiment désolé. ▷ *I'm sorry, I don't have any change.* Je suis désolé, je n'ai pas de monnaie. ▷ *I'm sorry I'm late.* Je suis désolée d'être en retard.; **sorry!** pardon!; **sorry?** pardon?; **I'm sorry about the noise.** Je m'excuse pour le bruit.; **You'll be sorry!** Tu le regretteras!; **to feel sorry for somebody** plaindre quelqu'un

sort [sɔːt] *n* sorte *f* ▷ *What sort of bike do you have?* Quelle sorte de vélo as-tu?

sort *vb* ❶ (*objects*) ranger ❷ (*problems*) résoudre

so-so ['səʊsəʊ] *adv* comme ci comme ça ▷ *"How are you feeling?" – "So-so."* « Comment est-ce que tu te sens? » – « Comme ci comme ça. »

sought [sɔːt] *vb* see **to seek**

soul [səʊl] *n* ❶ (*spirit*) âme *f* ❷ musique soul *f*

sound [saʊnd] *n* ❶ (*noise*) bruit *m* ▷ *Don't make a sound!* Pas un bruit! ▷ *The sound of footsteps* des bruits de pas ❷ son *m* ▷ *Can I turn the sound down?* Je peux baisser le son?
▶ *vb:* **That sounds interesting.** Ça a l'air intéressant.; **It sounds as if she's doing well**

at school. Elle a l'air de bien travailler à l'école.; **That sounds like a good idea.** C'est une bonne idée.
▶ *adj, adv* bon (*f* bonne) ▷ *That's sound advice.* C'est un bon conseil.; **sound asleep** profondément endormi

sound effects *npl* bruitage *m*; **sound effect specialist** le bruiteur ▷ *She's a sound effect specialist.* Elle est bruiteuse.

soundtrack ['saʊndtræk] *n* bande sonore *f*

soup [suːp] *n* soupe *f* ▷ *vegetable soup* la soupe aux légumes

sour ['saʊəʳ] *adj* aigre

south [saʊθ] *adj, adv* ❶ sud *m* (*f+pl* sud) ▷ *the south coast* la côte sud ❷ vers le sud ▷ *We were travelling south.* Nous allions vers le sud.; **south of** au sud de ▷ *It's south of Hearst.* C'est au sud de Hearst.; **South America** l'Amérique *f* du Sud ▶ *n* sud *m* ▷ *in the south* dans le sud ▷ *the south of Ontario* le sud de l'Ontario

southbound ['saʊθbaʊnd] *adj:* **Southbound traffic is moving very slowly.** La circulation en direction du sud est très ralentie.; **The suspect vehicle was southbound on the 400.** Le véhicule suspect se trouvait sur l'autoroute 400 en direction du sud.

southeast [saʊθ'iːst] *n* sud-est *m* ▷ *southeast Alberta* le sud-est de l'Alberta

southern ['sʌðən] *adj:* **the southern part of the island** la partie sud de l'île; **southern New Brunswick** le sud du Nouveau-Brunswick

South Pole *n* pôle Sud *m*

southwest [saʊθ'wɛst] *n* sud-ouest *m* ▷ *southwest Yukon* le sud-ouest du Yukon

souvenir [suːvə'nɪəʳ] *n* souvenir *m*; **a souvenir shop** une boutique de souvenirs

sovereigntist ['sɒvrɪntɪst] *n* souverainiste

sovereignty ['sɒvrɪntɪ] *n* souveraineté *f* ▷ *Are you in favour of Quebec sovereignty?* Êtes-vous en faveur de la souveraineté du Québec?

soya [sɔɪ] *n* soya *m*

soy sauce [sɔɪ-] *n* sauce soya *f*

space [speɪs] *n* ❶ place *f* ▷ *There isn't enough space.* Il n'y a pas suffisamment de place.; **a parking space** une place de stationnement ❷ (*universe, gap*) espace *m* ▷ *Leave a space after your answer.* Laissez un espace après votre réponse.; **a space shuttle** une navette spatiale

spacecraft ['speɪskrɑːft] *n* vaisseau spatial *m*

spade [speɪd] *n* pelle *f*; **spades** (*in cards*) le pique *m* ▷ *the ace of spades* l'as de pique

spam [spæm] *n* ❶ (*practice of spamming*) pollupostage *m* ▷ *Spam has become a real problem.* Le pollupostage est devenu un vrai problème. ❷ (*message*) polluriel *m* ▷ *I got some spam from that address.* J'ai reçu des polluriels de cette adresse.

spaniel ['spænjəl] *n* épagneul *m*

spank [spæŋk] *vb:* **to spank somebody** donner une fessée à quelqu'un

spare [spɛəʳ] *adj* de rechange ▷ *spare batteries* des piles de rechange ▷ *a spare part* une pièce de rechange; **a spare room** une chambre d'amis; **spare time** le temps libre ▷ *What do you do in your spare time?* Qu'est-ce que tu fais pendant ton temps libre?; **spare tire** un pneu de secours

▶ vb: **Can you spare a moment?** Vous pouvez m'accorder un instant?; **I can't spare the time.** Je n'ai pas le temps.; **There's no room to spare.** Il n'y a plus de place.; **We arrived with time to spare.** Nous sommes arrivés en avance.

▶ n: **a spare** un autre ▷ *"I've lost my key." — "Have you got a spare?"* « J'ai perdu ma clé. » — « En as-tu une autre? »

sparkling ['spɑːklɪŋ] adj (water) pétillant
sparrow ['spærəʊ] n moineau m (pl moineaux)
speak [spiːk] vb parler ▷ *Do you speak English?* Est-ce que vous parlez anglais?; **to speak to somebody** parler à quelqu'un ▷ *Have you spoken to him?* Tu lui as parlé? ▷ *She spoke to him about it.* Elle lui en a parlé.; **spoken French** le français parlé
speak up vb parler plus fort ▷ *Speak up, we can't hear you.* Parle plus fort, nous ne t'entendons pas.
speaker ['spiːkəʳ] n ❶ (loudspeaker) haut-parleur m (pl haut-parleurs) ❷ (in debate) intervenant m, intervenante f ❸ (at conference) conférencier m, conférencière f
special ['speʃl] adj spécial (mpl spéciaux)
specialist ['speʃəlɪst] n spécialiste
specialize ['speʃəlaɪz] vb se spécialiser ▷ *We specialize in skiing equipment.* Nous nous spécialisons dans les articles de ski.
specially ['speʃlɪ] adv spécialement ▷ *It's specially designed for teenagers.* C'est spécialement conçu pour les adolescents.
specialty ['speʃəltɪ] n spécialité f
species ['spiːʃiːz] n espèce f
specific [spə'sɪfɪk] adj ❶ (particular) particulier (f particulière) ▷ *certain specific issues* certains problèmes particuliers ❷ (precise) précis ▷ *Could you be more specific?* Est-ce que vous pourriez être plus précise?
specifically [spə'sɪfɪklɪ] adv ❶ spécialement ▷ *It's specifically designed for teenagers.* C'est spécialement conçu pour les adolescents. ❷ particulièrement ▷ *on the subject of snow sports, or more specifically snowboarding* au sujet des sports d'hiver, ou plus particulièrement de la planche à neige; **I specifically said that...** J'ai clairement dit que...
spectacular [spek'tækjʊləʳ] adj spectaculaire
spectator [spek'teɪtəʳ] n spectateur m, spectatrice f
speech [spiːtʃ] n discours m ▷ *to make a speech* faire un discours
speechless ['spiːtʃlɪs] adj muet (f muette) ▷ *speechless with admiration* muet d'admiration; **I was speechless.** Je suis resté sans voix.
speed [spiːd] n vitesse f ▷ *a ten-speed bike* un vélo à dix vitesses ▷ *at top speed* à toute vitesse; **speed limit** la limite de vitesse ▷ *The speed limit is 50 km/h here.* La limite de vitesse ici est de 50 kilomètres par heure. ▷ *to break the speed limit* faire un excès de vitesse
speedboat ['spiːdbəʊt] n hord-bord m (pl hors-bord)
speeding ['spiːdɪŋ] n excès m de vitesse

▷ *He was fined for speeding.* Il a reçu une contravention pour excès de vitesse.
speedometer [spɪ'dɒmɪtəʳ] n indicateur m de vitesse
speed up vb accélérer
spell [spel] vb ❶ (in writing) écrire ▷ *How do you spell that?* Comment est-ce que ça s'écrit? ❷ (out loud) épeler ▷ *Can you spell that please?* Est-ce que vous pouvez épeler, s'il vous plaît?; **I can't spell.** Je fais des fautes d'orthographe.
▶ n: **to cast a spell on somebody** jeter un sort à quelqu'un; **to be under somebody's spell** être sous le charme de quelqu'un
spelling ['spelɪŋ] n orthographe f ▷ *My spelling is terrible.* Je fais beaucoup de fautes d'orthographe.; **a spelling mistake** une faute d'orthographe
spend [spend] vb ❶ (money) dépenser ❷ (time) passer ▷ *She spent a month in Quebec.* Elle a passé un mois au Québec.
spice [spaɪs] n épice f
spicy ['spaɪsɪ] adj épicé
spider ['spaɪdəʳ] n araignée f
spill [spɪl] vb ❶ (tip over) renverser ▷ *He spilled his coffee on his pants.* Il a renversé son café sur son pantalon. ❷ (get spilled) se répandre ▷ *The soup spilled all over the table.* La soupe s'est répandue sur la table.
spinach ['spɪnɪtʃ] n épinards mpl
spine [spaɪn] n colonne vertébrale f
spire ['spaɪəʳ] n flèche f
spirit ['spɪrɪt] n ❶ esprit m ▷ *the human spirit* l'esprit humain ❷ (courage) courage m; **to be in good spirits** être de bonne humeur ❸ (energy) énergie f
spiritual ['spɪrɪtjʊəl] adj spirituel (f spirituelle) ▷ *the spiritual leader of Tibet* le chef spirituel du Tibet ▷ *spiritual development* la croissance spirituelle
spit [spɪt] n salive f
▶ vb cracher; **to spit something out** cracher quelque chose
spite [spaɪt] n: **in spite of** malgré; **out of spite** par méchanceté
▶ vb contrarier ▷ *She did it just to spite me.* Elle a fait ça juste pour me contrarier.
spiteful ['spaɪtful] adj ❶ (action) méchant ❷ (person) rancunier (f rancunière)
splash [splæʃ] vb éclabousser ▷ *Careful! Don't splash me!* Attention! Ne m'éclabousse pas!
▶ n plouf m ▷ *I heard a splash.* J'ai entendu un plouf.; **a splash of colour** une touche de couleur
splendid ['splendɪd] adj splendide
splint [splɪnt] n attelle f
splinter ['splɪntəʳ] n écharde f
split [splɪt] vb ❶ (break apart) fendre ▷ *He split the wood with an axe.* Il a fendu le bois avec une hache. ❷ se fendre ▷ *The ship hit a rock and split in two.* Le bateau a percuté un rocher et s'est fendu en deux. ❸ (divide up) partager ▷ *They decided to split the profits.* Ils ont décidé de partager les bénéfices.; **to split up (1)** (couple) rompre **(2)** (group) se disperser
spoil [spɔɪl] vb ❶ (object) abîmer ❷ (occasion, experience) gâcher ❸ (child) gâter ❹ (food) se

gâter ▷ *The fruit is beginning to spoil.* Les fruits commencent à se gâter.; **If you leave the milk on the counter it'll spoil.** Si tu laisses le lait sur le comptoir, il va tourner.

spoiled adj gâté ▷ *a spoiled child* une enfant gâtée

spoilsport ['spɔɪlspɔːt] n trouble-fête

spoke [spəʊk] vb see **speak**
▶ n (of wheel) rayon m

spoken ['spəʊkn] vb see **speak**

spokesperson ['spəʊkspɜːsn] n porte-parole (pl porte-parole)

sponge [spʌndʒ] n éponge f

sponsor ['spɒnsə'] n commanditaire
▶ vb commanditer ▷ *The festival was sponsored by...* Le festival a été commandité par...

spontaneous [spɒn'teɪnɪəs] adj spontané

spooky ['spuːkɪ] adj ❶ (eerie) sinistre; a **spooky story** une histoire qui fait froid dans le dos ❷ (strange) étrange ▷ *a spooky coincidence* une étrange coïncidence

spoon [spuːn] n cuillère f; **a spoonful** une cuillerée

sport [spɔːt] n sport m ▷ *What's your favourite sport?* Quel est ton sport préféré?; **a sports bag** un sac de sport; **a sports car** une voiture de sport; **a sports jacket** une veste sport; **Come on, be a sport!** Allez, sois sympa!

sportswear ['spɔːtswɛə'] n vêtements mpl de sport

sporty ['spɔːtɪ] adj sportif (f sportive) ▷ *I'm not very sporty.* Je ne suis pas très sportif.

spot [spɒt] n ❶ (mark) tache f ▷ *There's a spot on your shirt.* Il y a une tache sur ta chemise. ❷ (place) coin m ▷ *It's a lovely spot for a picnic.* C'est un coin agréable pour un pique-nique.; **on the spot** (immediately) sur-le-champ ▷ *They gave her the job on the spot.* Ils lui ont offert le poste sur-le-champ.
▶ vb repérer ▷ *I spotted a mistake.* J'ai repéré une faute.

spotless ['spɒtlɪs] adj immaculé

spotlight ['spɒtlaɪt] n projecteur m; **The universities have been in the spotlight recently.** Les universités ont été sous le feu des projecteurs ces derniers temps.

spouse [spauz] n époux m, épouse f

sprain [spreɪn] vb: **to sprain one's ankle** se faire une entorse à la cheville
▶ n entorse f ▷ *It's just a sprain.* C'est juste une entorse.

spray [spreɪ] n: **spray can** la bombe; **spray bottle** l'atomiseur m; **spray paint** la peinture en aérosol; **perfume spray** le parfum en atomiseur ▷ *Do you have this perfume in spray form?* Vous avez ce parfum en atomiseur?
▶ vb ❶ vaporiser ▷ *to spray perfume on one's hand* se vaporiser du parfum sur la main ❷ (crops) traiter ▷ *They sprayed their crops with fertilizer.* Ils ont traité leurs champs à l'engrais. ❸ (graffiti) peindre avec une bombe ▷ *Somebody had sprayed graffiti on the wall.* Quelqu'un avait peint des graffitis avec une bombe sur le mur.

spread [sprɛd] n: **cheese spread** le fromage à tartiner; **chocolate spread** le chocolat à tartiner
▶ vb ❶ étaler ▷ *to spread butter on a slice of bread* étaler du beurre sur une tranche de pain ❷ (disease, news) se propager ▷ *The news spread rapidly.* La nouvelle s'est propagée rapidement.; **to spread out** (people) se disperser ▷ *The soldiers spread out across the field.* Les soldats se sont dispersés dans le champ.

spreadsheet ['sprɛdʃiːt] n (computer program) tableur m

spring [sprɪŋ] n ❶ (season) printemps m; **in spring** au printemps ❷ (metal coil) ressort m ❸ (water hole) source f

spring cleaning [-kliːnɪŋ] n grand nettoyage du printemps m

sprinkler ['sprɪŋklə'] n (for lawn) arroseur m

sprint [sprɪnt] n sprint m
▶ vb courir à toute vitesse ▷ *He sprinted for the bus.* Il a couru à toute vitesse pour attraper le bus.

sprinter ['sprɪntə'] n sprinteur m, sprinteuse f

sprouts [sprauts] npl: **Brussels sprouts** les m choux de Bruxelles; **bean sprouts** les m germes de soya

spruce [spruːs] n épinette f

spy [spaɪ] n espion m, espionne f
▶ vb: **to spy on somebody** espionner quelqu'un

spying ['spaɪɪŋ] n espionnage m

squabble ['skwɒbl] vb se chamailler ▷ *Stop squabbling!* Arrêtez de vous chamailler!

square [skwɛə'] n ❶ carré m ▷ *a square and a triangle* un carré et un triangle ❷ place f ▷ *the town square* la place de l'hôtel de ville
▶ adj carré m ▷ *two square metres* deux mètres carrés; **It's 2 metres square.** Ça fait deux mètres sur deux.

squash [skwɒʃ] n (sport) squash m ▷ *I play squash.* Je joue au squash.; **a squash court** un court de squash; **a squash racquet** une raquette de squash
▶ vb écraser ▷ *You're squashing me.* Tu m'écrases.

squeak [skwiːk] vb ❶ (mouse, child) pousser un petit cri ❷ (creak) grincer

squeeze [skwiːz] vb ❶ (fruit, toothpaste) presser ❷ (hand, arm) serrer; **to squeeze into some tight jeans** rentrer tout juste dans des jeans serrés

squeeze in vb ❶ trouver une petite place ▷ *It was a tiny car, but we managed to squeeze in.* La voiture était toute petite, mais nous avons réussi à trouver une petite place. ❷ (for appointment) caser ▷ *I can squeeze you in at two o'clock.* Je peux vous caser demain à deux heures.

squint [skwɪnt] vb loucher

squirrel ['skwɪrəl] n écureuil m

stab [stæb] vb poignarder

stable ['steɪbl] n écurie f
▶ adj stable ▷ *a stable relationship* une relation stable

stack [stæk] n pile f ▷ *a stack of books* une pile de livres

stadium ['steɪdɪəm] n stade m

staff [stɑːf] n ❶ (in company) personnel m

❷ (in school) professeurs mpl

staffroom ['stɑːfruːm] n salon des professeurs m

stage [steɪdʒ] n ❶ (in plays) scène f ❷ (for speeches, lectures) estrade f; **at this stage (1)** à ce stade ▷ at this stage in the negotiations à ce stade des négociations **(2)** pour l'instant ▷ At this stage, it's too early to comment. Pour l'instant, il est trop tôt pour se prononcer.; **to do something in stages** faire quelque chose étape par étape

stagger ['stægə'] vb chanceler

stain [steɪn] n tache f
▶ vb tacher

stainless steel ['steɪnlɪs-] n acier m inoxydable

stain remover [-rɪ'muːvə'] n détachant m

stair [steə'] n (step) marche f

staircase ['steəkeɪs] n escalier m

stairs [steəz] npl escalier m

stale [steɪl] adj (bread) rassis

stalemate ['steɪlmeɪt] n ❶ (in chess) pat m ❷ impasse f ▷ Negotiations have reached a stalemate. Les négociations sont dans l'impasse.

stall [stɔːl] n stand m ▷ She has a stall at the market. Elle a un stand au marché.
▶ vb (car, engine) caler ▷ The school bus stalled. L'autobus scolaire a calé.

stamina ['stæmɪnə] n endurance f

stammer ['stæmə'] vb bégayer ▷ She stammered a reply. Elle a bégayé une réponse.

stamp [stæmp] vb ❶ (letter) affranchir ❷ tamponner ▷ The customs agent stamped my passport. Le douanier a tamponné mon passeport.; **to stamp one's foot** taper du pied
▶ n ❶ timbre m ▷ a 50-cent stamp un timbre de cinquante cents ▷ My hobby is stamp collecting. Je collectionne les timbres.; **a stamp album** un album de timbres; **a stamp collection** une collection de timbres ❷ (rubber stamp) timbre en caoutchouc m

stamped [stæmpt] adj affranchi ▷ The letter wasn't stamped. La lettre n'était pas affranchie.; **Enclose a stamped self-addressed envelope.** Joindre une enveloppe affranchie à vos nom et adresse.

stand [stænd] vb ❶ (be standing) être debout ▷ He was standing by the door. Il était debout à la porte. ❷ (stand up) se lever ❸ (tolerate, withstand) supporter ▷ I can't stand all this noise. Je ne peux pas tout ce bruit.; **to stand for (1)** (be short for) être l'abréviation de ▷ "GST" stands for "Goods and Services Tax". « TPS » est l'abréviation de « taxe sur les produits et services ». **(2)** (tolerate) supporter ▷ I won't stand for it! Je ne supporterai pas ça!; **to stand in for somebody** remplacer quelqu'un; **to stand one's ground** tenir bon ▷ If they try to persuade you, stand your ground. Si elles essaient de te persuader, tiens bon.; **to stand out** se distinguer ▷ All the contestants were good, but none of them stood out. Tous les concurrents étaient bons, mais aucun ne se distinguait.; **She really stands out in that orange coat.** Tout le monde la remarque avec

ce manteau orange.; **to stand up** (get up) se lever; **to stand up for** défendre ▷ Stand up for your rights! Défendez vos droits!

standard ['stændəd] adj ❶ courant ▷ standard French le français courant ❷ (equipment) ordinaire; **the standard procedure** la procédure normale; **standard time** l'heure normale ▷ We're back on standard time. On est revenu à l'heure normale.
▶ n niveau m (pl niveaux) ▷ The standard is very high. Le niveau est très haut.; **the standard of living** le niveau de vie; **She has very high standards.** Elle est très exigeante.

standby ticket ['stændbaɪ-] n billet sans réservation m

standpoint ['stændpɔɪnt] n point de vue m

stands [stændz] npl (at sports ground) tribune f

stank [stæŋk] vb see **stink**

staple ['steɪpl] n ❶ agrafe f ❷ (food) aliment m de base ▷ Rice is an important staple. Le riz est un aliment de base important.
▶ vb agrafer

stapler ['steɪplə'] n brocheuse f

star [stɑː'] n ❶ (in sky) étoile f ❷ (celebrity) vedette f ▷ He's a TV star. C'est une vedette de la télé.
▶ vb être la vedette ▷ to star in a film être la vedette d'un film; **The film stars Andrea Martin.** Le film a pour vedette Andrea Martin.; **...starring Kiefer Sutherland** ...avec Kiefer Sutherland

stare [steə'] vb: **to stare at something** fixer quelque chose

stark [stɑːk] adv: **stark naked** complètement nu

start [stɑːt] n ❶ début m ▷ It's not much, but it's a start. Ce n'est pas grand chose, mais c'est un début.; **Shall we make a start on the dishes?** On commence à faire la vaisselle? ❷ (of race) départ m
▶ vb ❶ commencer ▷ What time does it start? À quelle heure est-ce que ça commence?; **to start doing something** commencer à faire quelque chose ▷ I started learning French three years ago. J'ai commencé à apprendre le français il y a trois ans. ❷ (organization) créer ▷ He wants to start his own business. Il veut créer sa propre entreprise. ❸ (campaign) organiser ▷ She started a campaign against drugs. Elle a organisé une campagne contre la drogue. ❹ (car) démarrer ▷ He couldn't start the car. Il n'a pas réussi à démarrer la voiture. ▷ The car wouldn't start. La voiture ne voulait pas démarrer.; **to start off** (leave) partir ▷ We started off first thing in the morning. Nous sommes partis en début de matinée.

starve [stɑːv] vb mourir de faim ▷ People were literally starving. Les gens mouraient littéralement de faim.; **I'm starving!** Je meurs de faim!

state [steɪt] n état m; **he was in a real state** il était dans tous ses états; **the state** (government) l'État
▶ vb ❶ (say) déclarer ▷ She stated her intention to resign. Elle a déclaré son intention de démissionner. ❷ (give) donner ▷ Please state

your name and address. Veuillez donner vos nom et adresse.

statement ['steɪtmənt] n déclaration f

station ['steɪʃən] n (railway) gare f; **the bus station** la gare d'autobus; **a police station** un poste de police; **a radio station** une station de radio

station wagon [-wægən] n familiale f

statue ['stætjuː] n statue f

stay [steɪ] vb ❶ (remain) rester ▷ *Stay here!* Reste ici!; **to stay in** (not go out) rester à la maison; **to stay up** rester debout ▷ *We stayed up till midnight.* Nous sommes restés debout jusqu'à minuit. ❷ (spend the night) loger ▷ *to stay with friends* loger chez des amis ▷ *Where are you staying?* Où est-ce que vous logez?; **to stay the night** passer la nuit; **We stayed in Nova Scotia for a few days.** Nous avons passé quelques jours en Nouvelle-Écosse.
▶ n séjour m ▷ *my stay in the Gaspé* mon séjour en Gaspésie

steady ['stedɪ] adj ❶ régulier (f régulière) ▷ *steady progress* des progrès réguliers ❷ stable ▷ *a steady job* un emploi stable ❸ (voice, hand) ferme ❹ (person) calme; **a steady boyfriend** un copain; **a steady girlfriend** une copine; **Steady!** Doucement!

steak [steɪk] n (beef) steak m ▷ *"How would you like your steak?" — "Medium rare."* « Quelle cuisson, votre steak? » — « À point. »

steal [stiːl] vb voler

steam [stiːm] n vapeur f ▷ *a steam engine* une locomotive à vapeur

steel [stiːl] n acier m ▷ *a steel door* une porte en acier

steep [stiːp] adj (slope) raide

steeple ['stiːpl] n clocher m

steering wheel ['stɪərɪŋ-] n volant m

step [step] n ❶ (pace) pas m ▷ *He took a step forward.* Il a fait un pas en avant. ❷ (stair) marche f ▷ *She tripped over the step.* Elle a trébuché sur la marche.
▶ vb: **to step aside** faire un pas de côté; **to step back** faire un pas en arrière

stepbrother ['stepbrʌðəʳ] n demi-frère m (pl demi-frères)

stepdaughter ['stepdɔːtəʳ] n belle-fille f (pl belles-filles)

stepfather ['stepfɑːðəʳ] n beau-père m (pl beaux-pères)

stepladder ['steplædəʳ] n escabeau m (pl escabeaux)

stepmother ['stepmʌðəʳ] n belle-mère f (pl belles-mères)

stepsister ['stepsɪstəʳ] n demi-sœur f (pl demi-sœurs)

stepson ['stepsʌn] n beau-fils m (pl beaux-fils)

stereo ['steriəu] n chaîne stéréo f (pl chaînes stéréo)

stew [stjuː] n ragoût m

stick [stɪk] n ❶ bâton m ❷ (walking stick) canne f
▶ vb (with adhesive) coller ▷ *Stick the stamps on the envelope.* Collez les timbres sur l'enveloppe.

stick out vb (project) sortir ▷ *A pen was sticking out of his pocket.* Un stylo sortait de sa poche.;

to stick out one's tongue tirer la langue

sticker ['stɪkəʳ] n autocollant m

sticky ['stɪkɪ] adj ❶ poisseux (f poisseuse) ▷ *to have sticky hands* avoir les mains poisseuses ❷ adhésif (f adhésive) ▷ *a sticky label* une étiquette adhésive

stiff [stɪf] adj, adv (rigid) rigide; **to have a stiff back** avoir mal au dos; **to feel stiff** avoir des courbatures; **to be bored stiff** s'ennuyer à mourir; **to be frozen stiff** être mort de froid; **to be scared stiff** être mort de peur

still [stɪl] adv ❶ encore ▷ *I still haven't finished.* Je n'ai pas encore fini. ▷ *Are you still in bed?* Tu es encore au lit?; **better still** encore mieux ❷ (even so) quand même ▷ *She knows I don't like it, but she still does it.* Elle sait que je n'aime pas ça, mais elle le fait quand même. ❸ (after all) enfin ▷ *Still, it's the thought that counts.* Enfin, c'est l'intention qui compte.
▶ adj: **Keep still!** Ne bouge pas!; **Sit still!** Reste tranquille!

sting [stɪŋ] n piqûre f ▷ *a bee sting* une piqûre d'abeille
▶ vb piquer ▷ *I've been stung.* J'ai été piqué.

stingy ['stɪndʒɪ] adj pingre

stink [stɪŋk] vb puer ▷ *It stinks!* Ça pue!
▶ n puanteur f

stir [stɜːʳ] vb remuer

stir-fry ['stɜːˈfraɪ] n sauté m ▷ *a vegetable stir-fry* un sauté de légumes
▶ vb faire sauter ▷ *I stir-fried the vegetables.* J'ai fait sauter les légumes.

stitch [stɪtʃ] vb (cloth) coudre
▶ n ❶ (in sewing) point m ❷ (in wound) point de suture m ▷ *I had five stitches.* J'ai eu cinq points de suture.

stock [stɒk] n ❶ (supply) réserve f ❷ (in store) stock m ▷ *in stock* en stock; **out of stock** épuisé ❸ bouillon m ▷ *chicken stock* du bouillon de volaille
▶ vb (have in stock) avoir ▷ *Do you stock camping stoves?* Vous avez des réchauds de camping?; **to stock up** s'approvisionner ▷ *to stock up on something* s'approvisionner en quelque chose

stole, stolen vb see **steal**

stomach ['stʌmək] n estomac m

stomachache ['stʌməkeɪk] n: **to have a stomachache** avoir mal au ventre

stone [stəun] n ❶ (rock) pierre f ▷ *a stone wall* un mur en pierre ❷ (in fruit) noyau m (pl noyaux) ▷ *a peach stone* un noyau de pêche

stood [stud] vb see **stand**

stool [stuːl] n tabouret m

stop [stɒp] vb ❶ arrêter ▷ *a campaign to stop whaling* une campagne pour arrêter la chasse à la baleine ❷ s'arrêter ▷ *The bus doesn't stop there.* L'autobus ne s'arrête pas là. ▷ *I think the rain's going to stop.* Je pense qu'il va s'arrêter de pleuvoir.; **to stop doing something** arrêter de faire quelque chose ▷ *to stop smoking* arrêter de fumer; **to stop somebody from doing something** empêcher quelqu'un de faire quelque chose; **Stop!** Stop!
▶ n arrêt m ▷ *a bus stop* un arrêt d'autobus; **This is my stop.** Je descends ici.

stopwatch ['stɒpwɒtʃ] n chronomètre m

store [stɔːʳ] n magasin m ▷ *a furniture store* un magasin de meubles
▶ vb ❶ garder ▷ *They store potatoes in the cellar.* Ils gardent des pommes de terre dans la cave. ❷ (*information*) enregistrer

storey ['stɔːrɪ] n étage m ▷ *a three-storey building* un immeuble à trois étages

storm [stɔːm] n ❶ tempête f ❷ (*thunderstorm*) orage m

stormy ['stɔːmɪ] adj orageux (f orageuse)

story ['stɔːrɪ] n ❶ histoire f ❷ (*oral, traditional*) conte m ▷ *stories from the Cree tradition* des contes cris ▷ *a book of classic children's stories* un livre de contes pour enfants

storyteller ['stɔːrɪtɛləʳ] n conteur m, conteuse f

stove [stəʊv] n ❶ (*in kitchen*) cuisinière f ❷ (*camping stove*) réchaud m

straight [streɪt] adj, adv ❶ droit ▷ *a straight line* une ligne droite ▷ *He looked straight ahead.* Il a regardé droit devant lui. ▷ *Go straight ahead.* Allez tout droit. ❷ raide ▷ *straight hair* les cheveux raides ❸ (*heterosexual*) hétéro ❹ directement ▷ *I went straight home.* Je suis rentré directement chez moi.

straightforward [streɪt'fɔːwəd] adj simple m

strain [streɪn] n stress m; **It was a strain.** C'était éprouvant.
▶ vb se faire mal à ▷ *I strained my back.* Je me suis fait mal au dos.; **to strain a muscle** se froisser un muscle

strained [streɪnd] adj (*muscle*) froissé

stranded ['strændɪd] adj: **We were stranded.** Nous étions coincés.

strange [streɪndʒ] adj bizarre ▷ *That's strange!* C'est bizarre!

stranger ['streɪndʒəʳ] n inconnu m, inconnue f ▷ *Don't talk to strangers.* Ne parle pas aux inconnus.; **I'm a stranger here.** Je ne suis pas d'ici.

strangle ['stræŋgl] vb étrangler

strap [stræp] n ❶ (*of purse, camera, suitcase*) courroie f ❷ (*of bra, dress*) bretelle f ❸ (*on shoe*) bride f

straw [strɔː] n paille f; **That's the last straw!** Ça, c'est le comble!

strawberry ['strɔːbərɪ] n fraise f ▷ *strawberry jam* la confiture de fraises ▷ *strawberry ice cream* la crème glacée à la fraise

stray [streɪ] n: **a stray cat** un chat errant

stream [striːm] n ruisseau m (pl ruisseaux)

street [striːt] n rue f ▷ *in the street* dans la rue

streetcar ['striːtkaːʳ] n tramway m

streetlight ['striːtlaɪt] n réverbère m

street musician n musicien de rue m, musicienne de rue f ▷ *There are a lot of street musicians in Toronto.* Il y a beaucoup de musiciens de rue à Toronto.

street plan n plan de la ville m

streetwise ['striːtwaɪz] adj débrouillard

strength [strɛŋθ] n force f

stress [strɛs] vb souligner ▷ *I would like to stress that...* J'aimerais souligner que...
▶ n stress m

stretch [strɛtʃ] vb ❶ (*person, animal*) s'étirer ▷ *The dog woke up and stretched.* Le chien s'est

réveillé et s'est étiré. ❷ (*get bigger*) étirer ▷ *My sweater stretched when I washed it.* Mon chandail a étiré au lavage. ❸ (*stretch out*) tendre ▷ *They stretched a rope between two trees.* Ils ont tendu une corde entre deux arbres.; **to stretch out one's arms** tendre les bras

stretcher ['strɛtʃəʳ] n civière f

stretchy ['strɛtʃɪ] adj élastique

strict [strɪkt] adj strict

strike [straɪk] n grève f; **to be on strike** être en grève; **to go on strike** se mettre en grève
▶ vb ❶ (*hit*) frapper ❷ (*clock*) sonner ▷ *The clock struck three.* L'horloge a sonné trois heures. ❸ (*go on strike*) se mettre en grève; **to strike a match** frotter une allumette

striker ['straɪkəʳ] n (*person on strike*) gréviste

striking ['straɪkɪŋ] adj ❶ (*noticeable*) frappant ▷ *a striking difference* une différence frappante ❷ (*on strike*) en grève ▷ *striking miners* les mineurs en grève

string [strɪŋ] n ❶ ficelle f ▷ *a piece of string* un bout de ficelle ❷ (*of violin, guitar*) corde f

strip [strɪp] vb (*get undressed*) se déshabiller
▶ n bande f; **a comic strip** une bande dessinée

stripe [straɪp] n rayure f

striped [straɪpt] adj à rayures ▷ *a striped skirt* une jupe à rayures

stroke [strəʊk] vb caresser
▶ n attaque f ▷ *to have a stroke* avoir une attaque

stroll [strəʊl] n: **to go for a stroll** aller faire une petite promenade

stroller ['strəʊləʳ] n landau m

strong [strɒŋ] adj ❶ fort ▷ *She's very strong.* Elle est très forte. ❷ (*material*) résistant

strongly ['strɒŋlɪ] adv fortement ▷ *We recommend strongly that...* Nous recommandons fortement que...; **He smelt strongly of tobacco.** Il sentait fort le tabac.; **strongly built** solidement bâti; **I don't feel strongly about it.** Ça m'est égal.

struck [strʌk] vb see **strike**

struggle ['strʌgl] vb ❶ (*physically*) se débattre ▷ *She struggled, but she couldn't escape.* Elle s'est débattue, mais elle n'a pas pu s'échapper.; **to struggle to do something (1)** (*fight*) se battre pour faire quelque chose ▷ *He struggled to get custody of his daughter.* Il s'est battu pour obtenir la garde de sa fille. **(2)** (*have difficulty*) avoir du mal à faire quelque chose
▶ n (*for independence, equality*) lutte f; **It was a struggle.** Ça a été laborieux.

stub [stʌb] n ❶ talon m ▷ *Keep your ticket stub.* Garde le talon de ton billet.

stub vb: **to stub one's toe** se cogner l'orteil ▷ *I stubbed my toe on a stone.* Je me suis cogné l'orteil contre une pierre.

stubborn ['stʌbən] adj têtu

stuck [stʌk] vb see **stick**
▶ adj (*jammed*) coincé ▷ *It's stuck.* C'est coincé.; **to get stuck** rester coincé ▷ *We got stuck in a traffic jam.* Nous sommes restés coincés dans un embouteillage.

stuck-up [stʌk'ʌp] adj coincé (*informal*)

stud [stʌd] n ❶ (*earring*) boucle d'oreille f ❷ (*on football boots*) clou m

student ['stju:dənt] n étudiant m, étudiante f

student driver n apprenti-conducteur m, apprentie-conductrice f; **"Student Driver"** (on car) « Étudiant au volant »

studio ['stju:dɪəʊ] n studio m ▷ a TV studio un studio de télévision; **a studio apartment** un studio

study ['stʌdɪ] vb ❶ (at university) faire des études ▷ I plan to study biology. J'ai l'intention de faire des études en biologie. ❷ (do homework) travailler ▷ I have to study tonight. Je dois travailler ce soir.

stuff [stʌf] n ❶ (substance) chose f ▷ I need some stuff for hay fever. J'ai besoin de quelque chose contre le rhume des foins. ❷ (things) patentes fpl ▷ There's some stuff on the table for you. Il y a des patentes sur la table pour toi. ▷ I have a ton of stuff to do this weekend. J'ai plein de patentes à faire en fin de semaine. ❸ (possessions) affaires fpl ▷ Have you got all your stuff? Est-ce que tu as toutes tes affaires? ▶ vb ❶ (cram) fourrer ▷ He stuffed the notebook into his pack. Il a fourré le cahier dans son sac à dos. ❷ (turkey) farcir

stuffed [stʌft] adj: **stuffed animal** (1) (toy) l'animal en peluche (2) (real) l'animal empaillé; **No thanks, I'm stuffed!** Non, merci, j'ai l'estomac bien rempli!

stuffing ['stʌfɪŋ] n (in turkey) farce f

stuffy ['stʌfɪ] adj (room) mal aéré; **It's really stuffy in here.** On étouffe ici.

stumble ['stʌmbl] vb trébucher

stung [stʌŋ] vb see **sting**

stunk [stʌŋk] vb see **stink**

stunned [stʌnd] adj (amazed) sidéré ▷ I was stunned. J'étais sidérée.

stunning ['stʌnɪŋ] adj superbe

stunt [stʌnt] n (in film) cascade f

stunt actor n cascadeur m, cascadeuse f

stupid ['stju:pɪd] adj stupide ▷ a stupid joke une plaisanterie stupide; **Me, go jogging? Don't be stupid!** Moi, faire du jogging? Ne dis pas de niaiseries!

stutter ['stʌtər] vb bégayer

style [staɪl] n style m ▷ That's not his style. Ça n'est pas son style.

subject [səb'dʒɛkt] n ❶ sujet m ▷ The subject of my project was the Internet. Le sujet de mon projet était Internet. ❷ (at school) matière f ▷ What's your favourite subject? Quelle est ta matière préférée?

subjunctive [səb'dʒʌŋktɪv] n subjonctif m ▷ in the subjunctive au subjonctif

submarine [sʌbmə'ri:n] n sous-marin m; **submarine sandwich** le sous-marin

subscription [səb'skrɪpʃən] n (to paper, magazine) abonnement m; **to take out a subscription to** s'abonner à

subsidize ['sʌbsɪdaɪz] vb subventionner

substance ['sʌbstəns] n substance f; **substance abuse** l'abus m de substances toxiques

substitute ['sʌbstɪtju:t] n (person) remplaçant m, remplaçante f
▶ vb substituer ▷ to substitute A for B substituer A à B

subtitled ['sʌbtaɪtld] adj sous-titré

subtitles ['sʌbtaɪtlz] npl sous-titres mpl ▷ a French film with English subtitles un film français avec des sous-titres en anglais

subtle ['sʌtl] adj subtil

subtract [səb'trækt] vb soustraire ▷ to subtract 3 from 5 soustraire trois de cinq

suburb ['sʌbɜːb] n banlieue f ▷ a suburb of Vancouver une banlieue de Vancouver ▷ They live in the suburbs. Ils habitent en banlieue.

suburban [sə'bɜːbən] adj de banlieue ▷ a suburban home une maison de banlieue

subway ['sʌbweɪ] n métro m ▷ a subway station une station de métro

succeed [sək'si:d] vb réussir ▷ to succeed in doing something réussir à faire quelque chose

success [sək'sɛs] n succès m ▷ The play was a great success. La pièce a eu beaucoup de succès.

successful [sək'sɛsful] adj réussi ▷ a successful attempt une tentative réussie; **to be successful in doing something** réussir à faire quelque chose; **She's a successful entrepreneur.** Ses affaires marchent bien.

successfully [sək'sɛsfulɪ] adv avec succès

successor [sək'sɛsər] n successeur m, successeure f

such [sʌtʃ] adj, adv si ▷ such nice people des gens si gentils ▷ such a long journey un voyage si long; **such a lot of** tellement de ▷ such a lot of work tellement de travail; **such as** (like) comme ▷ spicy dishes, such as Creole shrimp les plats épicés, comme les crevettes à la créole; **not as such** pas exactement ▷ He's not an expert as such, but... Ce n'est pas exactement un expert, mais...; **There's no such thing.** Ça n'existe pas. ▷ There's no such thing as the Sasquatch. Le Sasquatch n'existe pas.

such-and-such ['sʌtʃənsʌtʃ] adj tel ou tel (f telle ou telle) ▷ such-and-such a place tel ou tel endroit

suck [sʌk] vb sucer ▷ to suck one's thumb sucer son pouce

sudden ['sʌdn] adj soudain ▷ a sudden change un changement soudain; **all of a sudden** tout à coup

suddenly ['sʌdnlɪ] adv ❶ (stop, leave, change) brusquement ❷ (die) subitement ❸ (at beginning of sentence) soudain ▷ Suddenly, the door opened. Soudain, la porte s'est ouverte.

suede [sweɪd] n suède m ▷ a suede jacket une veste en suède

suffer ['sʌfər] vb souffrir ▷ She was really suffering. Elle souffrait beaucoup.; **to suffer from a disease** avoir une maladie ▷ I suffer from hay fever. J'ai le rhume des foins.

suffocate ['sʌfəkeɪt] vb suffoquer

sugar ['ʃugər] n sucre m ▷ Do you take sugar? Est-ce que vous prenez du sucre?; **a sugar bush** une érablière; **a sugar shack** une cabane à sucre

sugaring off ['ʃugərɪŋ-] n temps des sucres m; **a sugaring-off party** une partie de sucre

suggest [sə'dʒɛst] vb suggérer ▷ I suggested they set off early. Je leur ai suggéré de partir de bonne heure.

suggestion [sə'dʒɛstʃən] n suggestion f ▷ to

make a suggestion faire une suggestion
suicide ['suːsaɪd] *n* suicide *m*; **to commit suicide** se suicider
suit [suːt] *n* ❶ *(man's)* costume *m* ❷ *(woman's)* tailleur *m*
▶ *vb* ❶ *(be convenient for)* convenir à ▷ *What time would it suit you?* Quelle heure vous conviendrait?; **That suits me fine.** Ça m'arrange.; **Suit yourself!** Comme tu veux! ❷ *(look good on)* aller bien à ▷ *That dress really suits you.* Cette robe te va vraiment bien.
suitable ['suːtəbl] *adj* ❶ convenable ▷ *a suitable time* une heure convenable ❷ *(clothes)* approprié ▷ *suitable clothing* des vêtements appropriés
suitcase ['suːtkeɪs] *n* valise *f*
suite [swiːt] *n* *(of rooms)* suite *f*; **a bedroom suite** le mobilier de chambre à coucher
sulk [sʌlk] *vb* bouder
sulky ['sʌlkɪ] *adj* boudeur *(f* boudeuse)
sum [sʌm] *n* *(amount)* somme *f* ▷ *a sum of money* une somme d'argent
sum up *vb* résumer
summarize ['sʌməraɪz] *vb* résumer
summary ['sʌmərɪ] *n* résumé *m*
summer ['sʌmə'] *n* été *m*; **in summer** en été; **summer clothes** les vêtements d'été; **the summer holidays** les vacances d'été; **a summer camp** un camp de vacances
summit ['sʌmɪt] *n* sommet *m*
sun [sʌn] *n* soleil *m* ▷ *in the sun* au soleil
sunbathe ['sʌnbeɪð] *vb* se bronzer
sunblock ['sʌnblɔk] *n* écran *m* solaire
sunburn ['sʌnbɜːn] *n* coup de soleil *m*
sunburned ['sʌnbɜːnt] *adj*: **I got sunburned.** J'ai attrapé un coup de soleil.
Sunday ['sʌndɪ] *n* dimanche *m* ▷ *on Sunday* dimanche ▷ *on Sundays* le dimanche ▷ *every Sunday* tous les dimanches ▷ *last Sunday* dimanche dernier ▷ *next Sunday* dimanche prochain
sunflower ['sʌnflauə'] *n* tournesol *m*
sung [sʌŋ] *vb see* **sing**
sunglasses ['sʌnglɑːsɪz] *npl* lunettes *fpl* de soleil
sunk [sʌŋk] *vb see* **sink**
sunlight ['sʌnlaɪt] *n* soleil *m*; **Avoid exposure to sunlight.** Évitez l'exposition au soleil.
sunny ['sʌnɪ] *adj* ensoleillé ▷ *a sunny morning* une matinée ensoleillée; **It's sunny.** Il fait du soleil.; **a sunny day** une belle journée
sunrise ['sʌnraɪz] *n* lever du soleil *m*
sunroof ['sʌnruːf] *n* toit ouvrant *m*
sunscreen ['sʌnskriːn] *n* écran *m* solaire
sunset ['sʌnsɛt] *n* coucher du soleil *m*
sunshine ['sʌnʃaɪn] *n* soleil *m*
sunstroke ['sʌnstrəuk] *n* insolation *f* ▷ *to get sunstroke* attraper une insolation
suntan ['sʌntæn] *n* bronzage *m*; **suntan lotion** le lait solaire; **suntan oil** l'huile *f* solaire
super ['suːpə'] *adj* formidable
superb [suː'pɜːb] *adj* superbe
supermarket ['suːpəmɑːkɪt] *n* supermarché *m*
supernatural [suːpə'nætʃərəl] *adj* surnaturel *(f* surnaturelle)

superstitious [suːpə'stɪʃəs] *adj* superstitieux *(f* superstitieuse)
supervise ['suːpəvaɪz] *vb* surveiller
supervisor ['suːpəvaɪzə'] *n* *(in factory)* superviseur *m*, superviseuse *f*
supper ['sʌpə'] *n* souper *m*
supplement [sʌplɪ'ment] *n* supplément *m* ▷ *a vitamin supplement* un supplément vitaminique
supplies [sə'plaɪz] *npl* ravitaillement *m*
supply [sə'plaɪ] *vb* *(provide)* fournir; **to supply somebody with something** fournir quelque chose à quelqu'un ▷ *The centre supplied us with all the equipment.* Le centre nous a fourni tout l'équipement.
▶ *n* provision *f* ▷ *a supply of paper* une provision de papier; **the water supply** *(to town)* l'approvisionnement *m* en eau
supply teacher *n* suppléant *m*, suppléante *f*
support [sə'pɔːt] *vb* ❶ *(encourage)* soutenir ▷ *My mom has always supported me.* Ma mère m'a toujours soutenu. ❷ *(agree with)* être en faveur de ▷ *I support the new rule.* Je suis en faveur du nouveau règlement. ❸ *(financially)* subvenir aux besoins de ▷ *She had to support five children on her own.* Elle a dû subvenir toute seule aux besoins de cinq enfants.
▶ *n* *(backing)* soutien *m*
supporter [sə'pɔːtə'] *n* ❶ sympathisant *m*, sympathisante *f* ▷ *a supporter of nuclear disarmament* un sympathisant du désarmement nucléaire ❷ *(donor)* donateur *m*, donatrice *f*
suppose [sə'pəuz] *vb* imaginer ▷ *I suppose he's late.* J'imagine qu'il est en retard. ▷ *Suppose you won the lottery.* Imaginez que vous gagniez à la loterie.; **I suppose so.** J'imagine.; **to be supposed to do something** être censé faire quelque chose ▷ *You're supposed to show your passport.* On est censé montrer son passeport.
supposing [sə'pəuzɪŋ] *conj* si ▷ *Supposing you won the lottery...* Si tu gagnais à la loterie...
supreme [suː'priːm] *adj* suprême ▷ *the Supreme Court* la Cour suprême
surcharge ['sɜːtʃɑːdʒ] *n* surcharge *f*
sure [ʃuə'] *adj* sûr ▷ *Are you sure?* Tu es sûr?; **Sure!** Bien sûr!; **to make sure that...** vérifier que... ▷ *I'm going to make sure the door's locked.* Je vais vérifier que la porte est fermée à clé.
surf [sɜːf] *n* ressac *m*
▶ *vb* surfer; **to go surfing** faire du surf; **to surf the Net** surfer sur Internet
surface ['sɜːfɪs] *n* surface *f*
surfboard ['sɜːfbɔːd] *n* planche de surf *f* *(pl* planches de surf)
surfing ['sɜːfɪŋ] *n* surf *m* ▷ *to go surfing* faire du surf
surgeon ['sɜːdʒən] *n* chirurgien *m*, chirurgienne *f* ▷ *She's a surgeon.* Elle est chirurgienne.
surgery ['sɜːdʒərɪ] *n* opération *f* ▷ *Surgery was required.* Il a fallu faire une opération. ▷ *The surgery is scheduled for Monday.* L'opération est prévue pour lundi.; **She underwent extensive surgery.** Elle a subi une grave intervention chirurgicale.

surname ['sə:neɪm] n nom de famille m (pl noms de famille)

surprise [sə'praɪz] n surprise f

surprised [sə'praɪzd] adj surpris ▷ I was surprised to see him. J'ai été surprise de le voir.

surprising [sə'praɪzɪŋ] adj surprenant

surrender [sə'rendə'] vb capituler

surrogate mother ['sʌrəgɪt-] n mère porteuse f

surround [sə'raund] vb encercler ▷ The police surrounded the house. La police a encerclé la maison. ▷ You're surrounded! Vous êtes encerclé!; **surrounded by** entouré de ▷ The house is surrounded by trees. La maison est entourée d'arbres.

surroundings [sə'raundɪŋz] npl cadre m ▷ a hotel in beautiful surroundings un hôtel situé dans un beau cadre

survey [sə:'veɪ] n (research) enquête f

survivor [sə'vaɪvə'] n survivant m, survivante f ▷ There were no survivors. Il n'y a pas eu de survivants.

suspect [səs'pekt] vb soupçonner
▶ n suspect m, suspecte f

suspend [səs'pend] vb ❶ (from school, team) exclure ▷ He's been suspended. Il s'est fait exclure. ❷ (from job) suspendre

suspenders [səs'pendəz] npl bretelles fpl

suspense [səs'pens] n ❶ (waiting) attente f ▷ The suspense was terrible. L'attente a été terrible. ❷ (in story) suspense m ▷ a film with lots of suspense un film avec beaucoup de suspense

suspension [səs'penʃən] n ❶ (from school, team) exclusion f ❷ (from job) suspension f

suspicious [səs'pɪʃəs] adj ❶ méfiant ▷ He was suspicious at first. Il était méfiant au début. ❷ (suspicious-looking) louche ▷ a suspicious person un individu louche

swallow ['swɔləu] vb avaler

swam [swæm] vb see **swim**

swan [swɔn] n cygne m

swap [swɔp] vb échanger ▷ Do you want to swap? Tu veux échanger?; **to swap A for B** échanger A contre B

swat [swɔt] vb écraser

sway [sweɪ] vb osciller

swear [sweə'] vb (make an oath, curse) sacrer

swearword ['sweəwə:d] n sacre m

sweat [swet] n transpiration f
▶ vb transpirer

sweater ['swetə'] n chandail m

sweatshirt ['swetʃə:t] n chandail en molleton m

sweaty ['swetɪ] adj ❶ (person, face) en sueur ▷ I'm all sweaty. Je suis en sueur. ❷ (hands) moite

sweep [swi:p] vb balayer; **to sweep the floor** balayer

sweet [swi:t] adj ❶ (taste) sucré ❷ (kind) gentil (f gentille) ▷ That was really sweet of you. C'était vraiment gentil de ta part. ❸ (cute) mignon (f mignonne) ▷ Isn't she sweet? Comme elle est mignonne!; **sweet and sour pork** le porc à la sauce aigre-douce

sweets [swi:ts] npl sucreries fpl

sweltering ['sweltərɪŋ] adj: **It was sweltering.** Il faisait une chaleur étouffante.

swept [swept] vb see **sweep**

swerve [swə:v] vb faire une embardée ▷ He swerved to avoid the cyclist. Il a fait une embardée pour éviter la cycliste.

swim [swɪm] n: **to go for a swim** aller se baigner
▶ vb nager ▷ Can you swim? Tu sais nager?; **She swam across the river.** Elle a traversé la rivière à la nage.

swimmer ['swɪmə'] n nageur m, nageuse f ▷ She's a good swimmer. C'est une bonne nageuse.

swimming ['swɪmɪŋ] n natation f ▷ Do you like swimming? Tu aimes la natation?; **to go swimming** (in a pool) aller à la piscine; **a swimming pool** une piscine; **swimming trunks** le maillot de bain

swimsuit ['swɪmsu:t] n maillot de bain m

swing [swɪŋ] n (in playground, garden) balançoire f
▶ vb ❶ se balancer ▷ A bunch of keys swung from his belt. Un trousseau de clés se balançait à sa ceinture.; **Sam was swinging an umbrella as he walked.** Sam balançait son parapluie en marchant. ❷ virer ▷ The canoe swung round sharply. Le canot a viré brusquement.

switch [swɪtʃ] n (for light, radio, etc.) interrupteur m
▶ vb changer de ▷ We switched partners. Nous avons changé de partenaire.

switch off vb ❶ (electrical appliance) éteindre ❷ (engine, machine) arrêter

switch on vb ❶ (electrical appliance) allumer ❷ (engine, machine) mettre en marche

swollen ['swəulən] adj (arm, leg) enflé

sword [sɔ:d] n épée f

swore, sworn vb see **swear**

swum [swʌm] vb see **swim**

swung [swʌŋ] vb see **swing**

symbol ['sɪmbl] n symbole m

sympathetic [sɪmpə'θetɪk] adj compréhensif (f compréhensive) ▷ The teacher was very sympathetic and allowed me to leave before the end of the class. La professeure a été très compréhensive et m'a permis de partir avant la fin du cours.

sympathize ['sɪmpəθaɪz] vb: **to sympathize with somebody** comprendre quelqu'un

sympathy ['sɪmpəθɪ] n compassion f

symptom ['sɪmptəm] n symptôme m

synagogue ['sɪnəgɔg] n synagogue f

syndrome n syndrome m; **Down syndrome** le syndrome de Down; **Severe Acute Respiratory Syndrome** le syndrome respiratoire aigu sévère; **chronic fatigue syndrome** le syndrome de fatigue chronique

synthetic [sɪn'θetɪk] adj synthétique ▷ synthetic fibres des fibres synthétiques

syringe [sɪ'rɪndʒ] n seringue f

system ['sɪstəm] n système m

table | 290

t

table ['teɪbl] n table f ▷ *to set the table* mettre la table

tablecloth ['teɪblklɔθ] n nappe f

tablespoon ['teɪblspuːn] n cuillère à soupe f; **a tablespoon of sugar** une cuillerée à soupe de sucre

table tennis n ping-pong m ▷ *to play table tennis* jouer au ping-pong

tabloid ['tæblɔɪd] n tabloïd m

tackle ['tækl] n (in football) tacle m; **fishing tackle** le matériel de pêche
▶ vb ❶ (in football) tacler ❷ (in rugby) plaquer; **to tackle a problem** s'attaquer à un problème

tact [tækt] n tact m

tactful ['tæktful] adj plein(e) de tact

tactics ['tæktɪks] npl tactique f

tactless ['tæktlɪs] adj: **to be tactless** manquer de tact ▷ *a tactless remark* une remarque qui manque de tact

tadpole ['tædpəʊl] n têtard m

tag [tæg] n (label) étiquette f

tail [teɪl] n queue f; **Heads or tails?** Pile ou face?

tailor ['teɪləʳ] n tailleur m

take [teɪk] vb ❶ prendre ▷ *Are you taking your new camera?* Tu prends ton nouvel appareil photo? ▷ *He took a plate from the cupboard.* Il a pris une assiette dans l'armoire. ▷ *It takes about an hour.* Ça prend environ une heure. ❷ (person) emmener ▷ *She goes to Toronto every week, but she never takes me.* Elle va à Toronto toutes les semaines, mais elle ne m'emmène jamais.; **to take something somewhere** emporter quelque chose quelque part ▷ *Do you take your notebooks home?* Vous emportez vos cahiers chez vous? ▷ *Don't take anything valuable with you.* N'emportez pas d'objets de valeur.; **I'm going to take my coat to the cleaner's.** Je vais porter mon manteau chez le nettoyeur. ❸ (effort, skill) demander ▷ *that takes a lot of courage* cela demande beaucoup de courage; **It takes a lot of money to do that.** Il faut beaucoup d'argent pour faire ça. ❹ (tolerate) supporter ▷ *He can't take being criticized.* Il ne supporte pas d'être critiqué. ❺ (test) passer ▷ *She's taking her driving test next week.* Elle passe le test de conduire la semaine prochaine. ❻ (subject) faire ▷ *I decided to take French instead of music.* J'ai décidé de faire du français au lieu de la musique.

take after vb ressembler à ▷ *She takes after her mother.* Elle ressemble à sa mère.

take apart vb: **to take something apart** démonter quelque chose

take away vb ❶ (object) emporter ❷ (person) emmener; **to take something away** (confiscate) confisquer quelque chose

take back vb rapporter ▷ *I took it back to the store.* Je l'ai rapporté au magasin.; **I take it all back!** Je n'ai rien dit!

take down vb ❶ (poster, sign) enlever ❷ (painting, curtains) décrocher ❸ (tent, scaffolding) démonter ❹ (make a note of) prendre en note ▷ *He took down the details in his notebook.* Il a pris tous les détails en note dans son carnet.

take in vb (understand) comprendre ▷ *I didn't really take it in.* Je n'ai pas bien compris.

take off vb ❶ (plane) décoller ▷ *The plane took off twenty minutes late.* L'avion a décollé avec vingt minutes de retard. ❷ (clothes) enlever ▷ *Take your coat off.* Enlevez votre manteau.

take out vb (from container, pocket) sortir; **They took us out to the movies.** Il nous ont emmenés au cinéma.; **hot meals to take out** des plats chauds à emporter

take over vb prendre la relève ▷ *I'll take over now.* Je vais prendre la relève.; **to take over from somebody** remplacer quelqu'un

taken ['teɪkən] vb see **take**

takeoff ['teɪkɔf] n (of plane) décollage m

takeout ['teɪkaʊt] n ❶ (meal) plat à emporter m ❷ (restaurant) restaurant qui vend des plats à emporter m ▷ *a Chinese takeout* un restaurant chinois qui vend des plats à emporter

tale [teɪl] n (story) conte f

talent ['tælnt] n talent m ▷ *He has lots of talent.* Il a beaucoup de talent.; **to have a talent for something** être doué pour quelque chose ▷ *He has a real talent for languages.* Il est vraiment doué pour les langues.

talented ['tæləntɪd] adj talentueux m (f talentueuse); **She's a talented pianist.** C'est une pianiste talentueuse.

talk [tɔːk] n ❶ (speech) exposé m ▷ *She gave a talk on rock climbing.* Elle a fait un exposé sur l'escalade. ❷ (conversation) conversation f ▷ *I had a talk with my dad about it.* J'ai eu une petite conversation avec mon père à ce sujet. ❸ (gossip) racontars mpl ▷ *It's just talk.* Ce sont des racontars.
▶ vb parler ▷ *to talk about something* parler de quelque chose; **to talk something over with somebody** discuter de quelque chose avec quelqu'un

talkative ['tɔːkətɪv] adj bavard

talk show n émission-débat f (pl émissions-débats)

tall [tɔːl] adj ❶ (person, tree) grand; **to be 2 metres tall** mesurer deux mètres ❷ (building) haut m

tame [teɪm] adj (animal) apprivoisé(e) ▷ *They have a tame ferret.* Ils ont un furet apprivoisé.

tampon ['tæmpɒn] n tampon m

tan [tæn] n bronzage m ▷ *to have an amazing tan.* avoir un bronzage superbe.

tangerine [tændʒəˈriːn] n mandarine f

tangle up ['tæŋgl-] vb emmêler ▷ *My hair is all tangled up.* Mes cheveux sont tout emmêlés.;

to get tangled up s'emmêler ▷ *His fishing line got tangled up with mine.* Sa ligne de pêche s'est emmêlée dans la mienne.

tank [tæŋk] n ❶ *(for water, gasoline)* réservoir m ❷ *(military)* char d'assaut m; **a fish tank** un aquarium

tanker ['tæŋkə'] n ❶ *(ship)* pétrolier m; **an oil tanker** un pétrolier ❷ *(truck)* camion-citerne m

tap [tæp] n ❶ *(water tap)* robinet m ❷ *(gentle touch)* petite tape f

tap-dancing ['tæpdɑ:nsɪŋ] n claquette f ▷ *I do tap-dancing.* Je danse la claquette.

tape [teɪp] vb *(record)* enregistrer ▷ *Did you tape that movie last night?* As-tu enregistré le film hier soir?
▶ n ❶ cassette f ▷ *a tape of Avril Lavigne* une cassette d'Avril Lavigne ❷ *(adhesive tape)* ruban adhésif m

tape measure n le galon à mesurer

target ['tɑ:gɪt] n cible f

tart [tɑ:t] n tartelette f ▷ *a butter tart* une tartelette aux raisins secs

tartan ['tɑ:tn] adj écossais ▷ *a tartan skirt* une jupe écossaise

task [tɑ:sk] n tâche f

taste [teɪst] n goût m ▷ *It has a really strange taste.* Ça a un goût vraiment bizarre. ▷ *a joke in bad taste* une plaisanterie de mauvais goût; **Would you like a taste?** Tu veux goûter?
▶ vb goûter ▷ *Would you like to taste it?* Vous voulez y goûter?; **to taste like something** avoir un goût de quelque chose ▷ *It tastes like fish.* Ça a un goût de poisson.; **You can taste the garlic in it.** Ça a bien le goût d'ail.

tasteful ['teɪstful] adj de bon goût

tasteless ['teɪstlɪs] adj ❶ *(food)* fade ❷ *(in bad taste)* de mauvais goût ▷ *a tasteless remark* une remarque de mauvais goût

tasty ['teɪstɪ] adj savoureux *(f* savoureuse)

tattoo [tə'tu:] n tatouage m

taught [tɔ:t] vb see **teach**

Taurus ['tɔ:rəs] n Taureau m ▷ *I'm a Taurus.* Je suis Taureau.

tax [tæks] n ❶ *(on income)* impôts mpl ❷ *(on goods, alcohol)* taxe f

taxi ['tæksɪ] n taxi m; **a taxi driver** un chauffeur de taxi; **a taxi stand** une station de taxi

TB n tuberculose f

tea [ti:] n thé m ▷ *a cup of tea* une tasse de thé; **a tea bag** un sachet de thé

teach [ti:tʃ] vb ❶ apprendre ▷ *My sister taught me to swim.* Ma sœur m'a appris à nager. ▷ *That'll teach you!* Ça t'apprendra! ❷ *(in school)* enseigner ▷ *She teaches physics.* Elle enseigne la physique.

teacher ['ti:tʃə'] n ❶ *(in secondary school)* professeur m, professeure f ▷ *a math teacher* un professeur de maths ▷ *She's a teacher.* Elle est professeure. ❷ *(in primary school)* enseignant m, enseignante f ▷ *He's a primary school teacher.* Il est enseignant.

teacher's pet ['ti:tʃəz-] n chouchou m, chouchoute f

teaching assistant ['ti:tʃɪŋ-] n aide-enseignant m, aide-enseignante f

team [ti:m] n équipe f ▷ *a football team* une équipe de football ▷ *She was on my team.* Elle était dans mon équipe.

teamwork ['ti:mwə:k] n travail d'équipe m ▷ *That's teamwork!* C'est ça, le travail d'équipe! ▷ *Teamwork makes all the difference.* Travailler en équipe fait toute la différence.

teapot ['ti:pɒt] n théière f

tear [n tɪə', vb tɛə'] n larme f ▷ *The child was in tears.* L'enfant était en larmes.
▶ vb ❶ déchirer ▷ *Be careful or you'll tear the page.* Fais attention, tu vas déchirer la page. ❷ se déchirer ▷ *It won't tear, it's very strong.* Ça ne se déchire pas, c'est très solide.; **to tear up** déchirer ▷ *He tore up the letter.* Il a déchiré la lettre.

tease [ti:z] vb ❶ *(unkindly)* tourmenter ▷ *Stop teasing that poor animal!* Arrête de tourmenter ce pauvre animal! ❷ *(jokingly)* taquiner ▷ *He's teasing you.* Il te taquine.; **I was only teasing.** Je plaisantais.

teaspoon ['ti:spu:n] n petite cuillère f; **a teaspoon of sugar** une cuillerée à thé de sucre

tea towel n torchon m

technical ['tɛknɪkl] adj technique f

technician [tɛk'nɪʃən] n technicien m, technicienne f

technique [tɛk'ni:k] n technique f

technological [tɛknə'lɒdʒɪkl] adj technologique

technology [tɛk'nɒlədʒɪ] n technologie f

teddy bear ['tɛdɪ-] n nounours m

teenage ['ti:neɪdʒ] adj ❶ pour les jeunes ▷ *a teenage magazine* un magazine pour les jeunes ❷ *(boys, girls)* adolescent ▷ *He has two teenage daughters.* Il a deux filles adolescentes.

teenager ['ti:neɪdʒə'] n adolescent m, adolescente f

teens [ti:nz] npl: **She's in her teens.** C'est une adolescente.

teeth [ti:θ] npl dents fpl

teethe [ti:ð] vb faire ses dents

teetotal ['ti:'təutl] adj: **I'm teetotal.** Je ne bois jamais d'alcool.

telecommunications ['tɛlɪkəmju:nɪ-'keɪʃənz] npl télécommunications fpl

telephone ['tɛlɪfəun] n téléphone m ▷ *on the telephone* au téléphone; **a telephone booth** une cabine téléphonique; **a telephone call** un coup de téléphone; **the telephone directory** l'annuaire m; **a telephone number** un numéro de téléphone

telescope ['tɛlɪskəup] n télescope m

television ['tɛlɪvɪʒən] n télévision f; **on television** à la télévision; **a television program** une émission de télévision

television ad n publicité télévisée f

tell [tɛl] vb dire; **to tell somebody something** dire quelque chose à quelqu'un ▷ *Did you tell your mother?* Tu l'as dit à ta mère? ▷ *I told him that I was going on holiday.* Je lui ai dit que je partais en vacances.; **to tell somebody to do something** dire à quelqu'un de faire quelque chose ▷ *He told me to wait a moment.* Il m'a dit d'attendre un moment.; **to tell lies** dire des mensonges; **to tell a story** raconter une histoire; **I can't tell the difference between them.** Je n'arrive pas à les distinguer.

tell off vb gronder

temper ['tɛmpə*] n caractère m ▷ **to have a bad temper**. avoir mauvais caractère.; **to lose one's temper** se mettre en colère ▷ I lost my temper. Je me suis mis en colère.

temperature ['tɛmprətʃə*] n (of oven, water, person) température f; **The temperature was 30 degrees.** Il faisait trente degrés.; **to have a temperature** avoir de la fièvre

temple ['tɛmpl] n temple m

temporary ['tɛmpərəri] adj temporaire

tempt [tɛmpt] vb tenter ▷ I'm very tempted! Je suis très tenté!; **to tempt somebody to do something** persuader quelqu'un de faire quelque chose

temptation [tɛmp'teɪʃən] n tentation f

tempting ['tɛmptɪŋ] adj tentant

ten [tɛn] num dix ▷ She's ten. Elle a dix ans.

tenant ['tɛnənt] n locataire m, locataire f

tend [tɛnd] vb: **to tend to do something** avoir tendance à faire quelque chose ▷ He tends to arrive late. Il a tendance à arriver en retard.

tender ['tɛndə*] adj ① (food) tendre ② (part of body) sensible ▷ My feet are really tender. J'ai les pieds très sensibles.

tennis ['tɛnɪs] n tennis m ▷ Do you play tennis? Vous jouez au tennis?; **a tennis ball** une balle de tennis; **a tennis court** un court de tennis; **a tennis racquet** une raquette de tennis

tense [tɛns] adj tendu
▶ n: **the present tense** le présent; **the future tense** le futur

tension ['tɛnʃən] n tension f

tent [tɛnt] n tente f; **a tent peg** un piquet de tente; **a tent pole** un montant de tente

tenth [tɛnθ] adj dixième ▷ the tenth floor le dixième étage; **the tenth of August** le dix août

term [tə:m] n ① (at school) trimestre m ② terme m ▷ a short-term solution une solution à court terme ▷ a technical term un terme technique; **to come to terms with something** accepter quelque chose

terminal ['tə:mɪnl] adj (illness, patient) incurable
▶ n (of computer) un terminal; **an airport terminal** une aérogare

terminally ['tə:mɪnlɪ] adv: **to be terminally ill** être condamné

terrace ['tɛrəs] n (patio) terrasse f

terrible ['tɛrɪbl] adj épouvantable ▷ He looks terrible. Il a une mine épouvantable.

terribly ['tɛrɪblɪ] adv ① terriblement ▷ He suffered terribly. Il souffre terriblement. ② vraiment ▷ I'm terribly sorry. Je suis vraiment désolé.

terrier ['tɛrɪə*] n terrier m

terrific [tə'rɪfɪk] adj (wonderful) super ▷ That's terrific! C'est super!; **You look terrific!** Tu es superbe!

terrified ['tɛrɪfaɪd] adj terrifié ▷ I was terrified! J'étais terrifié!

Territorial Council [tɛrɪ'tɔ:rɪəl-] n Conseil du territoire m

territory ['tɛrɪtərɪ] n territoire m

terrorism ['tɛrərɪzəm] n terrorisme m

terrorist ['tɛrərɪst] n terroriste; **a terrorist attack** un attentat terroriste

test [tɛst] n ① (at school: at school) test m ▷ I have a geography test today. J'ai un test de géographie aujourd'hui. ② (trial, check) essai m ▷ nuclear tests les essais nucléaires ③ (medical) analyse f ▷ a blood test une analyse de sang ▷ They're going to do some more tests. Ils vont faire d'autres analyses.; **driving test** l'examen du permis de conduire ▷ She's taking her driving test tomorrow. Elle subit son permis de conduire demain.
▶ vb ① essayer ▷ to test something out essayer quelque chose ② (class) interroger ▷ My teacher tested us on the vocabulary. Mon professeur nous a interrogés sur le vocabulaire.; **She was tested for drugs.** On lui a fait subir un contrôle antidopage.

test tube n éprouvette f

tetanus ['tɛtənəs] n tétanos m ▷ a tetanus injection un vaccin contre le tétanos

text [tɛkst] n ① texte m ② (mobile phone) minimessage m
▶ vb: **to text someone** envoyer un minimessage à quelqu'un

textbook ['tɛkstbuk] n manuel m ▷ a French textbook un manuel de français

than [ðæn, ðən] conj que ▷ She's taller than me. Elle est plus grande que moi. ▷ I have more books than him. J'ai plus de livres que lui.; **more than ten years** plus de dix ans; **more than once** plus d'une fois

thank [θæŋk] vb remercier ▷ Don't forget to write and thank them. N'oublie pas de leur écrire pour les remercier.; **thank you** merci; **thank you very much** merci beaucoup

thanks [θæŋks] excl merci; **thanks to** grâce à ▷ Thanks to her, everything went OK. Grâce à elle, tout s'est bien passé.

that [ðæt] adj, pron, conj ① ce ▷ that book ce livre, cet ▷ that man cet homme, cette ▷ that woman cette femme; **that road** cette route ▷ THAT road cette route-là; **that one** (1) (masculine) celui-là ▷ "This man?" — "No, that one." « Cet homme-ci? » — « Non, celui-là. » (2) (feminine) celle-là ▷ "Do you like this photo?" — "No, I prefer that one." « Tu aimes cette photo? » — « Non, je préfère celle-là. » ② ça ▷ You see that? Tu vois ça?; **What's that?** Qu'est-ce que c'est?; **Who's that?** C'est qui?; **Is that you?** C'est toi?; **That's...** C'est... ▷ That's my teacher. C'est mon prof. ▷ That's what she said. C'est ce qu'elle a dit. ③ qui ▷ the man that saw us l'homme qui nous a vus ▷ the woman that spoke to us la femme qui nous a parlé ④ que ▷ the man that we saw l'homme que nous avons vu ▷ the dog that she bought le chien qu'elle a acheté ▷ He thought that your brother was ill. Il pensait que ton frère était malade. ▷ I know that she likes chocolate. Je sais qu'elle aime le chocolat.; **the woman that we spoke to** la femme à qui nous avons parlé.; **It was that big.** Il était grand comme ça.; **It's about that high.** C'est à peu près haut comme ça.; **It's not that**

difficult. Ça n'est pas si difficile que ça.

thatched [θætʃt] adj : **a thatched cottage** une chaumière

the [ðiː, ðə] art le ▷ *the boy* le garçon, l' ▷ *the man* l'homme m ▷ *the air* l'air m ▷ *the habit* l'habitude f, la ▷ *the girl* la fille, les ▷ *the children* les enfants

theatre ['θɪətər] n théâtre m

theft [θeft] n vol m

their [ðeər] adj leur (pl leurs) ▷ *their house* leur maison ▷ *their parents* leurs parents

theirs [ðeəz] pron le + m leur, la + f leur, les + pl leurs ▷ *It's not our garage, it's theirs.* Ce n'est pas notre garage, c'est le leur. ▷ *It's not our car, it's theirs.* Ce n'est pas notre voiture, c'est la leur. ▷ *They're not our ideas, they're theirs.* Ce ne sont pas nos idées, ce sont les leurs.; **Is this theirs? (1)** (masculine owners) C'est à eux? ▷ *This car is theirs.* Cette voiture est à eux. ▷ *"Whose is this?" — "It's theirs."* « C'est à qui? » — « À eux. » **(2)** (feminine owners) C'est à elles?

them [ðem, ðəm] pron ❶ les ▷ *I didn't see them.* Je ne les ai pas vus. ❷ leur ▷ *I gave them some brochures.* Je leur ai donné des brochures. ▷ *I told them the truth.* Je leur ai dit la vérité. ❸ eux m, elles f ▷ *It's for them.* C'est pour eux. ▷ *My two sisters came, and my dad was with them.* Mes deux sœurs sont venues, et mon père était avec elles.

theme [θiːm] n thème m

theme park n parc d'attractions m

themselves [ðəm'selvz] pron ❶ se ▷ *Did they hurt themselves?* Est-ce qu'ils se sont fait mal? ❷ eux-mêmes m, elles-mêmes f ▷ *They did it themselves.* Ils l'ont fait eux-mêmes.

then [ðen] adv, conj ❶ (next) ensuite ▷ *I get dressed. Then I have breakfast.* Je m'habille. Ensuite je prends mon petit déjeuner. ❷ (in that case) alors ▷ *"My pen's run out."* — *"Use a pencil then!"* « Il n'y a plus d'encre dans mon stylo. » — « Alors utilise un crayon! » ❸ (at that time) à l'époque ▷ *There was no electricity then.* Il n'y avait pas l'électricité à l'époque.; **now and then** de temps en temps ▷ *"Do you play chess?" — "Now and then."* « Vous jouez aux échecs? » — « De temps en temps. »; **By then it was too late.** Il était déjà trop tard.

therapy ['θerəpɪ] n thérapie f

there [ðeər] adv ❶ là ▷ *Put it there, on the table.* Mets-le là, sur la table.; **over there** là-bas; **in there** là; **on there** là; **up there** là-haut; **down there** là-bas; **There he is!** Le voilà! ❷ y ▷ *She went there on Friday.* Elle y est allée vendredi. ▷ *Labrador? I've never been there.* Le Labrador? Je n'y suis jamais allé.; **There is…** Il y a… ▷ *There's a factory near my house.* Il y a une usine près de chez moi.; **There are…** Il y a… ▷ *There are five people in my family.* Il y a cinq personnes dans ma famille.; **There has been an accident.** Il y a eu un accident.

therefore ['ðeəfɔːr] adv donc

there's ['ðeəz]; = **there is**; **there has**

thermometer [θə'mɒmɪtər] n thermomètre m

Thermos® ['θə:məs] n thermos m

these [ðiːz] adj, pron ❶ ces ▷ *these shoes* ces chaussures; **THESE shoes** ces chaussures-là ❷ ceux-ci m ▷ *I want these!* Je veux ceux-ci!, celles-ci f ▷ *I'm looking for some sandals. Can I try these?* Je cherche des sandales. Je peux essayer celles-ci?

they [ðeɪ] pron ils, elles ▷ *"Are there any tickets left?" — "No, they're all sold."* « Est-ce qu'il reste des billets? » — « Non, ils sont tous vendus. » ▷ *"Do you like those shoes?" — "No, they're horrible."* « Tu aimes ces chaussures? » — « Non, elles sont affreuses. »; **They say that…** On dit que…

thick [θɪk] adj (not thin) épais (f épaisse); **The walls are one metre thick.** Les murs font un mètre d'épaisseur.

thief [θiːf] n voleur m, voleuse f; **Stop thief!** Au voleur!

thigh [θaɪ] n cuisse f

thin [θɪn] adj ❶ (person, slice) mince ❷ (skinny) maigre

thing [θɪŋ] n ❶ chose f ▷ *beautiful things* de belles choses ❷ (thingy) patente f ▷ *What's that thing called?* Comment s'appelle cette patente?; **my things** (belongings) mes f affaires; **You poor thing!** Mon pauvre!

think [θɪŋk] vb ❶ (believe) penser ▷ *I think you're wrong.* Je pense que vous avez tort. ▷ *What do you think about the war?* Que pensez-vous de la guerre? ❷ (spend time thinking) réfléchir ▷ *Think carefully before you reply.* Réfléchis bien avant de répondre. ▷ *I'll think about it.* Je vais y réfléchir.; **What are you thinking about?** À quoi tu penses? ❸ (imagine) imaginer ▷ *Think what life would be like without cars.* Imaginez la vie sans voitures.; **I think so.** Oui, je crois.; **I don't think so.** Je ne crois pas.; **I'll think it over.** Je vais y réfléchir.

third [θə:d] adj troisième ▷ *the third day* le troisième jour ▷ *the third time* la troisième fois ▷ *I came third.* Je suis arrivé troisième.; **the third of March** le trois mars ▷ n tiers m ▷ *a third of the population* un tiers de la population

thirdly ['θə:dlɪ] adv troisièmement

thirst [θə:st] n soif f

thirsty ['θə:stɪ] adj : **to be thirsty** avoir soif

thirteen [θə:'tiːn] num treize ▷ *I'm thirteen.* J'ai treize ans.

thirteenth [-'tiːnθ] adj treizième ▷ *her thirteenth birthday* son treizième anniversaire ▷ *the thirteenth floor* le treizième étage; **the thirteenth of August** le treize août

thirty ['θə:tɪ] num trente

this [ðɪs] adj, pron ❶ ce, cet, cette ▷ *this book* ce livre ▷ *this man* cet homme ▷ *this woman* cette femme; **this road** cette route; **THIS road** cette route-ci; **this one (1)** (masculine) celui-ci ▷ *"Pass me that pen." — "This one?"* « Passe-moi ce stylo. » — « Celui-ci? » **(2)** (feminine) celle-ci ▷ *Of the two photos, I prefer this one.* Des deux photos, c'est celle-ci que je préfère. ❷ ça ▷ *You see this?* Tu vois ça?; **What's this?** Qu'est-ce que c'est?; **This is my father.** (introduction) Je te présente mon père.; **This is Gavin speaking.** (on the phone) C'est Gavin à l'appareil.

thistle ['θɪsl] n chardon m

thorough ['θʌrə] adj minutieux (f minutieuse)

▷ *She's very thorough.* Elle est très minutieuse.

thoroughly ['θʌrəlɪ] *adv* (*examine*) à fond

those [ðəʊz] *adj, pron* ❶ ces ▷ *those shoes* ces chaussures; *those shoes* ces chaussures-là ❷ ceux-là m, celles-là f ▷ *I want those!* Je veux ceux-là! ▷ *I'm looking for some sandals. Can I try those?* Je cherche des sandales. Je peux essayer celles-là?

though [ðəʊ] *conj, adv* bien que ▷ *Though it's raining…* Bien qu'il pleuve…; *He's a nice person, though* he's not very outgoing. Il est sympathique, mais pas très extraverti.

thought [θɔːt] *vb see* **think**
▶ *n* (*idea*) idée f ▷ *I've just had a thought.* Je viens d'avoir une idée.; *It was a nice thought, thank you.* C'est gentil de ta part, merci.

thoughtful ['θɔːtful] *adj* ❶ (*deep in thought*) pensif (f pensive) ▷ *You look thoughtful.* Tu as l'air pensif. ❷ (*considerate*) prévenant ▷ *She's very thoughtful.* Elle est très prévenante.

thoughtless ['θɔːtlɪs] *adj*: *He's completely thoughtless.* Il ne pense absolument pas aux autres.

thousand ['θaʊzənd] *num*: *a thousand* mille ▷ *a thousand euros* mille euros; *$2000* deux mille dollars; *thousands of people* des milliers de personnes

thousandth ['θaʊzəntθ] *adj, n* millième m

thread [θred] *n* fil m

threat [θret] *n* menace f

threaten ['θretn] *vb* menacer ▷ *to threaten to do something* menacer de faire quelque chose

three [θriː] *num* trois ▷ *She's three.* Elle a trois ans.

three-dimensional [θriːdɪ'mɛnʃənl] *adj* à trois dimensions

threw [θruː] *vb see* **throw**

thrifty ['θrɪftɪ] *adj* économe

thrill [θrɪl] *n*: *What a thrill!* Quelle émotion

thrilled [θrɪld] *adj*: *I was thrilled.* (*pleased*) J'étais absolument ravi.

thrilling ['θrɪlɪŋ] *adj* palpitant

throat [θrəʊt] *n* gorge f ▷ *to have a sore throat* avoir mal à la gorge

throb [θrɒb] *vb*: *a throbbing pain* un élancement; *My arm's throbbing.* J'ai des élancements dans le bras.

throne [θrəʊn] *n* trône m

through [θruː] *prep, adj, adv* ❶ par ▷ *through the window* par la fenêtre ▷ *I know her through my sister.* Je la connais par ma sœur. ▷ *to go through Winnipeg* passer par Winnipeg; *to go through a tunnel* traverser un tunnel ❷ à travers ▷ *through the mist* à travers la brume ▷ *through the crowd* à travers la foule ▷ *The window was dirty and I couldn't see through.* La fenêtre était sale et je n'arrivais pas à voir à travers.; *a through train* un train direct; *"no through road"* « impasse »

throughout [θruː'aʊt] *prep*: **throughout** *Nova Scotia* dans toute la Nouvelle-Écosse; *throughout the year* pendant toute l'année

throw [θrəʊ] *vb* lancer ▷ *She threw the ball to me.* Elle m'a lancé le ballon.; *to throw a party* organiser une soirée; *That really threw him.* Ça l'a déconcentré.; *to throw away*

(1) (*garbage*) jeter (2) (*chance*) perdre; *to throw out* (1) (*throw away*) jeter (2) (*person*) mettre à la porte ▷ *I threw him out.* Je l'ai mis à la porte.; *to throw up* vomir

thug [θʌg] *n* voyou

thumb [θʌm] *n* pouce m

thumbtack ['θʌmtæk] *n* punaise f

thunder ['θʌndə'] *n* tonnerre m

thunderstorm ['θʌndəstɔːm] *n* orage m

Thursday ['θɜːzdɪ] *n* jeudi m ▷ *on Thursday* jeudi ▷ *on Thursdays* le jeudi ▷ *every Thursday* tous les jeudis ▷ *last Thursday* jeudi dernier ▷ *next Thursday* jeudi prochain

thyme [taɪm] *n* thym m

tick [tɪk] *n* (*of clock*) tic-tac m
▶ *vb* (*clock*) faire tic-tac

ticket ['tɪkɪt] *n* ❶ (*for bus, subway, movie, museum*) ticket m ▷ *a subway ticket* un ticket de métro ❷ (*for plane, train, theatre, concert*) billet m; *a parking ticket* une contravention (pour stationnement); *a speeding ticket* une contravention pour excès de vitesse

ticket office *n* guichet m

tickle ['tɪkl] *vb* chatouiller

ticklish ['tɪklɪʃ] *adj* chatouilleux (f chatouilleuse) ▷ *Are you ticklish?* Tu es chatouilleux?

tick off *vb*: *to tick something off* cocher quelque chose; *to tick somebody off* engueuler quelqu'un

tide [taɪd] *n* marée f; *high tide* la marée haute; *low tide* la marée basse

tidy ['taɪdɪ] *adj* ❶ (*room*) bien rangé ▷ *Your room's very tidy.* Ta chambre est bien rangée. ❷ (*person*) ordonné ▷ *She's very tidy.* Elle est très ordonnée.
▶ *vb* ranger ▷ *Go and tidy your room.* Va ranger ta chambre.; *to tidy up* ranger ▷ *Don't forget to tidy up afterwards.* N'oubliez pas de ranger après.

tie [taɪ] *n* (*necktie*) cravate f; *It was a tie.* (*in sport*) Ils ont fait match nul.
▶ *vb* ❶ (*ribbon, shoelaces*) nouer; *to tie a knot in something* faire un nœud à quelque chose ❷ (*in sport*) faire match nul ▷ *They tied three all.* Ils ont fait match nul, trois à trois.; *to tie up* (1) (*parcel*) ficeler (2) (*dog, boat*) attacher (3) (*prisoner*) ligoter

tiger ['taɪgə'] *n* tigre m

tight [taɪt] *adj* ❶ (*tight-fitting*) moulant ▷ *tight clothes* les vêtements moulants ❷ (*too tight*) serré(e) ▷ *These jeans are a bit tight.* Ces jeans sont un peu serrés.

tighten ['taɪtn] *vb* ❶ (*rope*) tendre ❷ (*screw*) resserrer

tightly ['taɪtlɪ] *adv* (*hold*) fort

tights [taɪts] *npl* collant m

tile [taɪl] *n* (*on wall, floor*) carreau m (pl carreaux)

tiled [taɪld] *adj* (*wall, floor, room*) carrelé

till [tɪl] *n* caisse f
▶ *prep, conj* ❶ jusqu'à ▷ *I waited till ten o'clock.* J'ai attendu jusqu'à dix heures.; *till now* jusqu'à présent; *till then* jusque-là ❷ avant ▷ *It won't be ready till next week.* Ça ne sera pas prêt avant la semaine prochaine. ▷ *Till last*

I'd never been to Gaspé. Avant l'année dernière, je n'étais jamais allé en Gaspésie.

time [taɪm] n ❶ (on clock) heure f ▷ *What time is it?* Quelle heure est-il? ▷ *What time do you get up?* À quelle heure tu te lèves? ▷ *It was two o'clock.* Il était deux heures, heure de Vancouver.; **on time** à l'heure ▷ *She never arrives on time.* Elle n'arrive jamais à l'heure. ❷ (amount of time) temps m ▷ *I'm sorry, I don't have time.* Je suis désolé, je n'ai pas le temps.; **from time to time** de temps en temps; **in time** à temps ▷ *We arrived in time for lunch.* Nous sommes arrivés à temps pour le dîner.; **just in time** juste à temps; **in no time** en un rien de temps ▷ *It was ready in no time.* Ça a été prêt en un rien de temps.; **It's time to go.** Il est temps de partir. ❸ (moment) moment m ▷ *This isn't a good time to ask him.* Ce n'est pas le bon moment pour lui demander.; **for the time being** pour le moment ❹ (occasion) fois f ▷ *this time* cette fois-ci ▷ *next time* la prochaine fois ▷ *two at a time* deux à la fois; **How many times?** Combien de fois?; **at times** parfois; **a long time** longtemps ▷ *Have you lived here for a long time?* Vous habitez ici depuis longtemps?; **in a week's time** dans une semaine ▷ *I'll come back in a month's time.* Je reviendrai dans un mois.; **Come and see us any time.** Venez nous voir quand vous voulez.; **to have a good time** bien s'amuser ▷ *Did you have a good time?* Vous vous êtes bien amusés?; **2 times 2 is 4** deux fois deux égalent quatre

time off n temps libre m

timer ['taɪmə^r] n minuterie f

time-share ['taɪmʃeə^r] n multipropriété f ▷ *We have a time-share ski chalet in Whistler.* Nous avons un chalet de ski en multipropriété à Whistler.

timetable ['taɪmteɪbl] n (for train, bus, school) horaire m

time zone n fuseau horaire m ▷ *Canada has six time zones.* Le Canada a six fuseaux horaires.

tin [tɪn] n (type of metal) étain m

tinsel ['tɪnsl] n guirlandes f

tinted ['tɪntɪd] adj (spectacles, glass) teinté

tiny ['taɪnɪ] adj minuscule

tip [tɪp] n ❶ (money) pourboire m ▷ *Shall I give him a tip?* Je lui donne un pourboire? ❷ (advice) conseil m ▷ *a useful tip* un bon conseil ❸ (informal: end) bout m ▷ *It's on the tip of my tongue.* Je l'ai sur le bout de la langue.
▷ vb donner un pourboire à ▷ *Don't forget to tip the taxi driver.* N'oubliez pas de donner un pourboire à la chauffeuse de taxi.; **to tip over** basculer ▷ *The vase tipped over.* Le vase a basculé.; **to tip something over** faire basculer quelque chose ▷ *She tipped over the vase.* Elle a fait basculer le vase.

tiptoe ['tɪptəʊ] n: **on tiptoe** sur la pointe des pieds

tire ['taɪə^r] n pneu m; **tire pressure** la pression des pneus

tired ['taɪəd] adj fatigué ▷ *I'm tired.* Je suis fatigué.; **to be tired of something** en avoir assez de quelque chose

tiring ['taɪərɪŋ] adj fatigant

tissue ['tɪʃuː] n mouchoir de papier m ▷ *Have you got a tissue?* Tu as un mouchoir de papier?

title ['taɪtl] n titre m

title role n rôle principal m

to [tuː, tə] prep ❶ à ▷ *to go to Toronto* aller à Toronto ▷ *to go to school* aller à l'école ▷ *a letter to his mother* une lettre à sa mère ▷ *the answer to the question* la réponse à la question, au ▷ *to go to the movies* aller au cinéma, aux ▷ *We said goodbye to the neighbours.* Nous avons dit au revoir aux voisins.; **ready to go** prêt à partir; **ready to eat** prêt à manger; **It's easy to do.** C'est facile à faire.; **something to drink** quelque chose à boire; **I've got things to do.** J'ai des choses à faire.; **from...to...** de... à... ▷ *from nine o'clock to half past three* de neuf heures à trois heures et demie ❷ de ▷ *the train to London* le train de London ▷ *the road to Saskatoon* la route de Saskatoon ▷ *the key to the front door* la clé de la porte d'entrée; **It's difficult to say.** C'est difficile à dire.; **It's easy to criticize.** C'est facile de critiquer. ❸ chez ▷ *to go to the doctor's* aller chez le docteur ▷ *Let's go to her house.* Si on allait chez elle. ❹ en ▷ *to go to France* aller en France, au ▷ *to go to Portugal* aller au Portugal ❺ (up to) jusqu'à ▷ *to count to ten* compter jusqu'à dix ❻ (in order to) pour ▷ *I did it to help you.* Je l'ai fait pour vous aider. ▷ *He's too young to go to school.* Il est trop jeune pour aller à l'école.

toad [təʊd] n crapaud m

toadstool ['təʊdstuːl] n champignon vénéneux m

toast [təʊst] n toast m ▷ *a piece of toast with peanut butter* un toast avec du beurre d'arachide

toaster ['təʊstə^r] n grille-pain m (pl grille-pain)

tobacco [tə'bækəʊ] n tabac m

toboggan [tə'bɒgən] n traîne sauvage f

tobogganing [tə'bɒgənɪŋ] n: **to go tobogganing** faire de la traîne sauvage

today [tə'deɪ] adv aujourd'hui ▷ *What did you do today?* Qu'est-ce tu as fait aujourd'hui?

toddler ['tɒdlə^r] n bambin m, bambine f

toe [təʊ] n orteil m

toffee ['tɒfɪ] n caramel m

together [tə'gɛðə^r] adv ❶ ensemble ▷ *Are they still together?* Ils sont toujours ensemble? ❷ (at the same time) en même temps ▷ *Don't all speak together!* Ne parlez pas tous en même temps!; **together with** (with person) avec

toilet ['tɔɪlət] n toilette f

toilet paper n papier hygiénique m

toiletries ['tɔɪlətrɪz] npl articles mpl de toilette

told [təʊld] vb see **tell**

tolerant ['tɒlərnt] adj tolérant

toll booth ['təʊlbuːθ] n (on bridge, highway) poste de péage m

tomato [tə'mɑːtəʊ] n tomate f ▷ *tomato sauce* la sauce tomate ▷ *tomato soup* la soupe aux tomates

tomorrow [tə'mɒrəʊ] adv demain ▷ *tomorrow morning* demain matin ▷ *tomorrow night* demain soir; **the day after tomorrow** après-demain

ton [tʌn] *n*: **a ton of homework** un tas de devoirs

tongue [tʌŋ] *n* langue *f*; **to say something tongue in cheek** dire quelque chose en plaisantant

tonic ['tɒnɪk] *n* (*tonic water*) soda tonique *m*

tonight [təˈnaɪt] *adv* ❶ (*this evening*) ce soir ▷ *Are you going out tonight?* Tu sors ce soir? ❷ (*during the night*) cette nuit ▷ *I'll sleep well tonight.* Je dormirai bien cette nuit.

tonne [tʌn] *n* tonne *f*

tonsillitis [ˌtɒnsɪˈlaɪtɪs] *n* amygdalite *f*

tonsils ['tɒnslz] *npl* amygdales *fpl*

too [tuː] *adv, adj* ❶ (*as well*) aussi ▷ *My sister came too.* Ma sœur est venue aussi. ❷ (*excessively*) trop ▷ *The water's too hot.* L'eau est trop chaude. ▷ *We arrived too late.* Nous sommes arrivés trop tard.; **too much (1)** (*with noun*) trop de ▷ *too much noise* trop de bruit **(2)** (*with verb*) trop ▷ *He talks too much.* Il parle trop. **(3)** (*too expensive*) trop cher ▷ *Fifty dollars? That's too much.* Cinquante dollars? C'est trop cher.; **too many** trop de ▷ *too many hamburgers* trop de hamburgers; **too bad!** tant pis!

took [tʊk] *vb see* **take**

tool [tuːl] *n* outil *m*; **a tool box** une boîte à outils

toolbar ['tuːlbɑːʳ] *n* barre d'outils *f*

toonie ['tuːni] *n* deux dollars *m*

tooth [tuːθ] *n* dent *f*

toothache ['tuːθeɪk] *n* mal de dents *m* ▷ *to have a toothache* avoir mal aux dents

toothbrush ['tuːθbrʌʃ] *n* brosse à dents *f*

toothpaste ['tuːθpeɪst] *n* dentifrice *m*

top [tɒp] *n* ❶ (*of page, ladder, garment*) haut *m* ▷ *at the top of the page* en haut de la page; **a bikini top** un haut de bikini ❷ (*of mountain*) sommet *m* ❸ (*of table*) dessus *m*; **on top of** (*on*) sur ▷ *on top of the fridge* sur le frigo; **to be on top of things** avoir la situation bien en main; **There's tax on top of that.** Il y a de la taxe en plus. ▷ *I searched the house from top to bottom.* J'ai fouillé la maison de fond en comble. ❹ (*of box, jar*) couvercle *m* ❺ (*of bottle*) bouchon *m* ▸ *adj* (*first-class*) grand ▷ *a top surgeon* une grande chirurgienne; **a top model** un mannequin vedette; **He always gets top marks in French.** Il a toujours d'excellentes notes en français.; **the top floor** le dernier étage ▷ *on the top floor* au dernier étage

topic ['tɒpɪk] *n* sujet *m* ▷ *The essay can be on any topic.* Cette dissertation peut être sur n'importe quel sujet.

topical ['tɒpɪkl] *adj* d'actualité ▷ *a topical issue* un sujet d'actualité

top-secret ['tɒp'siːkrɪt] *adj* très secret, très *f* secrète; **top-secret documents** des documents très secrets

tore, torn [tɔːʳ, tɔːn] *vb see* **tear**

tortoise ['tɔːtəs] *n* tortue *f*

torture ['tɔːtʃəʳ] *n* torture *f* ▷ *It was pure torture.* C'était une vraie torture. ▸ *vb* torturer ▷ *Stop torturing that poor animal!* Arrête de torturer ce pauvre animal!

toss [tɒs] *vb* lancer; **to toss a salad** brasser

une salade; **Shall we toss for it?** On joue à pile ou face?; **I tossed and turned all night.** Je n'ai pas arrêté de me tourner et de me retourner toute la nuit.

total ['tautl] *adj* total *m* (*mpl* totaux); **the total amount** le total ▸ *n* total *m* (*pl* totaux); **the grand total** le total

totally ['tautəlɪ] *adv* complètement ▷ *This thing is totally useless.* Cette chose est complètement inutile.

touch [tʌtʃ] *n*: **to get in touch with somebody** prendre contact avec quelqu'un; **to keep in touch with somebody** ne pas perdre contact avec quelqu'un; **Keep in touch!** Donne-moi de tes nouvelles!; **to lose touch** se perdre de vue; **to lose touch with somebody** perdre quelqu'un de vue ▸ *vb* toucher; **Don't touch that!** N'y touche pas!

touchdown ['tʌtʃdaun] *n* (*football*) essai *m*

touched [tʌtʃt] *adj* touché ▷ *I was really touched.* Ça m'a beaucoup touché.

touching ['tʌtʃɪŋ] *adj* touchant

touchpad ['tʌtʃpæd] *n* bloc à effleurement *m*

touchy ['tʌtʃɪ] *adj* susceptible ▷ *She's a bit touchy.* Elle est susceptible.

tough [tʌf] *adj* ❶ dur ▷ *It was tough, but I managed OK.* C'était dur, mais je m'en suis tiré. ▷ *It's a tough job.* C'est dur.; **The meat's tough.** La viande est coriace. ❷ (*strong*) solide ▷ *tough leather gloves* de solides gants en cuir ▷ *She's tough.* Elle est solide. Elle tiendra le coup. ❸ (*rough, violent*) dangereux (*f* dangereuse); **He thinks he's a tough guy.** Il se prend pour un dur.; **Tough luck!** C'est comme ça!

toupee ['tuːpeɪ] *n* postiche *m*

tour ['tuəʳ] *n* ❶ (*of town, museum*) tour *m* ▷ *We went on a tour of the city.* Nous avons fait le tour de la ville.; **a guided tour** une visite guidée; **a package tour** un voyage organisé ❷ (*by singer, group*) tournée *f* ▷ *on tour* en tournée; **to go on tour** faire une tournée ▸ *vb*: *Ashley MacIsaac is touring Europe.* (*singer, artiste*) Ashley MacIsaac est en tournée en Europe.

tour guide *n* guide *m*

tourism ['tuərɪzm] *n* tourisme *m*

tourist ['tuərɪst] *n* touriste; **tourist information office** le bureau d'information touristique

tournament ['tuənəmənt] *n* tournoi *m*

towards [təˈwɔːdz] *prep* ❶ (*in the direction of*) vers ▷ *She came towards me.* Elle est venue vers moi. ❷ (*of attitude*) envers ▷ *my feelings towards him* mes sentiments à son égard

towel ['tauəl] *n* serviette *f*

tower ['tauəʳ] *n* tour *f*

town [taun] *n* ville *f* ▷ *We went into town.* Nous sommes allés en ville.; **the town centre** le centre-ville; **the town hall** la mairie

tow truck ['tau-] *n* dépanneuse *f*

toy [tɔɪ] *n* jouet *m* ▷ *a toy store* un magasin de jouets; **a toy car** une petite voiture

trace [treɪs] *n* trace *f* ▷ *There was no trace of the robbers.* Il n'y avait pas de trace des voleurs.

▶ vb (draw) décalquer

tracing paper ['treɪsɪŋ-] n papier calque m

track [træk] n ❶ (dirt road) chemin m ❷ (railway line) voie ferrée f ❸ (sports) piste f ▷ two laps of the track deux tours de piste ❹ (song) chanson f ▷ This is my favourite track on the CD. C'est ma chanson préférée sur le CD. ❺ (trail) traces fpl ▷ They followed the tracks for miles. Ils ont suivi les traces pendant des kilomètres.

track down vb: **to track somebody down** retrouver quelqu'un ▷ The police never tracked down the killer. La police n'a jamais retrouvé l'assassin.

track and field n athlétisme m

tracksuit ['træksuːt] n survêtement m

tractor ['træktər] n tracteur m

trade [treɪd] n ❶ commerce m ▷ international trade le commerce international ❷ (skill, job) métier m ▷ to learn a trade apprendre un métier ▶ vb ❶ échanger ▷ Want to trade your apple for this orange? Veux-tu échanger ta pomme contre cette orange? ❷ faire du commerce ▷ Canada trades with many countries. Le Canada fait du commerce avec de nombreux pays.

tradition [trə'dɪʃən] n tradition f

traditional [trə'dɪʃənl] adj traditionnel (f traditionnelle)

traffic ['træfɪk] n circulation f ▷ The traffic was terrible. Il y avait une circulation épouvantable.

traffic jam n embouteillage m

traffic lights npl feux mpl

tragedy ['trædʒədɪ] n tragédie f

tragic ['trædʒɪk] adj tragique

trailer ['treɪlər] n ❶ (vehicle) remorque f ❷ (for movie) bande-annonce f

train [treɪn] n ❶ train m ❷ (on subway) rame f ▶ vb (sports) s'entraîner ▷ to train for a race s'entraîner pour une course; **to train as a teacher** suivre une formation d'enseignant; **to train an animal to do something** dresser un animal à faire quelque chose

trained [treɪnd] adj: **She's a trained nurse.** Elle est infirmière diplômée.

trainee [treɪ'niː] n ❶ (in profession) stagiaire ▷ He's a trainee. Il est stagiaire. ❷ (apprentice) apprenti m, apprentie f

trainer ['treɪnər] n ❶ (sports coach) entraîneur m, entraîneure f ❷ (of animals) dompteur m, dompteuse f

training ['treɪnɪŋ] n ❶ formation f ▷ a training course un stage de formation ❷ (sports) entraînement m

trampoline ['træmpəliːn] n trampoline m

tranquillizer ['træŋkwɪlaɪzər] n tranquillisant m ▷ He's on tranquillizers. Il prend des tranquillisants.

Trans-Canada highway ['træns'kænədə-] n Transcanadienne f

transfer [træns'fɜːr] n ❶ (sticker) décalque m ❷ transfert m ▷ a job transfer un transfert d'emploi

transfusion [træns'fjuːʒən] n transfusion f

transit ['trænzɪt] n transit m ▷ in transit en transit; **public transit** les transports publics; **the transit system** le système de transport

translate [trænz'leɪt] vb traduire ▷ to translate something into English traduire quelque chose en anglais

translation [trænz'leɪʃən] n traduction f

translator [trænz'leɪtər] n traducteur m, traductrice f ▷ She's a translator. Elle est traductrice.

transparency [træns'pɛərnsɪ] n transparent m ▷ Put the transparency on the overhead projector. Mets le transparent dans le rétroprojecteur.

transparent [træns'pærnt] adj transparent m

transplant ['trænsplɑːnt] n greffe f ▷ a heart transplant une greffe du cardiaque

transport [træns'pɔːt] n transport m ▷ public transport les transports publics ▶ vb transporter

trap [træp] n piège m

trapeze [trə'piːz] n trapèze m; **trapeze artist** le/la trapéziste

trash [træʃ] n ordures fpl; **the trash can** la poubelle

traumatic [trɔː'mætɪk] adj traumatisant ▷ It was a traumatic experience. Ça a été une expérience traumatisante.

traumatize ['trɔːmətaɪz] vb traumatiser

travel ['trævl] n voyages mpl ▶ vb voyager ▷ I prefer to travel by plane. Je préfère voyager en avion.; **I'd like to travel around the world.** J'aimerais faire le tour du monde.; **We travelled over 800 kilometres.** Nous avons fait plus de huit cents kilomètres.; **News travels fast!** Les nouvelles circulent vite!

travel agency n agence f de voyages

travel agent n agent m de voyages, agente f de voyages

traveller ['trævlər] n voyageur m, voyageuse f

traveller's cheque ['trævləz-] n chèque de voyage m

travelling ['trævlɪŋ] n: **I love travelling.** J'adore les voyages.

travel sickness n mal des transports m

tray [treɪ] n plateau m (pl plateaux)

treasure ['trɛʒər] n trésor m

treat [triːt] n ❶ (food) gâterie f; **to give somebody a treat** (not food) faire plaisir à quelqu'un ▶ vb (well, badly) traiter; **to treat somebody to something** offrir quelque chose à quelqu'un ▷ He treated us to an ice cream. Il nous a offert une crème glacée.

treatment ['triːtmənt] n traitement m

treaty ['triːtɪ] n traité m

tree [triː] n arbre m

tremble ['trɛmbl] vb trembler

tremendous [trɪ'mɛndəs] adj énorme ▷ a tremendous success un succès énorme

trend [trɛnd] n (fashion) mode f

trendy ['trɛndɪ] adj branché

trial ['traɪəl] n (in court) procès m

triangle ['traɪæŋgl] n triangle m

trick [trɪk] n ❶ tour ▷ to play a trick on somebody jouer un tour à quelqu'un ❷ (knack) truc f ▷ It's not easy: there's a trick to it. Ce n'est pas facile: il y a un truc.

▶ vb : **to trick somebody** rouler quelqu'un
tricky ['trɪkɪ] adj délicat
trim [trɪm] vb ❶ (hair) égaliser ❷ (grass)
tondre
▶ n (haircut) coupe d'entretien f ▷ **to get a trim**
se faire faire une coupe d'entretien
trip [trɪp] n voyage m ▷ **to go on a trip** faire un
voyage ▷ **Have a good trip!** Bon voyage!; **a day
trip** une excursion d'une journée
▶ vb (stumble) trébucher
triple ['trɪpl] adj triple
▶ vb tripler
triplets ['trɪplɪts] npl ❶ (boys) triplés mpl ❷
(girls), triplées fpl
trivial ['trɪvɪəl] adj insignifiant
trombone [trɒm'bəʊn] n trombone m ▷ **I play
the trombone.** Je joue du trombone.
troops [truːps] npl troupes fpl ▷ **Canadian
troops** les troupes canadiennes
trophy ['trəʊfɪ] n trophée m ▷ **to win a trophy**
gagner un trophée
tropical ['trɒpɪkl] adj tropical ▷ **The weather
was tropical.** Il faisait une chaleur tropicale.
tropics ['trɒpɪks] npl tropiques mpl ▷ **in the
tropics** sous les tropiques
trot [trɒt] vb trotter
trouble ['trʌbl] n problème m ▷ **The trouble is,
it's too expensive.** Le problème, c'est que c'est
trop cher.; **to be in trouble** avoir des ennuis;
What's the trouble? Qu'est-ce qui ne va pas?;
stomach trouble troubles gastriques; **to take
a lot of trouble over something** se donner
beaucoup de mal pour quelque chose; **Don't
worry, it's no trouble.** Mais non, ça ne me
dérange pas du tout.
troublemaker ['trʌblmeɪkəʳ] n perturbateur
m, perturbatrice f
trout [traʊt] n truite f
truck [trʌk] n camion m
trucker ['trʌkəʳ] n camionneur m,
camionneuse f
true [truː] adj vrai; **That's true.** C'est vrai.;
to come true se réaliser ▷ **I hope my dream will
come true.** J'espère que mon rêve se réalisera.;
true love le grand amour
truly ['truːlɪ] adv vraiment ▷ **It was a truly
remarkable victory.** C'était une victoire
remarquable.; **Yours truly.** Je vous prie
d'agréer mes salutations distinguées.
trumpet ['trʌmpɪt] n trompette f ▷ **She plays
the trumpet.** Elle joue de la trompette.
trunk [trʌŋk] n ❶ (of tree) tronc m ❷ (of
elephant) trompe f ❸ (of car) coffre m
trust [trʌst] n confiance f ▷ **to have trust in
somebody** avoir confiance en quelqu'un
▶ vb : **to trust somebody** faire confiance à
quelqu'un ▷ **Don't you trust me?** Tu ne me fais
pas confiance? ▷ **Trust me!** Fais-moi confiance!
trusting ['trʌstɪŋ] adj confiant
truth [truːθ] n vérité f
truthful ['truːθfʊl] adj : **She's a very truthful
person.** Elle dit toujours la vérité.
try [traɪ] n essai m ▷ **his third try** son troisième
essai; **to have a try** essayer; **It's worth a try.**
Ça vaut la peine d'essayer.; **to give something
a try** essayer quelque chose

▶ vb ❶ (attempt) essayer ▷ **to try to do something**
essayer de faire quelque chose; **to try again**
refaire un essai ❷ (taste) goûter ▷ **Would you
like to try some?** Voulez-vous goûter?; **to try
on** (clothes) essayer; **to try something out**
essayer quelque chose
T-shirt ['tiːʃəːt] n T-shirt m
tube [tjuːb] n tube m
tuberculosis [tjubɜːkju'ləʊsɪs] n
tuberculose f
Tuesday ['tjuːzdɪ] n mardi m ▷ **on Tuesday**
mardi ▷ **on Tuesdays** le mardi ▷ **every Tuesday**
tous les mardis ▷ **last Tuesday** mardi dernier
▷ **next Tuesday** mardi prochain
tug-of-war [tʌgəv'wɔːʳ] n lutte à la corde f
tulip ['tjuːlɪp] n tulipe f
tuna ['tjuːnə] n thon m; **tuna salad** la salade
de thon
tundra ['tʌndrə] n toundra f
tune [tjuːn] n (melody) air m; **to play in tune**
jouer juste; **to sing out of tune** chanter faux
▶ vb ❶ (instrument) accorder ▷ **You need to tune
your guitar.** Il faut que tu accordes ta guitare.
❷ (radio) syntoniser ▷ **I tuned the radio to CBC.**
J'ai syntonisé la radio sur Radio-Canada.
tunnel ['tʌnl] n tunnel m
tuque [tuːk] n tuque f
turkey ['tɜːkɪ] n ❶ (meat) dinde f ❷ (live bird)
dindon m
turn [tɜːn] n ❶ (bend in road) tournant m;
"no left turn" « défense de tourner à gauche »
❷ (in game) tour ▷ **It's my turn!** C'est à mon
tour!
▶ vb ❶ tourner ▷ **Turn right at the lights.**
Tournez à droite aux feux. ❷ (become) devenir
▷ **to turn red** devenir rouge; **to turn into
something** se transformer en quelque chose
▷ **The frog turned into a prince.** La grenouille s'est
transformée en prince.
turn around vb ❶ (car) faire demi-tour
❷ (person) se retourner
turn back vb faire demi-tour ▷ **We turned back.**
Nous avons fait demi-tour.
turn down vb ❶ (offer) refuser ❷ (radio, TV,
heating) baisser ▷ **Shall I turn the heating down?**
Je baisse le chauffage?
turn off vb ❶ (light, radio) éteindre ❷ (tap)
fermer ❸ (engine) arrêter
turn on vb ❶ (light, radio) allumer ❷ (tap)
ouvrir ❸ (engine) mettre en marche
turn out vb : **It turned out to be a mistake.**
Il s'est avéré que c'était une erreur.; **It turned
out that she was right.** Il s'est avéré qu'elle
avait raison.
turn up vb ❶ (arrive) arriver ❷ (increase)
monter; **Could you turn up the radio?** Tu peux
monter le son de la radio?
turnip ['tɜːnɪp] n navet m
turquoise ['tɜːkwɔɪz] adj (colour) turquoise
(f+pl turquoise)
turtle ['tɜːtl] n tortue f
tutor ['tjuːtəʳ] n (private teacher) professeur
m, professeure particulière f
TV [tiːˈviː] n télé f
tweezers ['twiːzəz] npl pince f à épiler
twelfth [twelfθ] adj douzième ▷ **the twelfth**

floor le douzième étage; **the twelfth of August** le douze août

twelve [twelv] *num* douze ▷ *He's twelve.* Il a douze ans.; **twelve o'clock (1)** *(midday)* midi **(2)** *(midnight)* minuit

twentieth ['twentɪɪθ] *adj* vingtième ▷ *the twentieth time* la vingtième fois; **the twentieth of May** le vingt mai

twenty ['twentɪ] *num* vingt ▷ *He's twenty.* Il a vingt ans.

twice [twaɪs] *adv* deux fois; **twice as much** deux fois plus ▷ *He gets twice as much allowance as me.* Il a deux fois plus d'argent de poche que moi.

twin [twɪn] *n (boy: girl)* jumeau *m*, jumelle *f* (*pl* jumeaux, *fpl* jumelles); **my twin brother** mon frère jumeau; **her twin sister** sa sœur jumelle; **identical twins** les vrais jumeaux; **a twin room** une chambre à deux lits

twinned [twɪnd] *adj* jumelé ▷ *Banff is twinned with Obama-cho.* Banff est jumelée avec Obama-cho.

twist [twɪst] *vb* ❶ *(bend)* tordre ❷ *(distort)* déformer ▷ *You're twisting my words.* Tu déformes ce que j'ai dit.

two [tuː] *num* deux ▷ *She's two.* Elle a deux ans.

type [taɪp] *n* type *m* ▷ *What type of camera do you have?* Quel type d'appareil photo as-tu? ▶ *vb* taper ▷ *Type your password.* Tape ton mot de passe.

typical ['tɪpɪkl] *adj* typique ▷ *That's just typical!* C'est typique!

tyrant ['taɪrənt] *n* tyran *m* ▷ *He's a real tyrant.* C'est un vrai tyran.

u

UFO ['juːfəʊ] *n* OVNI *m* (= *objet volant non identifié*)

ugh [əːh] *excl* yark!

ugly ['ʌglɪ] *adj* laid

ulcer ['ʌlsəʳ] *n* ulcère *m*

ultimate ['ʌltɪmət] *adj* suprême ▷ *the ultimate challenge* le défi suprême; **It was the ultimate adventure.** C'était la grande aventure.

ultimately ['ʌltɪmətlɪ] *adv* au bout du compte ▷ *Ultimately, it's your decision.* Au bout du compte, c'est votre décision.

umbrella [ʌm'brelə] *n* ❶ parapluie *m* ❷ *(for sun)* parasol *m*

umpire ['ʌmpaɪəʳ] *n* arbitre *mf*

UN *n* ONU *f* (= *Organisation des Nations unies*)

unable [ʌn'eɪbl] *adj*: **to be unable to do**

something ne pas pouvoir faire quelque chose ▷ *I was unable to come.* Je n'ai pas pu venir.

unacceptable [ʌnək'sɛptəbl] *adj* inacceptable

unanimous [juː'nænɪməs] *adj* unanime ▷ *a unanimous decision* une décision unanime

unattended [ʌnə'tɛndɪd] *adj*: **to leave something unattended** laisser quelque chose sans surveillance laissé sans surveillance ▷ *Never leave pets unattended in your car.* Ne laisser jamais d'animaux domestiques sans surveillance dans votre voiture.

unavoidable [ʌnə'vɔɪdəbl] *adj* inévitable

unaware [ʌnə'wɛəʳ] *adj*: **to be unaware (1)** *(not know about)* ignorer ▷ *I was unaware of the rules.* J'ignorais le règlement. **(2)** *(not notice)* ne pas se rendre compte ▷ *She was unaware that she was being filmed.* Elle ne s'était pas rendu compte qu'on la filmait.

unbearable [ʌn'bɛərəbl] *adj* insupportable

unbeatable [ʌn'biːtəbl] *adj* imbattable

unbelievable [ʌnbɪ'liːvəbl] *adj* incroyable

unborn [ʌn'bɔːn] *adj*: **the unborn child** le fœtus

unbreakable [ʌn'breɪkəbl] *adj* incassable

uncanny [ʌn'kænɪ] *adj* ❶ *That's uncanny!* C'est étrange!; **an uncanny resemblance** une ressemblance troublante

uncertain [ʌn'sɜːtn] *adj* incertain ▷ *The future is uncertain.* L'avenir est incertain.; **to be uncertain about something** ne pas être sûr de quelque chose

uncivilized [ʌn'sɪvɪlaɪzd] *adj* barbare

uncle ['ʌŋkl] *n* oncle *m* ▷ *my uncle* mon oncle

uncomfortable [ʌn'kʌmfətəbl] *adj* ❶ *(person)* mal à l'aise ▷ *I feel uncomfortable at their house.* Je me sens mal à l'aise chez eux. ❷ pas confortable ▷ *The seats are rather uncomfortable.* Les sièges ne sont pas très confortables.

unconscious [ʌn'kɔnʃəs] *adj* sans connaissance

uncontrollable [ʌnkən'trəʊləbl] *adj* incontrôlable

unconventional [ʌnkən'vɛnʃənl] *adj* peu conventionnel (*f* peu conventionnelle)

under ['ʌndəʳ] *prep* ❶ sous ▷ *The cat's under the table.* Le chat est sous la table. ▷ *The tunnel goes under the Fraser River.* Le tunnel passe sous le fleuve Fraser.; **under there** là-dessous ▷ *What's under there?* Qu'est-ce qu'il y a là-dessous? ❷ *(less than)* moins de ▷ *under 20 people* moins de vingt personnes ▷ *children under 10* les enfants de moins de dix ans

undercover [ʌndə'kʌvəʳ] *adj, adv* secret (*f* secrète) ▷ *an undercover agent* un agent d'infiltration; **He was working undercover.** Il travaillait sous une fausse identité.

underestimate ['ʌndər'estɪmeɪt] *vb* sous-estimer ▷ *I underestimated her.* Je l'ai sous-estimée.

undergo [ʌndə'gəʊ] *vb (operation, examination, change)* subir; **to be undergoing repairs** être en réparation

underground [ʌndəˈgraʊnd] *adj, adv* ❶ souterrain ▷ *an underground parking garage*

un stationnement souterrain ❷ sous terre
▷ *Moles live underground.* Les taupes vivent
sous terre.

underline [ˌʌndəˈlaɪn] vb souligner

underneath [ˌʌndəˈniːθ] prep, adv ❶ sous
▷ *underneath the carpet* sous le tapis ❷ dessous
▷ *I got out of the car and looked underneath.* Je suis
descendu de la voiture et j'ai regardé dessous.

underpaid [ˌʌndəˈpeɪd] adj sous-payé ▷ *I'm
underpaid.* Je suis sous-payé.

underpants [ˈʌndəpænts] npl ❶ *(women's)*
culotte f ❷ *(men's)* caleçon m ❸ *(all kinds,
informal)* bobettes

undershirt [ˈʌndəʃəːt] n camisole f

understand [ˌʌndəˈstænd] vb comprendre
▷ *Do you understand?* Vous comprenez? ▷ *I don't
understand this word.* Je ne comprends pas ce
mot. ▷ *Is that understood?* C'est compris?

understanding [ˌʌndəˈstændɪŋ] adj
compréhensif (f compréhensive) ▷ *She's very
understanding.* Elle est très compréhensive.

understood [ˌʌndəˈstʊd] vb see **understand**

undertaker [ˈʌndəteɪkə] n ❶ *(mortician)*
embaumeur m, embaumeuse f ❷ *(funeral
home director)* directeur de salon funéraire m,
directrice de salon funéraire f

underwater [ˌʌndəˈwɔːtə] adj, adv sous
l'eau ▷ *This sequence was filmed underwater.*
Cette séquence a été filmée sous l'eau.;
an underwater camera un appareil
photographique sous-marin; **underwater
photography** la photographie sous-marine

underwear [ˈʌndəwɛə] n sous-vêtements
mpl

underwent [ˌʌndəˈwɛnt] vb see **undergo**

undo [ʌnˈduː] vb *(buttons, knot)* défaire

undress [ʌnˈdrɛs] vb *(get undressed)* se
déshabiller ▷ *The doctor told me to undress.* Le
médecin m'a dit de me déshabiller.

unemployed [ˌʌnɪmˈplɔɪd] adj au chômage
▷ *He's unemployed.* Il est au chômage. ▷ *I've been
unemployed for a year.* Ça fait un an que je suis au
chômage.; **the unemployed** les m chômeurs

unemployment [ˌʌnɪmˈplɔɪmənt] n
chômage m

unexpected [ˌʌnɪkˈspɛktɪd] adj inattendu
▷ *an unexpected visitor* un visiteur inattendu

unexpectedly [ˌʌnɪkˈspɛktɪdlɪ] adv à
l'improviste ▷ *They arrived unexpectedly.* Ils sont
arrivés à l'improviste.

unfair [ʌnˈfɛə] adj injuste ▷ *It's unfair to
everybody.* C'est injuste pour tout le monde.

unfamiliar [ˌʌnfəˈmɪlɪə] adj: **I heard an
unfamiliar voice.** J'ai entendu une voix que je
ne connaissais pas.

unfold [ʌnˈfəʊld] vb déplier ▷ *She unfolded the
map.* Elle a déplié la carte.

unforgettable [ˌʌnfəˈɡɛtəbl] adj inoubliable

unfortunately [ʌnˈfɔːtʃnətlɪ] adv
malheureusement ▷ *Unfortunately, I arrived
late.* Malheureusement, je suis arrivé en retard.

unfriendly [ʌnˈfrɛndlɪ] adj pas aimable ▷ *The
waiters are a bit unfriendly.* Les serveurs ne sont
pas très aimables.

ungrateful [ʌnˈɡreɪtfʊl] adj ingrat

unhappy [ʌnˈhæpɪ] adj malheureux (f

malheureuse) ▷ *He was very unhappy as a child.*
Il était très malheureux quand il était petit.; **to
look unhappy** avoir l'air triste

unhealthy [ʌnˈhɛlθɪ] adj ❶ *(person)* maladif
(f maladive) ❷ *(place, habit)* malsain ❸ *(food)*
pas sain

uniform [ˈjuːnɪfɔːm] n uniforme m ▷ *the school
uniform* l'uniforme scolaire

unilingual [ˈjuːnɪˈlɪŋɡwəl] adj unilingue

uninhabited [ˌʌnɪnˈhæbɪtɪd] adj inhabité

union [ˈjuːnjən] n *(trade union)* syndicat m

unique [juːˈniːk] adj unique

unit [ˈjuːnɪt] n ❶ unité f ▷ *a unit of measurement*
une unité de mesure ❷ *(piece of furniture)*
élément m ▷ *a kitchen unit* un élément de
cuisine

United Nations [juːˈnaɪtɪd-] n O.N.U. f
(= Organisation des Nations Unies)

universe [ˈjuːnɪvəːs] n univers m

university [ˌjuːnɪˈvəːsɪtɪ] n université f ▷ *She's
in university.* Elle va à l'université. ▷ *Do you want
to go to university?* Tu veux aller à l'université?

unleaded [ʌnˈlɛdɪd] adj sans plomb

unless [ʌnˈlɛs] conj: **unless he leaves** à moins
qu'il ne parte ▷ *I won't come unless you phone
me.* Je ne viendrai pas à moins que tu ne me
téléphones.

unlike [ʌnˈlaɪk] prep contrairement à ▷ *Unlike
him, I really enjoy flying.* Contrairement à lui,
j'adore prendre l'avion.

unlikely [ʌnˈlaɪklɪ] adj peu probable ▷ *It's
possible, but unlikely.* C'est possible, mais peu
probable.

unlisted [ʌnˈlɪstɪd] adj: **an unlisted number**
un numéro confidentiel

unload [ʌnˈləʊd] vb décharger ▷ *We unloaded
the car.* Nous avons déchargé la voiture. ▷ *The
trucks go there to unload.* Les camions y vont
pour être déchargés.

unlock [ʌnˈlɒk] vb ouvrir ▷ *She unlocked the
door of the car.* Elle a ouvert la portière de la
voiture.

unlucky [ʌnˈlʌkɪ] adj: **to be unlucky
(1)** *(number, object)* porter malheur ▷ *They
say thirteen is an unlucky number.* On dit que le
nombre treize porte malheur. **(2)** *(person)* ne
pas avoir de chance ▷ *"Did you win?"—"No, I was
unlucky."* «Vous avez gagné?» — « Non, je n'ai
pas eu de chance.»

unmarried [ʌnˈmærɪd] adj *(person)* célibataire
▷ *an unmarried mother* une mère célibataire; **an
unmarried couple** un couple non marié

unnatural [ʌnˈnætʃrəl] adj pas naturel (f pas
naturelle)

unnecessary [ʌnˈnɛsəsərɪ] adj inutile

unofficial [ˌʌnəˈfɪʃl] adj *(meeting, leader)* non
officiel (f non officielle)

unpack [ʌnˈpæk] vb ❶ défaire ▷ *I unpacked my
suitcase.* J'ai défait ma valise. ❷ déballer ses
affaires ▷ *I went to my room to unpack.* Je suis allé
dans ma chambre pour déballer mes affaires.
▷ *I haven't unpacked my clothes yet.* Je n'ai pas
encore déballé mes vêtements.

unpleasant [ʌnˈplɛznt] adj désagréable

unplug [ʌnˈplʌɡ] vb débrancher

unpopular [ʌnˈpɒpjʊlə] adj impopulaire

unpredictable [ˌʌnprɪˈdɪktəbl] adj
imprévisible

unreal [ˌʌnˈrɪəl] adj (incredible) incroyable ▷ It
was unreal! C'était incroyable!

unrealistic [ˈʌnrɪəˈlɪstɪk] adj peu réaliste

unreasonable [ˌʌnˈriːznəbl] adj pas
raisonnable ▷ Her attitude was completely
unreasonable. Son attitude n'était pas du tout
raisonnable.

unreliable [ˌʌnrɪˈlaɪəbl] adj (car, machine)
pas fiable ▷ It's a nice car, but a bit unreliable.
C'est une belle voiture, mais il n'est pas très
fiable.; **He's completely unreliable.** On ne
peut pas du tout compter sur lui.

unroll [ʌnˈrəʊl] vb dérouler

unsatisfactory [ˈʌnsætɪsˈfæktərɪ] adj
insatisfaisant

unscrew [ʌnˈskruː] vb dévisser ▷ She
unscrewed the top of the bottle. Elle a dévissé le
bouchon de la bouteille.

unshaven [ʌnˈʃeɪvn] adj mal rasé

unstable [ʌnˈsteɪbl] adj instable

unsteady [ʌnˈstedɪ] adj (walk, voice) mal
assuré ▷ He was unsteady on his feet. Il
marchait d'un pas mal assuré.

unsuccessful [ˌʌnsəkˈsesful] adj (attempt)
vain; **to be unsuccessful in doing something**
ne pas réussir à faire quelque chose ▷ an
unsuccessful artist un artiste qui n'a pas réussi

unsuitable [ʌnˈsuːtəbl] adj (clothes,
equipment) inapproprié

untidy [ʌnˈtaɪdɪ] adj ⊕ en désordre ▷ My
bedroom's always untidy. Ma chambre est
toujours en désordre. ⊘ (appearance, person)
débraillé ▷ He's always untidy. Il est toujours
débraillé. ⊕ (in character) désordonné ▷ She's a
very untidy person. Elle est très désordonnée.

untie [ʌnˈtaɪ] vb ⊕ (knot, parcel) défaire
⊘ (animal) détacher

until [ənˈtɪl] prep, conj ⊕ jusqu'à ▷ I waited
until ten o'clock. J'ai attendu jusqu'à dix heures.;
until now jusqu'à présent ▷ It's never been a
problem until now. Ça n'a jamais été un
problème jusqu'à présent.; **until then** jusque-
là ▷ Until then I'd never been to Quebec. Jusque-là
je n'étais jamais allé au Québec. ⊘ avant ▷ It
won't be ready until next week. Ça ne sera pas prêt
avant la semaine prochaine. ▷ Until last year
I'd never been to New Brunswick. Avant l'année
dernière, je n'étais jamais allé au Nouveau-
Brunswick.

unusual [ʌnˈjuːʒʊəl] adj ⊕ insolite ▷ an
unusual shape une forme insolite ⊘ rare ▷ It's
unusual to get snow at this time of year. Il est rare
qu'il neige à cette époque de l'année.

unwilling [ʌnˈwɪlɪŋ] adj: **to be unwilling
to do something** ne pas être disposé à faire
quelque chose ▷ He was unwilling to help me. Il
n'était pas disposé à m'aider.

unwind [ʌnˈwaɪnd] vb (relax) se détendre

unwise [ʌnˈwaɪz] adj (person) imprudent
▷ That was rather unwise of you. C'était plutôt
imprudent de votre part.

unwound [ʌnˈwaʊnd] vb see **unwind**

unwrap [ʌnˈræp] vb déballer ▷ After the meal
we unwrapped the presents. Après le repas, nous

avons déballé les cadeaux.

up [ʌp] prep, adv en haut ▷ up on the hill en haut
de la colline; **up here** ici; **up there** là-haut;
up north dans le nord; **to be up** (out of bed)
être debout ▷ We were up at 6. Nous étions
debout à six heures. ▷ He's not up yet. Il n'est
pas encore debout.; **What's up?** Qu'est-ce
qu'il y a? ▷ What's up with him? Qu'est-ce qu'il
a?; **to get up** (in the morning) se lever ▷ What
time do you get up? À quelle heure est-ce que tu
te lèves?; **to go up** monter ▷ The bus went up
the hill. L'autobus a monté la colline.; **to go
up to somebody** s'approcher de quelqu'un ▷
She came up to me. Elle s'est approchée de
moi.; **up to** (as far as) jusqu'à ▷ to count up to
fifty compter jusqu'à cinquante ▷ up to three
hours jusqu'à trois heures ▷ up to now jusqu'à
présent; **It's up to you.** C'est à vous de décider.

upbringing [ˈʌpbrɪŋɪŋ] n éducation f

update [ʌpˈdeɪt] vb mettre à jour ▷ I've updated
the file. J'ai mis à jour le fichier.

uphill [ʌpˈhɪl] adv: **to go uphill** monter

upload [ˈʌpˈləʊd] vb télécharger vers le
serveur ▷ I uploaded the file without any trouble.
J'ai téléchargé le fichier vers le serveur sans
difficulté.
▶ n téléchargement vers le serveur m ▷ The
upload isn't finished yet. Le téléchargement vers
le serveur n'est pas encore terminé.

upper [ˈʌpə*] adj supérieur ▷ on the upper floor
à l'étage supérieur; **Upper Canada** le Haut-
Canada

upright [ˈʌpraɪt] adj: **to stand upright** se
tenir droit

upset [ʌpˈset] n: **a stomach upset** une
indigestion
▶ adj contrarié ▷ She's still a bit upset. Elle est
encore un peu contrariée.; **I had an upset
stomach.** J'avais l'estomac dérangé.
▶ vb: **to upset somebody** contrarier quelqu'un

upside down [ˈʌpsaɪd-] adv à l'envers ▷ That
painting is upside down. Ce tableau est à l'envers.

upstairs [ʌpˈsteəz] adv en haut ▷ "Where's your
coat?" — "It's upstairs." « Où est ton manteau?
» — « Il est en haut. »; **to go upstairs** monter

uptight [ʌpˈtaɪt] adj tendu ▷ She's really
uptight. Elle est très tendue.

up-to-date [ˈʌptəˈdeɪt] adj ⊕ (car, stereo)
moderne ⊘ (information) à jour ▷ an up-to-
date timetable un horaire à jour; **to bring
something up to date** moderniser quelque
chose

urgent [ˈɜːdʒənt] adj urgent ▷ Is it urgent? C'est
urgent?

urine [ˈjʊərɪn] n urine f

us [ʌs] pron nous ▷ They helped us. Ils nous ont
aidés. ▷ They gave us a map. Ils nous ont donné
une carte.

use [n juːs, vb juːz] n: **It's no use.** Ça ne sert à
rien. ▷ It's no use shouting, she's deaf. Ça ne sert
à rien de crier, elle est sourde.; **It's no use, I
can't do it.** Il n'y a rien à faire, je n'y arrive pas.;
to make use of something utiliser quelque
chose
▶ vb utiliser ▷ Can we use a dictionary on the
exam? Est-ce qu'on peut utiliser un dictionnaire

durant l'examen?; **Can I use your phone?** Je peux téléphoner?; **to use the washroom** aller aux toilettes; **to use up the paint.** Nous avons fini la peinture. (2) (money) dépenser; **I used to live in Timmins.** J'habitais à Timmins autrefois.; **I used to dislike math, but now…** Avant, je n'aimais pas les maths, mais maintenant…; **to be used to something** avoir l'habitude de quelque chose ▷ *He wasn't used to driving on the left.* Il n'avait pas l'habitude de conduire à gauche. ▷ *Don't worry, I'm used to it.* Ne t'inquiète pas, j'ai l'habitude.; **a used car** une voiture usagée

useful ['juːsful] *adj* utile

useless ['juːsləs] *adj* inutile ▷ *This map is just useless.* Cette carte est vraiment inutile.; **It's useless!** Ça ne sert à rien!

user ['juːzə'] *n* utilisateur *m*, utilisatrice *f*

user-friendly ['juːzə'frendli] *adj* facile à utiliser

usual ['juːʒuəl] *adj* habituel (f habituelle); **as usual** comme d'habitude

usually ['juːʒuəli] *adv* ❶ (generally) en général ▷ *I usually get to school at about half past eight.* En général, j'arrive à l'école vers huit heures et demie. ❷ (when making a contrast) d'habitude ▷ *Usually I don't wear make-up, but today is a special occasion.* D'habitude je ne me maquille pas, mais aujourd'hui c'est spécial.

utility room [juː'tɪlɪtɪ-] *n* (in institution) local d'entretien *m*

U-turn ['juː'təːn] *n* demi-tour *m* ▷ *to do a U-turn* faire demi-tour

vacancy ['veɪkənsɪ] *n* ❶ (job) poste vacant *m* ❷ (room in hotel) chambre disponible *f*; **"no vacancies"** (on sign) « complet »

vacant ['veɪkənt] *adj* libre

vacation [və'keɪʃən] *n* vacances *fpl* ▷ *to be on vacation* être en vacances ▷ *to take a vacation* prendre des vacances

vaccinate ['væksɪneɪt] *vb* vacciner

vacuum ['vækjum] *vb* passer l'aspirateur ▷ *to vacuum the hall* passer l'aspirateur dans le couloir

vacuum cleaner *n* ❶ aspirateur *m* ❷ balayeuse *f*

vagina [və'dʒaɪnə] *n* vagin *m*

vague [veɪg] *adj* vague

vain [veɪn] *adj* vaniteux (f vaniteuse) ▷ *He's so*

vain! Il est vraiment vaniteux!; **in vain** en vain

valentine ['væləntaɪn] *n* ❶ (person) valentin *m*, valentine *f* ▷ *Will you be my valentine?* Seras-tu ma valentine? ❷ carte de la Saint-Valentin *f* ▷ *I sent her a valentine.* Je lui ai envoyé une carte de la Saint-Valentin. ❸ (card)

Valentine's Day ['væləntaɪnz-] *n* Saint-Valentin *f*

valid ['vælɪd] *adj* valable ▷ *This ticket is valid for three months.* Ce billet est valable trois mois.

valley ['vælɪ] *n* vallée *f*

valuable ['væljuəbl] *adj* ❶ de valeur ▷ *a valuable picture* un tableau de valeur ❷ précieux (f précieuse) ▷ *valuable help* une aide précieuse

valuables ['væljuəblz] *npl* objets *mpl* de valeur ▷ *Don't take any valuables with you.* N'emportez pas d'objets de valeur.

value ['væljuː] *n* valeur *f*

van [væn] *n* camionnette *f*; **a moving van** un camion de déménagement

vandal ['vændl] *n* vandale

vandalism ['vændəlɪzəm] *n* vandalisme *m*

vandalize ['vændəlaɪz] *vb* vandaliser

vanilla [və'nɪlə] *n* vanille *f*; **vanilla ice cream** la crème glacée à la vanille

vanish ['vænɪʃ] *vb* disparaître

variable ['veərɪəbl] *adj* variable

varied ['veərɪd] *adj* varié

variety [və'raɪətɪ] *n* variété *f*

various ['veərɪəs] *adj* plusieurs ▷ *We visited various villages in the area.* Nous avons visité plusieurs villages de la région.

vary ['veərɪ] *vb* varier

vase [vaːz] *n* vase *m*

VCR *n* (= video cassette recorder) magnétoscope *m*

veal [viːl] *n* veau *m*

vegan ['viːgən] *n* végétalien *m*, végétalienne *f* ▷ *I'm a vegan.* Je suis végétalien.

vegetable ['vedʒtəbl] *n* légume *m* ▷ *vegetable soup* la soupe aux légumes

vegetarian [vedʒɪ'teərɪən] *adj* végétarien *m* (f végétarienne) ▷ *I'm vegetarian.* Je suis végétarien. ▷ *vegetarian lasagna* une lasagne végétarienne
▶ *n* végétarien *m*, végétarienne *f* ▷ *I'm a vegetarian.* Je suis végétarien.

vegetation [vedʒɪ'teɪʃən] *n* végétation *f*

vehicle ['viːɪkl] *n* véhicule *m*

vein [veɪn] *n* veine *f*

velvet ['vɛlvɪt] *n* velours *m*

vending machine ['vendɪŋ-] *n* distributrice automatique *f*

Venetian blind [vɪ'niːʃən-] *n* store vénitien *m*

verb [vəːb] *n* verbe *m*

verdict ['vəːdɪkt] *n* verdict *m*

vertical ['vəːtɪkl] *adj* vertical (*mpl* verticaux)

very ['verɪ] *adv* très ▷ *very tall* très grand ▷ *not very interesting* pas très intéressant; **very much** beaucoup

vest [vest] *n* veste *f*; **a fleece vest** une veste en polaire

vet [vet] *n* vétérinaire ▷ *She's a vet.* Elle est vétérinaire.

via ['vaɪə] *prep* en passant par ▷ *We went to*

Trois-Rivières via Québec City. Nous sommes allés à Trois-Rivières en passant par Québec.

vice-president [vaɪs'prezɪdənt] n vice-président m, vice-présidente f

vice-principal [vaɪs'prɪnsɪpl] n directeur-adjoint m, directrice-adjointe f

vice versa ['vaɪsɪ'vɜːsə] adv vice versa

vicious ['vɪʃəs] adj ⓵ brutal (mpl brutaux) ▷ a vicious attack une agression brutale ⓶ (dog, person) méchant m; **a vicious circle** un cercle vicieux

victim ['vɪktɪm] n victime f ▷ He was the victim of a mugging. Il a été victime d'une agression.

Victoria Day [vɪk'tɔːrɪə] n fête de la Reine f

victory ['vɪktərɪ] n victoire f

video ['vɪdɪəʊ] vb ⓵ (from TV) enregistrer ⓶ (with video camera) filmer
▶ n ⓵ (movie) vidéo f ▷ To watch a video regarder une vidéo ▷ a video of my family on holiday une vidéo de ma famille en vacances ▷ It's out on video. C'est sorti en vidéo. ⓶ (videocassette) vidéocassette f ▷ She lent me a video. Elle m'a prêté une vidéocassette.; **a video camera** une caméra vidéo; **a videocassette** une vidéocassette; **a video game** un jeu vidéo ▷ She likes playing video games. Elle aime les jeux vidéo.; **a video recorder** un magnétoscope; **a video rental store** un vidéoclub

videoconference ['vɪdɪəʊ'kɒnfərns] n vidéoconférence f

view [vjuː] n ⓵ vue f ▷ There's an amazing view when you get to the top. Il y a une vue extraordinaire quand on arrive au sommet. ⓶ (opinion) avis m ▷ in my view à mon avis

viewer ['vjuːə'] n (television) téléspectateur m, téléspectatrice f

viewpoint ['vjuːpɔɪnt] n point de vue m

vile [vaɪl] adj (smell, food) dégoûtant

village ['vɪlɪdʒ] n village m

villain ['vɪlən] n ⓵ (criminal) malfaiteur m, malfaitrice f ⓶ (in movie) méchant m, méchante f

vine [vaɪn] n vigne f

vinegar ['vɪnɪgə'] n vinaigre m

vineyard ['vɪnjɑːd] n vignoble m

viola [vɪ'əʊlə] n alto m ▷ I play the viola. Je joue de l'alto.

violence ['vaɪələns] n violence f

violent ['vaɪələnt] adj violent

violin [vaɪə'lɪn] n violon m ▷ I play the violin. Je joue du violon.

violinist [vaɪə'lɪnɪst] n violoniste

virgin ['vɜːdʒɪn] n vierge f ▷ To be a virgin être vierge

Virgo ['vɜːgəʊ] n Vierge f ▷ I'm a Virgo. Je suis Vierge.

virtual reality ['vɜːtjuəl-] n réalité virtuelle f

virus ['vaɪərəs] n (also computing) virus m

visa ['viːzə] n visa m

visible ['vɪzəbl] adj visible

visit ['vɪzɪt] n ⓵ (to museum) visite f ⓶ (to country) séjour m ▷ Did you enjoy your visit to Nova Scotia? Ton séjour en Nouvelle-Écosse s'est bien passé?; **my last visit to my grandmother** la dernière fois que je suis allé voir ma grand-mère
▶ vb ⓵ (person) rendre visite à ▷ To visit somebody rendre visite à quelqu'un ⓶ (place) visiter ▷ We'd like to visit the zoo. Nous voudrions visiter le zoo.

visitor ['vɪzɪtə'] n ⓵ (tourist) visiteur m, visiteuse f ⓶ (guest) invité m, invitée f; **to have visitors** avoir de la visite

visual ['vɪzjuəl] adj visuel (f visuelle)

visualize ['vɪzjuəlaɪz] vb imaginer

vital ['vaɪtl] adj vital (mpl vitaux); **vital signs** les signes vitaux

vitamin ['vɪtəmɪn] n vitamine f

vivid ['vɪvɪd] adj (colour) vif (f vive); **to have a vivid imagination** avoir une imagination débordante

vocabulary [vəʊ'kæbjʊlərɪ] n vocabulaire m

vocational [vəʊ'keɪʃənl] adj professionnel (f professionnelle); **a vocational course** un stage de formation professionnelle

voice [vɔɪs] n voix f (pl voix)

voice mail n messagerie vocale f

volcano [vɒl'keɪnəʊ] n volcan m

volleyball ['vɒlɪbɔːl] n volley-ball m ▷ To play volleyball jouer au volley-ball

volt [vəʊlt] n volt m

voltage ['vəʊltɪdʒ] n voltage m

voluntary ['vɒləntərɪ] adj (contribution, statement) volontaire; **to do voluntary work** travailler bénévolement

volunteer [vɒlən'tɪə'] n volontaire
▶ vb: **to volunteer to do something** se porter volontaire pour faire quelque chose

vomit ['vɒmɪt] vb vomir

vote [vəʊt] vb voter

voter ['vəʊtə'] n électeur m, électrice f

voucher ['vaʊtʃə'] n bon m ▷ a gift voucher un bon d'achat

vowel [vaʊəl] n voyelle f

vulgar ['vʌlgə'] adj vulgaire

W

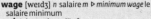

wage [weɪdʒ] n salaire m ▷ minimum wage le salaire minimum

waist [weɪst] n taille f

wait [weɪt] vb attendre; **to wait for something** attendre quelque chose; **to wait for somebody** attendre quelqu'un ▷ I'll wait for you. Je t'attendrai.; **Wait for me!** Attends-moi!; **Wait a minute!** Attends!; **to keep somebody waiting** faire attendre quelqu'un ▷ They kept us waiting for hours. Ils nous ont fait attendre pendant des heures.; **I can't wait for the**

holidays. J'ai hâte d'être en vacances.; **I can't wait to see him again.** J'ai hâte de le revoir.

wait up vb attendre pour se coucher ▷ *My mom always waits up till I get in.* Ma mère attend toujours que je rentre pour se coucher.

waiter ['weɪtəʳ] n serveur m

waiting list ['weɪtɪŋ-] n liste d'attente f

waiting room ['weɪtɪŋ-] n salle d'attente f

waitress ['weɪtrɪs] n serveuse f

wake up [weɪk-] vb se réveiller ▷ *I woke up at six o'clock.* Je me suis réveillé à six heures.; **to wake somebody up** réveiller quelqu'un ▷ *Please would you wake me up at seven o'clock?* Pourriez-vous me réveiller à sept heures?

walk [wɔːk] vb ❶ marcher ▷ *She walks fast.* Elle marche vite. ❷ *(go on foot)* aller à pied ▷ *Are you walking or going by bus?* Tu y vas à pied ou en autobus? ▷ *We walked 10 kilometres.* Nous avons fait dix kilomètres à pied.; **to walk the dog** promener le chien
▶ n promenade f ▷ *to go for a walk* faire une promenade; **It's 10 minutes' walk from here.** C'est à dix minutes d'ici à pied.

walkie-talkie ['wɔːkɪ'tɔːkɪ] n émetteur-récepteur m portatif

walking ['wɔːkɪŋ] n randonnée f ▷ *I did some walking in the Laurentians last summer.* J'ai fait de la randonnée dans les Laurentides l'été dernier.

walking stick n canne f

Walkman® ['wɔːkmən] n baladeur m

wall [wɔːl] n mur m

wallet ['wɔlɪt] n portefeuille m

walleye ['wɔːlaɪ] n doré m

wallpaper ['wɔːlpeɪpəʳ] n tapisserie f

walnut ['wɔːlnʌt] n noix f *(pl noix)*

wander ['wɔndəʳ] vb: **to wander around** flâner ▷ *I just wandered around for a while.* J'ai flâné un peu.

want [wɔnt] vb vouloir ▷ *Do you want some cake?* Tu veux du gâteau?; **to want to do something** vouloir faire quelque chose ▷ *I want to go to the movies.* Je veux aller au cinéma. ▷ *What do you want to do tomorrow?* Qu'est-ce que tu veux faire demain?

war [wɔːʳ] n guerre f

ward [wɔːd] n *(room in hospital)* salle f

wardrobe ['wɔːdrəub] n ❶ *(clothes)* garde-robe f ▷ *She has an extensive wardrobe.* Elle a une garde-robe bien fournie. ❷ *(piece of furniture)* armoire f

warehouse ['wɛəhaus] n entrepôt m

warm [wɔːm] adj ❶ chaud ▷ *warm water* l'eau chaude; **It's warm in here.** Il fait chaud ici.; **to be warm** *(person)* avoir chaud ▷ *I'm too warm.* J'ai trop chaud. ❷ chaleureux *(f* chaleureuse*)* ▷ *a warm welcome* un accueil chaleureux; **to warm up (1)** *(for sports)* s'échauffer **(2)** *(food)* réchauffer ▷ *I'll warm up some lasagna for you.* Je vais te réchauffer de la lasagne.

warn [wɔːn] vb prévenir ▷ *Well, I warned you!* Je t'avais prévenu.; **to warn somebody to do something** conseiller à quelqu'un de faire quelque chose

warning ['wɔːnɪŋ] n avertissement m

wart [wɔːt] n verrue f

was [wɔz] vb see **be**

wash [wɔʃ] vb ❶ laver ▷ *to wash something* laver quelque chose ❷ *(get washed)* se laver ▷ *Every morning I get up, wash and get dressed.* Tous les matins je me lève, je me lave et je m'habille.; **to wash one's hands** se laver les mains; **to wash one's hair** se laver les cheveux; **to wash the dishes** faire la vaisselle

washbasin ['wɔʃbeɪsn] n lavabo m

washcloth ['wɔʃklɔθ] n débarbouillette m

washing ['wɔʃɪŋ] n linge m ▷ *dirty washing* du linge sale; **Have you got any washing?** Tu as du linge à laver?; **to do the washing** faire le lavage

washing machine n laveuse f

wasn't ['wɔznt]; = **was not**

wasp [wɔsp] n guêpe f

waste [weɪst] n ❶ gaspillage m ▷ *It's such a waste!* C'est vraiment du gaspillage!; **It's a waste of time.** C'est une perte de temps. ❷ *(garbage)* déchets mpl ▷ *nuclear waste* les déchets nucléaires
▶ vb gaspiller ▷ *I don't like wasting money.* Je n'aime pas gaspiller de l'argent.; **to waste time** perdre du temps ▷ *There's no time to waste.* Il n'y a pas de temps à perdre.

wastepaper basket ['weɪstpeɪpə-] n poubelle f

watch [wɔtʃ] n montre f .
▶ vb ❶ regarder ▷ *to watch television* regarder la télévision ▷ *Watch me!* Regarde-moi! ❷ *(keep a watch on)* surveiller ▷ *The police were watching the house.* La police surveillait la maison.; **to watch out** faire attention; **Watch out!** Attention!

water ['wɔːtəʳ] n eau f
▶ vb arroser ▷ *He was watering his tulips.* Il arrosait ses tulipes.

waterfall ['wɔːtəfɔːl] n cascade f

watering can ['wɔːtərɪŋ-] n arrosoir m

watermelon ['wɔːtəmɛlən] n melon d'eau m

waterproof ['wɔːtəpruːf] adj imperméable ▷ *Is this coat waterproof?* Ce manteau est-il imperméable?; **a waterproof watch** une montre étanche

water-skiing ['wɔːtəskiːɪŋ] n ski nautique m ▷ *to go water-skiing* faire du ski nautique

wave [weɪv] n ❶ *(in water)* vague f ❷ *(of hand)* signe m ▷ *We gave him a wave.* Nous lui avons fait signe.
▶ vb faire un signe de la main ▷ *to wave at somebody* faire un signe de la main à quelqu'un; **to wave goodbye** faire au revoir de la main ▷ *I waved goodbye to her.* Je lui ai fait au revoir de la main.

wavy ['weɪvɪ] adj ondulé ▷ *wavy hair* les cheveux ondulés ▷ *a wavy line* une ligne ondulée

wax [wæks] n cire f

way [weɪ] n ❶ *(manner)* façon f ▷ *She looked at me in a strange way.* Elle m'a regardé d'une façon étrange.; **This book tells you the right way to do it.** Ce livre explique comment il faut faire.; **You're doing it the wrong way.** Ce n'est pas comme ça qu'il faut faire.; **in a way...** dans un sens...; **a way of life** un mode de vie ❷ *(route)* chemin m ▷ *I don't know the way.* Je ne connais pas le chemin.; **on the way** en chemin ▷ *We stopped on the way.* Nous nous sommes arrêtés en chemin.; **It's a long way.** C'est loin. ▷ *Kenora is a long way from Halifax.* Kenora est loin de Halifax.; **Which way is it?** C'est par où?; **The supermarket is this way.** Le supermarché est par ici.; **Do you know the way to the mall?** Vous savez comment aller au centre commercial?; **He's on his way.** Il arrive.; **the way in** l'entrée *f*; **the way out** la sortie; **by the way…** en passant…

we [wiː] *pron* nous ▷ *We're staying here for a week.* Nous restons une semaine ici.

weak [wiːk] *adj* faible

wealthy [ˈwɛlθɪ] *adj* riche

weapon [ˈwɛpən] *n* arme *f*

wear [wɛəʳ] *vb (clothes)* porter ▷ *He was wearing a hat.* Il portait un chapeau.; **She was wearing black.** Elle était en noir.

weather [ˈwɛðəʳ] *n* temps *m* ▷ *What was the weather like?* Quel temps a-t-il fait? ▷ *The weather was lovely.* Il a fait un temps magnifique.

weather forecast *n* météo *f*

Web [wɛb] *n* Web *m*

Web browser *n* navigateur Web *m*

webmaster [ˈwɛbmɑːstəʳ] *n* webmestre

webography [wɛˈbɒɡrəfɪ] *n* webographie *f*

website [ˈwɛbsaɪt] *n* site Web *m*

webzine [ˈwɛbziːn] *n* webzine *m*

we'd [wiːd]; = **we had**; = **we would**

wedding [ˈwɛdɪŋ] *n* mariage *m*; **wedding anniversary** l'anniversaire *m* de mariage; **wedding dress** la robe de mariée

Wednesday [ˈwɛnzdɪ] *n* mercredi *m* ▷ *on Wednesday* mercredi ▷ *on Wednesdays* le mercredi ▷ *every Wednesday* tous les mercredis ▷ *last Wednesday* mercredi dernier ▷ *next Wednesday* mercredi prochain

weed [wiːd] *n* mauvaise herbe *f* ▷ *The garden's full of weeds.* Le jardin est plein de mauvaises herbes.

week [wiːk] *n* semaine *f* ▷ *last week* la semaine dernière ▷ *every week* toutes les semaines ▷ *next week* la semaine prochaine; **a week from now** dans une semaine; **a week from Friday** vendredi dans une semaine

weekday [ˈwiːkdeɪ] *n*: **on weekdays** en semaine

weekend [wiːkˈɛnd] *n* fin de semaine *f* ▷ *on weekends* la fin de semaine ▷ *last weekend* la fin de semaine dernière ▷ *next weekend* la fin de semaine prochaine

weigh [weɪ] *vb* peser ▷ *How much do you weigh?* Combien est-ce que tu pèses? ▷ *They weighed my suitcase.* On a pesé ma valise.; **to weigh oneself** se peser

weight [weɪt] *n* poids *m*; **to lose weight** maigrir; **to put on weight** grossir

weightlifter [ˈweɪtlɪftəʳ] *n* haltérophile *mf*

weightlifting [ˈweɪtlɪftɪŋ] *n* haltérophilie *f*

weird [wɪəd] *adj* bizarre

welcome [ˈwɛlkəm] *n* accueil *m* ▷ *They gave her a warm welcome.* Ils lui ont fait un accueil chaleureux.; **Welcome!** Bienvenue! ▷ *Welcome to Nunavut!* Bienvenue au Nunavut!

▷ *vb*: **to welcome somebody** accueillir quelqu'un; **"Thank you!" — "You're welcome!"** «Merci!» — «De rien!»

well [wɛl] *adj, adv* ❶ bien ▷ *You did that really well.* Tu as très bien fait ça.; **to be well** réussir bien ▷ *He's doing really well at school.* Il réussit vraiment bien à l'école.; **to be well** *(in good health)* aller bien ▷ *I'm not very well at the moment.* Je ne vais pas très bien en ce moment.; **get well soon!** remets-toi vite!; **well done!** bravo! ▷ *It's enormous! Well, quite big anyway.* C'est énorme! Enfin, c'est assez grand.; **as well** aussi ▷ *We worked hard, but we had some fun as well.* Nous avons travaillé dur, mais nous nous sommes bien amusés aussi. ▷ *We went to Calgary as well as Edmonton.* Nous sommes allés à Edmonton et à Calgary aussi.

▷ *n* puits *m (pl* puits)

we'll [wiːl]; = **we will**

well-behaved [ˈwɛlbɪˈheɪvd] *adj* sage

well-dressed [ˈwɛlˈdrɛst] *adj* bien habillé

well-known [ˈwɛlˈnəʊn] *adj* célèbre ▷ *a well-known movie star* une vedette de cinéma célèbre

well-off [ˈwɛlˈɒf] *adj* aisé

went [wɛnt] *vb* see **go**

were [wəːʳ] *vb* see **be**

we're [wɪəʳ]; = **we are**

weren't [wəːnt]; = **were not**

west [wɛst] *n* ouest *m* ▷ *in the west* dans l'ouest; **the West** l'Occident *m*

▷ *adj, adv* ❷ ouest *(f+pl* ouest) ▷ *the West Coast* la côte Ouest; **west of** à l'ouest de ▷ *Toronto is west of Ottawa.* Toronto est à l'ouest d'Ottawa. ❷ vers l'ouest ▷ *We were travelling west.* Nous allions vers l'ouest.

westbound [ˈwɛstbaʊnd] *adj*: **The truck was westbound on the highway.** Le camion roulait sur l'autoroute en direction de l'ouest.; **Westbound traffic is moving very slowly.** La circulation en direction de l'ouest est très ralentie.

western [ˈwɛstən] *n* ❶ *(movie)* western *m* ❷ *(sandwich)* sandwich western *m*

▷ *adj*: **the western part of the island** la partie ouest de l'île; **Western Europe** l'Europe *f* de l'Ouest; **Western Canada** l'Ouest *m* du Canada

wet [wɛt] *adj* mouillé ▷ *wet clothes* les vêtements mouillés; **to get wet** se faire mouiller; **dripping wet** trempé; **wet weather** le temps pluvieux; **It was wet all week.** Il a plu toute la semaine.

wetsuit [ˈwɛtsuːt] *n* combinaison de plongée *f (pl* combinaisons de plongée)

we've [wiːv]; = **we have**

whale [weɪl] *n* baleine *f*

what [wɒt] *adj, pron* ❶ *(which)* quel *(f* quelle) ▷ *What subjects are you taking?* Quelles matières est-ce que tu fais? ▷ *What colour is it?* C'est de quelle couleur? ▷ *What's the capital of Canada?* Quelle est la capitale du Canada? ▷ *What a mess!* Quel fouillis! ❷ *est-ce que* ▷ *What are you doing?* Qu'est-ce que vous faites? ▷ *What did you say?* Qu'est-ce que vous avez dit? ▷ *What is it?* Qu'est-ce que c'est? ▷ *What's the matter?* Qu'est-ce qu'il y a? ❷ *qu'est-ce qui* ▷ *What*

happened? Qu'est-ce qui s'est passé? ▷ **What's bothering you?** Qu'est-ce qui te préoccupe? ❷ *(subject)* ce qui ▷ *I saw what happened.* J'ai vu ce qui est arrivé. ▷ *I know what's bothering you.* Je sais ce qui te préoccupe. ❸ *(object)* ce que ▷ *Tell me what you did.* Dites-moi ce que vous avez fait. ▷ *I heard what he said.* J'ai entendu ce qu'il a dit.; **What?** *(what did you say)* Comment?; **What!** *(shocked)* Quoi!

wheat [wi:t] *n* blé *m*

wheel [wi:l] *n* roue *f*; **the steering wheel** le volant

wheelchair ['wi:ltʃeə'] *n* fauteuil roulant *m*

when [wen] *adv, conj* quand ▷ *When did he leave?* Quand est-ce qu'il est parti? ▷ *She was reading when I came in.* Elle lisait quand je suis entré.

where [weə'] *adv, conj* où ▷ *Where's your sister today?* Où est ta sœur aujourd'hui? ▷ *Where do you live?* Où habites-tu? ▷ *Where are you going?* Où vas-tu? ▷ *a store where you can buy croissants* un magasin où l'on peut acheter des croissants

whether ['weðə'] *conj* si ▷ *I don't know whether to go or not.* Je ne sais pas si j'y vais ou non.

which [wɪtʃ] *adj, pron* ❶ quel (*f* quelle) ▷ *Which flavour do you want?* Quel parfum est-ce que tu veux?; **"I know her brother." — "Which one?"** « Je connais son frère. » — « Lequel? »; **"I know his sister." — "Which one?"** « Je connais sa sœur. » — « Laquelle? »; **Which would you like?** Lequel est-ce que vous voulez?; **Which of these are yours?** Lesquels sont à vous? ❷ *(subject)* qui ▷ *the CD which is playing now* le CD qui passe maintenant ❸ *(object)* que ▷ *the CD which I bought today* le CD que j'ai acheté hier

while [waɪl] *conj* ❶ pendant que ▷ *You hold the flashlight while I look inside.* Tiens la lampe de poche pendant que je regarde à l'intérieur. ❷ alors que ▷ *She is very dynamic, while he is more laid-back.* Elle est très dynamique, alors qu'il est plus relax.
▶ *n* moment *m* ▷ *after a while* au bout d'un moment; **a while ago** il y a un moment ▷ *He was here a while ago.* Il était là il y a un moment.; **for a while** pendant quelque temps ▷ *I lived in Thunder Bay for a while.* J'ai vécu à Thunder Bay pendant quelque temps.; **quite a while** longtemps ▷ *quite a while ago* il y a longtemps ▷ *I haven't seen him for quite a while.* Ça fait longtemps que je ne l'ai pas vu.

whip [wɪp] *n* ❶ fouet *m* ❷ *(parliament)* whip
▶ *vb* ❶ *(person, animal)* fouetter ❷ *(eggs)* battre

whipped cream [wɪpt-] *n* crème fouettée *f*

whisk [wɪsk] *n* fouet *m*

whiskers ['wɪskəz] *npl* moustaches *fpl*

whisper ['wɪspə'] *vb* chuchoter

whistle ['wɪsl] *n* sifflet *m*; **The referee blew her whistle.** L'arbitre a sifflé.
▶ *vb* siffler

white [waɪt] *adj* blanc (*f* blanche) ▷ *He has white hair.* Il a les cheveux blancs.; **white bread** le pain blanc; **a white man** un Blanc; **a white woman** une Blanche; **white people** les Blancs

whiteout ['waɪtaut] *n* voile blanc *m*

whiz [wɪz] *n* virtuose

who [hu:] *pron* ❶ qui ▷ *Who said that?* Qui a dit ça? ▷ *Who is Adrienne Clarkson?* Qui est Adrienne Clarkson? ❷ *(object)* qui ▷ *the woman who saw us* la femme qui nous a vus ▷ *the woman who spoke to us* la femme qui nous a parlé ❸ *(object)* que ▷ *the man who we saw* l'homme que nous avons vu ▷ *the man who she married* l'homme qu'elle a épousé

whole [həul] *adj* tout ▷ *the whole class* toute la classe ▷ *the whole afternoon* tout l'après-midi; **a whole box of chocolates** toute une boîte de chocolats; **the whole world** le monde entier; **whole wheat** le blé entier ▷ *whole wheat pasta* des pâtes au blé entier; **the whole works** le tout ▷ *I had a ton of assignments, but I finished the whole works in one evening.* J'avais un tas de devoirs, mais j'ai terminé le tout en une seule soirée.
▶ *n*: **The whole of Toronto was snowbound.** Toronto était complètement bloquée par la neige.; **The whole of Montréal was talking about it.** On en parlait dans tout Montréal.; **on the whole** dans l'ensemble

whom [hu:m] *pron* qui ▷ *Whom did you see?* Qui avez-vous vu? ▷ *the man to whom I spoke* l'homme à qui j'ai parlé

whose [hu:z] *pron, adj* ❶ à qui ▷ *Whose is this?* À qui est-ce? ▷ *I know whose it is.* Je sais à qui c'est. ▷ *Whose book is this?* À qui est ce livre? ❷ *(after noun)* dont ▷ *the girl whose picture was in the paper* la jeune fille dont la photo était dans le journal

why [waɪ] *adv* pourquoi ▷ *Why did you do that?* Pourquoi avez-vous fait ça? ▷ *That's why he did it.* Voilà pourquoi il a fait ça. ▷ *Tell me why.* Dis-moi pourquoi.; **"I've never been to Saskatchewan." — "Why not?"** « Je ne suis jamais allé en Saskatchewan. » — « Pourquoi? »; **All right, why not?** D'accord, pourquoi pas?

wicked ['wɪkɪd] *adj* ❶ *(evil)* méchant ❷ *(really great)* génial (*mpl* géniaux)

wide [waɪd] *adj, adv* large ▷ *a wide road* une route large; **wide open** grand ouvert ▷ *The door was wide open.* La porte était grande ouverte. ▷ *The windows were wide open.* Les fenêtres étaient grandes ouvertes.; **wide awake** complètement réveillé

widow ['wɪdəu] *n* veuve *f* ▷ *She's a widow.* Elle est veuve.

widower ['wɪdəuə'] *n* veuf *m* ▷ *He's a widower.* Il est veuf.

width [wɪdθ] *n* largeur *f*

wife [waɪf] *n* femme *f* ▷ *She's his wife.* C'est sa femme.

wig [wɪg] *n* perruque *f*

wild [waɪld] *adj* ❶ *(not tame)* sauvage ▷ *a wild animal* un animal sauvage ❷ *(crazy)* fou (*f* folle)

wilderness ['wɪldənɪs] *n* région sauvage *f*; **wilderness camping** le camping sauvage

wildlife ['waɪldlaɪf] *n* nature *f* ▷ *I'm interested in wildlife.* Je m'intéresse à la nature.

will [wɪl] *n* testament *m* ▷ *She left me some money in her will.* Elle m'a laissé de l'argent dans son testament.
▶ *vb*: **I'll show you your room.** Je vais te montrer ta chambre.; **I'll give you a hand.**

Je vais t'aider.; **I will finish it tomorrow.** Je le finirai demain.; **It won't take long.** Ça ne prendra pas longtemps.; **"Will you wash the dishes?" — "No, I won't."** « Est-ce que tu peux faire la vaisselle?» — « Non. »; **Will you help me?** Est-ce que tu peux m'aider?; **Will you be quiet!** Voulez-vous bien vous taire!; **That will be the paperboy.** Ça doit être le livreur de journaux.

willing ['wɪlɪŋ] *adj*: **to be willing to do something** être prêt à faire quelque chose

win [wɪn] *vb* gagner ▷ *Did you win?* Est-ce que tu as gagné?; **to win a prize** remporter un prix
▶ *n* victoire *f*

wind [waɪnd] *vb* ❶ (*rope, wool, wire*) enrouler ❷ (*river, path*) serpenter ▷ *The road winds through the valley.* La route serpente à travers la vallée.
▶ *n* [wɪnd] vent *m* ▷ *There was a strong wind.* Il y avait beaucoup de vent.; **a wind instrument** un instrument à vent; **wind power** l'énergie *f* éolienne

wind chill ['wɪnd-] *n* refroidissement éolien *m* ▷ *The wind chill factor is -10 today.* Le facteur de refroidissement éolien est de moins dix degrés aujourd'hui.

windmill ['wɪndmɪl] *n* moulin à vent *m* (*pl* moulins à vent)

window ['wɪndəʊ] *n* ❶ fenêtre *f* ❷ (*in car, train*) vitre *f*; **a store window** une vitrine

windshield ['wɪndʃi:ld] *n* pare-brise *m* (*pl* pare-brise)

windshield wiper [-'waɪpə^r] *n* essuie-glace *m* (*pl* essuie-glace)

windy ['wɪndɪ] *adj* (*place*) venteux (*f* venteuse); **It's windy.** Il y a du vent.

wing [wɪŋ] *n* aile *f*

wink [wɪŋk] *vb*: **to wink at somebody** faire un clin d'œil à quelqu'un ▷ *He winked at me.* Il m'a fait un clin d'œil.

winner ['wɪnə^r] *n* gagnant *m*, gagnante *f*

winning ['wɪnɪŋ] *adj*: **the winning team** l'équipe gagnante; **the winning goal** le but décisif

winter ['wɪntə^r] *n* hiver *m*; **in winter** en hiver

winterize ['wɪntəraɪz] *vb* hivériser ▷ *We have to winterize our cottage.* Nous devons hivériser le chalet.

winter sports *npl* sports *mpl* d'hiver

wipe [waɪp] *vb* essuyer; **to wipe one's feet** s'essuyer les pieds ▷ *Wipe your feet!* Essuie-toi les pieds!; **to wipe up** essuyer

wire ['waɪə^r] *n* fil *m*

wireless ['waɪəlɪs] *adj* sans fil

wisdom tooth ['wɪzdəm-] *n* dent de sagesse *f* (*pl* dents de sagesse)

wise [waɪz] *adj* sage

wish [wɪʃ] *vb*: **to wish for something** souhaiter quelque chose ▷ *What more could you wish for?* Que pourrais-tu souhaiter de plus?; **to wish to do something** désirer faire quelque chose ▷ *I wish to make a complaint.* Je désire porter plainte.; **I wish you were here!** Si seulement tu étais ici!; **I wish you'd told me!** Si seulement tu m'en avais parlé!
▶ *n* vœu *m* (*pl* vœux) ▷ *to make a wish* faire

un vœu; **"best wishes"** (*on greeting card*) « meilleurs vœux »; **"with best wishes, Kathy"** « bien amicalement, Kathy »

with [wɪð, wɪθ] *prep* ❶ avec ▷ *Come with me.* Venez avec moi. ▷ *He walks with a stick.* Il marche avec une canne.; **a woman with blue eyes** une femme aux yeux bleus ❷ (*at the home of*) chez ▷ *We stayed with friends.* Nous sommes restés chez des amis. ❸ de ▷ *green with envy* vert de jalousie ▷ *to shake with fear* trembler de peur ▷ *Fill the jug with water.* Remplis la carafe d'eau.

within [wɪð'ɪn] *prep*: **The stores are within easy reach.** Les magasins sont à proximité.; **within a week** avant la fin d'une semaine

without [wɪð'aʊt] *prep* sans ▷ *without a coat* sans manteau ▷ *without speaking* sans parler

witness ['wɪtnɪs] *n* témoin ▷ *There were no witnesses.* Il n'y a pas eu de témoins.

witty ['wɪtɪ] *adj* spirituel (*f* spirituelle)

wives ['waɪvz] *npl* see **wife**

wizard ['wɪzəd] *n* magicien *m*

wok [wɔk] *n* wok *m*

woke up, woken up [wəʊk-, 'wəʊkən-] *vb* see **wake up**

wolf [wʊlf] *n* loup *m*; **a wolf cub** un louveteau

wolverine ['wʊlvəri:n] *n* carcajou *m*

woman ['wʊmən] *n* femme *f* ▷ *a woman doctor* une femme médecin

won [wʌn] *vb* see **win**

wonder ['wʌndə^r] *vb* se demander ▷ *I wonder why he said that.* Je me demande pourquoi il a dit ça. ▷ *I wonder what that means.* Je me demande ce que ça veut dire. ▷ *I wonder where my sister is.* Je me demande où est ma sœur.

wonderful ['wʌndəful] *adj* formidable

won't [wəʊnt] = **will not**

wood [wʊd] *n* bois *m* ▷ *It's made of wood.* C'est en bois.

wooden ['wʊdn] *adj* en bois ▷ *a wooden chair* une chaise en bois

woods [wʊdz] *npl* bois *m* ▷ *We went for a walk in the woods.* Nous sommes allés nous promener dans le bois.

woodworking ['wʊdwə:kɪŋ] *n* menuiserie *f* ▷ *My hobby is woodworking.* Je fais de la menuiserie.

wool [wʊl] *n* laine *f* ▷ *a wool sweater* un chandail de laine

word [wə:d] *n* mot *m* ▷ *a difficult word* un mot difficile; **What's the word for "store" in German?** Comment dit-on « magasin » en allemand?; **in other words** en d'autres termes; **to have a word with somebody** parler avec quelqu'un; **the words** (*lyrics*) les paroles ▷ *I really like the words of this song.* J'adore les paroles de cette chanson.

word processing [-'prəʊsɛsɪŋ] *n* traitement de texte *m*

wore [wɔː^r] *vb* see **wear**

work [wə:k] *n* travail *m* (*pl* travaux) ▷ *She's looking for work.* Elle cherche du travail. ▷ *He's at work at the moment.* Il est au travail en ce moment.; **It's hard work.** C'est dur.; **to be off work** (*sick*) être malade ▷ *He's been off work for a week.* Il est malade depuis une semaine.; **He's**

out of work. Il est sans emploi.
▶ vb ❶ (person) travailler ▷ She works in a store.
Elle travaille dans un magasin. ▷ to work hard
travailler dur ❷ (machine, plan) marcher ▷ The
heat isn't working. Le chauffage ne marche pas.
▷ My plan worked perfectly. Mon plan a marché
à merveille.; **to work out (1)** (exercise) faire de
l'exercice ▷ I work out twice a week. Je fais de
l'exercice deux fois par semaine. **(2)** (turn out)
marcher ▷ In the end it worked out really well.
Au bout du compte, ça a très bien marché.
(3) (figure out) arriver à comprendre ▷ I just
couldn't work it out. Je n'arrivais pas du tout à
comprendre.; **It works out to $10 each.** Ça
fait dix dollars chacun.

workaholic [wə:kə'hɒlɪk] n bourreau de
travail

worker ['wə:kə'] n ❶ (in factory) ouvrier
m, ouvrière f; **He's a factory worker.** Il est
ouvrier. ❷ (general) travailleur m, travailleuse
f; **She's a good worker.** Elle travaille bien.

workforce ['wə:kfɔːs] n population active f

workout ['wə:kaut] n séance d'entraînement f

works [wə:ks] n: **the whole works** le tout ▷ I
had a ton of assignments, but I finished the whole
works in one evening. J'avais un tas de devoirs,
mais j'ai terminé le tout en une seule soirée.;
a hamburger with the works un hamburger
tout garni

worksheet ['wə:kʃiːt] n feuille d'exercices f

workshop ['wə:kʃɒp] n atelier m ▷ a drama
workshop un atelier de théâtre

workspace ['wə:kspeɪs] n (computing) espace
m de travail

workstation ['wə:ksteɪʃən] n poste de travail
m (pl postes de travail)

world [wə:ld] n monde m; **He's the world
champion.** Il est champion du monde.

worm [wə:m] n ver m

worn [wɔːn] vb see **wear**
▶ adj usé ▷ The carpet is a bit worn. Le tapis est
un peu usé.; **worn out** (tired) épuisé

worne [wɔːn] vb see **wear**

worried ['wʌrɪd] adj inquiet (f inquiète)
▷ She's very worried. Elle est très inquiète.; **to
be worried about something** s'inquiéter pour
quelque chose ▷ I'm worried about the exams. Je
m'inquiète pour les examens.; **to look worried**
avoir l'air inquiet ▷ She looks a bit worried. Elle a
l'air un peu inquiète.

worry ['wʌrɪ] vb s'inquiéter; **Don't worry!** Ne
t'inquiète pas!

worse [wə:s] adj, adv ❶ pire m ▷ It was even
worse than that. C'était encore pire que ça. ▷ My
marks were bad, but his were even worse. Mes
notes étaient mauvaises, mais les siennes
étaient encore pires. ❷ plus mal ▷ I'm feeling
worse. Je me sens plus mal.

worship ['wə:ʃɪp] vb (God) vénérer; **He really
worships her.** Il est en adoration devant elle.

worst [wə:st] adj: **the worst** le plus mauvais
▷ the worst student in the class le plus mauvais
élève de la classe ▷ She got the worst mark in
the whole class. Elle a eu la plus mauvaise note
de toute la classe.; **my worst enemy** mon
pire ennemi; **Math is my worst subject.** Les

maths sont ma matière faible.
▶ n pire m ▷ The worst of it is that... Le pire c'est
que...; **at worst** au pire; **if worst comes to
worst** au pire

worth [wə:θ] adj: **to be worth** valoir ▷ It's
worth a lot of money. Ça vaut très cher. ▷ How
much is it worth? Ça vaut combien?; **It's worth
it.** Ça vaut la peine. ▷ Is it worth it? Est-ce que
ça vaut la peine? ▷ It's not worth it. Ça ne vaut
pas la peine.

would [wud] vb: **Would you like a cookie?**
Vous voulez un biscuit?; **Would you like to
go see a movie?** Est-ce que tu veux aller voir
un film?; **Would you close the door please?**
Vous pouvez fermer la porte, s'il vous plaît?;
I'd like... j'aimerais... ▷ I'd like to go to Labrador.
J'aimerais aller au Labrador. ▷ "Shall we go see a
movie?" — "Yes, I'd like that." « Si on allait voir un
film? » — « Oui, j'aimerais bien. »; **I said I would
do it.** J'ai dit que je le ferais.; **If you asked
her, she'd do it.** Si vous le lui demandiez, elle
le ferait.; **If you had asked him he would
have done it.** Si vous le lui aviez demandé, il
l'aurait fait.

wouldn't ['wudnt]; = **would not**

wound [wuːnd] n blessure f
▶ vb blesser ▷ He was wounded in the leg. Il a été
blessé à la jambe.

wound [waund] vb see **wind**

wrap [ræp] vb emballer ▷ She's wrapping your
birthday presents. Elle est en train d'emballer
tes cadeaux de fête.; **Can you wrap it for
me please?** (in store) Vous pouvez me faire un
emballage cadeau, s'il vous plaît?; **to wrap up**
emballer

wrapping paper ['ræpɪŋ-] n papier
emballage m

wreck [rɛk] n ❶ (vehicle, machine) tas de
ferraille m ▷ That car is a wreck! Cette voiture
est un tas de ferraille! ❷ (person) loque f ▷ After
the tournament I was a complete wreck. Après le
tournoi, j'étais une véritable loque.
▶ vb ❶ (building, vehicle) démolir ▷ The explosion
wrecked the whole house. L'explosion a démoli
toute la maison. ❷ (plan, holiday) ruiner ▷ The
trip was wrecked by bad weather. Le voyage a été
ruiné par le mauvais temps.

wreckage ['rɛkɪdʒ] n ❶ (of vehicle) débris mpl
❷ (of building) décombres mpl

wrench [rɛntʃ] n clé anglaise f

wrestler ['rɛslə'] n lutteur m, lutteuse f

wrestling ['rɛslɪŋ] n lutte f

wrinkled ['rɪŋkld] adj ridé

wrist [rɪst] n poignet m

write [raɪt] vb écrire ▷ to write a letter écrire
une lettre; **to write to somebody** écrire à
quelqu'un ▷ I'm going to write to him in French.
Je vais lui écrire en français.; **to write down**
noter ▷ I wrote down the address. J'ai noté
l'adresse.; **Can you write it down for me,
please?** Vous pouvez me l'écrire, s'il vous plaît?

writer ['raɪtə'] n écrivain m, écrivaine f ▷ She's a
writer. Elle est écrivaine.

writing ['raɪtɪŋ] n écriture f ▷ I can't read your
writing. Je n'arrive pas à lire ton écriture.; **in
writing** par écrit

written ['rɪtn] *vb see* **write**

wrong [rɒŋ] *adj, adv* ❶ (*incorrect*) faux (*f* fausse) ▷ *The information they gave us was wrong.* Les renseignements qu'ils nous ont donnés étaient faux.; **the wrong answer** la mauvaise réponse; **You've got the wrong number.** Vous vous êtes trompé de numéro. ❷ (*morally bad*) mal ▷ *Some people think hunting is wrong.* Certains pensent que c'est mal de chasser.; **to be wrong** (*mistaken*) se tromper ▷ *You're wrong about that.* Tu te trompes.; **to do something wrong** se tromper ▷ *You've done it wrong.* Tu t'es trompé.; **to go wrong** (*plan*) mal tourner ▷ *The robbery went wrong and they got caught.* Le cambriolage a mal tourné et ils ont été pris.; **What's wrong?** Qu'est-ce qu'il y a?; **What's wrong with her?** Qu'est-ce qu'elle a?

wrote [rəʊt] *vb see* **write**

X-ray ['ɛksreɪ] *vb:* **to X-ray something** faire une radio de quelque chose ▷ *They X-rayed my arm.* Ils ont fait une radio de mon bras.
▶ *n* radio *f* ▷ **to have an X-ray** passer une radio

yacht [jɒt] *n* ❶ (*sailing boat*) voilier *m* ❷ (*luxury motorboat*) yacht *m*

yard [jɑːd] *n* ❶ (*of building*) cour *f* ▷ *in the yard* dans la cour ❷ (*of house*) jardin *m*

yawn [jɔːn] *vb* bâiller

year [jɪəʳ] *n* ❶ an *m* ▷ *last year* l'an dernier ▷ *next year* l'an prochain; **to be 15 years old** avoir quinze ans; **an eight-year-old child** un enfant de huit ans ❷ (*duration*) année *f* ▷ *Mom has been sick for several years.* Maman a été malade pendant plusieurs années. ▷ *throughout the year* à longueur d'année

yell [jɛl] *vb* hurler

yellow ['jɛləʊ] *adj* jaune

yes [jɛs] *adv* oui ▷ *"Do you like it?" — "Yes."* «Tu aimes ça?» — «Oui.» ▷ *"You don't like it?" — "Yes I do!"* «Tu n'aimes pas ça?» — «Mais oui, j'aime ça!»; *"Would you like a cup of tea?" — "Yes please."* «Voulez-vous une tasse de thé?» — «Je veux bien.»

yesterday ['jɛstədɪ] *adv* hier ▷ *yesterday morning* hier matin ▷ *yesterday afternoon* hier après-midi ▷ *yesterday evening* hier soir ▷ *all day yesterday* toute la journée d'hier

yet [jɛt] *adv, conj* ❶ encore; **not yet** pas encore ▷ *It's not finished yet.* Ce n'est pas encore fini.; **not as yet** pas encore ▷ *There's no news as yet.* Nous n'avons pas encore de nouvelles.; **Have you finished yet?** Vous avez fini? ❷ (*nevertheless*) pourtant ▷ *It's nearly impossible, and yet it has to be done.* C'est presque impossible, et pourtant il faut le faire.

yield [jiːld] *vb* (*on road sign*) céder le passage

yogurt *n* yogourt *m*

yolk [jəʊk] *n* jaune d'œuf *m* (*pl* jaunes d'œuf)

you [juː] *pron* ❶ (*polite form or plural*) vous ▷ *Do you like basketball?* Est-ce que vous aimez le basket-ball? ▷ *Can I help you?* Est-ce que je peux vous aider? ▷ *It's for you.* C'est pour vous. ❷ (*familiar singular*) tu ▷ *Do you like basketball?* Tu aimes le basket-ball? ❸ te, t' ▷ *I know you.* Je te connais. ▷ *I gave it to you.* Je te l'ai donné. ▷ *I saw you.* Je t'ai vu. ▷ *I'll help you.* Je vais t'aider. ❹ toi ▷ *It's for you.* C'est pour toi. ▷ *I'll come with you.* Je viens avec toi. ▷ *She's younger than you.* Elle est plus jeune que toi.

young [jʌŋ] *adj* jeune; **young people** les jeunes

younger [jʌŋgəʳ] *adj* plus jeune ▷ *He's younger than me.* Il est plus jeune que moi.; **my younger brother** mon frère cadet; **my younger sister** ma sœur cadette

youngest ['jʌŋgəst] *adj* le plus jeune, la plus jeune ▷ *my youngest brother* mon plus jeune frère ▷ *She's the youngest.* C'est la plus jeune.

your [jɔːʳ] *adj* ❶ votre, vos *pl* ▷ *your house* votre maison ❷ (*polite form or plural*) vos ▷ *your seats* vos places ❸ ton *m*, ta *f*, tes *pl* ▷ *your brother* ton frère ❹ (*familiar singular*) ▷ *your sister* ta sœur ▷ *your parents* tes parents; **your friend (1)** (*male*) ton ami **(2)** (*female*) ton amie ▷ *Would you like to wash your hands?* Est-ce que vous voulez vous laver les mains? ▷ *Do you want to wash your hair?* Tu veux te laver les cheveux?

yours [jɔːz] *pron* ❶ le + *m* vôtre, la + *f* vôtre, les + *pl* vôtres ▷ *I've lost my pen. Can I use yours?* J'ai perdu mon stylo. Je peux utiliser le vôtre? ▷ *I like that car. Is it yours?* J'aime cette voiture-là. C'est la vôtre? ❷ *my parents and yours* mes parents et les vôtres; **Is this yours?** C'est à vous? ▷ *This book is yours.* Ce livre est à vous. ▷ *"Whose is this?" — "It's yours."* «C'est à qui?» — «À vous.»; **Yours sincerely...** Veuillez agréer l'expression de mes sentiments les plus distingués... ❸ le + *m* tien, la + *f* tienne, les + *m* tiens, les + *f* tiennes ▷ *I've lost my pen. Can I use yours?* J'ai perdu mon stylo. Je peux utiliser le tien? ▷ *I like that car. Is it yours?* J'aime cette voiture-là. C'est la tienne? ▷ *my parents and yours* mes parents et les tiens ▷ *My hands are dirty, yours are clean.* Mes mains sont sales, les tiennes sont propres.; **Is this yours?** C'est à toi? ▷ *This book is yours.* Ce livre est à toi. ▷ *"Whose is this?" —"It's yours."* « C'est à qui? » — « À toi. »

yourself [jɔː'sɛlf] *pron* ❶ *(polite form)* vous ▷ *Have you hurt yourself?* Est-ce que vous vous êtes fait mal? ▷ *Tell me about yourself!* Parlez-moi de vous! ❷ *(familiar form)* te ▷ *Have you hurt yourself?* Est-ce que tu t'es fait mal? ❸ *(familiar form)* toi ▷ *Tell me about yourself!* Parle-moi de toi! ❹ toi-même ▷ *Do it yourself!* Fais-le toi-même! ❺ vous-même ▷ *Do it yourself!* Faites-le vous-même!

yourselves [jɔː'sɛlvz] *pron* ❶ vous ▷ *Did you enjoy yourselves?* Vous vous êtes bien amusés? ❷ vous-mêmes ▷ *Did you make it yourselves?* Vous l'avez fait vous-mêmes?

youth club *n* centre de jeunes *m*

youth hostel *n* auberge *f* de jeunesse *(pl* auberges de jeunesse)

Yukon ['juːkɔn] *n* Yukon *m*

Zamboni® [zæm'bəunɪ] *n* surfaceuse *f*

zany ['zeɪnɪ] *adj* loufoque

zebra ['ziːbrə] *n* zèbre *m*

zero ['zɪərəu] *n* zéro *m*

zipper ['zɪpəʳ] *n* fermeture éclair® *f (pl* fermetures éclair)

zip up [zɪp-] *vb* fermer ▷ *Zip up your coat.* Ferme ton manteau.; **The dress zips up the back.** La robe se ferme avec une fermeture éclair au dos.

zit [zɪt] *n* bouton *m*

zodiac ['zəudɪæk] *n* zodiaque *m* ▷ *the signs of the zodiac* les signes du zodiaque

zone [zəun] *n* zone *f*

zoo [zuː] *n* zoo *m*

zoom lens ['zuːm-] *n* zoom *m*

zucchini [zuː'kiːnɪ] *n* courgette *f*

Grammar
Grammaire

—— USING THE GRAMMAR ——

The Grammar section deals systematically and comprehensively with all the information you will need in order to communicate accurately in French. The boxed numbers, → 1 etc, direct you to the relevant example in every case.

—— ABBREVIATIONS ——

ctd.	continued	**p(p)**	page(s)	**qn**	quelqu'un
fem.	feminine	**perf.**	perfect	**sb**	somebody
infin.	infinitive	**plur.**	plural	**sing.**	singular
masc.	masculine	**qch**	quelque chose	**sth**	something

CONTENTS

❑ Simple Tenses: Formation of Regular Verbs

Simple tenses are one-word tenses which are formed by adding endings to a verb stem. The endings show the number and person of the subject of the verb. The stem and endings of regular verbs are totally predictable.

There are three regular patterns (called conjugations), each identifiable by the ending of the infinitive. For irregular verbs see pp 50 ff.

❑ Simple Tenses: First Conjugation

◆ First conjugation verbs end in **-er**, e.g. **donner** to give. The stem is formed as follows:

TENSE	FORMATION	EXAMPLE
Present Imperfect Past Historic Present Subjunctive	infinitive minus **-er**	**donn-**
Future Conditional	infinitive	**donner-**

◆ To the appropriate stem add the following endings

		PRESENT → 1	IMPERFECT → 2	PAST HISTORIC → 3
sing.	1st person	**-e**	**-ais**	**-ai**
	2nd person	**-es**	**-ais**	**-as**
	3rd person	**-e**	**-ait**	**-a**
plur.	1st person	**-ons**	**-ions**	**-âmes**
	2nd person	**-ez**	**-iez**	**-âtes**
	3rd person	**-ent**	**-aient**	**-èrent**

		PRESENT SUBJUNCTIVE → 4	FUTURE → 5	CONDITIONAL → 6
sing.	1st person	**-e**	**-ai**	**-ais**
	2nd person	**-es**	**-as**	**-ais**
	3rd person	**-e**	**-a**	**-ait**
plur.	1st person	**-ions**	**-ons**	**-ions**
	2nd person	**-iez**	**-ez**	**-iez**
	3rd person	**-ent**	**-ont**	**-aient**

	1 PRESENT			**2** IMPERFECT
je	donne		je	donnais
tu	donnes		tu	donnais
il	donne		il	donnait
elle	donne		elle	donnait
nous	donnons		nous	donnions
vous	donnez		vous	donniez
ils	donnent		ils	donnaient
elles	donnent		elles	donnaient

I give, I am giving, I do give *etc*

I gave, I was giving, I used to give *etc*

	3 PAST HISTORIC			**4** PRESENT SUBJUNCTIVE
je	donnai		je	donne
tu	donnas		tu	donnes
il	donna		il	donne
elle	donna		elle	donne
nous	donnâmes		nous	donnions
vous	donnâtes		vous	donniez
ils	donnèrent		ils	donnent
elles	donnèrent		elles	donnent

I gave *etc*

I give/gave *etc*

	5 FUTURE			**6** CONDITIONAL
je	donnerai		je	donnerais
tu	donneras		tu	donnerais
il	donnera		il	donnerait
elle	donnera		elle	donnerait
nous	donnerons		nous	donnerions
vous	donnerez		vous	donneriez
ils	donneront		ils	donneraient
elles	donneront		elles	donneraient

I shall give, I shall be giving *etc*

I should/would give,
I should/would be giving *etc*

❏ Simple Tenses: Second Conjugation

◆ Second conjugation verbs end in **-ir**, e.g. **finir** to finish. The stem is formed as follows:

TENSE	FORMATION	EXAMPLE
Present Imperfect Past Historic Present Subjunctive	infinitive minus **-ir**	**fin-**
Future Conditional	infinitive	**finir-**

◆ To the appropriate stem add the following endings:

		PRESENT → 1	IMPERFECT → 2
sing.	1st person	**-is**	**-issais**
	2nd person	**-is**	**-issais**
	3rd person	**-it**	**-issait**
plur.	1st person	**-issons**	**-issions**
	2nd person	**-issez**	**-issiez**
	3rd person	**-issent**	**-issaient**

		PAST HISTORIC → 3	PRESENT SUBJUNCTIVE → 4
sing.	1st person	**-is**	**-isse**
	2nd person	**-is**	**-isses**
	3rd person	**-it**	**-isse**
plur.	1st person	**-îmes**	**-issions**
	2nd person	**-îtes**	**-issiez**
	3rd person	**-irent**	**-issent**

		FUTURE → 5	CONDITIONAL → 6
sing.	1st person	**-ai**	**-ais**
	2nd person	**-as**	**-ais**
	3rd person	**-a**	**-ait**
plur.	1st person	**-ons**	**-ions**
	2nd person	**-ez**	**-iez**
	3rd person	**-ont**	**-aient**

EXAMPLES

	1 PRESENT		**2 IMPERFECT**
je	fin**is**	je	fin**issais**
tu	fin**is**	tu	fin**issais**
il	fin**it**	il	fin**issait**
elle	fin**it**	elle	fin**issait**
nous	fin**issons**	nous	fin**issions**
vous	fin**issez**	vous	fin**issiez**
ils	fin**issent**	ils	fin**issaient**
elles	fin**issent**	elles	fin**issaient**

I finish, I am finishing, I do finish *etc*

I finished, I was finishing, I used to finish *etc*

	3 PAST HISTORIC		**4 PRESENT SUBJUNCTIVE**
je	fin**is**	je	fin**isse**
tu	fin**is**	tu	fin**isses**
il	fin**it**	il	fin**isse**
elle	fin**it**	elle	fin**isse**
nous	fin**îmes**	nous	fin**issions**
vous	fin**îtes**	vous	fin**issiez**
ils	fin**irent**	ils	fin**issent**
elles	fin**irent**	elles	fin**issent**

I finished *etc*

I finish/finished *etc*

	5 FUTURE		**6 CONDITIONAL**
je	fin**irai**	je	fin**irais**
tu	fin**iras**	tu	fin**irais**
il	fin**ira**	il	fin**irait**
elle	fin**ira**	elle	fin**irait**
nous	fin**irons**	nous	fin**irions**
vous	fin**irez**	vous	fin**iriez**
ils	fin**iront**	ils	fin**iraient**
elles	fin**iront**	elles	fin**iraient**

I shall finish, I shall be finishing *etc*

I should/would finish, I should/would be finishing *etc*

❒ Simple Tenses: Third Conjugation

◆ Third conjugation verbs end in **-re**, e.g. **vendre** to sell. The stem is formed as follows:

TENSE	FORMATION	EXAMPLE
Present Imperfect Past Historic Present Subjunctive	} infinitive minus **-re**	**vend-**
Future Conditional	} infinitive minus **-e**	**vendr-**

◆ To the appropriate stem add the following endings:

		PRESENT → 1	IMPERFECT → 2
	1st person	**-s**	**-ais**
sing.	2nd person	**-s**	**-ais**
	3rd person	—	**-ait**
	1st person	**-ons**	**-ions**
plur.	2nd person	**-ez**	**-iez**
	3rd person	**-ent**	**-aient**

		PAST HISTORIC → 3	PRESENT SUBJUNCTIVE → 4
	1st person	**-is**	**-e**
sing.	2nd person	**-is**	**-es**
	3rd person	**-it**	**-e**
	1st person	**-imes**	**-ions**
plur.	2nd person	**-ites**	**-iez**
	3rd person	**-irent**	**-ent**

		FUTURE → 5	CONDITIONAL → 6
	1st person	**-ai**	**-ais**
sing.	2nd person	**-as**	**-ais**
	3rd person	**-a**	**-ait**
	1st person	**-ons**	**-ions**
plur.	2nd person	**-ez**	**-iez**
	3rd person	**-ont**	**-aient**

	1 **PRESENT**		**2** **IMPERFECT**
je	vend**s**	je	vend**ais**
tu	vend**s**	tu	vend**ais**
il	vend	il	vend**ait**
elle	vend	elle	vend**ait**
nous	vend**ons**	nous	vend**ions**
vous	vend**ez**	vous	vend**iez**
ils	vend**ent**	ils	vend**aient**
elles	vend**ent**	elles	vend**aient**

I sell, I am selling, I do sell *etc*

I sold, I was selling, I used to sell *etc*

	3 **PAST HISTORIC**		**4** **PRESENT SUBJUNCTIVE**
je	vend**is**	je	vend**e**
tu	vend**is**	tu	vend**es**
il	vend**it**	il	vend**e**
elle	vend**it**	elle	vend**e**
nous	vend**îmes**	nous	vend**ions**
vous	vend**îtes**	vous	vend**iez**
ils	vend**irent**	ils	vend**ent**
elles	vend**irent**	elles	vend**ent**

I sold *etc*

I sell/sold *etc*

	5 **FUTURE**		**6** **CONDITIONAL**
je	vend**rai**	je	vend**rais**
tu	vend**ras**	tu	vend**rais**
il	vend**ra**	il	vend**rait**
elle	vend**ra**	elle	vend**rait**
nous	vend**rons**	nous	vend**rions**
vous	vend**rez**	vous	vend**riez**
ils	vend**ront**	ils	vend**raient**
elles	vend**ront**	elles	vend**raient**

I shall sell, I shall be selling *etc*

I should/would sell,
I should/would be selling *etc*

❐ First Conjugation Spelling Irregularities

Before certain endings, the stems of some '-er' verbs may change slightly.

Verbs ending:	**-cer**
Change:	**c** becomes **ç** before **a** or **o** to retain its soft [s] pronunciation
Tenses affected:	Present, Imperfect, Past Historic; Present Participle
Model:	**lancer** *to throw* → [1]

Verbs ending:	**-ger**
Change:	**g** becomes **ge** before **a** or **o** to retain its soft [ʒ] pronunciation
Tenses affected:	Present, Imperfect, Past Historic; Present Participle
Model:	**manger** *to eat* → [2]

Verbs ending	**-eler**
Change:	**-l** doubles before **-e, -es, -ent** and throughout the Future and Conditional tenses
Tenses affected:	Present, Present Subjunctive, Future, Conditional
Model:	**appeler** *to call* → [3]

◆   EXCEPTIONS: **geler** *to freeze* } like **mener** (p 14)
                peler *to peel* }

Grammar

1 INFINITIVE   PRESENT PARTICIPLE
     lancer   **lançant**

PRESENT		IMPERFECT		PAST HISTORIC	
je	lance	**je**	**lançais**	**je**	**lançai**
tu	lances	**tu**	**lançais**	**tu**	**lanças**
il/elle	lance	**il/elle**	**lançait**	**il/elle**	**lança**
nous	**lançons**	nous	lancions	**nous**	**lançâmes**
vous	lancez	vous	lanciez	**vous**	**lançâtes**
ils/elles	lancent	**ils/elles**	**lançaient**	ils/elles	lancèrent

2 INFINITIVE   PRESENT PARTICIPLE
     manger   **mangeant**

PRESENT		IMPERFECT		PAST HISTORIC	
je	mange	**je**	**mangeais**	**je**	**mangeai**
tu	manges	**tu**	**mangeais**	**tu**	**mangeas**
il/elle	mange	**il/elle**	**mangeait**	**il/elle**	**mangea**
nous	**mangeons**	nous	mangions	**nous**	**mangeâmes**
vous	mangez	vous	mangiez	**vous**	**mangeâtes**
ils/elles	mangent	**ils/elles**	**mangeaient**	ils/elles	mangèrent

3 PRESENT (+ SUBJUNCTIVE)   FUTURE

	j'appelle		**j'appellerai**
tu	**appelles**	**tu**	**appelleras**
il/elle	**appelle**	**il**	**appellera** *etc*
nous	appelons		
	(appelions)		CONDITIONAL
vous	appelez		**j'appellerais**
	(appeliez)	**tu**	**appellerais**
ils/elles	**appellent**	**il**	**appellerait** *etc*

Verbs ending	**-eter**
Change:	**-t** doubles before **-e, -es, -ent** and throughout the Future and Conditional tenses
Tenses affected:	Present, Present Subjunctive, Future, Conditional
Model:	**jeter** *to throw* → ①

♦ EXCEPTIONS: **acheter** *to buy* ⎫ like **mener** *(see below)*
   haleter *to pant* ⎭

Verbs ending	**-yer**
Change:	**y** changes to **i** before **-e, -es, -ent** and throughout the Future and Conditional tenses
Tenses affected:	Present, Present Subjunctive, Future, Conditional
Model:	**essuyer** *to wipe* → ②

♦ The change described is optional for verbs ending in **-ayer** e.g. **payer** *to pay*, **essayer** *to try*.

Verbs like:	**mener, peser, lever** etc
Change:	**e** changes to **è** before **-e, -es, -ent** and throughout the Future and Conditional tenses
Tenses affected:	Present, Present Subjunctive, Future, Conditional
Model:	**mener** *to lead* → ③

Verbs like:	**céder, régler, espérer** etc
Change:	**é** changes to **è** before **-e, -es, -ent**
Tenses affected:	Present, Present Subjunctive
Model:	**céder** *to yield* → ④

Grammar

	1	PRESENT (+ SUBJUNCTIVE)	FUTURE	
	je	**jette**	**je**	**jetterai**
	tu	**jettes**	**tu**	**jetteras**
	il/elle	**jette**	**il**	**jettera** *etc*
	nous	jetons		
		(jetions)	CONDITIONAL	
	vous	jetez	**je**	**jetterais**
		(jetiez)	**tu**	**jetterais**
	ils/elles	**jettent**	**il**	**jetterait** *etc*

	2	PRESENT (+ SUBJUNCTIVE)	FUTURE	
		j'essuie		**j'essuierai**
	tu	**essuies**	**tu**	**essuieras**
	il/elle	**essuie**	**il**	**essuiera** *etc*
	nous	essuyons		
		(essuyions)	CONDITIONAL	
	vous	essuyez		**j'essuierais**
		(essuyiez)	**tu**	**essuierais**
	ils/elles	**essuient**	**il**	**essuierait** *etc*

	3	PRESENT (+ SUBJUNCTIVE)	FUTURE	
	je	**mène**	**je**	**mènerai**
	tu	**mènes**	**tu**	**mèneras**
	il/elle	**mène**	**il**	**mènera** *etc*
	nous	menons		
		(menions)	CONDITIONAL	
	vous	menez	**je**	**mènerais**
		(meniez)	**tu**	**mènerais**
	ils/elles	**mènent**	**il**	**mènerait** *etc*

	4	PRESENT (+ SUBJUNCTIVE)
	je	**cède**
	tu	**cèdes**
	il/elle	**cède**
	nous	cédons
		(cédions)
	vous	cédez
		(cédiez)
	ils/elles	**cèdent**

☐ The Imperative

The imperative is the form of the verb used to give commands or orders. It can be used politely, as in English 'Shut the door, please'.

The imperative is the same as the present tense **tu, nous** and **vous** forms without the subject pronouns:

donne*	**finis**	**vends**
give	*finish*	*sell*

*The final 's' of the present tense of first conjugation verbs is dropped, except before **y** and **en** → ①

donnons	**finissons**	**vendons**
let's give	*let's finish*	*let's sell*

donnez	**finissez**	**vendez**
give	*finish*	*sell*

- The imperative of irregular verbs is given in the verb tables, pp 50 ff.

- Position of object pronouns with the imperative:
  in POSITIVE commands: they follow the verb and are attached to it by hyphens → ②
  in NEGATIVE commands: they precede the verb and are not attached to it → ③

- For the order of object pronouns, see p 102.

- For reflexive verbs – e.g. **se lever** *to get up* – the object pronoun is the reflexive pronoun → ④

Grammar

1   Compare: **Tu donnes de l'argent à Paul**
             You give (some) money to Paul
  and: **Donne de l'argent à Paul**
             Give (some) money to Paul

2   **Excusez-moi**
Excuse me
Crois-nous
Believe us
Attendons-la
Let's wait for her/it

Envoyons-les-leur
Let's send them to them
Expliquez-le-moi
Explain it to me
Rends-la-lui
Give it back to him/her

3   **Ne me dérange pas**
Don't disturb me
Ne les négligeons pas
Let's not neglect them
Ne leur répondez pas
Don't answer them

Ne leur en parlons pas
Let's not speak to them about it
N'y pense plus
Don't think about it any more
Ne la lui rends pas
Don't give it back to him/her

4   **Lève-toi**
Get up
Dépêchons-nous
Let's hurry
Levez-vous
Get up

Ne te lève pas
Don't get up
Ne nous affolons pas
Let's not panic
Ne vous levez pas
Don't get up

☐ Compound Tenses: Formation of Regular Verbs

Compound tenses consist of the past participle of the verb together with an auxiliary verb. Most verbs take the auxiliary **avoir,** but some take **être** (see p 22).

Compound tenses are formed in exactly the same way for both regular and irregular verbs, the only difference being that irregular verbs may have an irregular past participle. The past participle of irregular verbs is given for each verb in the verb tables, pp 50 ff.

The past participle

For all compound tenses you need to know how to form the past participle of the verb. For regular verbs this is as follows:

◆　1st conjugation: replace the **-er** of the infinitive by **-é:**

donner	→	**donné**
to give	→	given

◆　2nd conjugation: replace the **-ir** of the infinitive by **-i:**

finir	→	**fini**
to finish	→	finished

◆　3rd conjugation: replace the **-re** of the infinitive by **-u:**

vendre	→	**vendu**
to sell	→	sold

◆　See p 40 for agreement of past participles.

☐ **Compound Tenses** (Continued)

Perfect tense: the present tense of **avoir** or **être** plus the past
                            participle → ① (see pp 20–21)

Pluperfect tense: the imperfect tense of **avoir** or **être** plus the
                            past participle → ② (see pp 20–21)

Future Perfect: the future tense of **avoir** or **être** plus the past
                            participle → ③ (see pp 20–21)

Conditional Perfect: the conditional of **avoir** or **être** plus the past
                            participle → ④ (see pp 20–21)

Perfect Subjunctive: the present subjunctive of **avoir** or **être** plus
                            the past participle → ⑤ (see pp 20–21)

◆   Examples of a verb that takes **avoir** and one that takes **être** are
    conjugated on pp 20 and 21.

◆   For a list of verbs and verb types that take the auxiliary **être,** see
    p 22.

1 PERFECT

j'ai donné	nous avons donné
tu as donné	vous avez donné
il/elle a donné	ils/elles ont donné

I gave, have given *etc*

2 PLUPERFECT

j'avais donné	nous avions donné
tu avais donné	vous aviez donné
il/elle avait donné	ils/elles avaient donné

I had given *etc*

3 FUTURE PERFECT

j'aurai donné	nous aurons donné
tu auras donné	vous aurez donné
il/elle aura donné	ils/elles auront donné

I shall have given *etc*

4 CONDITIONAL PERFECT

j'aurais donné	nous aurions donné
tu aurais donné	vous auriez donné
il/elle aurait donné	ils/elles auraient donné

I should/would have given *etc*

5 PERFECT SUBJUNCTIVE

j'aie donné	nous ayons donné
tu aies donné	vous ayez donné
il/elle ait donné	ils/elles aient donné

I gave/have given *etc*

1 PERFECT

je suis tombé(e)	nous sommes tombé(e)s
tu es tombé(e)	vous êtes tombé(e)(s)
il est tombé	ils sont tombés
elle est tombée	elles sont tombées

I fell, have fallen *etc*

2 PLUPERFECT

j'étais tombé(e)	nous étions tombé(e)s
tu étais tombé(e)	vous étiez tombé(e)(s)
il était tombé	ils étaient tombés
elle était tombée	elles étaient tombées

I had fallen *etc*

3 FUTURE PERFECT

je serai tombé(e)	nous serons tombé(e)s
tu seras tombé(e)	vous serez tombé(e)(s)
il sera tombé	ils seront tombés
elle sera tombée	elles seront tombées

I shall have fallen *etc*

4 CONDITIONAL PERFECT

je serais tombé(e)	nous serions tombé(e)s
tu serais tombé(e)	vous seriez tombé(e)(s)
il serait tombé	ils seraient tombés
elle serait tombée	elles seraient tombées

I should/would have fallen *etc*

5 PERFECT SUBJUNCTIVE

je sois tombé(e)	nous soyons tombé(e)s
tu sois tombé(e)	vous soyez tombé(e)(s)
il soit tombé	ils soient tombés
elle soit tombée	elles soient tombées

I fell/have fallen *etc*

❏ **Compound Tenses** (Continued)

Verbs which take the auxiliary être

◆ Reflexive verbs (see p 24) → 1️⃣

◆ The following intransitive verbs (i.e. verbs which cannot take a direct object), largely expressing motion or a change of state:

aller	to go → 2️⃣	**passer**	to pass
arriver	to arrive; to happen	**rentrer**	to go back/in
descendre	to go/come down	**rester**	to stay → 5️⃣
devenir	to become	**retourner**	to go back
entrer	to go/come in	**revenir**	to come back
monter	to go/come up	**sortir**	to go/come out
mourir	to die → 3️⃣	**tomber**	to fall
naître	to be born	**venir**	to come → 6️⃣
partir	to leave → 4️⃣		

◆ Of these, the following are conjugated with **avoir** when used transitively (i.e. with a direct object):

descendre	to bring/take down
entrer	to bring/take in
monter	to bring/take up → 7️⃣
passer	to pass; to spend → 8️⃣
rentrer	to bring/take in
retourner	to turn over
sortir	to bring/take out → 9️⃣

⚠️ NOTE that the past participle must show an agreement in number and gender whenever the auxiliary is **être** EXCEPT FOR REFLEXIVE VERBS WHERE THE REFLEXIVE PRONOUN IS THE INDIRECT OBJECT (see p 40).

1. **je me suis arrêté(e)**
I stopped
tu t'es levé(e)
you got up

   elle s'est trompée
she made a mistake
ils s'étaient battus
they had fought (one another)

2. **elle est allée**
she went

3. **ils sont morts**
they died

4. **vous êtes partie**
you left *(addressing a female person)*
vous êtes parties
you left *(addressing more than one female person)*

5. **nous sommes resté(e)s**
we stayed

6. **elles étaient venues**
they *(female)* had come

7. **Il a monté les valises**
He's taken up the cases

8. **Nous avons passé trois semaines chez elle**
We spent three weeks at her place

9. **Avez-vous sorti la voiture?**
Have you taken the car out?

☐ Reflexive Verbs

A reflexive verb is one accompanied by a reflexive pronoun, e.g. **se lever** *to get up;* **se laver** *to wash (oneself).* The pronouns are:

PERSON	SINGULAR	PLURAL
1st	**me (m')**	**nous**
2nd	**te (t')**	**vous**
3rd	**se (s')**	**se (s')**

The forms shown in brackets are used before a vowel, an **h** 'mute', or the pronoun **y** → ①

♦ In positive commands, **te** changes to **toi** → ②

♦ The reflexive pronoun 'reflects back' to the subject, but it is not always translated in English → ③

The plural pronouns are sometimes translated as *one another, each other* (the 'reciprocal' meaning). The reciprocal meaning may be emphasized by **l'un(e) l'autre (les un(e)s les autres)** → ④

♦ In constructions other than the imperative affirmative the pronoun comes before the verb → ⑤

♦ In the imperative affirmative, the pronoun follows the verb and is attached to it by a hyphen → ⑥

Past participle agreement

♦ In most reflexive verbs the reflexive pronoun is a DIRECT object pronoun → ⑦

♦ When a direct object accompanies the reflexive verb the pronoun is then the INDIRECT object → ⑧

♦ The past participle of a reflexive verb agrees in number and gender with a direct object which *precedes* the verb (usually, but not always, the reflexive pronoun) → ⑨

The past participle does not change if the direct object follows the verb → ⑩

1	**Je m'ennuie** I'm bored	**Ils s'y intéressent** They are interested in it
2	**Assieds-toi** Sit down	**Tais-toi** Be quiet
3	**Je me prépare** I'm getting (myself) ready	**Elle se lève** She gets up
4	**Nous nous parlons** We speak to each other **Ils se regardent l'un l'autre** They are looking at each other	**Ils se ressemblent** They resemble one another
5	**Je me couche tôt** I go to bed early **Il ne s'est pas rasé** He hasn't shaved	**Comment vous appelez-vous?** What is your name? **Ne te dérange pas pour nous** Don't put yourself out on our account
6	**Renseignons-nous** Let's find out	**Asseyez-vous** Sit down
7	**Je m'appelle** I'm called *(literally: I call myself)*	**Ils se lavent** They wash (themselves)
8	**Elle se lave les mains** She's washing her hands *(literally: She's washing to herself the hands)* **Nous nous envoyons des cadeaux à Noël** We send presents to each other at Christmas	
9	**'Je me suis endormi' s'est-il excusé** 'I fell asleep', he apologized **Pauline s'est dirigée vers la sortie** Pauline made her way towards the exit **Ils se sont levés vers dix heures** They got up around ten o'clock **Elles se sont excusées de leur erreur** They apologized for their mistake	
10	**Elle s'est lavé les cheveux** She (has) washed her hair **Nous nous sommes serré la main** We shook hands	

❐ Reflexive Verbs (Continued)

Conjugation of: **se laver** *to wash (oneself)*

I SIMPLE TENSES

Simple tenses of reflexive verbs are conjugated in exactly the same way as those of non-reflexive verbs except that the reflexive pronoun is always used.

PRESENT

je me lave	**nous nous lavons**
tu te laves	**vous vous lavez**
il/elle se lave	**ils/elles se lavent**

IMPERFECT

je me lavais	**nous nous lavions**
tu te lavais	**vous vous laviez**
il/elle se lavait	**ils/elles se lavaient**

FUTURE

je me laverai	**nous nous laverons**
tu te laveras	**vous vous laverez**
il/elle se lavera	**ils/elles se laveront**

CONDITIONAL

je me laverais	**nous nous laverions**
tu te laverais	**vous vous laveriez**
il/elle se laverait	**ils/elles se laveraient**

PAST HISTORIC

je me lavai	**nous nous lavâmes**
tu te lavas	**vous vous lavâtes**
il/elle se lava	**ils/elles se lavèrent**

PRESENT SUBJUNCTIVE

je me lave	**nous nous lavions**
tu te laves	**vous vous laviez**
il/elle se lave	**ils/elles se lavent**

☐ **Reflexive Verbs** (Continued)

Conjugation of: **se laver** *to wash (oneself)*

II COMPOUND TENSES

Compound tenses of reflexive verbs are formed with the auxiliary **être**.

PERFECT

je me suis lavé(e)	nous nous sommes lavé(e)s
tu t'es lavé(e)	vous vous êtes lavé(e)(s)
il/elle s'est lavé(e)	ils/elles se sont lavé(e)s

PLUPERFECT

je m'étais lavé(e)	nous nous étions lavé(e)s
tu t'étais lavé(e)	vous vous étiez lavé(e)(s)
il/elle s'était lavé(e)	ils/elles s'étaient lavé(e)s

FUTURE PERFECT

je me serai lavé(e)	nous nous serons lavé(e)s
tu te seras lavé(e)	vous vous serez lavé(e)(s)
il/elle se sera lavé(e)	ils/elles se seront lavé(e)s

CONDITIONAL PERFECT

je me serais lavé(e)	nous nous serions lavé(e)s
tu te serais lavé(e)	vous vous seriez lavé(e)(s)
il/elle se serait lavé(e)	ils/elles se seraient lavé(e)s

PERFECT SUBJUNCTIVE

je me sois lavé(e)	nous nous soyons lavé(e)s
tu te sois lavé(e)	vous vous soyez lavé(e)(s)
il/elle se soit lavé(e)	ils/elles se soient lavé(e)s

❏ The Passive

In the passive, the subject *receives* the action (e.g. *I was hit*) as opposed to *performing* it (e.g. *I hit him*). In English the verb 'to be' is used with the past participle. In French the passive is formed in exactly the same way, i.e.:

a tense of **être** + past participle.

The past participle agrees in number and gender with the subject → ①

A sample verb is conjugated in the passive voice on pp 30 and 31.

◆ The indirect object in French cannot become the subject in the passive:

in **quelqu'un m'a donné un livre** the indirect object **m'** cannot become the subject of a passive verb (unlike English: *someone gave me a book* → *I was given a book*).

◆ The passive meaning is often expressed in French by:

– **on** plus a verb in the active voice → ②
– a reflexive verb (see p 24) → ③

1. **Philippe a été récompensé**
   Philip has been rewarded

   Cette peinture est très admirée
   This painting is greatly admired

   Ils le feront pourvu qu'ils soient payés
   They'll do it provided they're paid

   Les enfants seront félicités
   The children will be congratulated

   Cette mesure aurait été critiquée si ...
   This measure would have been criticized if ...

   Les portes avaient été fermées
   The doors had been closed

2. **On leur a envoyé une lettre**
   They were sent a letter

   On nous a montré le jardin
   We were shown the garden

   On m'a dit que ...
   I was told that ...

3. **Ils se vendent 30 francs (la) pièce**
   They are sold for 30 francs each

   Ce mot ne s'emploie plus
   This word is no longer used

❑ The Passive (Continued)

Conjugation of: **être aimé** to *be liked*

PRESENT
je suis aimé(e)   **nous sommes aimé(e)s**
tu es aimé(e)   **vous êtes aimé(e)(s)**
il/elle est aimé(e)   **ils/elles sont aimé(e)s**

IMPERFECT
j'étais aimé(e)   **nous étions aimé(e)s**
tu étais aimé(e)   **vous étiez aimé(e)(s)**
il/elle était aimé(e)   **ils/elles étaient aimé(e)s**

FUTURE
je serai aimé(e)   **nous serons aimé(e)s**
tu seras aimé(e)   **vous serez aimé(e)(s)**
il/elle sera aimé(e)   **ils/elles seront aimé(e)s**

CONDITIONAL
je serais aimé(e)   **nous serions aimé(e)s**
tu serais aimé(e)   **vous seriez aimé(e)(s)**
il/elle serait aimé(e)   **ils/elles seraient aimé(e)s**

PAST HISTORIC
je fus aimé(e)   **nous fûmes aimé(e)s**
tu fus aimé(e)   **vous fûtes aimé(e)(s)**
il/elle fut aimé(e)   **ils/elles furent aimé(e)s**

PRESENT SUBJUNCTIVE
je sois aimé(e)   **nous soyons aimé(e)s**
tu sois aimé(e)   **vous soyez aimé(e)(s)**
il/elle soit aimé(e)   **ils/elles soient aimé(e)s**

☐ The Passive (Continued)

Conjugation of: **être aimé** to *be liked*

PERFECT

j'ai été aimé(e)	nous avons été aimé(e)s
tu as été aimé(e)	vous avez été aimé(e)(s)
il/elle a été aimé(e)	ils/elles ont été aimé(e)s

PLUPERFECT

j'avais été aimé(e)	nous avions été aimé(e)s
tu avais été aimé(e)	vous aviez été aimé(e)(s)
il/elle avait été aimé(e)	ils/elles avaient été aimé(e)s

FUTURE PERFECT

j'aurai été aimé(e)	nous aurons été aimé(e)s
tu auras été aimé(e)	vous aurez été aimé(e)(s)
il/elle aura été aimé(e)	ils/elles auront été aimé(e)s

CONDITIONAL PERFECT

j'aurais été aimé(e)	nous aurions été aimé(e)s
tu aurais été aimé(e)	vous auriez été aimé(e)(s)
il/elle aurait été aimé(e)	ils/elles auraient été aimé(e)s

PERFECT SUBJUNCTIVE

j'aie été aimé(e)	nous ayons été aimé(e)s
tu aies été aimé(e)	vous ayez été aimé(e)(s)
il/elle ait été aimé(e)	ils/elles aient été aimé(e)s

❏ Impersonal Verbs

Impersonal verbs are used only in the infinitive and in the third person singular with the subject pronoun **il**, generally translated *it*.

e.g. **il pleut**
it's raining
il est facile de dire que ...
it's easy to say that ...

The most common impersonal verbs are:

INFINITIVE	CONSTRUCTIONS
s'agir	**il s'agit de** + noun → 1
	il s'agit de + infinitive → 2
falloir	**il faut** + noun object (+ indirect object) → 3
	il faut + infinitive (+ indirect object) → 4
	il faut que + subjunctive → 5
neiger, pleuvoir	**il neige/il pleut** → 6
valoir mieux	**il vaut mieux** + infinitive → 7
	il vaut mieux que + subjunctive → 8

The following are also commonly used in impersonal constructions:

INFINITIVE	CONSTRUCTIONS
avoir	**il y a** + noun → 9
être	**il est** + noun → 10
	il est + adjective + **de** + infinitive → 11
faire	**il fait** + adjective or noun of weather → 12
manquer	**il manque** + noun (+ indirect object) → 13
paraître	**il paraît que** + subjunctive → 14
	il paraît + indirect object + **que** + indicative → 15
rester	**il reste** + noun (+ indirect object) → 16
sembler	**il semble que** + subjunctive → 17
	il semble + indirect object + **que** + indicative → 18
suffire	**il suffit de** + infinitive → 19

1 **Il ne s'agit pas d'argent**
It isn't a question/matter of money

2 **Il s'agit de faire vite**
We must act quickly

3 **Il me faut une chaise de plus**
I need an extra chair

4 **Il me fallait prendre une décision**
I had to make a decision

5 **Il faut que vous partiez**
You have to leave/You must leave

6 **Il neige/Il pleuvait à verse**
It's snowing/It was raining heavily/It was pouring

7 **Il vaut mieux refuser**
It's better to refuse; You/He/I had better refuse *(depending on context)*

8 **Il vaudrait mieux que nous ne venions pas**
It would be better if we didn't come; We'd better not come

9 **Il y a du pain (qui reste)**   **Il n'y avait pas de lettres ce matin**
There is some bread (left)   There were no letters this morning

10 **Il est dix heures**
It's ten o'clock

11 **Il était inutile de protester**   **Il est facile de critiquer**
It was useless to protest   Criticizing is easy

12 **Il fait beau/mauvais**   **Il faisait nuit/du soleil**
It's lovely/horrible weather   It was dark/sunny

13 **Il manque deux tasses**
There are two cups missing; Two cups are missing

14 **Il paraît qu'ils partent demain**
It appears they are leaving tomorrow

15 **Il nous paraît certain qu'il aura du succès**
It seems certain to us that he'll be successful

16 **Il lui restait cinquante francs**
He/She had fifty francs left

17 **Il semble que vous ayez raison**
It seems/appears that you are right

18 **Il me semblait qu'il conduisait trop vite**
It seemed to me (that) he was driving too fast

19 **Il suffit de téléphoner pour réserver une place**
You need only phone to reserve a seat

20 **Il suffit d'une seule erreur pour tout gâcher**
One single error is enough to ruin everything

❐ The Infinitive

The infinitive is the form of the verb found in dictionary entries meaning 'to …', e.g. **donner** *to give,* **vivre** *to live.*

There are three main types of verbal construction involving the infinitive:

- with the linking preposition **de**
- with the linking preposition **à**
- with no linking preposition

Examples of verbs governing de

s'apercevoir de qch	*to notice sth* → ①
changer de qch	*to change sth* → ②
décider de + infin.	*to decide to* → ③
essayer de + infin.	*to try to do* → ④
finir de + infin.	*to finish doing* → ⑤
s'occuper de qch/qn	*to look after sth/sb* → ⑥
oublier de + infin.	*to forget to do* → ⑦
regretter de + perf. infin.*	*to regret doing, having done* → ⑧
se souvenir de qn/qch/de + perf. infin.*	*to remember sb/sth/doing, having done* → ⑨
venir de + infin.	*to have just done* → ⑩

Examples of verbs governing à

conseiller à qn de + infin.	*to advise sb to do* → ⑪
défendre à qn de + infin.	*to forbid sb to do* → ⑫
dire à qn de + infin.	*to tell sb to do* → ⑬
s'intéresser à qn/qch/à + infin.	*to be interested in sb/sth/in doing* → ⑭
manquer à qn	*to be missed by sb* → ⑮
penser à qn/qch	*to think about sb/sth* → ⑯
réussir à + infin.	*to manage to do* → ⑰

1. **Il ne s'est pas aperçu de son erreur**
   He didn't notice his mistake
2. **J'ai changé d'avis**
   I changed my mind
3. **Qu'est-ce que vous avez décidé de faire?**
   What have you decided to do?
4. **Essayez d'arriver à l'heure**
   Try to arrive on time
5. **Avez-vous fini de lire ce journal?**
   Have you finished reading this newspaper?
6. **Je m'occupe de ma nièce**
   I'm looking after my niece
7. **J'ai oublié d'appeler ma mère**
   I forgot to ring my mother
8. **Je regrette de ne pas vous avoir écrit plus tôt**
   I'm sorry for not writing to you sooner
9. **Vous vous souvenez de Lucienne?**
   Do you remember Lucienne?
10. **Nous venions d'arriver**
    We had just arrived
11. **Il leur a conseillé d'attendre**
    He advised them to wait
12. **Je leur ai défendu de sortir**
    I've forbidden them to go out
13. **Dites-leur de se taire**
    Tell them to be quiet
14. **Elle s'intéresse beaucoup au sport**
    She's very interested in sport
15. **Tu manques à tes parents**
    Your parents miss you
16. **Je pense souvent à toi**
    I often think about you
17. **Vous avez réussi à me convaincre**
    You've managed to convince me
18. **avoir fini** **être allé** **s'être levé**
    to have finished to have gone to have got up
    Après être sorties, elles se sont dirigées vers le parking
    After leaving/having left, they headed for the car park

❐ The Infinitive (Continued)

Verbs followed by an infinitive with no linking preposition

- the modal auxiliary verbs:

devoir	*to have to, must* →	1
	to be due to →	2
	in the conditional/conditional perfect:	
	should/should have, ought/ought to have →	3
pouvoir	*to be able to, can* →	4
	to be allowed to, can, may →	5
	indicating possibility: *may/might/could* →	6
savoir	*to know how to, can* →	7
vouloir	*to want/wish to* →	8
	to be willing to, will →	9
	in polite phrases →	10
falloir	*to be necessary:* see p 32.	

- verbs of seeing or hearing e.g. **voir** *to see*, **entendre** *to hear* → 11

- intransitive verbs of motion e.g. **aller** *to go*, **descendre** *to come/go down* → 12

- The following common verbs:

adorer	*to love*
aimer	*to like, love*
aimer mieux	*to prefer* → 13
compter	*to expect*
désirer	*to wish, want*
détester	*to hate*
envoyer	*to send*
espérer	*to hope*
faillir	→ 14
faire	→ 15
laisser	*to let, allow* → 16
oser	*to dare*
préférer	*to prefer*
sembler	*to seem* → 17
souhaiter	*to wish*
valoir mieux	see p 32.

1. **Je dois leur rendre visite**   **Elle a dû partir**
   I must visit them   She (has) had to leave
   Il a dû regretter d'avoir parlé
   He must have been sorry he spoke

2. **Je devais attraper le train de neuf heures mais …**
   I was (supposed) to catch the nine o'clock train but …

3. **Je devrais le faire**   **J'aurais dû m'excuser**
   I ought to do it   I ought to have apologized

4. **Il ne peut pas lever le bras**
   He can't raise his arm

5. **Puis-je les accompagner?**
   May I go with them?

6. **Il peut encore changer d'avis**   **Cela pourrait être vrai**
   He may change his mind yet   It could/might be true

7. **Savez-vous conduire?**
   Can you drive?

8. **Elle veut rester encore un jour**
   She wants to stay another day

9. **Ils ne voulaient pas le faire**
   They wouldn't do it/They weren't willing to do it
   Ma voiture ne veut pas démarrer
   My car won't start

10. **Voulez-vous boire quelque chose?**
    Would you like something to drink?

11. **Il nous a vus arriver**   **On les entend chanter**
    He saw us arriving   You can hear them singing

12. **Allez voir Nicolas**   **Descends leur demander**
    Go and see Nicholas   Go down and ask them

13. **J'aimerais mieux le choisir moi-même**
    I'd rather choose it myself

14. **J'ai failli tomber**
    I almost fell

15. **Ne me faites pas rire!**   **J'ai fait réparer ma valise**
    Don't make me laugh!   I've had my case repaired

16. **Laissez-moi passer**
    Let me pass

17. **Vous semblez être inquiet**
    You seem to be worried

❏ The Present Participle

Formation

◆ 1st conjugation
Replace the **-er** of the infinitive by **-ant** → 1

– Verbs ending in **-cer**: **c** changes to **ç** → 2
– Verbs ending in **-ger**: **g** changes to **ge** → 3

◆ 2nd conjugation
Replace the **-ir** of the infinitive by **-issant** → 4

◆ 3rd conjugation
Replace the **-re** of the infinitive by **-ant** → 5

◆ For irregular present participles, see irregular verbs, pp 50 ff.

Uses

The present participle has a more restricted use in French than in English.

◆ Used as a verbal form, the present participle is invariable. It is found:

– on its own, where it corresponds to the English present participle → 6
– following the preposition **en** → 7

⚠ NOTE, in particular, the construction:

verb + **en** + present participle

which is often translated by an English phrasal verb, i.e. one followed by a preposition like *to run down, to bring up* → 8

◆ Used as an adjective, the present participle agrees in number and gender with the noun or pronoun → 9

⚠ NOTE, in particular, the use of **ayant** and **étant** – the present participles of the auxiliary verbs **avoir** and **être** – with a past participle → 10

Grammar

1. **donner** → **donnant**
   to give / giving
2. **lancer** → **lançant**
   to throw / throwing
3. **manger** → **mangeant**
   to eat / eating
4. **finir** → **finissant**
   to finish / finishing
5. **vendre** → **vendant**
   to sell / selling
6. **David, habitant près de Paris, a la possibilité de …**
   David, living near Paris, has the opportunity of…
   Elle, pensant que je serais fâché, a dit '…'
   She, thinking that I would be angry, said '…'
   Ils m'ont suivi, criant à tue-tête
   They followed me, shouting at the top of their voices
7. **En attendant sa sœur, Richard s'est endormi**
   While waiting for his sister, Richard fell asleep
   Téléphone-nous an arrivant chez toi
   Telephone us when you get home
   En appuyant sur ce bouton, on peut …
   By pressing this button, you can …
   Il s'est blessé en essayant de sauver un chat
   He hurt himself trying to rescue a cat
8. **sortir en courant**
   to run out (literally: to go out running)
   avancer en boîtant
   to limp along (literally: to go forward limping)
9. **le soleil couchant**   **une lumière éblouissante**
   the setting sun   a dazzling light
   ils sont déroutants   **elles étaient étonnantes**
   they are disconcerting   they were surprising
10. **Ayant mangé plus tôt, il a pu …**
    Having eaten earlier, he was able to …
    Étant arrivée en retard, elle a dû …
    Having arrived late, she had to …

☐ Past Participle Agreement

Like adjectives, a past participle must sometimes agree in number and gender with a noun or pronoun. For the rules of agreement, see below. Example: **donné**

	MASCULINE	FEMININE
SING.	donné	donnée
PLUR.	donnés	données

◆ When the masculine singular form already ends in **-s**, no further **s** is added in the masculine plural, e.g. **pris** *taken*.

Rules of agreement in compound tenses

◆ When the auxiliary verb is **avoir**

   The past participle remains in the masculine singular form, unless a direct object precedes the verb. The past participle then agrees in number and gender with the preceding direct object → 1

◆ When the auxiliary verb is **être**

   The past participle of a non-reflexive verb agrees in number and gender with the subject → 2

   The past participle of a reflexive verb agrees in number and gender with the reflexive pronoun, if the pronoun is a direct object → 3

   No agreement is made if the reflexive pronoun is an indirect object → 4

The past participle as an adjective

The past participle agrees in number and gender with the noun or pronoun → 5

① **Voici le livre que vous avez demandé**
Here's the book you asked for
Laquelle avaient-elles choisie?
Which one had they chosen?
Ces amis? Je les ai rencontrés à Édimbourg
Those friends? I met them in Edinburgh
Il a gardé toutes les lettres qu'elle a écrites
He has kept all the letters she wrote

② **Est-ce que ton frère est allé à l'étranger?**
Did your brother go abroad?
Elle était restée chez elle
She had stayed at home
Ils sont partis dans la matinée
They left in the morning
Mes cousines sont revenues hier
My cousins came back yesterday

③ **Tu t'es rappelé d'acheter du pain, Georges?**
Did you remember to buy bread, George?
Martine s'est demandée pourquoi il l'appelait
Martine wondered why he was calling her
'Lui et moi nous nous sommes cachés' a-t-elle dit
'He and I hid,' she said
Les vendeuses se sont mises en grève
Shop assistants have gone on strike
Vous vous êtes brouillés?
Have you fallen out with each other?
Les ouvrières s'étaient entraidées
The workers had helped one another

④ **Elle s'est lavé les mains**
She washed her hands
Ils se sont parlé pendant des heures
They talked to each other for hours

⑤ **à un moment donné**   **la porte ouverte**
at a certain point   the open door
ils sont bien connus   **elles semblent fatiguées**
they are well-known   they seem tired

❏ Use of Tenses

The present

- Unlike English, French does not distinguish between the simple present (e.g. *I smoke, he reads, we live*) and the continuous present (e.g. *I am smoking, he is reading, we are living*) → 1

- To emphasize continuity, the following constructions may be used:

  être en train de faire
  être à faire } *to be doing* → 2

- French uses the present tense where English uses the perfect in the following cases:

  – with certain prepositions of time – notably **depuis** *for/since* – when an action begun in the past is continued in the present → 3
  Note, however, that the perfect is used as in English when the verb is negative or the action has been completed → 4

  – in the construction **venir de faire** *to have just done* → 5

The future

The future is generally used as in English, but note the following:

- Immediate future time is often expressed by means of the present tense of **aller** plus an infinitive → 6

- In time clauses expressing future action, French uses the future where English uses the present → 7

The future perfect

- Used as in English to mean *shall/will have done* → 8

- In time clauses expressing future action, where English uses the perfect tense → 9

1. **Je fume**
   I smoke OR I am smoking
   Il lit
   He reads OR He is reading
   Nous habitons
   We live OR We are living

2. **Il est en train de travailler**
   He's (busy) working

3. **Paul apprend à nager depuis six mois**
   Paul's been learning to swim for six months *(and still is)*
   Je suis debout depuis sept heures
   I've been up since seven
   Il y a longtemps que vous attendez?
   Have you been waiting long?
   Voilà deux semaines que nous sommes ici
   That's two weeks we've been here (now)

4. **Ils ne se sont pas vus depuis des mois**
   They haven't seen each other for months
   Elle est revenue il y a un an
   She came back a year ago

5. **Élisabeth vient de partir**
   Elizabeth has just left

6. **Tu vas tomber si tu ne fais pas attention**
   You'll fall if you're not careful
   Il va manquer le train
   He's going to miss the train
   Ça va prendre une demi-heure
   It'll take half an hour

7. **Quand il viendra vous serez en vacances**
   When he comes you'll be on holiday
   Faites-nous savoir aussitôt qu'elle arrivera
   Let us know as soon as she arrives

8. **J'aurai fini dans une heure**
   I shall have finished in an hour

9. **Quand tu auras lu ce roman, rends-le-moi**
   When you've read the novel, give it back to me
   Je partirai dès que j'aurai fini
   I'll leave as soon as I've finished

❏ Use of Tenses (Continued)

The imperfect

- The imperfect describes:
  - an action (or state) in the past without definite limits in time → 1
  - habitual action(s) in the past (often translated by means of *would* or *used to*) → 2

- French uses the imperfect tense where English uses the pluperfect in the following cases:
  - with certain prepositions of time – notably **depuis** *for/since* – when an action begun in the remoter past was continued in the more recent past → 3

  Note, however, that the pluperfect is used as in English, when the verb is negative or the action has been completed → 4
  - in the construction **venir de faire** *to have just done* → 5

The perfect

- The perfect is used to recount a completed action or event in the past. Note that this corresponds to a perfect tense or a simple past tense in English → 6

The past historic

- Only ever used in *written, literary* French, the past historic recounts a completed action in the past, corresponding to a simple past tense in English → 7

The subjunctive

- In spoken French, the present subjunctive generally replaces the imperfect subjunctive. See also pp 46 ff.

1. **Elle regardait par la fenêtre**
   She was looking out of the window
   Il pleuvait quand je suis sorti de chez moi
   It was raining when I left the house
   Nos chambres donnaient sur la plage
   Our rooms overlooked the beach

2. **Dans sa jeunesse, il se levait à l'aube**
   In his youth he got up at dawn
   Nous causions des heures entières
   We would talk for hours on end
   Elle te taquinait, n'est-ce pas?
   She used to tease you, didn't she?

3. **Nous habitions à Londres depuis deux ans**
   We had been living in London for two years (*and still were*)
   Il était malade depuis 1985
   He had been ill since 1985
   Il y avait assez longtemps qu'il le faisait
   He had been doing it for quite a long time

4. **Voilà un an que je ne l'avais pas vu**
   I hadn't seen him for a year
   Il y avait une heure qu'elle était arrivée
   She had arrived one hour before

5. **Je venais de les rencontrer**
   I had just met them

6. **Nous sommes allés au bord de la mer**
   We went/have been to the seaside
   Il a refusé de nous aider
   He (has) refused to help us
   La voiture ne s'est pas arrêtée
   The car didn't stop/hasn't stopped

7. **Le roi mourut en 1592**
   The king died in 1592

☐ The subjunctive: when to use it

(For how to form the subjunctive see pp 6 ff.)

◆ After certain conjunctions

quoique ⎱ bien que ⎰	*although* → 1
pour que⎱ afin que ⎰	*so that* → 2
pourvu que	*provided that* → 3
jusqu'à ce que	*until* → 4
avant que (... ne)	*before* → 5
à moins que (... ne)	*unless* → 6
de peur que (... ne) ⎱ de crainte que (... ne) ⎰	*for fear that, lest* → 7
de sorte que de façon que de manière que	*so that* (indicating a *purpose*; when they introduce a *result* the indicative is used) → 8

⚠ NOTE that **ne** in examples 5 to 7 has no translation value. It is often omitted in spoken informal French.

◆ After impersonal constructions which express necessity, possibility etc

il faut que ⎱ il est nécessaire que ⎰	*it is necessary that* → 9
il est possible que	*it is possible that* → 10
il semble que	*it seems that* → 11

| il vaut mieux que | *it is better that* → 12 |
| il est dommage que | *it's a pity that* → 13 |

◆ After a superlative → 14

◆ After certain adjectives expressing some sort of 'uniqueness'

dernier ... qui/que	*last ... who/that*
premier ... qui/que	*first ... who/that*
meilleur ... qui/que	*best ... who/that* ⎫ → 15
seul unique ⎰ ... qui/que	*only ... who/that* ⎭

1. **Bien qu'il fasse beaucoup d'efforts, il est peu récompensé**
   Although he makes a lot of effort, he isn't rewarded for it

2. **Demandez un reçu afin que vous puissiez être remboursé**
   Ask for a receipt so that you can get a refund

3. **Nous partirons ensemble pourvu que Sylvie soit d'accord**
   We'll leave together provided Sylvie agrees

4. **Reste ici jusqu'à ce que nous revenions**
   Stay here until we come back

5. **Je le ferai avant que tu ne partes**
   I'll do it before you leave

6. **Ce doit être Paul, à moins que je ne me trompe**
   That must be Paul, unless I'm mistaken

7. **Parlez bas de peur qu'on ne vous entende**
   Speak softly lest anyone hears you

8. **Retournez-vous de sorte que je vous voie**
   Turn round so that I can see you

9. **Il faut que je vous parle immédiatement**
   I must speak to you right away/It is necessary that I speak …

10. **Il est possible qu'ils aient raison**
    They may be right/It's possible that they are right

11. **Il semble qu'elle ne soit pas venue**
    It appears that she hasn't come

12. **Il vaut mieux que vous restiez chez vous**
    It's better that you stay at home

13. **Il est dommage qu'elle ait perdu cette adresse**
    It's a shame/a pity that she's lost the address

14. **la personne la plus sympathique que je connaisse**
    the nicest person I know
    l'article le moins cher que j'aie jamais acheté
    the cheapest item I have ever bought

15. **Voici la dernière lettre qu'elle m'ait écrite**
    This is the last letter she wrote to me
    David est la seule personne qui puisse me conseiller
    David is the only person who can advise me

16. **Vive le roi!**   **Que Dieu vous bénisse!**
    Long live the king!   God bless you!

☐ The subjunctive: when to use it (Continued)

◆ After verbs of:
  – 'wishing'
     vouloir que
     désirer que ⎫ *to wish that, want* → 1
     souhaiter que ⎭

  – 'fearing'
     craindre que ⎫
     avoir peur que ⎭ *to be afraid that* → 2

  ⚠ NOTE that **ne** in example 2 has no translation value. It is often omitted in spoken informal French.

  – 'ordering', 'forbidding', 'allowing'
     ordonner que   *to order that*
     défendre que   *to forbid that*
     permettre que   *to allow that* → 3

  – opinion, expressing uncertainty
     croire que ⎫
     penser que ⎭ *to think that* → 4
     douter que   *to doubt that*

  – emotion (e.g. regret, shame, pleasure)
     regretter que *to be sorry that* → 5
     être content/surpris etc **que** *to be pleased/surprised* etc *that* → 6

◆ After   **si (...) que**   *however*   → 7
                 qui que   *whoever*   → 8
                 quoi que   *whatever*   → 9

◆ After **que** in the following:
  – to form the 3rd person imperative or to express a wish → 10
  – when **que** has the meaning *if*, replacing **si** in a clause → 11
  – when **que** has the meaning *whether* → 12
◆ In relative clauses following certain types of indefinite and negative construction → 13

1. **Nous voulons qu'elle soit contente**
   We want her to be happy *(literally: We want that she is happy)*

2. **Il craint qu'il ne soit trop tard**
   He's afraid it may be too late

3. **Permettez que nous vous aidions**
   Allow us to help you

4. **Je ne pense pas qu'ils soient venus**
   I don't think they came

5. **Je regrette que vous ne puissiez pas venir**
   I'm sorry that you cannot come

6. **Je suis content que vous les aimiez**
   I'm pleased that you like them

7. **si courageux qu'il soit**   **si peu que ce soit**
   however brave he may be   however little it is

8. **Qui que vous soyez, allez-vous-en!**
   Whoever you are, go away!

9. **Quoi que nous fassions, ...**
   Whatever we do, ...

10. **Qu'il entre!**   **Que cela vous serve de leçon!**
    Let him come in!   Let that be a lesson to you!

11. **S'il fait beau et que tu te sentes mieux, nous irons ...**
    If it's nice and you're feeling better, we'll go ...

12. **Que tu viennes ou non, je ...**
    Whether you come or not, I ...

13. **Il cherche une maison qui ait deux caves**
    He's looking for a house which has two cellars
    (subjunctive used since such a house may or may not exist)
    J'ai besoin d'un livre qui décrive l'art du mime
    I need a book which describes the art of mime
    (subjunctive used since such a book may or may not exist)

    Je n'ai rencontré personne qui la connaisse
    I haven't met anyone who knows her

❏ Irregular Verb Tables

The verbs on the following pages provide the main patterns for irregular verbs. They are given in their most common simple tenses, together with the imperative and the present participle. The auxiliary (*avoir* or *être*) is also shown, together with the past participle, to enable you to form the compound tenses (see pp 18ff). *Falloir* and *pleuvoir*, which are only used in the 'il' form, are given below. The rest follow in alphabetical order.

falloir *to be necessary* // pleuvoir *to rain*		Auxiliary: avoir
PAST PARTICIPLE fallu // plu	**PRESENT PARTICIPLE** *not used* // **pleuvant**	**IMPERATIVE** *not used*
PRESENT	**FUTURE**	**IMPERFECT**
il **faut** // il **pleut**	il **faudra** // il **pleuvra**	il **fallait** // il **pleuvait**
PRESENT SUBJUNCTIVE	**CONDITIONAL**	**PAST HISTORIC**
il **faille** // il **pleuve**	il **faudrait** // il **pleuvrait**	il **fallut** // il **plut**

acquérir *to acquire*		Auxiliary: avoir
PAST PARTICIPLE acquis	**PRESENT PARTICIPLE** acquérant	**IMPERATIVE** acquiers acquérons acquérez
PRESENT	**FUTURE**	**IMPERFECT**
j'acquiers tu acquiers il acquiert nous acquérons vous acquérez ils acquièrent	j'acquerrai tu acquerras il acquerra nous acquerrons vous acquerrez ils acquerront	j'acquérais tu acquérais il acquérait nous acquérions vous acquériez ils acquéraient
PRESENT SUBJUNCTIVE	**CONDITIONAL**	**PAST HISTORIC**
j'acquière tu acquières il acquière nous acquérions vous acquériez ils acquièrent	j'acquerrais tu acquerrais il acquerrait nous acquerrions vous acquerriez ils acquerraient	j'acquis tu acquis il acquit nous acquîmes vous acquîtes ils acquirent

VERBS: IRREGULAR

---

aller *to go* — Auxiliary: **être**

PAST PARTICIPLE	PRESENT PARTICIPLE	IMPERATIVE
allé	allant	va
		allons
		allez

PRESENT	FUTURE	IMPERFECT
je **vais**	j'**irai**	j'allais
tu **vas**	tu **iras**	tu allais
il **va**	il **ira**	il allait
nous allons	nous **irons**	nous allions
vous allez	vous **irez**	vous alliez
ils **vont**	ils **iront**	ils allaient

PRESENT SUBJUNCTIVE	CONDITIONAL	PAST HISTORIC
j'**aille**	j'**irais**	j'allai
tu **ailles**	tu **irais**	tu allas
il **aille**	il **irait**	il alla
nous allions	nous **irions**	nous allâmes
vous alliez	vous **iriez**	vous allâtes
ils **aillent**	ils **iraient**	ils allèrent

··

s'asseoir *to sit down* — Auxiliary: **être**

PAST PARTICIPLE	PRESENT PARTICIPLE	IMPERATIVE
assis	s'asseyant	assieds-toi
		asseyons-nous
		asseyez-vous

PRESENT	FUTURE	IMPERFECT
je **m'assieds** or **assois**	je **m'assiérai**	je **m'asseyais**
tu **t'assieds** or **assois**	tu **t'assiéras**	tu **t'asseyais**
il **s'assied** or **assoit**	il **s'assiéra**	il **s'asseyait**
nous **nous asseyons**	nous **nous assiérons**	nous **nous asseyions**
or **assoyons**		
vous **vous asseyez** or **assoyez**	vous **vous assiérez**	vous **vous asseyiez**
ils **s'asseyent** or **assoient**	ils **s'assiéront**	ils **s'asseyaient**

PRESENT SUBJUNCTIVE	CONDITIONAL	PAST HISTORIC
je **m'asseye**	je **m'assiérais**	je **m'assis**
tu **t'asseyes**	tu **t'assiérais**	tu **t'assis**
il **s'asseye**	il **s'assiérait**	il **s'assit**
nous **nous asseyions**	nous **nous assiérions**	nous **nous assîmes**
vous **vous asseyiez**	vous **vous assiériez**	vous **vous assîtes**
ils **s'asseyent**	ils **s'assiéraient**	ils **s'assirent**

avoir to have   Auxiliary: avoir

PAST PARTICIPLE	PRESENT PARTICIPLE	IMPERATIVE
eu	ayant	aie
		ayons
		ayez

PRESENT	FUTURE	IMPERFECT
j'ai	j'aurai	j'avais
tu as	tu auras	tu avais
il a	il aura	il avait
nous avons	nous aurons	nous avions
vous avez	vous aurez	vous aviez
ils ont	ils auront	ils avaient

PRESENT SUBJUNCTIVE	CONDITIONAL	PAST HISTORIC
j'aie	j'aurais	j'eus
tu aies	tu aurais	tu eus
il ait	il aurait	il eut
nous ayons	nous aurions	nous eûmes
vous ayez	vous auriez	vous eûtes
ils aient	ils auraient	ils eurent

battre to beat   Auxiliary: avoir

PAST PARTICIPLE	PRESENT PARTICIPLE	IMPERATIVE
battu	battant	bats
		battons
		battez

PRESENT	FUTURE	IMPERFECT
je bats	je battrai	je battais
tu bats	tu battras	tu battais
il bat	il battra	il battait
nous battons	nous battrons	nous battions
vous battez	vous battrez	vous battiez
ils battent	ils battront	ils battaient

PRESENT SUBJUNCTIVE	CONDITIONAL	PAST HISTORIC
je batte	je battrais	je battis
tu battes	tu battrais	tu battis
il batte	il battrait	il battit
nous battions	nous battrions	nous battîmes
vous battiez	vous battriez	vous battîtes
ils battent	ils battraient	ils battirent

boire *to drink*   Auxiliary: **avoir**

PAST PARTICIPLE	PRESENT PARTICIPLE	IMPERATIVE
bu	**buvant**	bois
		buvons
		buvez

PRESENT	FUTURE	IMPERFECT
je **bois**	je boirai	je **buvais**
tu **bois**	tu boiras	tu **buvais**
il **boit**	il boira	il **buvait**
nous **buvons**	nous boirons	nous **buvions**
vous **buvez**	vous boirez	vous **buviez**
ils **boivent**	ils boiront	ils **buvaient**

PRESENT SUBJUNCTIVE	CONDITIONAL	PAST HISTORIC
je **boive**	je boirais	je **bus**
tu **boives**	tu boirais	tu **bus**
il **boive**	il boirait	il **but**
nous **buvions**	nous boirions	nous **bûmes**
vous **buviez**	vous boiriez	vous **bûtes**
ils **boivent**	ils boiraient	ils **burent**

connaître *to know*   Auxiliary: **avoir**

PAST PARTICIPLE	PRESENT PARTICIPLE	IMPERATIVE
connu	**connaissant**	**connais**
		connaissons
		connaissez

PRESENT	FUTURE	IMPERFECT
je **connais**	je connaîtrai	je **connaissais**
tu **connais**	tu connaîtras	tu **connaissais**
il connaît	il connaîtra	il **connaissait**
nous **connaissons**	nous connaîtrons	nous **connaissions**
vous **connaissez**	vous connaîtrez	vous **connaissiez**
ils **connaissent**	ils connaîtront	ils **connaissaient**

PRESENT SUBJUNCTIVE	CONDITIONAL	PAST HISTORIC
je **connaisse**	je connaîtrais	je **connus**
tu **connaisses**	tu connaîtrais	tu **connus**
il **connaisse**	il connaîtrait	il **connut**
nous **connaissions**	nous connaîtrions	nous **connûmes**
vous **connaissiez**	vous connaîtriez	vous **connûtes**
ils **connaissent**	ils connaîtraient	ils **connurent**

coudre to sew   Auxiliary: avoir

PAST PARTICIPLE	PRESENT PARTICIPLE	IMPERATIVE
cousu	cousant	couds
		cousons
		cousez

PRESENT	FUTURE	IMPERFECT
je couds	je coudrai	je cousais
tu couds	tu coudras	tu cousais
il coud	il coudra	il cousait
nous cousons	nous coudrons	nous cousions
vous cousez	vous coudrez	vous cousiez
ils cousent	ils coudront	ils cousaient

PRESENT SUBJUNCTIVE	CONDITIONAL	PAST HISTORIC
je couse	je coudrais	je cousis
tu couses	tu coudrais	tu cousis
il couse	il coudrait	il cousit
nous cousions	nous coudrions	nous cousîmes
vous cousiez	vous coudriez	vous cousîtes
ils cousent	ils coudraient	ils cousirent

courir to run   Auxiliary: avoir

PAST PARTICIPLE	PRESENT PARTICIPLE	IMPERATIVE
couru	courant	cours
		courons
		courez

PRESENT	FUTURE	IMPERFECT
je cours	je courrai	je courais
tu cours	tu courras	tu courais
il court	il courra	il courait
nous courons	nous courrons	nous courions
vous courez	vous courrez	vous couriez
ils courent	ils courront	ils couraient

PRESENT SUBJUNCTIVE	CONDITIONAL	PAST HISTORIC
je coure	je courrais	je courus
tu coures	tu courrais	tu courus
il coure	il courrait	il courut
nous courions	nous courrions	nous courûmes
vous couriez	vous courriez	vous courûtes
ils courent	ils courraient	ils coururent

craindre to fear

Auxiliary: avoir

PAST PARTICIPLE	PRESENT PARTICIPLE	IMPERATIVE
craint	**craignant**	**crains**
		craignons
		craignez

PRESENT	FUTURE	IMPERFECT
je **crains**	je craindrai	je **craignais**
tu **crains**	tu craindras	tu **craignais**
il **craint**	il craindra	il **craignait**
nous **craignons**	nous craindrons	nous **craignions**
vous **craignez**	vous craindrez	vous **craigniez**
ils **craignent**	ils craindront	ils **craignaient**

PRESENT SUBJUNCTIVE	CONDITIONAL	PAST HISTORIC
je **craigne**	je craindrais	je **craignis**
tu **craignes**	tu craindrais	tu **craignis**
il **craigne**	il craindrait	il **craignit**
nous **craignions**	nous craindrions	nous **craignîmes**
vous **craigniez**	vous craindriez	vous **craignîtes**
ils **craignent**	ils craindraient	ils **craignirent**

Verbs ending in **-eindre** and **-oindre** are conjugated similarly

croire to believe

Auxiliary: avoir

PAST PARTICIPLE	PRESENT PARTICIPLE	IMPERATIVE
cru	**croyant**	crois
		croyons
		croyez

PRESENT	FUTURE	IMPERFECT
je crois	je croirai	je **croyais**
tu crois	tu croiras	tu **croyais**
il **croit**	il croira	il **croyait**
nous **croyons**	nous croirons	nous **croyions**
vous **croyez**	vous croirez	vous **croyiez**
ils croient	ils croiront	ils **croyaient**

PRESENT SUBJUNCTIVE	CONDITIONAL	PAST HISTORIC
je croie	je croirais	je **crus**
tu croies	tu croirais	tu **crus**
il croie	il croirait	il **crut**
nous **croyions**	nous croirions	nous **crûmes**
vous **croyiez**	vous croiriez	vous **crûtes**
ils croient	ils croiraient	ils **crurent**

croître to grow		Auxiliary: avoir
PAST PARTICIPLE	PRESENT PARTICIPLE	IMPERATIVE
crû	croissant	crois croissons croissez

PRESENT	FUTURE	IMPERFECT
je crois	je croîtrai	je croissais
tu crois	tu croîtras	tu croissais
il croît	il croîtra	il croissait
nous croissons	nous croîtrons	nous croissions
vous croissez	vous croîtrez	vous croissiez
ils croissent	ils croîtront	ils croissaient

PRESENT SUBJUNCTIVE	CONDITIONAL	PAST HISTORIC
je croisse	je croîtrais	je crûs
tu croisses	tu croîtrais	tu crûs
il croisse	il croîtrait	il crût
nous croissions	nous croîtrions	nous crûmes
vous croissiez	vous croîtriez	vous crûtes
ils croissent	ils croîtraient	ils crûrent

cueillir to pick		Auxiliary: avoir
PAST PARTICIPLE	PRESENT PARTICIPLE	IMPERATIVE
cueilli	cueillant	cueille cueillons cueillez

PRESENT	FUTURE	IMPERFECT
je cueille	je cueillerai	je cueillais
tu cueilles	tu cueilleras	tu cueillais
il cueille	il cueillera	il cueillait
nous cueillons	nous cueillerons	nous cueillions
vous cueillez	vous cueillerez	vous cueilliez
ils cueillent	ils cueilleront	ils cueillaient

PRESENT SUBJUNCTIVE	CONDITIONAL	PAST HISTORIC
je cueille	je cueillerais	je cueillis
tu cueilles	tu cueillerais	tu cueillis
il cueille	il cueillerait	il cueillit
nous cueillions	nous cueillerions	nous cueillîmes
vous cueilliez	vous cueilleriez	vous cueillîtes
ils cueillent	ils cueilleraient	ils cueillirent

cuire *to cook*   Auxiliary: **avoir**

PAST PARTICIPLE	PRESENT PARTICIPLE	IMPERATIVE
cuit	**cuisant**	cuis
		cuisons
		cuisez

PRESENT	FUTURE	IMPERFECT
je **cuis**	je **cuirai**	je **cuisais**
tu **cuis**	tu **cuiras**	tu **cuisais**
il **cuit**	il **cuira**	il **cuisait**
nous **cuisons**	nous **cuirons**	nous **cuisions**
vous **cuisez**	vous **cuirez**	vous **cuisiez**
ils **cuisent**	ils **cuiront**	ils **cuisaient**

PRESENT SUBJUNCTIVE	CONDITIONAL	PAST HISTORIC
je **cuise**	je cuirais	je **cuisis**
tu **cuises**	tu cuirais	tu **cuisis**
il **cuise**	il cuirait	il **cuisit**
nous **cuisions**	nous cuirions	nous **cuisîmes**
vous **cuisiez**	vous cuiriez	vous **cuisîtes**
ils **cuisent**	ils cuiraient	ils **cuisirent**

nuire *to harm*, conjugated similarly, but past participle **nui**

devoir *to have to; to owe*   Auxiliary: **avoir**

PAST PARTICIPLE	PRESENT PARTICIPLE	IMPERATIVE
dû, due	**devant**	dois
		devons
		devez

PRESENT	FUTURE	IMPERFECT
je **dois**	je **devrai**	je **devais**
tu **dois**	tu **devras**	tu **devais**
il **doit**	il **devra**	il **devait**
nous **devons**	nous **devrons**	nous **devions**
vous **devez**	vous **devrez**	vous **deviez**
ils **doivent**	ils **devront**	ils **devaient**

PRESENT SUBJUNCTIVE	CONDITIONAL	PAST HISTORIC
je **doive**	je **devrais**	je **dus**
tu **doives**	tu **devrais**	tu **dus**
il **doive**	il **devrait**	il **dut**
nous **devions**	nous **devrions**	nous **dûmes**
vous **deviez**	vous **devriez**	vous **dûtes**
ils **doivent**	ils **devraient**	ils **durent**

dire *to say, tell* — Auxiliary: **avoir**

PAST PARTICIPLE	PRESENT PARTICIPLE	IMPERATIVE
dit	**disant**	dis
		disons
		dites

PRESENT	FUTURE	IMPERFECT
je dis	je dirai	**je disais**
tu dis	tù diras	**tu disais**
il **dit**	il dira	**il disait**
nous disons	nous dirons	**nous disions**
vous dites	vous direz	**vous disiez**
ils disent	ils diront	**ils disaient**

PRESENT SUBJUNCTIVE	CONDITIONAL	PAST HISTORIC
je dise	je dirais	**je dis**
tu dises	tu dirais	**tu dis**
il dise	il dirait	**il dit**
nous disions	nous dirions	**nous dîmes**
vous disiez	vous diriez	**vous dîtes**
ils disent	ils diraient	**ils dirent**

interdire *to forbid*, conjugated similarly, but 2nd person plural of the present tense is **vous interdisez**

dormir *to sleep* — Auxiliary: **avoir**

PAST PARTICIPLE	PRESENT PARTICIPLE	IMPERATIVE
dormi	**dormant**	dors
		dormons
		dormez

PRESENT	FUTURE	IMPERFECT
je dors	je dormirai	**je dormais**
tu dors	tu dormiras	**tu dormais**
il dort	il dormira	**il dormait**
nous dormons	nous dormirons	**nous dormions**
vous dormez	vous dormirez	**vous dormiez**
ils dorment	ils dormiront	**ils dormaient**

PRESENT SUBJUNCTIVE	CONDITIONAL	PAST HISTORIC
je dorme	je dormirais	je dormis
tu dormes	tu dormirais	tu dormis
il dorme	il dormirait	il dormit
nous dormions	nous dormirions	nous dormîmes
vous dormiez	vous dormiriez	vous dormîtes
ils dorment	ils dormiraient	ils dormirent

écrire to write   Auxiliary: **avoir**

PAST PARTICIPLE	PRESENT PARTICIPLE	IMPERATIVE
écrit	**écrivant**	écris
		écrivons
		écrivez

PRESENT	FUTURE	IMPERFECT
j'écris	j'écrirai	**j'écrivais**
tu écris	tu écriras	**tu écrivais**
il écrit	il écrira	**il écrivait**
nous écrivons	nous écrirons	**nous écrivions**
vous écrivez	vous écrirez	**vous écriviez**
ils écrivent	ils écriront	**ils écrivaient**

PRESENT SUBJUNCTIVE	CONDITIONAL	PAST HISTORIC
j'écrive	j'écrirais	**j'écrivis**
tu écrives	tu écrirais	**tu écrivis**
il écrive	il écrirait	**il écrivit**
nous écrivions	nous écririons	**nous écrivîmes**
vous écriviez	vous écririez	**vous écrivîtes**
ils écrivent	ils écriraient	**ils écrivirent**

---

envoyer to send   Auxiliary: **avoir**

PAST PARTICIPLE	PRESENT PARTICIPLE	IMPERATIVE
envoyé	envoyant	envoie
		envoyons
		envoyez

PRESENT	FUTURE	IMPERFECT
j'envoie	**j'enverrai**	j'envoyais
tu envoies	**tu enverras**	tu envoyais
il envoie	**il enverra**	il envoyait
nous envoyons	**nous enverrons**	nous envoyions
vous envoyez	**vous enverrez**	vous envoyiez
ils envoient	**ils enverront**	ils envoyaient

PRESENT SUBJUNCTIVE	CONDITIONAL	PAST HISTORIC
j'envoie	**j'enverrais**	j'envoyai
tu envoies	**tu enverrais**	tu envoyas
il envoie	**il enverrait**	il envoya
nous envoyions	**nous enverrions**	nous envoyâmes
vous envoyiez	**vous enverriez**	vous envoyâtes
ils envoient	**ils enverraient**	ils envoyèrent

être *to be*

Auxiliary: avoir

PAST PARTICIPLE	PRESENT PARTICIPLE	IMPERATIVE
été	étant	sois
		soyons
		soyez

PRESENT	FUTURE	IMPERFECT
je suis	je serai	j'étais
tu es	tu seras	tu étais
il est	il sera	il était
nous sommes	nous serons	nous étions
vous êtes	vous serez	vous étiez
ils sont	ils seront	ils étaient

PRESENT SUBJUNCTIVE	CONDITIONAL	PAST HISTORIC
je sois	je serais	je fus
tu sois	tu serais	tu fus
il soit	il serait	il fut
nous soyons	nous serions	nous fûmes
vous soyez	vous seriez	vous fûtes
ils soient	ils seraient	ils furent

faire *to do; to make*

Auxiliary: avoir

PAST PARTICIPLE	PRESENT PARTICIPLE	IMPERATIVE
fait	faisant	fais
		faisons
		faites

PRESENT	FUTURE	IMPERFECT
je fais	je ferai	je faisais
tu fais	tu feras	tu faisais
il fait	il fera	il faisait
nous faisons	nous ferons	nous faisions
vous faites	vous ferez	vous faisiez
ils font	ils feront	ils faisaient

PRESENT SUBJUNCTIVE	CONDITIONAL	PAST HISTORIC
je fasse	je ferais	je fis
tu fasses	tu ferais	tu fis
il fasse	il ferait	il fit
nous fassions	nous ferions	nous fîmes
vous fassiez	vous feriez	vous fîtes
ils fassent	ils feraient	ils firent

fuir to flee
Auxiliary: avoir

PAST PARTICIPLE	PRESENT PARTICIPLE	IMPERATIVE
fui	**fuyant**	fuis
		fuyons
		fuyez

PRESENT	FUTURE	IMPERFECT
je fuis	je fuirai	**je fuyais**
tu fuis	tu fuiras	**tu fuyais**
il fuit	il fuira	**il fuyait**
nous fuyons	nous fuirons	**nous fuyions**
vous fuyez	vous fuirez	**vous fuyiez**
ils fuient	ils fuiront	**ils fuyaient**

PRESENT SUBJUNCTIVE	CONDITIONAL	PAST HISTORIC
je fuie	je fuirais	je fuis
tu fuies	tu fuirais	tu fuis
il fuie	il fuirait	il fuit
nous fuyions	nous fuirions	nous fuîmes
vous fuyiez	vous fuiriez	vous fuîtes
ils fuient	ils fuiraient	ils fuirent

haïr to hate
Auxiliary: avoir

PAST PARTICIPLE	PRESENT PARTICIPLE	IMPERATIVE
haï	**haïssant**	hais
		haïssons
		haïssez

PRESENT	FUTURE	IMPERFECT
je hais	je haïrai	**je haïssais**
tu hais	tu haïras	**tu haïssais**
il hait	il haïra	**il haïssait**
nous haïssons	nous haïrons	**nous haïssions**
vous haïssez	vous haïrez	**vous haïssiez**
ils haïssent	ils haïront	**ils haïssaient**

PRESENT SUBJUNCTIVE	CONDITIONAL	PAST HISTORIC
je haïsse	je haïrais	**je haïs**
tu haïsses	tu haïrais	**tu haïs**
il haïsse	il haïrait	**il haït**
nous haïssions	nous haïrions	**nous haïmes**
vous haïssiez	vous haïriez	**vous haïtes**
ils haïssent	ils haïraient	**ils haïrent**

lire *to read*   Auxiliary: **avoir**

PAST PARTICIPLE	PRESENT PARTICIPLE	IMPERATIVE
lu	**lisant**	lis
		lisons
		lisez

PRESENT	FUTURE	IMPERFECT
je lis	je lirai	je lisais
tu lis	tu liras	tu lisais
il lit	il lira	il lisait
nous lisons	nous lirons	nous lisions
vous lisez	vous lirez	vous lisiez
ils lisent	ils liront	ils lisaient

PRESENT SUBJUNCTIVE	CONDITIONAL	PAST HISTORIC
je lise	je lirais	je lus
tu lises	tu lirais	tu lus
il lise	il lirait	il lut
nous lisions	nous lirions	nous lûmes
vous lisiez	vous liriez	vous lûtes
ils lisent	ils liraient	ils lurent

mettre *to put*   Auxiliary: **avoir**

PAST PARTICIPLE	PRESENT PARTICIPLE	IMPERATIVE
mis	mettant	**mets**
		mettons
		mettez

PRESENT	FUTURE	IMPERFECT
je mets	je mettrai	je mettais
tu mets	tu mettras	tu mettais
il met	il mettra	il mettait
nous mettons	nous mettrons	nous mettions
vous mettez	vous mettrez	vous mettiez
ils mettent	ils mettront	ils mettaient

PRESENT SUBJUNCTIVE	CONDITIONAL	PAST HISTORIC
je mette	je mettrais	je mis
tu mettes	tu mettrais	tu mis
il mette	il mettrait	il mit
nous mettions	nous mettrions	nous mîmes
vous mettiez	vous mettriez	vous mîtes
ils mettent	ils mettraient	ils mirent

mourir *to die*   Auxiliary: être

PAST PARTICIPLE	PRESENT PARTICIPLE	IMPERATIVE
mort	mourant	meurs
		mourons
		mourez

PRESENT	FUTURE	IMPERFECT
je meurs	je mourrai	je mourais
tu meurs	tu mourras	tu mourais
il meurt	il mourra	il mourait
nous mourons	nous mourrons	nous mourions
vous mourez	vous mourrez	vous mouriez
ils meurent	ils mourront	ils mouraient

PRESENT SUBJUNCTIVE	CONDITIONAL	PAST HISTORIC
je meure	je mourrais	je mourus
tu meures	tu mourrais	tu mourus
il meure	il mourrait	il mourut
nous mourions	nous mourrions	nous mourûmes
vous mouriez	vous mourriez	vous mourûtes
ils meurent	ils mourraient	ils moururent

naître *to be born*   Auxiliary: être

PAST PARTICIPLE	PRESENT PARTICIPLE	IMPERATIVE
né	naissant	nais
		naissons
		naissez

PRESENT	FUTURE	IMPERFECT
je nais	je naîtrai	je naissais
tu nais	tu naîtras	tu naissais
il naît	il naîtra	il naissait
nous naissons	nous naîtrons	nous naissions
vous naissez	vous naîtrez	vous naissiez
ils naissent	ils naîtront	ils naissaient

PRESENT SUBJUNCTIVE	CONDITIONAL	PAST HISTORIC
je naisse	je naîtrais	je naquis
tu naisses	tu naîtrais	tu naquis
il naisse	il naîtrait	il naquit
nous naissions	nous naîtrions	nous naquîmes
vous naissiez	vous naîtriez	vous naquîtes
ils naissent	ils naîtraient	ils naquirent

ouvrir *to open* — Auxiliary: avoir

PAST PARTICIPLE	PRESENT PARTICIPLE	IMPERATIVE
ouvert	ouvrant	ouvre
		ouvrons
		ouvrez

PRESENT	FUTURE	IMPERFECT
j'ouvre	j'ouvrirai	j'ouvrais
tu ouvres	tu ouvriras	tu ouvrais
il ouvre	il ouvrira	il ouvrait
nous ouvrons	nous ouvrirons	nous ouvrions
vous ouvrez	vous ouvrirez	vous ouvriez
ils ouvrent	ils ouvriront	ils ouvraient

PRESENT SUBJUNCTIVE	CONDITIONAL	PAST HISTORIC
j'ouvre	j'ouvrirais	j'ouvris
tu ouvres	tu ouvrirais	tu ouvris
il ouvre	il ouvrirait	il ouvrit
nous ouvrions	nous ouvririons	nous ouvrîmes
vous ouvriez	vous ouvririez	vous ouvrîtes
ils ouvrent	ils ouvriraient	ils ouvrirent

offrir *to offer*, **souffrir** *to suffer* are conjugated similarly

paraître *to appear* — Auxiliary: avoir

PAST PARTICIPLE	PRESENT PARTICIPLE	IMPERATIVE
paru	paraissant	parais
		paraissons
		paraissez

PRESENT	FUTURE	IMPERFECT
je parais	je paraîtrai	je paraissais
tu parais	tu paraîtras	tu paraissais
il paraît	il paraîtra	il paraissait
nous paraissons	nous paraîtrons	nous paraissions
vous paraissez	vous paraîtrez	vous paraissiez
ils paraissent	ils paraîtront	ils paraissaient

PRESENT SUBJUNCTIVE	CONDITIONAL	PAST HISTORIC
je paraisse	je paraîtrais	je parus
tu paraisses	tu paraîtrais	tu parus
il paraisse	il paraîtrait	il parut
nous paraissions	nous paraîtrions	nous parûmes
vous paraissiez	vous paraîtriez	vous parûtes
ils paraissent	ils paraîtraient	ils parurent

VERBS: IRREGULAR

partir *to leave*

Auxiliary: **être**

PAST PARTICIPLE	PRESENT PARTICIPLE	IMPERATIVE
parti	**partant**	pars
		partons
		partez

PRESENT	FUTURE	IMPERFECT
je **pars**	je partirai	je **partais**
tu **pars**	tu partiras	tu **partais**
il **part**	il partira	il **partait**
nous **partons**	nous partirons	nous **partions**
vous **partez**	vous partirez	vous **partiez**
ils **partent**	ils partiront	ils **partaient**

PRESENT SUBJUNCTIVE	CONDITIONAL	PAST HISTORIC
je **parte**	je partirais	je partis
tu **partes**	tu partirais	tu partis
il **parte**	il partirait	il partit
nous **partions**	nous partirions	nous **partîmes**
vous **partiez**	vous partiriez	vous **partîtes**
ils **partent**	ils partiraient	ils partirent

....

plaire *to please*

Auxiliary: **avoir**

PAST PARTICIPLE	PRESENT PARTICIPLE	IMPERATIVE
plu	**plaisant**	plais
		plaisons
		plaisez

PRESENT	FUTURE	IMPERFECT
je plais	je plairai	je **plaisais**
tu plais	tu plairas	tu **plaisais**
il **plaît**	il plaira	il **plaisait**
nous **plaisons**	nous plairons	nous **plaisions**
vous **plaisez**	vous plairez	vous **plaisiez**
ils **plaisent**	ils plairont	ils **plaisaient**

PRESENT SUBJUNCTIVE	CONDITIONAL	PAST HISTORIC
je **plaise**	je plairais	je **plus**
tu **plaises**	tu plairais	tu **plus**
il **plaise**	il plairait	il **plut**
nous **plaisions**	nous plairions	nous **plûmes**
vous **plaisiez**	vous plairiez	vous **plûtes**
ils **plaisent**	ils plairaient	ils **plurent**

pouvoir *to be able to* — Auxiliary: avoir

PAST PARTICIPLE	PRESENT PARTICIPLE	IMPERATIVE
pu	**pouvant**	*not used*

PRESENT	FUTURE	IMPERFECT
je peux*	je pourrai	je pouvais
tu peux	tu pourras	tu pouvais
il peut	il pourra	il pouvait
nous pouvons	nous pourrons	nous pouvions
vous pouvez	vous pourrez	vous pouviez
ils peuvent	ils pourront	ils pouvaient

PRESENT SUBJUNCTIVE	CONDITIONAL	PAST HISTORIC
je puisse	je pourrais	je pus
tu puisses	tu pourrais	tu pus
il puisse	il pourrait	il put
nous puissions	nous pourrions	nous pûmes
vous puissiez	vous pourriez	vous pûtes
ils puissent	ils pourraient	ils purent

*In questions: **puis-je?**

prendre *to take* — Auxiliary: avoir

PAST PARTICIPLE	PRESENT PARTICIPLE	IMPERATIVE
pris	**prenant**	prends
		prenons
		prenez

PRESENT	FUTURE	IMPERFECT
je prends	je prendrai	je prenais
tu prends	tu prendras	tu prenais
il prend	il prendra	il prenait
nous prenons	nous prendrons	nous prenions
vous prenez	vous prendrez	vous preniez
ils prennent	ils prendront	ils prenaient

PRESENT SUBJUNCTIVE	CONDITIONAL	PAST HISTORIC
je prenne	je prendrais	je pris
tu prennes	tu prendrais	tu pris
il prenne	il prendrait	il prit
nous prenions	nous prendrions	nous prîmes
vous preniez	vous prendriez	vous prîtes
ils prennent	ils prendraient	ils prirent

recevoir *to receive* — Auxiliary: **avoir**

PAST PARTICIPLE	PRESENT PARTICIPLE	IMPERATIVE
reçu	recevant	reçois
		recevons
		recevez

PRESENT	FUTURE	IMPERFECT
je reçois	je recevrai	je recevais
tu reçois	tu recevras	tu recevais
il reçoit	il recevra	il recevait
nous recevons	nous recevrons	nous recevions
vous recevez	vous recevrez	vous receviez
ils reçoivent	ils recevront	ils recevaient

PRESENT SUBJUNCTIVE	CONDITIONAL	PAST HISTORIC
je reçoive	je recevrais	je reçus
tu reçoives	tu recevrais	tu reçus
il reçoive	il recevrait	il reçut
nous recevions	nous recevrions	nous reçûmes
vous receviez	vous recevriez	vous reçûtes
ils reçoivent	ils recevraient	ils reçurent

résoudre *to solve* — Auxiliary: **avoir**

PAST PARTICIPLE	PRESENT PARTICIPLE	IMPERATIVE
résolu	résolvant	résous
		résolvons
		résolvez

PRESENT	FUTURE	IMPERFECT
je résous	je résoudrai	je résolvais
tu résous	tu résoudras	tu résolvais
il résout	il résoudra	il résolvait
nous résolvons	nous résoudrons	nous résolvions
vous résolvez	vous résoudrez	vous résolviez
ils résolvent	ils résoudront	ils résolvaient

PRESENT SUBJUNCTIVE	CONDITIONAL	PAST HISTORIC
je résolve	je résoudrais	je résolus
tu résolves	tu résoudrais	tu résolus
il résolve	il résoudrait	il résolut
nous résolvions	nous résoudrions	nous résolûmes
vous résolviez	vous résoudriez	vous résolûtes
ils résolvent	ils résoudraient	ils résolurent

rire *to laugh*   Auxiliary: avoir

PAST PARTICIPLE	PRESENT PARTICIPLE	IMPERATIVE
ri	riant	ris
		rions
		riez

PRESENT	FUTURE	IMPERFECT
je ris	je rirai	je riais
tu ris	tu riras	tu riais
il **rit**	il rira	il riait
nous rions	nous rirons	nous riions
vous riez	vous rirez	vous riiez
ils rient	ils riront	ils riaient

PRESENT SUBJUNCTIVE	CONDITIONAL	PAST HISTORIC
je rie	je rirais	**je ris**
tu ries	tu rirais	**tu ris**
il rie	il rirait	**il rit**
nous riions	nous ririons	**nous rîmes**
vous riiez	vous ririez	**vous rîtes**
ils rient	ils riraient	**ils rirent**

rompre *to break*   Auxiliary: avoir

PAST PARTICIPLE	PRESENT PARTICIPLE	IMPERATIVE
rompu	rompant	romps
		rompons
		rompez

PRESENT	FUTURE	IMPERFECT
je romps	je romprai	je rompais
tu romps	tu rompras	tu rompais
il rompt	il rompra	il rompait
nous rompons	nous romprons	nous rompions
vous rompez	vous romprez	vous rompiez
ils rompent	ils rompront	ils rompaient

PRESENT SUBJUNCTIVE	CONDITIONAL	PAST HISTORIC
je rompe	je romprais	je rompis
tu rompes	tu romprais	tu rompis
il rompe	il romprait	il rompit
nous rompions	nous romprions	nous rompîmes
vous rompiez	vous rompriez	vous rompîtes
ils rompent	ils rompraient	ils rompirent

savoir to know   Auxiliary: avoir

PAST PARTICIPLE	PRESENT PARTICIPLE	IMPERATIVE
su	sachant	sache
		sachons
		sachez

PRESENT	FUTURE	IMPERFECT
je sais	je saurai	je savais
tu sais	tu sauras	tu savais
il sait	il saura	il savait
nous savons	nous saurons	nous savions
vous savez	vous saurez	vous saviez
ils savent	ils sauront	ils savaient

PRESENT SUBJUNCTIVE	CONDITIONAL	PAST HISTORIC
je sache	je saurais	je sus
tu saches	tu saurais	tu sus
il sache	il saurait	il sut
nous sachions	nous saurions	nous sûmes
vous sachiez	vous sauriez	vous sûtes
ils sachent	ils sauraient	ils surent

sentir to feel; to smell   Auxiliary: avoir

PAST PARTICIPLE	PRESENT PARTICIPLE	IMPERATIVE
senti	sentant	sens
		sentons
		sentez

PRESENT	FUTURE	IMPERFECT
je sens	je sentirai	je sentais
tu sens	tu sentiras	tu sentais
il sent	il sentira	il sentait
nous sentons	nous sentirons	nous sentions
vous sentez	vous sentirez	vous sentiez
ils sentent	ils sentiront	ils sentaient

PRESENT SUBJUNCTIVE	CONDITIONAL	PAST HISTORIC
je sente	je sentirais	je sentis
tu sentes	tu sentirais	tu sentis
il sente	il sentirait	il sentit
nous sentions	nous sentirions	nous sentîmes
vous sentiez	vous sentiriez	vous sentîtes
ils sentent	ils sentiraient	ils sentirent

servir to serve — Auxiliary: avoir

PAST PARTICIPLE	PRESENT PARTICIPLE	IMPERATIVE
servi	**servant**	**sers**
		servons
		servez

PRESENT	FUTURE	IMPERFECT
je **sers**	je servirai	je **servais**
tu **sers**	tu serviras	tu **servais**
il **sert**	il servira	il **servait**
nous **servons**	nous servirons	nous **servions**
vous **servez**	vous servirez	vous **serviez**
ils **servent**	ils serviront	ils **servaient**

PRESENT SUBJUNCTIVE	CONDITIONAL	PAST HISTORIC
je **serve**	je servirais	je servis
tu **serves**	tu servirais	tu servis
il **serve**	il servirait	il servit
nous **servions**	nous servirions	nous servîmes
vous **serviez**	vous serviriez	vous servîtes
ils **servent**	ils serviraient	ils servirent

sortir to go/come out — Auxiliary: être

PAST PARTICIPLE	PRESENT PARTICIPLE	IMPERATIVE
sorti	**sortant**	**sors**
		sortons
		sortez

PRESENT	FUTURE	IMPERFECT
je **sors**	je sortirai	je **sortais**
tu **sors**	tu sortiras	tu **sortais**
il **sort**	il sortira	il **sortait**
nous **sortons**	nous sortirons	nous **sortions**
vous **sortez**	vous sortirez	vous **sortiez**
ils **sortent**	ils sortiront	ils **sortaient**

PRESENT SUBJUNCTIVE	CONDITIONAL	PAST HISTORIC
je **sorte**	je sortirais	je sortis
tu **sortes**	tu sortirais	tu sortis
il **sorte**	il sortirait	il sortit
nous **sortions**	nous sortirions	nous sortîmes
vous **sortiez**	vous sortiriez	vous sortîtes
ils **sortent**	ils sortiraient	ils sortirent

suffire *to be enough*   Auxiliary: avoir

PAST PARTICIPLE	PRESENT PARTICIPLE	IMPERATIVE
suffi	**suffisant**	suffis
		suffisons
		suffisez

PRESENT	FUTURE	IMPERFECT
je suffis	je suffirai	je **suffisais**
tu suffis	tu suffiras	tu **suffisais**
il suffit	il suffira	il **suffisait**
nous suffisons	nous suffirons	**nous suffisions**
vous suffisez	vous suffirez	**vous suffisiez**
ils suffisent	ils suffiront	**ils suffisaient**

PRESENT SUBJUNCTIVE	CONDITIONAL	PAST HISTORIC
je suffise	je suffirais	**je suffis**
tu suffises	tu suffirais	**tu suffis**
il suffise	il suffirait	**il suffit**
nous suffisions	nous suffirions	**nous suffîmes**
vous suffisiez	vous suffiriez	**vous suffîtes**
ils suffisent	ils suffiraient	**ils suffirent**

suivre *to follow*   Auxiliary: avoir

PAST PARTICIPLE	PRESENT PARTICIPLE	IMPERATIVE
suivi	suivant	**suis**
		suivons
		suivez

PRESENT	FUTURE	IMPERFECT
je suis	je suivrai	je suivais
tu suis	tu suivras	tu suivais
il suit	il suivra	il suivait
nous suivons	nous suivrons	nous suivions
vous suivez	vous suivrez	vous suiviez
ils suivent	ils suivront	ils suivaient

PRESENT SUBJUNCTIVE	CONDITIONAL	PAST HISTORIC
je suive	je suivrais	je suivis
tu suives	tu suivrais	tu suivis
il suive	il suivrait	il suivit
nous suivions	nous suivrions	nous suivîmes
vous suiviez	vous suivriez	vous suivîtes
ils suivent	ils suivraient	ils suivirent

se taire *to stop talking*   Auxiliary: être

PAST PARTICIPLE	PRESENT PARTICIPLE	IMPERATIVE
tu	se taisant	tais-toi
		taisons-nous
		taisez-vous

PRESENT	FUTURE	IMPERFECT
je me tais	je me tairai	je me taisais
tu te tais	tu te tairas	tu te taisais
il se tait	il se taira	il se taisait
nous nous taisons	nous nous tairons	nous nous taisions
vous vous taisez	vous vous tairez	vous vous taisiez
ils se taisent	ils se tairont	ils se taisaient

PRESENT SUBJUNCTIVE	CONDITIONAL	PAST HISTORIC
je me taise	je me tairais	je me tus
tu te taises	tu te tairais	tu te tus
il se taise	il se tairait	il se tut
nous nous taisions	nous nous tairions	nous nous tûmes
vous vous taisiez	vous vous tairiez	vous vous tûtes
ils se taisent	ils se tairaient	ils se turent

tenir *to hold*   Auxiliary: avoir

PAST PARTICIPLE	PRESENT PARTICIPLE	IMPERATIVE
tenu	tenant	tiens
		tenons
		tenez

PRESENT	FUTURE	IMPERFECT
je tiens	je tiendrai	je tenais
tu tiens	tu tiendras	tu tenais
il tient	il tiendra	il tenait
nous tenons	nous tiendrons	nous tenions
vous tenez	vous tiendrez	vous teniez
ils tiennent	ils tiendront	ils tenaient

PRESENT SUBJUNCTIVE	CONDITIONAL	PAST HISTORIC
je tienne	je tiendrais	je tins
tu tiennes	tu tiendrais	tu tins
il tienne	il tiendrait	il tint
nous tenions	nous tiendrions	nous tînmes
vous teniez	vous tiendriez	vous tîntes
ils tiennent	ils tiendraient	ils tinrent

vaincre to defeat · Auxiliary: avoir

PAST PARTICIPLE	PRESENT PARTICIPLE	IMPERATIVE
vaincu	**vainquant**	vaincs
		vainquons
		vainquez

PRESENT	FUTURE	IMPERFECT
je vaincs	je vaincrai	je **vainquais**
tu vaincs	tu vaincras	tu **vainquais**
il vainc	il vaincra	il **vainquait**
nous **vainquons**	nous vaincrons	nous **vainquions**
vous **vainquez**	vous vaincrez	vous **vainquiez**
ils **vainquent**	ils vaincront	ils **vainquaient**

PRESENT SUBJUNCTIVE	CONDITIONAL	PAST HISTORIC
je **vainque**	je vaincrais	je **vainquis**
tu **vainques**	tu vaincrais	tu **vainquis**
il **vainque**	il vaincrait	il **vainquit**
nous **vainquions**	nous vaincrions	nous **vainquîmes**
vous **vainquiez**	vous vaincriez	vous **vainquîtes**
ils **vainquent**	ils vaincraient	ils **vainquirent**

valoir to be worth · Auxiliary: avoir

PAST PARTICIPLE	PRESENT PARTICIPLE	IMPERATIVE
valu	**valant**	**vaux**
		valons
		valez

PRESENT	FUTURE	IMPERFECT
je vaux	je vaudrai	je valais
tu vaux	tu vaudras	tu valais
il vaut	il vaudra	il valait
nous valons	nous vaudrons	nous valions
vous valez	vous vaudrez	vous valiez
ils valent	ils vaudront	ils valaient

PRESENT SUBJUNCTIVE	CONDITIONAL	PAST HISTORIC
je **vaille**	je **vaudrais**	je valus
tu **vailles**	tu **vaudrais**	tu valus
il **vaille**	il **vaudrait**	il valut
nous valions	nous **vaudrions**	nous valûmes
vous valiez	vous **vaudriez**	vous valûtes
ils **vaillent**	ils **vaudraient**	ils valurent

venir *to come* — Auxiliary: être

PAST PARTICIPLE	PRESENT PARTICIPLE	IMPERATIVE
venu	venant	viens
		venons
		venez

PRESENT	FUTURE	IMPERFECT
je viens	je viendrai	je venais
tu viens	tu viendras	tu venais
il vient	il viendra	il venait
nous venons	nous viendrons	nous venions
vous venez	vous viendrez	vous veniez
ils viennent	ils viendront	ils venaient

PRESENT SUBJUNCTIVE	CONDITIONAL	PAST HISTORIC
je vienne	je viendrais	je vins
tu viennes	tu viendrais	tu vins
il vienne	il viendrait	il vint
nous venions	nous viendrions	nous vînmes
vous veniez	vous viendriez	vous vîntes
ils viennent	ils viendraient	ils vinrent

vivre *to live* — Auxiliary: avoir

PAST PARTICIPLE	PRESENT PARTICIPLE	IMPERATIVE
vécu	vivant	vis
		vivons
		vivez

PRESENT	FUTURE	IMPERFECT
je vis	je vivrai	je vivais
tu vis	tu vivras	tu vivais
il vit	il vivra	il vivait
nous vivons	nous vivrons	nous vivions
vous vivez	vous vivrez	vous viviez
ils vivent	ils vivront	ils vivaient

PRESENT SUBJUNCTIVE	CONDITIONAL	PAST HISTORIC
je vive	je vivrais	je vécus
tu vives	tu vivrais	tu vécus
il vive	il vivrait	il vécut
nous vivions	nous vivrions	nous vécûmes
vous viviez	vous vivriez	vous vécûtes
ils vivent	ils vivraient	ils vécurent

voir to see		Auxiliary: **avoir**
PAST PARTICIPLE	PRESENT PARTICIPLE	IMPERATIVE
vu	voyant	vois
		voyons
		voyez

PRESENT	FUTURE	IMPERFECT
je vois	je verrai	je voyais
tu vois	tu verras	tu voyais
il voit	il verra	il voyait
nous voyons	nous verrons	nous voyions
vous voyez	vous verrez	vous voyiez
ils voient	ils verront	ils voyaient

PRESENT SUBJUNCTIVE	CONDITIONAL	PAST HISTORIC
je voie	je verrais	je vis
tu voies	tu verrais	tu vis
il voie	il verrait	il vit
nous voyions	nous verrions	nous vîmes
vous voyiez	vous verriez	vous vîtes
ils voient	ils verraient	ils virent

vouloir to wish, want		Auxiliary: **avoir**
PAST PARTICIPLE	PRESENT PARTICIPLE	IMPERATIVE
voulu	voulant	veuille
		veuillons
		veuillez

PRESENT	FUTURE	IMPERFECT
je veux	je voudrai	je voulais
tu veux	tu voudras	tu voulais
il veut	il voudra	il voulait
nous voulons	nous voudrons	nous voulions
vous voulez	vous voudrez	vous vouliez
ils veulent	ils voudront	ils voulaient

PRESENT SUBJUNCTIVE	CONDITIONAL	PAST HISTORIC
je veuille	je voudrais	je voulus
tu veuilles	tu voudrais	tu voulus
il veuille	il voudrait	il voulut
nous voulions	nous voudrions	nous voulûmes
vous vouliez	vous voudriez	vous voulûtes
ils veuillent	ils voudraient	ils voulurent

❐ The Gender of Nouns

In French, all nouns are either masculine or feminine, whether denoting people, animals or things. Unlike English, there is no neuter gender for inanimate objects and abstract nouns.

Gender is largely unpredictable and has to be learnt for each noun. However, the following guidelines will help you determine the gender for certain types of nouns.

◆ Nouns denoting male people and animals are usually – but not always – masculine, e.g.

un homme	**un taureau**
a man	*a bull*
un infirmier	**un cheval**
a (male) nurse	*a horse*

◆ Nouns denoting female people and animals are usually – but not always – feminine, e.g.

une fille	**une vache**
a girl	*a cow*
une infirmière	**une brebis**
a nurse	*a ewe*

◆ Some nouns are masculine OR feminine depending on the sex of the person to whom they refer, e.g.

un camarade	**une camarade**
a (male) friend	*a (female) friend*
un Belge	**une Belge**
a Belgian (man)	*a Belgian (woman)*

◆ Other nouns referring to either men or women have only one gender which applies to both, e.g.

un professeur	**une personne**	**une sentinelle**
a teacher	*a person*	*a sentry*
un témoin	**une victime**	**une recrue**
a witness	*a victim*	*a recruit*

Grammar

◆ Sometimes the ending of the noun indicates its gender. Shown below are some of the most important to guide you:

Masculine endings

-age	**le courage** *courage*, **le rinçage** *rinsing*
	EXCEPTIONS: **une cage** *a cage*, **une image** *a picture*, **la nage** *swimming*, **une page** *a page*, **une plage** *a beach*, **une rage** *a rage*
-ment	**le commencement** *the beginning*
	EXCEPTION: **une jument** *a mare*
-oir	**un couloir** *a corridor*, **un miroir** *a mirror*
-sme	**le pessimisme** *pessimism*, **l'enthousiasme** *enthusiasm*

Feminine endings

-ance, anse	**la confiance** *confidence*, **la danse** *dancing*
-ence, -ense	**la prudence** *caution*, **la défense** *defence*
	EXCEPTION: **le silence** *silence*
-ion	**une région** *a region*, **une addition** *a bill*
	EXCEPTIONS: **un pion** *a pawn*, **un espion** *a spy*
-oire	**une baignoire** *a bath(tub)*
-té, -tié	**la beauté** *beauty*, **la moitié** *half*

◆ Suffixes which differentiate between male and female are shown on p 78.

◆ The following words have different meanings depending on gender:

le crêpe	*crêpe*	**la crêpe**	*pancake*
le livre	*book*	**la livre**	*pound*
le manche	*handle*	**la manche**	*sleeve*
le mode	*method*	**la mode**	*fashion*
le moule	*mould*	**la moule**	*mussel*
le page	*page(boy)*	**la page**	*page (in book)*
le physique	*physique*	**la physique**	*physics*
le poêle	*stove*	**la poêle**	*frying pan*
le somme	*nap*	**la somme**	*sum*
le tour	*turn*	**la tour**	*tower*
le voile	*veil*	**la voile**	*sail*

❏ Gender: the Formation of Feminines

As in English, male and female are sometimes differentiated by the use of two quite separate words, e.g. **mon oncle/ma tante** *my uncle/my aunt*. There are, however, some words in French which show this distinction by the form of their ending.

♦ Some nouns add an **e** to the masculine singular form to form the feminine → ①

♦ If the masculine singular form already ends in **-e**, no further **e** is added in the feminine → ②

♦ Some nouns undergo a further change when **e** is added.

MASC. SING.	FEM. SING.	
-f	-ve	→ ③
-x	-se	→ ④
-eur	-euse	→ ⑤
-teur	⌠-teuse	→ ⑥
	⌡-trice	→ ⑦

Some nouns double the final consonant before adding **e:**

MASC. SING.	FEM. SING.	
-an	-anne	→ ⑧
-en	-enne	→ ⑨
-on	-onne	→ ⑩
-et	-ette	→ ⑪
-el	-elle	→ ⑫

Some nouns add an accent to the final syllable before adding **e:**

MASC. SING.	FEM. SING.	
-er	-ère	→ ⑬

♦ Some nouns have unusual feminine forms → ⑭

1	**un ami** a (male) friend	**une amie** a (female) friend	
2	**un élève** a (male) pupil	**une élève** a (female) pupil	
3	**un veuf** a widower	**une veuve** a widow	
4	**un époux** a husband	**une épouse** a wife	
5	**un danseur** a dancer	**une danseuse** a dancer	
6	**un menteur** a liar	**une menteuse** a liar	
7	**un conducteur** a driver	**une conductrice** a driver	
8	**un paysan** a countryman	**une paysanne** a countrywoman	
9	**un Parisien** a Parisian	**une Parisienne** a Parisian (woman)	
10	**un baron** a baron	**une baronne** a baroness	
11	**le cadet** the youngest (child)	**la cadette** the youngest (child)	
12	**un intellectuel** an intellectual	**une intellectuelle** an intellectual	
13	**un étranger** a foreigner	**une étrangère** a foreigner	
14	**le comte/la comtesse** count/countess	**le duc/la duchesse** duke/duchess	
	le maître/la maîtresse master/mistress	**le prince/la princesse** prince/princess	
	le fou/la folle madman/madwoman	**le Turc/la Turque** Turk	
	un hôte/une hôtesse host/hostess	**le vieux/la vieille** old man/old woman	

❏ The Formation of Plurals

- Most nouns add **s** to the singular form → 1

- When the singular form already ends in **-s**, **-x** or **-z**, no further **s** is added → 2

- For nouns ending in **-au**, **-eau** or **-eu**, the plural ends in **-aux**, **-eaux** or **-eux** → 3
  EXCEPTIONS: **pneu** *tyre* (plur: **pneus**)
  bleu *bruise* (plur: **bleus**)

- For nouns ending in **-al** or **-ail**, the plural ends in **-aux** → 4
  EXCEPTIONS: **bal** *ball* (plur: **bals**)
  festival *festival* (plur: **festivals**)
  chandail *sweater* (plur: **chandails**)
  détail *detail* (plur: **détails**)

- Forming the plural of compound nouns is complicated and you are advised to check each one individually in a dictionary.

- A word which is singular in English may be plural in French, or vice versa → 5

Irregular plural forms

- Some masculine nouns ending in **-ou** add **x** in the plural. These are:

bijou	*jewel*	**genou**	*knee*	**joujou**	*toy*
caillou	*pebble*	**hibou**	*owl*	**pou**	*louse*
chou	*cabbage*				

- Some other nouns are totally unpredictable. Chief among these are:

SINGULAR		PLURAL
œil	*eye*	**yeux**
ciel	*sky*	**cieux**
Monsieur	*Mr*	**Messieurs**
Madame	*Mrs*	**Mesdames**
Mademoiselle	*Miss*	**Mesdemoiselles**

1 **le jardin**	**les jardins**
the garden	the gardens
une voiture	**des voitures**
a car	(some) cars
l'hôtel	**les hôtels**
the hotel	the hotels
2 **un tas**	**des tas**
a heap	(some) heaps
une voix	**des voix**
a voice	(some) voices
le gaz	**les gaz**
the gas	the gases
3 **un tuyau**	**des tuyaux**
a pipe	(some) pipes
le chapeau	**les chapeaux**
the hat	the hats
le feu	**les feux**
the fire	the fires
4 **le journal**	**les journaux**
the newspaper	the newspapers
un travail	**des travaux**
a job	(some) jobs
5 **les bagages**	**ses cheveux**
the luggage	his/her hair
le bétail	**mon pantalon**
the cattle	my trousers

☐ **The Definite Article**

	WITH MASC. NOUN	WITH FEM. NOUN	
SING.	**le (l')**	**la (l')**	*the*
PLUR.	**les**	**les**	*the*

♦ The gender and number of the noun determines the form of the article → ☐1

♦ **le** and **la** change to **l'** before a vowel or an **h** 'mute' → ☐2

♦ While the French definite article is used in much the same way as in English, it is also found:

 – with abstract nouns, except after certain prepositions → ☐3

 – in generalizations, especially with plural or uncountable nouns (those which cannot be used in the plural or with an indefinite article, e.g. **le lait** *milk*) → ☐4

 – with names of countries, except after **en** *to/in* → ☐5

 – with parts of the body; 'ownership' is often indicated by an indirect object pronoun or a reflexive pronoun → ☐6

 – in expressions of quantity/rate/price → ☐7

 – with titles/ranks/professions followed by a proper name → ☐8

 – The definite article is NOT used with nouns in apposition → ☐9

♦ **à + le/la (l'), à + les; de + le/la (l'), de + les**

	à WITH MASC. NOUN	**à** WITH FEM. NOUN	**de** WITH MASC. NOUN	**de** WITH FEM. NOUN
SING.	**au (à l')**	**à la (à l')** → ☐10	**du (de l')**	**de la (de l')** → ☐11
PLUR.	**aux**	**aux**	**des**	**des**

♦ The definite article combines with the prepositions **à** and **de**, as shown above. You should pay particular attention to the masculine singular forms **au** and **du**, and plural forms **aux** and **des**, since these are not visually the sum of their parts.

1 **le garçon** the boy	**la fille** the girl
les hôtels the hotels	**les écoles** the schools
2 **l'acteur** the actor	**l'actrice** the actress
l'hôpital the hospital	**l'heure** the time
3 **Les prix montent** Prices are rising	**L'amour rayonne dans ses yeux** Love shines in his eyes
BUT **avec plaisir** with pleasure	**sans espoir** without hope
4 **Je n'aime pas le café** I don't like coffee	**Les enfants ont besoin d'être aimés** Children need to be loved
5 **le Japon** Japan	**les Pays-Bas** The Netherlands
BUT **aller en Écosse** to go to Scotland	

6 **Tournez la tête à gauche**   **J'ai mal à la gorge**
Turn your head to the left   My throat is sore, I have a sore throat
La tête me tourne   **Elle s'est brossé les dents**
My head is spinning   She brushed her teeth

7 **40 francs le mètre/le kilo/rouler à 80 km à l'heure**
40 francs a metre/a kilo/to go at 50 mph

8 **le roi Georges III**   **Monsieur le président**
King George III   Mr Chairman/President

9 **Victor Hugo, grand écrivain du dix-neuvième siècle**
Victor Hugo, a great author of the nineteenth century

10 **au cinéma**   **à la bibliothèque**   **à l'hôpital**
at/to the cinema   at/to the library   at/to the hospital
à l'hôtesse   **aux étudiants**   **aux maisons**
to the hostess   to the students   to the houses

11 **du bureau**   **de la réunion**
from/of the office   from/of the meeting
de l'auteur   **de l'Italienne**
from/of the author   from/of the Italian woman
des États-Unis   **des vendeuses**
from/of the United States   from/of the saleswomen

⬚ The Partitive Article

The partitive article has the sense of *some* or *any*, although the French is not always translated in English.

	WITH MASC. NOUN	WITH FEM. NOUN	
SING.	**du (de l')**	**de la (de l')**	some, any
PLUR.	**des**	**des**	some, any

- The gender and number of the noun determines the form of the partitive → 1

- The forms shown in brackets in the above table are used before a vowel or an **h** 'mute' → 2

- **des** becomes **de** (**d'** + vowel) before an adjective → 3, unless the adjective and noun are seen as forming one unit → 4

- In negative sentences **de** (**d'** + vowel) is used → 5
  EXCEPTION: after **ne ... que** *only*, the positive forms above are used → 6

⬚ The Indefinite Article

	WITH MASC. NOUN	WITH FEM. NOUN	
SING.	**un**	**une**	*a*
PLUR.	**des**	**des**	some

- In negative sentences, **de** (**d'** + vowel) is used → 7

- The indefinite article is used in French largely as it is in English EXCEPT:

  – there is no article when a person's profession is being stated → 8
    The article *is* present, however, following **ce** (**c'** + vowel) → 9

  – the English article is not translated by **un/une** in constructions like *what a surprise, what an idiot* → 10

  – in structures of the type given in example 11 the article **un/une** is

1   **Avez-vous du sucre?**   **J'ai acheté de la farine**
Do you have any sugar?   I bought (some) flour
Il a mangé des gâteaux
He ate some cakes
Est-ce qu'il y a des lettres pour moi?
Are there (any) letters for me?

2   **Il me doit de l'argent**   **C'est de l'histoire ancienne**
He owes me (some) money   That's ancient history

3   **Cette région a de belles églises**
This region has some beautiful churches

4   **des grandes vacances**   **des jeunes gens**
summer holidays   young people

5   **Vous n'avez pas de timbres/d'œufs?**
Have you no stamps/eggs?
Je ne mange jamais de viande/d'omelettes
I never eat meat/omelettes

6   **Il ne boit que du thé/de la bière/de l'eau**
He only drinks tea/beer/water
Je n'ai que des problèmes avec cette machine
I have nothing but problems with this machine

7   **Je n'ai pas de livre/d'enfants**
I don't have a book/(any) children

8   **Il est professeur**   **Ma mère est infirmière**
He's a teacher   My mother's a nurse

9   **C'est un médecin**   **Ce sont des acteurs**
He's/She's a doctor   They're actors

10   **Quelle surprise!**   **Quel dommage!**
What a surprise!   What a shame!

11   **avec une grande sagesse/un courage admirable**
with great wisdom/admirable courage
un produit d'une qualité incomparable
a product of incomparable quality

❐ Adjectives

Most adjectives agree in number and in gender with the noun or pronoun.

The formation of feminines

◆ Most adjectives add an **e** to the masculine singular form → ①

◆ If the masculine singular form already ends in **-e,** no further **e** is added → ②

◆ Some adjectives undergo a further change when **e** is added. These changes occur regularly and are shown on p 88.

◆ Irregular feminine forms are shown on p 90.

The formation of plurals

◆ The plural of both regular and irregular adjectives is formed by adding an **s** to the masculine or feminine singular form, as appropriate → ③

◆ When the masculine singular form already ends in **-s** or **-x,** no further **s** is added → ④

◆ For masculine singulars ending in **-au** and **-eau,** the masculine plural is **-aux** and **-eaux** → ⑤

◆ For masculine singulars ending in **-al,** the masculine plural is **-aux** → ⑥

    EXCEPTIONS: **final**   (masculine plural **finals**)
                      fatal   (masculine plural **fatals**)
                      naval   (masculine plural **navals**)

1. **mon frère aîné**
my elder brother
le petit garçon
the little boy
un sac gris
a grey bag
un bruit fort
a loud noise

     ma sœur aînée
my elder sister
la petite fille
the little girl
une chemise grise
a grey shirt
une voix forte
a loud voice

2. **un jeune homme**
a young man
l'autre verre
the other glass

     une jeune femme
a young woman
l'autre assiette
the other plate

3. **le dernier train**
the last train
une vieille maison
an old house
un long voyage
a long journey
la rue étroite
the narrow street

     les derniers trains
the last trains
de vieilles maisons
old houses
de longs voyages
long journeys
les rues étroites
the narrow streets

4. **un diplomate français**
a French diplomat
un homme dangereux
a dangerous man

     des diplomates français
French diplomats
des hommes dangereux
dangerous men

5. **le nouveau professeur**
the new teacher
un chien esquimau
a husky (Fr. = an Eskimo dog)

     les nouveaux professeurs
the new teachers
des chiens esquimaux
huskies (Fr. = Eskimo dogs)

6. **un ami loyal**
a loyal friend
un geste amical
a friendly gesture

     des amis loyaux
loyal friends
des gestes amicaux
friendly gestures

❏ Regular Feminine Endings

MASC. SING.	FEM. SING.	EXAMPLES	
-f	-ve	**neuf, vif**	→ 1
-x	-se	**heureux, jaloux**	→ 2
-eur	-euse	**travailleur, flâneur**	→ 3
-teur	{ -teuse	**flatteur, menteur**	→ 4
	-trice	**destructeur, séducteur**	→ 5

EXCEPTIONS:

> **bref**: see p 90
>
> **doux, faux, roux, vieux:** see p 90
>
> **extérieur, inférieur, intérieur, meilleur, supérieur:** all add **e** to the masculine
>
> **enchanteur**: fem. = **enchanteresse**

MASC. SING.	FEM. SING.	EXAMPLES	
-an	-anne	**paysan**	→ 6
-en	-enne	**ancien, parisien**	→ 7
-on	-onne	**bon, breton**	→ 8
-as	-asse	**bas, las**	→ 9
-et*	-ette	**muet, violet**	→ 10
-el	-elle	**annuel, mortel**	→ 11
-eil	-eille	**pareil, vermeil**	→ 12

EXCEPTION:

> **ras**: fem. = **rase**

MASC. SING.	FEM. SING.	EXAMPLES	
-et*	-ète	**secret, complet**	→ 13
-er	-ère	**étranger, fier**	→ 14

*Note that there are two feminine endings for masculine adjectives ending in -et.

1. **un résultat positif**
   a positive result

   une attitude positive
   a positive attitude

2. **d'un ton sérieux**
   in a serious tone (of voice)

   une voix sérieuse
   a serious voice

3. **un enfant trompeur**
   a deceitful child

   une déclaration trompeuse
   a misleading statement

4. **un tableau flatteur**
   a flattering picture

   une comparaison flatteuse
   a flattering comparison

5. **un geste protecteur**
   a protective gesture

   une couche protectrice
   a protective layer

6. **un problème paysan**
   a farming problem

   la vie paysanne
   country life

7. **un avion égyptien**
   an Egyptian plane

   une statue égyptienne
   an Egyptian statue

8. **un bon repas**
   a good meal

   de bonne humeur
   in a good mood

9. **un plafond bas**
   a low ceiling

   à voix basse
   in a low voice

10. **un travail net**
    a clean piece of work

    une explication nette
    a clear explanation

11. **un homme cruel**
    a cruel man

    une remarque cruelle
    a cruel remark

12. **un livre pareil**
    such a book

    en pareille occasion
    on such an occasion

13. **un regard inquiet**
    an anxious look

    une attente inquiète
    an anxious wait

14. **un goût amer**
    a bitter taste

    une amère déception
    a bitter disappointment

☐ Irregular Feminine Forms

MASC. SING.	FEM. SING.		
aigu	aiguë	*sharp; high-pitched*	→ ①
ambigu	ambiguë	*ambiguous*	
beau (bel*)	belle	*beautiful*	
bénin	bénigne	*benign*	
blanc	blanche	*white*	
bref	brève	*brief, short*	→ ②
doux	douce	*soft; sweet*	
épais	épaisse	*thick*	
faux	fausse	*wrong*	
favori	favorite	*favourite*	→ ③
fou (fol*)	folle	*mad*	
frais	fraîche	*fresh*	→ ④
franc	franche	*frank*	
gentil	gentille	*kind*	
grec	grecque	*Greek*	
gros	grosse	*big*	
jumeau	jumelle	*twin*	→ ⑤
long	longue	*long*	
malin	maligne	*malignant*	
mou (mol*)	molle	*soft*	
nouveau (nouvel*)	nouvelle	*new*	
nul	nulle	*no*	
public	publique	*public*	→ ⑥
roux	rousse	*red-haired*	
sec	sèche	*dry*	
sot	sotte	*foolish*	
turc	turque	*Turkish*	
vieux (vieil*)	vieille	*old*	

*This form is used when the following word begins with a vowel or an **h** 'mute' → ⑦

1	**un son aigu** a high-pitched sound	**une douleur aiguë** a sharp pain
2	**un bref discours** a short speech	**une brève rencontre** a short meeting
3	**mon sport favori** my favourite sport	**ma chanson favorite** my favourite song
4	**du pain frais** fresh bread	**de la crème fraîche** fresh cream
5	**mon frère jumeau** my twin brother	**ma sœur jumelle** my twin sister
6	**un jardin public** a (public) park	**l'opinion publique** public opinion

7   **un bel appartement**
a beautiful flat
le nouvel inspecteur
the new inspector
un vieil arbre
an old tree

un bel habit
a beautiful outfit
un nouvel harmonica
a new harmonica
un vieil hôtel
an old hotel

❏ Comparatives and Superlatives

Comparatives

These are formed using the following constructions:

plus ... (que)	*more ... (than)*	→ 1
moins ... (que)	*less ... (than)*	→ 2
aussi ... que	*as ... as*	→ 3
si ... que*	*as ... as*	→ 4

*used mainly after a negative

Superlatives

These are formed using the following constructions:

le/la/les plus ... (que)	*the most ... (that)*	→ 5
le/la/les moins ... (que)	*the least ... (that)*	→ 6

- When the possessive adjective is present, two constructions are possible → 7

- After a superlative the preposition **de** is often translated as *in* → 8

- If a clause follows a superlative, the verb is in the subjunctive → 9

Adjectives with irregular comparatives/superlatives

ADJECTIVE	COMPARATIVE	SUPERLATIVE
bon *good*	**meilleur** *better*	**le meilleur** *the best*
mauvais *bad*	**pire** OR **plus mauvais** *worse*	**le pire** OR **le plus mauvais** *the worst*
petit *small*	**moindre*** OR **plus petit** *smaller; lesser*	**le moindre*** OR **le plus petit** *the smallest; the least*

*used only with abstract nouns

- Comparative and superlative adjectives agree in number and in gender with the noun, just like any other adjective → 10

Grammar

1. **une raison plus grave**
   a more serious reason
   Elle est plus petite que moi
   She is smaller than me

2. **un film moins connu**
   a less well-known film
   C'est moins cher qu'il ne pense
   It's cheaper than he thinks

3. **Robert était aussi inquiet que moi**
   Robert was as worried as I was
   Cette ville n'est pas aussi grande que Bordeaux
   This town isn't as big as Bordeaux

4. **Ils ne sont pas si contents que ça**
   They aren't as happy as all that

5. **le guide le plus utile**   **la voiture la plus petite**
   the most useful guidebook   the smallest car
   les plus grandes maisons
   the biggest houses

6. **le mois le moins agréable**   **la fille la moins forte**
   the least pleasant month   the weakest girl
   les moins belles peintures
   the least attractive paintings

7. **Mon désir le plus cher** } **est de voyager**
   Mon plus cher désir
   My dearest wish is to travel

8. **la plus grande gare de Londres**
   the biggest station in London
   l'habitant le plus âgé du village/de la région
   the oldest inhabitant in the village/in the area

9. **la personne la plus gentille que je connaisse**
   the nicest person I know

10. **les moindres difficultés**
    the least difficulties
    la meilleure qualité
    the best quality

☐ Demonstrative Adjectives

	MASCULINE	FEMININE	
SING.	**ce (cet)**	**cette**	*this; that*
PLUR.	**ces**	**ces**	*these; those*

- ◆ Demonstrative adjectives agree in number and gender with the noun → ①

- ◆ **cet** is used when the following word begins with a vowel or an **h** 'mute' → ②

- ◆ For emphasis or in order to distinguish between people or objects, **-ci** or **-là** is added to the noun: **-ci** indicates proximity (usually translated *this*) and **-là** distance *(that)* → ③

☐ Interrogative Adjectives

	MASCULINE	FEMININE	
SING.	**quel?**	**quelle?**	*what?; which?*
PLUR.	**quels?**	**quelles?**	*what?; which?*

- ◆ Interrogative adjectives agree in number and gender with the noun → ④

- ◆ The forms shown above are also used in indirect questions → ⑤

☐ Exclamatory Adjectives

	MASCULINE	FEMININE	
SING.	**quel!**	**quelle!**	*what (a)!*
PLUR.	**quels!**	**quelles!**	*what!*

- ◆ Exclamatory adjectives agree in number and gender with the noun → ⑥

- ◆ For other exclamations, see p 128.

EXAMPLES

1. **Ce stylo ne marche pas**
   This/That pen isn't working
   Comment s'appelle cette entreprise?
   What's this/that company called?
   Ces livres sont les miens
   These/Those books are mine
   Ces couleurs sont plus jolies
   These/Those colours are nicer

2. **cet oiseau**   **cet homme**
   this/that bird   this/that man

3. **Combien coûte ce manteau-ci?**
   How much is this coat?
   Je voudrais cinq de ces pommes-là
   I'd like five of those apples
   Est-ce que tu reconnais cette personne-là?
   Do you recognize that person?
   Mettez ces vêtements-ci dans cette valise-là
   Put these clothes in that case

4. **Quel genre d'homme est-ce?**
   What type of man is he?
   Quelle est leur décision?
   What is their decision?
   Vous jouez de quels instruments?
   What instruments do you play?
   Quelles offres avez-vous reçues?
   What offers have you received?

5. **Je ne sais pas à quelle heure il est arrivé**
   I don't know what time he arrived
   Dites-moi quels sont les livres les plus intéressants
   Tell me which books are the most interesting

6. **Quel dommage!**   **Quelle idée!**
   What a pity!   What an idea!
   Quels beaux livres vous avez!   **Quelles jolies fleurs!**
   What fine books you have!   What nice flowers!

❑ Position of Adjectives

- French adjectives usually follow the noun → 1

- Adjectives of colour or nationality *always* follow the noun → 2

- As in English, demonstrative, possessive, numerical and interrogative adjectives precede the noun → 3

- The adjectives **autre** *other* and **chaque** *each*, *every* precede the noun → 4

- The following common adjectives can precede the noun:

beau	*beautiful*	**jeune**	*young*
bon	*good*	**joli**	*pretty*
court	*short*	**long**	*long*
dernier	*last*	**mauvais**	*bad*
grand	*great*	**petit**	*small*
gros	*big*	**tel**	*such (a)*
haut	*high*	**vieux**	*old*

- The meaning of the following adjectives varies according to their position:

	BEFORE NOUN	AFTER NOUN	
ancien	*former*	*old, ancient*	→ 5
brave	*good*	*brave*	→ 6
cher	*dear (beloved)*	*expensive*	→ 7
grand	*great*	*tall*	→ 8
même	*same*	*very*	→ 9
pauvre	*poor* *(wretched)*	*poor* *(not rich)*	→ 10
propre	*own*	*clean*	→ 11
seul	*single, sole*	*on one's own*	→ 12
simple	*mere, simple*	*simple, easy*	→ 13

1	**le chapitre suivant** the following chapter	**l'heure exacte** the right time
2	**une cravate rouge** a red tie	**un mot français** a French word
3	**ce dictionnaire** this dictionary	**mon père** my father
	le premier étage the first floor	**deux exemples** two examples
	quel homme? which man?	
4	**une autre fois** another time	**chaque jour** every day
5	**un ancien collègue** a former colleague	**l'histoire ancienne** ancient history
6	**un brave homme** a good man	**un homme brave** a brave man
7	**mes chers amis** my dear friends	**une robe chère** an expensive dress
8	**un grand peintre** a great painter	**un homme grand** a tall man
9	**la même réponse** the same answer	**vos paroles mêmes** your very words
10	**cette pauvre femme** that poor woman	**une nation pauvre** a poor nation
11	**ma propre vie** my own life	**une chemise propre** a clean shirt
12	**une seule réponse** a single reply	**une femme seule** a woman on her own
13	**un simple regard** a mere look	**un problème simple** a simple problem
14	**la vraie raison** the real reason	**les faits vrais** the true facts
15	**un acte lâche et trompeur** a cowardly, deceitful act	
	un acte lâche, trompeur et ignoble a cowardly, deceitful and ignoble act	

❑ **Possessive Adjectives**

WITH SING. NOUN		WITH PLUR. NOUN	
MASC.	FEM.	MASC./FEM.	
mon	**ma (mon)**	**mes**	*my*
ton	**ta (ton)**	**tes**	*your*
son	**sa (son)**	**ses**	*his; her; its*
notre	**notre**	**nos**	*our*
votre	**votre**	**vos**	*your*
leur	**leur**	**leurs**	*their*

◆ Possessive adjectives agree in number and gender with the noun, NOT WITH THE OWNER → ①

◆ The forms shown in brackets are used when the following word begins with a vowel or an **h** 'mute' → ②

◆ **son, sa, ses** have the additional meaning of *one's* → ③

---

① **Catherine a oublié son parapluie**
Catherine has left her umbrella
Paul cherche sa montre
Paul's looking for his watch
Mon frère et ma sœur habitent à Glasgow
My brother and sister live in Glasgow
Est-ce que tes voisins ont vendu leur voiture?
Did your neighbours sell their car?
Rangez vos affaires
Put your things away

② **mon appareil-photo**   **ton histoire**
my camera   your story
son erreur   **mon autre sœur**
his/her mistake   my other sister

③ **perdre son équilibre**   **présenter ses excuses**
to lose one's balance   to offer one's apologies

☐ Personal Pronouns: Subject

PERSON	SINGULAR	PLURAL
1st	**je (j')** *I*	**nous** *we*
2nd	**tu** *you*	**vous** *you*
3rd (masc.)	**il** *he; it*	**ils** *they*
(fem.)	**elle** *she; it*	**elles** *they*

je changes to **j'** before a vowel, an **h** 'mute', or the pronoun **y** → ①

◆ **Vous**, as well as being the second person plural, is also used when addressing one person. As a general rule, use **tu** only when addressing a friend, a child, a relative, someone you know very well, or when invited to do so. In all other cases use **vous**. For singular and plural uses of **vous**, see example ②

◆ The form of the third person pronouns (**il/elle; ils/elles**) reflects the number and gender of the noun(s) they replace, referring to animals and things as well as to people. **Ils** also replaces a combination of masculine and feminine nouns → ③

◆ Sometimes stressed pronouns replace the subject pronouns, see p 103.

①	**J'arrive!**	**J'en ai trois**
	I'm just coming!	I've got 3 of them
	J'hésite à le déranger	**J'y pense souvent**
	I hesitate to disturb him	I often think about it
②	Compare:	**Vous êtes certain, Monsieur Leclerc?**
		Are you sure, Mr Leclerc?
	and:	**Vous êtes certains, les enfants?**
		Are you sure, children?
③	**Où logent ton père et ta mère quand ils vont à Rome?**	
	Where do your father and mother stay when they go to Rome?	
	Donne-moi le journal et les lettres quand ils arriveront	
	Give me the newspaper and the letters when they arrive	

❑ Personal Pronouns: Object

	DIRECT OBJECT PRONOUNS		INDIRECT OBJECT PRONOUNS	
PERSON	SINGULAR	PLURAL	SINGULAR	PLURAL
1st	**me (m')**	**nous**	**me (m')**	**nous**
	me	*us*	*to me*	*to us*
2nd	**te (t')**	**vous**	**te (t')**	**vous**
	you	*you*	*to you*	*to you*
3rd (masc.)	**le (l')**	**les**	**lui**	**leur**
	him; it	*them*	*to him; to it*	*to them*
(fem.)	**la (l')**	**les**	**lui**	**leur**
	her; it	*them*	*to her; to it*	*to them*

The forms shown in brackets are used before a vowel, an **h** 'mute', or the pronoun **y** → ①

- In positive commands **me** and **te** change to **moi** and **toi** except before **en** or **y** → ②

- **le** sometimes functions as a 'neuter' pronoun, referring to an idea or information contained in a previous statement or question. It is often not translated → ③

- The indirect object pronouns replace the preposition **à** + noun, where the noun is a person or an animal → ④

- The verbal construction affects the translation of the pronoun → ⑤

Position of object pronouns

- In constructions other than the imperative affirmative the pronoun comes before the verb → ⑥
  The same applies when the verb is in the infinitive → ⑦
  In the imperative affirmative, the pronoun follows the verb and is attached to it by a hyphen → ⑧

- For further information, see Order of Object Pronouns, p 102.

Reflexive pronouns

These are dealt with under reflexive verbs, p 24.

1. **Il m'a vu**   **Ils t'ont caché les faits**
He saw me   They hid the facts from you

2. **Avertis-moi de ta décision** → **Avertis-m'en**
Inform me of your decision   Inform me of it
Donnez-moi du sucre   → **Donnez-m'en**
Give me some sugar   Give me some

3. **Il n'est pas là. – Je le sais bien.**
He isn't there. – I know that.
Elle viendra demain. – Je l'espère bien.
She'll come tomorrow. – I hope so.

4. **J'écris à Suzanne**   → **Je lui écris**
I'm writing to Suzanne   I'm writing to her

5. **arracher qch à qn: Un voleur m'a arraché mon porte-monnaie**
           A thief snatched my purse from me
promettre qch à qn: Il leur a promis un cadeau
           He promised them a present
demander à qn de faire: Elle nous avait demandé de revenir
           She had asked us to come back

6. **Je t'aime**   **Les voyez-vous?**
I love you   Can you see them?
Ne me faites pas rire   **Elle ne nous connaît pas**
Don't make me laugh   She doesn't know us
Elle vous a écrit   **Vous a-t-elle écrit?**
She's written to you   Has she written to you?
Il ne nous parle pas   **Ne leur répondez pas**
He doesn't speak to us   Don't answer them

7. **Puis-je vous aider?**
May I help you?
Voulez-vous leur envoyer l'adresse?
Do you want to send them the address?

8. **Aidez-moi**   **Donnez-nous la réponse**
Help me   Tell us the answer

☐ Personal Pronouns: Order of Object Pronouns

◆ When two object pronouns of different persons come before the verb, the order is: indirect before direct, i.e.

me te nous vous	before	le la les	→ ①

◆ When two third person object pronouns come before the verb, the order is: direct before indirect, i.e.

le la les	before	lui leur	→ ②

◆ When two object pronouns come after the verb (i.e. in the imperative affirmative), the order is: direct before indirect, i.e.

le la les	before	moi toi lui nous vous leur	→ ③

◆ The pronouns **en** and **y** (see pp 104 and 105) always come last → ④

①	**Dominique vous l'envoie demain** Dominique's sending it to you tomorrow **Est-ce qu'il te les a montrés?** Has he shown them to you?	
②	**Elle le leur a emprunté** She borrowed it from them	**Ne la leur donne pas** Don't give it to them
③	**Rends-les-moi** Give them back to me	**Donnez-le-nous** Give it to us
④	**Donnez-leur-en** Give them some	**Je l'y ai déposé** I dropped him there

❏ Personal Pronouns: Stressed or Disjunctive Forms

PERSON	SINGULAR	PLURAL
1st	**moi** *me*	**nous** *us*
2nd	**toi** *you*	**vous** *you*
3rd (masc.)	**lui** *him; it*	**eux** *them*
(fem.)	**elle** *her; it*	**elles** *them*
('reflexive')	**soi** *oneself*	

◆ These pronouns are used:

– after prepositions → 1
– on their own → 2
– following **c'est, ce sont** *it is* → 3
– for emphasis, especially to show contrast; for particular emphasis **-même** (singular) or **-mêmes** (plural) is added to the pronoun → 4
– when the subject consists of two or more pronouns, or a pronoun and a noun → 5
– in comparisons → 6
– before relative pronouns → 7

---

1 **Je pense à toi**   **Partez sans eux**
   I think about you   Leave without them

2 **Qui a fait cela? – Lui**   **Qui est-ce qui gagne? – Moi**
   Who did that? – He did   Who's winning? – Me

3 **C'est toi, Simon? – Non, c'est moi, David**
   Is that you, Simon? – No, it's me, David

4 **Toi, tu ressembles à ton père, eux pas**
   You look like your father, *they* don't
   Je l'ai fait moi-même
   I did it myself

5 **Lui et moi partons demain**
   He and I are leaving tomorrow
   Mon père et elle ne s'entendent pas
   My father and she don't get on

6 **plus jeune que moi**   **Il est moins grand que toi**
   younger than me   He's smaller than you (are)

7 **Ce sont eux qui font du bruit, pas nous**
   They're the ones making the noise, not us

☐ The Pronoun *en*

◆ **en** replaces the preposition **de** + noun → 1
  The verbal construction can affect the translation → 2

◆ **en** also replaces the partitive article *(English = some, any)* + noun
  → 3

In expressions of quantity **en** represents the noun → 4

◆ Position:
  en comes before the verb, except in positive commands when it
  follows and is attached to the verb by a hyphen → 5

◆ **en** follows other object pronouns → 6

---

1   **Il est fier de son succès** → **Il en est fier**
    He's proud of his success   He's proud of it

    Elle est sortie du cinéma → **Elle en est sortie**
    She came out of the cinema   She came out (of it)

    Je suis couvert de peinture → **J'en suis couvert**
    I'm covered in paint   I'm covered in it

2   **avoir besoin de qch: J'en ai besoin**
        I need it/them
    avoir peur de qch: J'en ai peur
        I'm afraid of it/them

3   **Avez-vous de l'argent?** → **En avez-vous?**
    Have you any money?   Do you have any?

    Je veux acheter des timbres → **Je veux en acheter**
    I want to buy some stamps   I want to buy some

4   **Combien de sœurs as-tu? – J'en ai trois**
    How many sisters do you have? – I have three

5   **Elle en a discuté avec moi**   **En êtes-vous content?**
    She discussed it with me   Are you pleased with it/them?

    N'en parlez plus   **Prenez-en**
    Don't talk about it any more   Take some

6   **Donnez-leur-en**   **Il m'en a parlé**
    Give them some   •He spoke to me about it

❐ The Pronoun *y*

- **y** replaces the preposition **à** + noun → ①
  The verbal construction can affect the translation → ②

- **y** also replaces the prepositions **dans** and **sur** + noun → ③

- **y** can also mean *there* → ④

- Position:
  y comes before the verb, except in positive commands when it follows and is attached to the verb by a hyphen → ⑤

- **y** follows other object pronouns → ⑥

---

① **Ne touchez pas à ce bouton** → **N'y touchez pas**
Don't touch this switch   Don't touch it
Il participe aux concerts → **Il y participe**
He takes part in the concerts   He takes part (in them)

② **penser à qch: J'y pense souvent**
     I often think about it
consentir à qch: Tu y as consenti?
     Have you agreed to it?

③ **Mettez-les dans la boîte** → **Mettez-les-y**
Put them in the box   Put them in it
Il les a mis sur les étagères → **Il les y a mis**
He put them on the shelves   He put them on them

④ **Elle y passe tout l'été**
She spends the whole summer there

⑤ **Il y a ajouté du sucre**   **Elle n'y a pas écrit son nom**
He added sugar to it   She hasn't written her name on it
Comment fait-on pour y aller?
How do you get there?
N'y pense plus!   **Réfléchissez-y**
Don't give it another thought!   Think it over

⑥ **Elle m'y a conduit**   **Menez-nous-y**
She drove me there   Take us there

❏ Relative Pronouns

qui	*who; which*
que	*who(m); which*

These are subject and direct object pronouns that introduce a clause and refer to people or things.

	PEOPLE	THINGS
SUBJECT	**qui** → ①	**qui** → ③
	who, that	*which, that*
DIRECT OBJECT	**que (qu')** → ②	**que (qu')** → ④
	who(m), that	*which, that*

- **que** changes to **qu'** before a vowel → ②/④

- You cannot omit the object relative pronoun in French as you can in English → ②/④

After a preposition:
- When referring to people, use **qui** → ⑤
  EXCEPTIONS: after **parmi** *among* and **entre** *between* use **lesquels/lesquelles** (see below) → ⑥
- When referring to things, use forms of **lequel**:

	MASCULINE	FEMININE	
SING.	**lequel**	**laquelle**	*which*
PLUR.	**lesquels**	**lesquelles**	*which*

The pronoun agrees in number and gender with the noun → ⑦

- After the prepositions **à** and **de, lequel** and **lesquel(le)s** contract as follows:
  à + lequel → auquel
  à + lesquels → auxquels   → ⑧
  à + lesquelles → auxquelles

  de + lequel → duquel
  de + lesquels → desquels   → ⑨
  de + lesquelles → desquelles

1   **Mon frère, qui a vingt ans, est à l'université**
My brother, who's twenty, is at university

2   **Les amis que je vois le plus sont …**
The friends (that) I see most are …
Lucienne, qu'il connaît depuis longtemps, est …
Lucienne, whom he has known for a long time, is …

3   **Il y a un escalier qui mène au toit**
There's a staircase which leads to the roof

4   **La maison que nous avons achetée a …**
The house (which) we've bought has …
Voici le cadeau qu'elle m'a envoyé
This is the present (that) she sent me

5   **la personne à qui il parle**
the person he's talking to
la personne avec qui je voyage
the person with whom I travel
les enfants pour qui je l'ai acheté
the children for whom I bought it

6   **Il y avait des jeunes, parmi lesquels Robert**
There were some young people, Robert among them
les filles entre lesquelles j'étais assis
the girls between whom I was sitting

7   **le torchon avec lequel il l'essuie**
the cloth he's wiping it with
la table sur laquelle je l'ai mis
the table on which I put it
les moyens par lesquels il l'accomplit
the means by which he achieves it
les pièces pour lesquelles elle est connue
the plays for which she is famous

8   **le magasin auquel il livre ces marchandises**
the shop to which he delivers these goods

9   **les injustices desquelles il se plaint**
the injustices he's complaining about

❏ Relative Pronouns (Continued)

quoi *which, what*

◆ When the relative pronoun does not refer to a specific noun, **quoi** is used after a preposition → ①

dont *whose, of whom, of which*

◆ **dont** often (but not always) replaces **de qui, duquel, de laquelle**, and **desquel(le)s** → ②

◆ It cannot replace **de qui, duquel** etc in the construction preposition + noun + **de qui/duquel** → ③

◆ If the person (or object) 'owned' is the *object* of the verb, word order is: **dont** + verb + noun → ④
If the person (or object) 'owned' is the *subject* of the verb, word order is: **dont** + noun + verb → ⑤

ce qui, ce que *that which, what*

These are used when the relative pronoun does not refer to a specific noun, and they are often translated as *what* (literally: *that which*)

    ce qui   is used as the subject → ⑥
    ce que*   is used as the direct object → ⑦

    ***que** changes to **qu'** before a vowel → ⑦

◆ Note the construction

    tout ce qui ⎫
    tout ce que ⎬ *everything/all that* → ⑧

◆ **de + ce que** → **ce dont** → ⑨

◆ preposition + **ce que** → **ce** + preposition + **quoi** → ⑩

◆ When **ce qui, ce que** etc, refers to a previous CLAUSE the translation is *which* → ⑪

1   **C'est en quoi vous vous trompez**
That's where you're wrong
À quoi, j'ai répondu '...'
To which I replied, '...'

2   **la femme dont (= de qui) la voiture est garée en face**
the woman whose car is parked opposite
un prix dont (= de qui) je suis fier
an award I am proud of

3   **une personne sur l'aide de qui on peut compter**
a person whose help one can rely on
les enfants aux parents de qui j'écris
the children to whose parents I'm writing
la maison dans le jardin de laquelle il y a ...
the house in whose garden there is ...

4   **un homme dont je connais la fille**
a man whose daughter I know

5   **un homme dont la fille me connaît**
a man whose daughter knows me

6   **Je n'ai pas vu ce qui s'est passé**
I didn't see what happened

7   **Ce que j'aime c'est la musique classique**
What I like is classical music
Montrez-moi ce qu'il vous a donné
Show me what he gave you

8   **Tout ce qui reste c'est ...**
All that's left is ...
Donnez-moi tout ce que vous avez
Give me everything you have

9   **Voilà ce dont il s'agit**
That's what it's about

10   **Ce n'est pas ce à quoi je m'attendais**
It's not what I was expecting
Ce à quoi je m'intéresse particulièrement c'est ...
What I'm particularly interested in is ...

11   **Il est d'accord, ce qui m'étonne**
He agrees, which surprises me
Il a dit qu'elle ne venait pas, ce que nous savions déjà
He said she wasn't coming, which we already knew

❏ Interrogative Pronouns

In direct questions

qui?	*who; whom?*
que?	*what?*
quoi?	*what?*

These pronouns are used in direct questions. Their form depends on:
- whether it refers to people or to things
- whether it is the subject or object of the verb, or if it comes after a preposition

Qui and **que** have longer forms, as shown in the tables below.

- Referring to people:

SUBJECT	**qui?**	
	qui est-ce qui?	→ ①
	who?	
OBJECT	**qui?**	
	qui est-ce que*?	→ ②
	who(m)?	
AFTER PREPOSITIONS	**qui?**	→ ③
	who(m)?	

- Referring to things:

SUBJECT	**qu'est-ce qui?**	→ ④
	what?	
OBJECT	**que*?**	
	qu'est-ce que*?	→ ⑤
	what?	
AFTER PREPOSITIONS	**quoi?**	→ ⑥
	what?	

*que changes to **qu'** before a vowel → ②, ⑤

1. **Qui vient?**
   Qui est-ce qui vient?
   Who's coming?

2. **Qui vois-tu?**
   Qui est-ce que tu vois?
   Who(m) can you see?
   Qui a-t-elle rencontré?
   Qui est-ce qu'elle a rencontré?
   Who(m) did she meet?

3. **De qui parle-t-il?**
   Who's he talking about?
   Pour qui est ce livre?
   Who's this book for?
   À qui avez-vous écrit?
   To whom did you write?

4. **Qu'est-ce qui se passe?**
   What's happening?
   Qu'est-ce qui a vexé Paul?
   What upset Paul?

5. **Que faites-vous?**
   Qu'est-ce que vous faites?
   What are you doing?
   Qu'a-t-il dit?
   Qu'est-ce qu'il a dit?
   What did he say?

6. **À quoi cela sert-il?**
   What's that used for?
   De quoi a-t-on parlé?
   What was the discussion about?
   Sur quoi vous basez-vous?
   What do you base it on?

❑ Interrogative Pronouns (Continued)

In indirect questions

qui	*who; whom*
ce qui	*what*
ce que	*what*
quoi	*what*

These pronouns are used in indirect questions.
The form of the pronoun depends on:
- whether it refers to people or to things
- whether it is the subject or object of the verb, or if it comes after a preposition

- Referring to people: use **qui** in all instances → ①
- Referring to things:

SUBJECT	**ce qui** *what*	→ ②
OBJECT	**ce que*** *what*	→ ③
AFTER PREPOSITIONS	**quoi** *what*	→ ④

*que** changes to **qu'** before a vowel → ③

lequel?, laquelle?; lesquels?, lesquelles?

	MASCULINE	FEMININE	
SING.	**lequel?**	**laquelle?**	*which (one)?*
PLUR.	**lesquels?**	**lesquelles?**	*which (ones)?*

- The pronoun agrees in number and gender with the noun it refers to → ⑤
- The same forms are used in indirect questions → ⑥
- After **à** and **de**, **lequel** and **lesquel(le)s** contract as shown on p 106.

EXAMPLES

1 **Demande-lui qui est venu**
Ask him who came
Je me demande qui ils ont vu
I wonder who they saw
Dites-moi qui vous préférez
Tell me who you prefer
Elle ne sait pas à qui s'adresser
She doesn't know who to apply to
Demandez-leur pour qui elles travaillent
Ask them who they work for

2 **Il se demande ce qui se passe**
He's wondering what's happening
Je ne sais pas ce qui vous fait croire que ...
I don't know what makes you think that ...

3 **Raconte-nous ce que tu as fait**
Tell us what you did
Je me demande ce qu'elle pense
I wonder what she's thinking

4 **On ne sait pas de quoi vivent ces animaux**
We don't know what these animals live on
Je vais lui demander à quoi il fait allusion
I'm going to ask him what he's hinting at

5 **J'ai choisi un livre – Lequel?**
I've chosen a book – Which one?
Laquelle de ces valises est la vôtre?
Which of these cases is yours?
Amenez quelques amis – Lesquels?
Bring some friends – Which ones?
Lesquelles de vos sœurs sont mariées?
Which of your sisters are married?

6 **Je me demande laquelle des maisons est la leur**
I wonder which is their house
Dites-moi lesquels d'entre eux étaient là
Tell me which of them were there

☐ Possessive Pronouns

SINGULAR		
MASCULINE	FEMININE	
le mien	**la mienne**	*mine*
le tien	**la tienne**	*yours*
le sien	**la sienne**	*his; hers; its*
le nôtre	**la nôtre**	*ours*
le vôtre	**la vôtre**	*yours*
le leur	**la leur**	*theirs*

PLURAL		
MASCULINE	FEMININE	
les miens	**les miennes**	*mine*
les tiens	**les tiennes**	*yours*
les siens	**les siennes**	*his; hers; its*
les nôtres	**les nôtres**	*ours*
les vôtres	**les vôtres**	*yours*
les leurs	**les leurs**	*theirs*

◆ The pronoun agrees in number and gender with the noun it replaces, NOT WITH THE OWNER → ①

◆ Alternative translations are *my own, your own* etc; **le sien, la sienne** etc may also mean *one's own* → ②

◆ After the prepositions **à** and **de** the articles **le** and **les** are contracted in the normal way (see p 82):

à + le mien → au mien
à + les miens → aux miens → ③
à + les miennes → aux miennes

de + le mien → du mien
de + les miens → des miens → ④
de + les miennes → des miennes

1. **Demandez à Carole si ce stylo est le sien**
   Ask Carole if this pen is hers
   Quelle équipe a gagné – la leur ou la nôtre?
   Which team won – theirs or ours?
   Mon stylo marche mieux que le tien
   My pen writes better than yours
   Richard a pris mes affaires pour les siennes
   Richard mistook my belongings for his
   Si tu n'as pas de disques, emprunte les miens
   If you don't have any records, borrow mine
   Nos maisons sont moins grandes que les vôtres
   Our houses are smaller than yours

2. **Est-ce que leur entreprise est aussi grande que la vôtre?**
   Is their company as big as your own?
   Leurs prix sont moins élevés que les nôtres
   Their prices are lower than our own
   Le bonheur des autres importe plus que le sien
   Other people's happiness matters more than one's own

3. **Pourquoi préfères-tu ce manteau au mien?**
   Why do you prefer this coat to mine?
   Quelles maisons ressemblent aux leurs?
   Which houses resemble theirs?

4. **Leur car est garé à côté du nôtre**
   Their coach is parked beside ours
   Vos livres sont au-dessus des miens
   Your books are on top of mine

☐ Demonstrative Pronouns

celui, celle; ceux, celles

	MASCULINE	FEMININE	
SING.	**celui**	**celle**	*the one*
PLUR.	**ceux**	**celles**	*the ones*

◆ **Celui** agrees in number and gender with the noun it replaces → ①

◆ Uses:
  – preceding a relative pronoun, meaning *the one(s) who/which* → ①
  – preceding **de**, meaning *the one(s) belonging to, the one(s) of* → ②
  – with **-ci** and **-là**, for emphasis or to distinguish between two things:

	MASCULINE	FEMININE		
SING.	**celui-ci**	**celle-ci**	*this (one)*	→ ③
PLUR.	**ceux-ci**	**celles-ci**	*these (ones)*	
SING.	**celui-là**	**celle-là**	*that(one)*	→ ③
PLUR.	**ceux-là**	**celles-là**	*those (ones)*	

  – **celui-ci/celui-là** etc can also mean *the former/the latter*.

ce (c')   *it, that*

◆ **Ce** is usually found in the expressions **c'est, ce sont** etc. Note the spelling **ç** when followed by the letter **a** → ④

◆ Uses:
  – to identify a person or object → ⑤
  – for emphasis → ⑥
  – as a neuter pronoun, referring to a statement, idea etc → ⑦

ce qui, ce que, ce dont etc

  See Relative Pronouns (p 108), Interrogative Pronouns (p 112).

cela, ça   *it, that*

◆ **cela** and **ça** are used as 'neuter' pronouns, referring to a statement, an idea, an object. In everyday spoken language **ça** is preferred → ⑧

ceci   *this* → ⑨

◆ **ceci** is not used as often as 'this' in English; **cela, ça** are used instead.

1 **Cet article n'est pas celui dont vous m'avez parlé**
This article isn't the one you spoke to me about
Quelle robe désirez-vous? – Celle qui est en vitrine
Which dress do you want? – The one which is in the window
Est-ce que ces livres sont ceux qu'il t'a donnés?
Are these the books that he gave you?
Quelles filles? – Celles que nous avons vues hier
Which girls? – The ones we saw yesterday

2 **Comparez vos réponses à celles de votre voisin**
Compare your answers with your neighbour's (answers)
les montagnes d'Écosse et celles du pays de Galles
the mountains of Scotland and those of Wales

3 **Quel tailleur préférez-vous: celui-ci ou celui-là?**
Which suit do you prefer: this one or that one?
De toutes mes jupes, celle-ci me va le mieux
Of all my skirts, this one fits me best

4 **Ç'a été la cause de …**   **C'était moi**
It has been the cause of…   It was me

5 **Qui est-ce?**
Who is it?; Who's this/that?; Who's he/she?
C'est mon frère   **C'est une infirmière***
It's/That's my brother   She's a nurse
Qu'est-ce que c'est?   **Ce sont des trombones**
What's this/that?   They're paper clips

6 **C'est moi qui ai téléphoné**
It was me who phoned

7 **C'est très intéressant**   **Ce serait dangereux**
That's/It's very interesting   That/It would be dangerous

8 **Ça ne fait rien**   **Cela ne compte pas**
It doesn't matter   That doesn't count

9 **À qui est ceci?**   **Ouvrez-le comme ceci**
Whose is this?   Open it like this

* See p 85 for the use of the article with professions

❏ Adverbs

Formation

- Most adverbs are formed by adding **-ment** to the feminine form of the adjective → ☐1

- **-ment** is added to the *masculine* form when the masculine form ends in **-é, -i** or **-u** → ☐2
  EXCEPTION: **gai** → ☐3
  Occasionally the **u** changes to **û** before **-ment** is added → ☐4

- If the adjective ends in **-ant** or **-ent**, the adverb ends in **-amment** or **-emment** → ☐5
  EXCEPTIONS: **lent, présent** → ☐6

Irregular adverbs

ADJECTIVE		ADVERB		
aveugle	*blind*	**aveuglément**	blindly	
bon	*good*	**bien**	well	→ ☐7
bref	*brief*	**brièvement**	briefly	
énorme	*enormous*	**énormément**	enormously	
exprès	*express*	**expressément**	expressly	→ ☐8
gentil	*kind*	**gentiment**	kindly	
mauvais	*bad*	**mal**	badly	→ ☐9
meilleur	*better*	**mieux**	better	
pire	*worse*	**pis**	worse	
précis	*precise*	**précisément**	precisely	
profond	*deep*	**profondément**	deeply	→ ☐10
traître	*treacherous*	**traîtreusement**	treacherously	

Adjectives used as adverbs

Certain adjectives are used adverbially. These include: **bas, bon, cher, clair, court, doux, droit, dur, faux, ferme, fort, haut, mauvais** and **net** → ☐11

1 MASC./FEM. ADJECTIVE	ADVERB
heureux/heureuse fortunate	**heureusement** fortunately
franc/franche frank	**franchement** frankly
extrême/extrême extreme	**extrêmement** extremely
2 MASC. ADJECTIVE	ADVERB
désespéré desperate	**désespérément** desperately
vrai true	**vraiment** truly
résolu resolute	**résolument** resolutely
3 **gai** cheerful	**gaiement** OR **gaîment** cheerfully
4 **continu** continuous	**continûment** continuously
5 **constant** constant	**constamment** constantly
courant fluent	**couramment** fluently
évident obvious	**évidemment** obviously
fréquent frequent	**fréquemment** frequently
6 **lent** slow	**lentement** slowly
présent present	**présentement** presently

7 **Elle travaille bien**
She works well

8 **Il a expressément défendu qu'on parte**
He has expressly forbidden us to leave

9 **Un emploi mal payé**
A badly paid job

10 **J'ai été profondément ému**
I was deeply moved

11 **parler bas/haut**
to speak softly/loudly
coûter cher
to be expensive
voir clair
to see clearly
travailler dur
to work hard
chanter faux
to sing off key
sentir bon/mauvais
to smell nice/horrible

☐ Position of Adverbs

◆ When the adverb accompanies a verb in a simple tense, it generally follows the verb → ①

◆ When the adverb accompanies a verb in a compound tense, it generally comes between the auxiliary verb and the past participle → ②
Some adverbs, however, follow the past participle → ③

◆ When the adverb accompanies an adjective or another adverb it generally precedes the adjective/adverb → ④

☐ Comparatives and Superlatives of Adverbs

◆ Comparatives are formed using the following constructions:

plus ... (que)	more ... (than)	→ ⑤
moins ... (que)	less ... (than)	→ ⑥
aussi ... que	as ... as	→ ⑦
si ... que*	as ... as	→ ⑧

*used mainly after a negative

◆ Superlatives are formed using the following constructions:

| le plus ... (que) | the most ... (that) | → ⑨ |
| le moins ... (que) | the least ... (that) | → ⑩ |

Adverbs with irregular comparatives/superlatives

ADVERB	COMPARATIVE	SUPERLATIVE
beaucoup	**plus**	**le plus**
a lot	*more*	*(the) most*
bien	**mieux**	**le mieux**
well	*better*	*(the) best*
mal	**pis** OR **plus mal**	**le pis** OR **le plus mal**
badly	*worse*	*(the) worst*
peu	**moins**	**le moins**
little	*less*	*(the) least*

1	**Il dort encore**	**Je pense souvent à toi**
	He's still asleep	I often think about you
2	**Ils sont déjà partis**	**J'ai toujours cru que …**
	They've already gone	I've always thought that …
	J'ai presque fini	**Il a trop mangé**
	I've almost finished	He's eaten too much
3	**On les a vus partout**	**Elle est revenue hier**
	We saw them everywhere	She came back yesterday
4	**un très beau chemisier**	**une femme bien habillée**
	a very nice blouse	a well-dressed woman
	beaucoup plus vite	**peu souvent**
	much faster	not very often
5	**plus vite**	**plus régulièrement**
	more quickly	more regularly
	Elle chante plus fort que moi	
	She sings louder than I do	
6	**moins facilement**	**moins souvent**
	less easily	less often
	Nous nous voyons moins fréquemment qu'auparavant	
	We see each other less frequently than before	
7	**Faites-le aussi vite que possible**	
	Do it as quickly as possible	
	Il en sait aussi long que nous	
	He knows as much about it as we do	
8	**Ce n'est pas si loin que je pensais**	
	It's not as far as I thought	
9	**Marianne court le plus vite**	
	Marianne runs fastest	
	Le plus tôt que je puisse venir c'est samedi	
	The earliest that I can come is Saturday	
10	**C'est l'auteur que je connais le moins bien**	
	It's the writer I'm least familiar with	

❏ Prepositions

◆ It is often difficult to give an English equivalent for French prepositions, since usage varies so much between the two languages. The French preposition may not always be the one that the English sentence leads you to expect, and vice versa. A good dictionary will help you here → ①

◆ English verbal constructions often contain a preposition where none exists in French, and vice versa → ②

◆ English phrasal verbs (i.e. verbs followed by a preposition e.g. *to run away*, *to fall down*) are often translated by one word in French → ③

---

① **Il y a beaucoup de restaurants à Londres**
There are lots of restaurants in London
Elle est allée à Londres
She went/has gone to London
donner qch à qn
to give sth to sb, to give sb sth

lancer qch à qn	**prendre qch à qn**
to throw sth at sb	to take sth from sb
à pied **une tasse à thé**	
on foot a teacup	
venir de Paris	**une boîte d'allumettes**
to come from Paris	a box of matches
une robe de soie	**d'une façon irrégulière**
a silk dress	in an irregular way
la plus belle ville du monde	**plus de cent personnes**
The most beautiful city in the world	more than a hundred people
je vais en ville	**en janvier**
I'm going (in)to town	in January
déguisé en cowboy	**je suis venue en voiture**
dressed up as a cowboy	I came by car

②	**payer**	**regarder**	**écouter**
	to pay for	to look at	to listen to
	obéir à	**nuire à**	**manquer de**
	to obey	to harm	to lack
③	**s'enfuir**	**tomber**	**céder**
	to run away	to fall down	to give in

☐ Conjunctions

Some conjunctions introduce a main clause, e.g. **et** *and*, **mais** *but*, and some introduce subordinate clauses e.g. **parce que** *because*, **pendant que** *while*. They are used in much the same way as in English, but:

- Some conjunctions in French require a following subjunctive, see p 46
- Some conjunctions are 'split' in French:

et ... et	*both ... and*	→ ⒈
ni ... ni ... ne	*neither ... nor*	→ ⒉
ou (bien) ... ou (bien)	*either ... or (else)*	→ ⒊
soit ... soit	*either ... or*	→ ⒋

- **si + il(s) → s'il(s)** → ⒌

- **que**
  - meaning *that* → ⒍
  - replacing another conjunction → ⒎
  - replacing **si**, see p 48
  - in comparisons, see pp 92 and 120
  - followed by the subjunctive, see p 48

- **aussi** *so*, *therefore*: the subject and verb are inverted if the subject is a pronoun → ⒏

⒈ **Ces fleurs poussent et en été et en hiver**
These flowers grow in both summer and winter

⒉ **Ni lui ni elle ne sont venus**
Neither he nor she came

⒊ **Ou bien il m'évite ou bien il ne me reconnaît pas**
Either he's avoiding me or else he doesn't recognize me

⒋ **Il faut choisir soit l'un soit l'autre**
You have to choose either one or the other

⒌ **Je ne sais pas s'il vient/s'ils viennent**
I don't know if he's coming/if they're coming

⒍ **Il dit qu'il t'a vu**
He says (that) he saw you

⒎ **Comme il pleuvait et que je n'avais pas de parapluie, ...**
As it was raining and I didn't have an umbrella, ...

⒏ **Ceux-ci sont plus rares, aussi coûtent-ils cher**
These ones are rarer, so they're expensive

☐ Negatives

ne ... pas	*not*
ne ... point (literary)	*not*
ne ... rien	*nothing*
ne ... personne	*nobody*
ne ... plus	*no longer, no more*
ne ... jamais	*never*
ne ... que	*only*
ne ... aucun(e)	*no*
ne ... nul(le)	*no*
ne ... nulle part	*nowhere*
ne ... ni (... ni)	*neither ... nor*

◆ **Word order**

– In simple tenses and the imperative:
ne precedes the verb (and any object pronouns) and the second element follows the verb → ☐1

– In compound tenses:

i **ne ... pas, ne ... point, ne ... rien, ne ... plus, ne ... jamais, ne... guère** follow the pattern:
ne + auxiliary verb + **pas** + past participle → ☐2

ii **ne ... personne, ne ... que, ne ... aucun(e), ne ... nul(le), ne ... nulle part, ne ... ni (... ni)** follow the pattern:
ne + auxiliary verb + past participle + **personne** → ☐3

– With a verb in the infinitive:
ne ... pas, ne ... point (etc; see i above) come together → ☐4

◆ **Rien, personne** and **aucun** can also be used as pronouns. When they are the subject or object of the verb, **ne** is placed immediately before the verb. **Aucun** also needs the pronoun **en** when used as an object → ☐5

◆ **Jamais** and **plus** can be combined with some of the negative particles listed above → ☐6

1   **Je ne fume pas**   **Ne changez rien**
I don't smoke   Don't change anything
Je ne vois personne
I can't see anybody
Nous ne nous verrons plus
We won't see each other any more
Il n'arrive jamais à l'heure   **Il n'avait qu'une valise**
He never arrives on time   He only had one suitcase
Il ne boit ni ne fume
He neither drinks nor smokes
Ni mon fils ni ma fille ne les connaissaient
Neither my son nor my daughter knew them

2   **Elle n'a pas fait ses devoirs**
She hasn't done her homework
Ne vous a-t-il rien dit?
Didn't he say anything to you?
Tu n'as guère changé
You've hardly changed

3   **Je n'ai vu personne**
I haven't seen anybody
Il n'avait mangé que la moitié du repas
He had only eaten half the meal
Elle ne les a trouvés nulle part
She couldn't find them anywhere

4   **Il essayait de ne pas rire**
He was trying not to laugh

5   **Je ne vois personne**   **Rien ne lui plaît**
I can't see anyone   Nothing pleases him/her
Aucune des entreprises ne veut …   **Il n'en a aucun**
None of the companies wants …   He hasn't any (of them)

6   **Je ne le ferai plus jamais**
I'll never do it again
Ces marchandises ne valaient plus rien
Those goods were no longer worth anything
Ils ne font jamais rien d'intéressant
They never do anything interesting
Je n'ai jamais parlé qu'à sa femme
I've only ever spoken to his wife

❏ Question Forms

Direct questions

There are four ways of forming direct questions in French:

- by inverting the normal word order so that *pronoun subject + verb*
  → *verb + pronoun subject*. A hyphen links the verb and pronoun → ①

  - When the subject is a noun, a pronoun is inserted after the verb
    and linked to it by a hyphen → ②

  - When the verb ends in a vowel in the third person singular, **-t-** is
    inserted before the pronoun → ③

- by maintaining the word order *subject + verb* and using a rising
  intonation at the end of the sentence → ④

- by inserting **est-ce que** before the construction *subject + verb* → ⑤

- by using an interrogative word at the beginning of the sentence,
  together with inversion *or* the **est-ce que** form above → ⑥

Indirect questions

An indirect question is one that is 'reported', e.g. he asked me *what the
time was*, tell me *which way to go*. Word order in indirect questions is as
follows:

- *interrogative word* + subject + verb → ⑦

- when the subject is a noun, and not a pronoun, the subject and verb
  are often inverted → ⑧

n'est-ce pas

This is used wherever English would use *isn't it?*, *don't they?*, *weren't we?*, *is
it?* etc tagged on to the end of a sentence → ⑨

1. **Aimez-vous la France?**   **Avez-vous fini?**
   Do you like France?   Have you finished?
   Est-ce possible?   **Est-elle restée?**
   Is it possible?   Did she stay?

2. **Tes parents sont-ils en vacances?**
   Are your parents on holiday?

3. **A-t-elle de l'argent?**
   Does she have any money?
   La pièce dure-t-elle longtemps?
   Does the play last long?

4. **Robert va venir**   **Robert va venir?**
   Robert's coming   Is Robert coming?

5. **Est-ce que tu la connais?**
   Do you know her?
   Est-ce que tes parents sont revenus d'Italie?
   Have your parents come back from Italy?

6. **Quel train** { **prends-tu?**
                 { **est-ce que tu prends?**
   What train are you getting?

   Pourquoi { **ne sont-ils pas venus?**
              { **est-ce qu'ils ne sont pas venus?**
   Why haven't they come?

7. **Je me demande s'il viendra**
   I wonder if he'll come
   Dites-moi quel autobus va à la gare
   Tell me which bus goes to the station

8. **Elle nous a demandé comment allait notre père**
   She asked us how our father was
   Je ne sais pas ce que veulent dire ces mots
   I don't know what these words mean

9. **Il fait chaud, n'est-ce pas?**
   It's warm, isn't it?
   Vous n'oublierez pas, n'est-ce pas?
   You won't forget, will you?

❑ Word Order

Word order in French is largely the same as in English, except:

- ◆ Object pronouns nearly always come before the verb (see p 100)
- ◆ Certain adjectives come after the noun (see p 96)
- ◆ Adverbs accompanying a verb in a simple tense usually follow the verb (see p 120)
- ◆ After **aussi** *so, therefore,* **à peine** *hardly,* **peut-être** *perhaps,* the verb and subject are inverted → ①
- ◆ After the relative pronoun **dont** *whose* certain rules apply (see p 108)
- ◆ In exclamations, **que** and **comme** do not affect the normal word order → ②
- ◆ Following direct speech:
  - the *verb + subject* order is inverted to become *subject + verb* → ③
  - with a pronoun subject, the verb and pronoun are linked by a hyphen → ④
  - when the verb ends in a vowel in the third person singular, **-t-** is inserted between the pronoun and the verb → ⑤

For word order in negative sentences, see p 124.
For word order in interrogative sentences, see pp 126 and 128.

---

① **Il vit tout seul, aussi fait-il ce qu'il veut**
He lives alone, so he does what he likes
À peine la pendule avait-elle sonné trois heures que …
Hardly had the clock struck three when …
Peut-être avez-vous raison
Perhaps you're right

② **Qu'il fait chaud!**   **Comme c'est cher**
How warm it is!   How expensive it is!

③ **'Je pense que oui' a dit Luc**   **'Ça ne fait rien' répondit Jean**
' I think so', said Luke   'It doesn't matter', John replied

④ **'Quelle horreur!' me suis-je exclamé**
'How awful!' I exclaimed

⑤ **'Pourquoi pas?' a-t-elle demandé**
'Why not?' she asked